S0-ALG-728

CLAMP

TRANSLATED AND ADAPTED BY
William Flanagan

LETTERED BY
Dana Hayward

KODANSHA COMICS

Tsubasa Omnibus volume 8 is a work of fiction. Names, characters, places, and incidents are the products of the author's imagination or are used fictitiously. Any resemblance to actual events, locales, or persons, living or dead, is entirely coincidental.

A Kodansha Comics Trade Paperback Original.

Published in the United States by Kodansha Comics, an imprint of Kodansha USA Publishing, LLC, New York.

Publication rights for this English edition arranged through Kodansha Ltd., Tokyo.

First published in Japan in 2008 by Kodansha Ltd., Tokyo, as *Tsubasa*, volumes 22, 23 and 24.

ISBN 978-1-63236-219-3

Printed in the United States of America.

www.kodanshacomics.com

9 8 7 6 5 4 3 2 1

Translation: William Flanagan
Lettering: Dana Hayward
Kodansha Comics edition cover design: Phil Balsman

Contents

Tsubasa crosses over with *xxxHOLiC*. Although it isn't necessary to read *xxxHOLiC* to understand the events in *Tsubasa*, you'll get to see the same events from different perspectives if you read both series!

Honorifics Explained

Throughout Kodansha Comics books, you will find Japanese honorifics left intact in the translations. For those not familiar with how the Japanese use honorifics and, more important, how they differ from American honorifics, we present this brief overview.

Politeness has always been a critical facet of Japanese culture. Ever since the feudal era, when Japan was a highly stratified society, use of honorifics—which can be defined as polite speech that indicates relationship or status—has played an essential role in the Japanese language. When you address someone in Japanese, an honorific usually takes the form of a suffix attached to one's name (example: "Asuna-san"), is used as a title at the end of one's name, or appears in place of the name itself (example: "Negi-sensei," or simply "Sensei!").

Honorifics can be expressions of respect or endearment. In the context of manga and anime, honorifics give insight into the nature of the relationship between characters. Many English translations leave out these important honorifics and therefore distort the feel of the original Japanese. Because Japanese honorifics contain nuances that English honorifics lack, it is our policy at Kodansha Comics not to translate them. Here, instead, is a guide to some of the honorifics you may encounter in Kodansha Comics manga.

-san: This is the most common honorific and is equivalent to Mr., Miss, Ms., or Mrs. It is the all-purpose honorific and can be used in any situation where politeness is required.

-sama: This is one level higher than "-san" and is used to confer great respect.

-dono: This comes from the word "tono," which means "lord." It is an even higher level than "-sama" and confers utmost respect.

-kun: This suffix is used at the end of boys' names to express familiarity or endearment. It is also sometimes used by men among friends, or when addressing someone younger or of a lower station.

-chan: This is used to express endearment, mostly toward girls. It is also used for little boys, pets, and even among lovers. It gives a sense of childish cuteness.

Bozu: This is an informal way to refer to a boy, similar to the English terms "kid" and "squirt."

Sempai/Senpai: This title suggests that the addressee is one's senior in a group or organization. It is most often used in a school setting, where underclassmen refer to their upperclassmen as "sempai." It can also be used in the workplace, such as when a newer employee addresses an employee who has seniority in the company.

Kohai: This is the opposite of "sempai" and is used toward underclassmen in school or newcomers in the workplace. It connotes that the addressee is of a lower station.

Sensei: Literally meaning "one who has come before," this title is used for teachers, doctors, or masters of any profession or art.

-[blank]: This is usually forgotten in these lists, but it is perhaps the most significant difference between Japanese and English. The lack of honorific means that the speaker has permission to address the person in a very intimate way. Usually, only family, spouses, or very close friends have this kind of permission. Known as *yobisute*, it can be gratifying when someone who has earned the intimacy starts to call one by one's name without an honorific. But when that intimacy hasn't been earned, it can be very insulting.

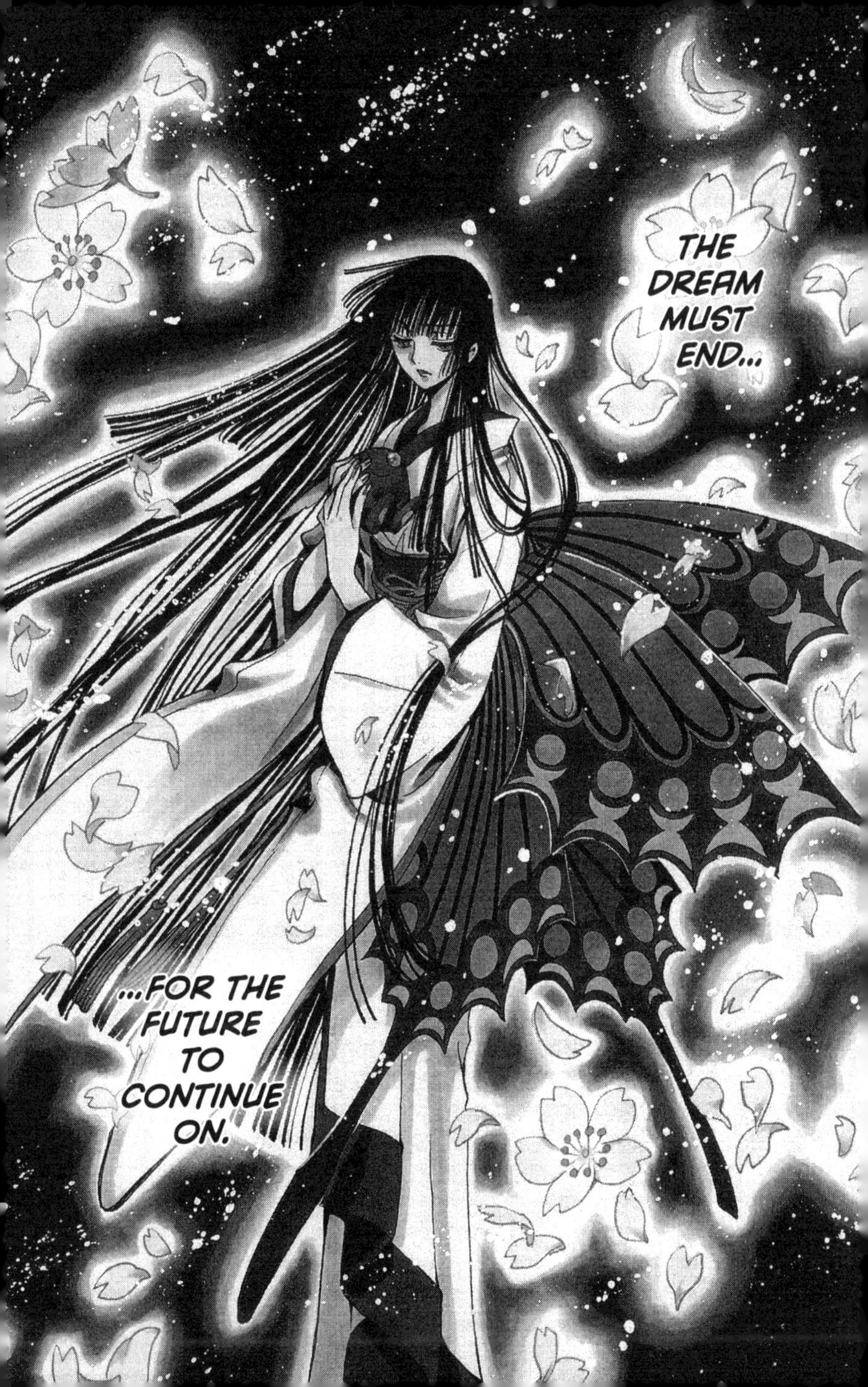
THE DREAM MUST END...
...FOR THE FUTURE TO CONTINUE ON.

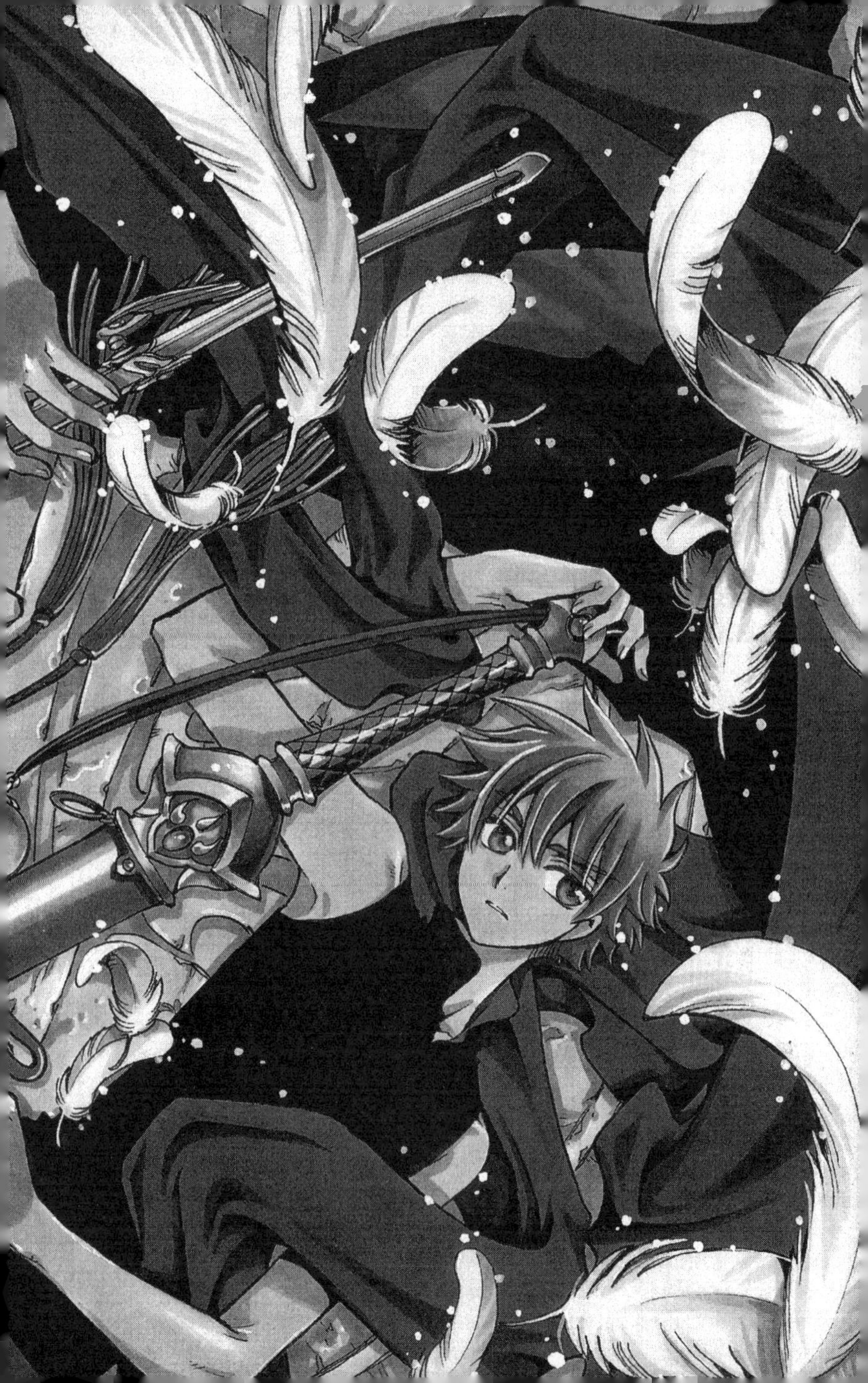

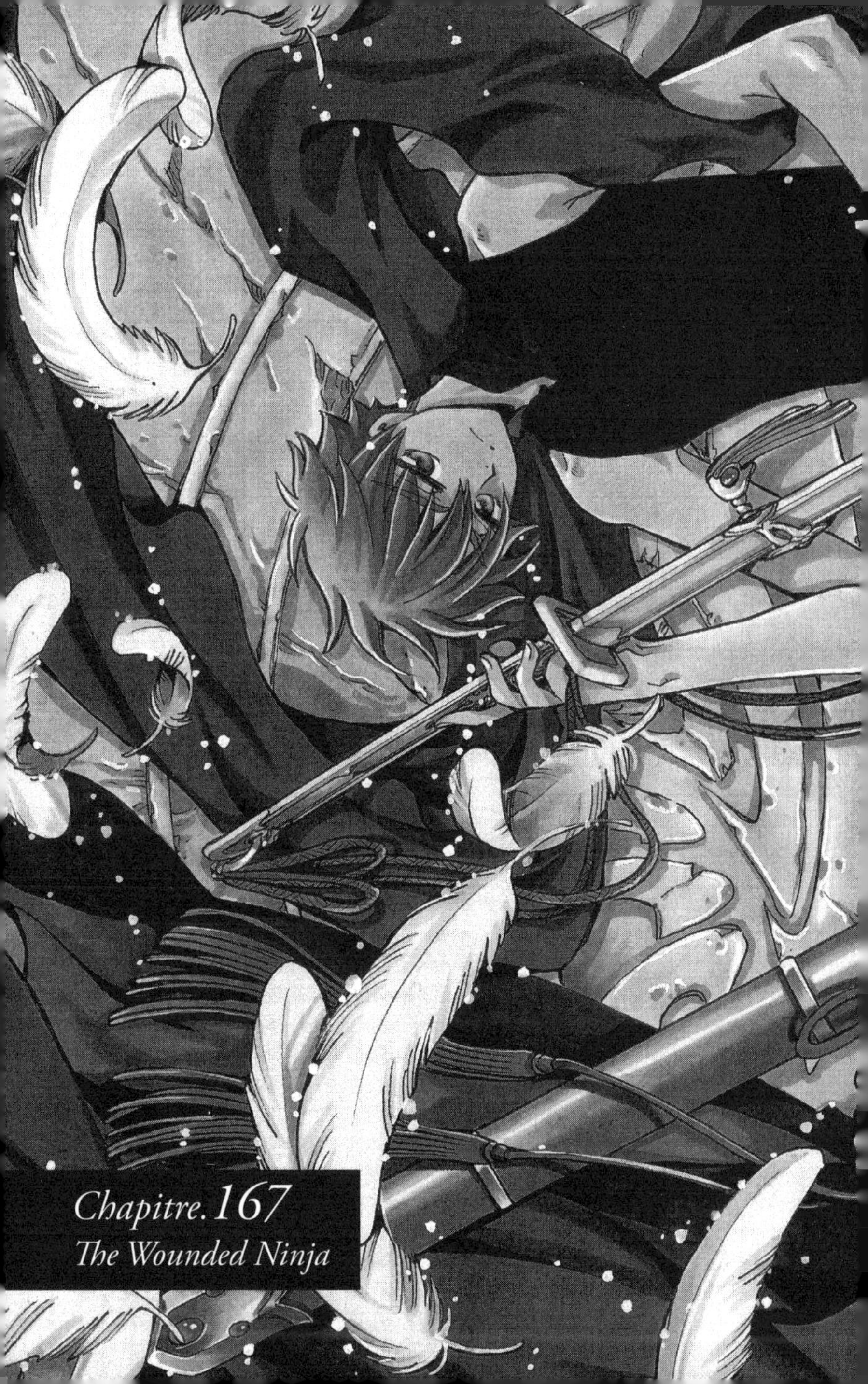
Chapitre. 167
The Wounded Ninja

ツバサ

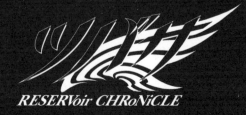

RESERVoir CHRoNiCLE

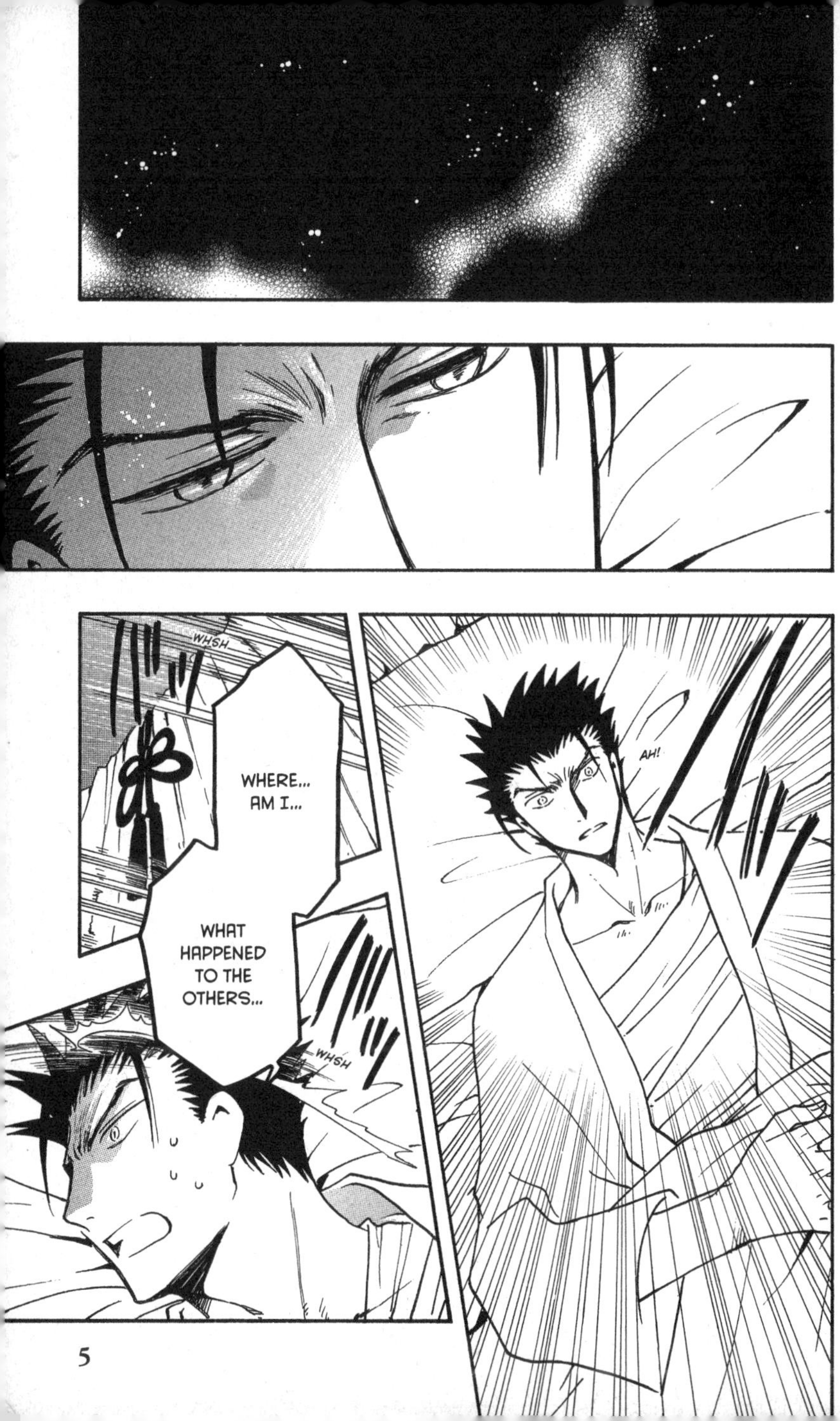
AH!
WHSH
WHERE... AM I...
WHAT HAPPENED TO THE OTHERS...
WHSH

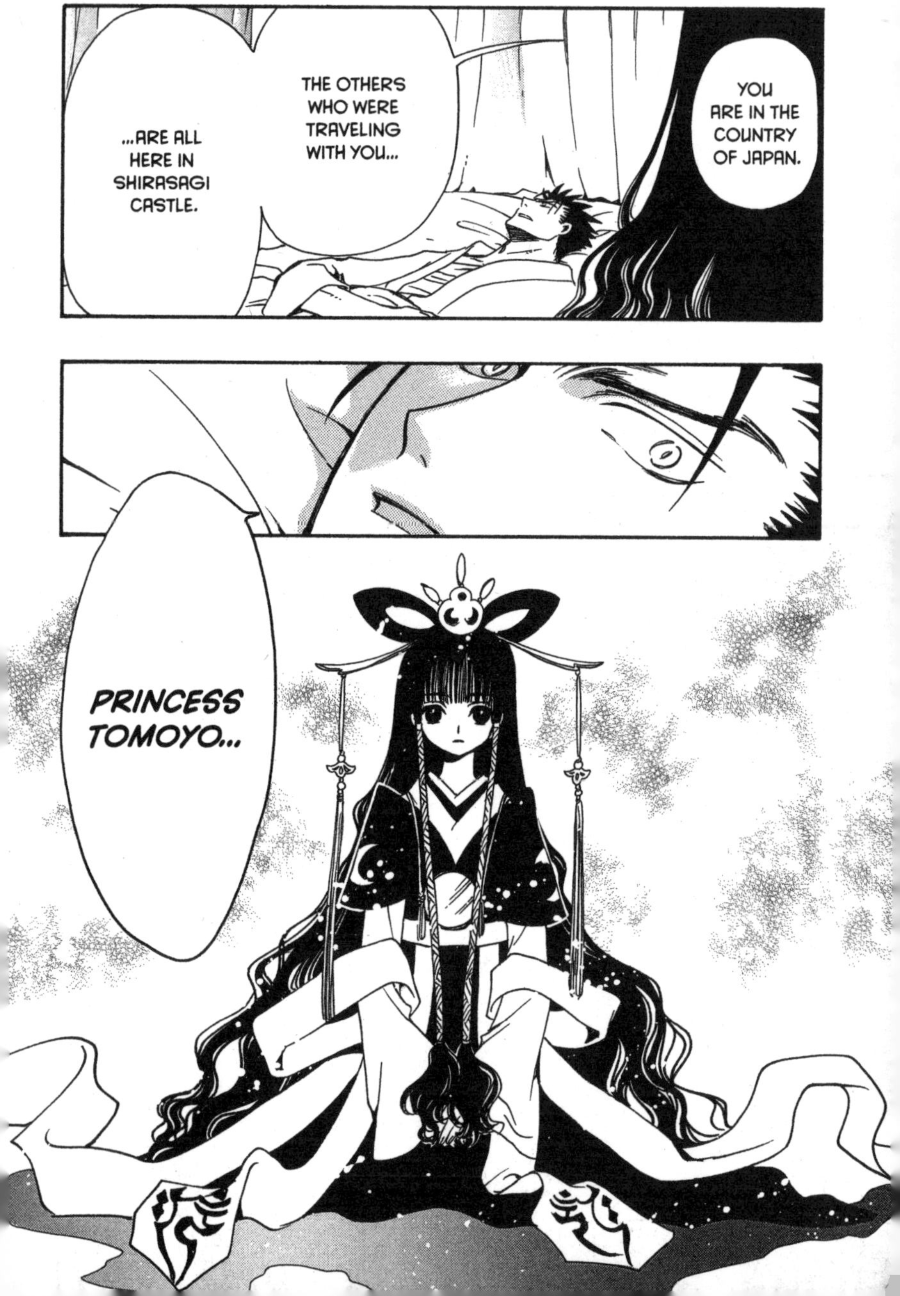
YOU ARE IN THE COUNTRY OF JAPAN.
THE OTHERS WHO WERE TRAVELING WITH YOU...
...ARE ALL HERE IN SHIRASAGI CASTLE.
PRINCESS TOMOYO...

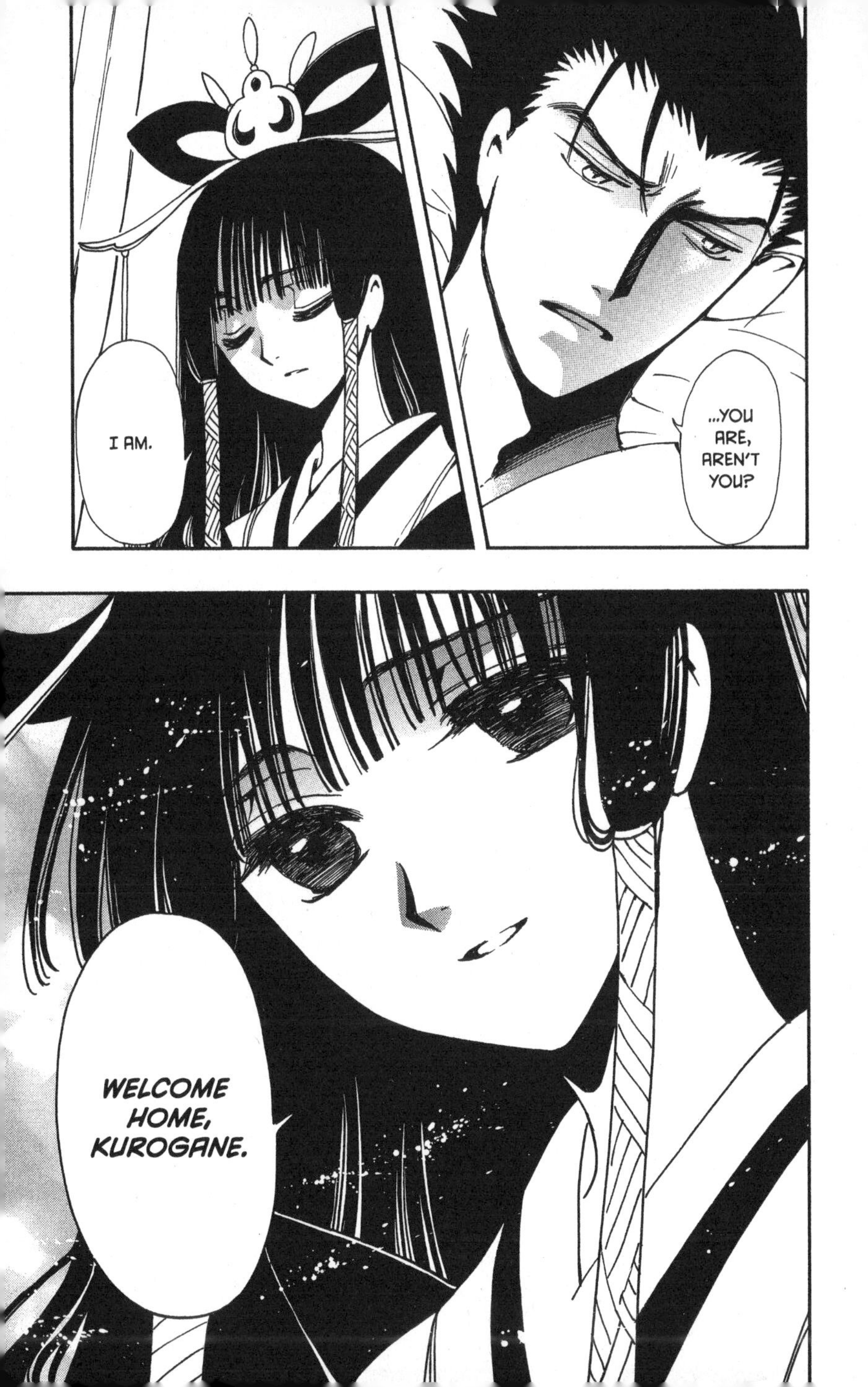
...YOU ARE, AREN'T YOU?
I AM.
WELCOME HOME, KUROGANE.

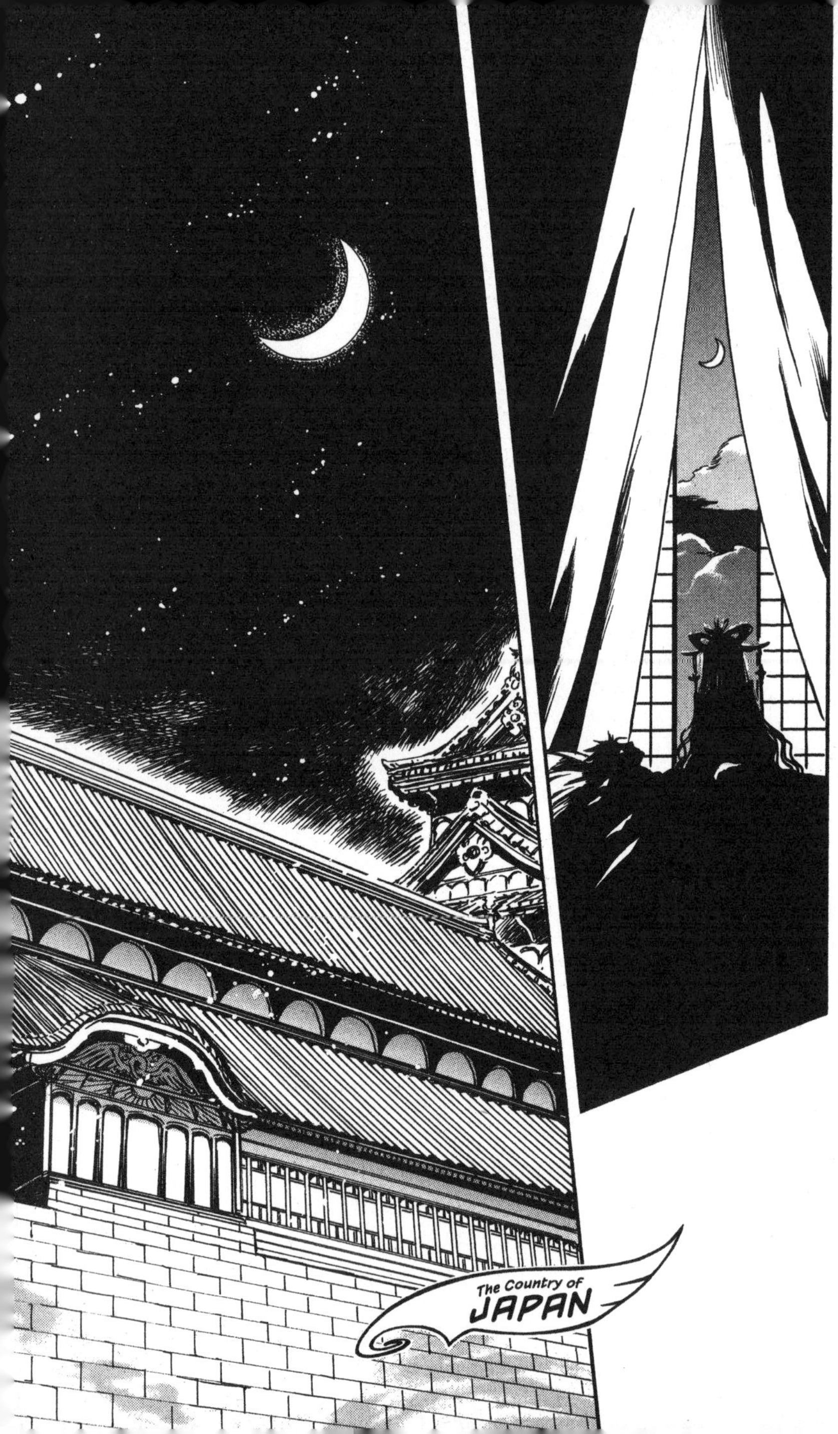
The Country of
JAPAN

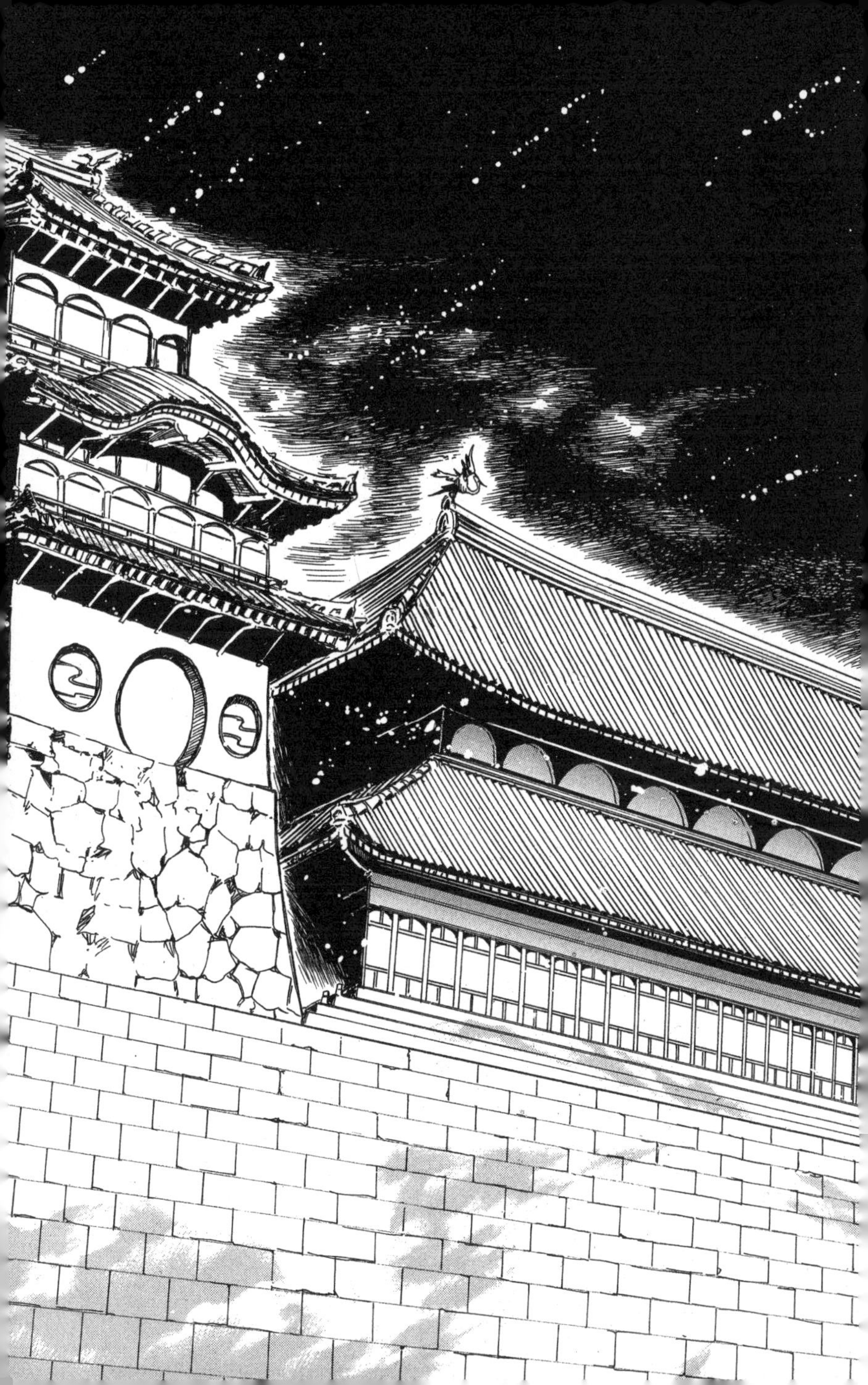

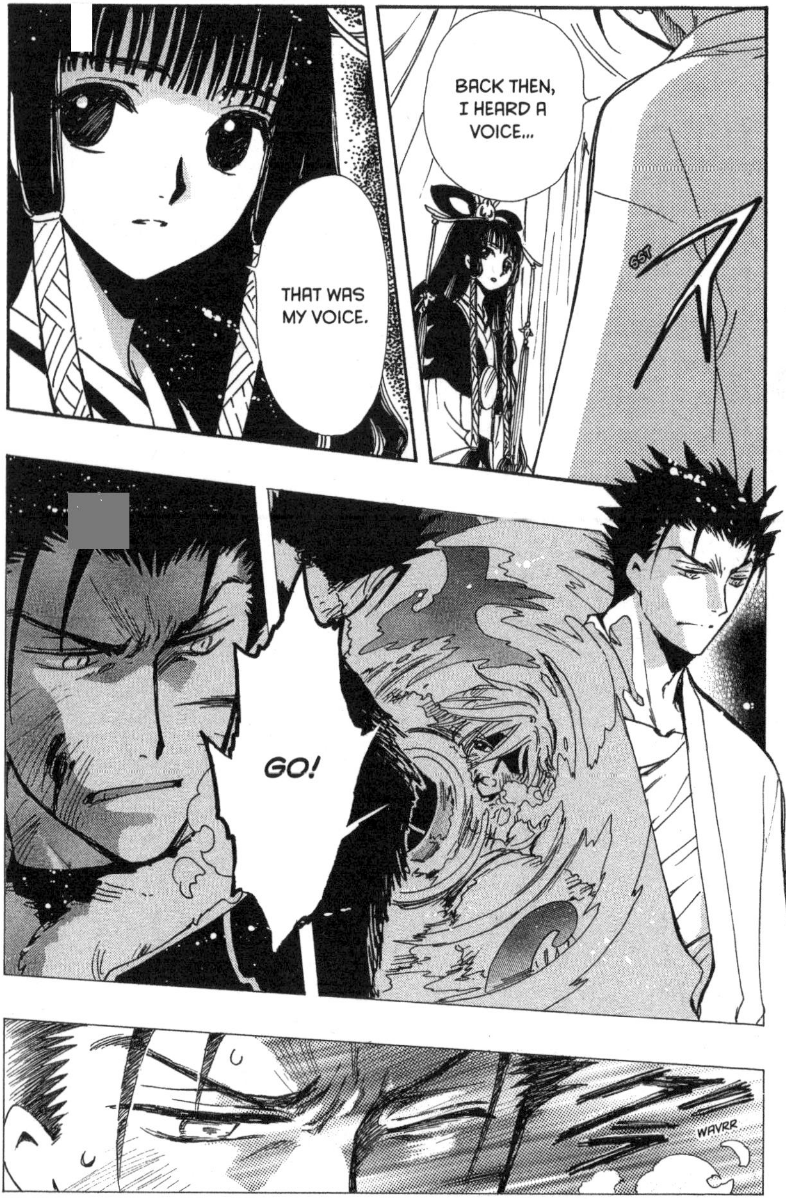
BACK THEN, I HEARD A VOICE...
SST
THAT WAS MY VOICE.
GO!
WAVRR

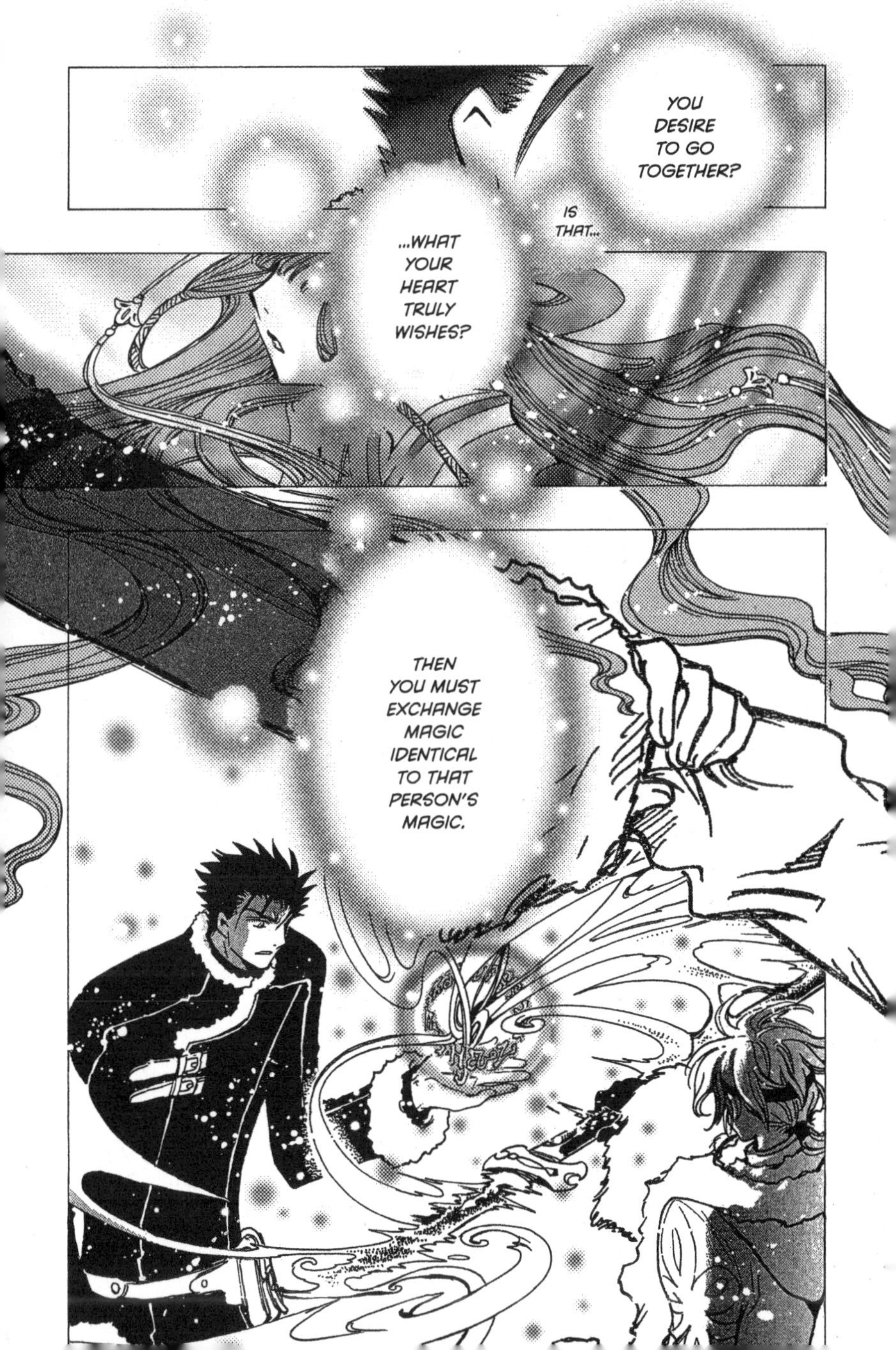
YOU DESIRE TO GO TOGETHER?
IS THAT...
...WHAT YOUR HEART TRULY WISHES?
THEN YOU MUST EXCHANGE MAGIC IDENTICAL TO THAT PERSON'S MAGIC.

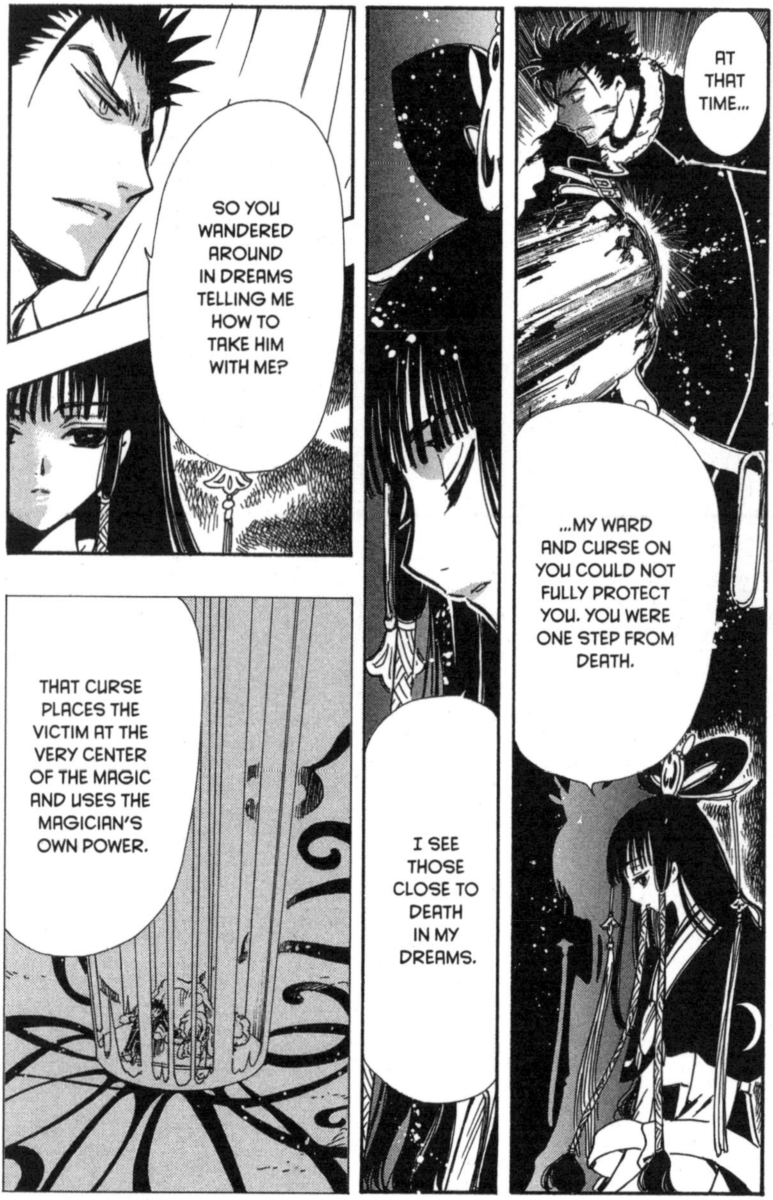
AT THAT TIME...
...MY WARD AND CURSE ON YOU COULD NOT FULLY PROTECT YOU. YOU WERE ONE STEP FROM DEATH.
I SEE THOSE CLOSE TO DEATH IN MY DREAMS.
SO YOU WANDERED AROUND IN DREAMS TELLING ME HOW TO TAKE HIM WITH ME?
THAT CURSE PLACES THE VICTIM AT THE VERY CENTER OF THE MAGIC AND USES THE MAGICIAN'S OWN POWER.

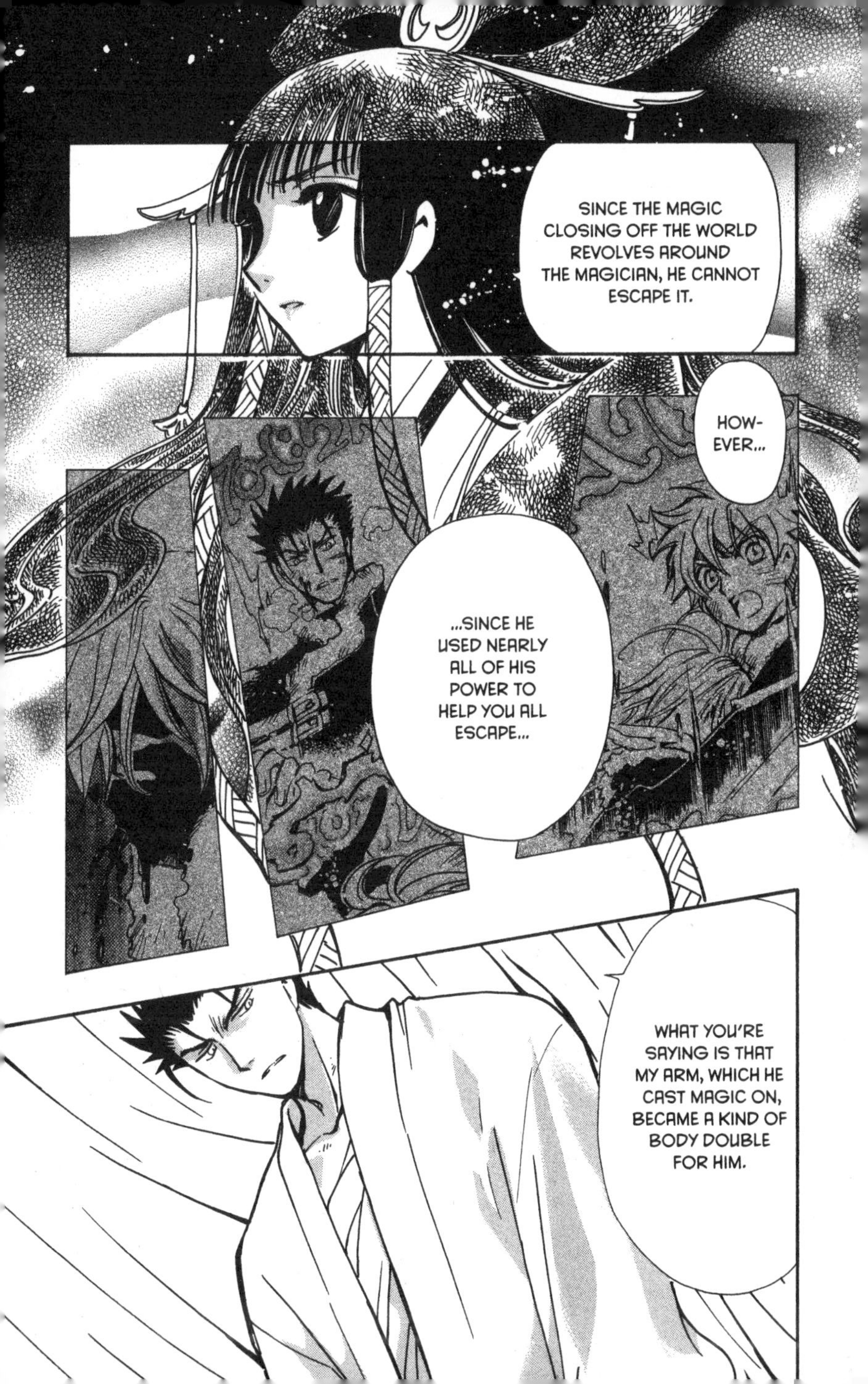
SINCE THE MAGIC CLOSING OFF THE WORLD REVOLVES AROUND THE MAGICIAN, HE CANNOT ESCAPE IT.
HOW-EVER...
...SINCE HE USED NEARLY ALL OF HIS POWER TO HELP YOU ALL ESCAPE...
WHAT YOU'RE SAYING IS THAT MY ARM, WHICH HE CAST MAGIC ON, BECAME A KIND OF BODY DOUBLE FOR HIM.

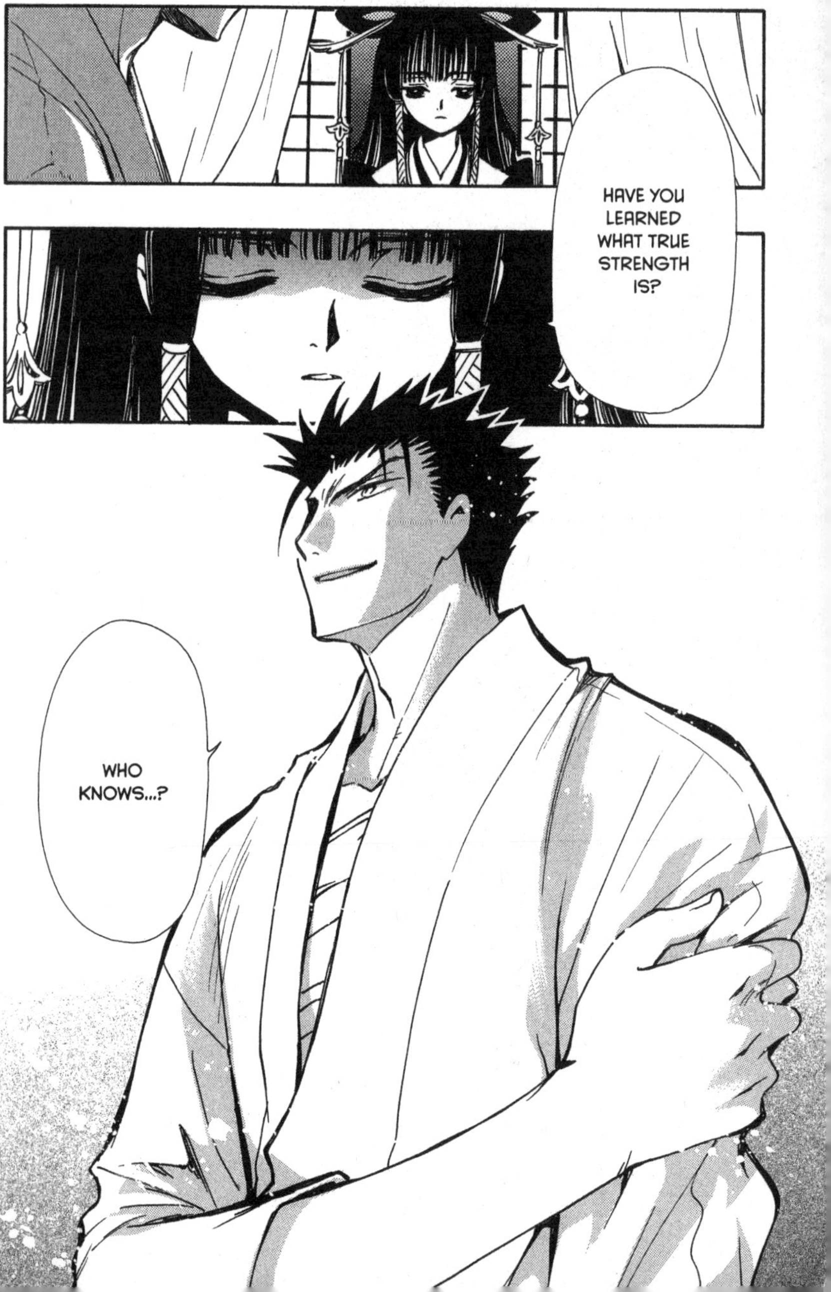
HAVE YOU LEARNED WHAT TRUE STRENGTH IS?
WHO KNOWS...?

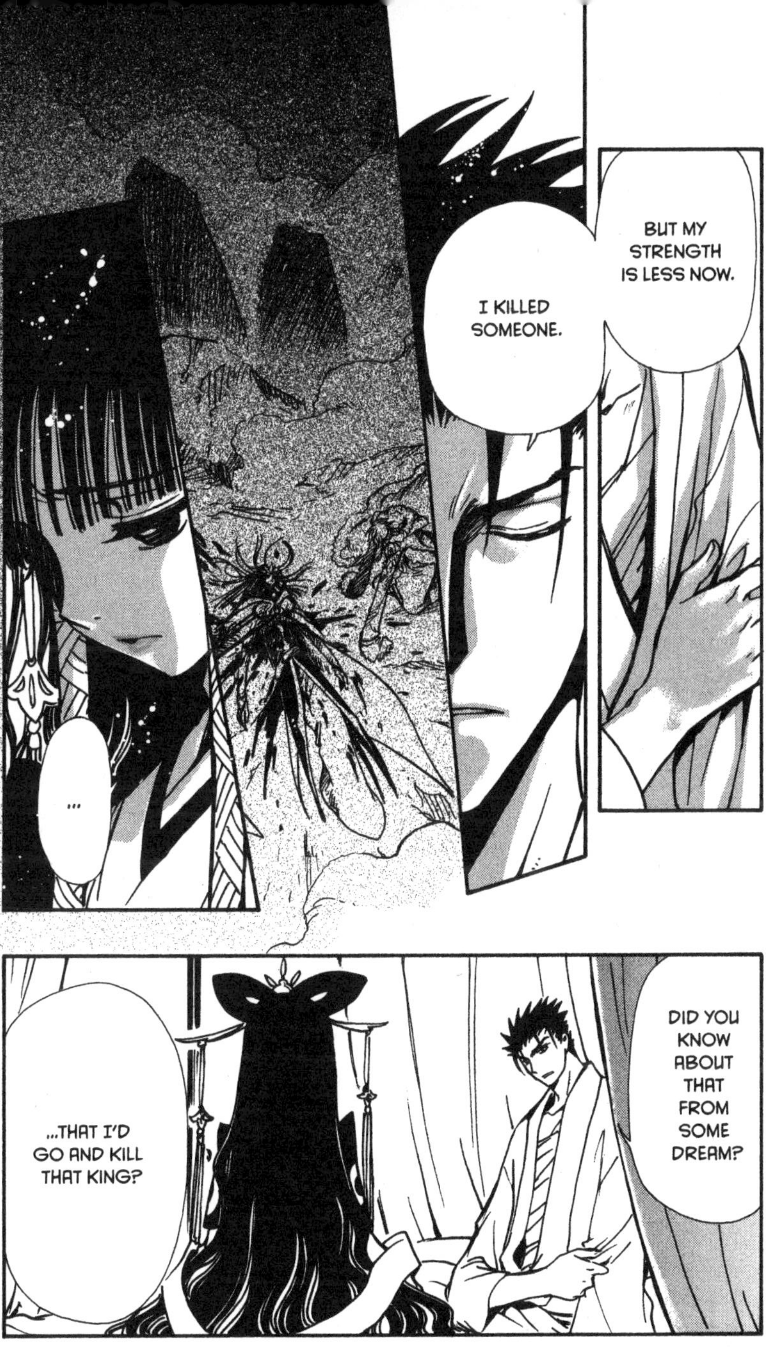
BUT MY STRENGTH IS LESS NOW.
I KILLED SOMEONE.
...
DID YOU KNOW ABOUT THAT FROM SOME DREAM?
...THAT I'D GO AND KILL THAT KING?

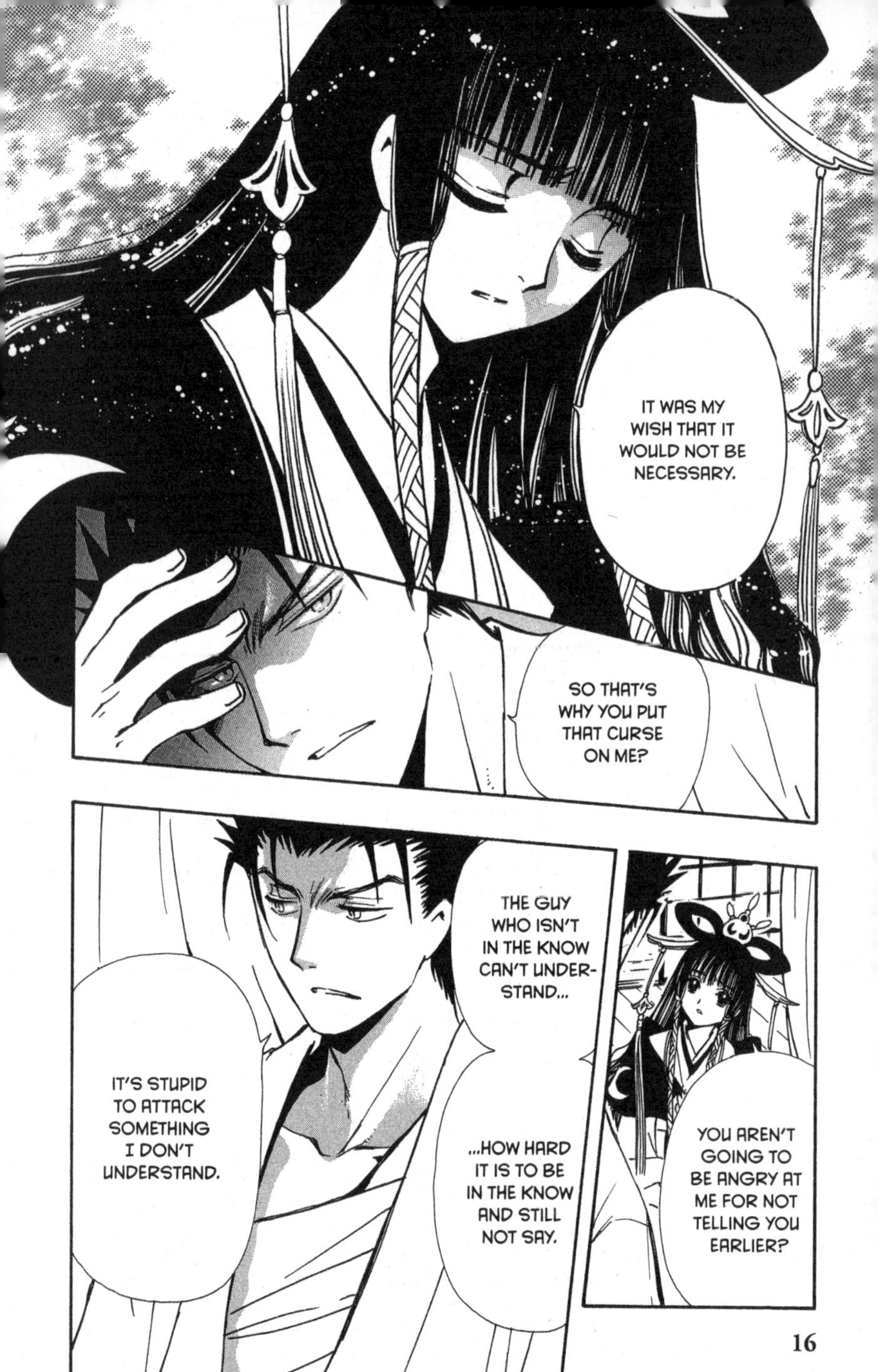
IT WAS MY WISH THAT IT WOULD NOT BE NECESSARY.
SO THAT'S WHY YOU PUT THAT CURSE ON ME?
YOU AREN'T GOING TO BE ANGRY AT ME FOR NOT TELLING YOU EARLIER?
THE GUY WHO ISN'T IN THE KNOW CAN'T UNDER-STAND...
...HOW HARD IT IS TO BE IN THE KNOW AND STILL NOT SAY.
IT'S STUPID TO ATTACK SOMETHING I DON'T UNDERSTAND.

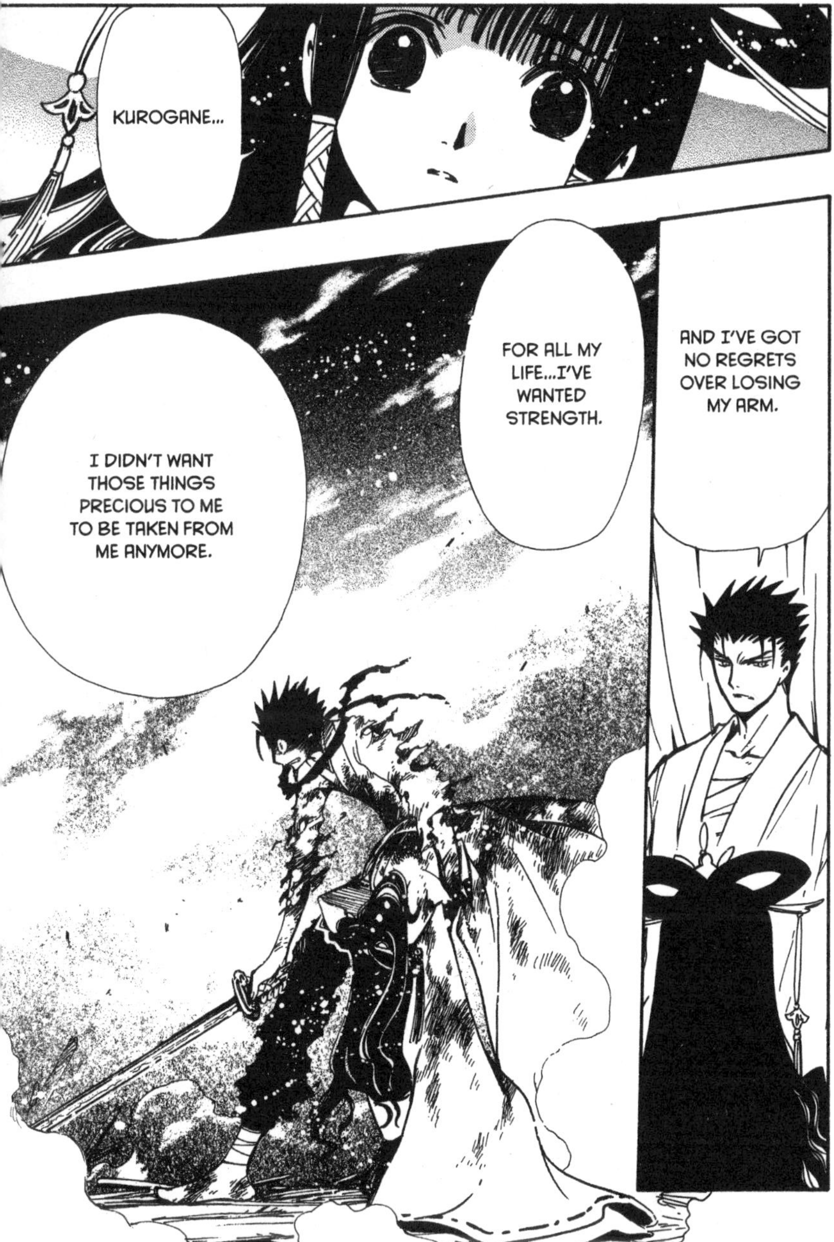
KUROGANE...
FOR ALL MY LIFE...I'VE WANTED STRENGTH.
I DIDN'T WANT THOSE THINGS PRECIOUS TO ME TO BE TAKEN FROM ME ANYMORE.
AND I'VE GOT NO REGRETS OVER LOSING MY ARM.

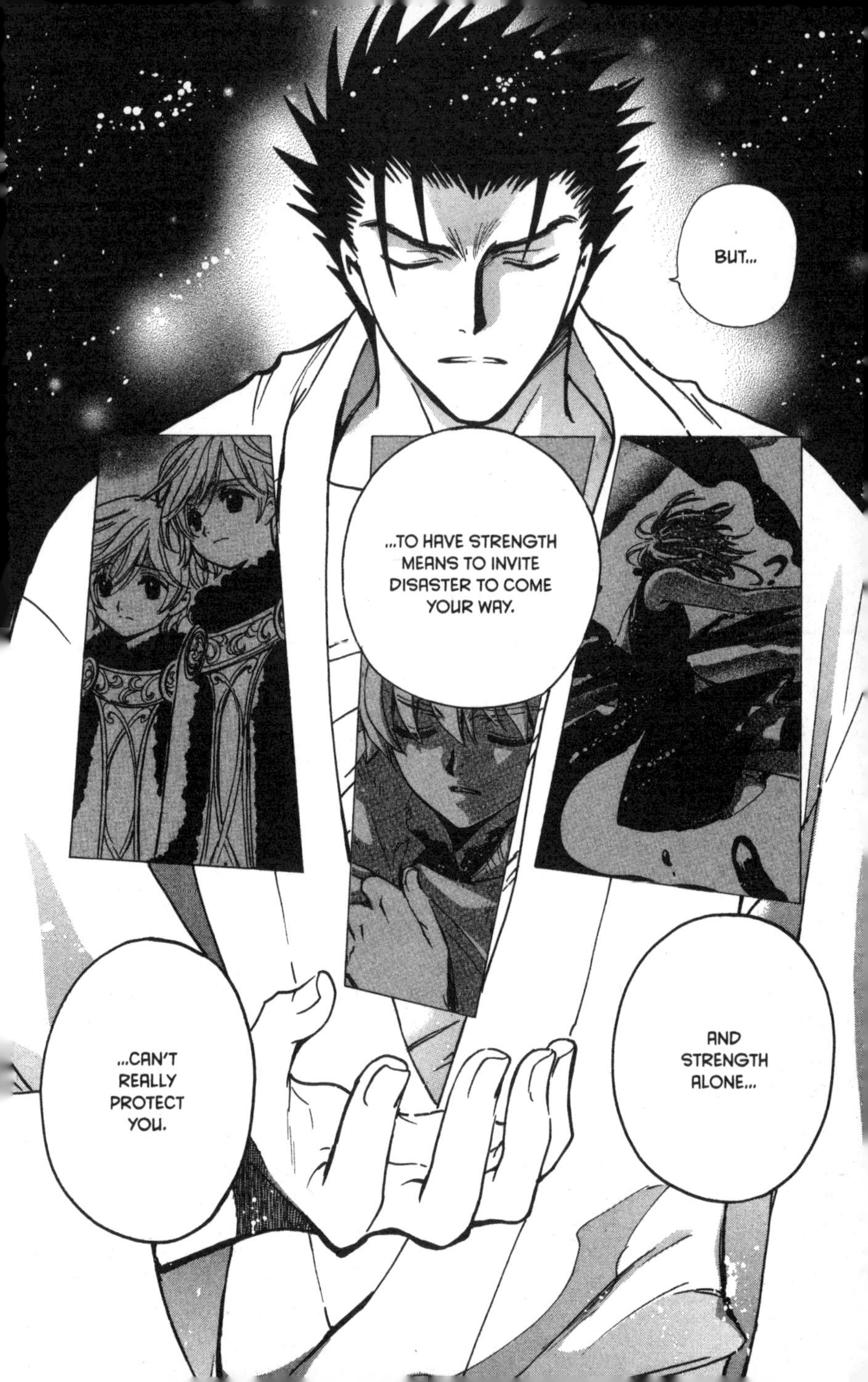
BUT...
...TO HAVE STRENGTH MEANS TO INVITE DISASTER TO COME YOUR WAY.
AND STRENGTH ALONE...
...CAN'T REALLY PROTECT YOU.

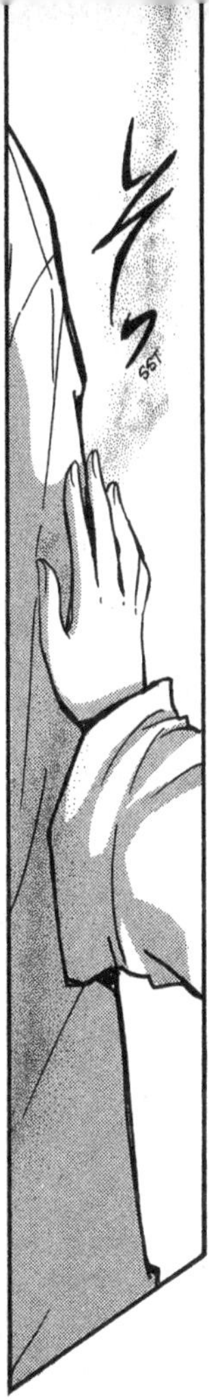
SST
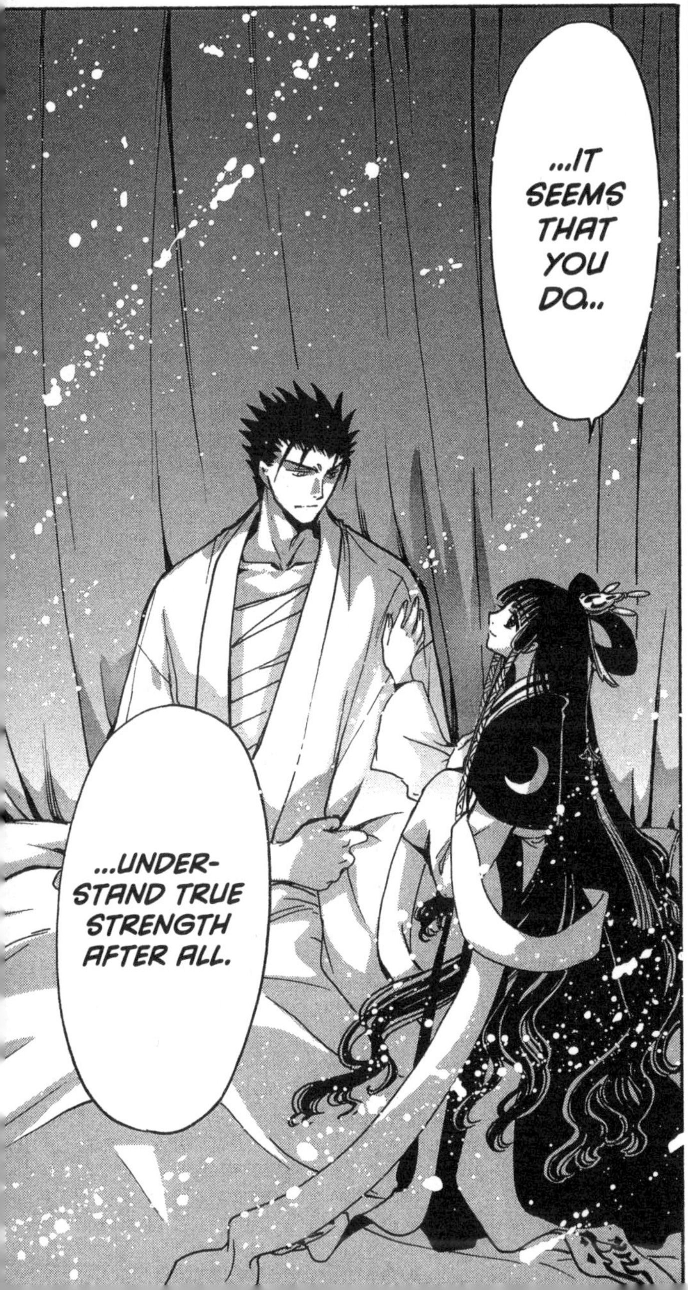
...IT SEEMS THAT YOU DO...
...UNDER-STAND TRUE STRENGTH AFTER ALL.

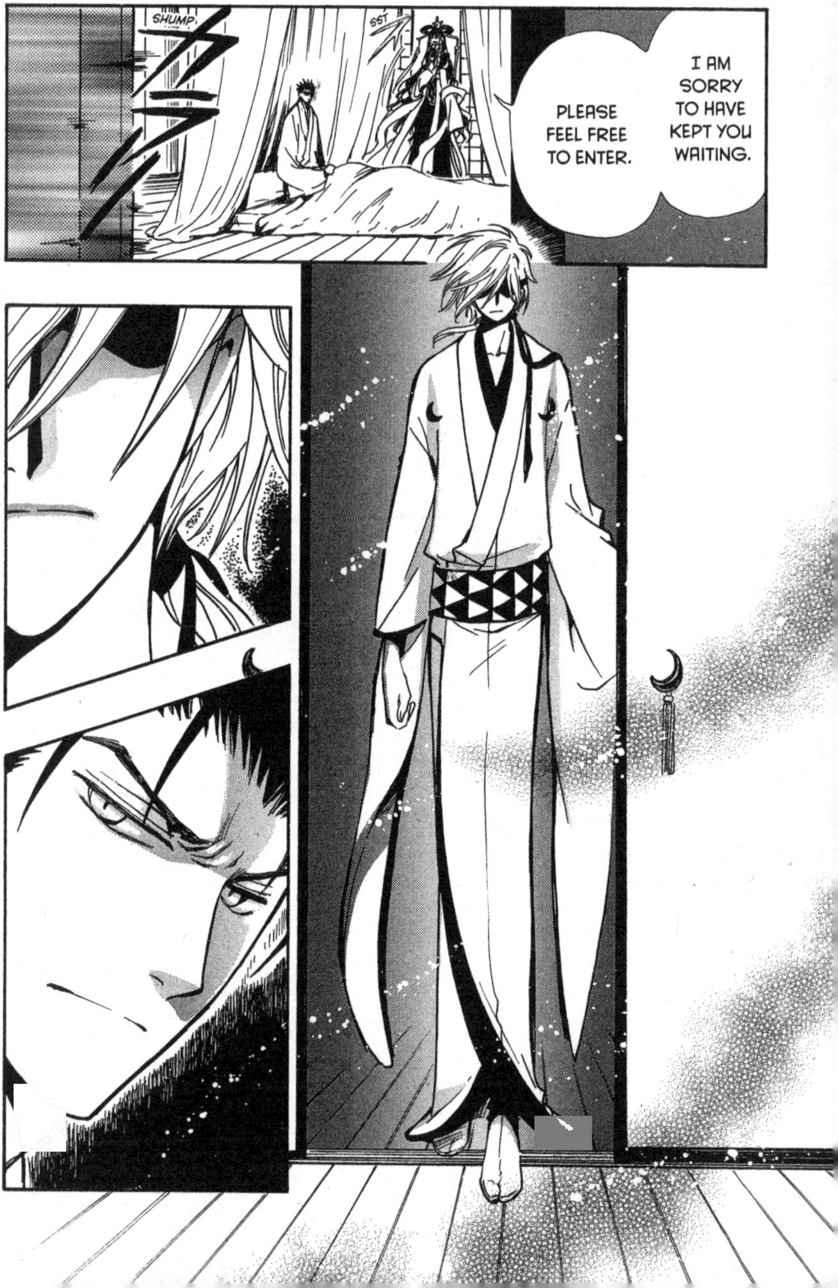
I AM SORRY TO HAVE KEPT YOU WAITING.
PLEASE FEEL FREE TO ENTER.
SST
SHUMP

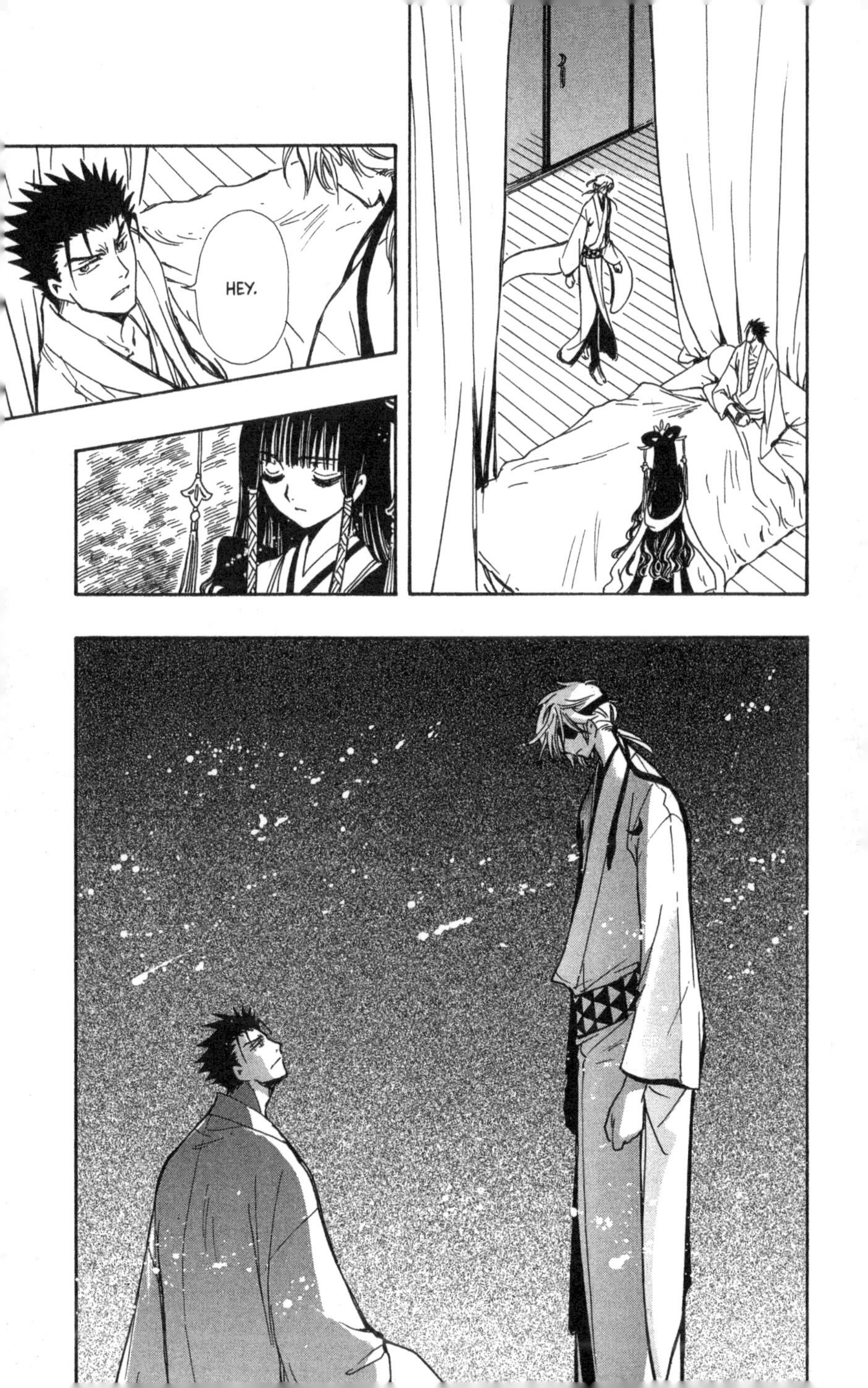
HEY.

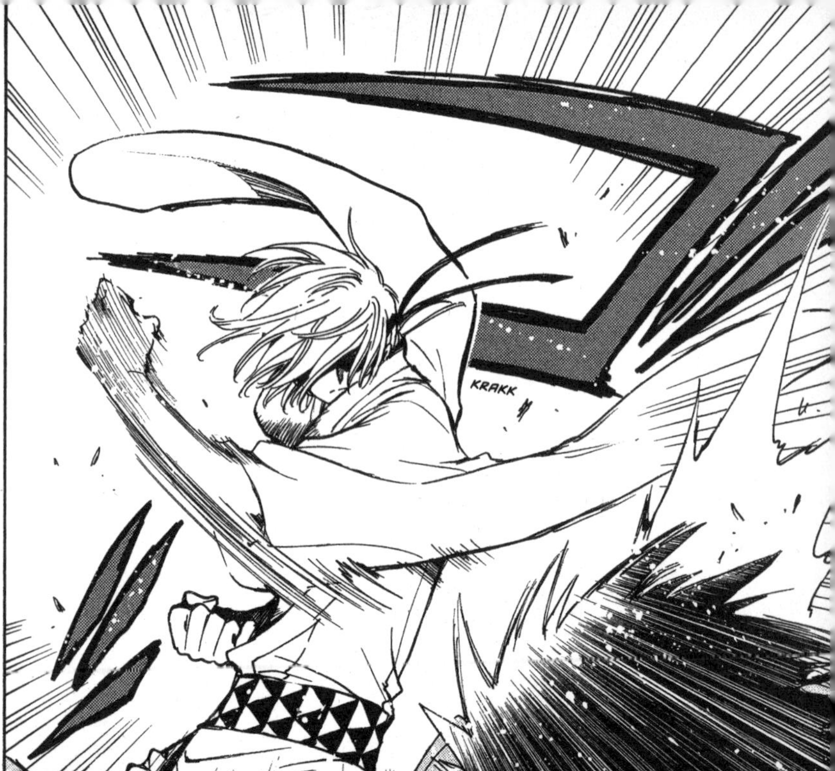
KRAKK
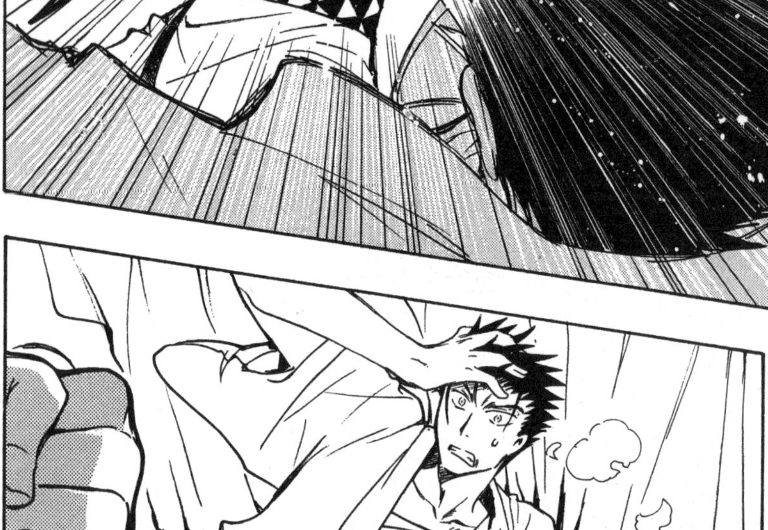

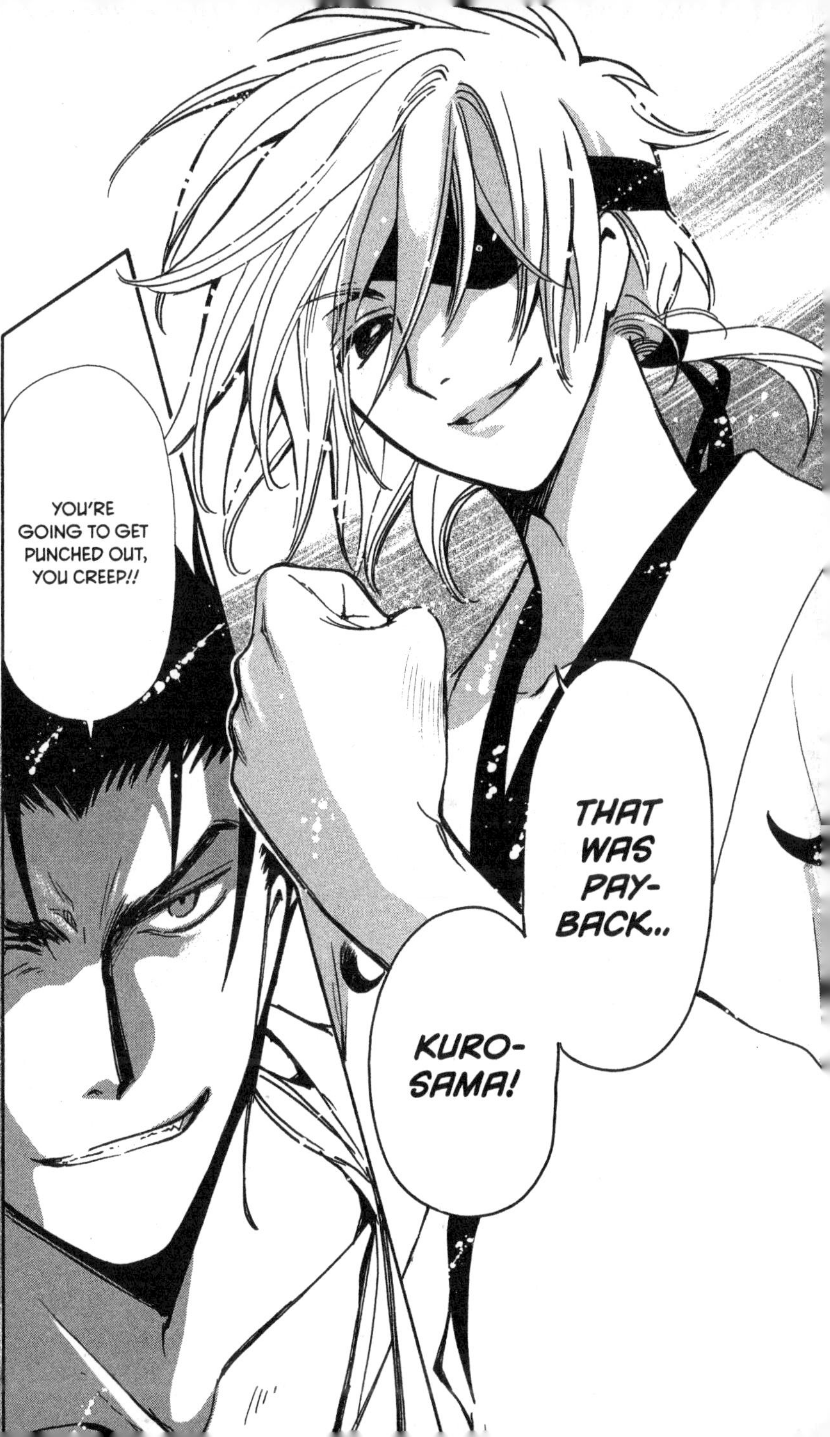
THAT WAS PAY-BACK..
KURO-SAMA!
YOU'RE GOING TO GET PUNCHED OUT, YOU CREEP!!

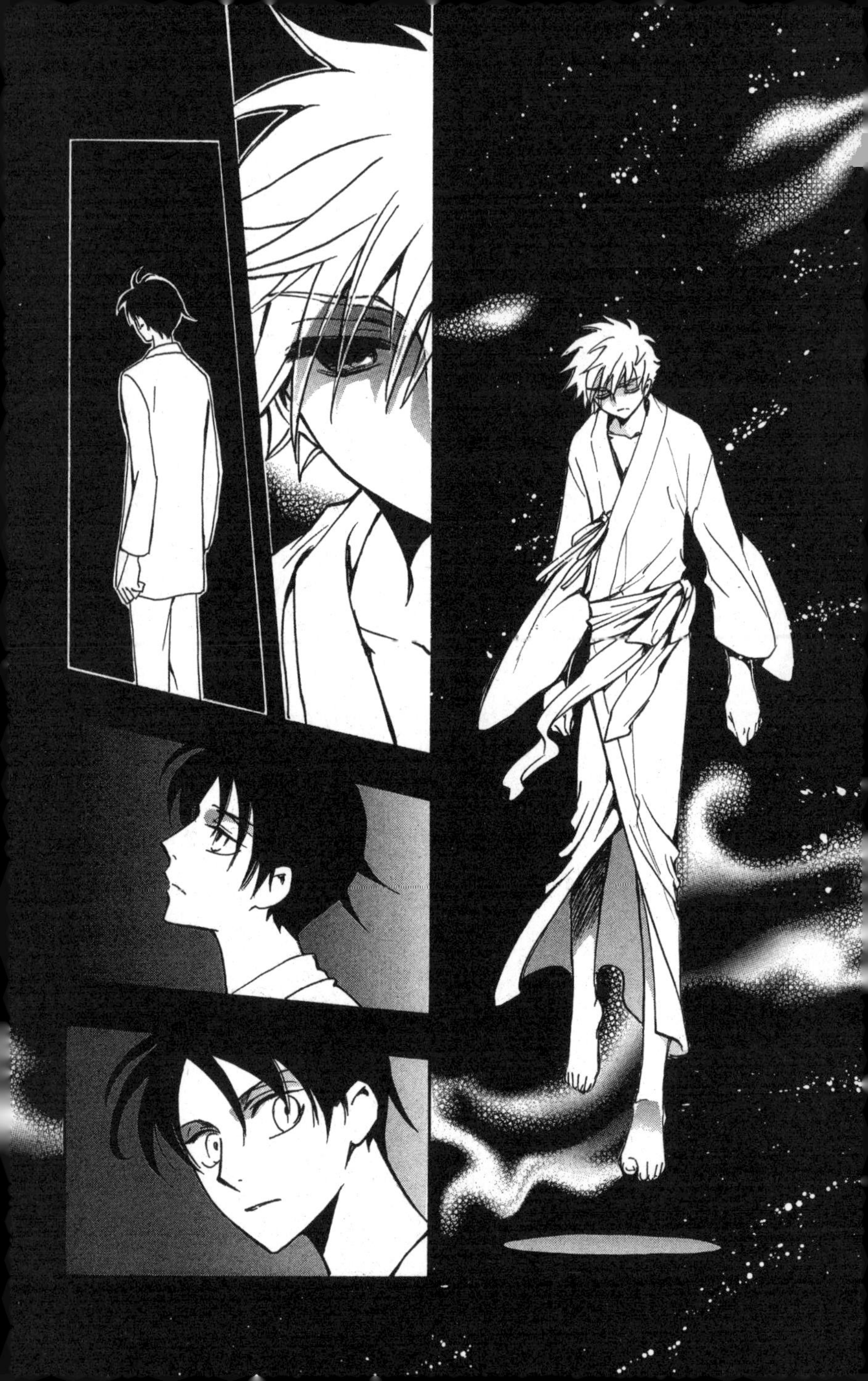

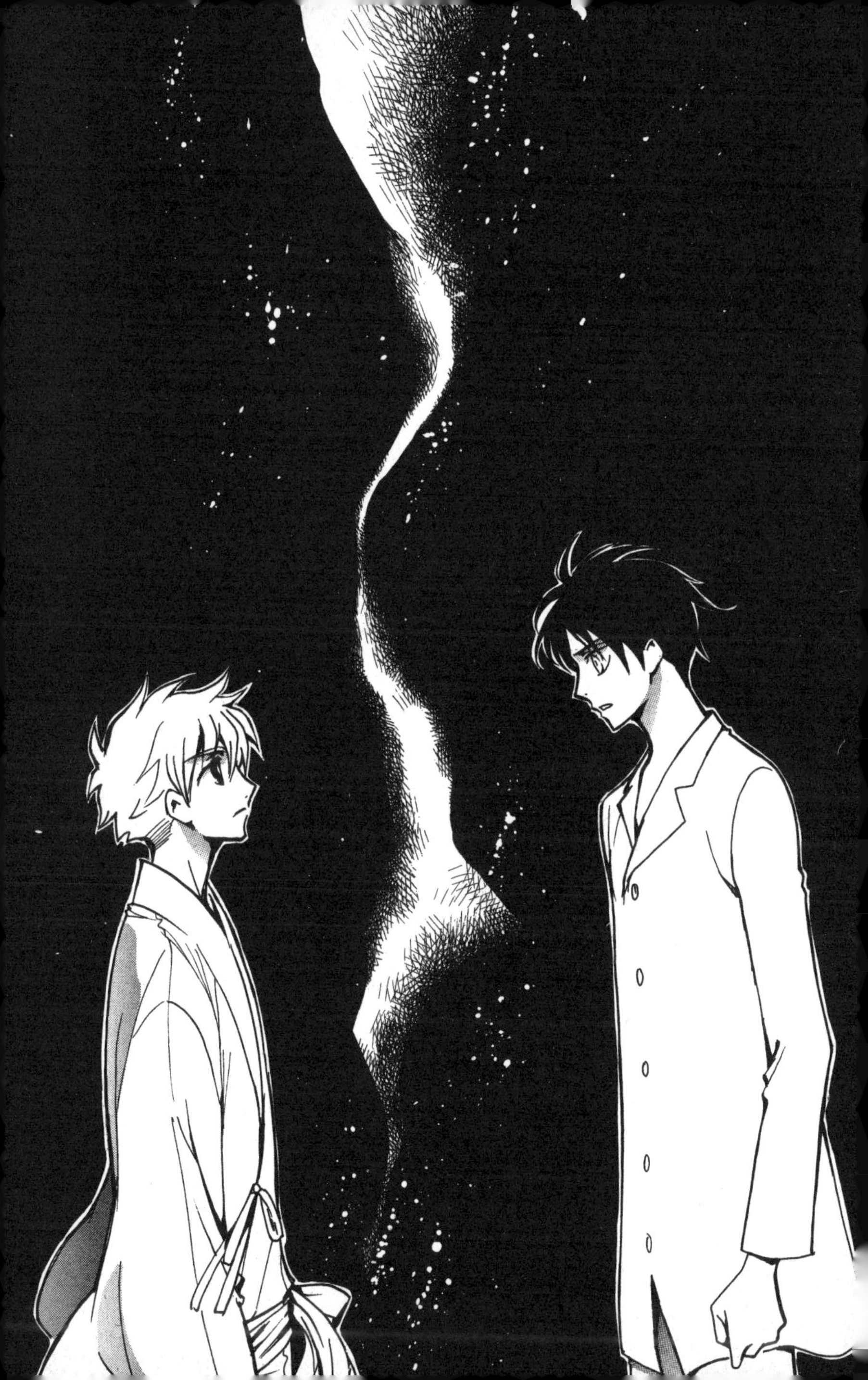

ツバサ

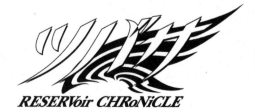

RESERVoir CHRoNiCLE

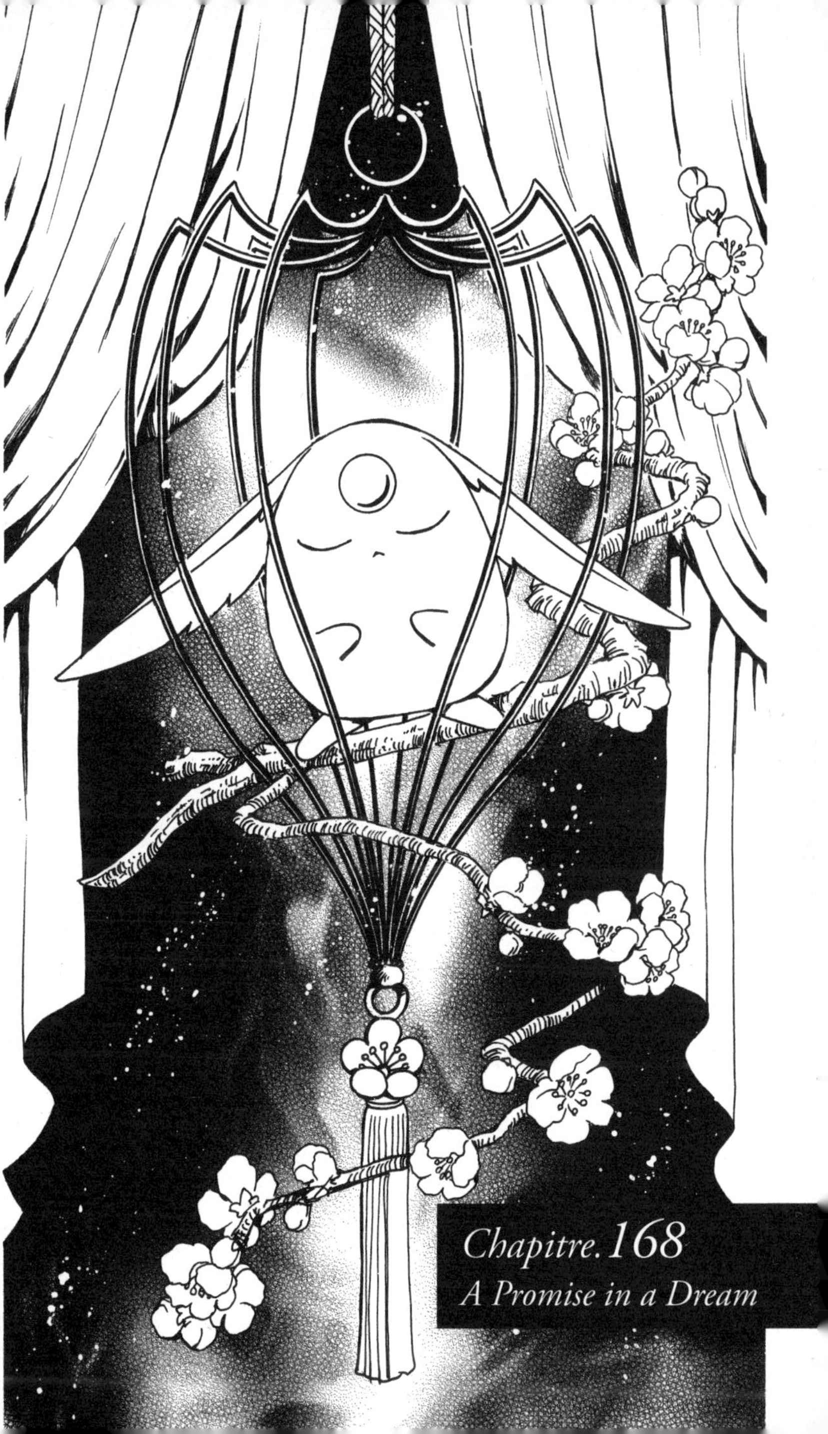
Chapitre.168
A Promise in a Dream

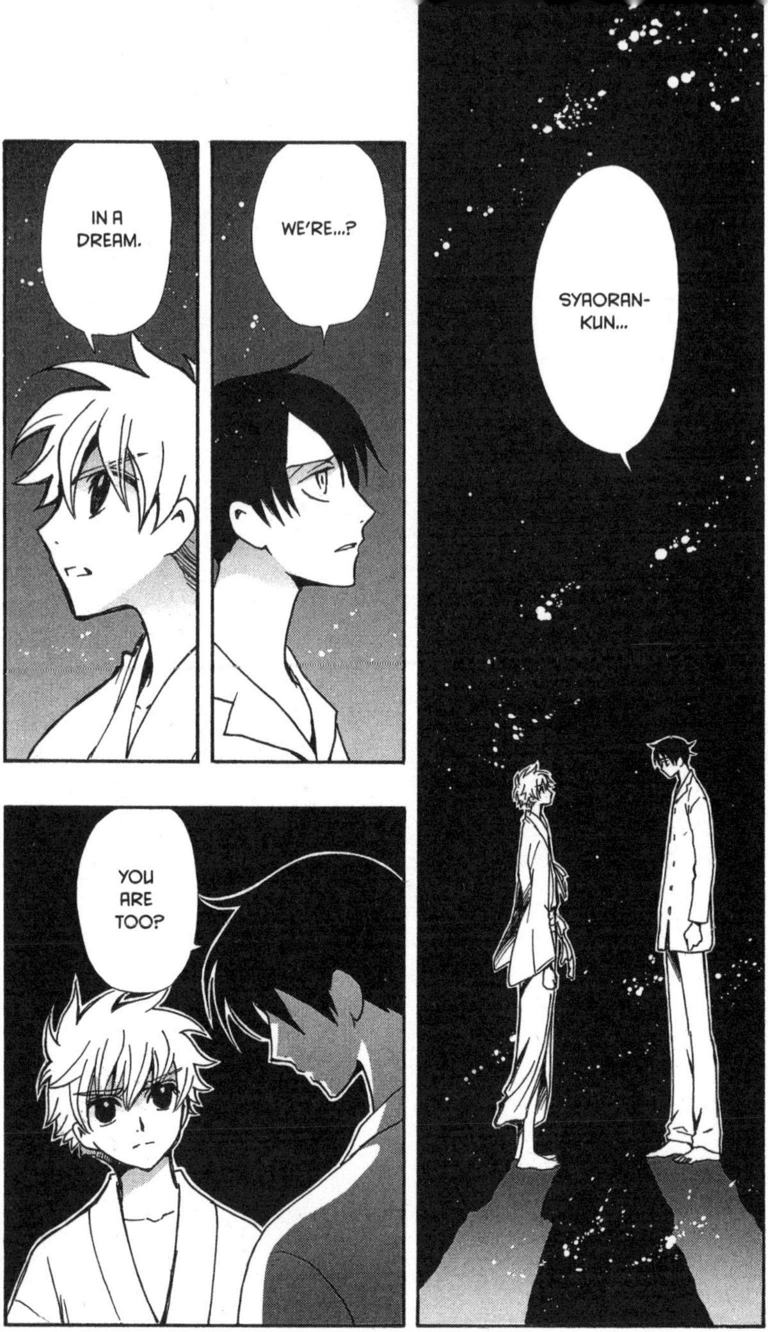
SYAORAN-KUN...
WE'RE...?
IN A DREAM.
YOU ARE TOO?

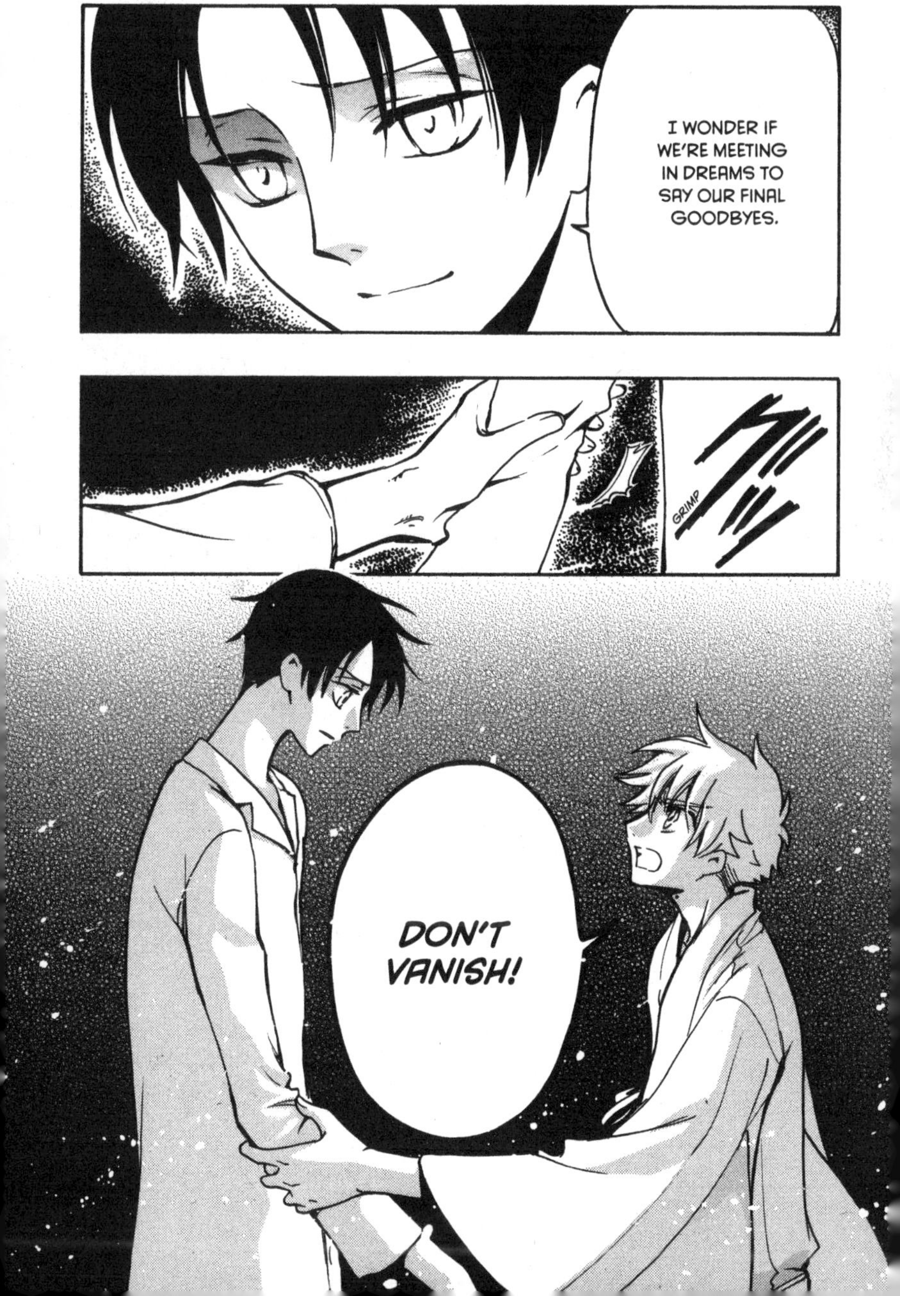
I WONDER IF WE'RE MEETING IN DREAMS TO SAY OUR FINAL GOODBYES.
GRIMP
DON'T VANISH!

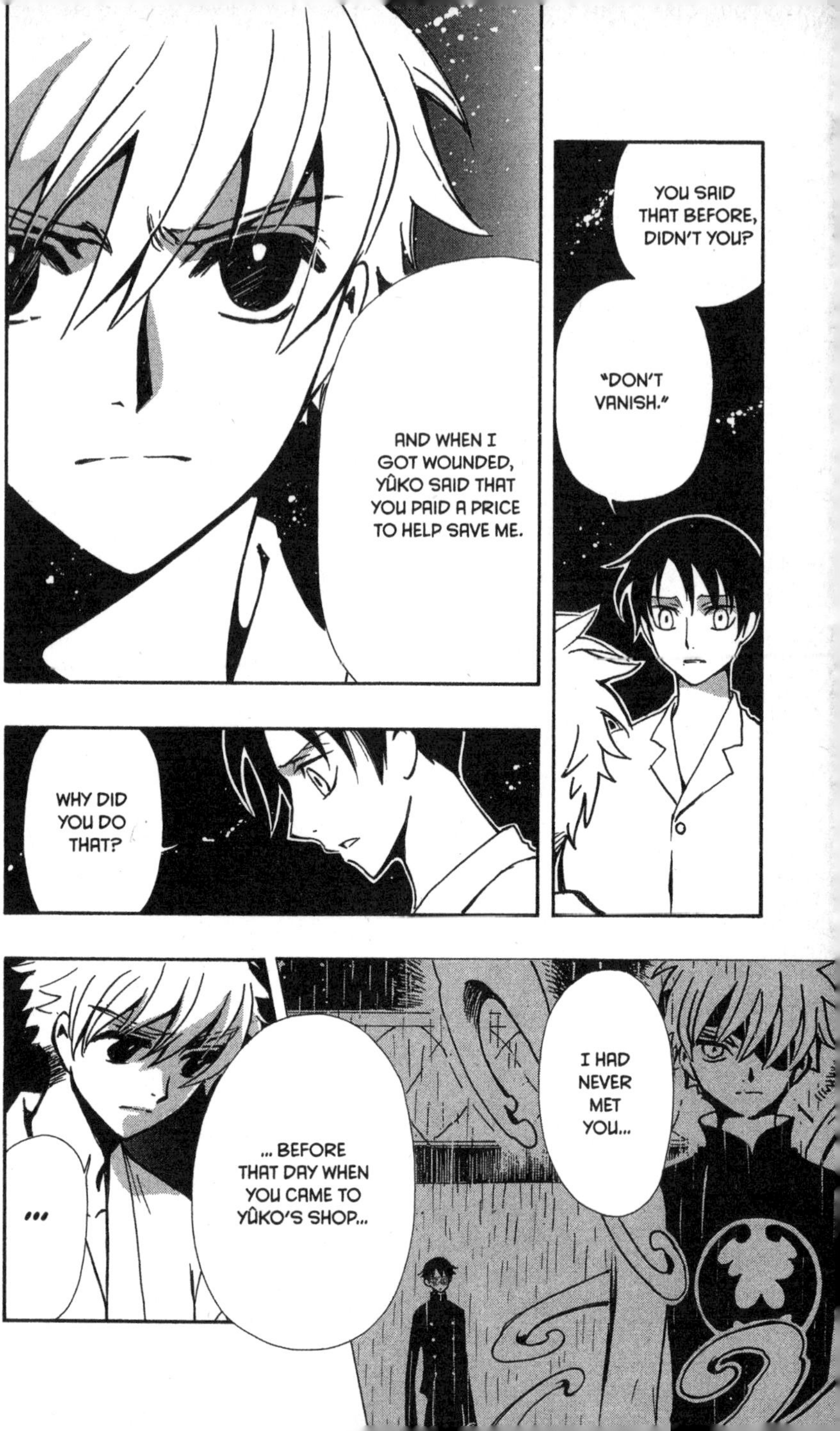
YOU SAID THAT BEFORE, DIDN'T YOU?
"DON'T VANISH."
AND WHEN I GOT WOUNDED, YÛKO SAID THAT YOU PAID A PRICE TO HELP SAVE ME.
WHY DID YOU DO THAT?
I HAD NEVER MET YOU...
... BEFORE THAT DAY WHEN YOU CAME TO YÛKO'S SHOP...
...

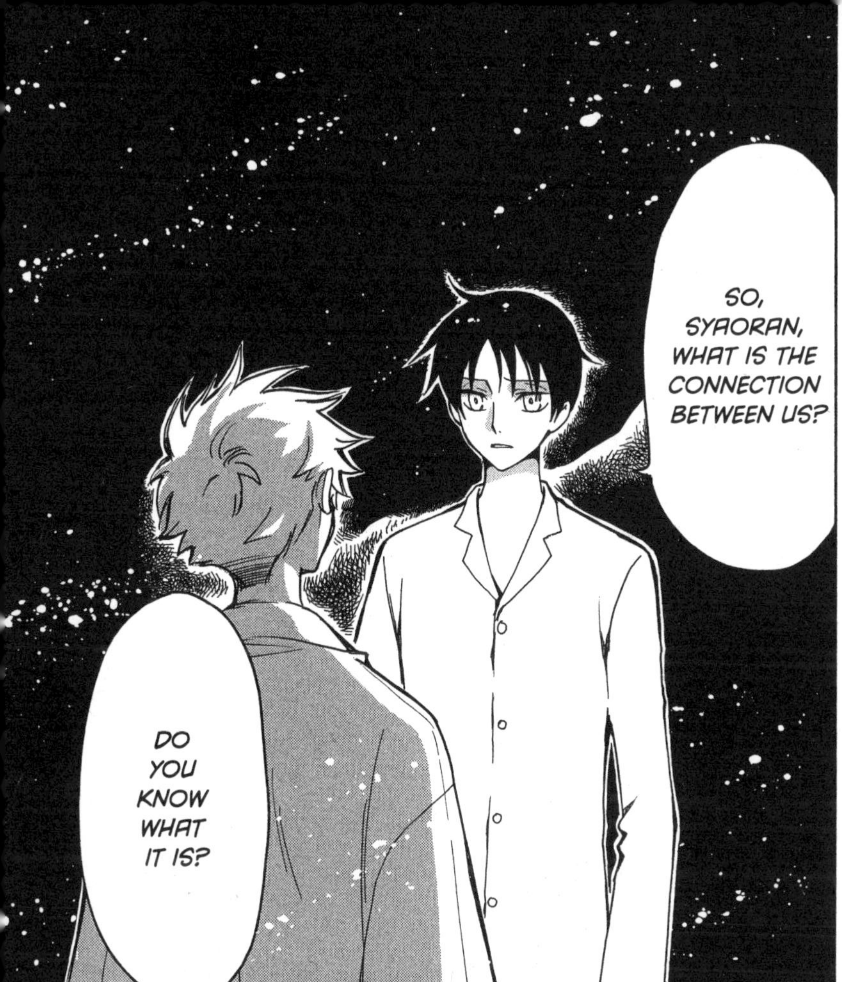
SO, SYAORAN, WHAT IS THE CONNECTION BETWEEN US?
DO YOU KNOW WHAT IT IS?

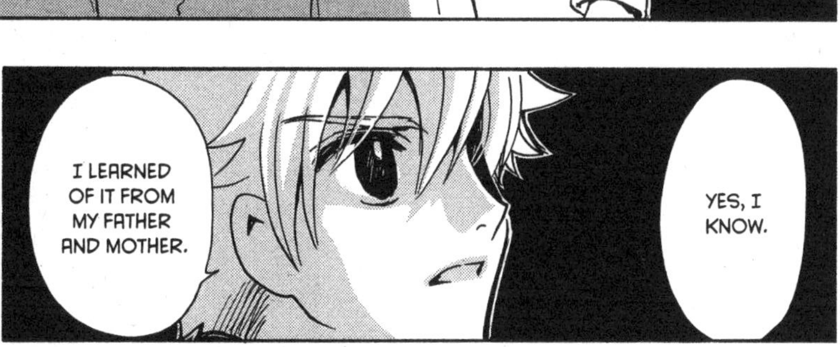
YES, I KNOW.
I LEARNED OF IT FROM MY FATHER AND MOTHER.

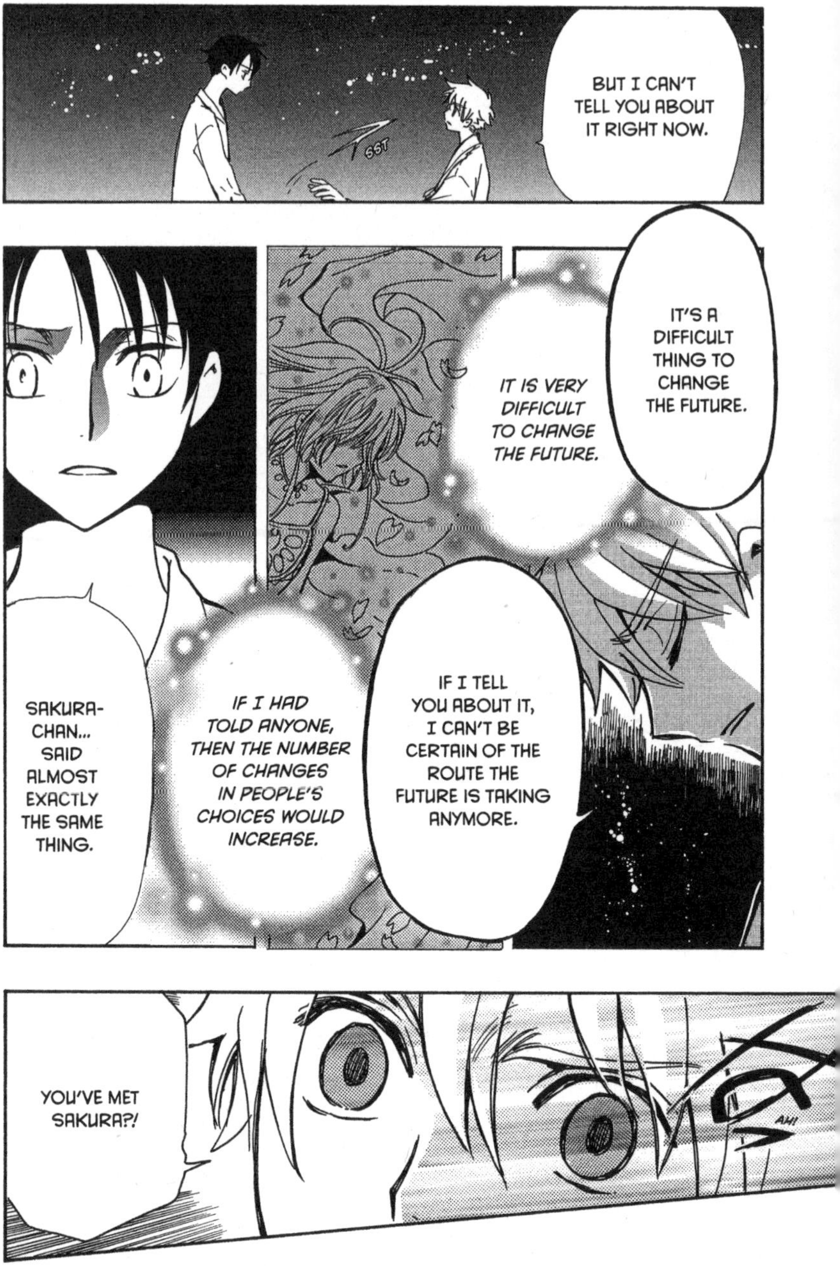
BUT I CAN'T TELL YOU ABOUT IT RIGHT NOW.
SST
IT'S A DIFFICULT THING TO CHANGE THE FUTURE.
IT IS VERY DIFFICULT TO CHANGE THE FUTURE.
IF I TELL YOU ABOUT IT, I CAN'T BE CERTAIN OF THE ROUTE THE FUTURE IS TAKING ANYMORE.
IF I HAD TOLD ANYONE, THEN THE NUMBER OF CHANGES IN PEOPLE'S CHOICES WOULD INCREASE.
SAKURA-CHAN... SAID ALMOST EXACTLY THE SAME THING.
AH!
YOU'VE MET SAKURA?!

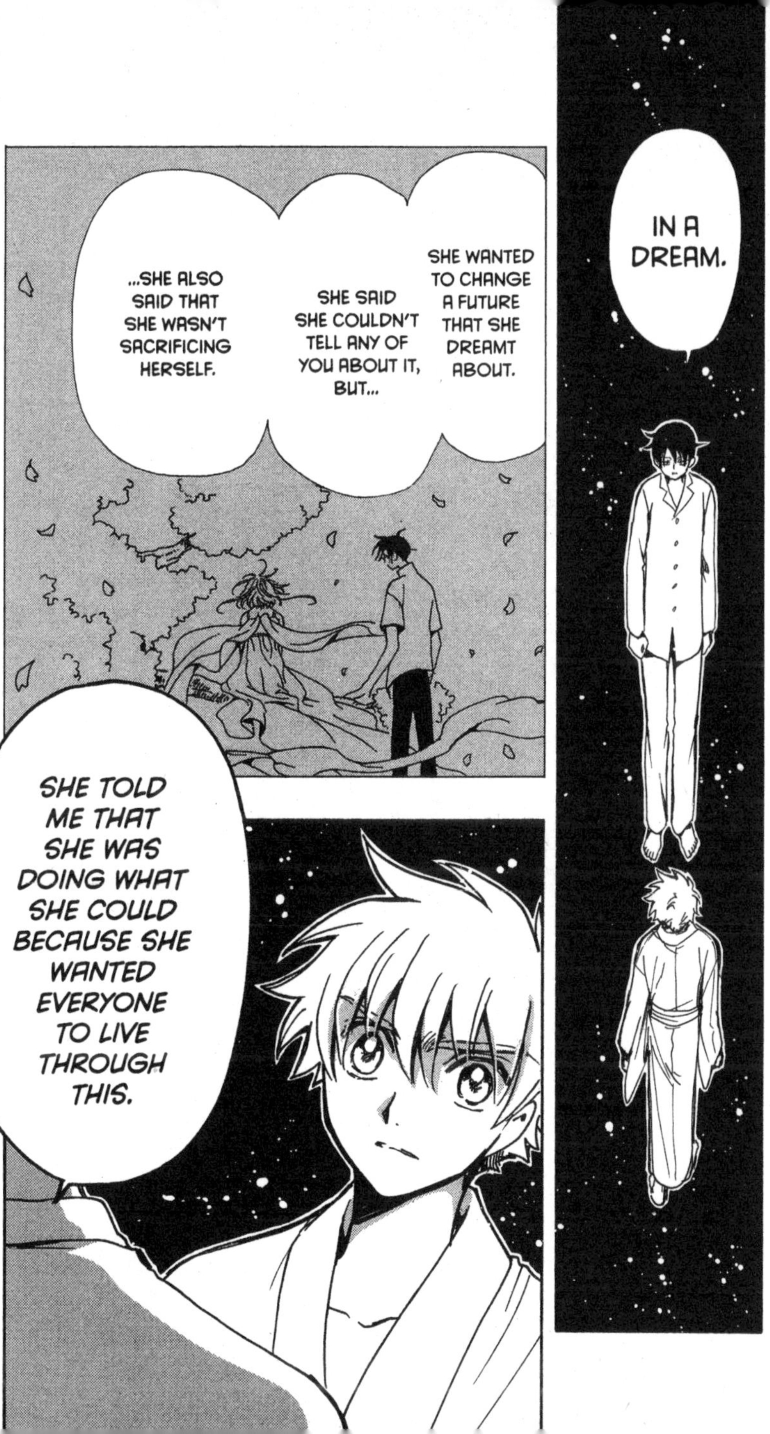
IN A DREAM.
SHE WANTED TO CHANGE A FUTURE THAT SHE DREAMT ABOUT.
SHE SAID SHE COULDN'T TELL ANY OF YOU ABOUT IT, BUT...
...SHE ALSO SAID THAT SHE WASN'T SACRIFICING HERSELF.
SHE TOLD ME THAT SHE WAS DOING WHAT SHE COULD BECAUSE SHE WANTED EVERYONE TO LIVE THROUGH THIS.

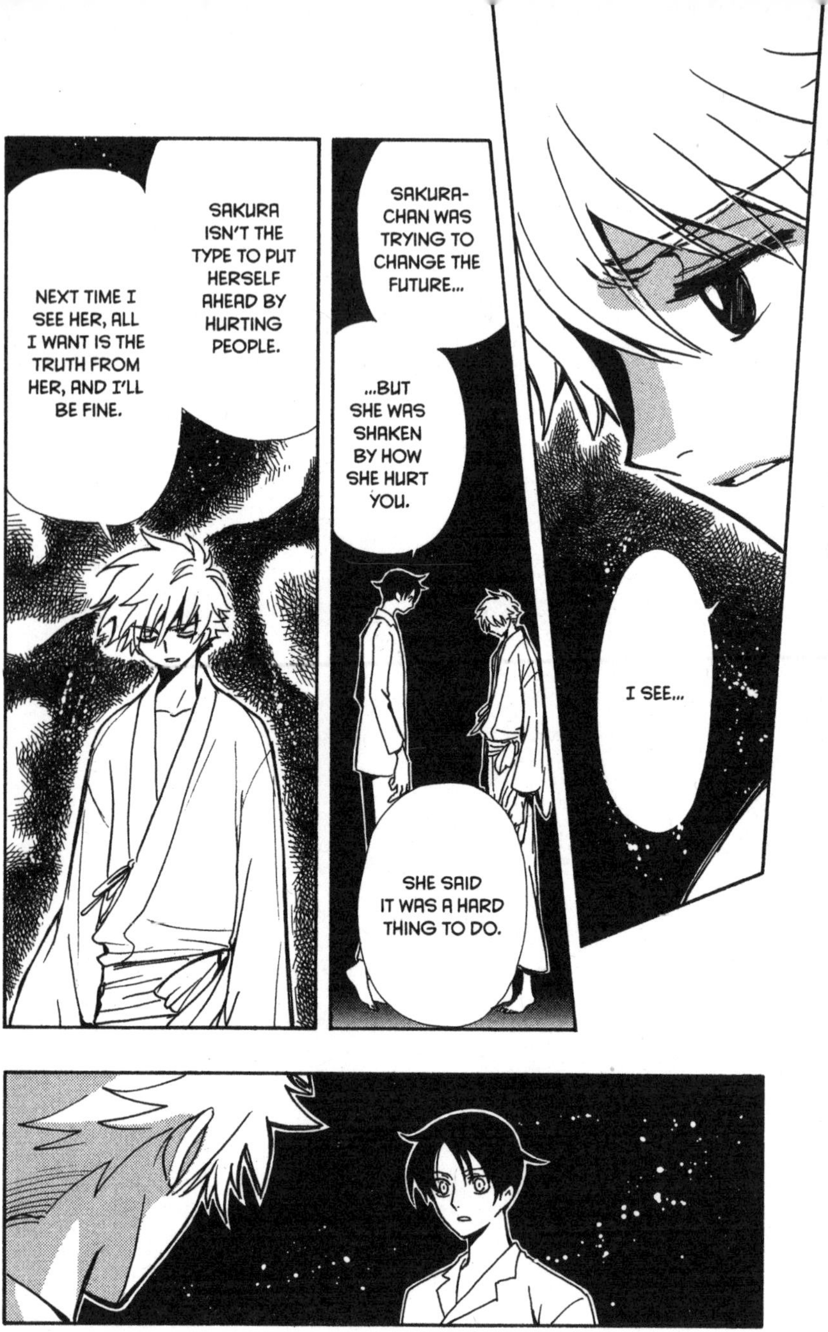
I SEE...
SAKURA-CHAN WAS TRYING TO CHANGE THE FUTURE...
...BUT SHE WAS SHAKEN BY HOW SHE HURT YOU.
SHE SAID IT WAS A HARD THING TO DO.
SAKURA ISN'T THE TYPE TO PUT HERSELF AHEAD BY HURTING PEOPLE.
NEXT TIME I SEE HER, ALL I WANT IS THE TRUTH FROM HER, AND I'LL BE FINE.

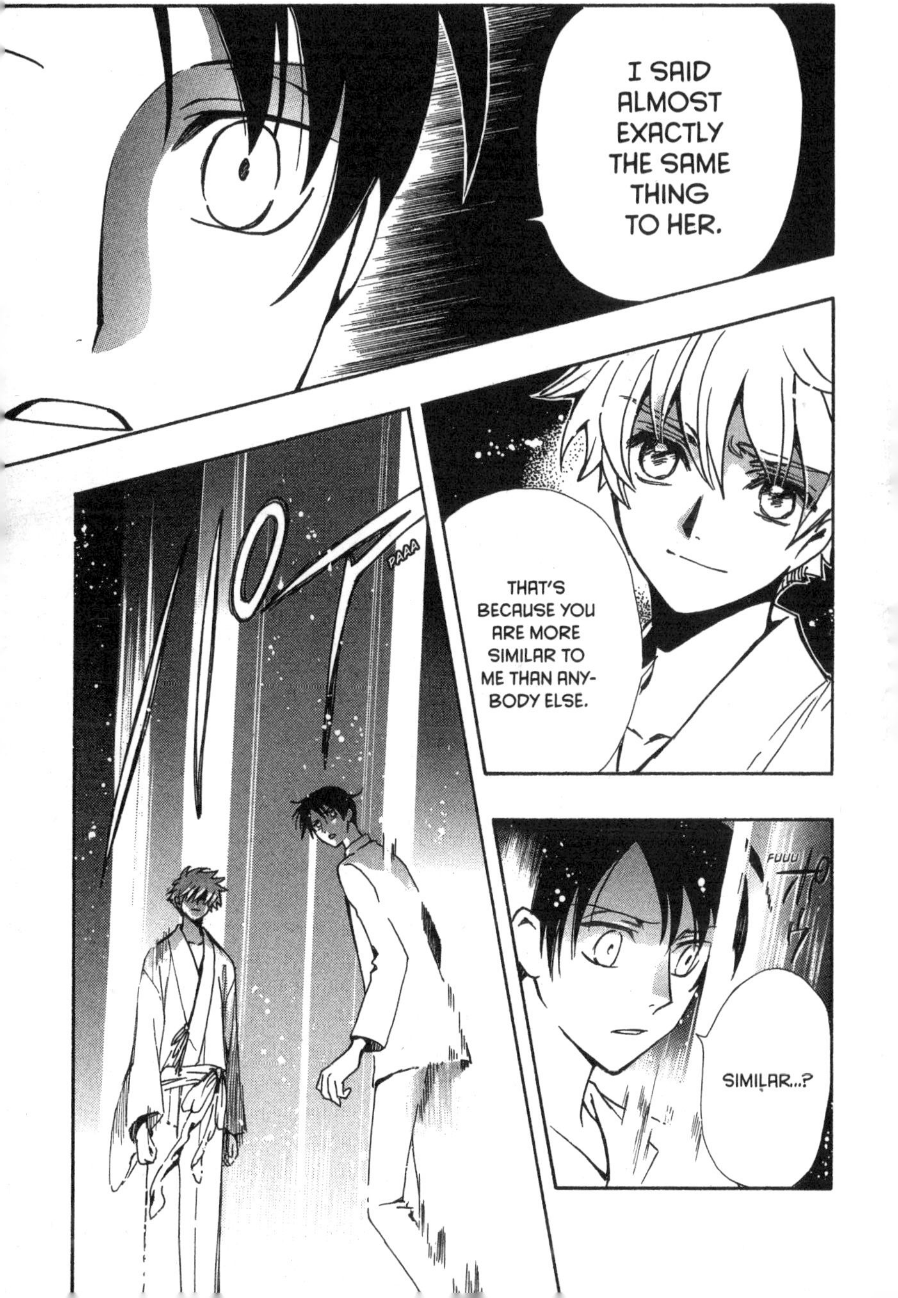
I SAID ALMOST EXACTLY THE SAME THING TO HER.
THAT'S BECAUSE YOU ARE MORE SIMILAR TO ME THAN ANY-BODY ELSE.
PAAA
FUUU
SIMILAR...?

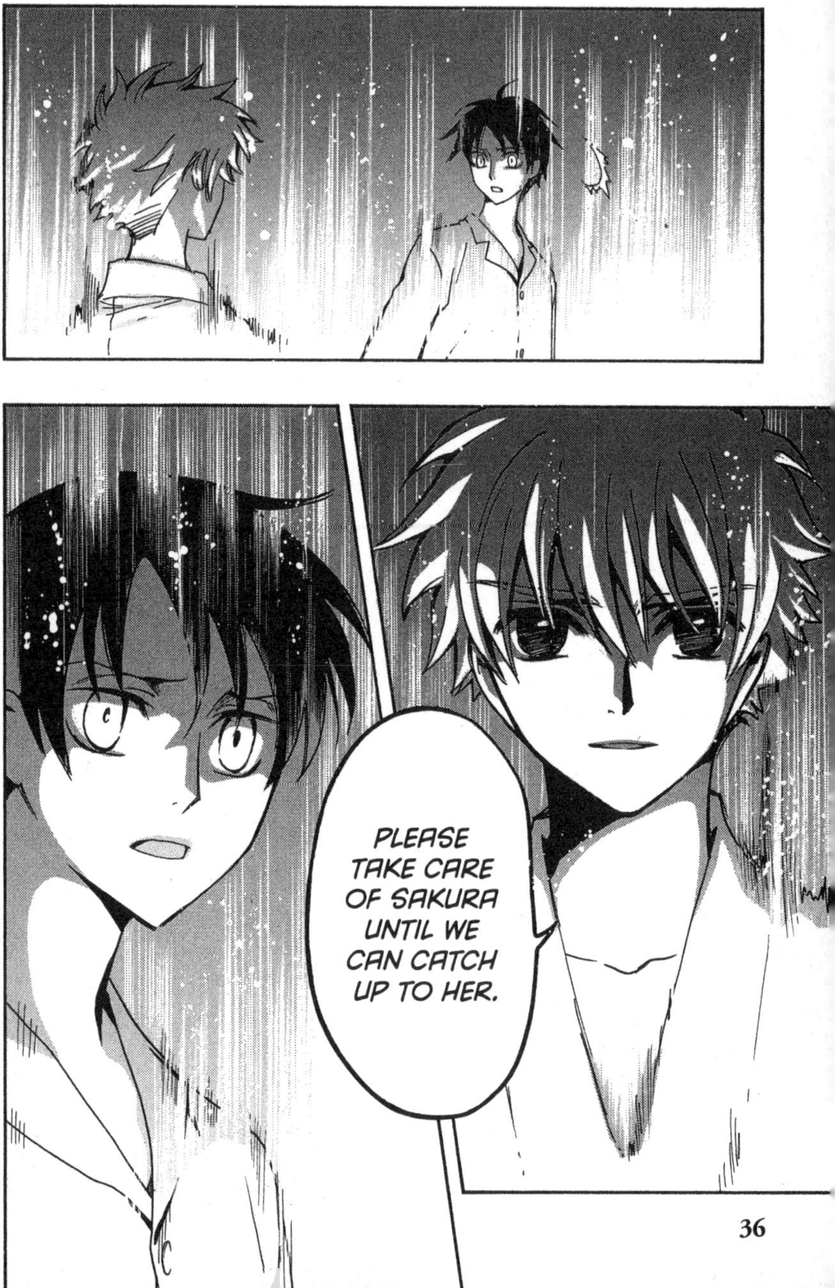
PLEASE TAKE CARE OF SAKURA UNTIL WE CAN CATCH UP TO HER.

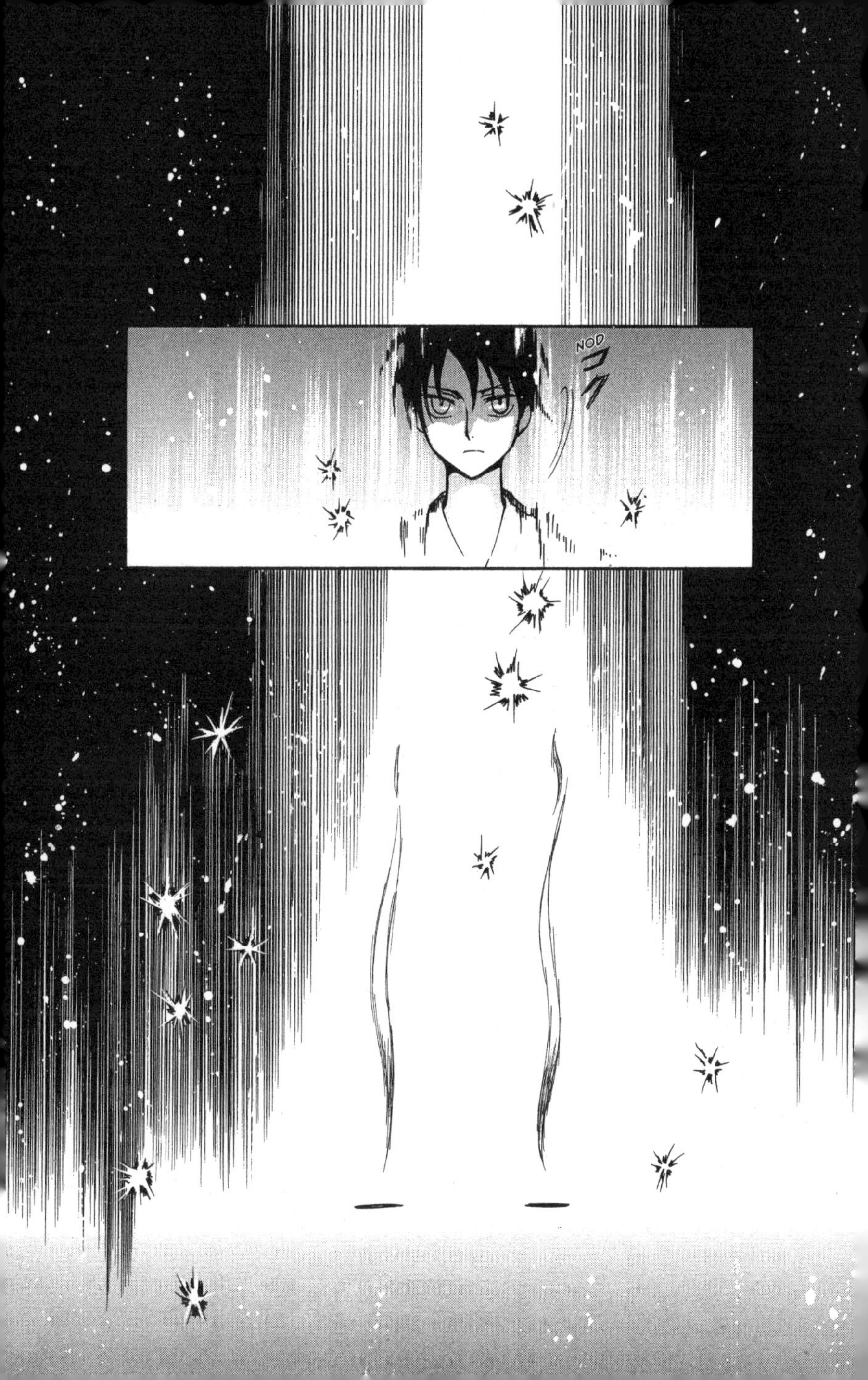
NOD
コク

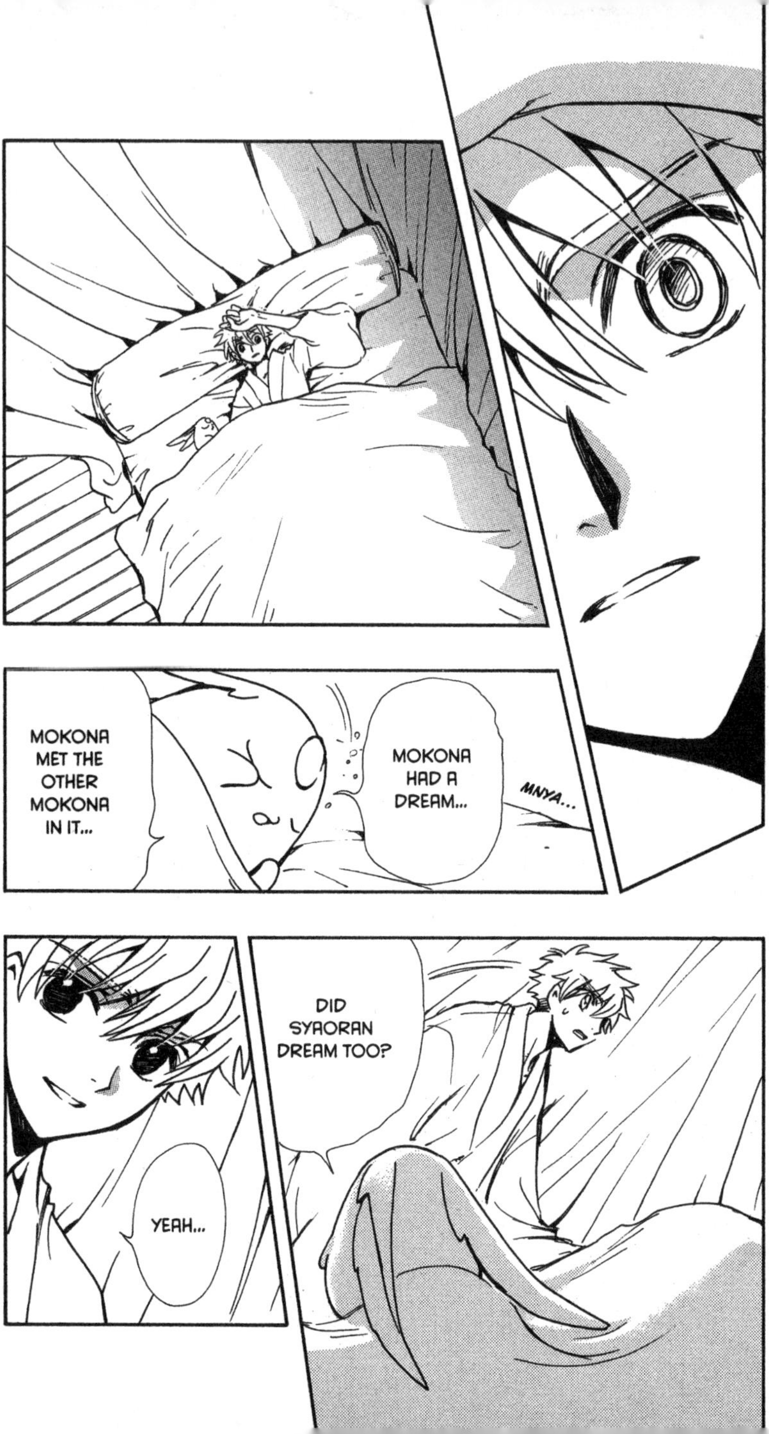
MNYA...
MOKONA HAD A DREAM...
MOKONA MET THE OTHER MOKONA IN IT...
DID SYAORAN DREAM TOO?
YEAH...

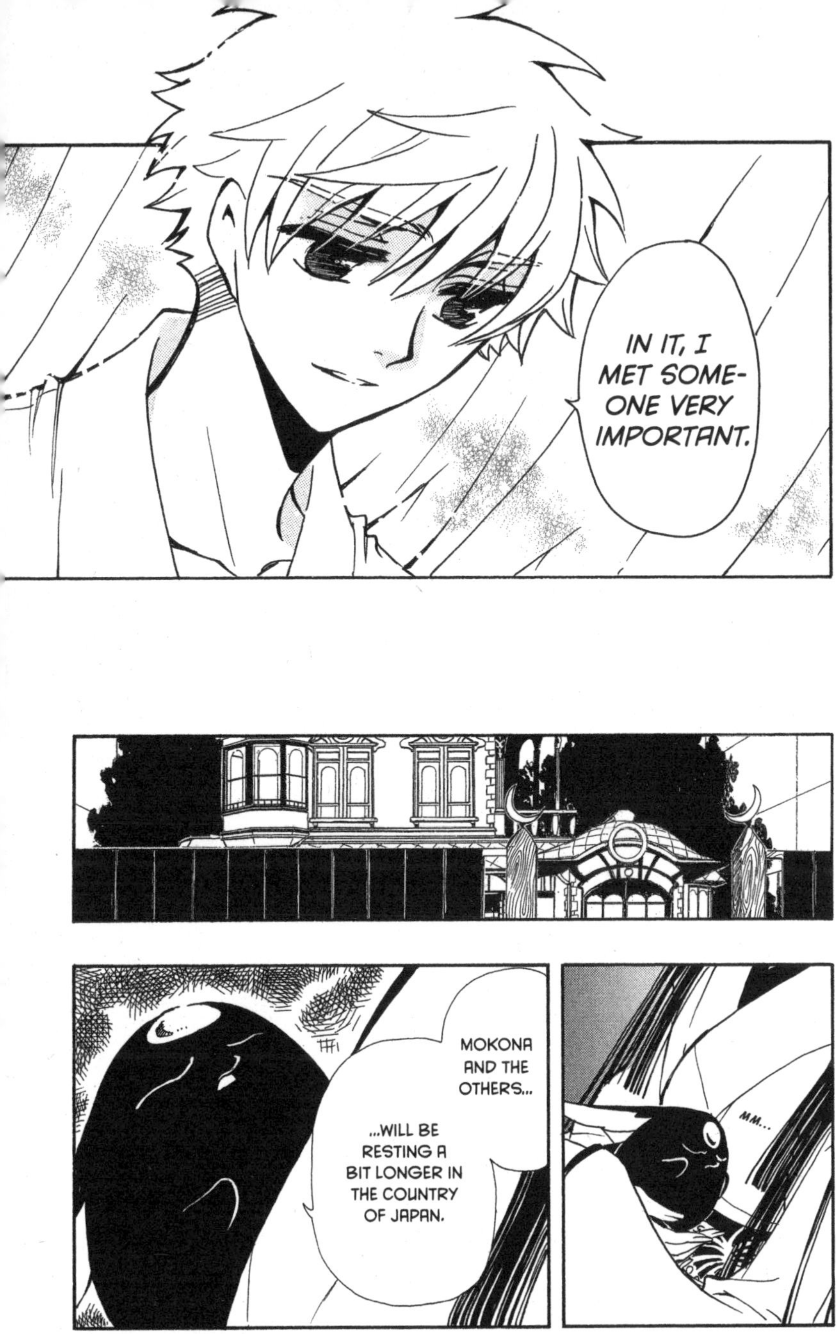
IN IT, I MET SOME-ONE VERY IMPORTANT.
MOKONA AND THE OTHERS...
...WILL BE RESTING A BIT LONGER IN THE COUNTRY OF JAPAN.
MM...

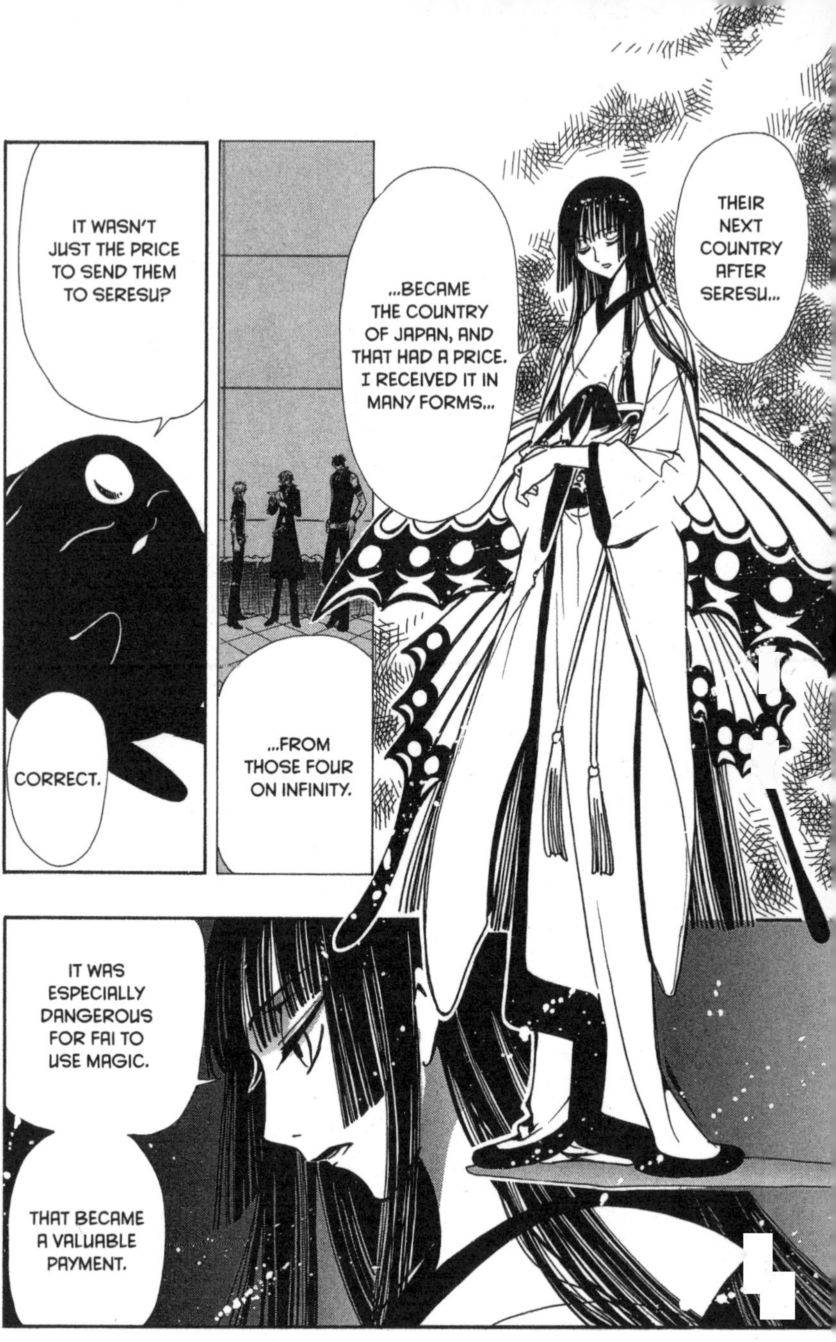
THEIR NEXT COUNTRY AFTER SERESU...
...BECAME THE COUNTRY OF JAPAN, AND THAT HAD A PRICE. I RECEIVED IT IN MANY FORMS...
...FROM THOSE FOUR ON INFINITY.
IT WASN'T JUST THE PRICE TO SEND THEM TO SERESU?
CORRECT.
IT WAS ESPECIALLY DANGEROUS FOR FAI TO USE MAGIC.
THAT BECAME A VALUABLE PAYMENT.

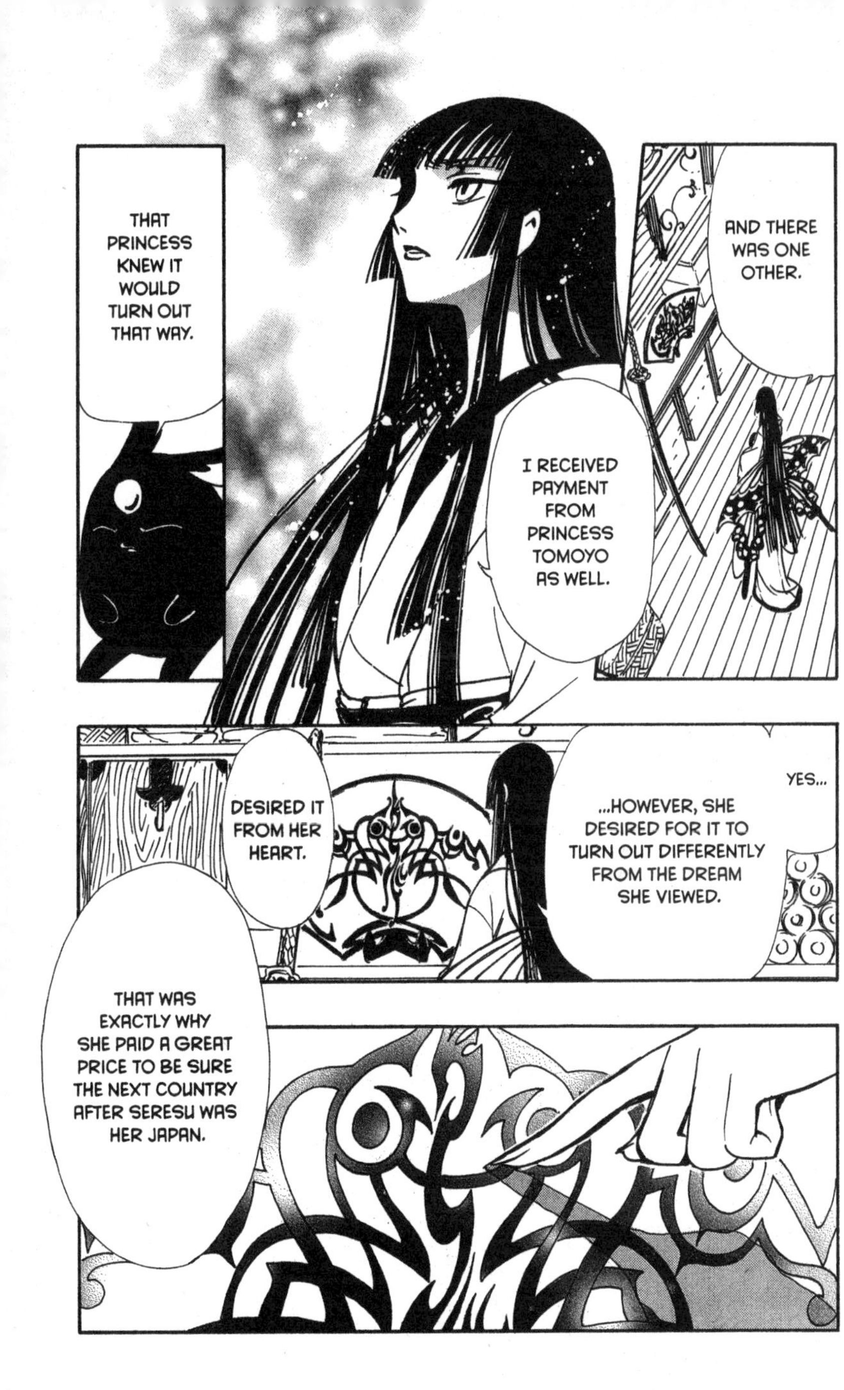
AND THERE WAS ONE OTHER.
I RECEIVED PAYMENT FROM PRINCESS TOMOYO AS WELL.
THAT PRINCESS KNEW IT WOULD TURN OUT THAT WAY.
YES...
...HOWEVER, SHE DESIRED FOR IT TO TURN OUT DIFFERENTLY FROM THE DREAM SHE VIEWED.
DESIRED IT FROM HER HEART.
THAT WAS EXACTLY WHY SHE PAID A GREAT PRICE TO BE SURE THE NEXT COUNTRY AFTER SERESU WAS HER JAPAN.

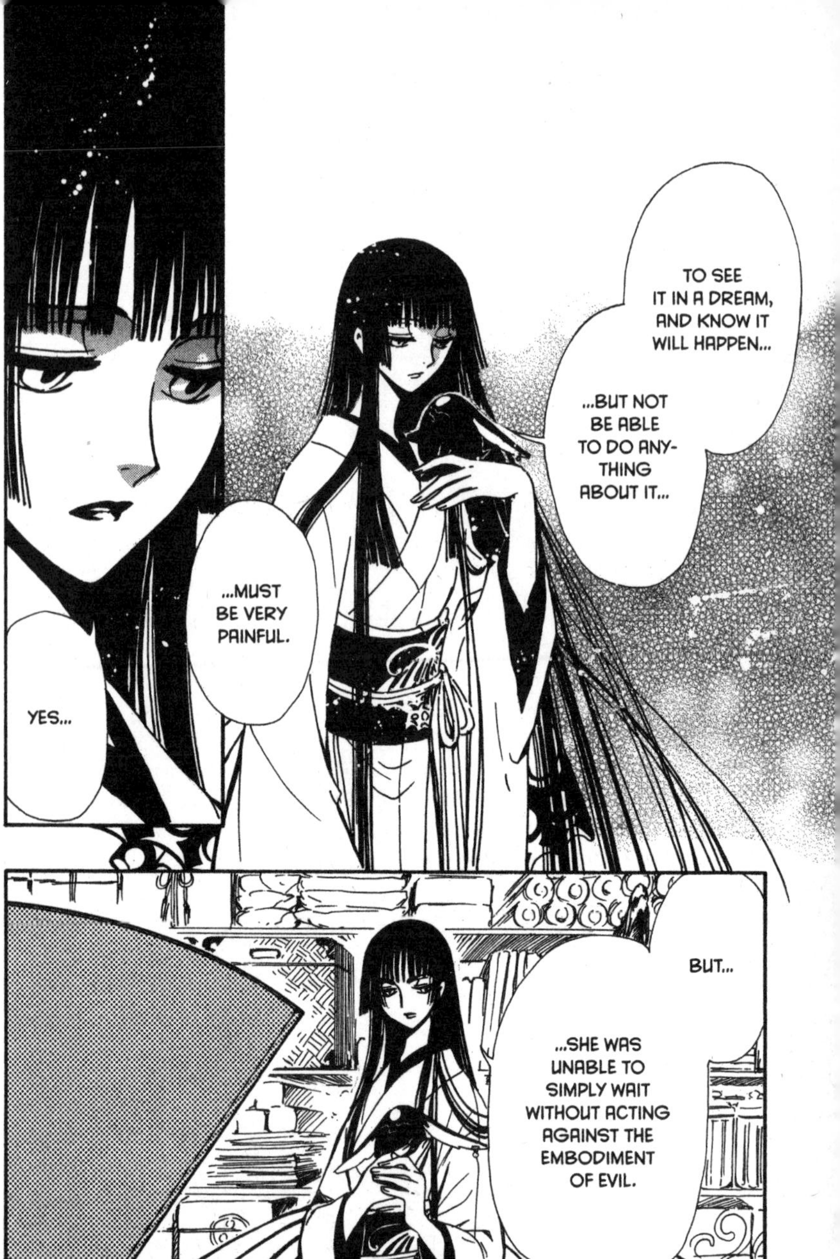
TO SEE IT IN A DREAM, AND KNOW IT WILL HAPPEN...
...BUT NOT BE ABLE TO DO ANY-THING ABOUT IT...
...MUST BE VERY PAINFUL.
YES...
BUT...
...SHE WAS UNABLE TO SIMPLY WAIT WITHOUT ACTING AGAINST THE EMBODIMENT OF EVIL.

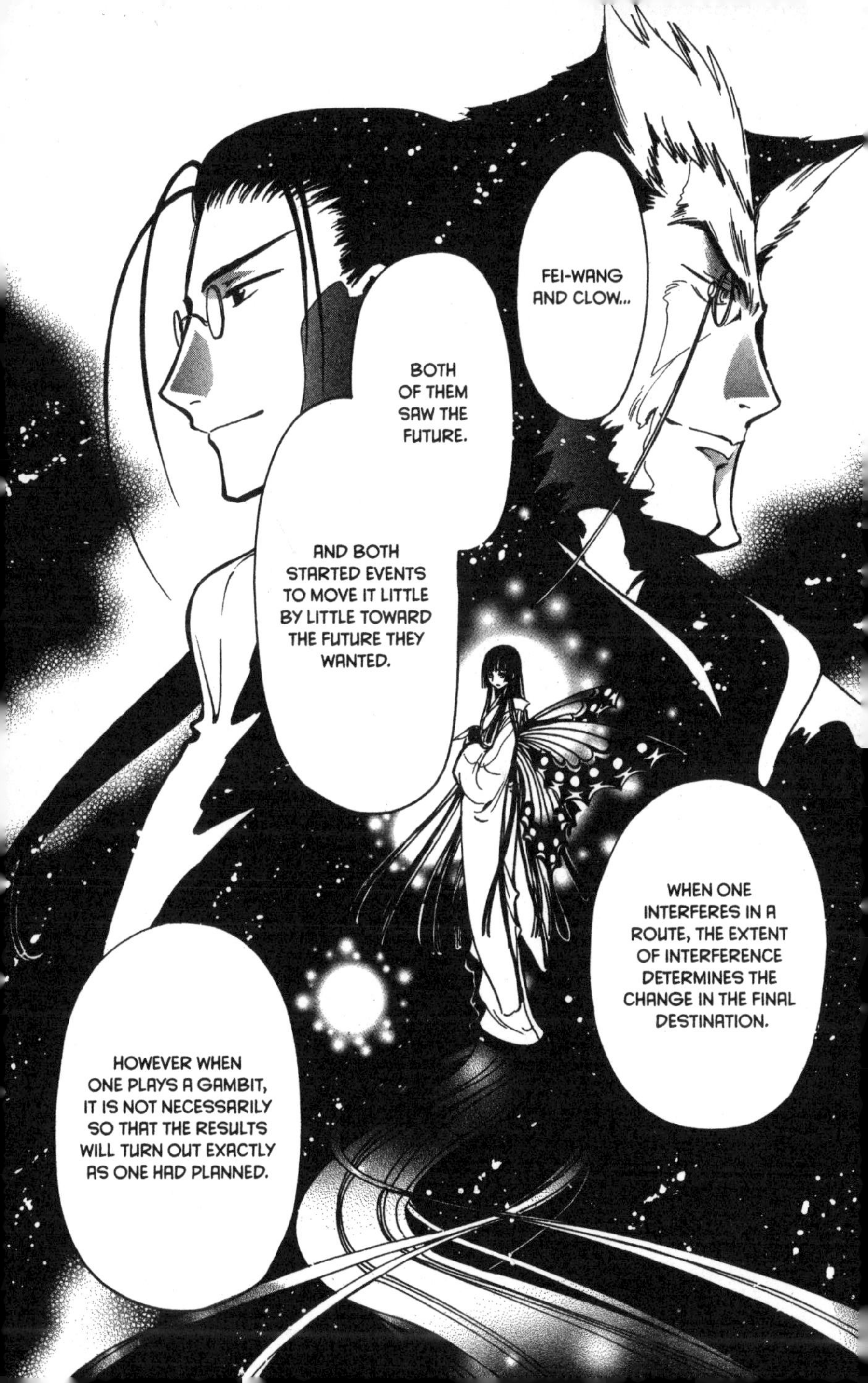
FEI-WANG AND CLOW...
BOTH OF THEM SAW THE FUTURE.
AND BOTH STARTED EVENTS TO MOVE IT LITTLE BY LITTLE TOWARD THE FUTURE THEY WANTED.
WHEN ONE INTERFERES IN A ROUTE, THE EXTENT OF INTERFERENCE DETERMINES THE CHANGE IN THE FINAL DESTINATION.
HOWEVER WHEN ONE PLAYS A GAMBIT, IT IS NOT NECESSARILY SO THAT THE RESULTS WILL TURN OUT EXACTLY AS ONE HAD PLANNED.

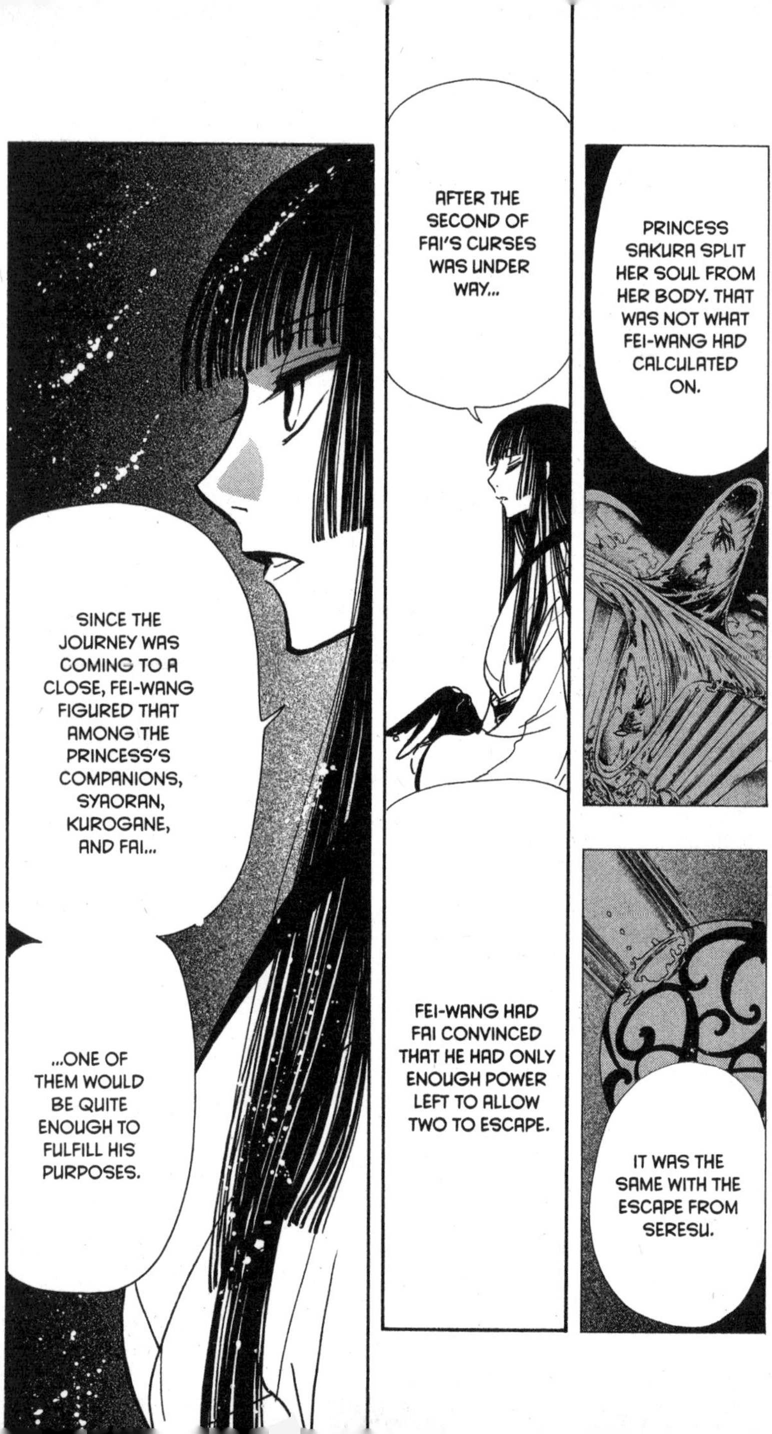
PRINCESS SAKURA SPLIT HER SOUL FROM HER BODY. THAT WAS NOT WHAT FEI-WANG HAD CALCULATED ON.
IT WAS THE SAME WITH THE ESCAPE FROM SERESU.
AFTER THE SECOND OF FAI'S CURSES WAS UNDER WAY...
FEI-WANG HAD FAI CONVINCED THAT HE HAD ONLY ENOUGH POWER LEFT TO ALLOW TWO TO ESCAPE.
SINCE THE JOURNEY WAS COMING TO A CLOSE, FEI-WANG FIGURED THAT AMONG THE PRINCESS'S COMPANIONS, SYAORAN, KUROGANE, AND FAI...
...ONE OF THEM WOULD BE QUITE ENOUGH TO FULFILL HIS PURPOSES.

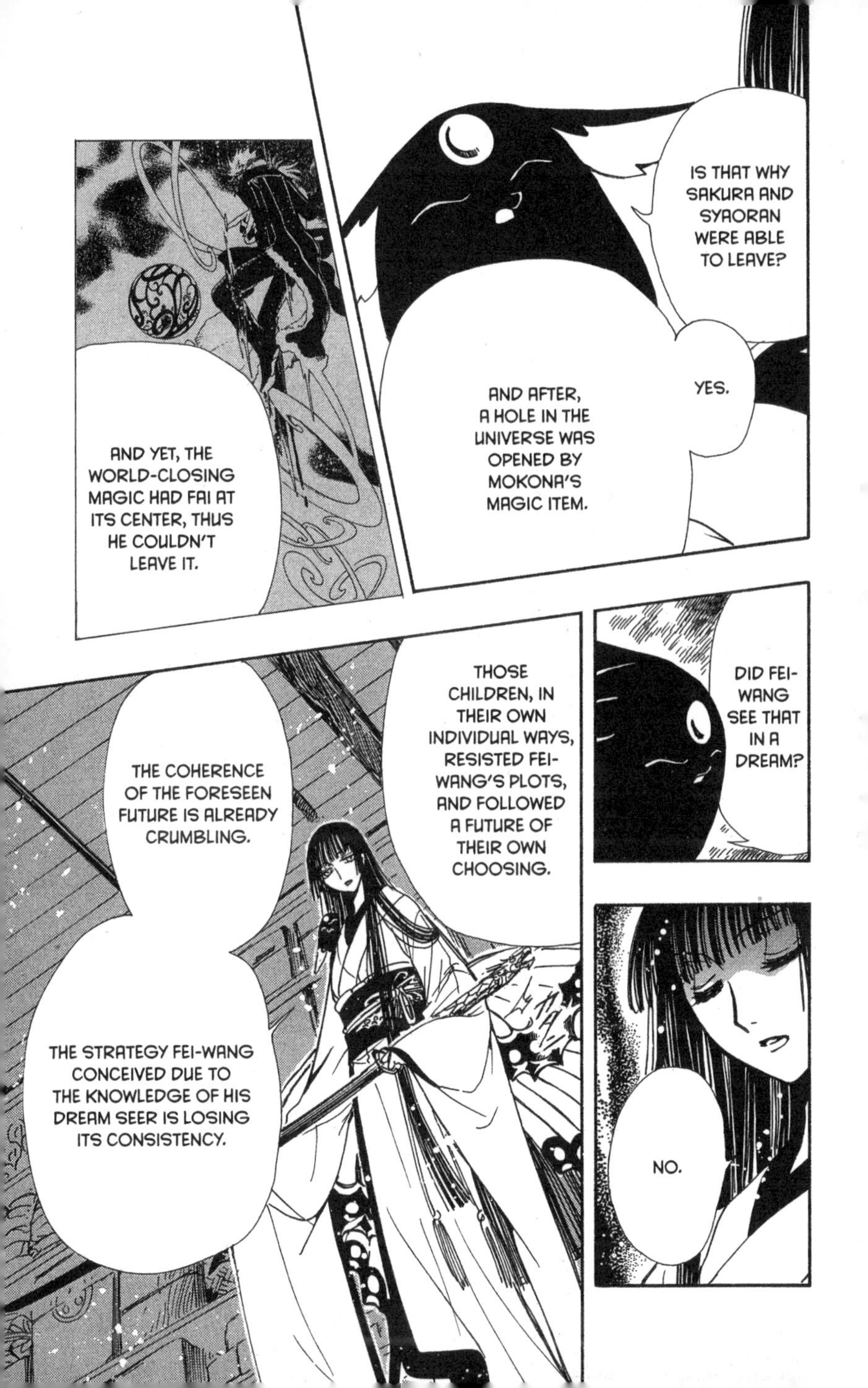
IS THAT WHY SAKURA AND SYAORAN WERE ABLE TO LEAVE?
YES.
AND AFTER, A HOLE IN THE UNIVERSE WAS OPENED BY MOKONA'S MAGIC ITEM.
AND YET, THE WORLD-CLOSING MAGIC HAD FAI AT ITS CENTER, THUS HE COULDN'T LEAVE IT.
DID FEI-WANG SEE THAT IN A DREAM?
NO.
THOSE CHILDREN, IN THEIR OWN INDIVIDUAL WAYS, RESISTED FEI-WANG'S PLOTS, AND FOLLOWED A FUTURE OF THEIR OWN CHOOSING.
THE COHERENCE OF THE FORESEEN FUTURE IS ALREADY CRUMBLING.
THE STRATEGY FEI-WANG CONCEIVED DUE TO THE KNOWLEDGE OF HIS DREAM SEER IS LOSING ITS CONSISTENCY.

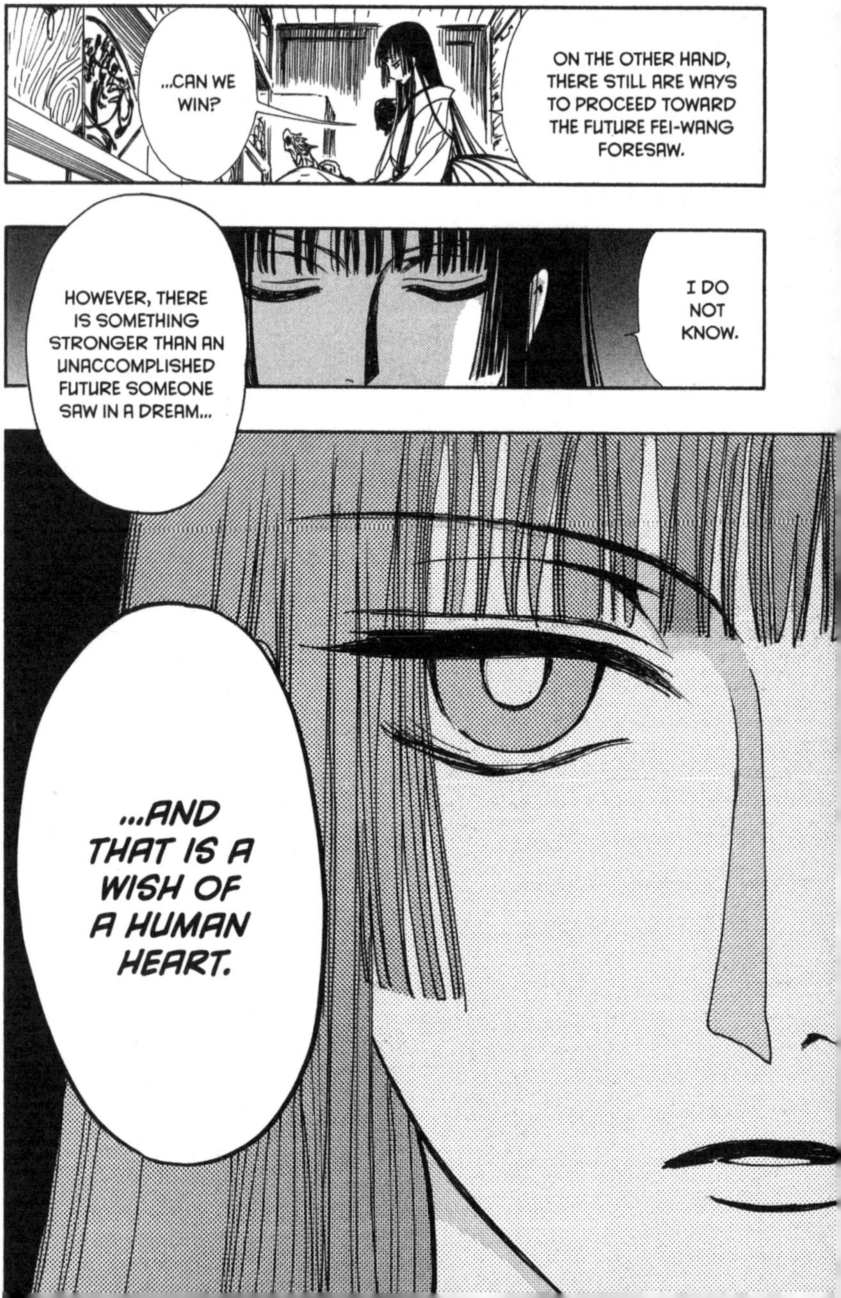
ON THE OTHER HAND, THERE STILL ARE WAYS TO PROCEED TOWARD THE FUTURE FEI-WANG FORESAW.
...CAN WE WIN?
I DO NOT KNOW.
HOWEVER, THERE IS SOMETHING STRONGER THAN AN UNACCOMPLISHED FUTURE SOMEONE SAW IN A DREAM...
...AND THAT IS A WISH OF A HUMAN HEART.

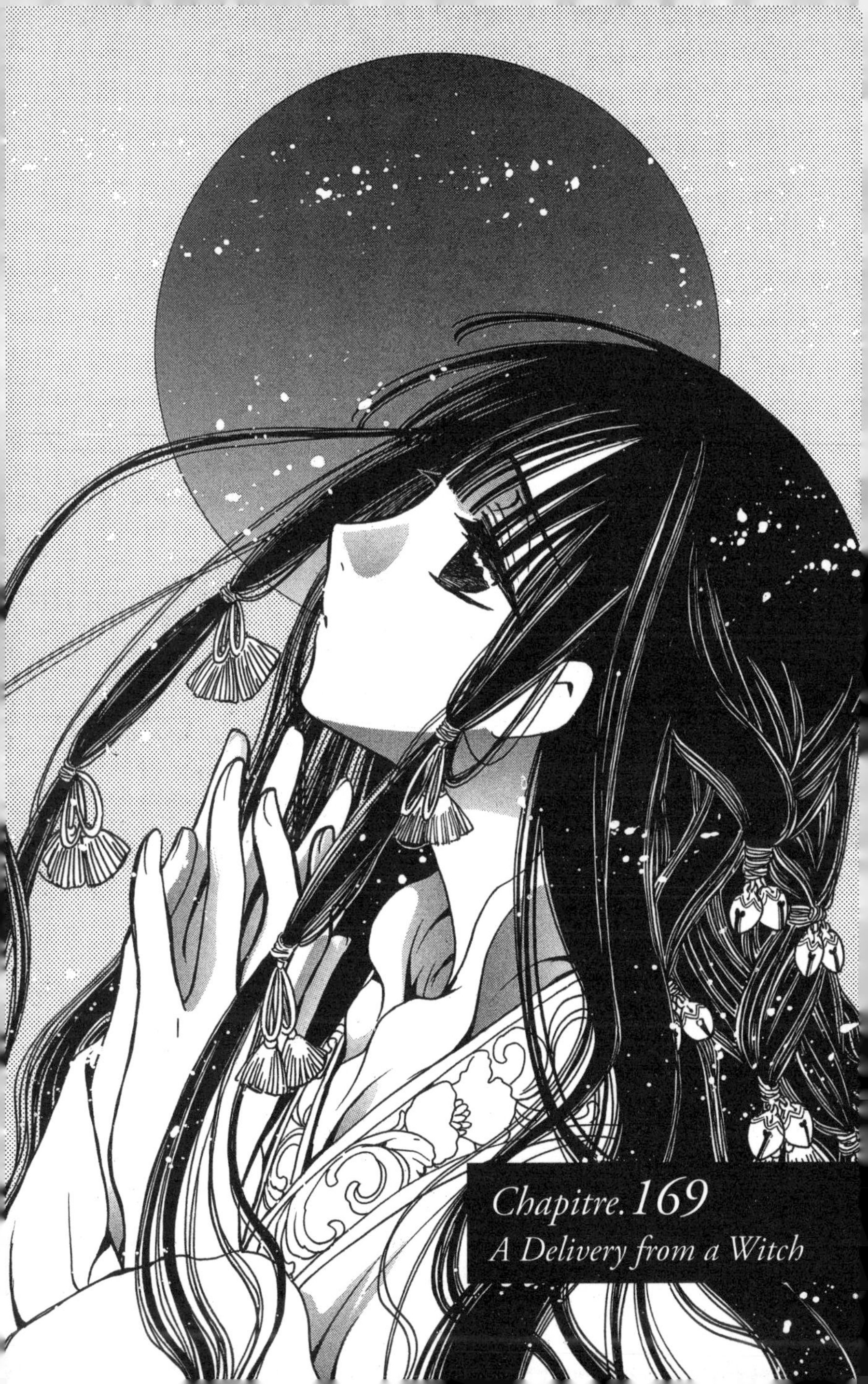
Chapitre. 169
A Delivery from a Witch

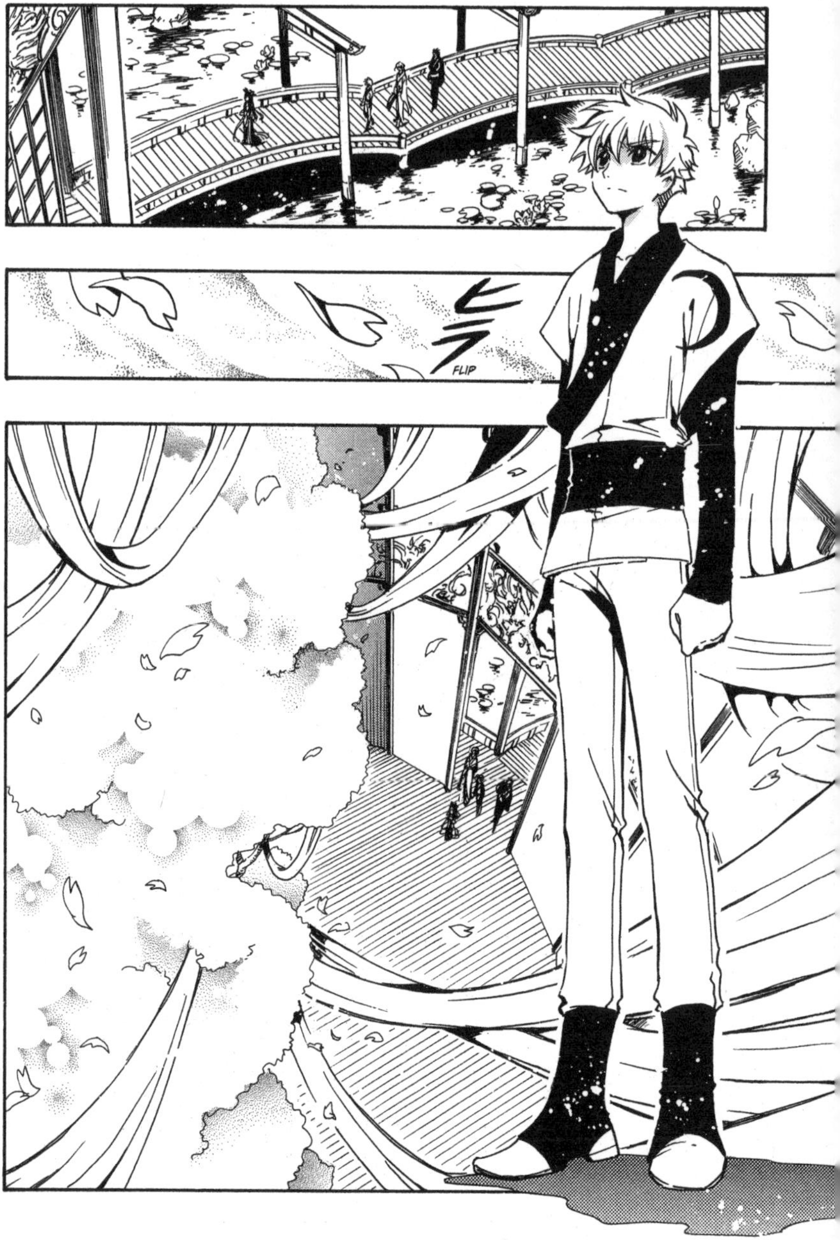
ヒラ
FLIP

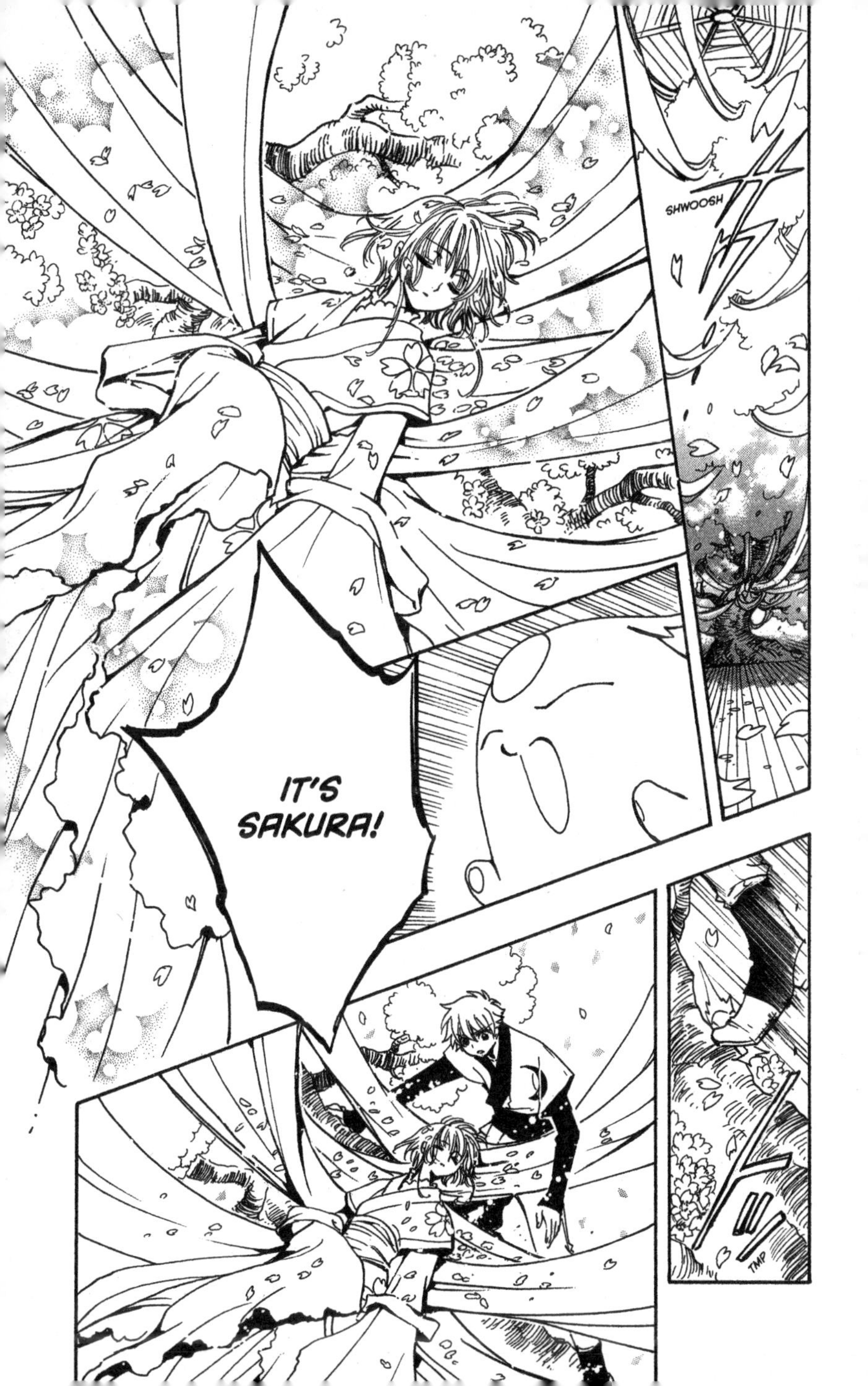
SHWOOSH
IT'S SAKURA!
TMP

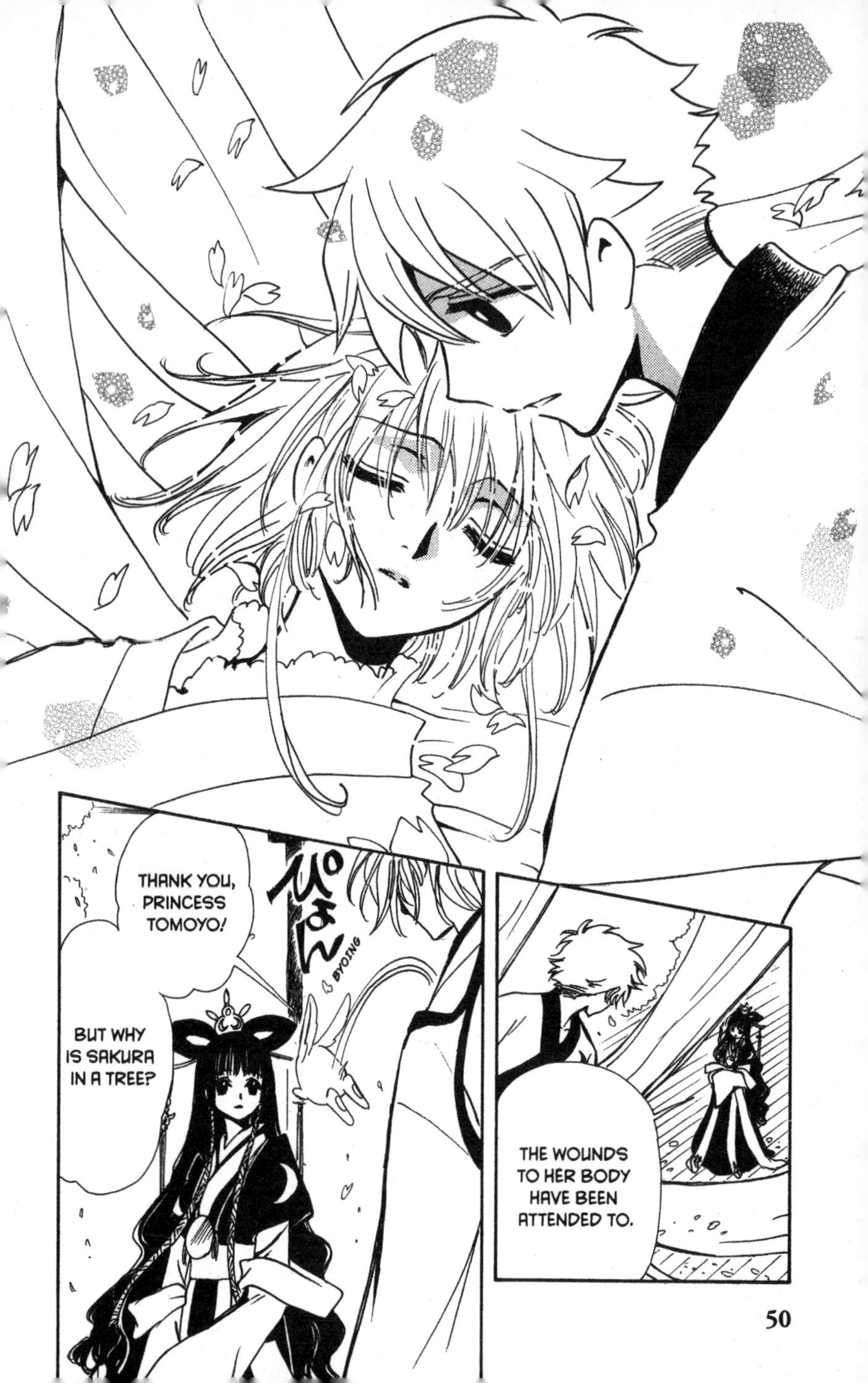
THE WOUNDS TO HER BODY HAVE BEEN ATTENDED TO.
THANK YOU, PRINCESS TOMOYO!
BYOING
BUT WHY IS SAKURA IN A TREE?

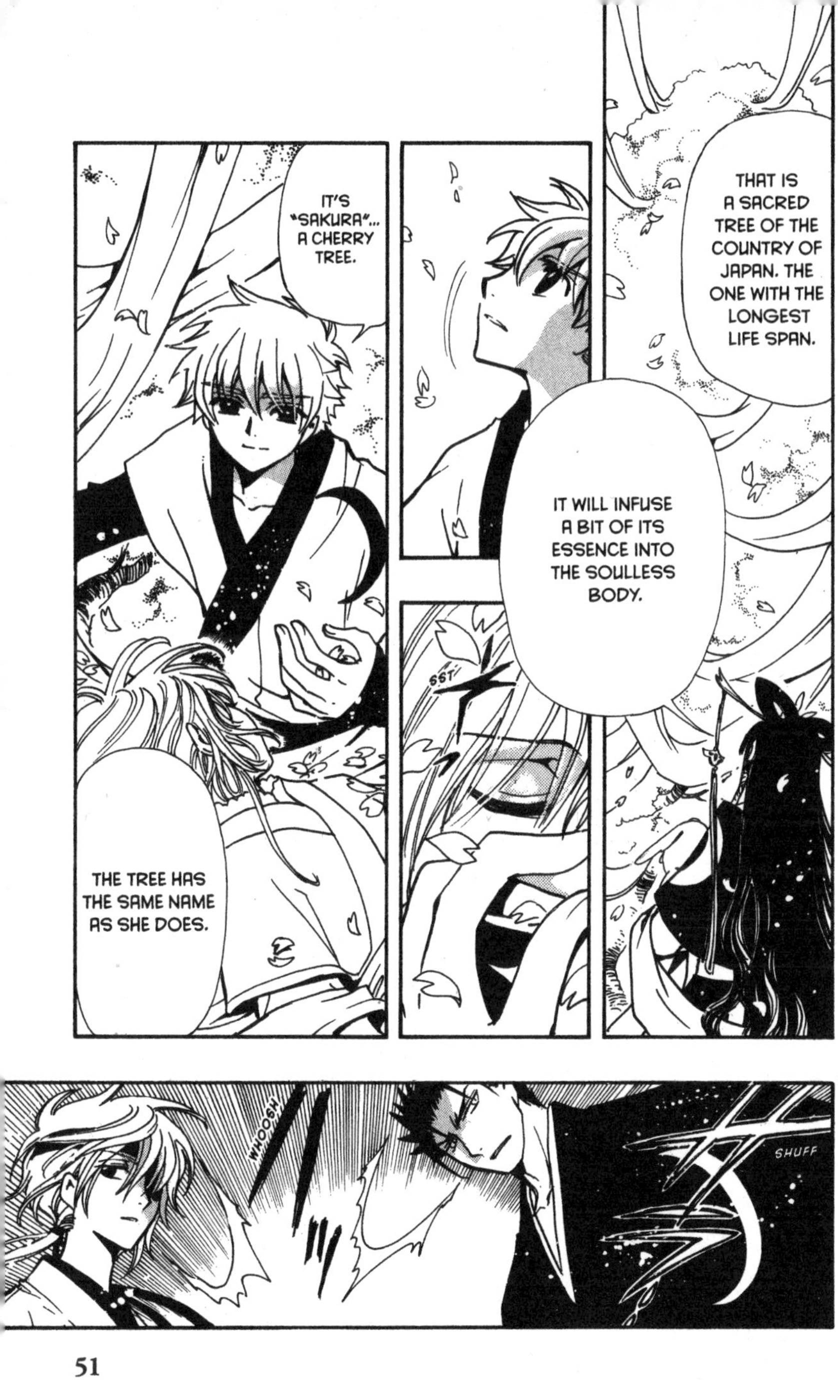
THAT IS A SACRED TREE OF THE COUNTRY OF JAPAN. THE ONE WITH THE LONGEST LIFE SPAN.
IT WILL INFUSE A BIT OF ITS ESSENCE INTO THE SOULLESS BODY.
SST
IT'S "SAKURA"... A CHERRY TREE.
THE TREE HAS THE SAME NAME AS SHE DOES.
SHUFF
WHOOSH

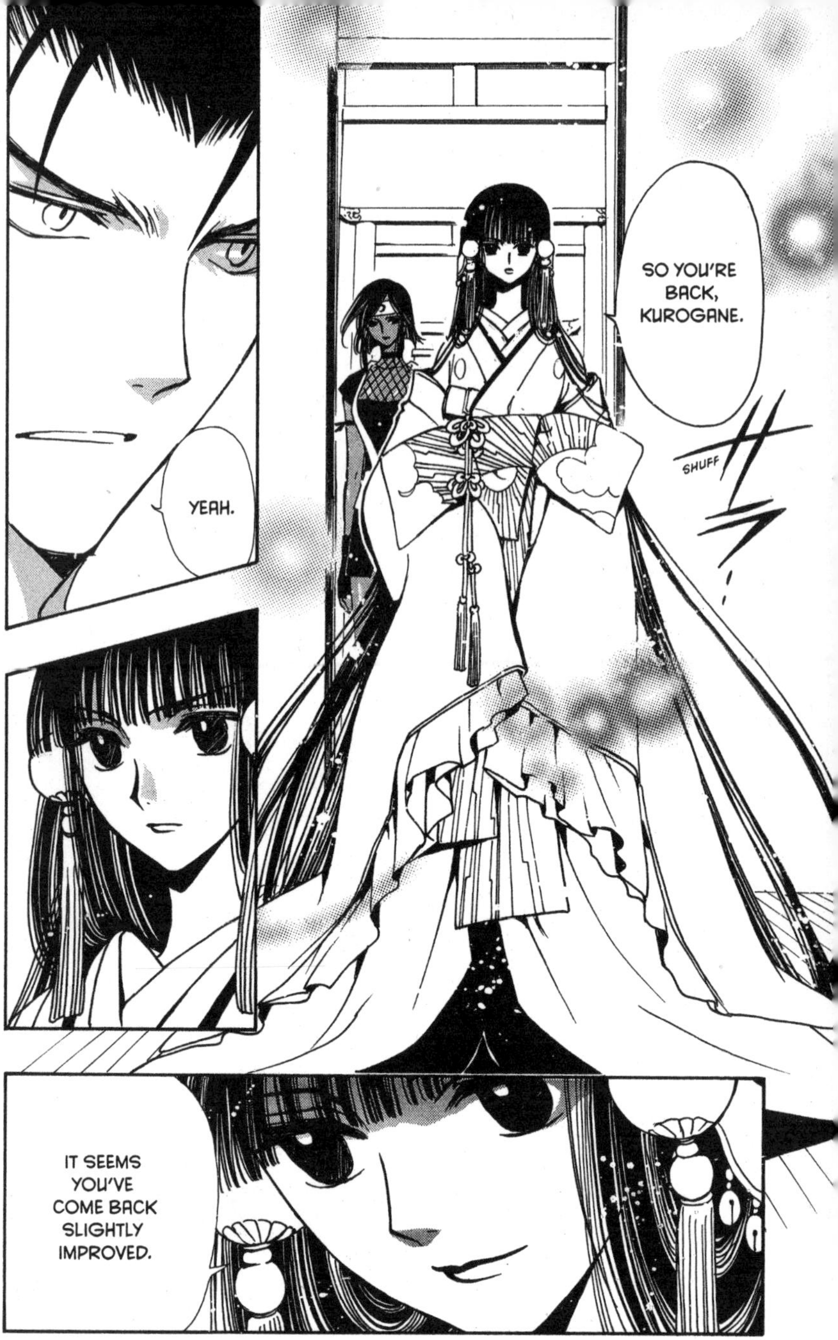
SO YOU'RE BACK, KUROGANE.
SHUFF
YEAH.
IT SEEMS YOU'VE COME BACK SLIGHTLY IMPROVED.

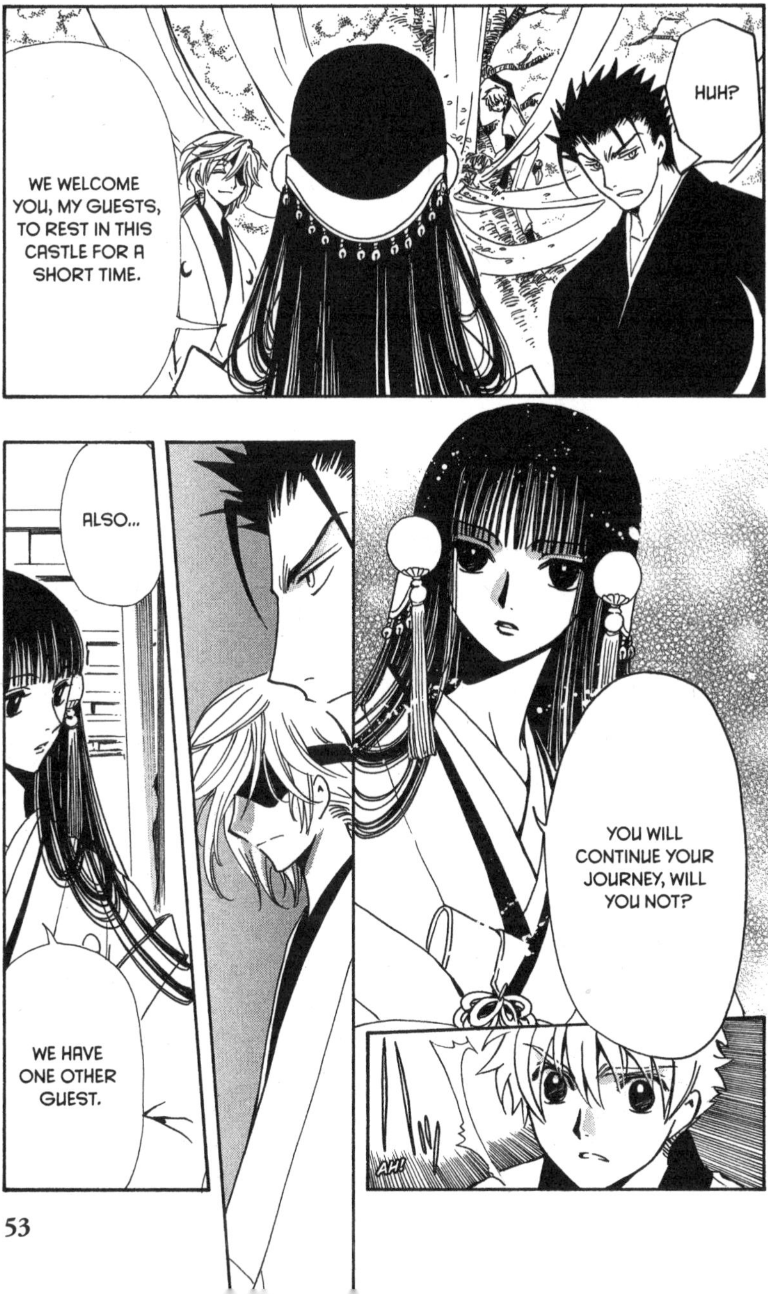
HUH?
WE WELCOME YOU, MY GUESTS, TO REST IN THIS CASTLE FOR A SHORT TIME.
YOU WILL CONTINUE YOUR JOURNEY, WILL YOU NOT?
AH!
ALSO...
WE HAVE ONE OTHER GUEST.

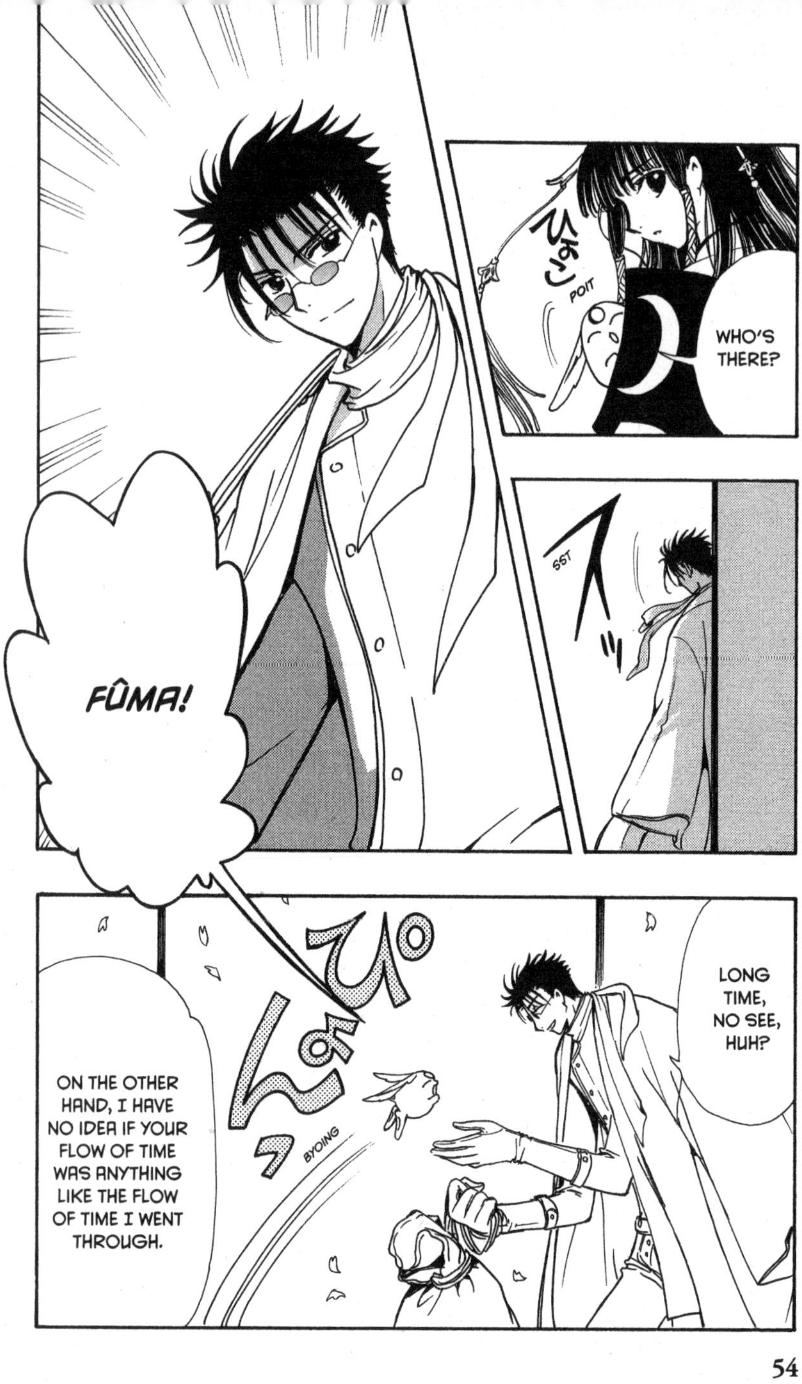
ひょこ
POIT
WHO'S THERE?
SST
FÛMA!
ぴょん
BYOING
LONG TIME, NO SEE, HUH?
ON THE OTHER HAND, I HAVE NO IDEA IF YOUR FLOW OF TIME WAS ANYTHING LIKE THE FLOW OF TIME I WENT THROUGH.

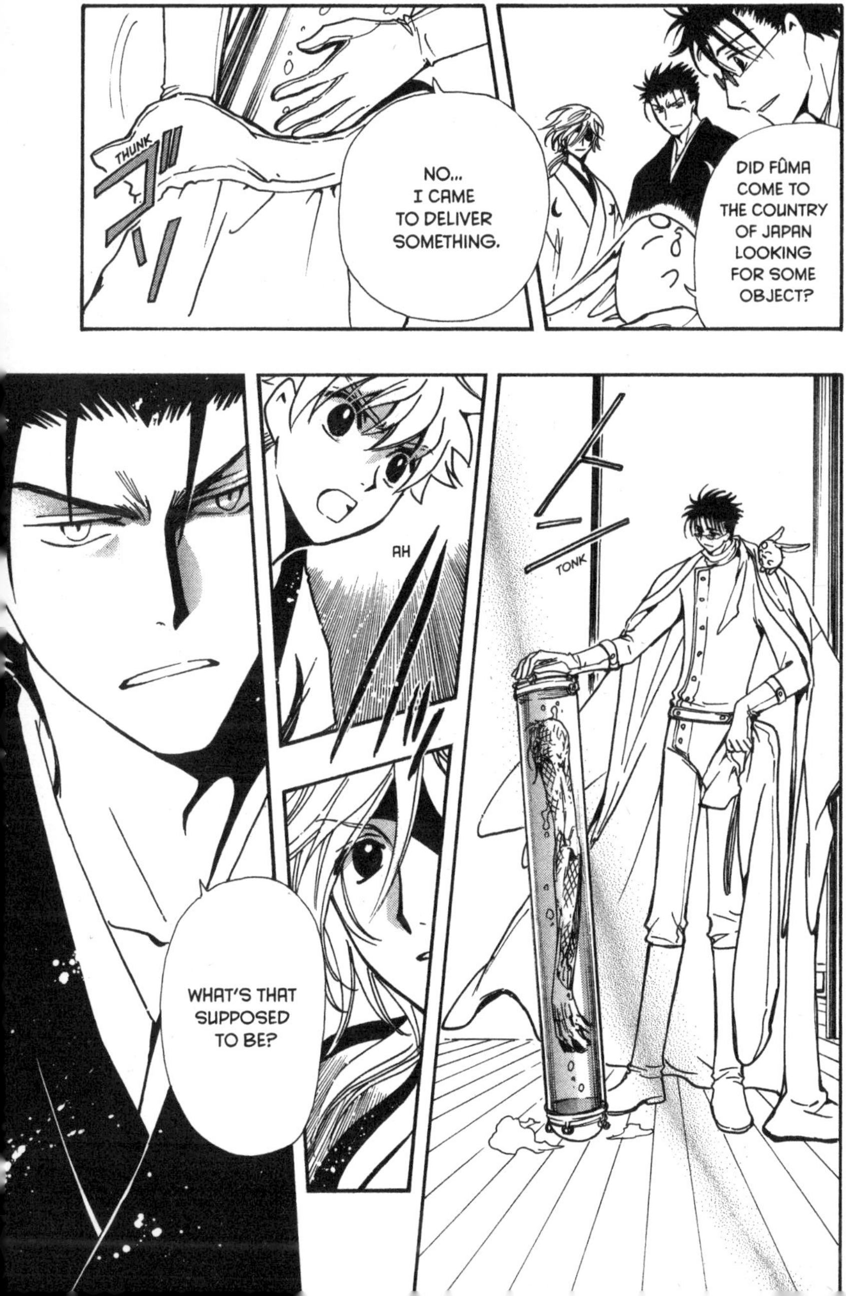
DID FÛMA COME TO THE COUNTRY OF JAPAN LOOKING FOR SOME OBJECT?
NO... I CAME TO DELIVER SOMETHING.
THUNK
TONK
AH
WHAT'S THAT SUPPOSED TO BE?

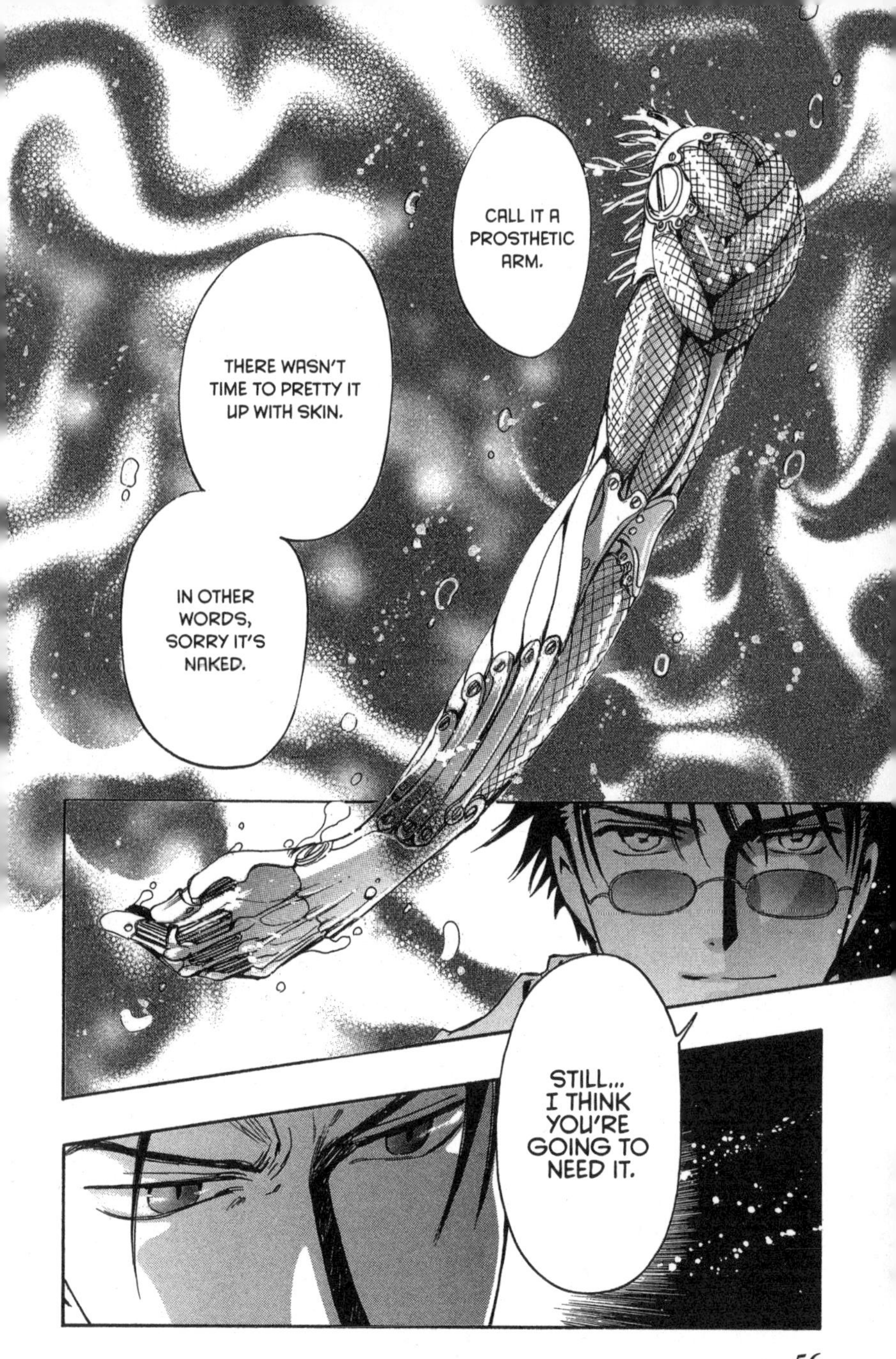
CALL IT A PROSTHETIC ARM.
THERE WASN'T TIME TO PRETTY IT UP WITH SKIN.
IN OTHER WORDS, SORRY IT'S NAKED.
STILL... I THINK YOU'RE GOING TO NEED IT.

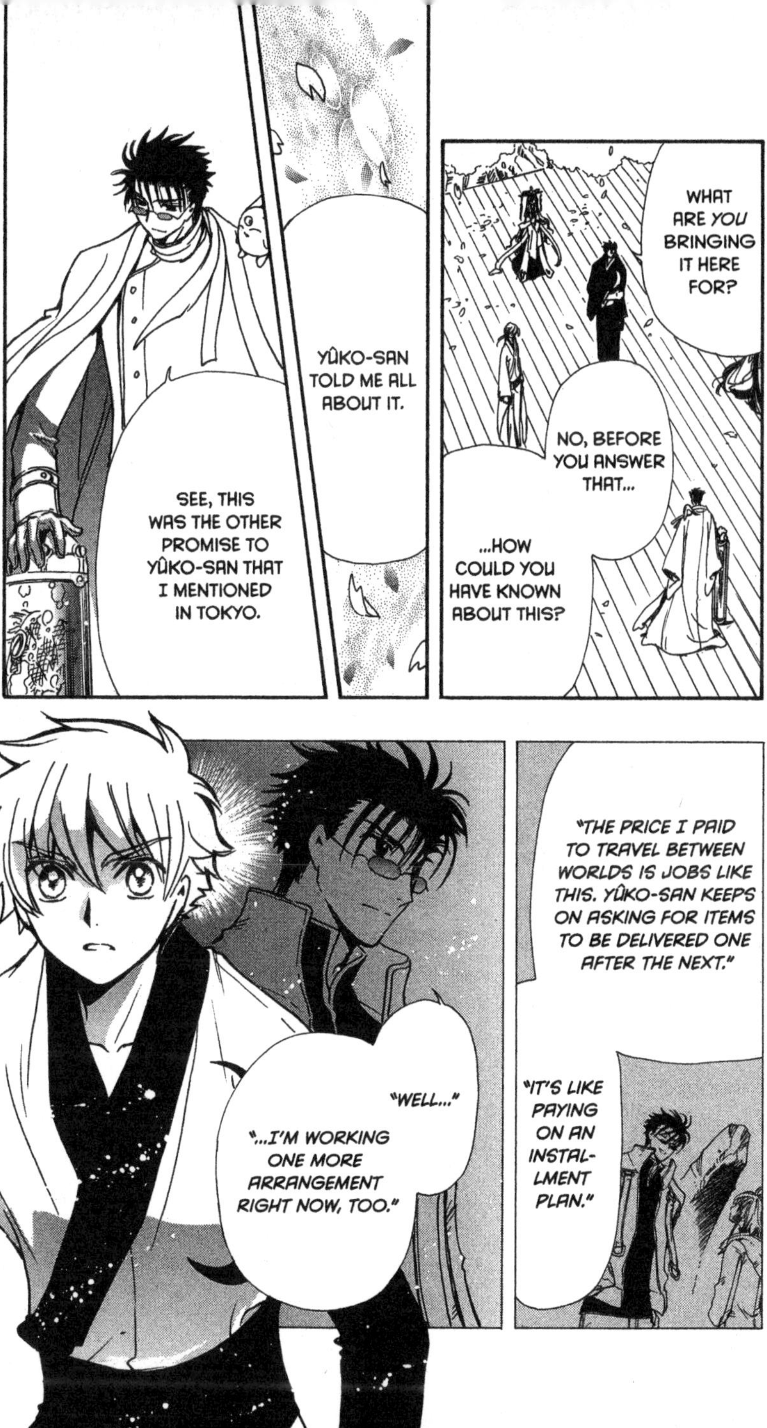
WHAT ARE *YOU* BRINGING IT HERE FOR?
NO, BEFORE YOU ANSWER THAT...
...HOW COULD YOU HAVE KNOWN ABOUT THIS?
YÛKO-SAN TOLD ME ALL ABOUT IT.
SEE, THIS WAS THE OTHER PROMISE TO YÛKO-SAN THAT I MENTIONED IN TOKYO.
"THE PRICE I PAID TO TRAVEL BETWEEN WORLDS IS JOBS LIKE THIS. YÛKO-SAN KEEPS ON ASKING FOR ITEMS TO BE DELIVERED ONE AFTER THE NEXT."
"IT'S LIKE PAYING ON AN INSTAL-LMENT PLAN."
"WELL..."
"...I'M WORKING ONE MORE ARRANGEMENT RIGHT NOW, TOO."

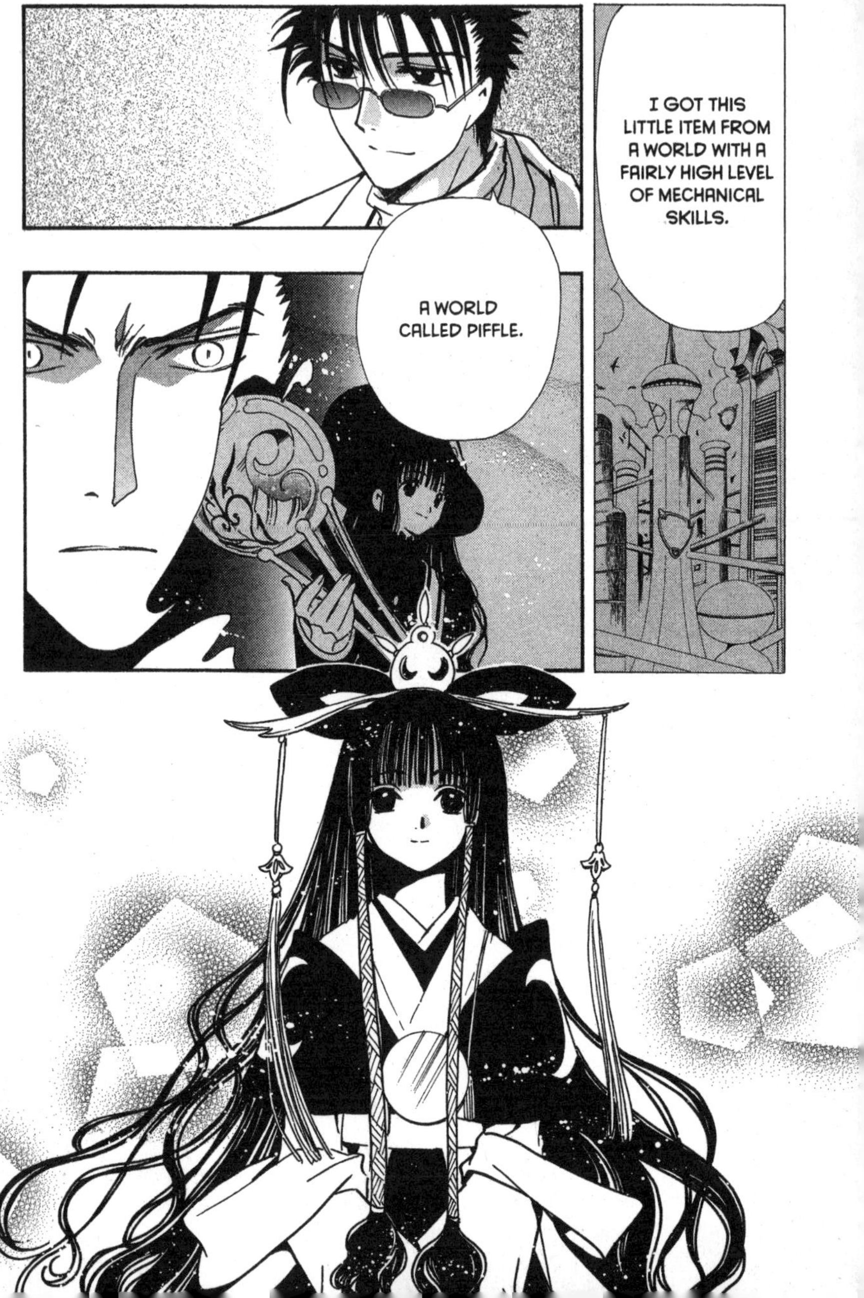
I GOT THIS LITTLE ITEM FROM A WORLD WITH A FAIRLY HIGH LEVEL OF MECHANICAL SKILLS.
A WORLD CALLED PIFFLE.

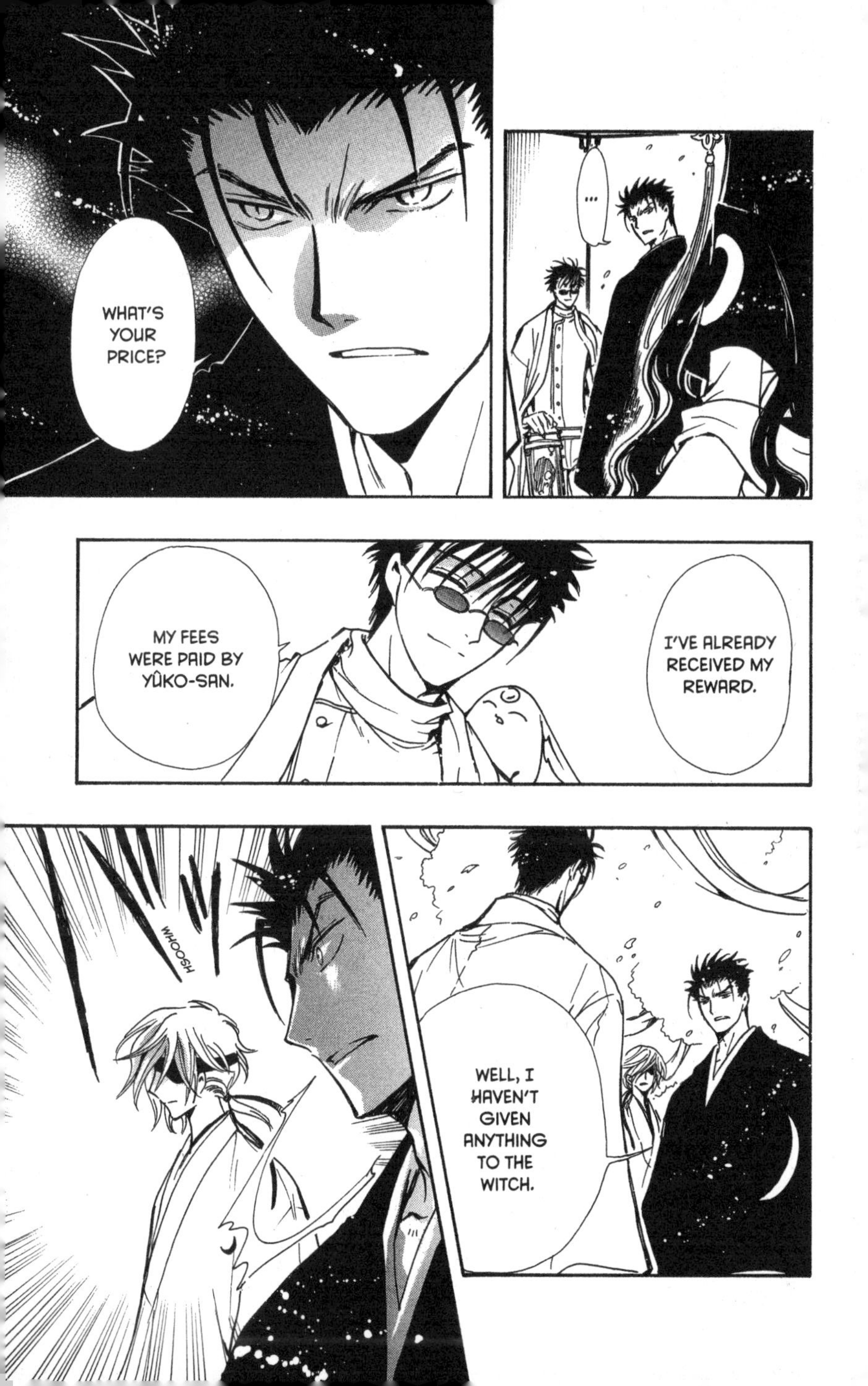
...
WHAT'S YOUR PRICE?
I'VE ALREADY RECEIVED MY REWARD.
MY FEES WERE PAID BY YÛKO-SAN.
WELL, I HAVEN'T GIVEN ANYTHING TO THE WITCH.
WHOOSH

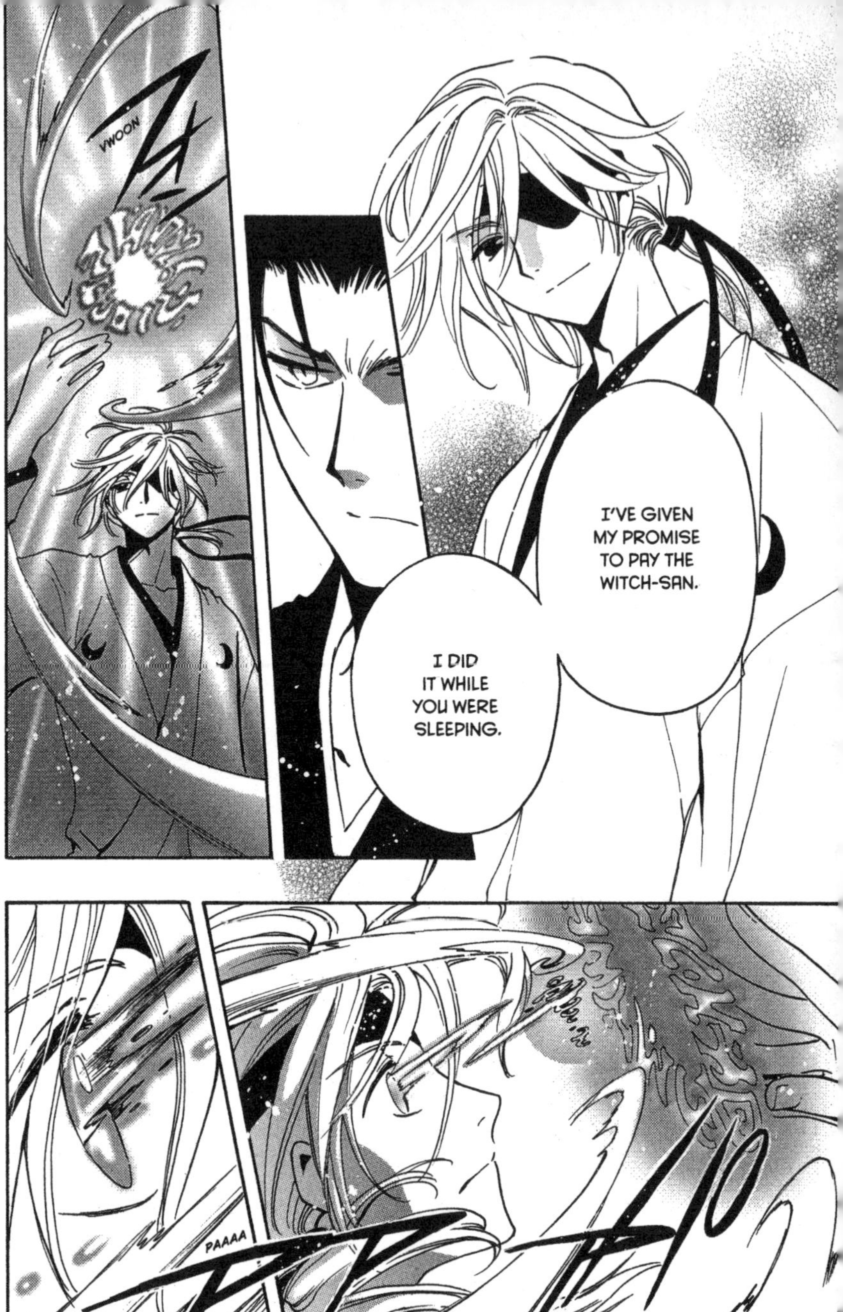
I'VE GIVEN MY PROMISE TO PAY THE WITCH-SAN.
I DID IT WHILE YOU WERE SLEEPING.
VWOON
PAAAA

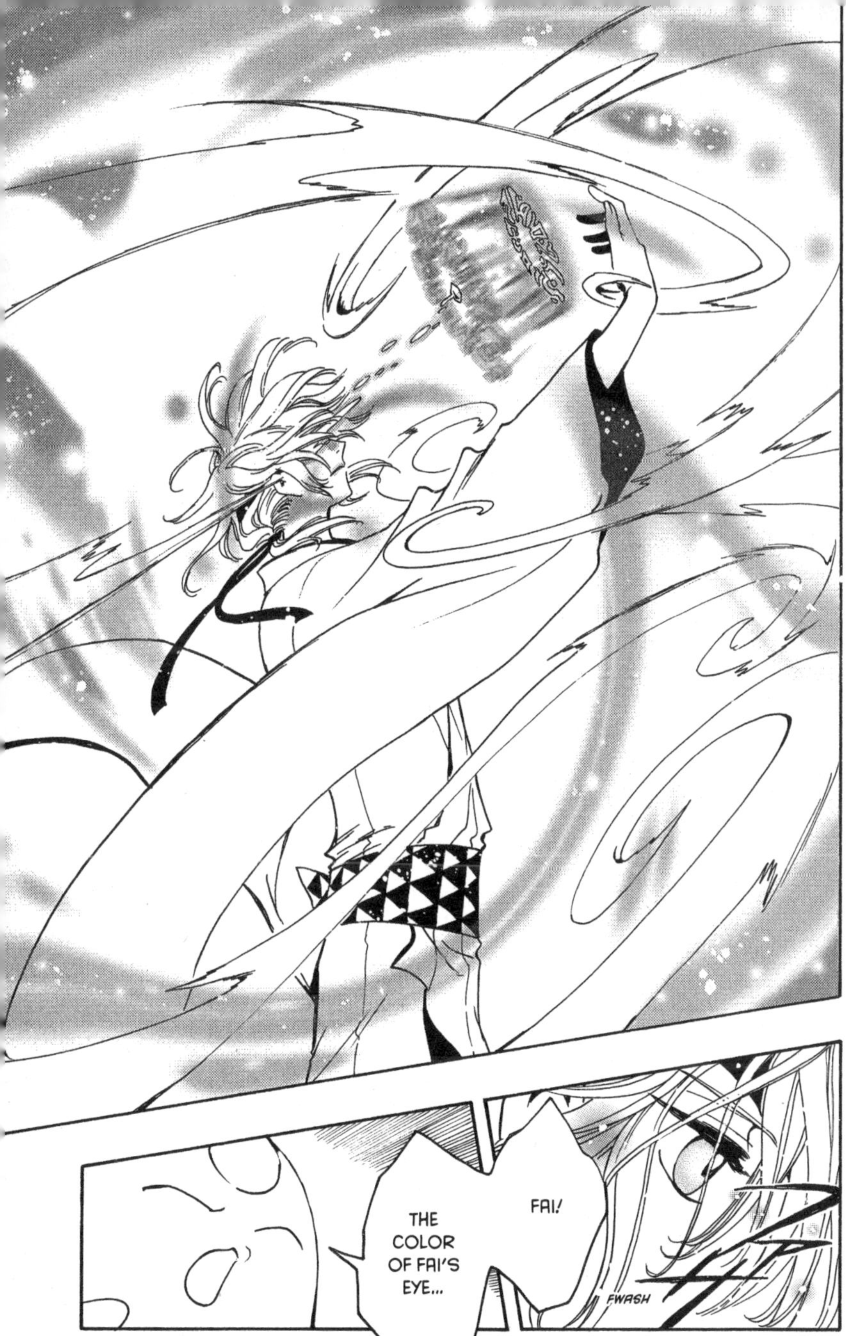
FWASH
FAI!
THE COLOR OF FAI'S EYE...

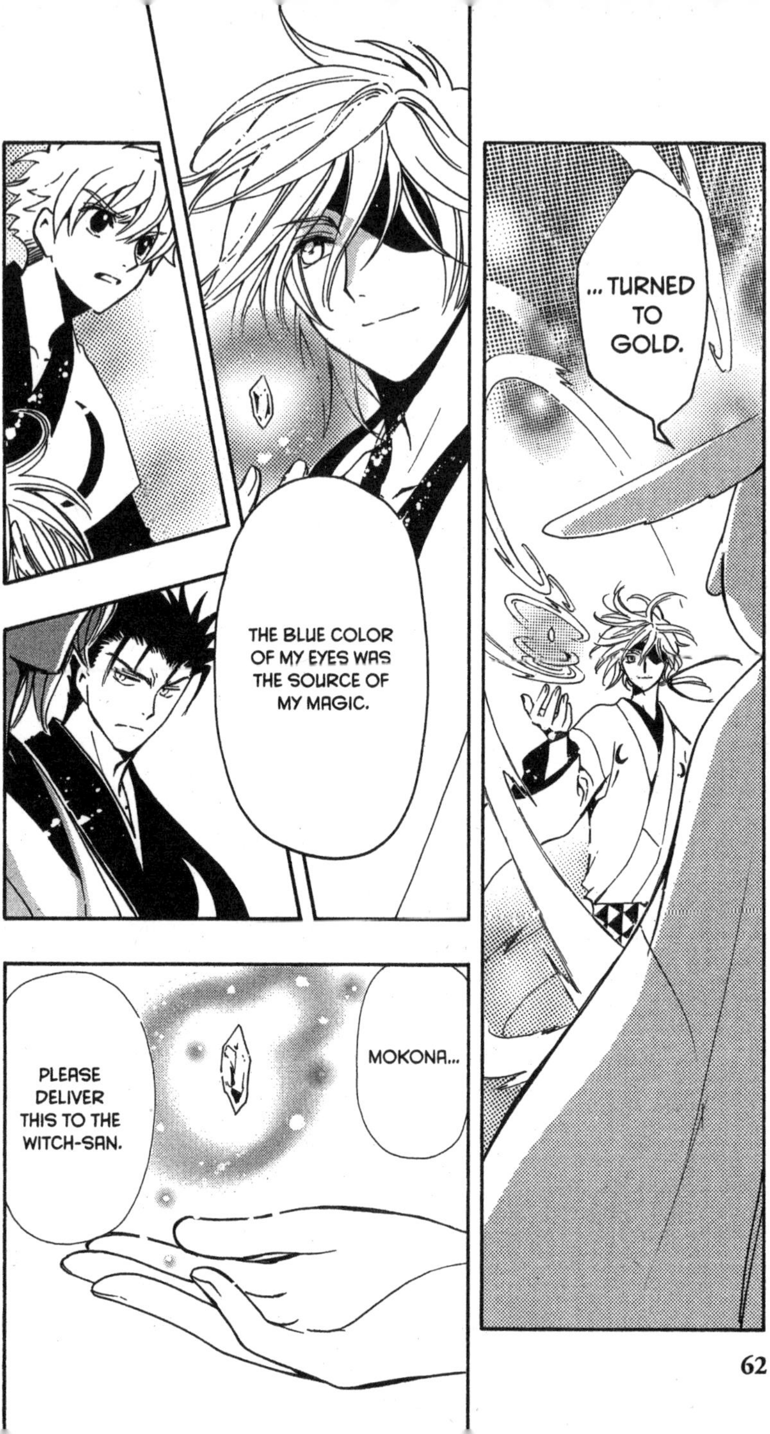
...TURNED TO GOLD.
THE BLUE COLOR OF MY EYES WAS THE SOURCE OF MY MAGIC.
MOKONA...
PLEASE DELIVER THIS TO THE WITCH-SAN.

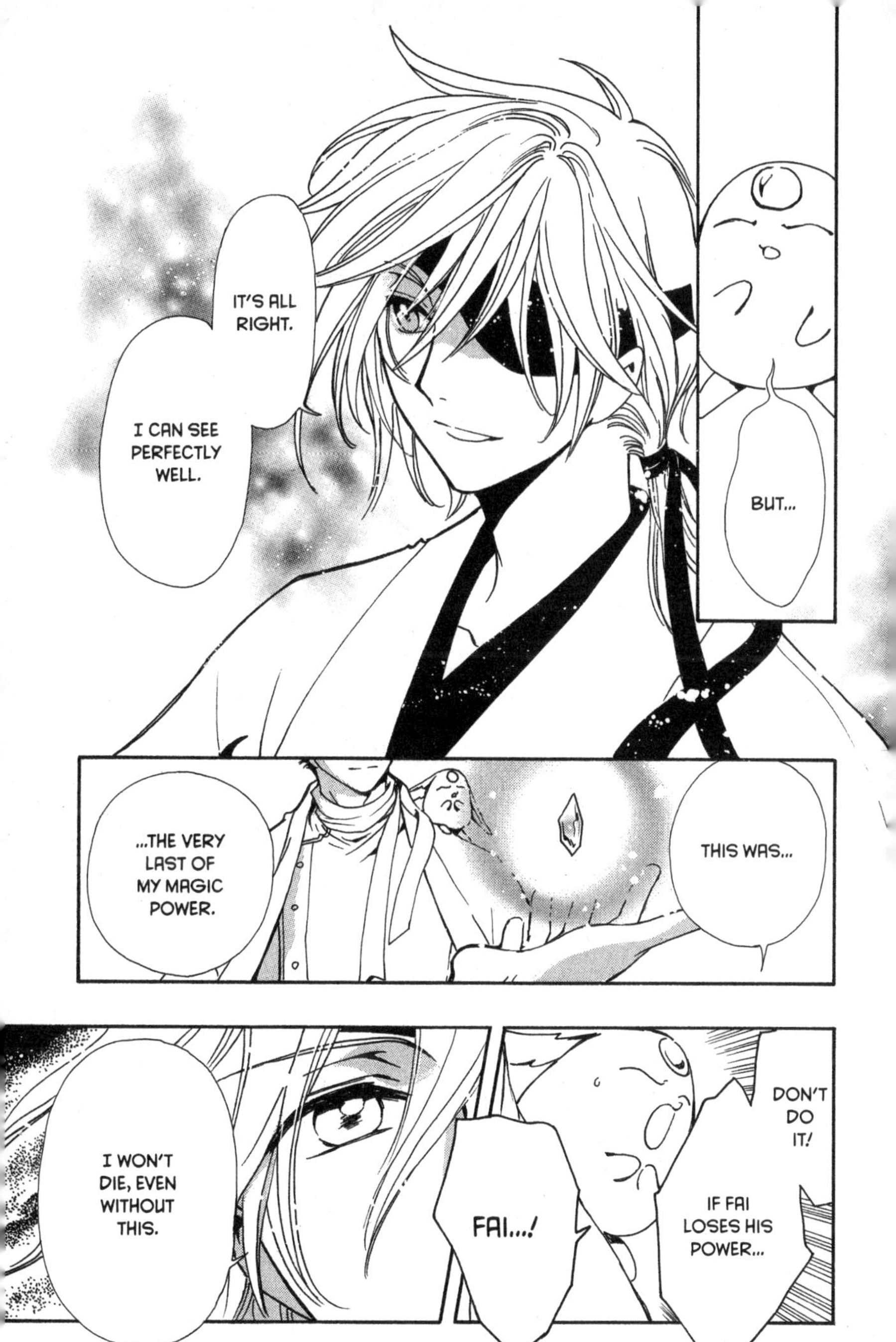
BUT...
IT'S ALL RIGHT.
I CAN SEE PERFECTLY WELL.
THIS WAS...
...THE VERY LAST OF MY MAGIC POWER.
DON'T DO IT!
IF FAI LOSES HIS POWER...
FAI...!
I WON'T DIE, EVEN WITHOUT THIS.

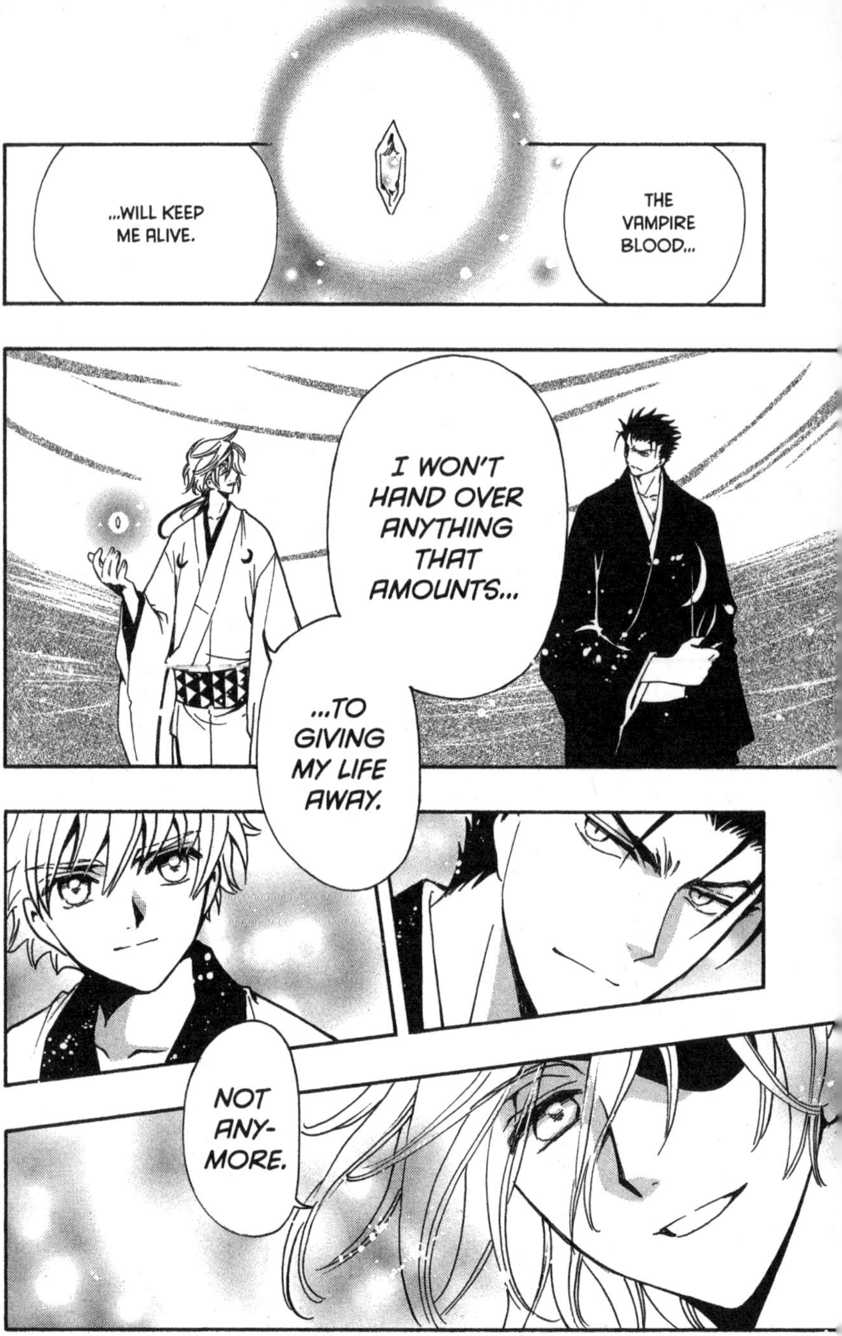
THE VAMPIRE BLOOD...
...WILL KEEP ME ALIVE.
I WON'T HAND OVER ANYTHING THAT AMOUNTS...
...TO GIVING MY LIFE AWAY.
NOT ANY-MORE.

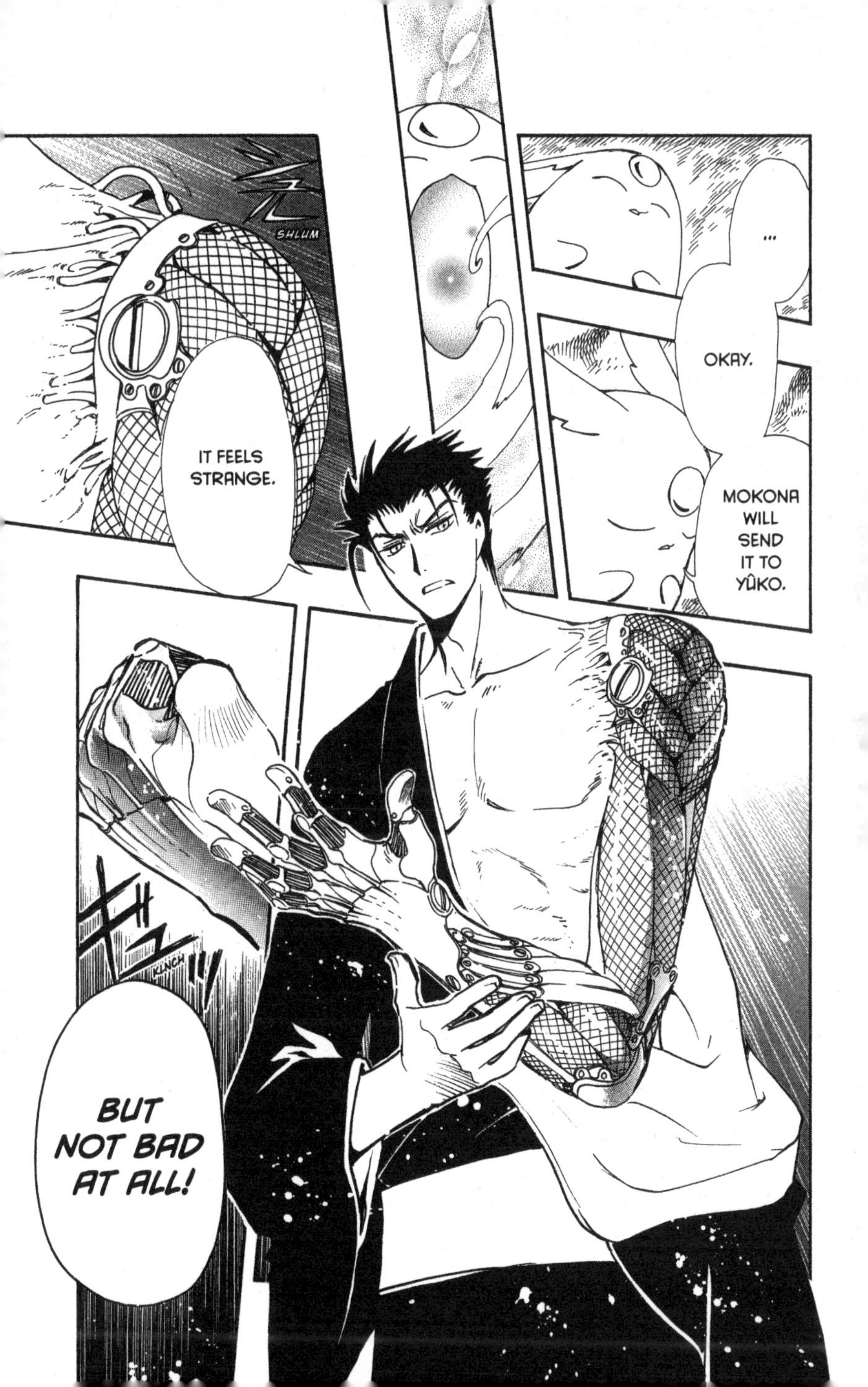
...
OKAY.
MOKONA WILL SEND IT TO YÛKO.
SHLUM
IT FEELS STRANGE.
KLNCH
BUT NOT BAD AT ALL!

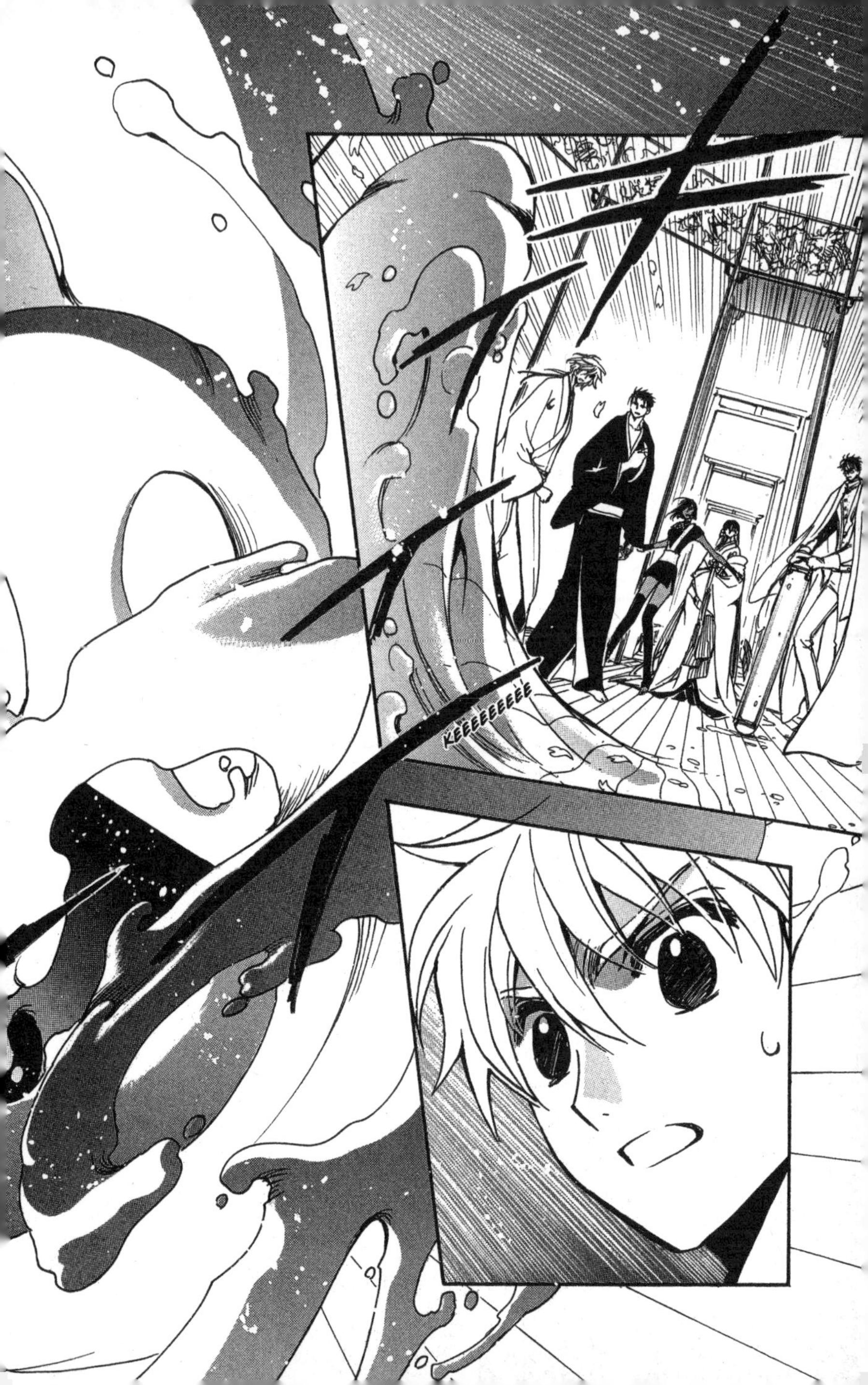
KEEEEEEEEE

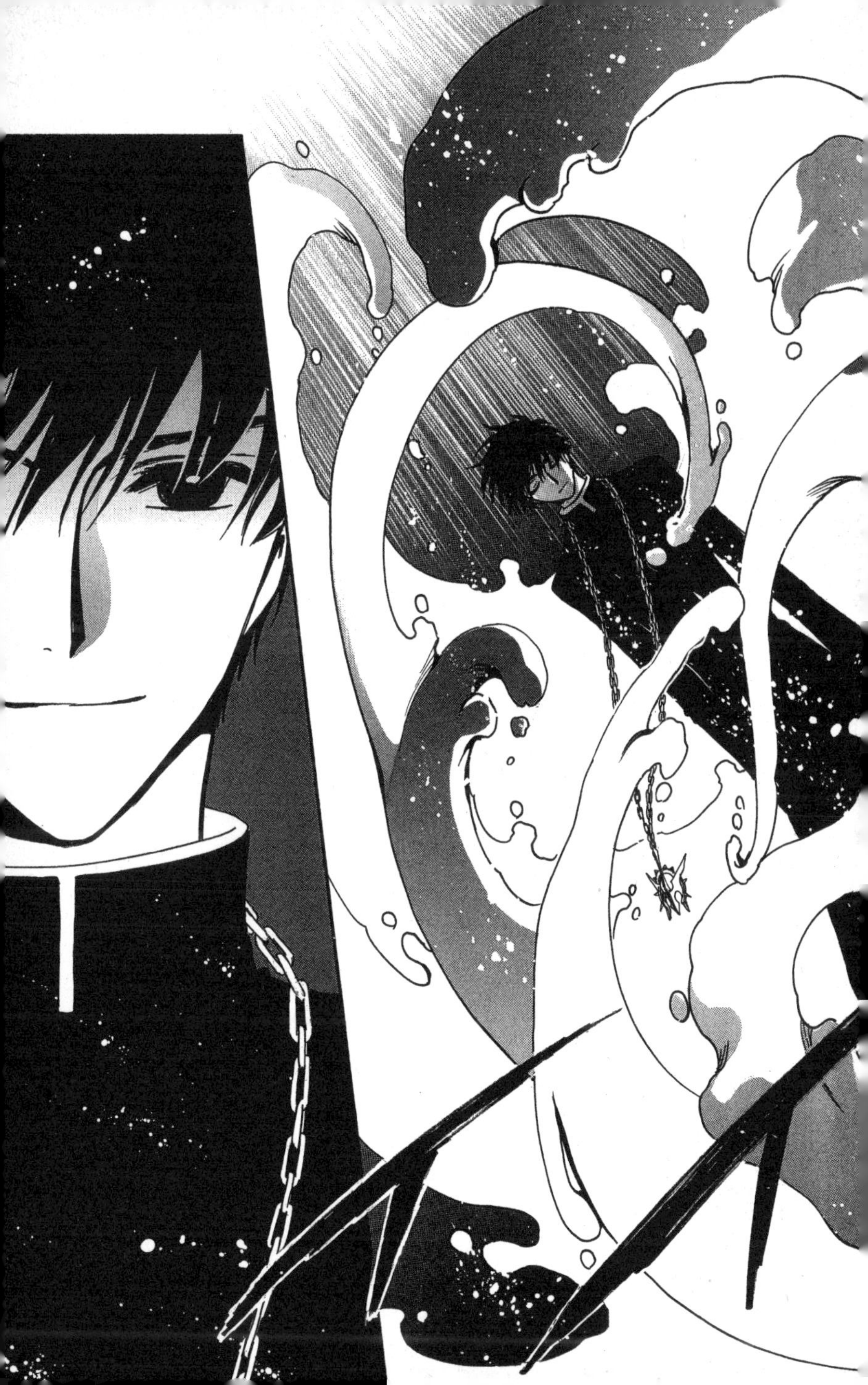

ツバサ

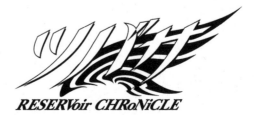

RESERVoir CHRoNiCLE

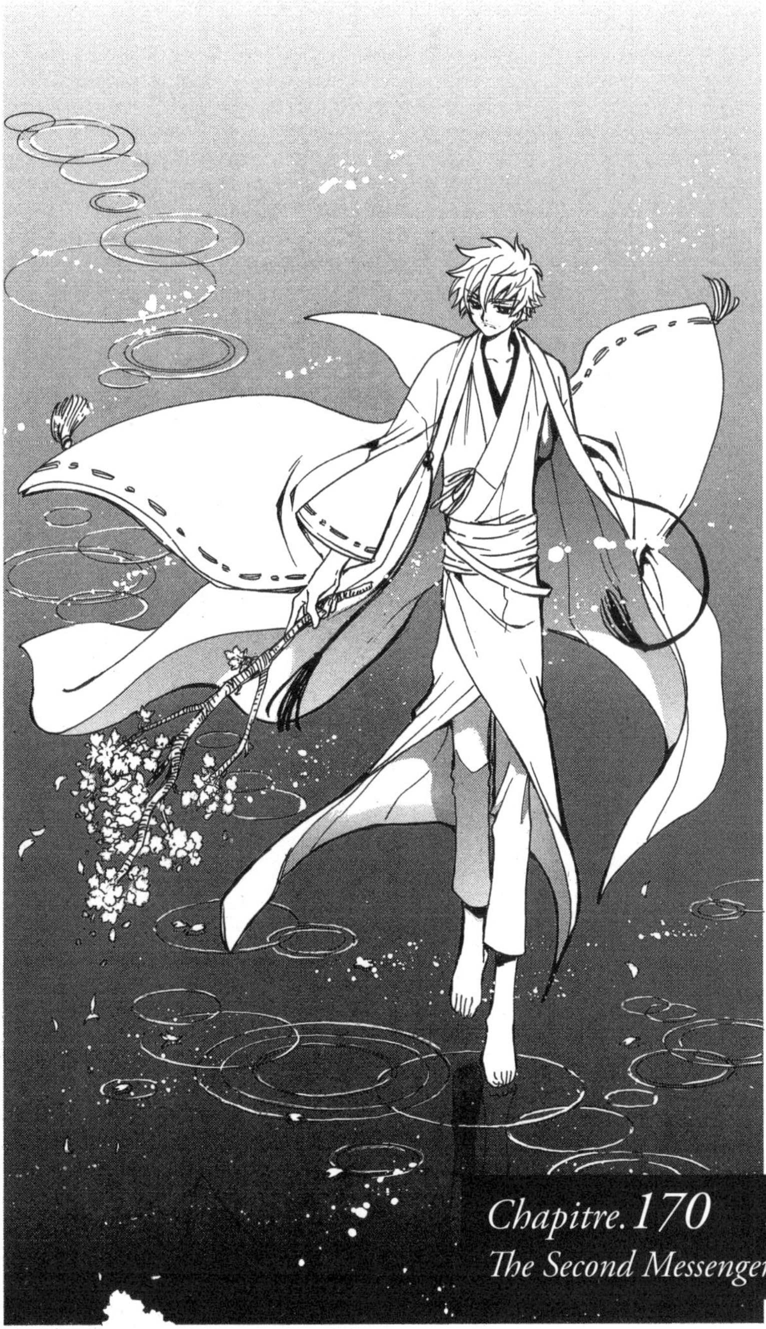
Chapitre. 170
The Second Messenger

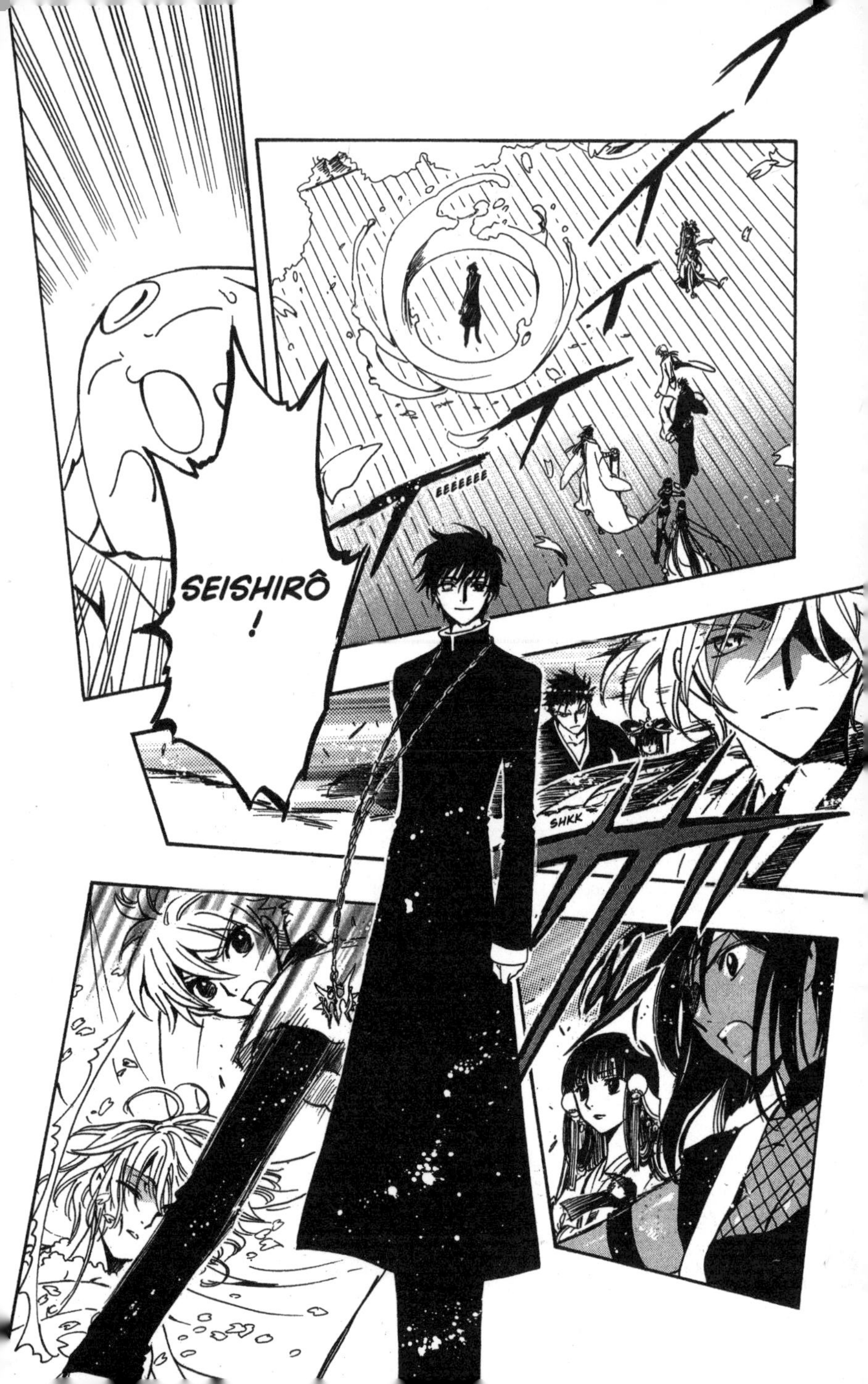
EEEEEEE
SEISHIRÔ
!
SHKK

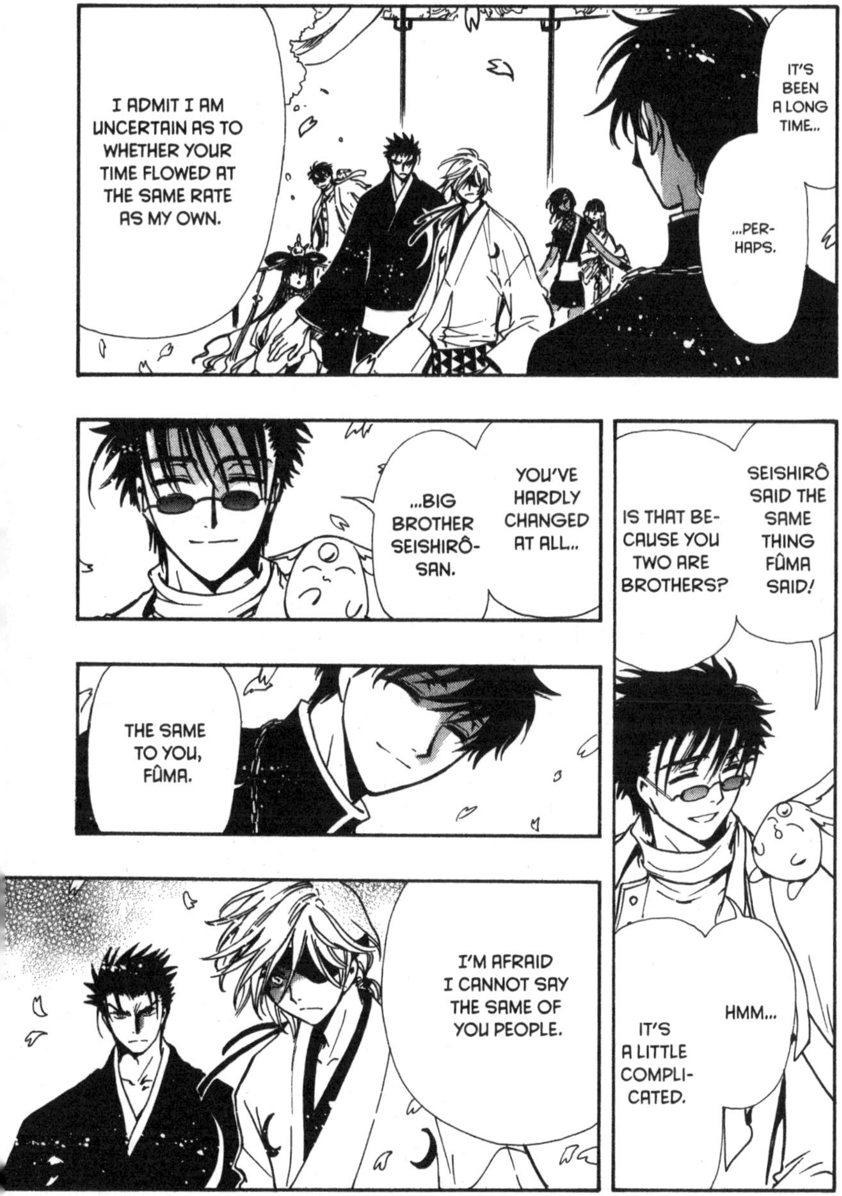
IT'S BEEN A LONG TIME...
...PERHAPS.
I ADMIT I AM UNCERTAIN AS TO WHETHER YOUR TIME FLOWED AT THE SAME RATE AS MY OWN.
YOU'VE HARDLY CHANGED AT ALL...
...BIG BROTHER SEISHIRÔ-SAN.
THE SAME TO YOU, FÛMA.
SEISHIRÔ SAID THE SAME THING FÛMA SAID!
IS THAT BE-CAUSE YOU TWO ARE BROTHERS?
HMM...
IT'S A LITTLE COMPLI-CATED.
I'M AFRAID I CANNOT SAY THE SAME OF YOU PEOPLE.

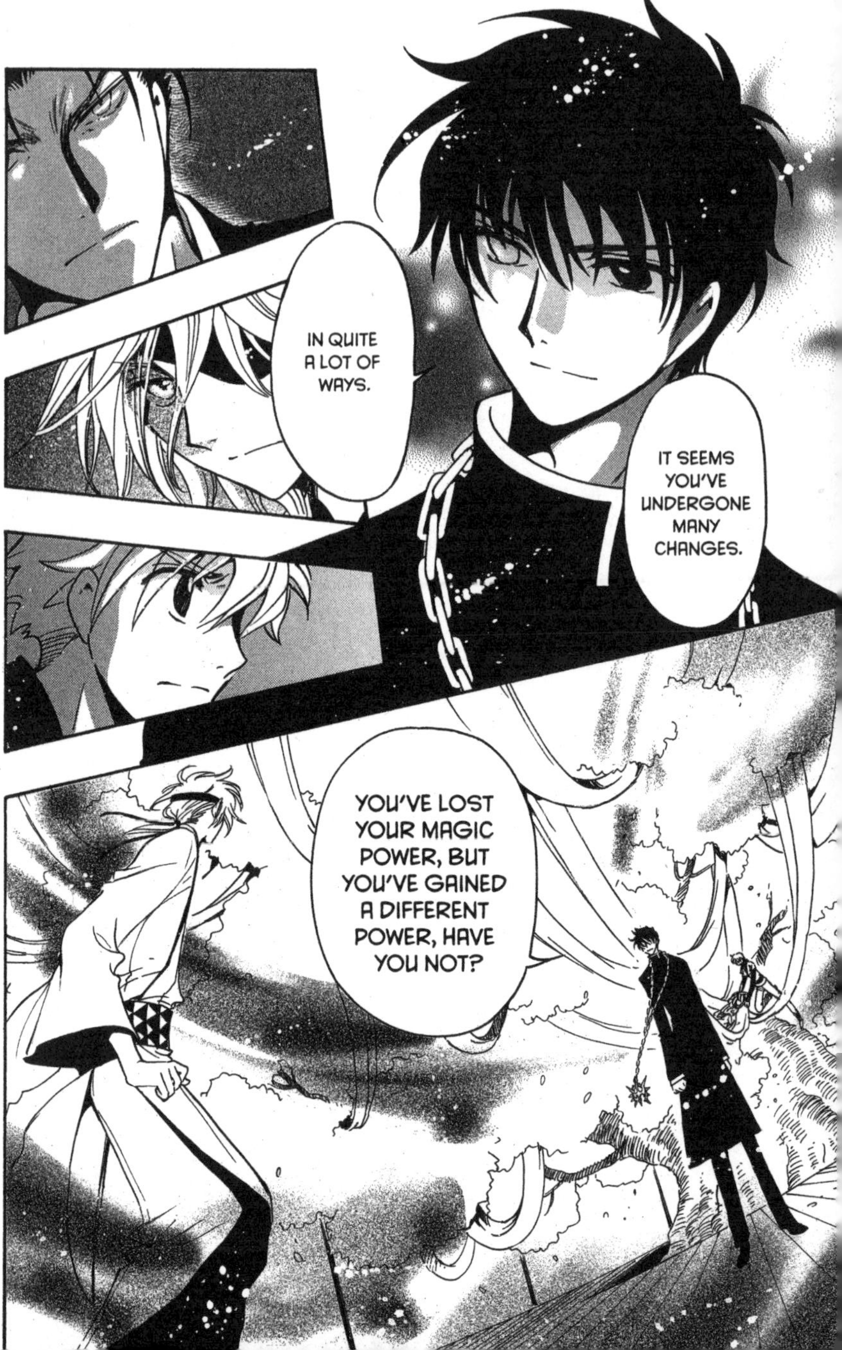
IT SEEMS YOU'VE UNDERGONE MANY CHANGES.
IN QUITE A LOT OF WAYS.
YOU'VE LOST YOUR MAGIC POWER, BUT YOU'VE GAINED A DIFFERENT POWER, HAVE YOU NOT?

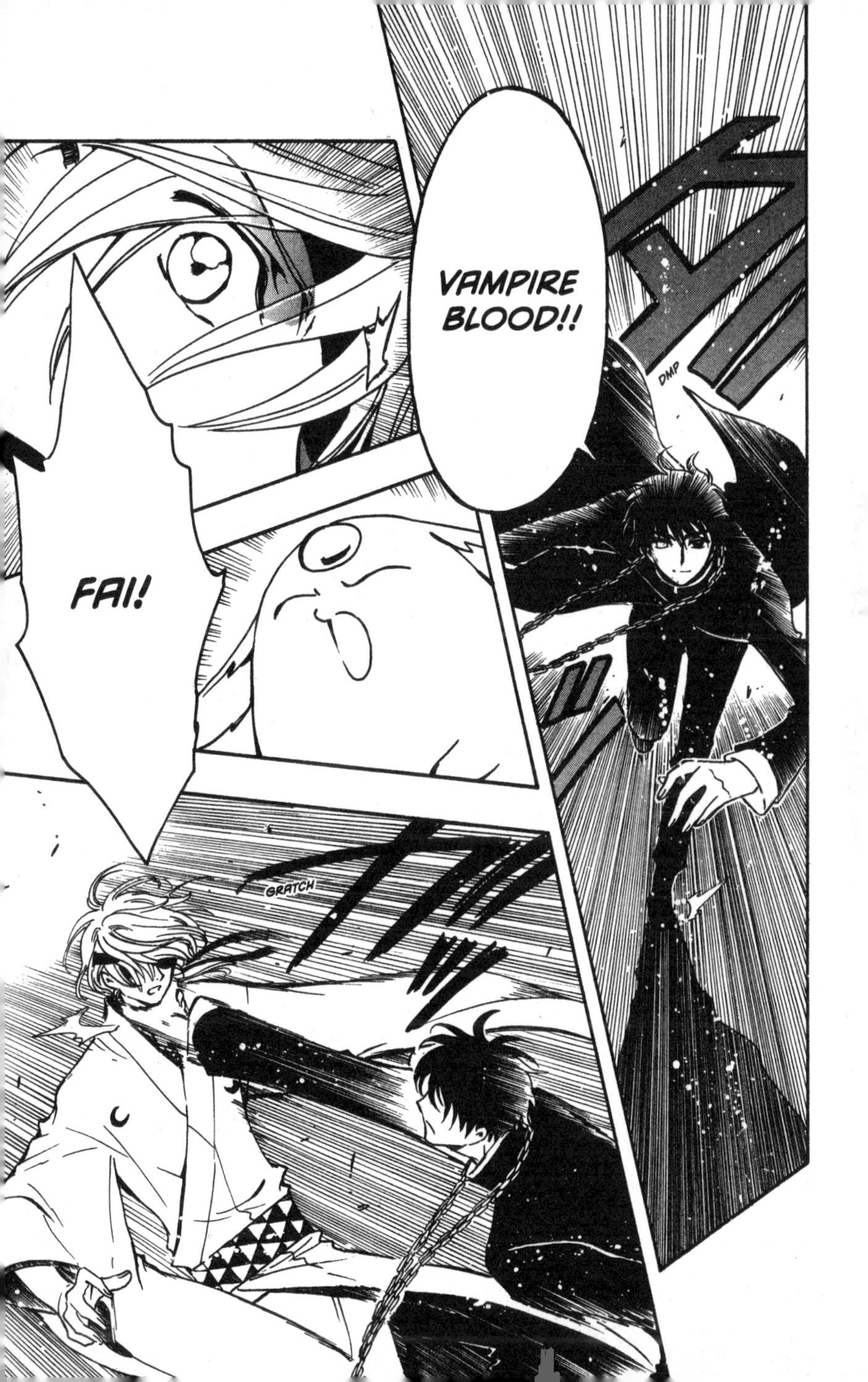
VAMPIRE BLOOD!!
DMP
FAI!
GRATCH

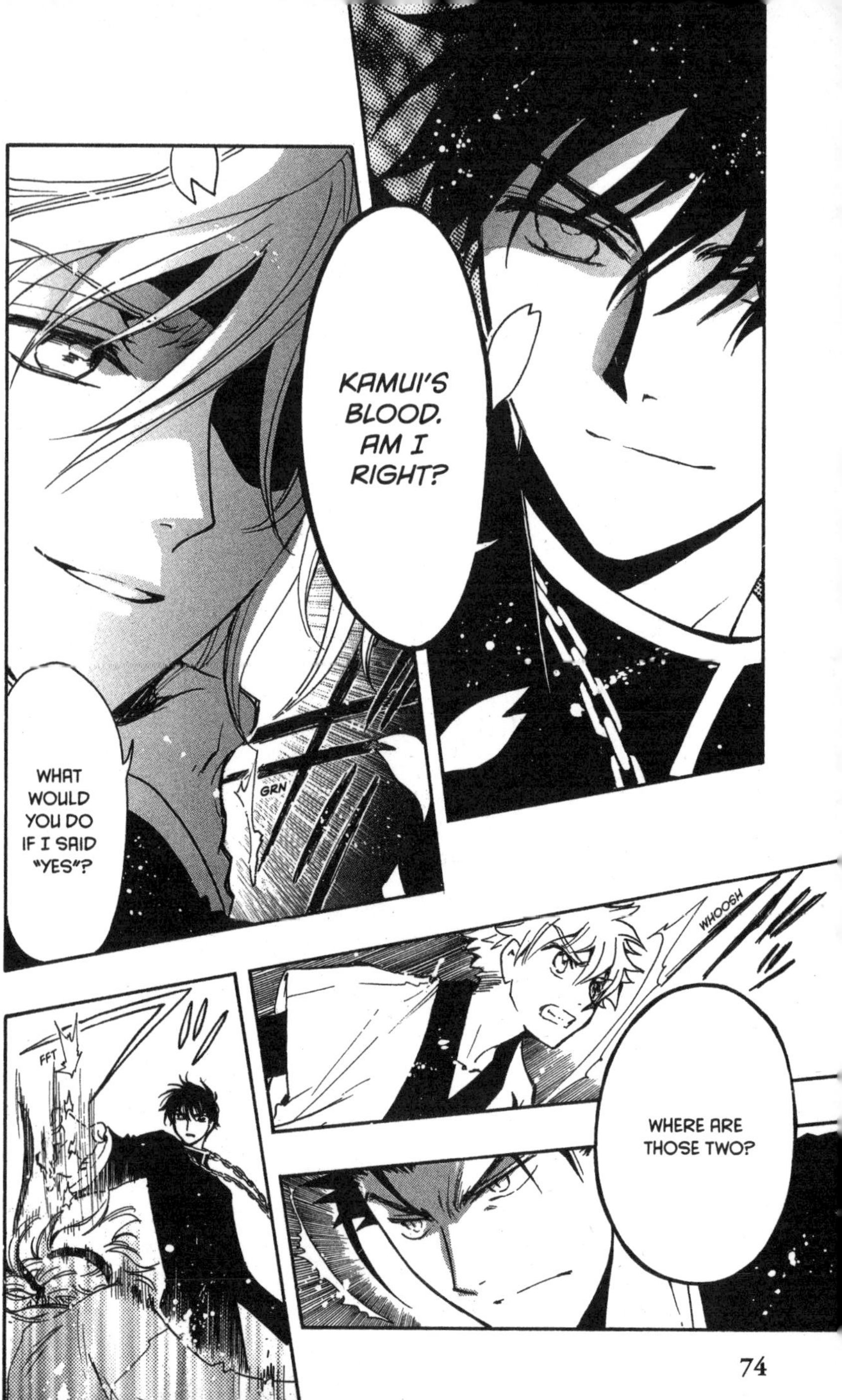
KAMUI'S BLOOD. AM I RIGHT?
WHAT WOULD YOU DO IF I SAID "YES"?
GRN
WHOOSH
WHERE ARE THOSE TWO?
FFT

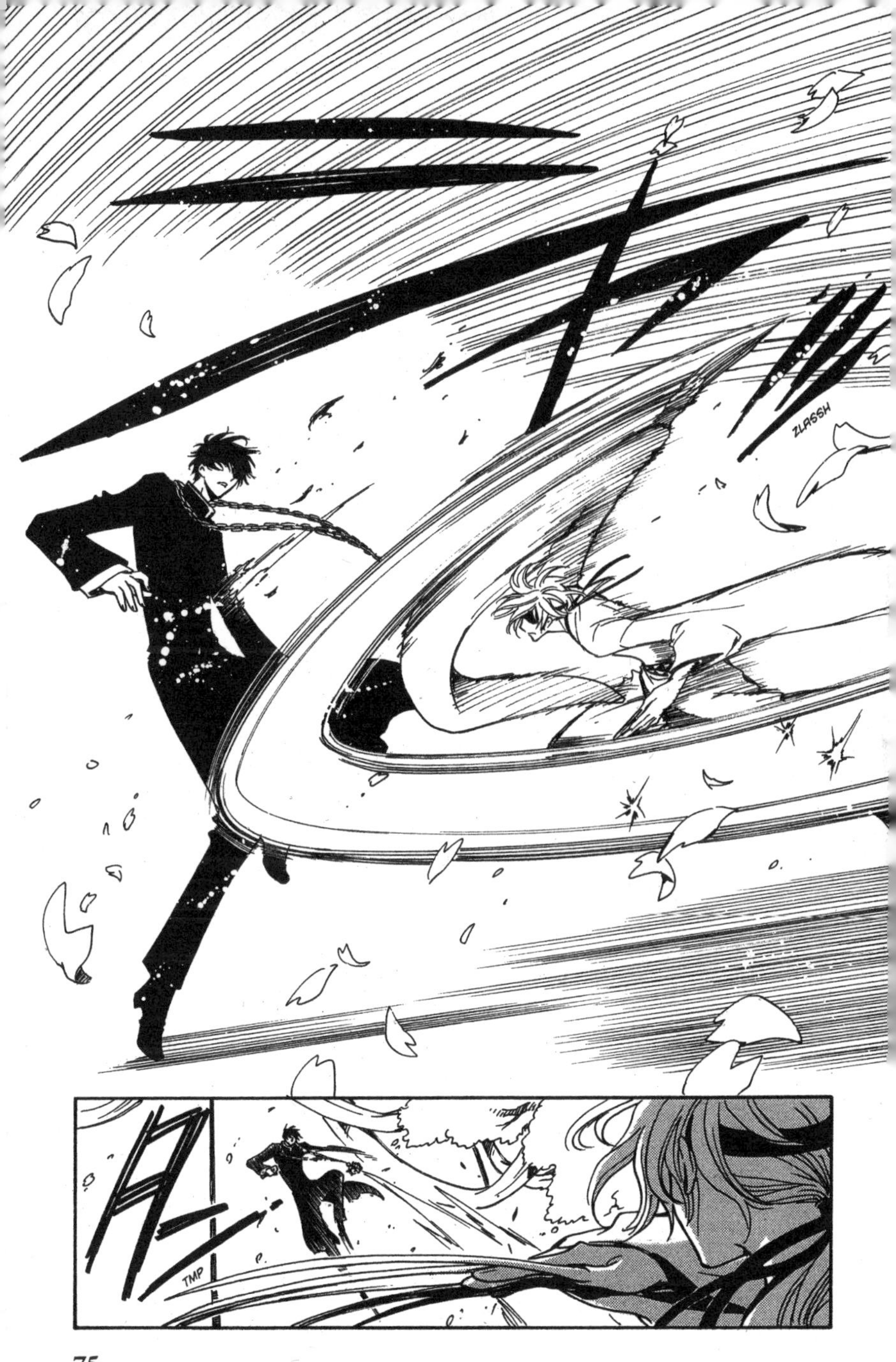
ZLASSH
TMP

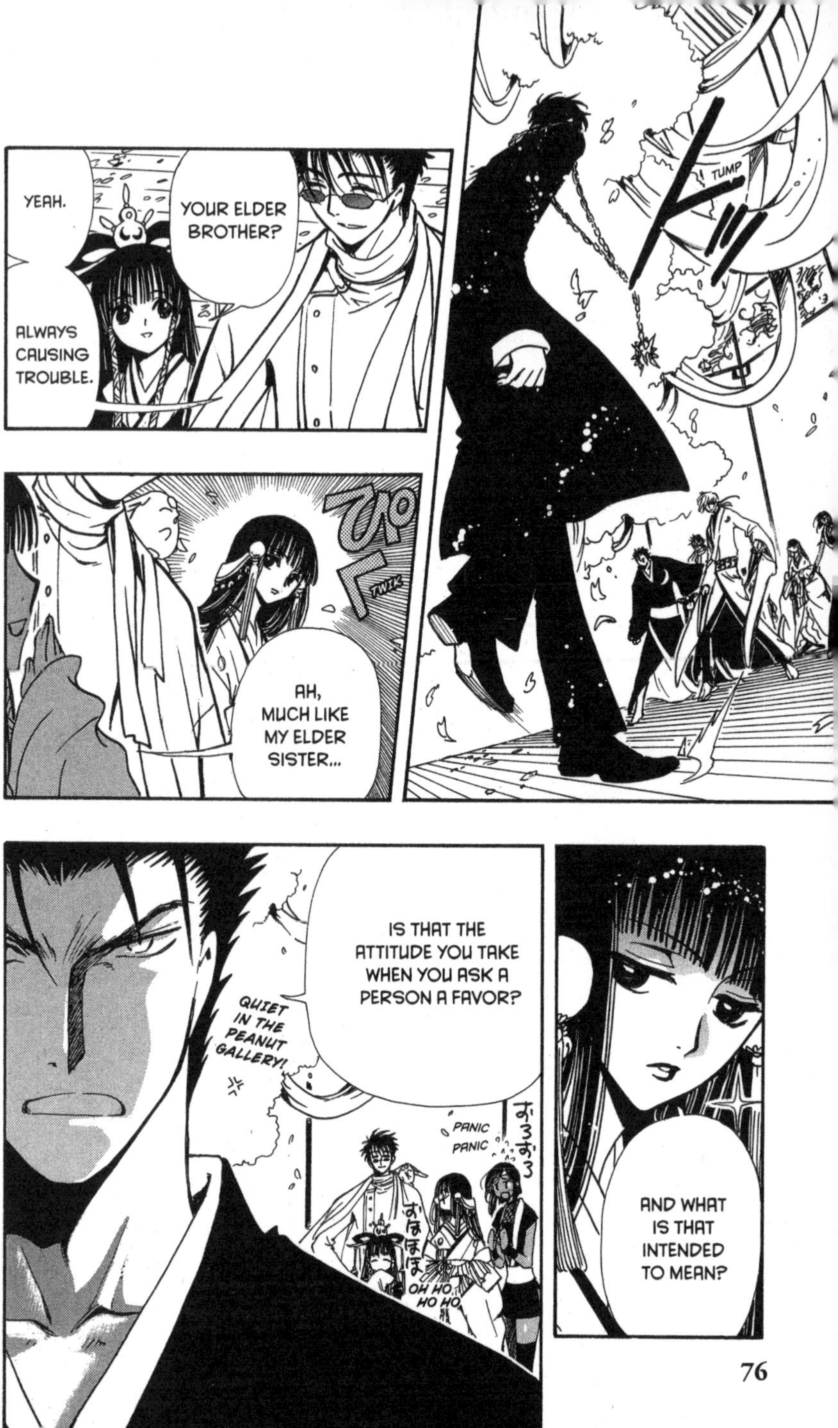
TUMP
YOUR ELDER BROTHER?
YEAH.
ALWAYS CAUSING TROUBLE.
TWIK
AH, MUCH LIKE MY ELDER SISTER...
AND WHAT IS THAT INTENDED TO MEAN?
IS THAT THE ATTITUDE YOU TAKE WHEN YOU ASK A PERSON A FAVOR?
QUIET IN THE PEANUT GALLERY!
PANIC PANIC
OH HO HO HO

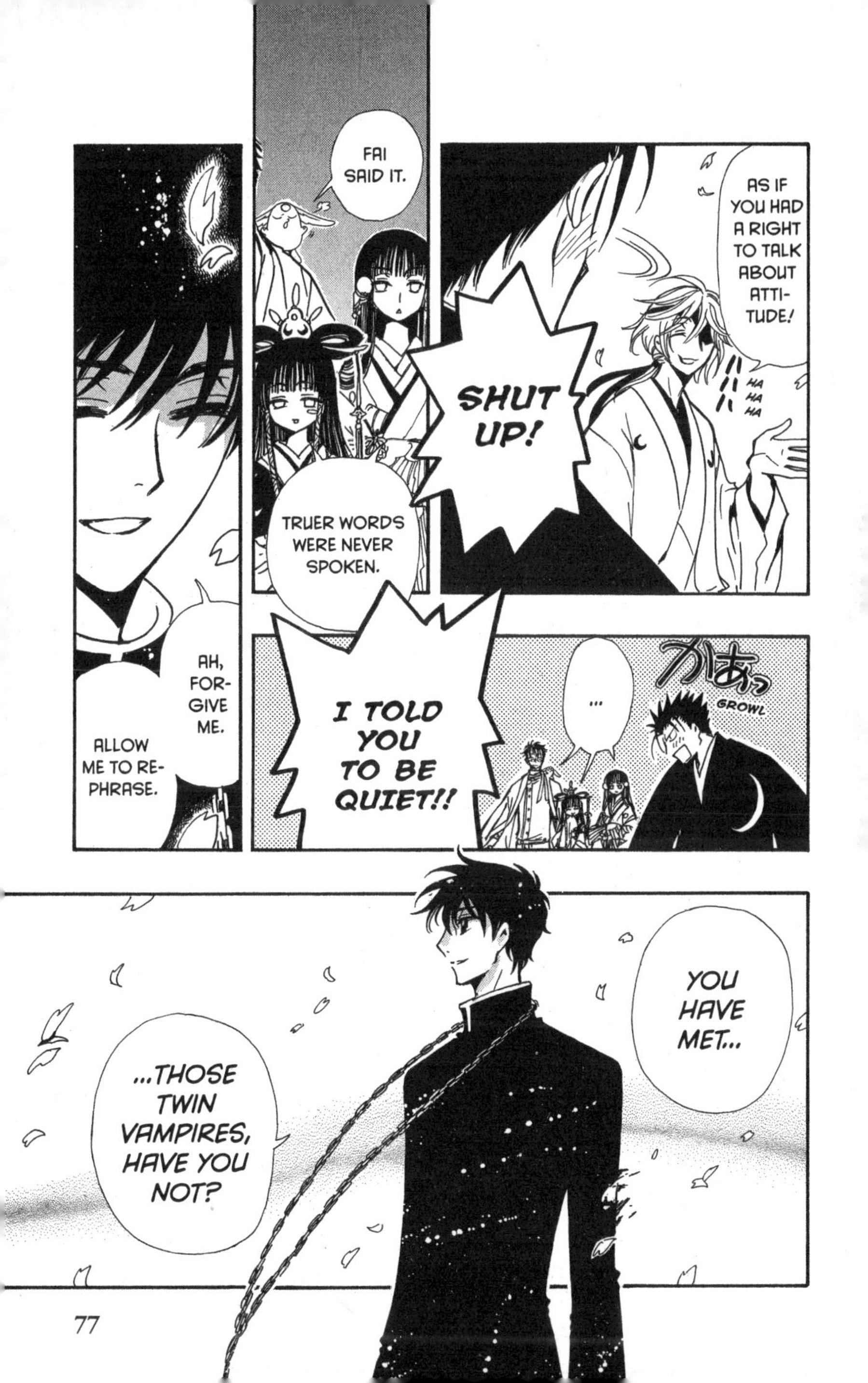
AS IF YOU HAD A RIGHT TO TALK ABOUT ATTI-TUDE!
HA HA HA
SHUT UP!
FAI SAID IT.
TRUER WORDS WERE NEVER SPOKEN.
I TOLD YOU TO BE QUIET!!
...
かあっ
GROWL
AH, FOR-GIVE ME.
ALLOW ME TO RE-PHRASE.
YOU HAVE MET...
...THOSE TWIN VAMPIRES, HAVE YOU NOT?

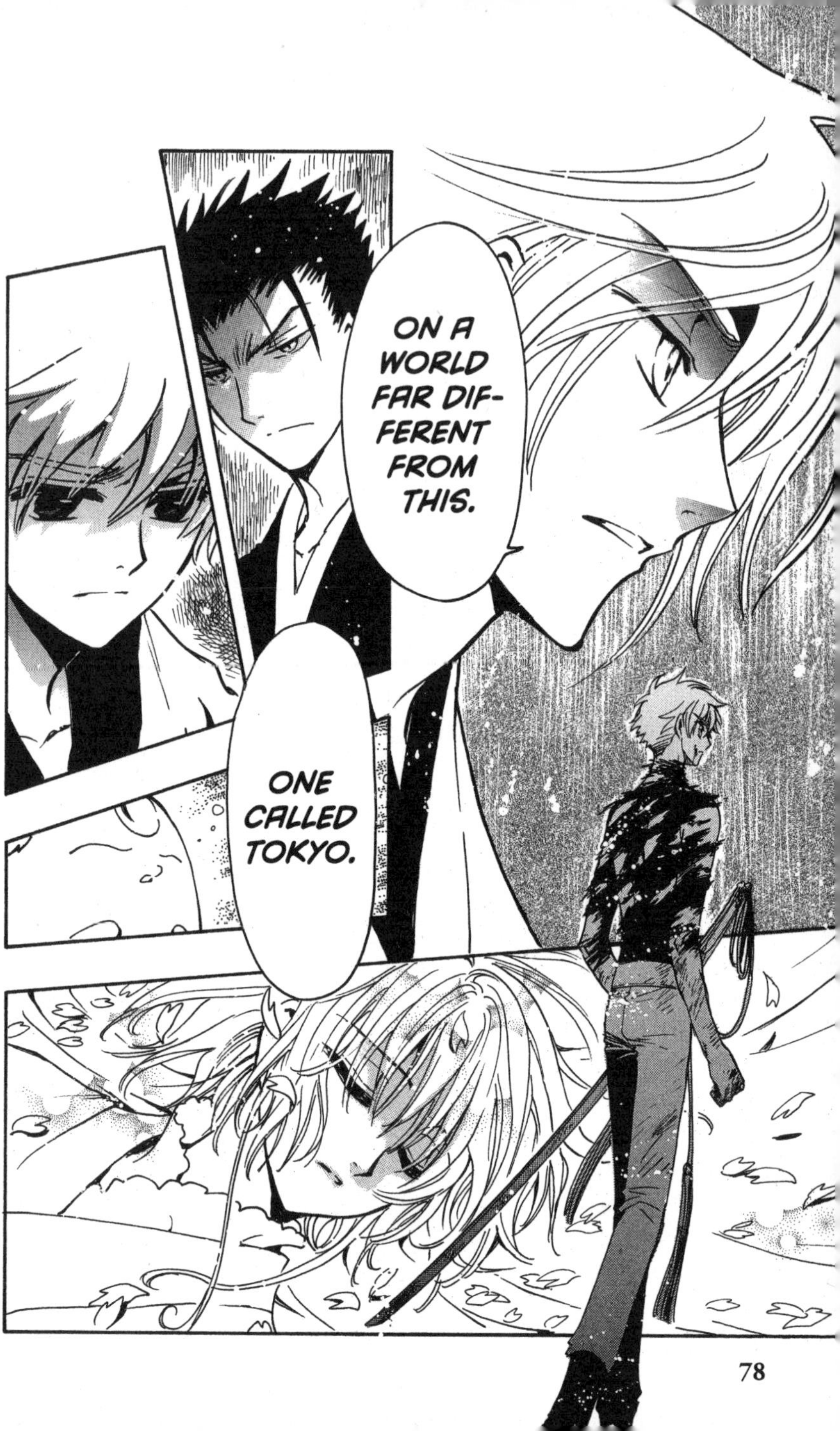
ON A WORLD FAR DIF- FERENT FROM THIS.
ONE CALLED TOKYO.

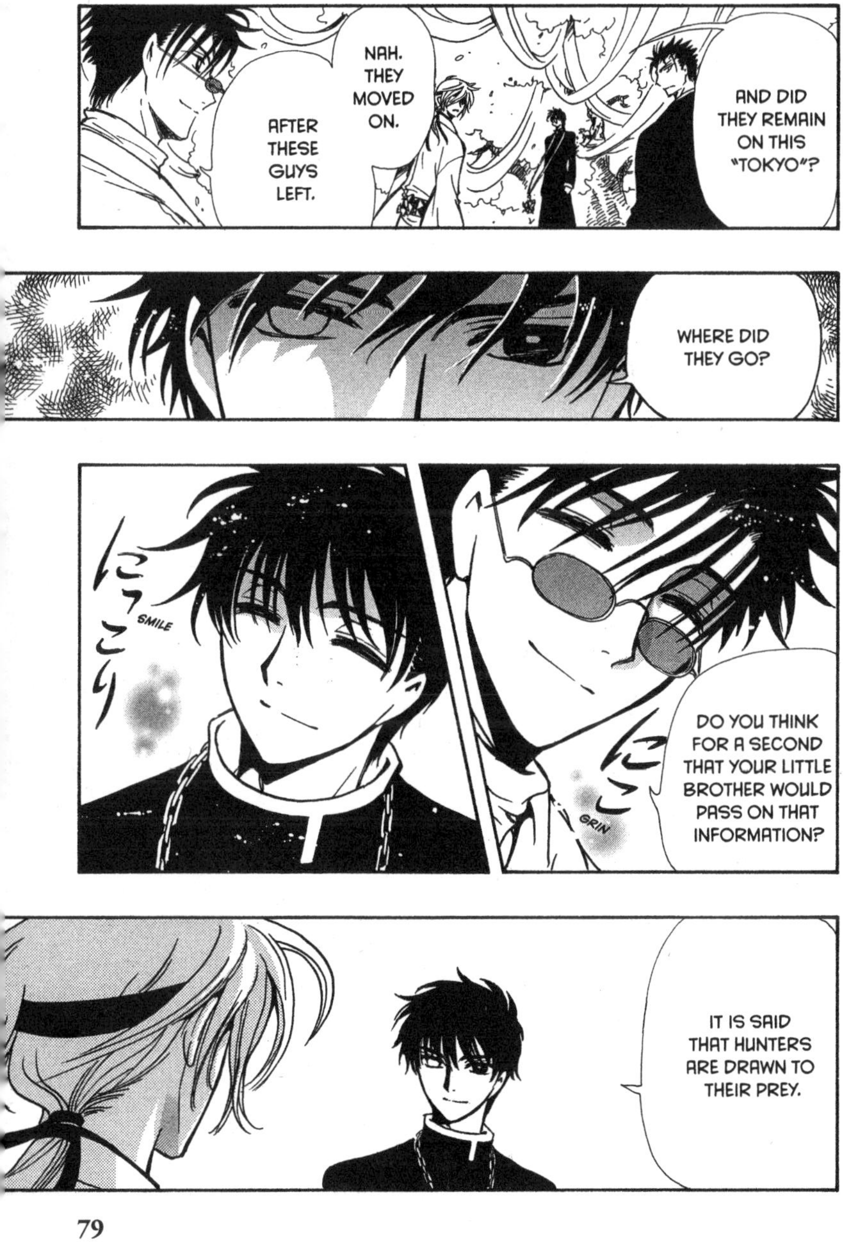
AND DID THEY REMAIN ON THIS "TOKYO"?
NAH. THEY MOVED ON.
AFTER THESE GUYS LEFT.
WHERE DID THEY GO?
DO YOU THINK FOR A SECOND THAT YOUR LITTLE BROTHER WOULD PASS ON THAT INFORMATION?
GRIN
にっこり
SMILE
IT IS SAID THAT HUNTERS ARE DRAWN TO THEIR PREY.

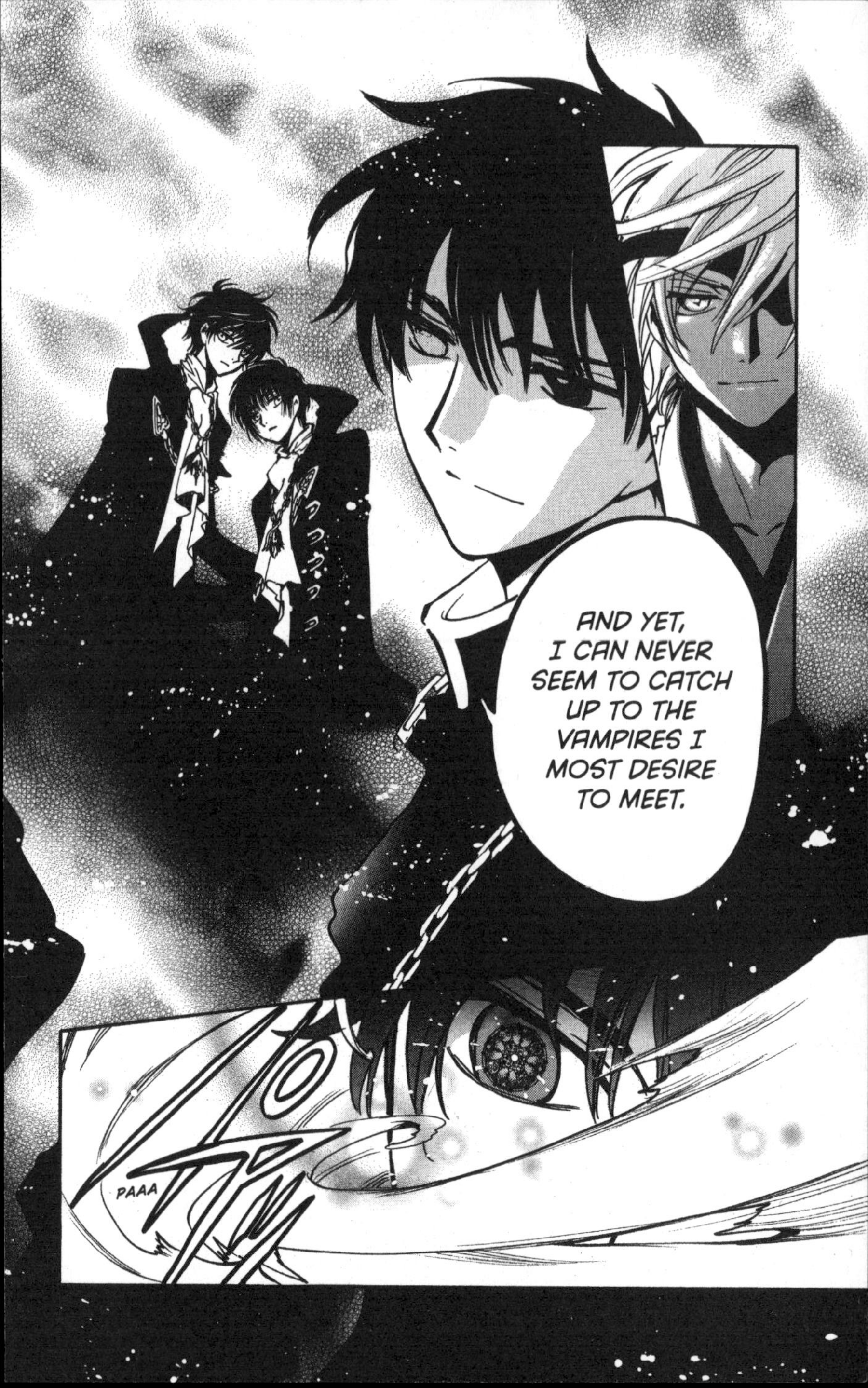
AND YET, I CAN NEVER SEEM TO CATCH UP TO THE VAMPIRES I MOST DESIRE TO MEET.
PAAA

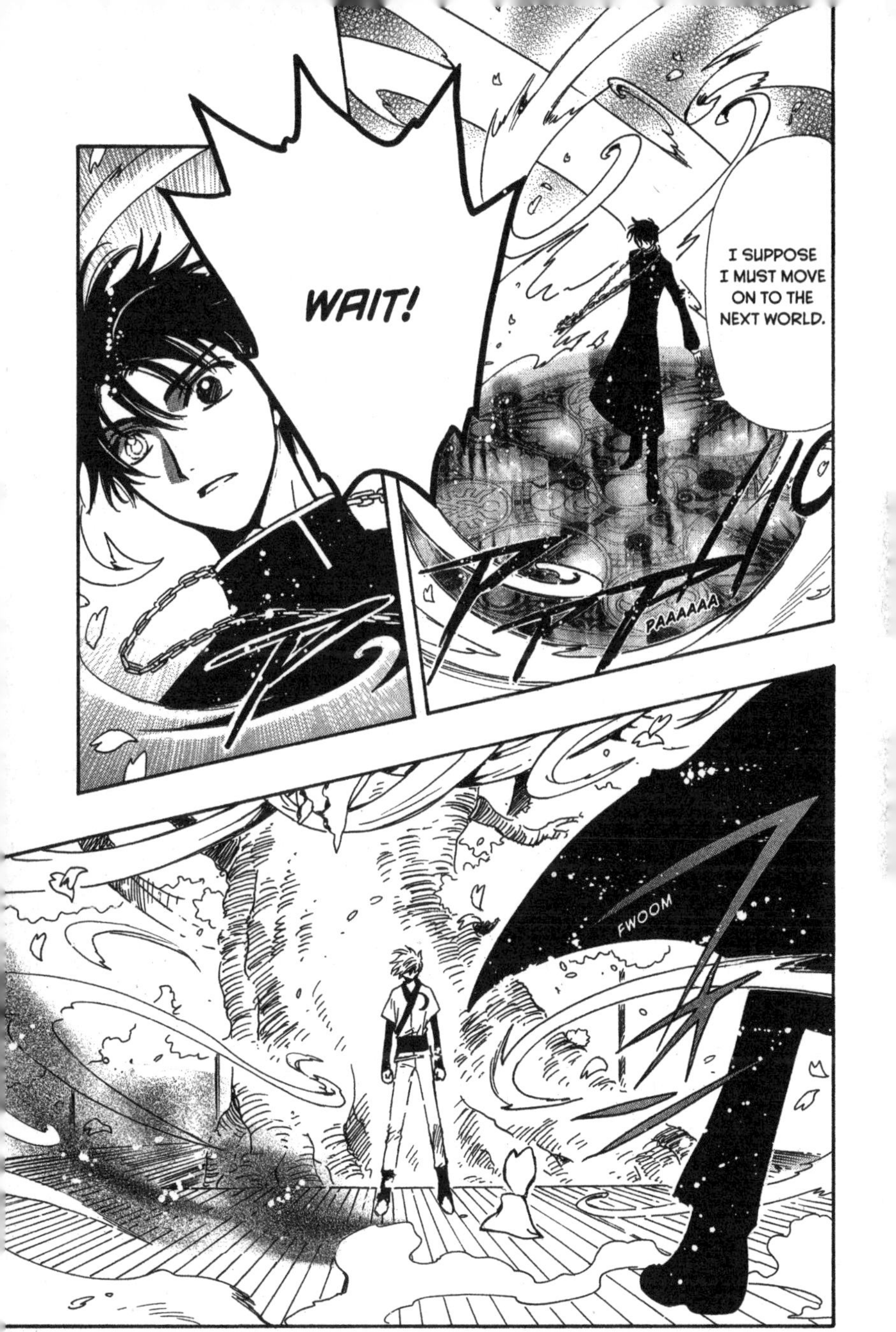
I SUPPOSE I MUST MOVE ON TO THE NEXT WORLD.
WAIT!
PAAAAAA
FWOOM

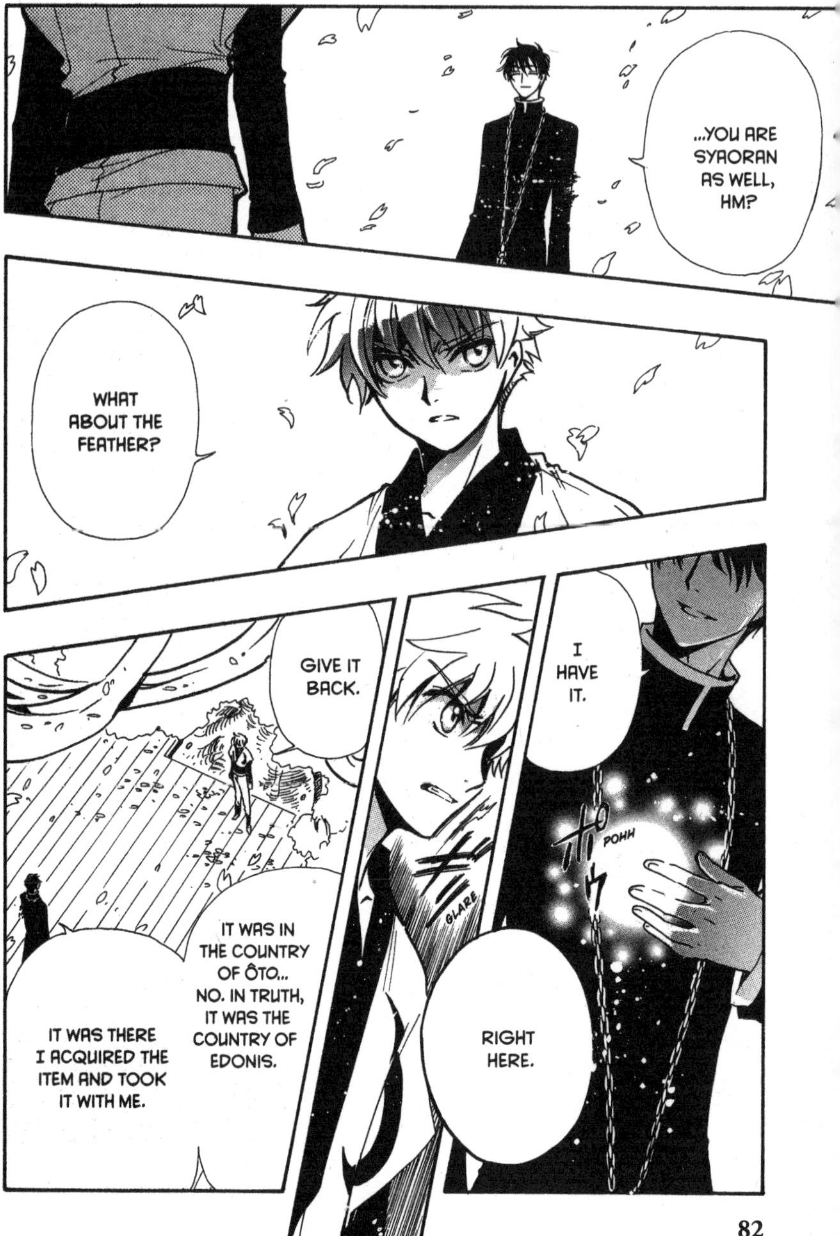
...YOU ARE SYAORAN AS WELL, HM?
WHAT ABOUT THE FEATHER?
I HAVE IT.
POHH
RIGHT HERE.
GIVE IT BACK.
GLARE
IT WAS IN THE COUNTRY OF ÔTO... NO. IN TRUTH, IT WAS THE COUNTRY OF EDONIS.
IT WAS THERE I ACQUIRED THE ITEM AND TOOK IT WITH ME.

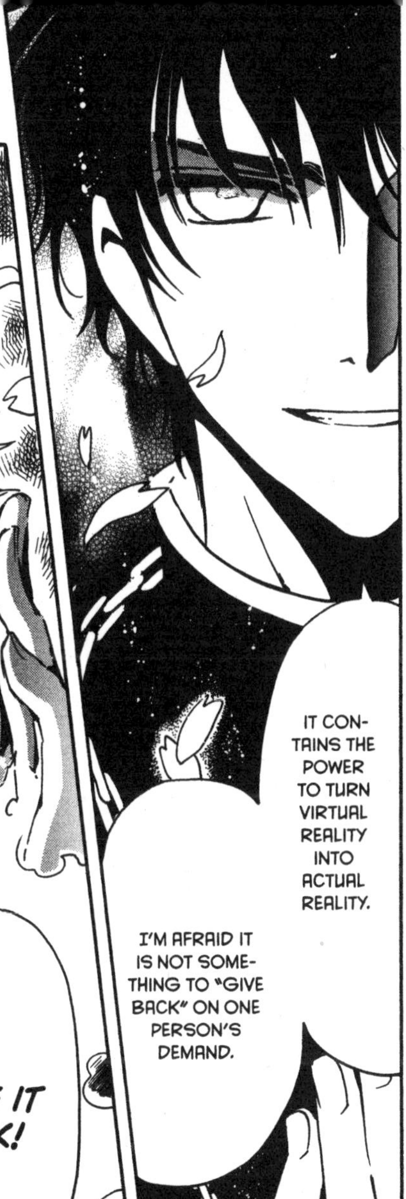
IT CONTAINS THE POWER TO TURN VIRTUAL REALITY INTO ACTUAL REALITY.
I'M AFRAID IT IS NOT SOMETHING TO "GIVE BACK" ON ONE PERSON'S DEMAND.
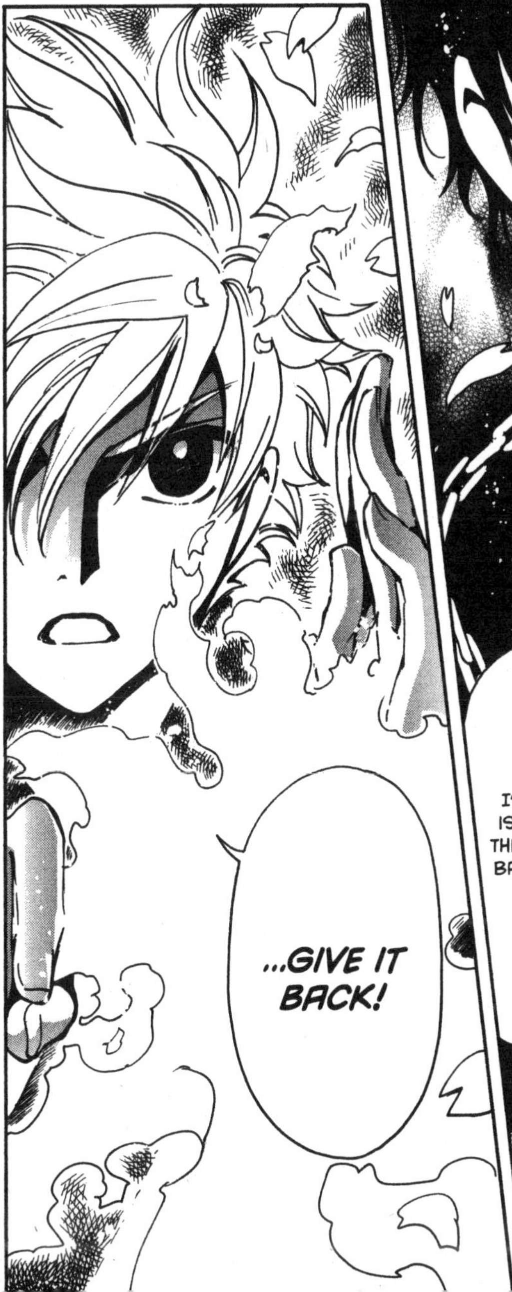
...GIVE IT BACK!

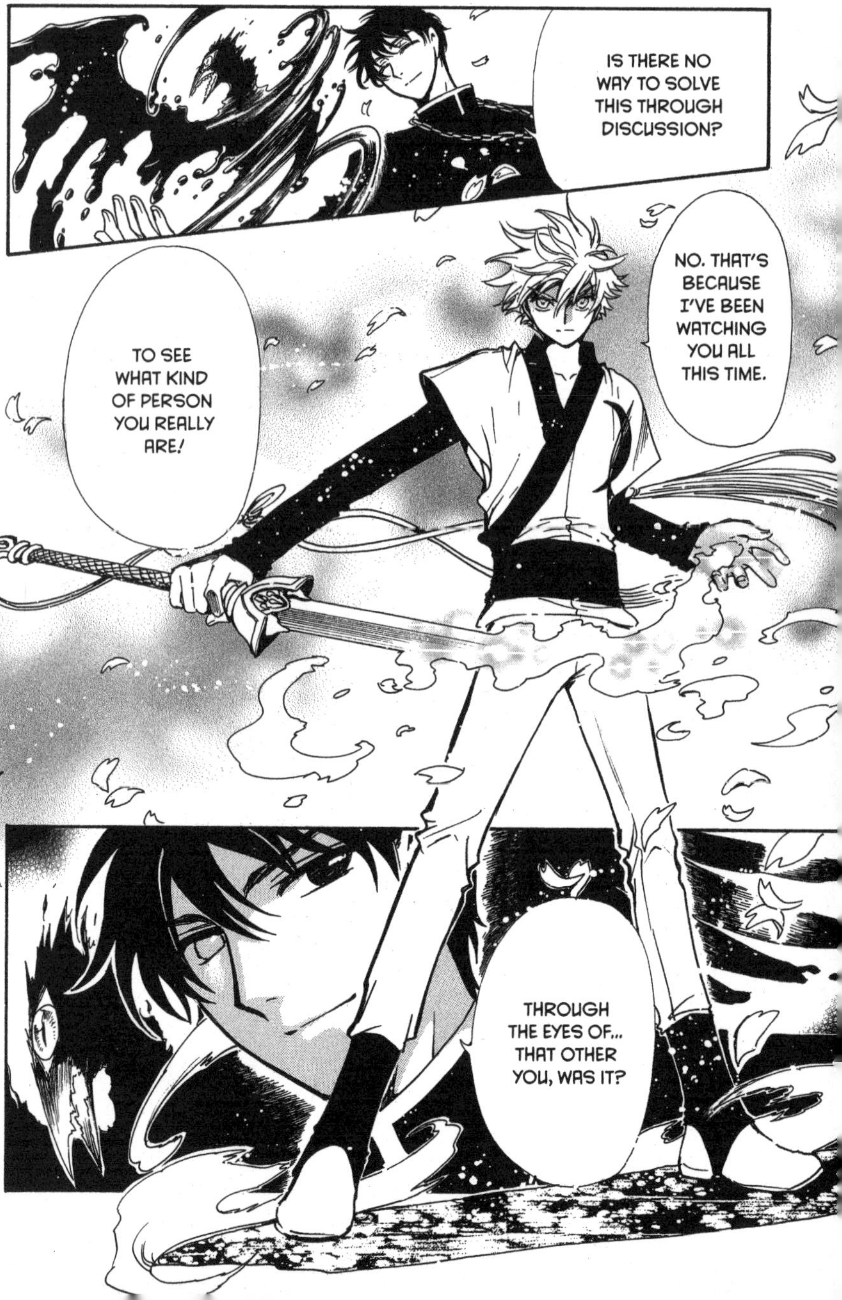
IS THERE NO WAY TO SOLVE THIS THROUGH DISCUSSION?
NO. THAT'S BECAUSE I'VE BEEN WATCHING YOU ALL THIS TIME.
TO SEE WHAT KIND OF PERSON YOU REALLY ARE!
THROUGH THE EYES OF... THAT OTHER YOU, WAS IT?

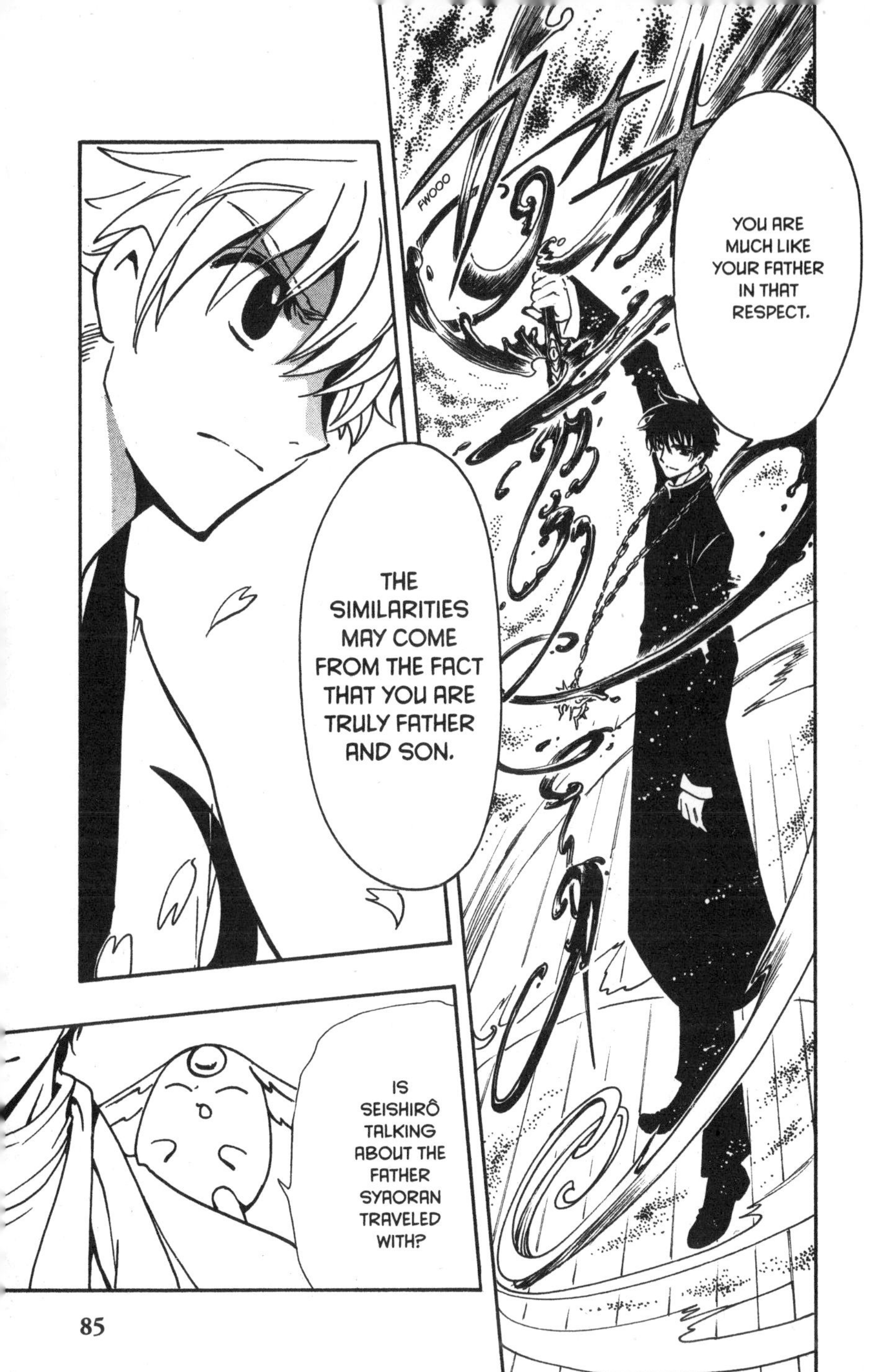
FWOOO
YOU ARE MUCH LIKE YOUR FATHER IN THAT RESPECT.
THE SIMILARITIES MAY COME FROM THE FACT THAT YOU ARE TRULY FATHER AND SON.
IS SEISHIRÔ TALKING ABOUT THE FATHER SYAORAN TRAVELED WITH?

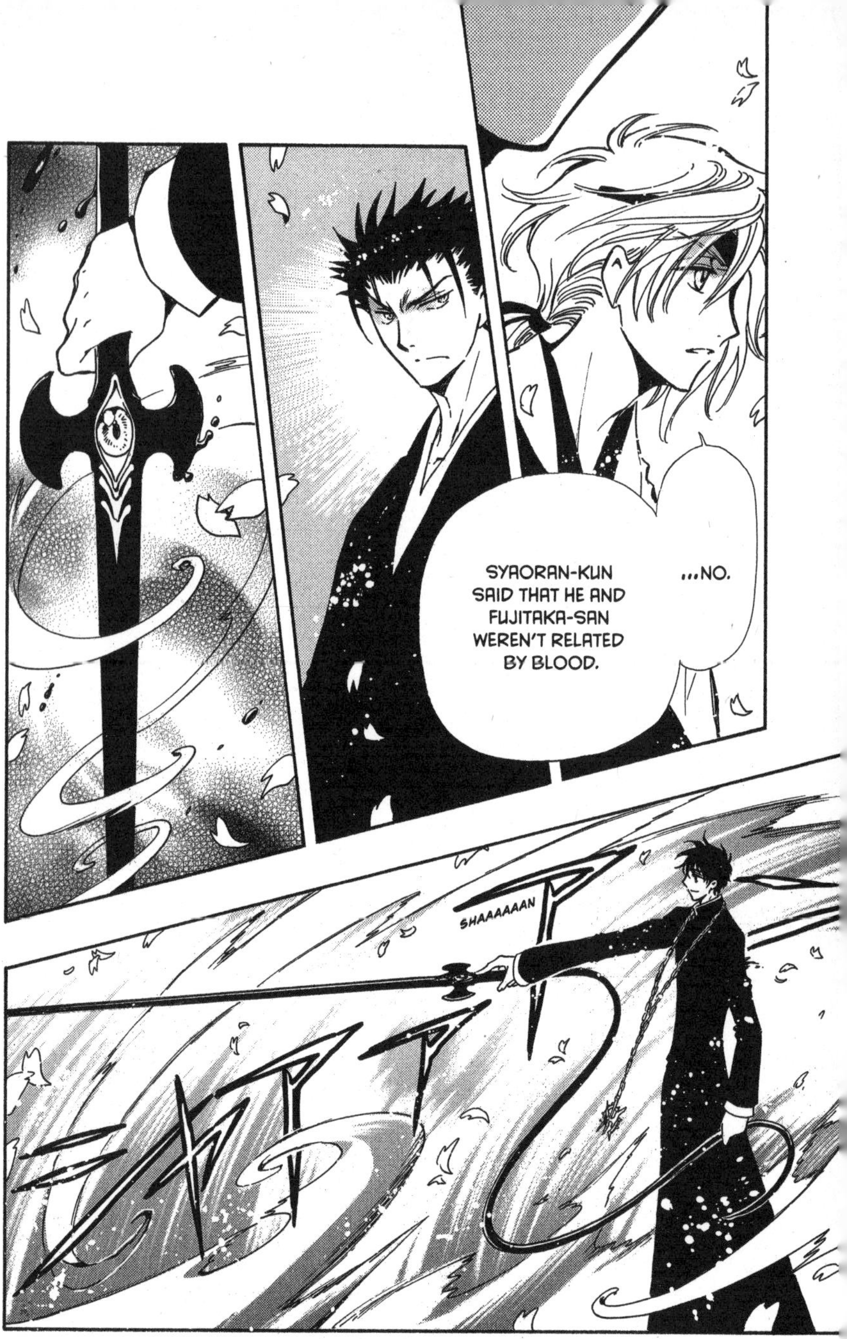
...NO.
SYAORAN-KUN SAID THAT HE AND FUJITAKA-SAN WEREN'T RELATED BY BLOOD.
SHAAAAAAN

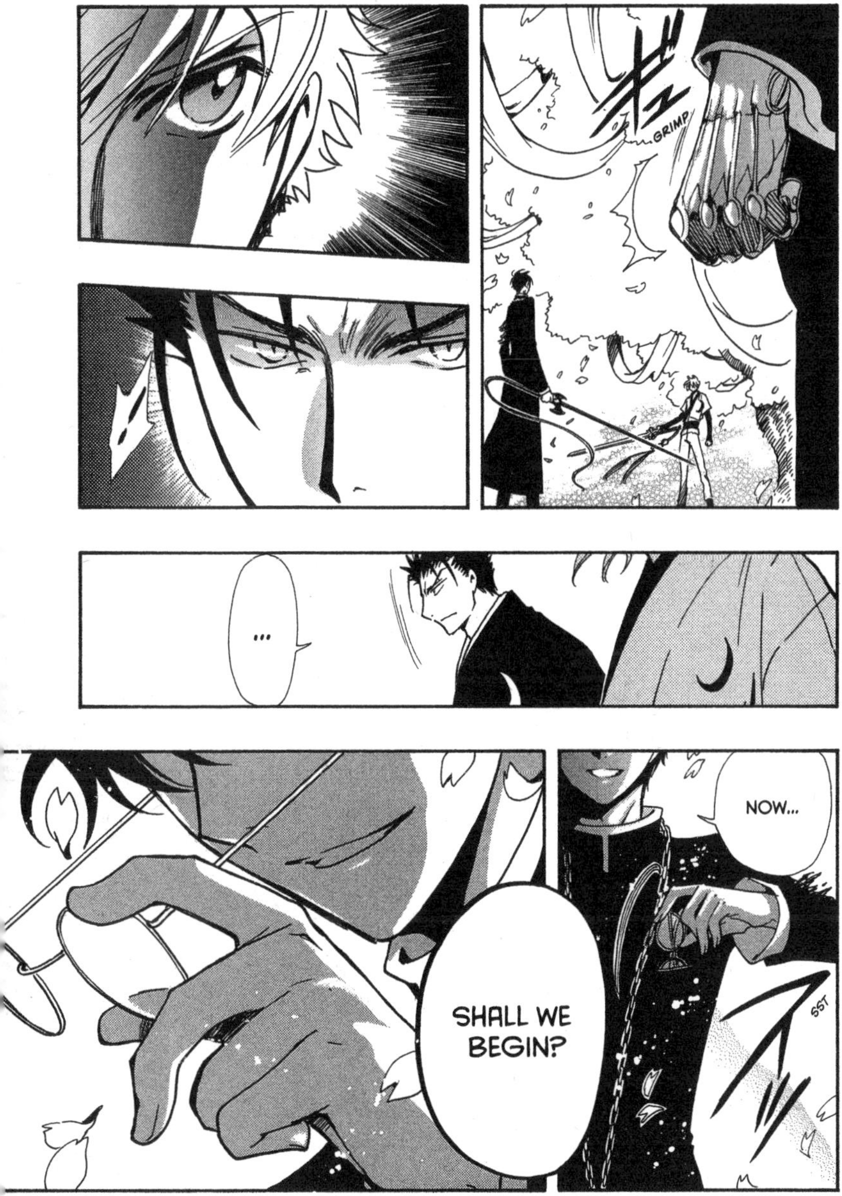
GRIMP
...
NOW...
SST
SHALL WE BEGIN?

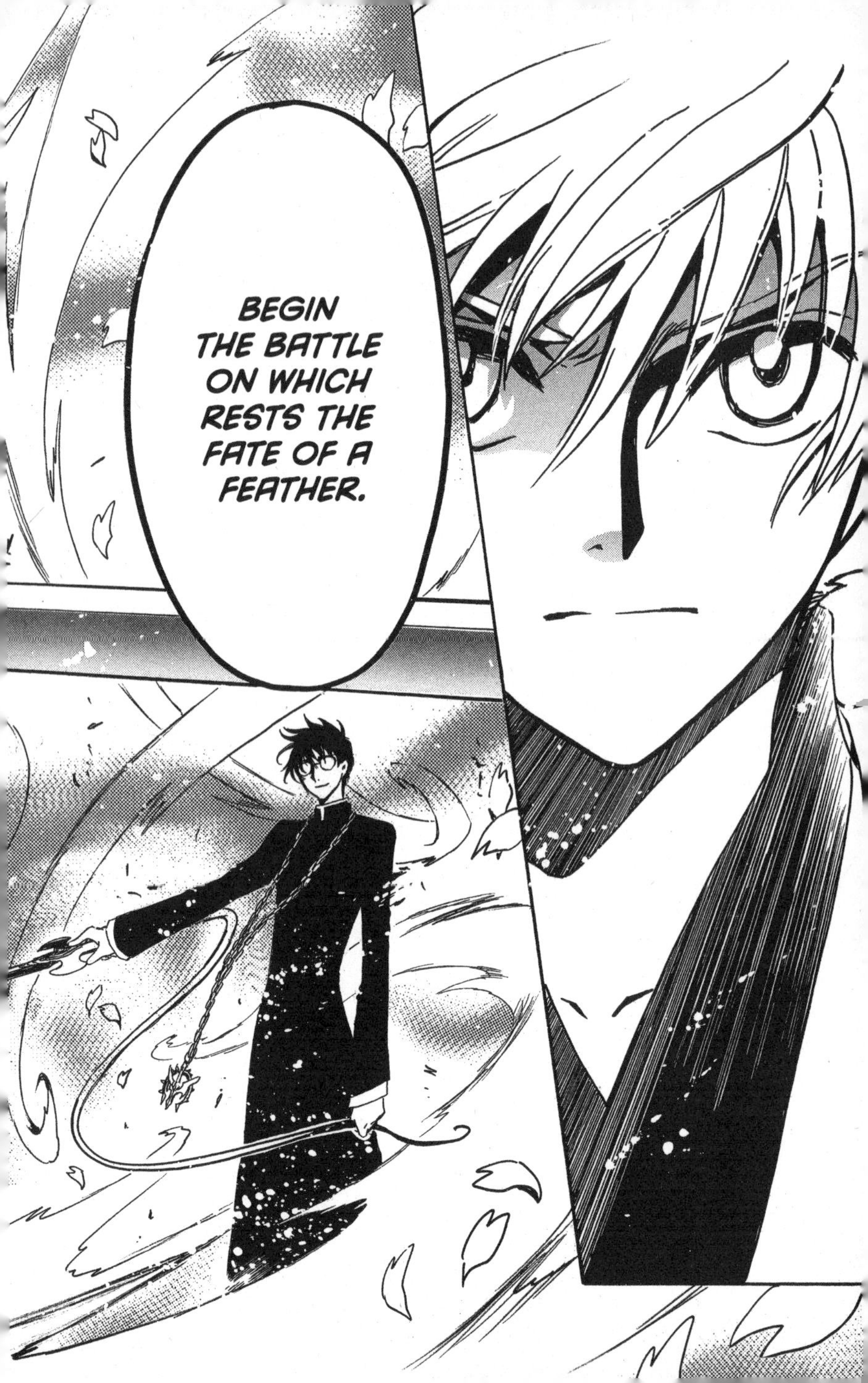
BEGIN THE BATTLE ON WHICH RESTS THE FATE OF A FEATHER.

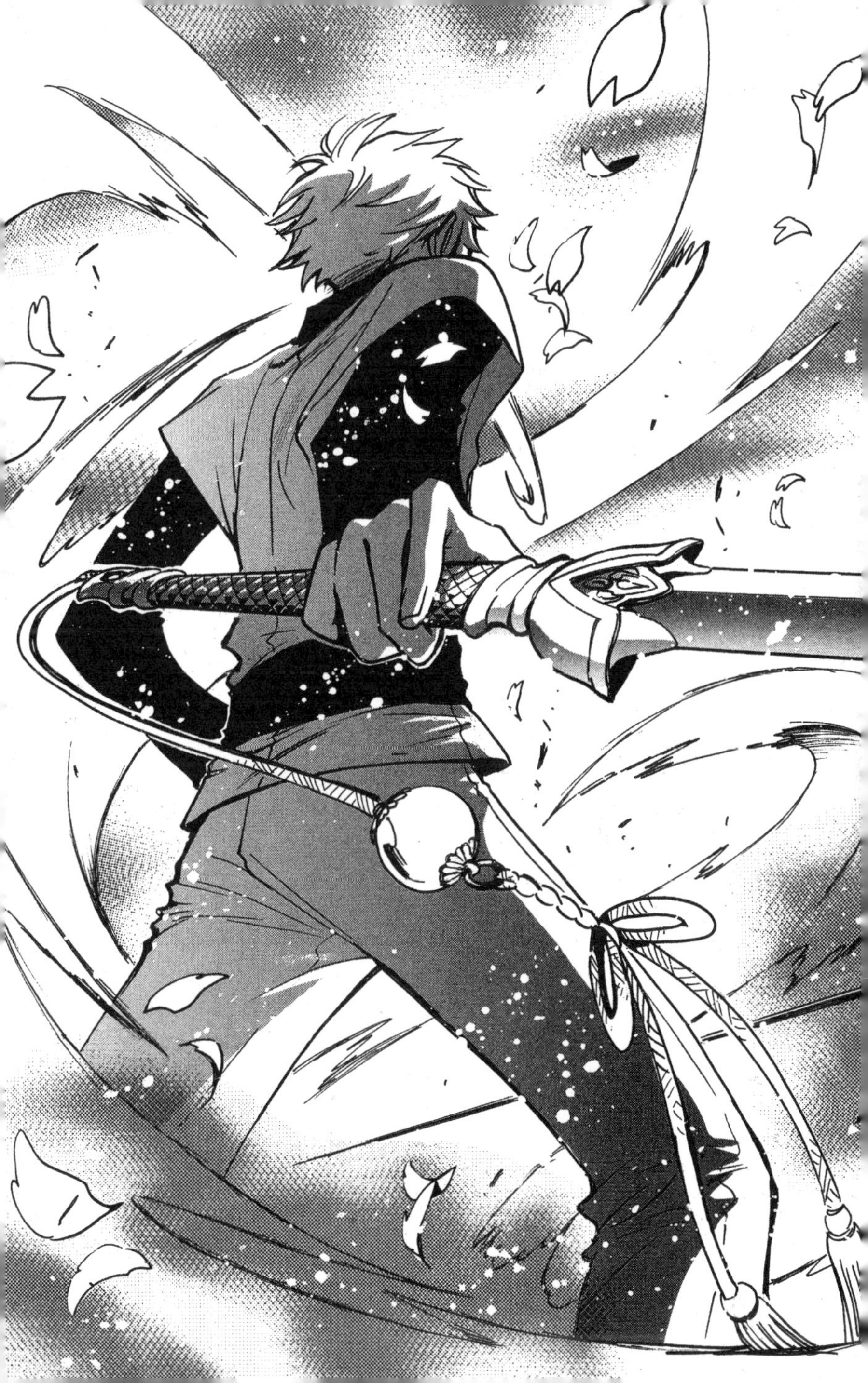

ツバサ

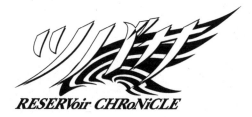

RESERVoir CHRoNiCLE

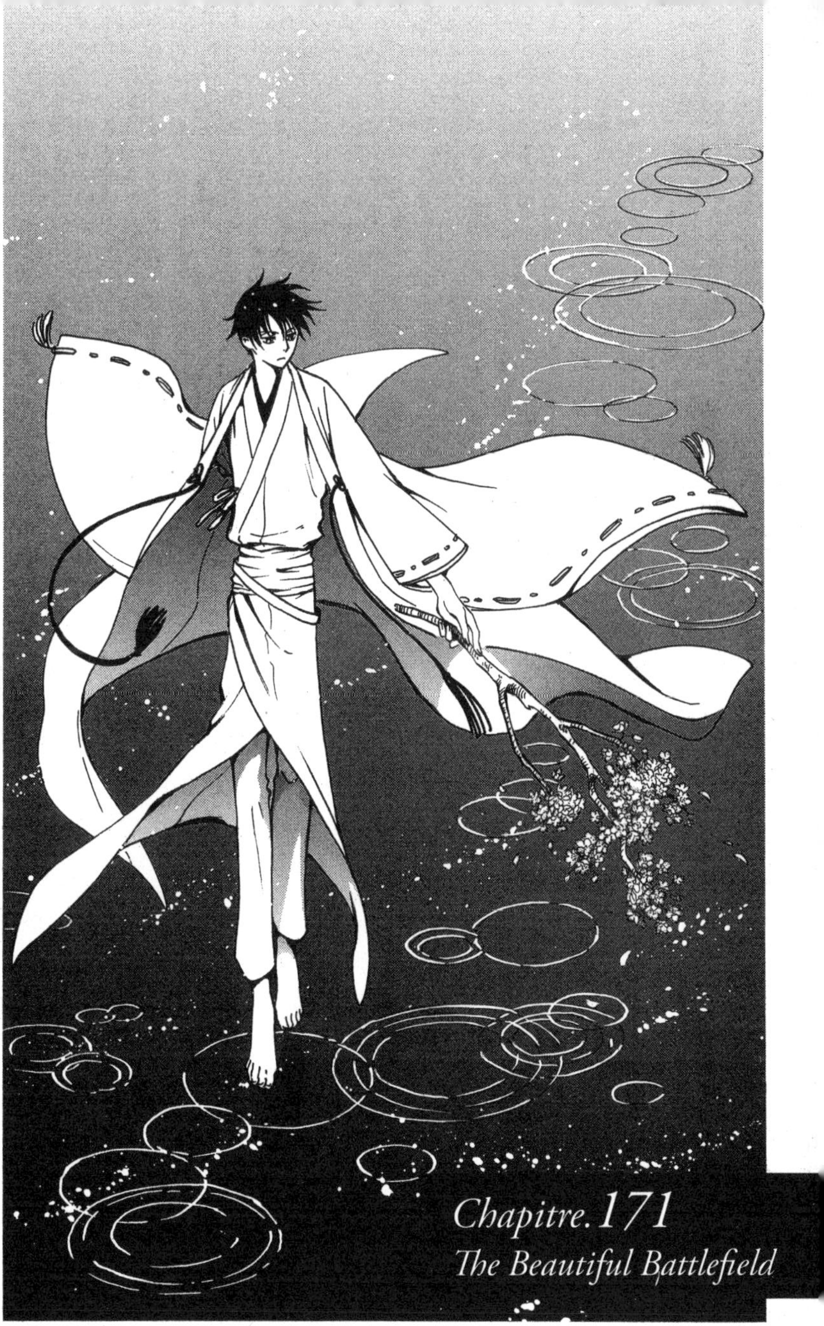
Chapitre.171
The Beautiful Battlefield

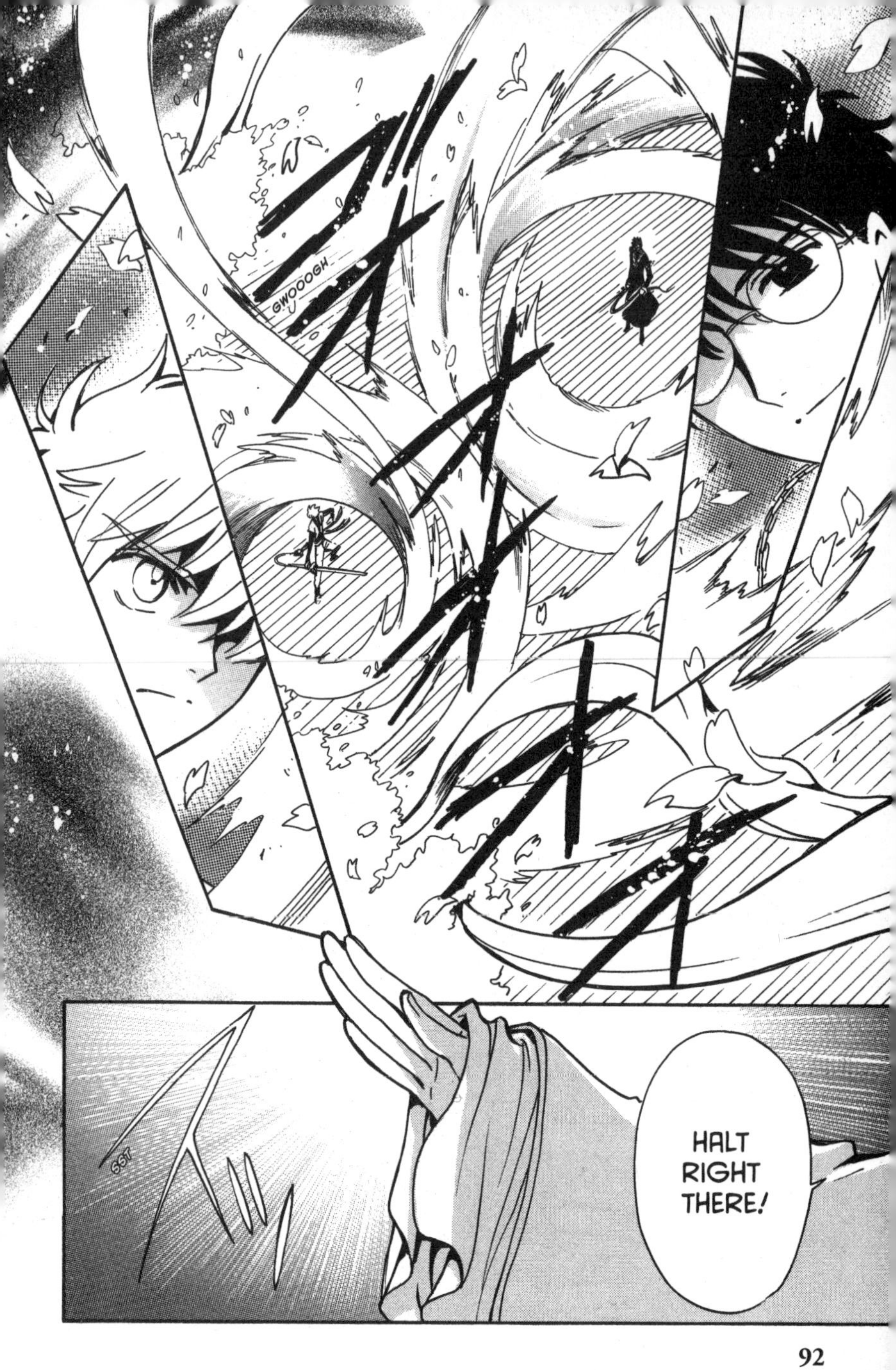
GWOOOGH
SST
HALT RIGHT THERE!

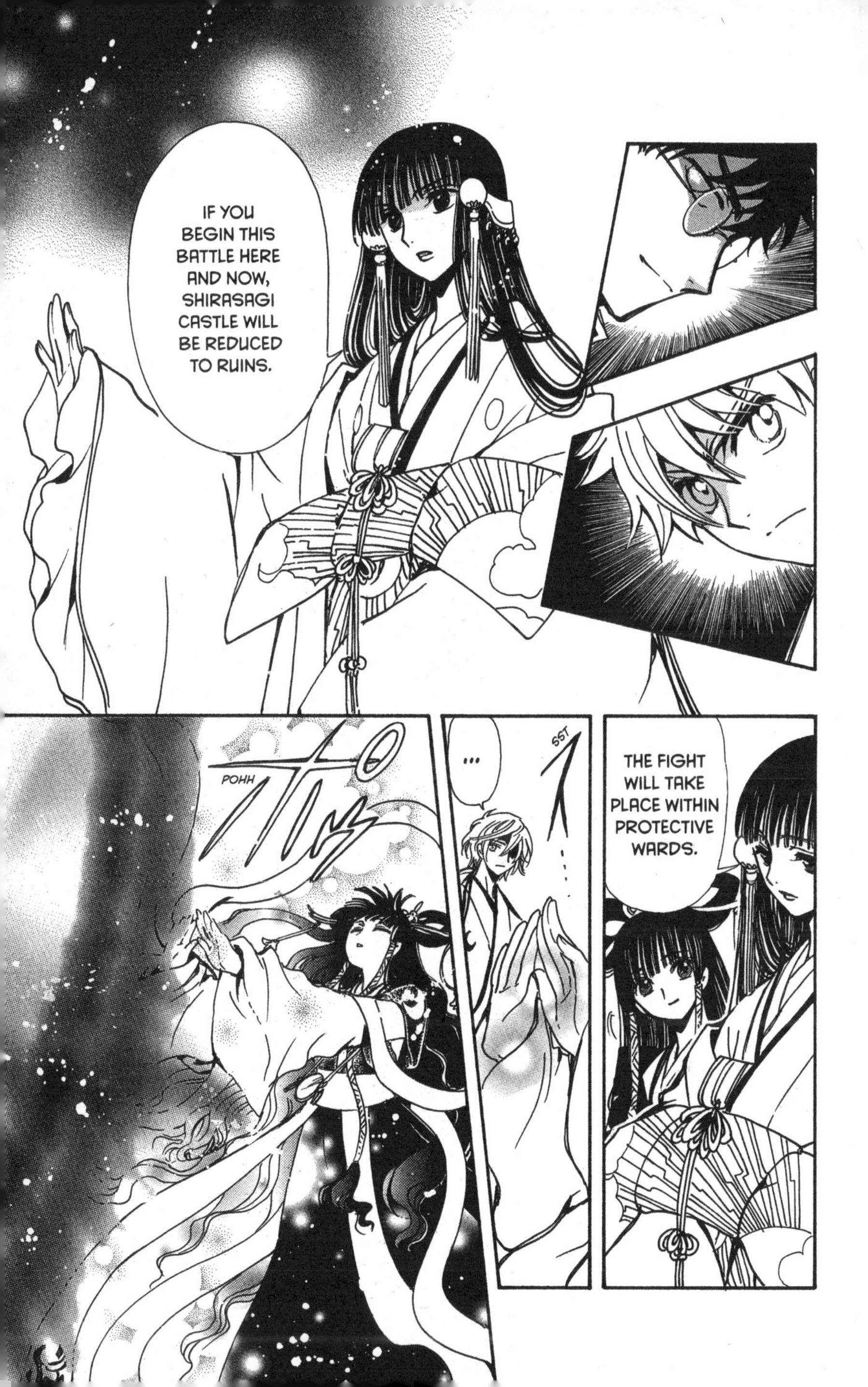
IF YOU BEGIN THIS BATTLE HERE AND NOW, SHIRASAGI CASTLE WILL BE REDUCED TO RUINS.
THE FIGHT WILL TAKE PLACE WITHIN PROTECTIVE WARDS.
...
SST
POHH

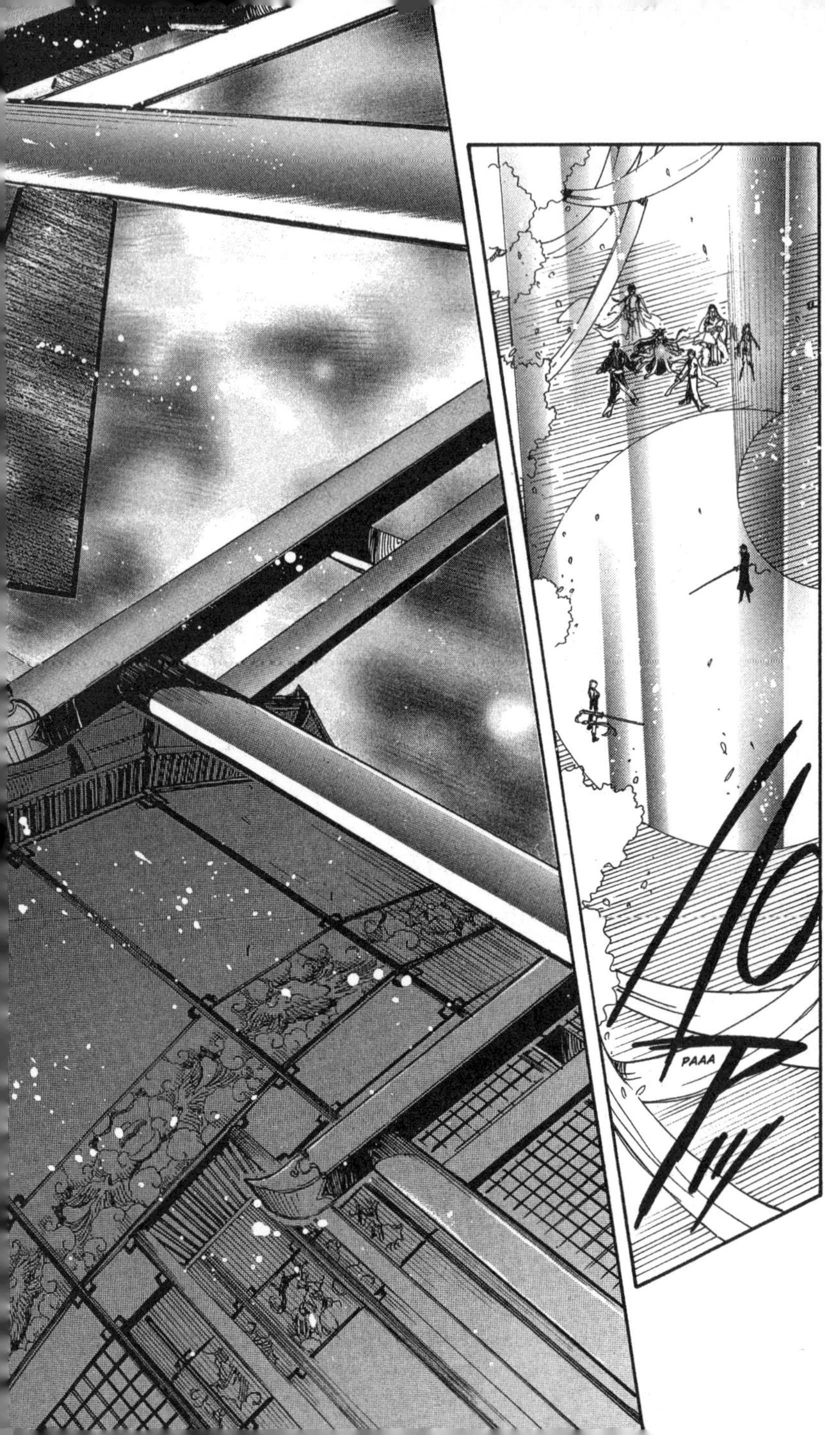
PAAA

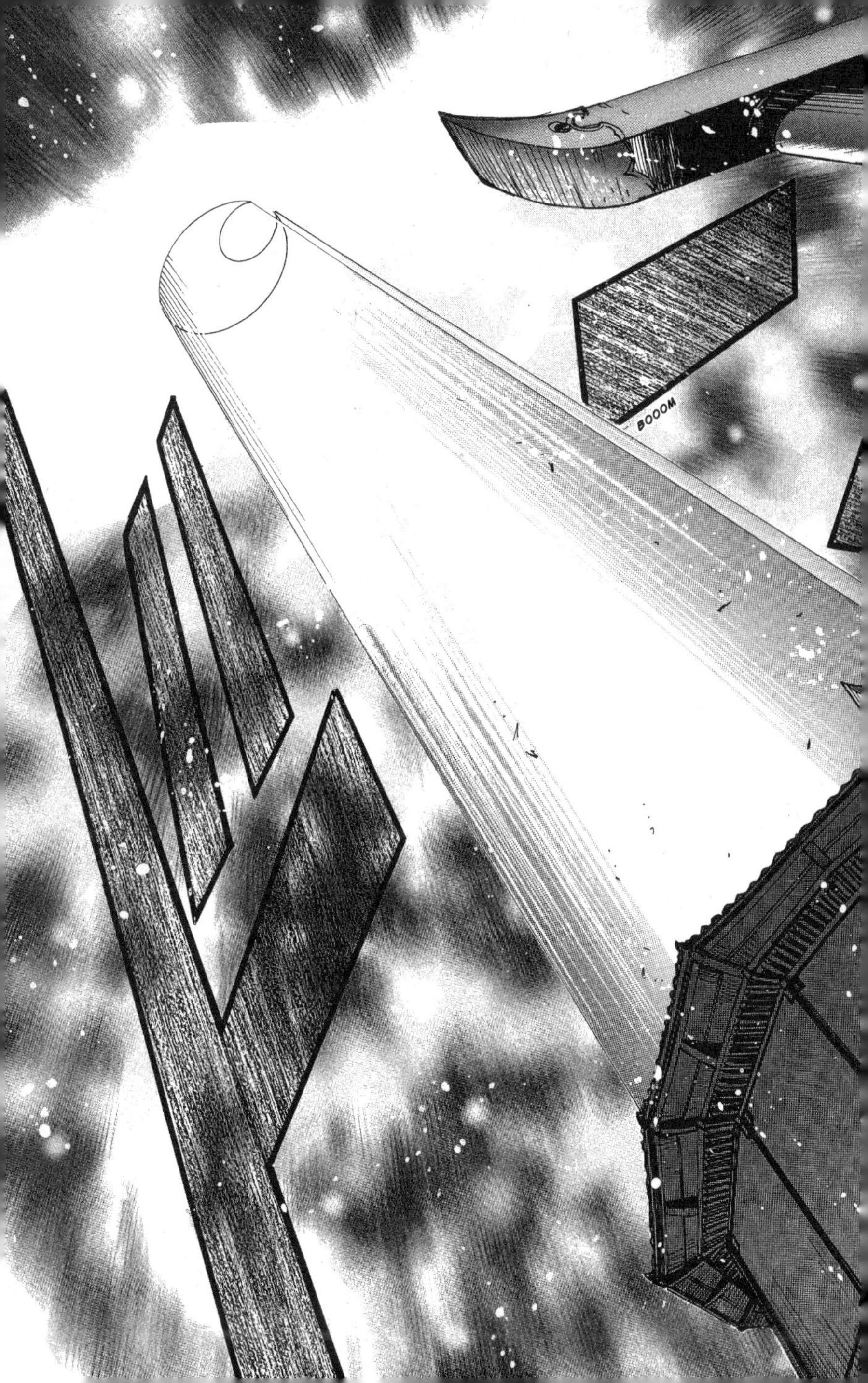
BOOOM

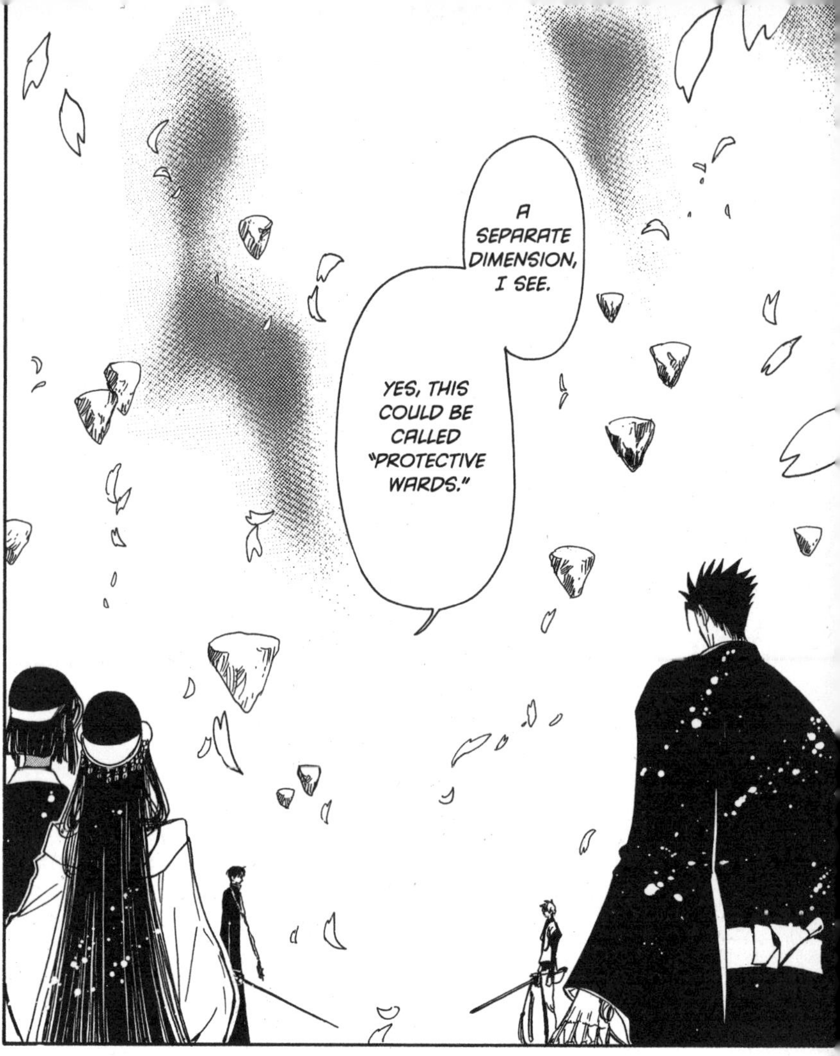
A SEPARATE DIMENSION, I SEE.
YES, THIS COULD BE CALLED "PROTECTIVE WARDS."
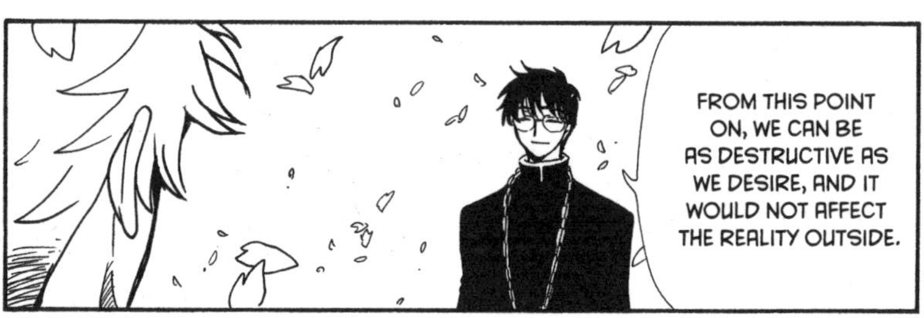
FROM THIS POINT ON, WE CAN BE AS DESTRUCTIVE AS WE DESIRE, AND IT WOULD NOT AFFECT THE REALITY OUTSIDE.

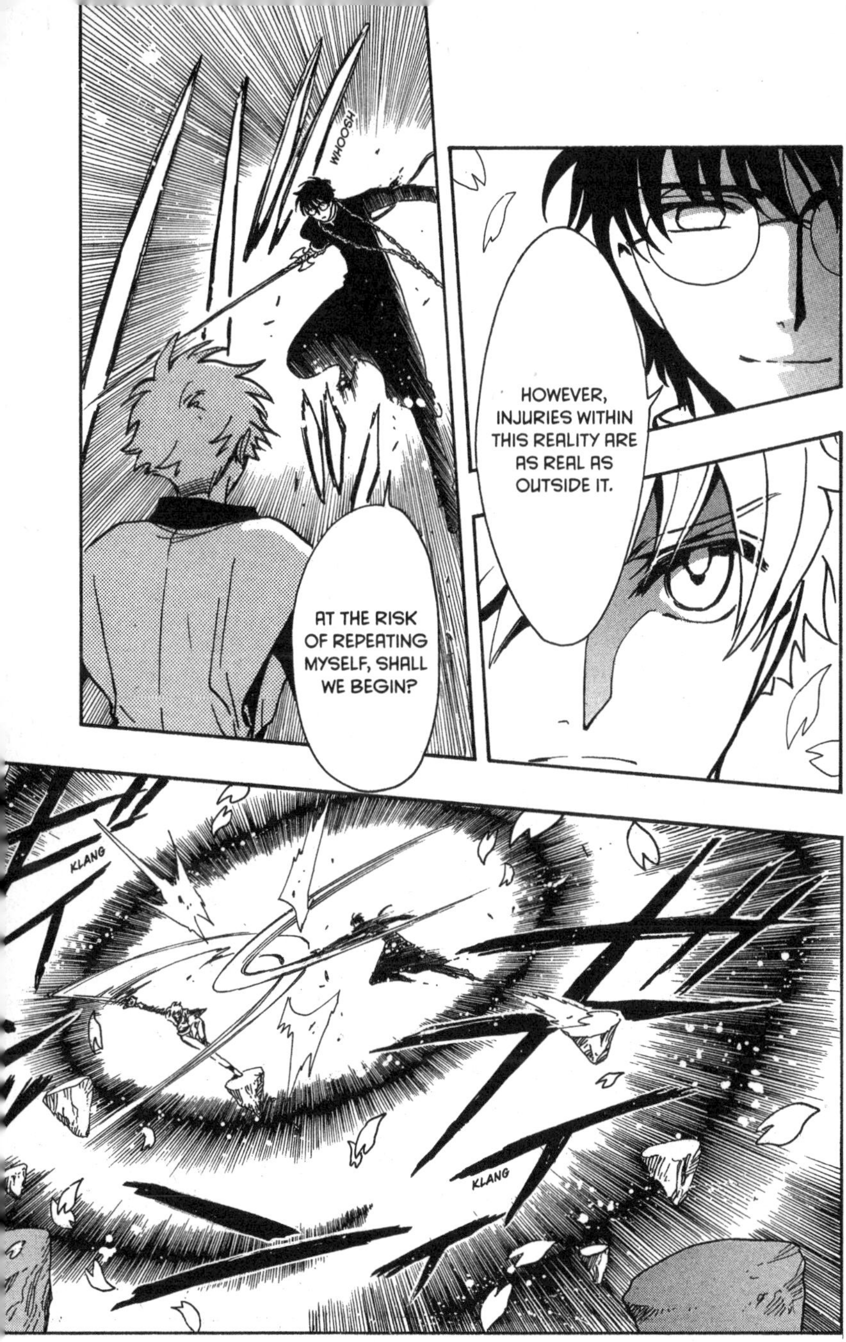
HOWEVER, INJURIES WITHIN THIS REALITY ARE AS REAL AS OUTSIDE IT.
WHOOSH
AT THE RISK OF REPEATING MYSELF, SHALL WE BEGIN?
KLANG
KLANG

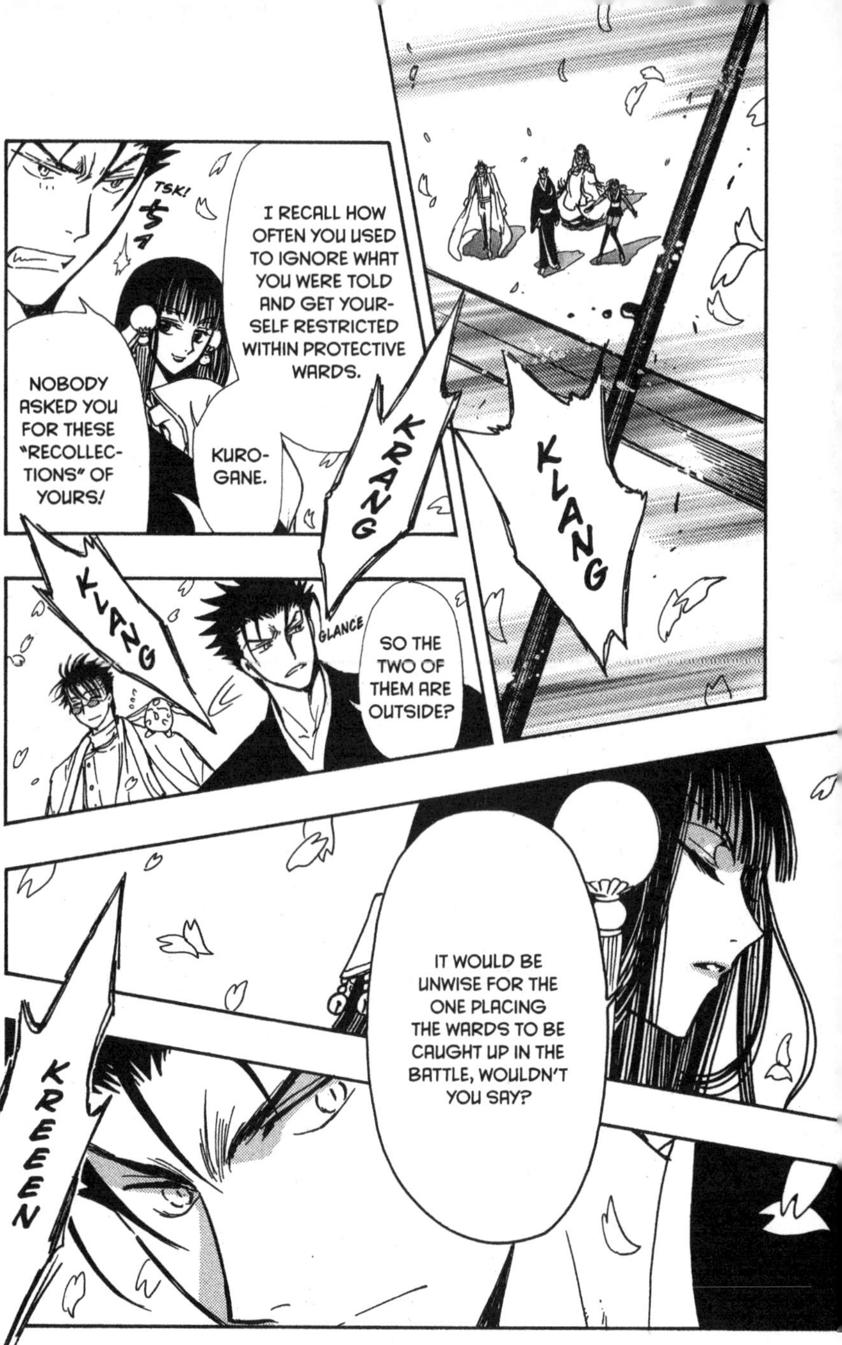
KLANG
I RECALL HOW OFTEN YOU USED TO IGNORE WHAT YOU WERE TOLD AND GET YOUR-SELF RESTRICTED WITHIN PROTECTIVE WARDS.
KURO-GANE.
TSK!
NOBODY ASKED YOU FOR THESE "RECOLLEC-TIONS" OF YOURS!
KRANG
KLANG
GLANCE
SO THE TWO OF THEM ARE OUTSIDE?
IT WOULD BE UNWISE FOR THE ONE PLACING THE WARDS TO BE CAUGHT UP IN THE BATTLE, WOULDN'T YOU SAY?
KREEEN

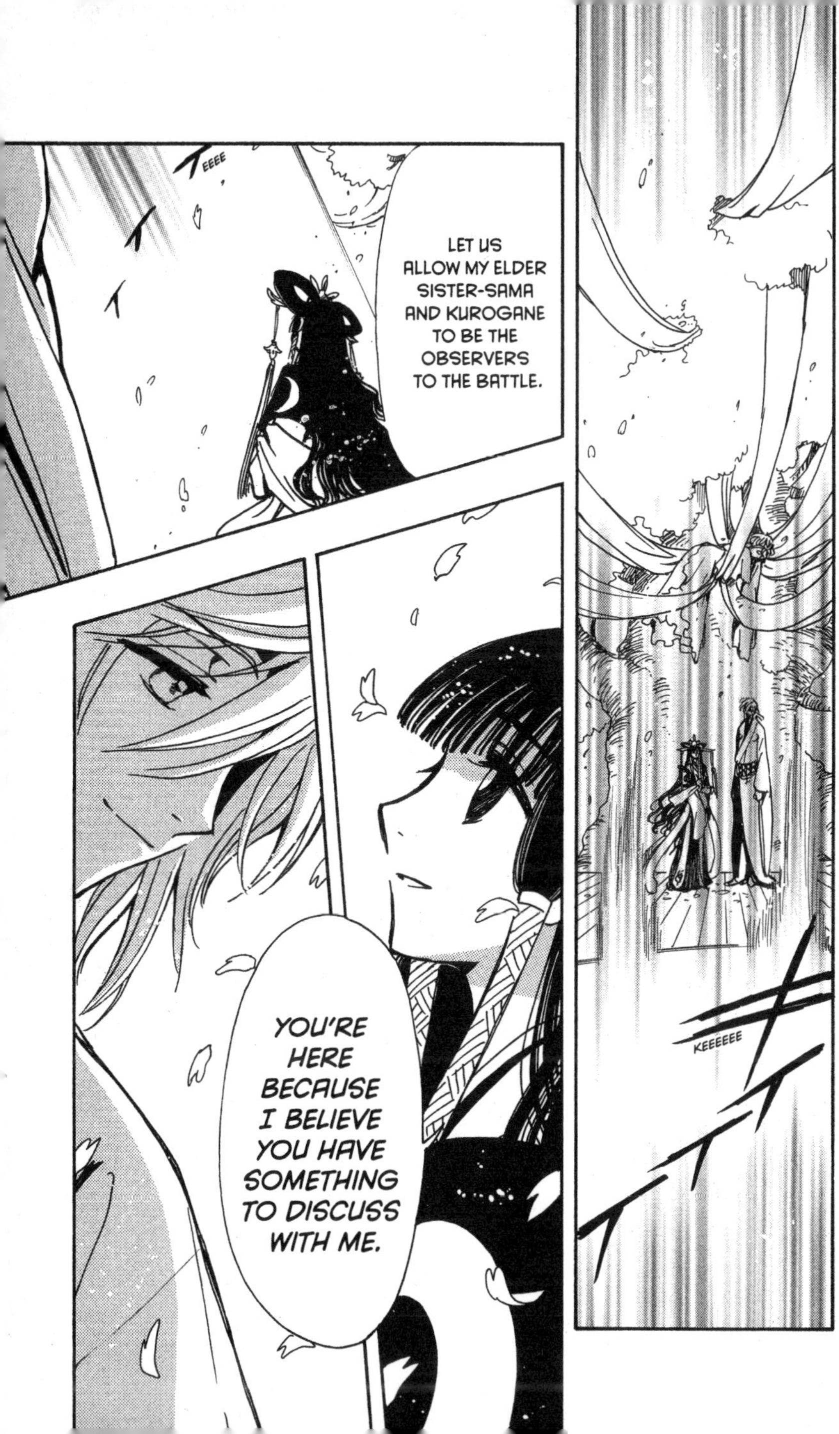
KEEEEEE
TEEEE
LET US ALLOW MY ELDER SISTER-SAMA AND KUROGANE TO BE THE OBSERVERS TO THE BATTLE.
YOU'RE HERE BECAUSE I BELIEVE YOU HAVE SOMETHING TO DISCUSS WITH ME.

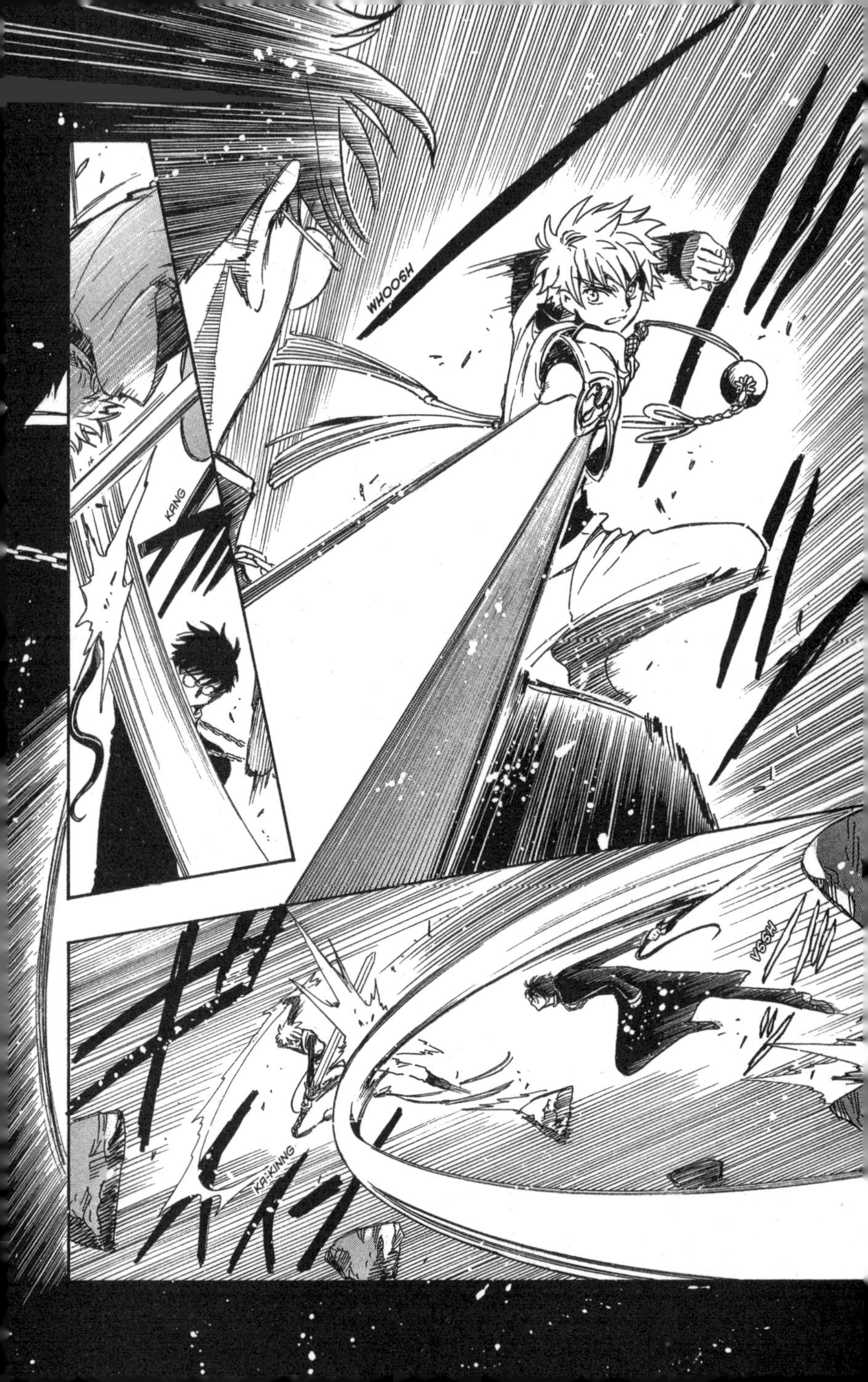
WHOOSH
KANG
VSSH
KA-KING

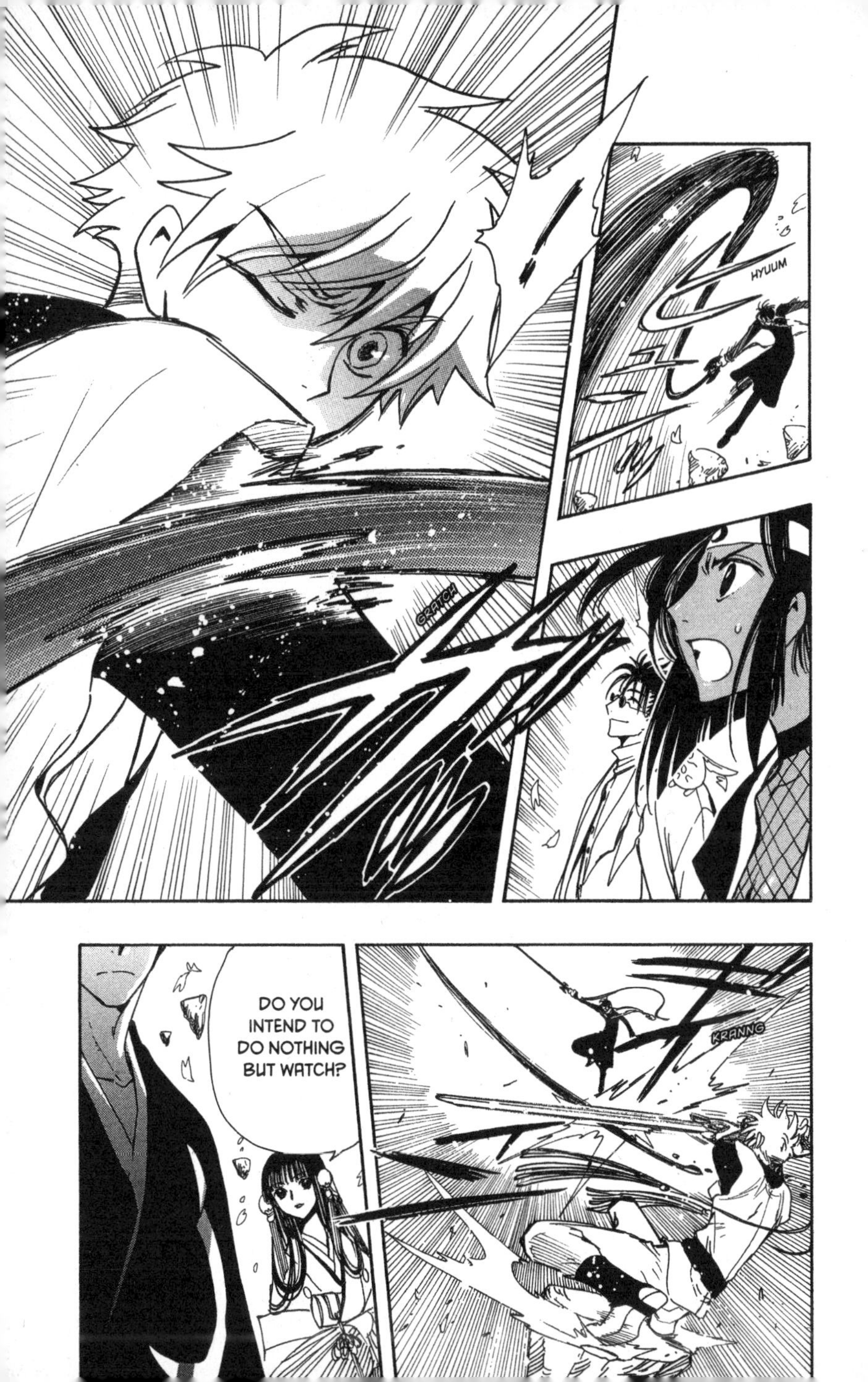
HYUUM
GRATCH
KRANNG
DO YOU INTEND TO DO NOTHING BUT WATCH?

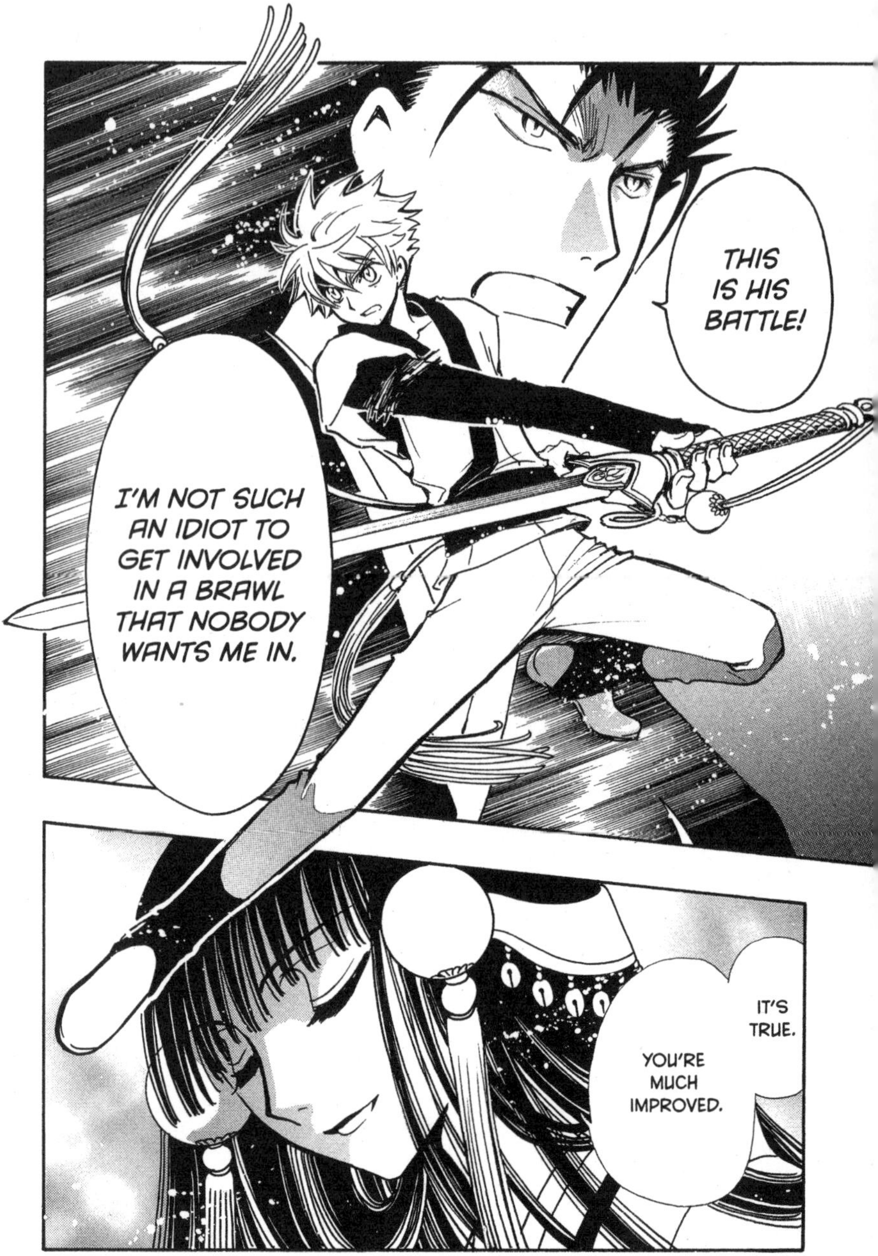
THIS IS HIS BATTLE!
I'M NOT SUCH AN IDIOT TO GET INVOLVED IN A BRAWL THAT NOBODY WANTS ME IN.
IT'S TRUE.
YOU'RE MUCH IMPROVED.

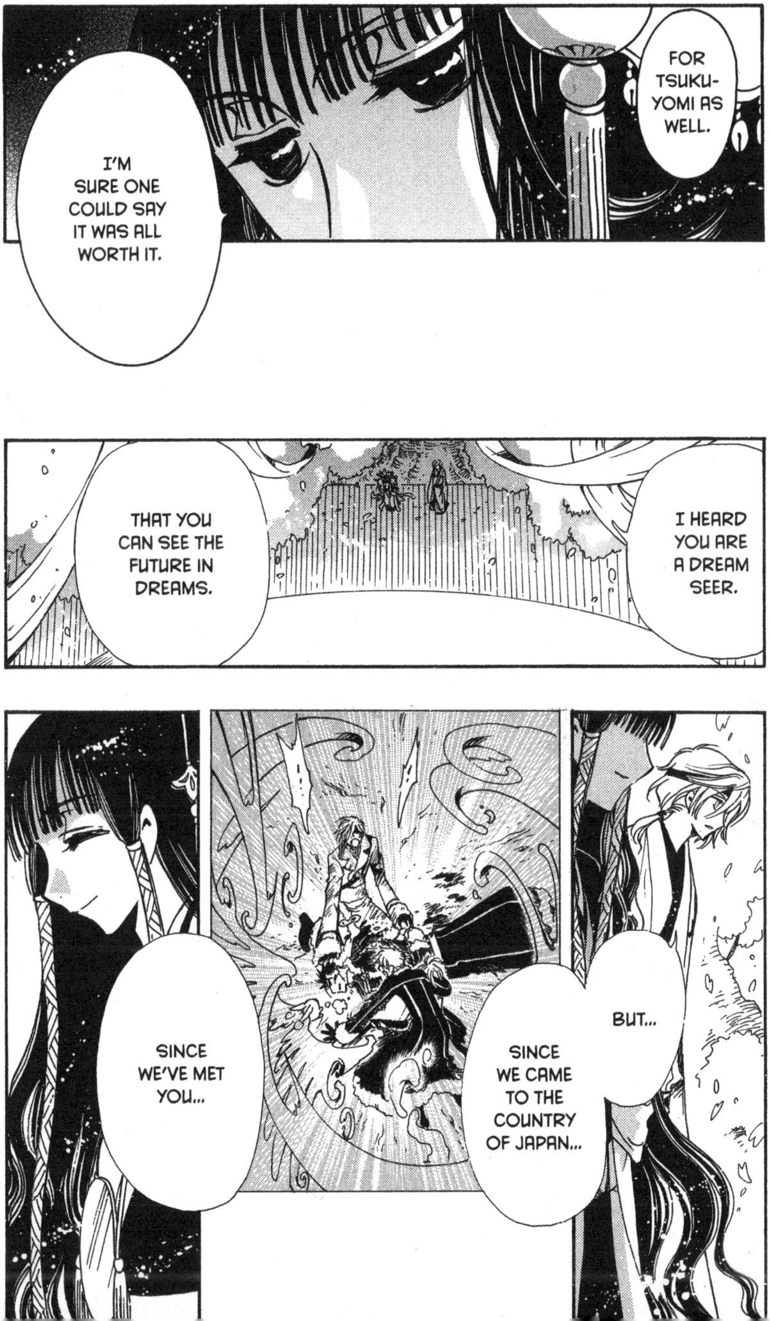
FOR TSUKU-YOMI AS WELL.
I'M SURE ONE COULD SAY IT WAS ALL WORTH IT.
I HEARD YOU ARE A DREAM SEER.
THAT YOU CAN SEE THE FUTURE IN DREAMS.
BUT...
SINCE WE CAME TO THE COUNTRY OF JAPAN...
SINCE WE'VE MET YOU...

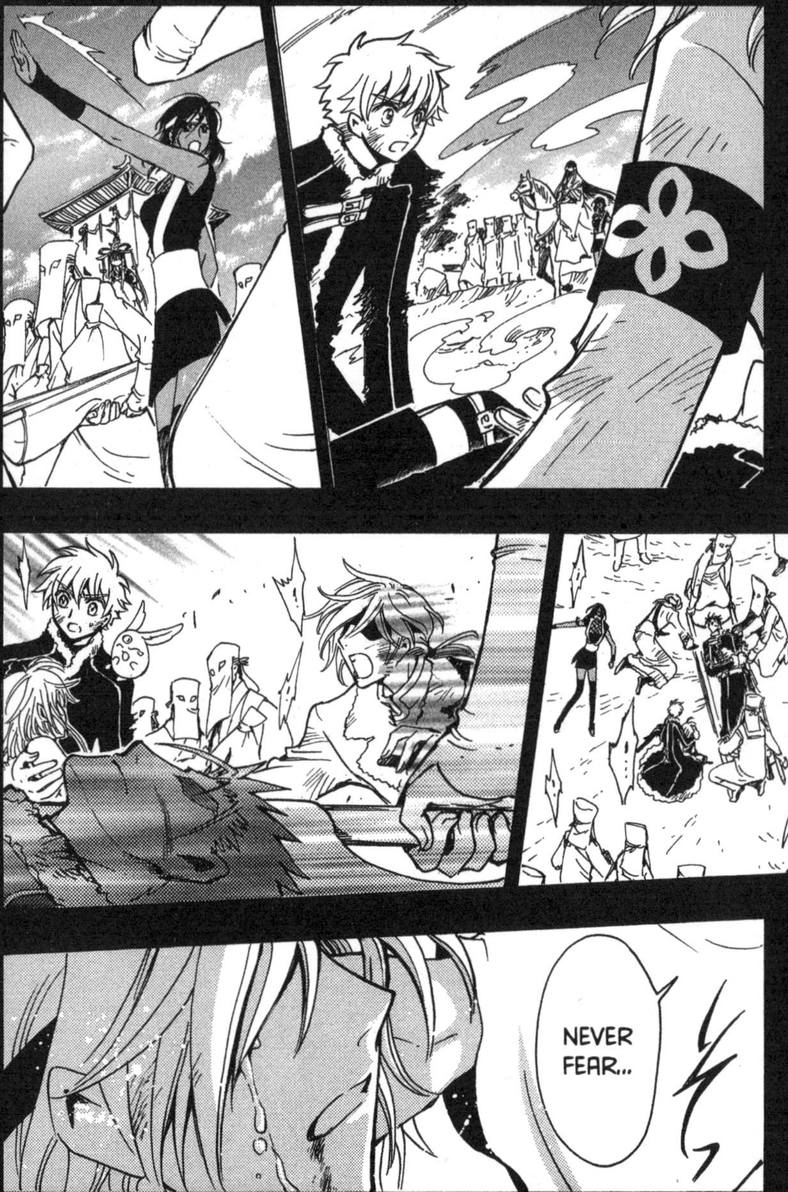
NEVER FEAR...

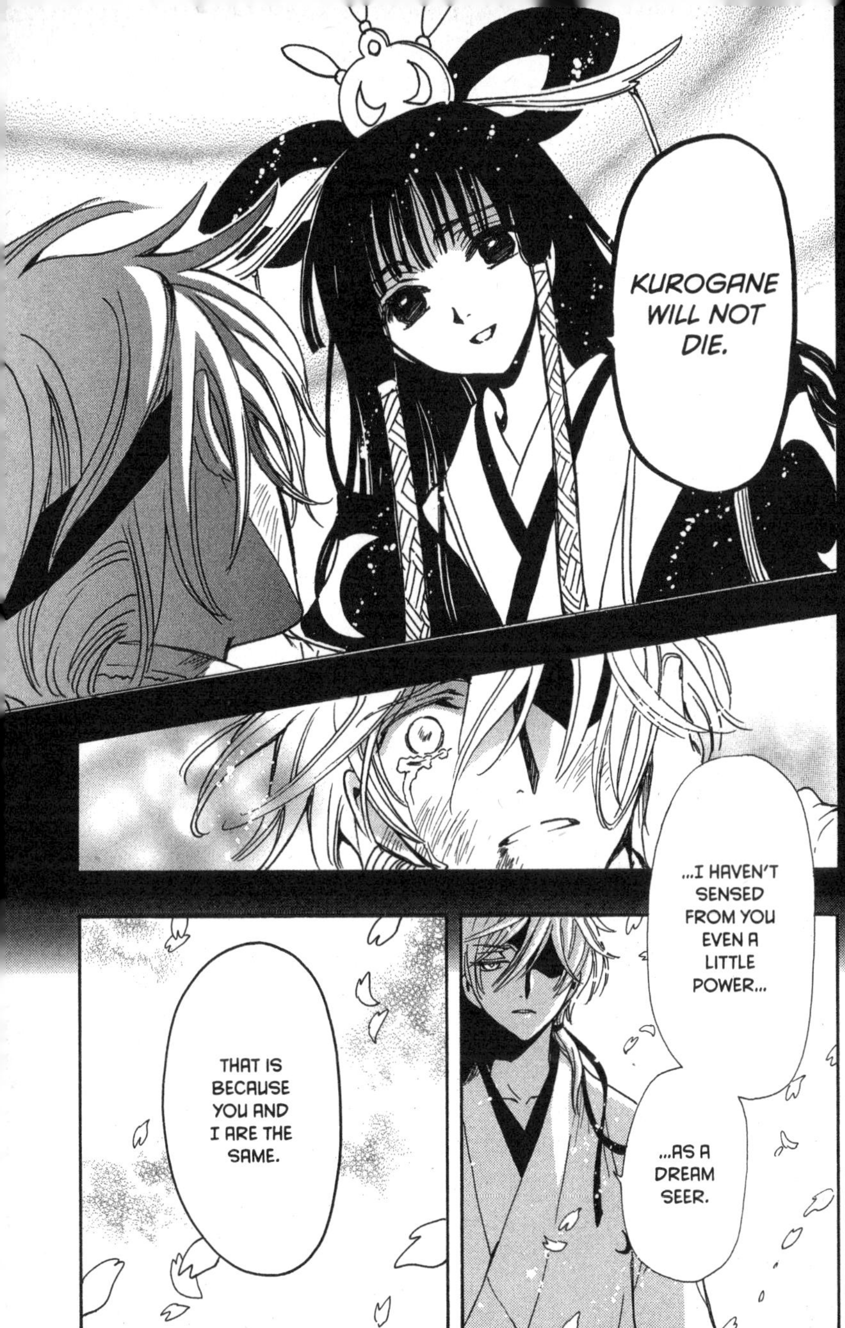
KUROGANE WILL NOT DIE.
...I HAVEN'T SENSED FROM YOU EVEN A LITTLE POWER...
...AS A DREAM SEER.
THAT IS BECAUSE YOU AND I ARE THE SAME.

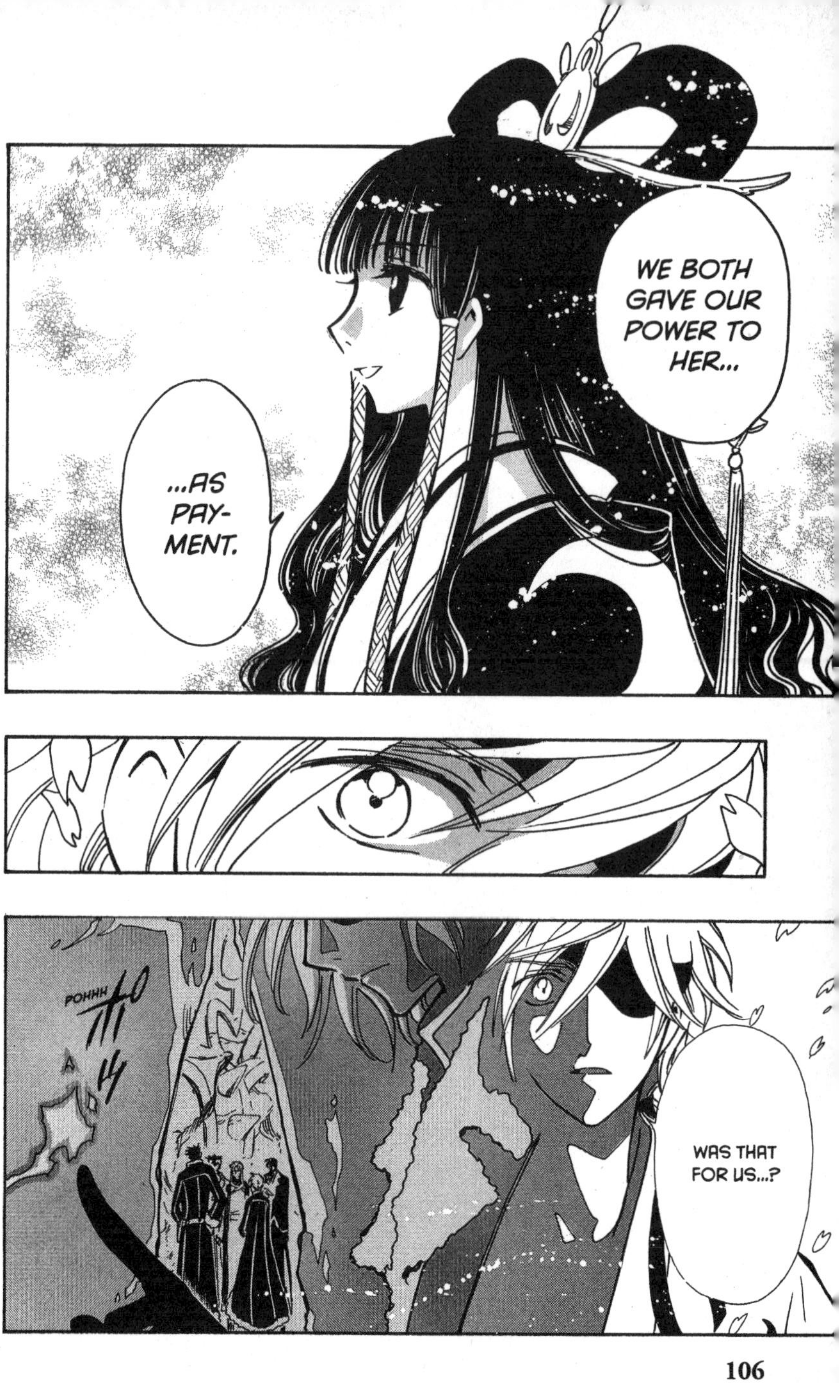
WE BOTH GAVE OUR POWER TO HER...
...AS PAY-MENT.
POHHH
WAS THAT FOR US...?

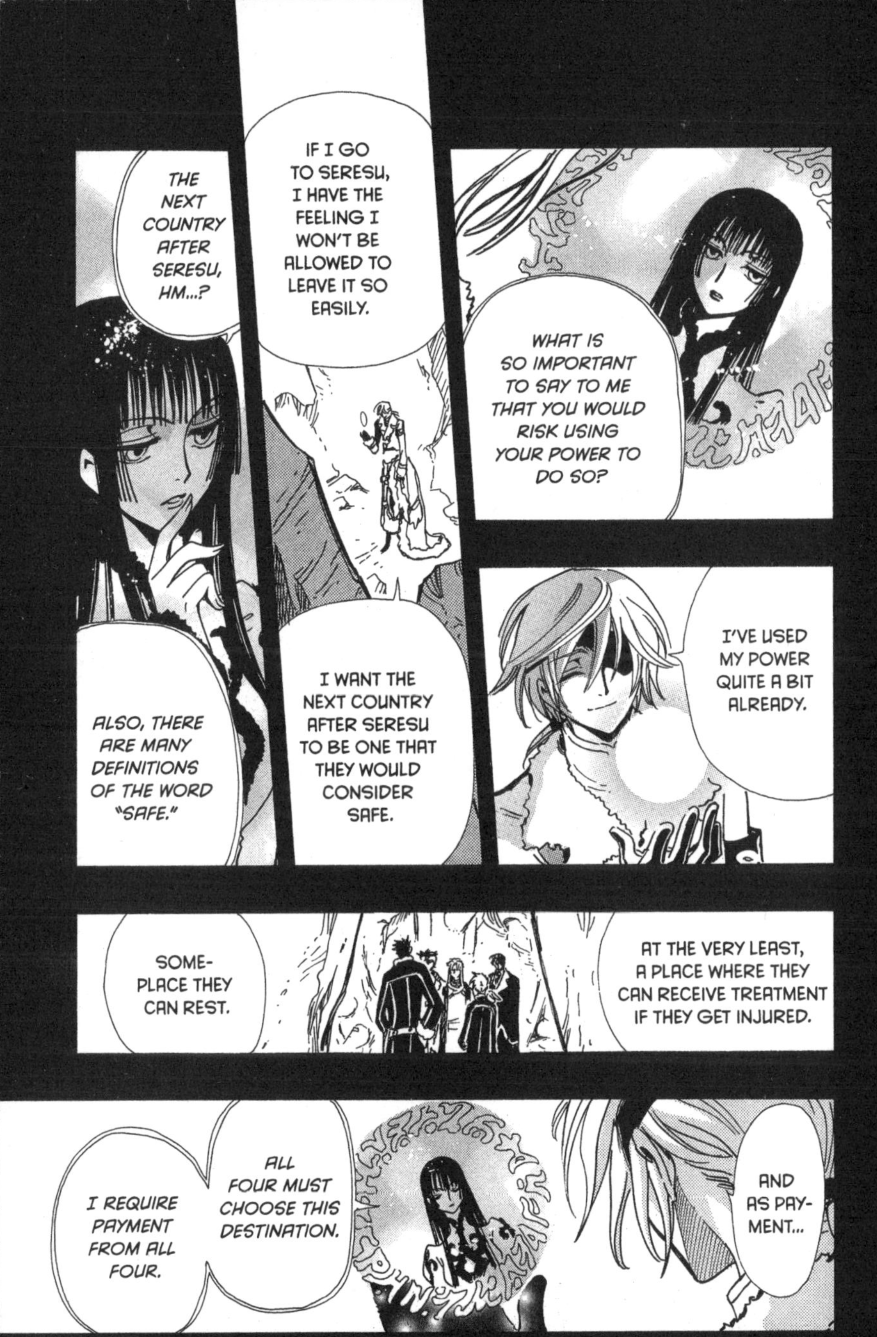
WHAT IS SO IMPORTANT TO SAY TO ME THAT YOU WOULD RISK USING YOUR POWER TO DO SO?
I'VE USED MY POWER QUITE A BIT ALREADY.
IF I GO TO SERESU, I HAVE THE FEELING I WON'T BE ALLOWED TO LEAVE IT SO EASILY.
I WANT THE NEXT COUNTRY AFTER SERESU TO BE ONE THAT THEY WOULD CONSIDER SAFE.
THE NEXT COUNTRY AFTER SERESU, HM...?
ALSO, THERE ARE MANY DEFINITIONS OF THE WORD "SAFE."
AT THE VERY LEAST, A PLACE WHERE THEY CAN RECEIVE TREATMENT IF THEY GET INJURED.
SOME-PLACE THEY CAN REST.
AND AS PAY-MENT...
ALL FOUR MUST CHOOSE THIS DESTINATION.
I REQUIRE PAYMENT FROM ALL FOUR.

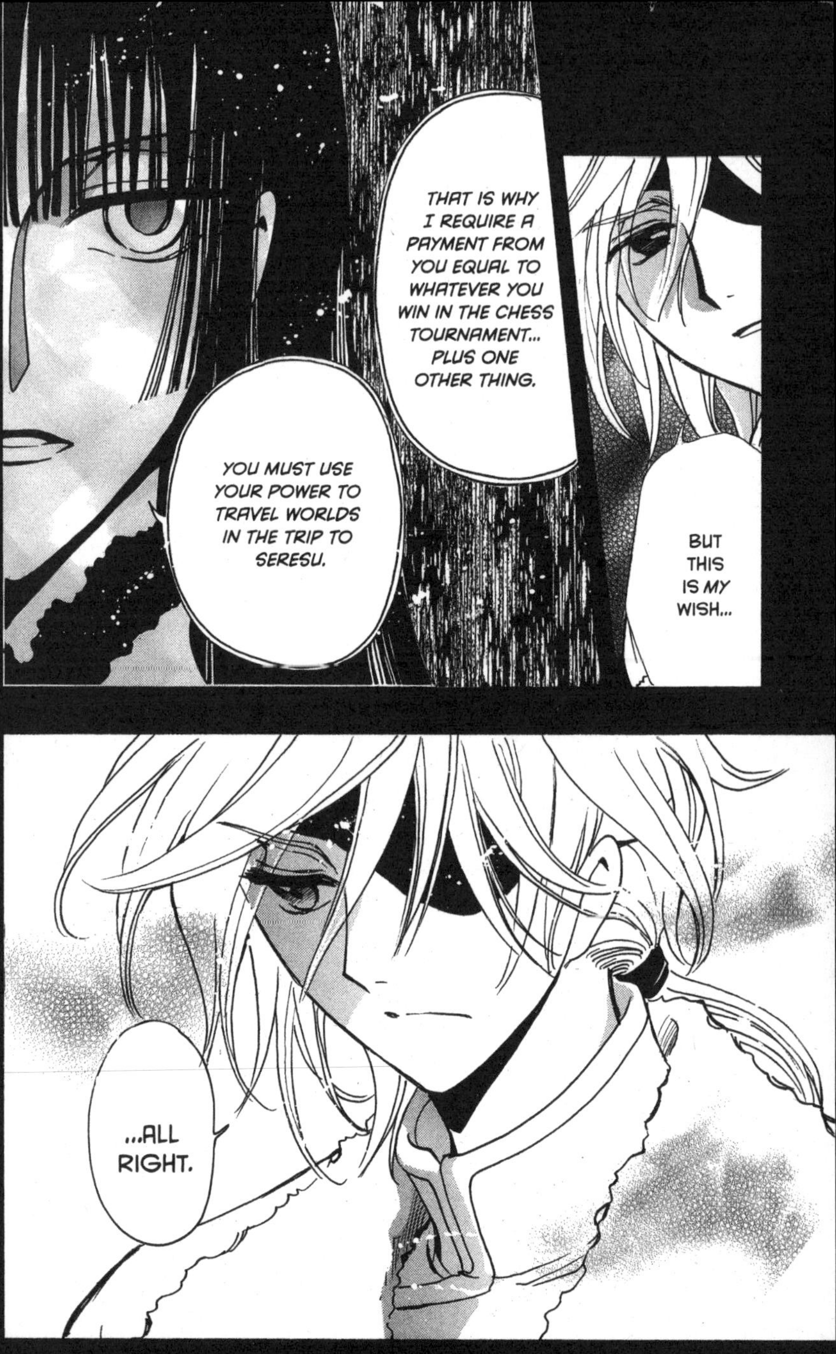
BUT THIS IS MY WISH...
THAT IS WHY I REQUIRE A PAYMENT FROM YOU EQUAL TO WHATEVER YOU WIN IN THE CHESS TOURNAMENT... PLUS ONE OTHER THING.
YOU MUST USE YOUR POWER TO TRAVEL WORLDS IN THE TRIP TO SERESU.
...ALL RIGHT.

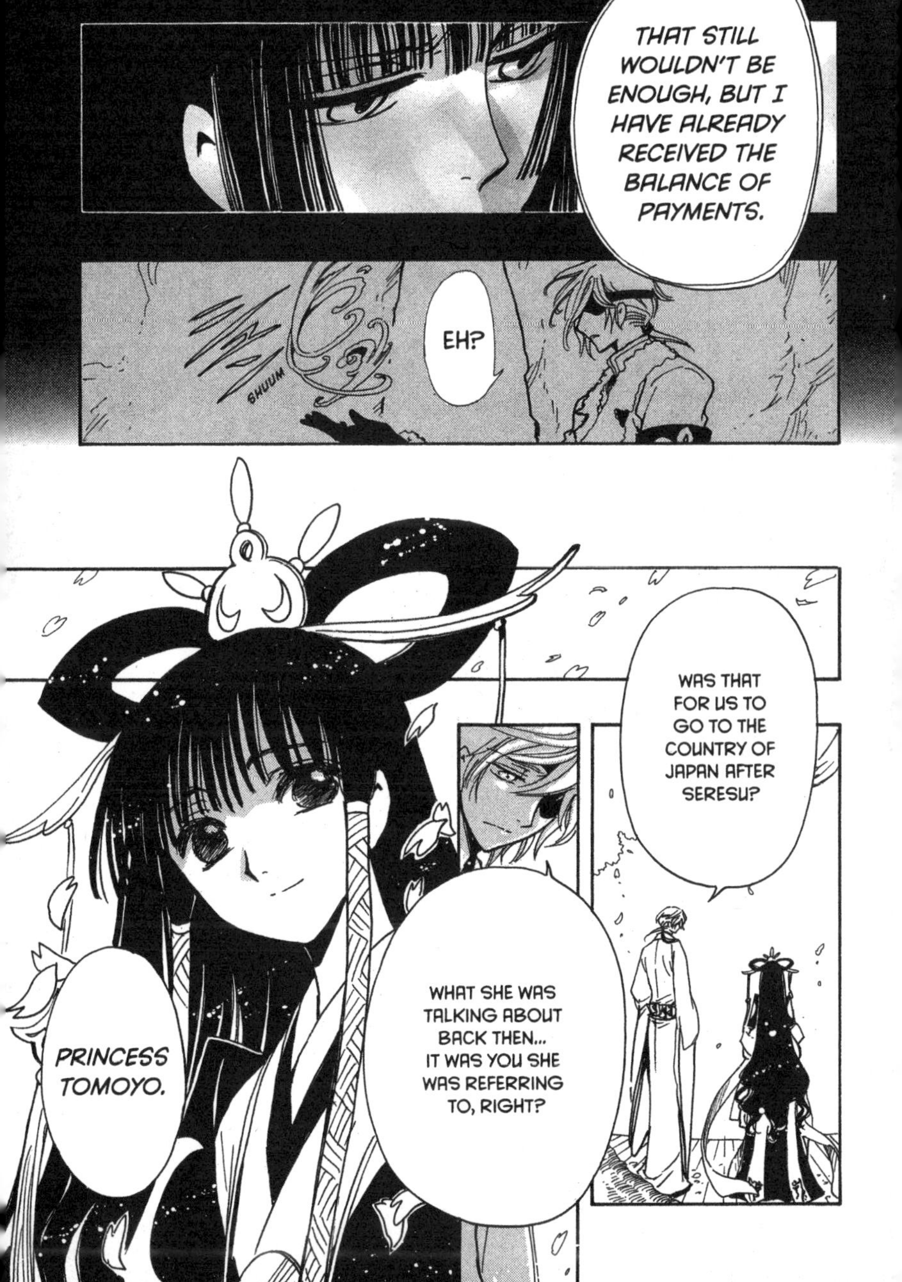
THAT STILL WOULDN'T BE ENOUGH, BUT I HAVE ALREADY RECEIVED THE BALANCE OF PAYMENTS.
EH?
SHUUM
WAS THAT FOR US TO GO TO THE COUNTRY OF JAPAN AFTER SERESU?
WHAT SHE WAS TALKING ABOUT BACK THEN... IT WAS YOU SHE WAS REFERRING TO, RIGHT?
PRINCESS TOMOYO.

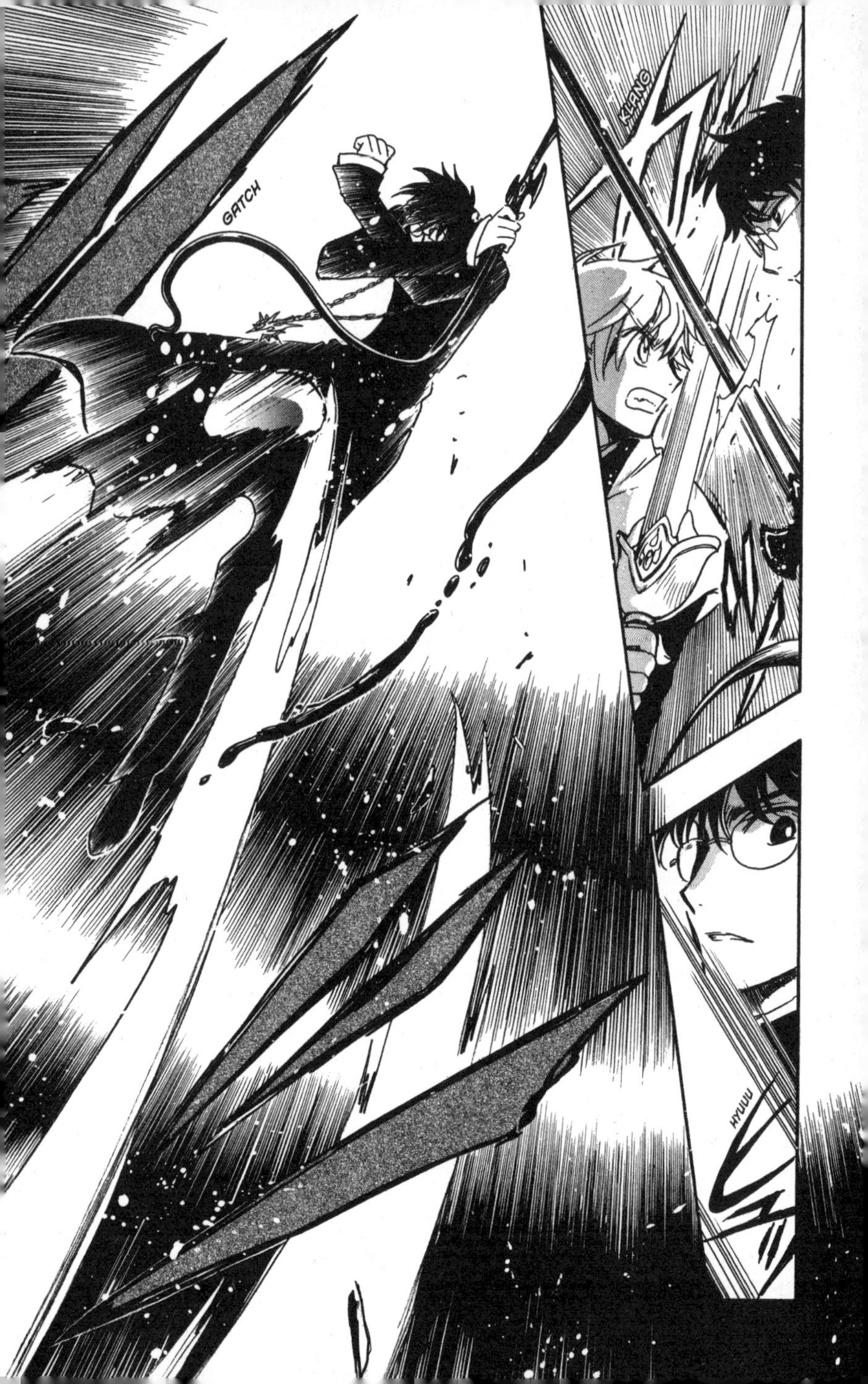
KLANG
GATCH
HYUUU

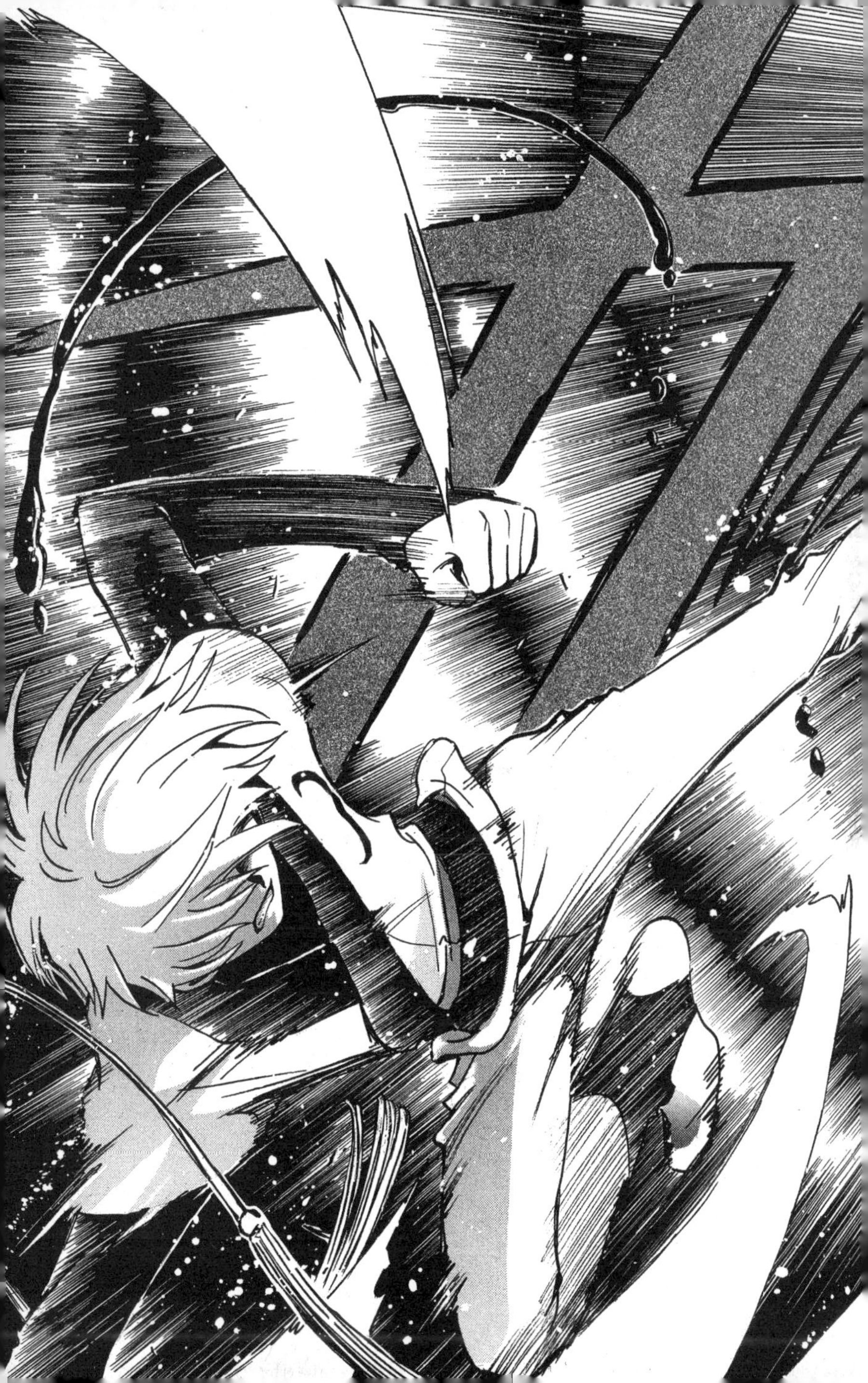

ツバサ
RESERVoir CHRoNiCLE

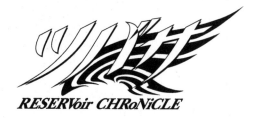

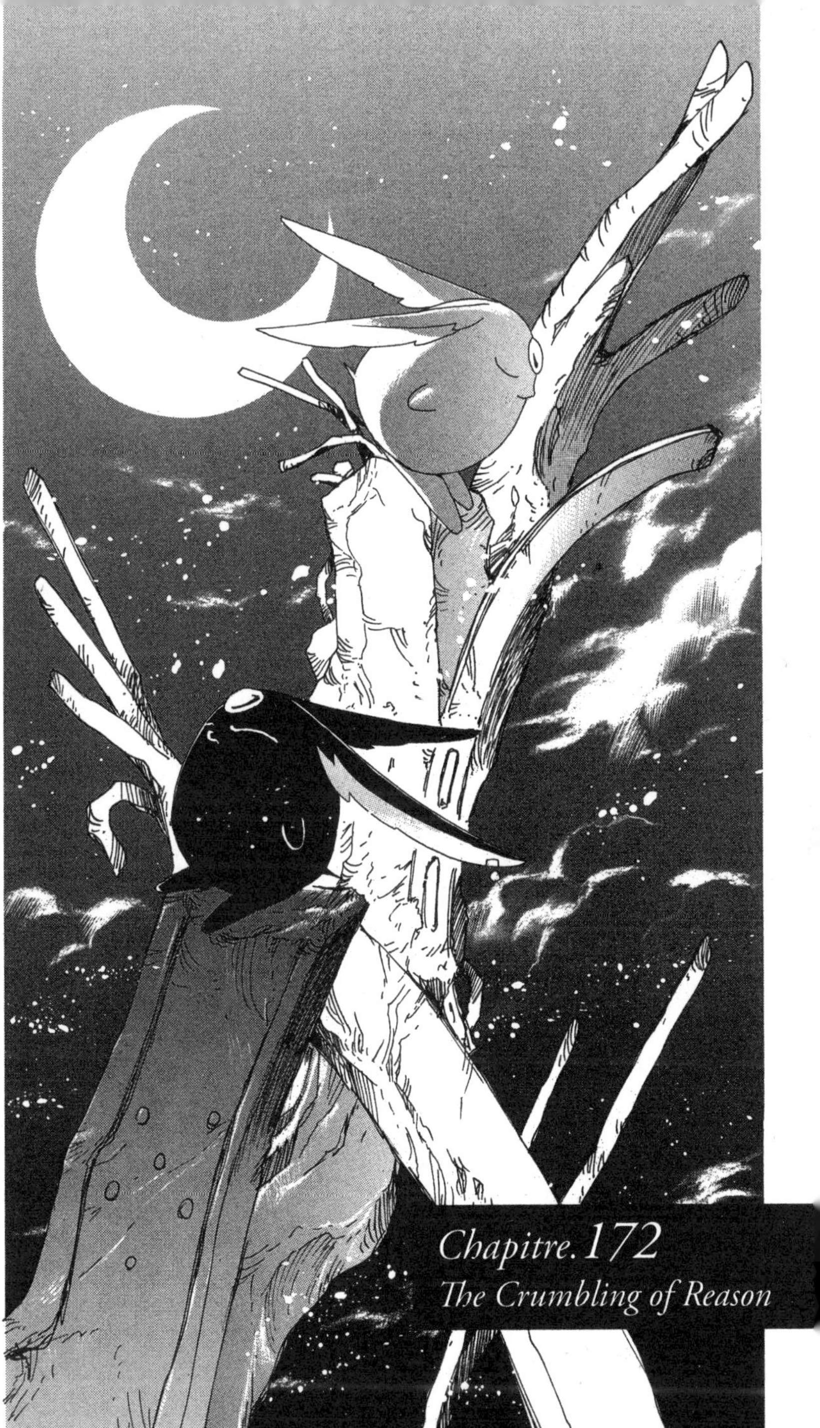

Chapitre. 172
The Crumbling of Reason

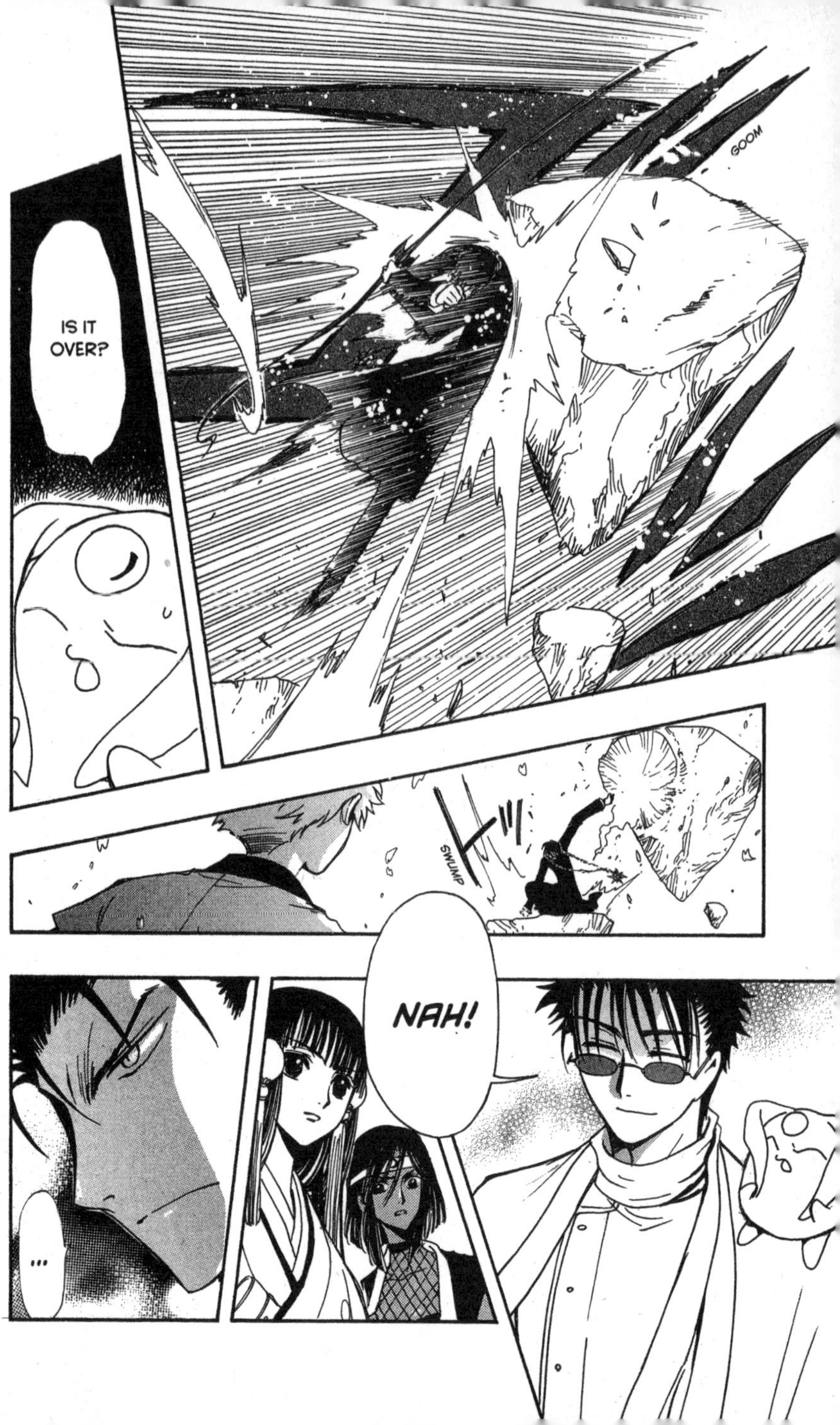
GOOM
IS IT OVER?
SWUMP
NAH!
...

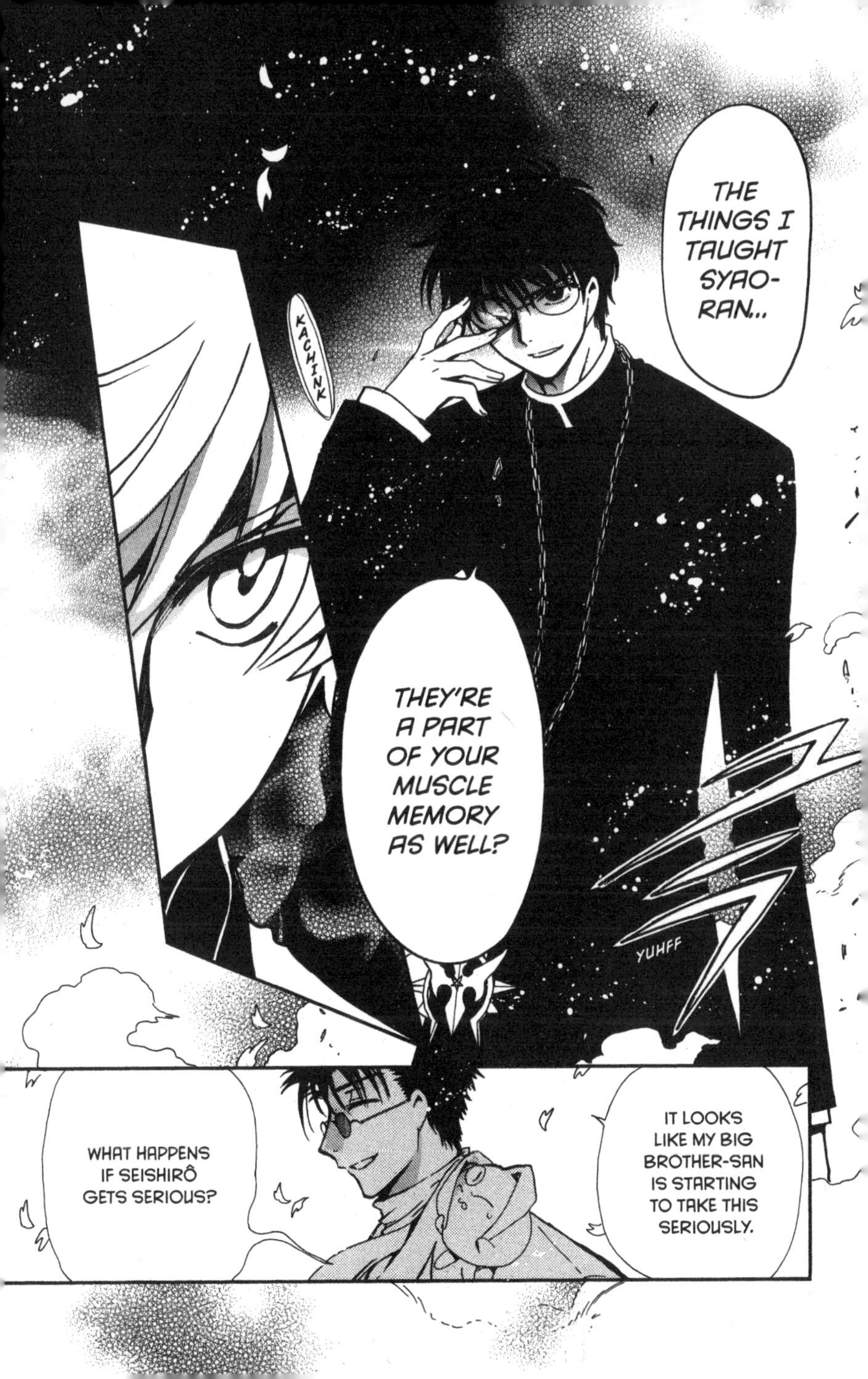
THE THINGS I TAUGHT SYAO-RAN...
KACHINK
THEY'RE A PART OF YOUR MUSCLE MEMORY AS WELL?
YUHFF
IT LOOKS LIKE MY BIG BROTHER-SAN IS STARTING TO TAKE THIS SERIOUSLY.
WHAT HAPPENS IF SEISHIRÔ GETS SERIOUS?

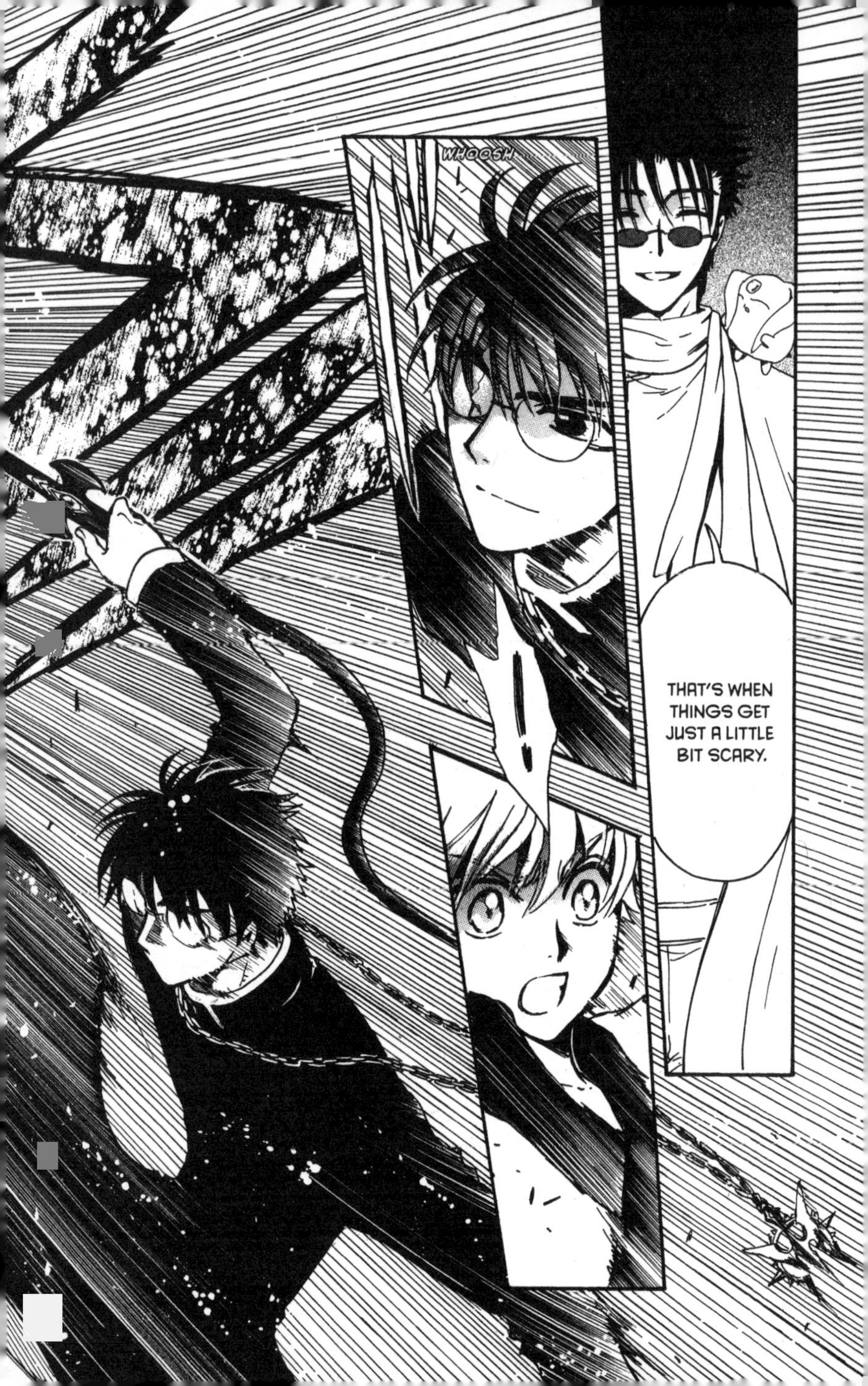
WHOOSH
THAT'S WHEN THINGS GET JUST A LITTLE BIT SCARY.

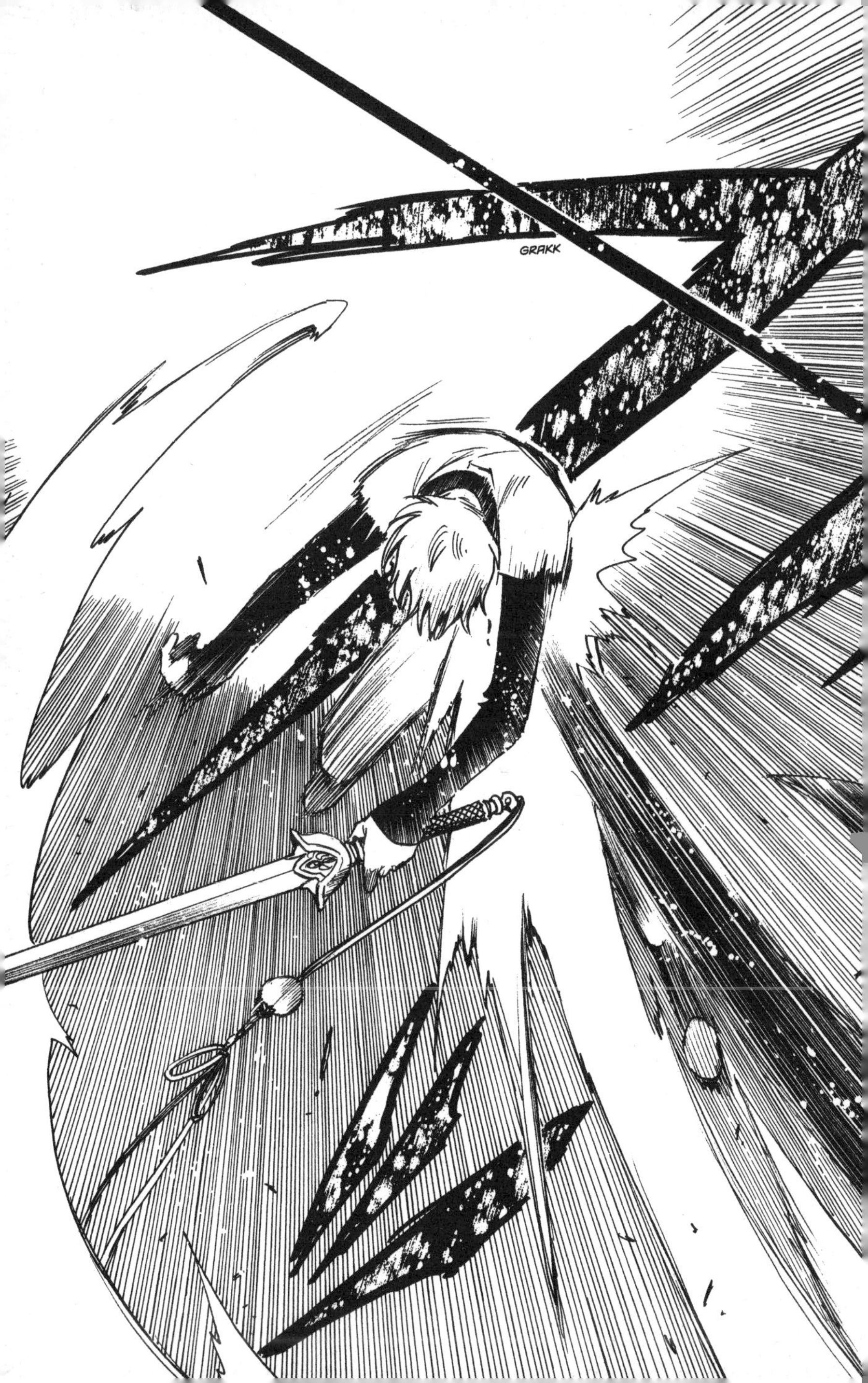
GRAKK

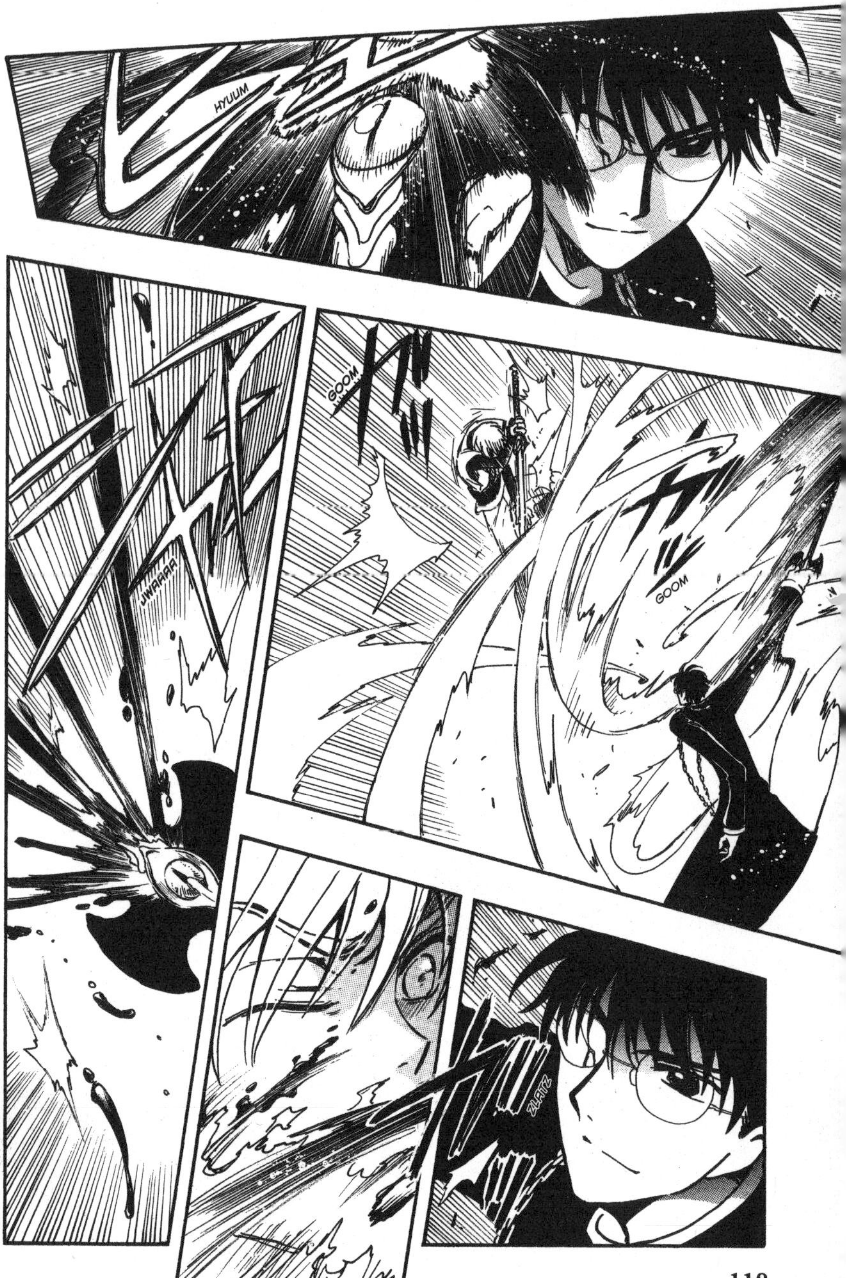
HYUUM
GOOM
GOOM
ZLATZ
JWARRR

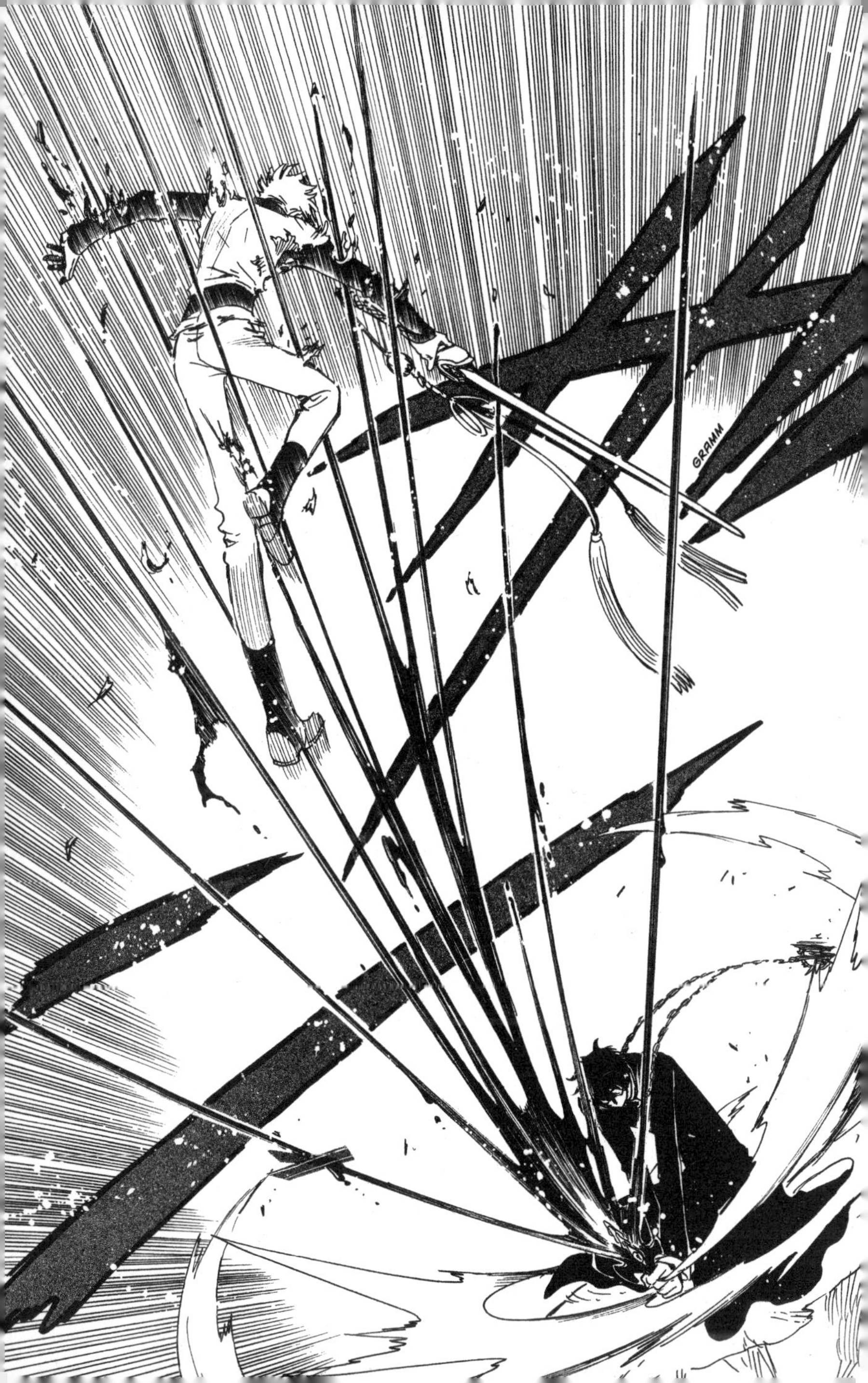
GRAMM

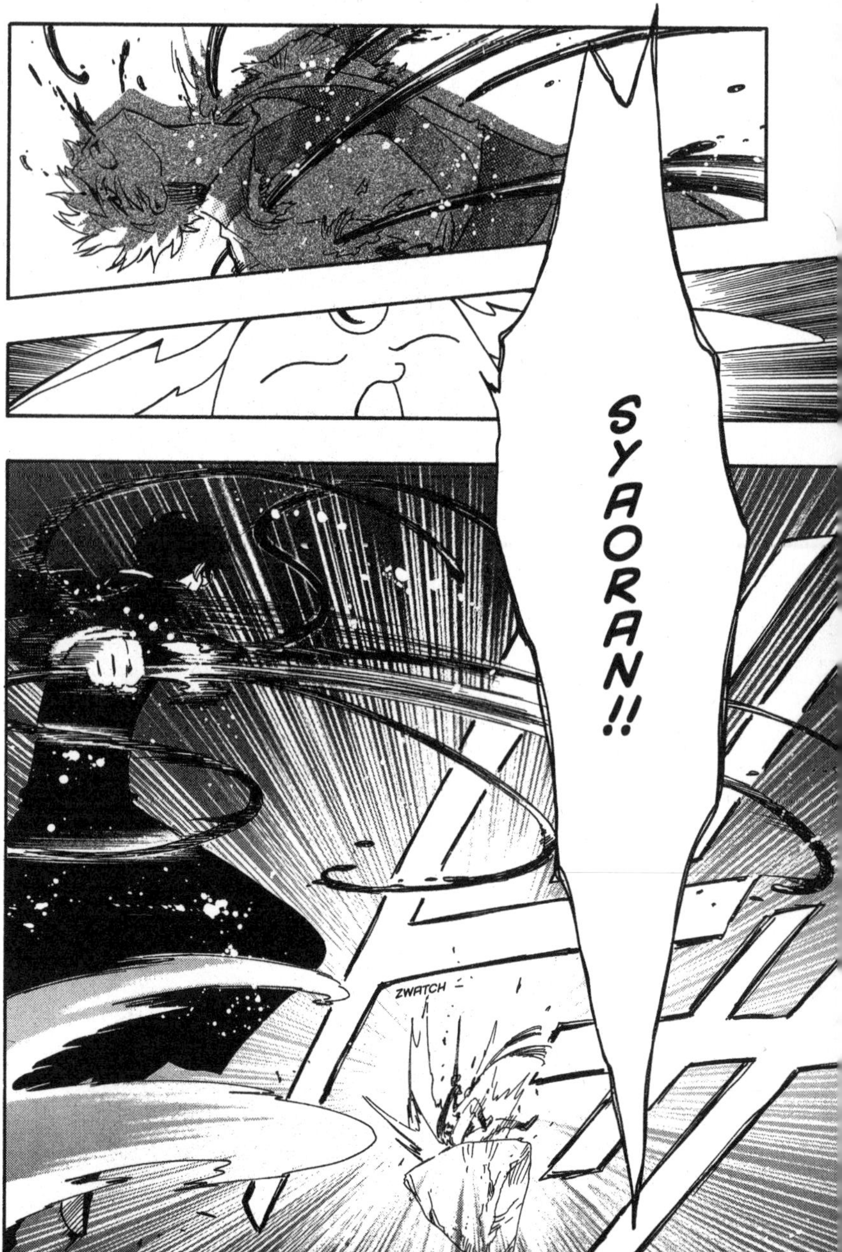
SYAORAN!!
ZWATCH

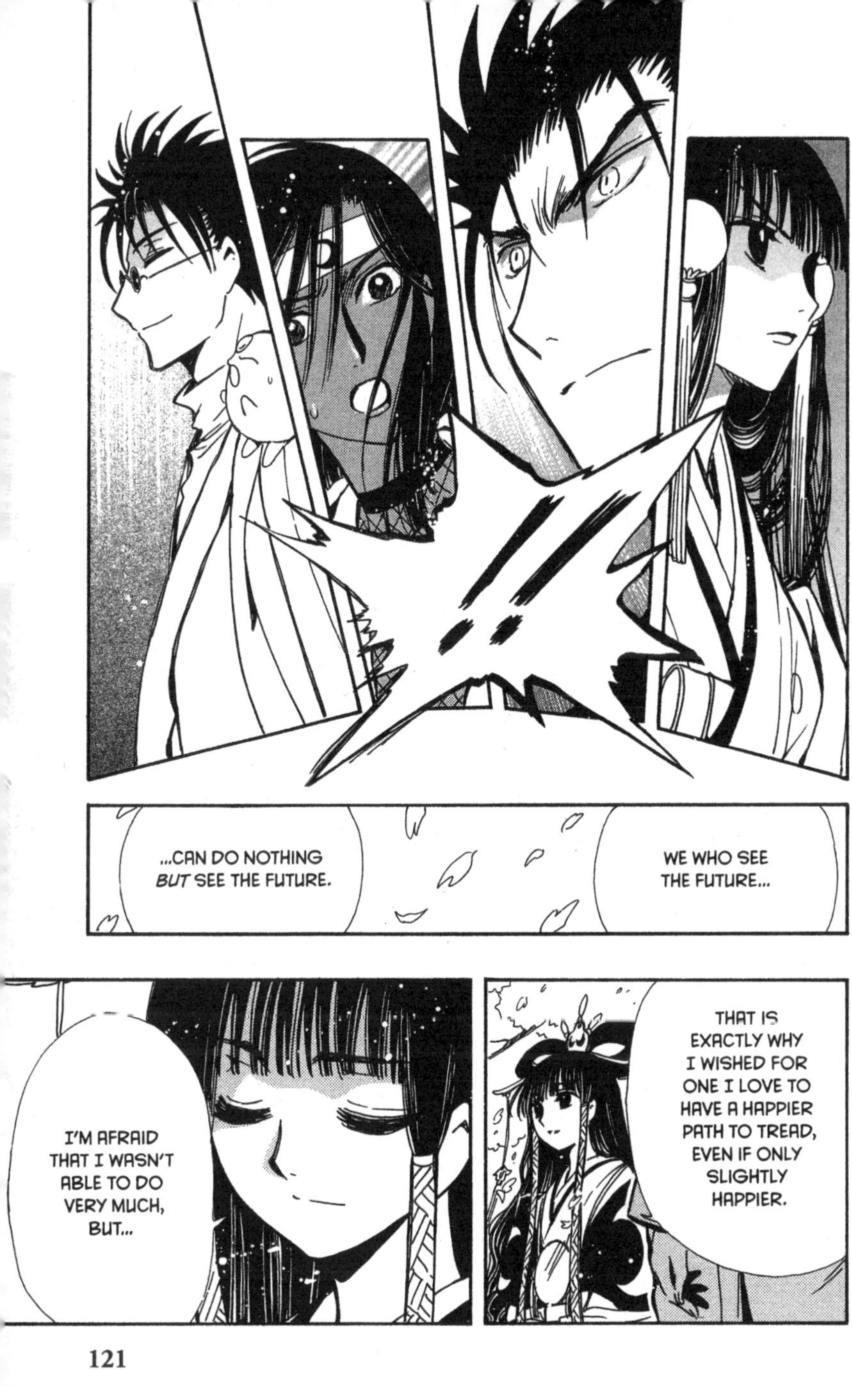
WE WHO SEE THE FUTURE...
...CAN DO NOTHING *BUT* SEE THE FUTURE.
THAT IS EXACTLY WHY I WISHED FOR ONE I LOVE TO HAVE A HAPPIER PATH TO TREAD, EVEN IF ONLY SLIGHTLY HAPPIER.
I'M AFRAID THAT I WASN'T ABLE TO DO VERY MUCH, BUT...

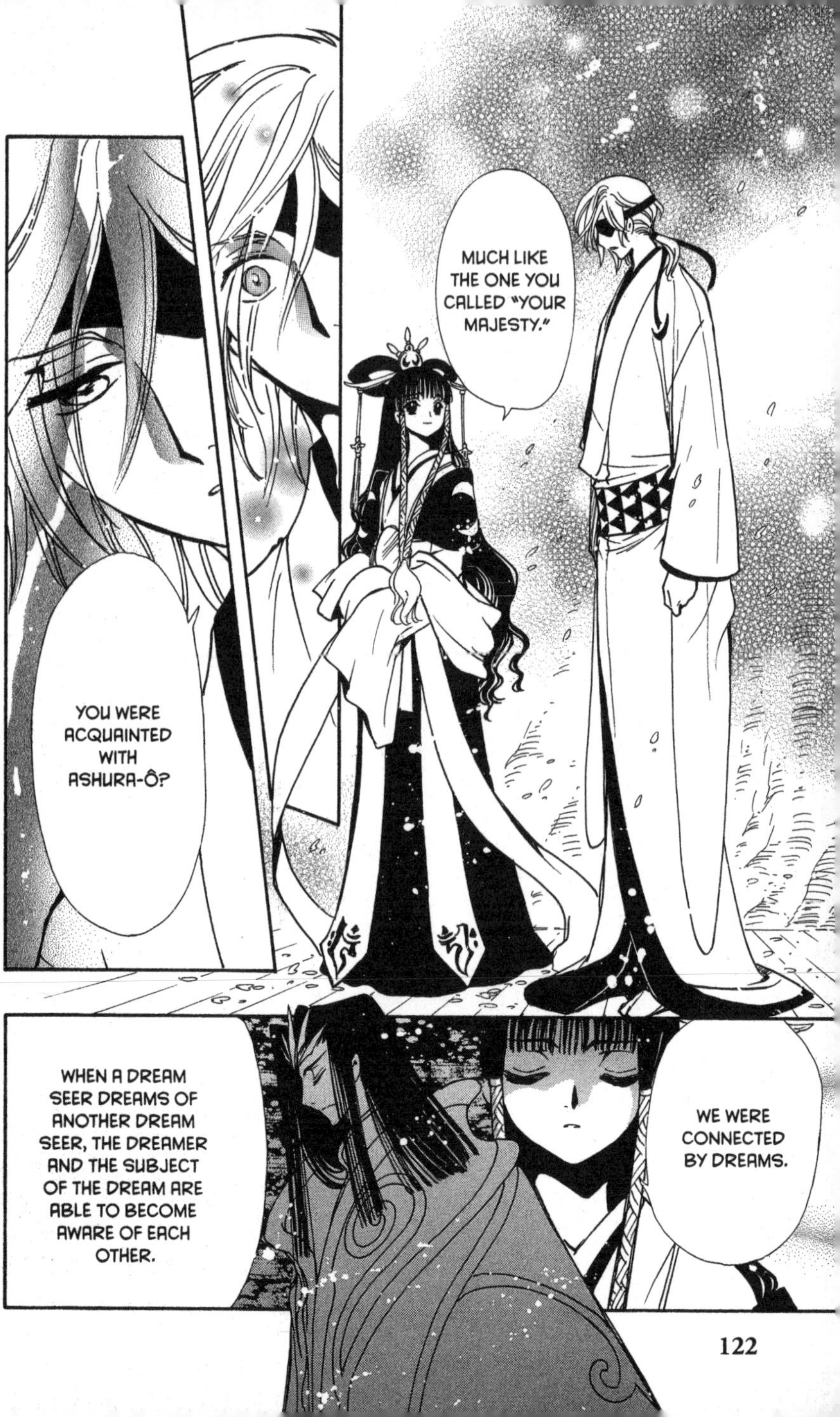
MUCH LIKE THE ONE YOU CALLED "YOUR MAJESTY."
YOU WERE ACQUAINTED WITH ASHURA-Ô?
WE WERE CONNECTED BY DREAMS.
WHEN A DREAM SEER DREAMS OF ANOTHER DREAM SEER, THE DREAMER AND THE SUBJECT OF THE DREAM ARE ABLE TO BECOME AWARE OF EACH OTHER.

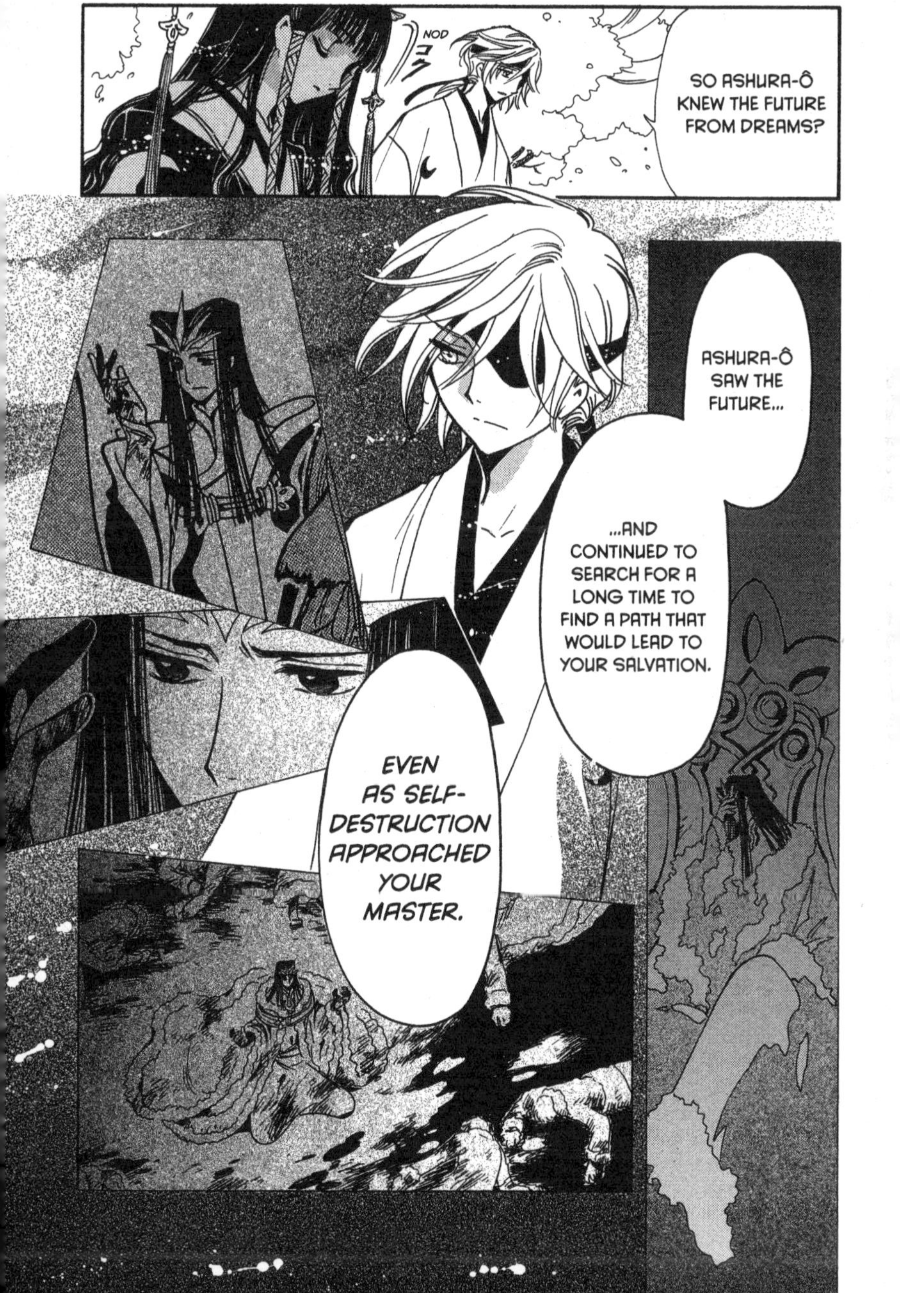
SO ASHURA-Ô KNEW THE FUTURE FROM DREAMS?
NOD
ASHURA-Ô SAW THE FUTURE...
...AND CONTINUED TO SEARCH FOR A LONG TIME TO FIND A PATH THAT WOULD LEAD TO YOUR SALVATION.
EVEN AS SELF-DESTRUCTION APPROACHED YOUR MASTER.

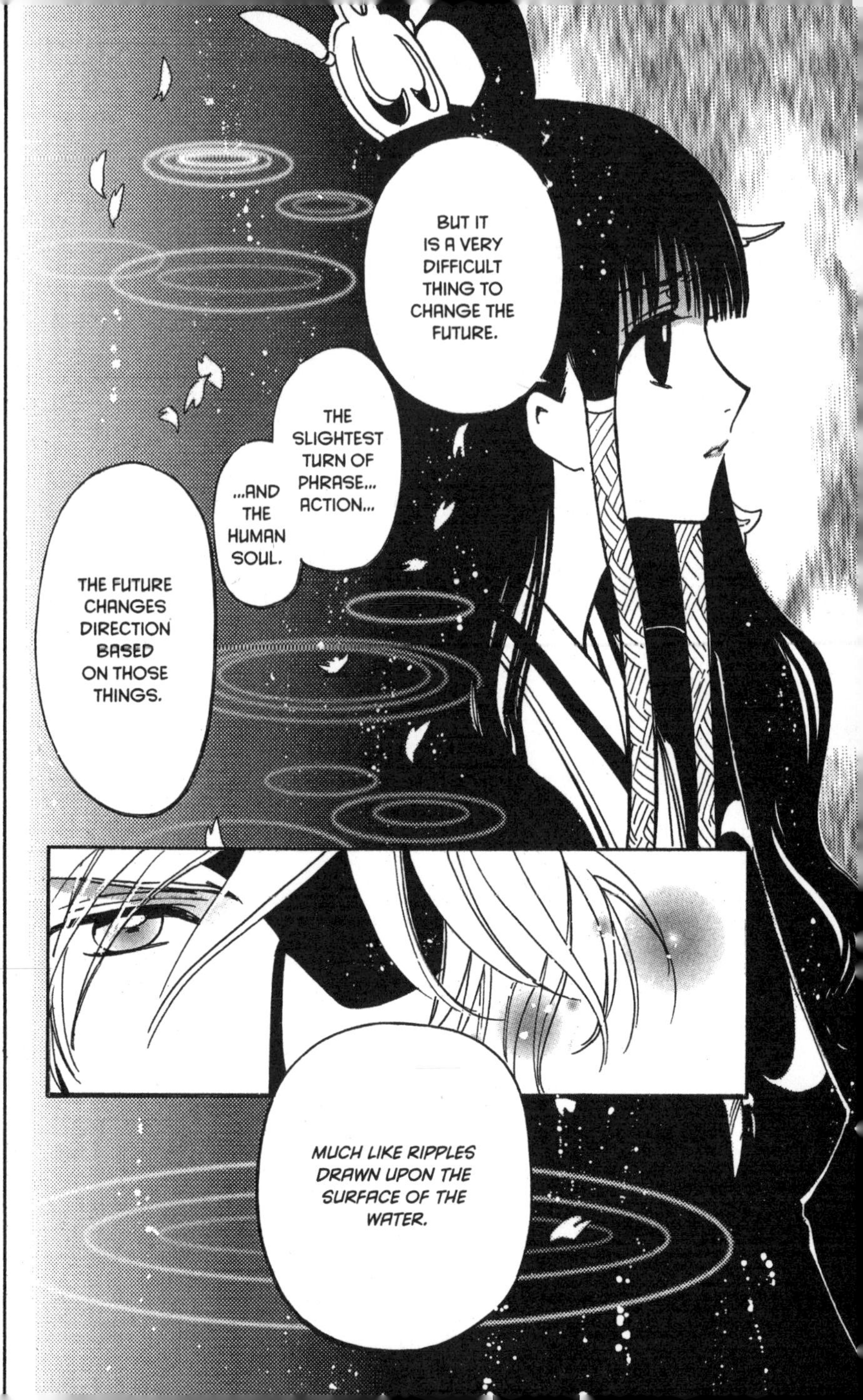
BUT IT IS A VERY DIFFICULT THING TO CHANGE THE FUTURE.
THE SLIGHTEST TURN OF PHRASE... ACTION...
...AND THE HUMAN SOUL.
THE FUTURE CHANGES DIRECTION BASED ON THOSE THINGS.
MUCH LIKE RIPPLES DRAWN UPON THE SURFACE OF THE WATER.

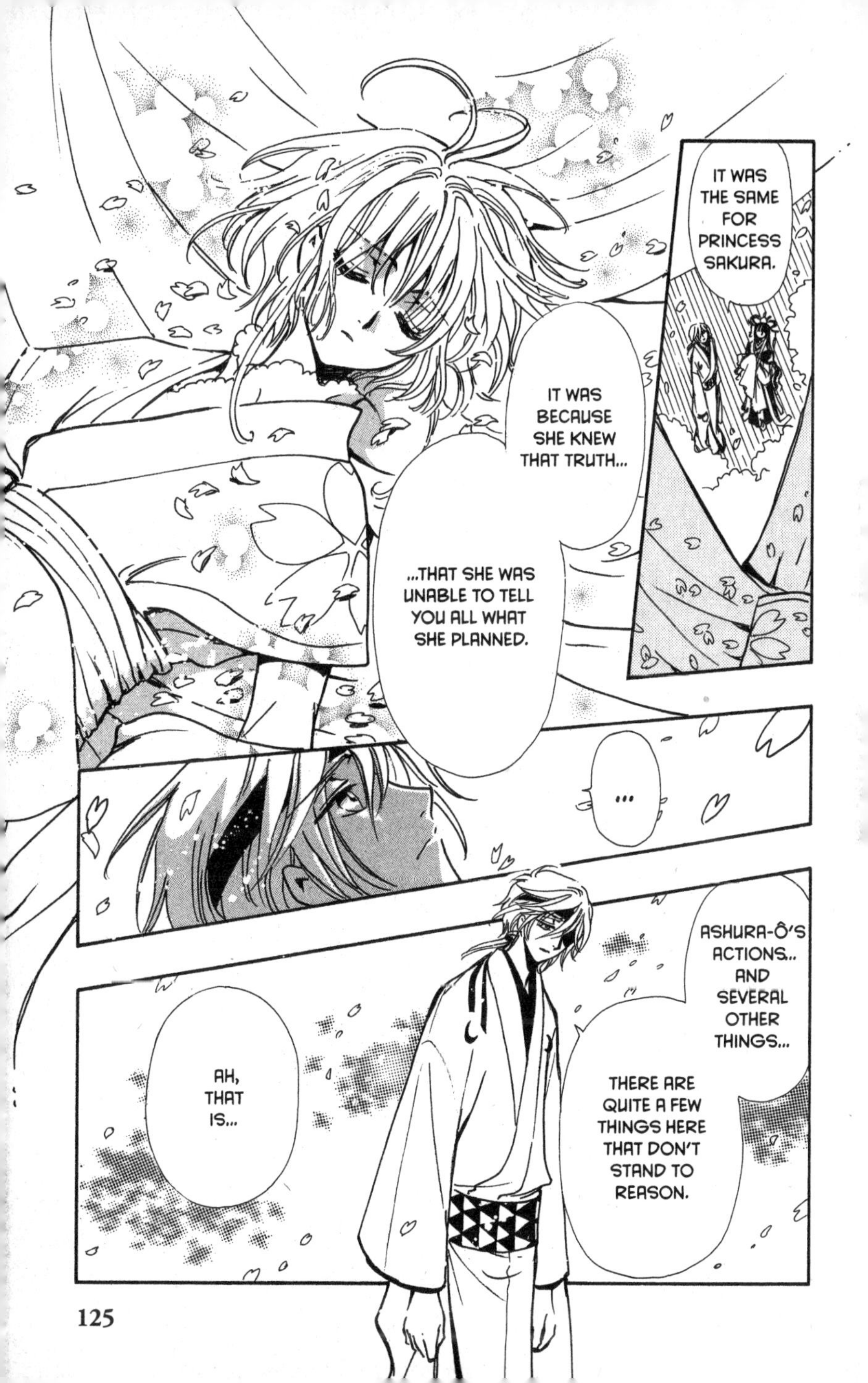
IT WAS THE SAME FOR PRINCESS SAKURA.
IT WAS BECAUSE SHE KNEW THAT TRUTH...
...THAT SHE WAS UNABLE TO TELL YOU ALL WHAT SHE PLANNED.
...
ASHURA-Ô'S ACTIONS... AND SEVERAL OTHER THINGS...
THERE ARE QUITE A FEW THINGS HERE THAT DON'T STAND TO REASON.
AH, THAT IS...

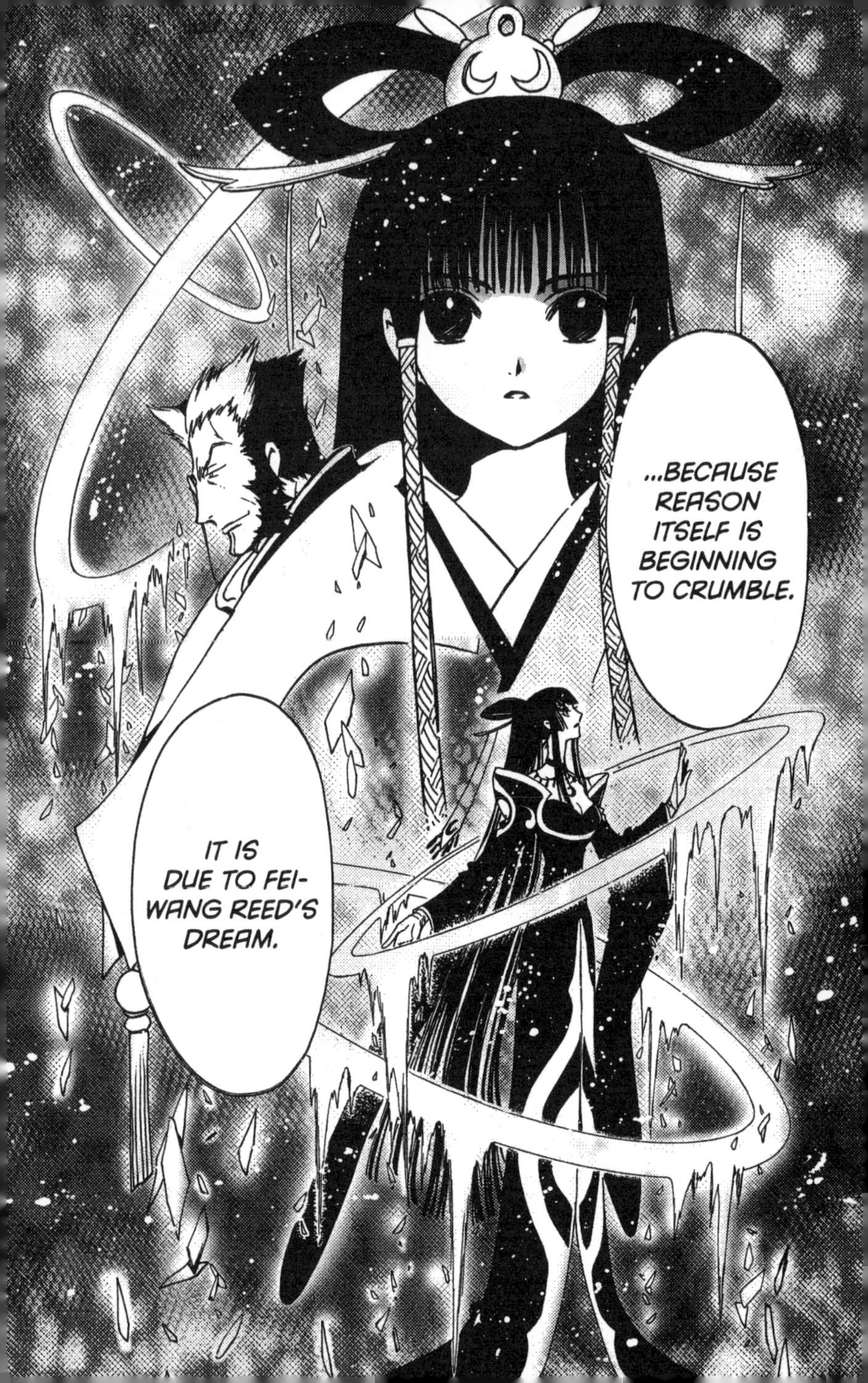
...BECAUSE REASON ITSELF IS BEGINNING TO CRUMBLE.
IT IS DUE TO FEI-WANG REED'S DREAM.

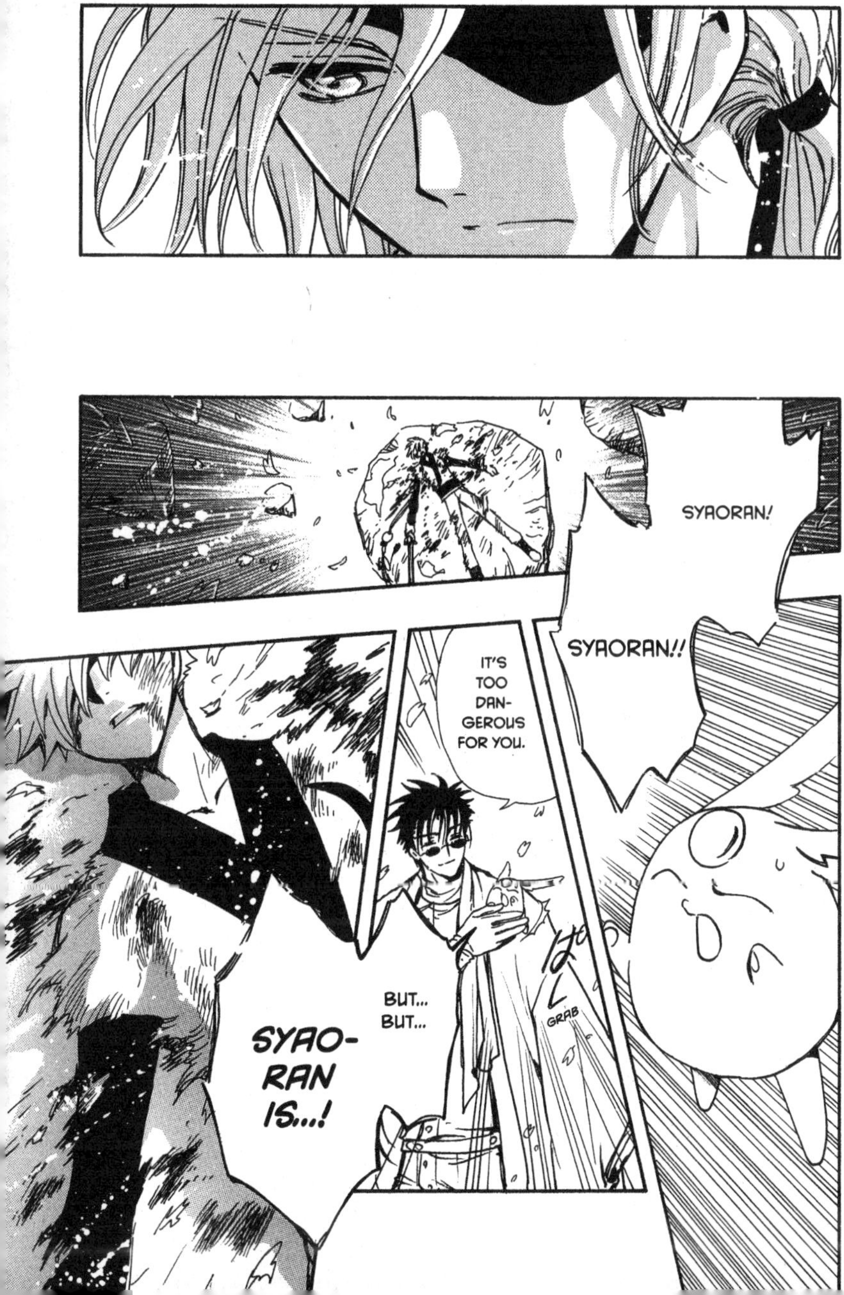
SYAORAN!
SYAORAN!!
IT'S TOO DAN-GEROUS FOR YOU.
GRAB
BUT... BUT...
SYAO-RAN IS...!

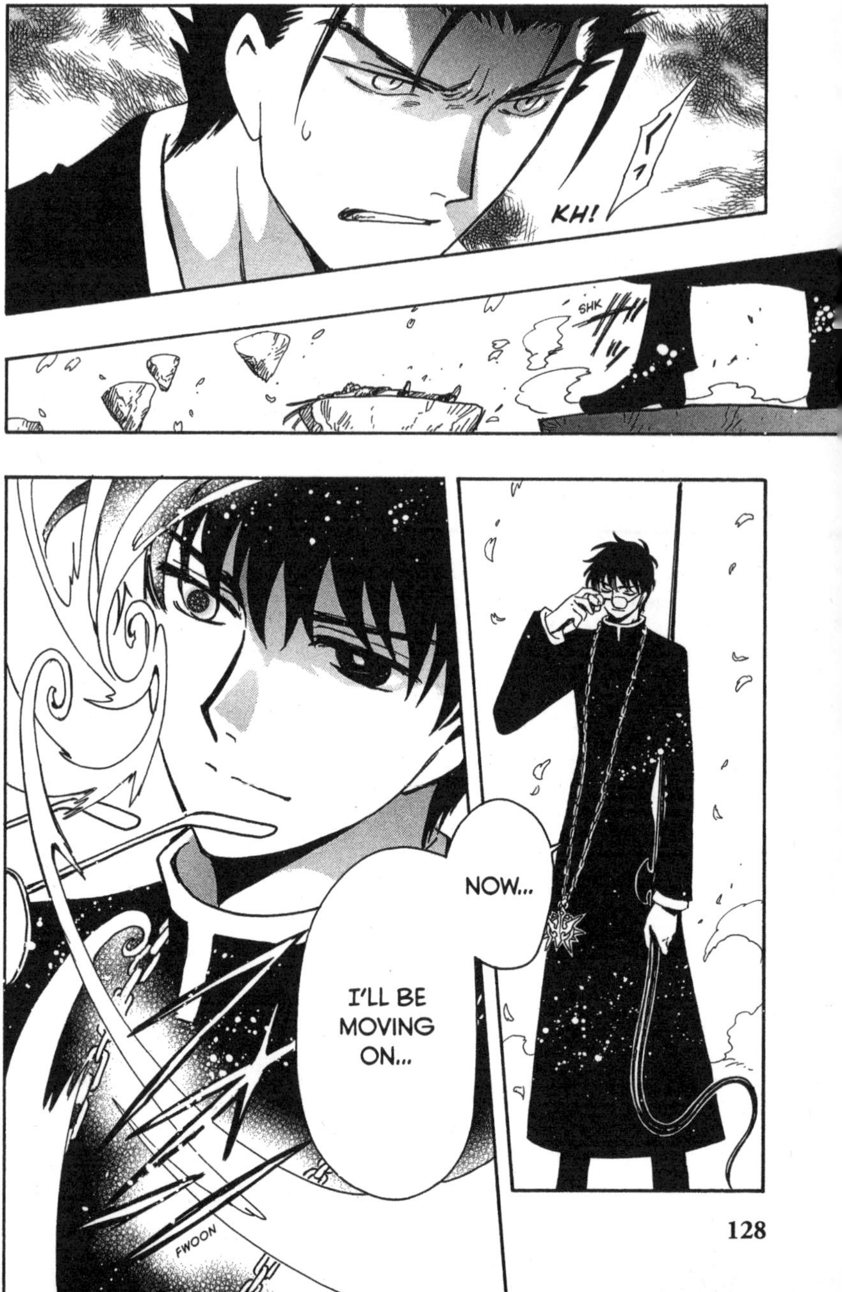
KH!
SHK
NOW...
I'LL BE MOVING ON...
FWOON

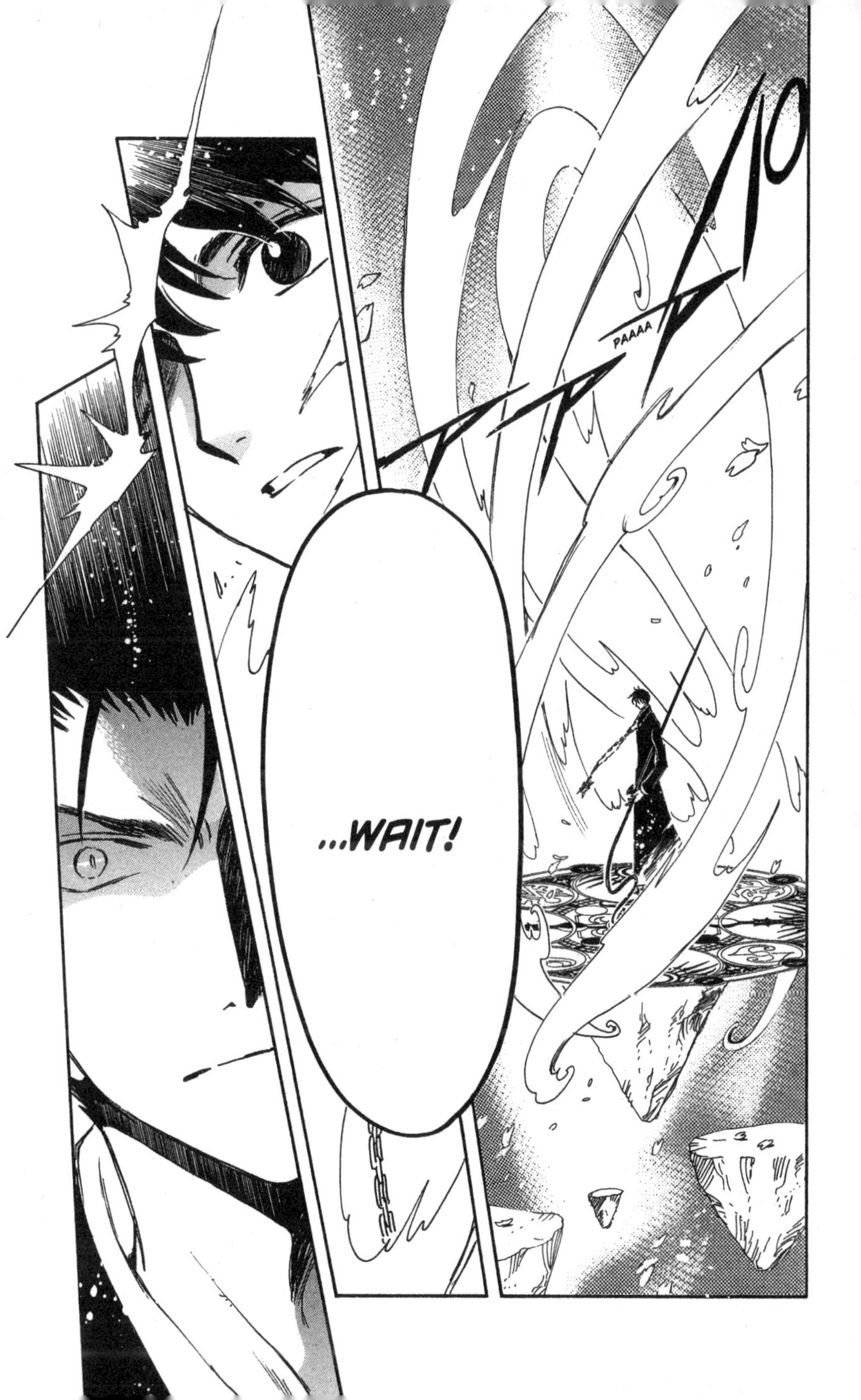
PAAAA
...WAIT!

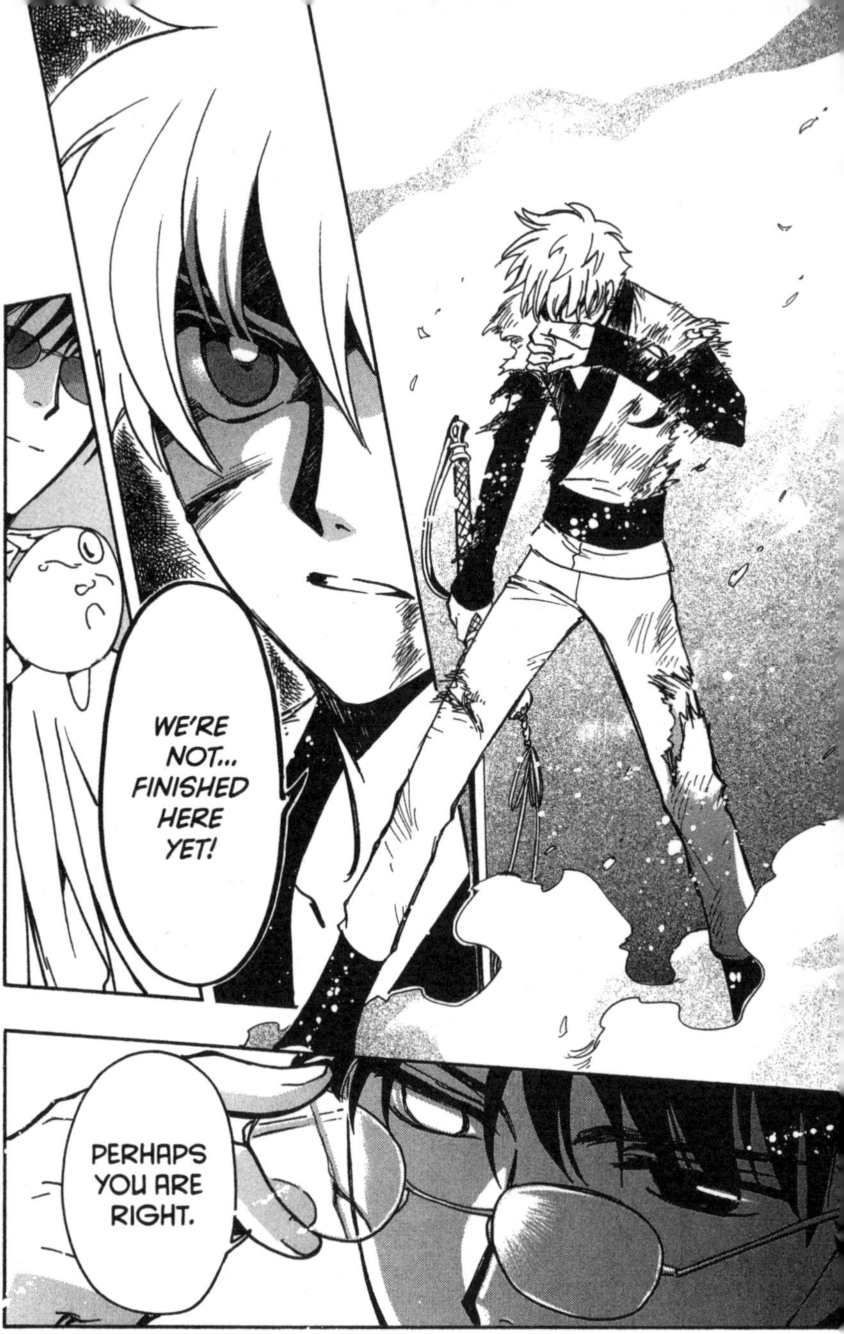
WE'RE NOT... FINISHED HERE YET!
PERHAPS YOU ARE RIGHT.

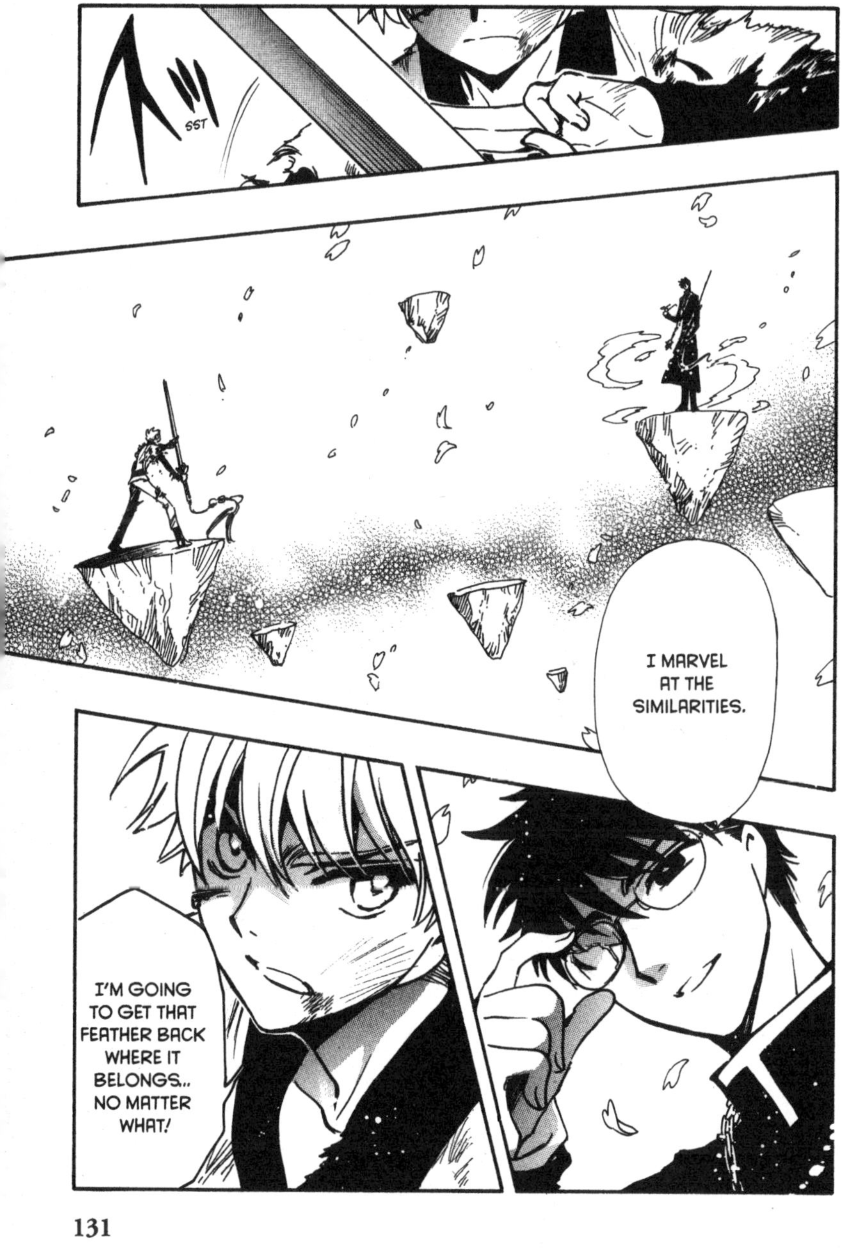
SST
I MARVEL AT THE SIMILARITIES.
I'M GOING TO GET THAT FEATHER BACK WHERE IT BELONGS... NO MATTER WHAT!

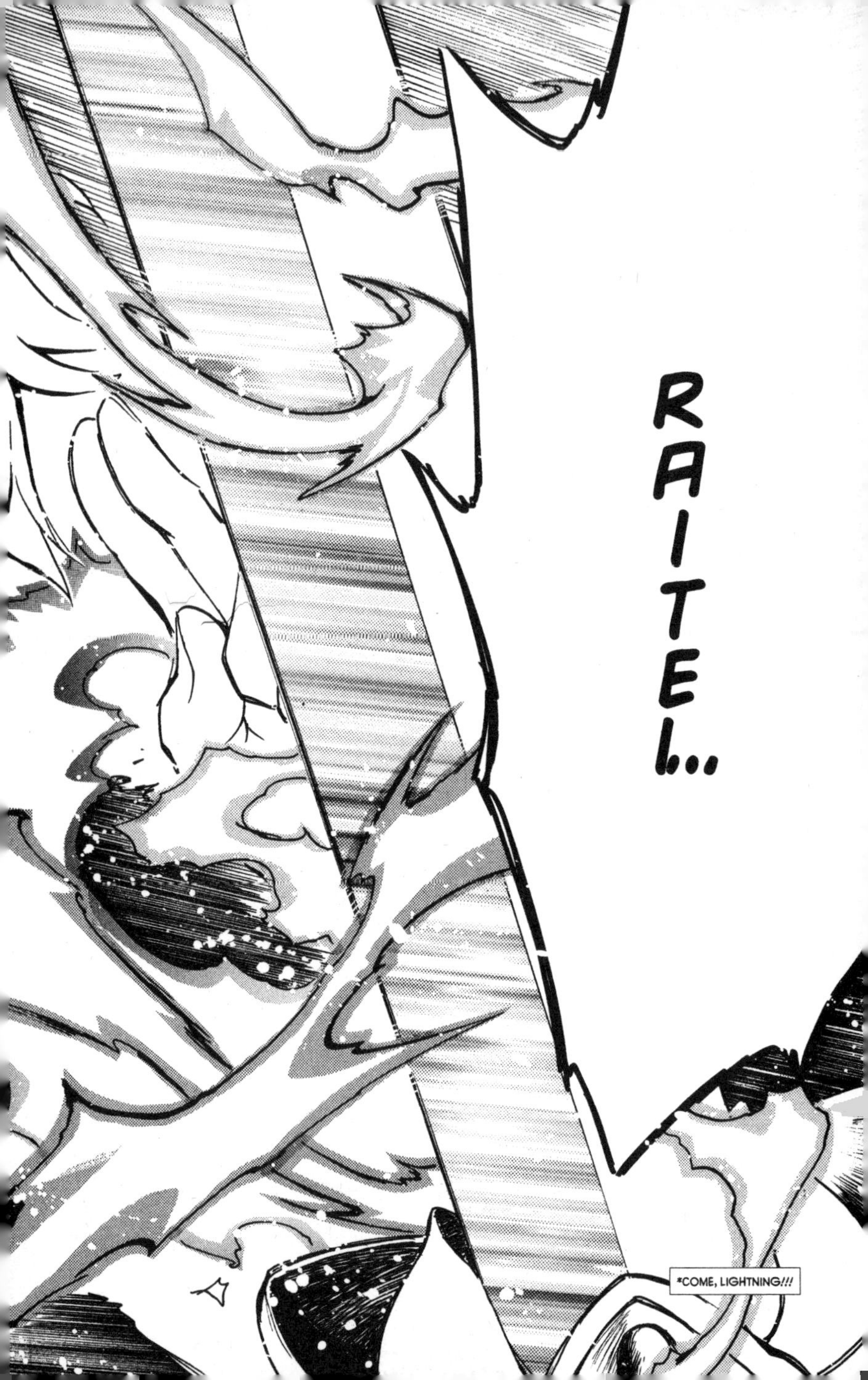
RAITEI...
*COME, LIGHTNING!!!

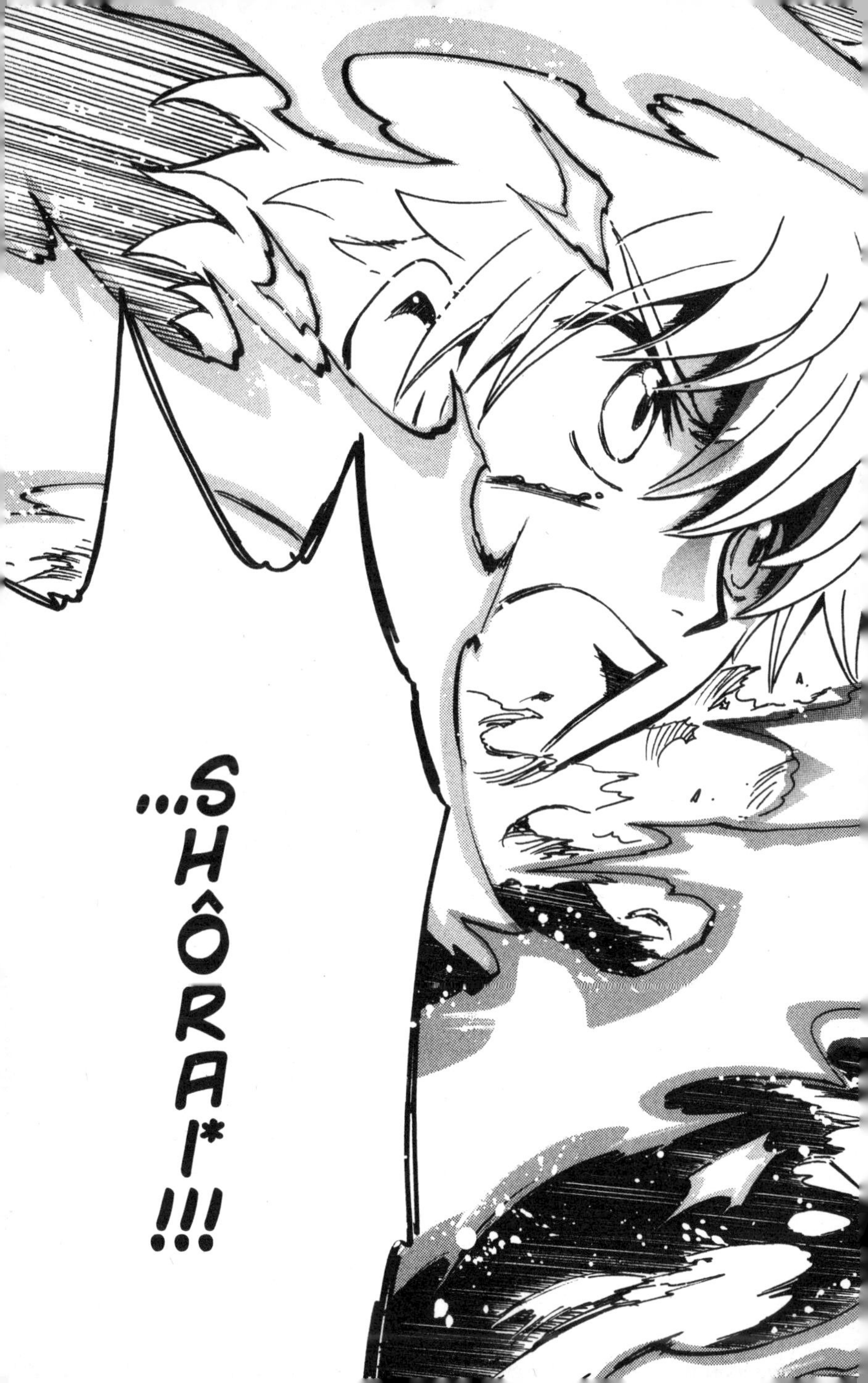
...SHÔRA*!!!

ツバサ
RESERVoir CHRoNiCLE

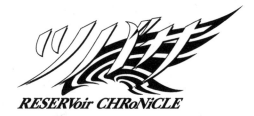

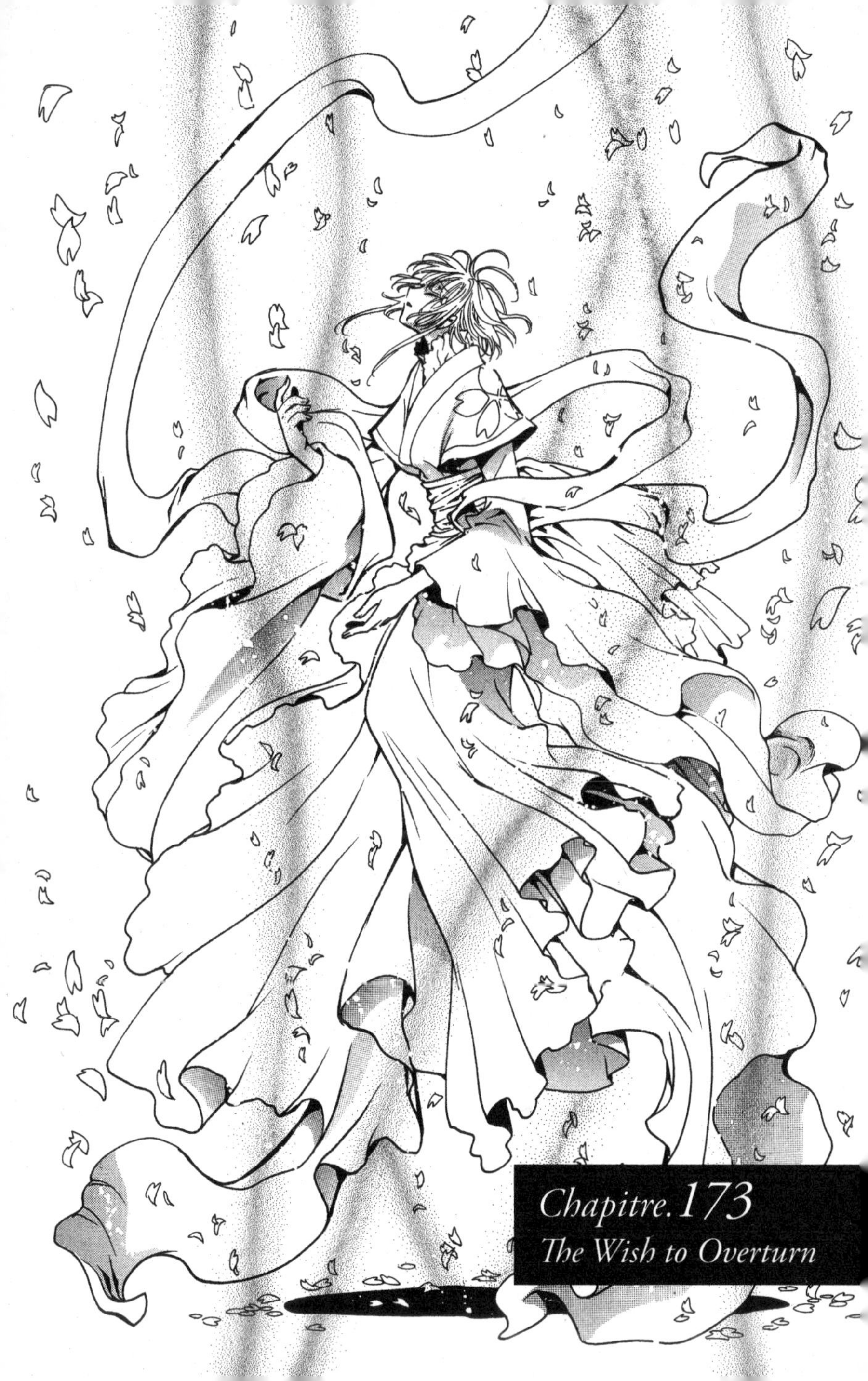
Chapitre.173
The Wish to Overturn

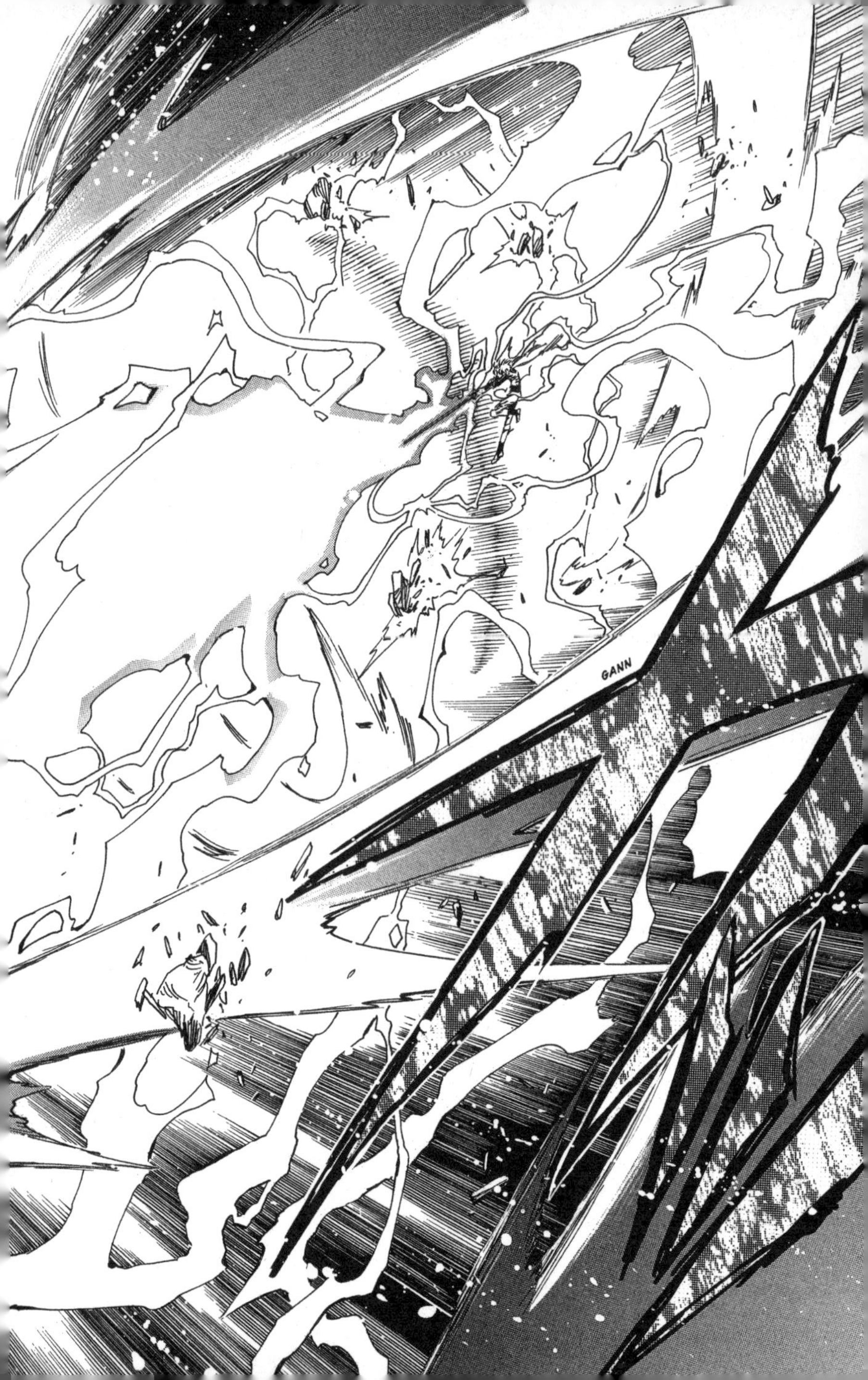
GANN

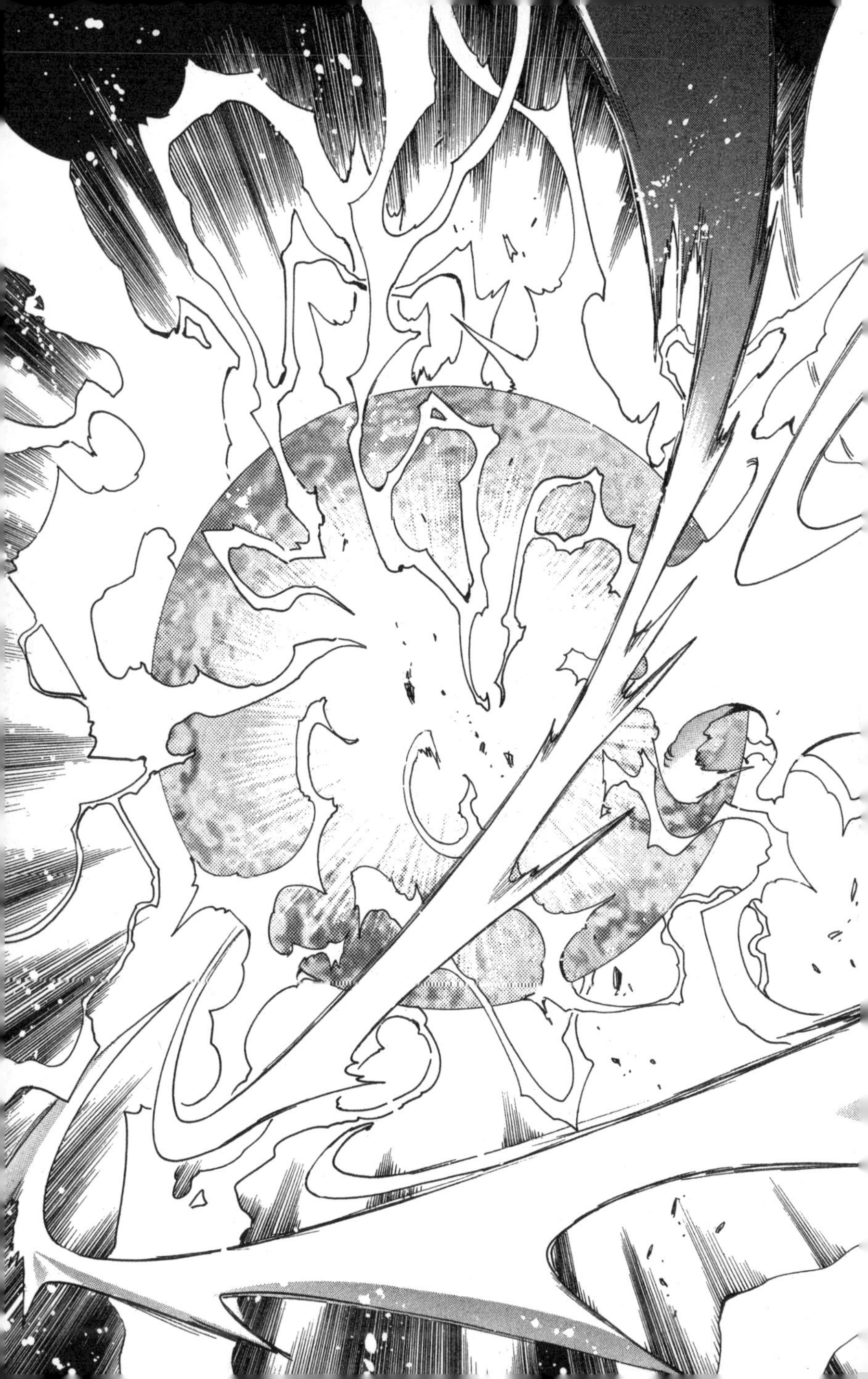

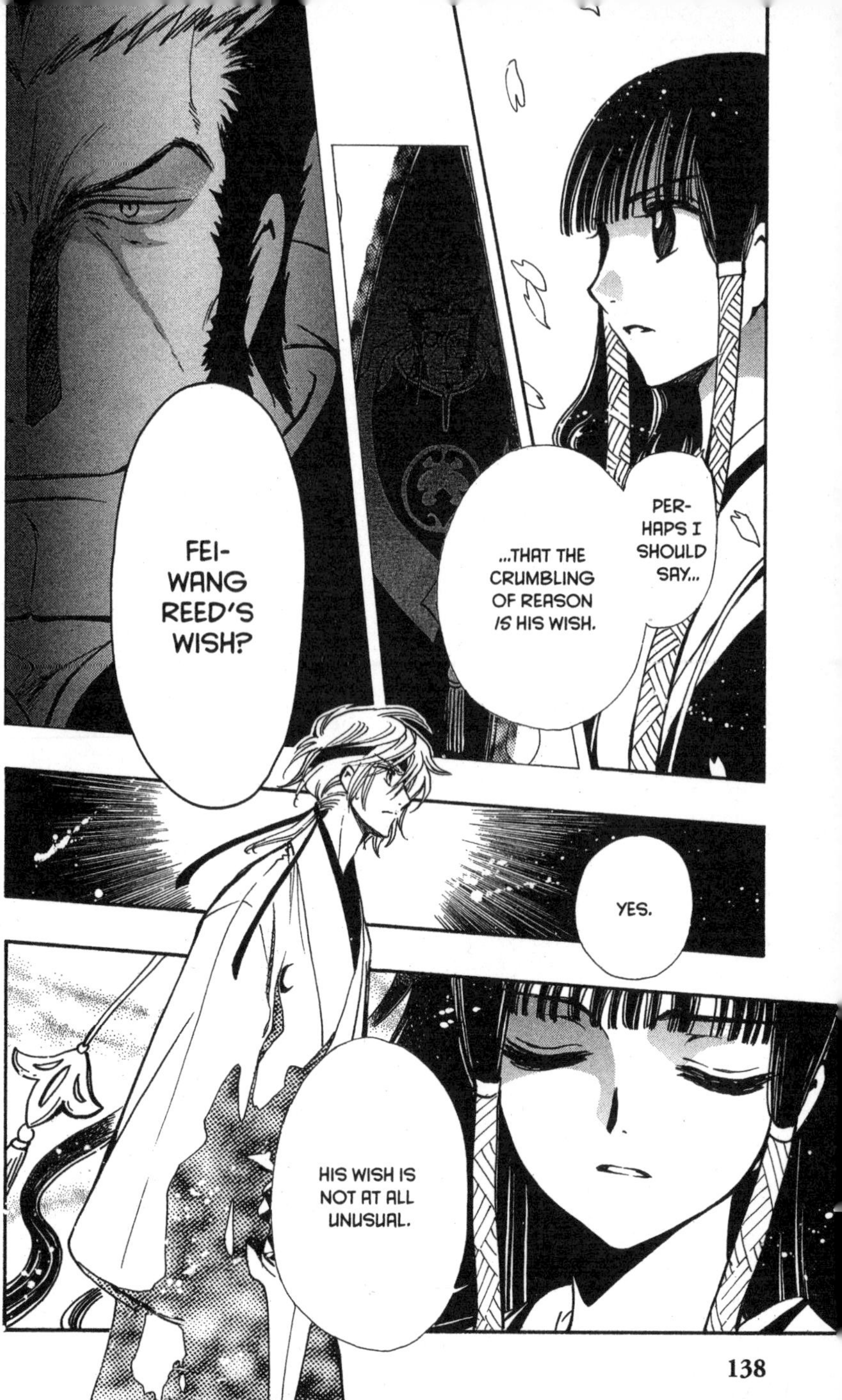
PER-HAPS I SHOULD SAY...
...THAT THE CRUMBLING OF REASON *IS* HIS WISH.
FEI-WANG REED'S WISH?
YES.
HIS WISH IS NOT AT ALL UNUSUAL.

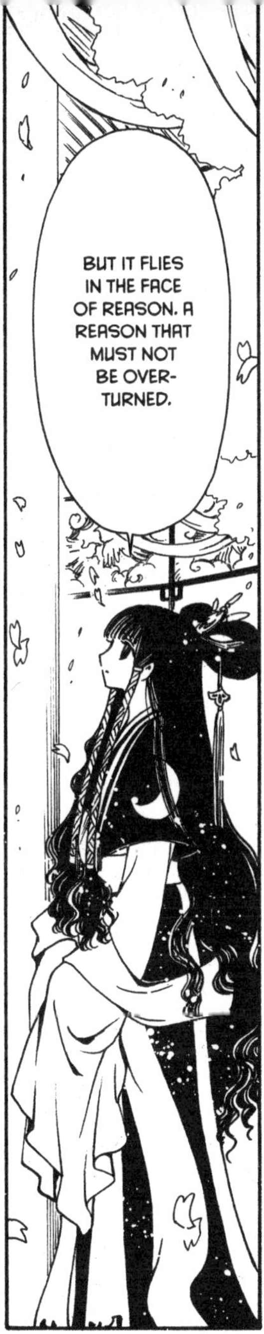
BUT IT FLIES IN THE FACE OF REASON. A REASON THAT MUST NOT BE OVER-TURNED.
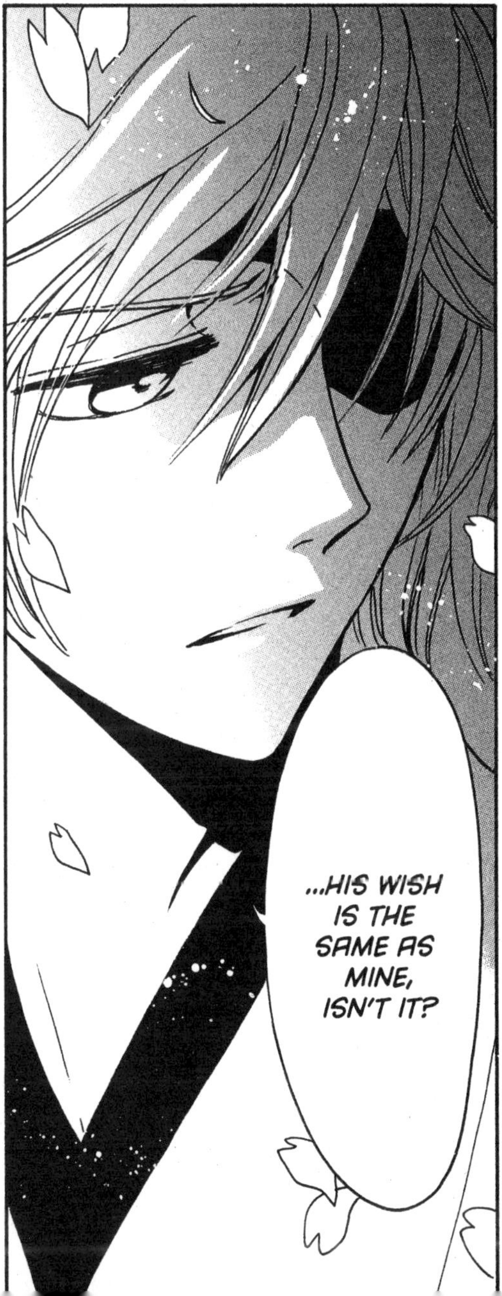
...HIS WISH IS THE SAME AS MINE, ISN'T IT?

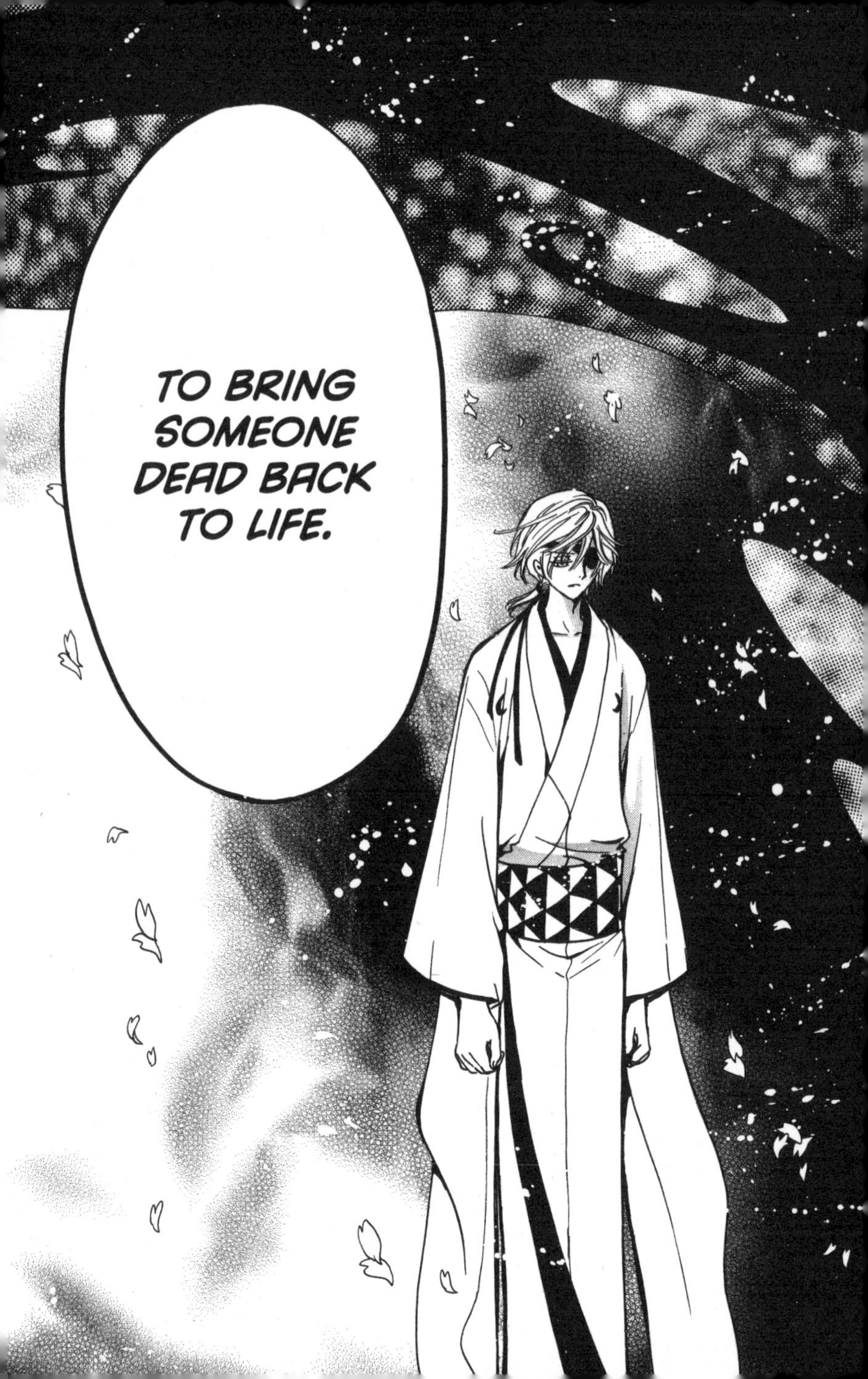
TO BRING SOMEONE DEAD BACK TO LIFE.

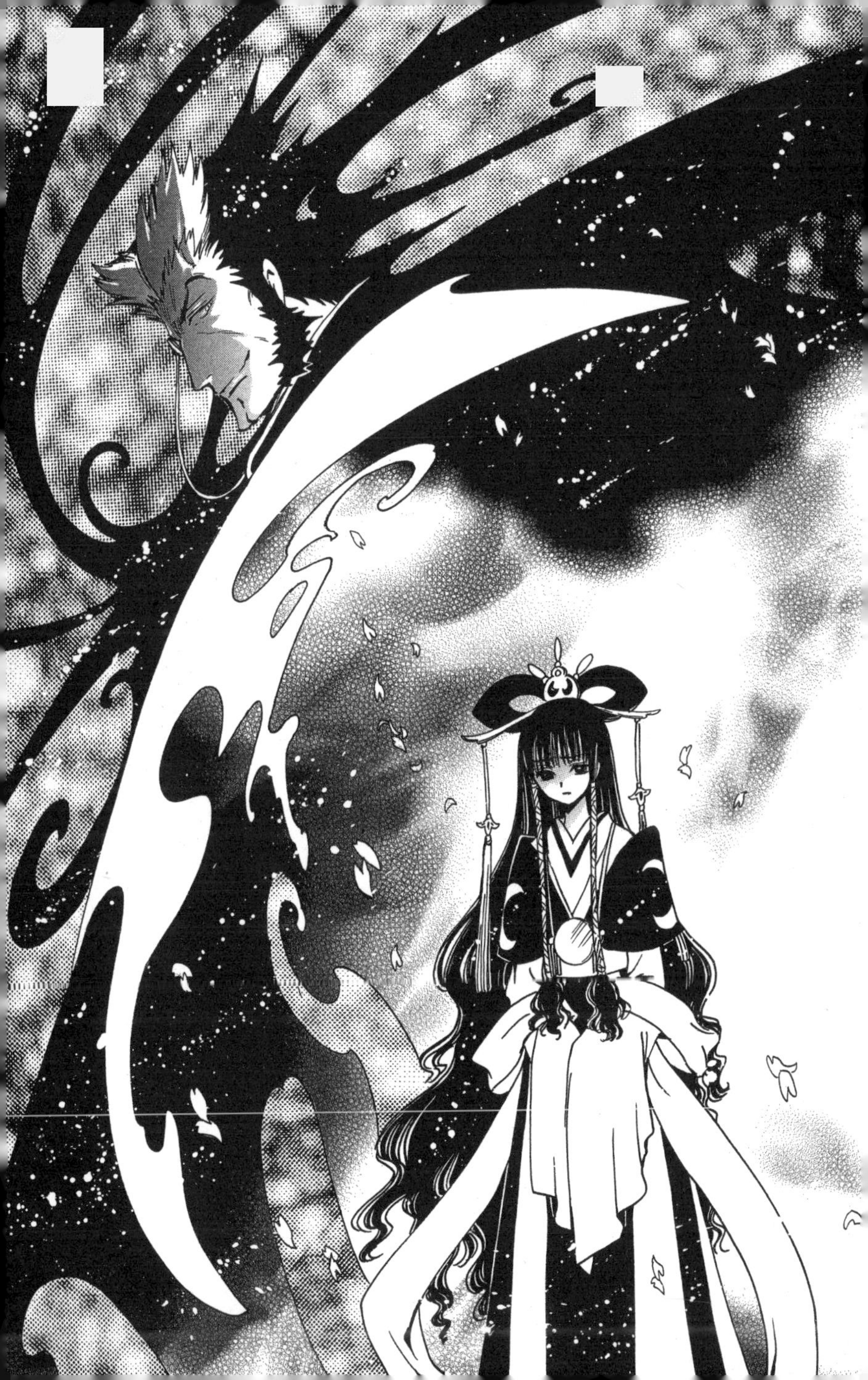

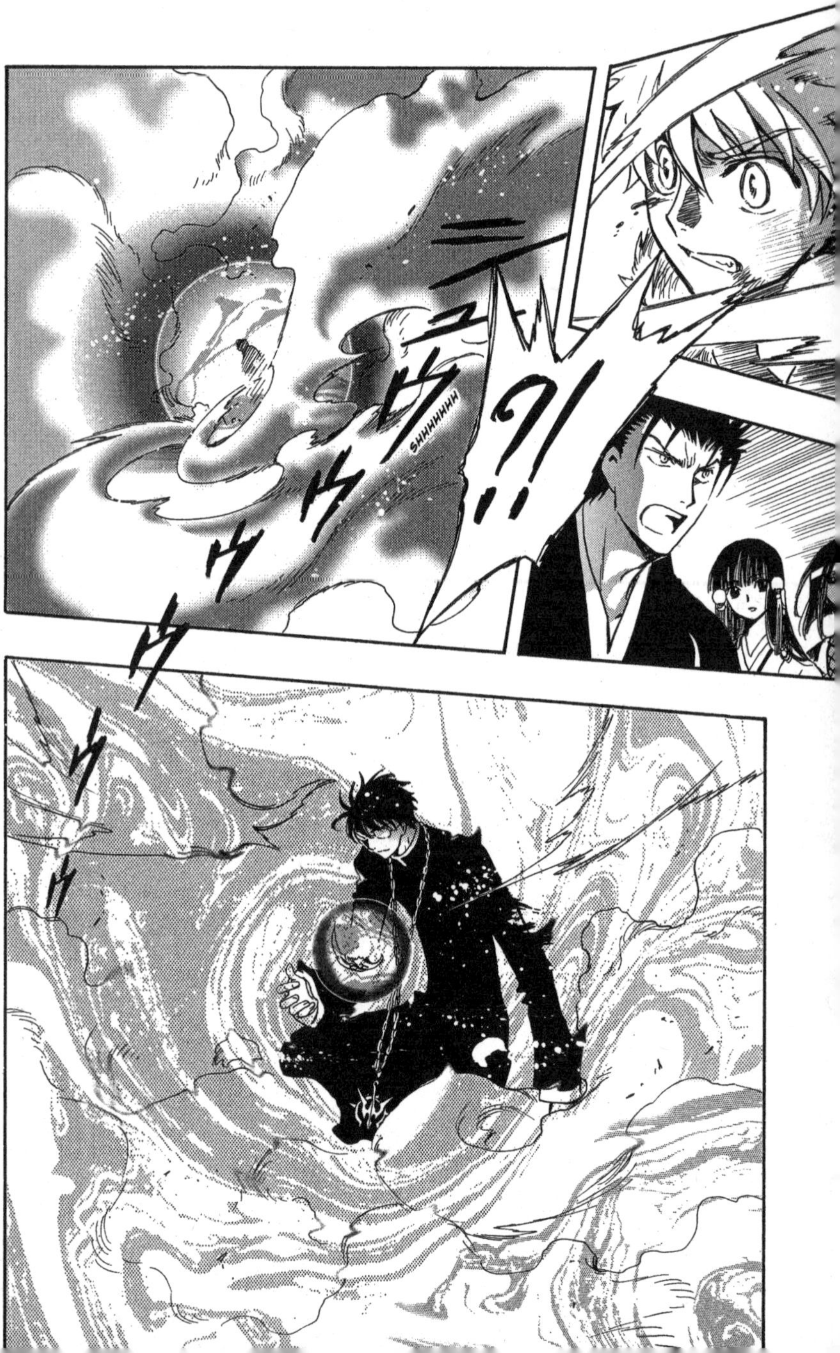
?!!
SHHHHHHH

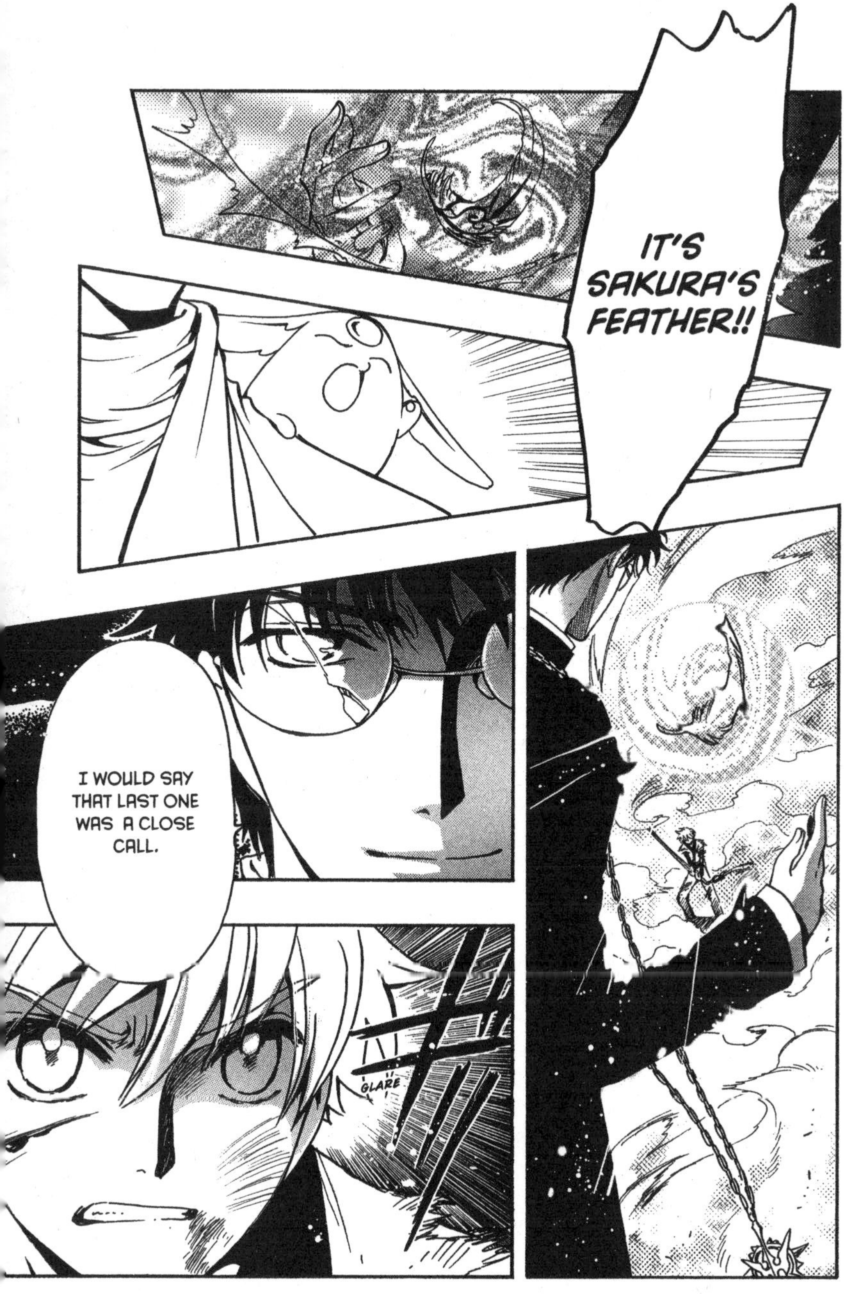
IT'S SAKURA'S FEATHER!!
I WOULD SAY THAT LAST ONE WAS A CLOSE CALL.
GLARE

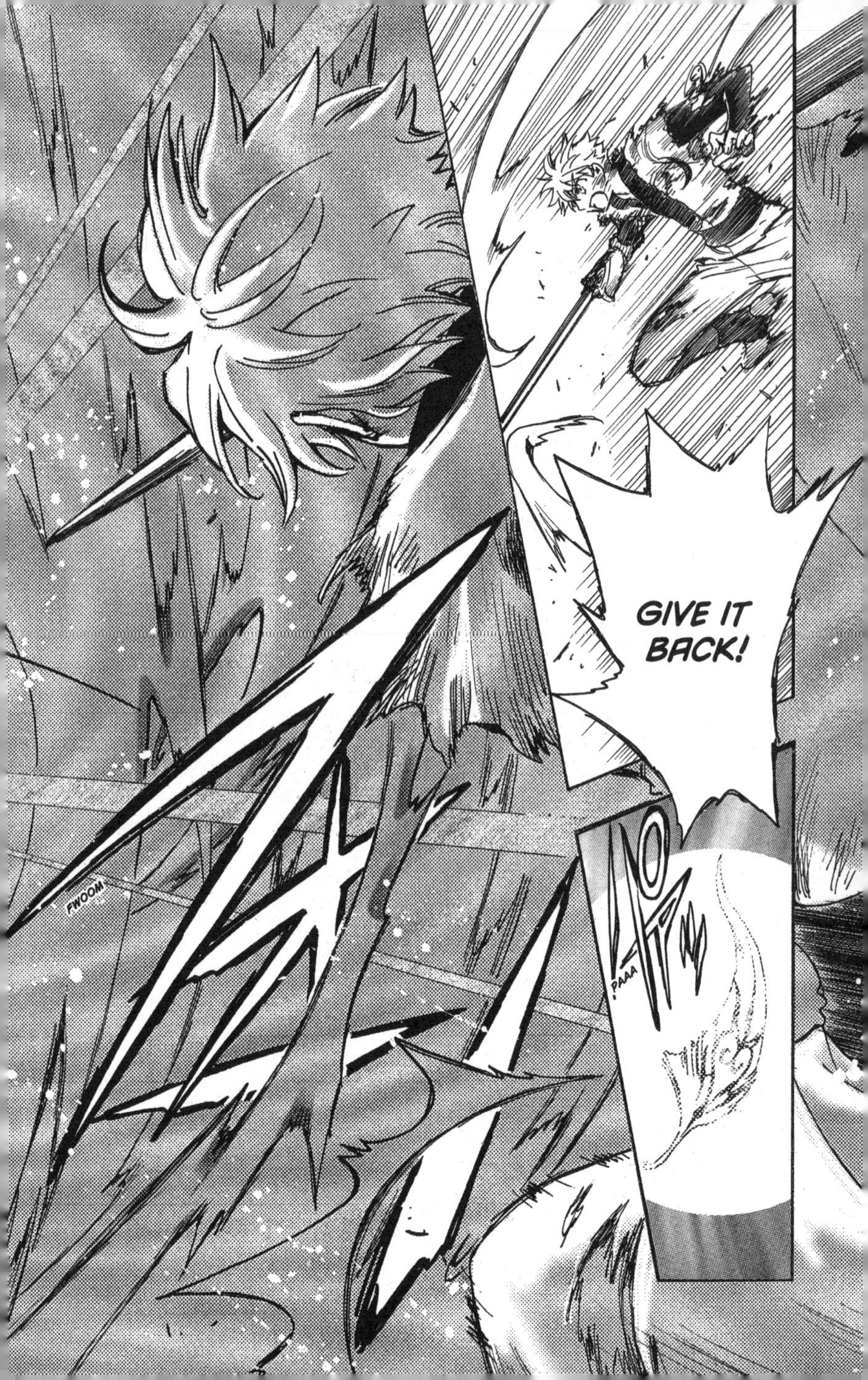
GIVE IT BACK!
PAAA
FWOOM

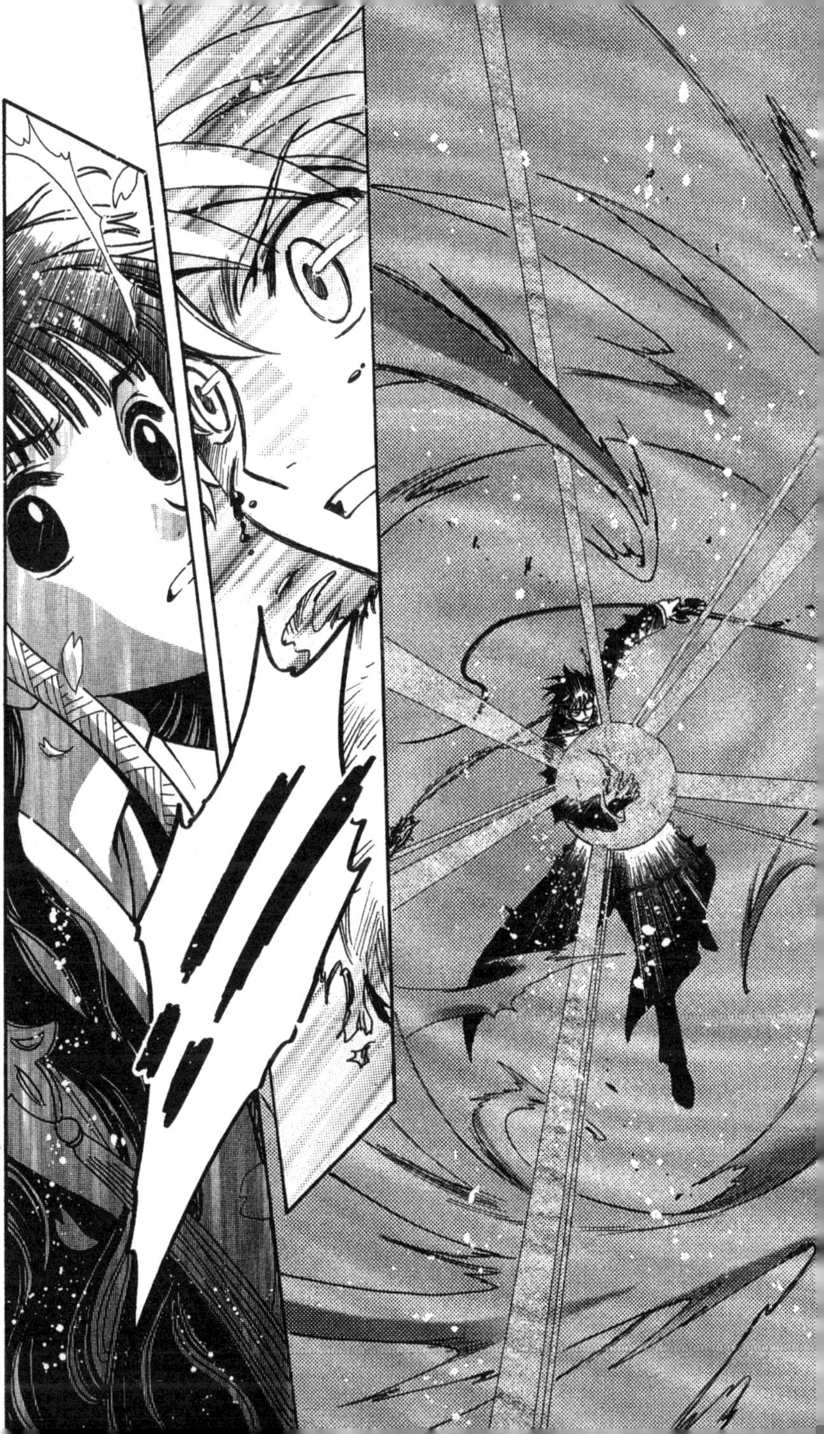

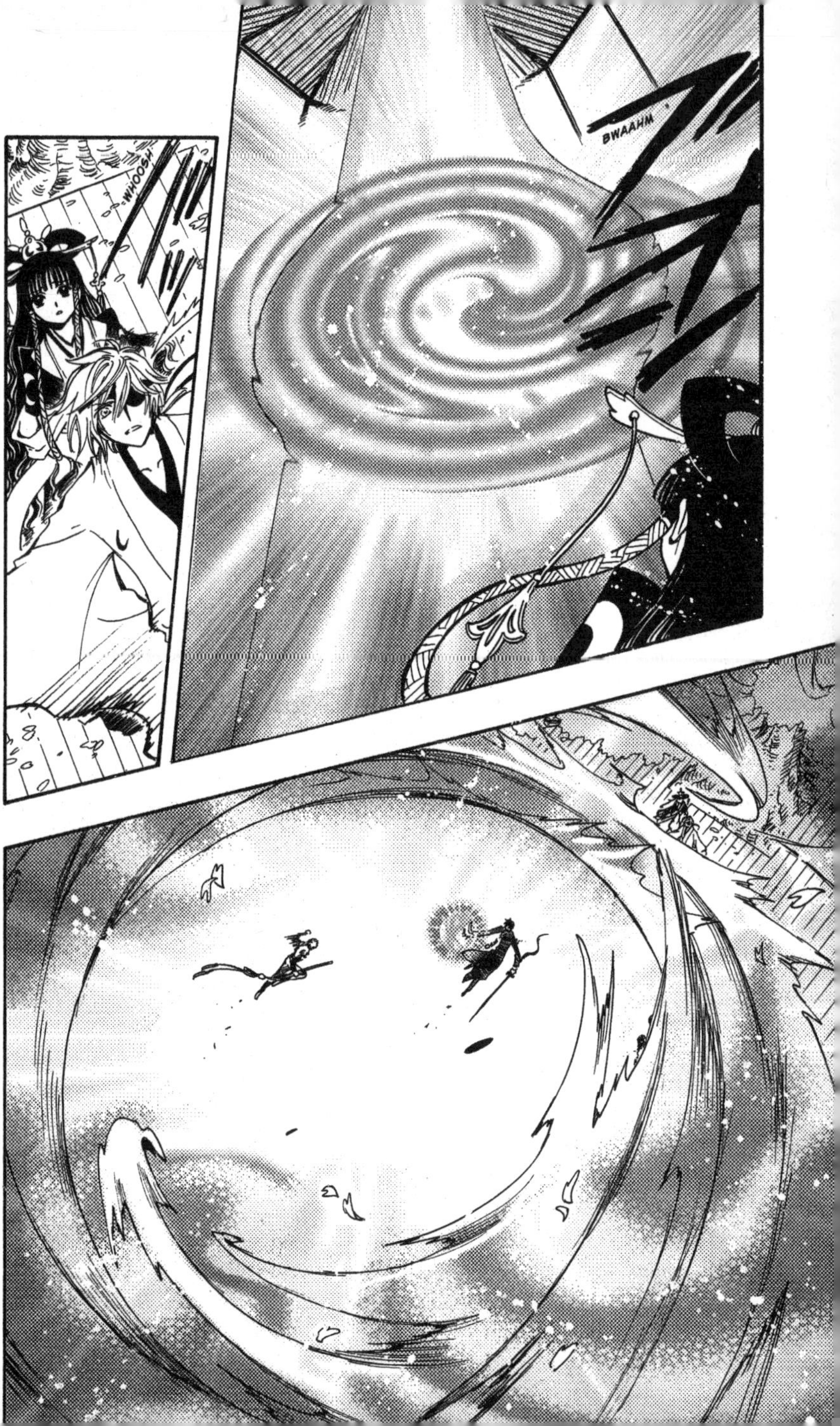
BWAAHM
WHOOSH

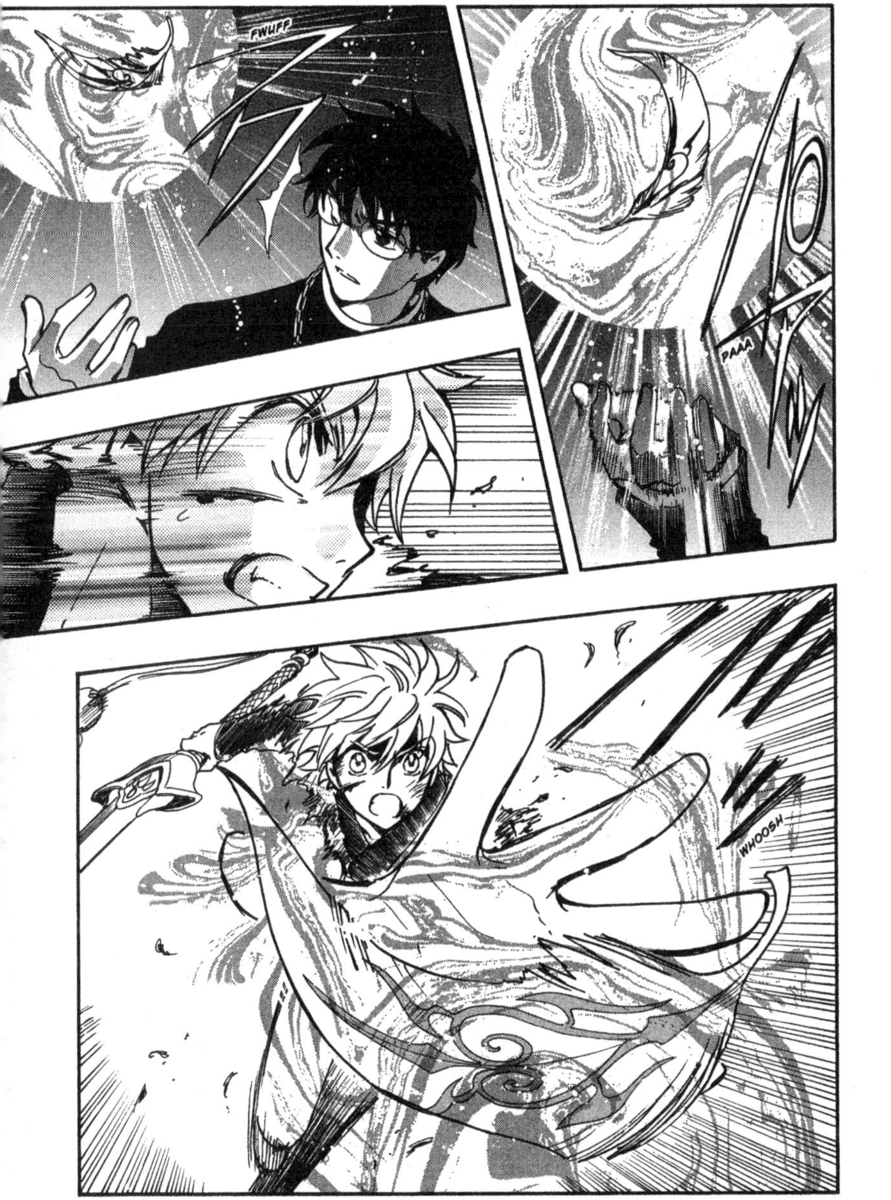
PAAA
FWUFF
WHOOSH

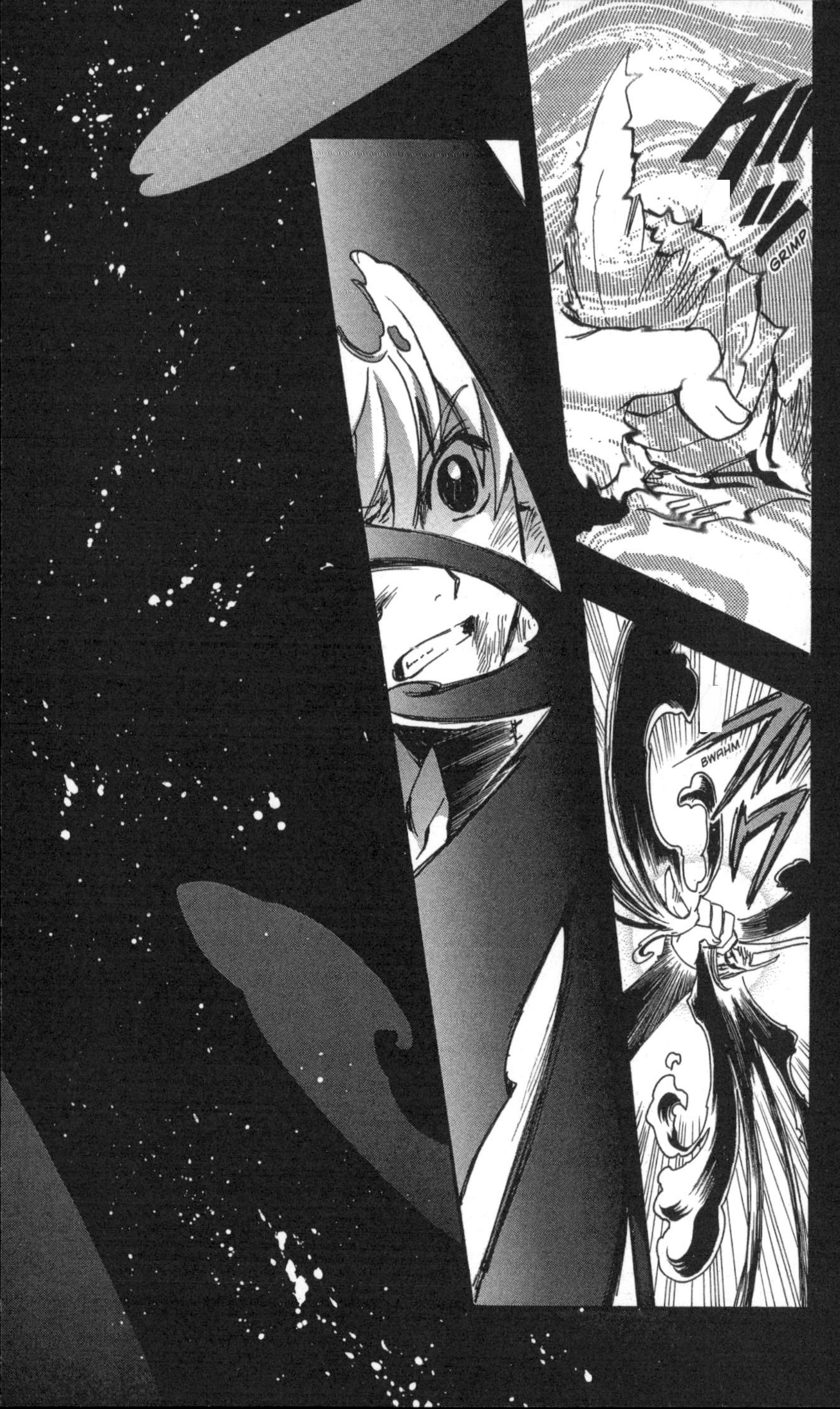
GRIMP
BWAHM

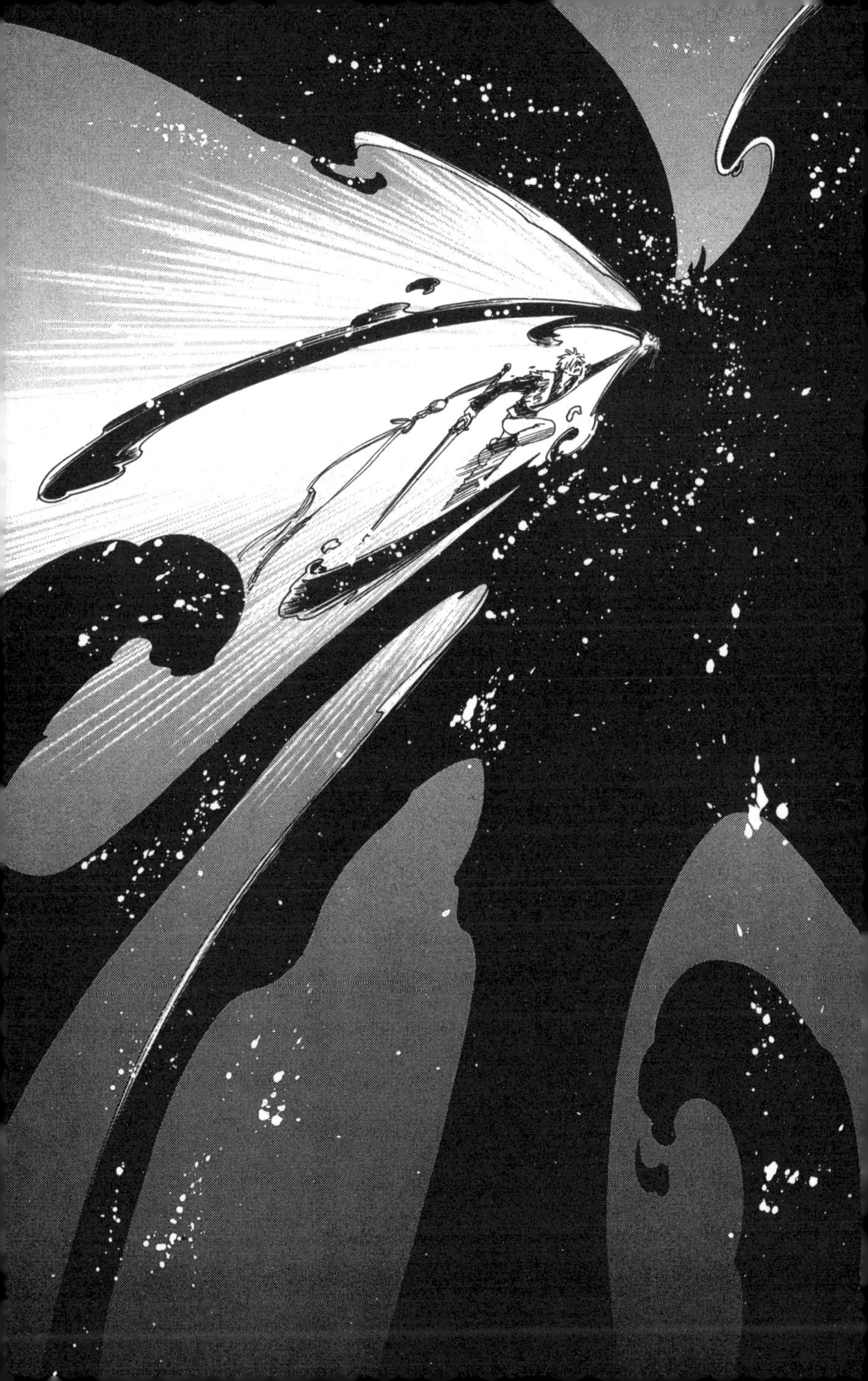

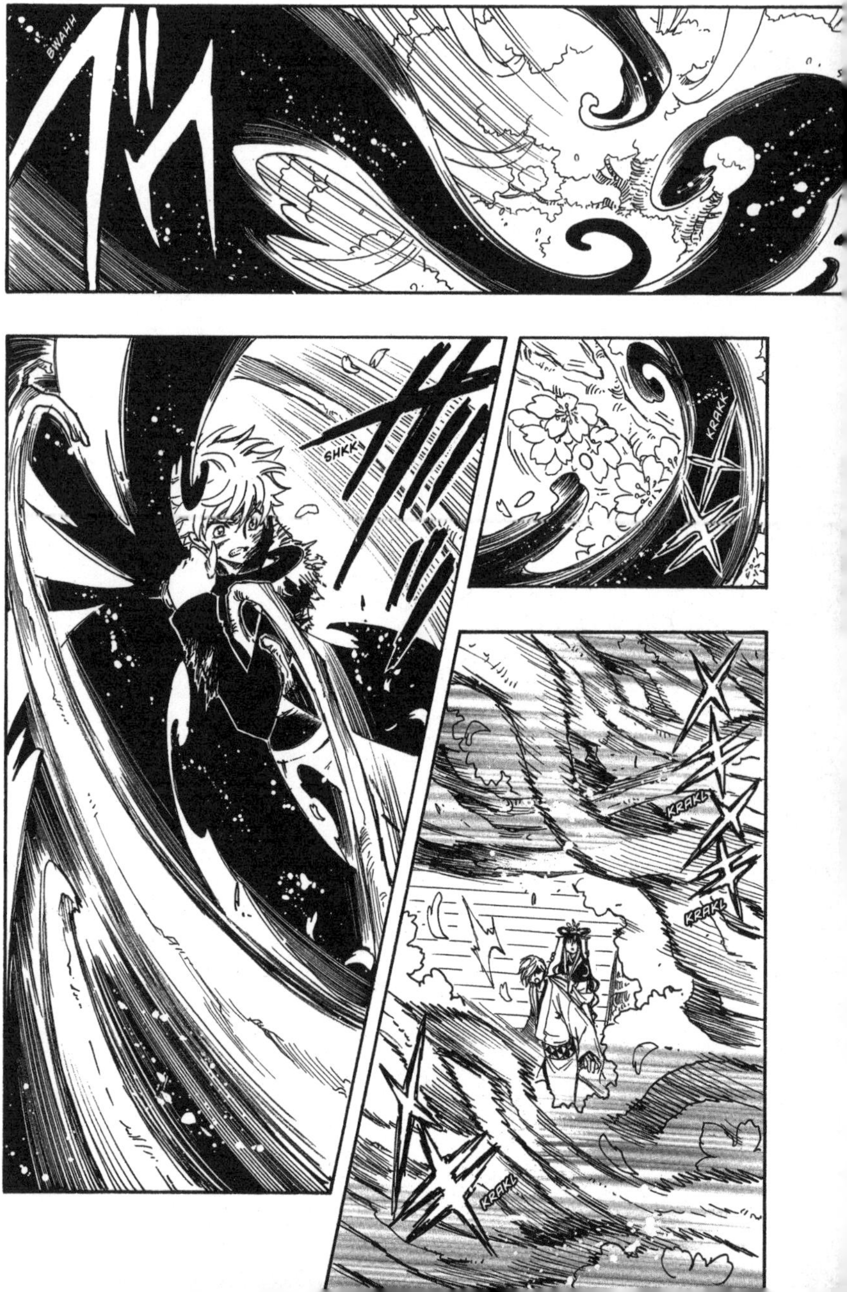
BWAHH
KRAKK
KRAKL
KRAKL
KRAKL
SHKK

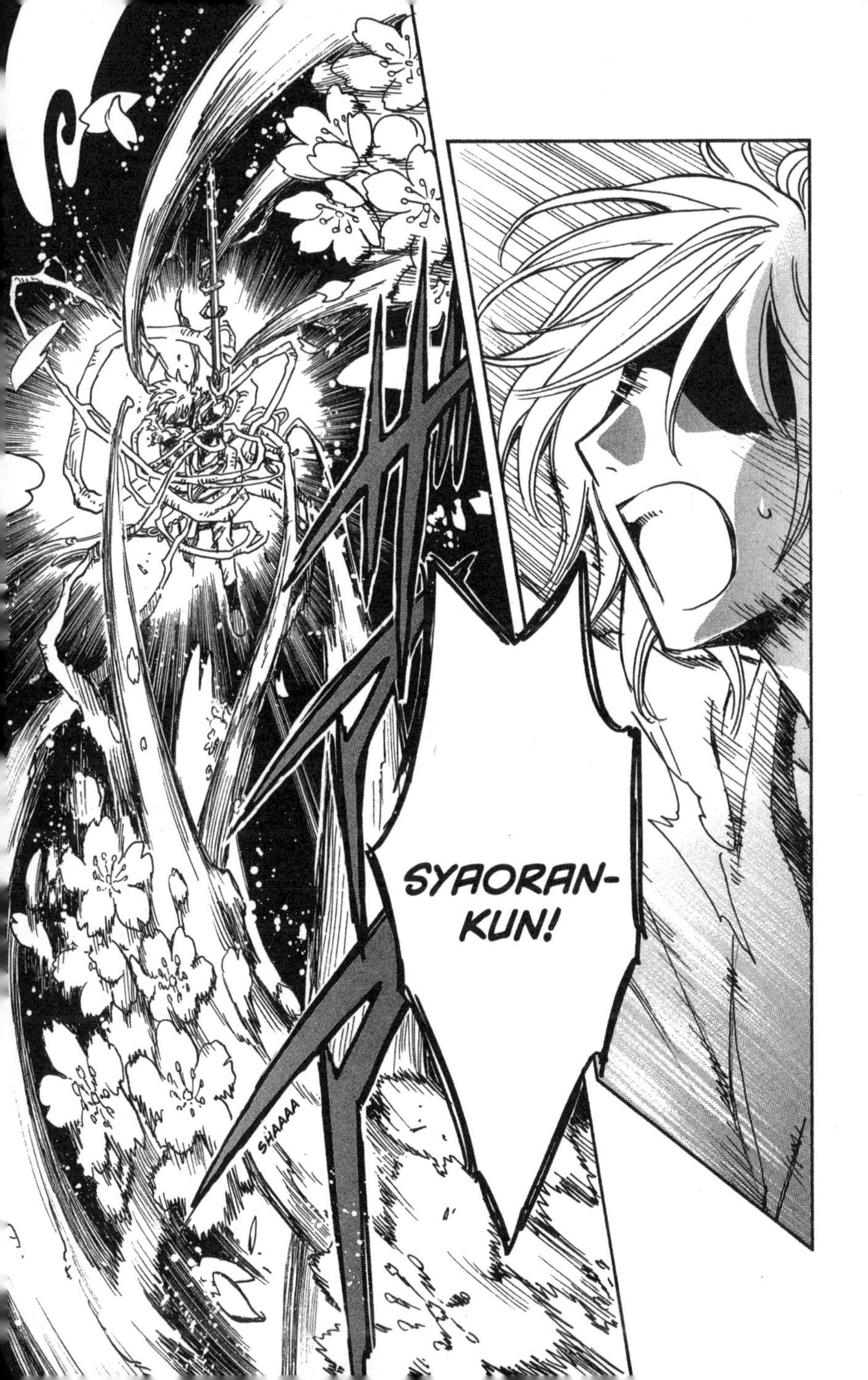
SYAORAN-KUN!
SHAAAA

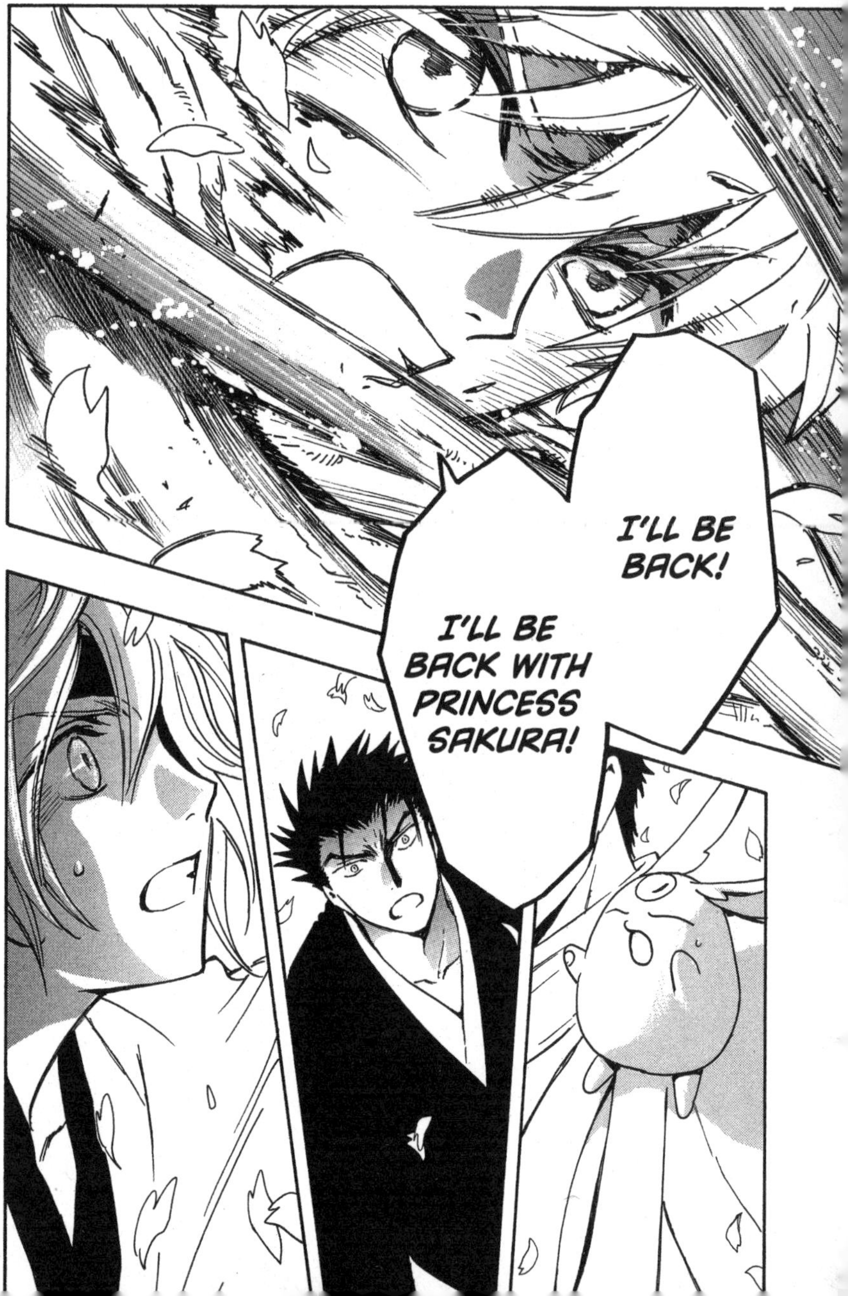
I'LL BE BACK!
I'LL BE BACK WITH PRINCESS SAKURA!

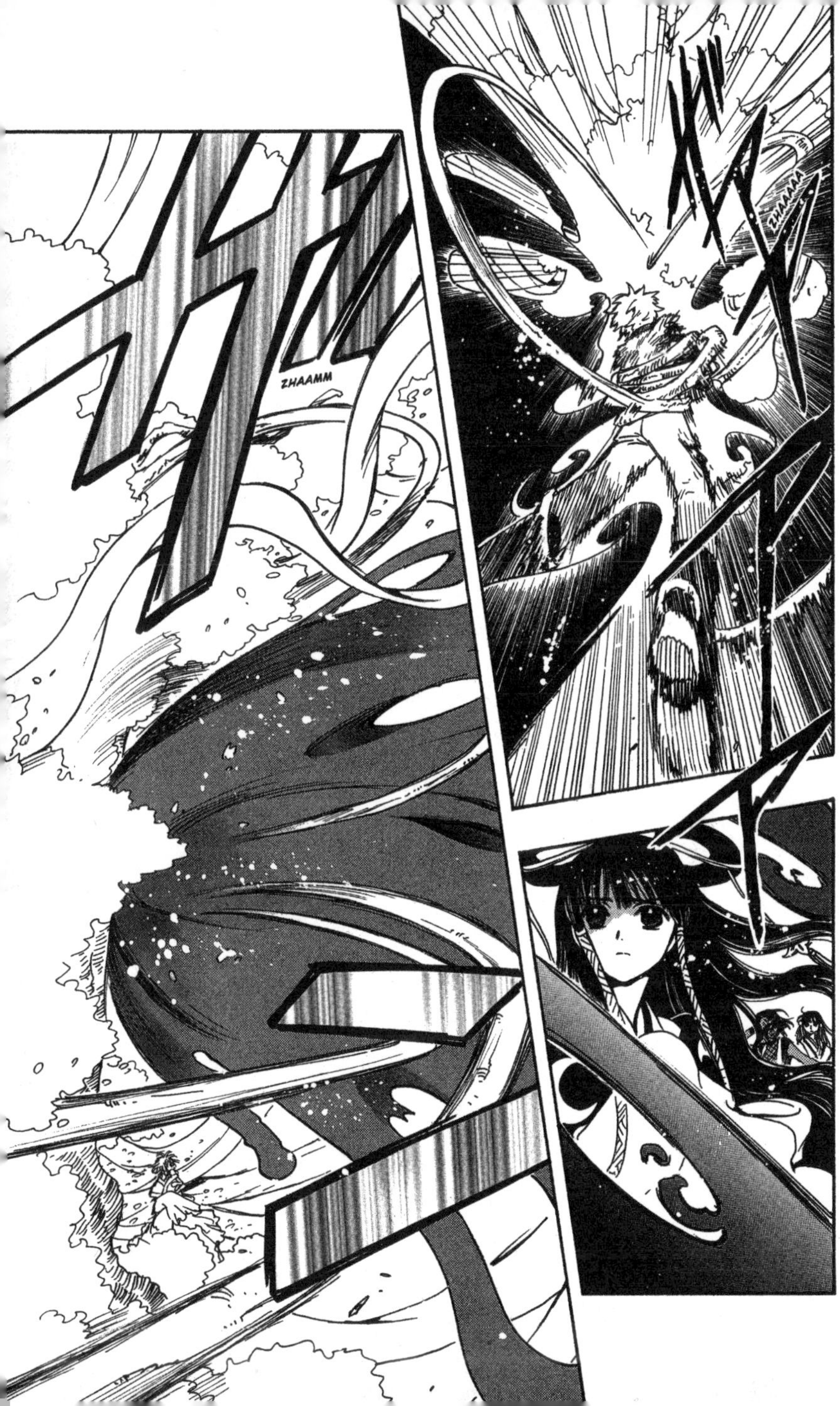
ZHAAAAA
ZHAAMM

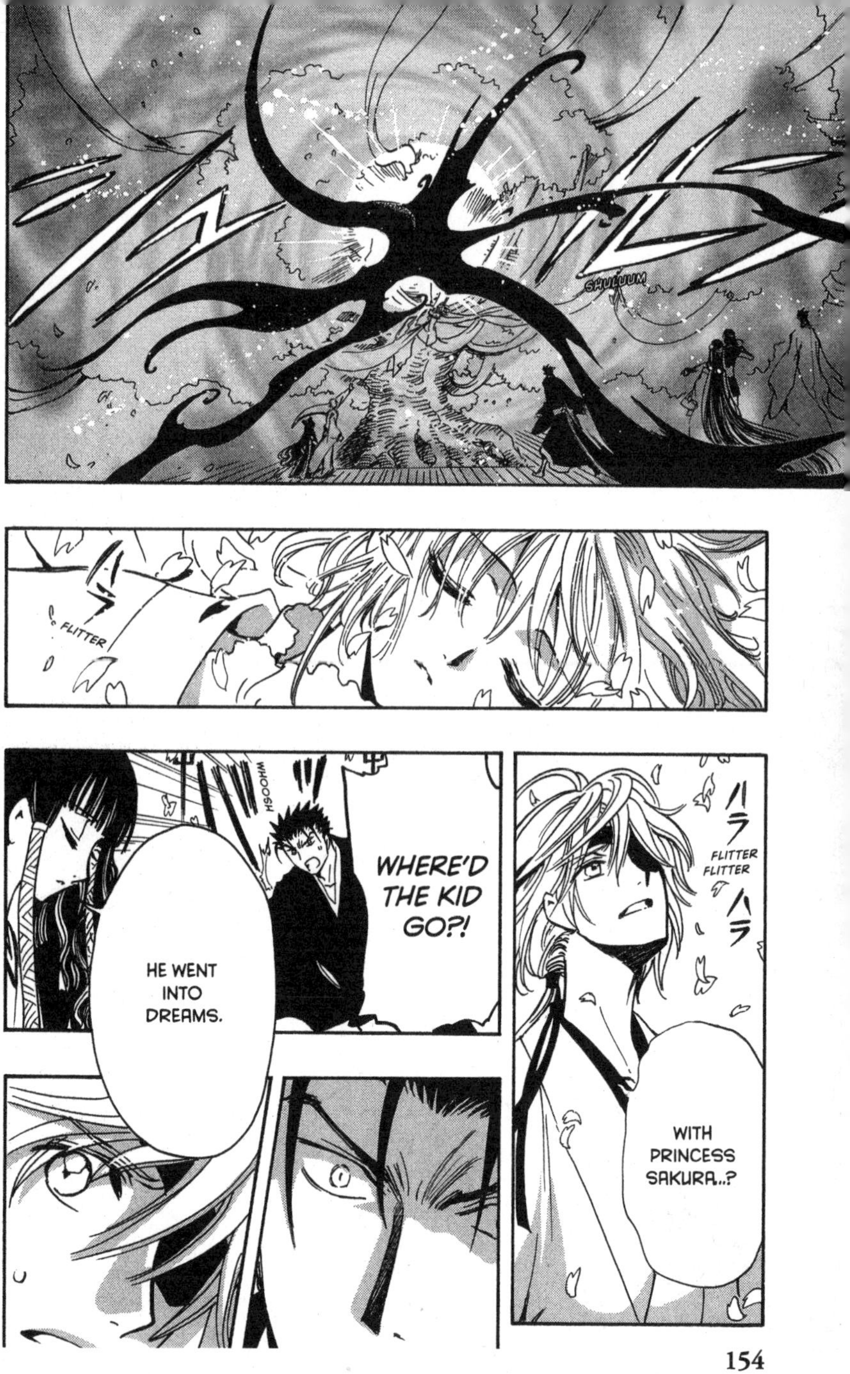
SHULUUM
FLITTER
WHOOSH
WHERE'D THE KID GO?!
HE WENT INTO DREAMS.
FLITTER FLITTER
WITH PRINCESS SAKURA..?

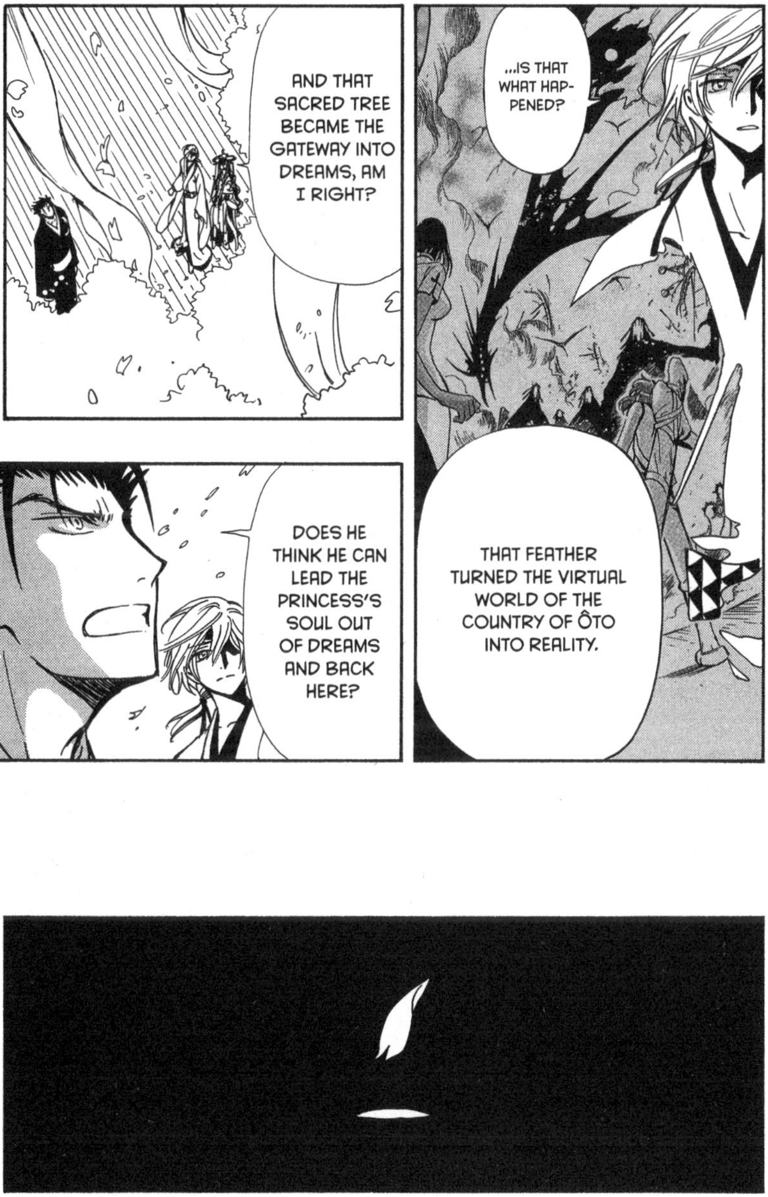
...IS THAT WHAT HAP-PENED?
THAT FEATHER TURNED THE VIRTUAL WORLD OF THE COUNTRY OF ÔTO INTO REALITY.
AND THAT SACRED TREE BECAME THE GATEWAY INTO DREAMS, AM I RIGHT?
DOES HE THINK HE CAN LEAD THE PRINCESS'S SOUL OUT OF DREAMS AND BACK HERE?

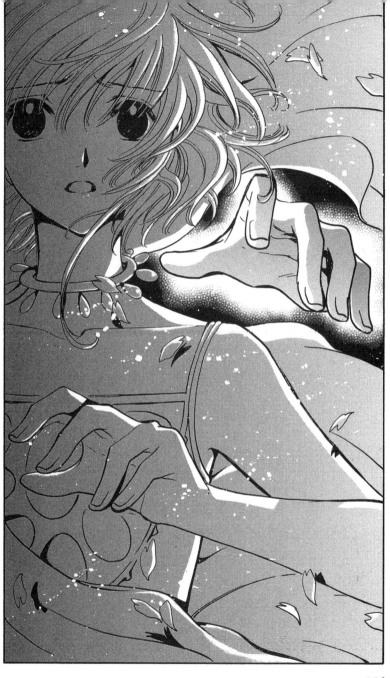

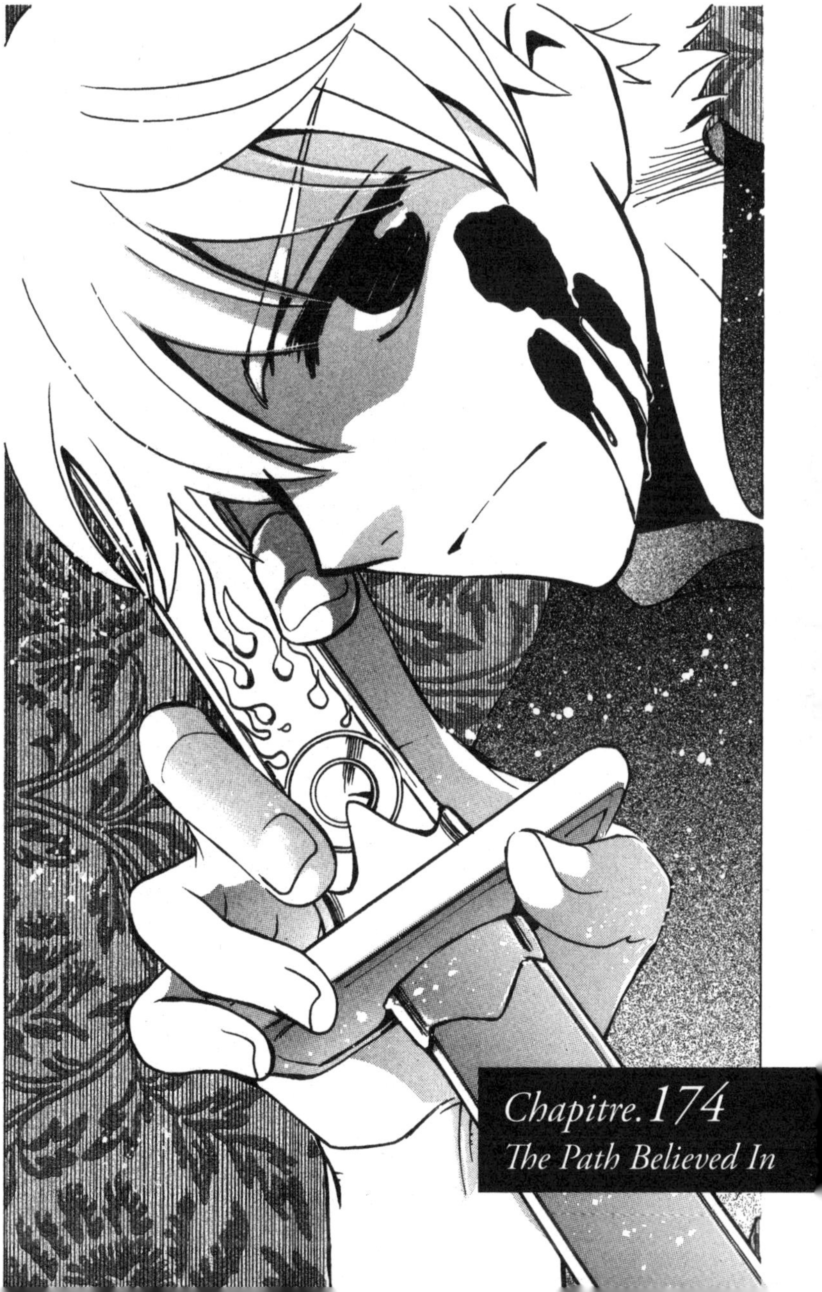
Chapitre.174
The Path Believed In

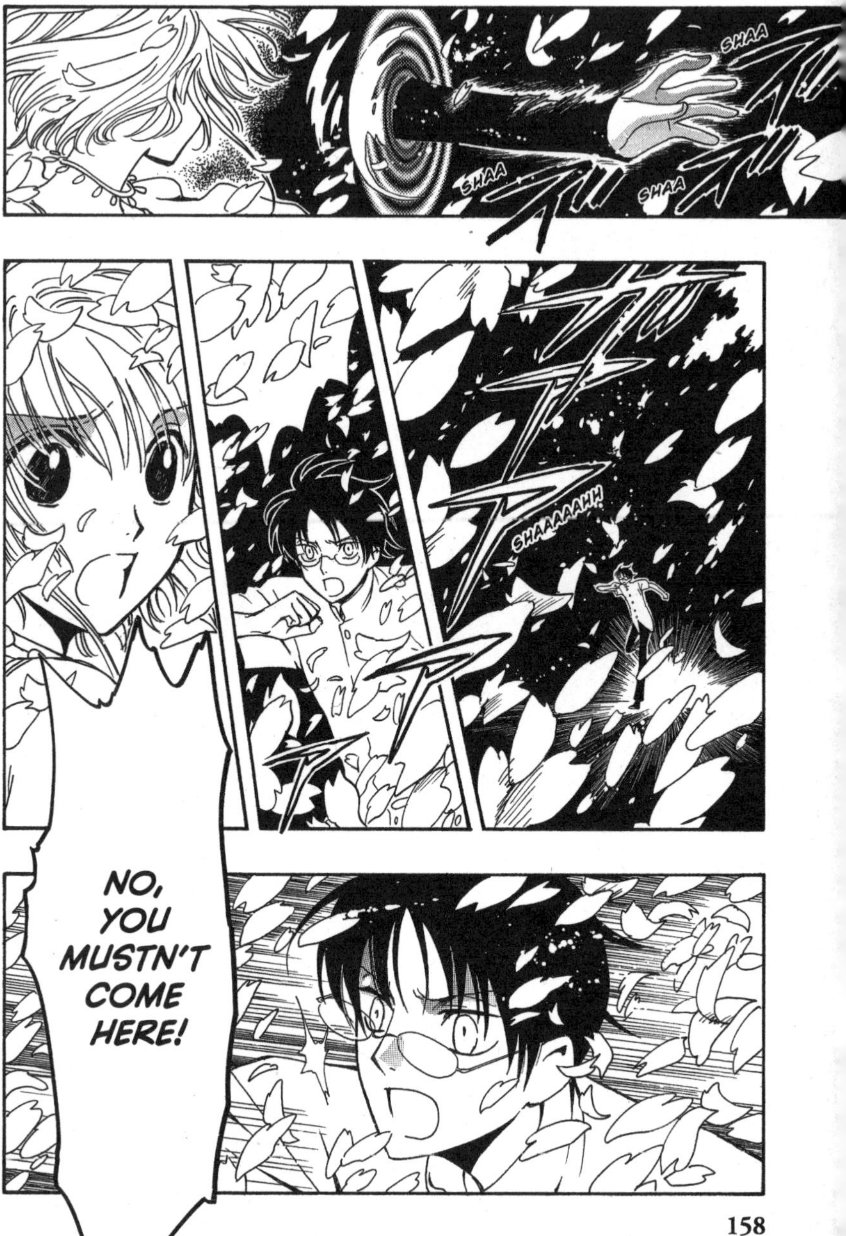
SHAA
SHAA
SHAA
SHAAAAAHH
NO, YOU MUSTN'T COME HERE!

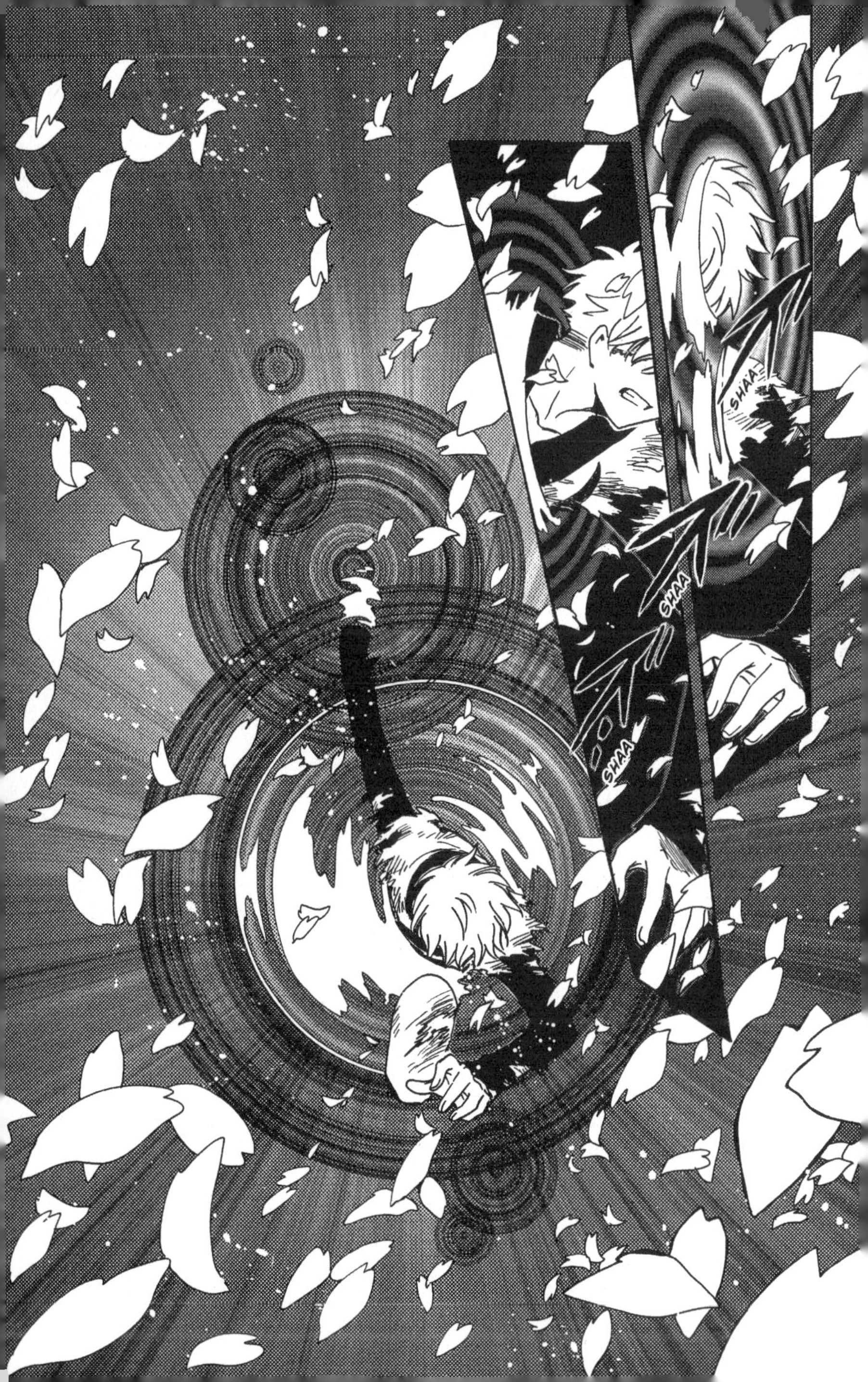
SHAA
SHAA
SHAA

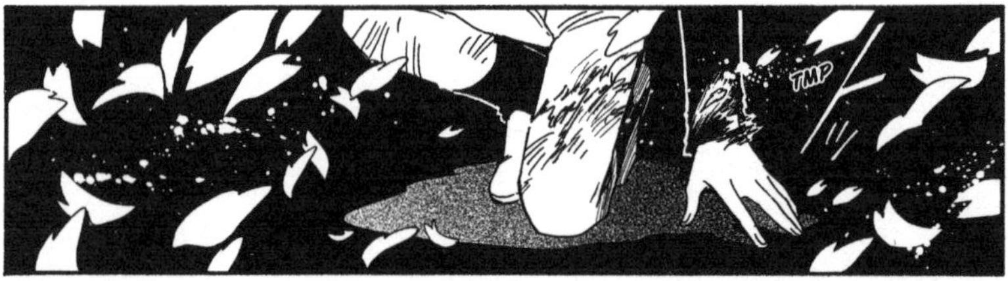
TMP
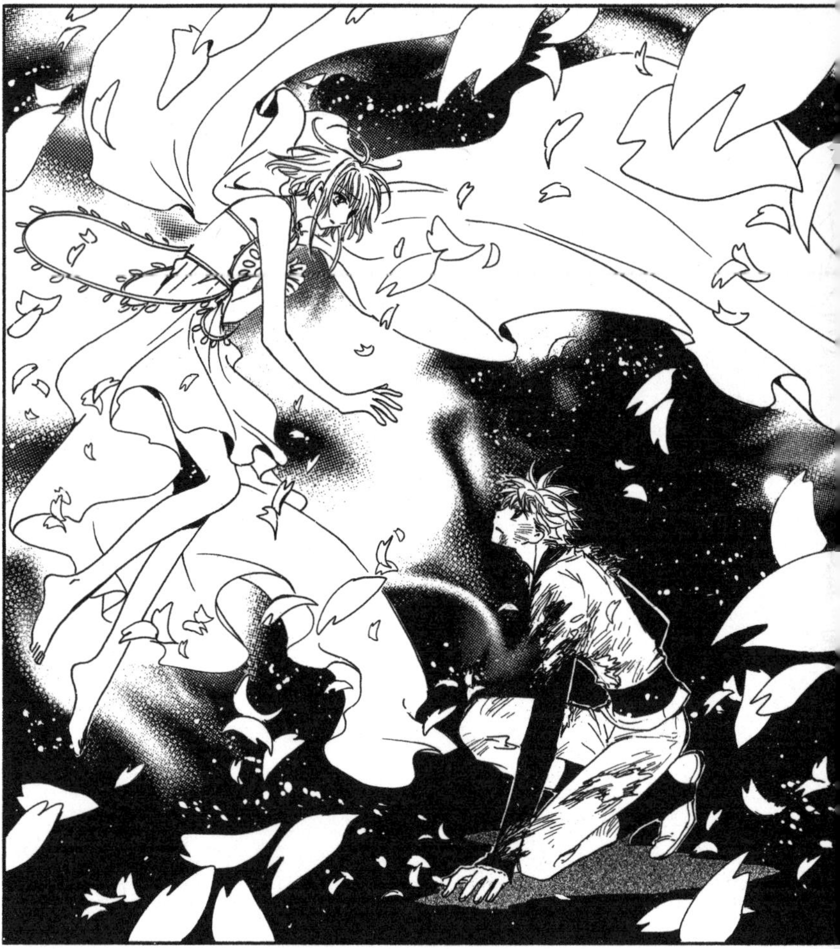

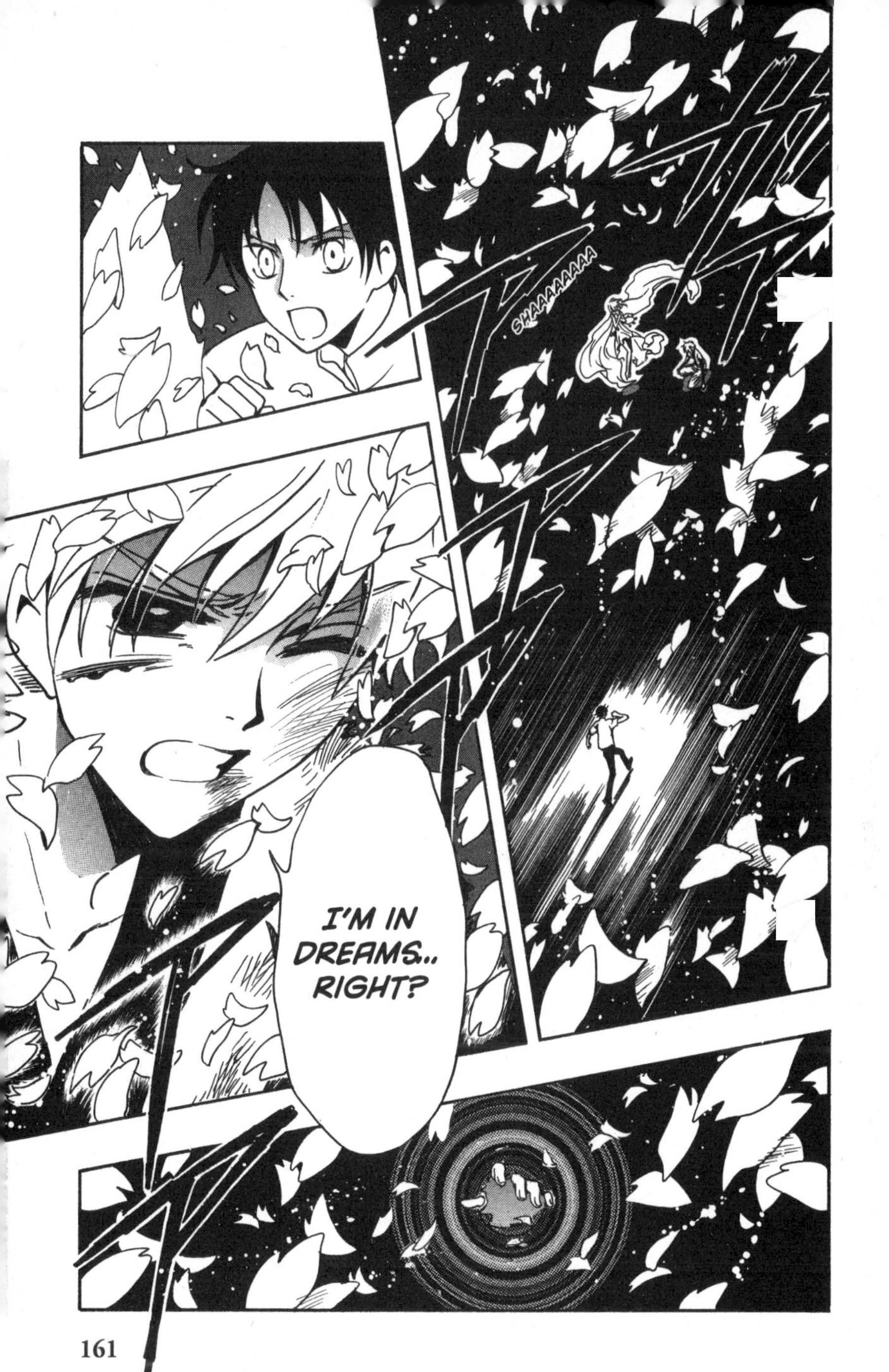
SHAAAAAAA
I'M IN DREAMS.. RIGHT?

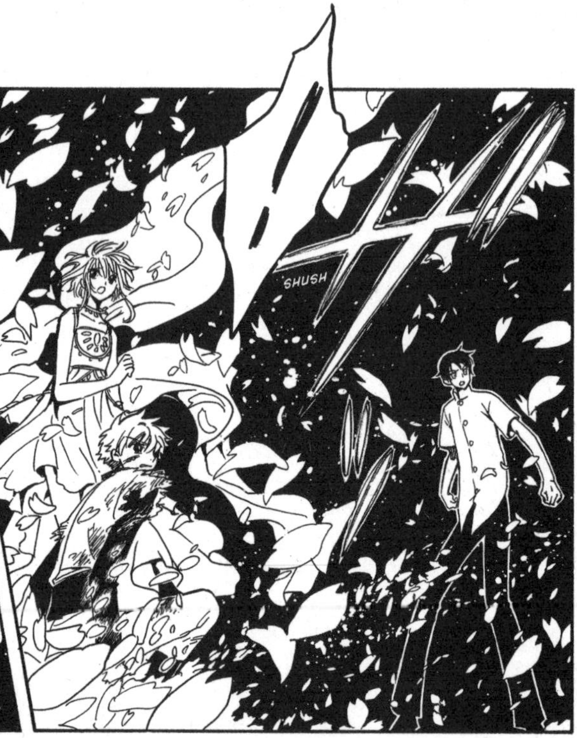
SHUSH
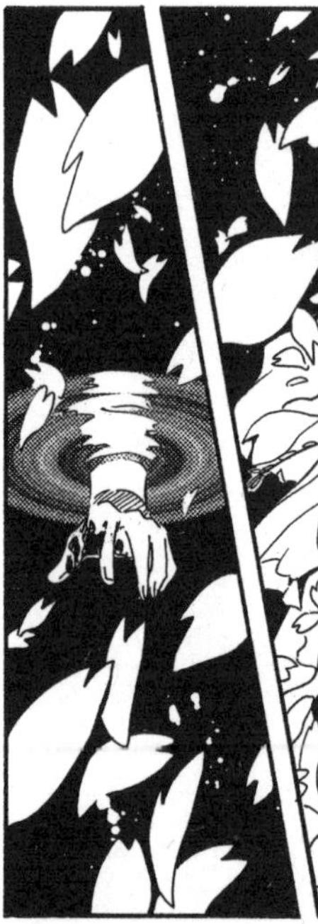
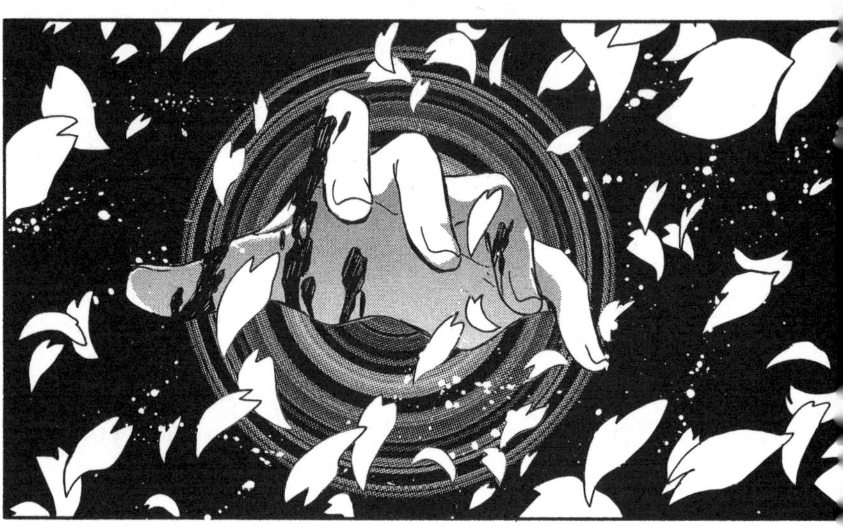

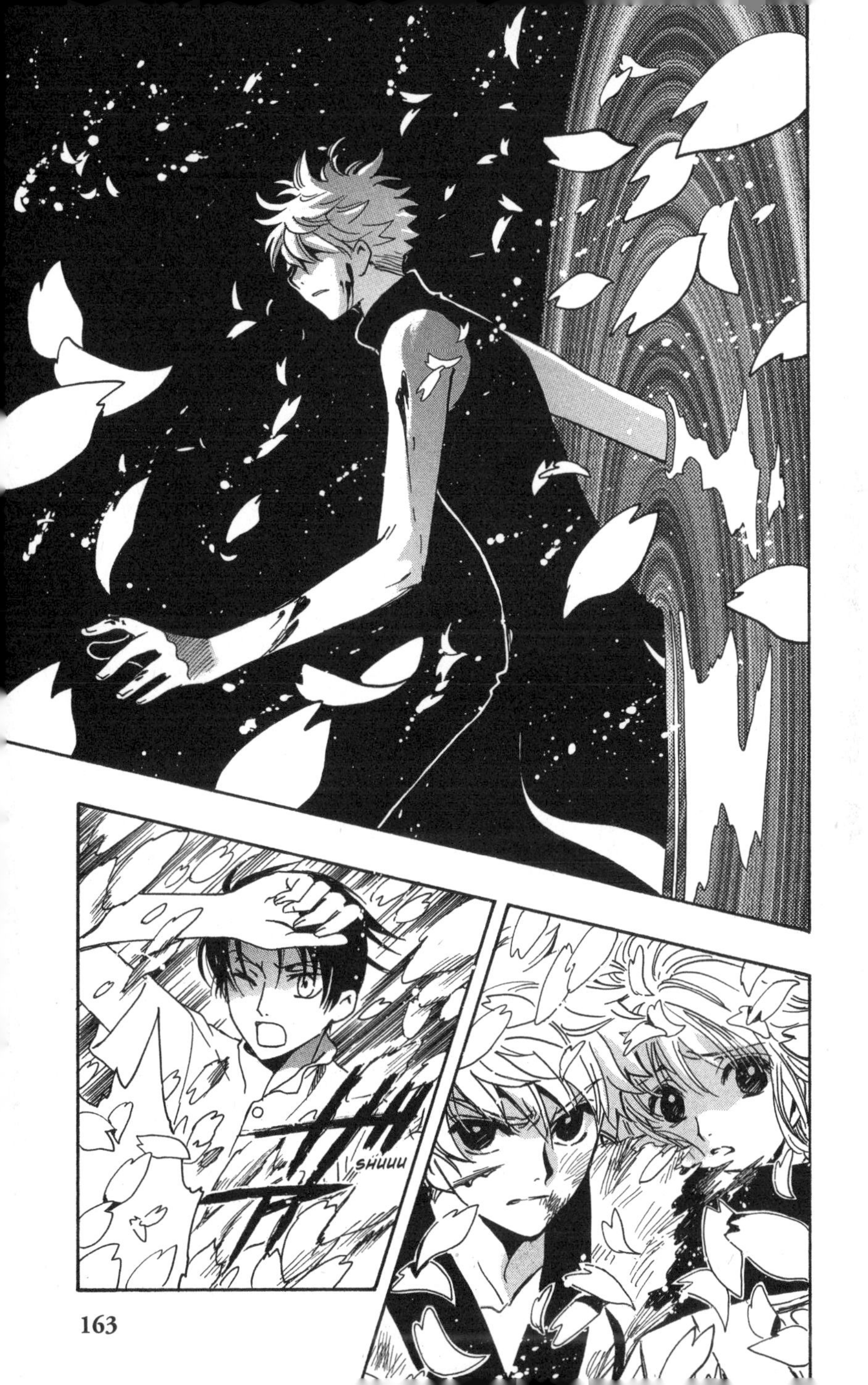
SHUUU

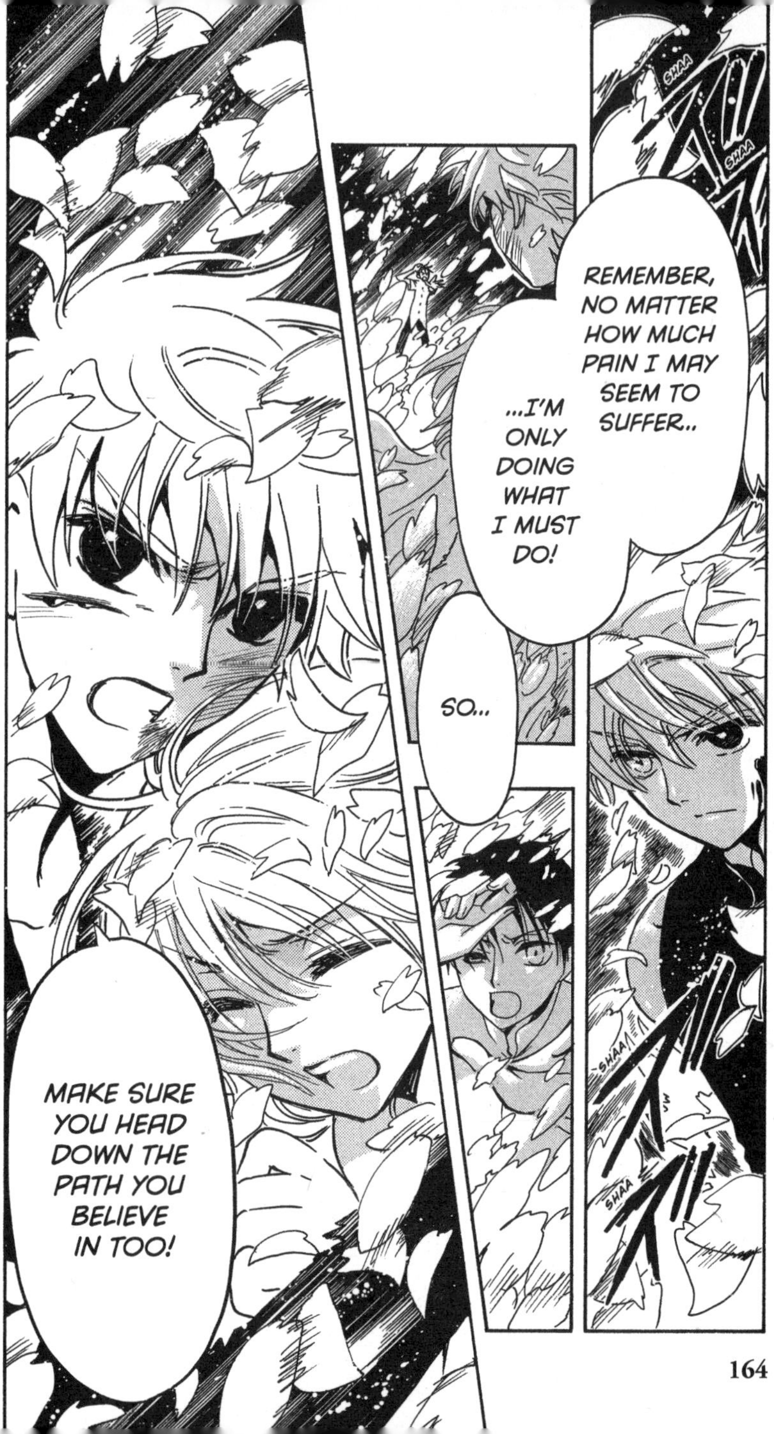
SHAA
SHAA
REMEMBER, NO MATTER HOW MUCH PAIN I MAY SEEM TO SUFFER..
...I'M ONLY DOING WHAT I MUST DO!
SO...
SHAA
SHAA
MAKE SURE YOU HEAD DOWN THE PATH YOU BELIEVE IN TOO!

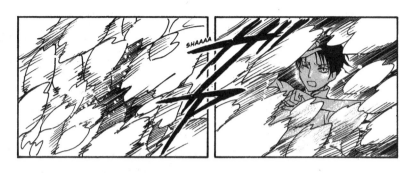

SHAAAA

165

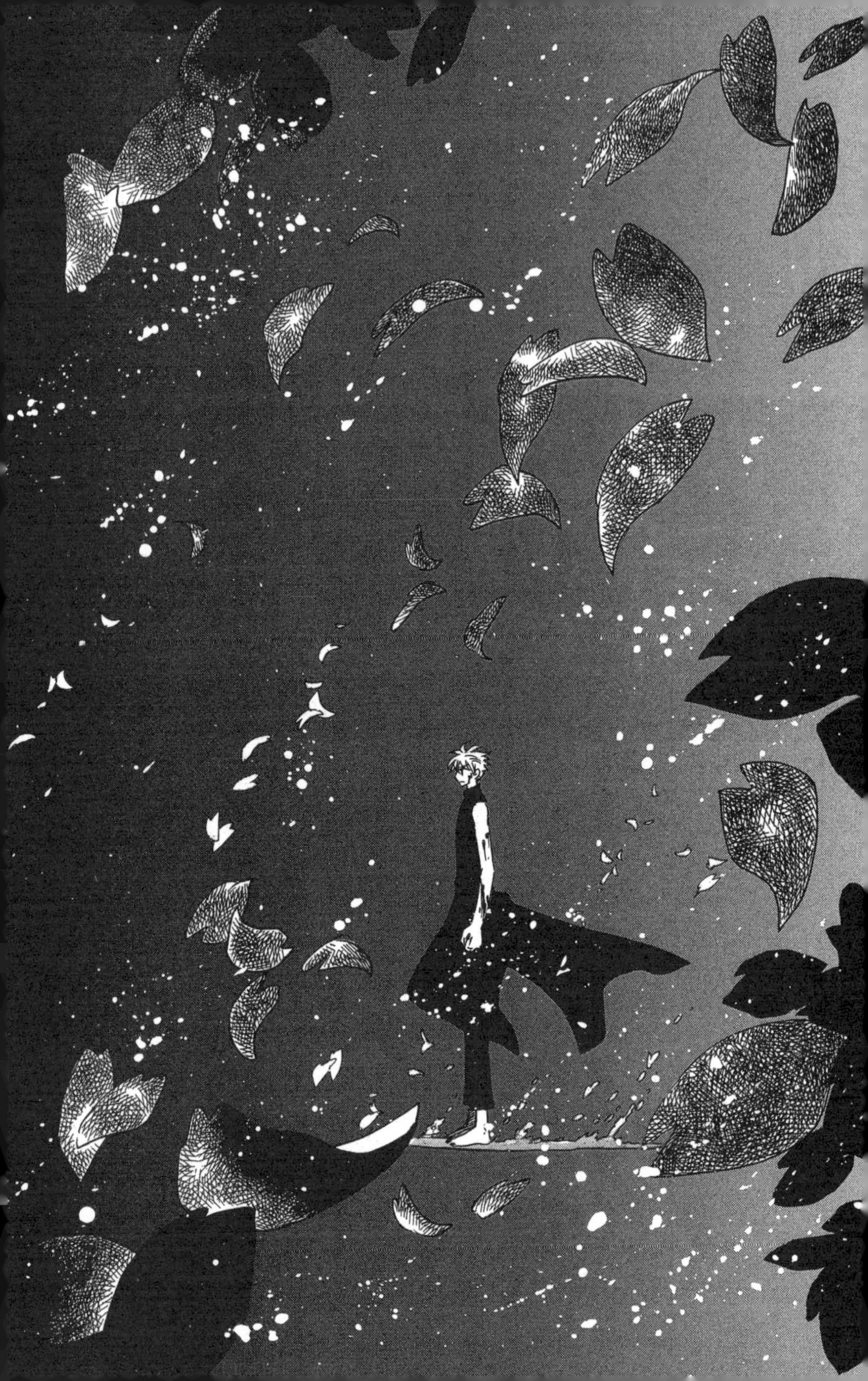

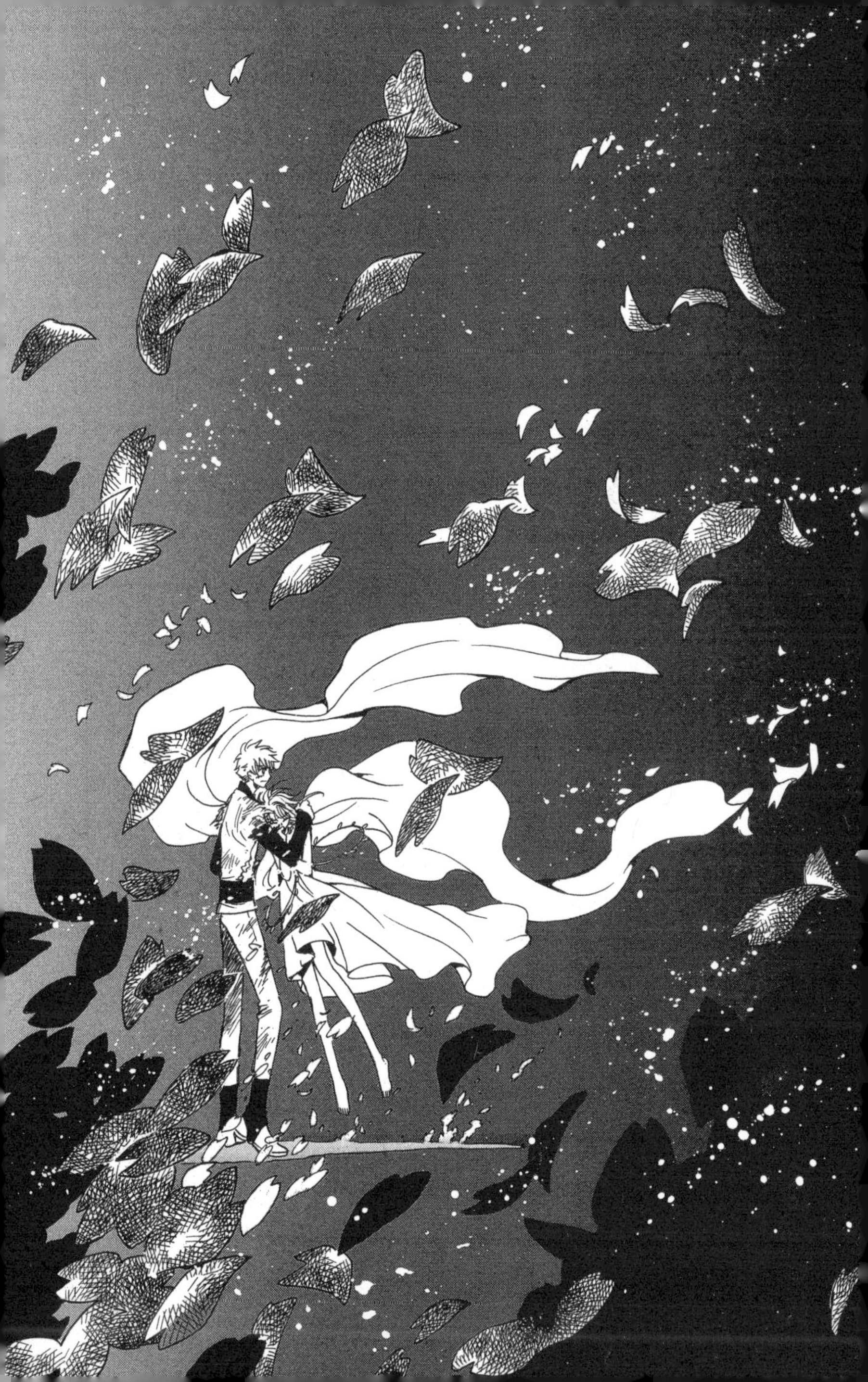

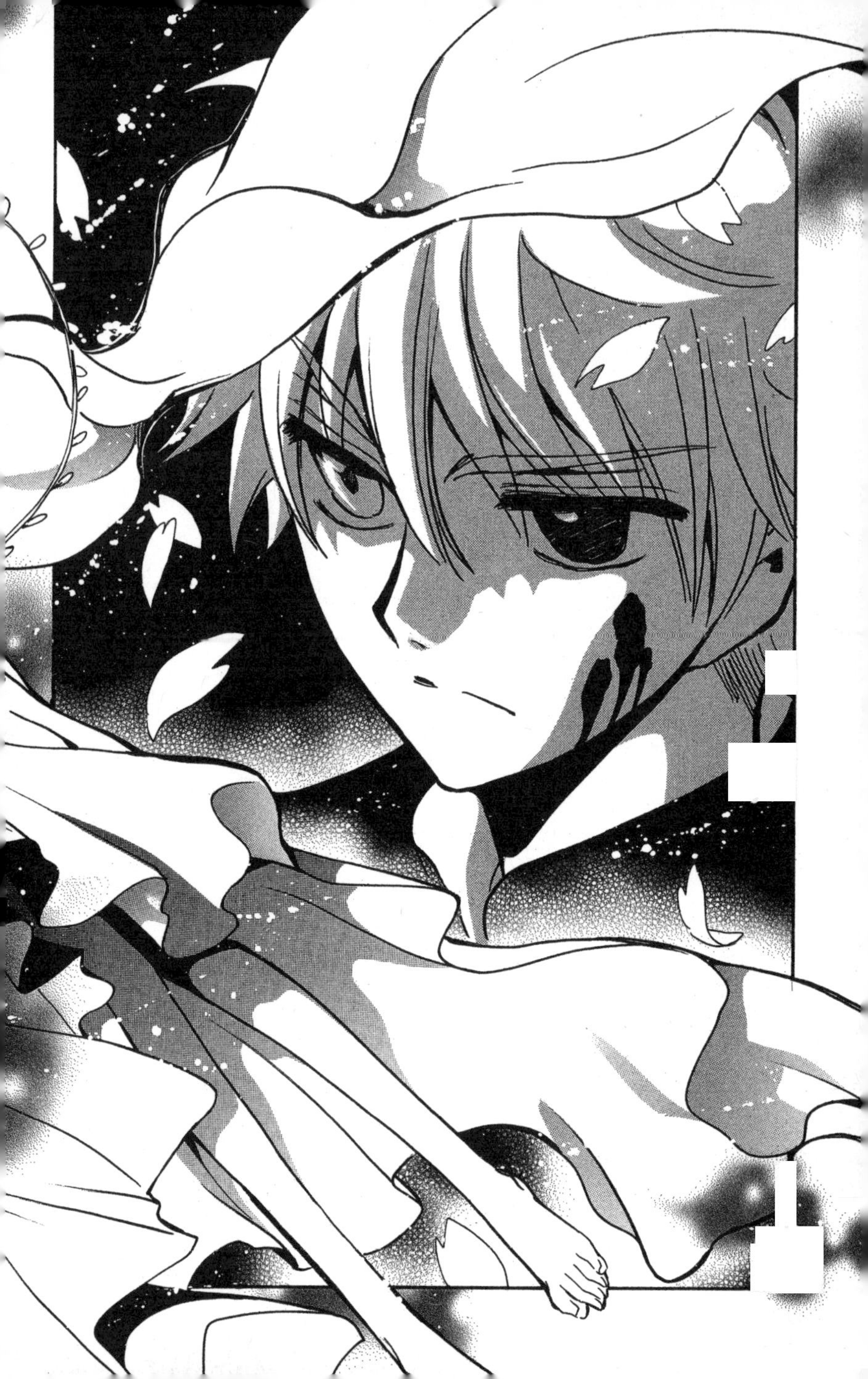

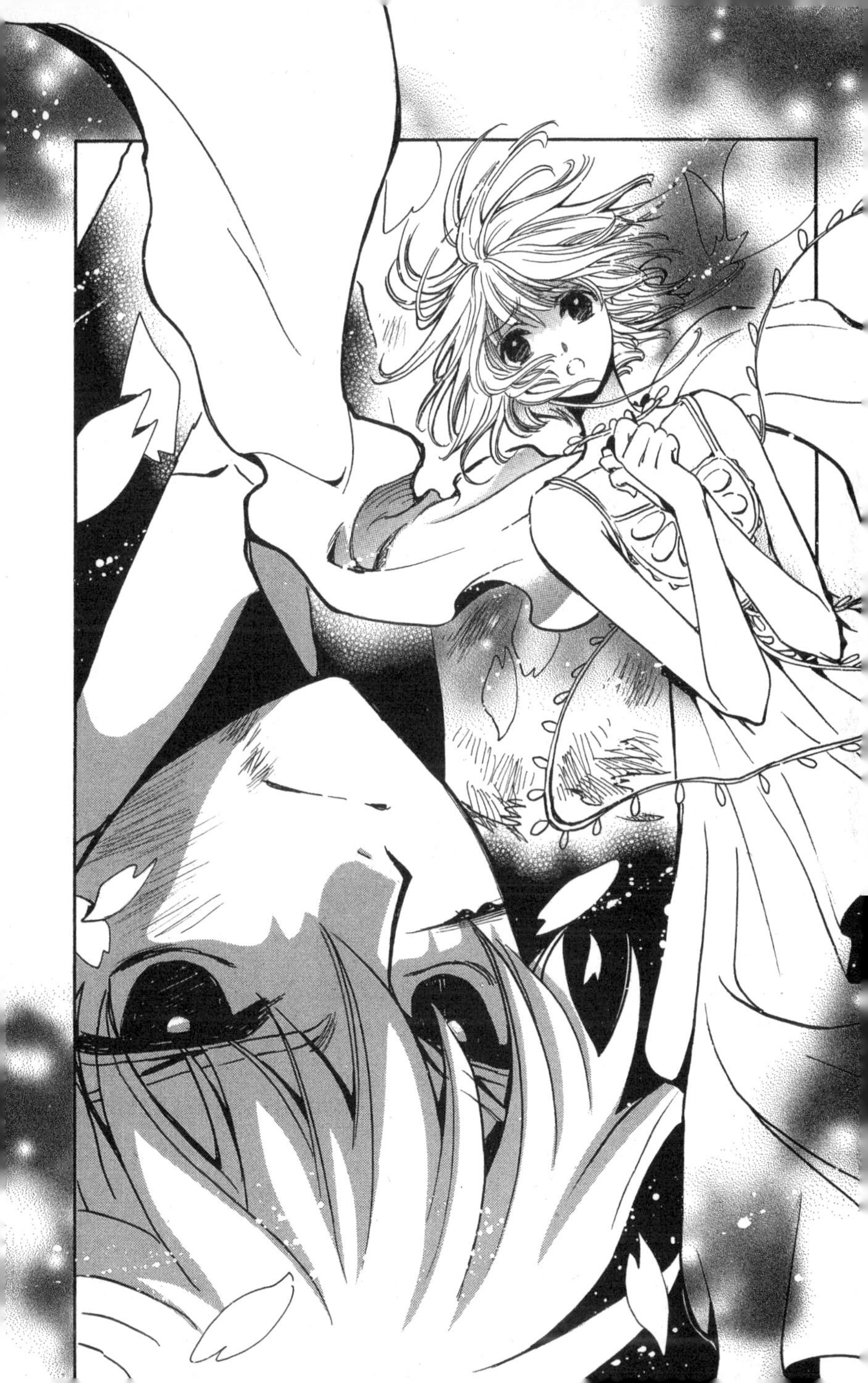

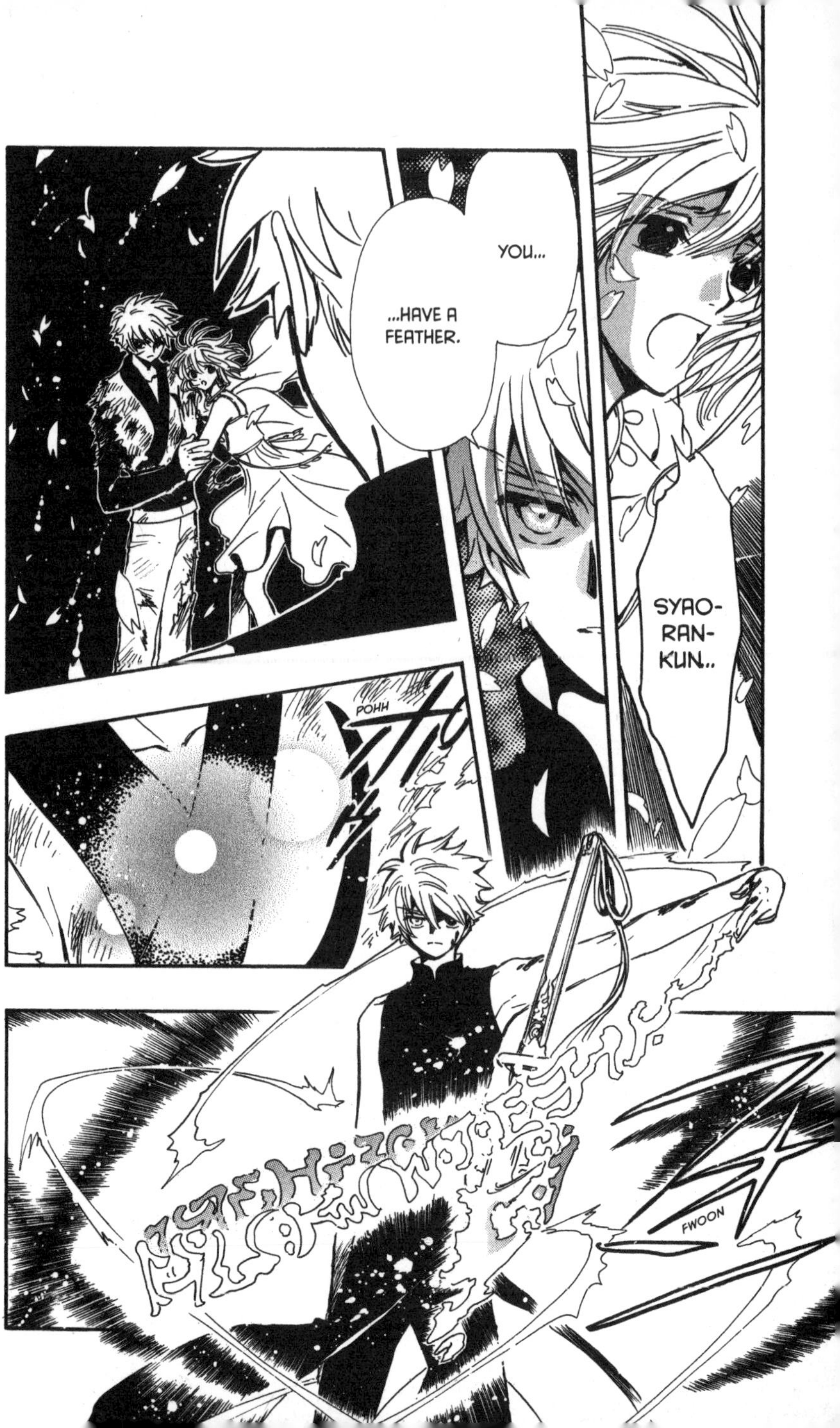
SYAO-RAN-KUN..
YOU...
...HAVE A FEATHER.
POHH
FWOON

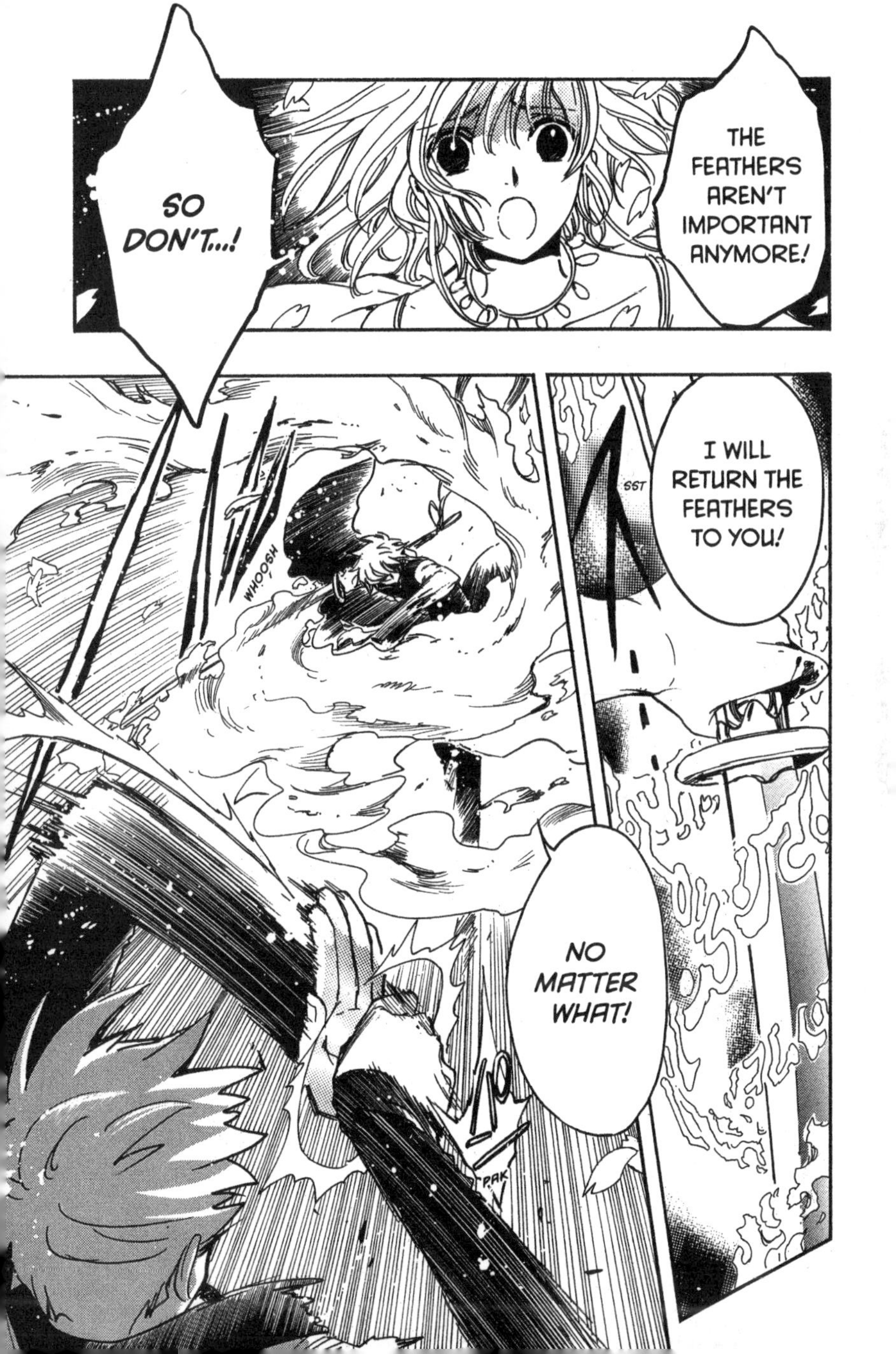
THE FEATHERS AREN'T IMPORTANT ANYMORE!
SO DON'T...!
I WILL RETURN THE FEATHERS TO YOU!
SST
WHOOSH
NO MATTER WHAT!
PAK

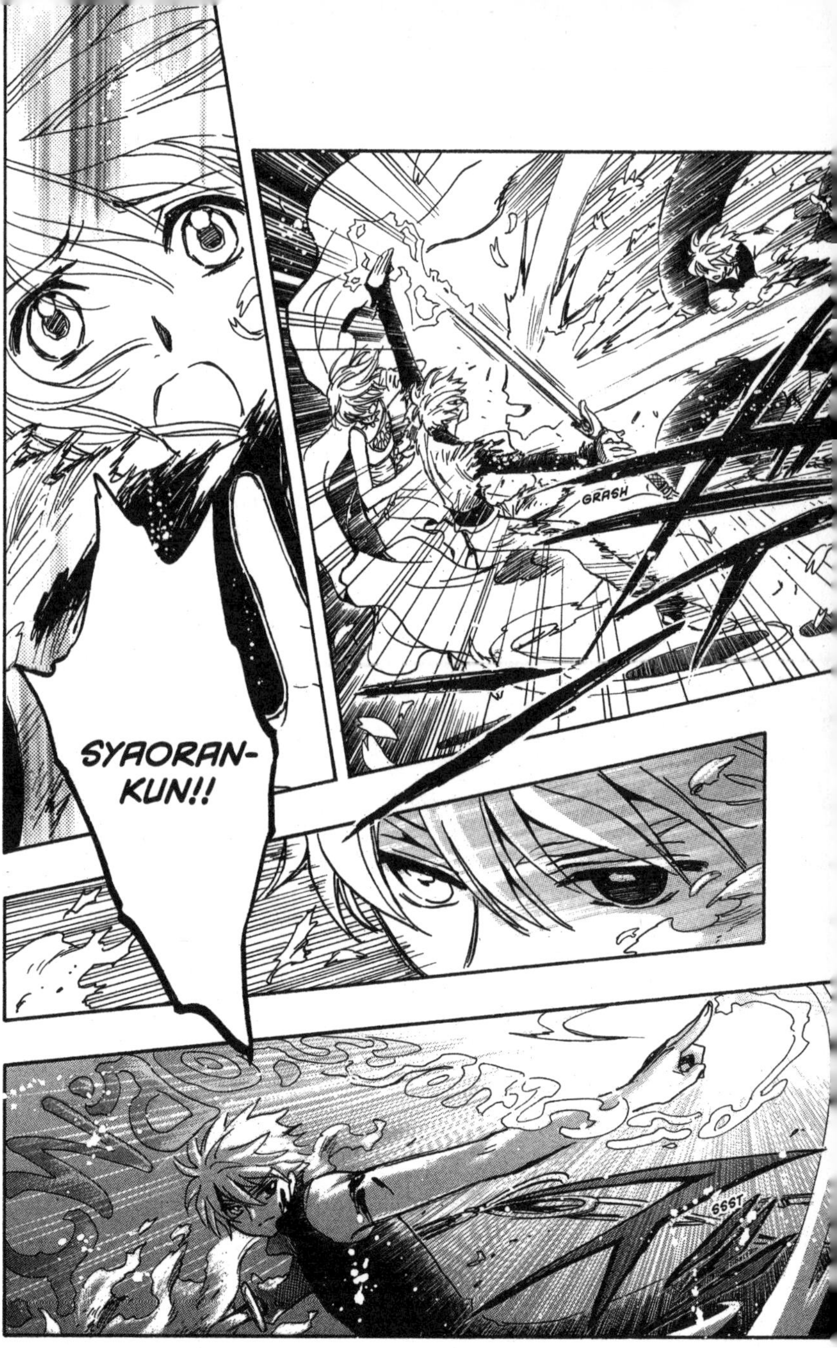
GRASH
SYAORAN-KUN!!
SSST

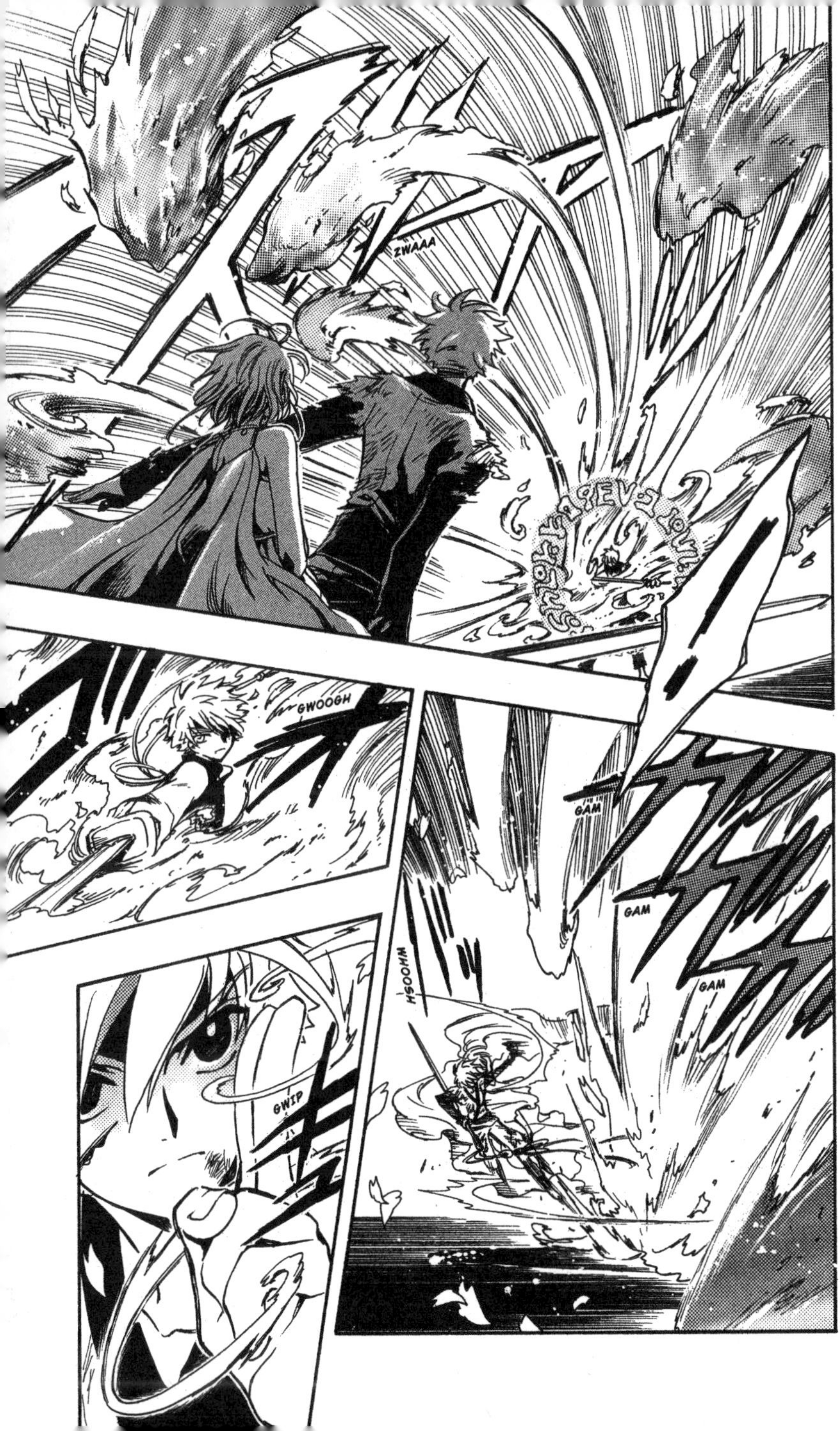
ZWAAA
GAM
GAM
GAM
WHOOSH
GWOOGH
GWIP

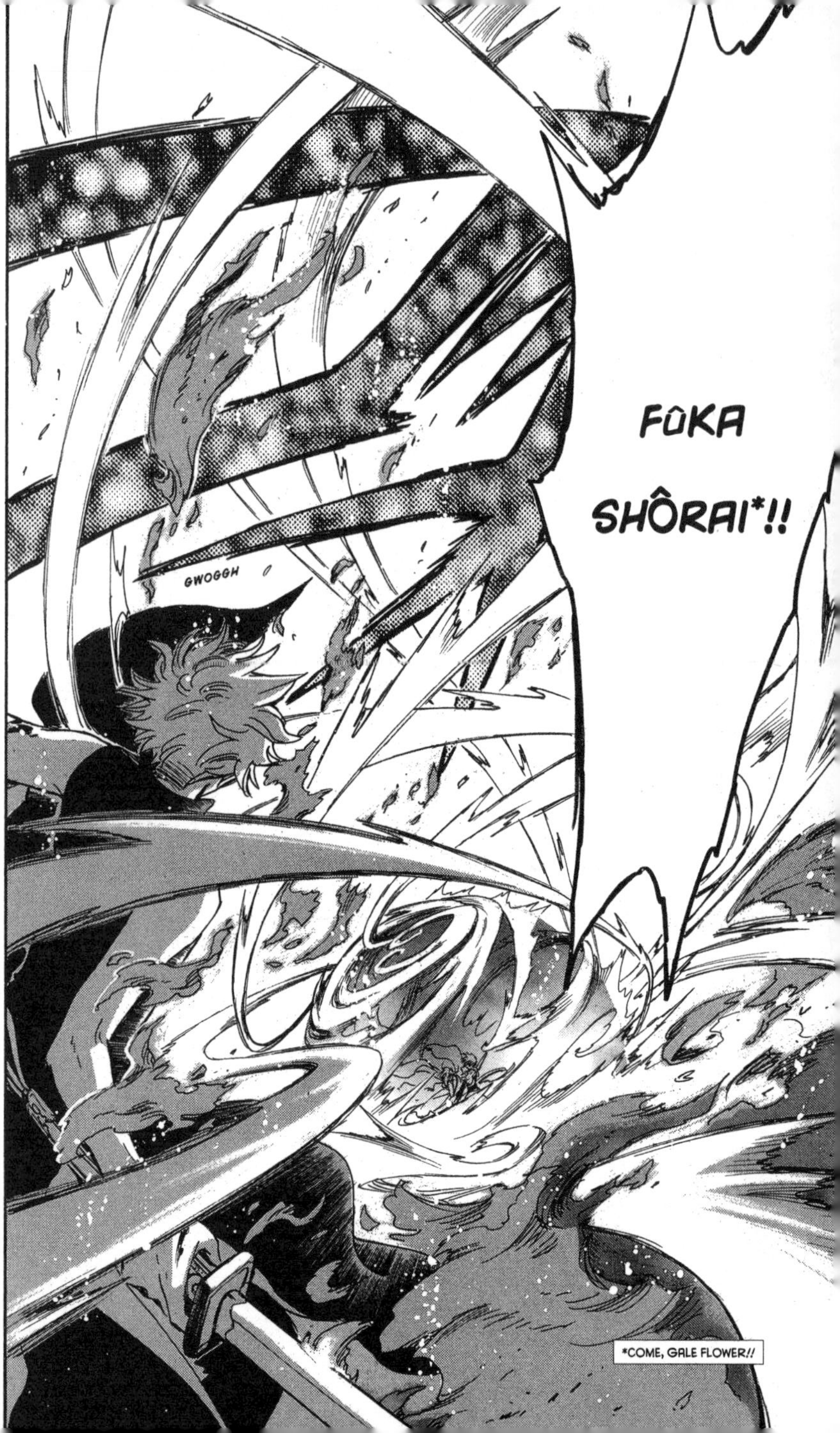
FÛKA SHÔRAI*!!
GWOGGH
*COME, GALE FLOWER!!

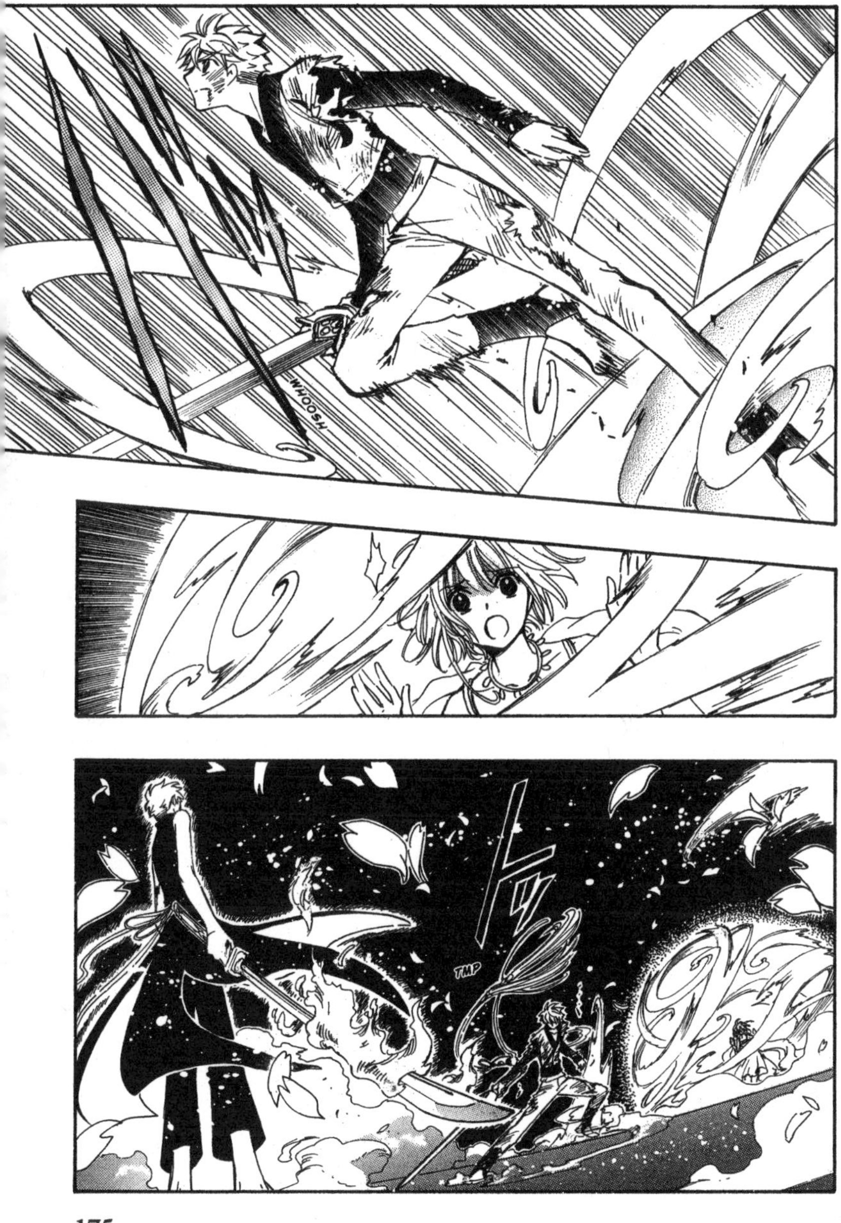
WHOOSH
TMP

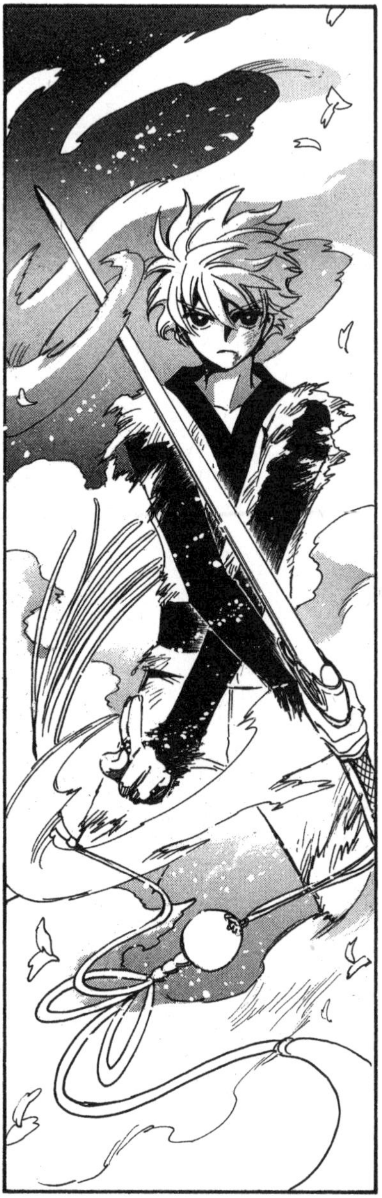
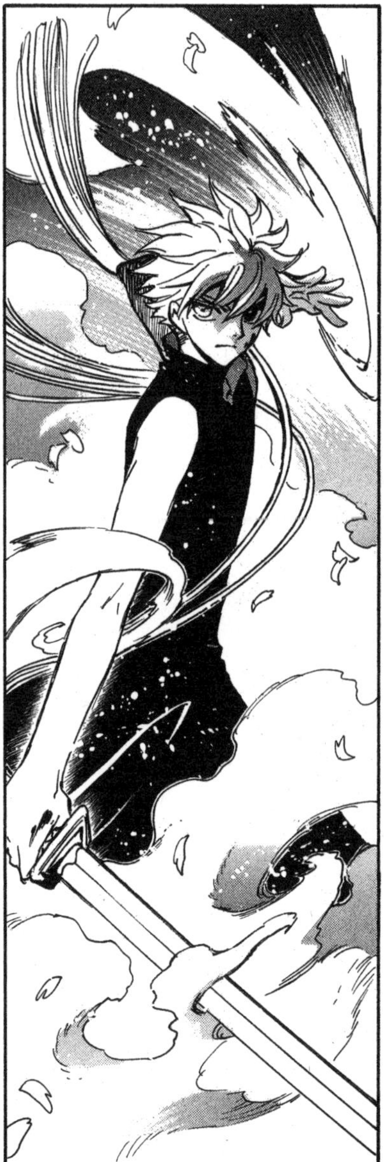

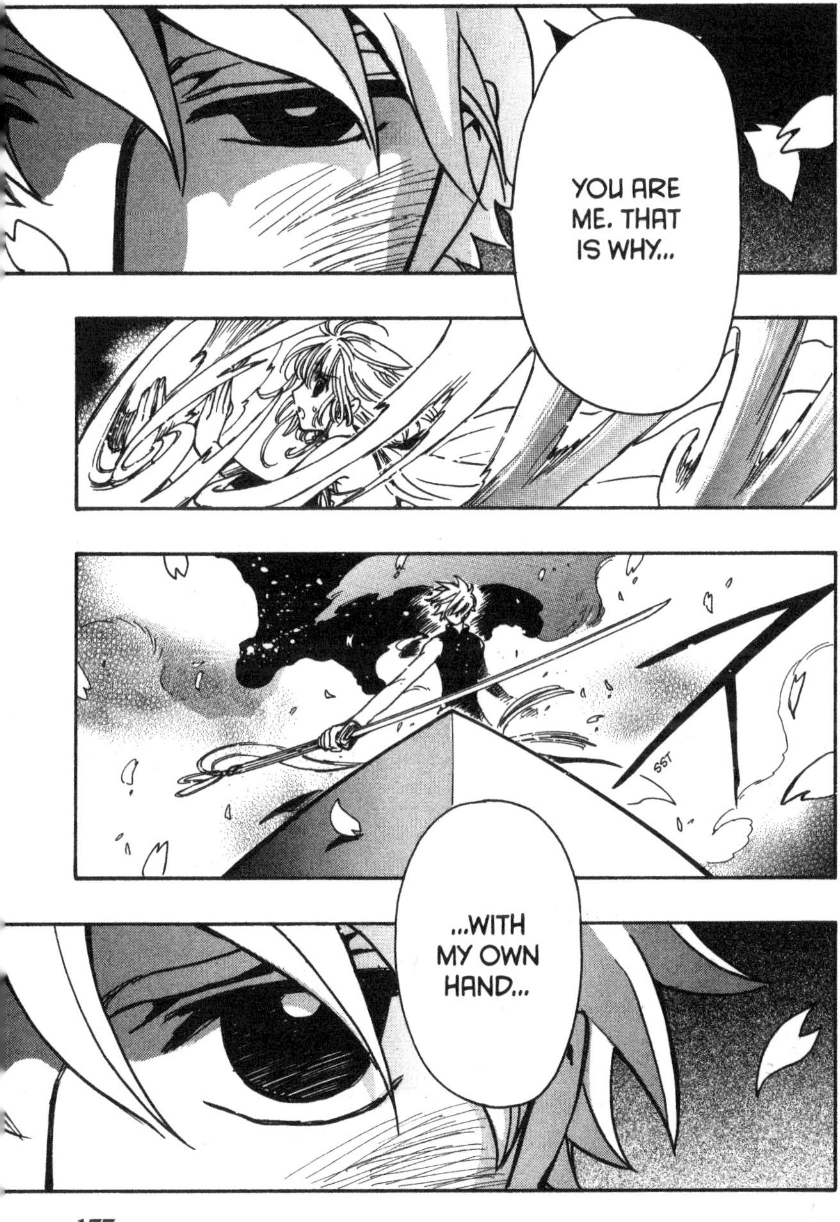
YOU ARE ME. THAT IS WHY...
SST
...WITH MY OWN HAND...

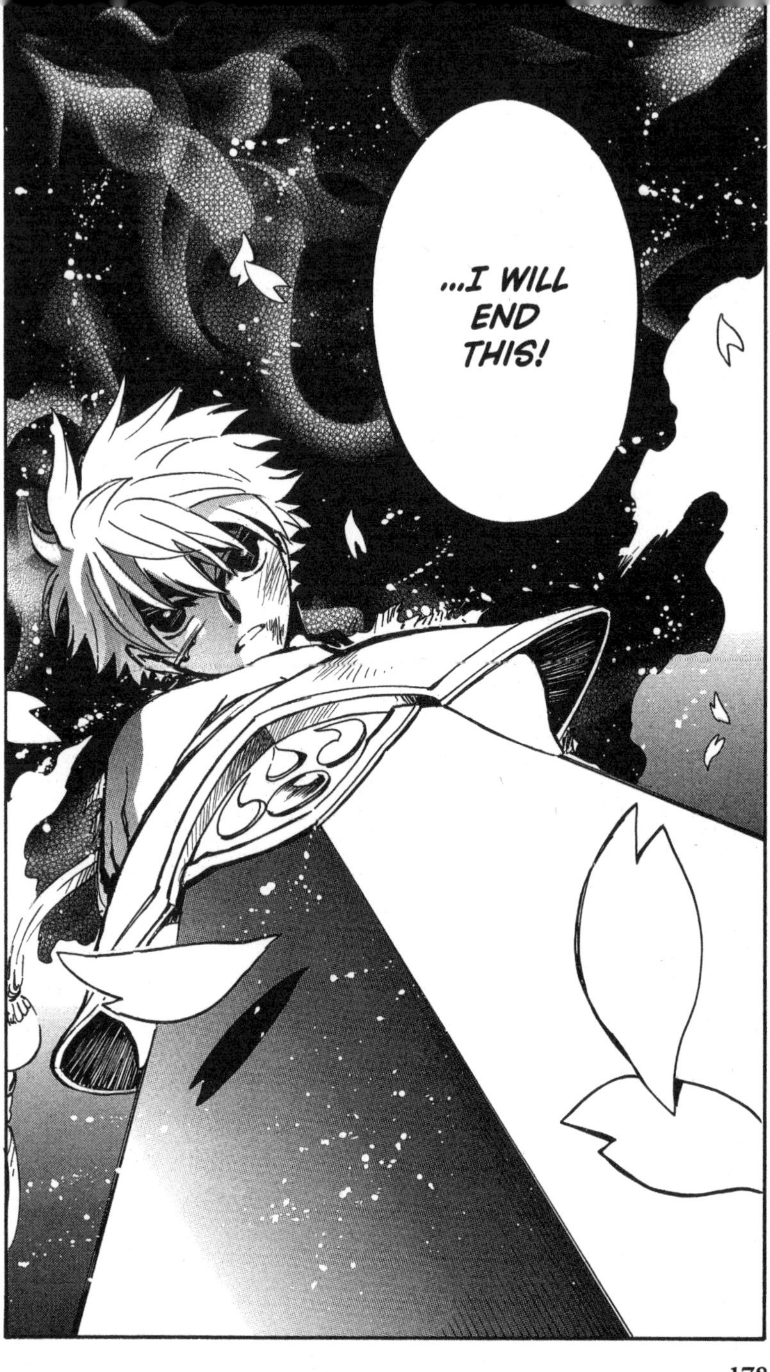
...I WILL END THIS!

About the Creators

CLAMP is a group of four women who have become some of the most popular manga artists in America—Nanase Ohkawa, Mokona, Satsuki Igarashi, and Tsubaki Nekoi. They started out as *doujinshi* (fan comics) creators, but their skill and craft brought them to the attention of publishers very quickly. Their first work from a major publisher was *RG Veda*, but their first mass success was with *Magic Knight Rayearth*. From there, they went on to write many series, including *Cardcaptor Sakura* and *Chobits*, two of the most popular manga in the United States. Like many Japanese manga artists, they prefer to avoid the spotlight, and little is known about them personally.

Translation Notes

Japanese is a tricky language for most Westerners, and translation is often more art than science. For your edification and reading pleasure, here are notes on some of the places where we could have gone in a different direction in our translation of the work, or where a Japanese cultural reference is used.

Body Double, page 13

In the original Japanese, Kurogane referred to a term that isn't exactly "body double" (which is *kagemusha* in Japanese), but instead a ninja technique called *migawari*, where the ninja disguises some other object to look like him and take the attack for him. In concept, it's very much like a body double; however, this decoy need not necessarily be a living person.

WHAT YOU'RE SAYING IS THAT MY ARM, THAT HE CAST MAGIC ON, BECAME A KIND OF BODY DOUBLE FOR HIM.

Flashback to Fûma's dialogue, page 57

Attentive readers with early printings of Tsubasa, volume 18 will notice that the dialog doesn't quite match. This is because volume 18 was printed in the United States before the translator could get his paws on this volume (vol. 22) to read it and correct the translation. CLAMP writes dialogue the meaning of which only becomes clear with flashbacks to the dialogue in later volumes. In this case the original dialogue in volume 18 included a sentence in which it wasn't clear just who Fûma was doing the other work for. Taken on its own, my original translation is not a bad interpretation. But given the new information, it is clear that my original translation is in error. Later printings of Tsubasa 18 will reflect this new, more accurate translation.

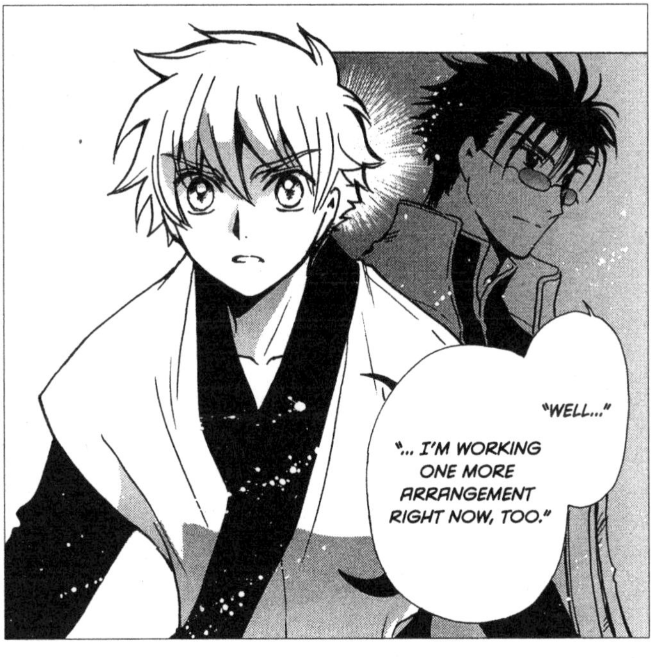
"WELL..."
"... I'M WORKING ONE MORE ARRANGEMENT RIGHT NOW, TOO."

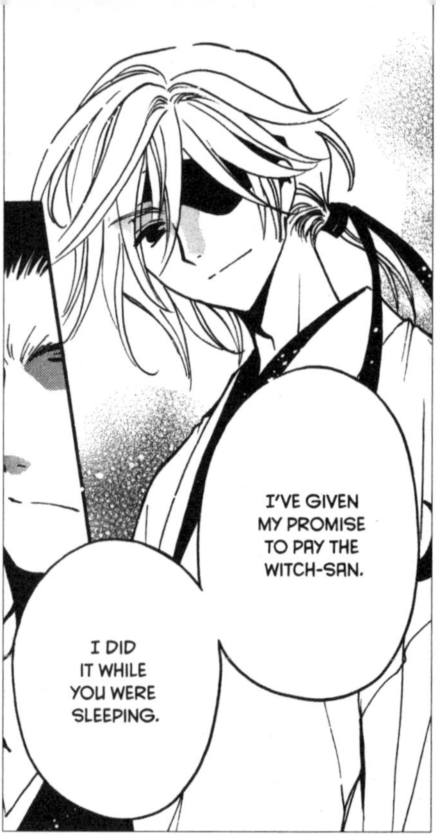
I'VE GIVEN MY PROMISE TO PAY THE WITCH-SAN.
I DID IT WHILE YOU WERE SLEEPING.

Witch-san, page 60

Honorifics can go at the end of job titles as a means of address just as they can go at the end of names. If you work in an electronics store, you could be referred to as *denkiya-san*. Of course, this doesn't work where the job title is an honorific in itself such as the word sensei for teachers, doctors, and artists. One would never say *Sensei-san*. In this case, the original was *majo-san* (witch-san).

Haven't changed, page 71

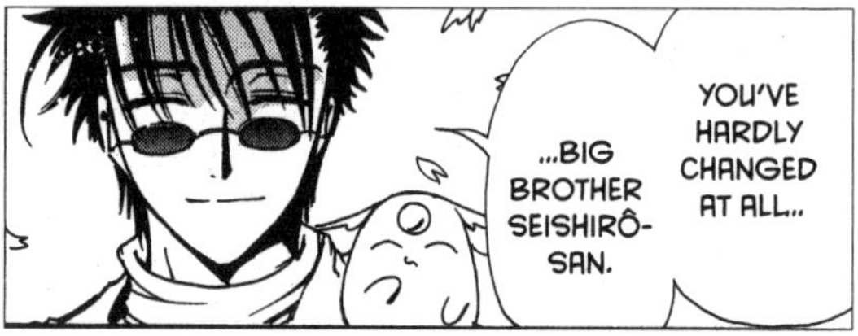
YOU'VE HARDLY CHANGED AT ALL...
...BIG BROTHER SEISHIRÔ-SAN.

This is a standard greeting in Japan when one meets up with a person again after a long time. Like "how are you doing" in English, the phrase is hardly noticed for its real meaning in Japanese—it is simply a greeting. But the fact that the main characters of Tsubasa have changed so much since the Country of Ôto/Edonis, the idea of who has changed and who hasn't becomes very significant.

Peanut Gallery (anachronism), page 76

Some may balk at Kurogane, who comes from a feudal-Japan-style world, using slang like "peanut gallery" in his dialogue. Normally, I wouldn't translate his dialogue using words the character wouldn't know, but in this case, the Japanese version of his line of dialogue was about criticisms being shouted from the outfield—a baseball reference. Since the Japanese was anachronistic, it left room for the English to be equally anachronistic. That being the case, aside from the fact that the Japanese was a reference to baseball, and the English translation was a reference to vaudeville, "peanut gallery" is a near exact translation of the original Japanese line.

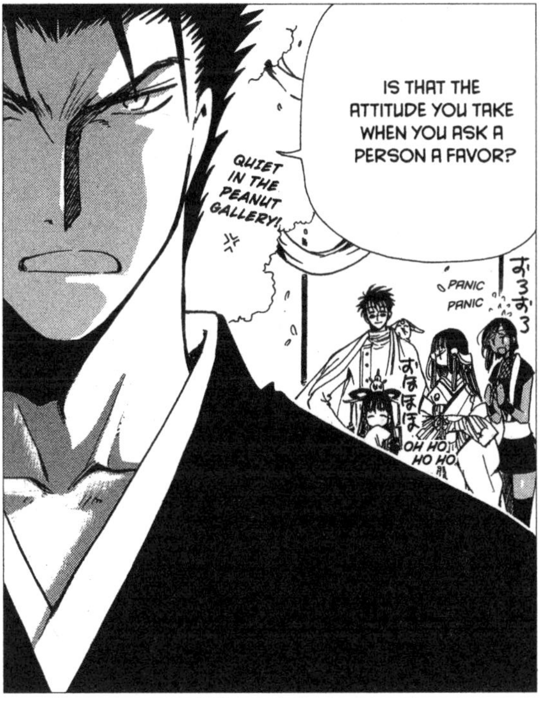
IS THAT THE ATTITUDE YOU TAKE WHEN YOU ASK A PERSON A FAVOR?
QUIET IN THE PEANUT GALLERY!
PANIC
PANIC
OH HO HO HO

Contents

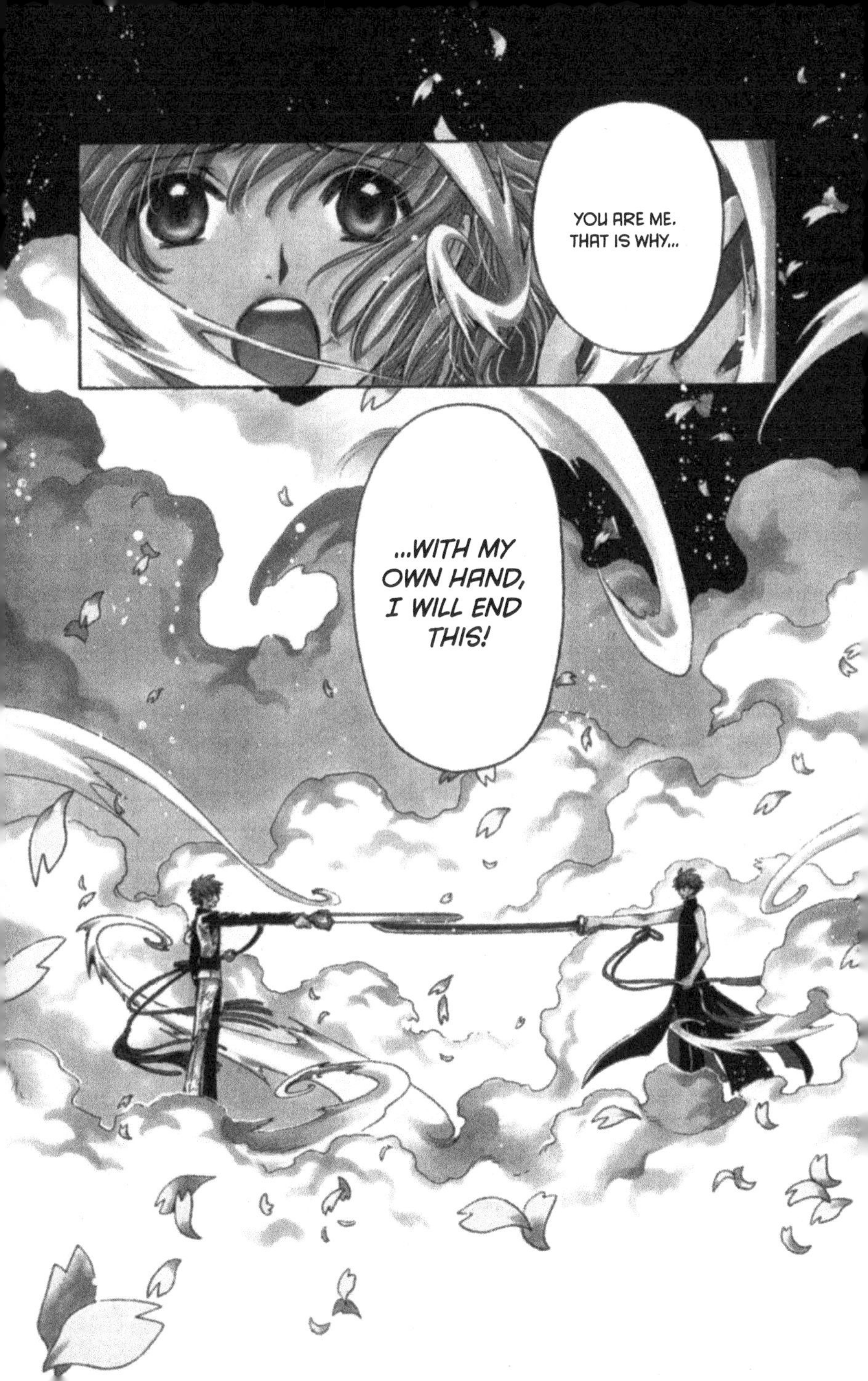
YOU ARE ME. THAT IS WHY...
...WITH MY OWN HAND, I WILL END THIS!

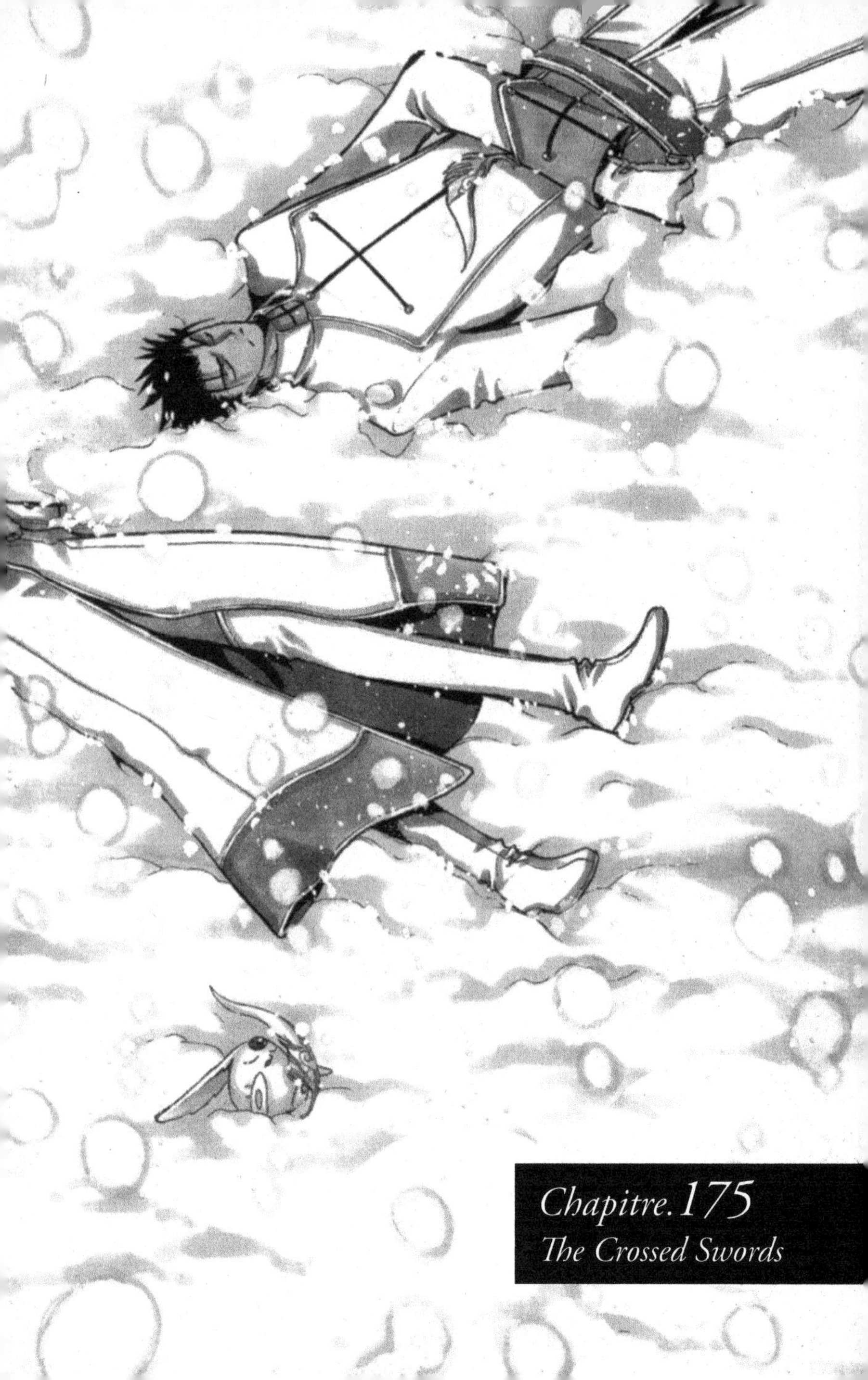

Chapitre. 175
The Crossed Swords

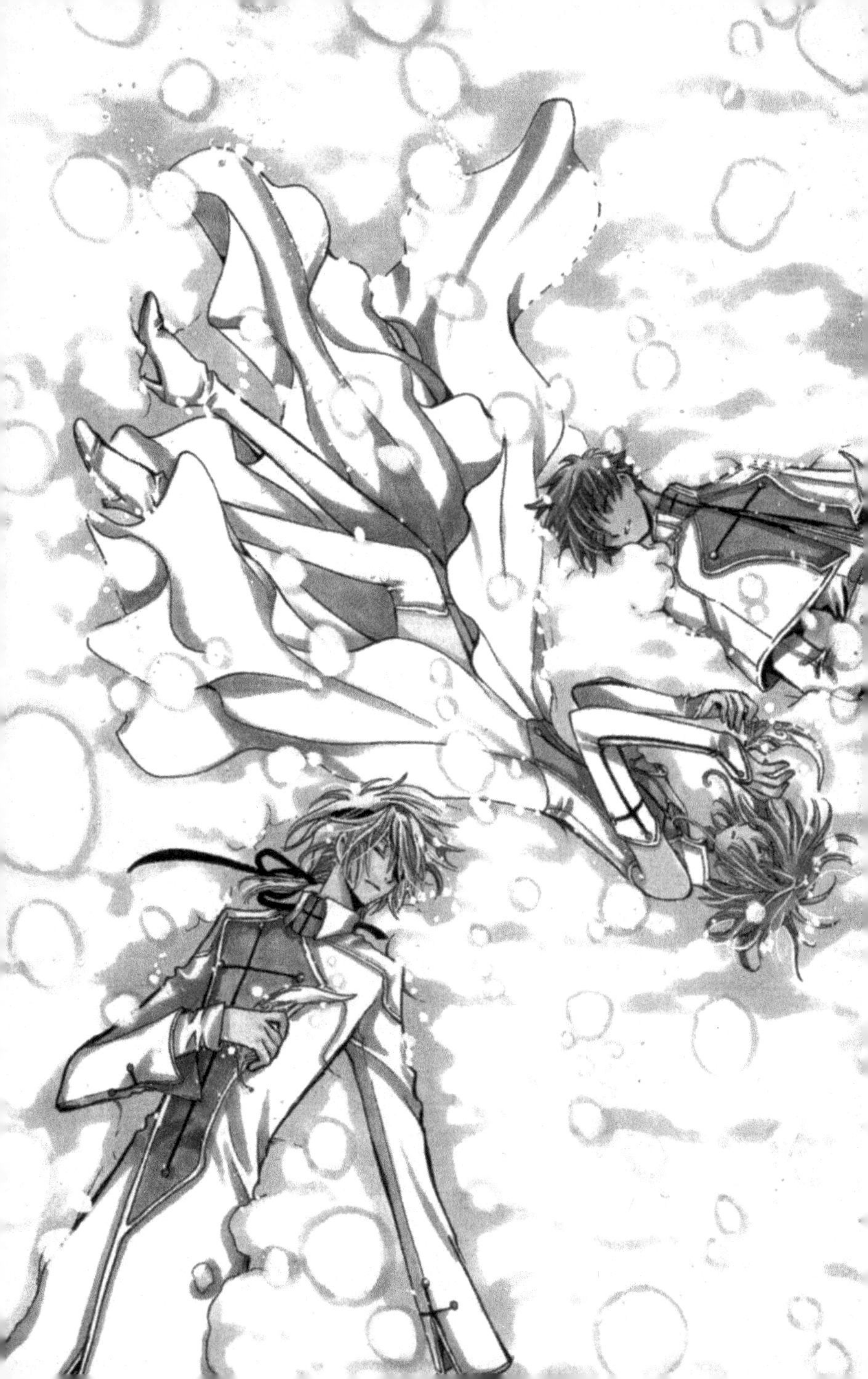

ツバサ
RESERVoir CHRoNiCLE

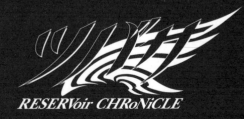

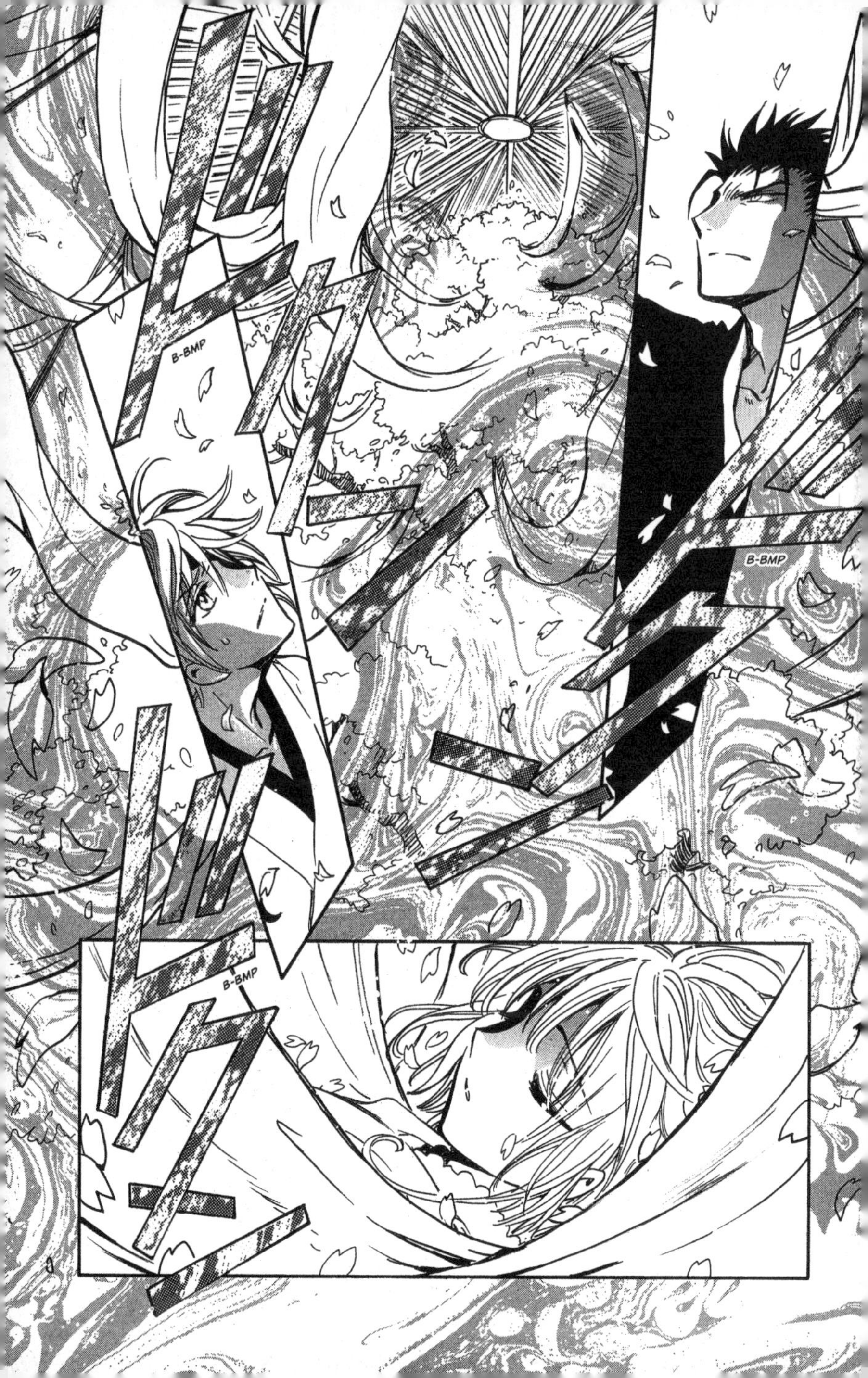
B-BMP
B-BMP
B-BMP

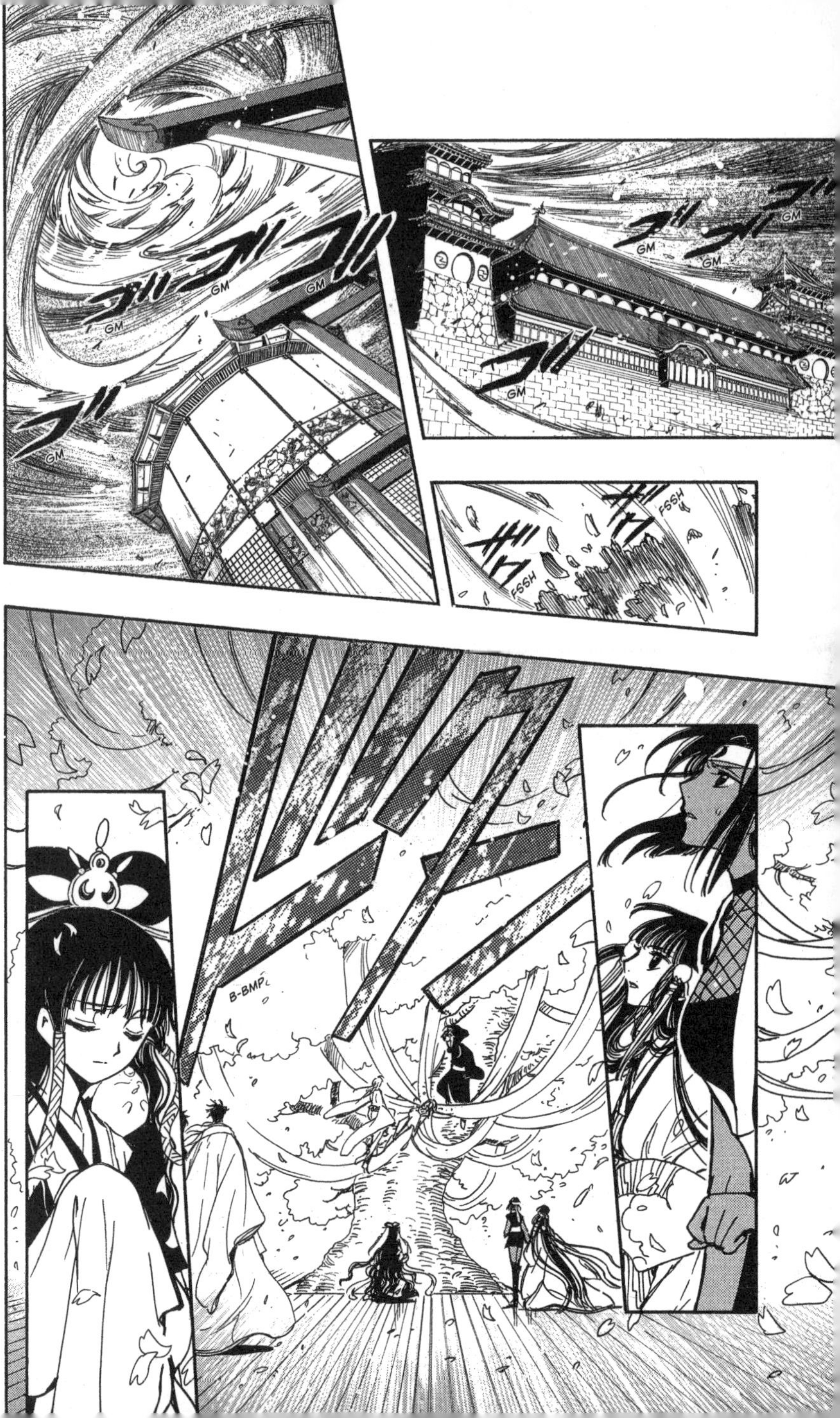
GM
GM
GM
GM
FSSH
FSSH
GM
GM
GM
B-BMP

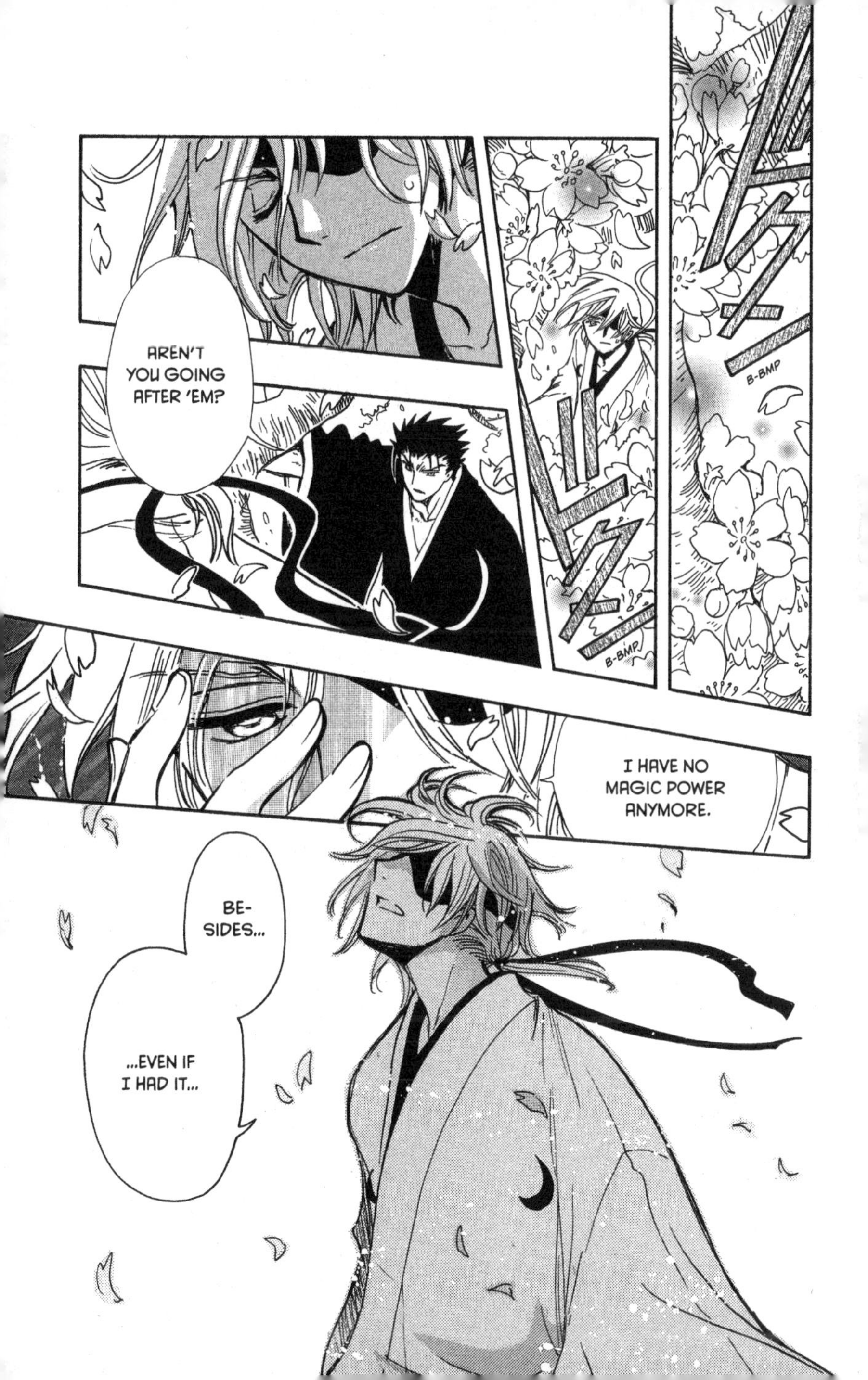
B-BMP
B-BMP
AREN'T YOU GOING AFTER 'EM?
I HAVE NO MAGIC POWER ANYMORE.
BE-SIDES...
...EVEN IF I HAD IT...

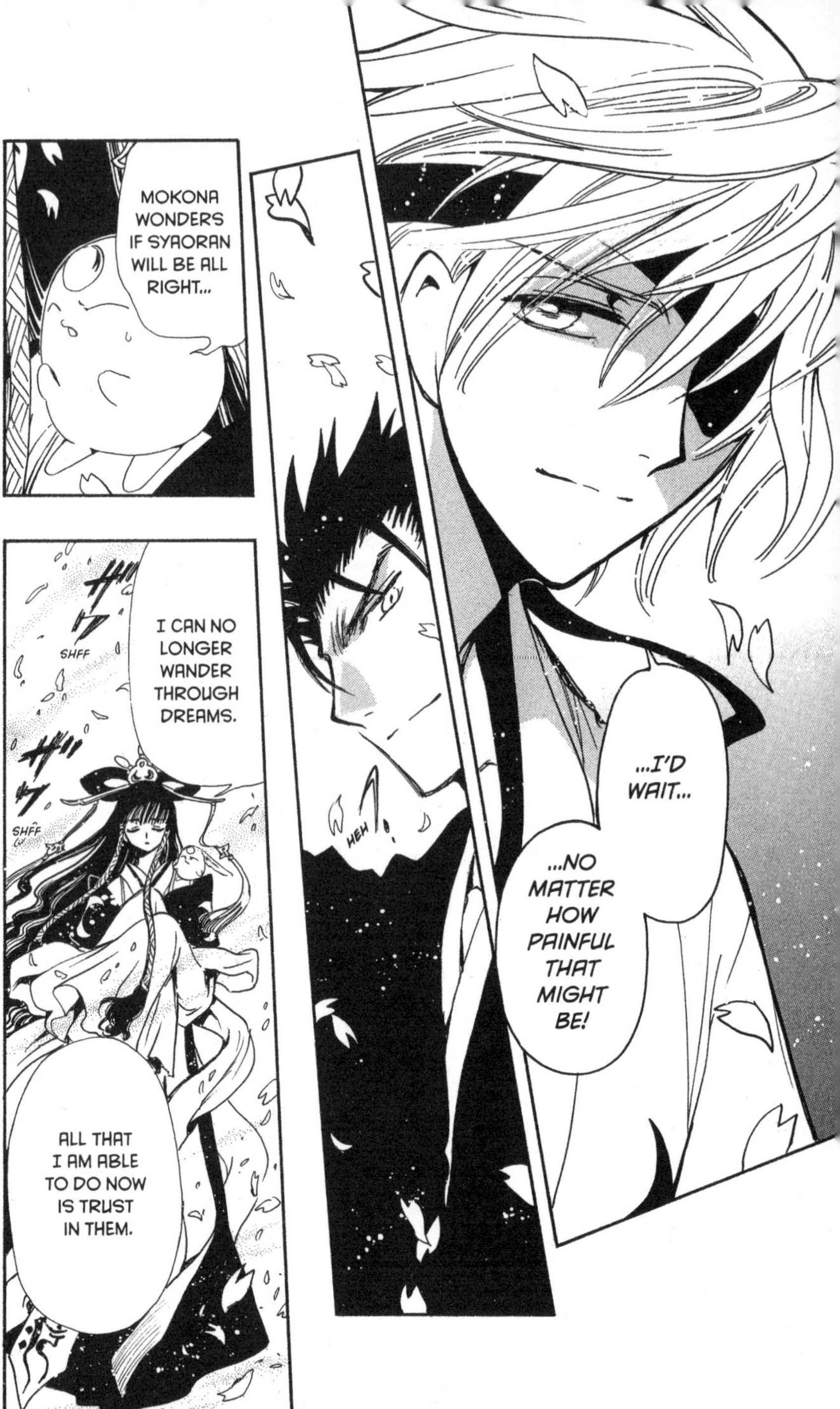
...I'D WAIT...
...NO MATTER HOW PAINFUL THAT MIGHT BE!
HEH
MOKONA WONDERS IF SYAORAN WILL BE ALL RIGHT...
I CAN NO LONGER WANDER THROUGH DREAMS.
SHFF
SHFF
ALL THAT I AM ABLE TO DO NOW IS TRUST IN THEM.

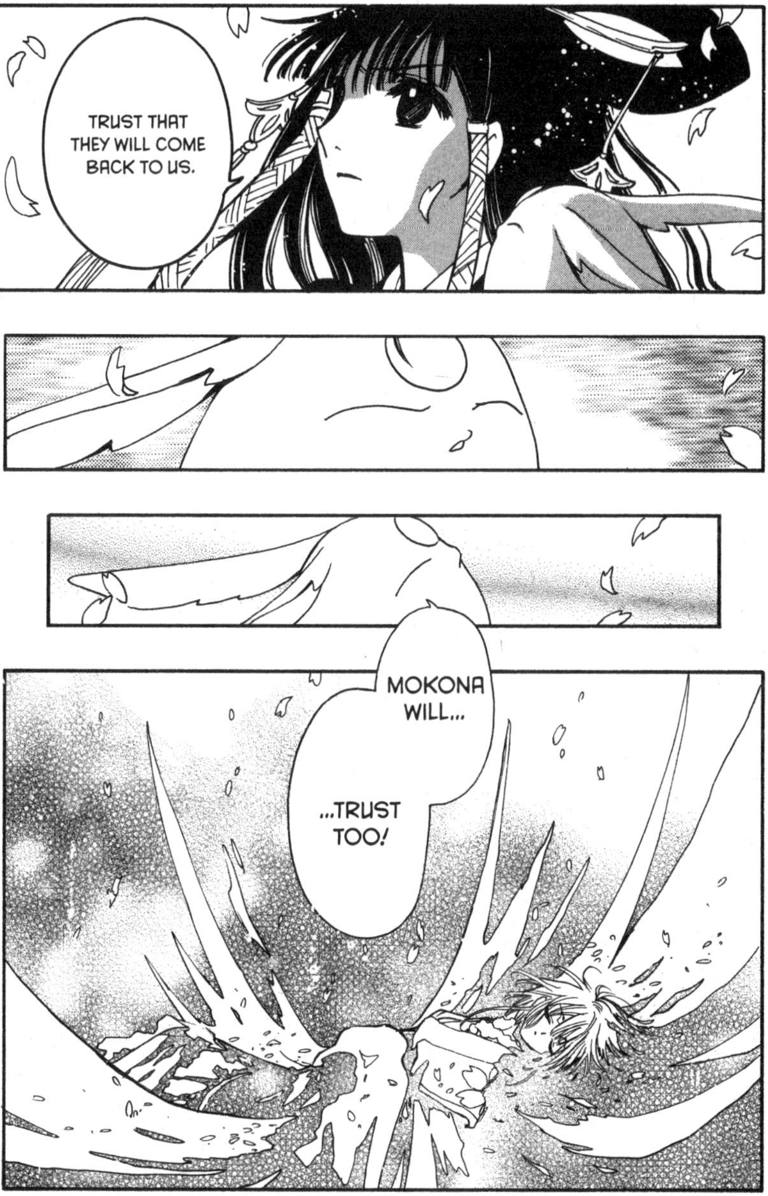
TRUST THAT THEY WILL COME BACK TO US.
MOKONA WILL...
...TRUST TOO!

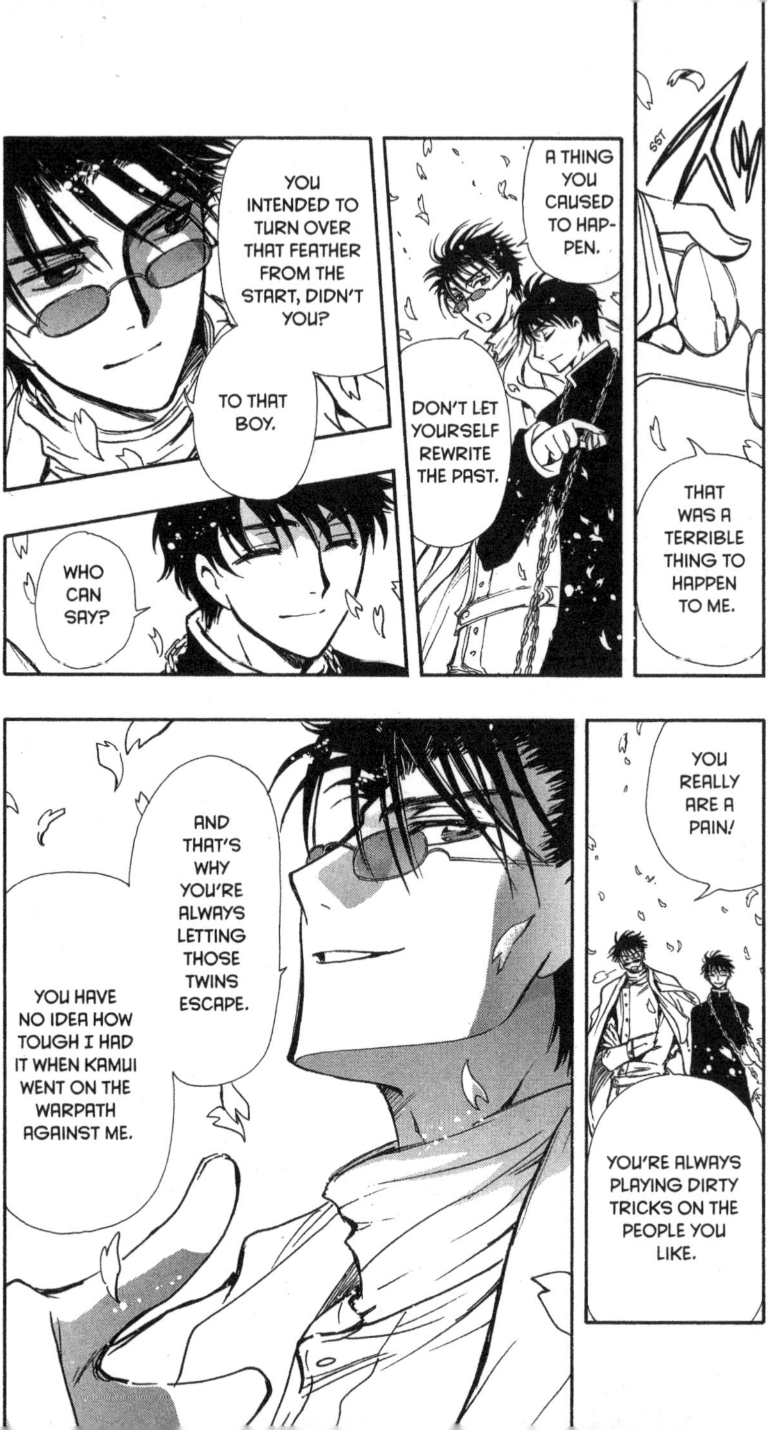
SST
THAT WAS A TERRIBLE THING TO HAPPEN TO ME.
A THING YOU CAUSED TO HAP-PEN.
DON'T LET YOURSELF REWRITE THE PAST.
YOU INTENDED TO TURN OVER THAT FEATHER FROM THE START, DIDN'T YOU?
TO THAT BOY.
WHO CAN SAY?
YOU REALLY ARE A PAIN!
YOU'RE ALWAYS PLAYING DIRTY TRICKS ON THE PEOPLE YOU LIKE.
AND THAT'S WHY YOU'RE ALWAYS LETTING THOSE TWINS ESCAPE.
YOU HAVE NO IDEA HOW TOUGH I HAD IT WHEN KAMUI WENT ON THE WARPATH AGAINST ME.

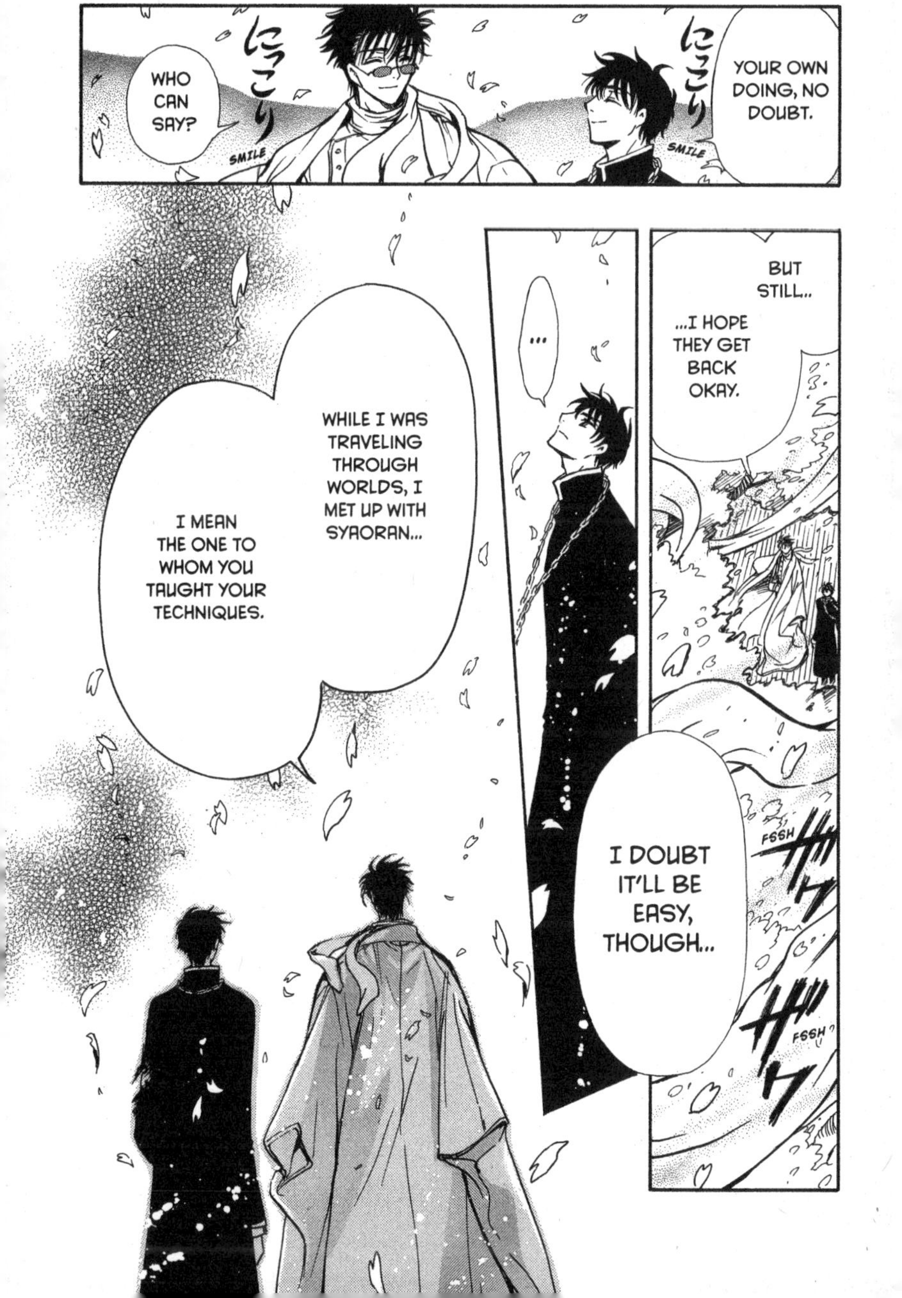
にっこり
SMILE
YOUR OWN DOING, NO DOUBT.
にっこり
SMILE
WHO CAN SAY?
BUT STILL...
...I HOPE THEY GET BACK OKAY.
FSSH
FSSH
I DOUBT IT'LL BE EASY, THOUGH...
...
WHILE I WAS TRAVELING THROUGH WORLDS, I MET UP WITH SYAORAN...
I MEAN THE ONE TO WHOM YOU TAUGHT YOUR TECHNIQUES.

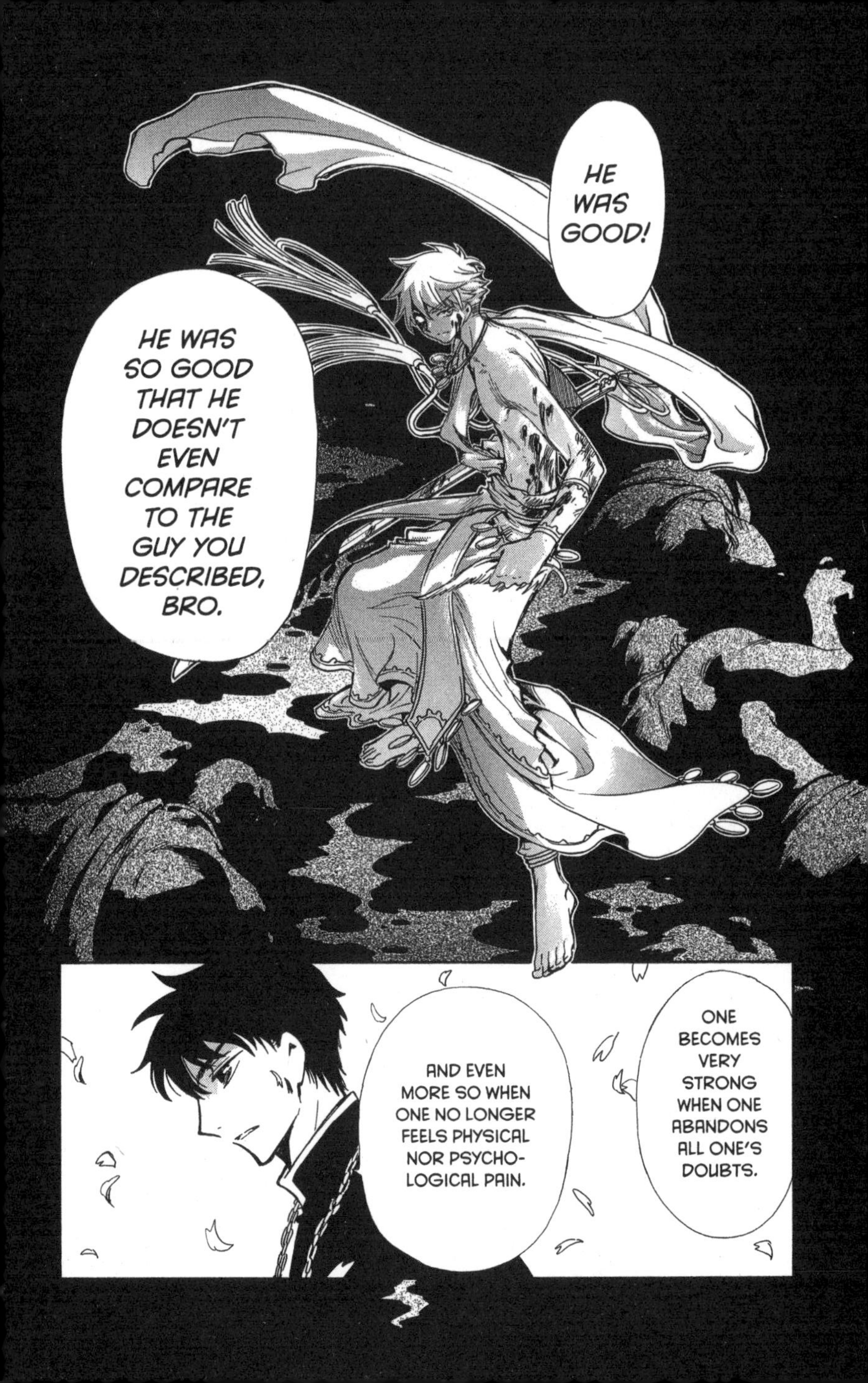
HE WAS GOOD!
HE WAS SO GOOD THAT HE DOESN'T EVEN COMPARE TO THE GUY YOU DESCRIBED, BRO.
ONE BECOMES VERY STRONG WHEN ONE ABANDONS ALL ONE'S DOUBTS.
AND EVEN MORE SO WHEN ONE NO LONGER FEELS PHYSICAL NOR PSYCHO-LOGICAL PAIN.

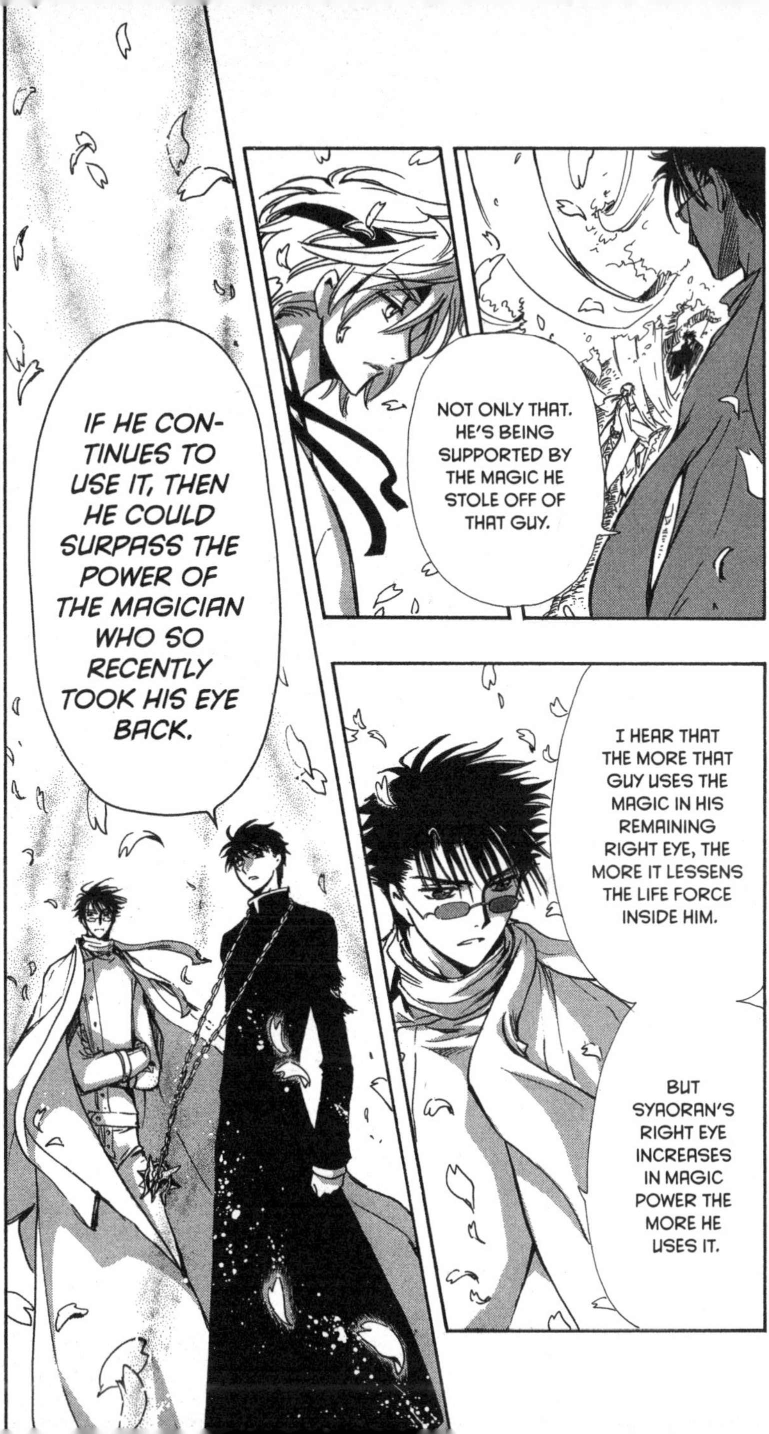
I HEAR THAT THE MORE THAT GUY USES THE MAGIC IN HIS REMAINING RIGHT EYE, THE MORE IT LESSENS THE LIFE FORCE INSIDE HIM.
BUT SYAORAN'S RIGHT EYE INCREASES IN MAGIC POWER THE MORE HE USES IT.
NOT ONLY THAT. HE'S BEING SUPPORTED BY THE MAGIC HE STOLE OFF OF THAT GUY.
IF HE CON-TINUES TO USE IT, THEN HE COULD SURPASS THE POWER OF THE MAGICIAN WHO SO RECENTLY TOOK HIS EYE BACK.

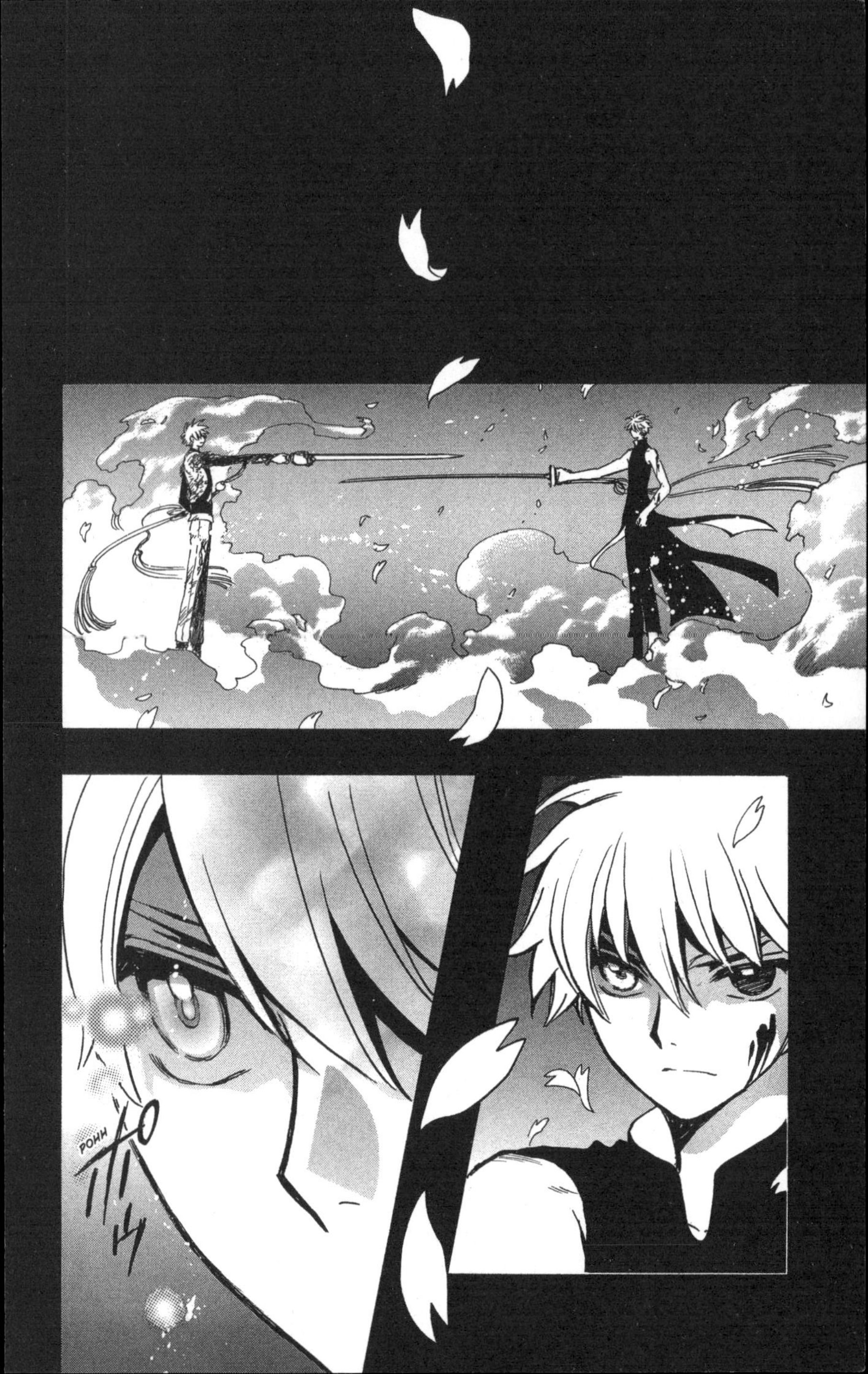
POHH

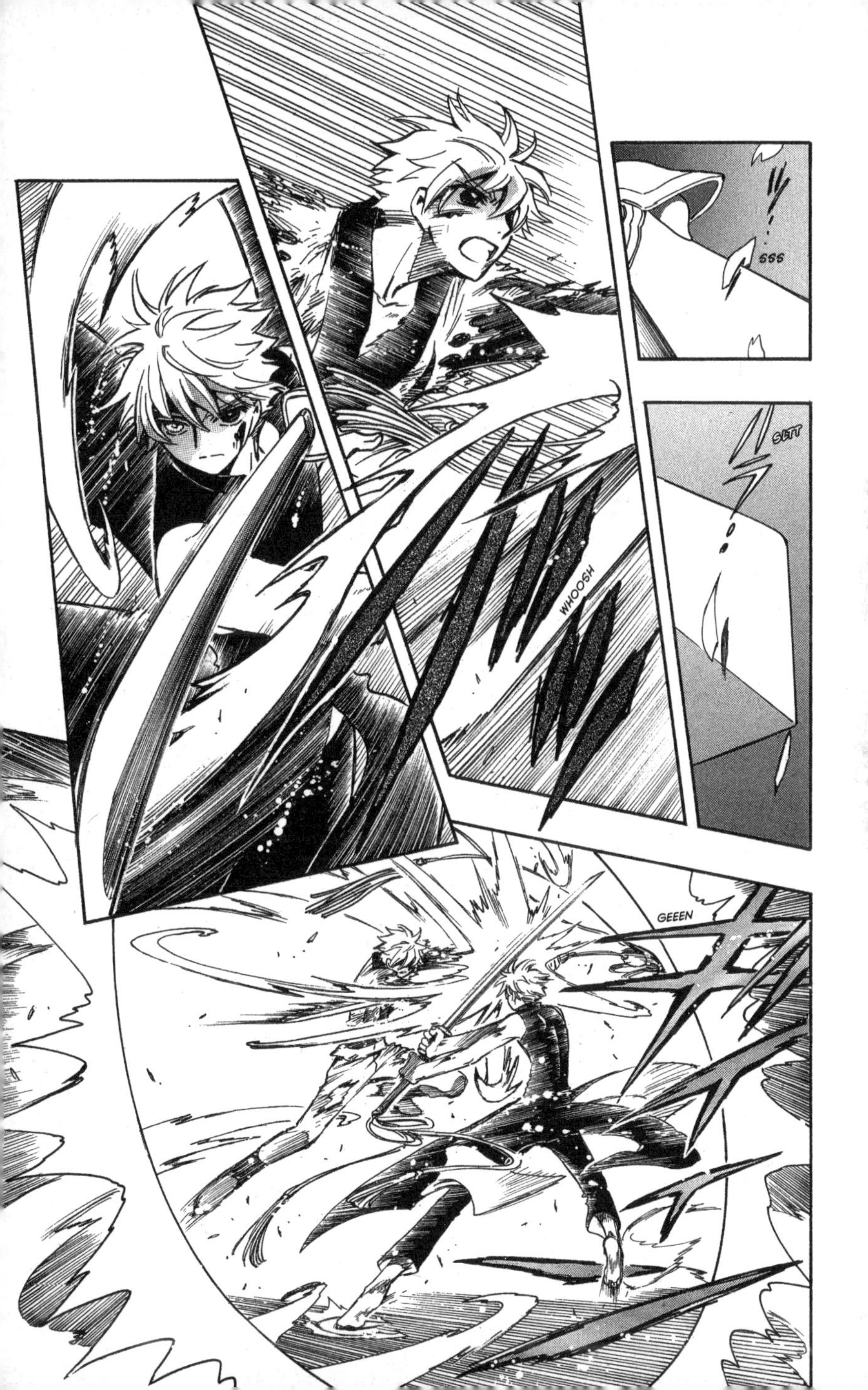
SSS
SLTT
WHOOSH
GEEN

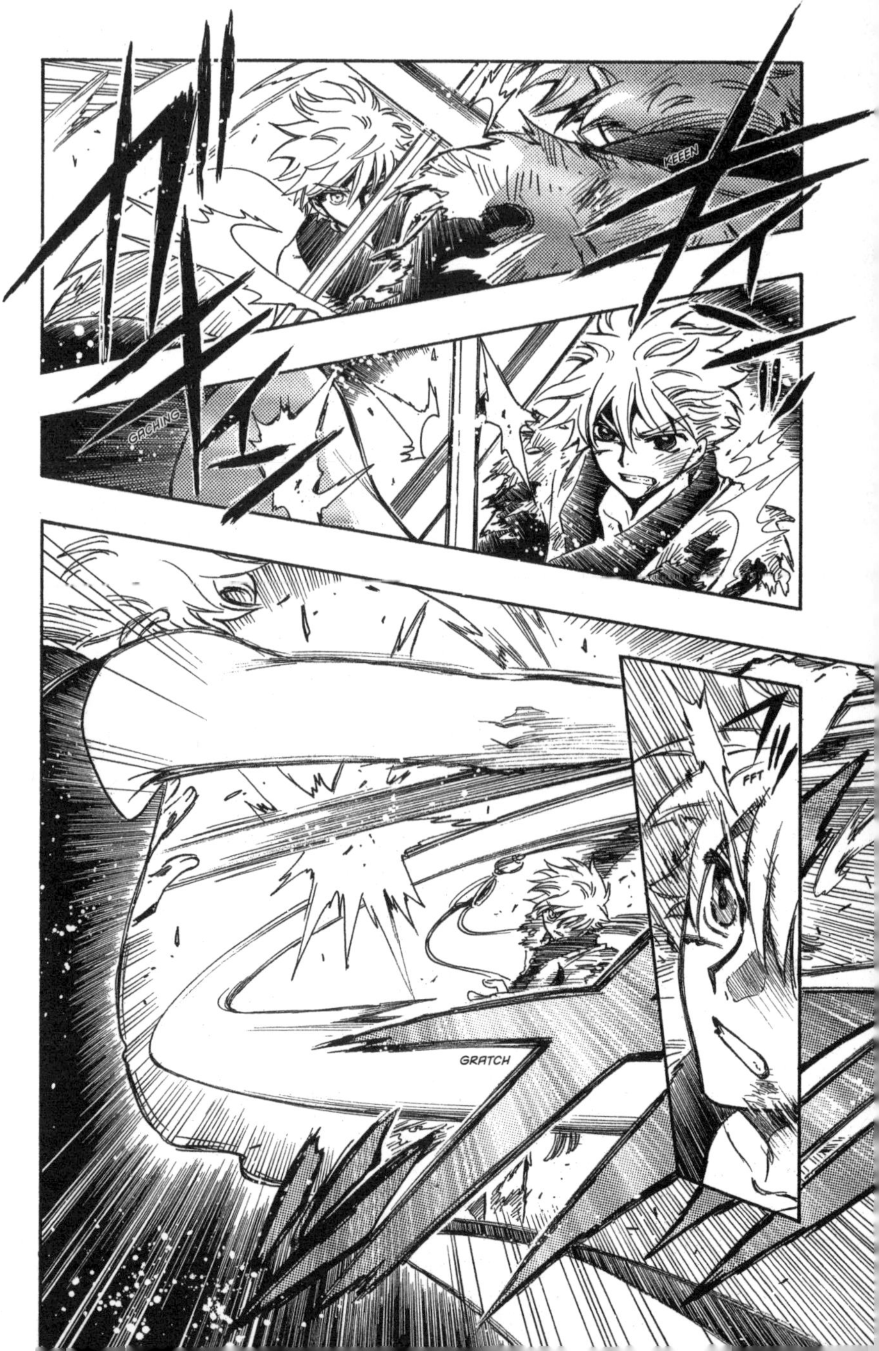
KEEEN
GACHING
FFT
GRATCH

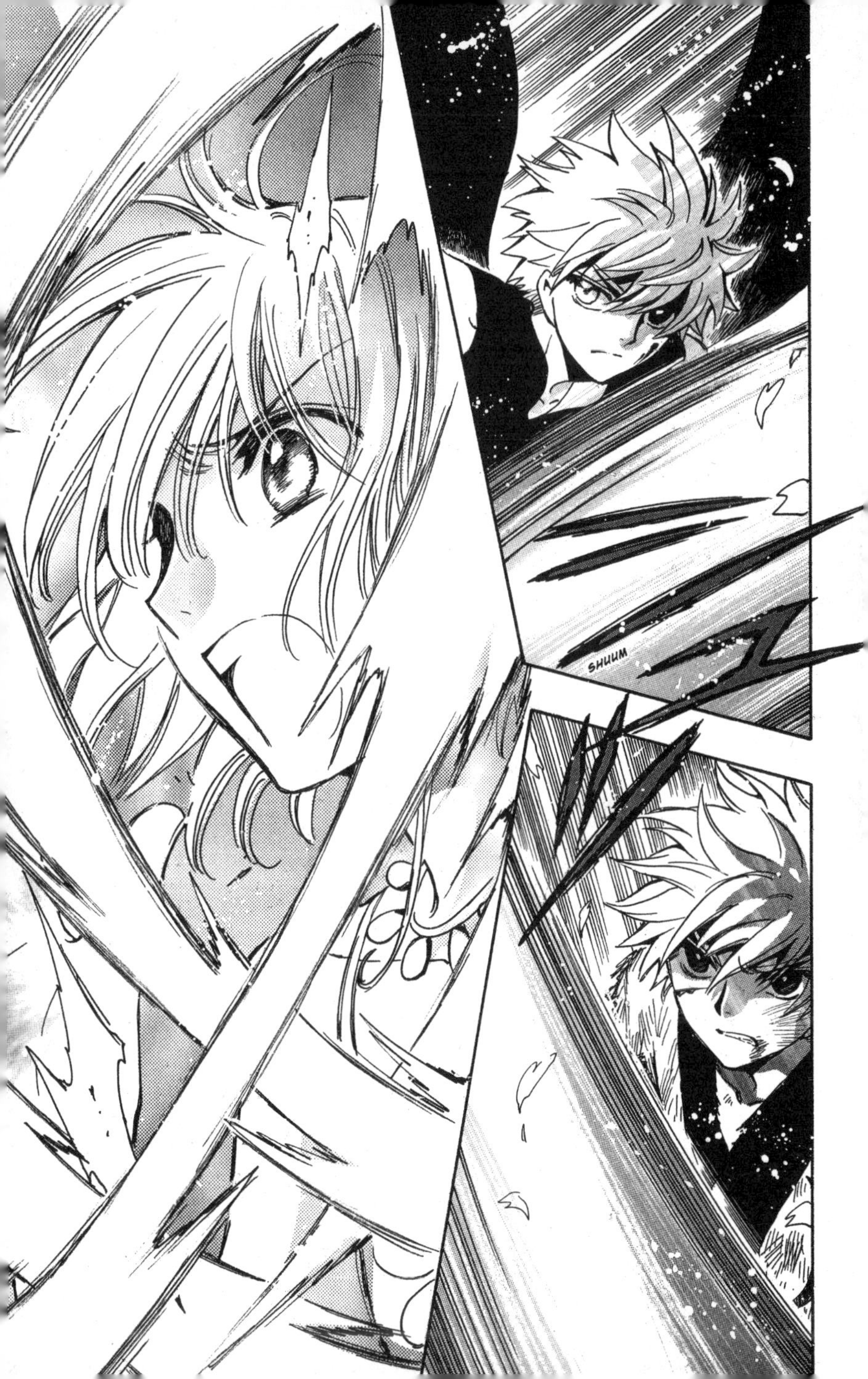
SHUUM

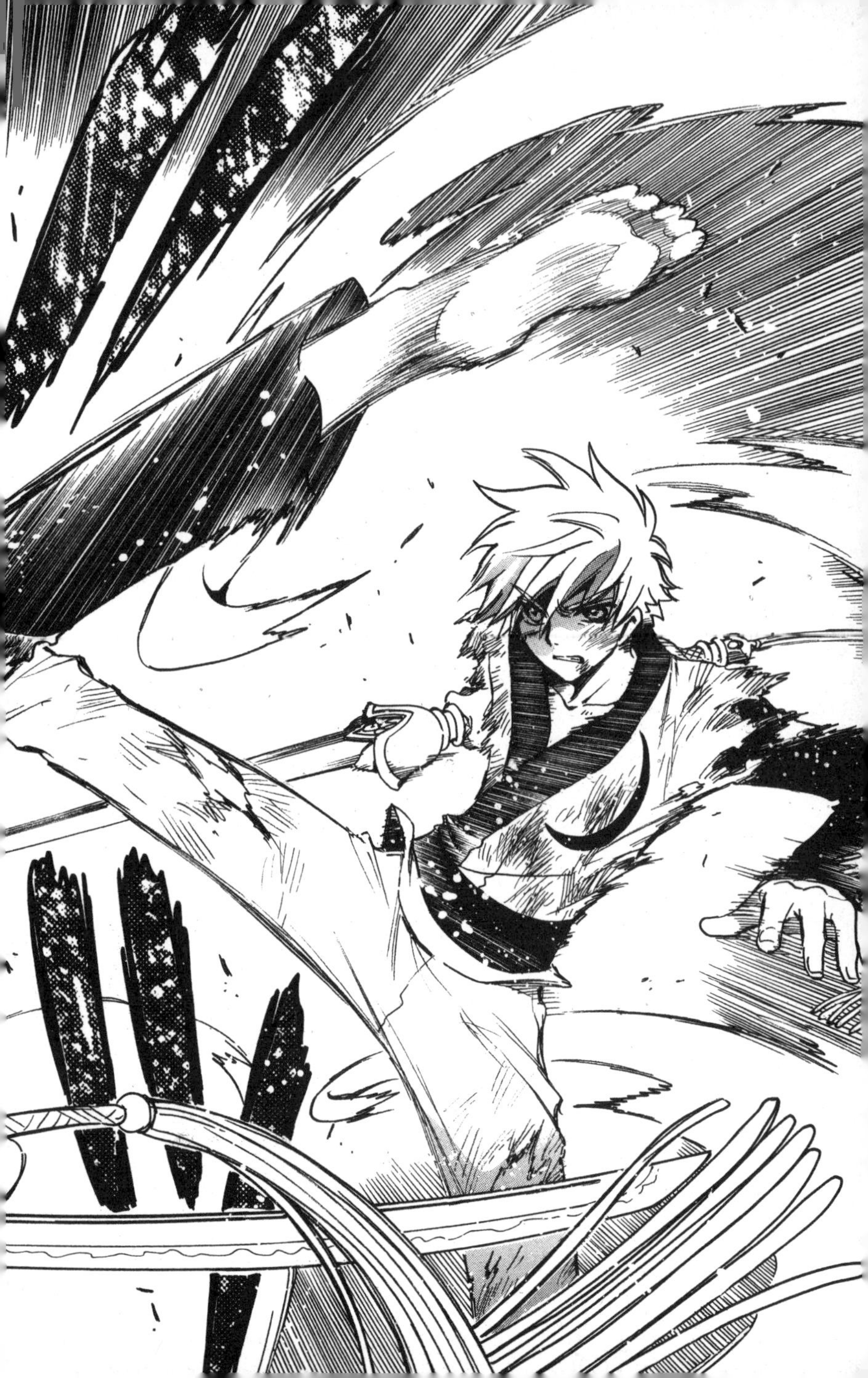

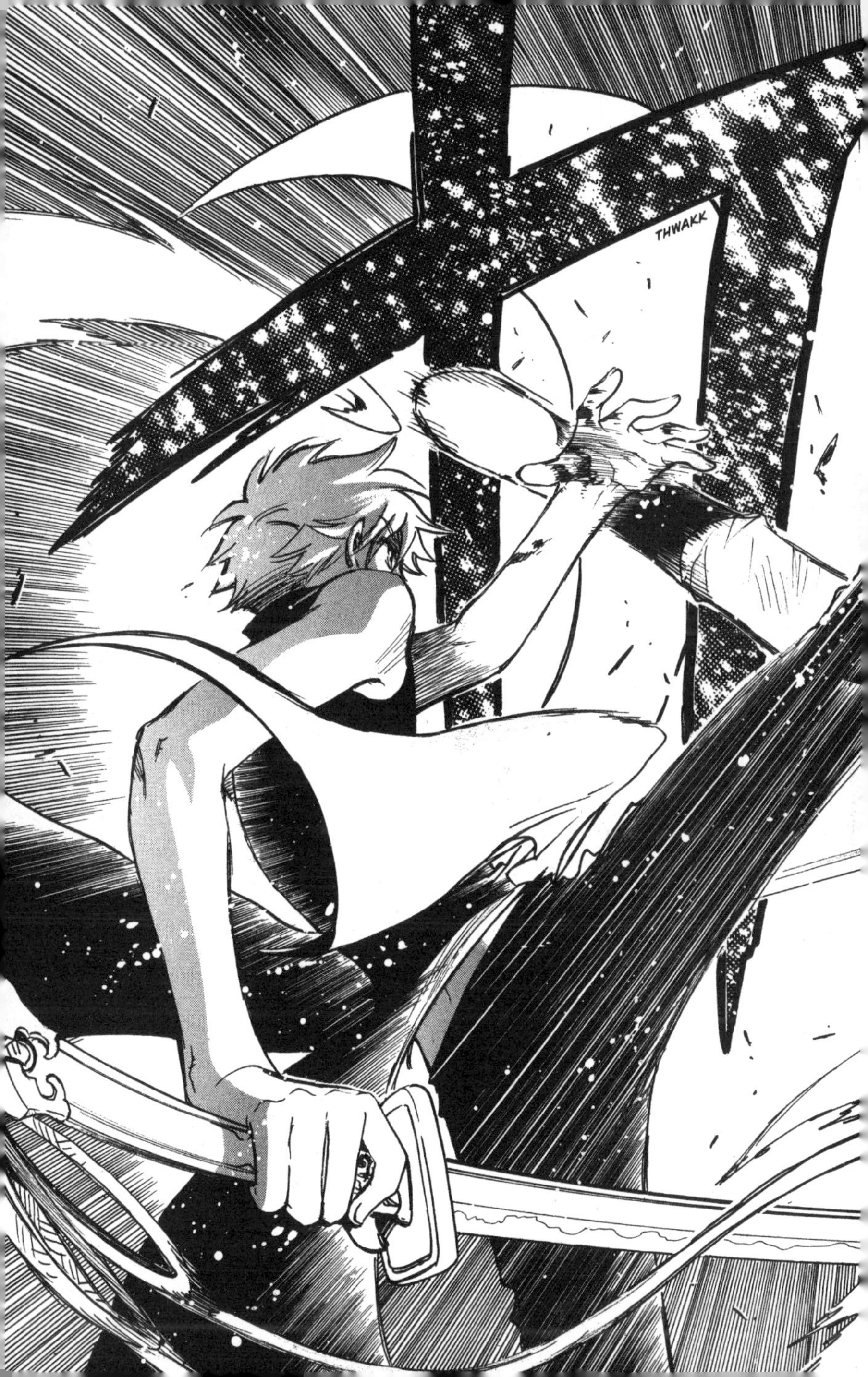
THWAKK

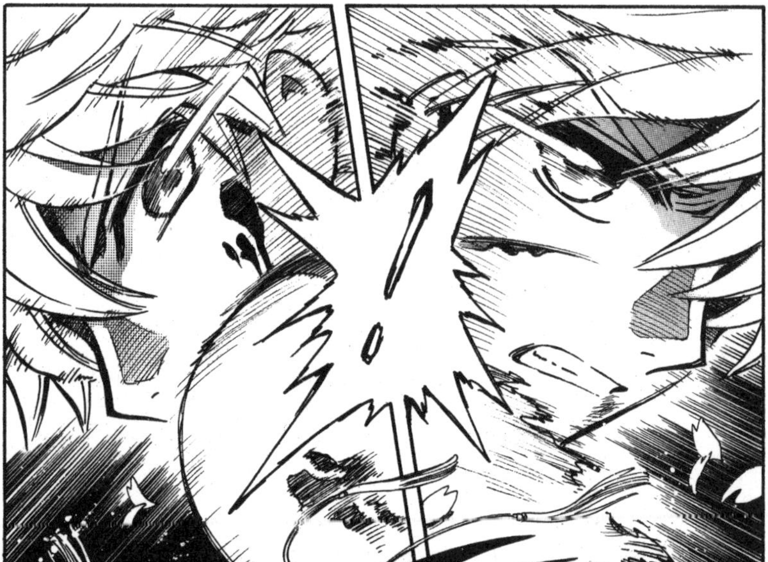

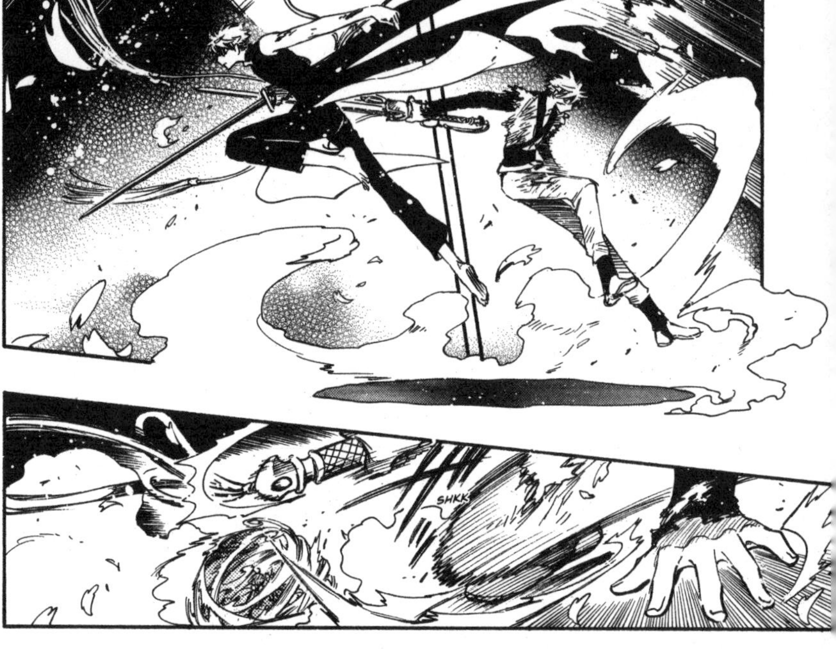
SHKK

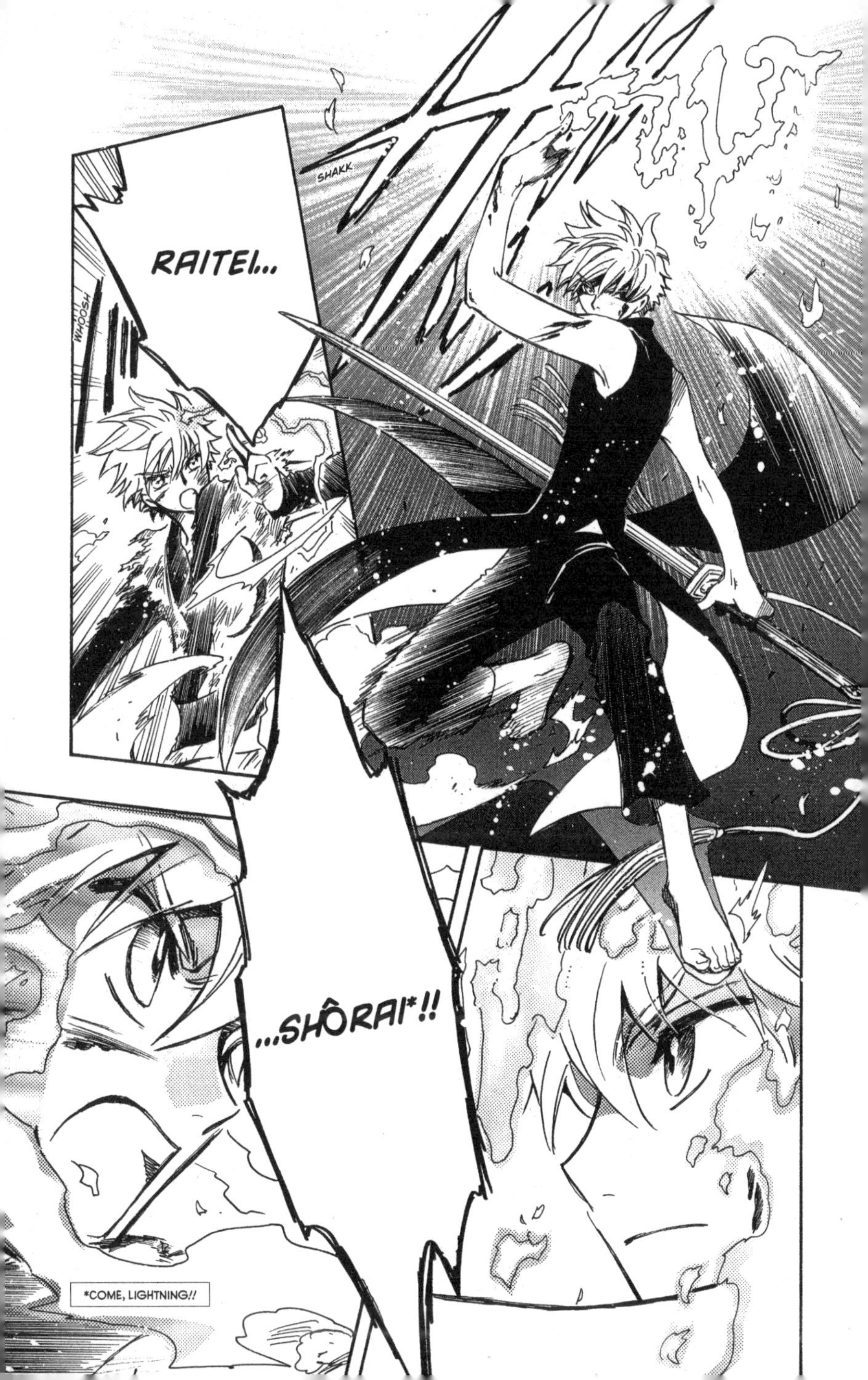
SHAKK
RAITEI...
WHOOSH
...SHÔRAI*!!
*COME, LIGHTNING!!

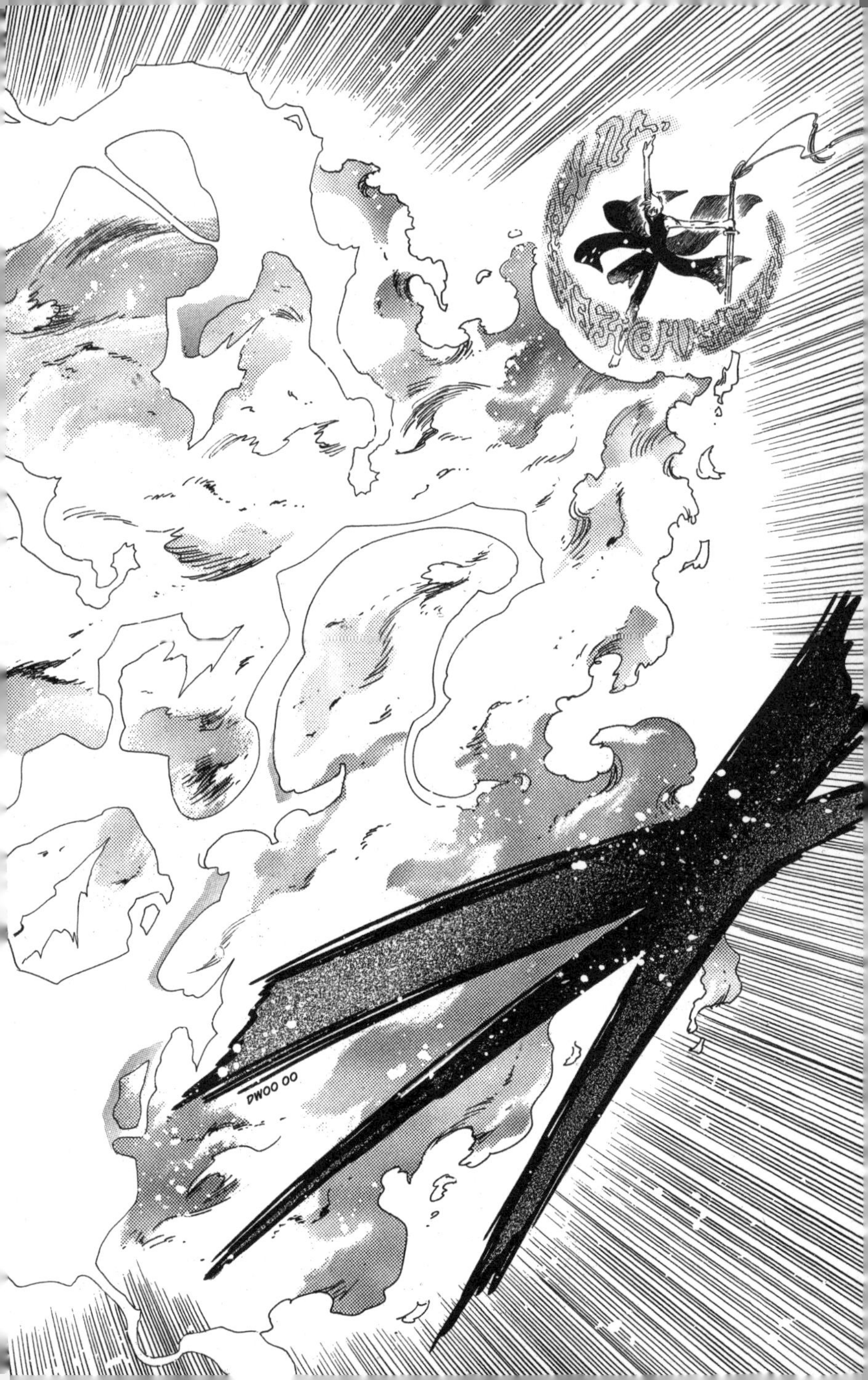
DWOO OO

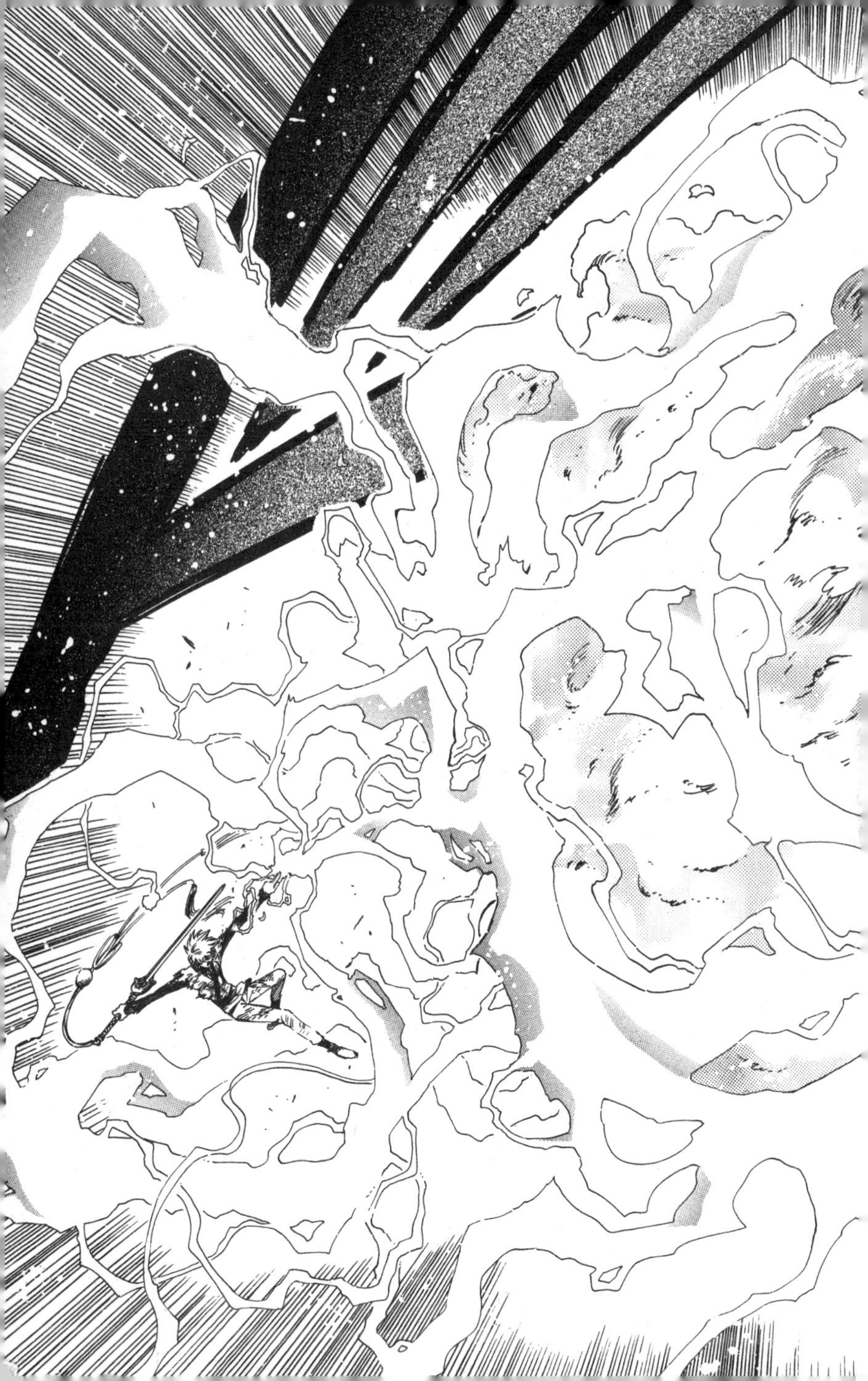

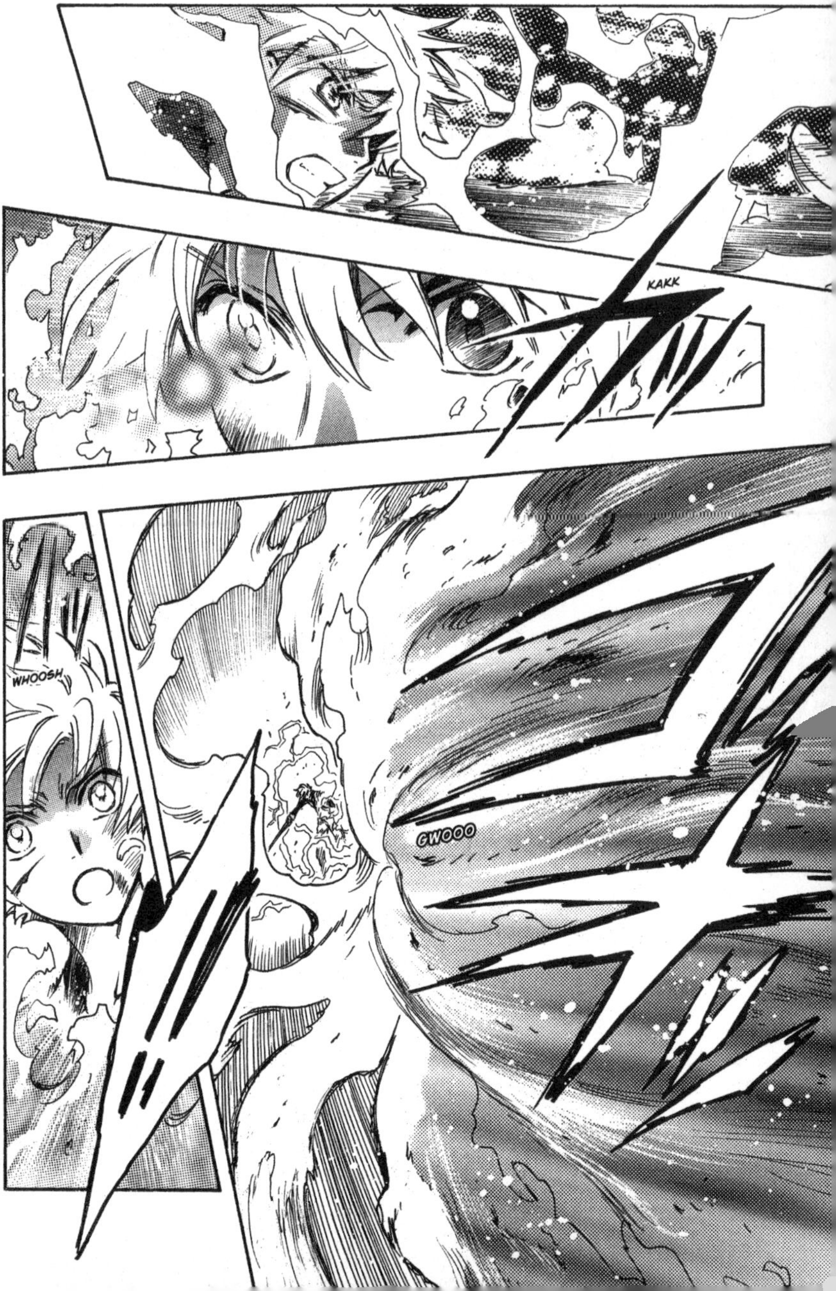
KAKK
GWOOO
WHOOSH

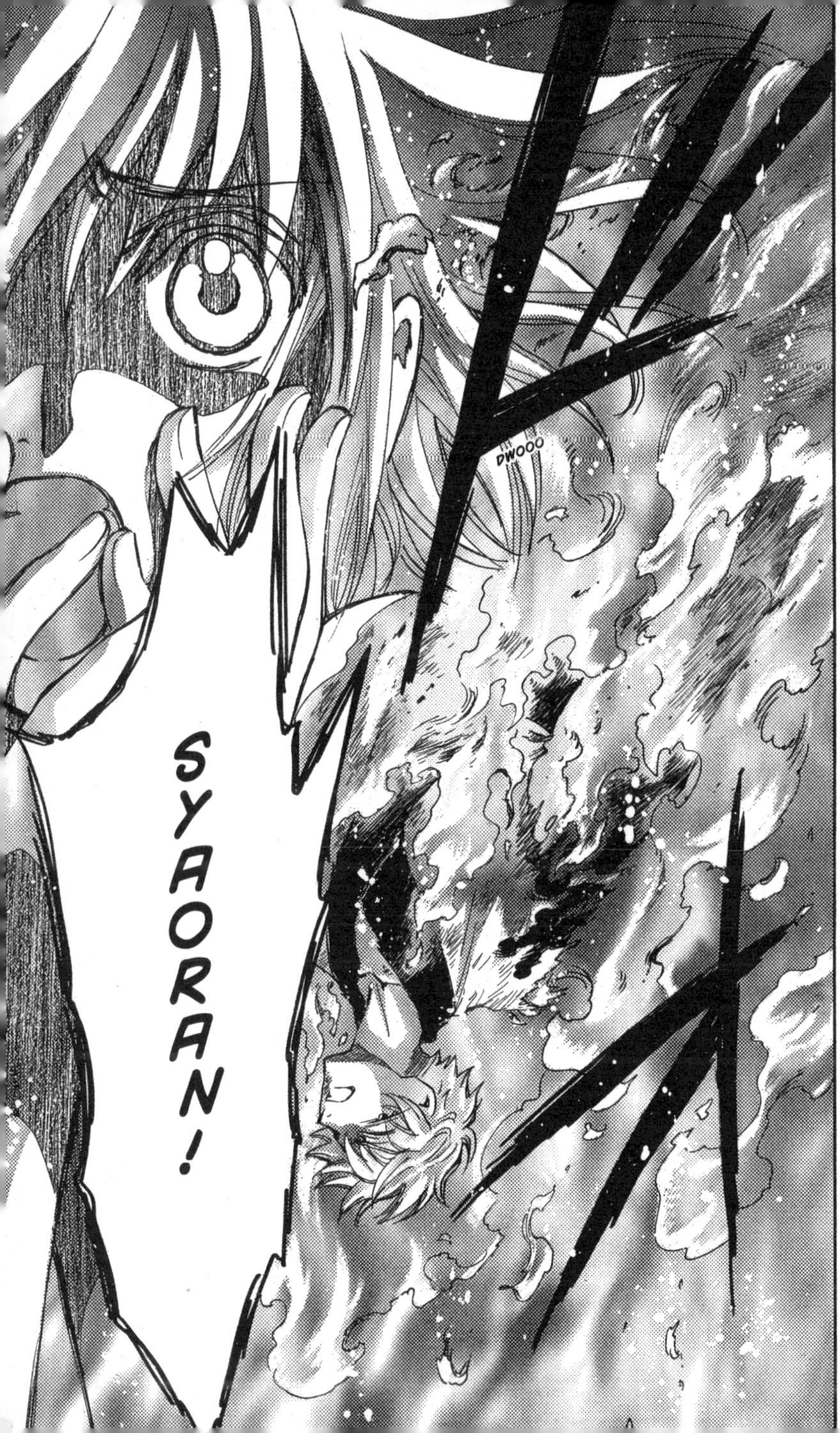
DWOOO
SYAORAN!

ツバサ
RESERVoir CHRoNiCLE

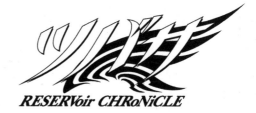

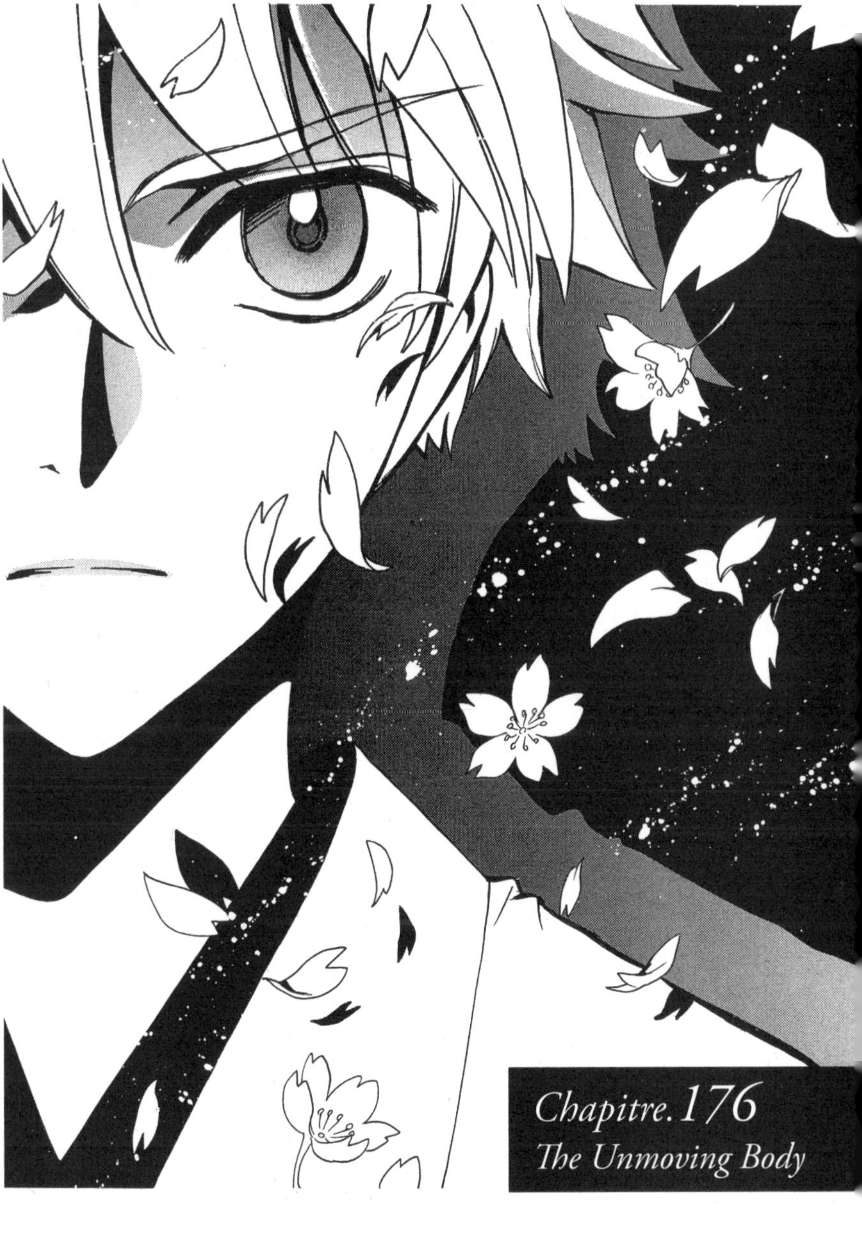

Chapitre. 176
The Unmoving Body

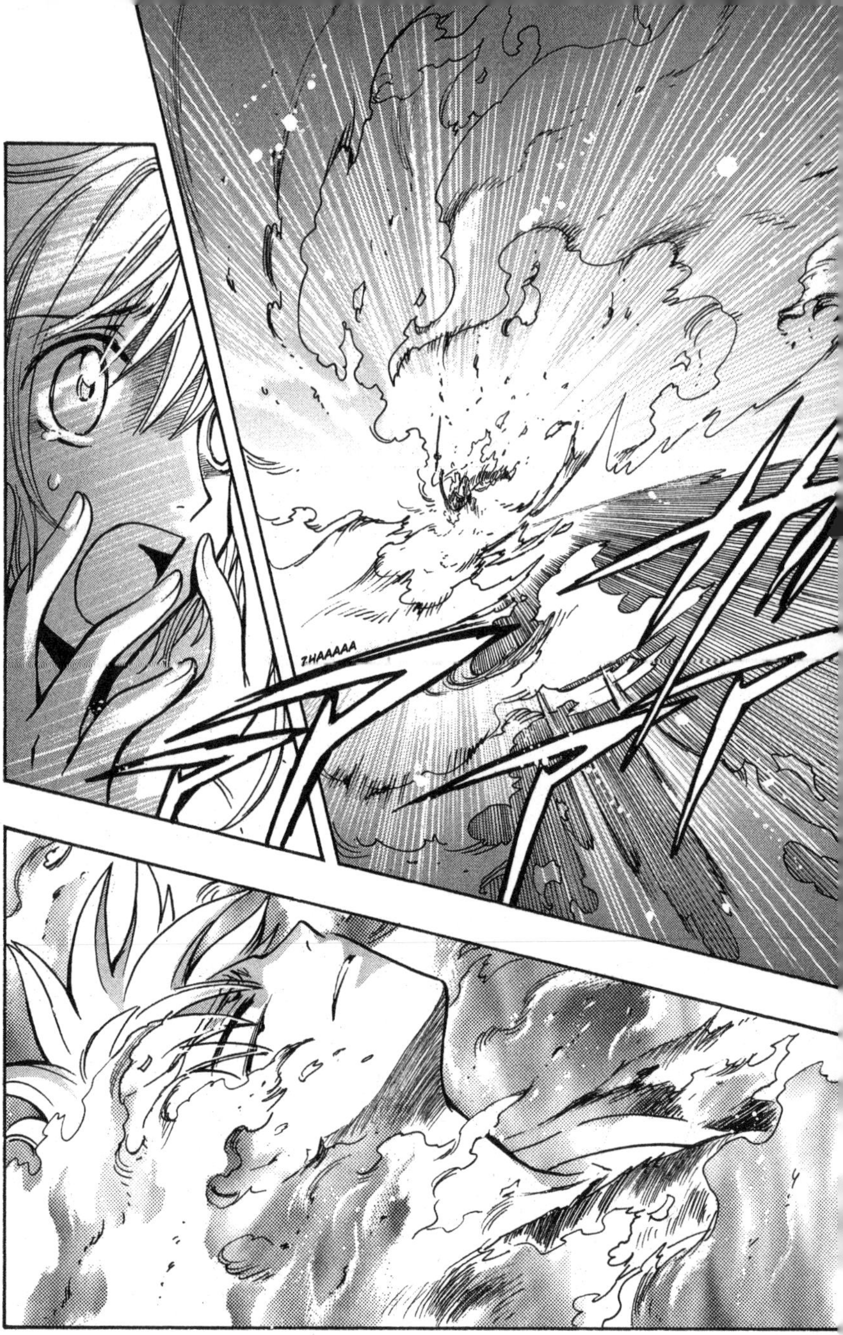
ZHAAAAA

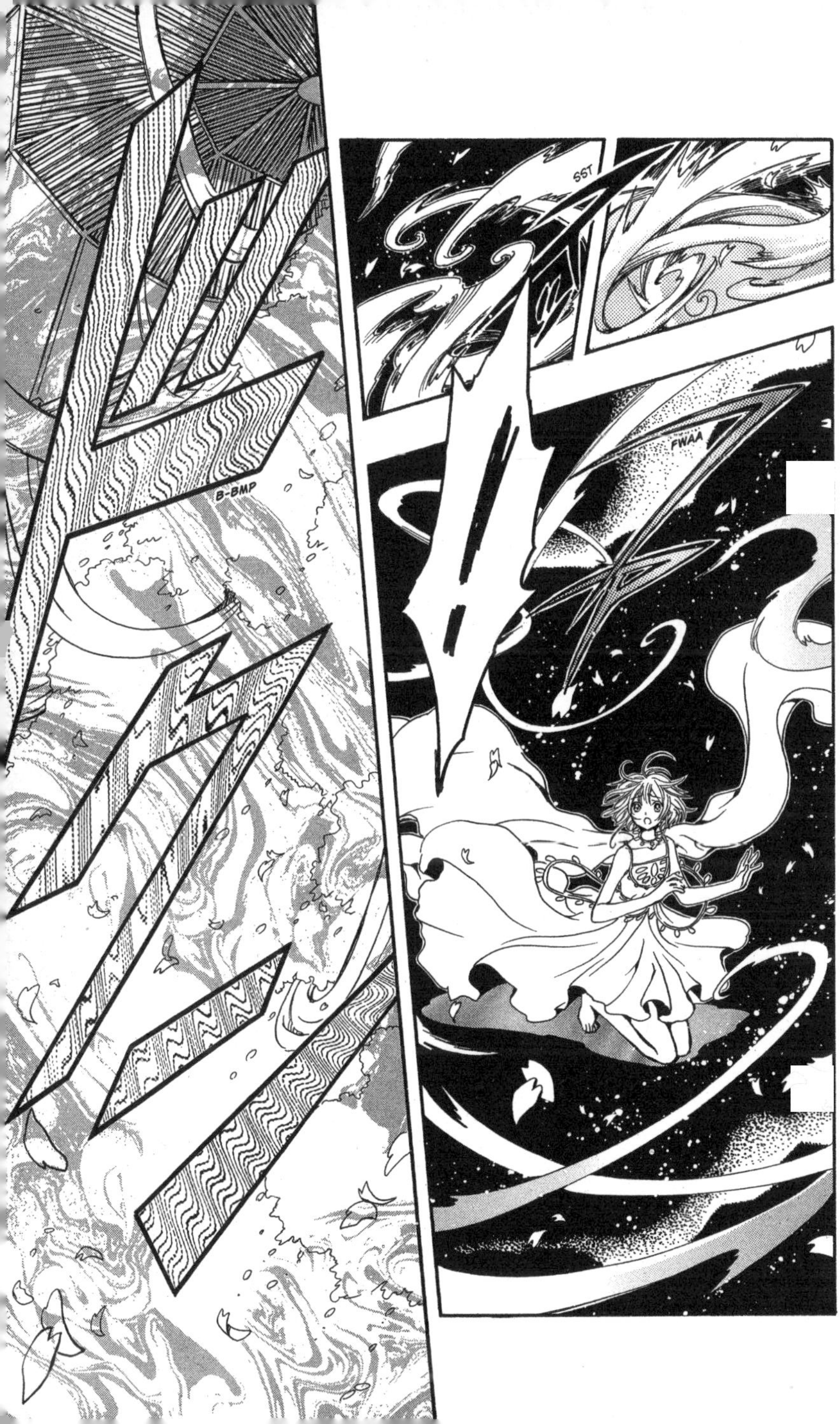
SST
FWAA
B-BMP

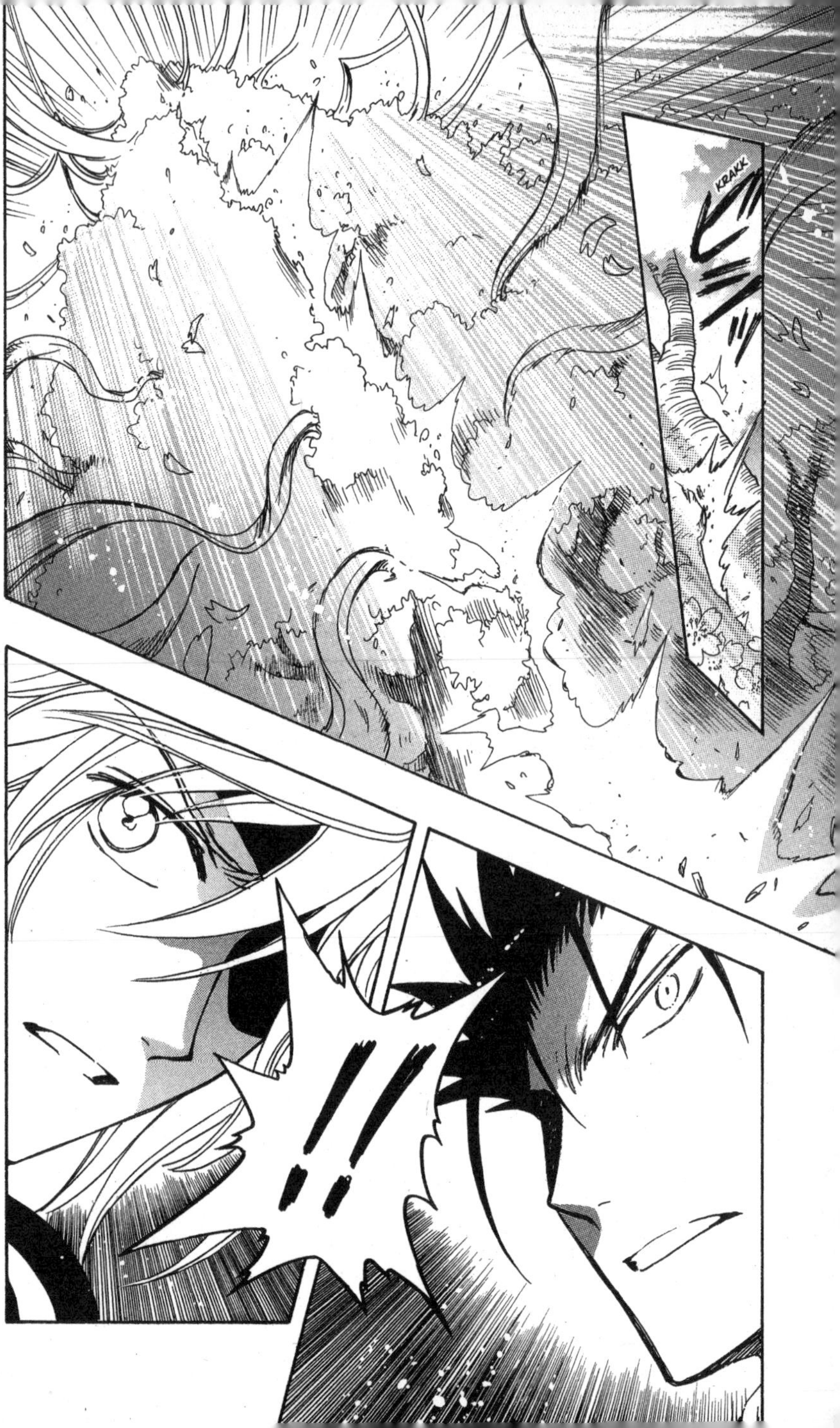
KRAKK

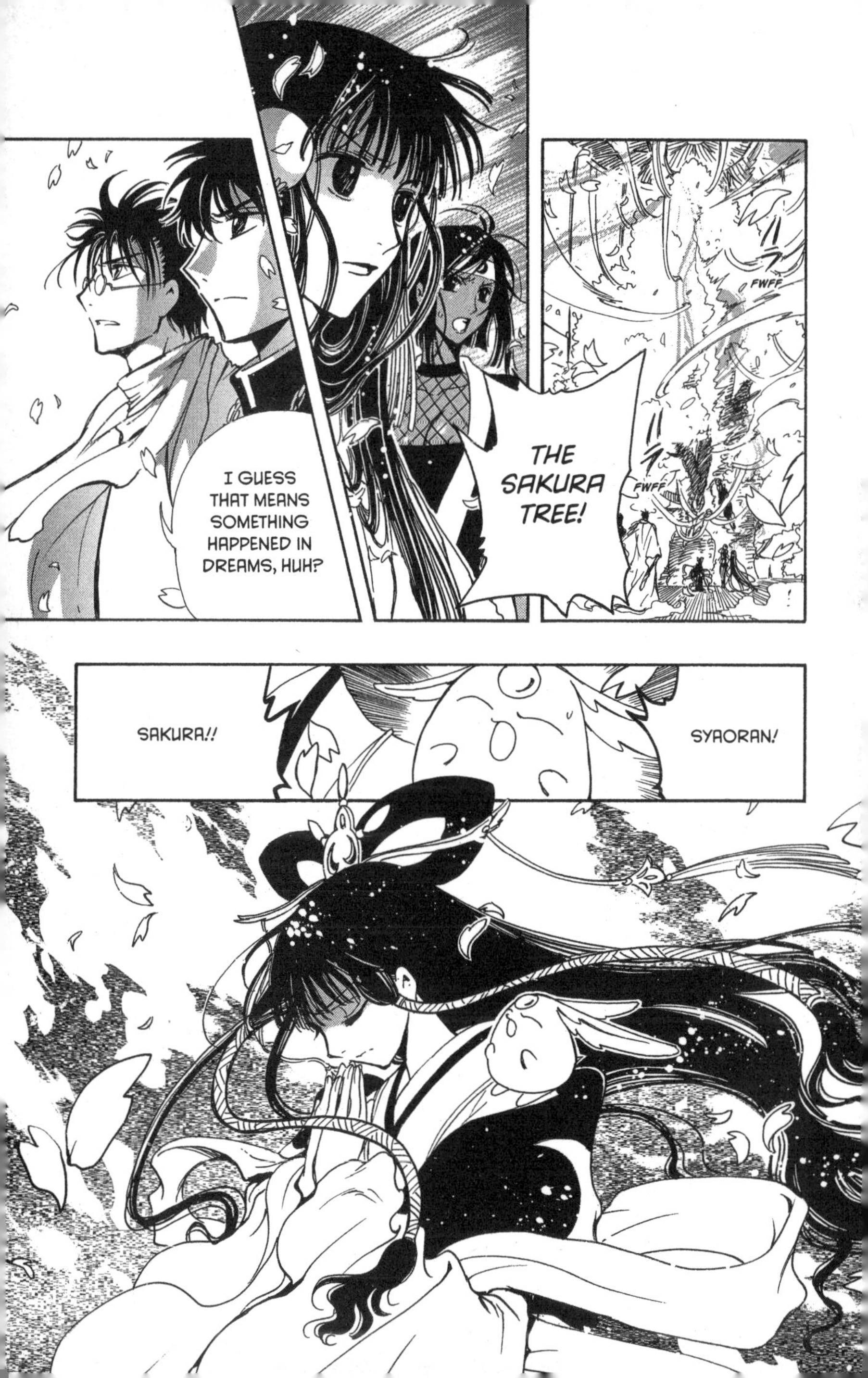
FWFF
THE SAKURA TREE!
FWFF
I GUESS THAT MEANS SOMETHING HAPPENED IN DREAMS, HUH?
SYAORAN!
SAKURA!!

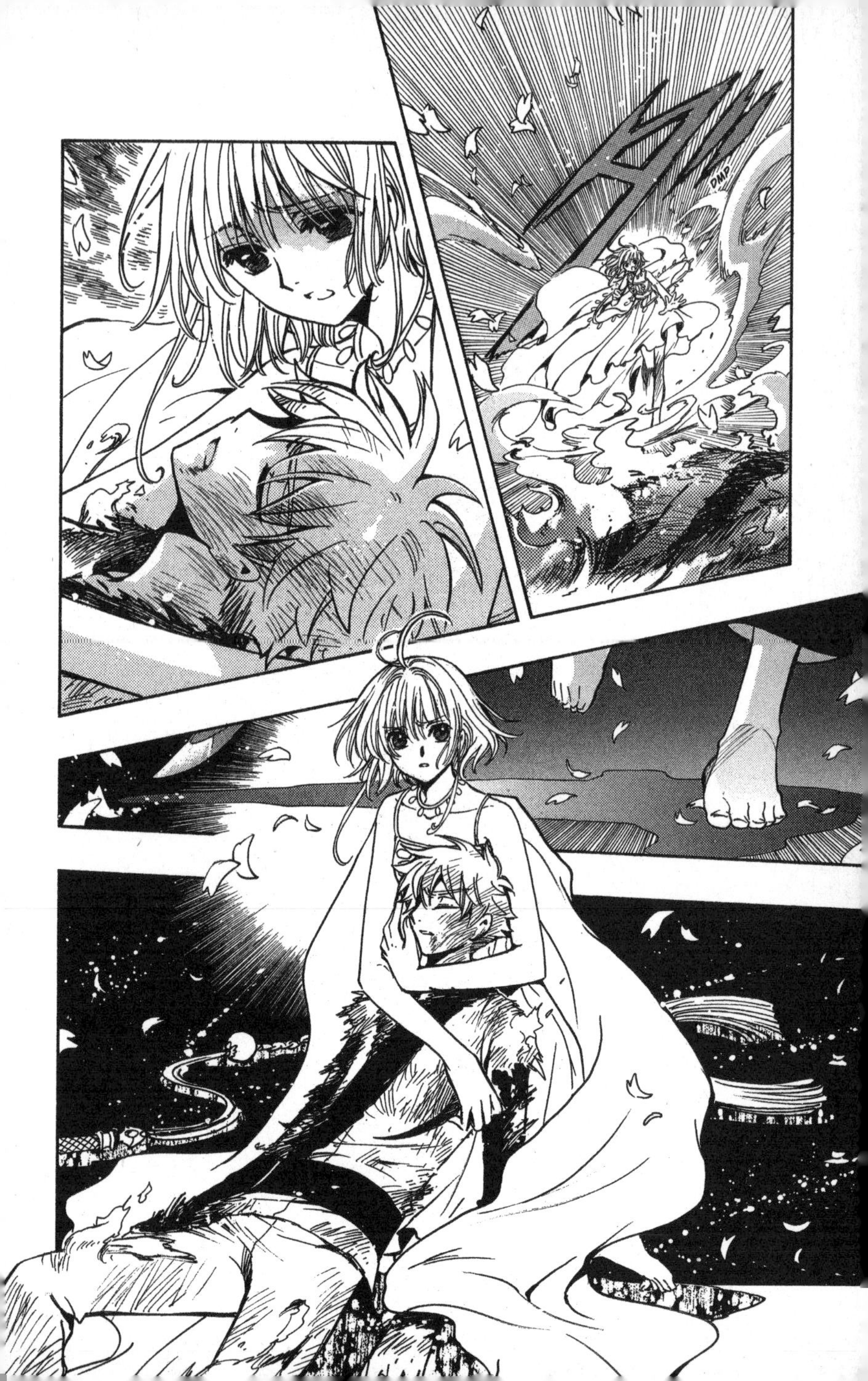
DMP

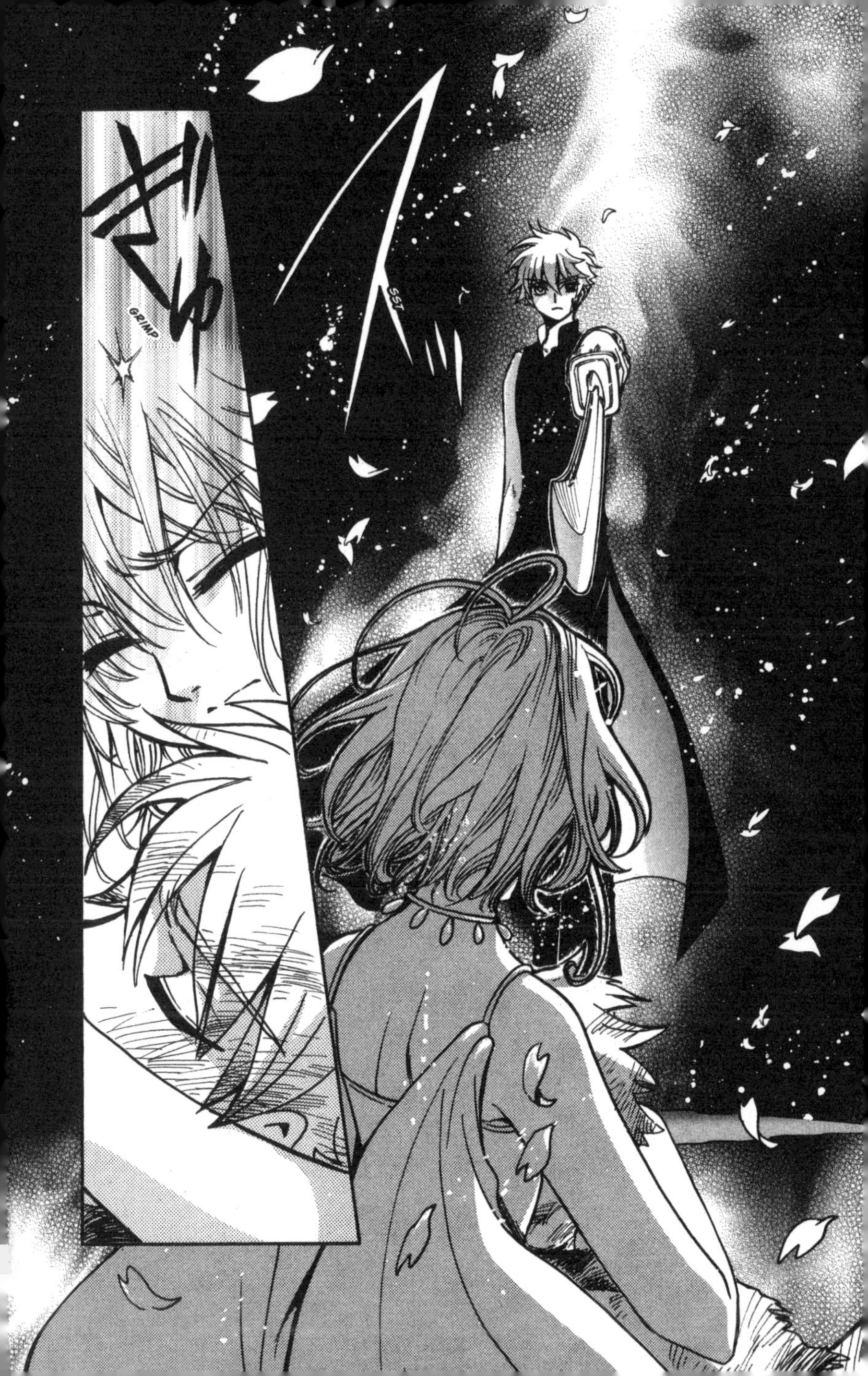
SST
ぎゅ
GRIMP

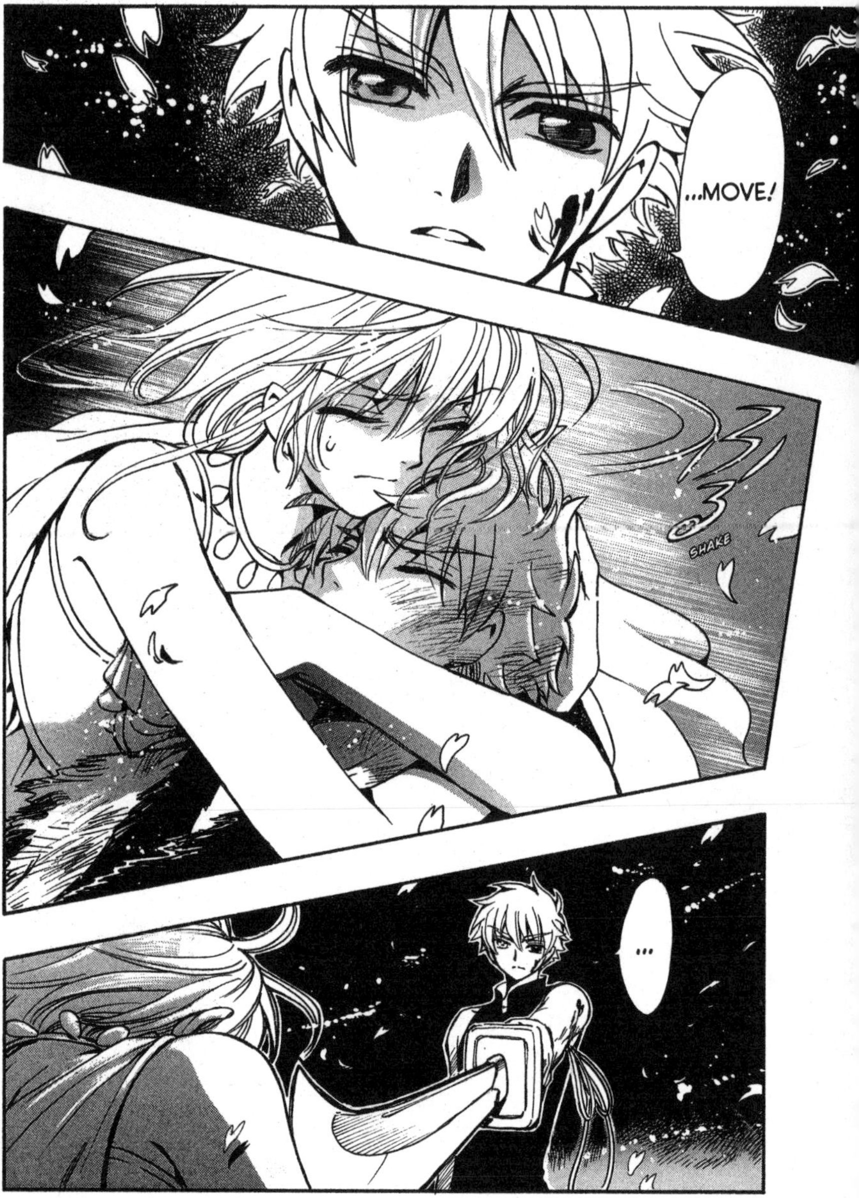
...MOVE!
SHAKE
...

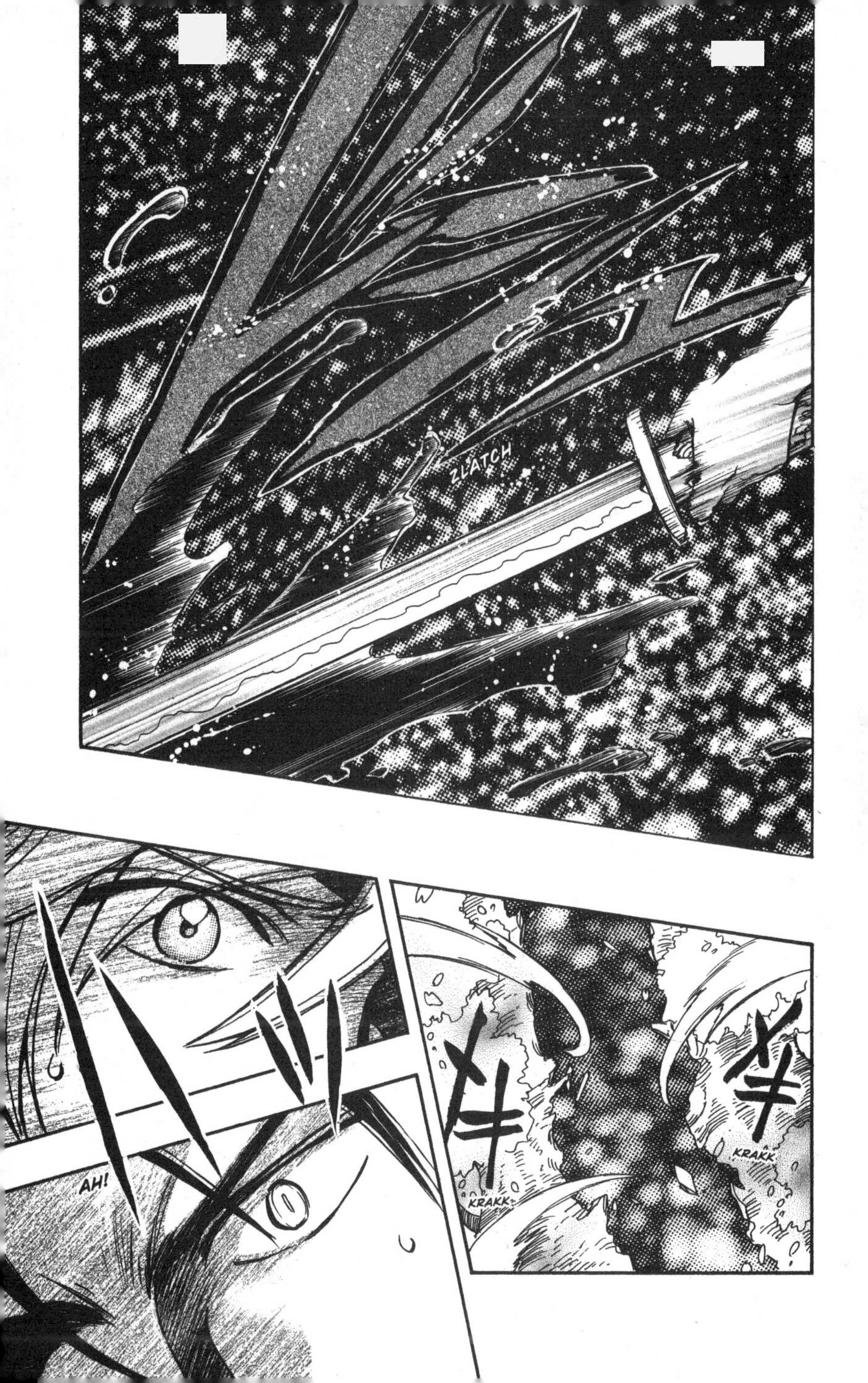
ZLATCH
KRAKK
KRAKK
AH!

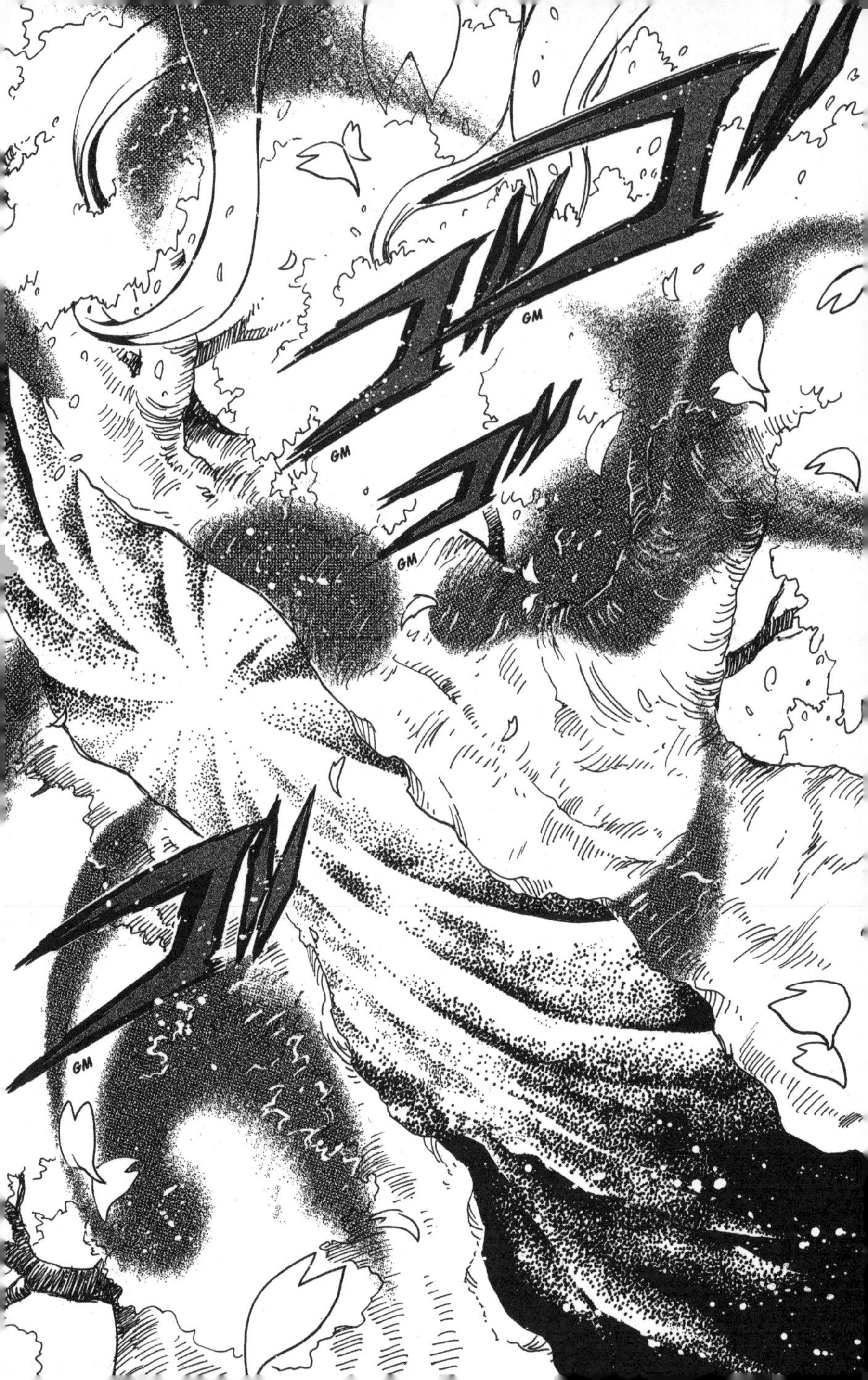
GM
GM
GM
GM

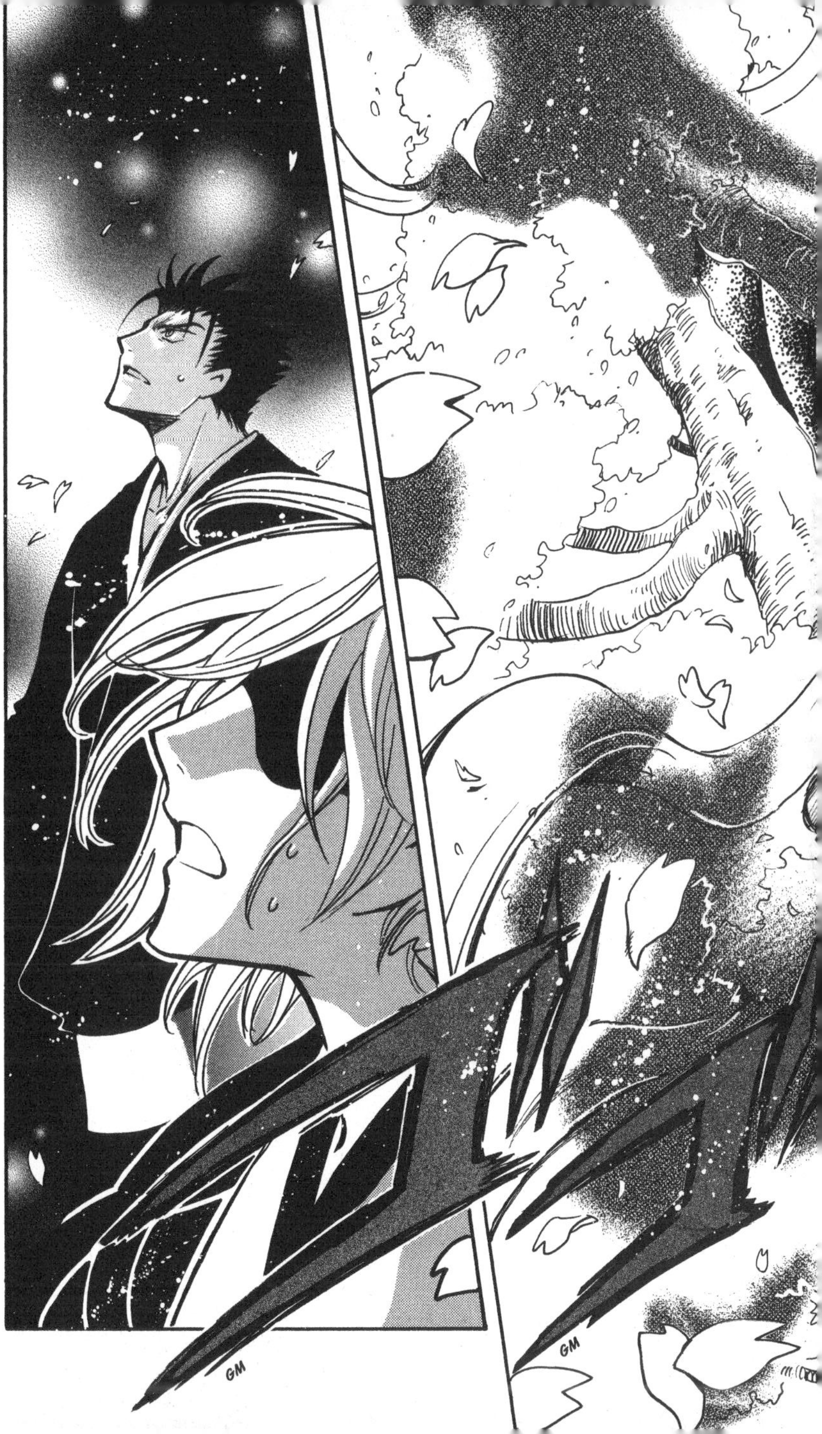
GM
GM

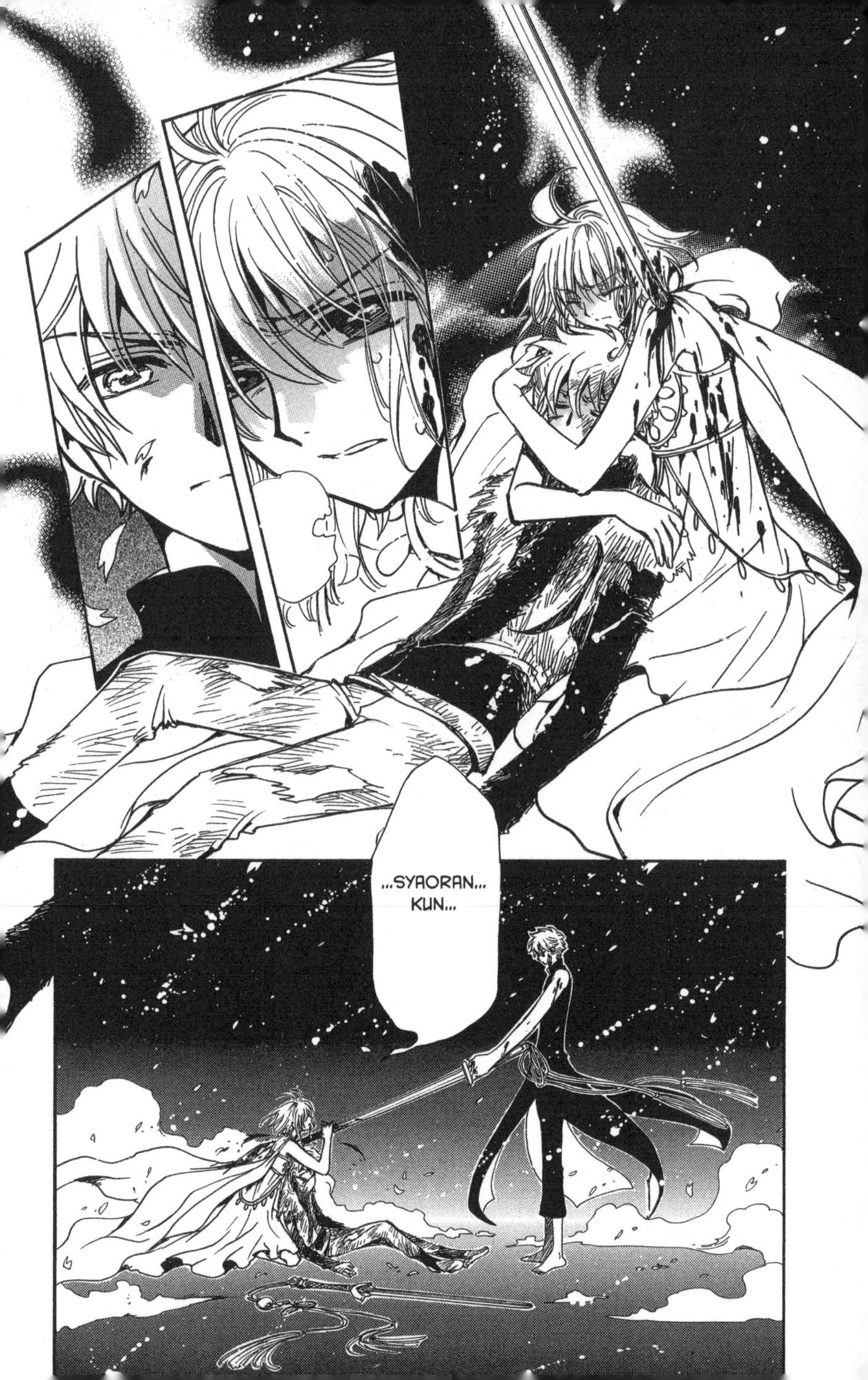
...SYAORAN... KUN...

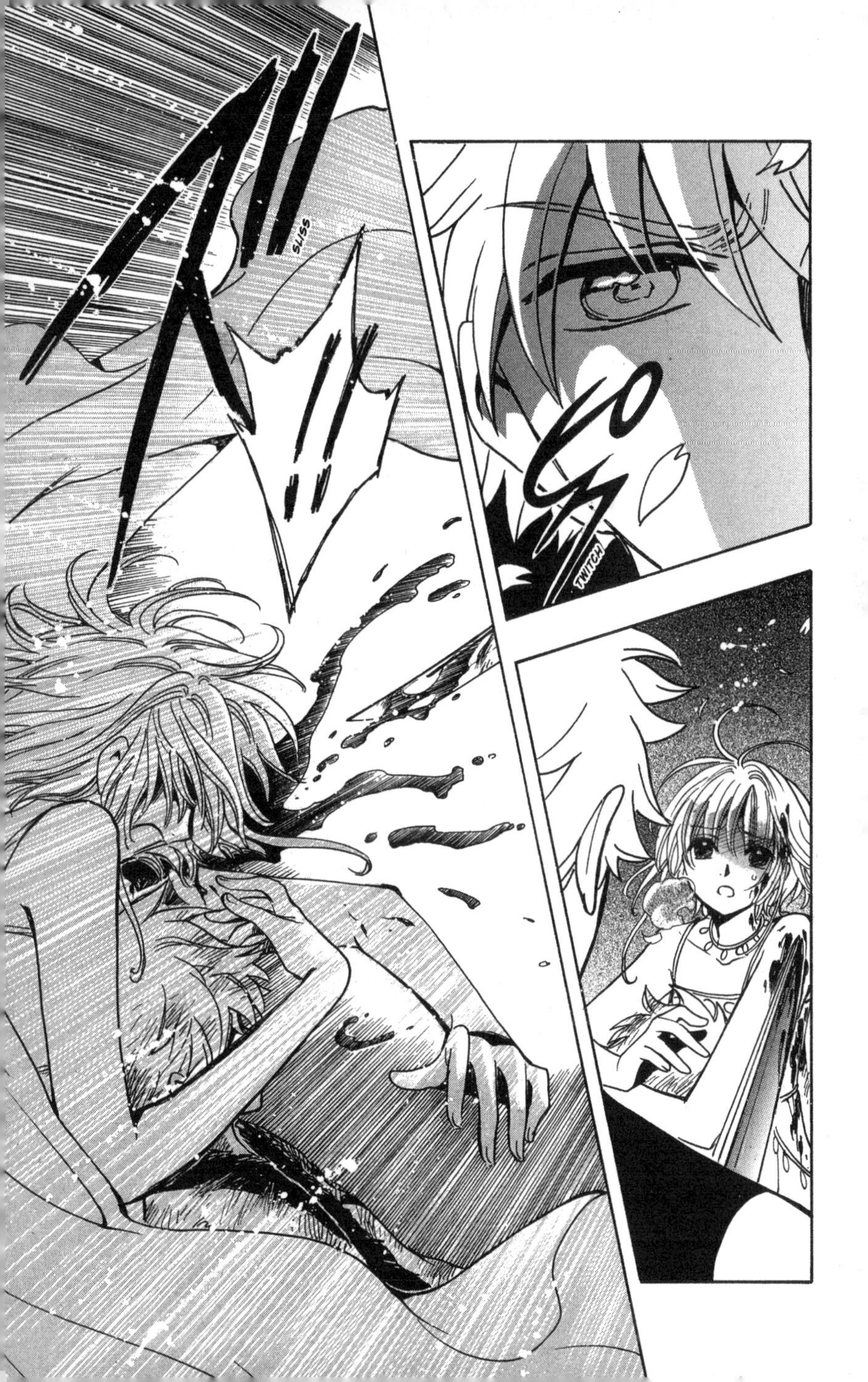
TWITCH
SLISS

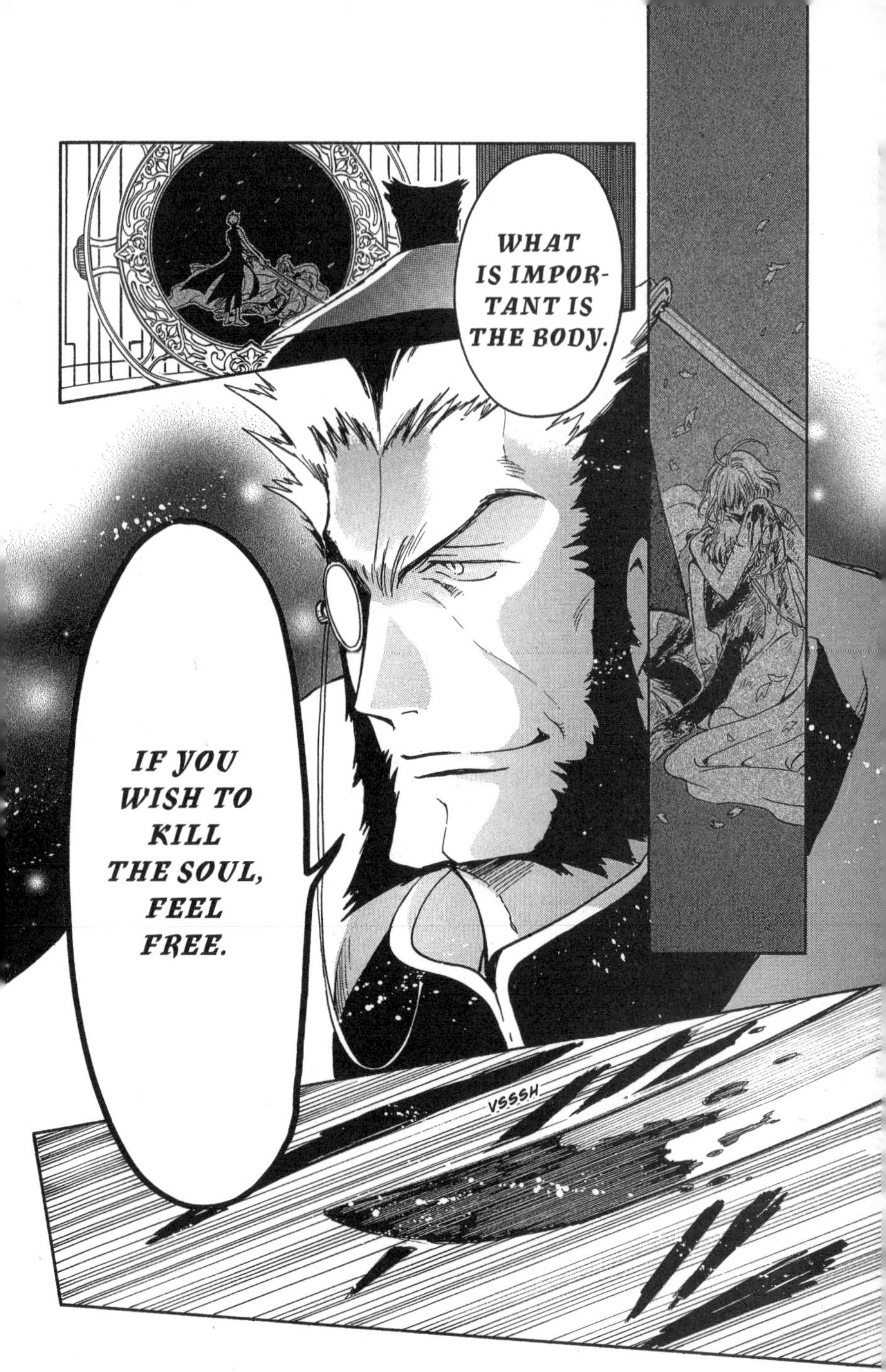
WHAT IS IMPORTANT IS THE BODY.
IF YOU WISH TO KILL THE SOUL, FEEL FREE.
VSSSH

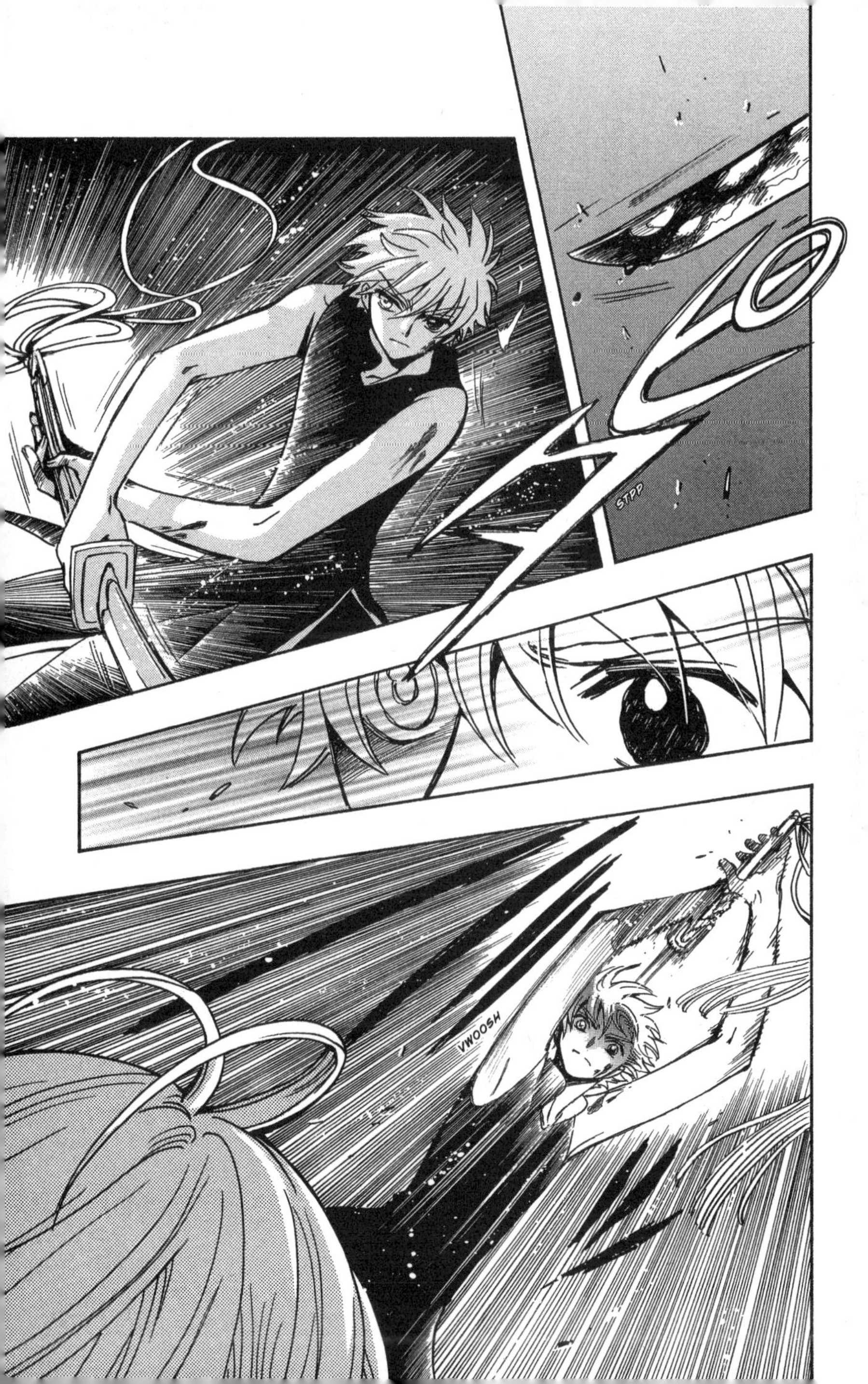
STPP
VWOOSH

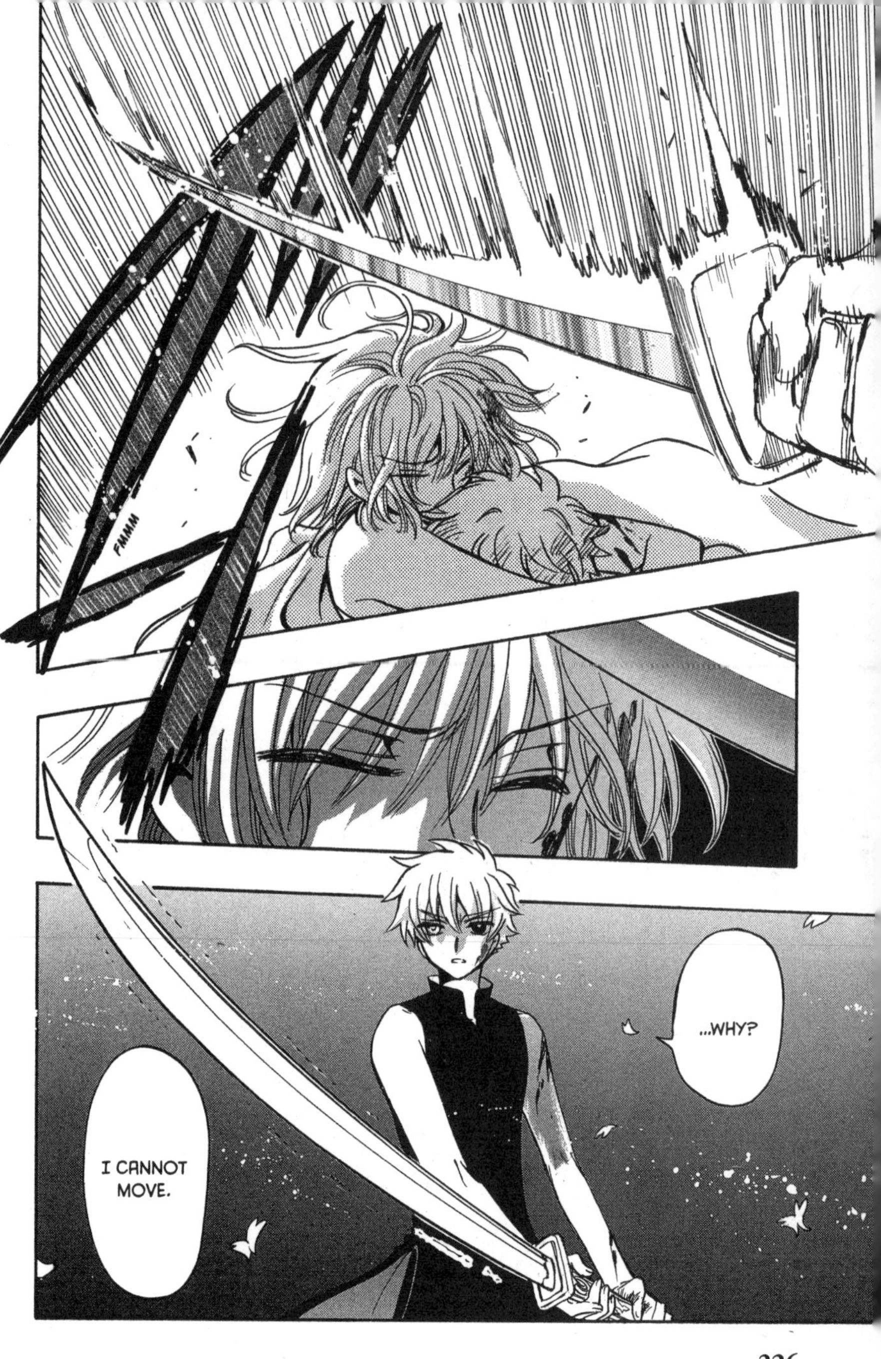
FMMM
...WHY?
I CANNOT MOVE.

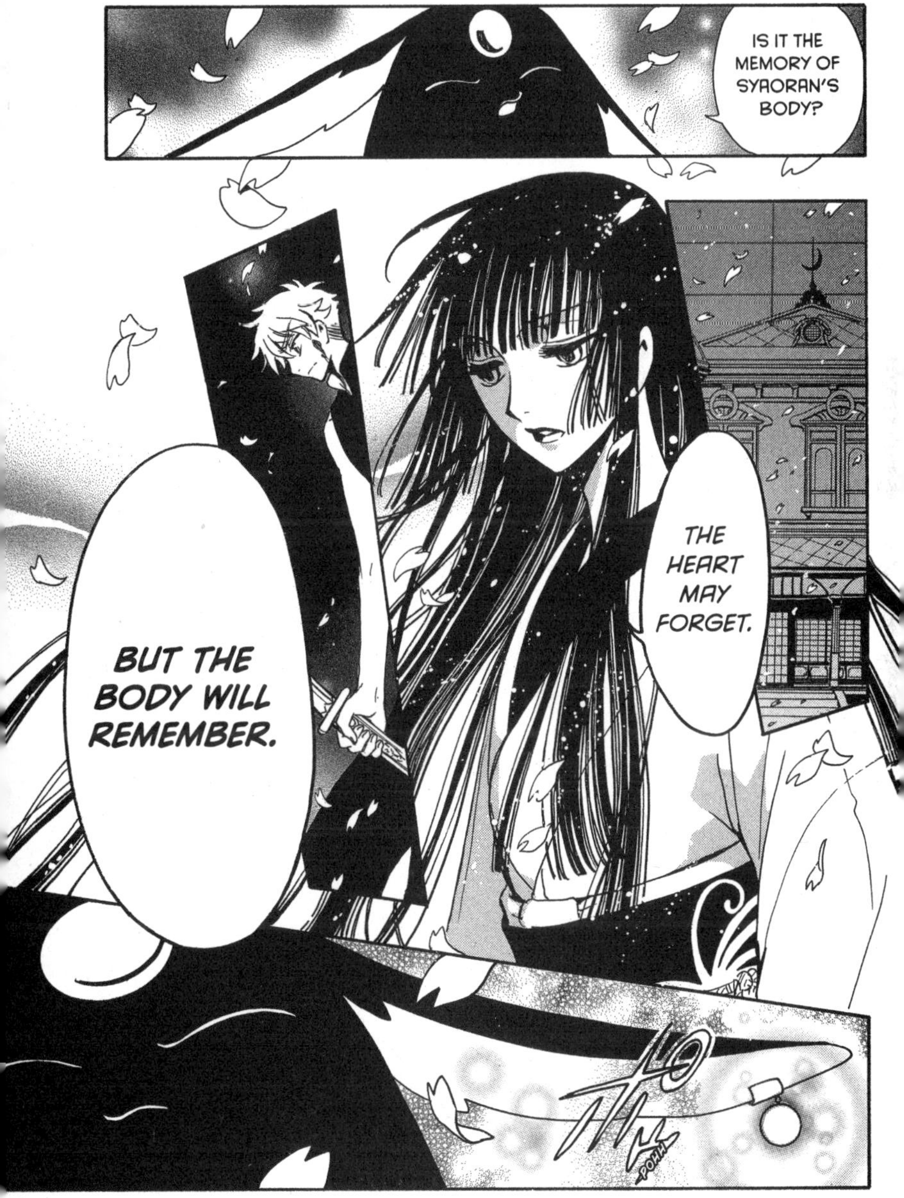
IS IT THE MEMORY OF SYAORAN'S BODY?
THE HEART MAY FORGET.
BUT THE BODY WILL REMEMBER.

ツバサ

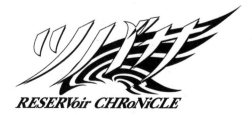

RESERVoir CHRoNiCLE

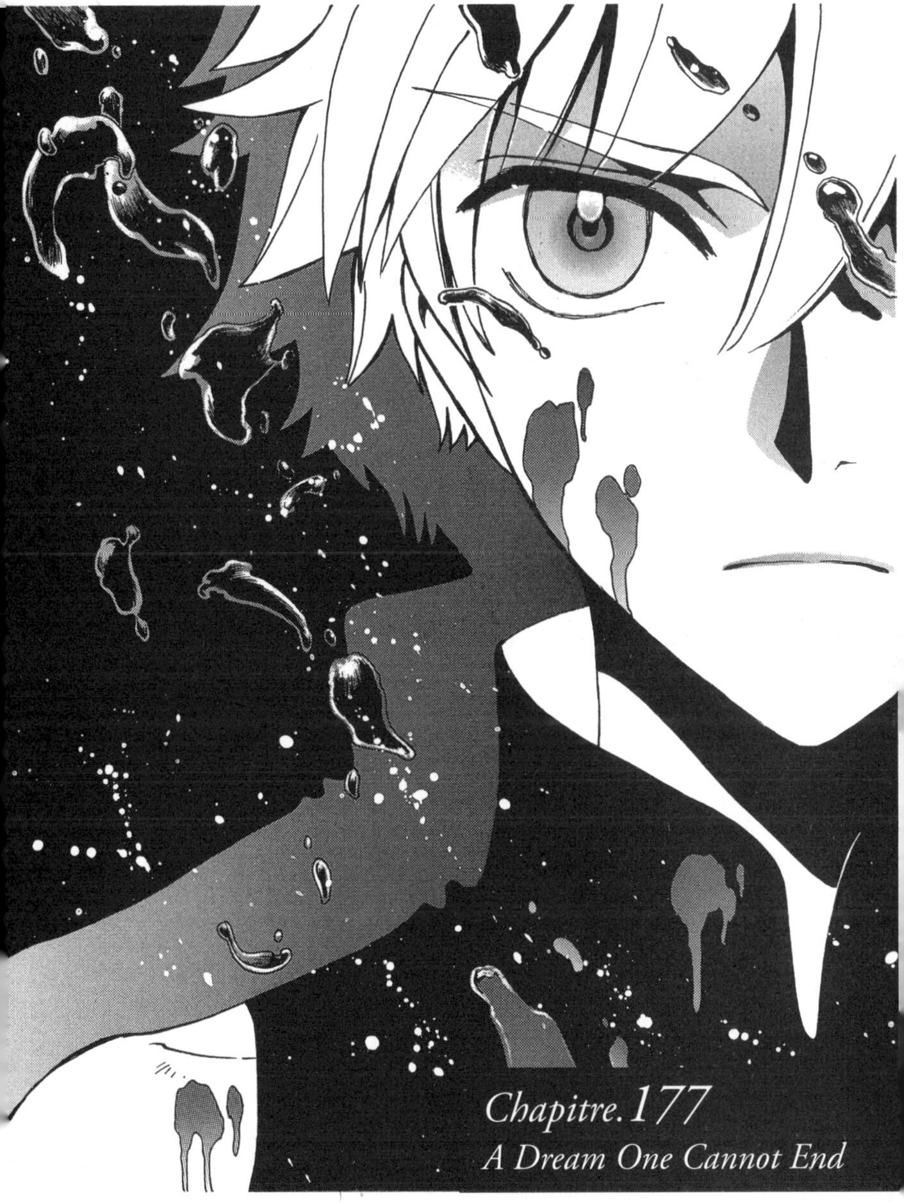
Chapitre. 177
A Dream One Cannot End

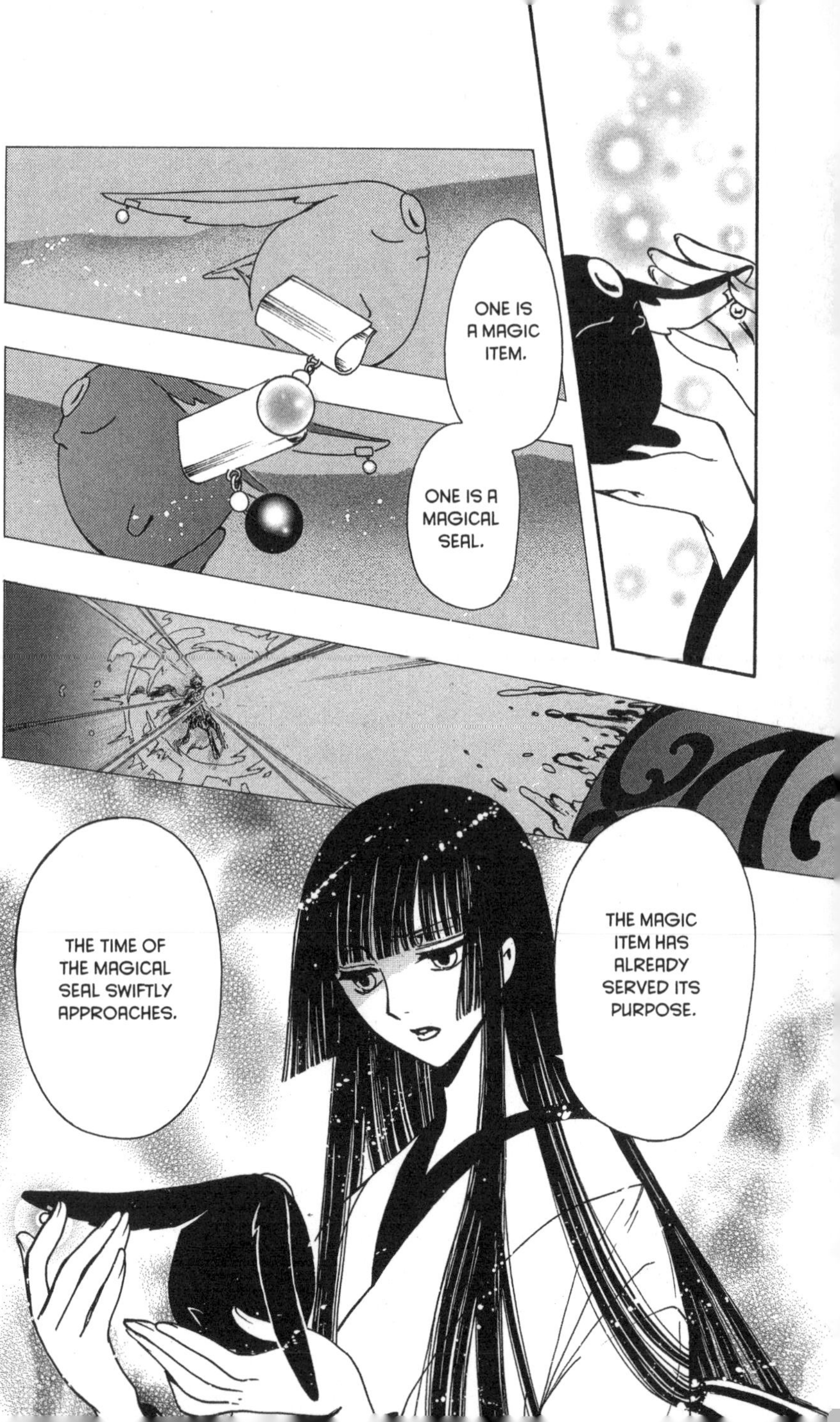
ONE IS A MAGIC ITEM.
ONE IS A MAGICAL SEAL.
THE MAGIC ITEM HAS ALREADY SERVED ITS PURPOSE.
THE TIME OF THE MAGICAL SEAL SWIFTLY APPROACHES.

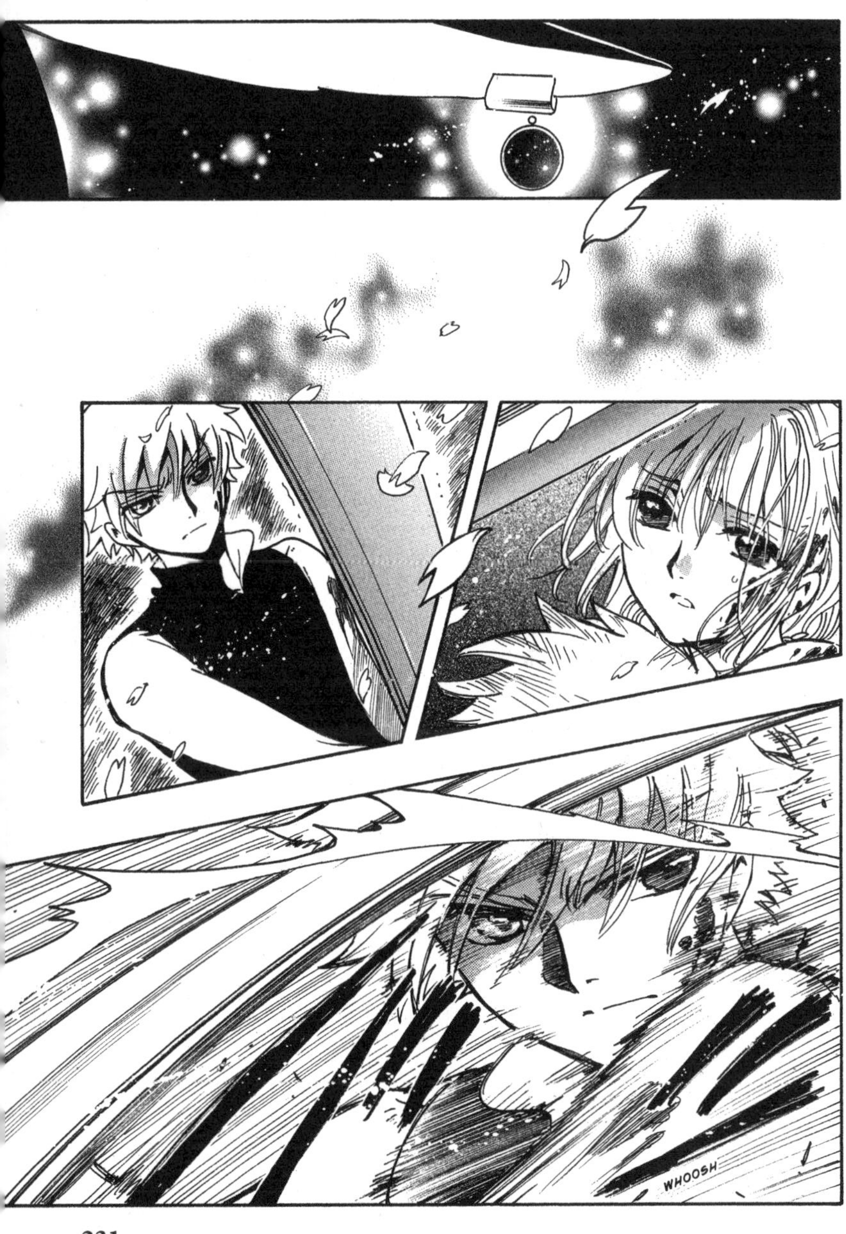
WHOOSH

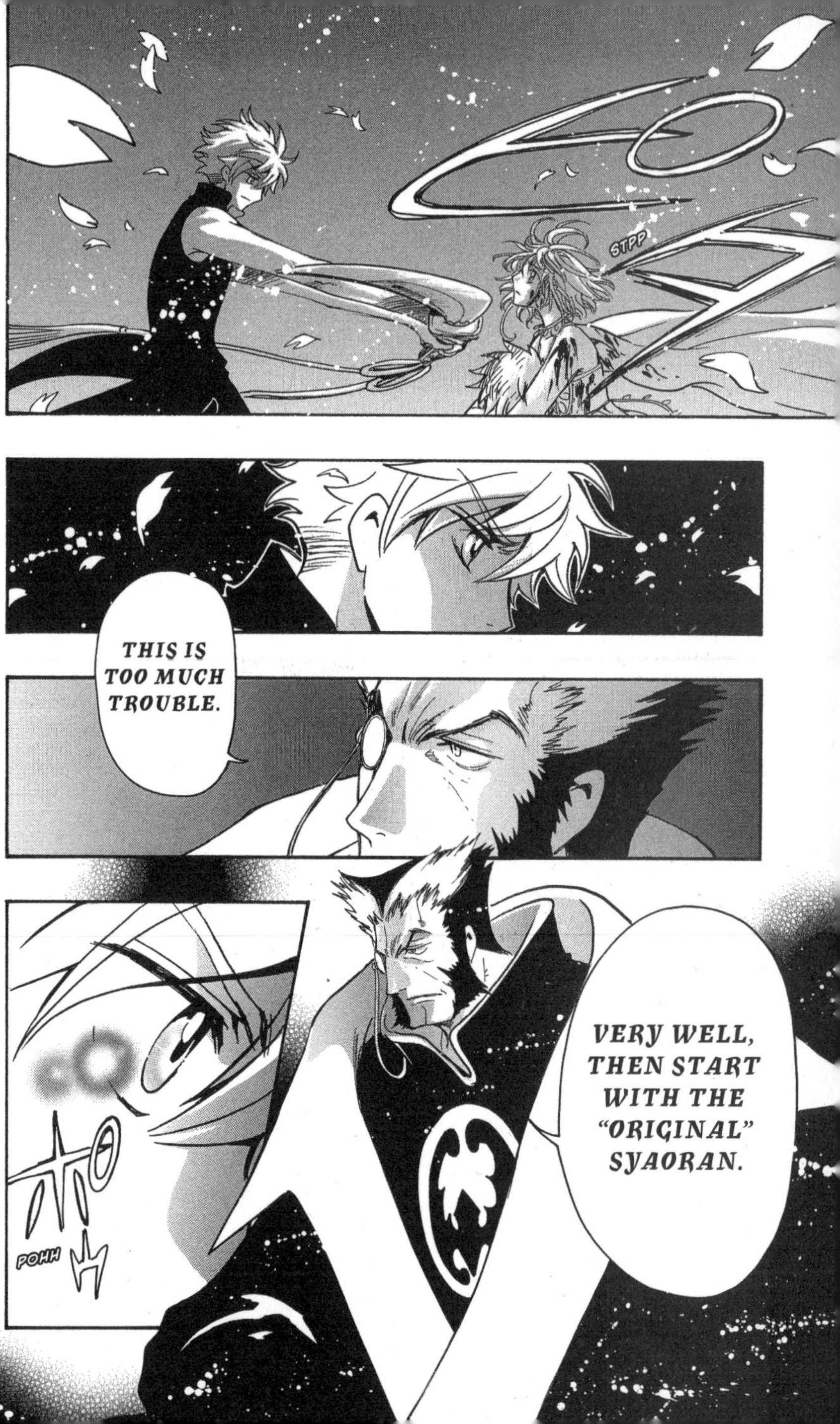
STPP
THIS IS TOO MUCH TROUBLE.
VERY WELL, THEN START WITH THE "ORIGINAL" SYAORAN.
POHH

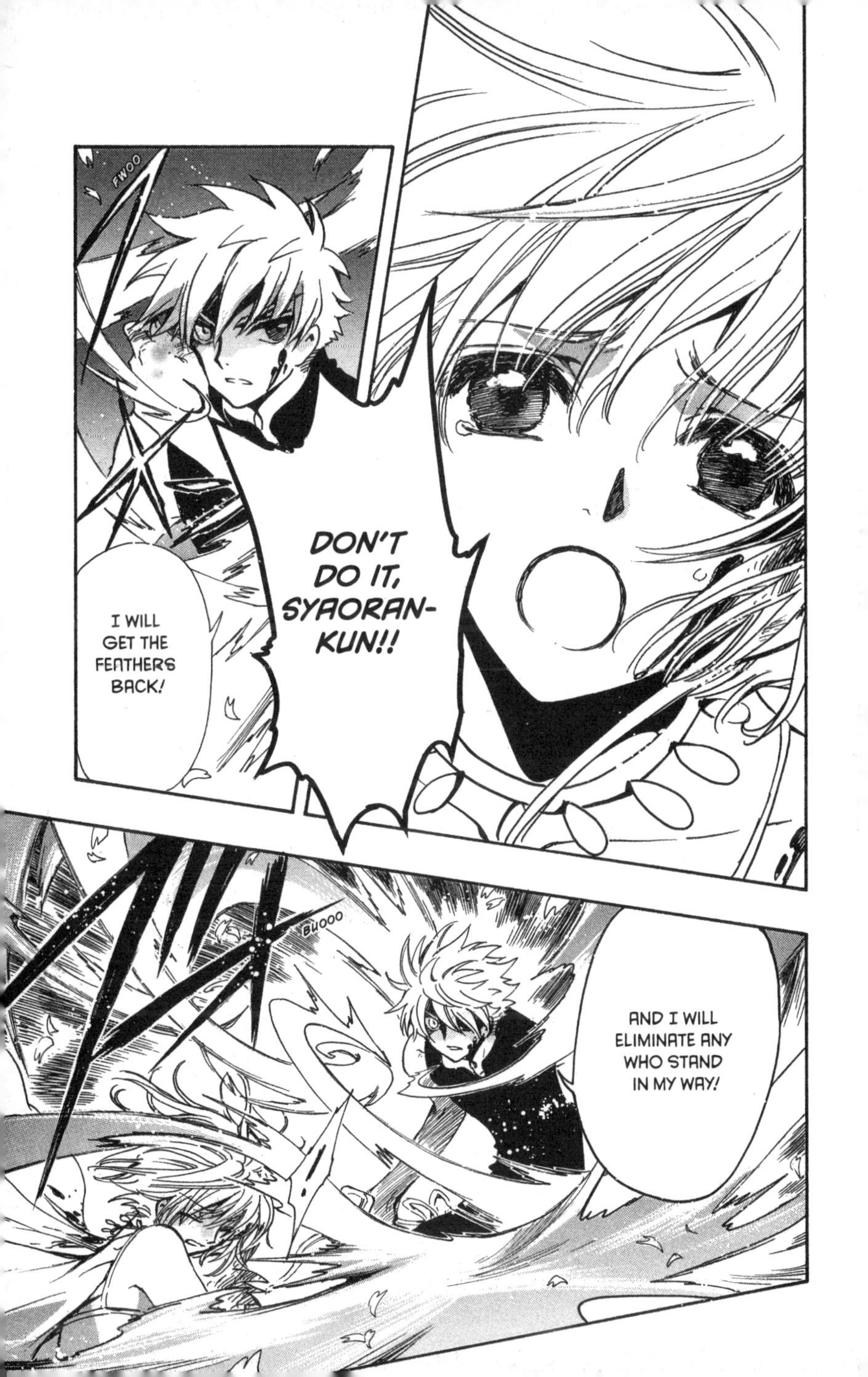
DON'T DO IT, SYAORAN-KUN!!
FWOO
I WILL GET THE FEATHERS BACK!
BUOOO
AND I WILL ELIMINATE ANY WHO STAND IN MY WAY!

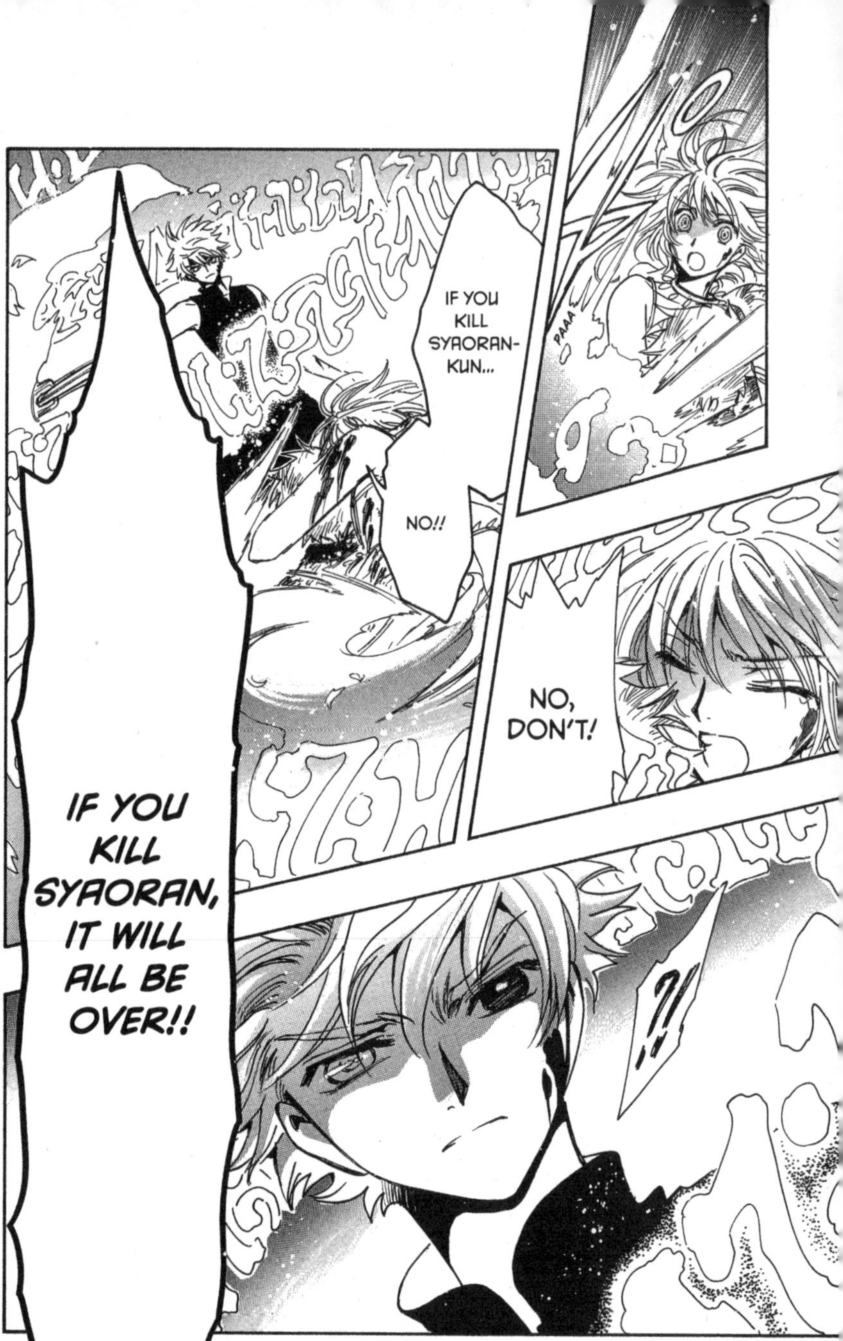
PAAA
IF YOU KILL SYAORAN-KUN...
NO!!
NO, DON'T!
IF YOU KILL SYAORAN, IT WILL ALL BE OVER!!

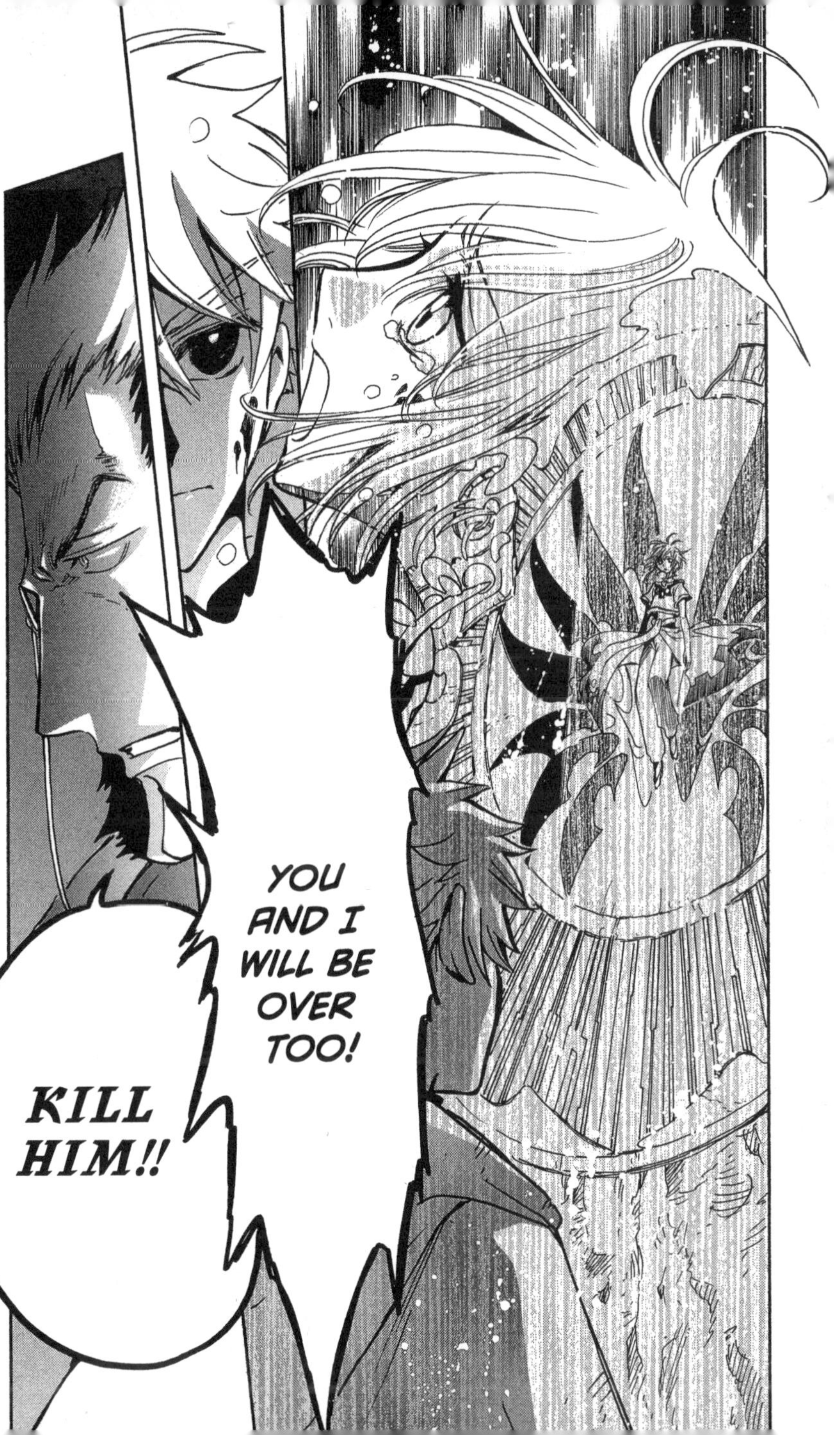
YOU AND I WILL BE OVER TOO!
KILL HIM!!

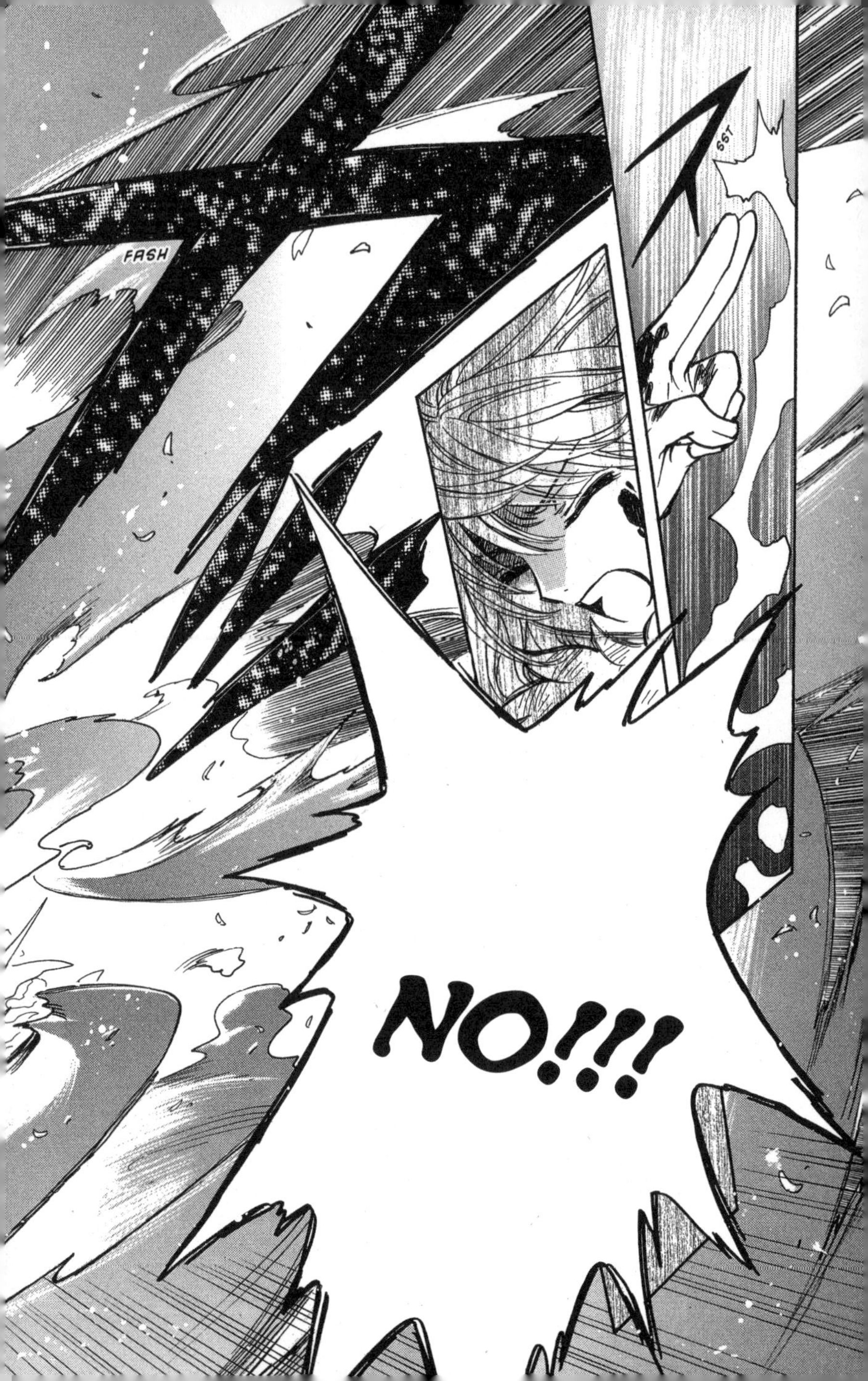
SST
FASH
NO!!!

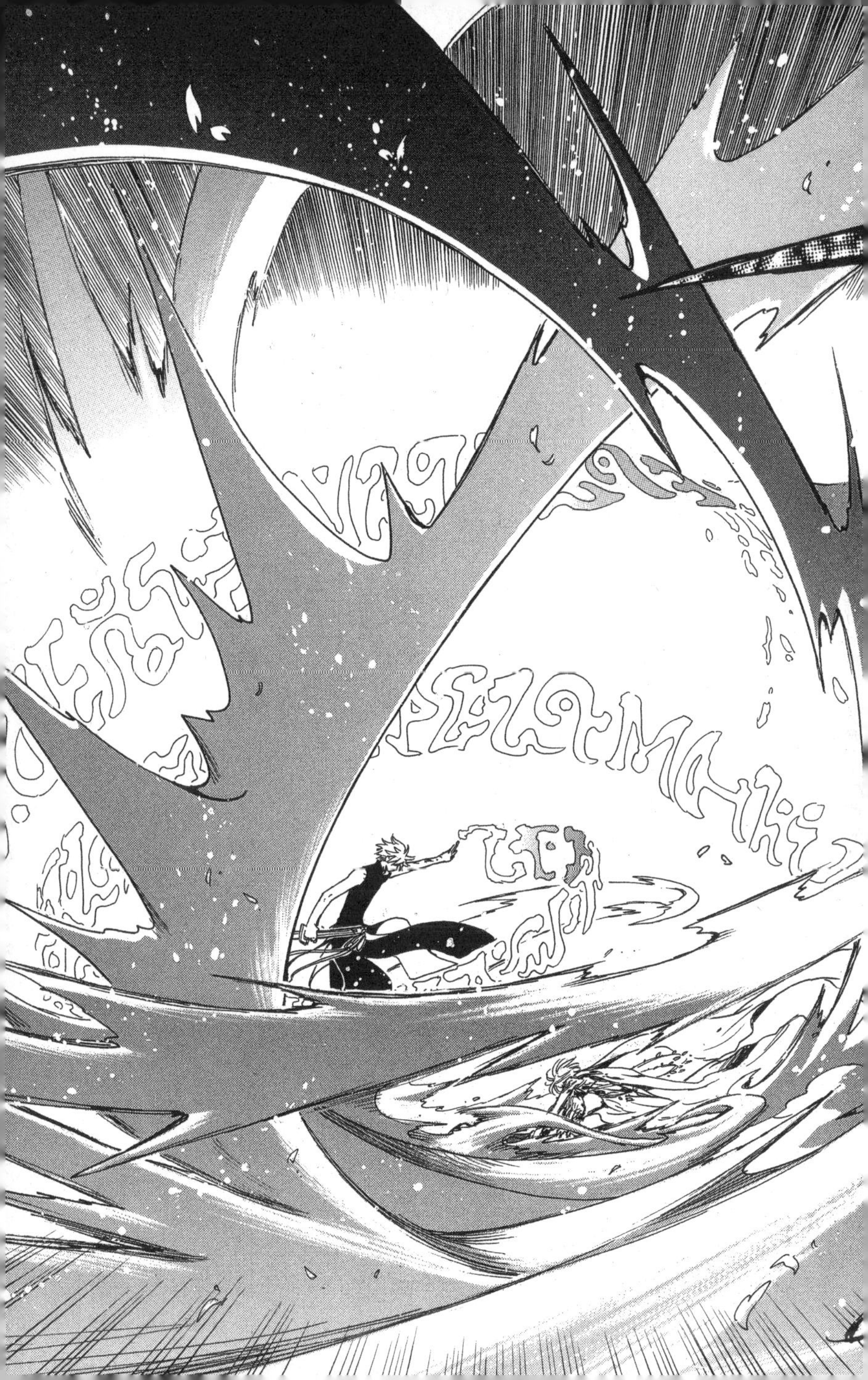

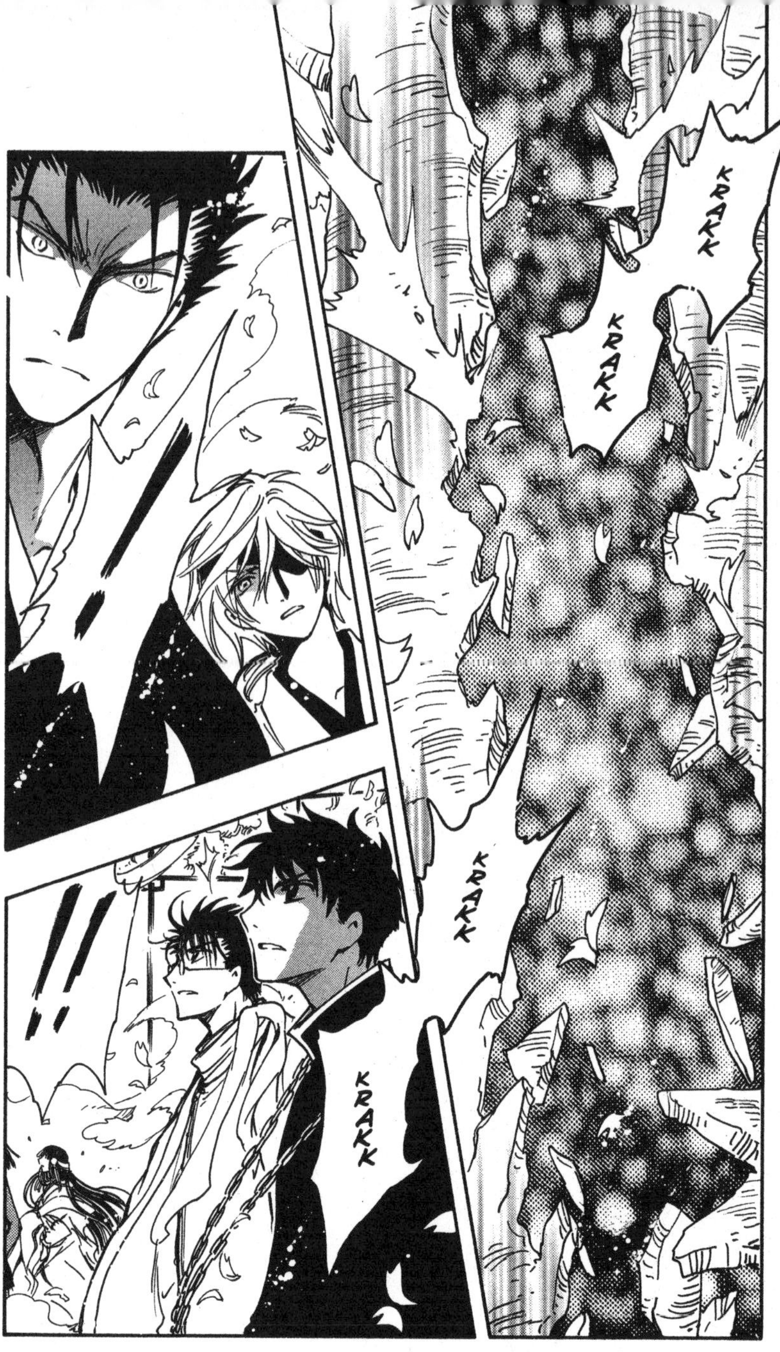
KRAKK
KRAKK
KRAKK
KRAKK
!!

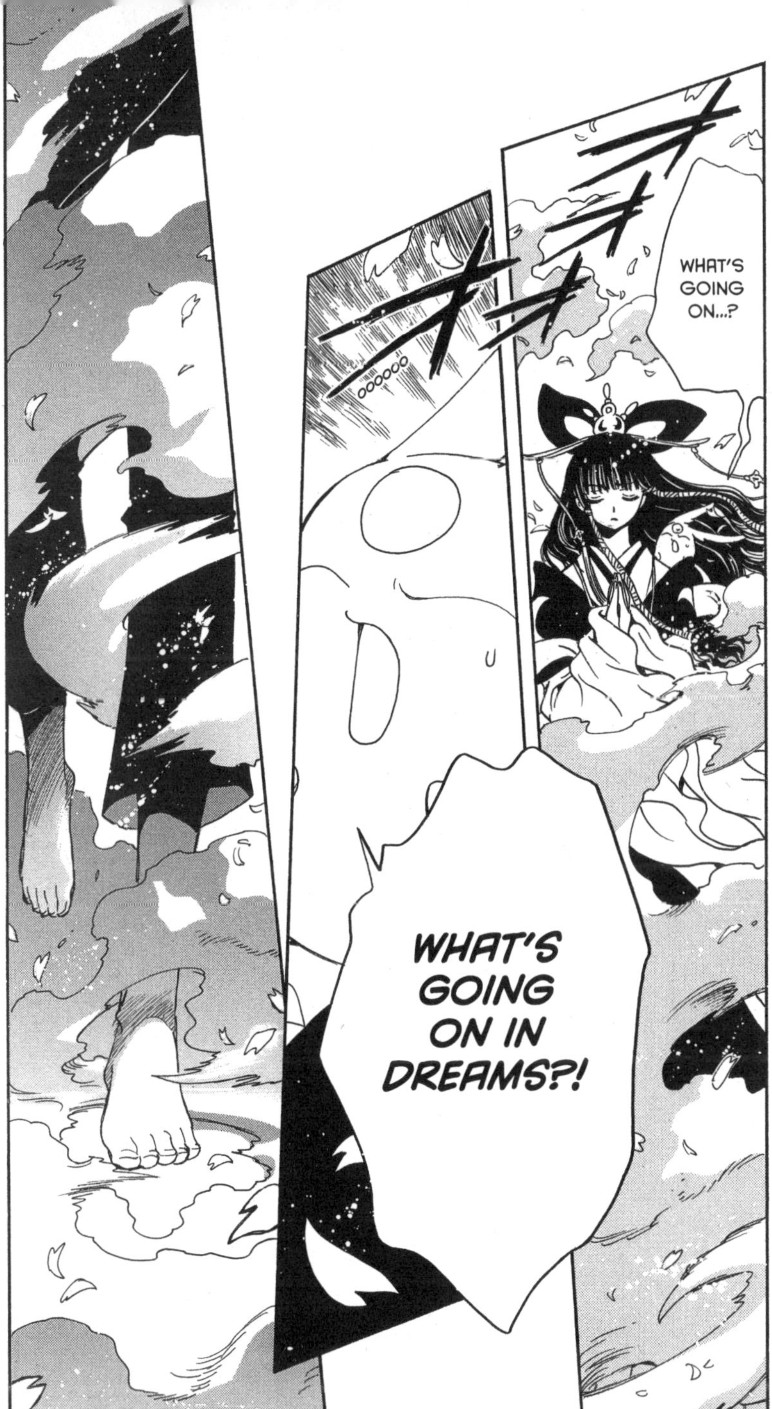
WHAT'S GOING ON...?
OOOOOO
WHAT'S GOING ON IN DREAMS?!

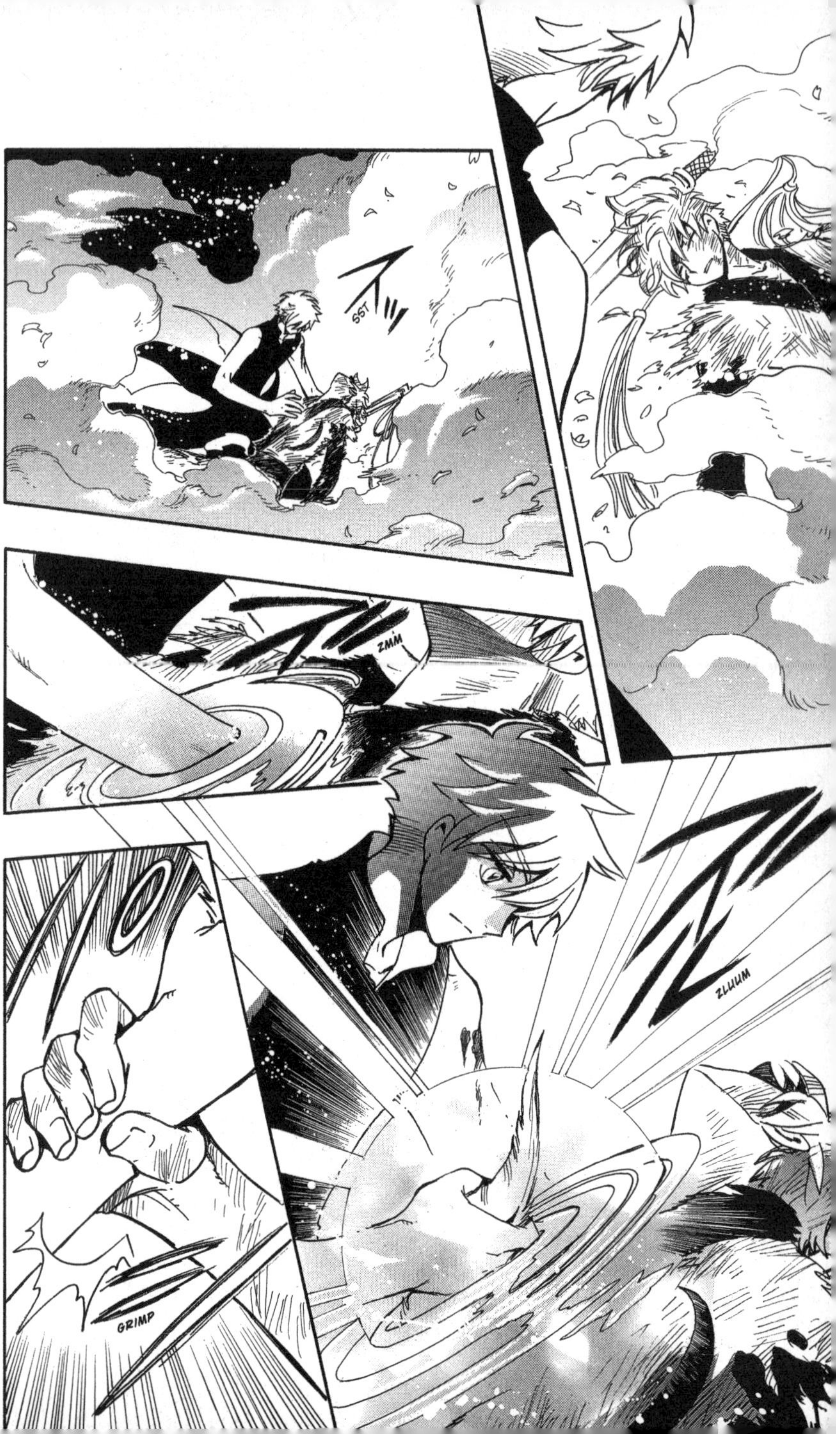
SST
ZMM
ZLUUM
GRIMP

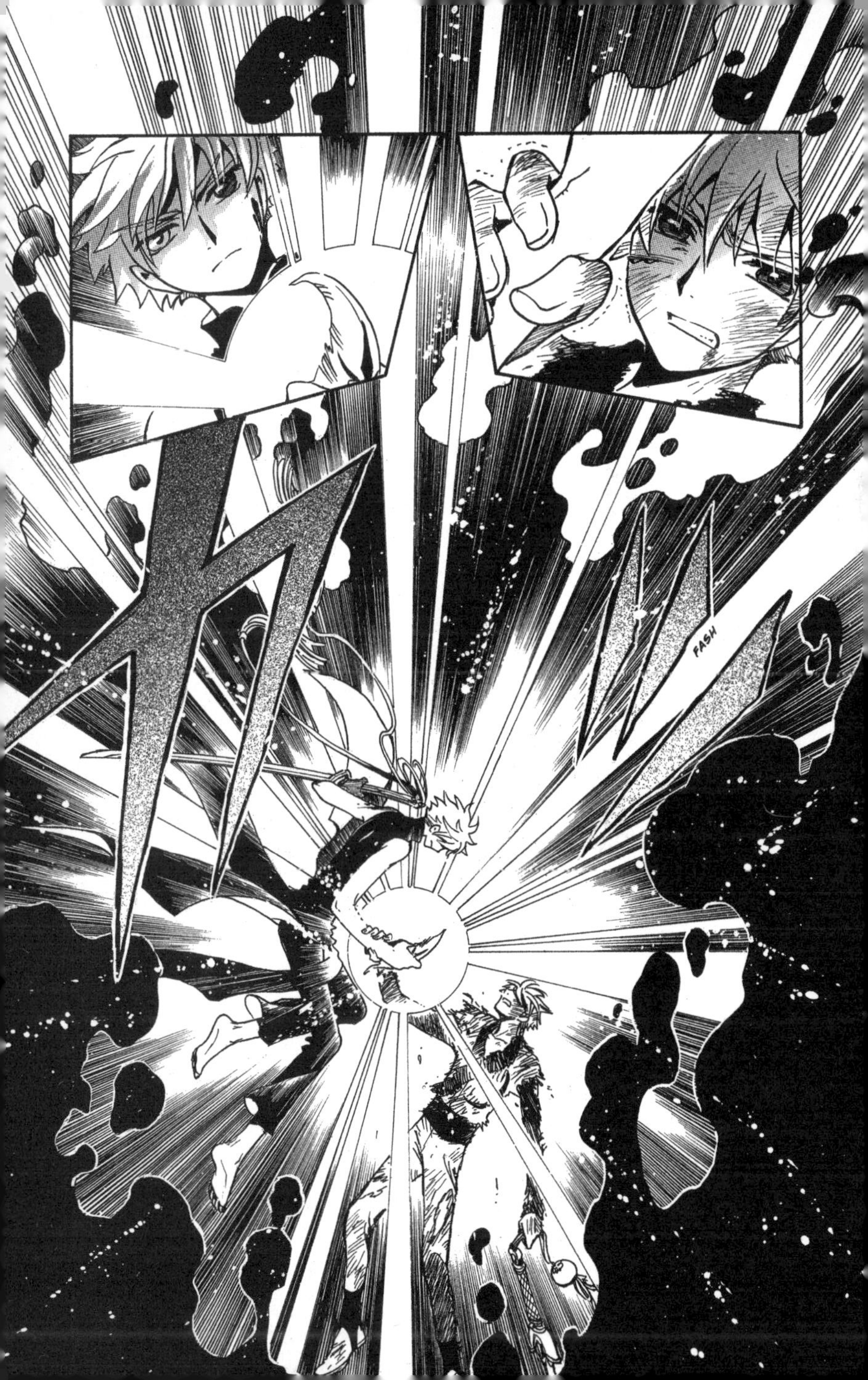
FASH

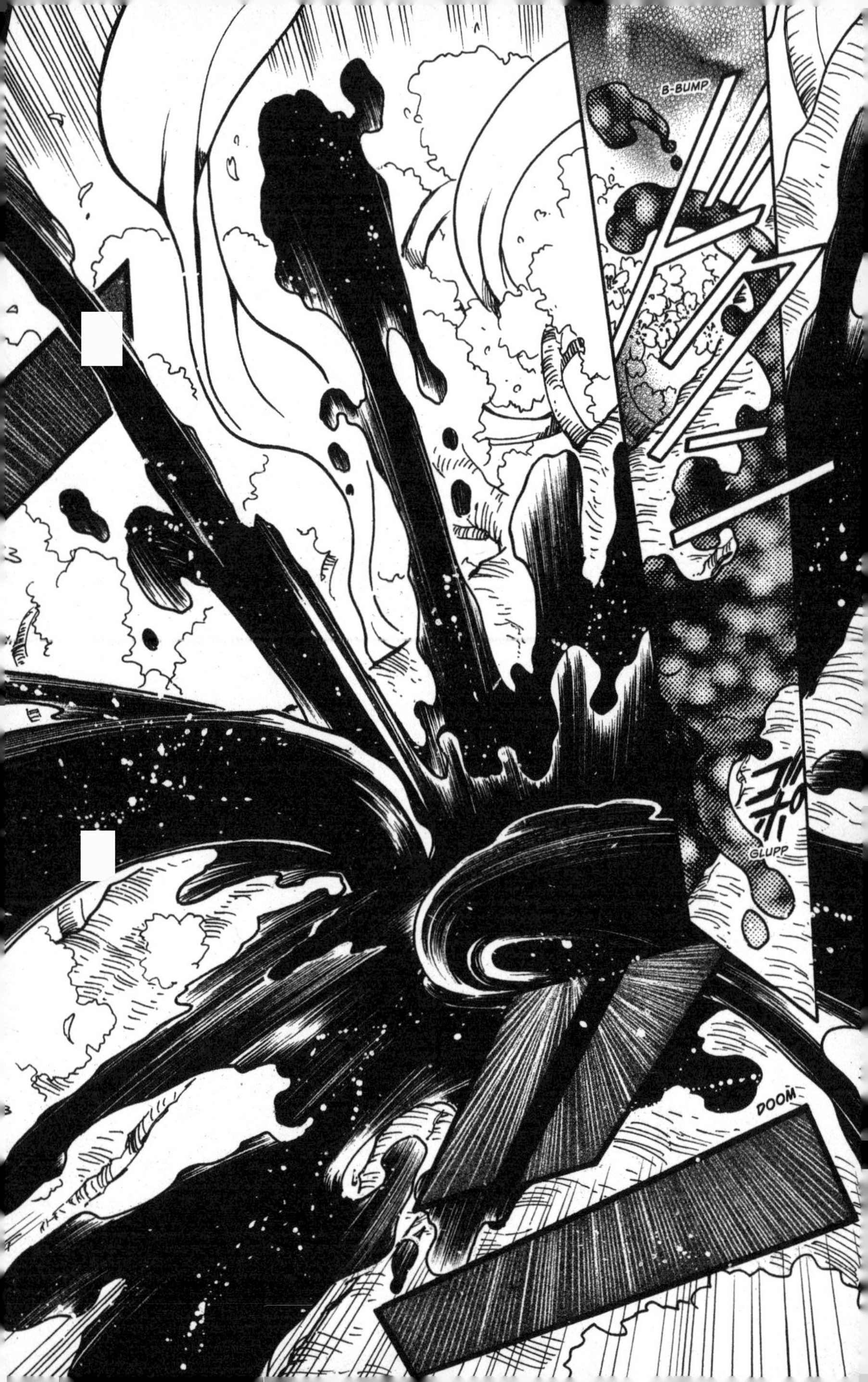
B-BUMP
GLUPP
DOOM

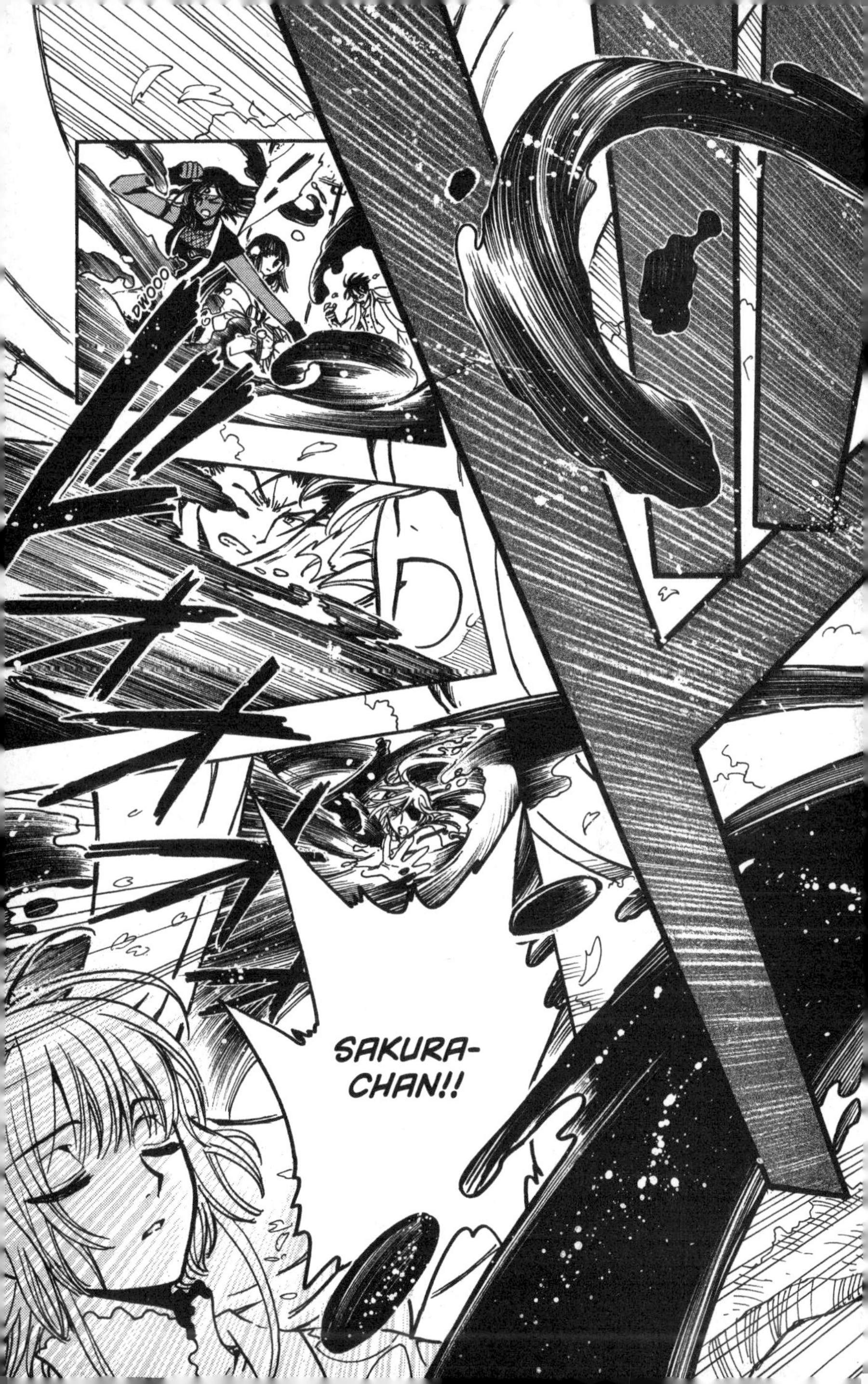
DWOOO
SAKURA-
CHAN!!

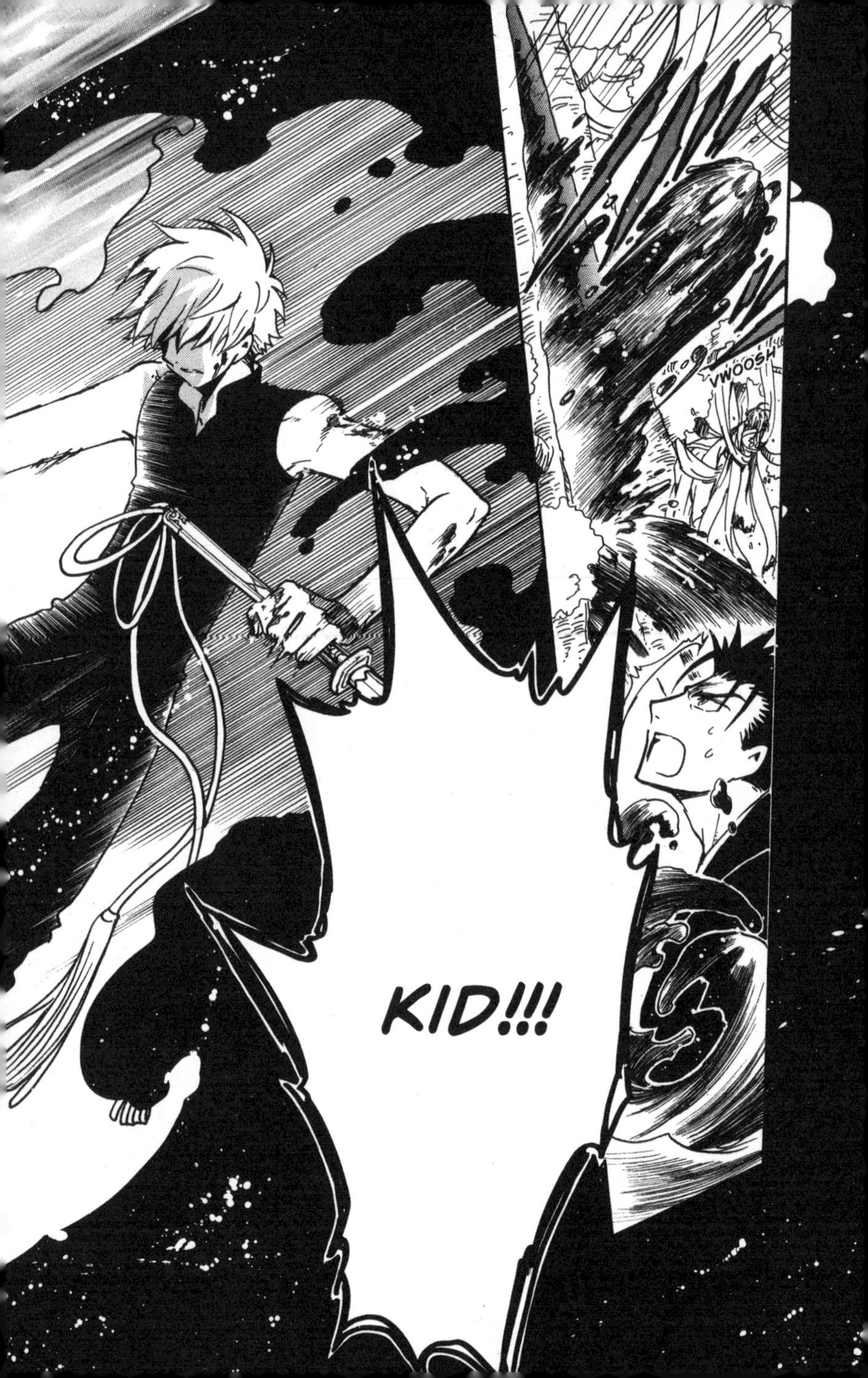
VWOOSH
KID!!!

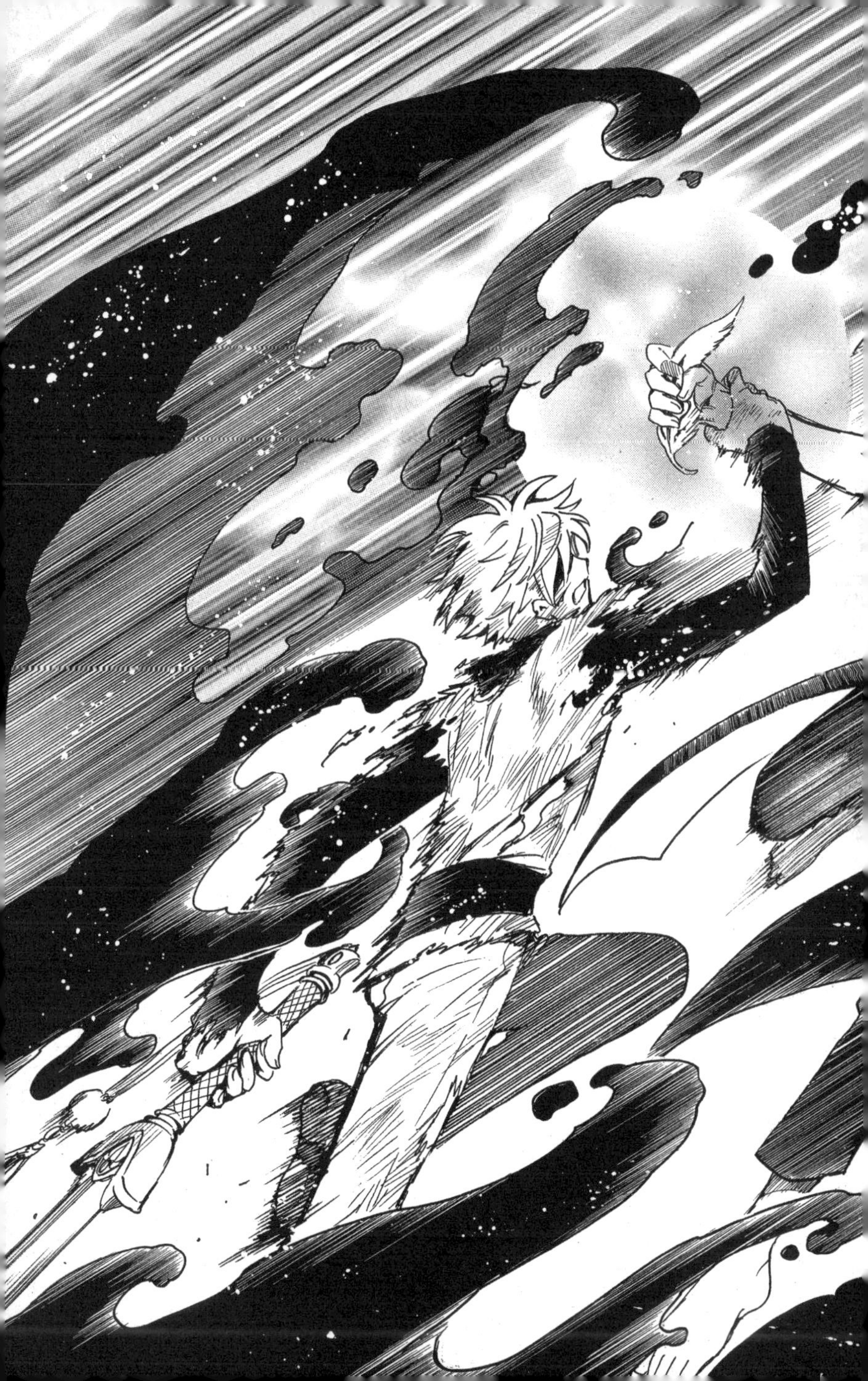

ツバサ

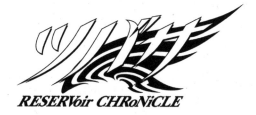

RESERVoir CHRoNiCLE

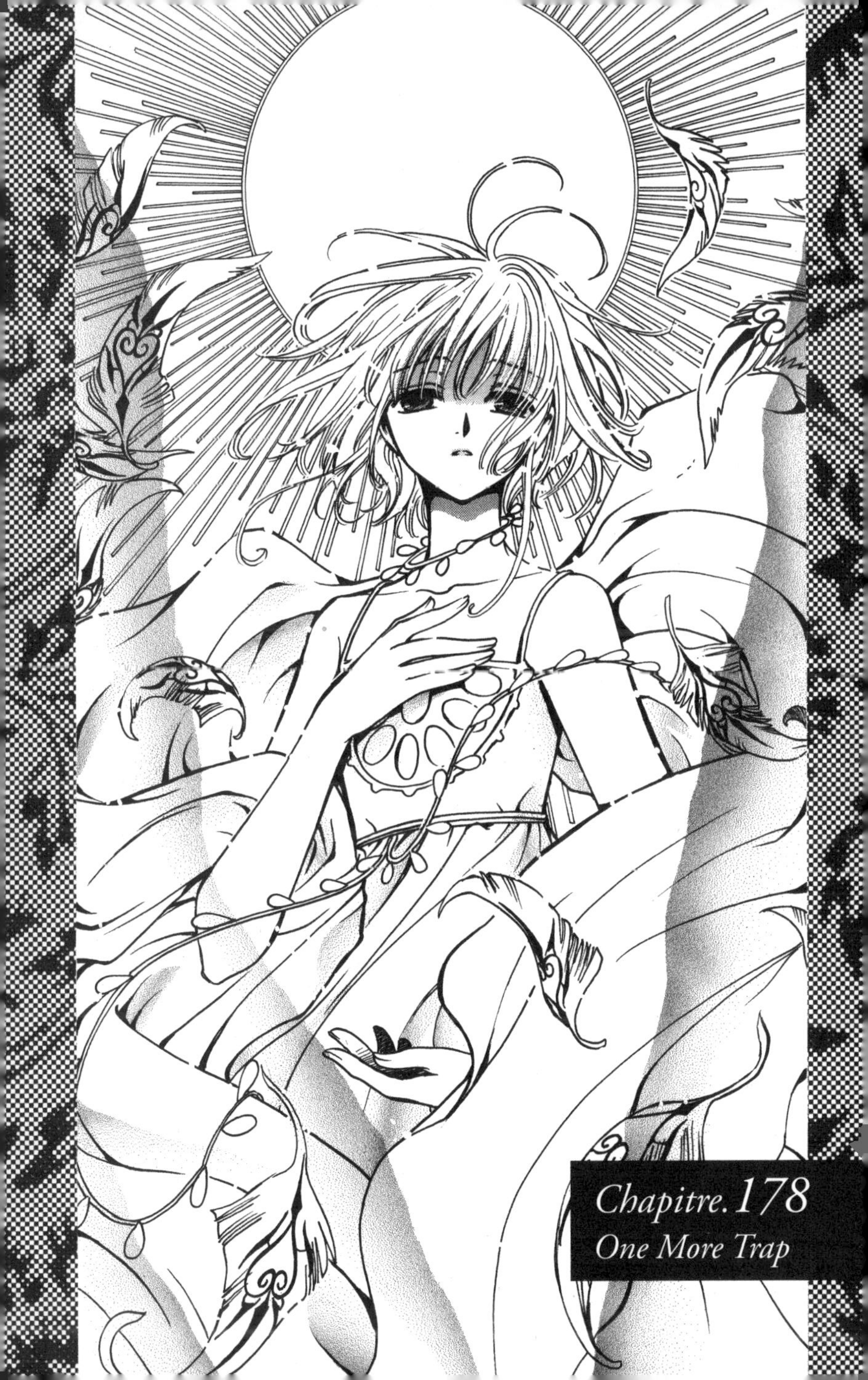
Chapitre.178
One More Trap

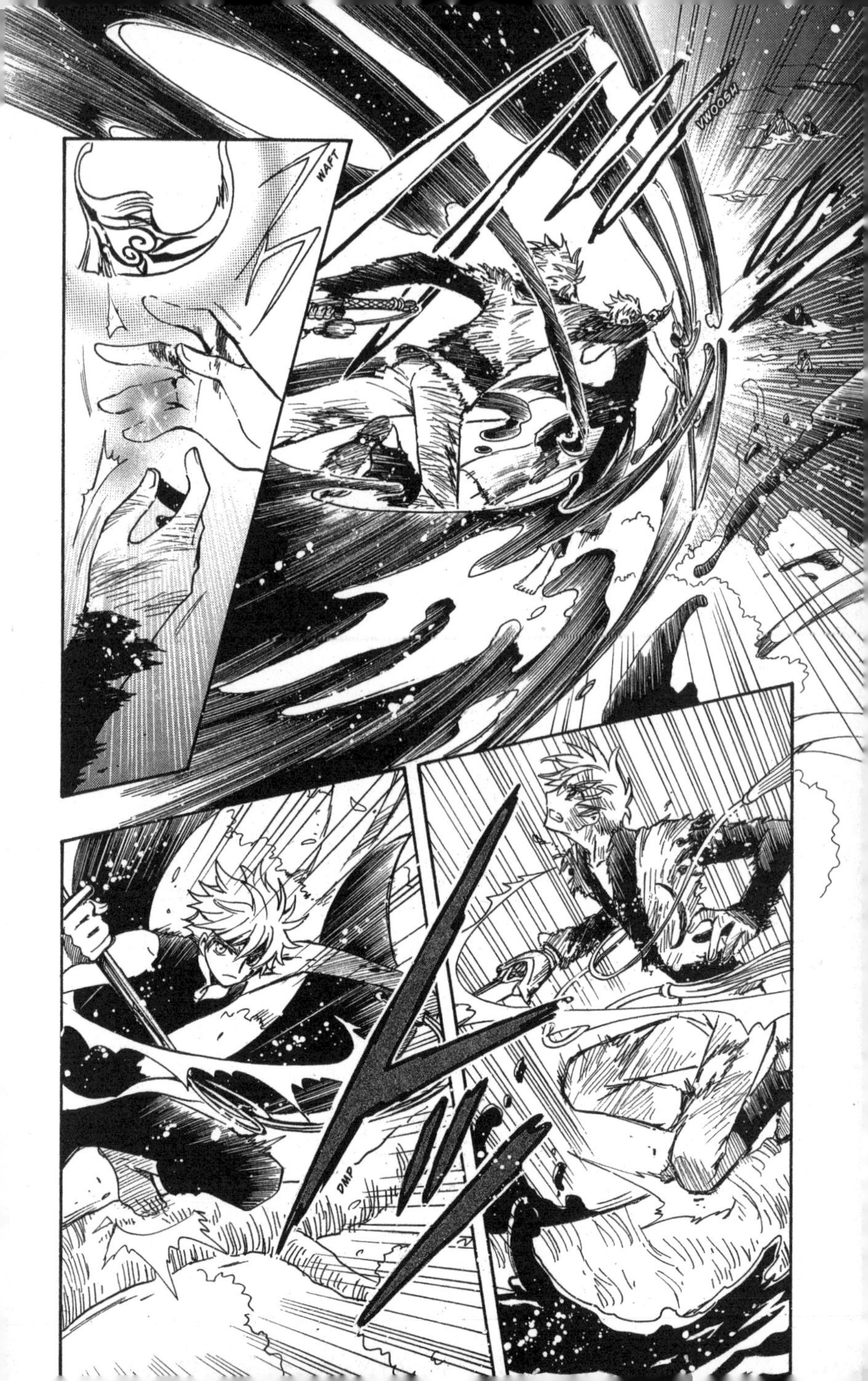
VWOOSH
WAFT
DMP

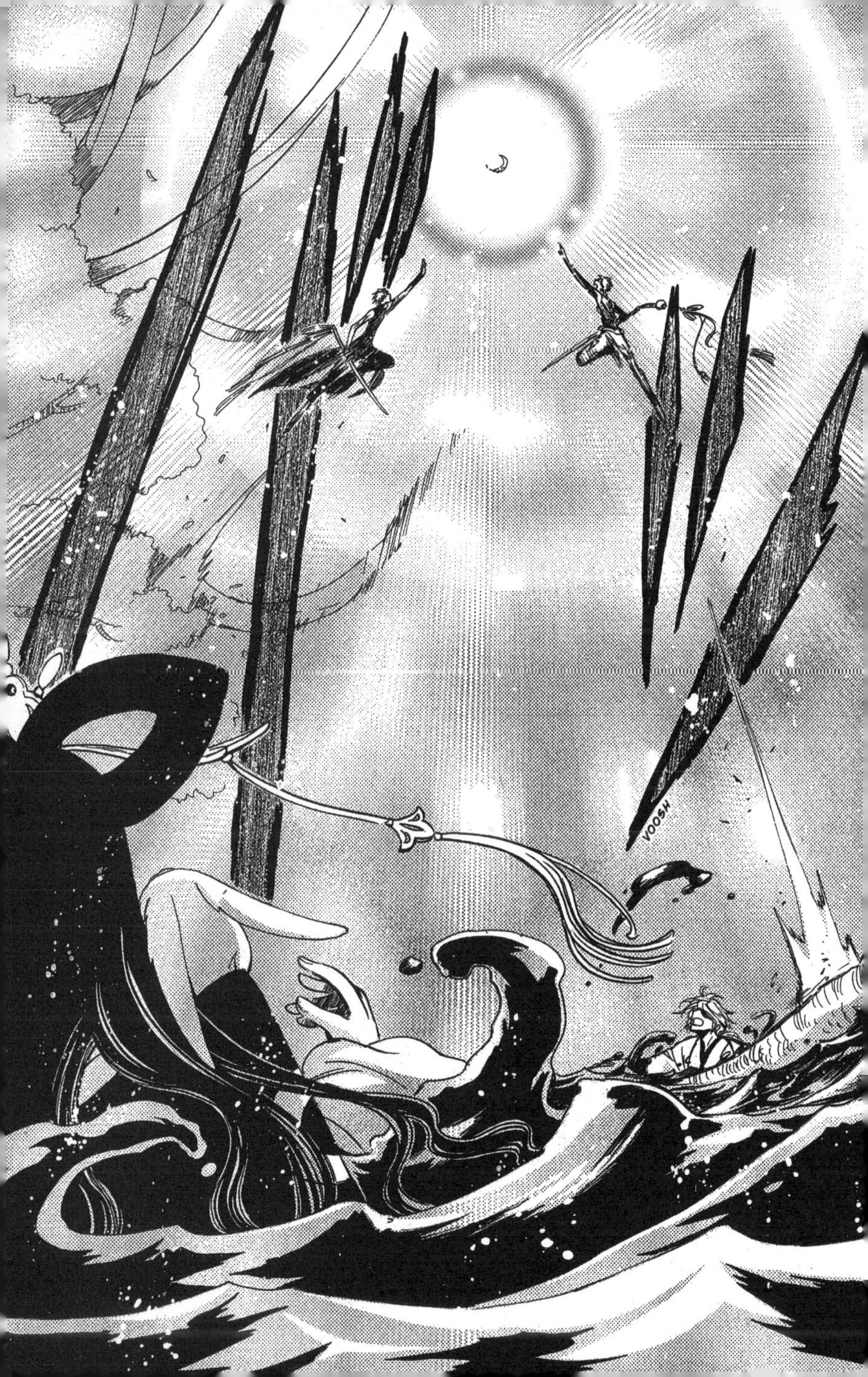
VOOSH

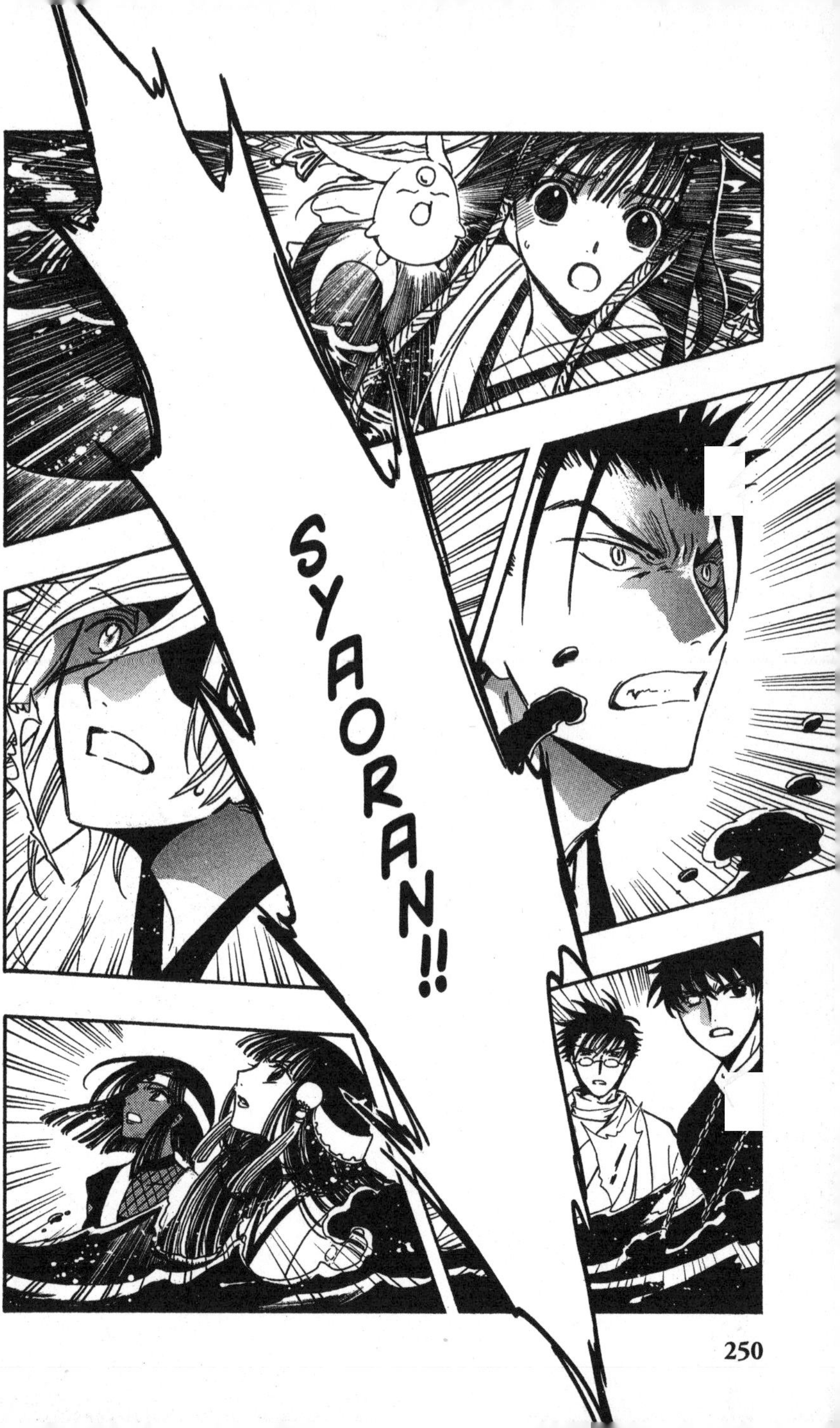
SYAORAN!!

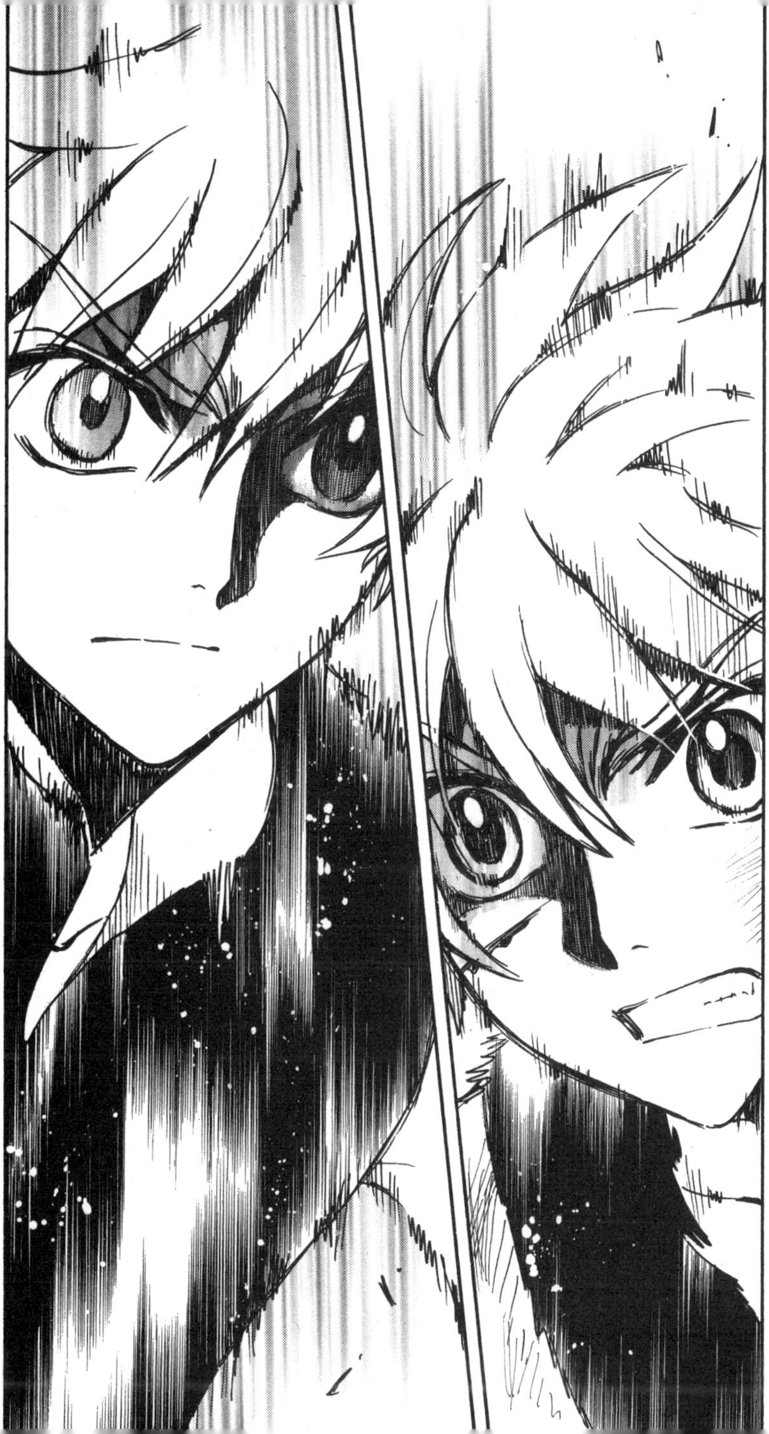

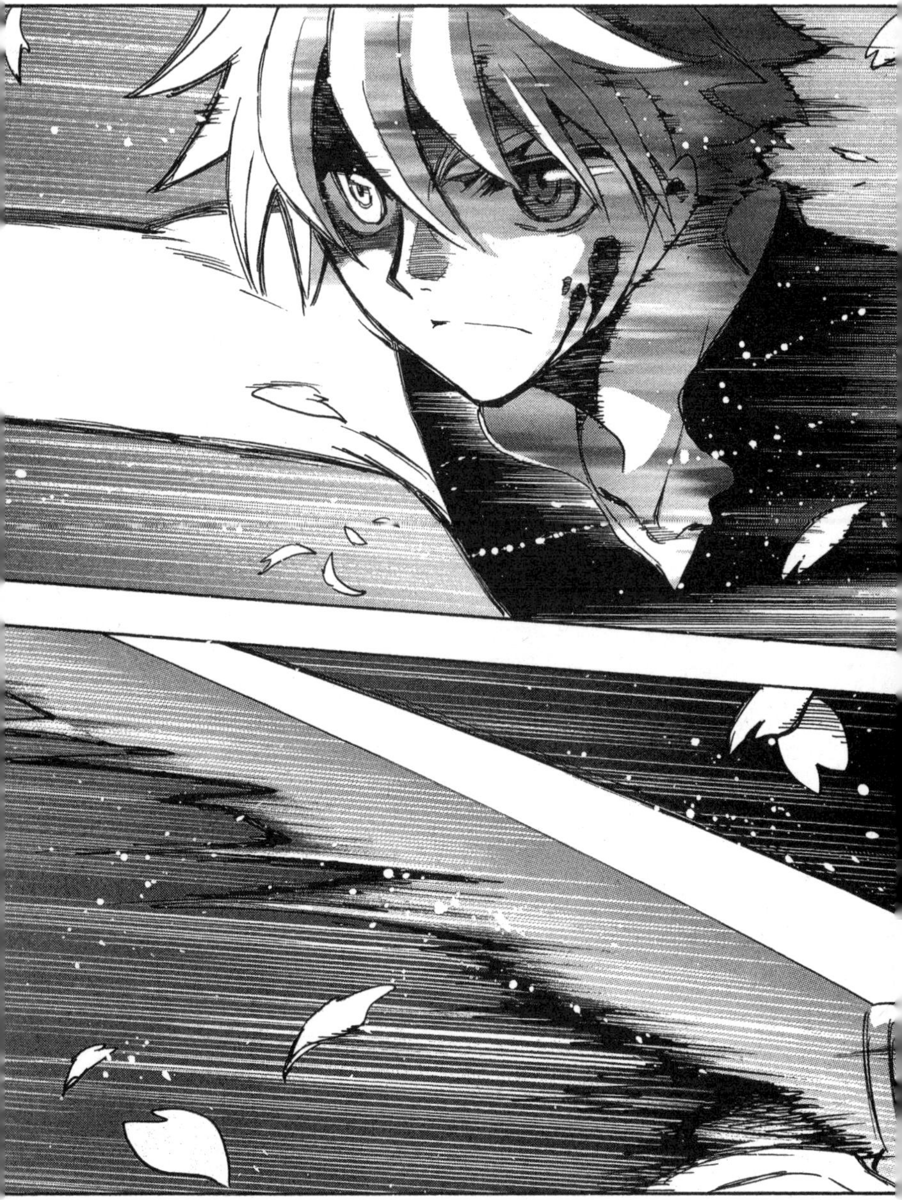

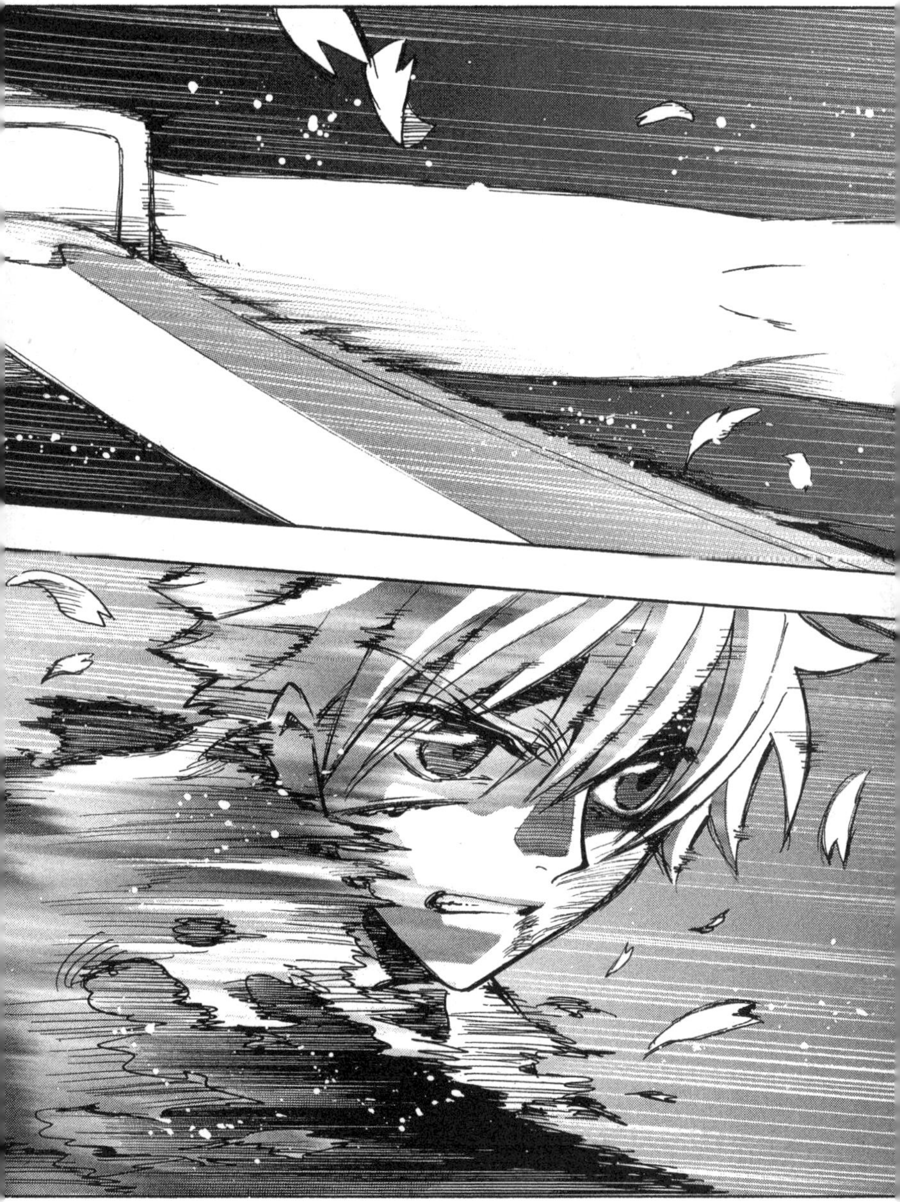

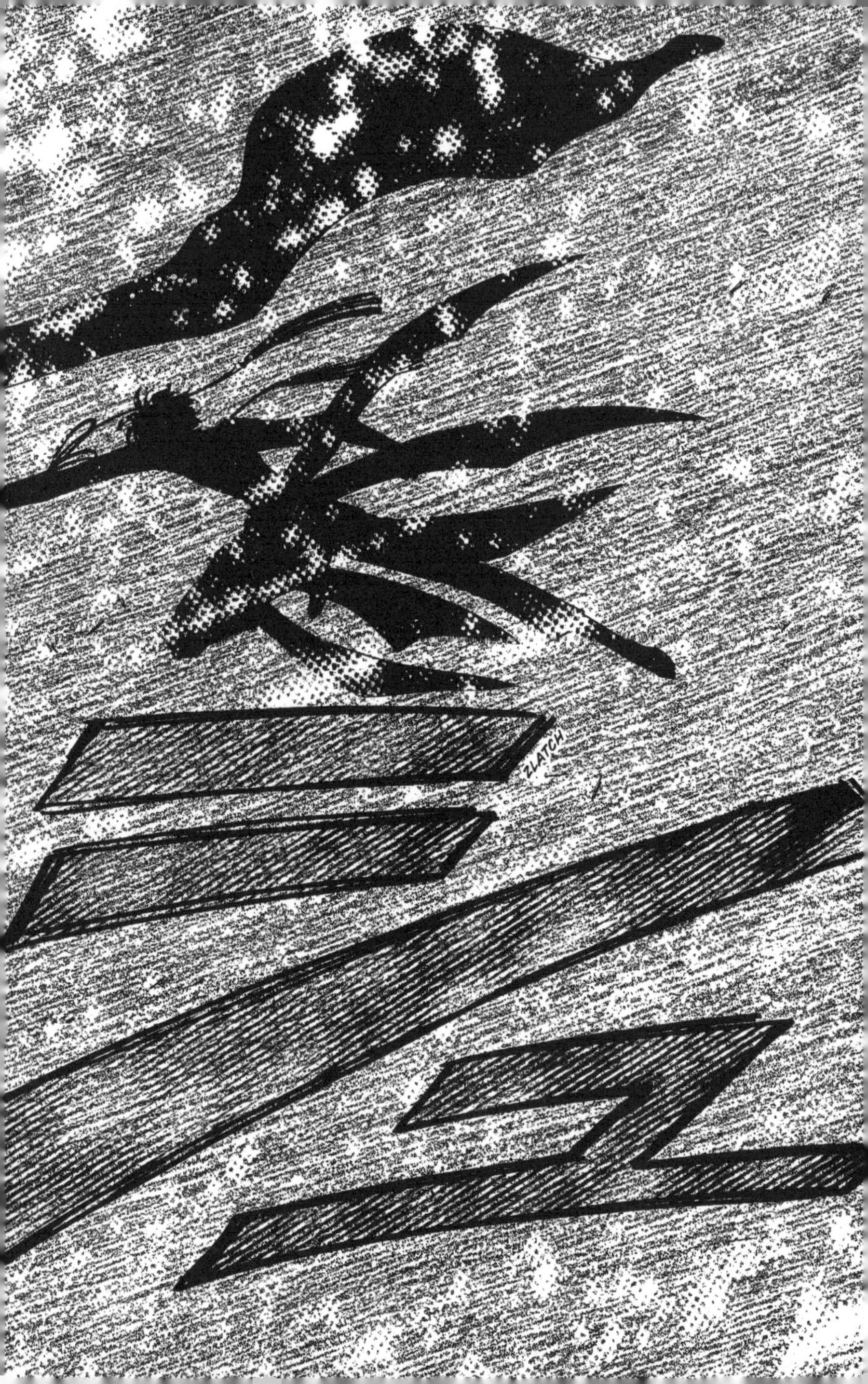
ZLATCH

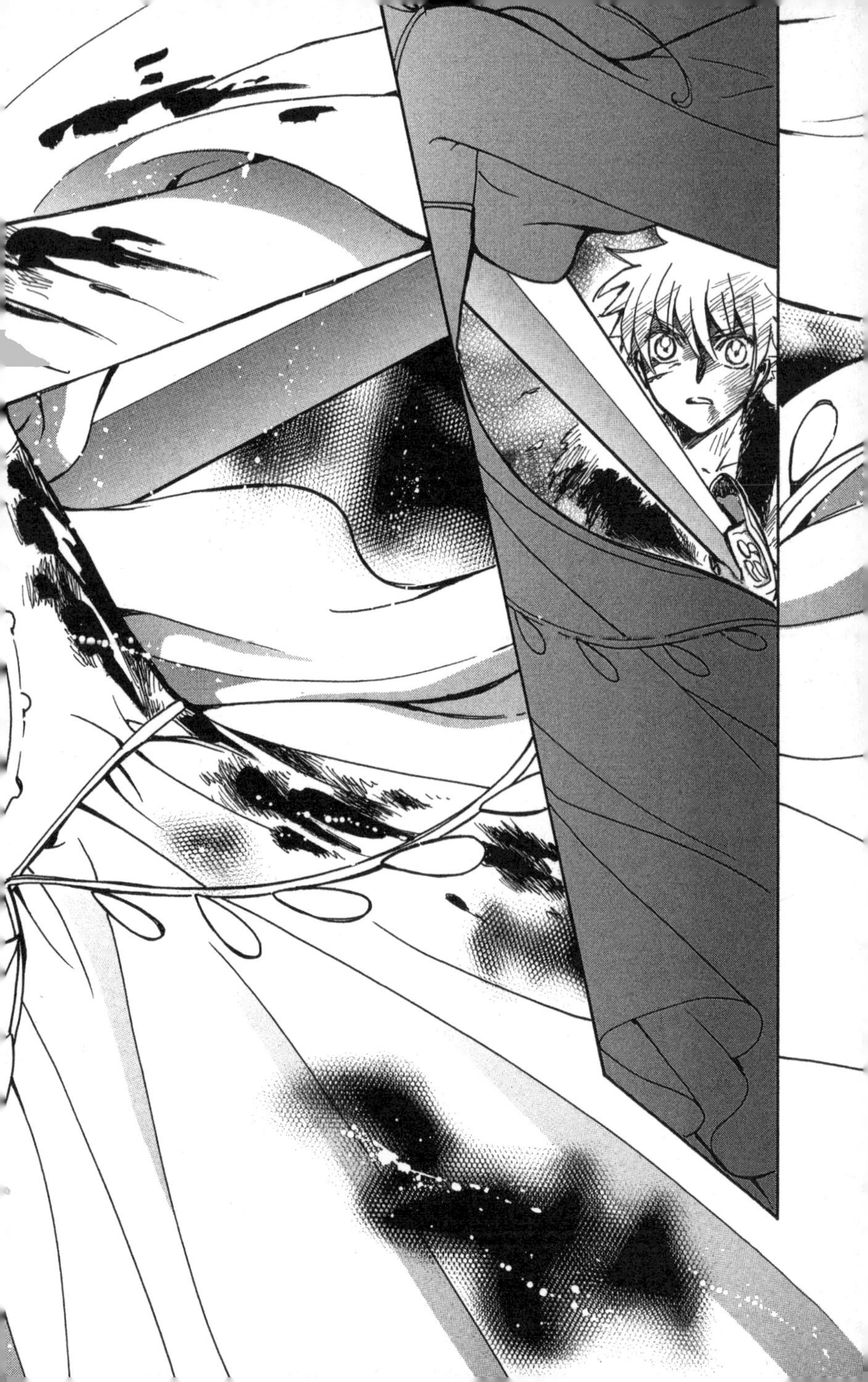

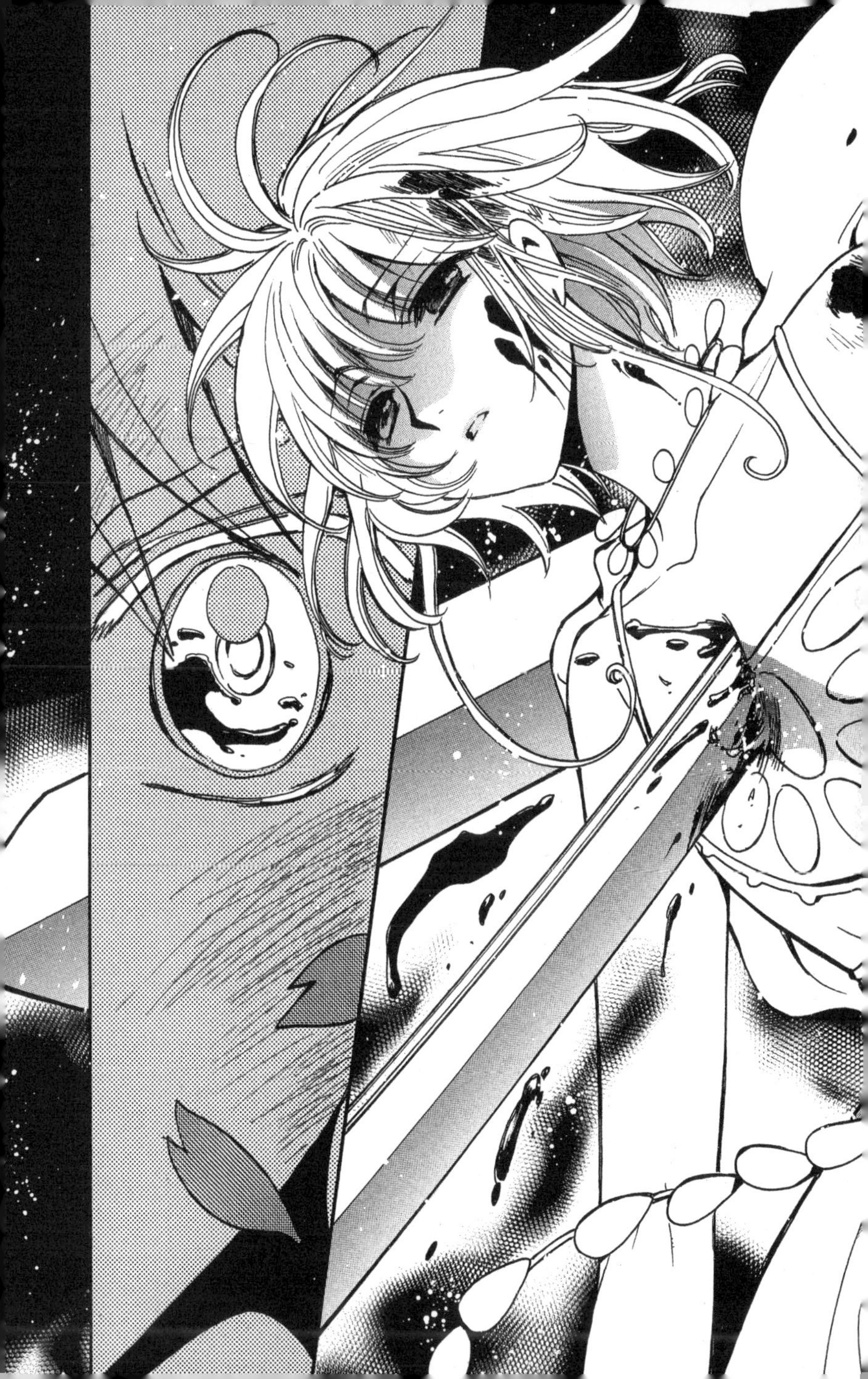

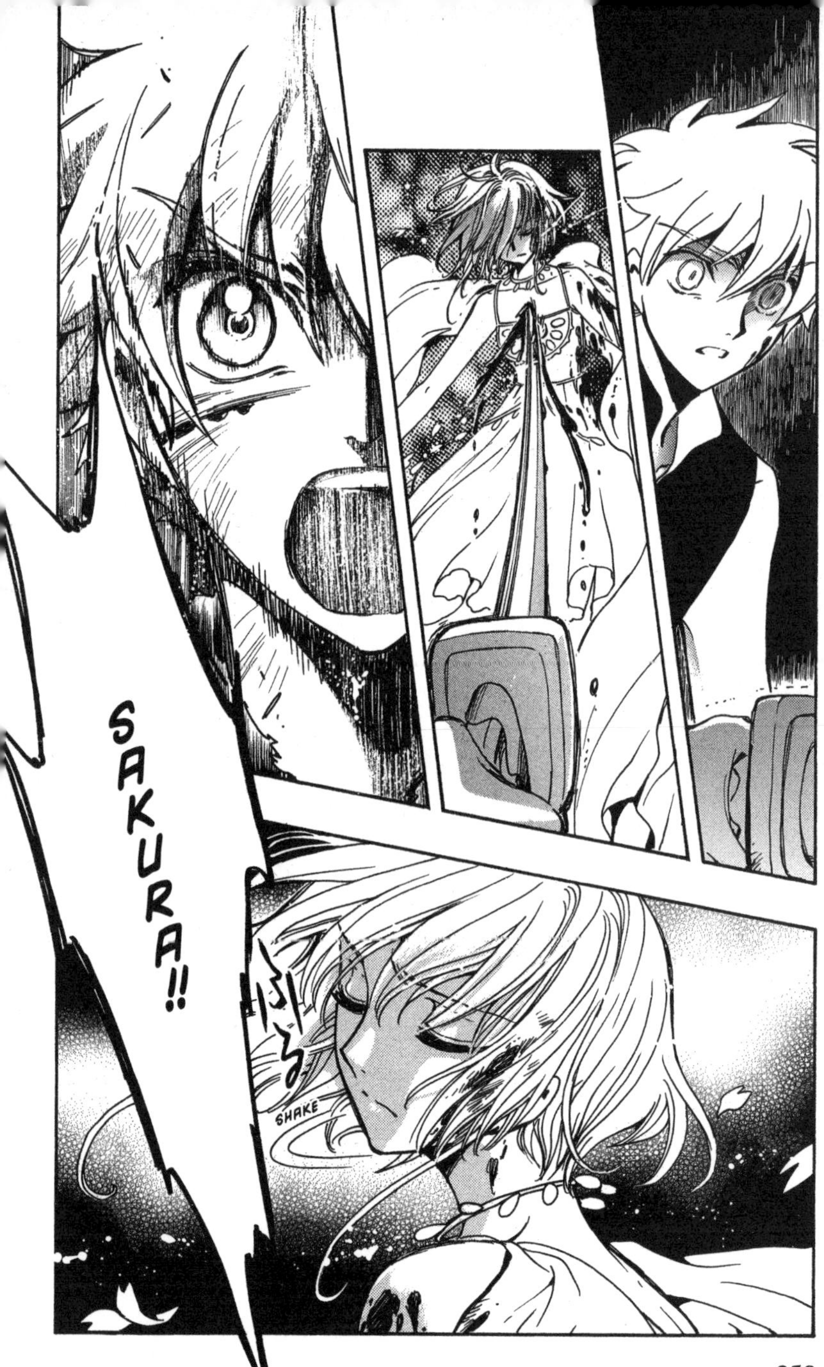
SAKURA!!
SHAKE

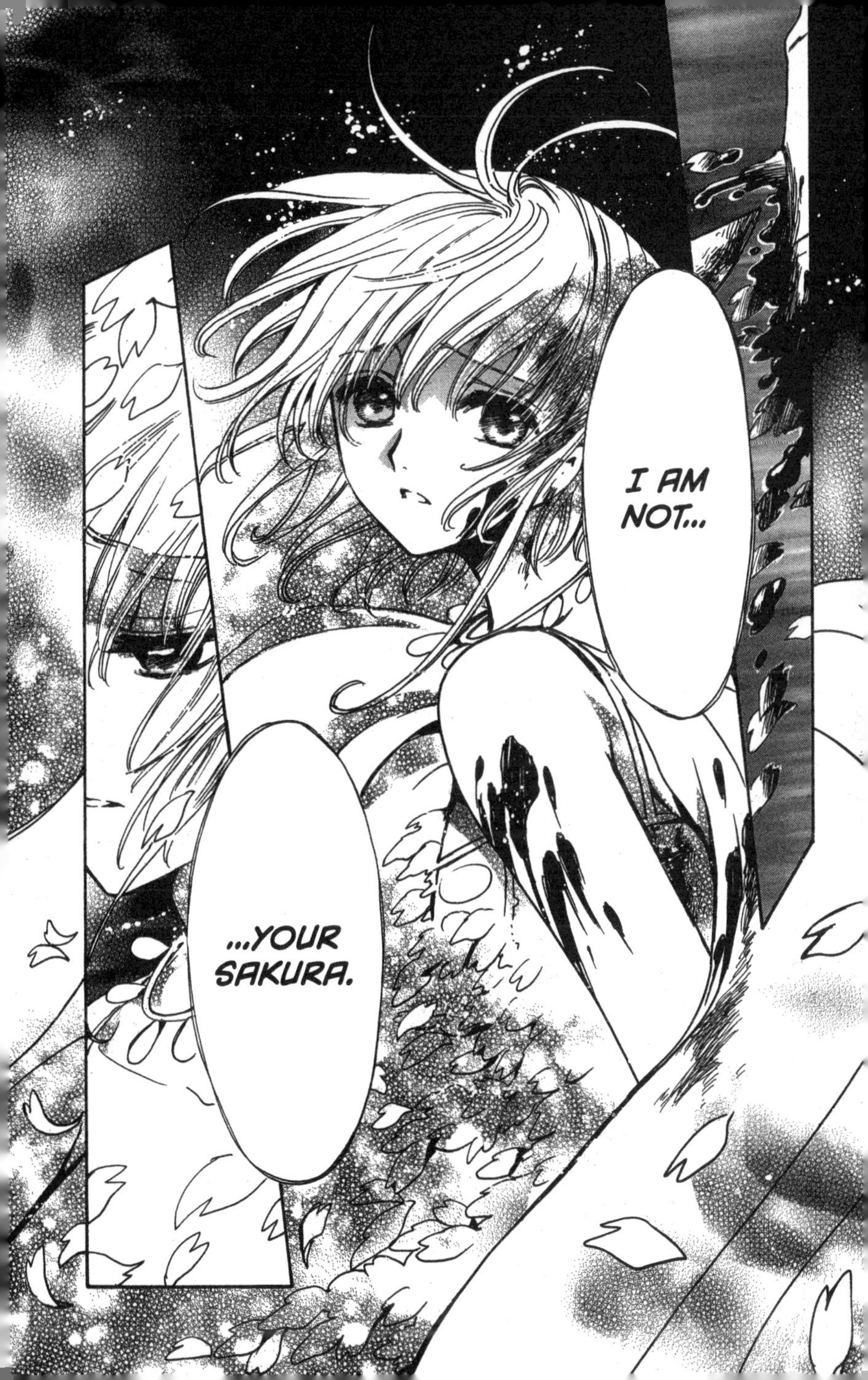
I AM NOT...
...YOUR SAKURA.

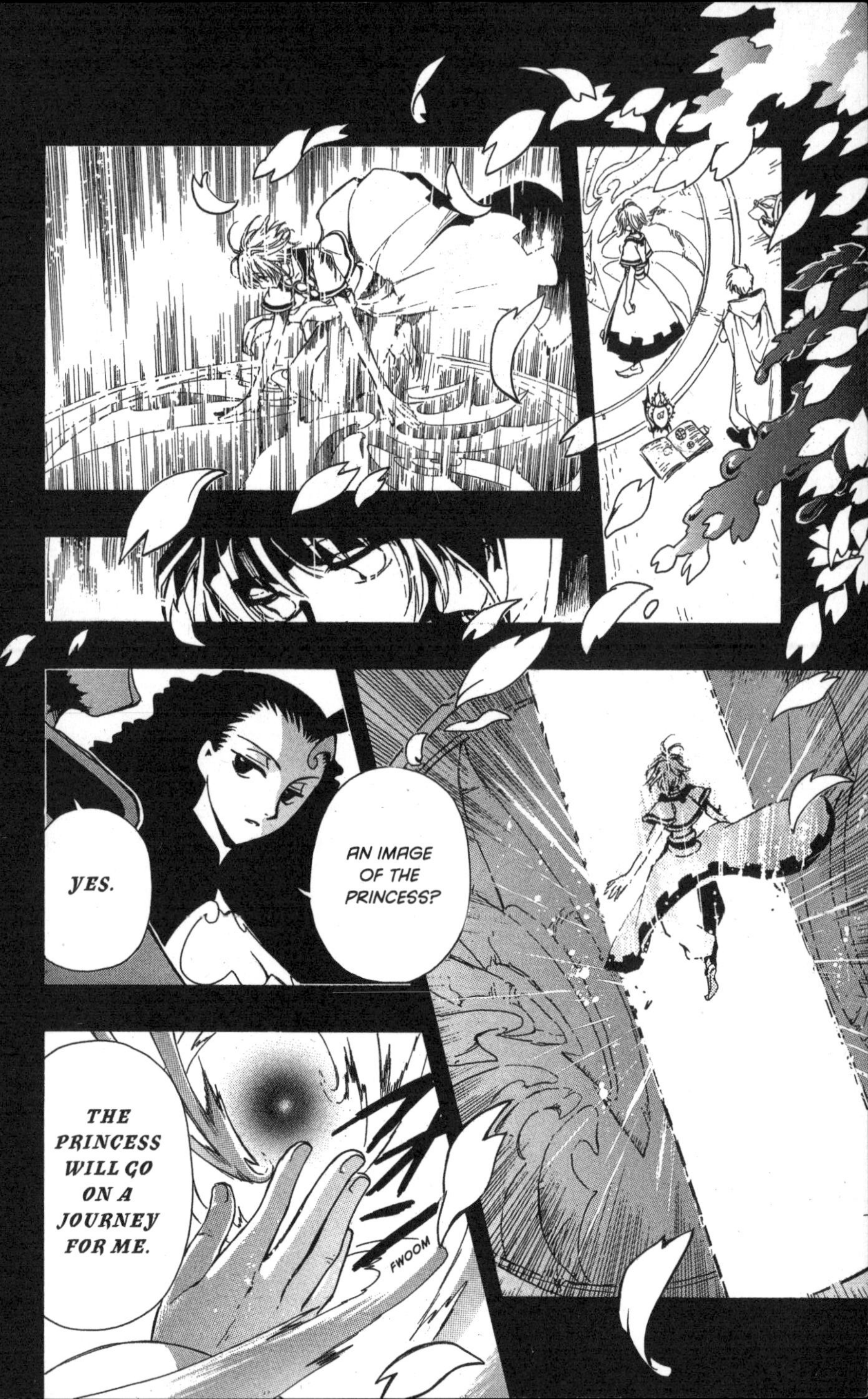
AN IMAGE OF THE PRINCESS?
YES.
THE PRINCESS WILL GO ON A JOURNEY FOR ME.
FWOOM

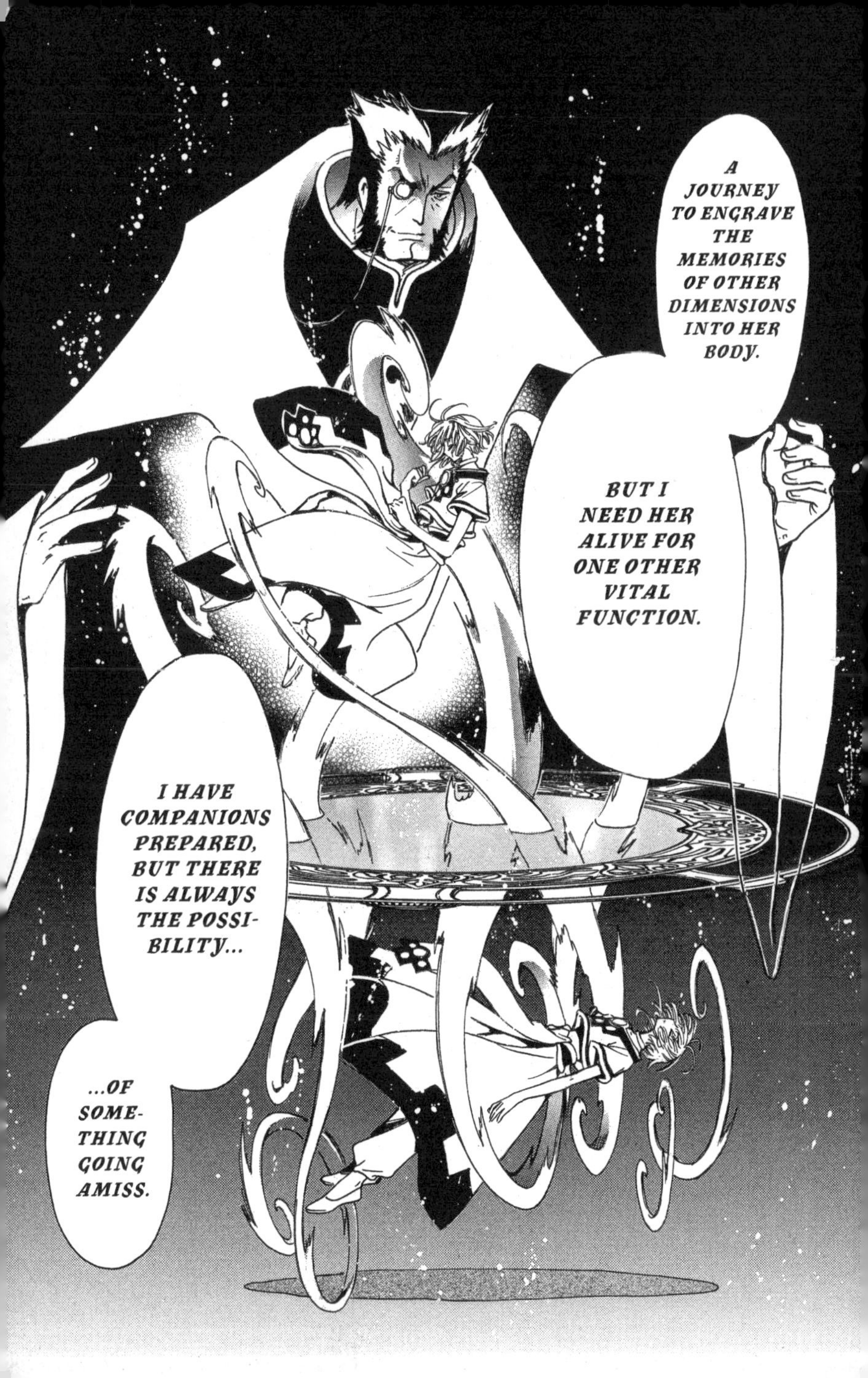
A JOURNEY TO ENGRAVE THE MEMORIES OF OTHER DIMENSIONS INTO HER BODY.
BUT I NEED HER ALIVE FOR ONE OTHER VITAL FUNCTION.
I HAVE COMPANIONS PREPARED, BUT THERE IS ALWAYS THE POSSI-BILITY...
...OF SOME-THING GOING AMISS.

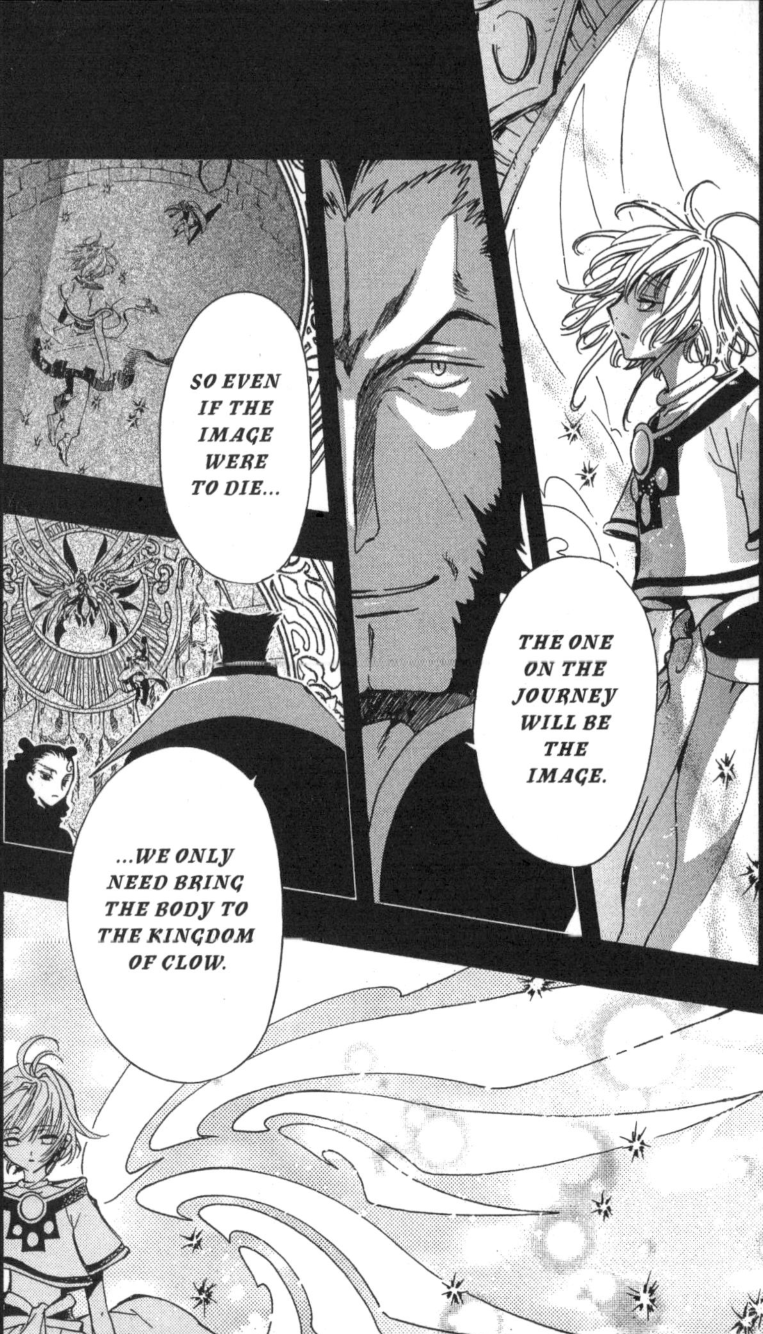
THE ONE ON THE JOURNEY WILL BE THE IMAGE.
SO EVEN IF THE IMAGE WERE TO DIE...
...WE ONLY NEED BRING THE BODY TO THE KINGDOM OF CLOW.

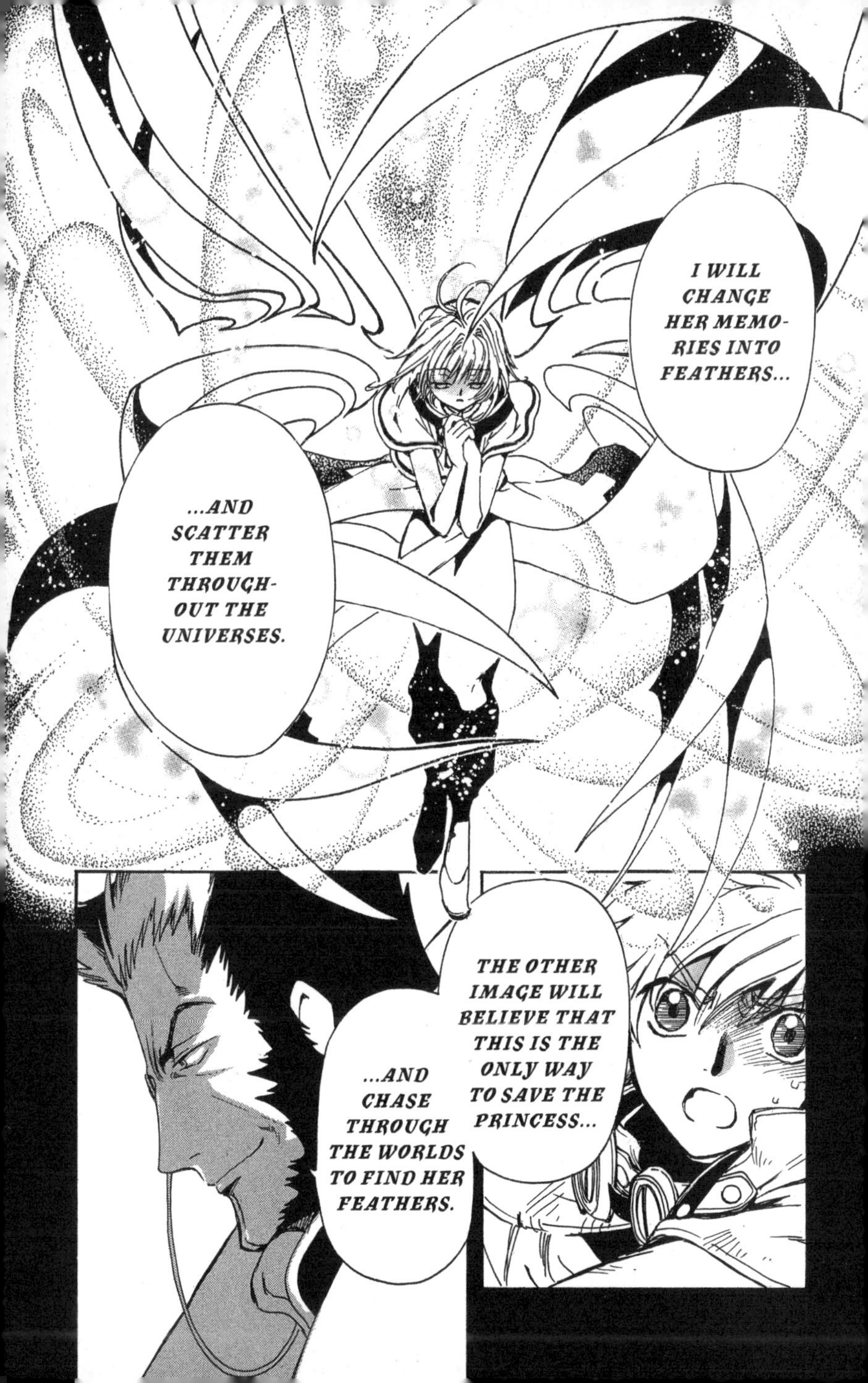
I WILL CHANGE HER MEMORIES INTO FEATHERS...
...AND SCATTER THEM THROUGHOUT THE UNIVERSES.
THE OTHER IMAGE WILL BELIEVE THAT THIS IS THE ONLY WAY TO SAVE THE PRINCESS...
...AND CHASE THROUGH THE WORLDS TO FIND HER FEATHERS.

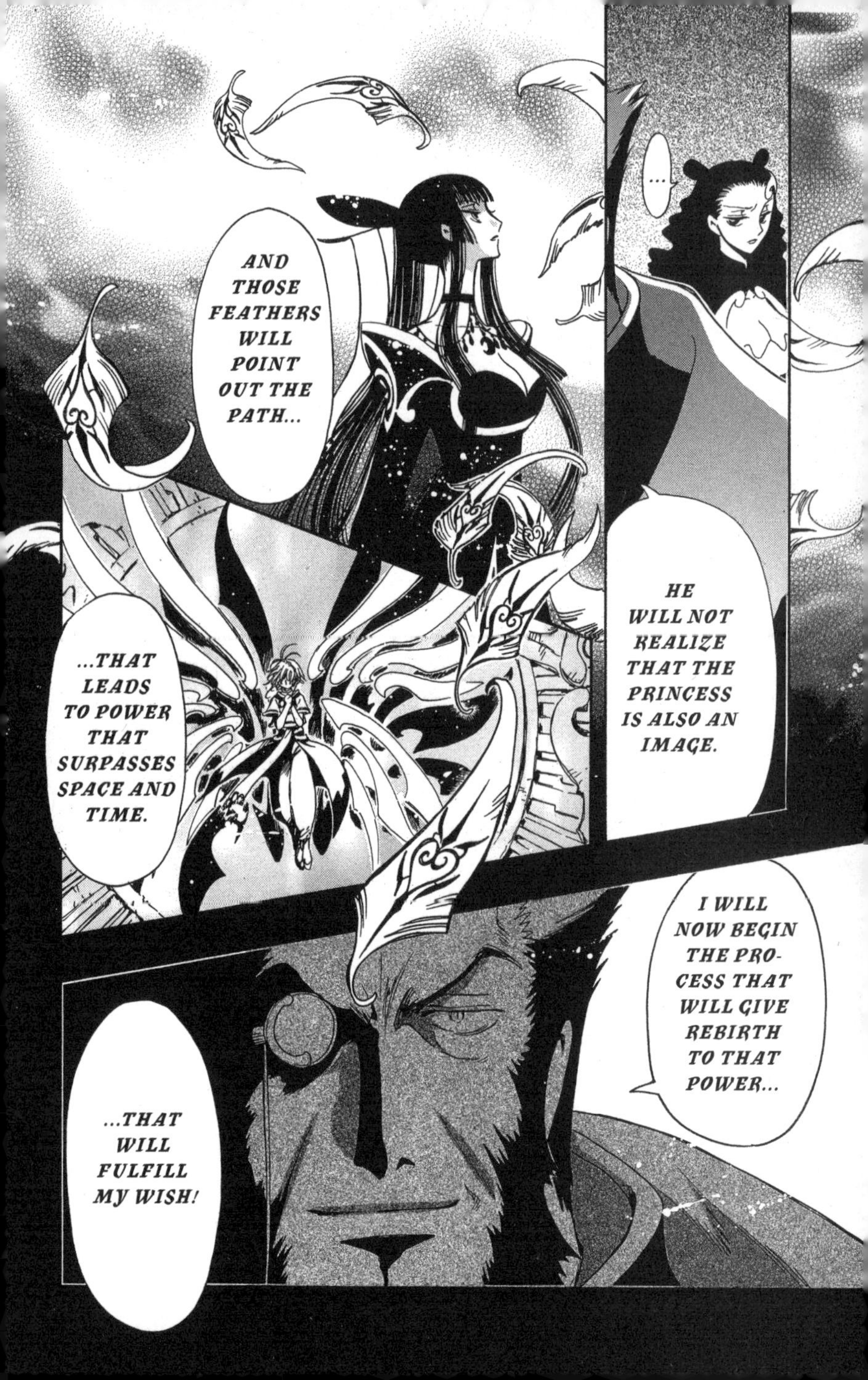
...
HE WILL NOT REALIZE THAT THE PRINCESS IS ALSO AN IMAGE.
AND THOSE FEATHERS WILL POINT OUT THE PATH...
...THAT LEADS TO POWER THAT SURPASSES SPACE AND TIME.
I WILL NOW BEGIN THE PRO-CESS THAT WILL GIVE REBIRTH TO THAT POWER...
...THAT WILL FULFILL MY WISH!

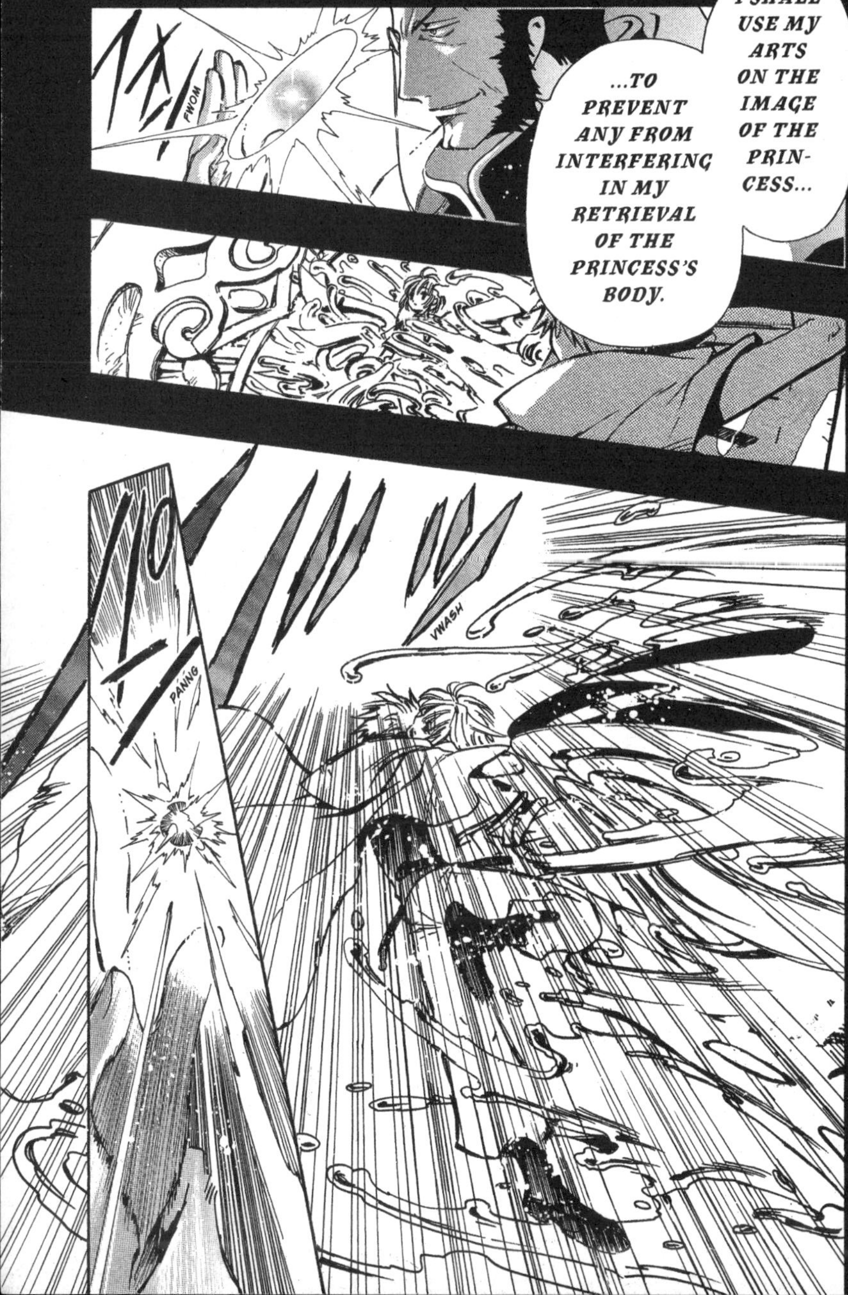
I SHALL USE MY ARTS ON THE IMAGE OF THE PRINCESS...
FWOM
...TO PREVENT ANY FROM INTERFERING IN MY RETRIEVAL OF THE PRINCESS'S BODY.
VWASH
PANNG

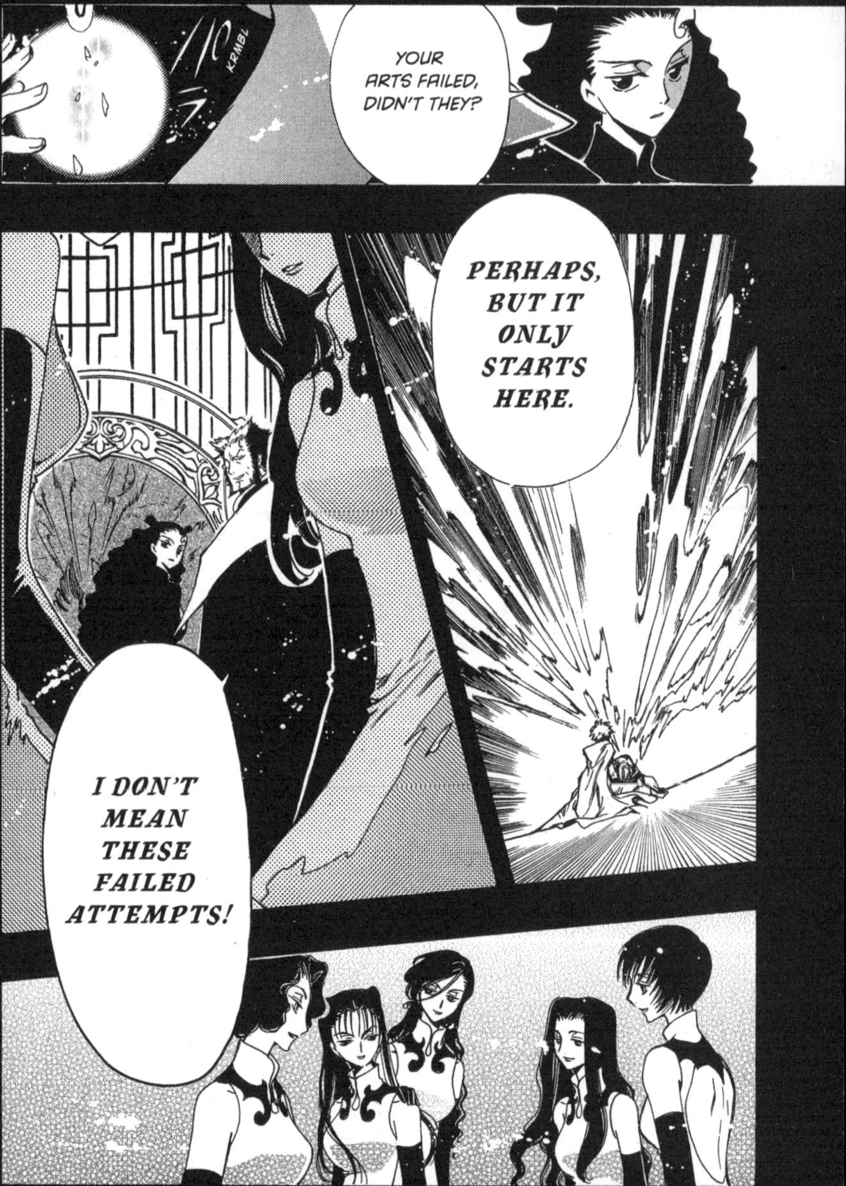
YOUR ARTS FAILED, DIDN'T THEY?
KRMBL
PERHAPS, BUT IT ONLY STARTS HERE.
I DON'T MEAN THESE FAILED ATTEMPTS!

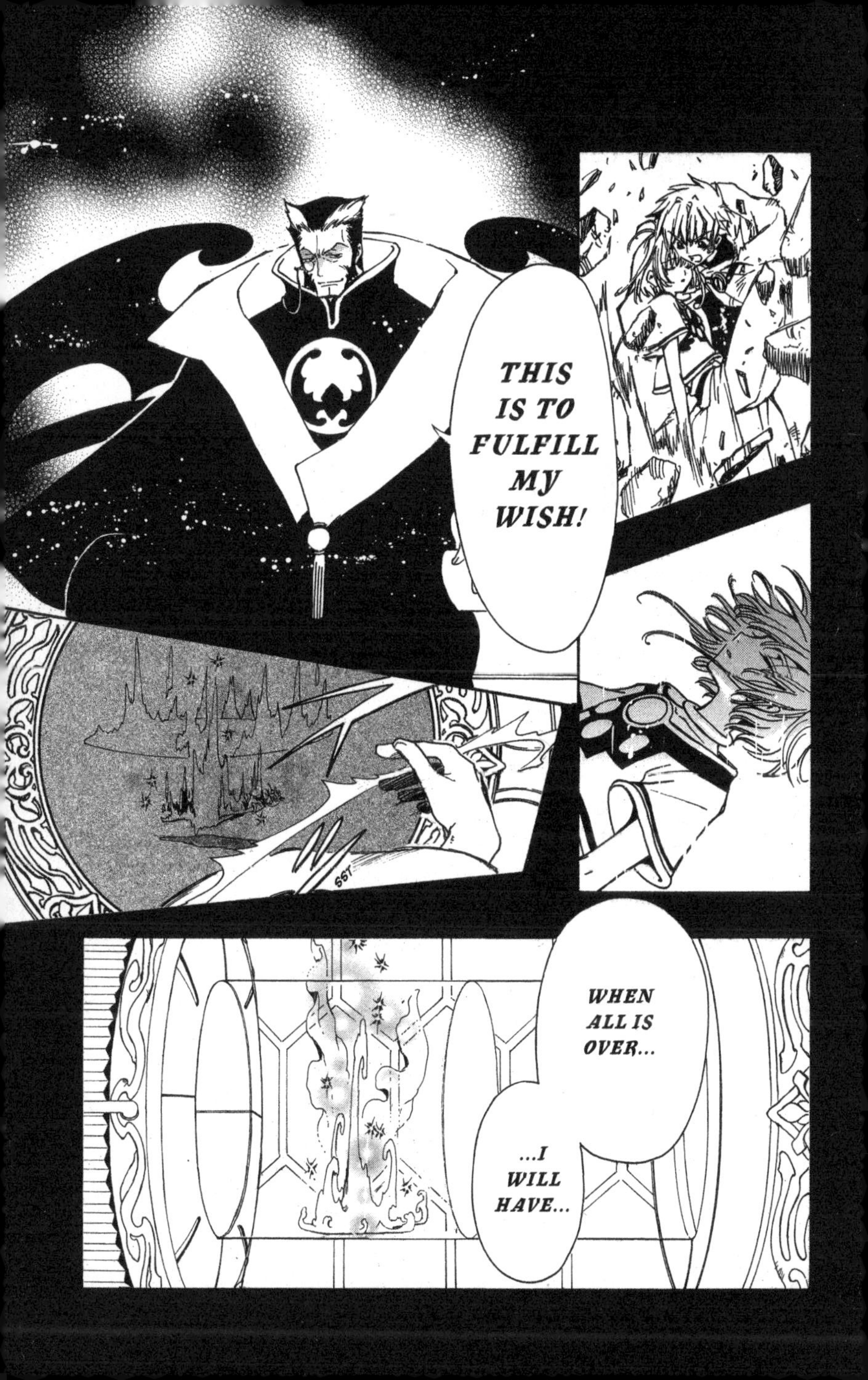
THIS IS TO FULFILL MY WISH!
WHEN ALL IS OVER...
...I WILL HAVE...

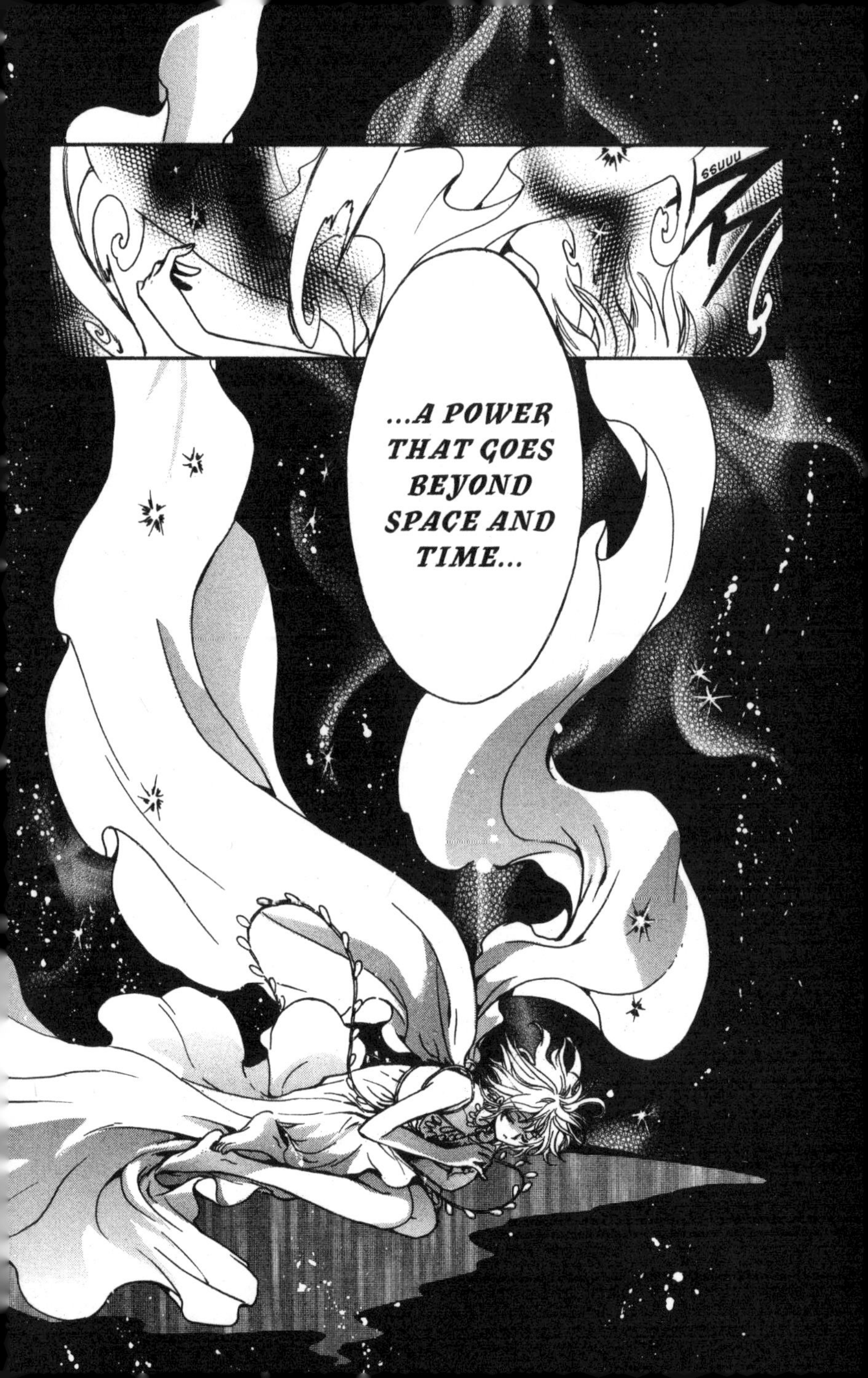
ssuuu
...A POWER THAT GOES BEYOND SPACE AND TIME...

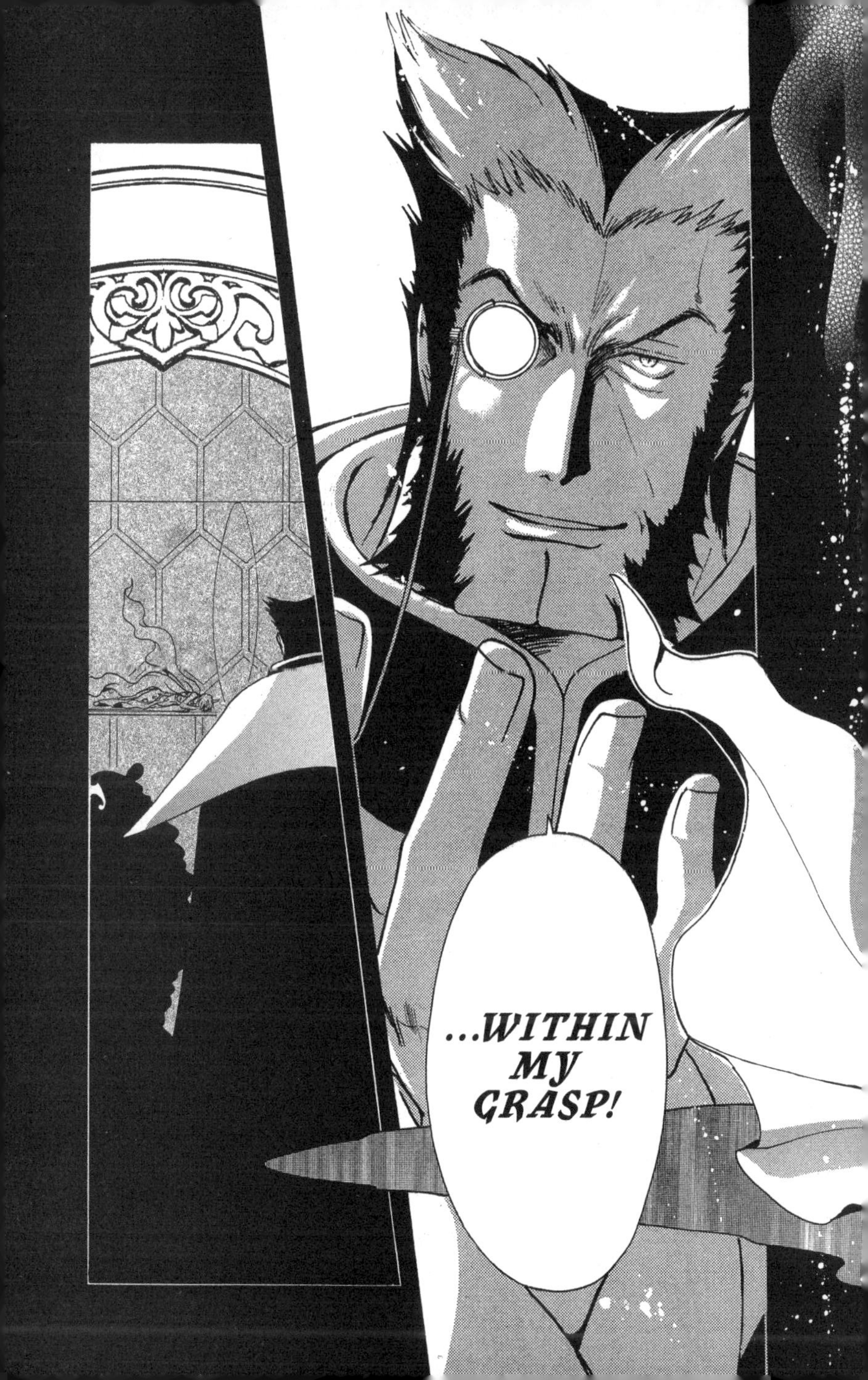
...WITHIN MY GRASP!

ツバサ

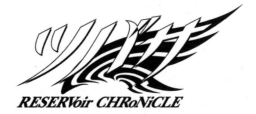

RESERVoir CHRoNiCLE

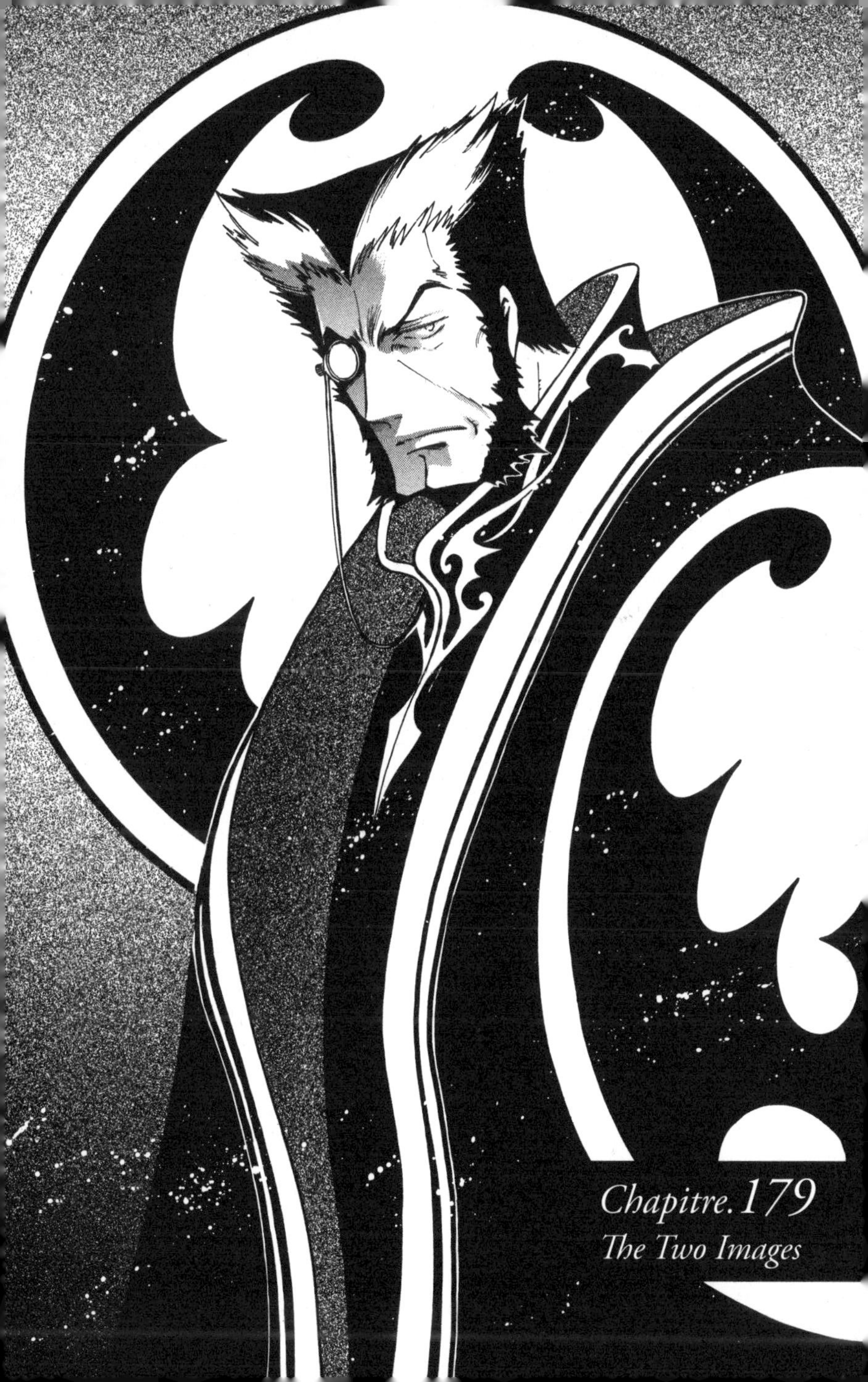
Chapitre. 179
The Two Images

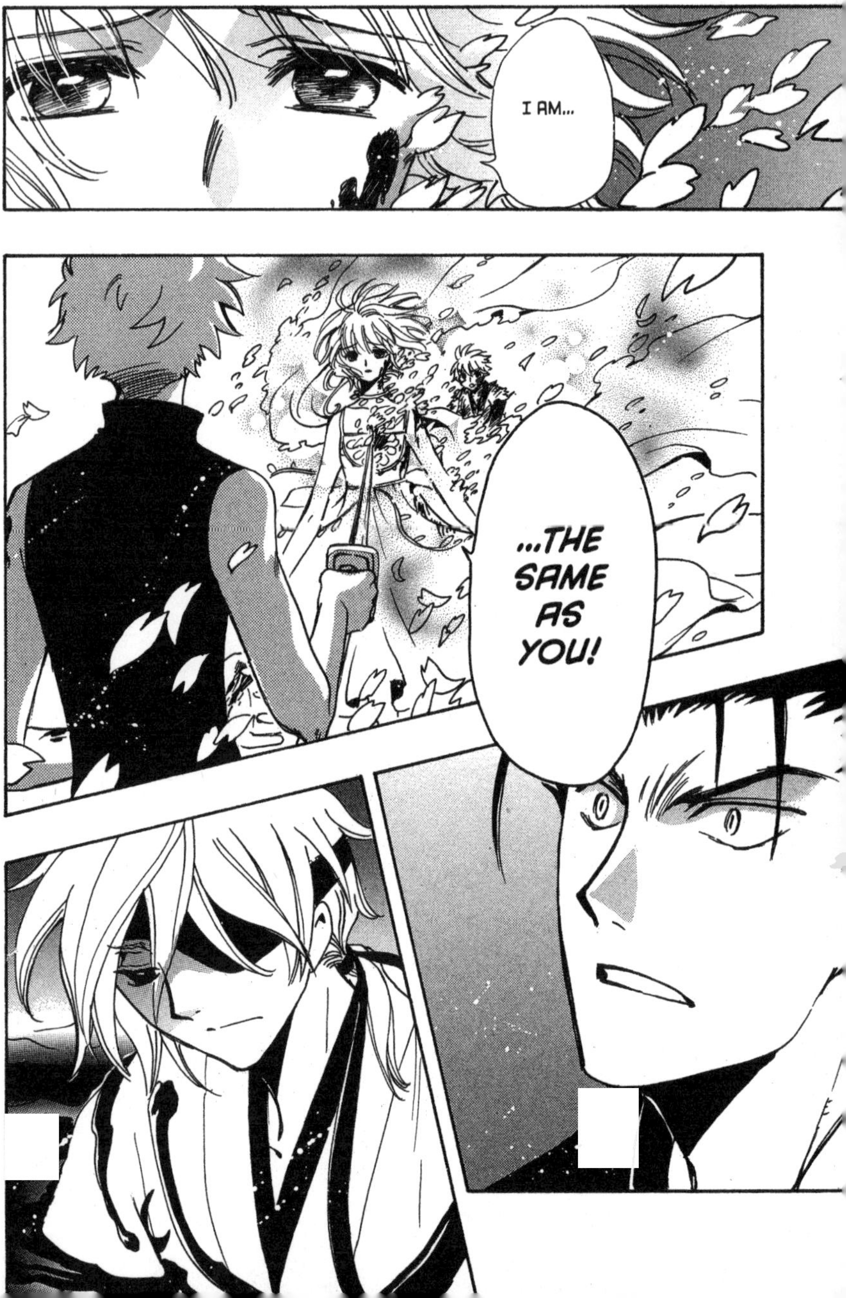
I AM...
...THE SAME AS YOU!

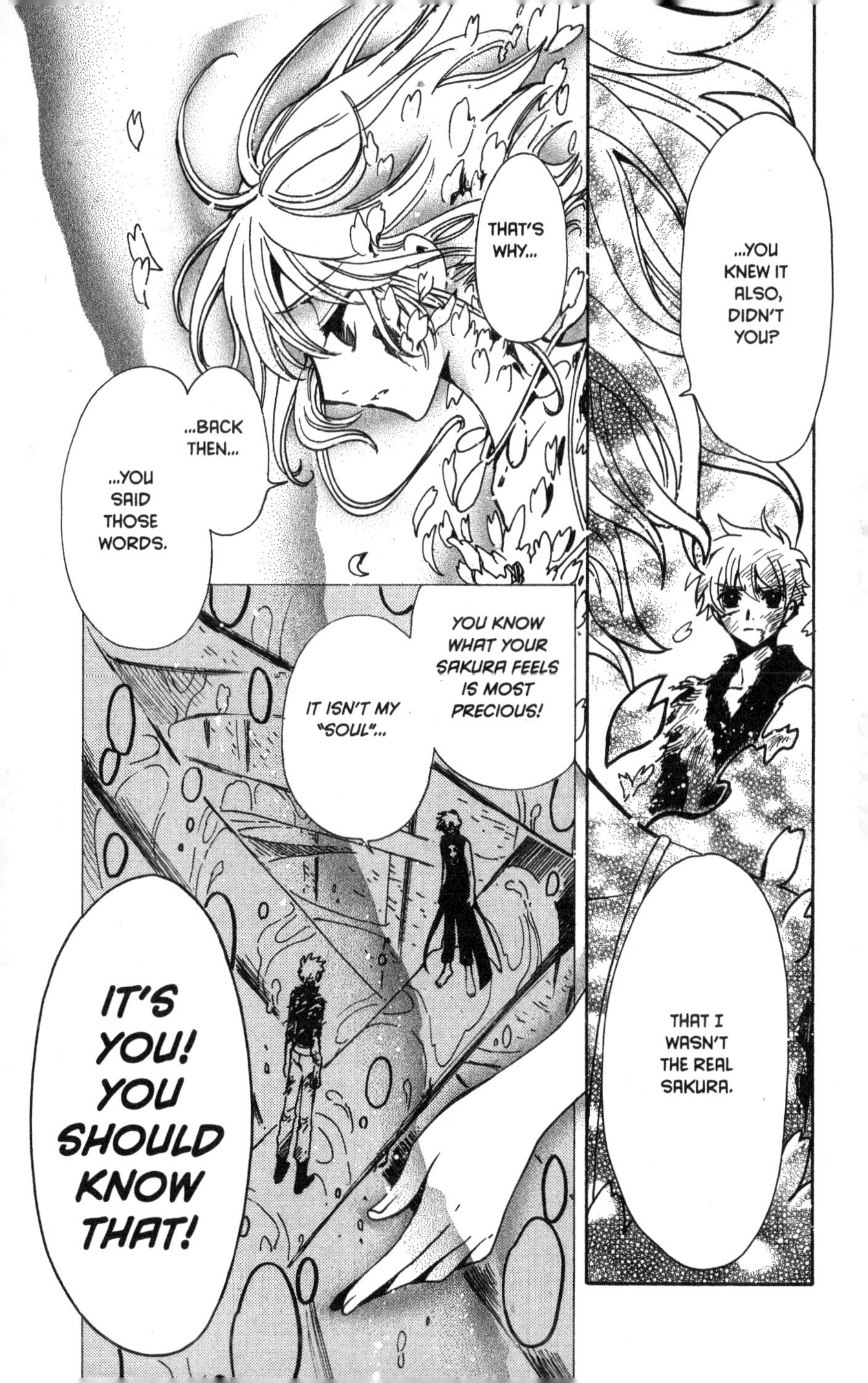
...YOU KNEW IT ALSO, DIDN'T YOU?
THAT I WASN'T THE REAL SAKURA.
THAT'S WHY...
...BACK THEN...
...YOU SAID THOSE WORDS.
YOU KNOW WHAT YOUR SAKURA FEELS IS MOST PRECIOUS!
IT ISN'T MY "SOUL"...
IT'S YOU! YOU SHOULD KNOW THAT!

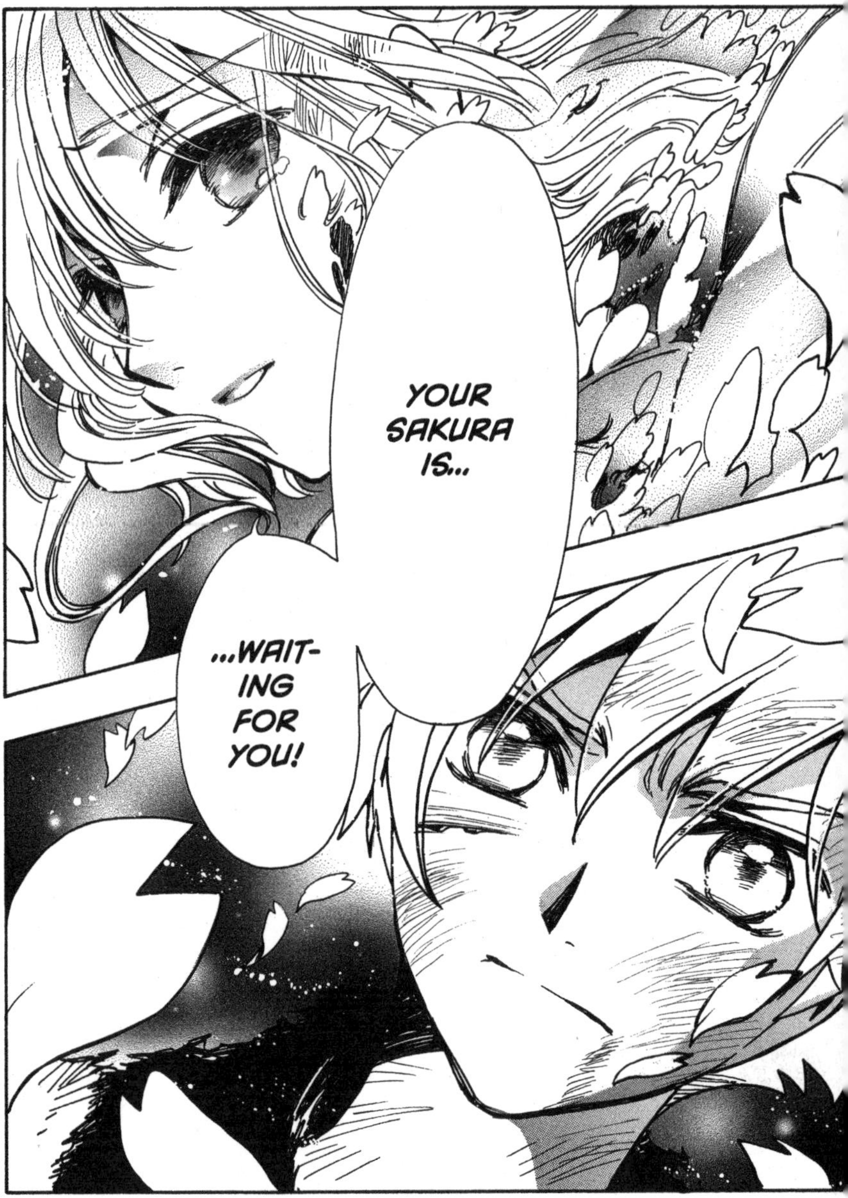
YOUR SAKURA IS...
...WAIT-ING FOR YOU!

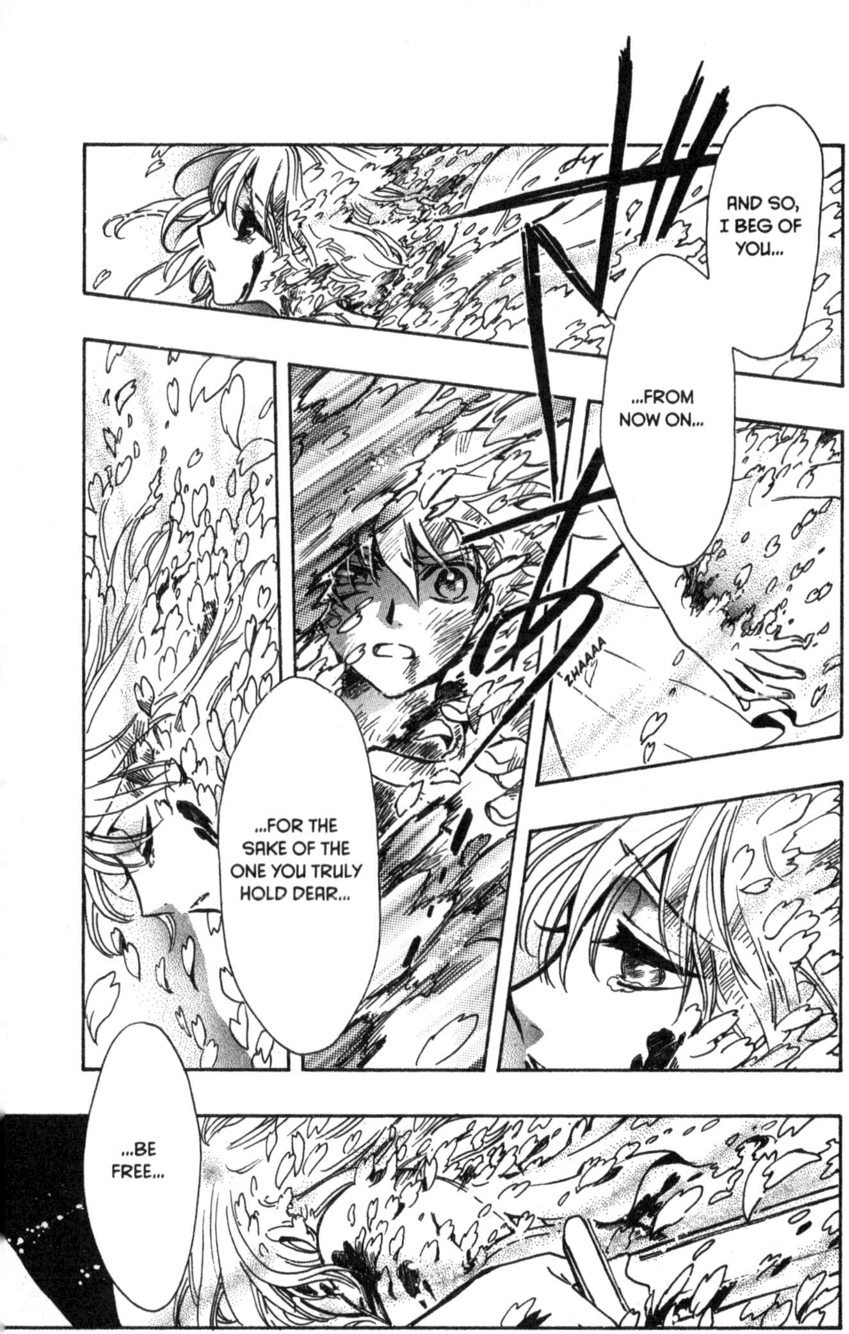
AND SO, I BEG OF YOU...
...FROM NOW ON...
ZHAAAA
...FOR THE SAKE OF THE ONE YOU TRULY HOLD DEAR...
...BE FREE...

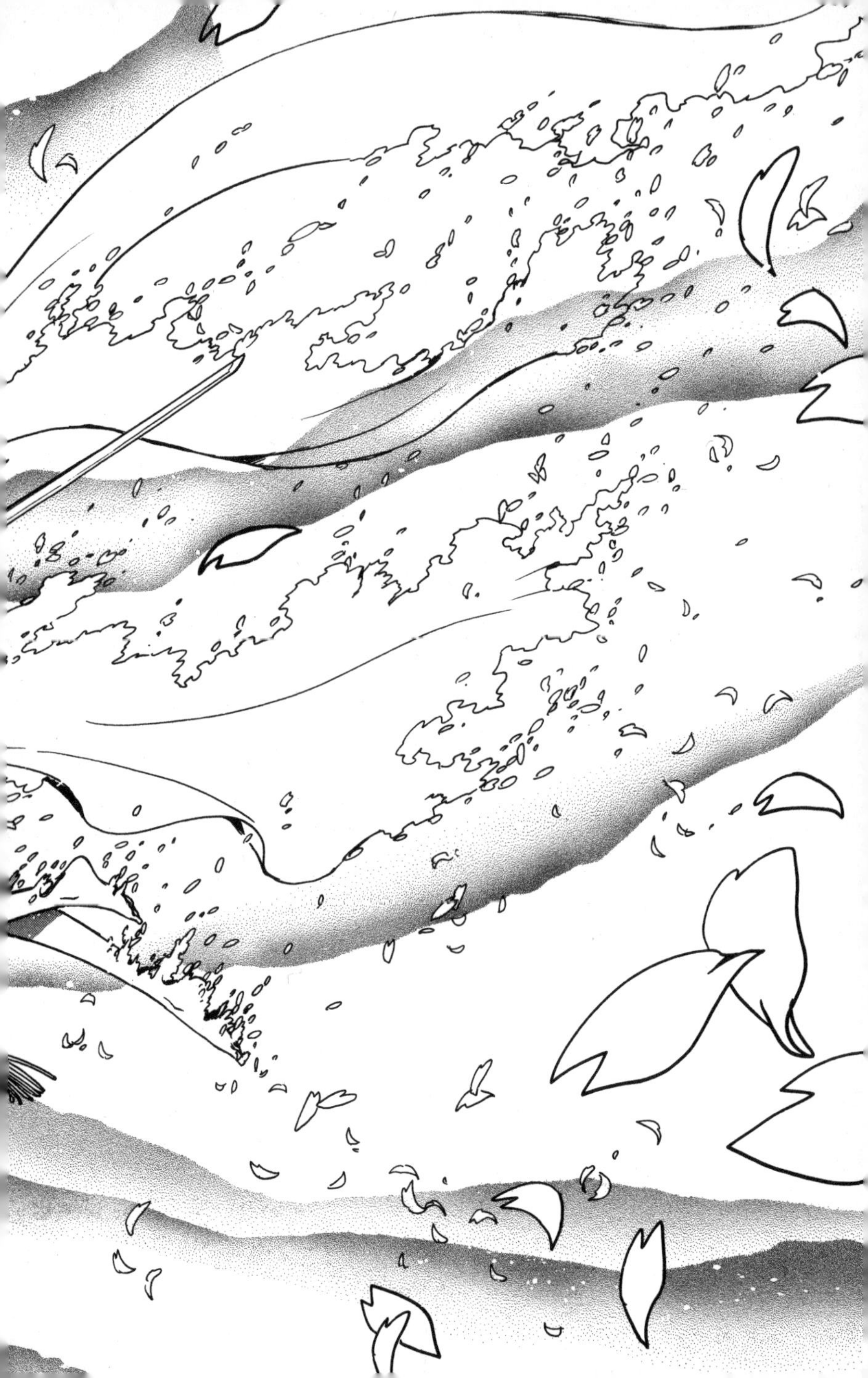

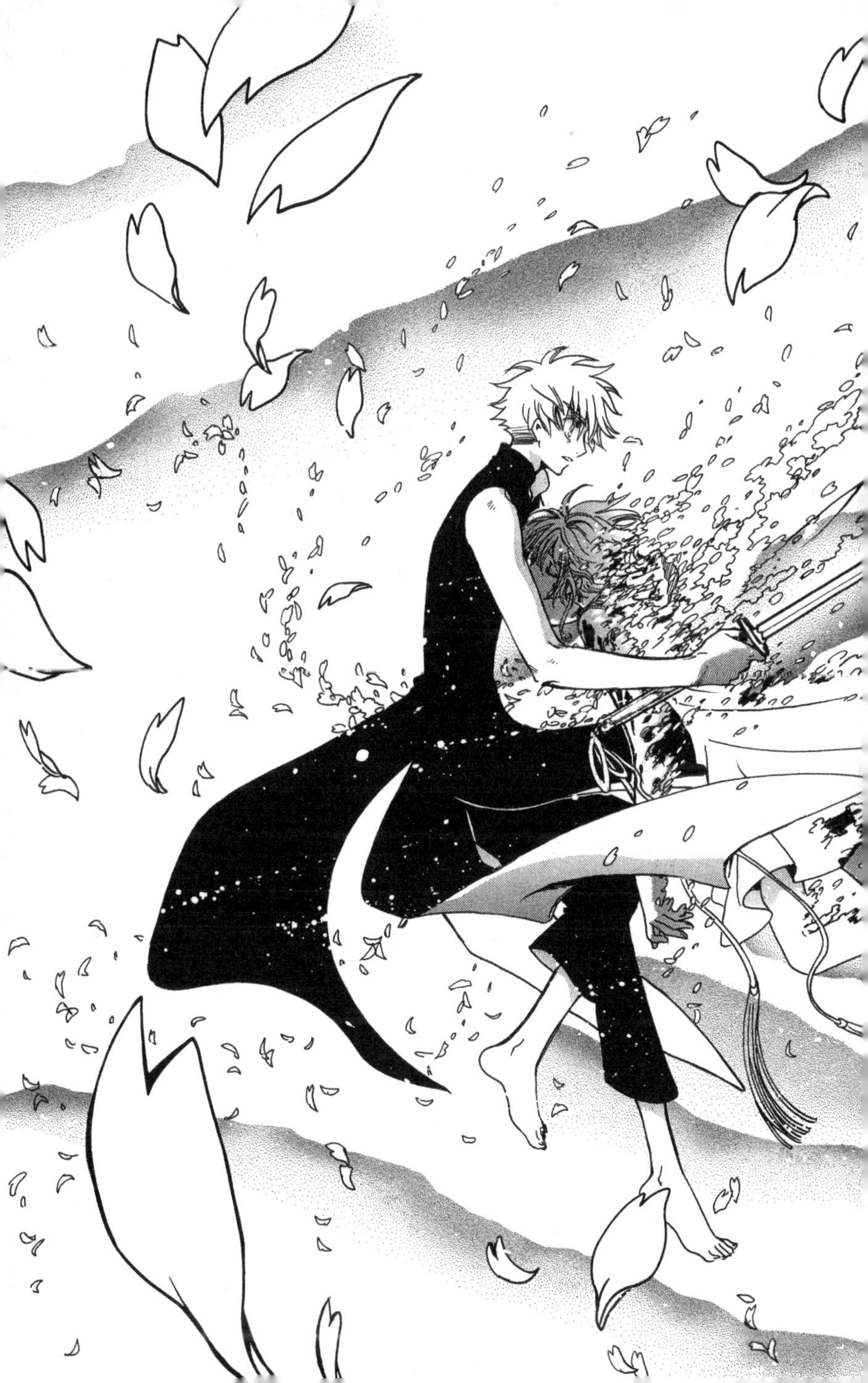

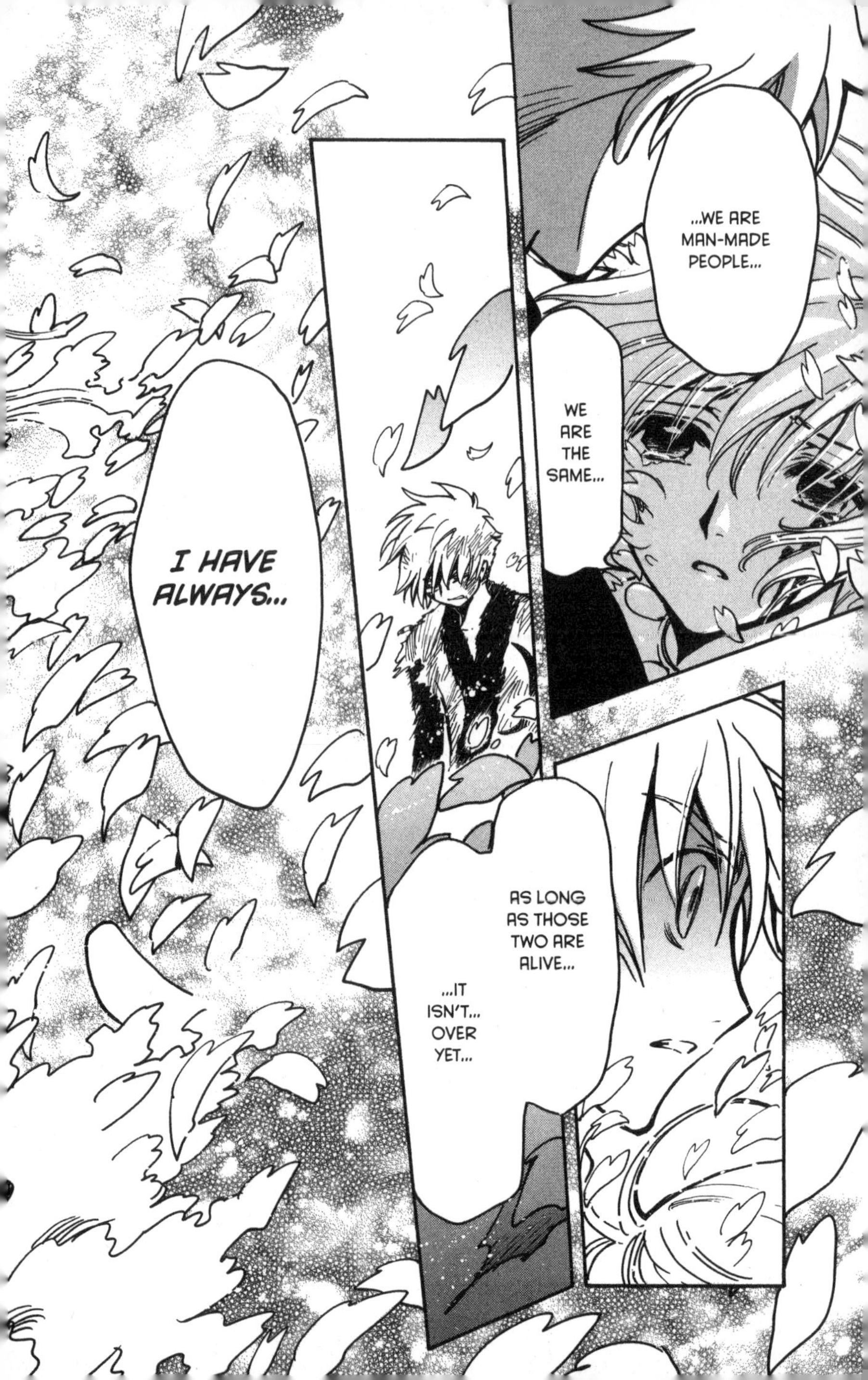
...WE ARE MAN-MADE PEOPLE...
WE ARE THE SAME...
AS LONG AS THOSE TWO ARE ALIVE...
...IT ISN'T... OVER YET...
I HAVE ALWAYS...

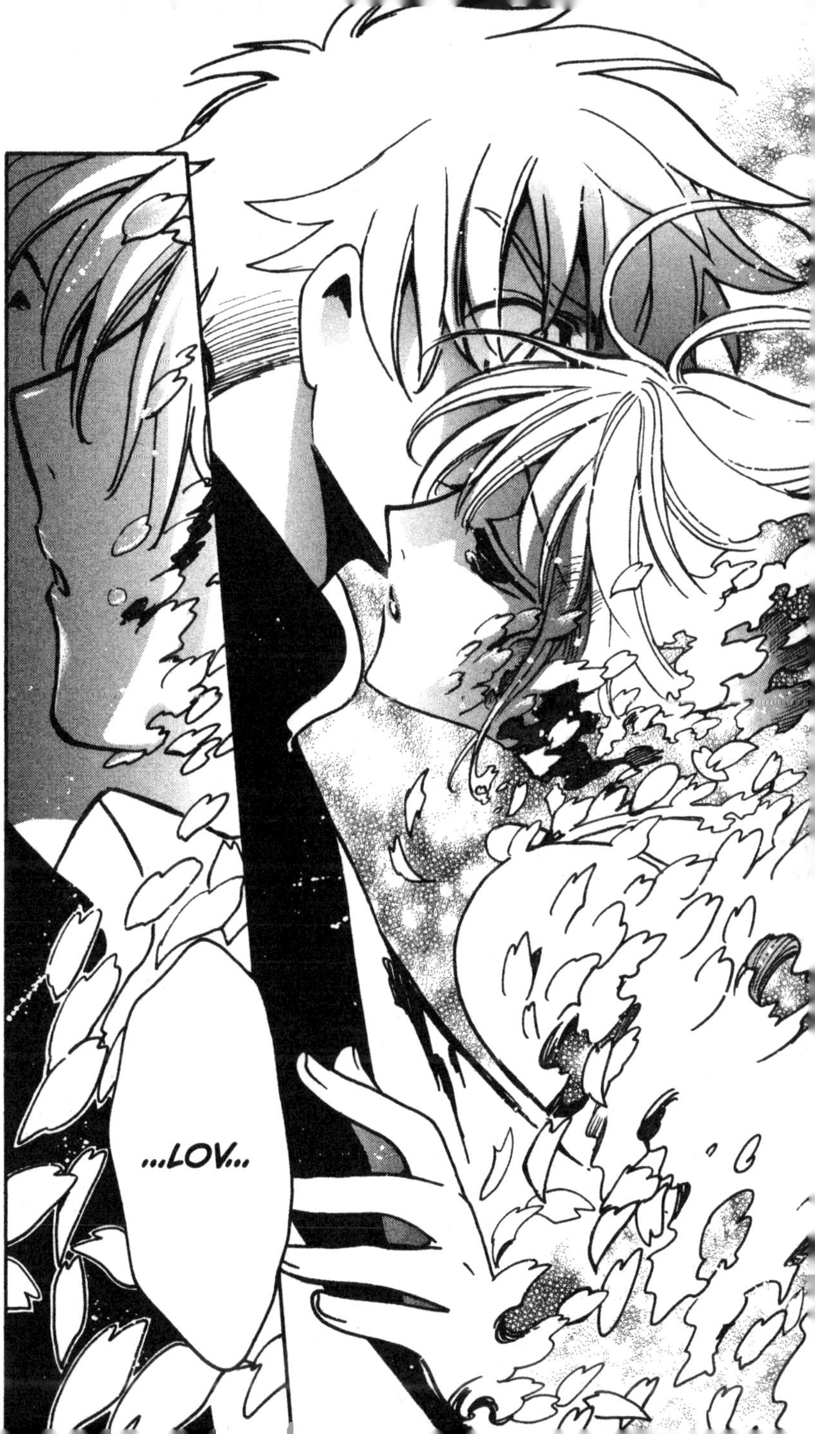
...LOV...

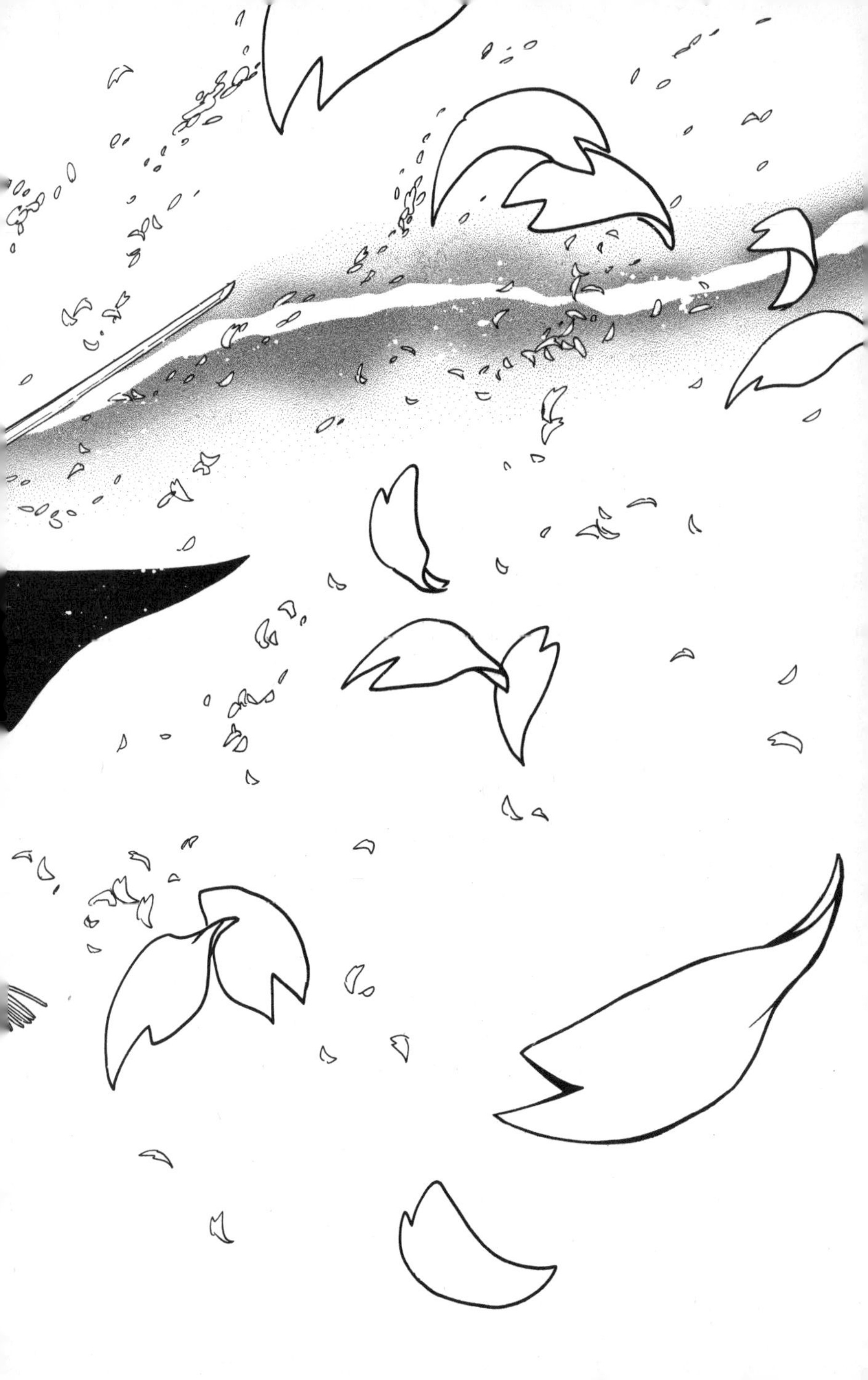

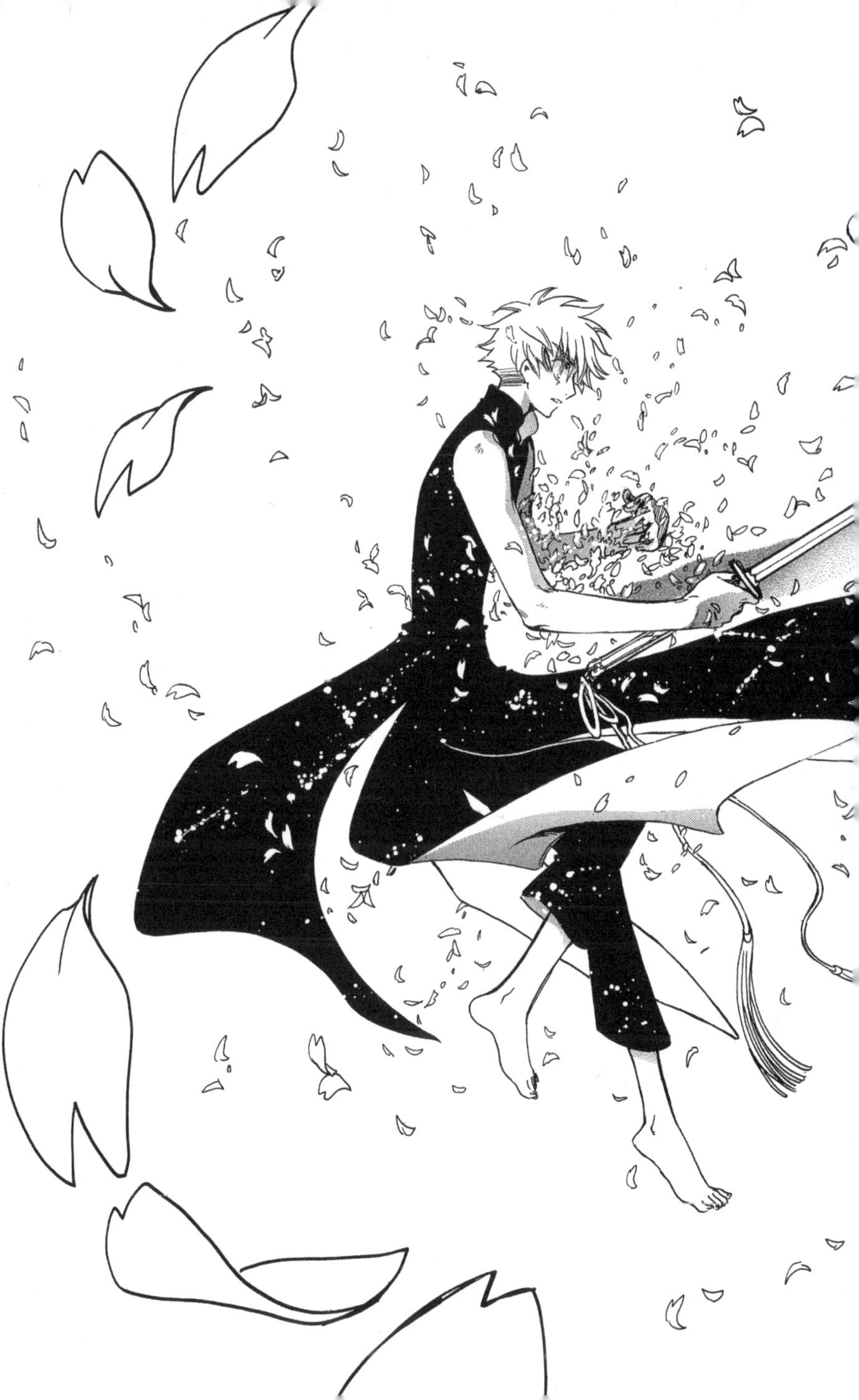

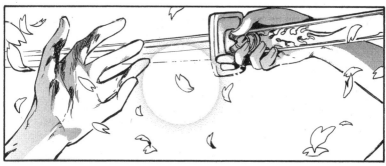

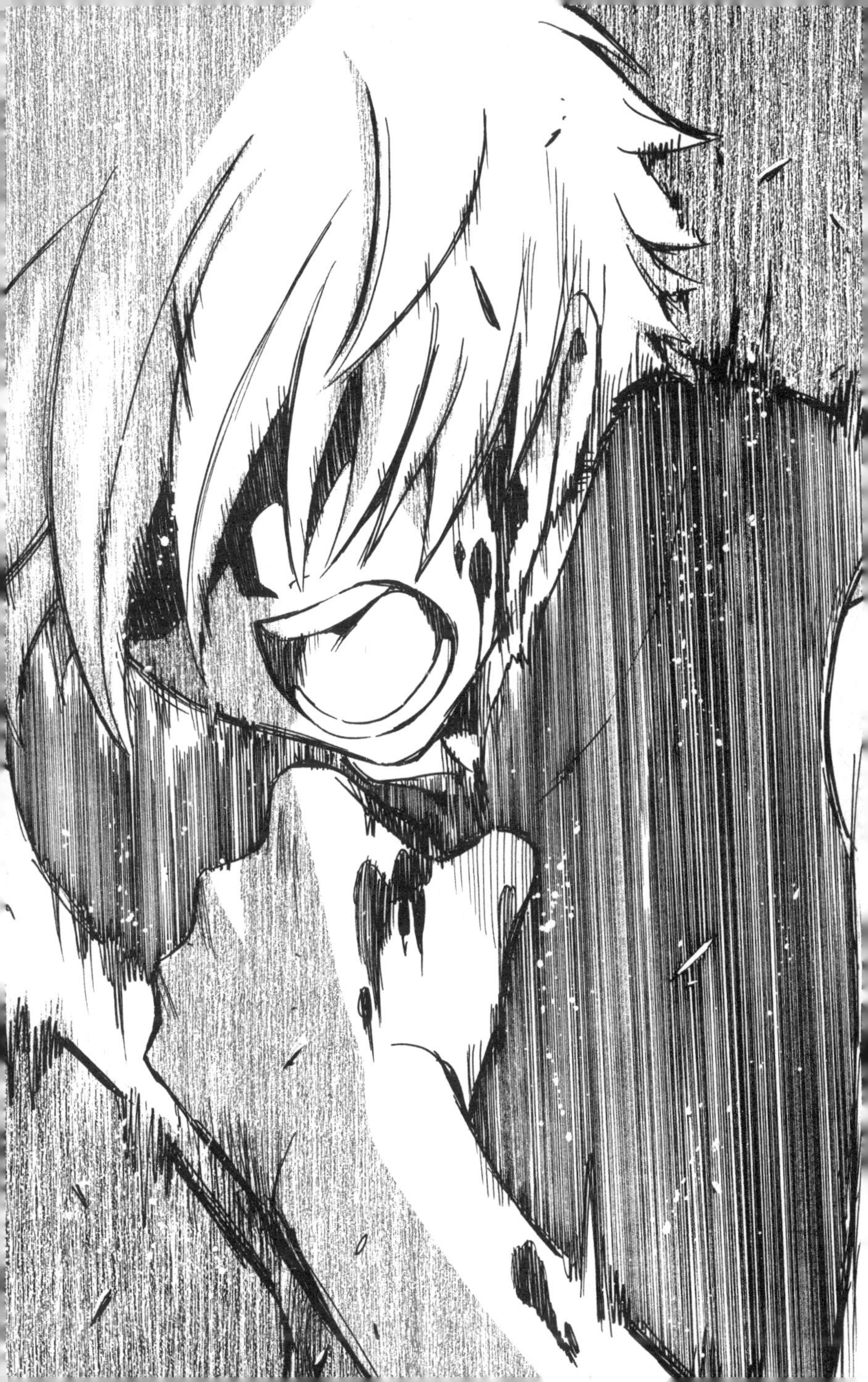

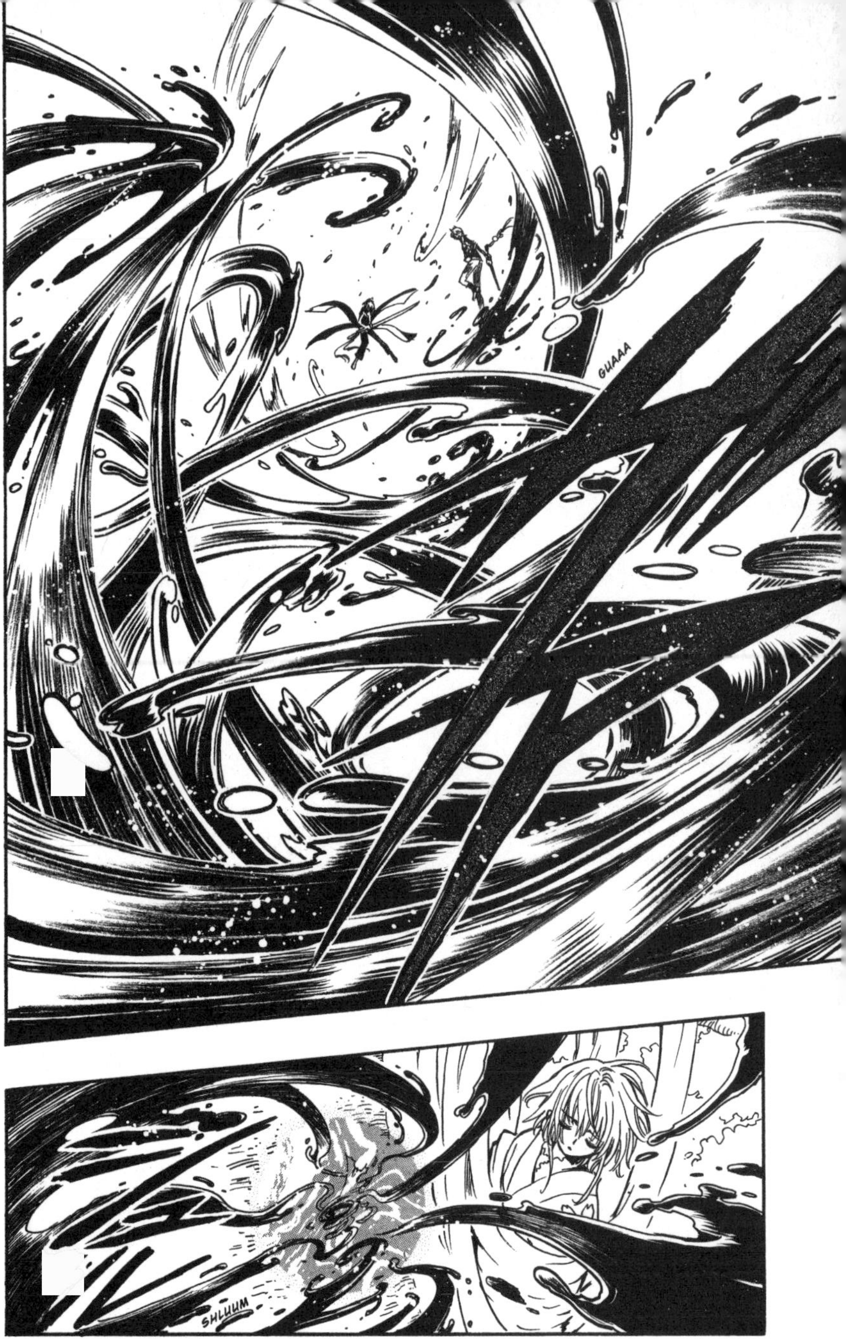
GUAAA
SHLUUM

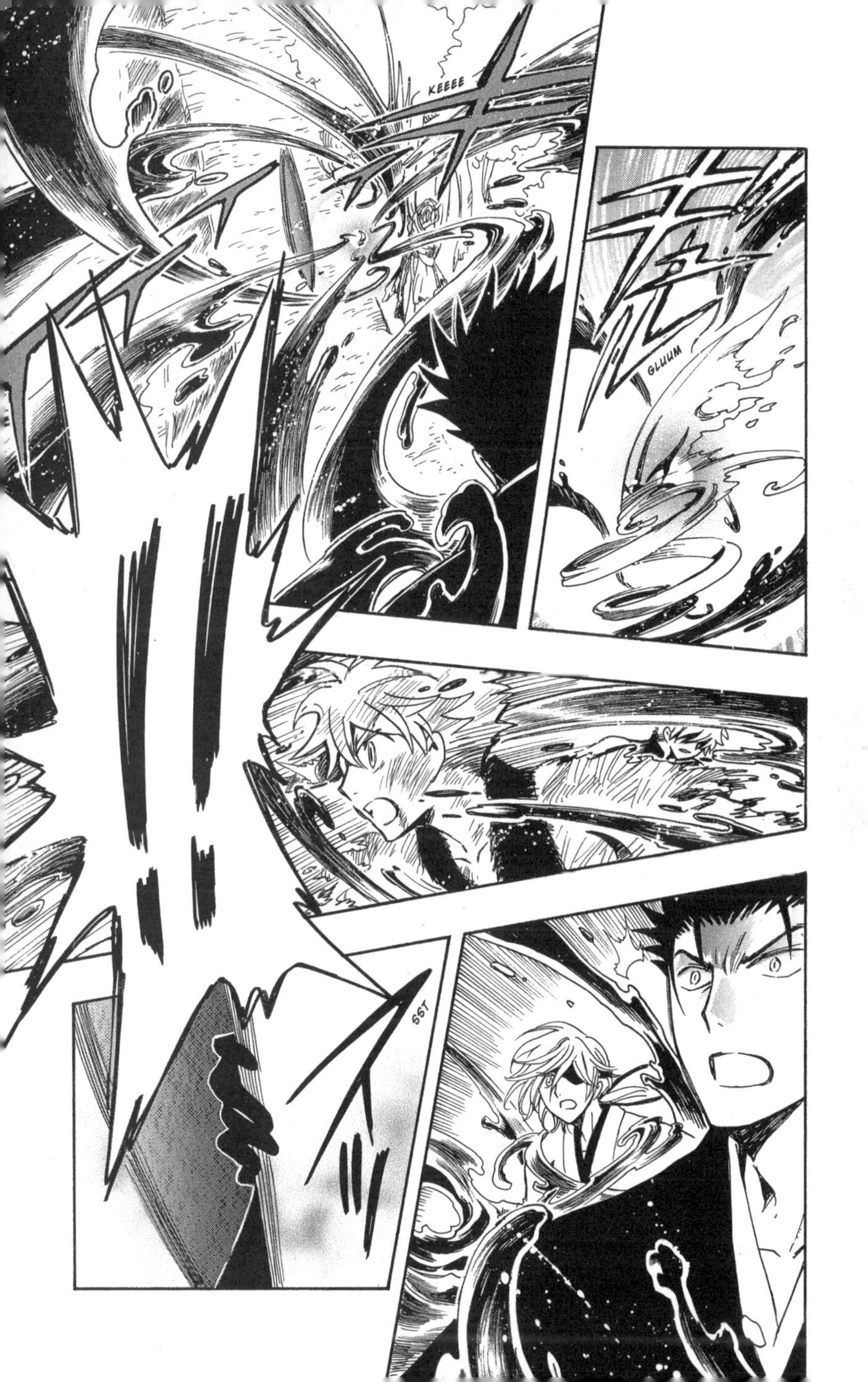
KEEEE
GLUUM
SST

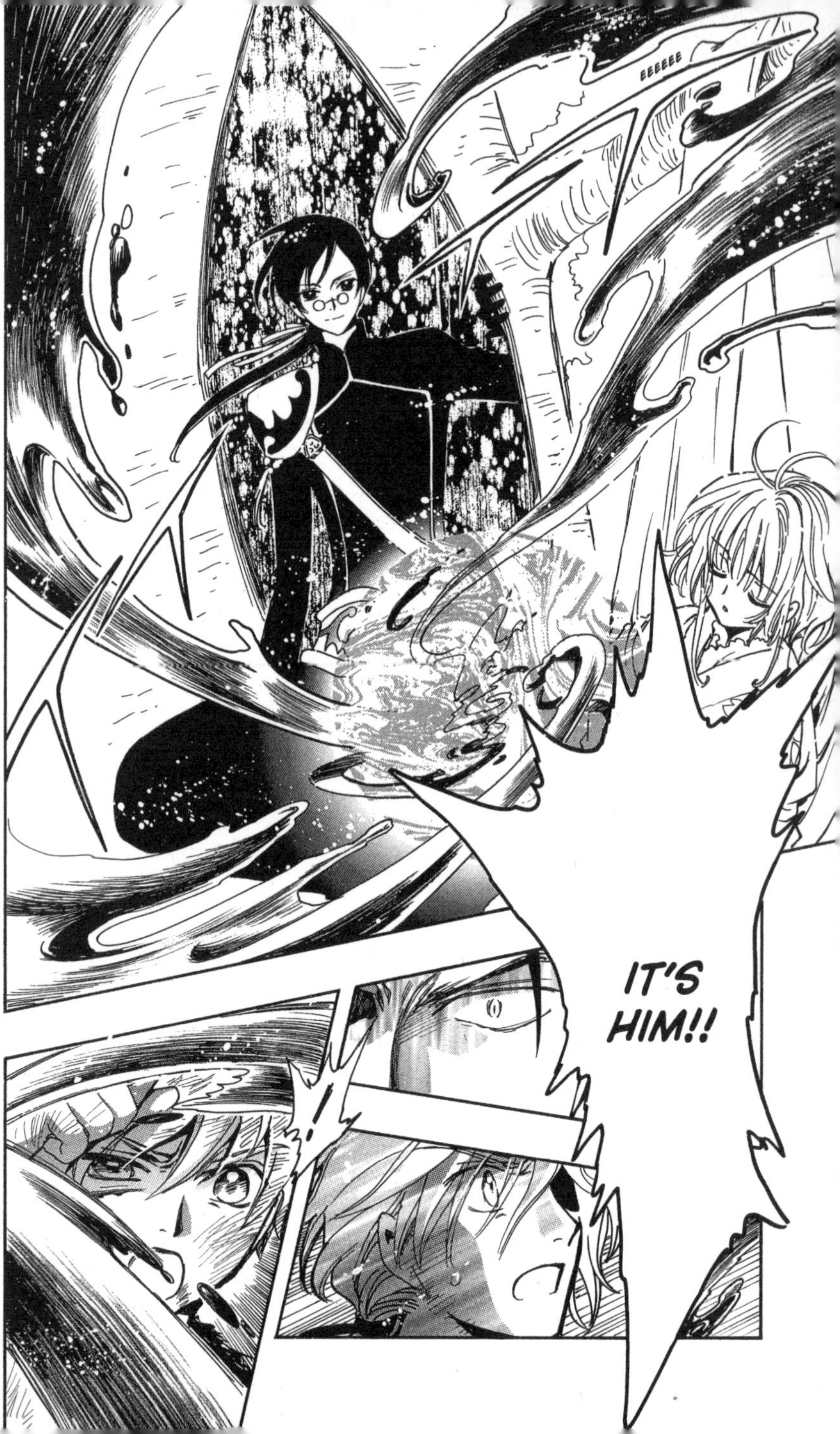
IT'S HIM!!

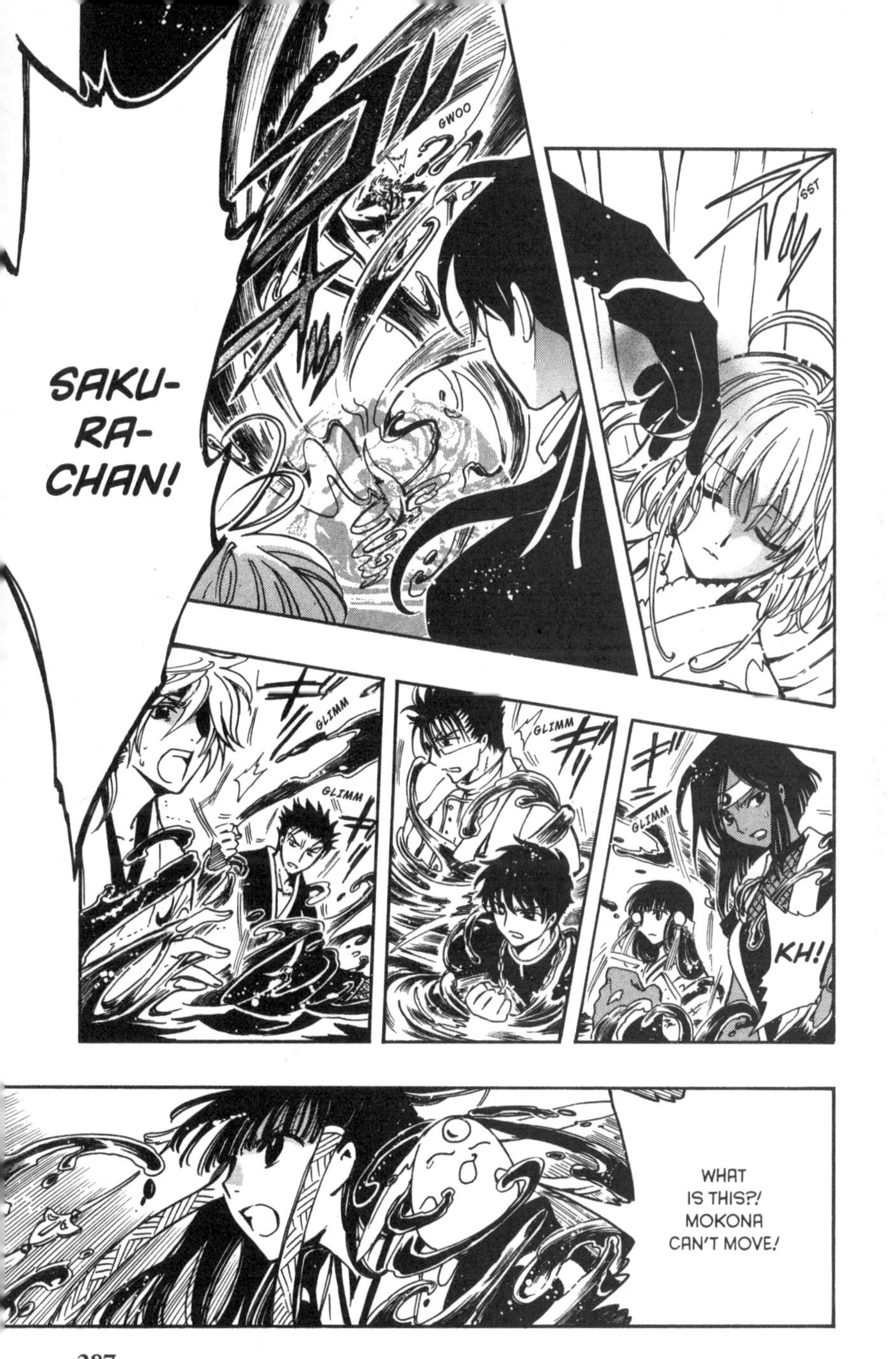
SST
GWOO
SAKU-RA-CHAN!
GLIMM
KH!
GLIMM
GLIMM
GLIMM
WHAT IS THIS?! MOKONA CAN'T MOVE!

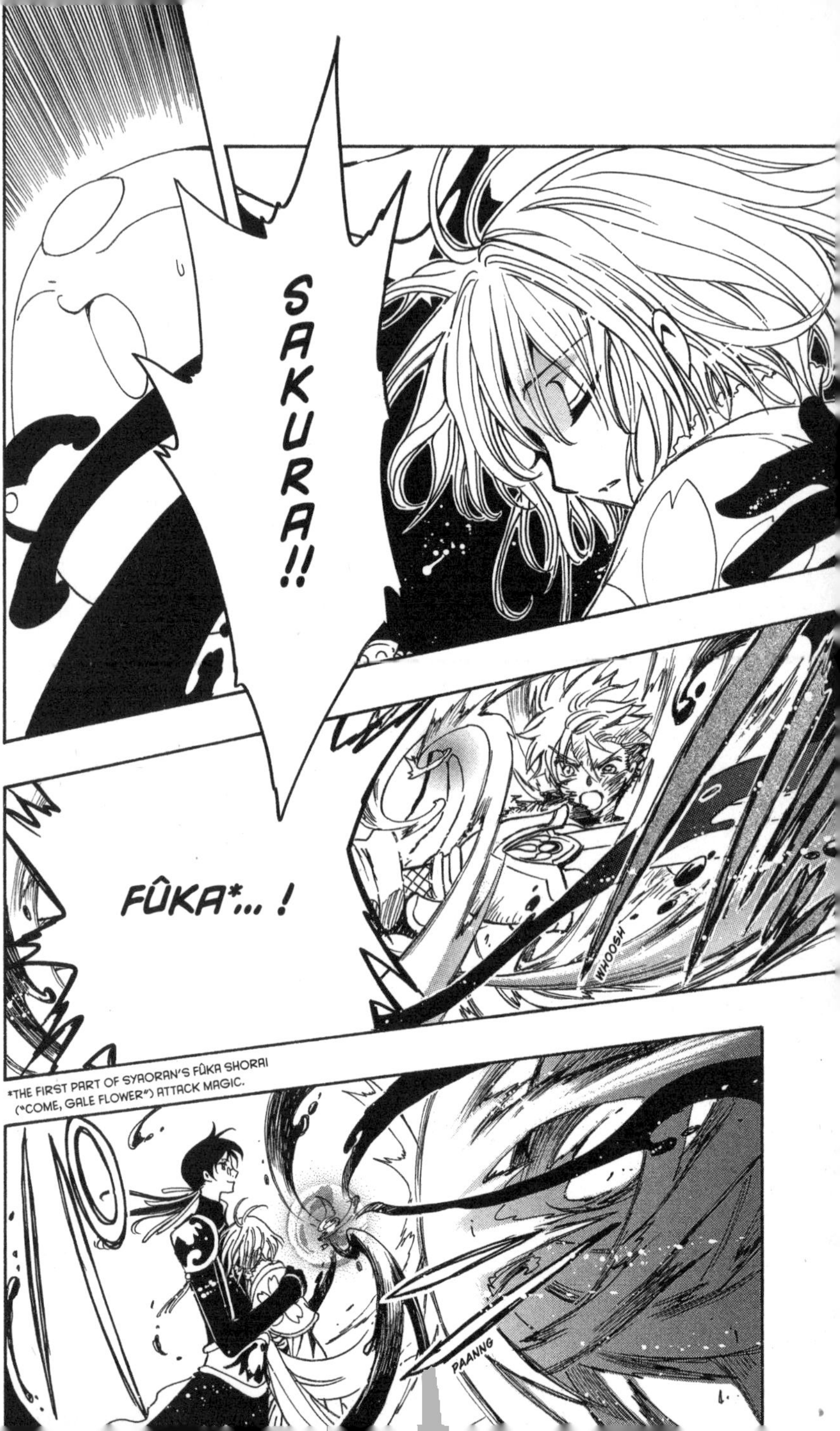
SAKURA!!
FÛKA*... !
WHOOSH
*THE FIRST PART OF SYAORAN'S FÛKA SHORAI ("COME, GALE FLOWER") ATTACK MAGIC.
PAANNG

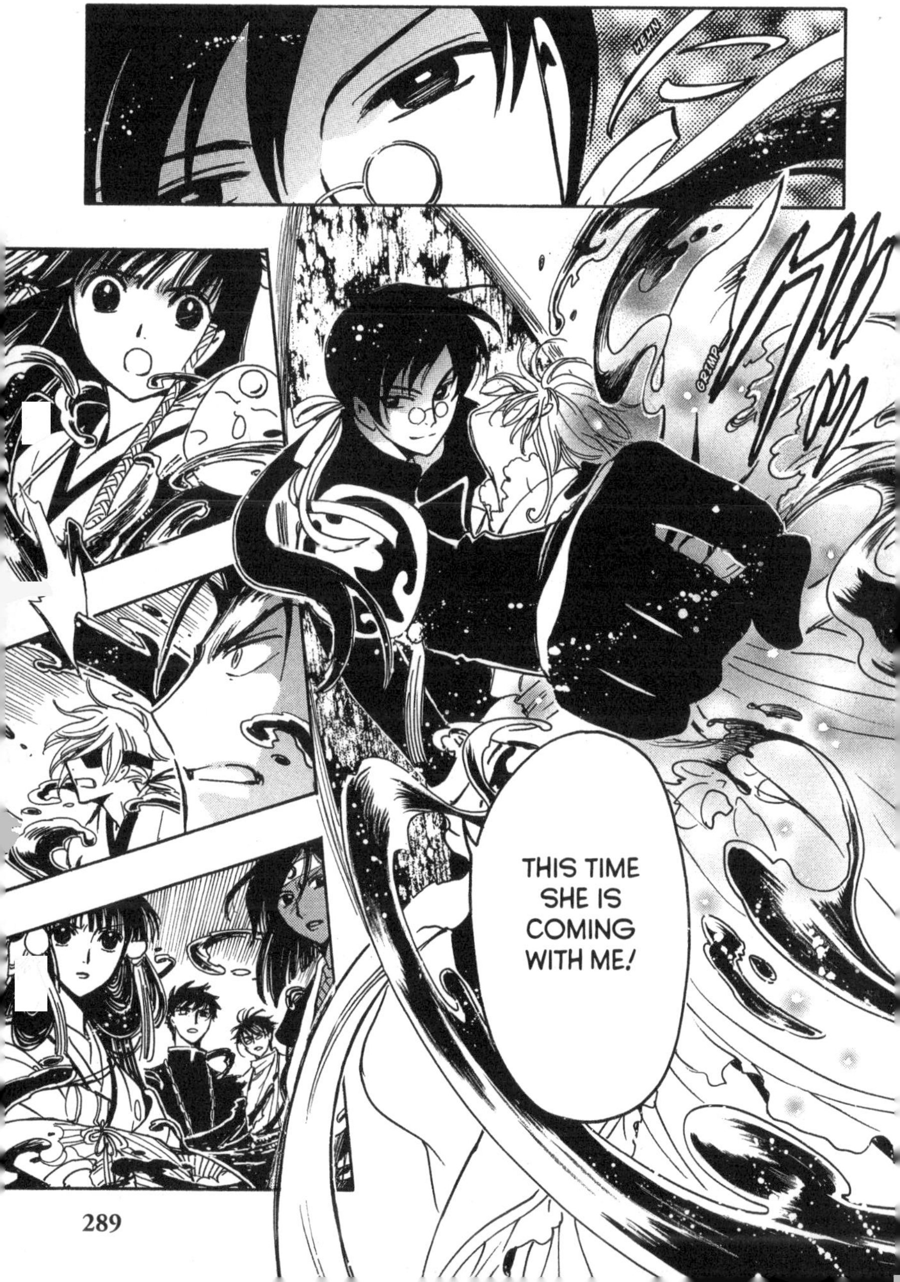
HEHN
GRIMP
THIS TIME SHE IS COMING WITH ME!

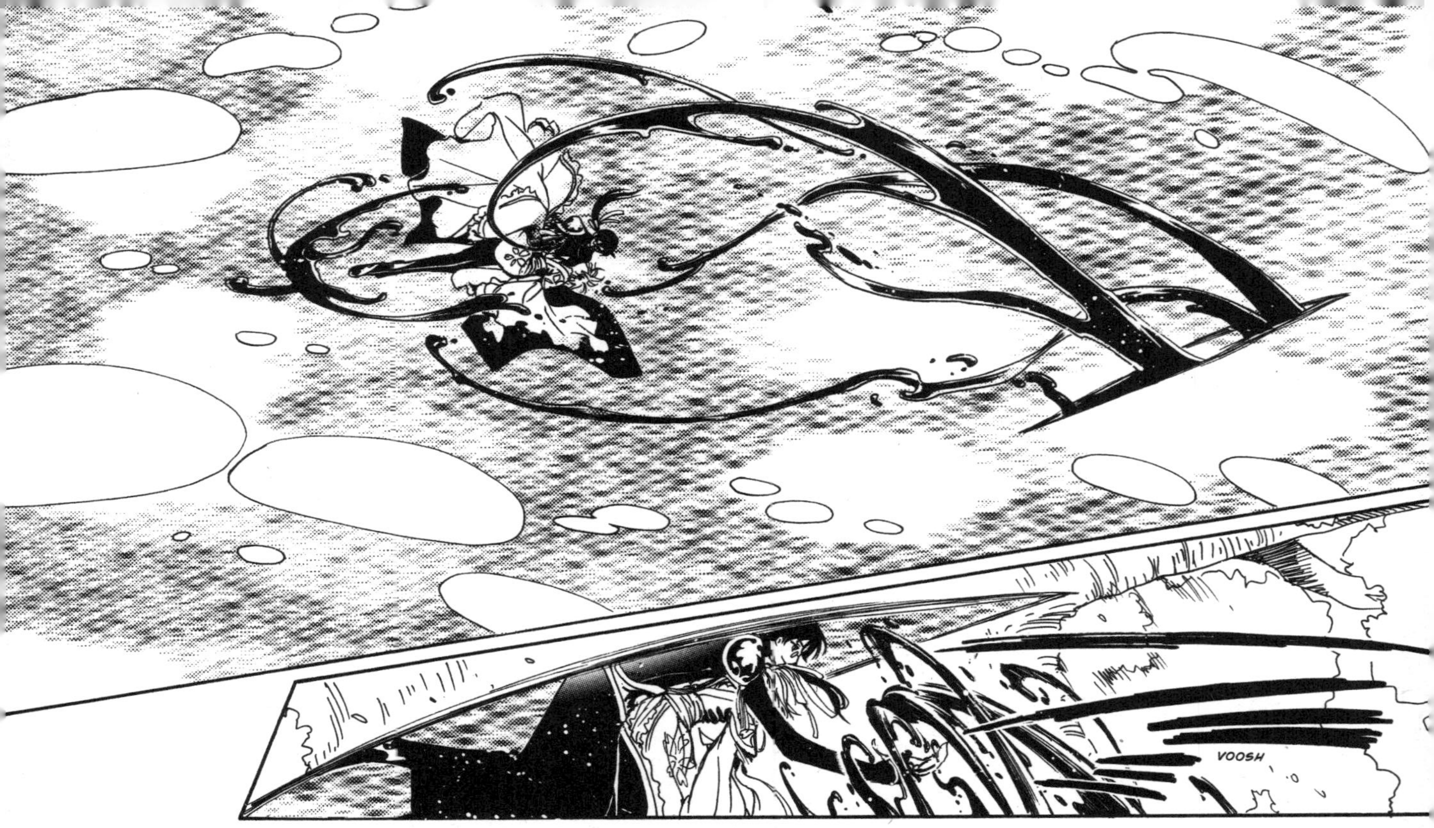
VOOSH

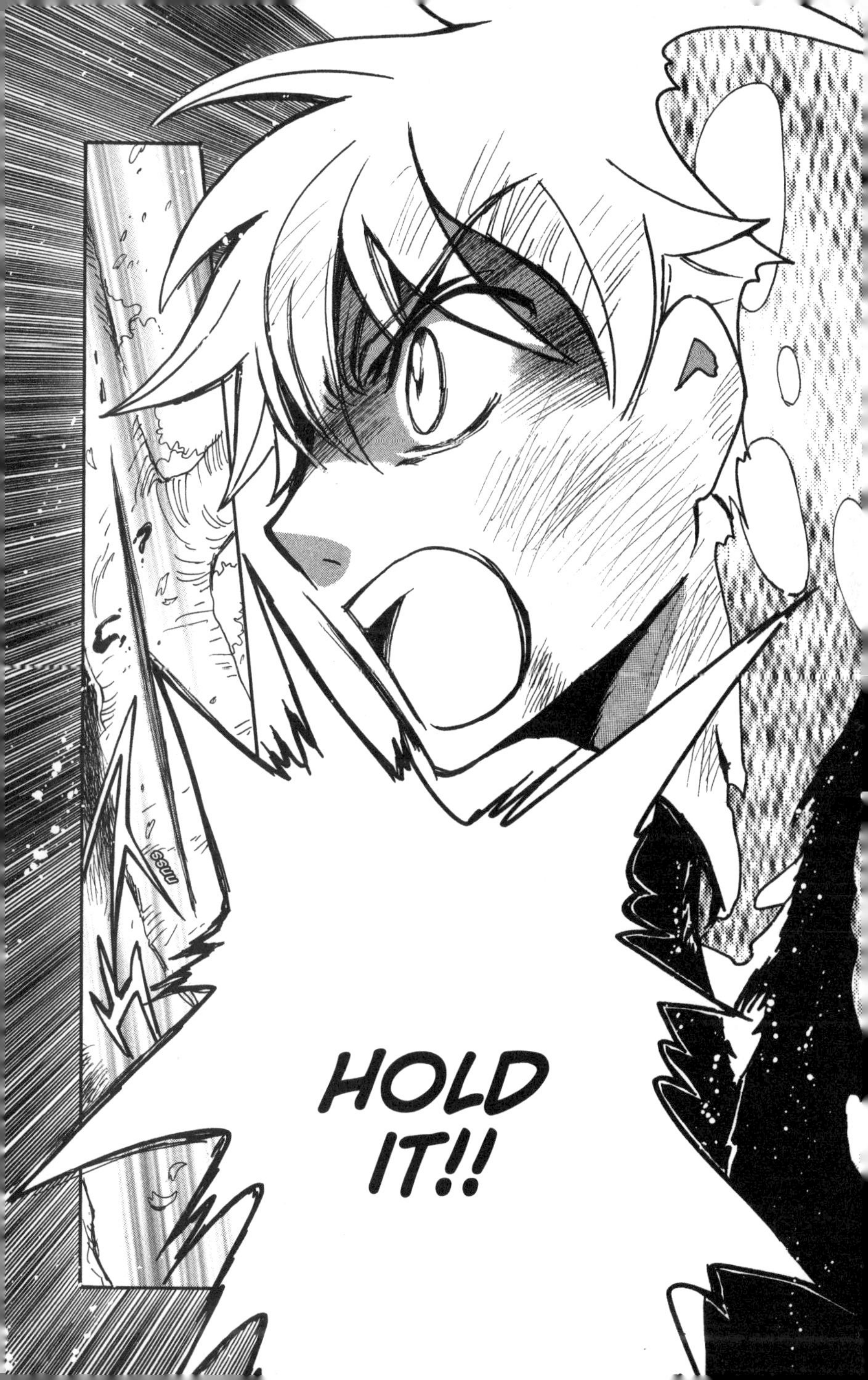
HOLD IT!!

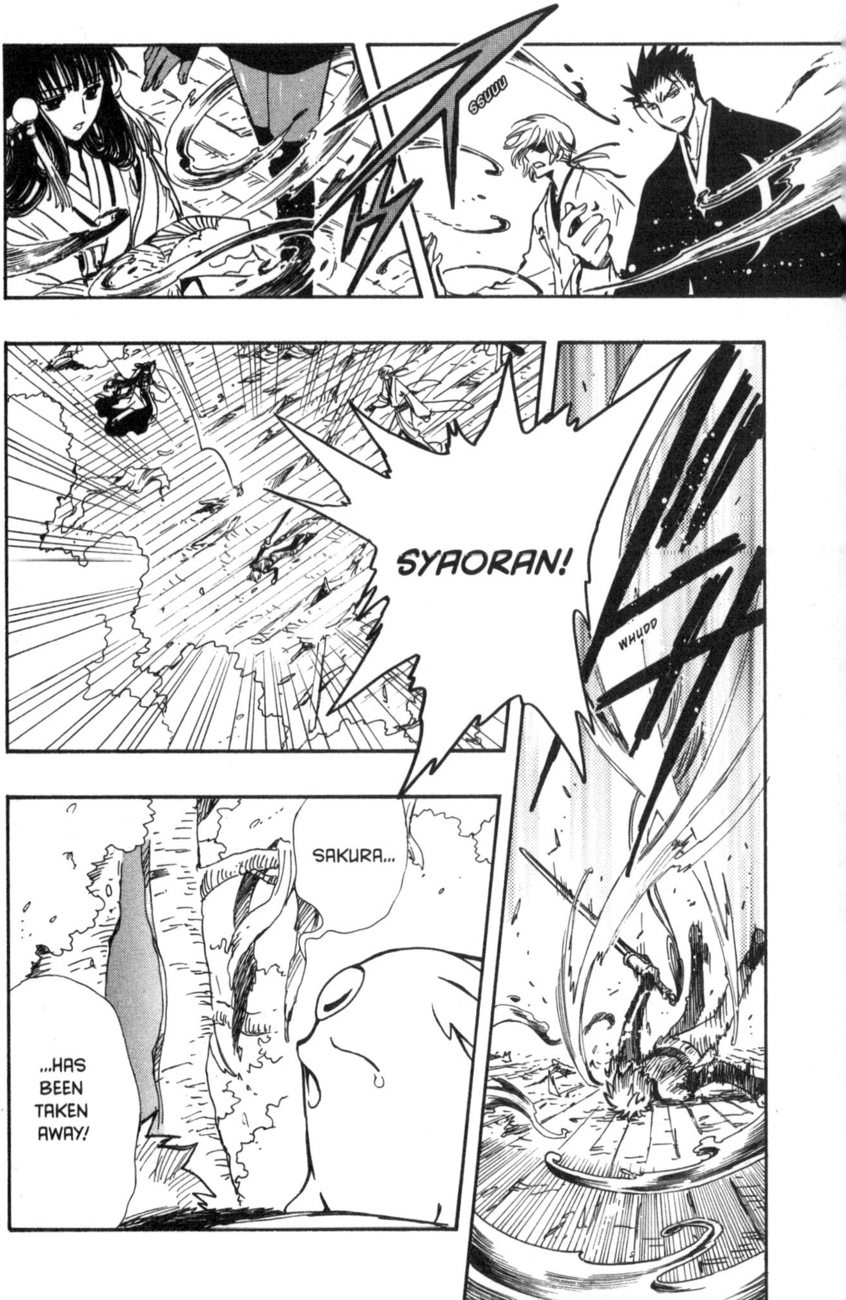
SSUUU
SYAORAN!
WHUDD
SAKURA...
...HAS BEEN TAKEN AWAY!

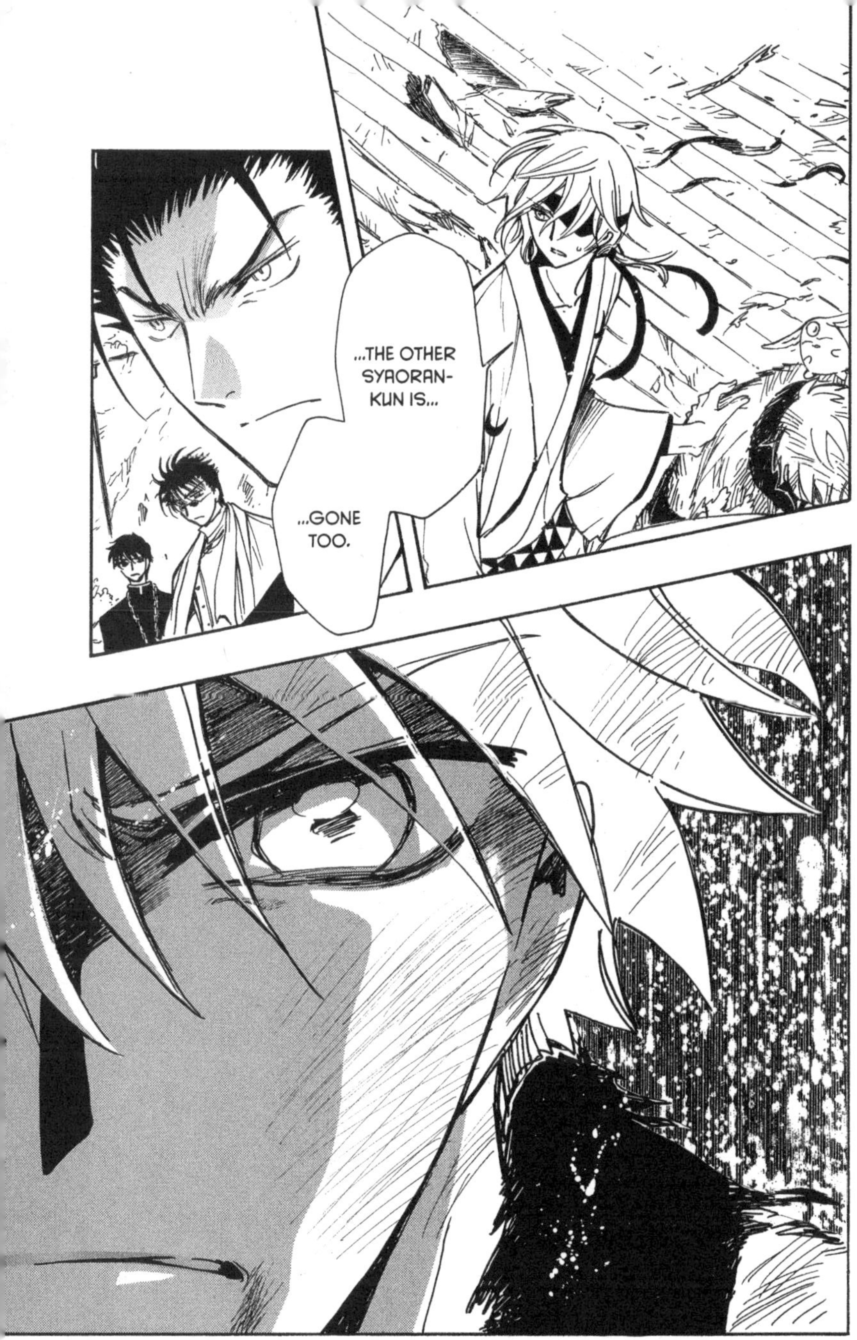
...THE OTHER SYAORAN-KUN IS...
...GONE TOO.

ツバサ
RESERVoir CHRoNiCLE

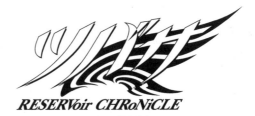

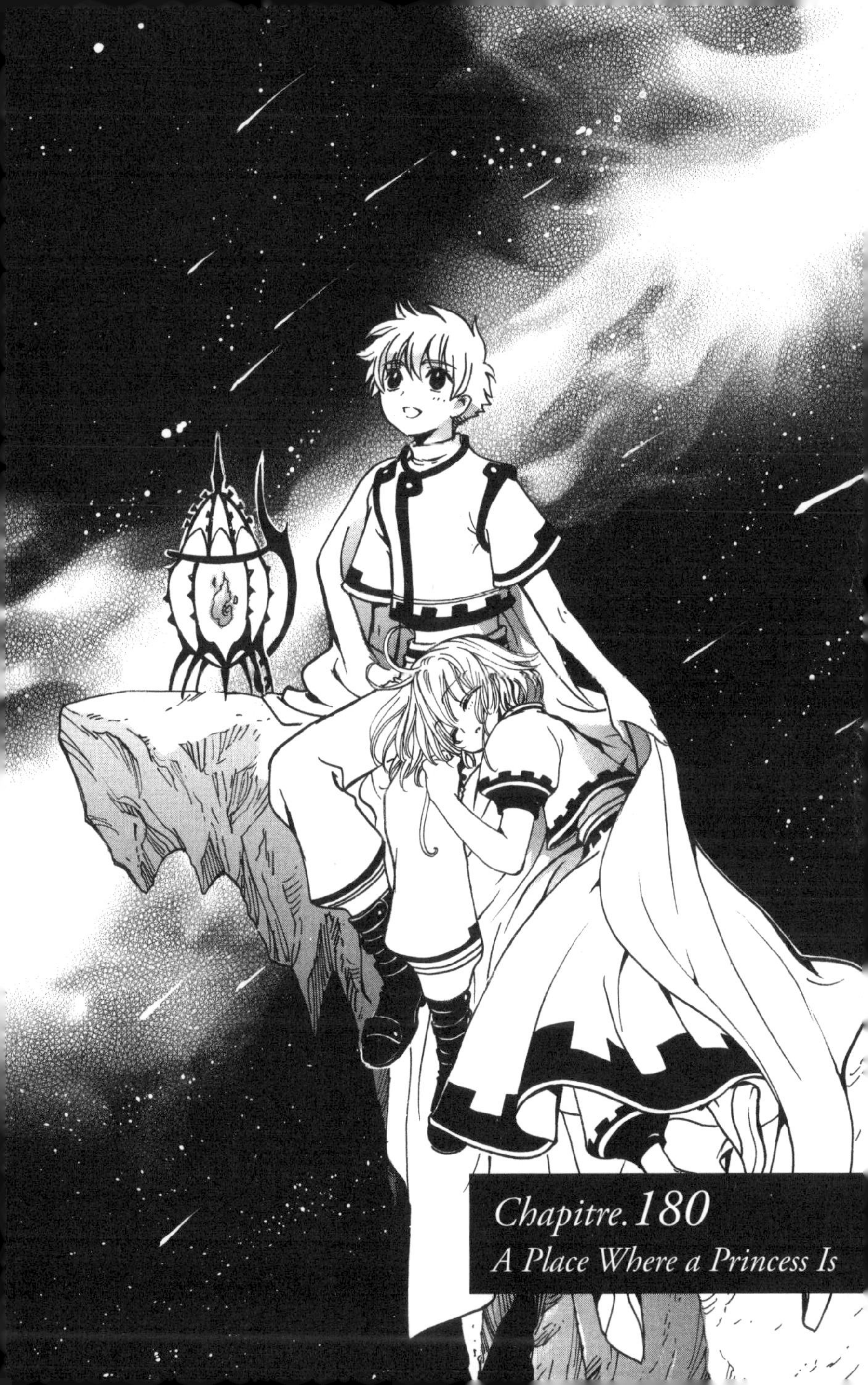
Chapitre.180
A Place Where a Princess Is

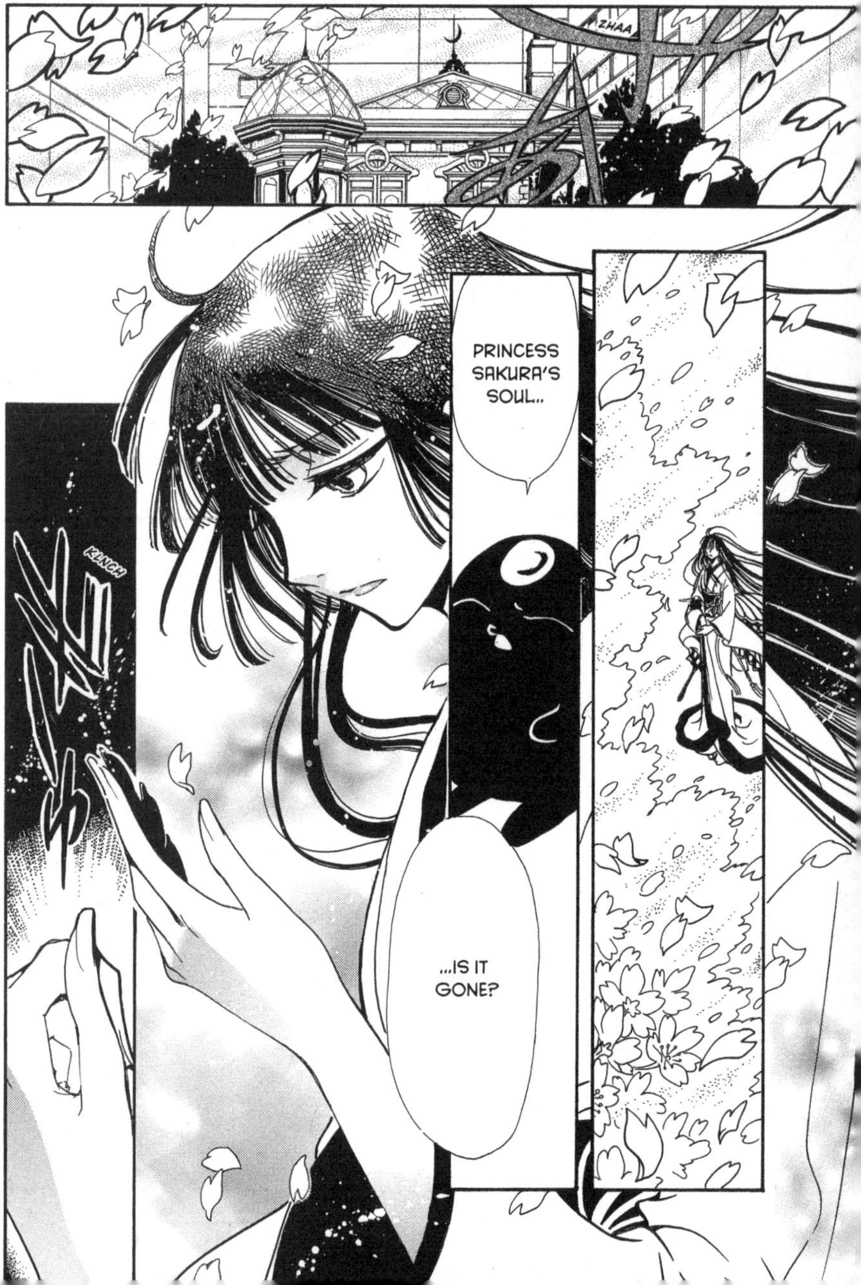
ZHAA
PRINCESS SAKURA'S SOUL...
...IS IT GONE?
KLINCH

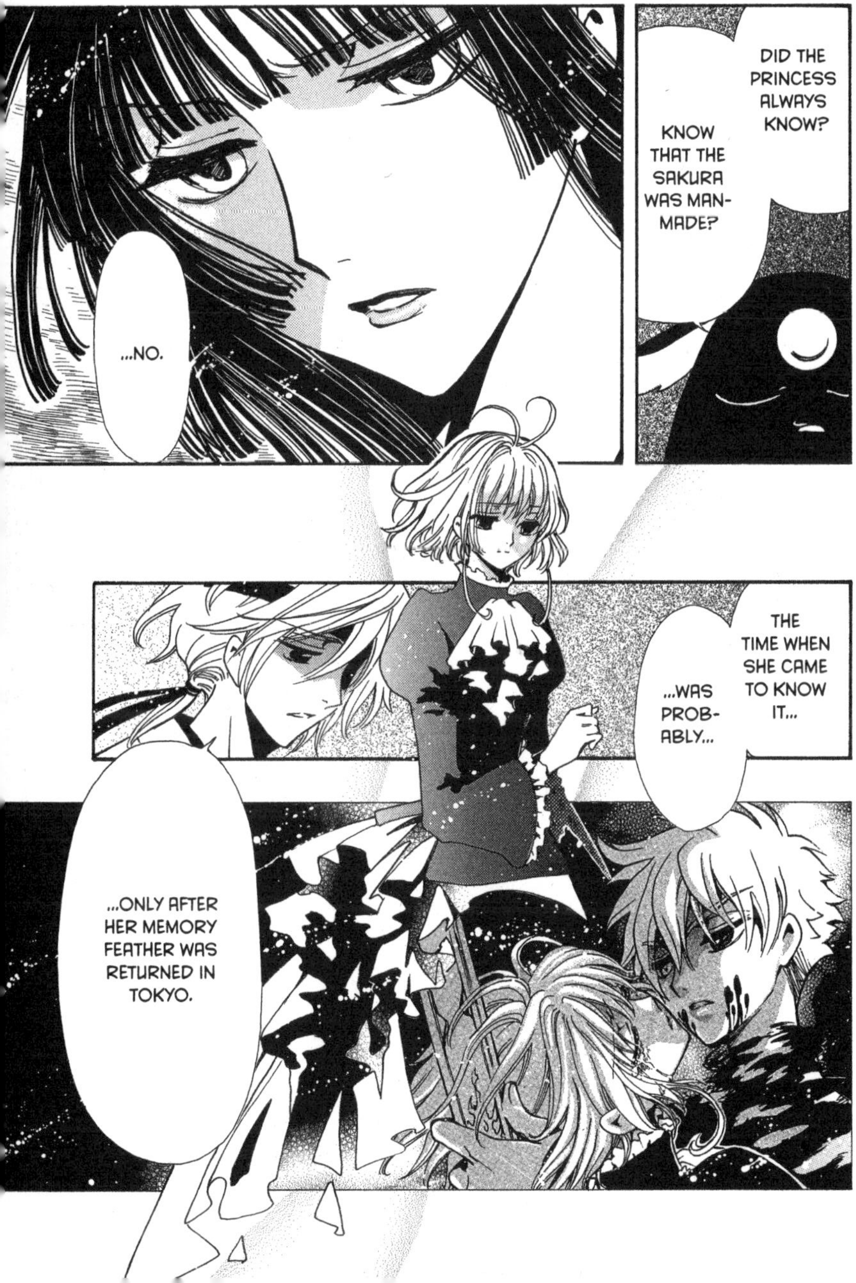
DID THE PRINCESS ALWAYS KNOW?
KNOW THAT THE SAKURA WAS MAN-MADE?
...NO.
THE TIME WHEN SHE CAME TO KNOW IT...
...WAS PROBABLY...
...ONLY AFTER HER MEMORY FEATHER WAS RETURNED IN TOKYO.

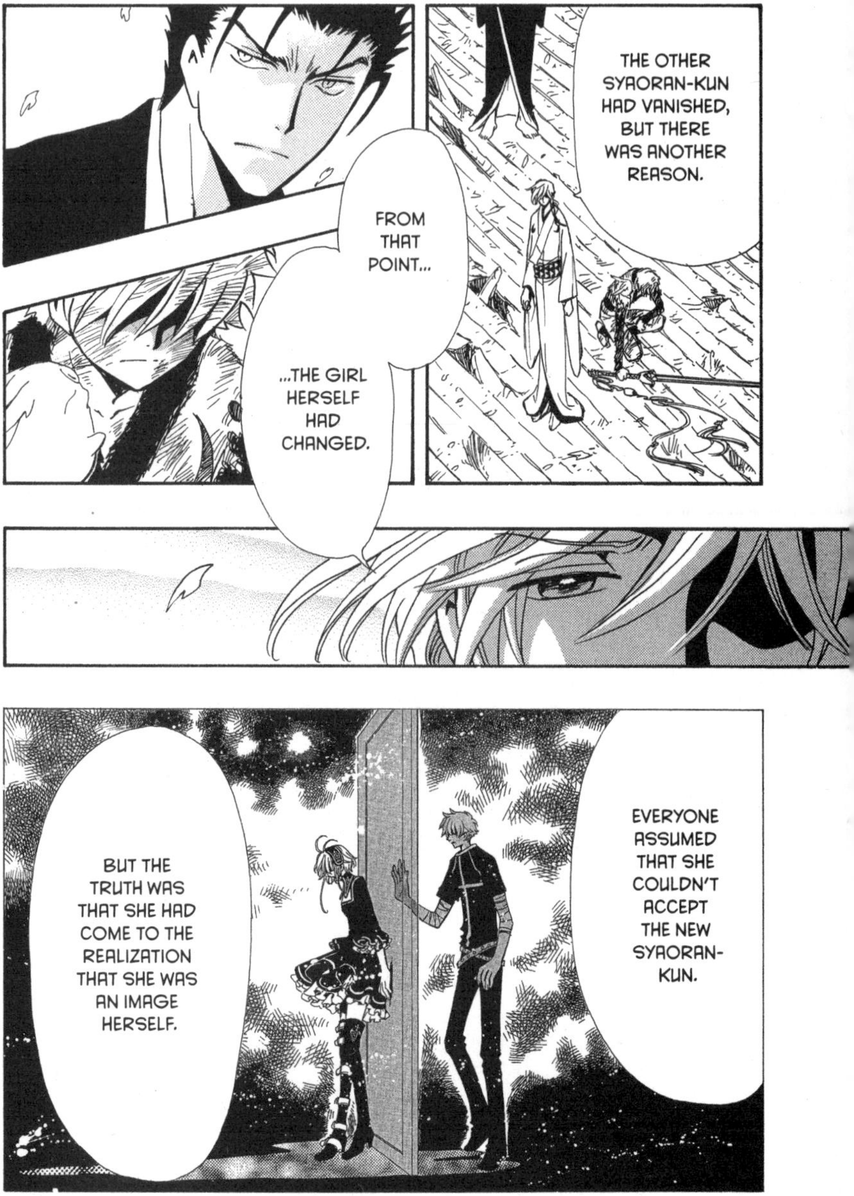
THE OTHER SYAORAN-KUN HAD VANISHED, BUT THERE WAS ANOTHER REASON.
FROM THAT POINT...
...THE GIRL HERSELF HAD CHANGED.
EVERYONE ASSUMED THAT SHE COULDN'T ACCEPT THE NEW SYAORAN-KUN.
BUT THE TRUTH WAS THAT SHE HAD COME TO THE REALIZATION THAT SHE WAS AN IMAGE HERSELF.

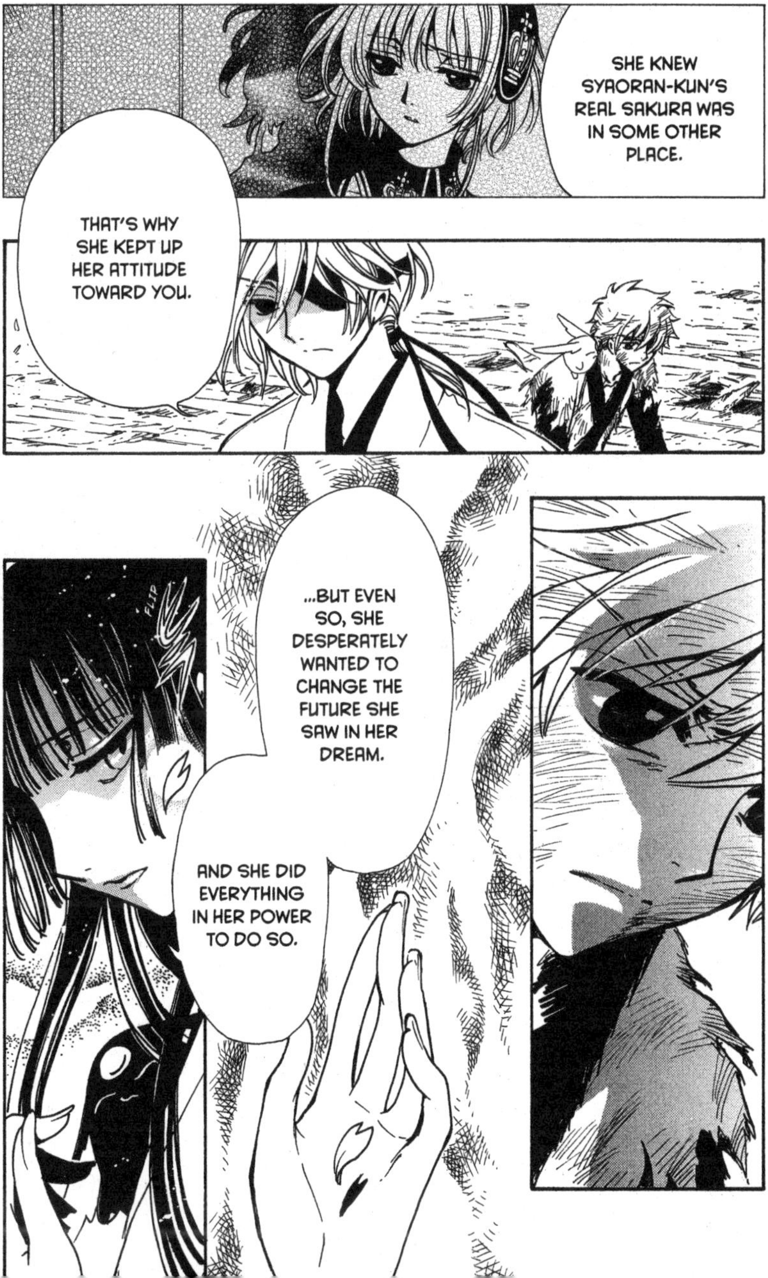
SHE KNEW SYAORAN-KUN'S REAL SAKURA WAS IN SOME OTHER PLACE.
THAT'S WHY SHE KEPT UP HER ATTITUDE TOWARD YOU.
...BUT EVEN SO, SHE DESPERATELY WANTED TO CHANGE THE FUTURE SHE SAW IN HER DREAM.
AND SHE DID EVERYTHING IN HER POWER TO DO SO.
FLIP

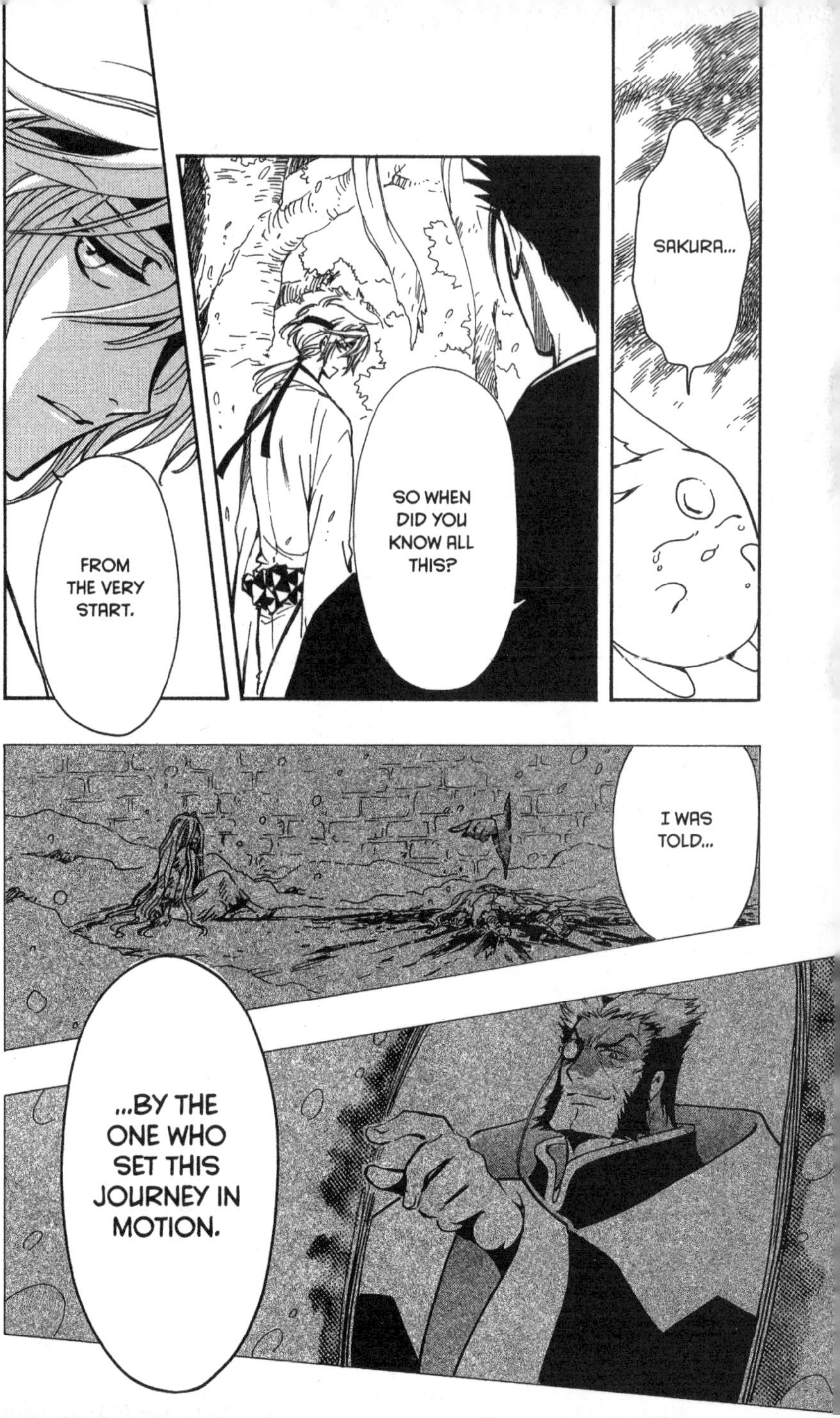
SAKURA...
SO WHEN DID YOU KNOW ALL THIS?
FROM THE VERY START.
I WAS TOLD...
...BY THE ONE WHO SET THIS JOURNEY IN MOTION.

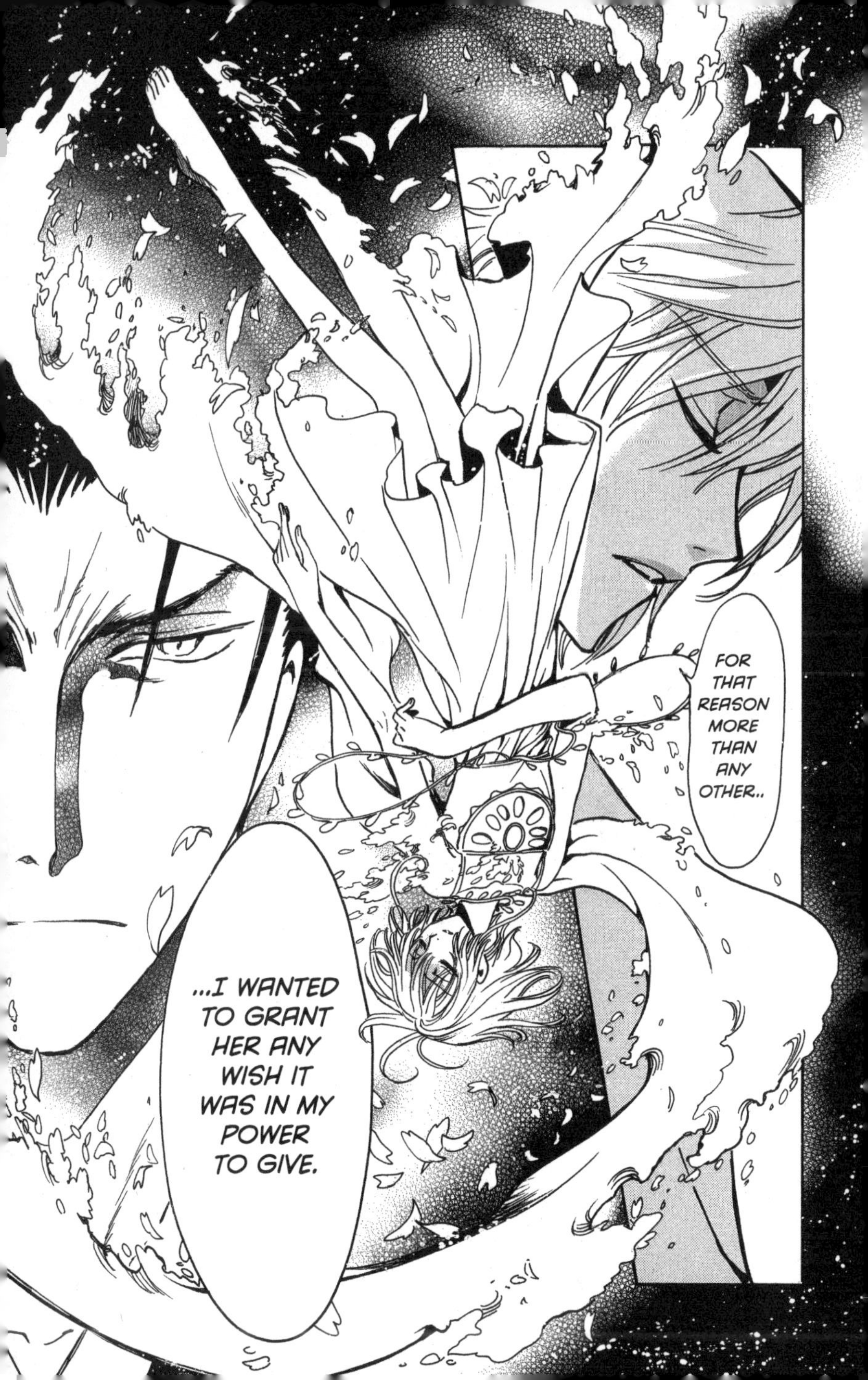
FOR THAT REASON MORE THAN ANY OTHER..
...I WANTED TO GRANT HER ANY WISH IT WAS IN MY POWER TO GIVE.

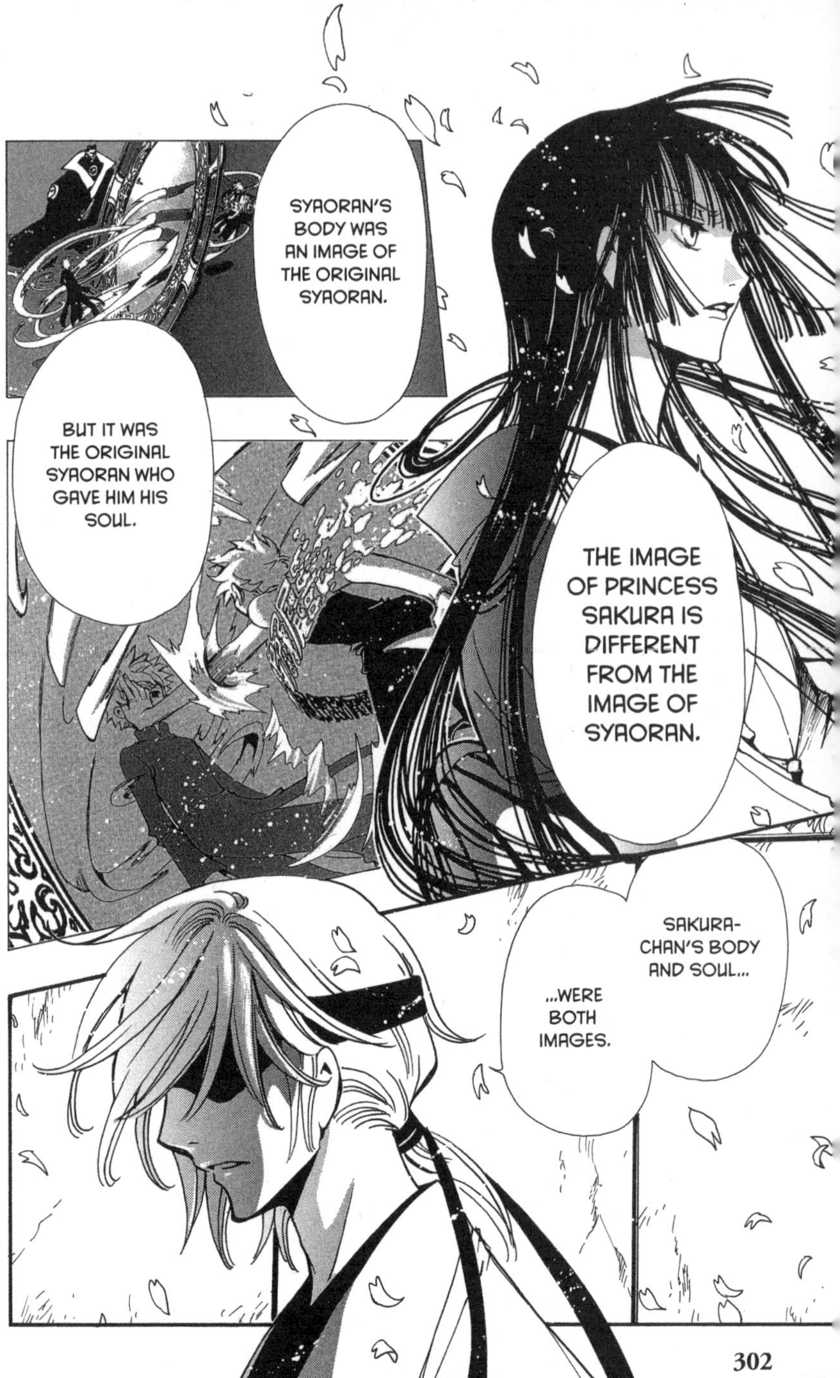
SYAORAN'S BODY WAS AN IMAGE OF THE ORIGINAL SYAORAN.
BUT IT WAS THE ORIGINAL SYAORAN WHO GAVE HIM HIS SOUL.
THE IMAGE OF PRINCESS SAKURA IS DIFFERENT FROM THE IMAGE OF SYAORAN.
SAKURA-CHAN'S BODY AND SOUL...
...WERE BOTH IMAGES.

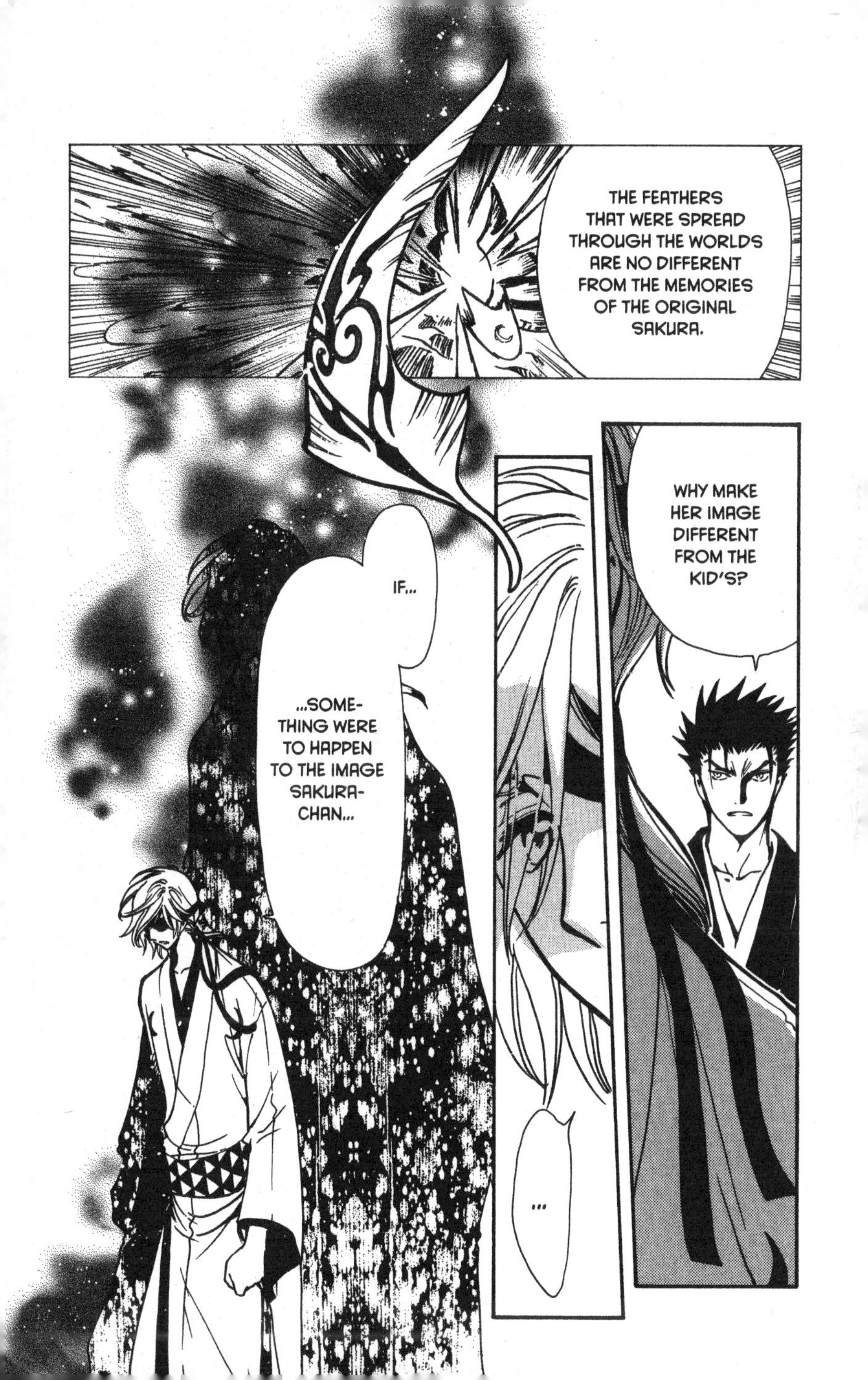
THE FEATHERS THAT WERE SPREAD THROUGH THE WORLDS ARE NO DIFFERENT FROM THE MEMORIES OF THE ORIGINAL SAKURA.
WHY MAKE HER IMAGE DIFFERENT FROM THE KID'S?
...
IF...
...SOME-THING WERE TO HAPPEN TO THE IMAGE SAKURA-CHAN...

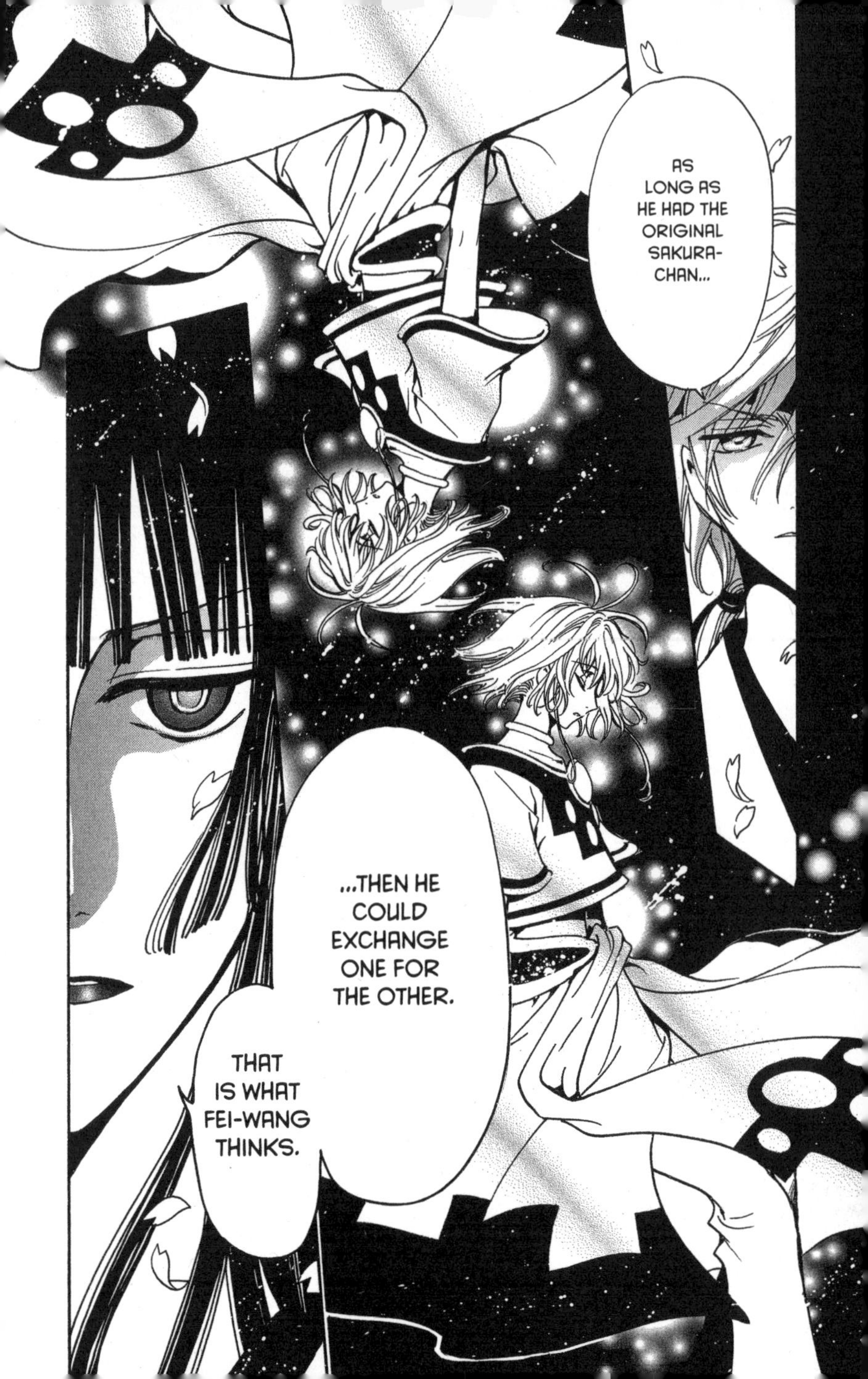
AS LONG AS HE HAD THE ORIGINAL SAKURA-CHAN...
...THEN HE COULD EXCHANGE ONE FOR THE OTHER.
THAT IS WHAT FEI-WANG THINKS.

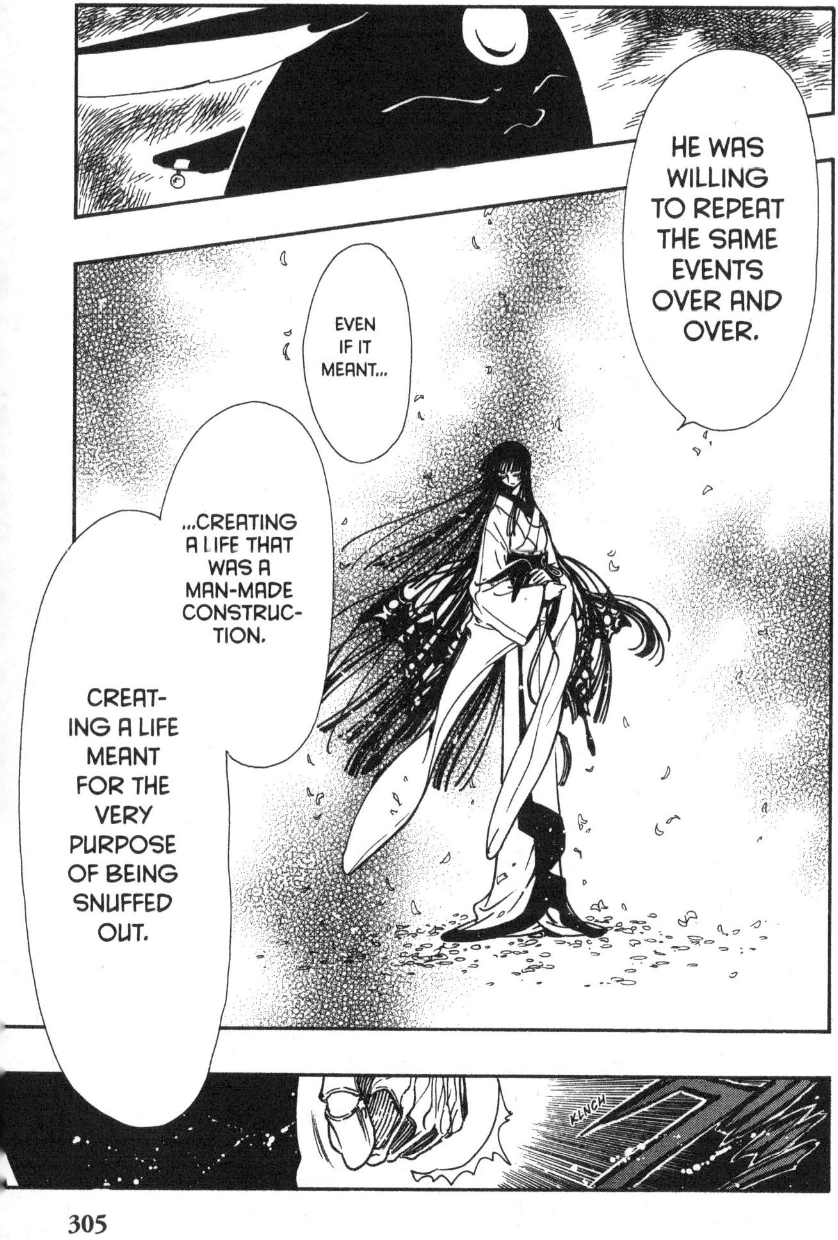
HE WAS WILLING TO REPEAT THE SAME EVENTS OVER AND OVER.
EVEN IF IT MEANT...
...CREATING A LIFE THAT WAS A MAN-MADE CONSTRUCTION.
CREATING A LIFE MEANT FOR THE VERY PURPOSE OF BEING SNUFFED OUT.
KLNCH

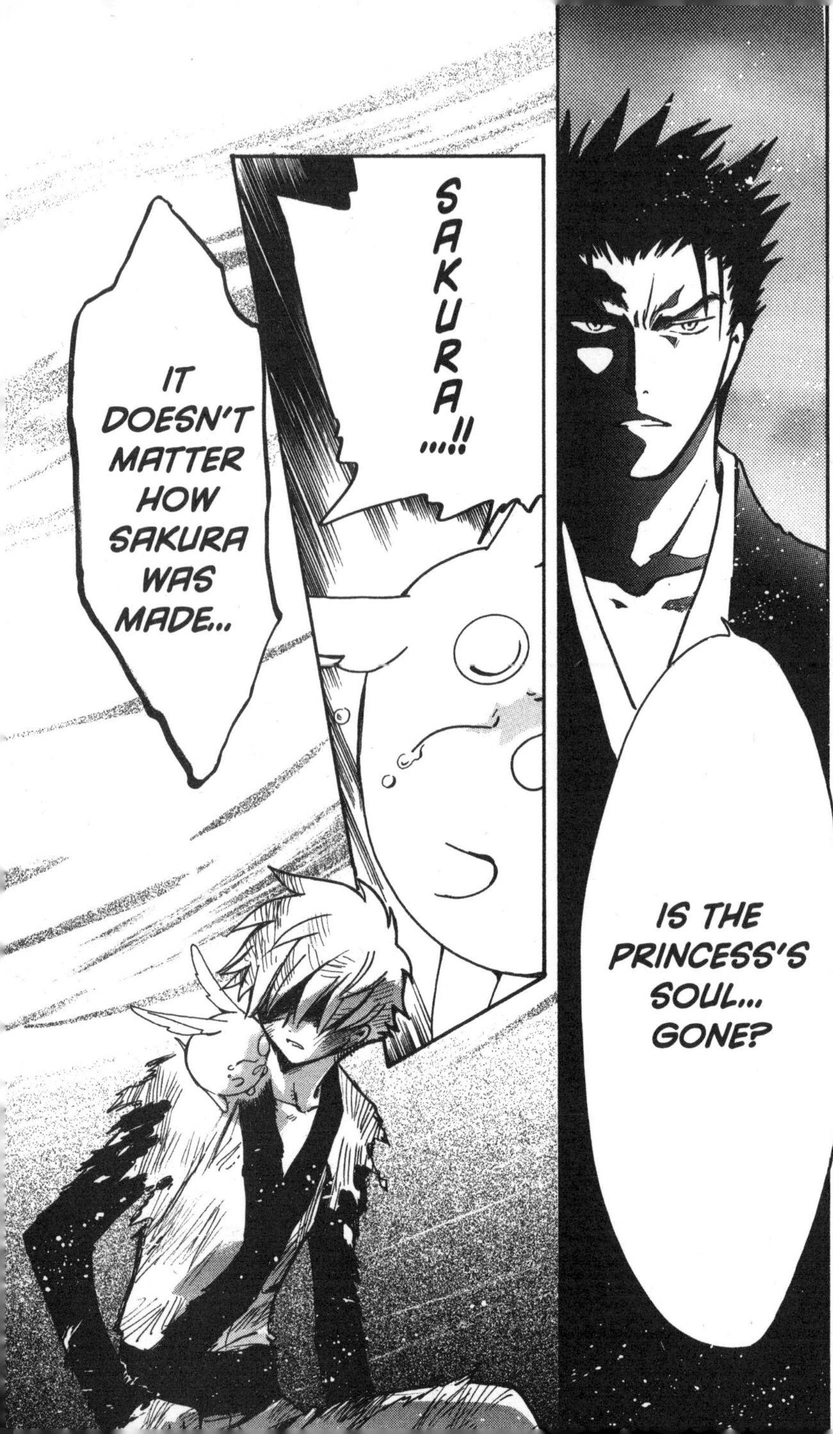
IS THE PRINCESS'S SOUL... GONE?
SAKURA ....!!
IT DOESN'T MATTER HOW SAKURA WAS MADE...

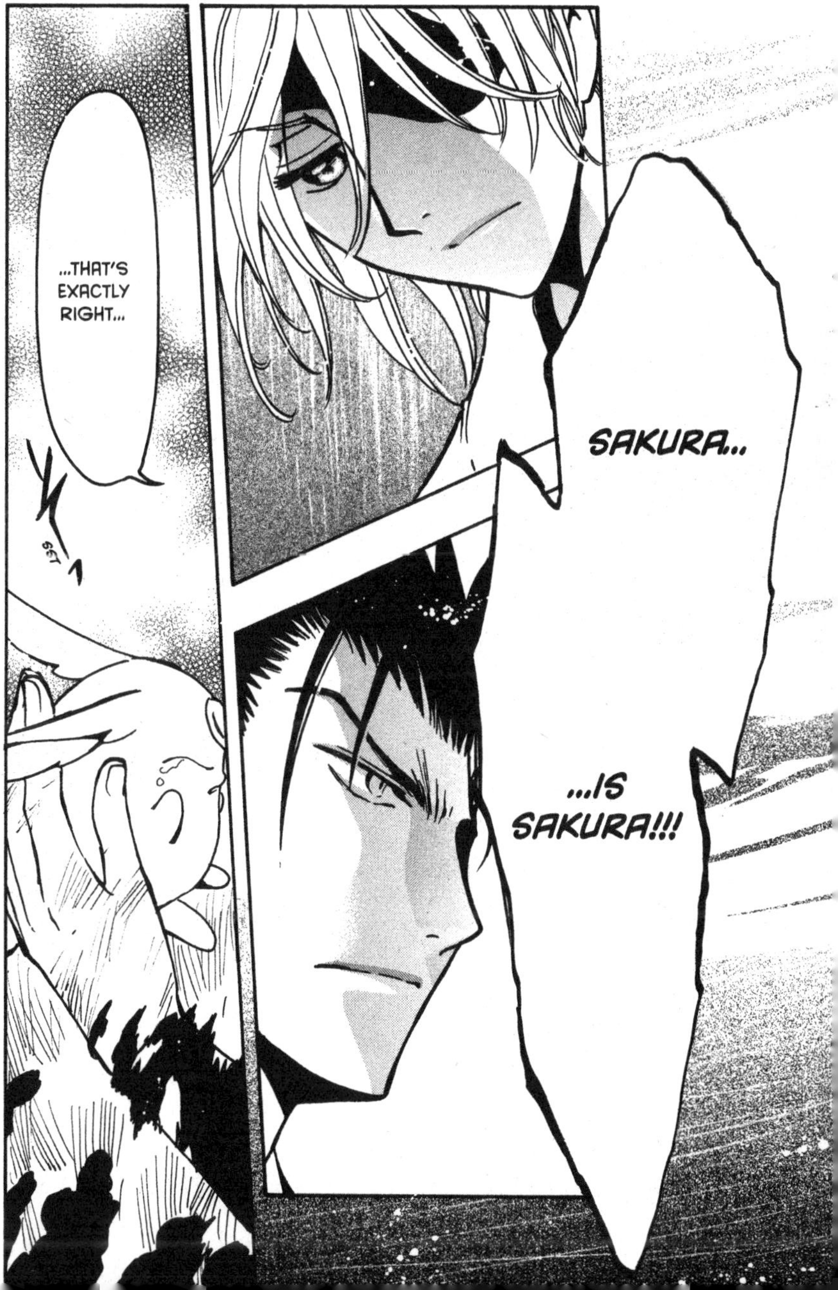
SAKURA...
...IS SAKURA!!!
...THAT'S EXACTLY RIGHT...

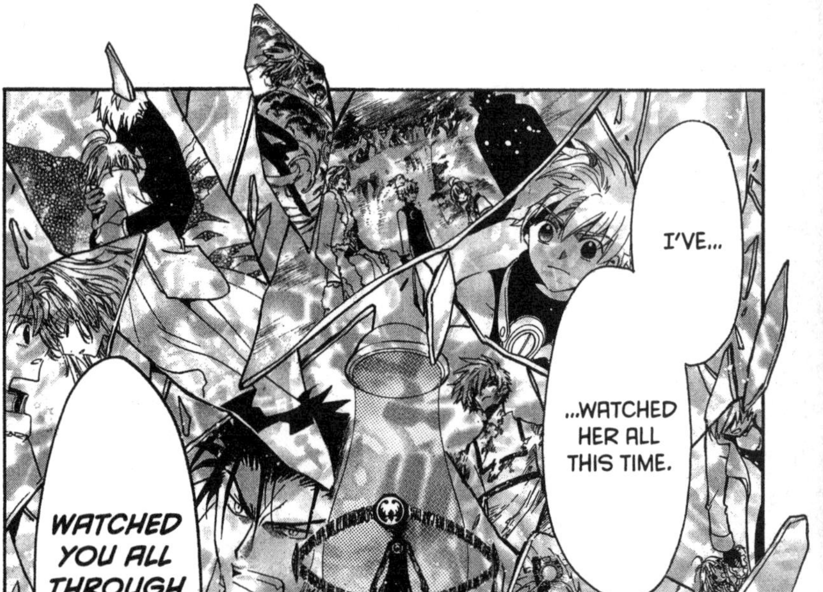
I'VE...
...WATCHED HER ALL THIS TIME.
WATCHED YOU ALL THROUGH YOUR JOURNEYS.
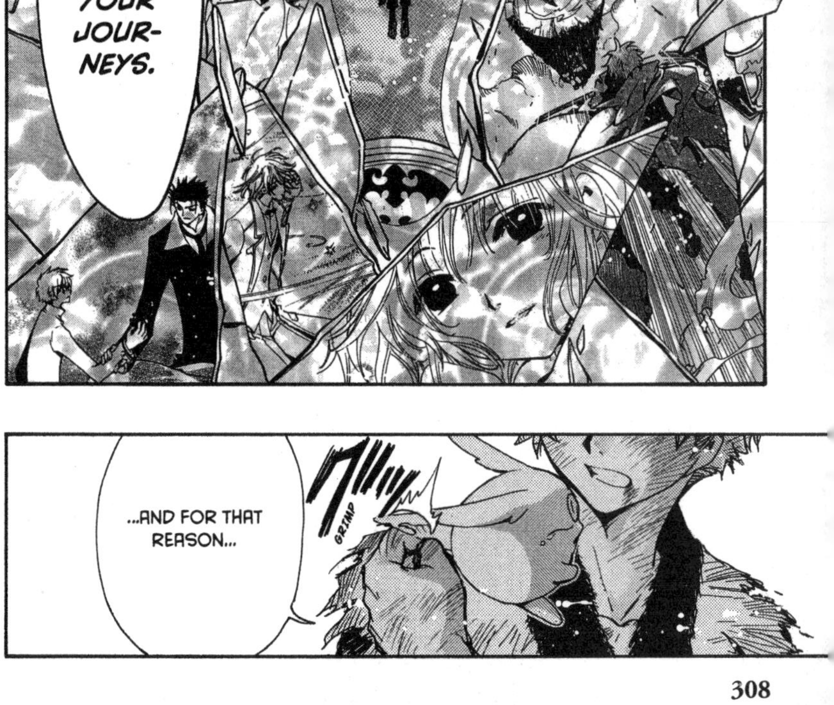
GRIMP
...AND FOR THAT REASON...

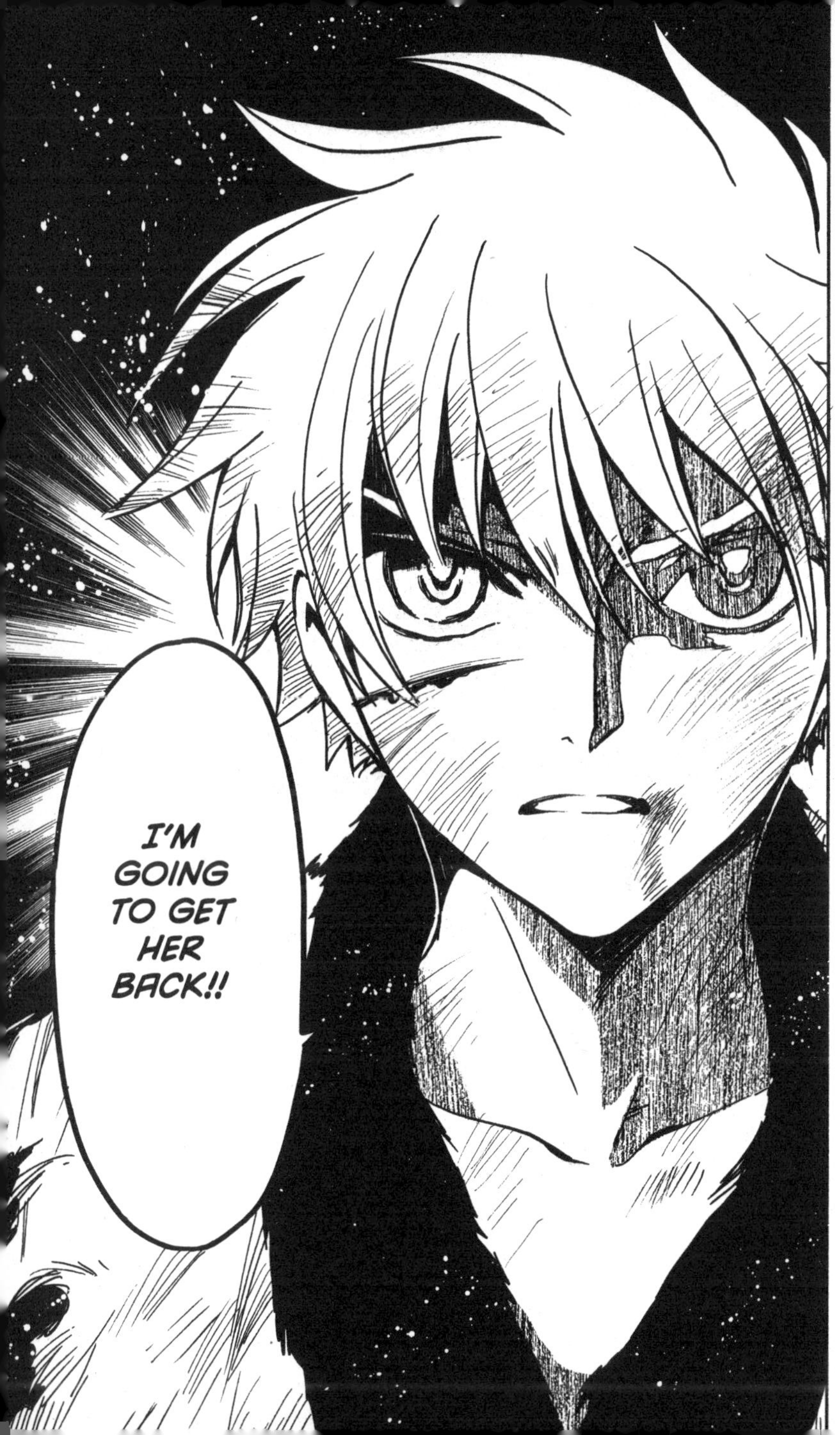
I'M GOING TO GET HER BACK!!

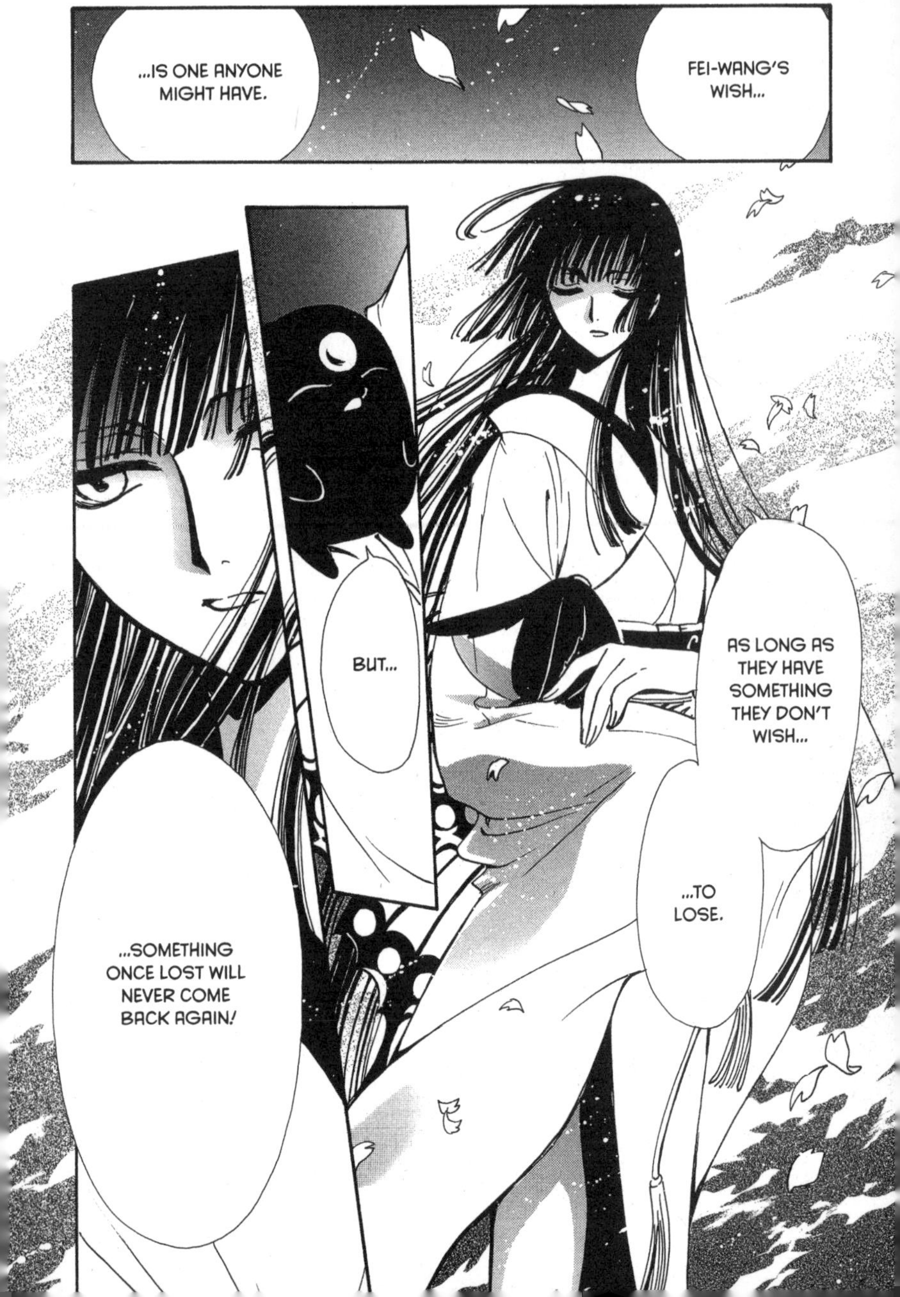
FEI-WANG'S WISH...
...IS ONE ANYONE MIGHT HAVE.
AS LONG AS THEY HAVE SOMETHING THEY DON'T WISH...
...TO LOSE.
BUT...
...SOMETHING ONCE LOST WILL NEVER COME BACK AGAIN!

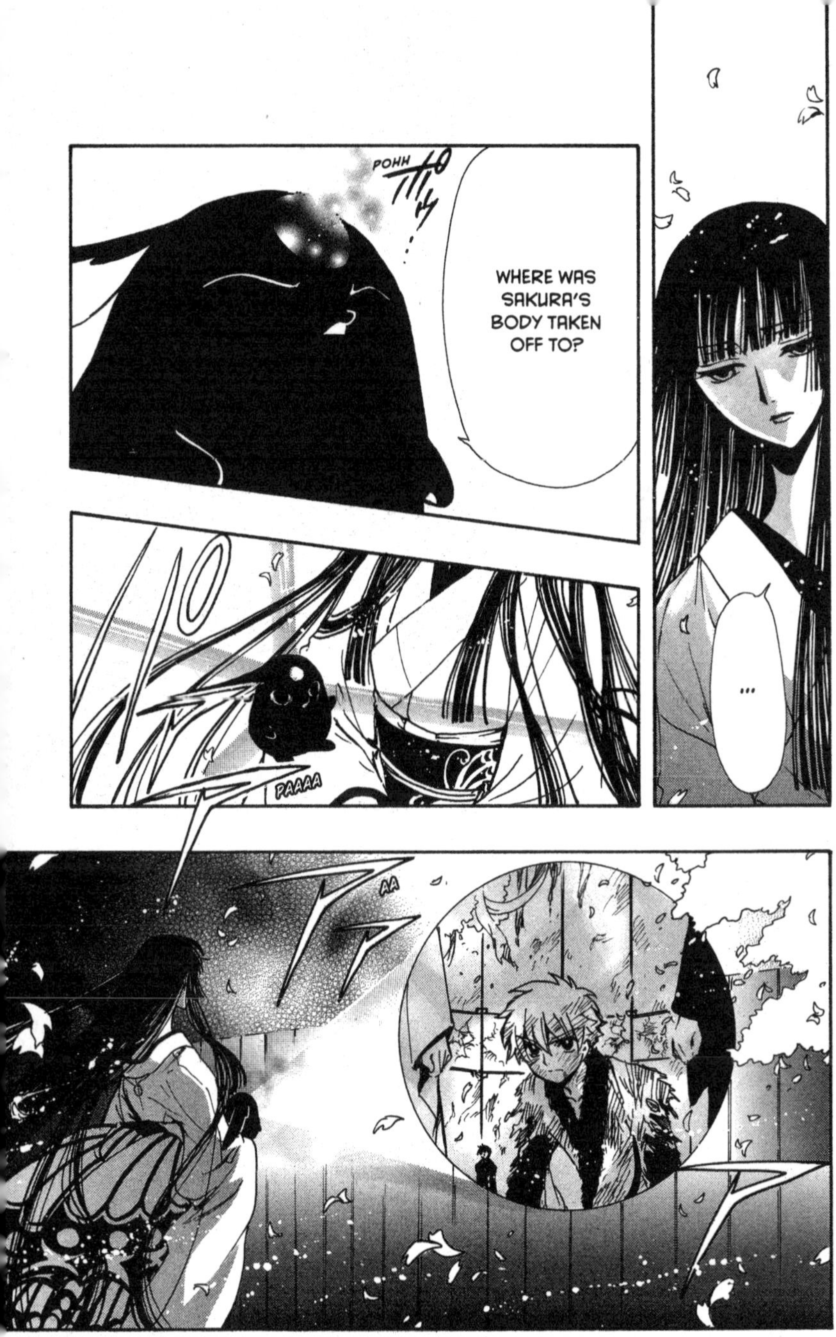
POHH
WHERE WAS SAKURA'S BODY TAKEN OFF TO?
...
PAAAA
AA

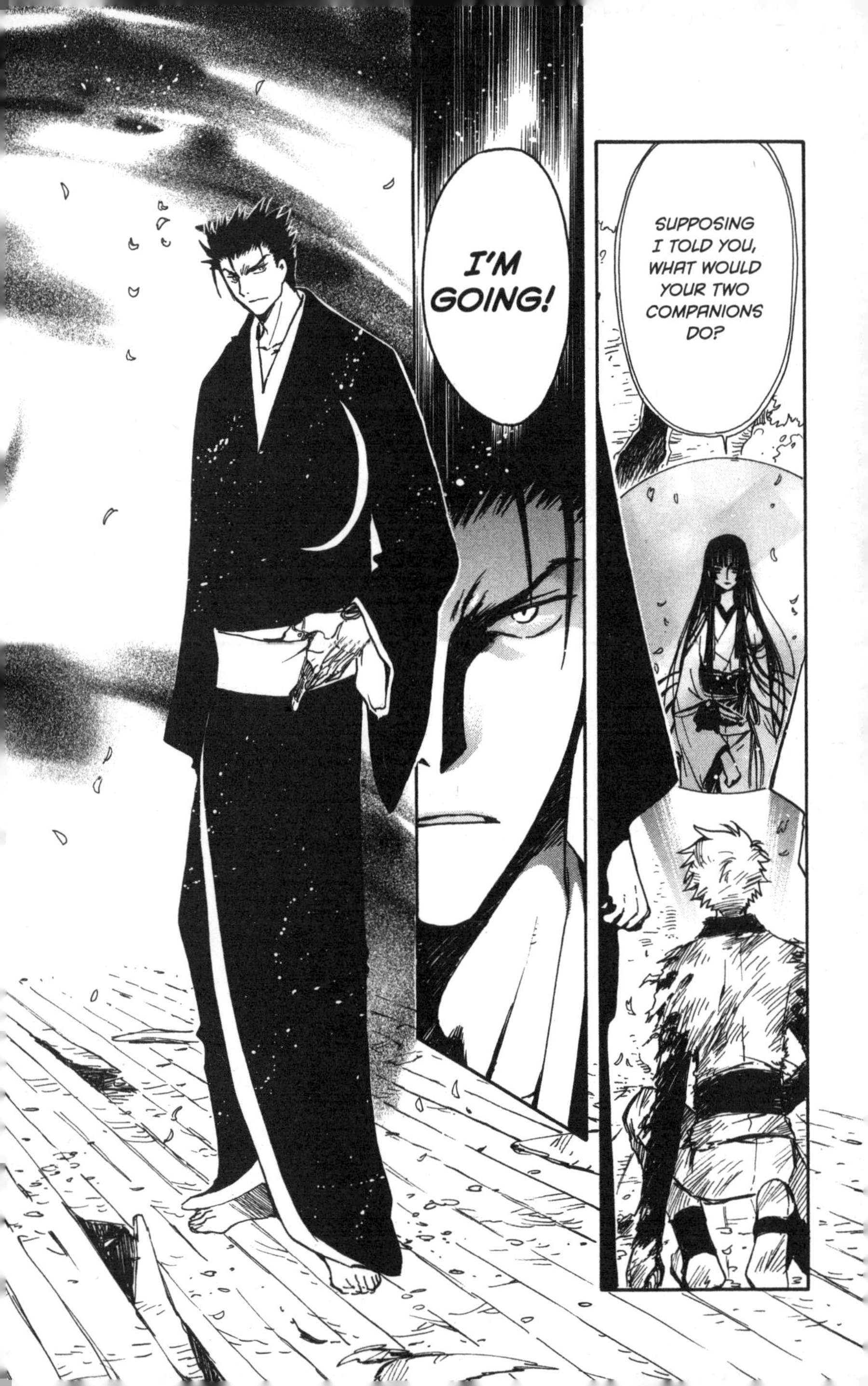
SUPPOSING I TOLD YOU, WHAT WOULD YOUR TWO COMPANIONS DO?
I'M GOING!

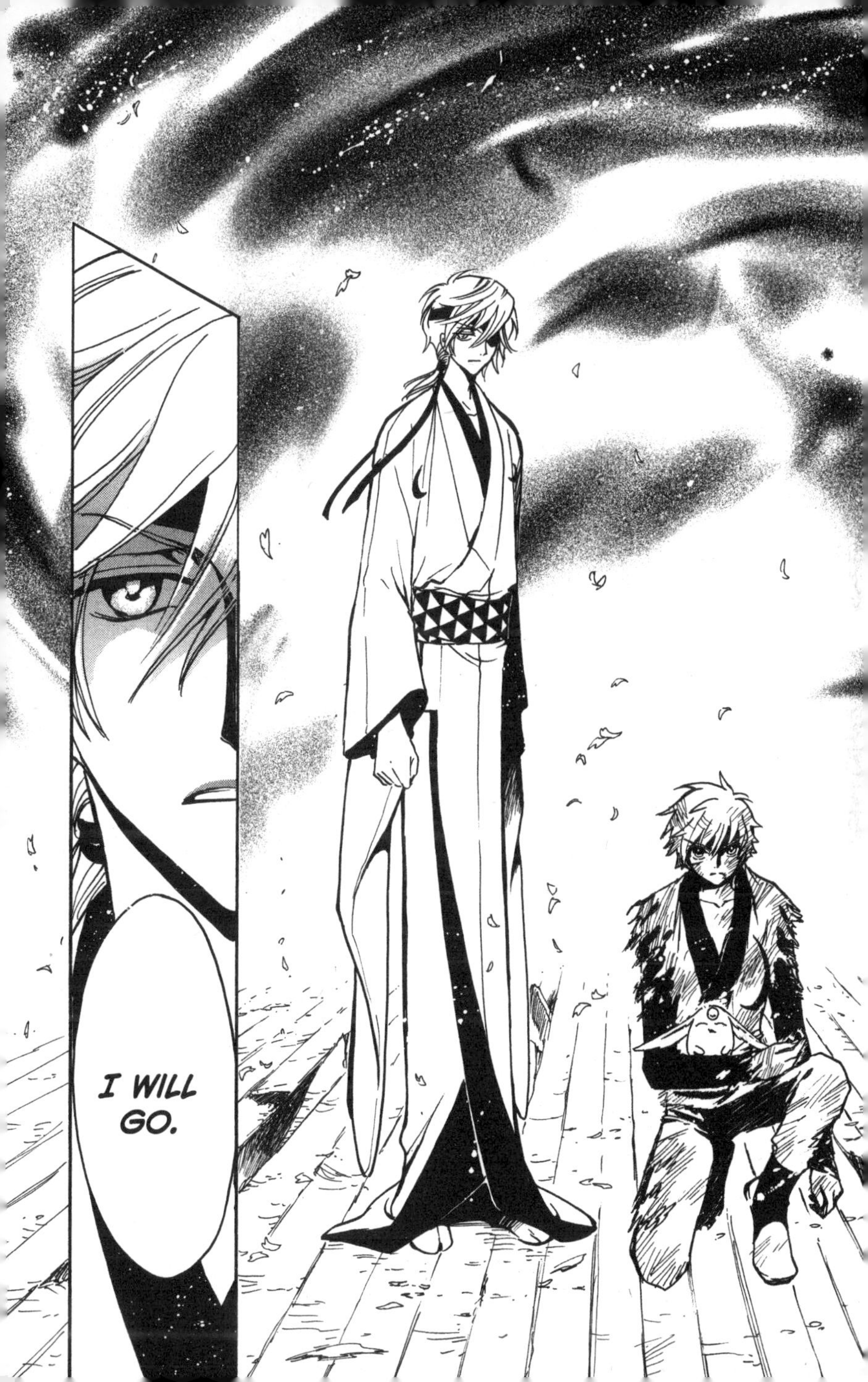
I WILL GO.

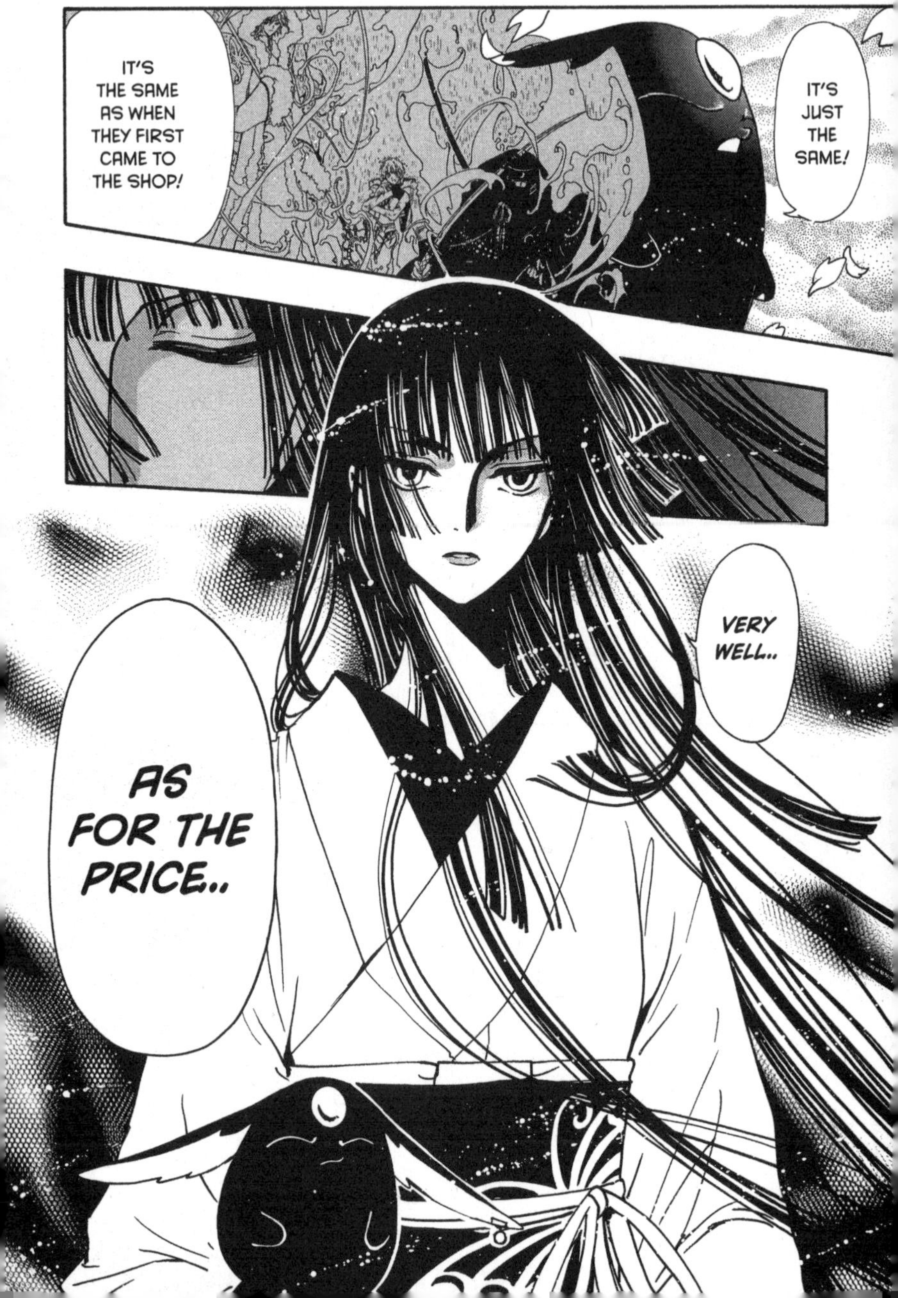
IT'S JUST THE SAME!
IT'S THE SAME AS WHEN THEY FIRST CAME TO THE SHOP!
VERY WELL..
AS FOR THE PRICE..

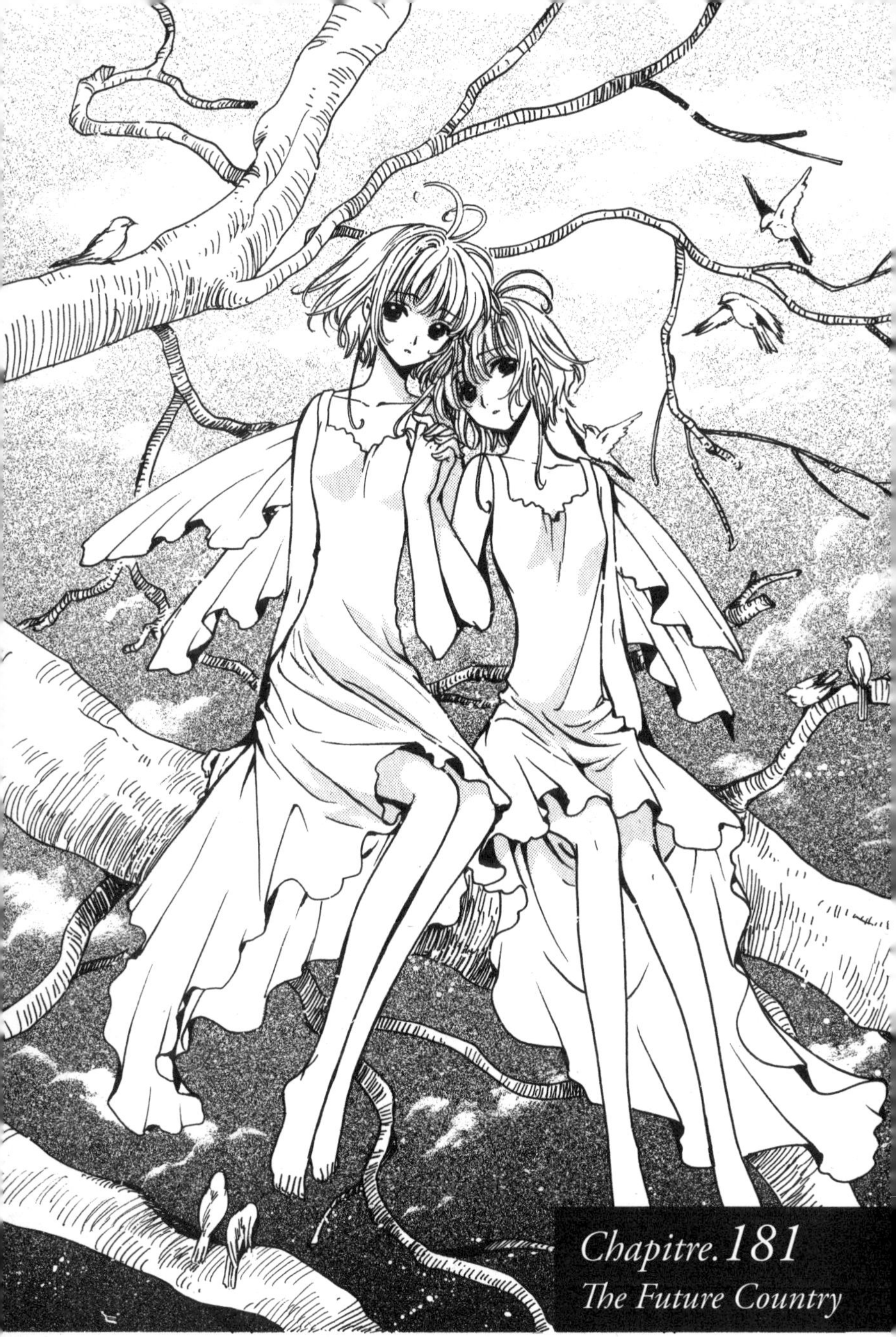
Chapitre. 181
The Future Country

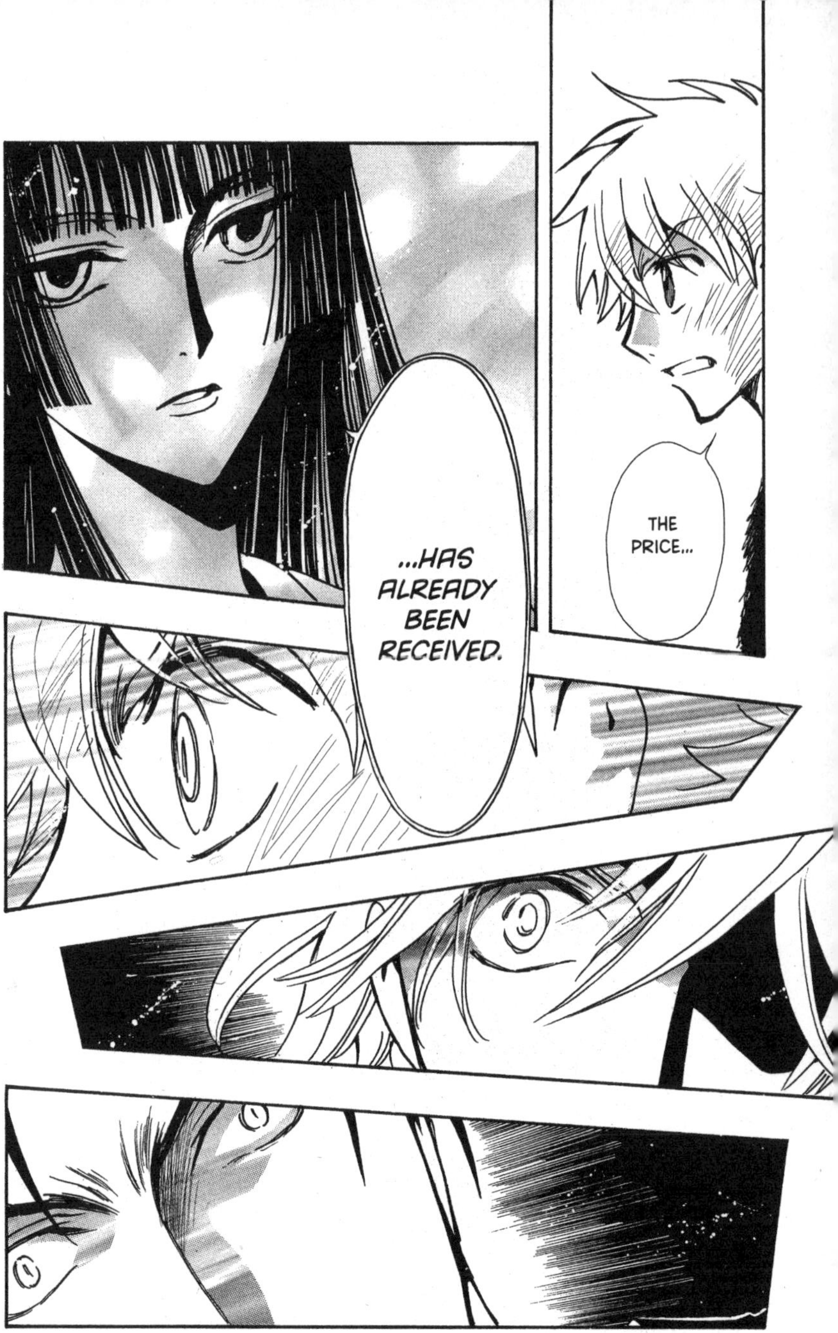
THE PRICE...
...HAS ALREADY BEEN RECEIVED.

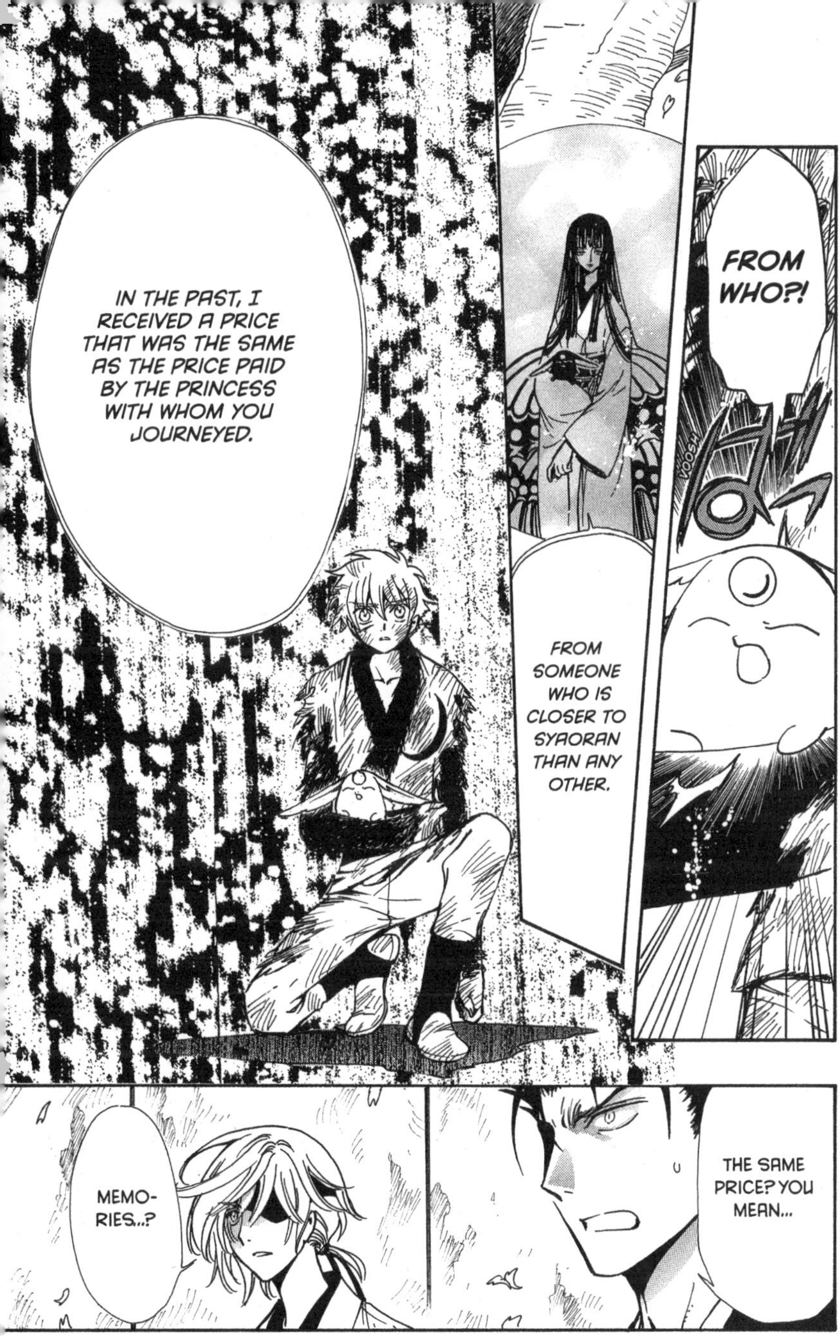
FROM WHO?!
VOOSH
FROM SOMEONE WHO IS CLOSER TO SYAORAN THAN ANY OTHER.
IN THE PAST, I RECEIVED A PRICE THAT WAS THE SAME AS THE PRICE PAID BY THE PRINCESS WITH WHOM YOU JOURNEYED.
THE SAME PRICE? YOU MEAN...
MEMO-RIES...?

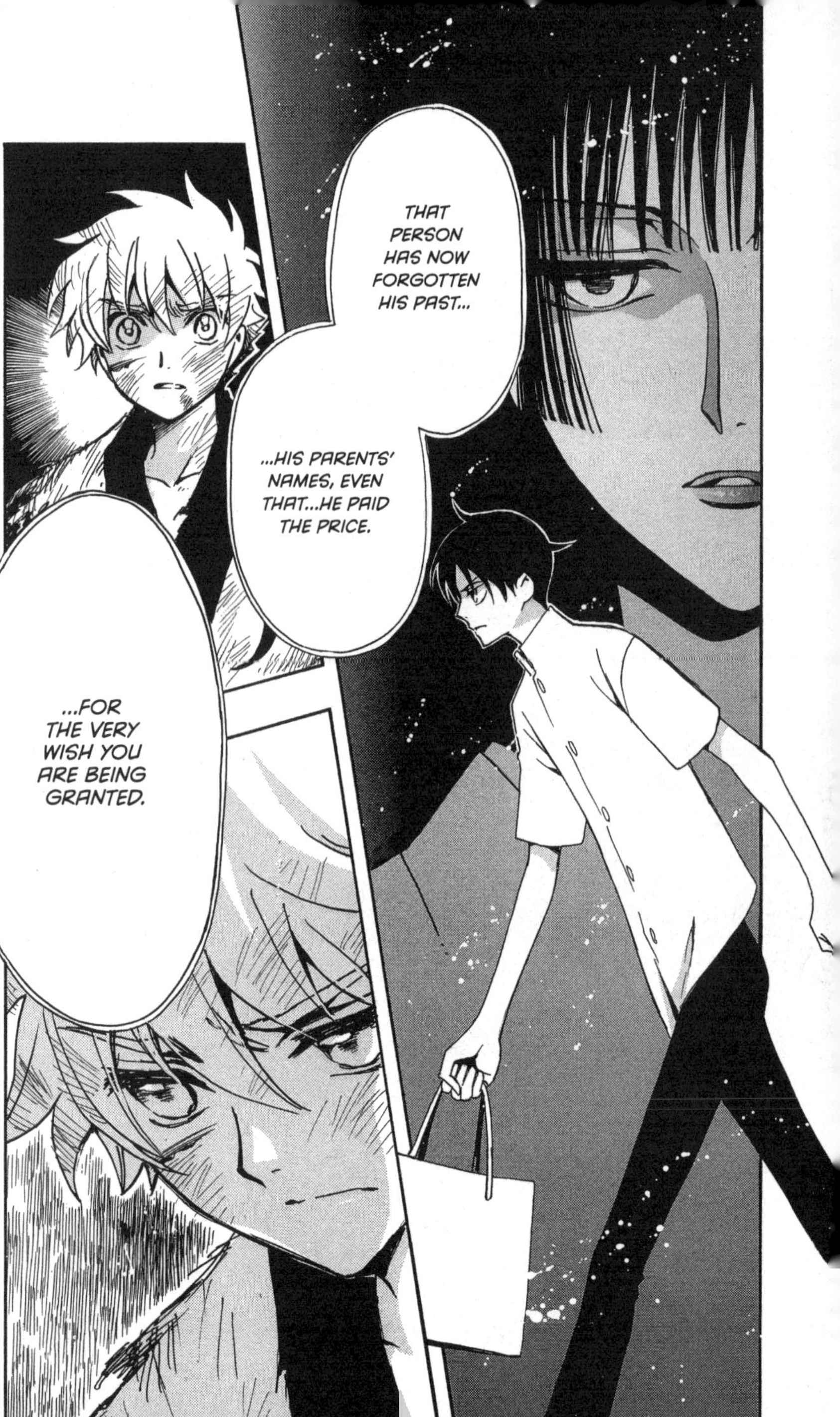
THAT PERSON HAS NOW FORGOTTEN HIS PAST...
...HIS PARENTS' NAMES, EVEN THAT...HE PAID THE PRICE.
...FOR THE VERY WISH YOU ARE BEING GRANTED.

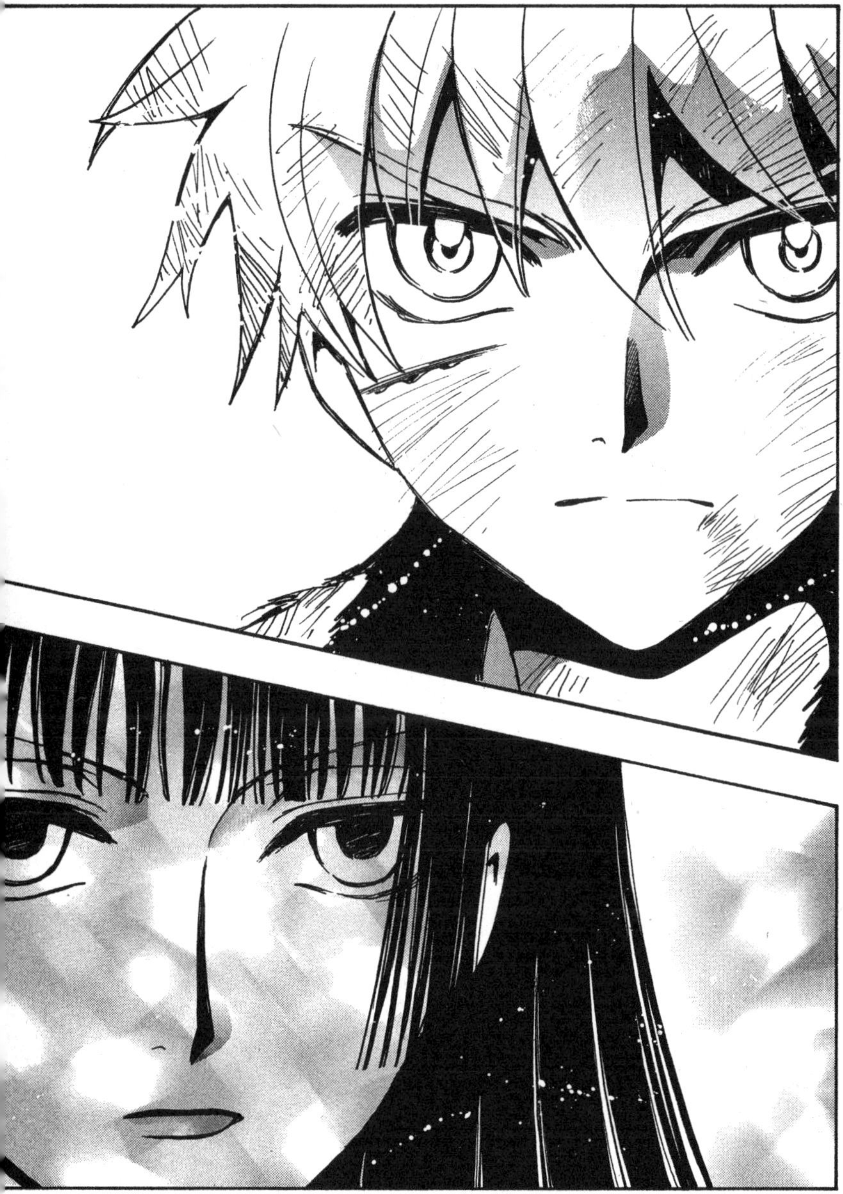

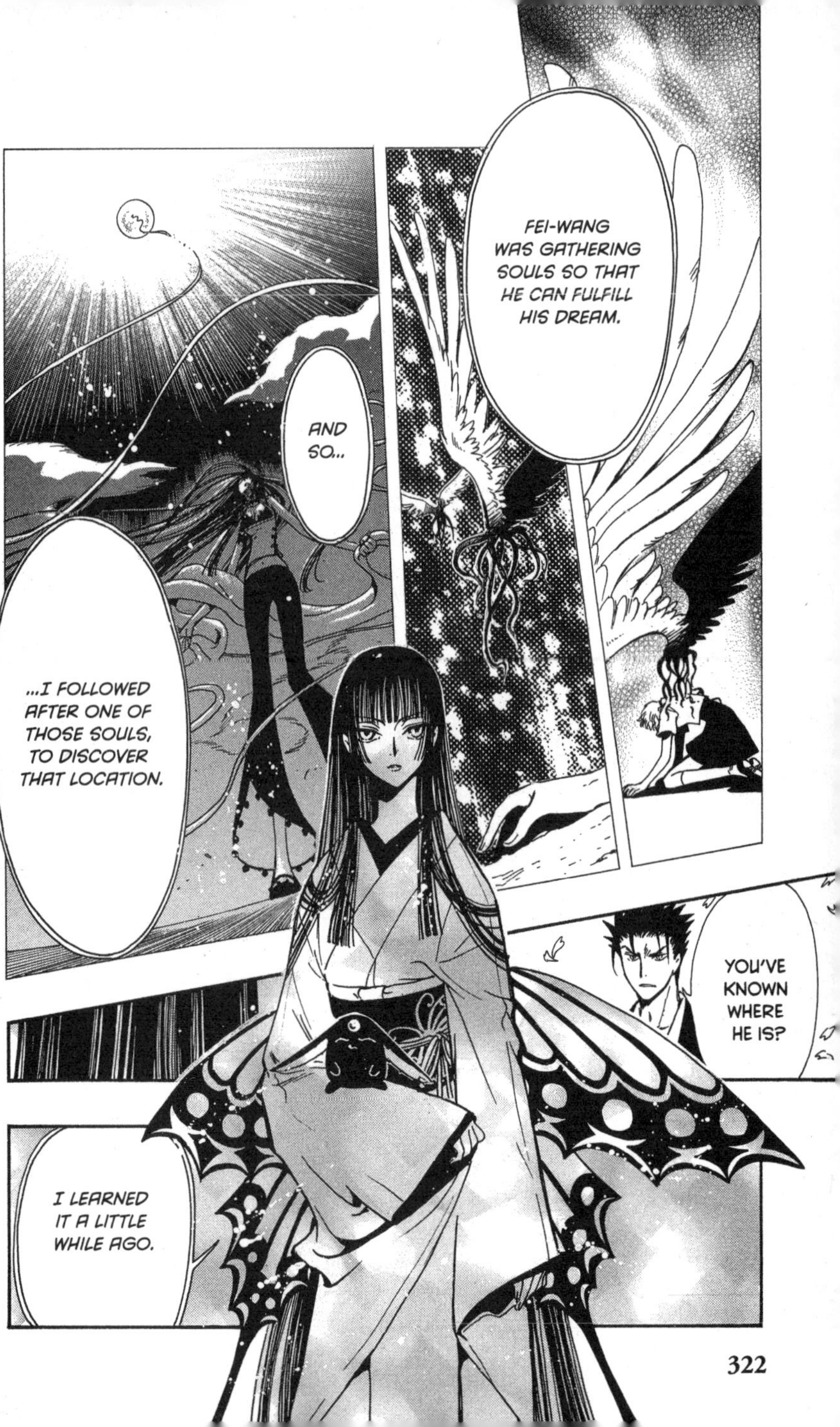
FEI-WANG WAS GATHERING SOULS SO THAT HE CAN FULFILL HIS DREAM.
AND SO...
...I FOLLOWED AFTER ONE OF THOSE SOULS, TO DISCOVER THAT LOCATION.
YOU'VE KNOWN WHERE HE IS?
I LEARNED IT A LITTLE WHILE AGO.

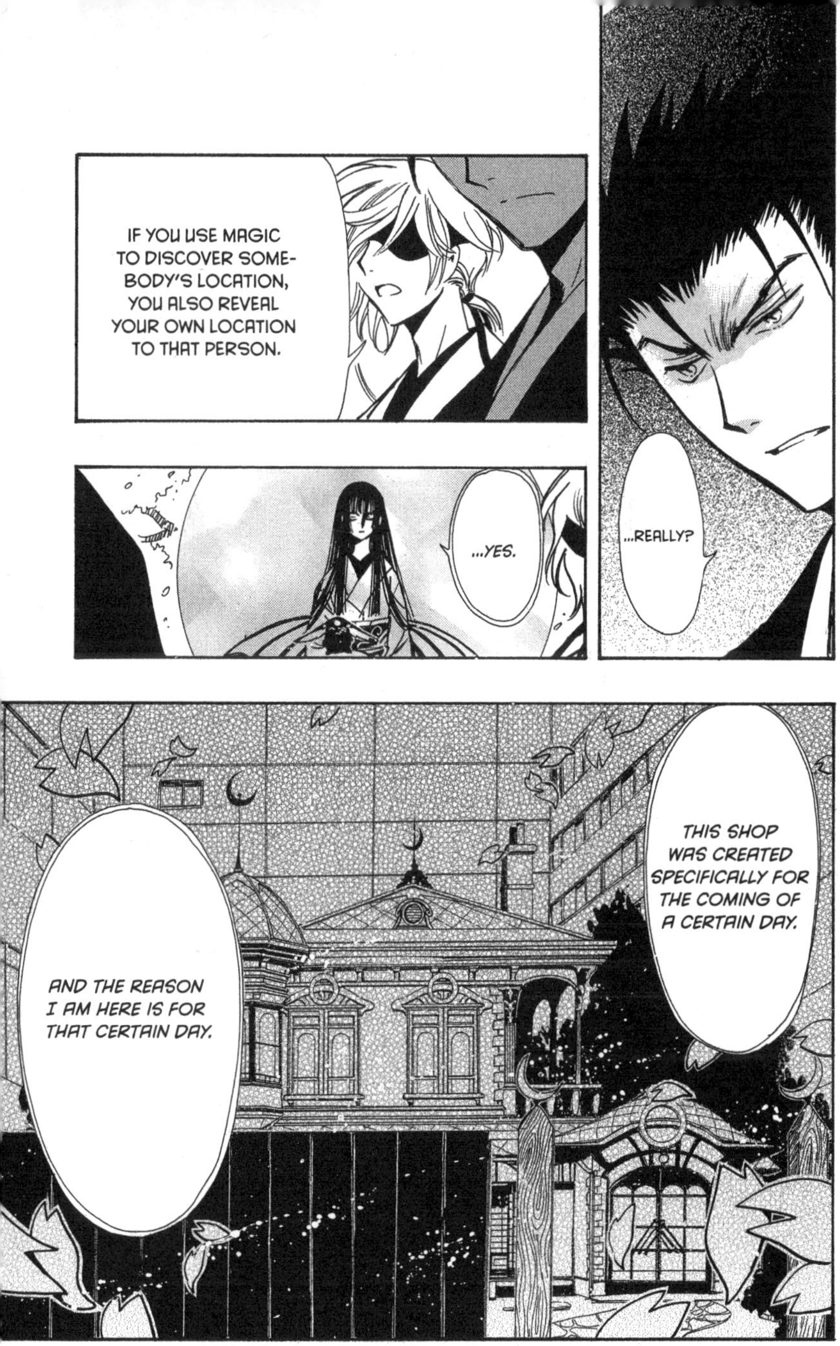
IF YOU USE MAGIC TO DISCOVER SOME-BODY'S LOCATION, YOU ALSO REVEAL YOUR OWN LOCATION TO THAT PERSON.
...REALLY?
...YES.
THIS SHOP WAS CREATED SPECIFICALLY FOR THE COMING OF A CERTAIN DAY.
AND THE REASON I AM HERE IS FOR THAT CERTAIN DAY.

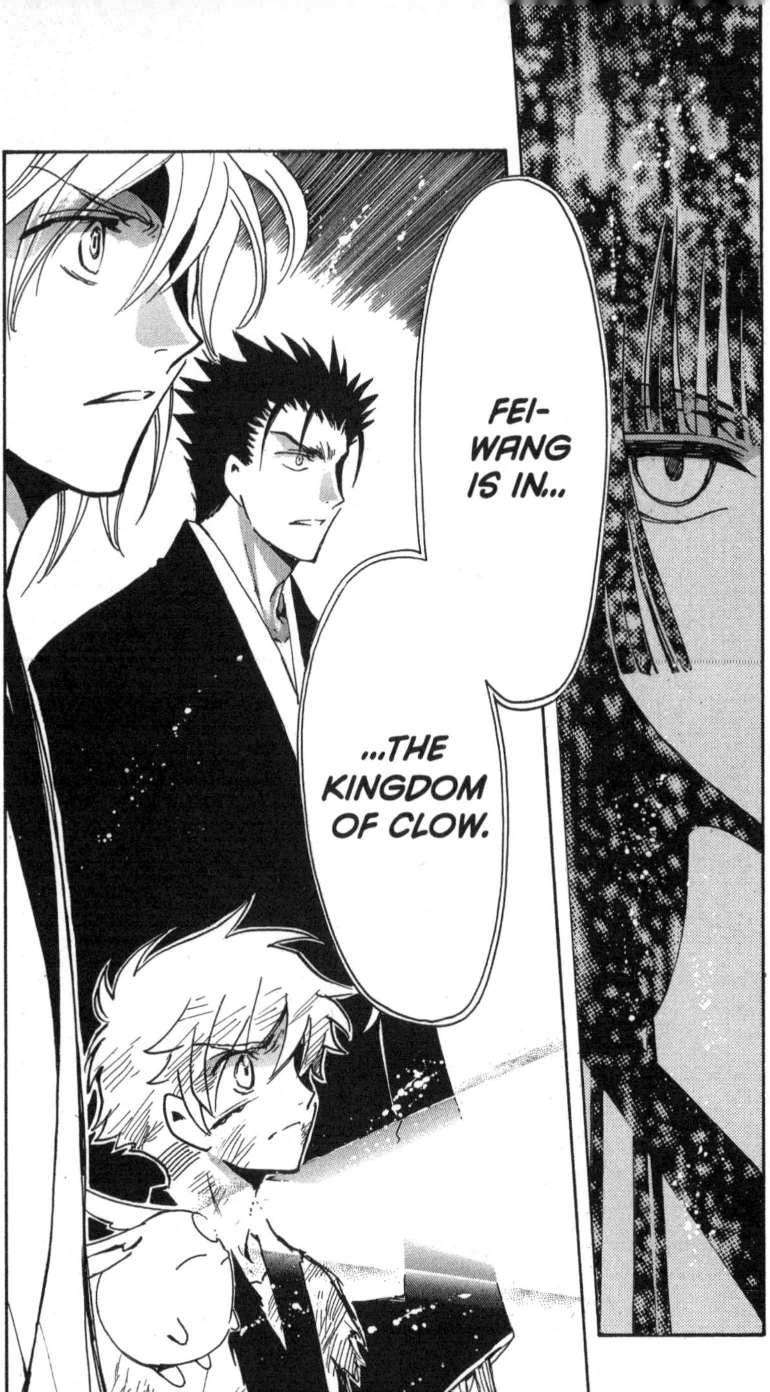
FEI-WANG IS IN...
...THE KINGDOM OF CLOW.

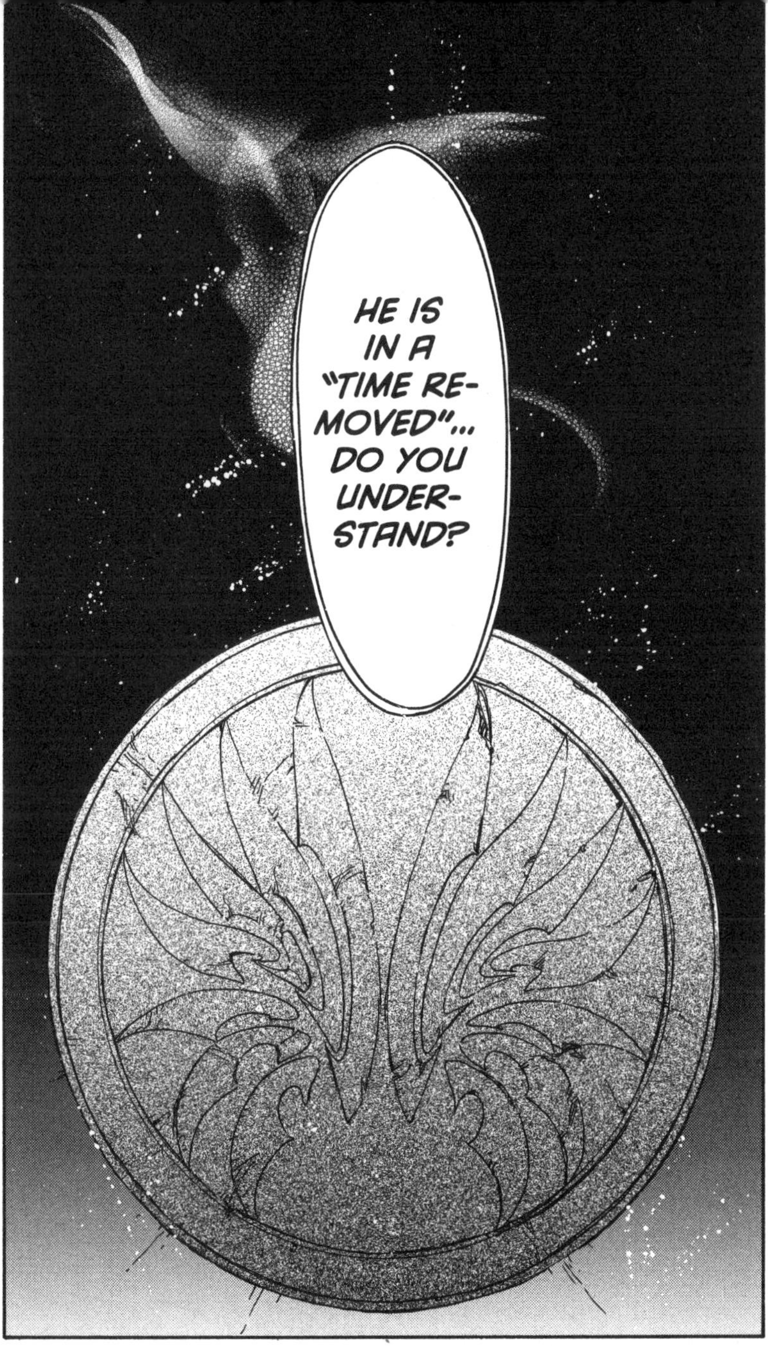
HE IS IN A "TIME RE-MOVED"... DO YOU UNDER-STAND?

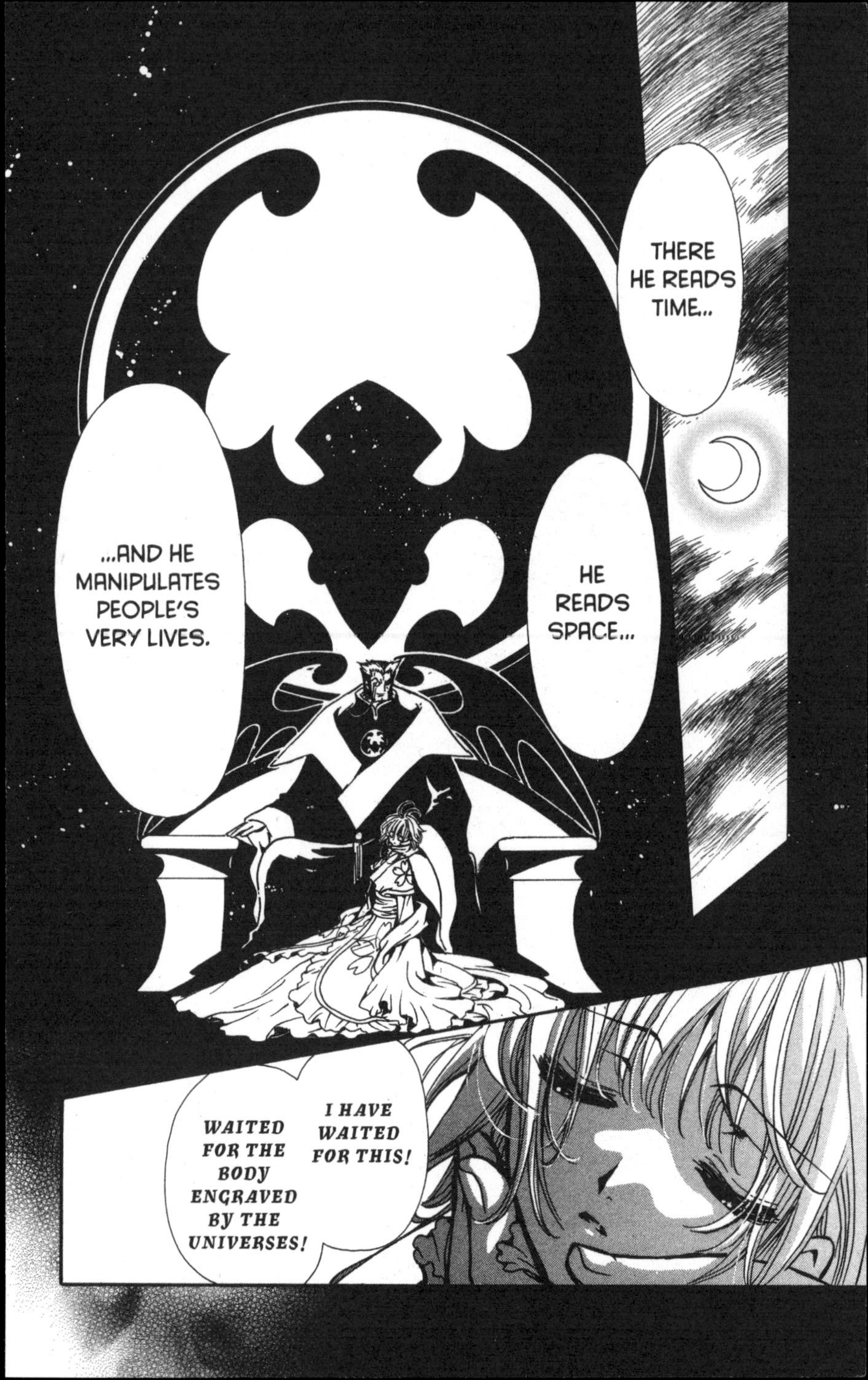
THERE HE READS TIME...
HE READS SPACE...
...AND HE MANIPULATES PEOPLE'S VERY LIVES.
I HAVE WAITED FOR THIS!
WAITED FOR THE BODY ENGRAVED BY THE UNIVERSES!

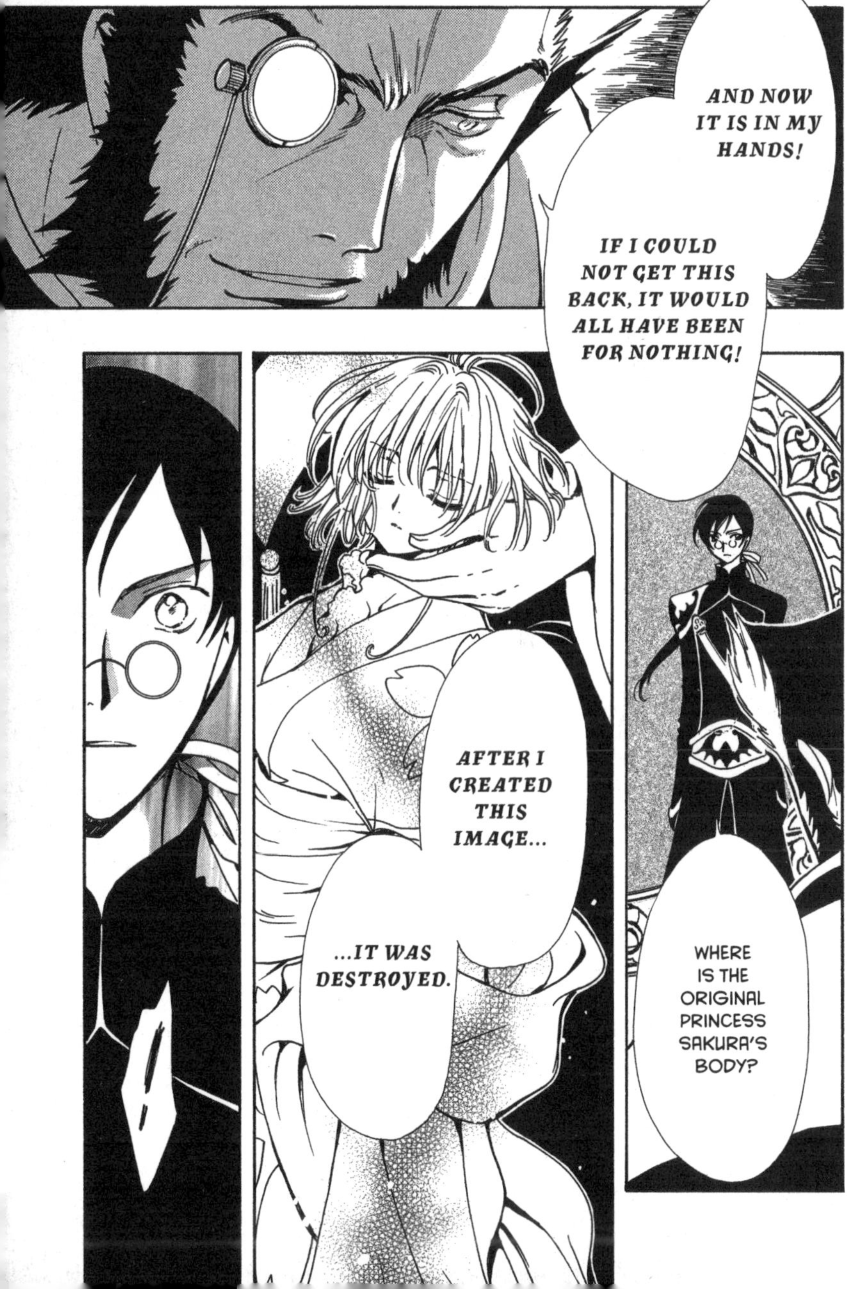
AND NOW IT IS IN MY HANDS!
IF I COULD NOT GET THIS BACK, IT WOULD ALL HAVE BEEN FOR NOTHING!
WHERE IS THE ORIGINAL PRINCESS SAKURA'S BODY?
AFTER I CREATED THIS IMAGE...
...IT WAS DESTROYED.

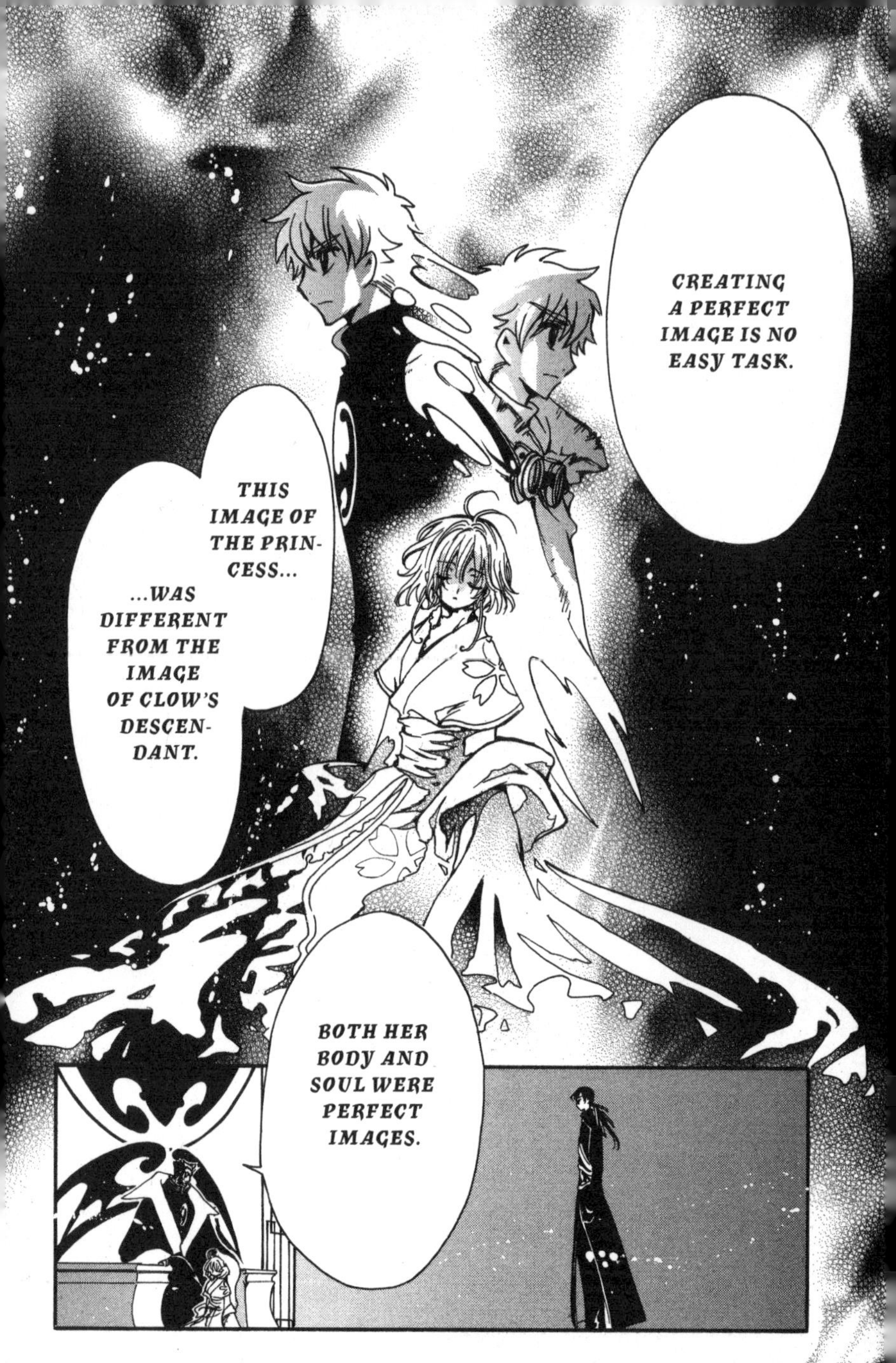
CREATING A PERFECT IMAGE IS NO EASY TASK.
THIS IMAGE OF THE PRINCESS...
...WAS DIFFERENT FROM THE IMAGE OF CLOW'S DESCENDANT.
BOTH HER BODY AND SOUL WERE PERFECT IMAGES.

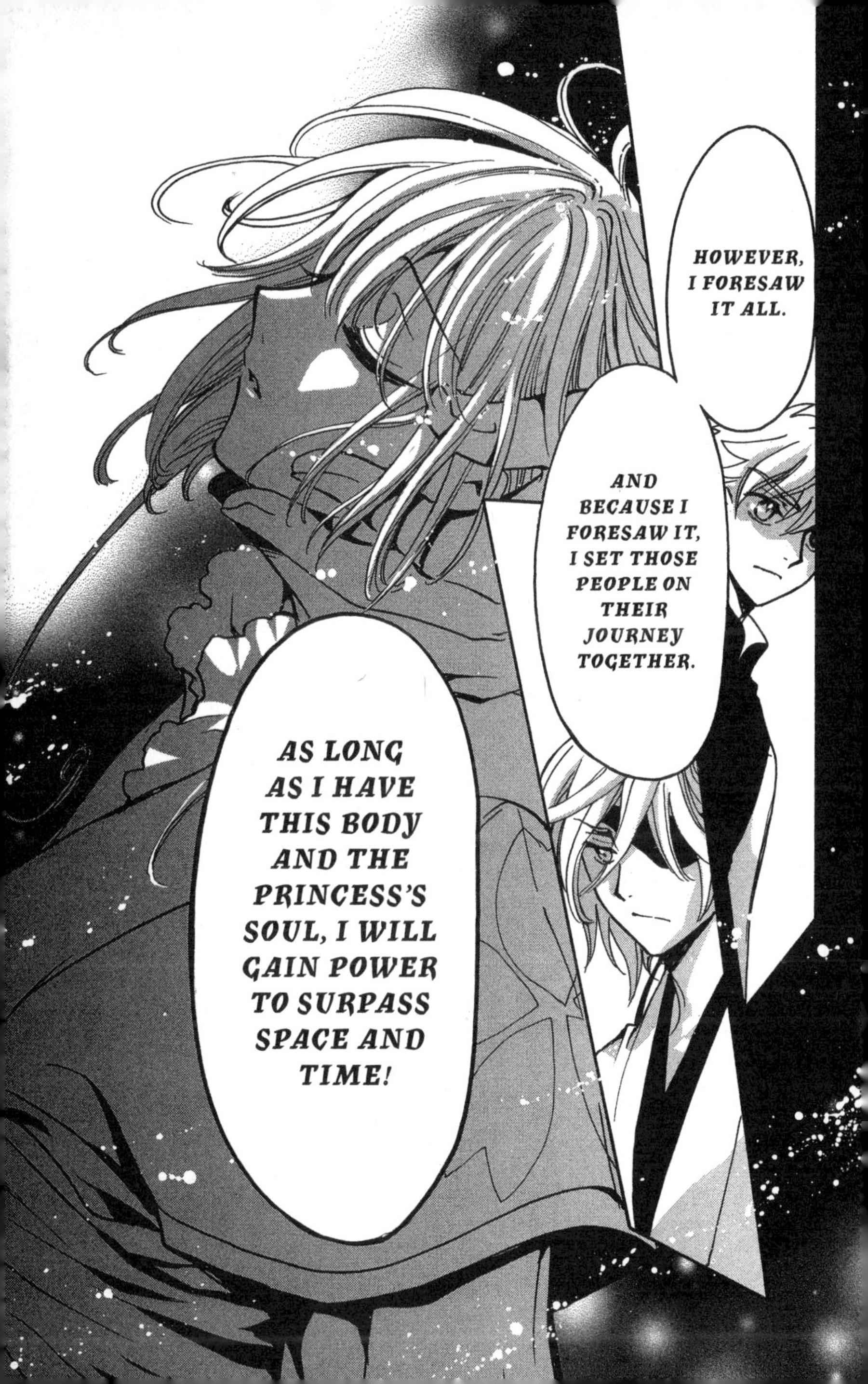
HOWEVER, I FORESAW IT ALL.
AND BECAUSE I FORESAW IT, I SET THOSE PEOPLE ON THEIR JOURNEY TOGETHER.
AS LONG AS I HAVE THIS BODY AND THE PRINCESS'S SOUL, I WILL GAIN POWER TO SURPASS SPACE AND TIME!

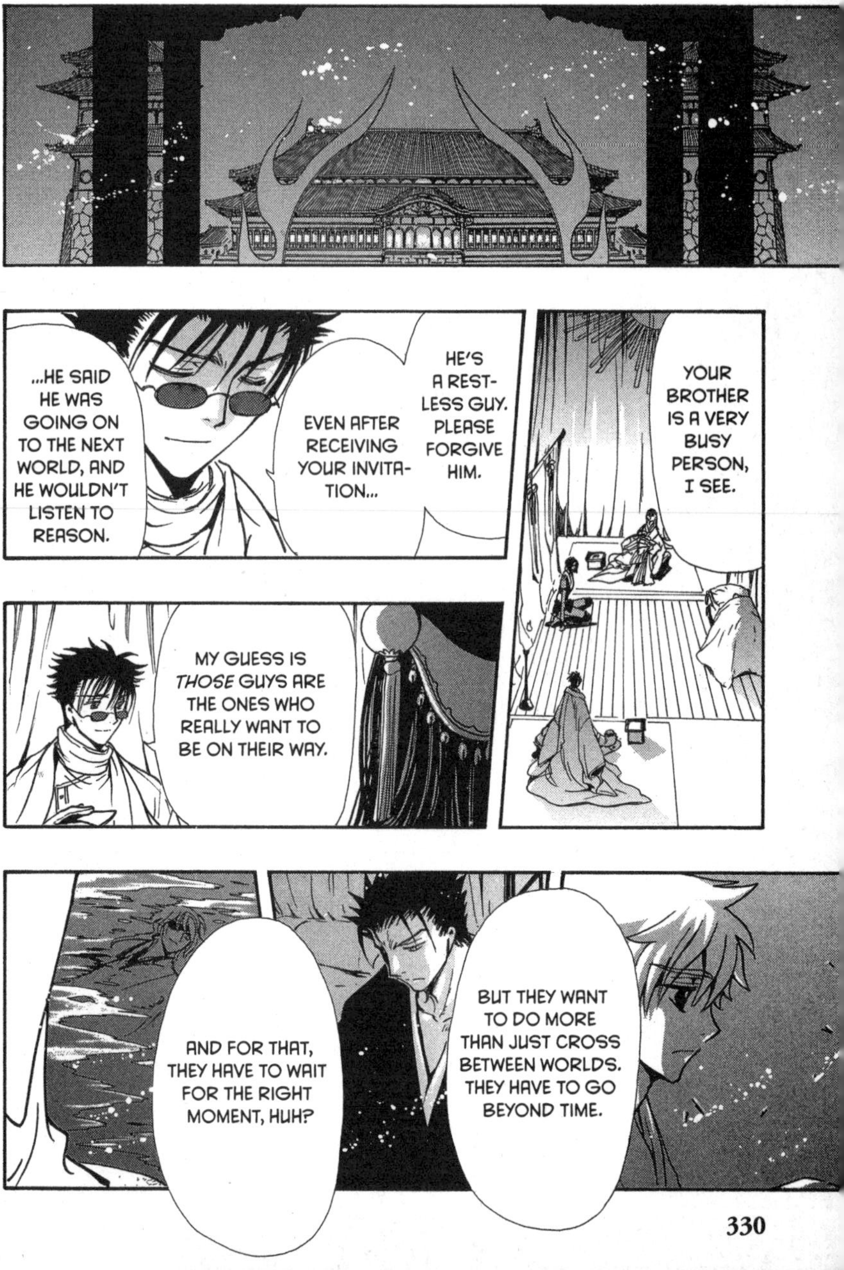
YOUR BROTHER IS A VERY BUSY PERSON, I SEE.
HE'S A RESTLESS GUY. PLEASE FORGIVE HIM.
EVEN AFTER RECEIVING YOUR INVITATION...
...HE SAID HE WAS GOING ON TO THE NEXT WORLD, AND HE WOULDN'T LISTEN TO REASON.
MY GUESS IS *THOSE* GUYS ARE THE ONES WHO REALLY WANT TO BE ON THEIR WAY.
BUT THEY WANT TO DO MORE THAN JUST CROSS BETWEEN WORLDS. THEY HAVE TO GO BEYOND TIME.
AND FOR THAT, THEY HAVE TO WAIT FOR THE RIGHT MOMENT, HUH?

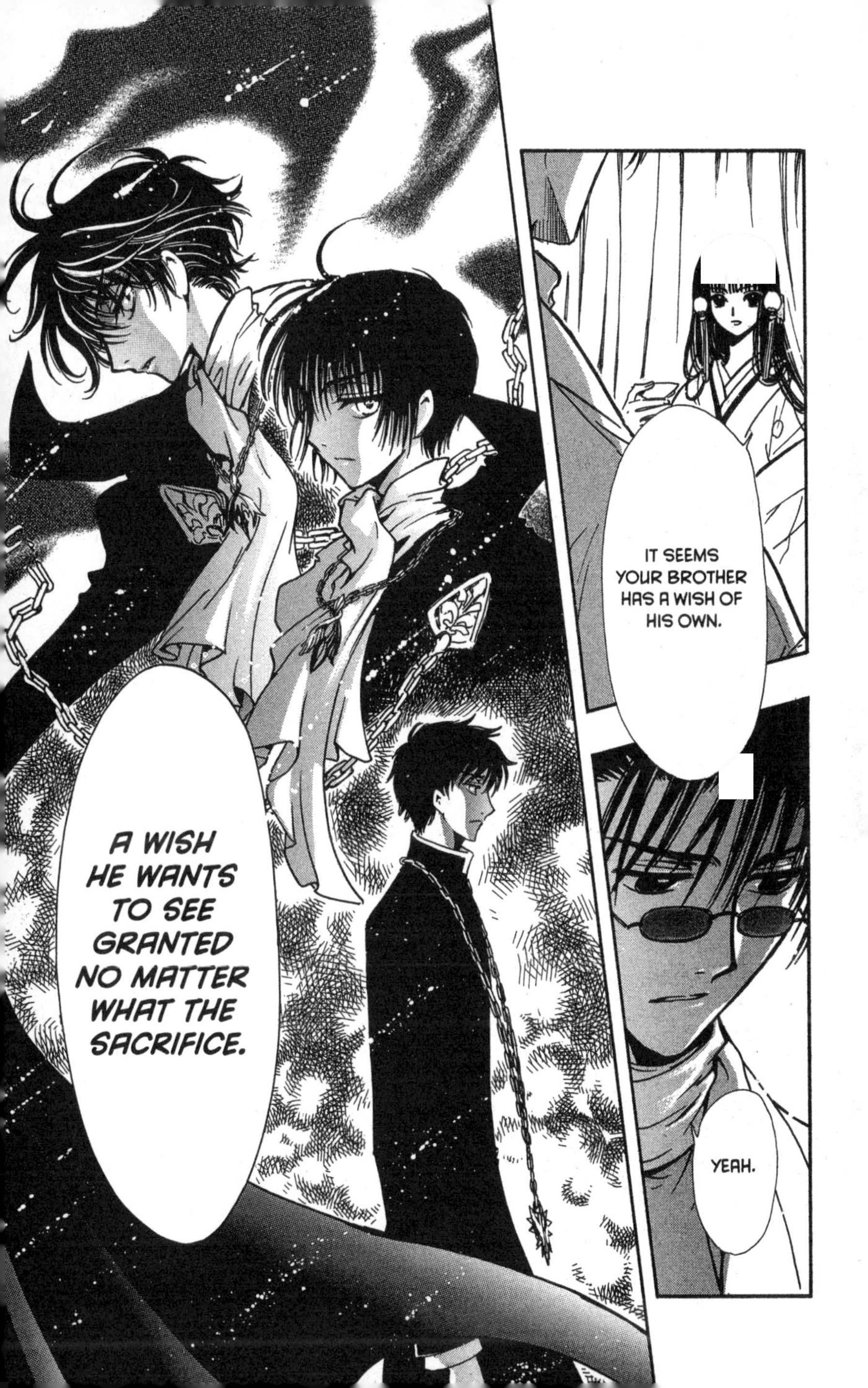
IT SEEMS YOUR BROTHER HAS A WISH OF HIS OWN.
YEAH.
A WISH HE WANTS TO SEE GRANTED NO MATTER WHAT THE SACRIFICE.

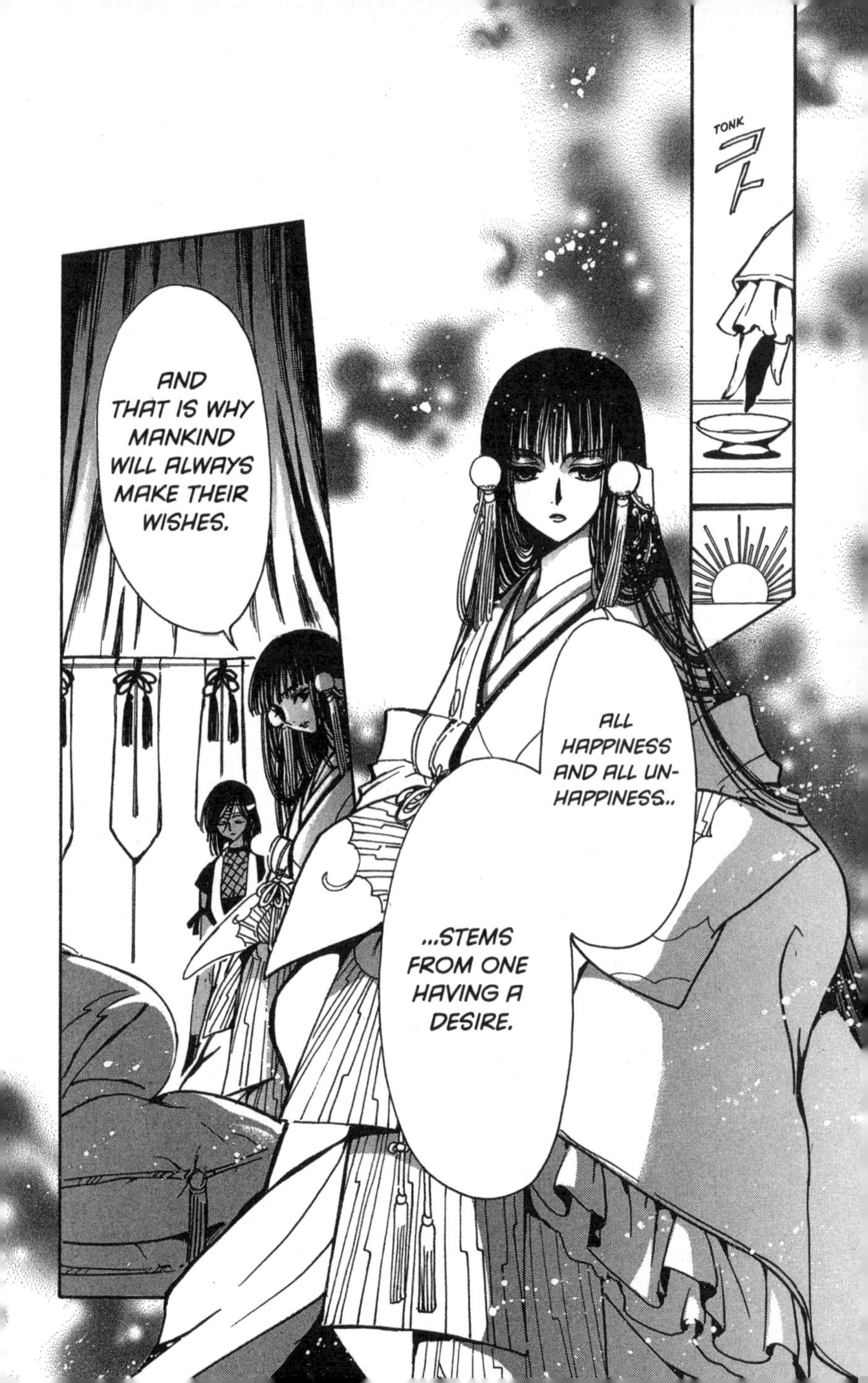
TONK
ALL HAPPINESS AND ALL UN-HAPPINESS...
...STEMS FROM ONE HAVING A DESIRE.
AND THAT IS WHY MANKIND WILL ALWAYS MAKE THEIR WISHES.

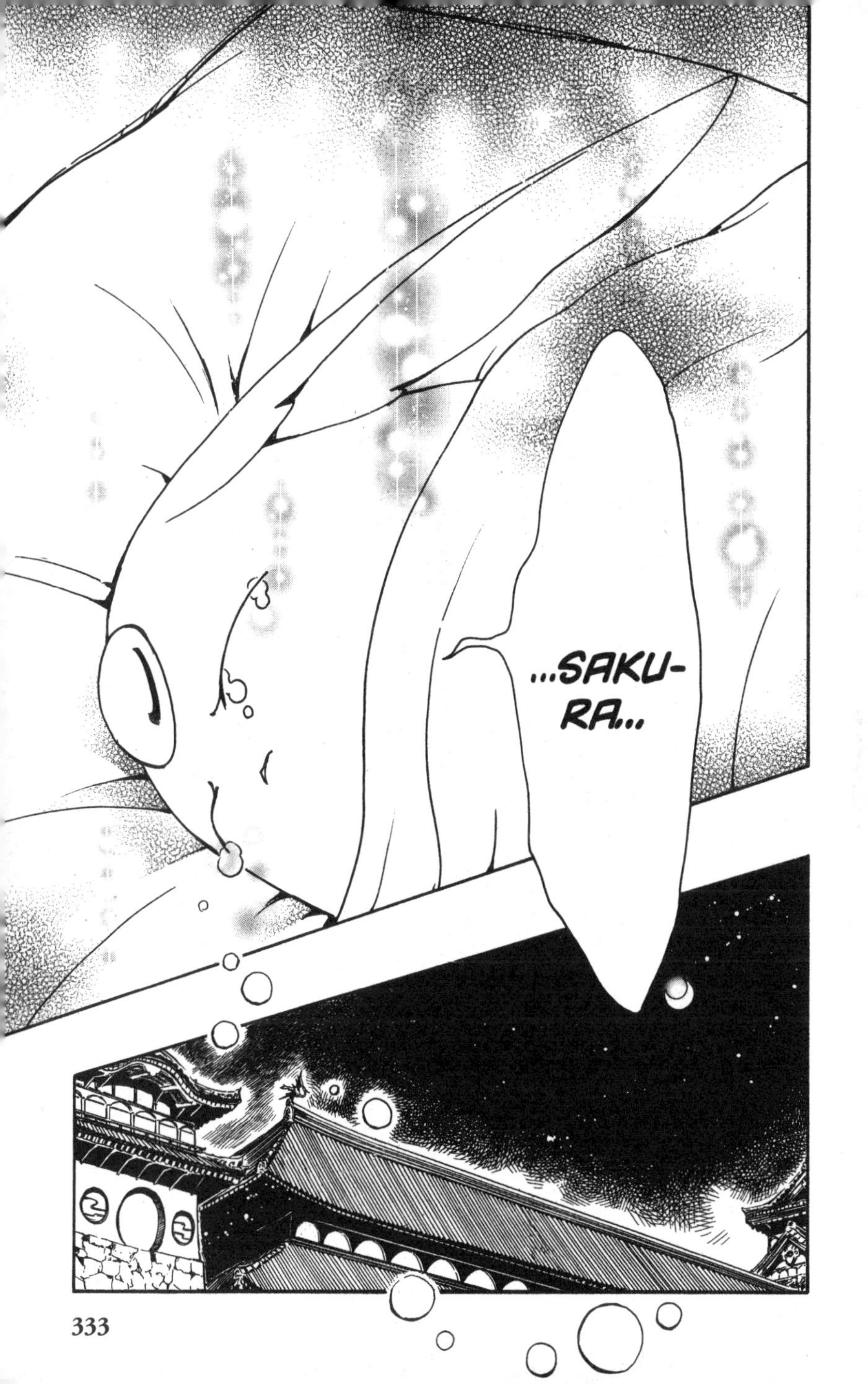
...SAKU-
RA...

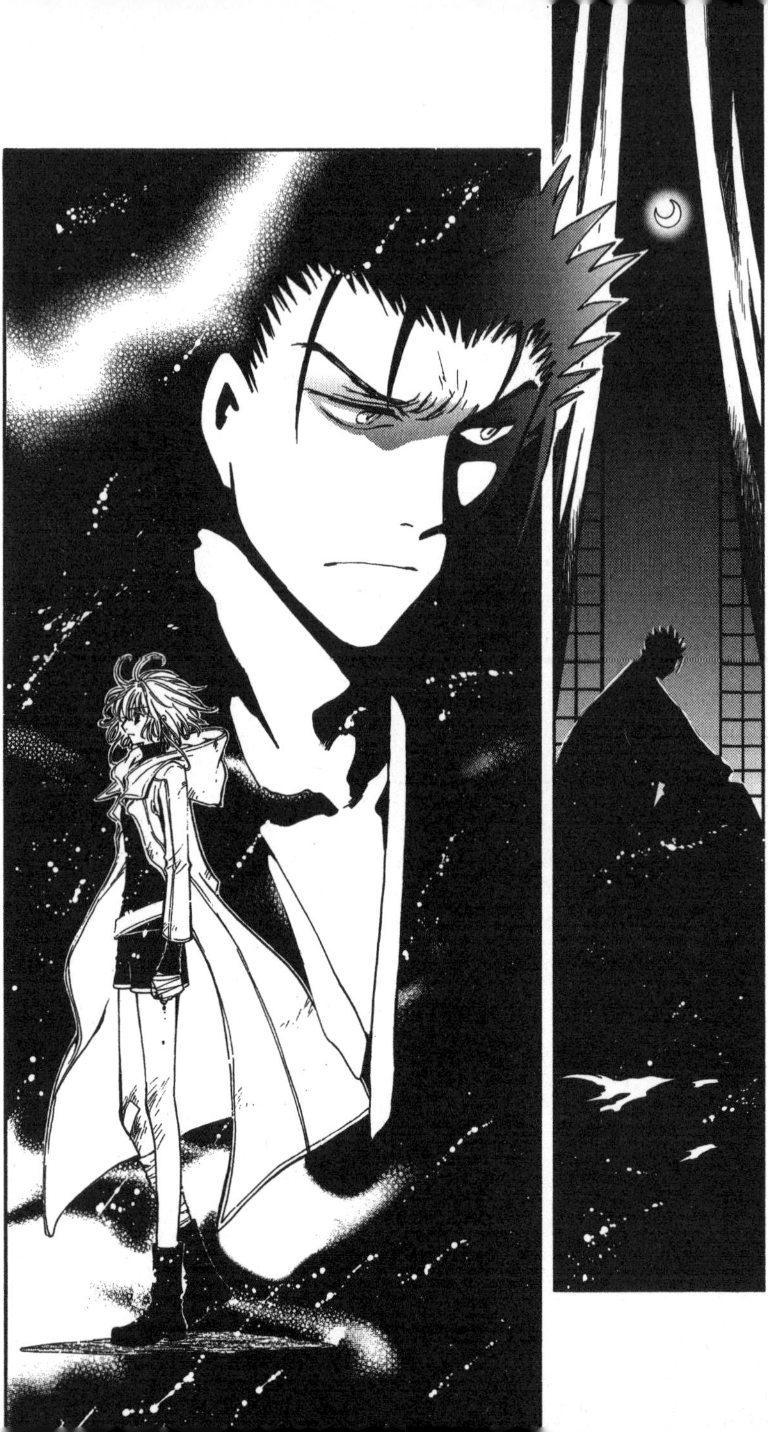

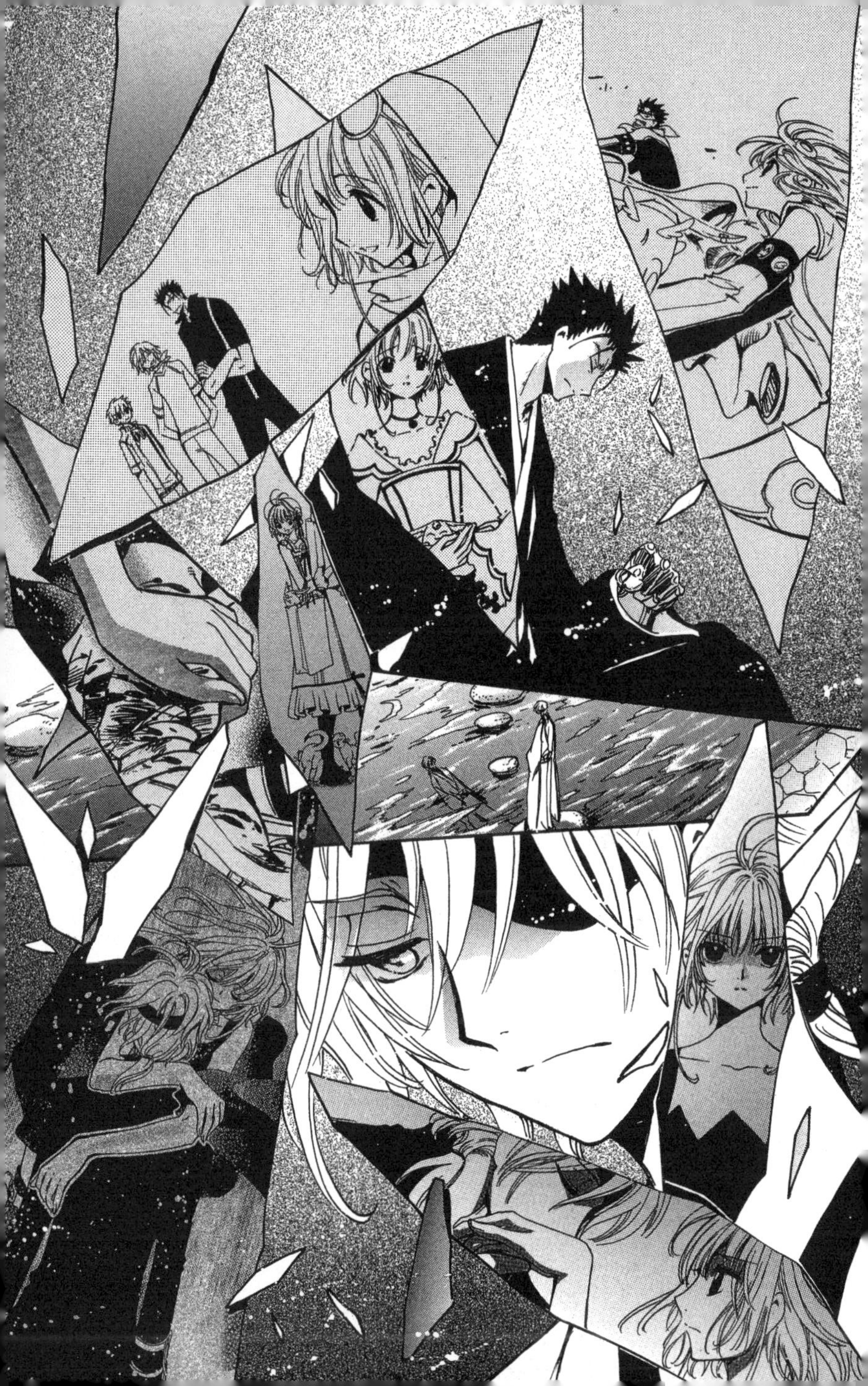

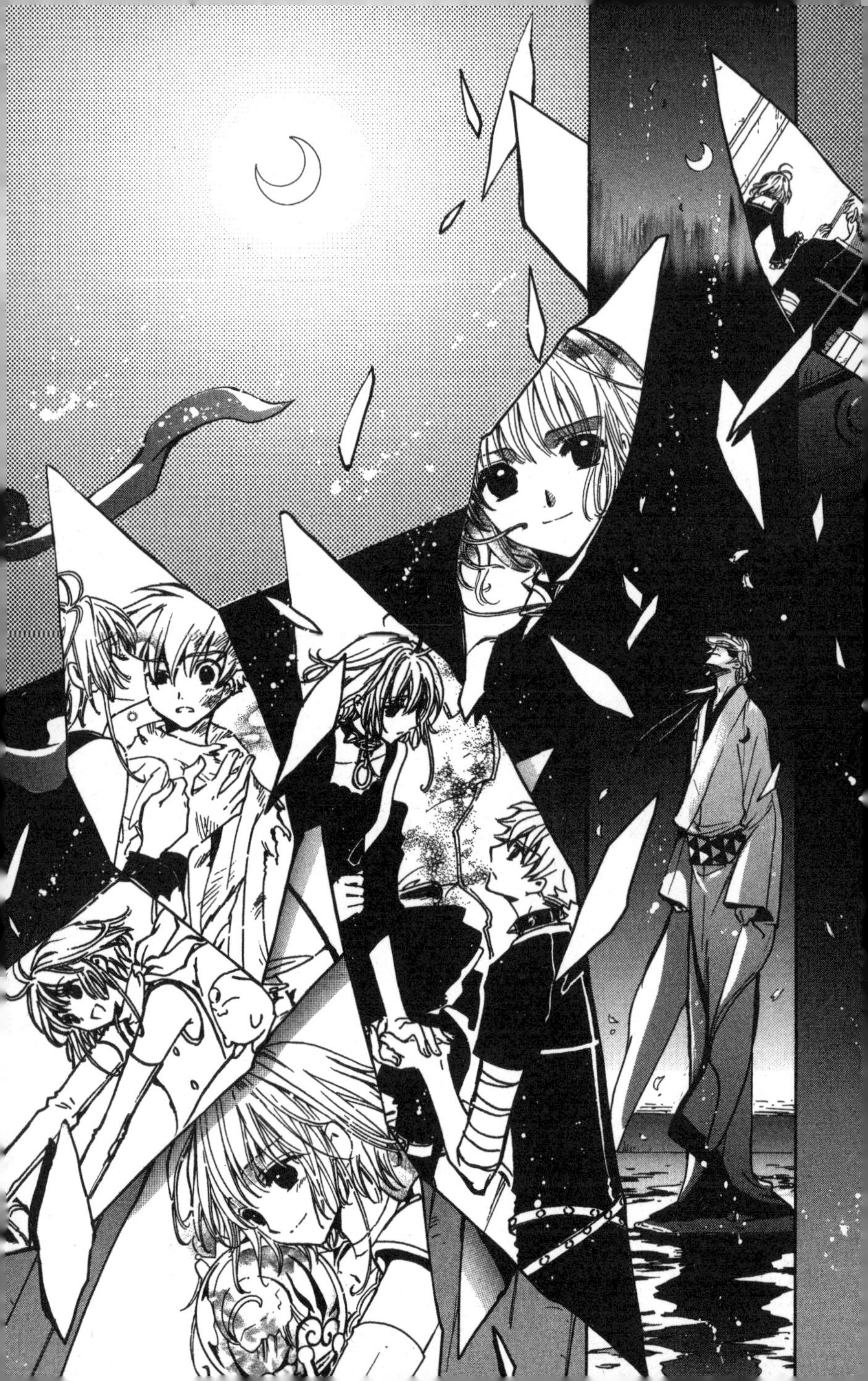

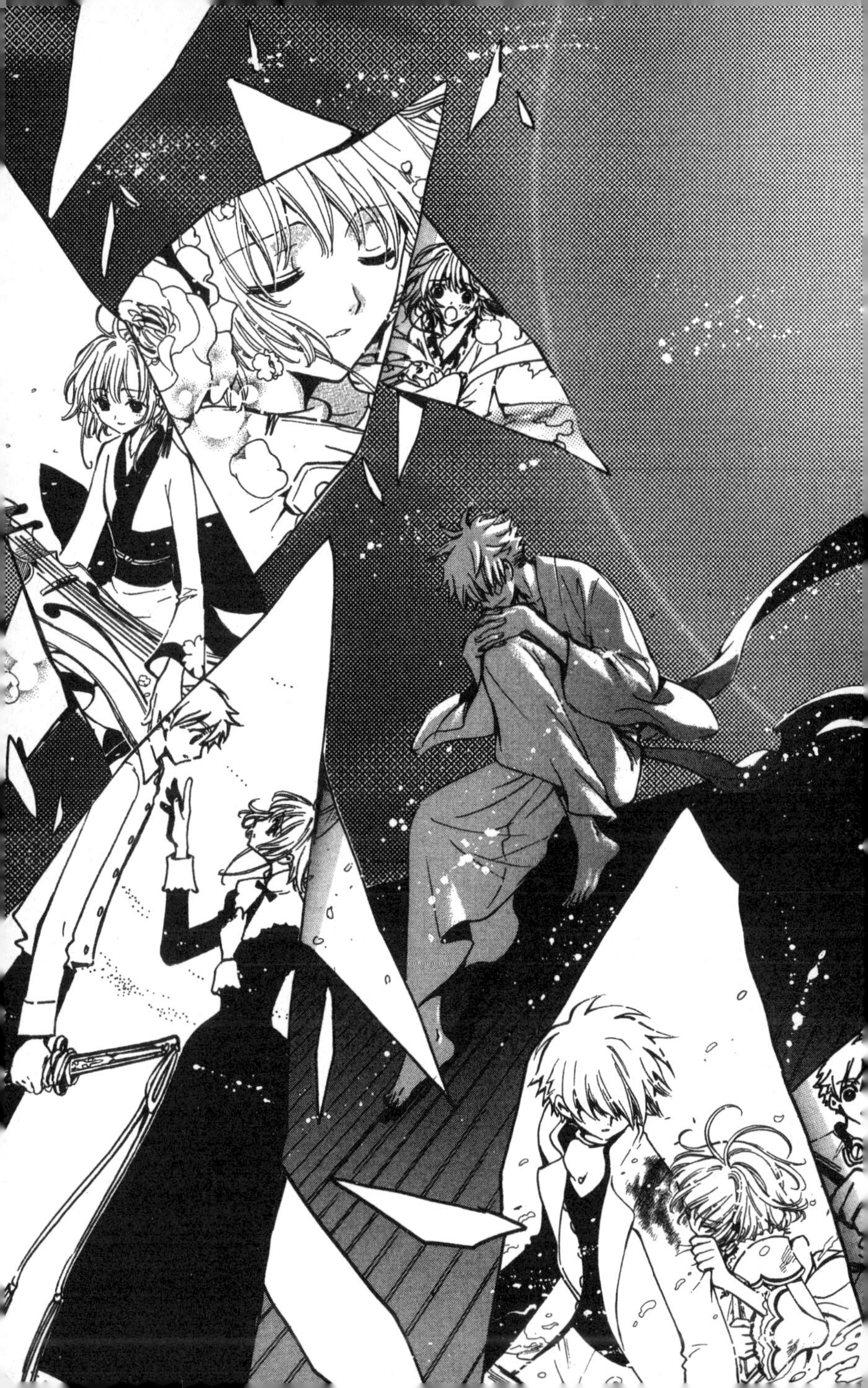

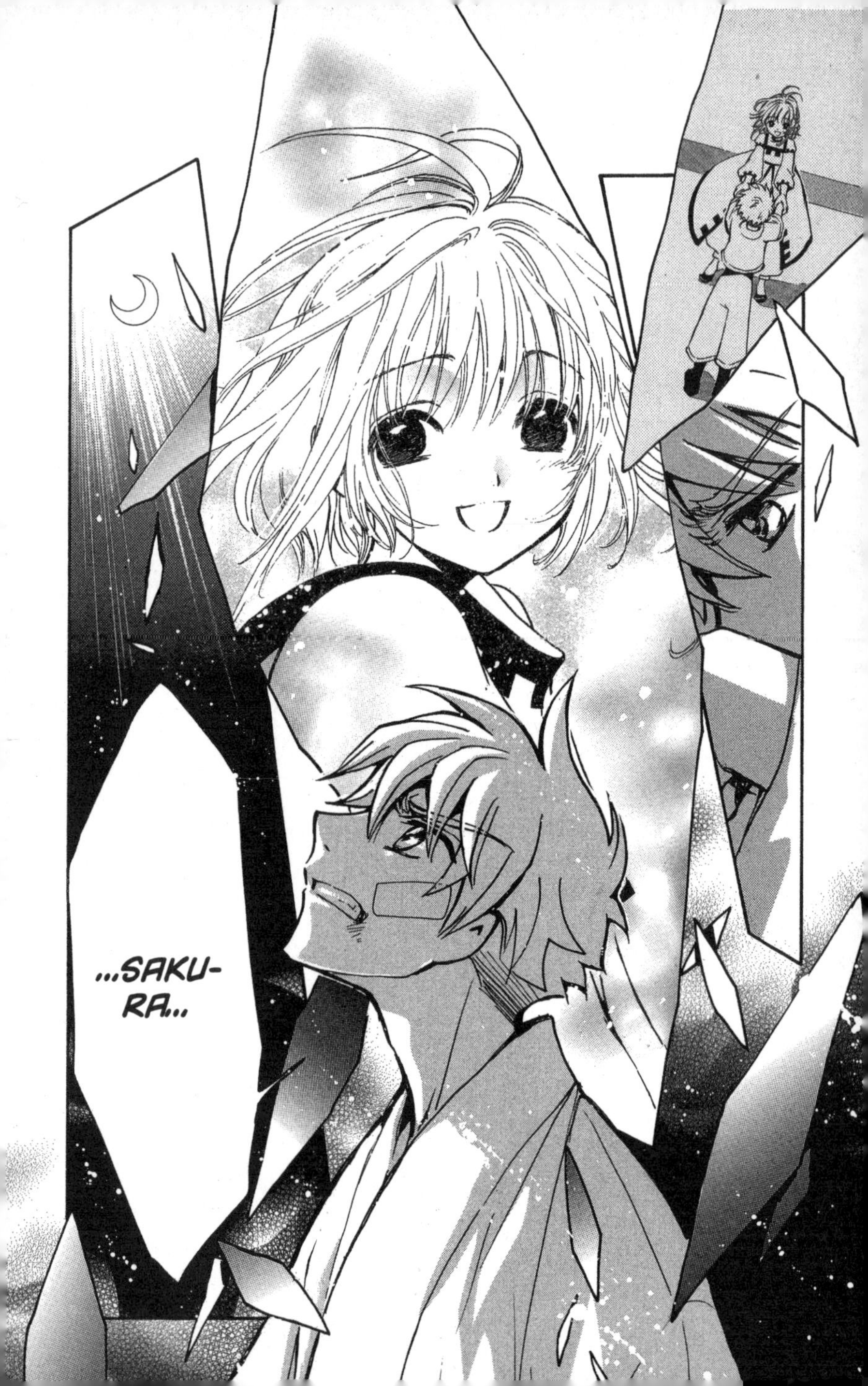
...SAKU-RA...

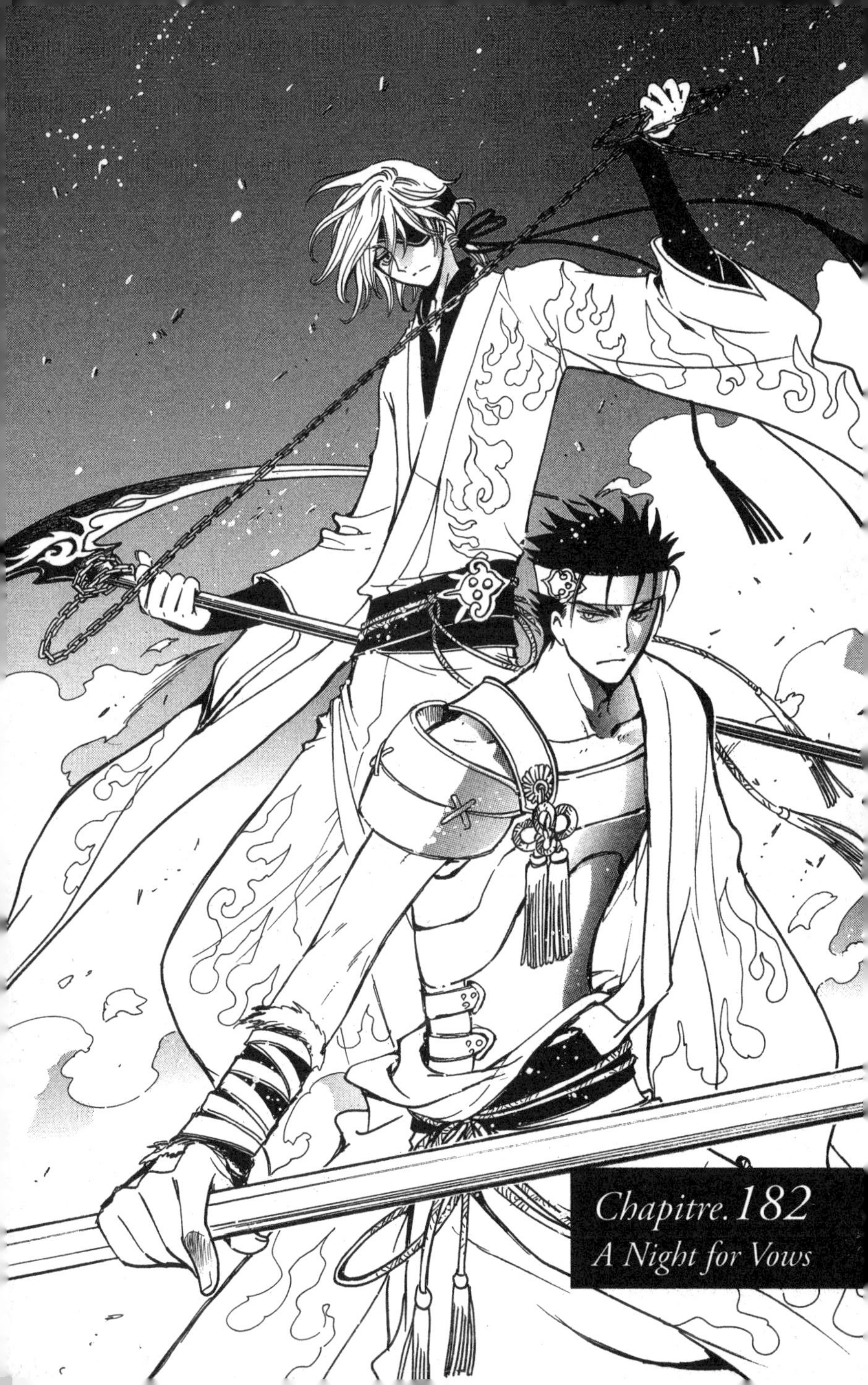
Chapitre. 182
A Night for Vows

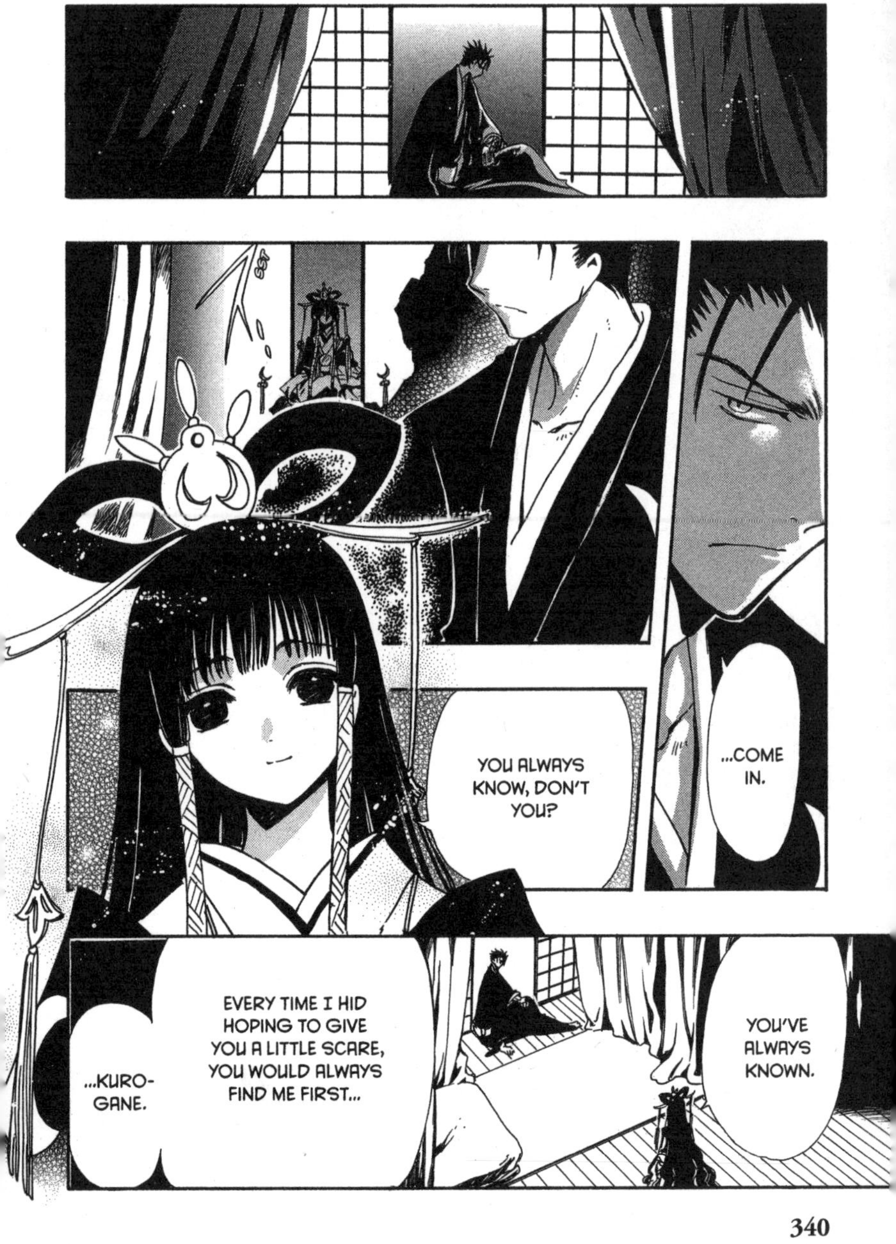
...COME IN.
YOU ALWAYS KNOW, DON'T YOU?
YOU'VE ALWAYS KNOWN.
EVERY TIME I HID HOPING TO GIVE YOU A LITTLE SCARE, YOU WOULD ALWAYS FIND ME FIRST...
...KURO-GANE.

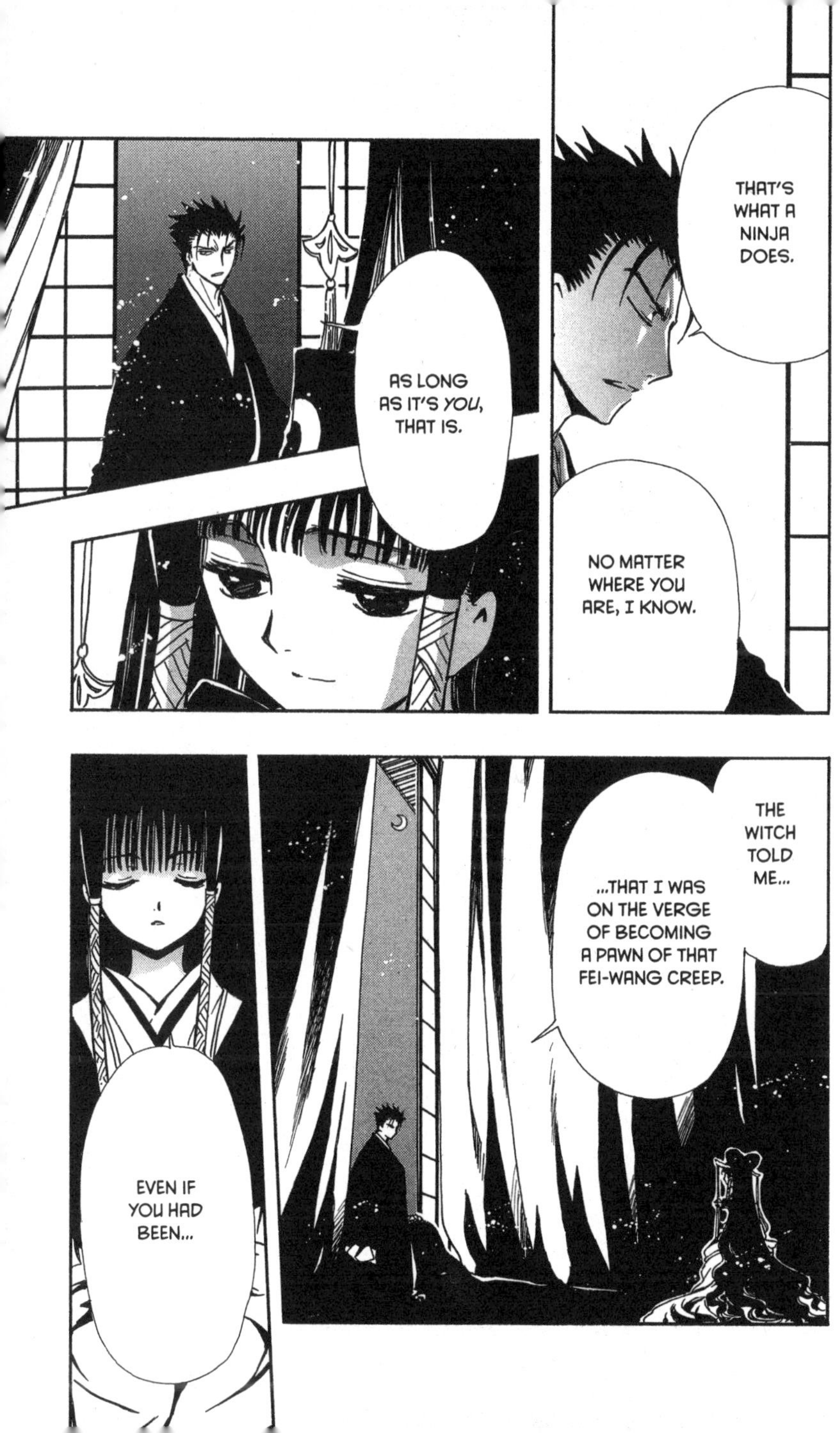
THAT'S WHAT A NINJA DOES.
NO MATTER WHERE YOU ARE, I KNOW.
AS LONG AS IT'S *YOU*, THAT IS.
THE WITCH TOLD ME...
...THAT I WAS ON THE VERGE OF BECOMING A PAWN OF THAT FEI-WANG CREEP.
EVEN IF YOU HAD BEEN...

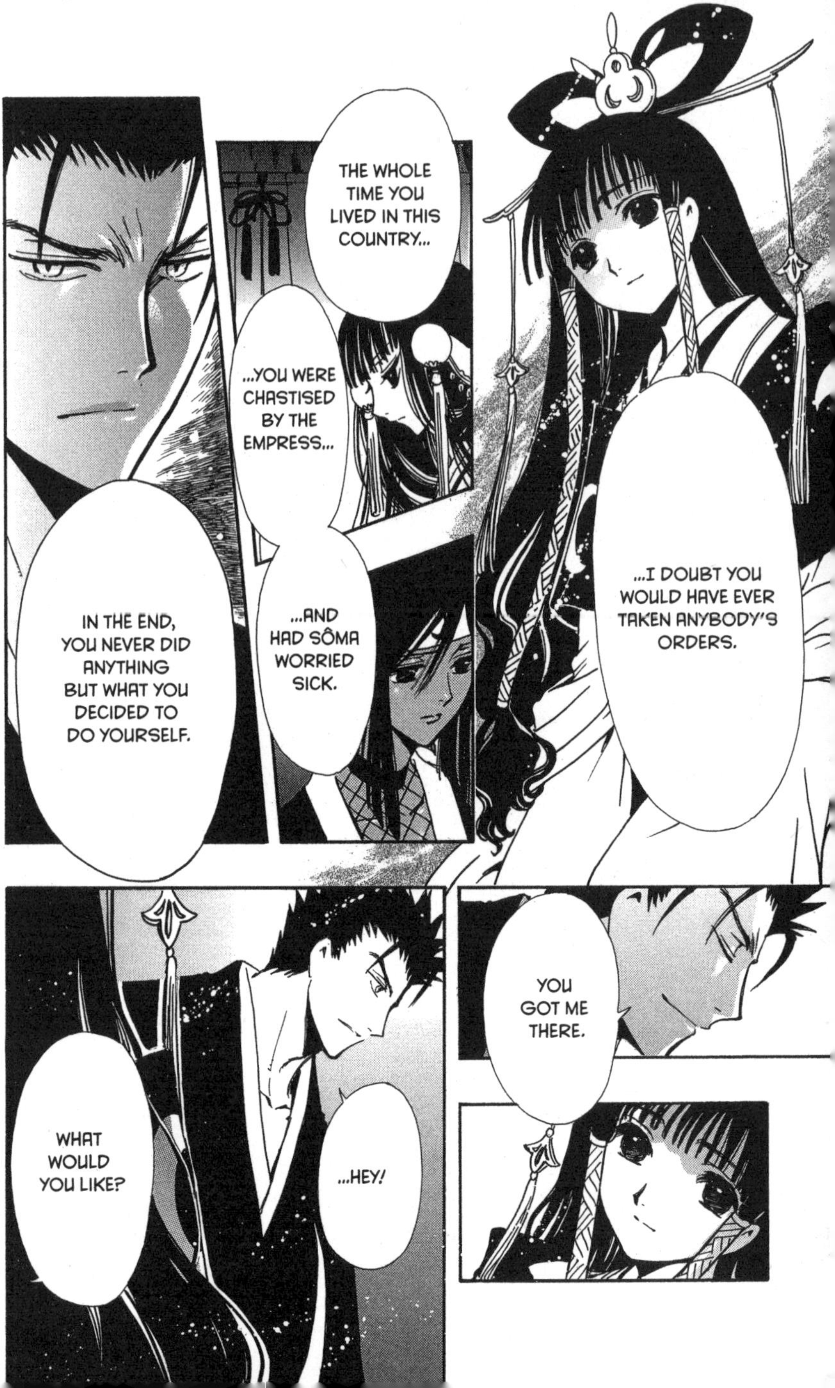
THE WHOLE TIME YOU LIVED IN THIS COUNTRY...
...YOU WERE CHASTISED BY THE EMPRESS...
...AND HAD SÔMA WORRIED SICK.
IN THE END, YOU NEVER DID ANYTHING BUT WHAT YOU DECIDED TO DO YOURSELF.
...I DOUBT YOU WOULD HAVE EVER TAKEN ANYBODY'S ORDERS.
YOU GOT ME THERE.
...HEY!
WHAT WOULD YOU LIKE?

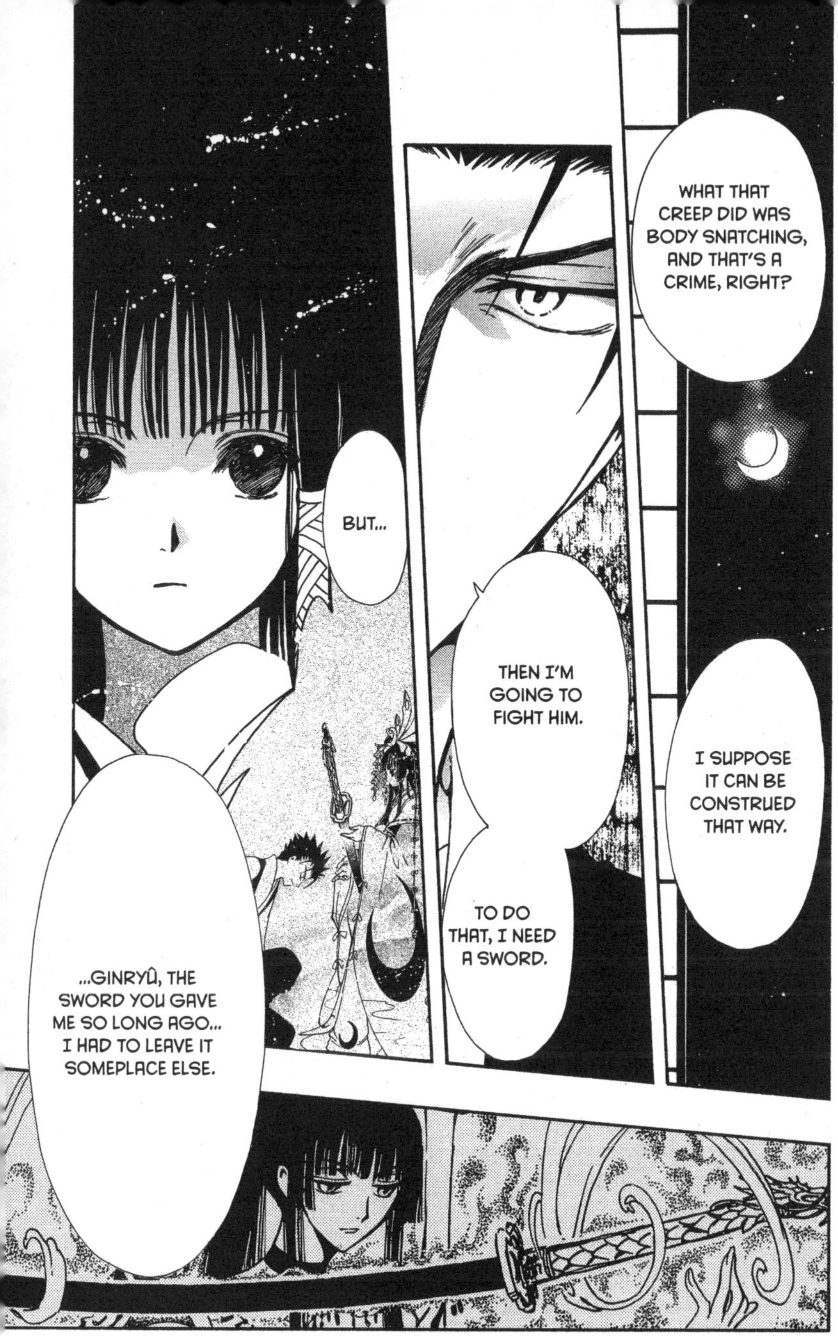
WHAT THAT CREEP DID WAS BODY SNATCHING, AND THAT'S A CRIME, RIGHT?
I SUPPOSE IT CAN BE CONSTRUED THAT WAY.
THEN I'M GOING TO FIGHT HIM.
TO DO THAT, I NEED A SWORD.
BUT...
...GINRYÛ, THE SWORD YOU GAVE ME SO LONG AGO... I HAD TO LEAVE IT SOMEPLACE ELSE.

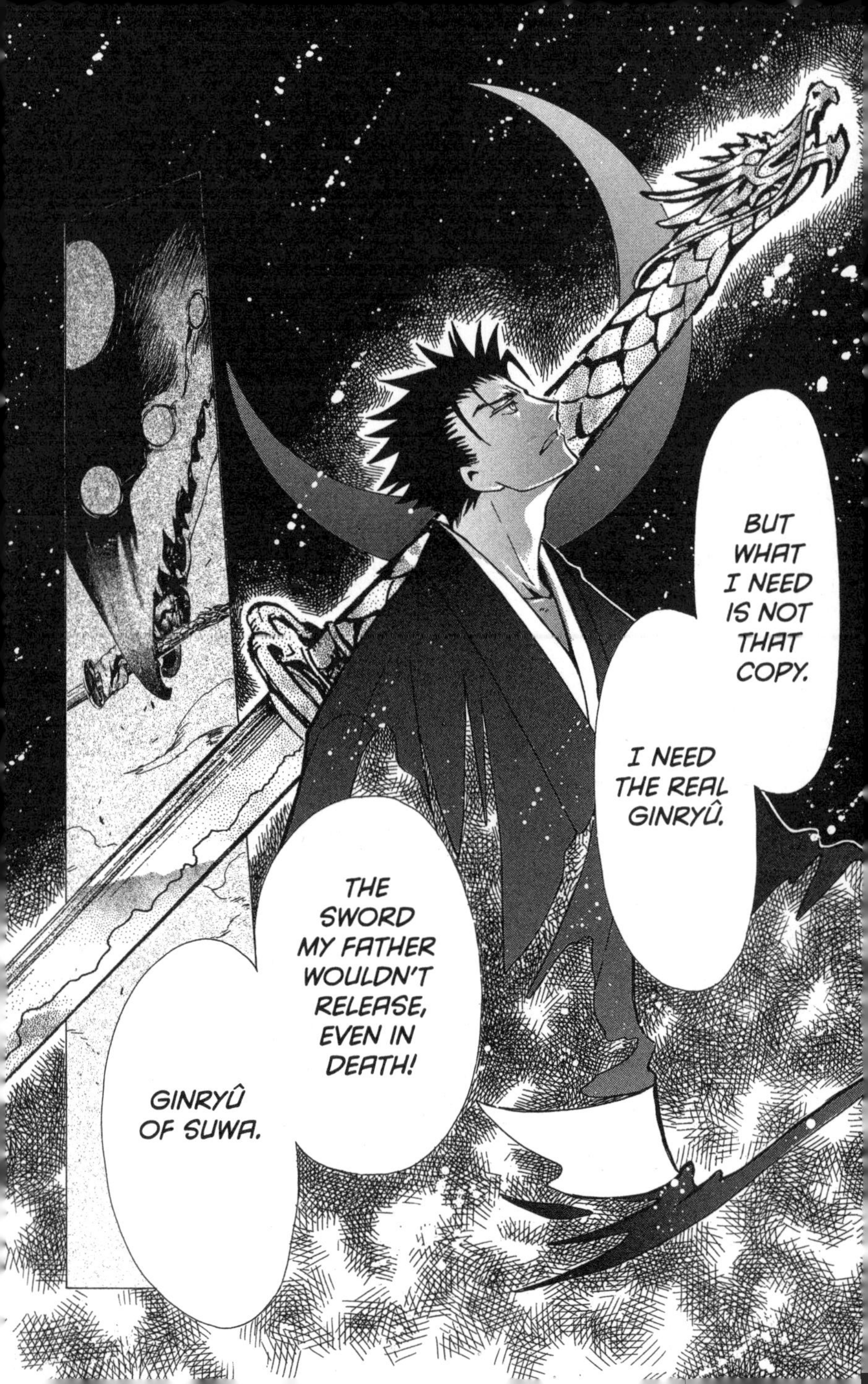
BUT WHAT I NEED IS NOT THAT COPY.
I NEED THE REAL GINRYÛ.
THE SWORD MY FATHER WOULDN'T RELEASE, EVEN IN DEATH!
GINRYÛ OF SUWA.

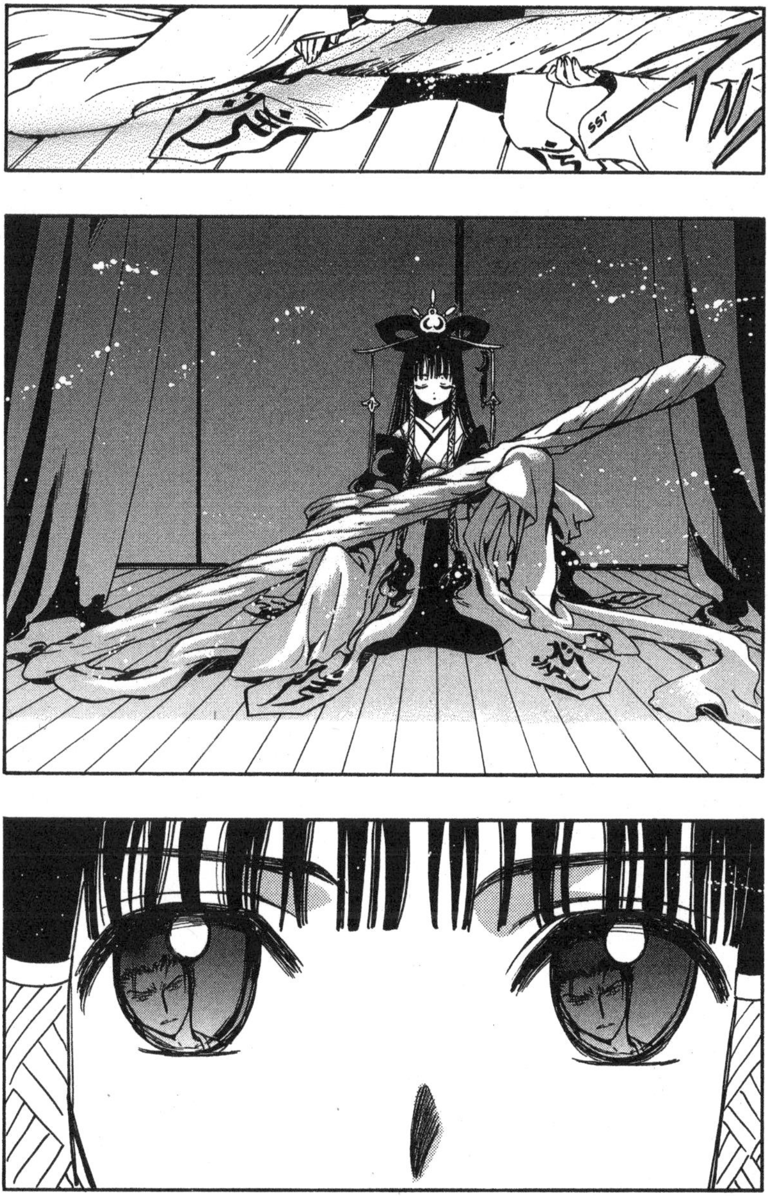
SST

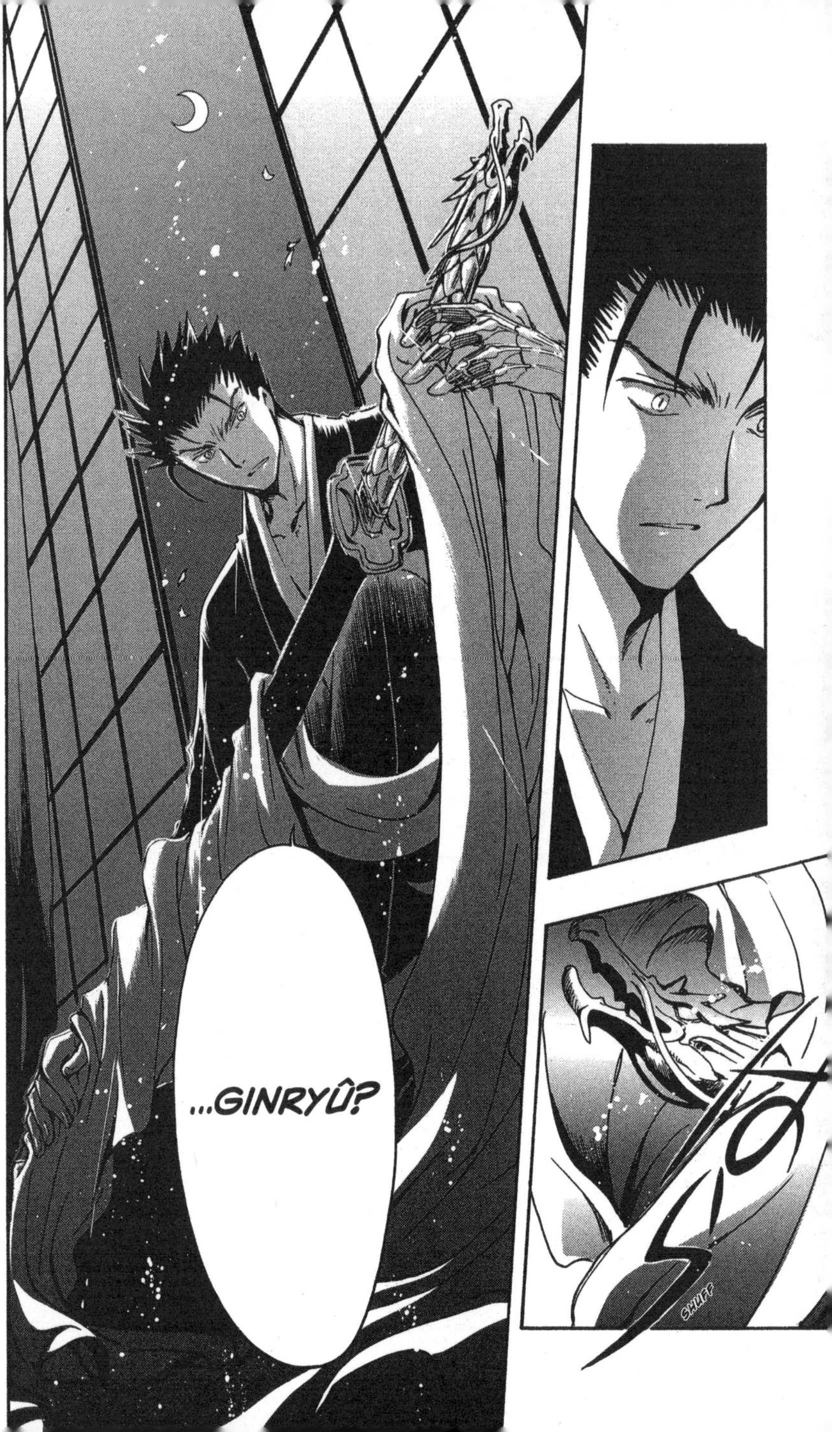
...GINRYÛ?
SHUFF

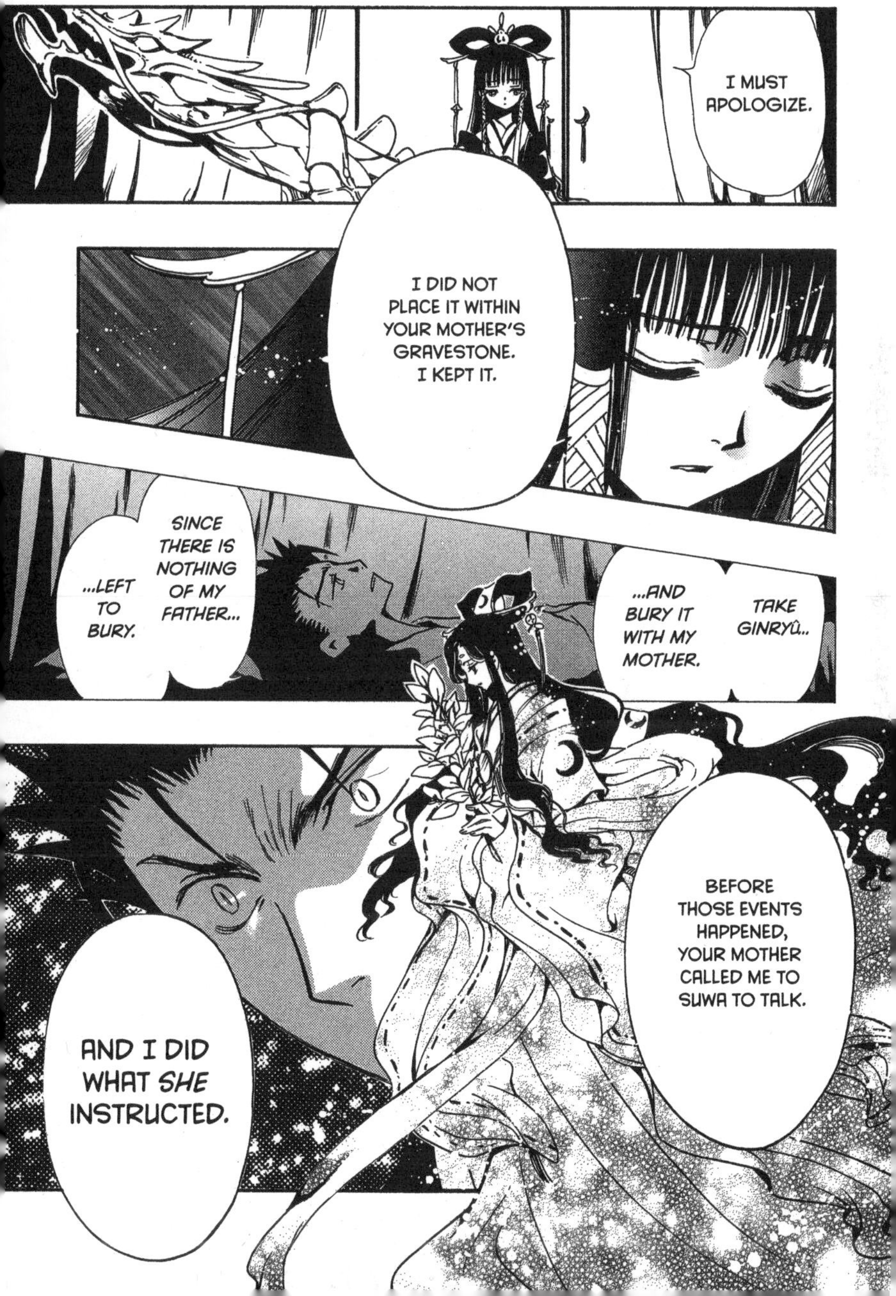
I MUST APOLOGIZE.
I DID NOT PLACE IT WITHIN YOUR MOTHER'S GRAVESTONE. I KEPT IT.
TAKE GINRYÛ...
...AND BURY IT WITH MY MOTHER.
SINCE THERE IS NOTHING OF MY FATHER...
...LEFT TO BURY.
BEFORE THOSE EVENTS HAPPENED, YOUR MOTHER CALLED ME TO SUWA TO TALK.
AND I DID WHAT SHE INSTRUCTED.

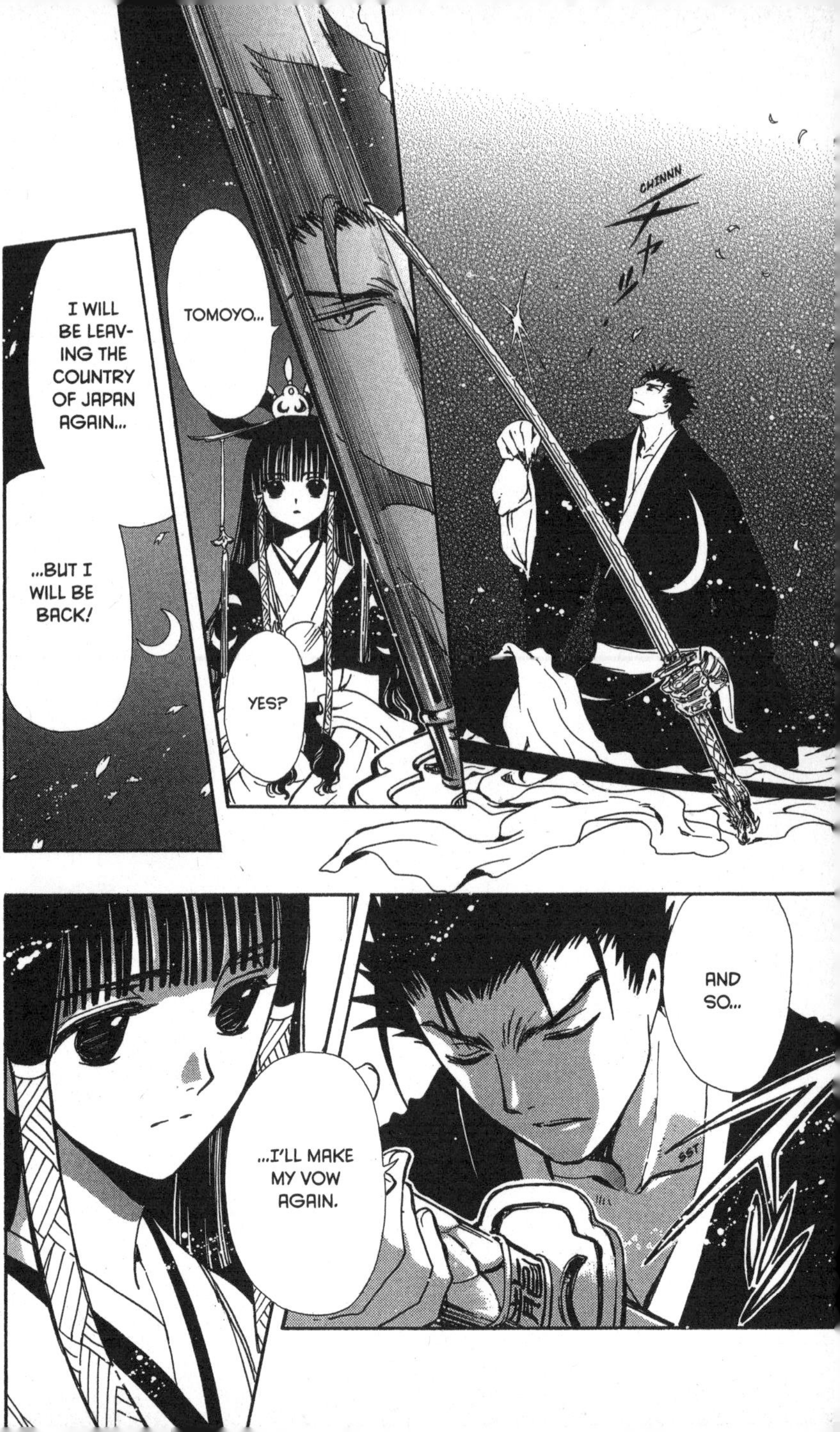
CHINNN
TOMOYO...
YES?
I WILL BE LEAVING THE COUNTRY OF JAPAN AGAIN...
...BUT I WILL BE BACK!
AND SO...
SST
...I'LL MAKE MY VOW AGAIN.

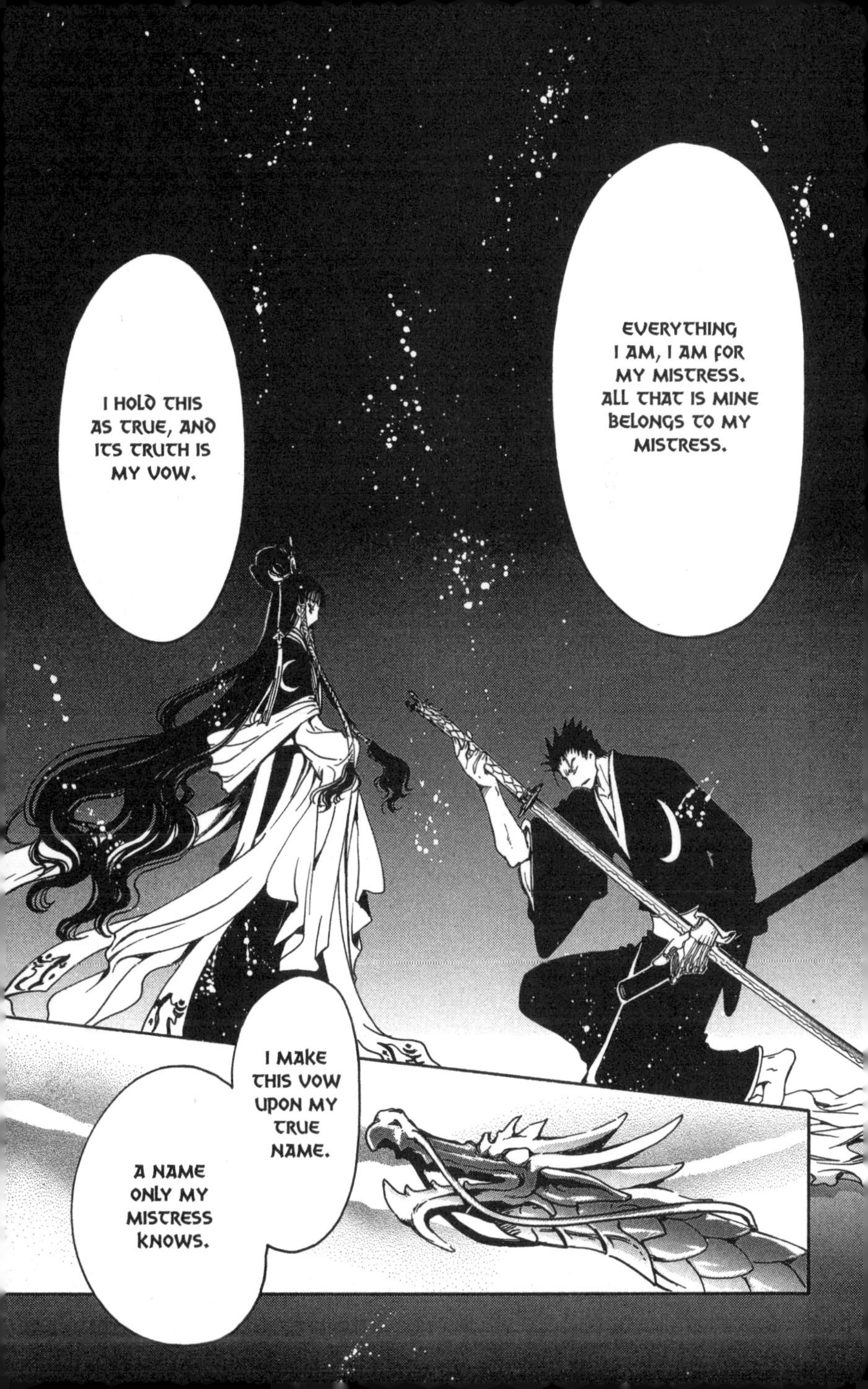
EVERYTHING I AM, I AM FOR MY MISTRESS. ALL THAT IS MINE BELONGS TO MY MISTRESS.
I HOLD THIS AS TRUE, AND ITS TRUTH IS MY VOW.
I MAKE THIS VOW UPON MY TRUE NAME.
A NAME ONLY MY MISTRESS KNOWS.

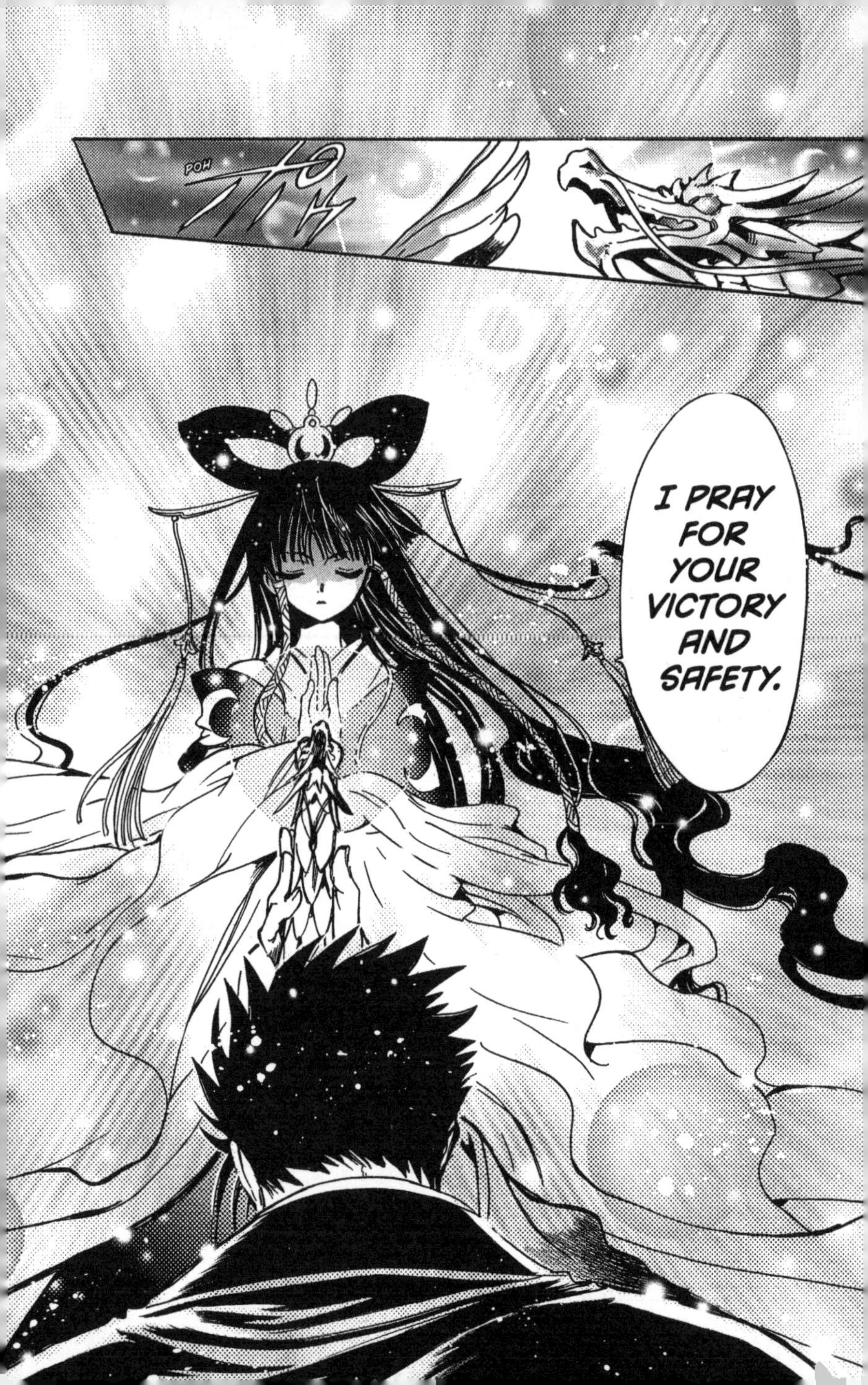
POH
I PRAY FOR YOUR VICTORY AND SAFETY.

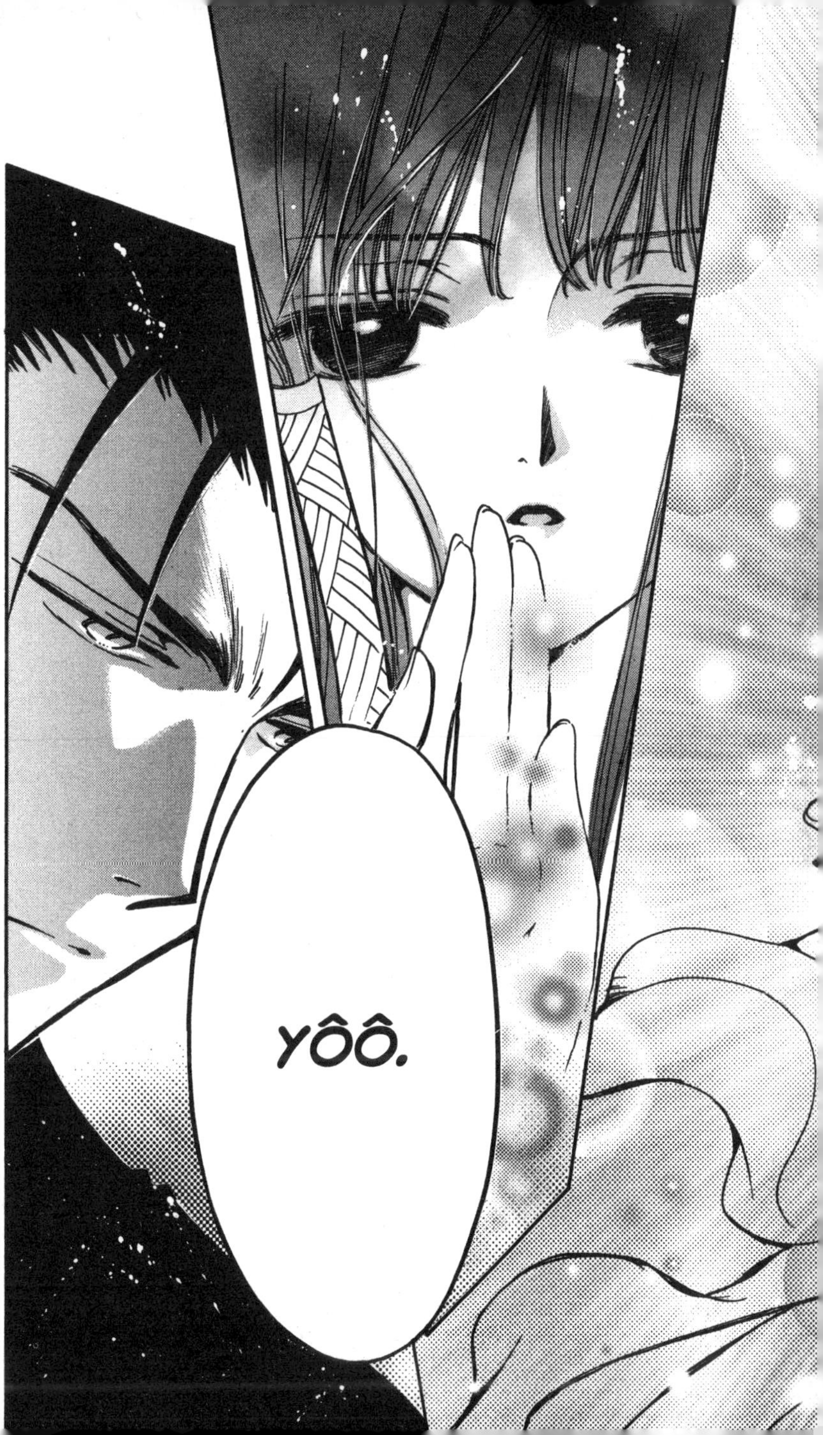
YÔÔ.

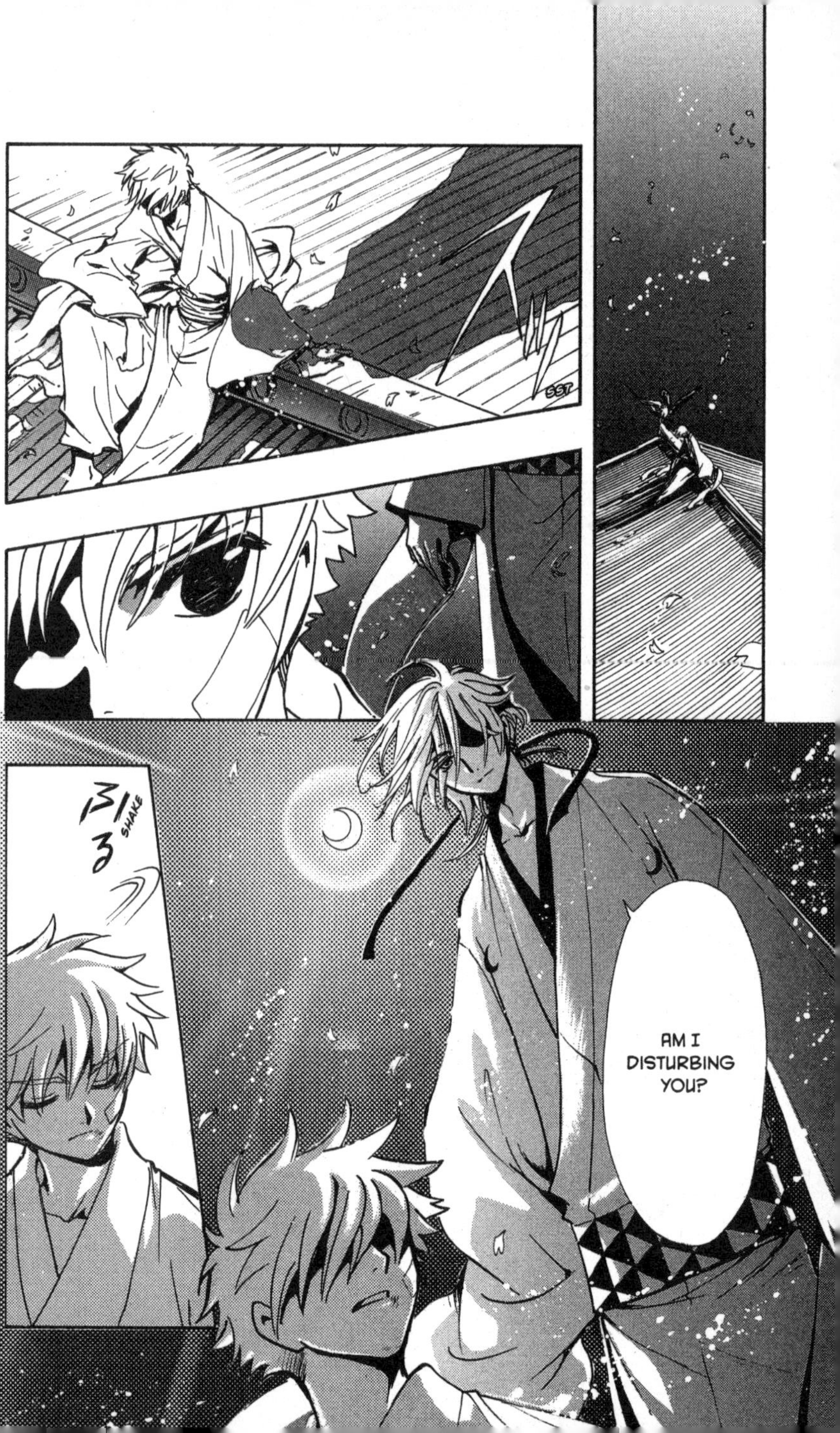
SST
ふる SHAKE
AM I DISTURBING YOU?

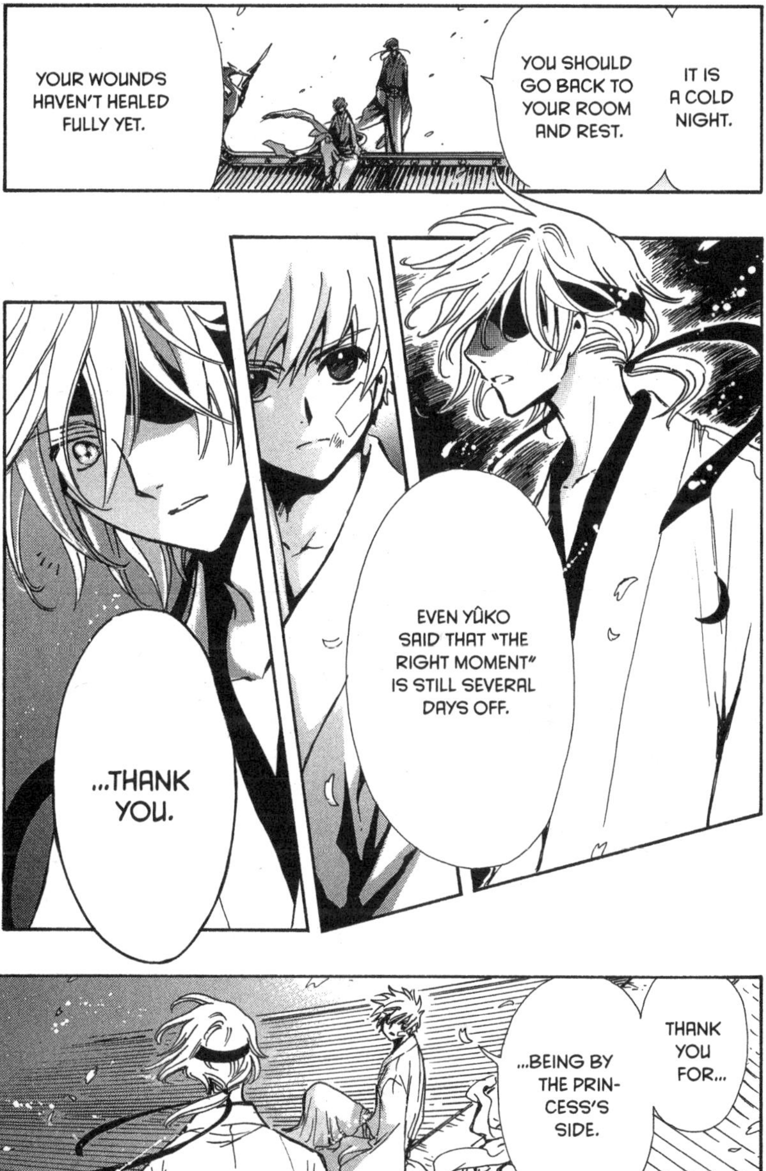
IT IS A COLD NIGHT.
YOU SHOULD GO BACK TO YOUR ROOM AND REST.
YOUR WOUNDS HAVEN'T HEALED FULLY YET.
EVEN YÛKO SAID THAT "THE RIGHT MOMENT" IS STILL SEVERAL DAYS OFF.
...THANK YOU.
THANK YOU FOR...
...BEING BY THE PRIN-CESS'S SIDE.

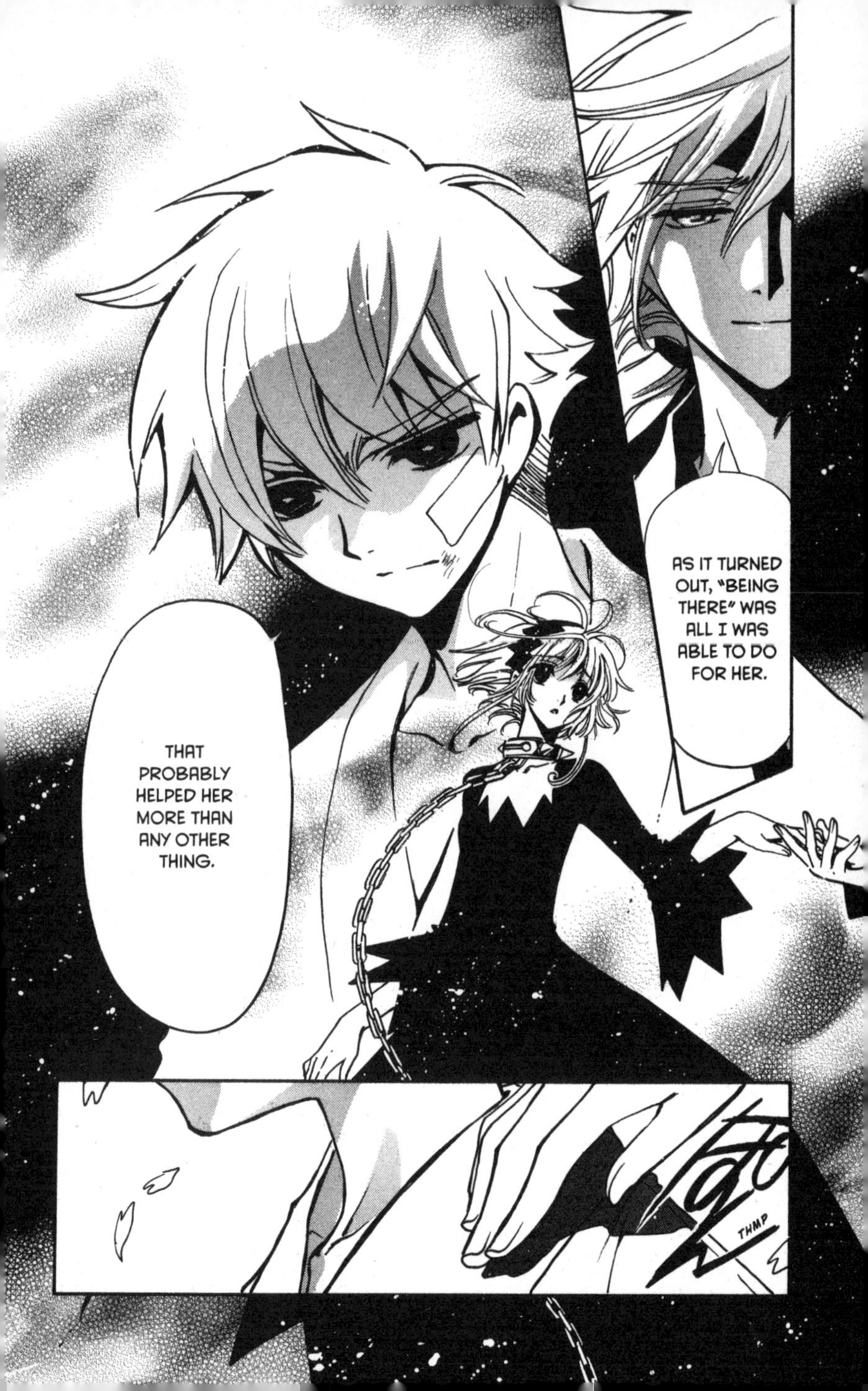
AS IT TURNED OUT, "BEING THERE" WAS ALL I WAS ABLE TO DO FOR HER.
THAT PROBABLY HELPED HER MORE THAN ANY OTHER THING.
THMP

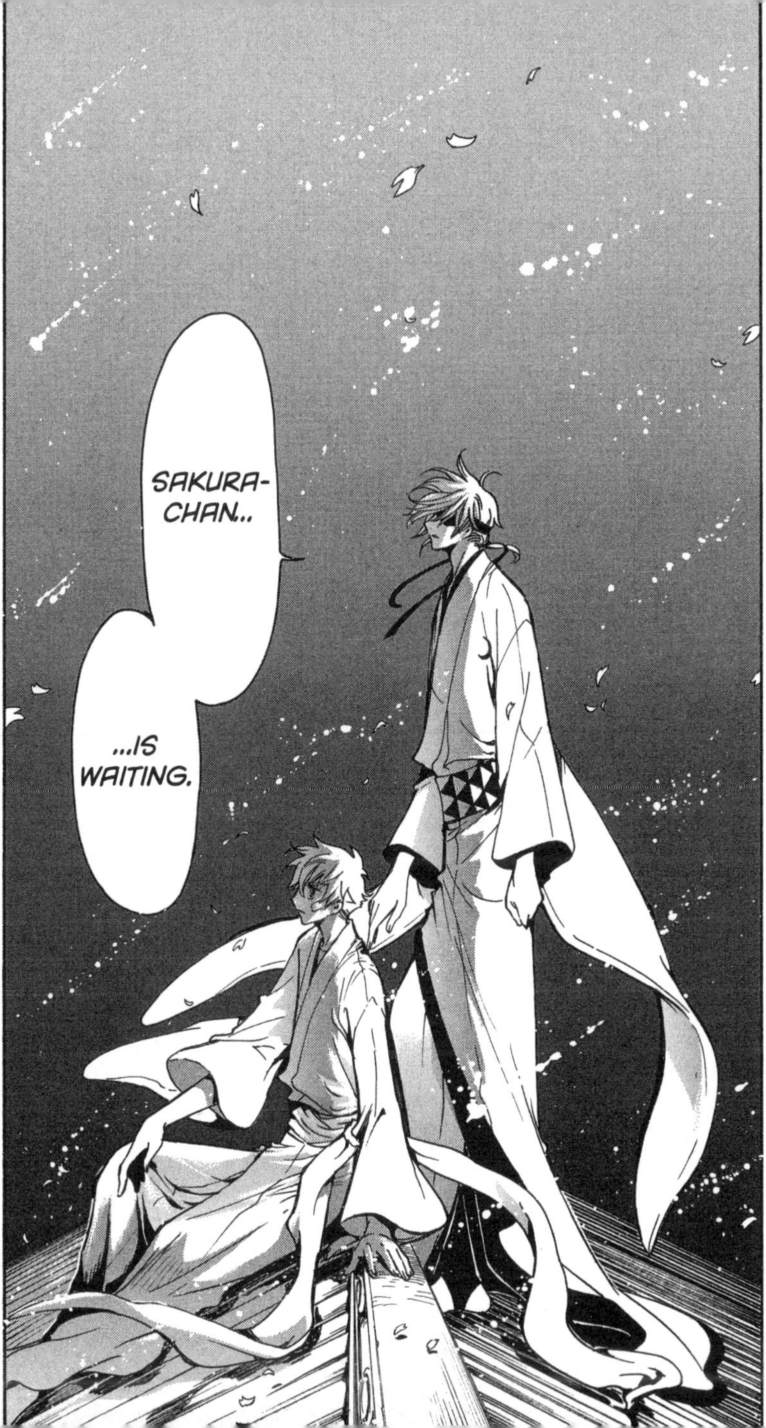
SAKURA-CHAN...
...IS WAITING.

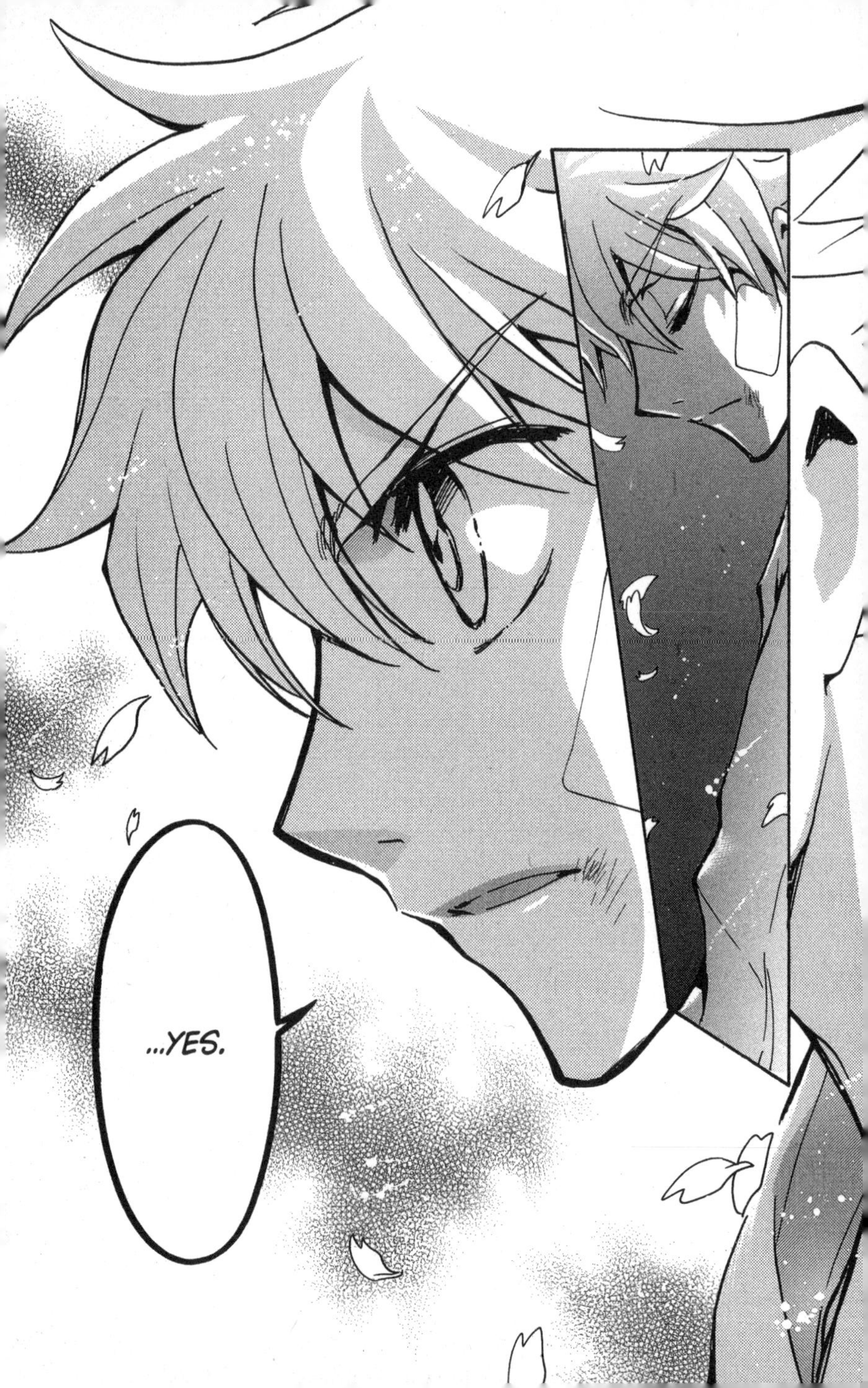
...YES.

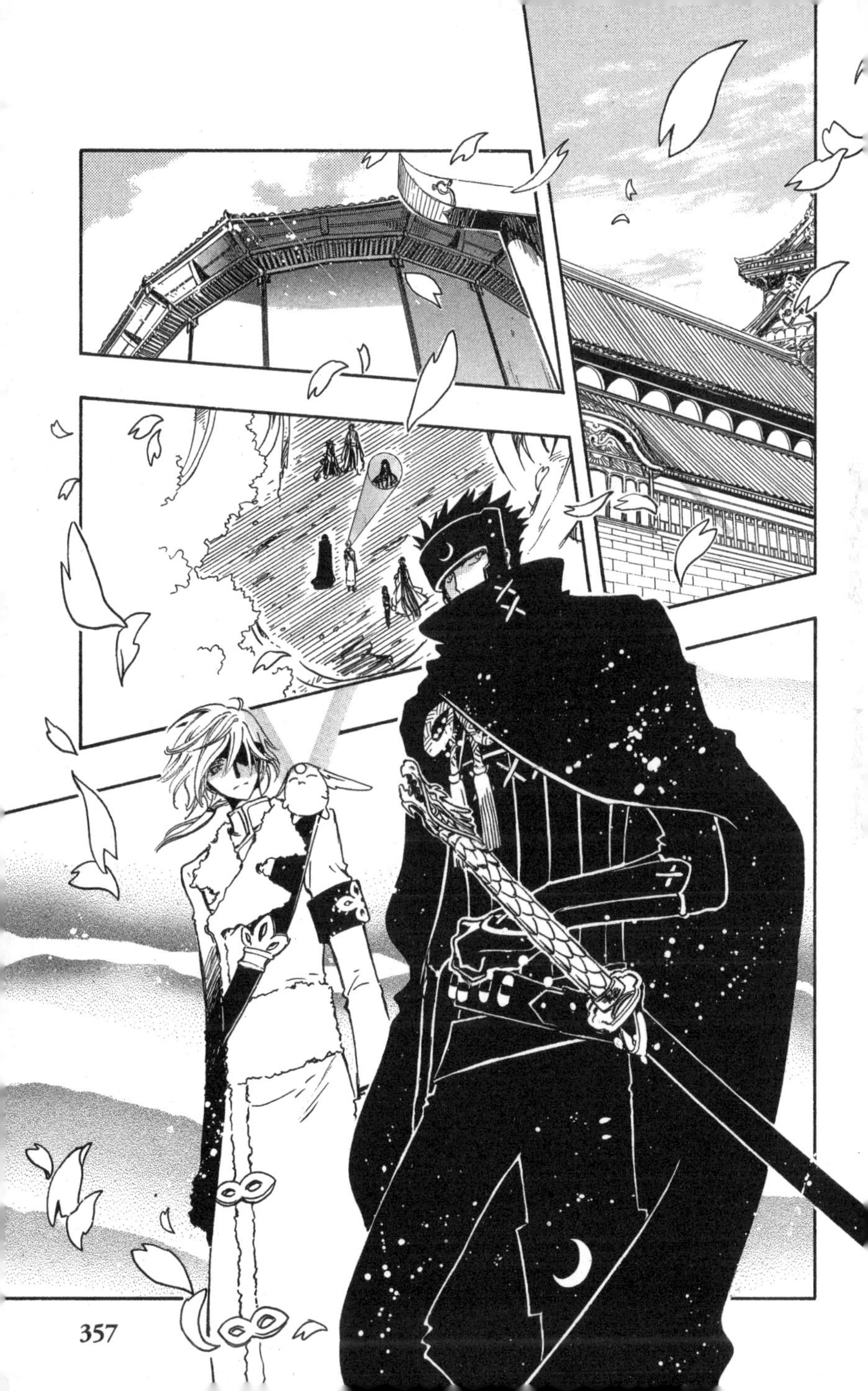

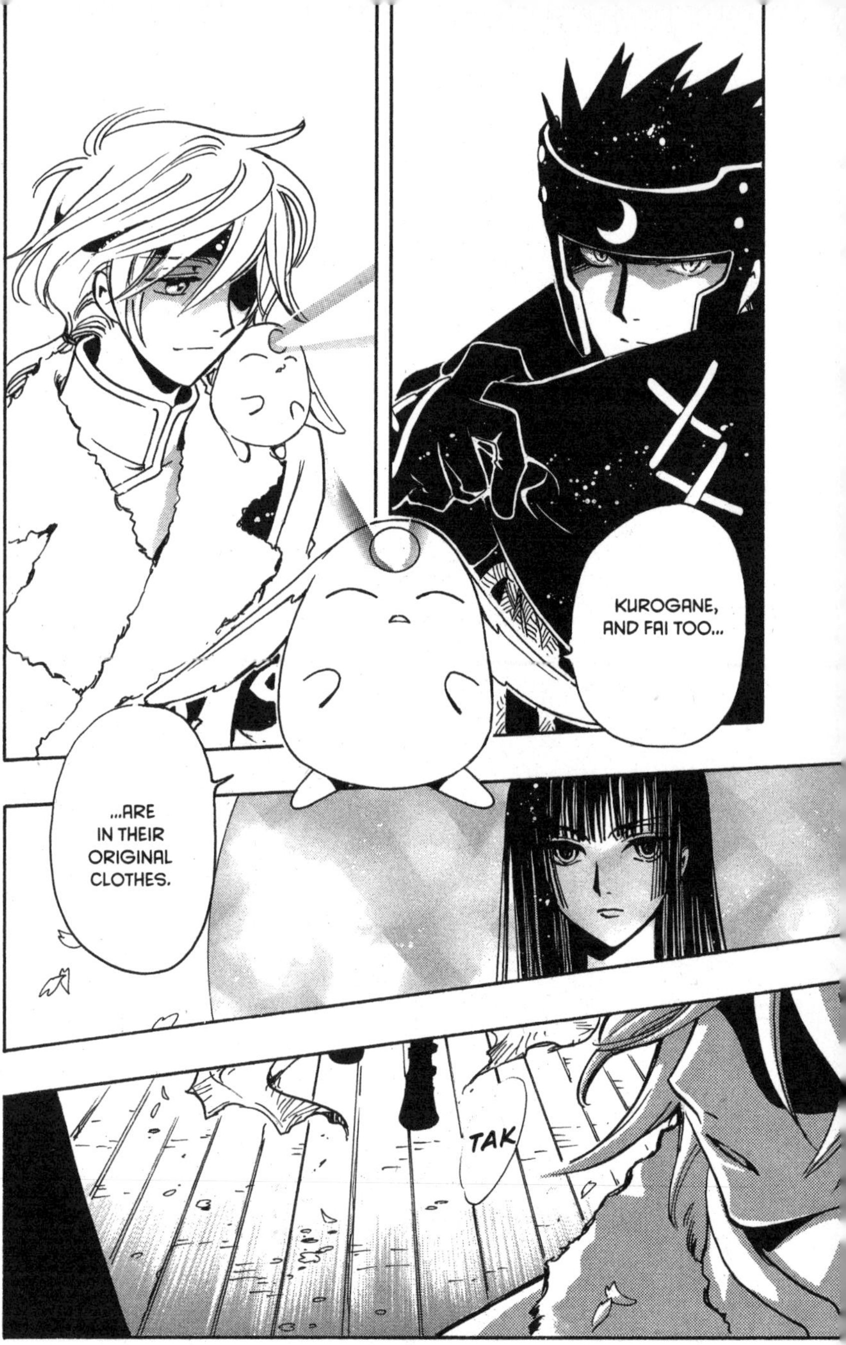
KUROGANE, AND FAI TOO...
...ARE IN THEIR ORIGINAL CLOTHES.
TAK

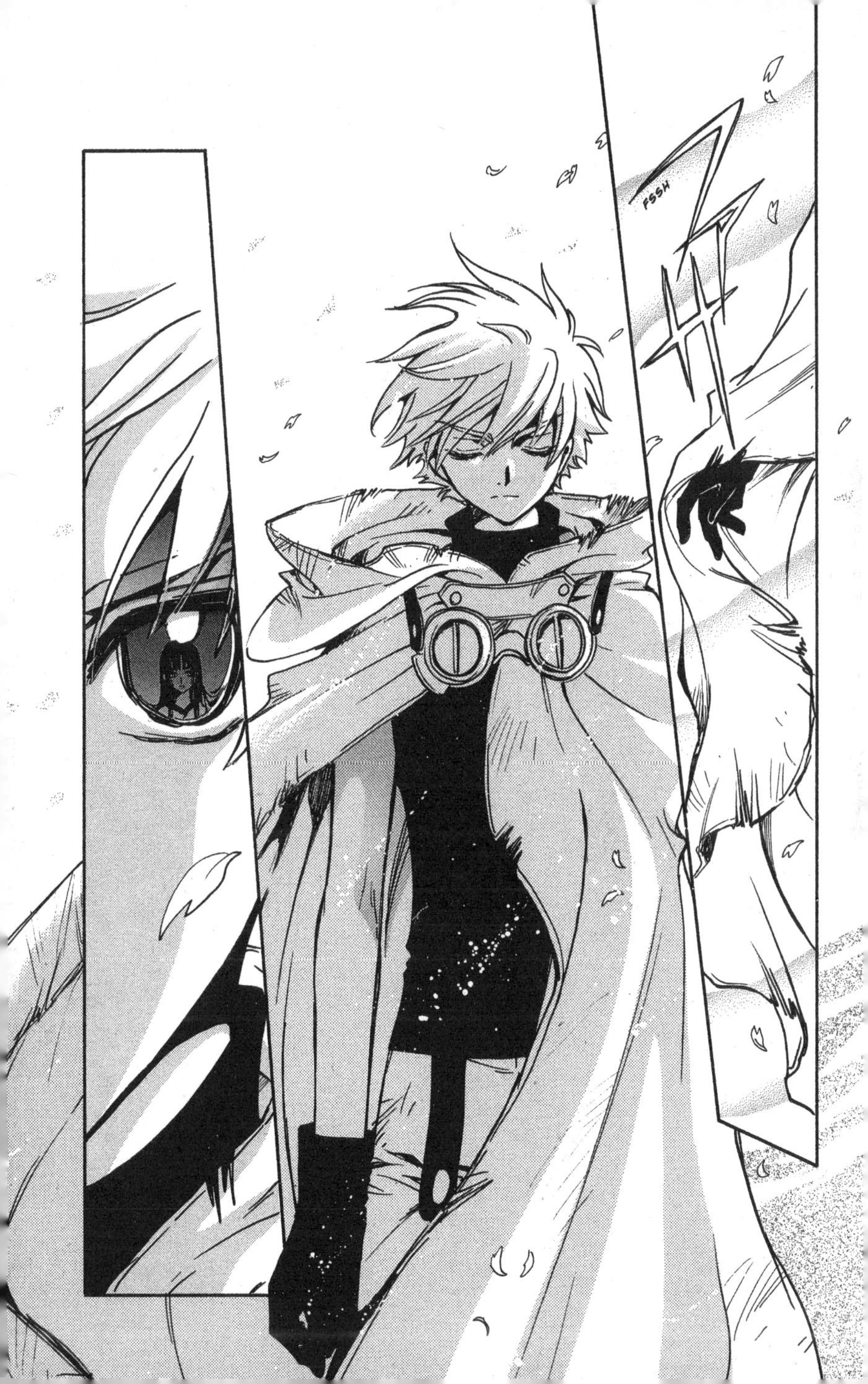
FSSH

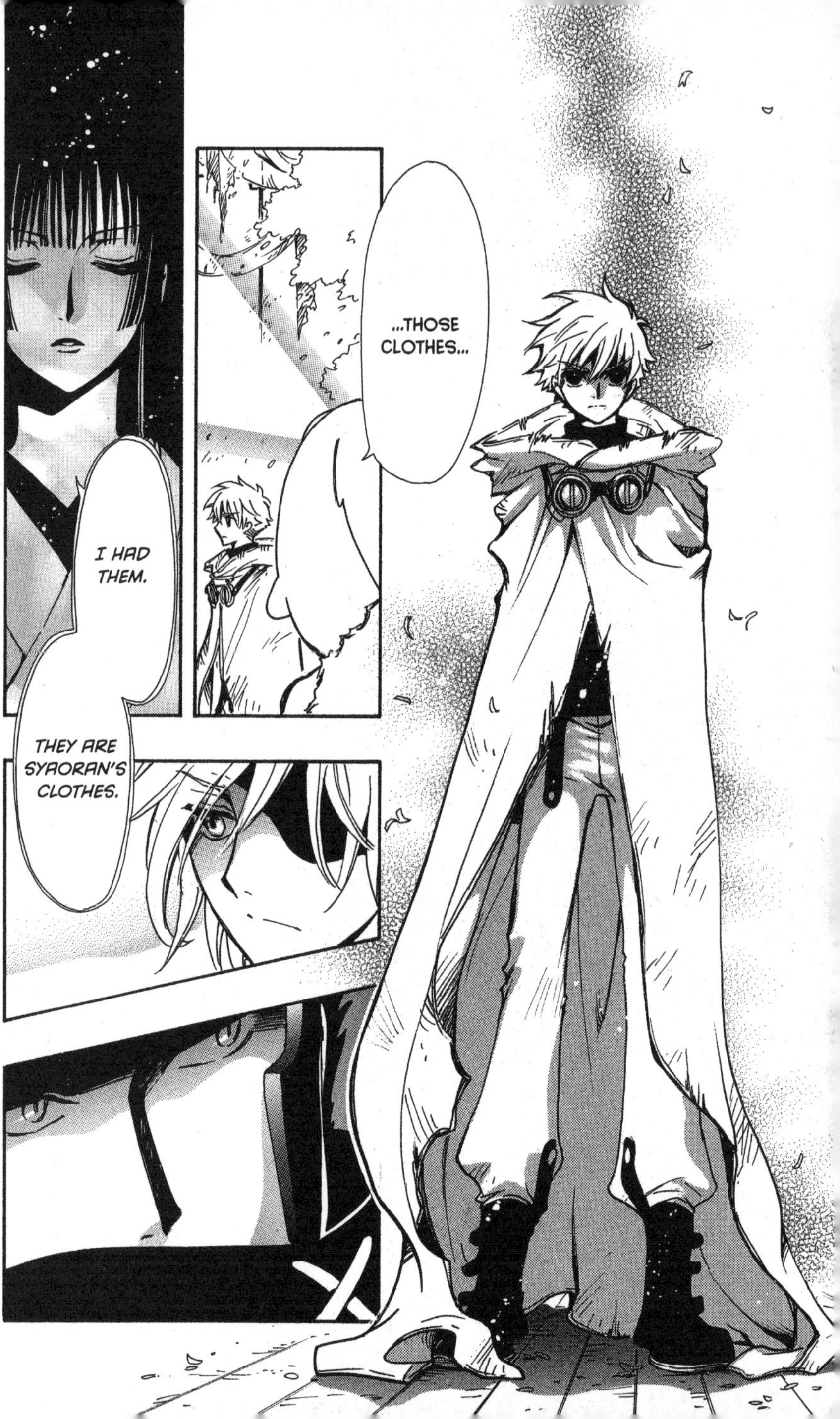
...THOSE CLOTHES...
I HAD THEM.
THEY ARE SYAORAN'S CLOTHES.

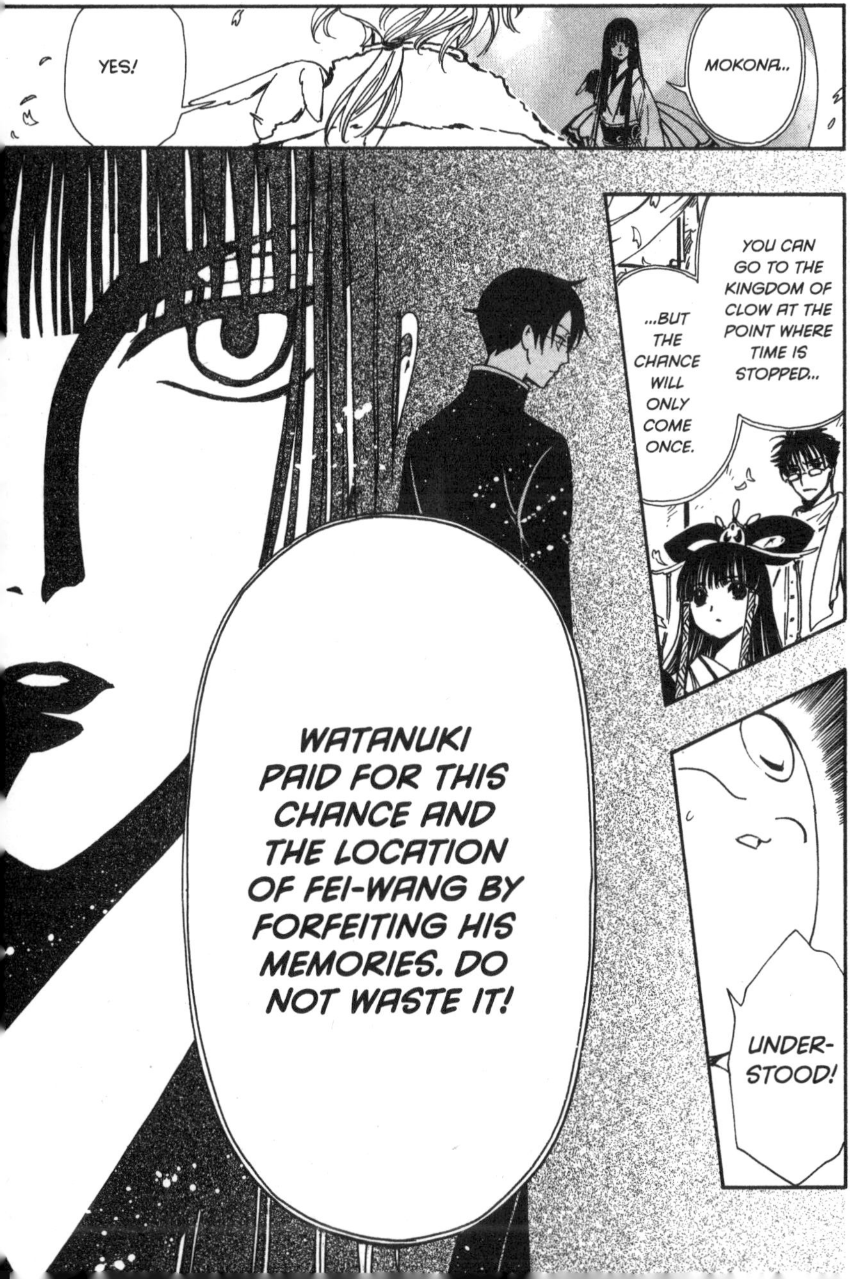
MOKONA...
YES!
YOU CAN GO TO THE KINGDOM OF CLOW AT THE POINT WHERE TIME IS STOPPED...
...BUT THE CHANCE WILL ONLY COME ONCE.
UNDER-STOOD!
WATANUKI PAID FOR THIS CHANCE AND THE LOCATION OF FEI-WANG BY FORFEITING HIS MEMORIES. DO NOT WASTE IT!

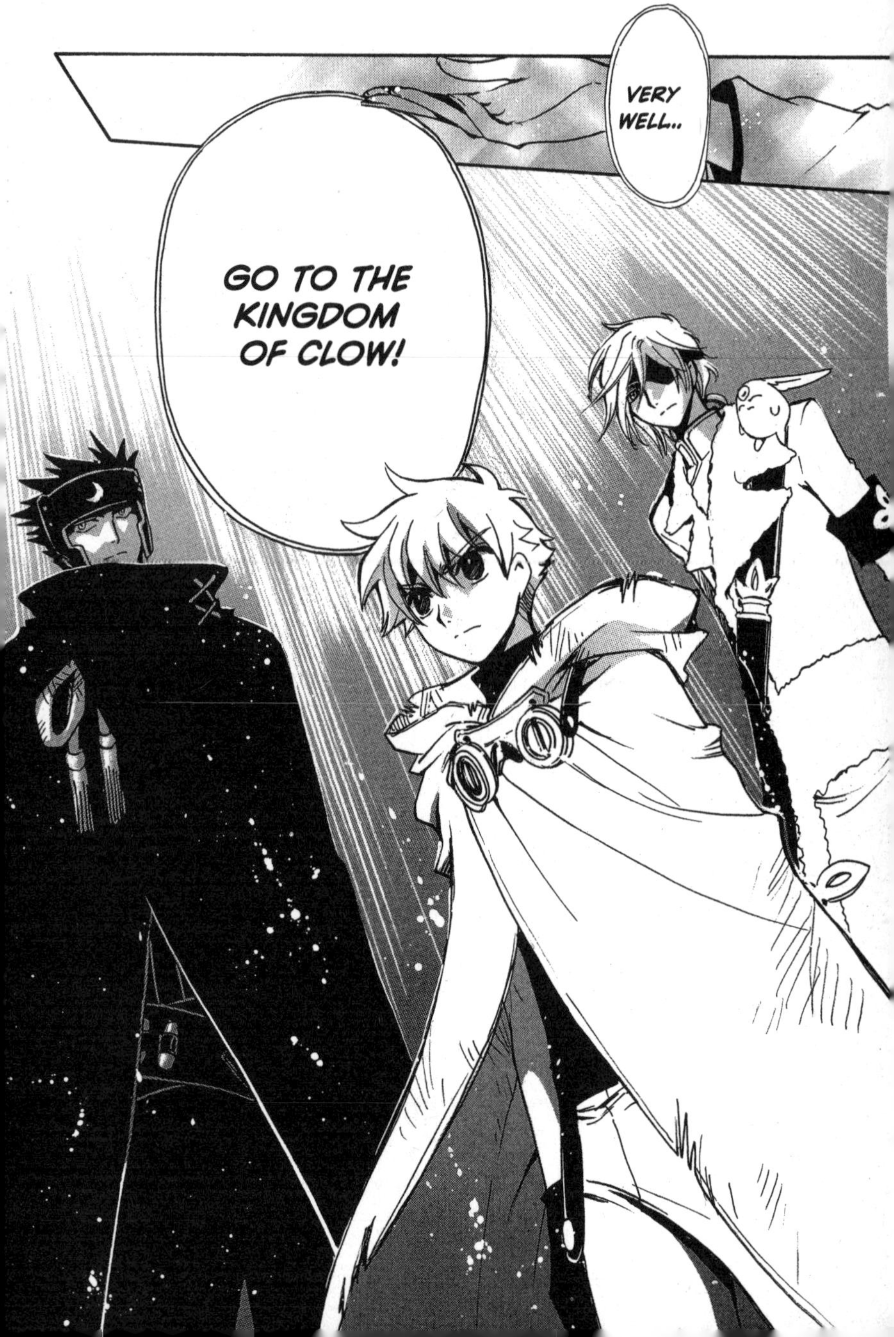
VERY WELL..
GO TO THE KINGDOM OF CLOW!

To Be Continued

Translation Notes

Japanese is a tricky language for most Westerners, and translation is often more art than science. For your edification and reading pleasure, here are notes on some of the places where we could have gone in a different direction in our translation of the work, or where a Japanese cultural reference is used.

IF HE CONTINUES TO USE IT, THEN HE COULD SURPASS THE POWER OF THE MAGICIAN WHO SO RECENTLY TOOK HIS EYE BACK.

Magician who took his eye back, page 197

Those readers who are reading this without having to pause three months between volumes will have no trouble figuring out who Seishirô is talking about in this passage. But the rest of us would have to recall volume 16, or omnibus 6, to get the reference. The original Syaoran gave the image Syaoran his eye hoping that it would lead the image to develop a soul of his own. Unfortunately that hope seems to have been in vain, and in volume 16, he took his eye back.

You know what your Sakura feels..., page 273

As sometimes happens in these books, later revelations modify the translations of previous volumes. In this volume, it is finally revealed that Sakura is not the original, but an image of the original, and the original Syaoran knew it. Unfortunately, I, as translator, didn't know it (this volume had yet to be published in Japan at the time that I was translating volume 16). So the line was slightly mistranslated in volume 16. Syaoran's term in the original translation, "my heart," seems to refer to the soul in the form of an eye that the original Syaoran gave to his image. The image of Syaoran assumed that Sakura was the original and that she was only attracted to the piece of the original Syaoran that he possessed. In fact, Sakura was herself an image, and she was honestly attracted to the image Syaoran. I have asked for the line in volume 16 to be modified to reflect the new translation in future printings. If there is no discrepancy between this volume and volume 16, then you have a corrected volume 16.

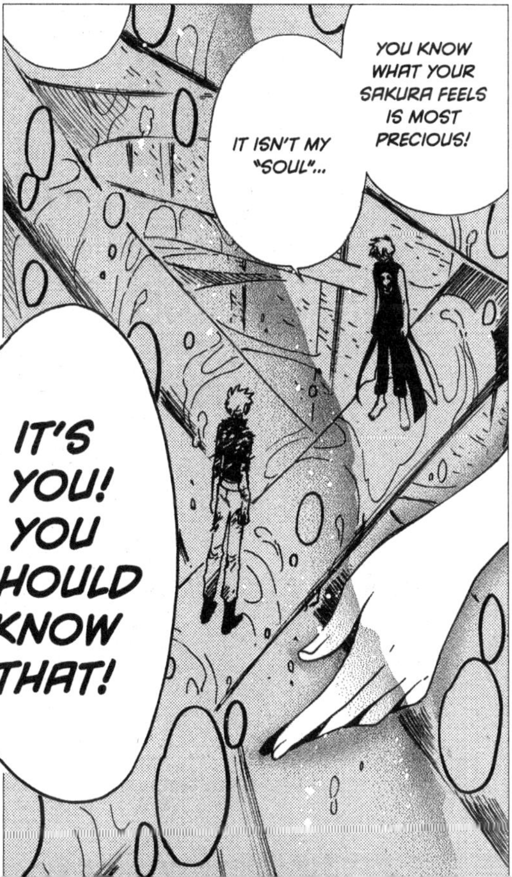
YOU KNOW WHAT YOUR SAKURA FEELS IS MOST PRECIOUS!
IT ISN'T MY "SOUL"...
IT'S YOU! YOU SHOULD KNOW THAT!

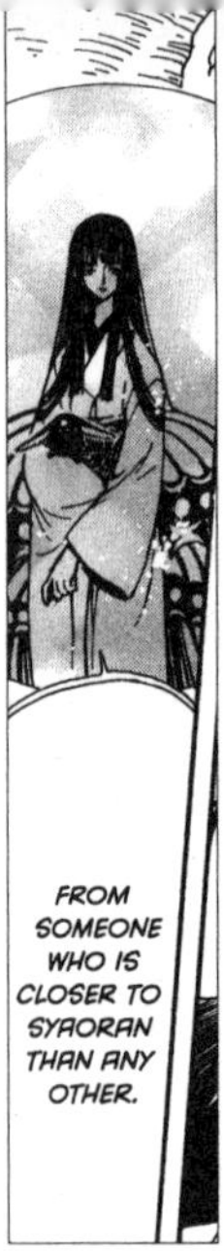
FROM SOMEONE WHO IS CLOSER TO SYAORAN THAN ANY OTHER.

Closer to Syaoran, page 319
It has been stated in both *xxxHOLiC* and *Tsubasa* that Kimihiro Watanuki's personality is close to Syaoran's. There seems to be a close connection between them, and both have paid high prices to the witch Yûko for the other's sake. As is becoming more obvious in *xxxHOLiC*, Watanuki is missing memories. He cannot remember his parents' names, for example, and he is seriously beginning to wonder whether his life with Yûko is real or a part of dreams.

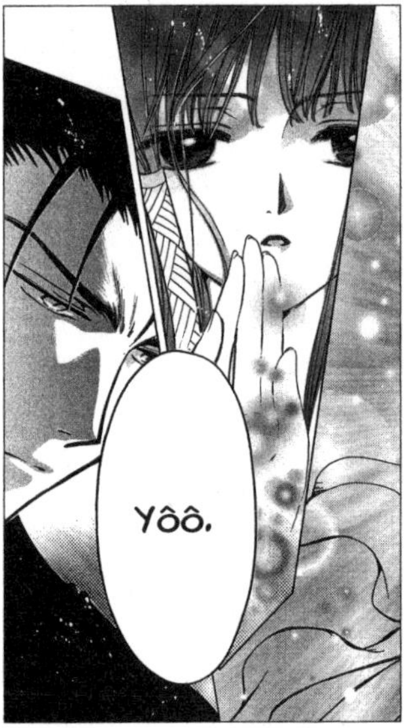
YÔÔ.

Yôô, page 351
This is Kurogane's true name, the one that only he and Princess Tomoyo know. It is made up of two kanji, one of which is *yô*, which means "hawk," and another kanji to which *Tsubasa* readers should be familiar, *ô*, which means "king."

Contents

ツバサ

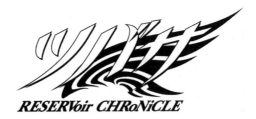

RESERVoir CHRoNiCLE

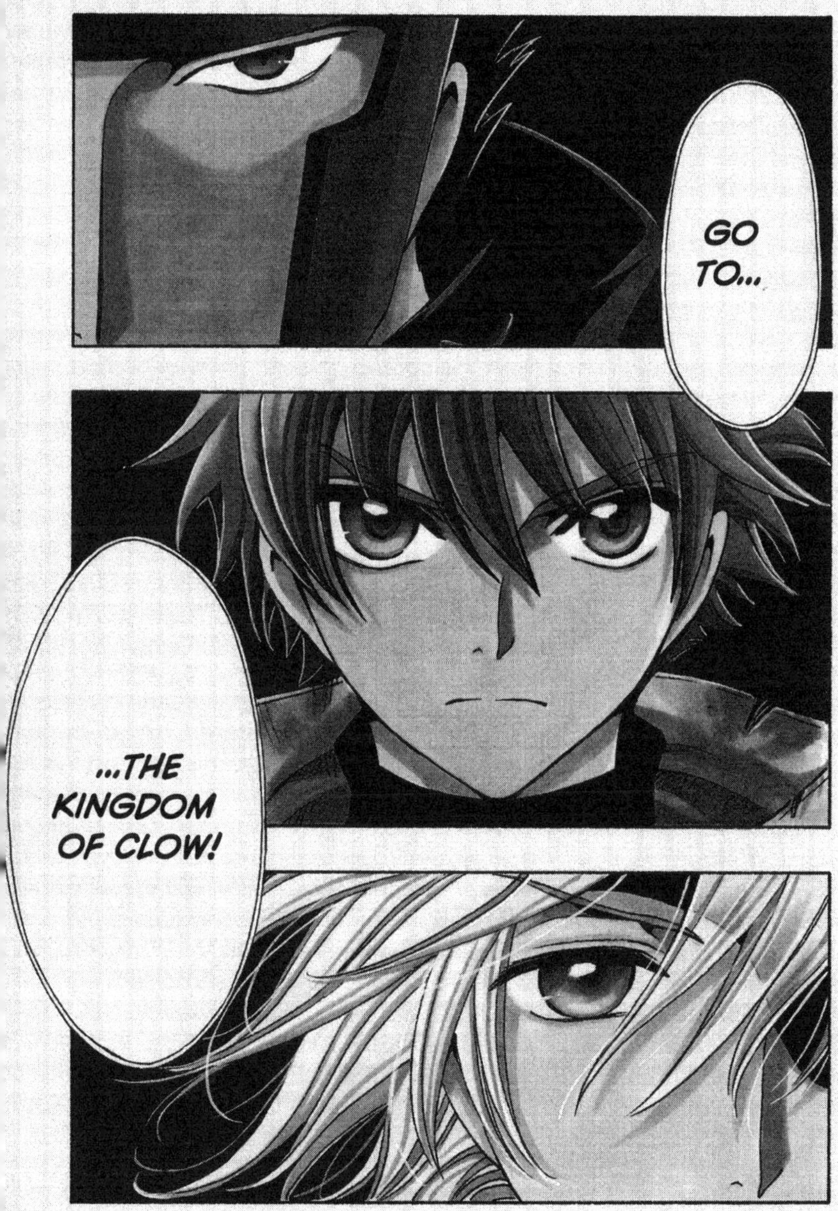
GO TO...
...THE KINGDOM OF CLOW!

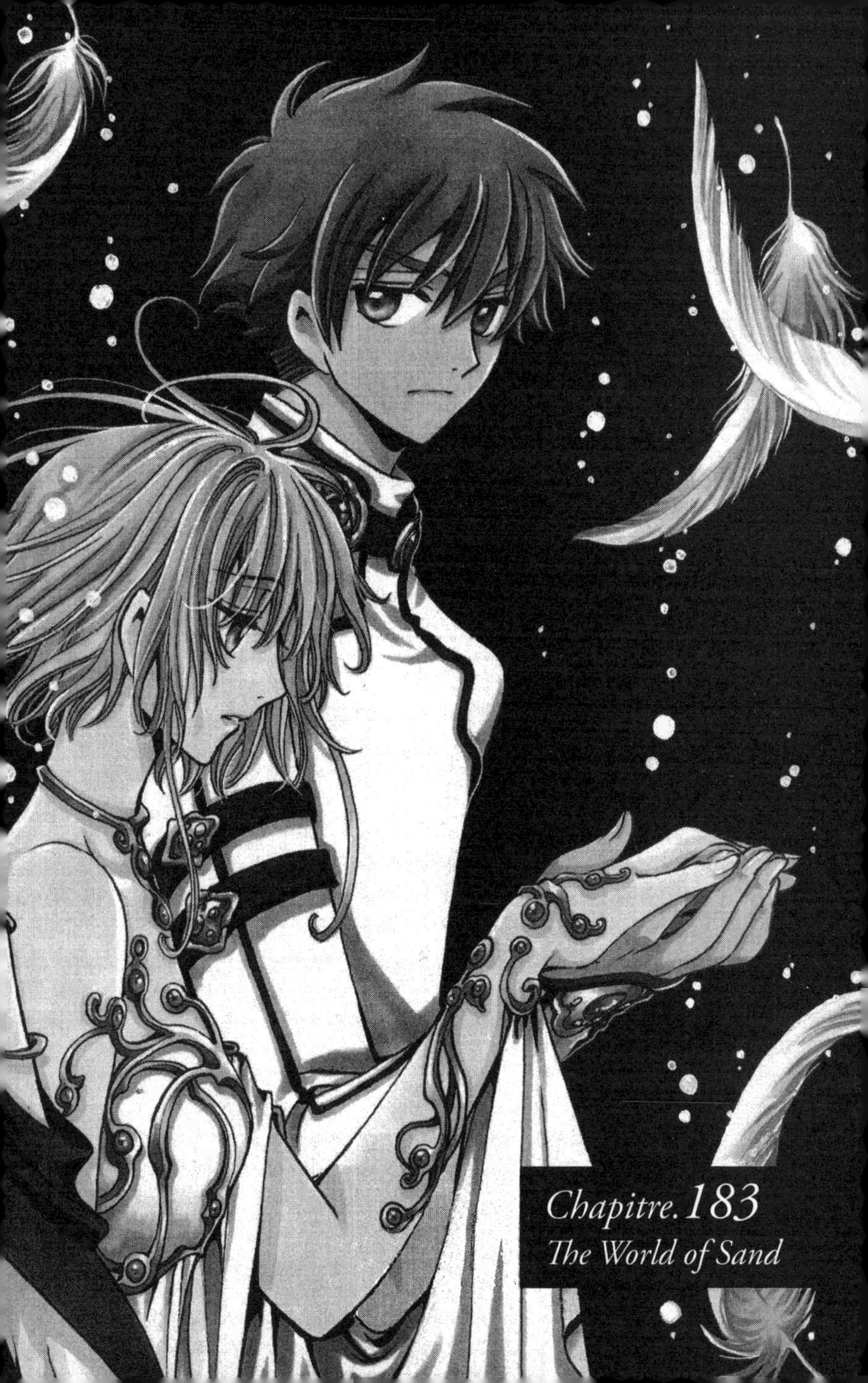
Chapitre. 183
The World of Sand

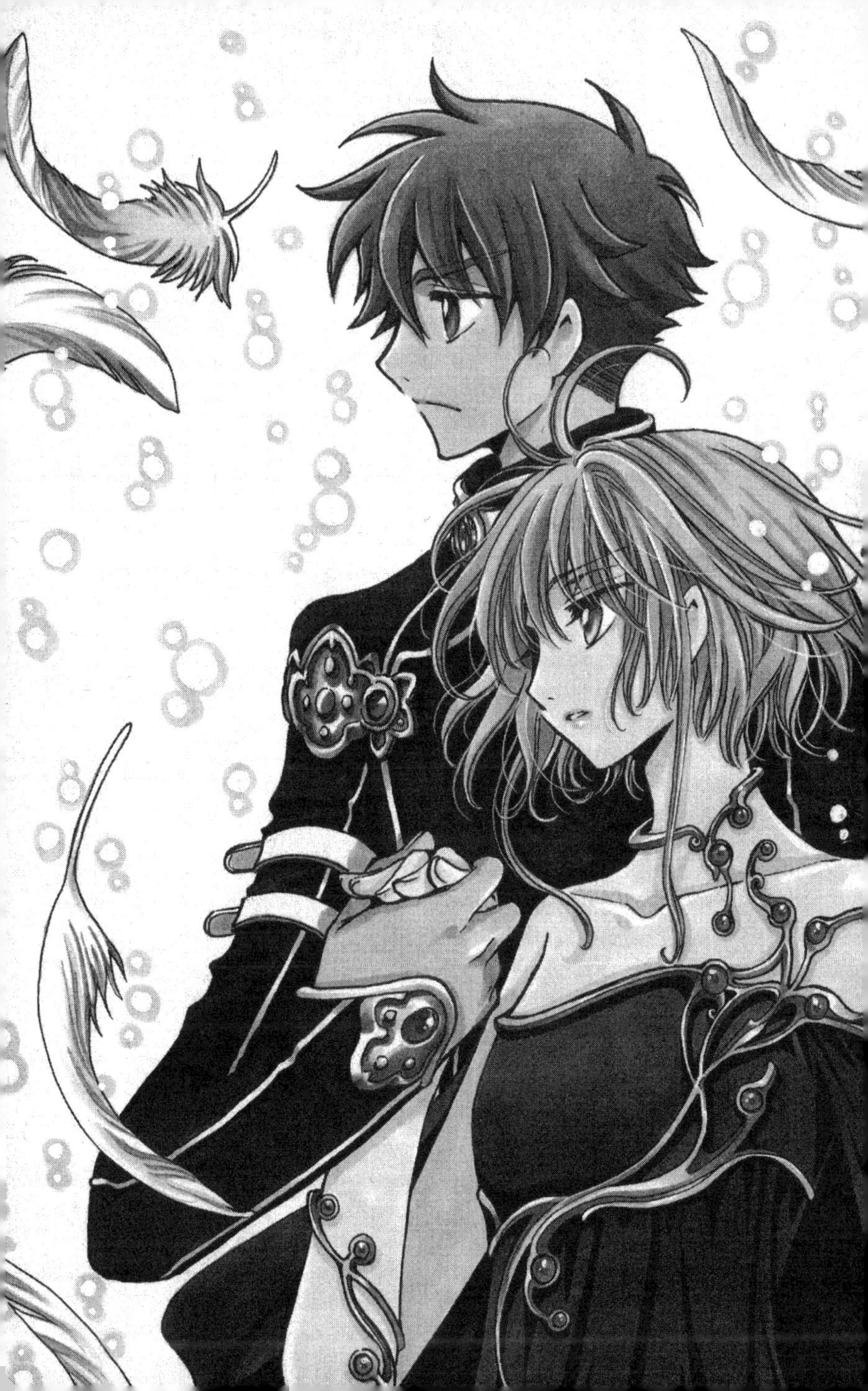

ツバサ
RESERVoir CHRoNiCLE

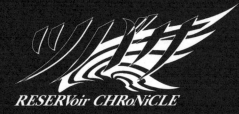

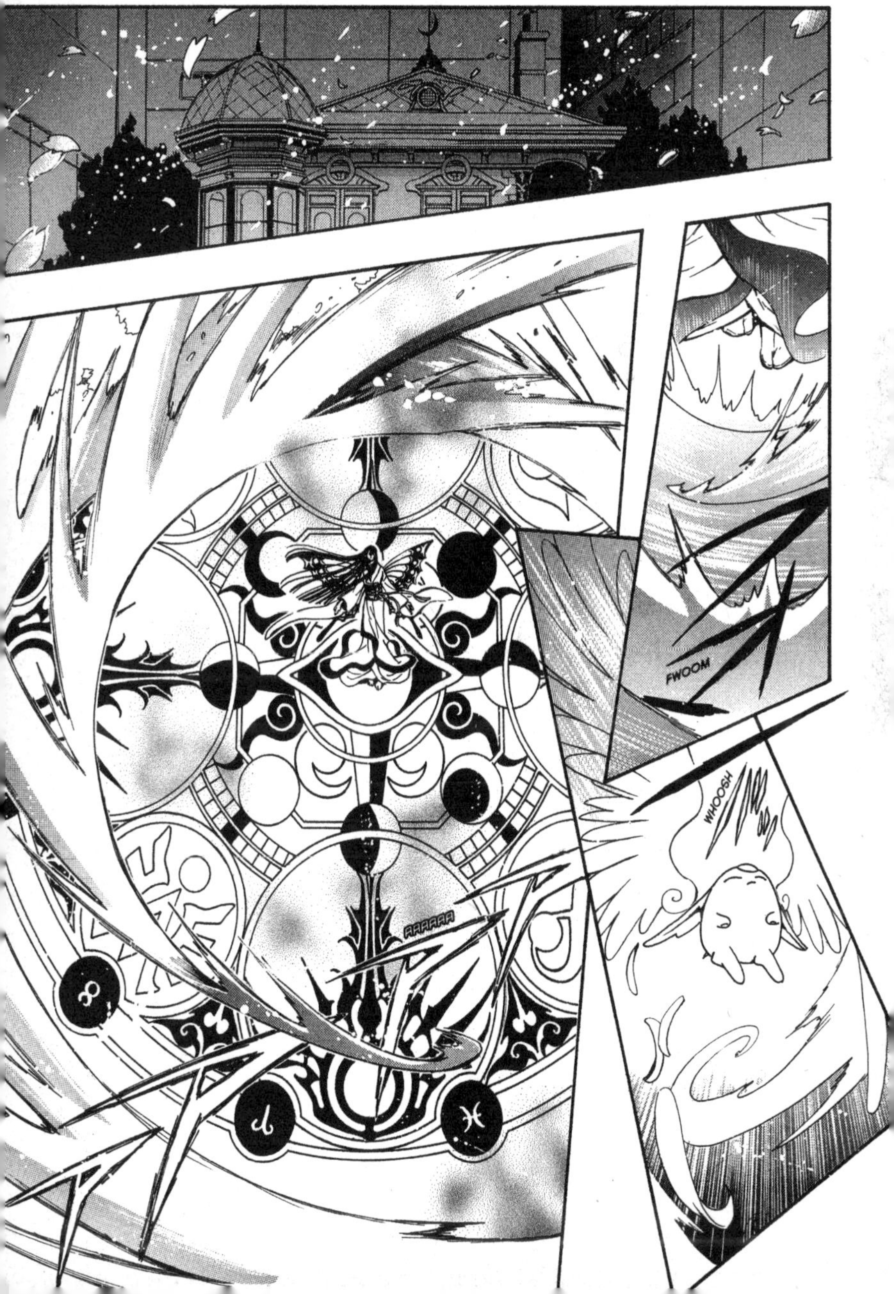
FWOOM
WHOOSH
AAAAAA

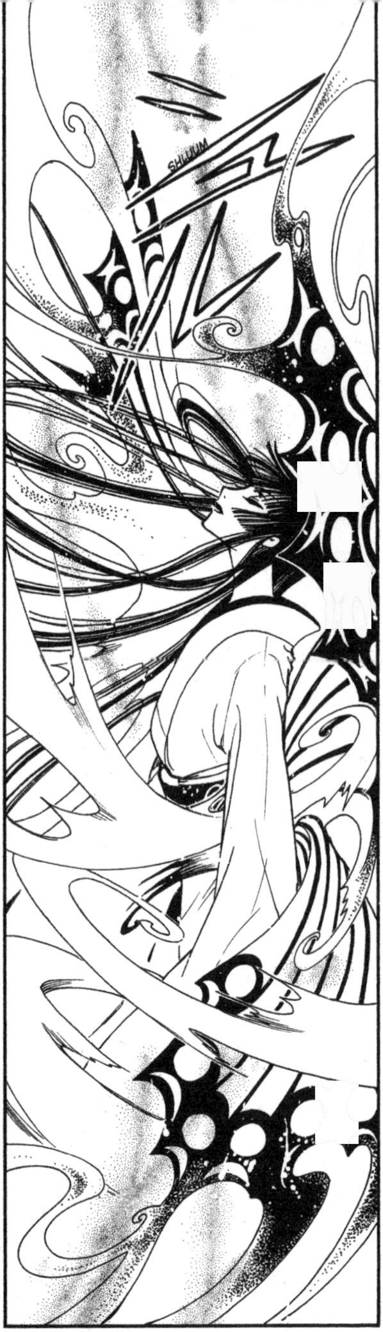
SHLUUM
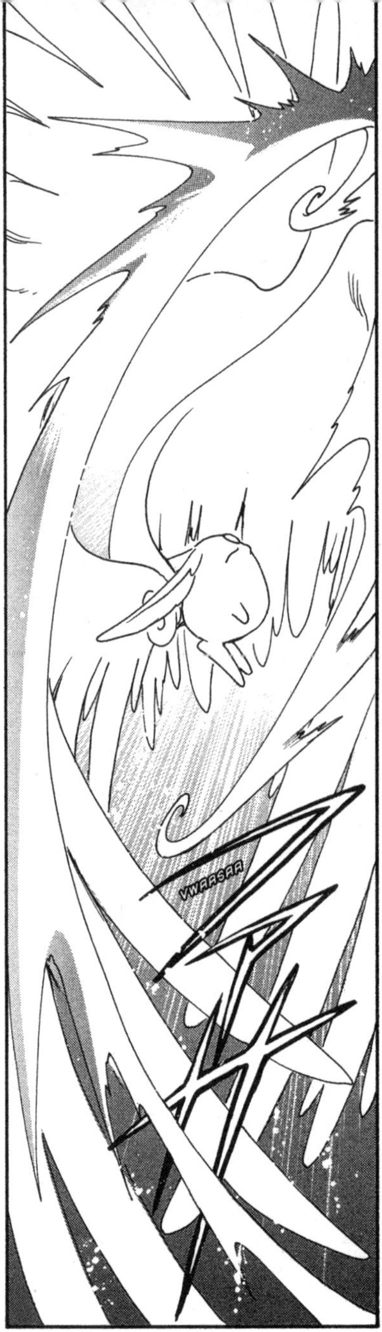
VWAASAA

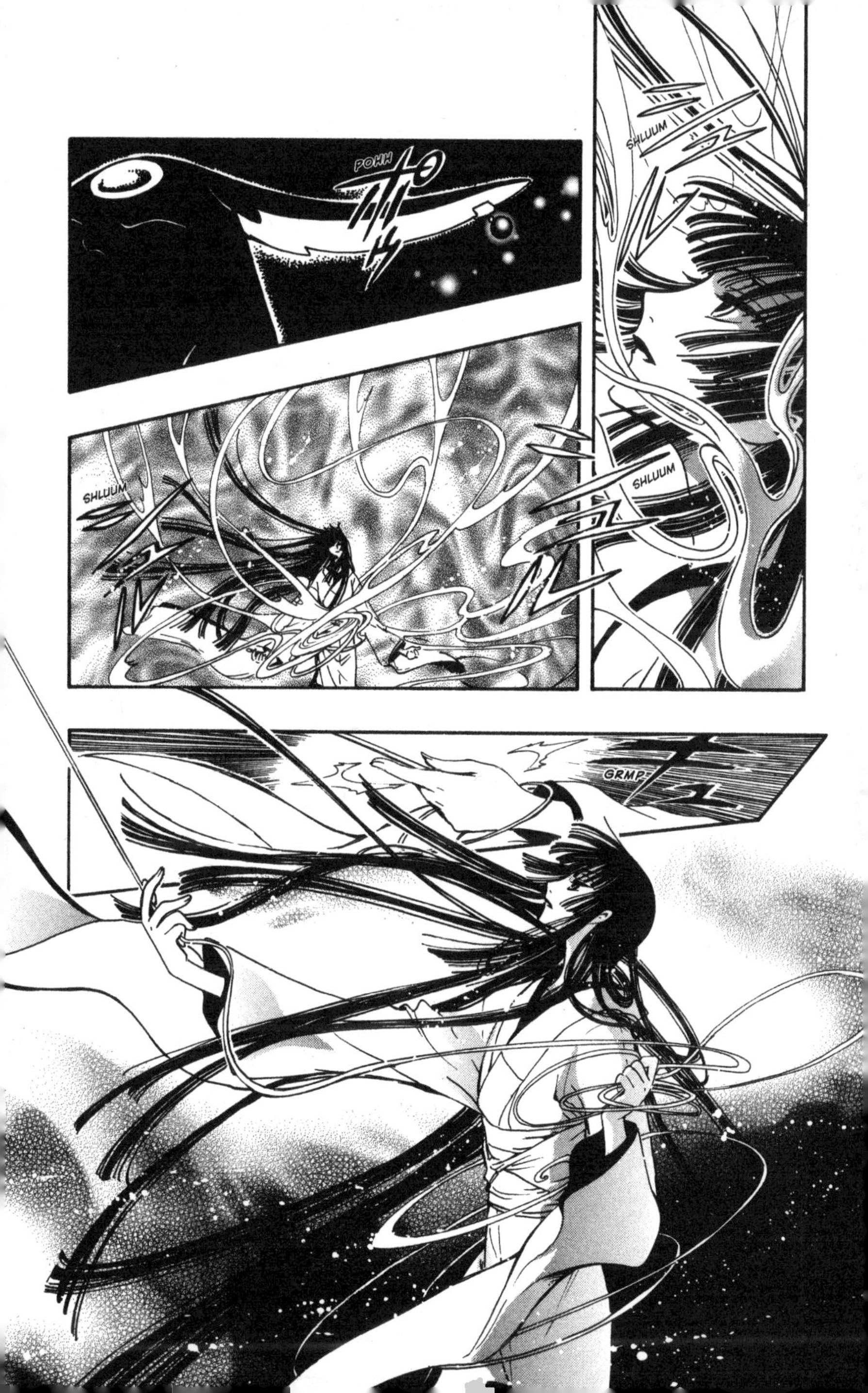
SHLUUM
POHH
SHLUUM
SHLUUM
GRMP

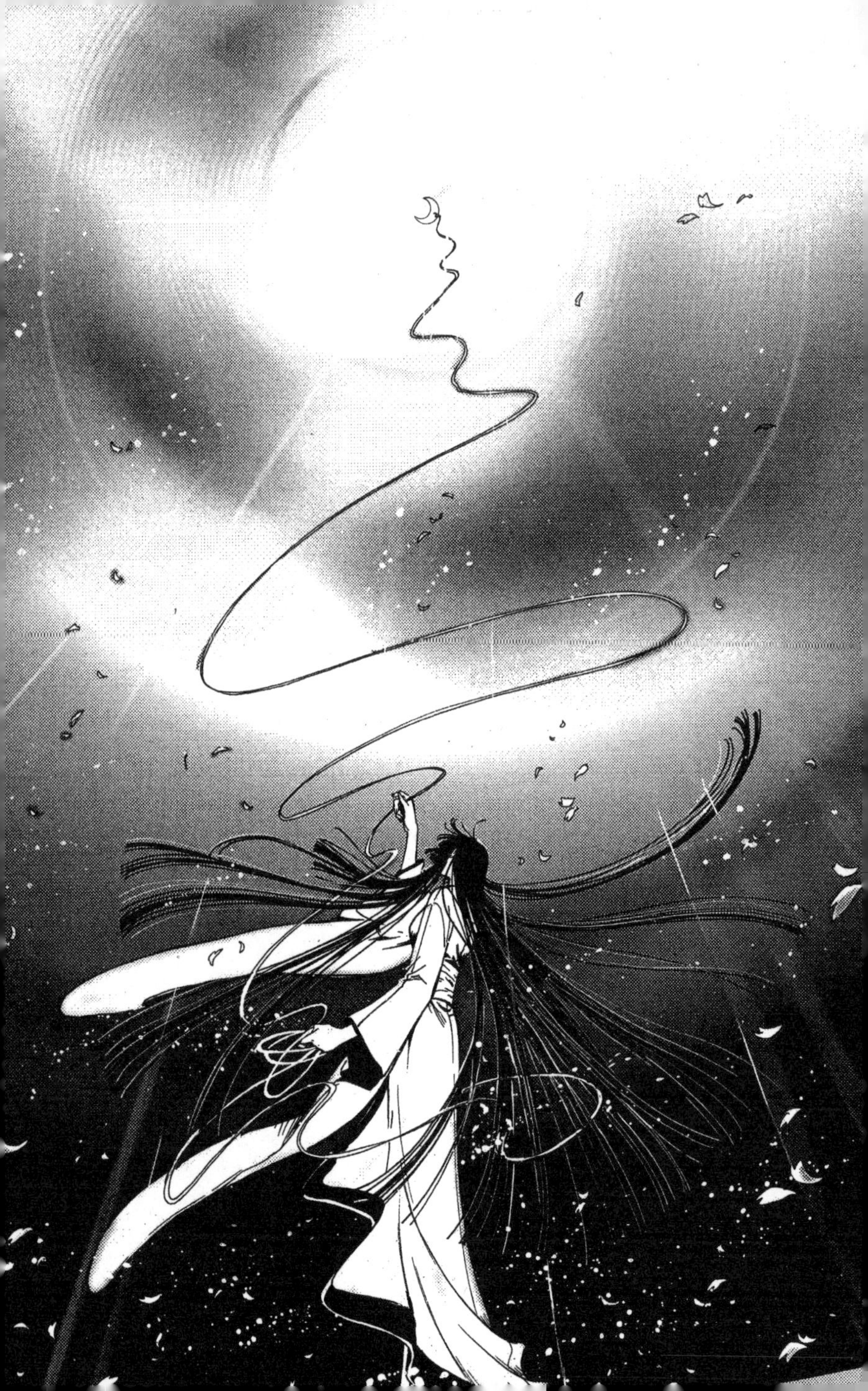

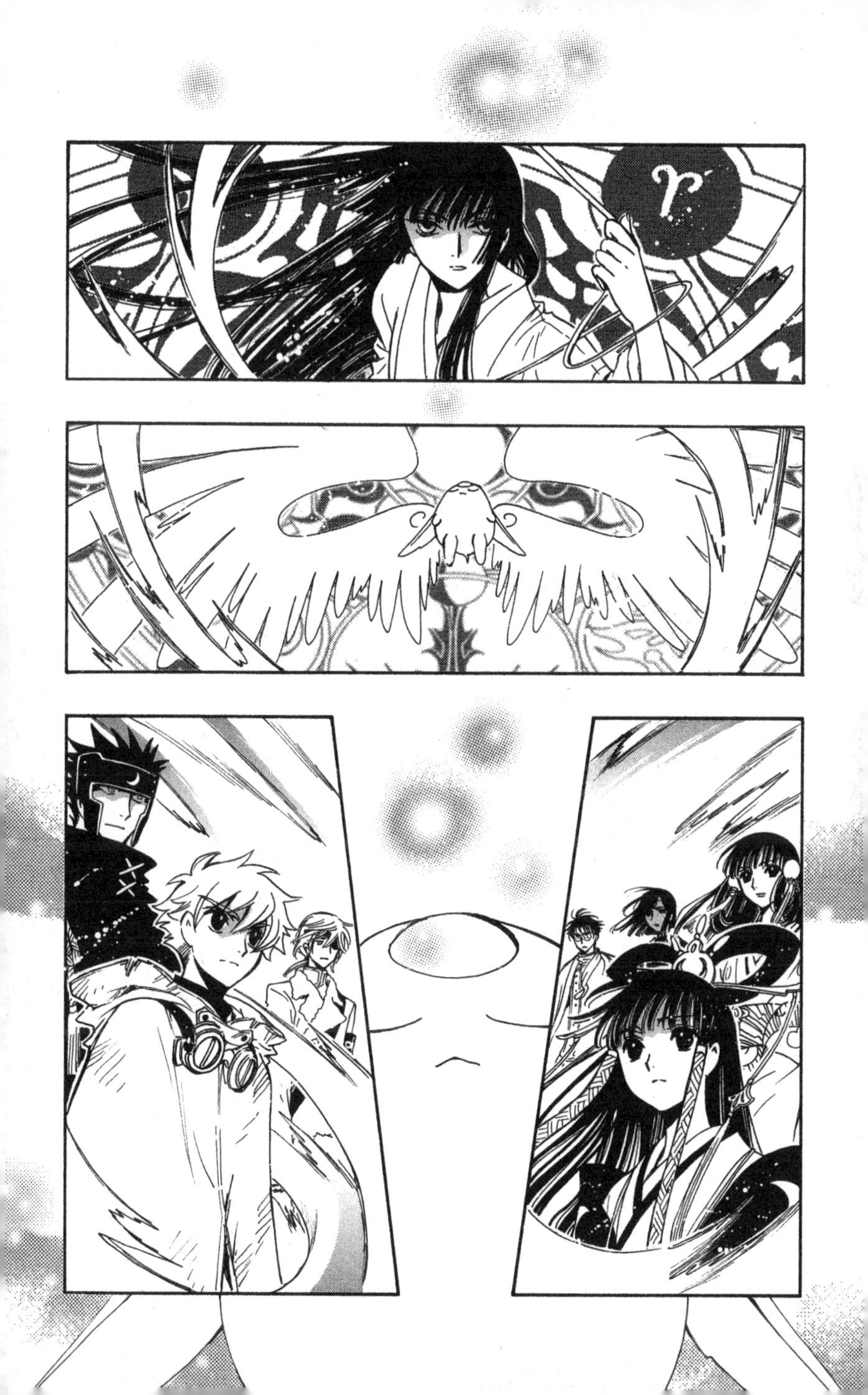

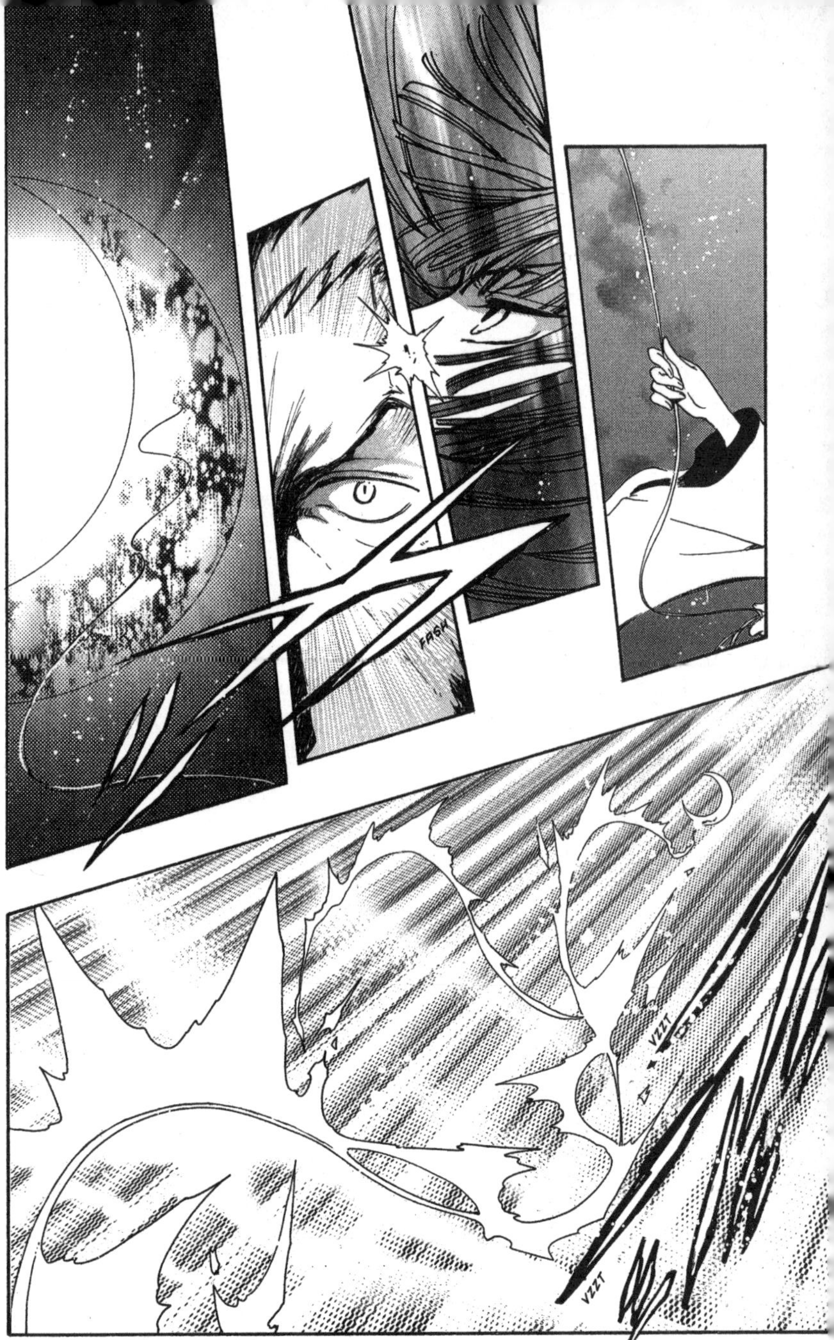
FASH
VZZT
VZZT

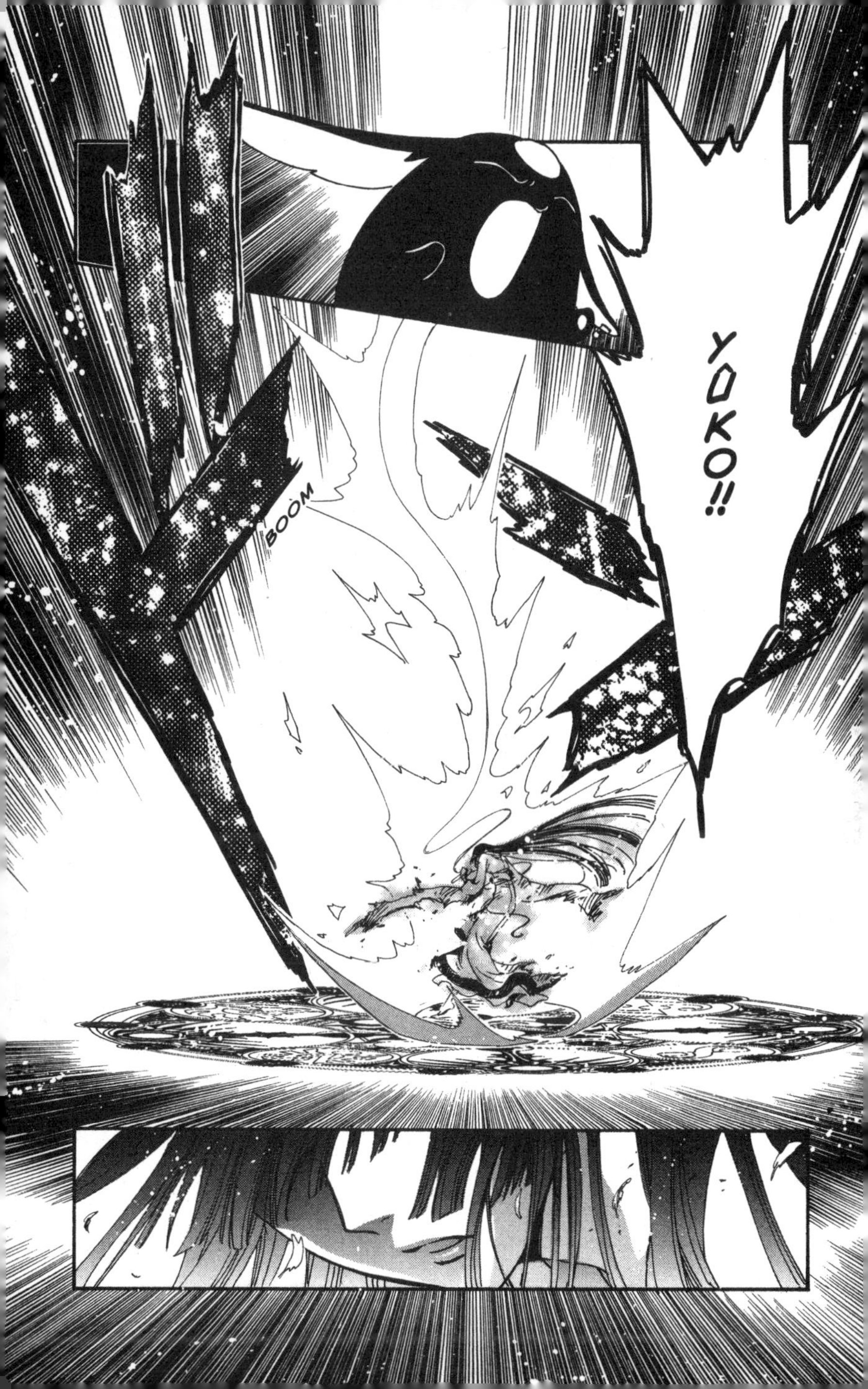
YOKO!!
BOOM

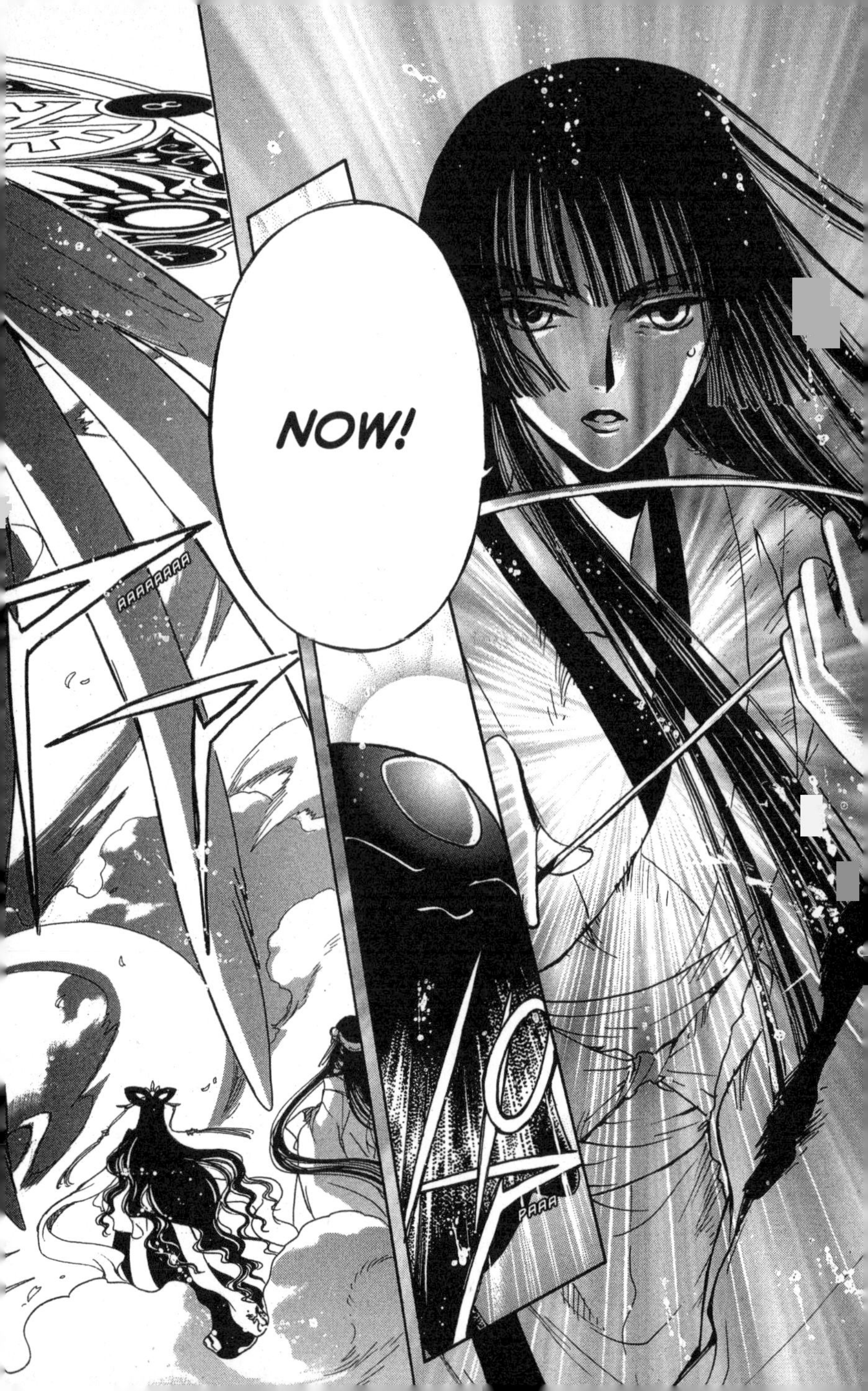
NOW!
AAAAAAAAA
PAAA

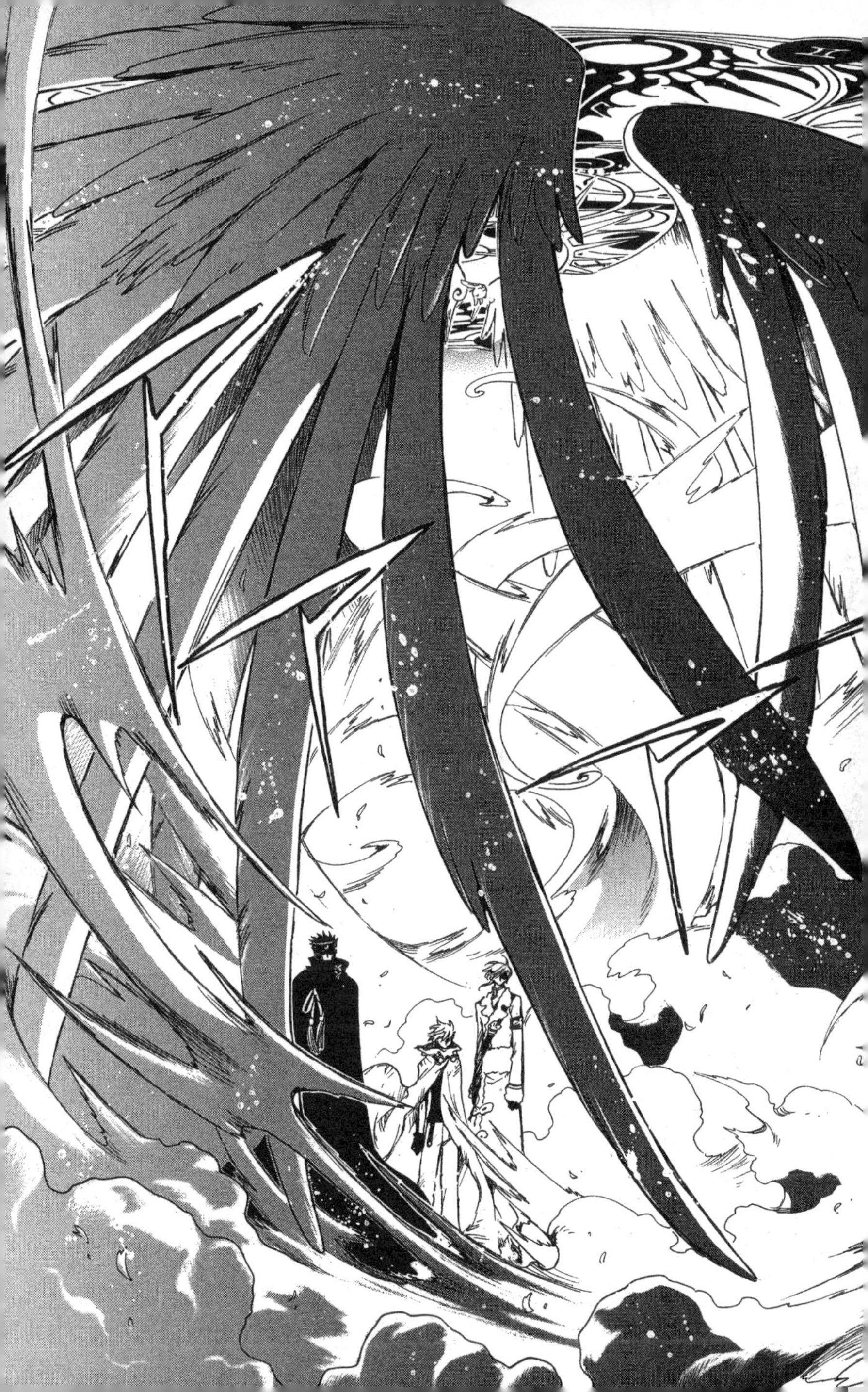

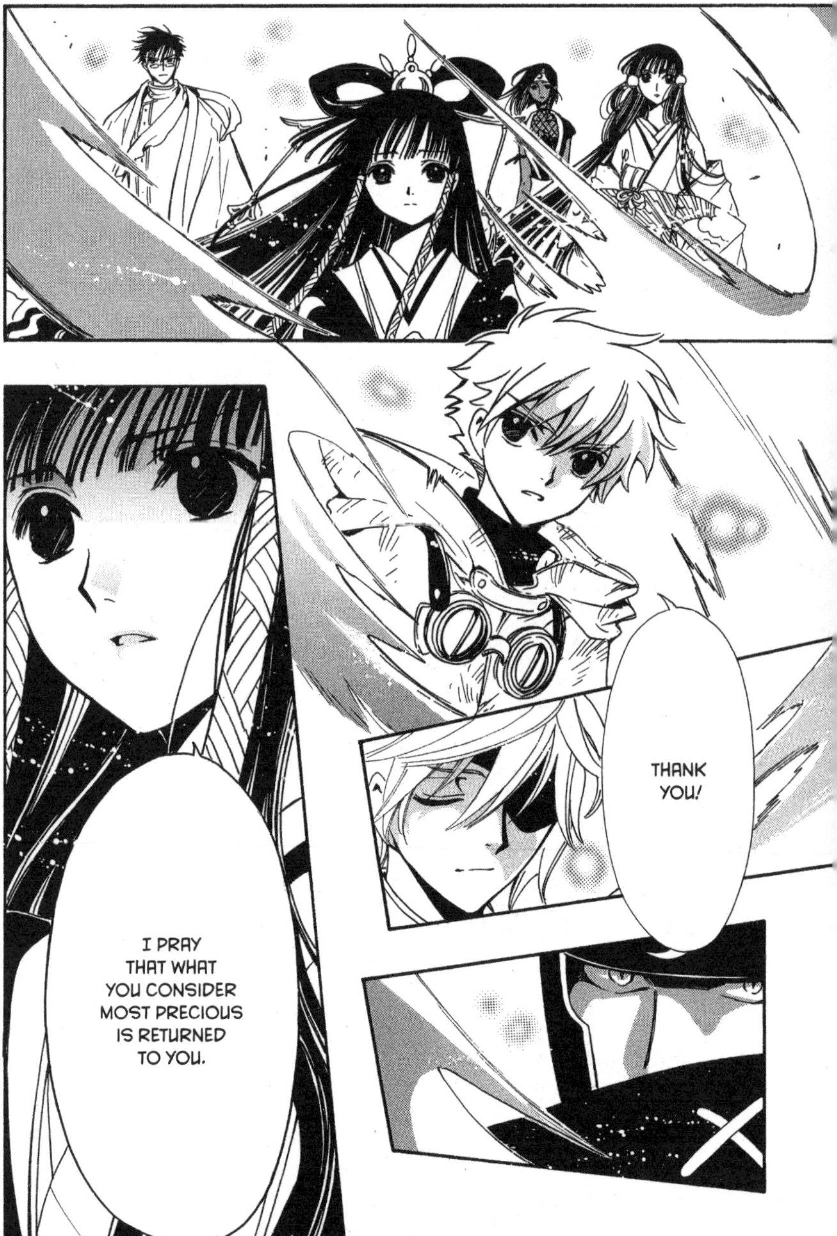
THANK YOU!
I PRAY THAT WHAT YOU CONSIDER MOST PRECIOUS IS RETURNED TO YOU.

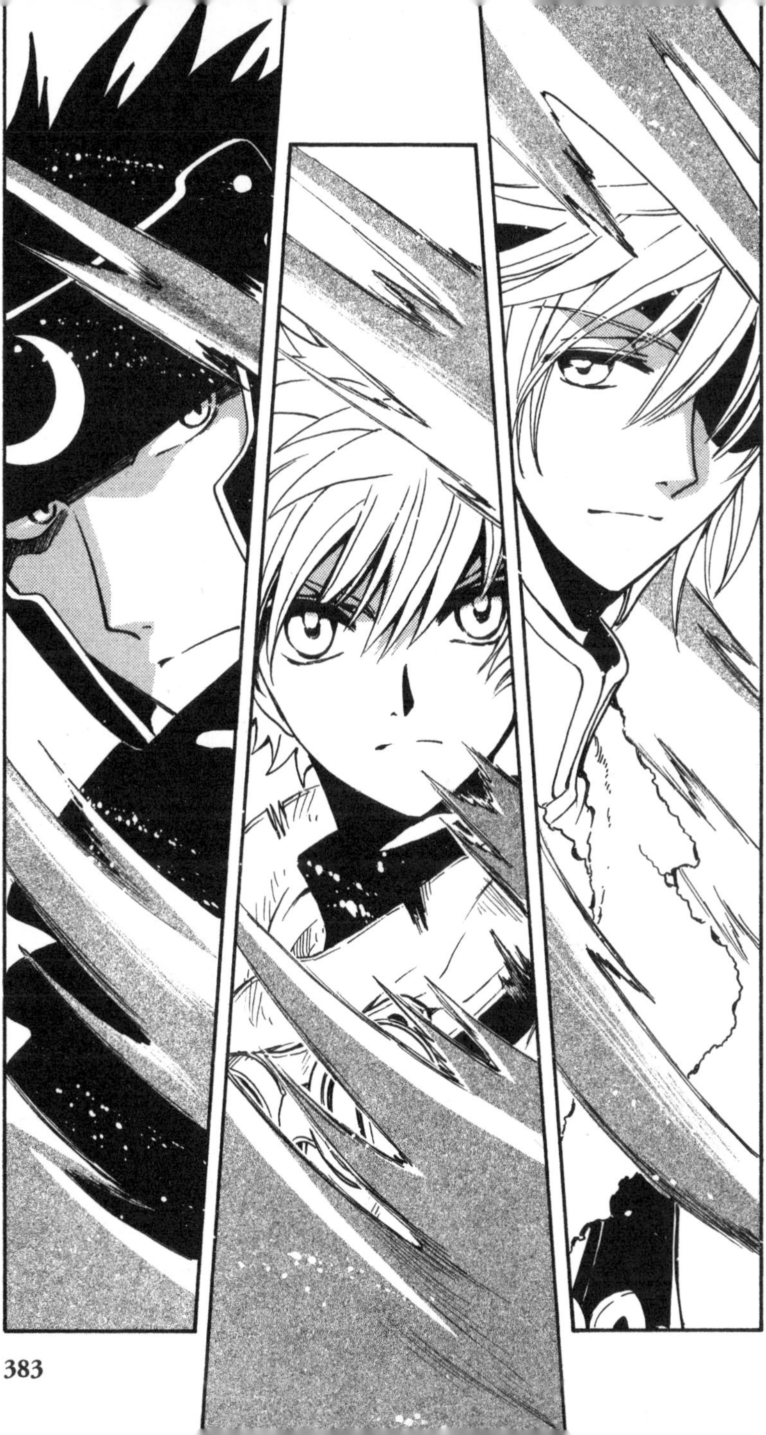

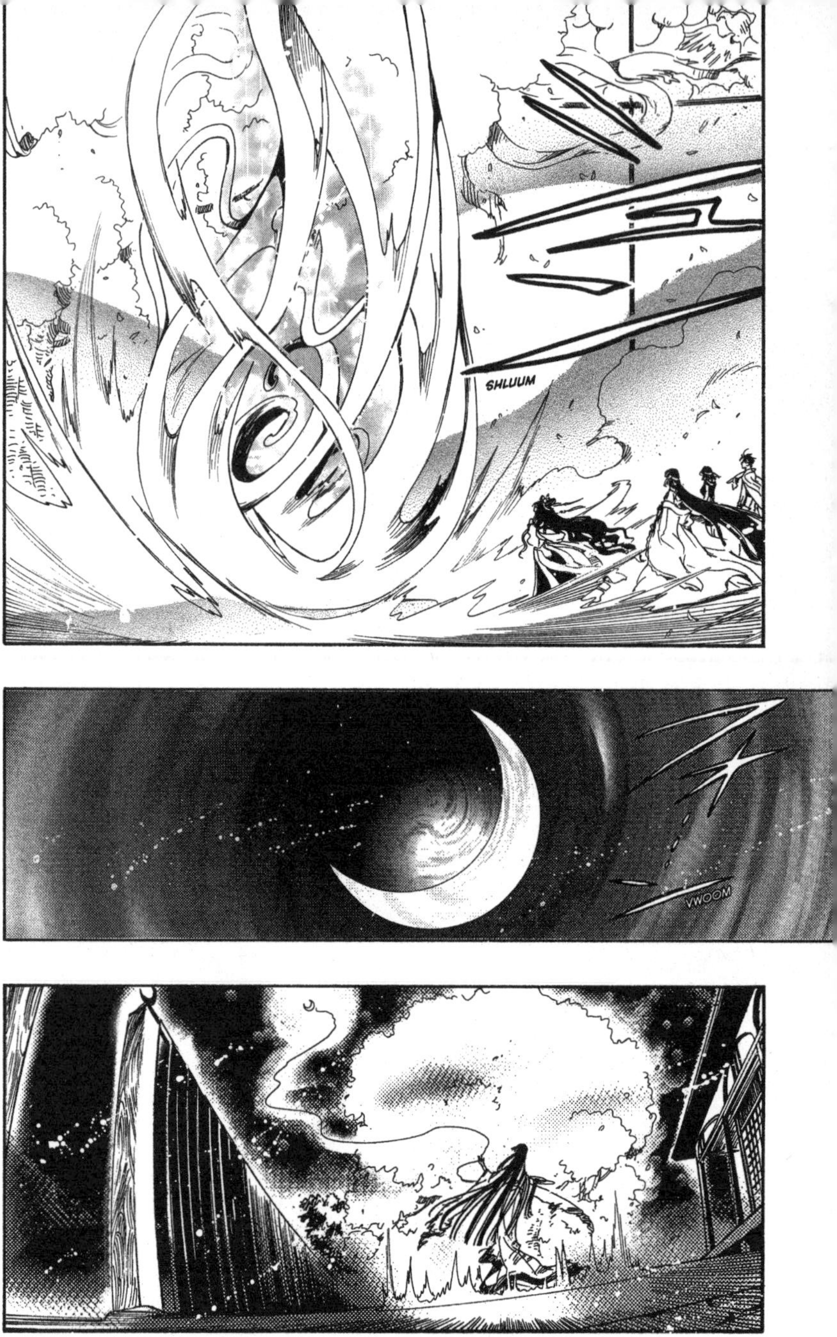
SHLUUM
VWOOM

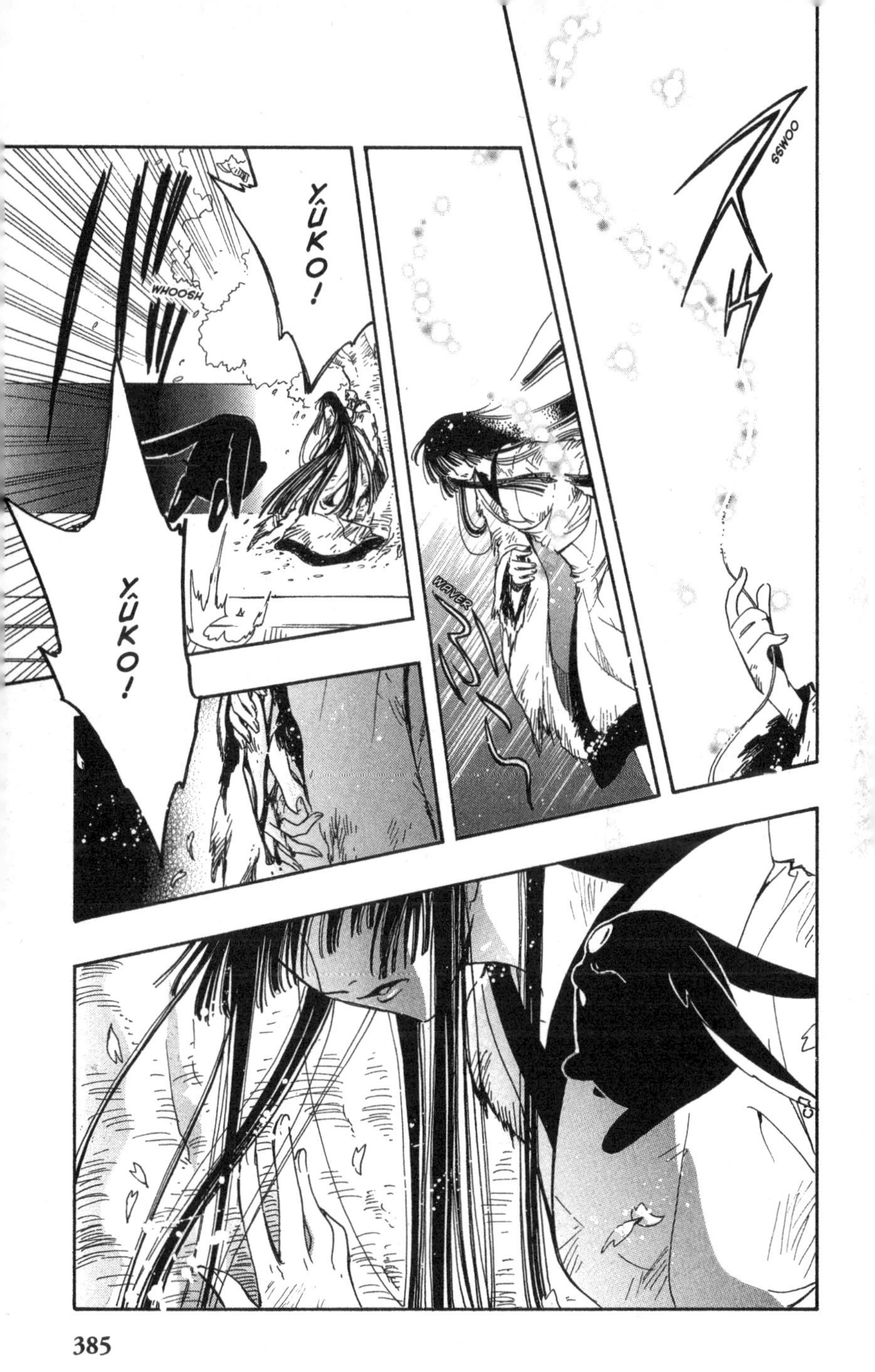
SSWOO
WAVER
YÛKO!
WHOOSH
YÛKO!

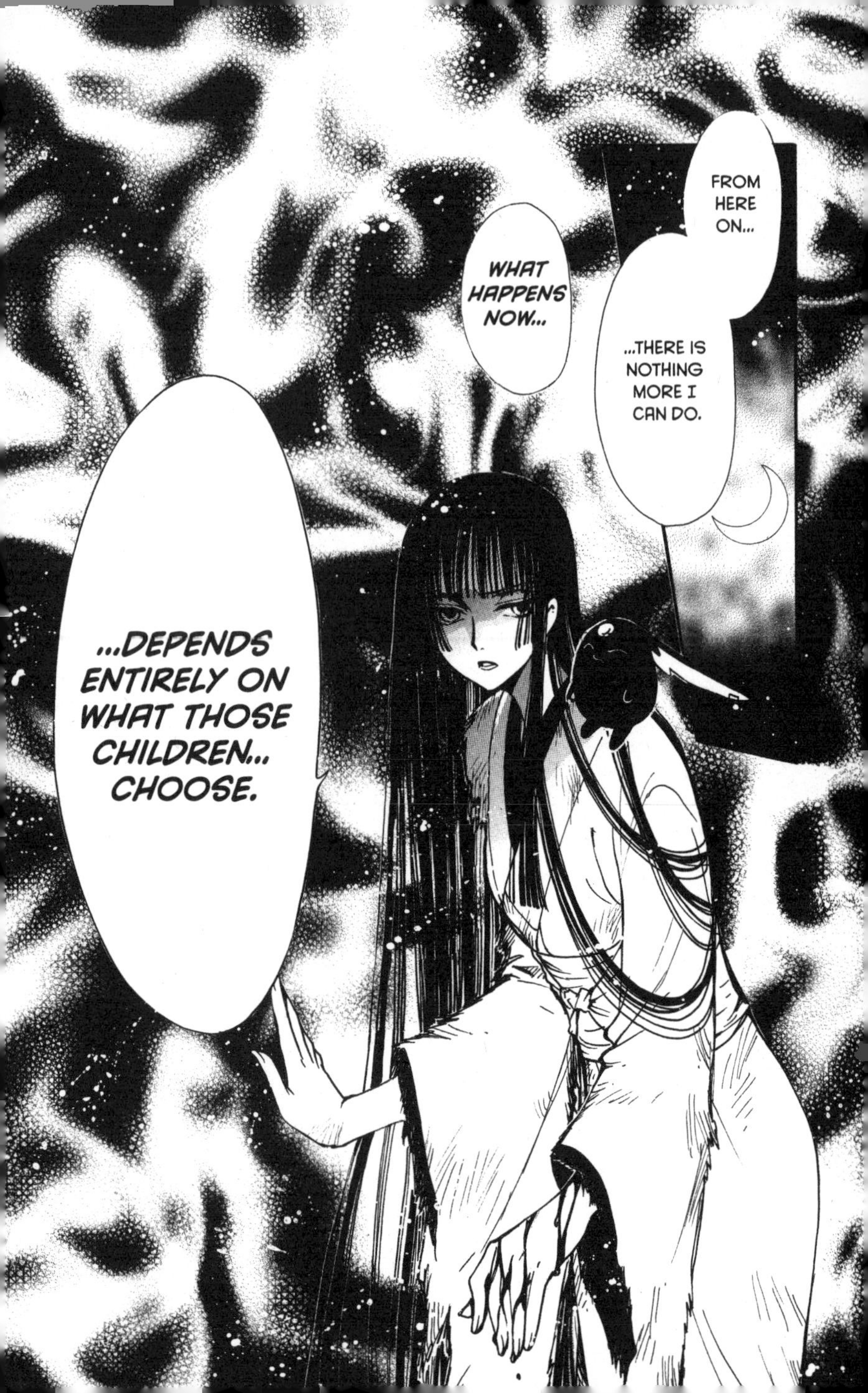
FROM HERE ON...
...THERE IS NOTHING MORE I CAN DO.
WHAT HAPPENS NOW...
...DEPENDS ENTIRELY ON WHAT THOSE CHILDREN... CHOOSE.

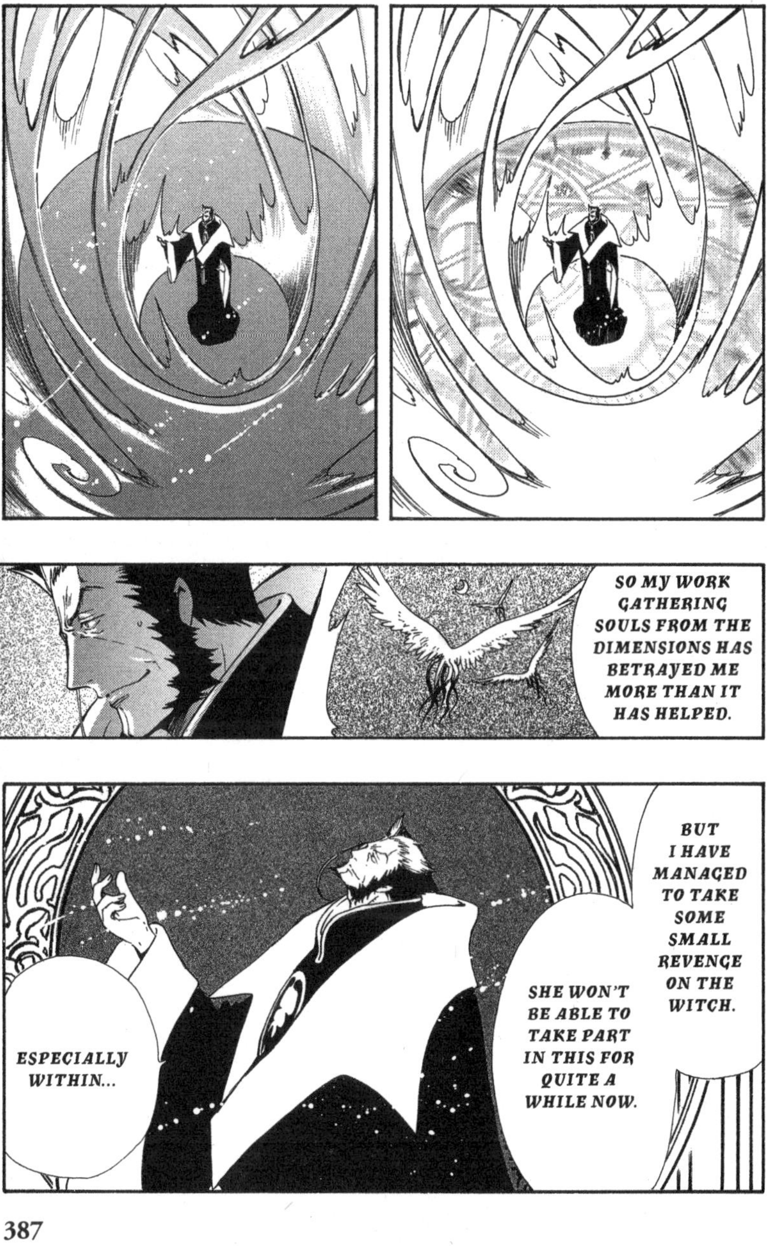
SO MY WORK GATHERING SOULS FROM THE DIMENSIONS HAS BETRAYED ME MORE THAN IT HAS HELPED.
BUT I HAVE MANAGED TO TAKE SOME SMALL REVENGE ON THE WITCH.
SHE WON'T BE ABLE TO TAKE PART IN THIS FOR QUITE A WHILE NOW.
ESPECIALLY WITHIN...

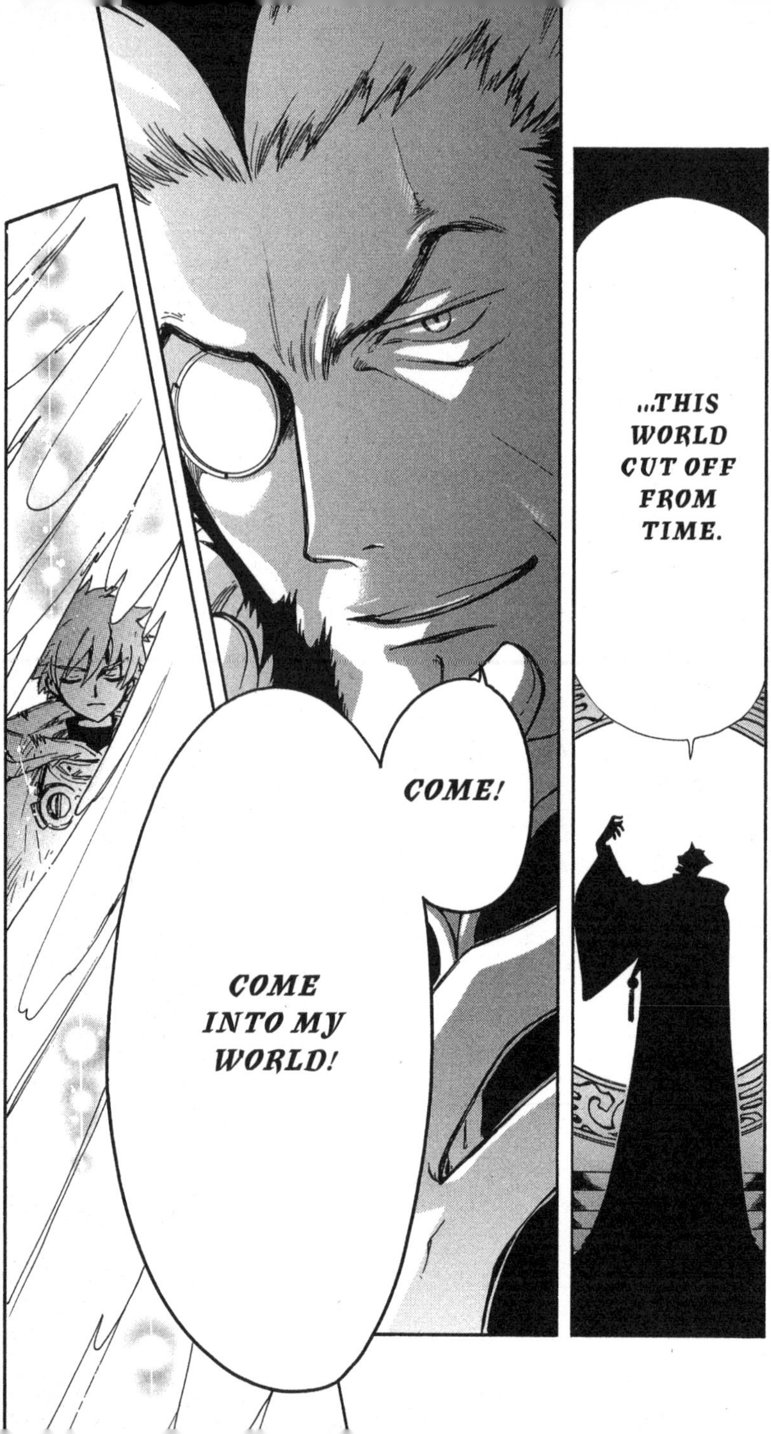
...THIS WORLD CUT OFF FROM TIME.
COME!
COME INTO MY WORLD!

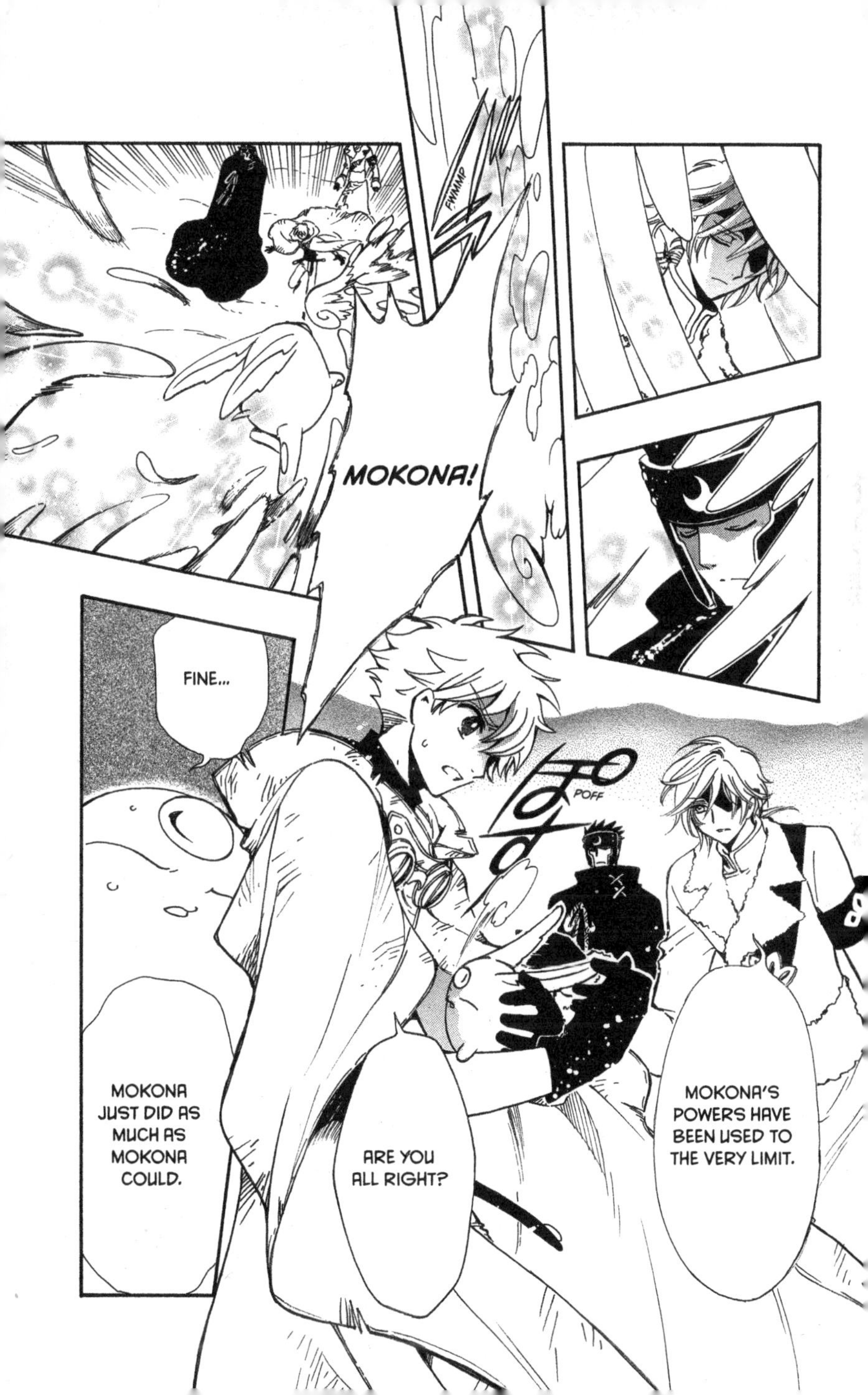
FWMMP
MOKONA!
POFF
MOKONA'S POWERS HAVE BEEN USED TO THE VERY LIMIT.
ARE YOU ALL RIGHT?
FINE...
MOKONA JUST DID AS MUCH AS MOKONA COULD.

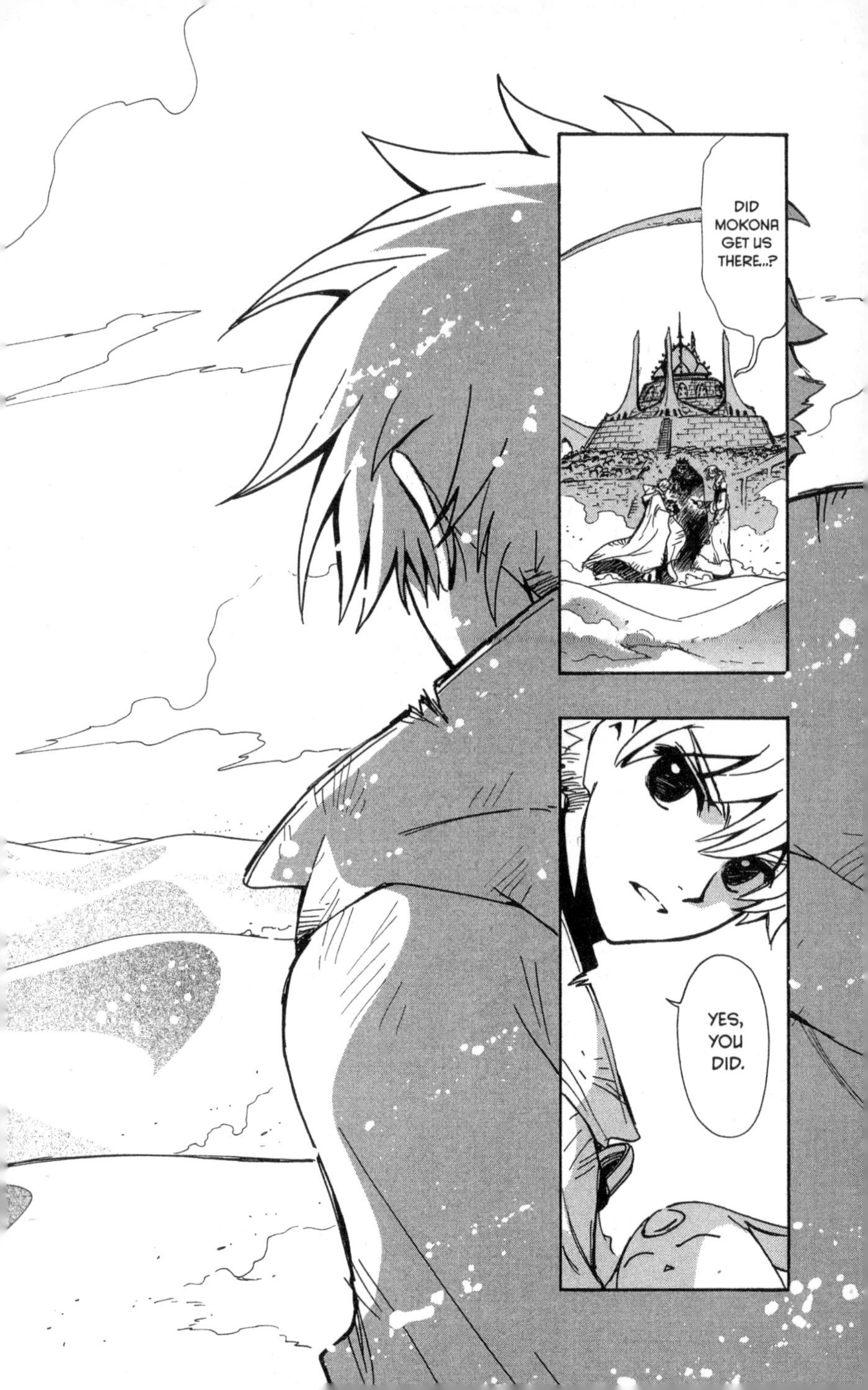
DID MOKONA GET US THERE...?
YES, YOU DID.

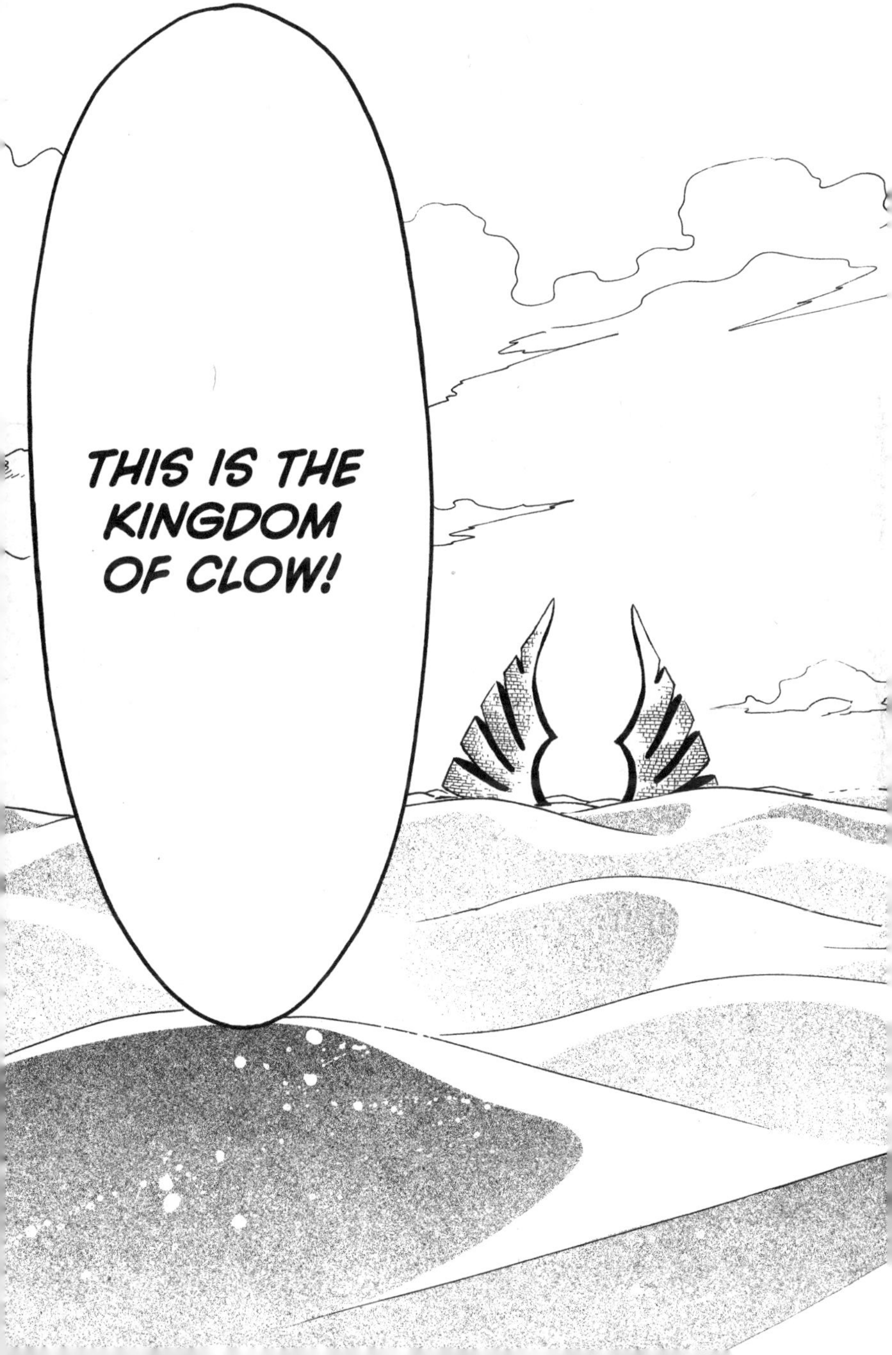
THIS IS THE KINGDOM OF CLOW!

ツバサ

RESERVoir CHRoNiCLE

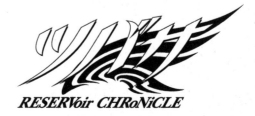

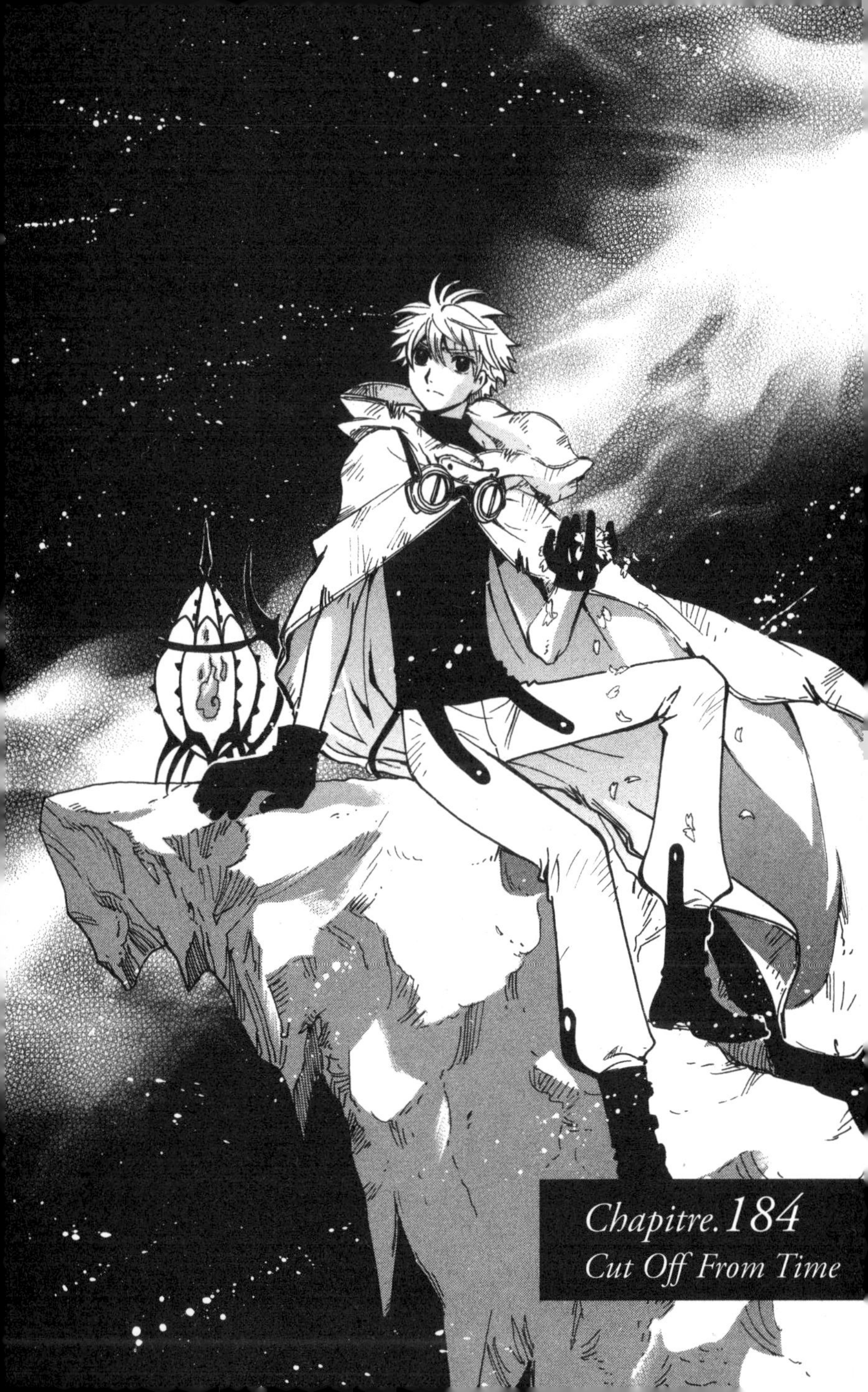
Chapitre. 184
Cut Off From Time

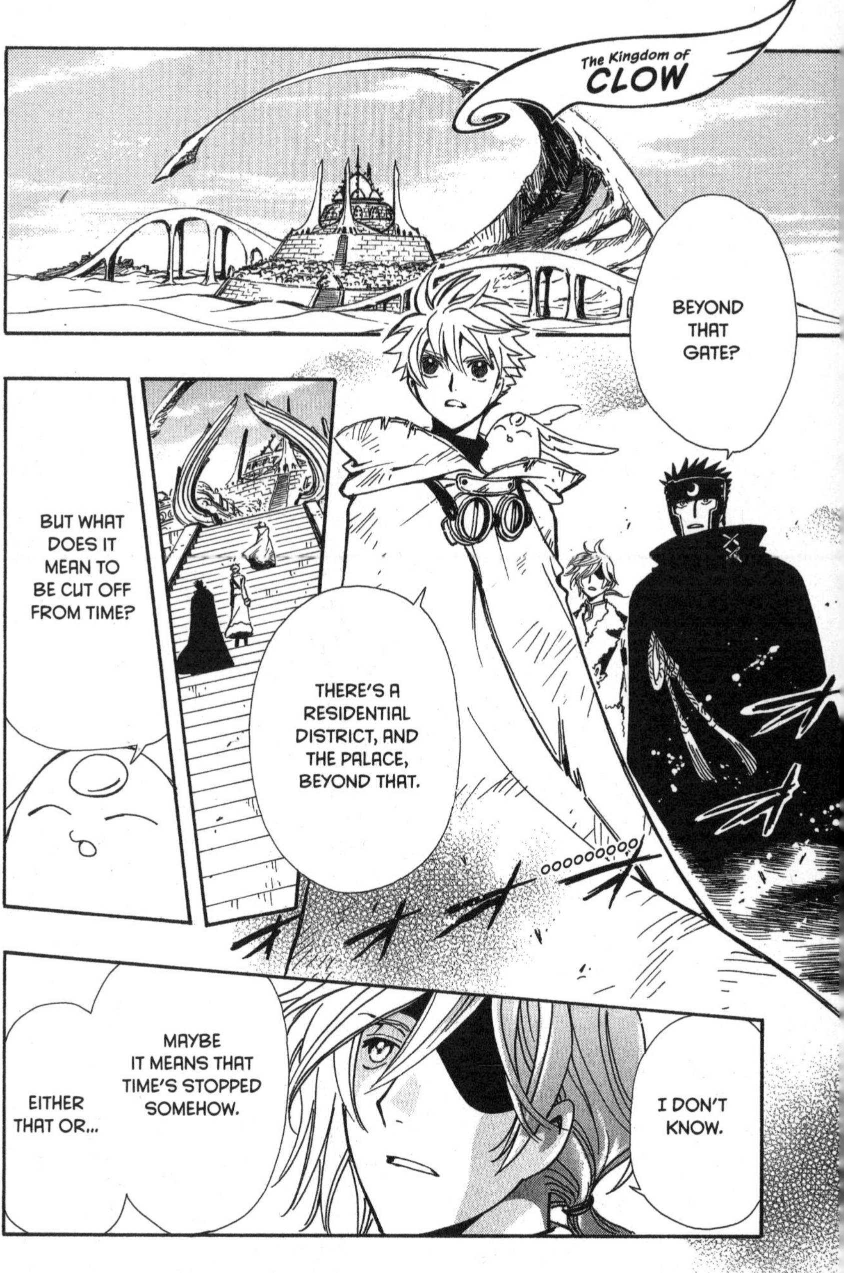
The Kingdom of CLOW
BEYOND THAT GATE?
THERE'S A RESIDENTIAL DISTRICT, AND THE PALACE, BEYOND THAT.
BUT WHAT DOES IT MEAN TO BE CUT OFF FROM TIME?
I DON'T KNOW.
MAYBE IT MEANS THAT TIME'S STOPPED SOMEHOW.
EITHER THAT OR...

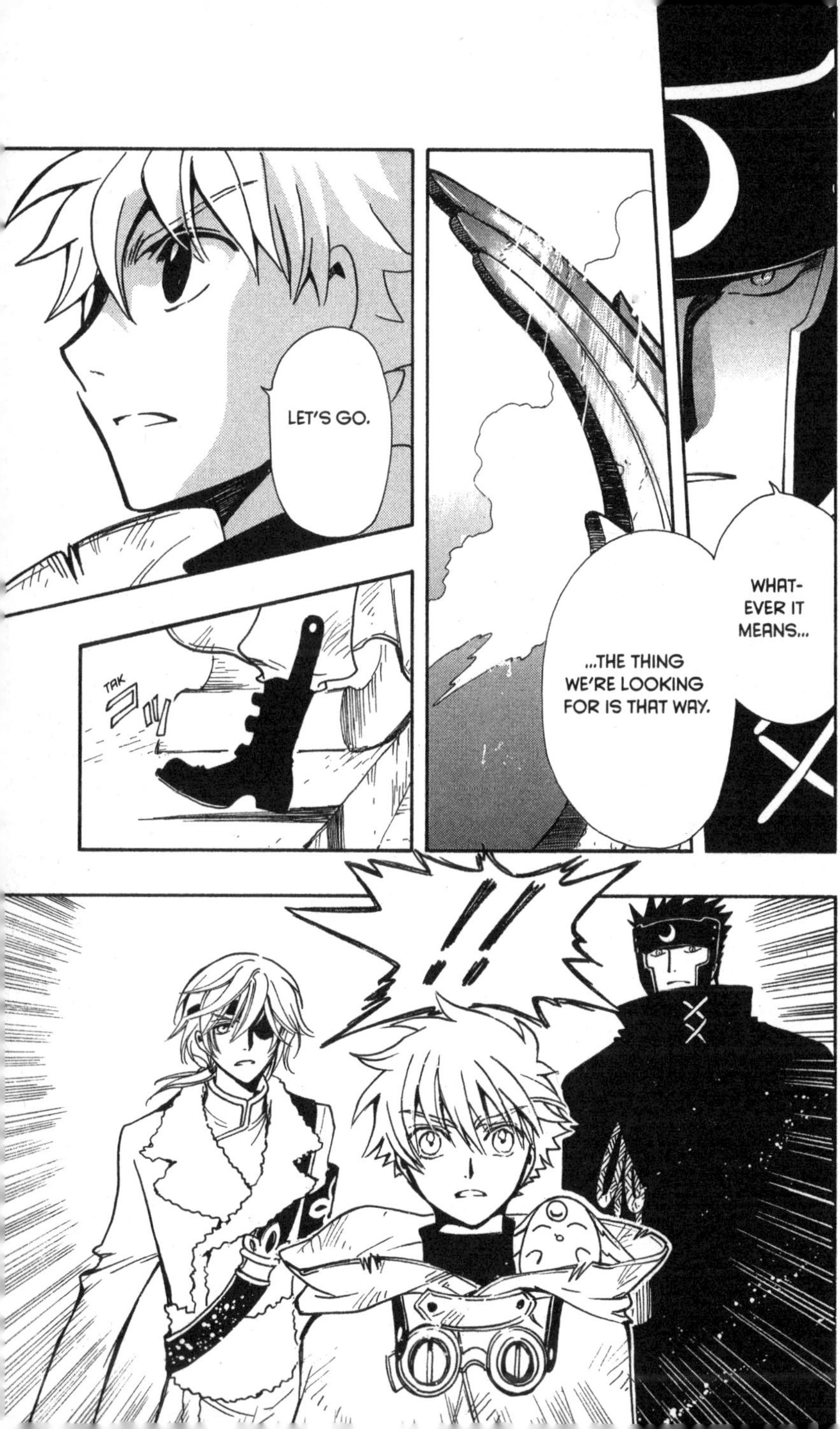
WHAT-EVER IT MEANS...
...THE THING WE'RE LOOKING FOR IS THAT WAY.
LET'S GO.
TAK
!!

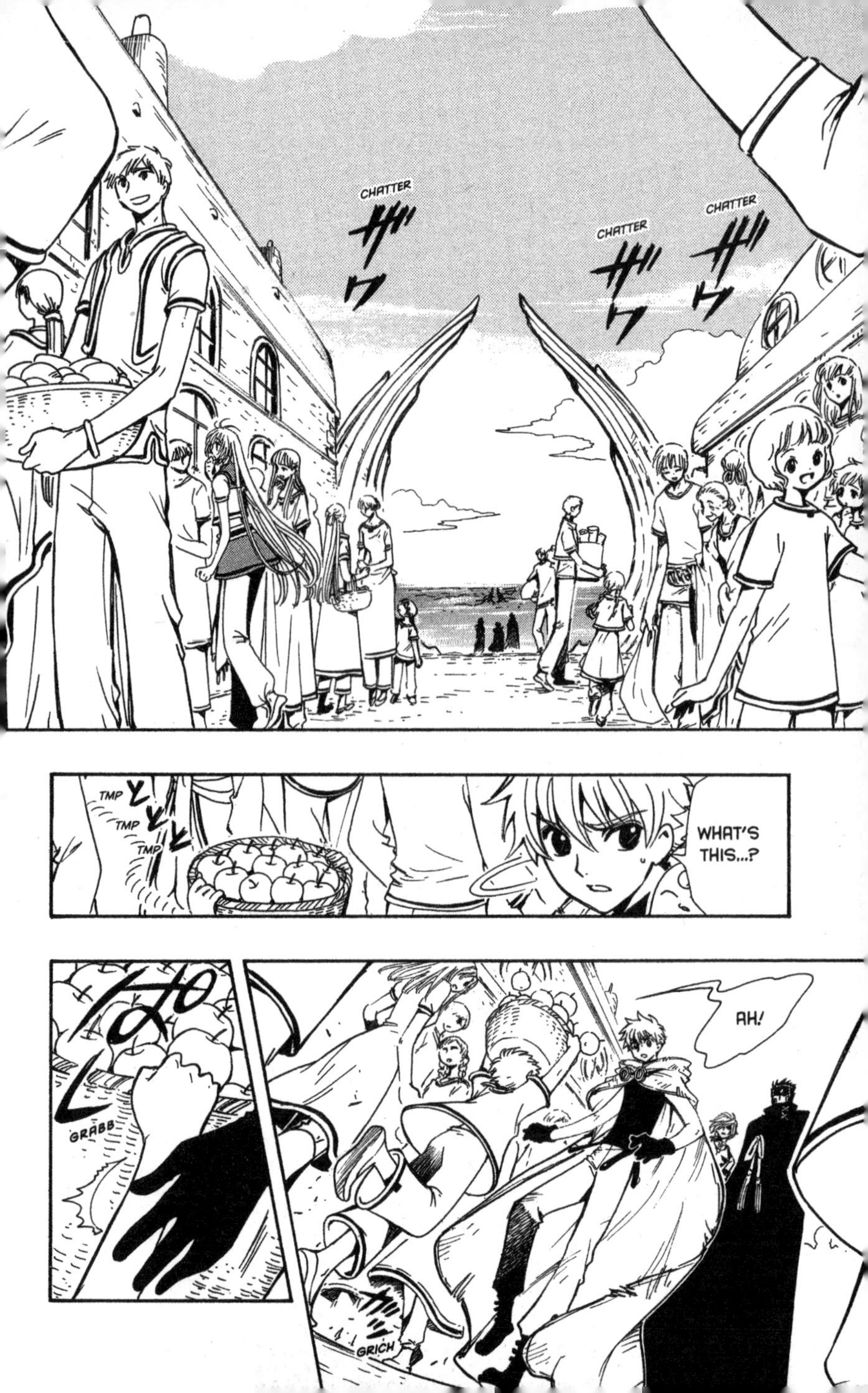
CHATTER
ザワ
CHATTER
ザワ
CHATTER
ザワ
WHAT'S THIS...?
TMP
TMP
TMP
AH!
GRICH
GRABB

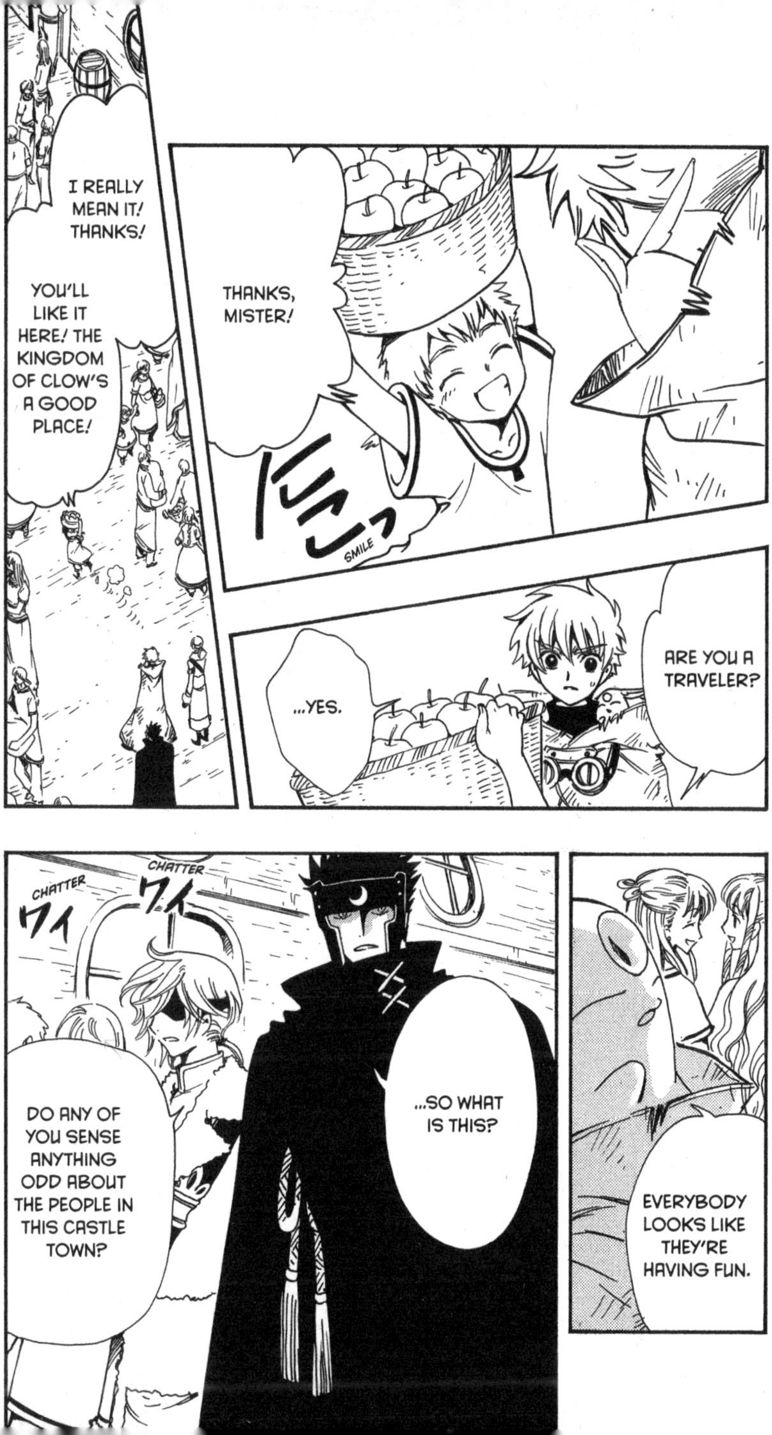
THANKS, MISTER!
SMILE
ARE YOU A TRAVELER?
...YES.
I REALLY MEAN IT! THANKS!
YOU'LL LIKE IT HERE! THE KINGDOM OF CLOW'S A GOOD PLACE!
EVERYBODY LOOKS LIKE THEY'RE HAVING FUN.
CHATTER
CHATTER
...SO WHAT IS THIS?
DO ANY OF YOU SENSE ANYTHING ODD ABOUT THE PEOPLE IN THIS CASTLE TOWN?

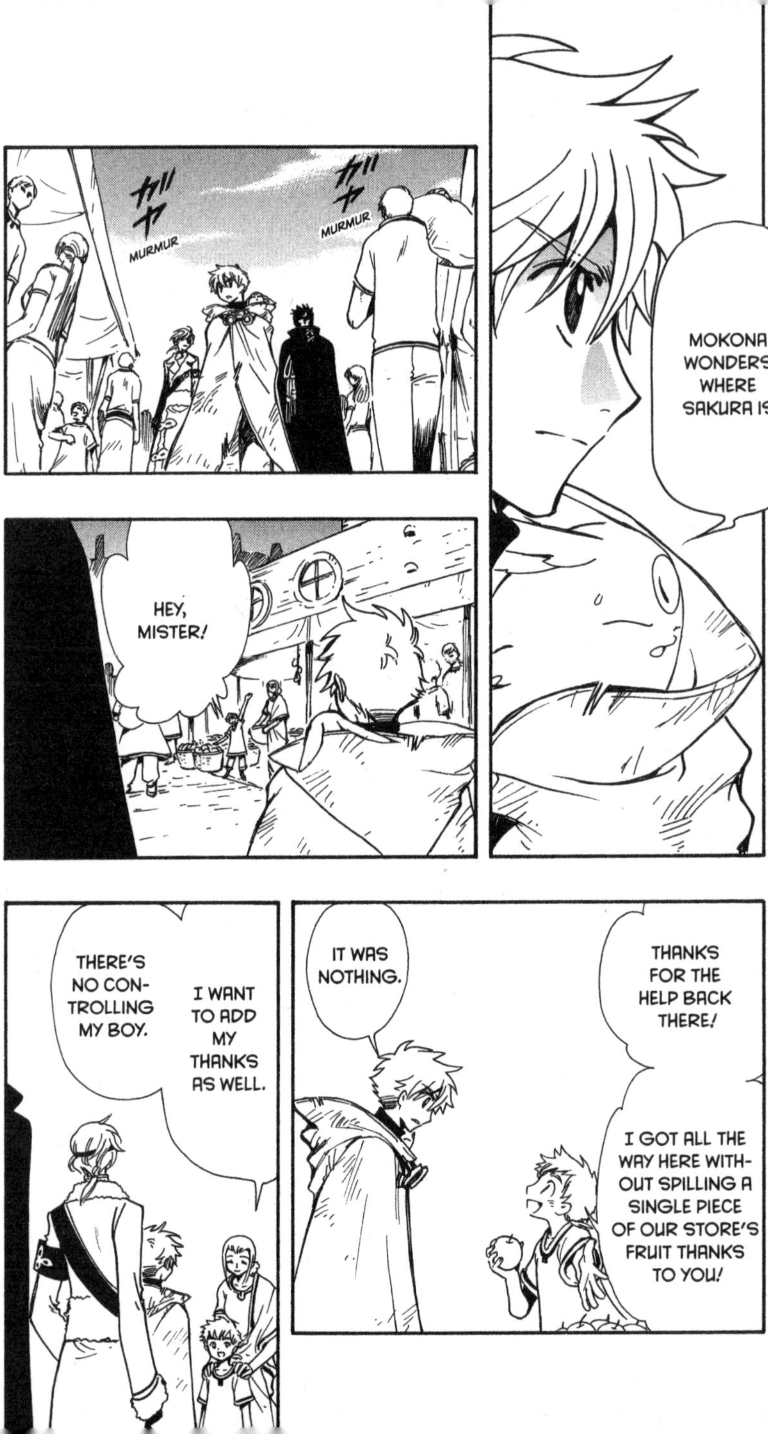
MOKONA WONDERS WHERE SAKURA IS.
ガヤ
MURMUR
ガヤ
MURMUR
HEY, MISTER!
THANKS FOR THE HELP BACK THERE!
I GOT ALL THE WAY HERE WITH-OUT SPILLING A SINGLE PIECE OF OUR STORE'S FRUIT THANKS TO YOU!
IT WAS NOTHING.
I WANT TO ADD MY THANKS AS WELL.
THERE'S NO CON-TROLLING MY BOY.

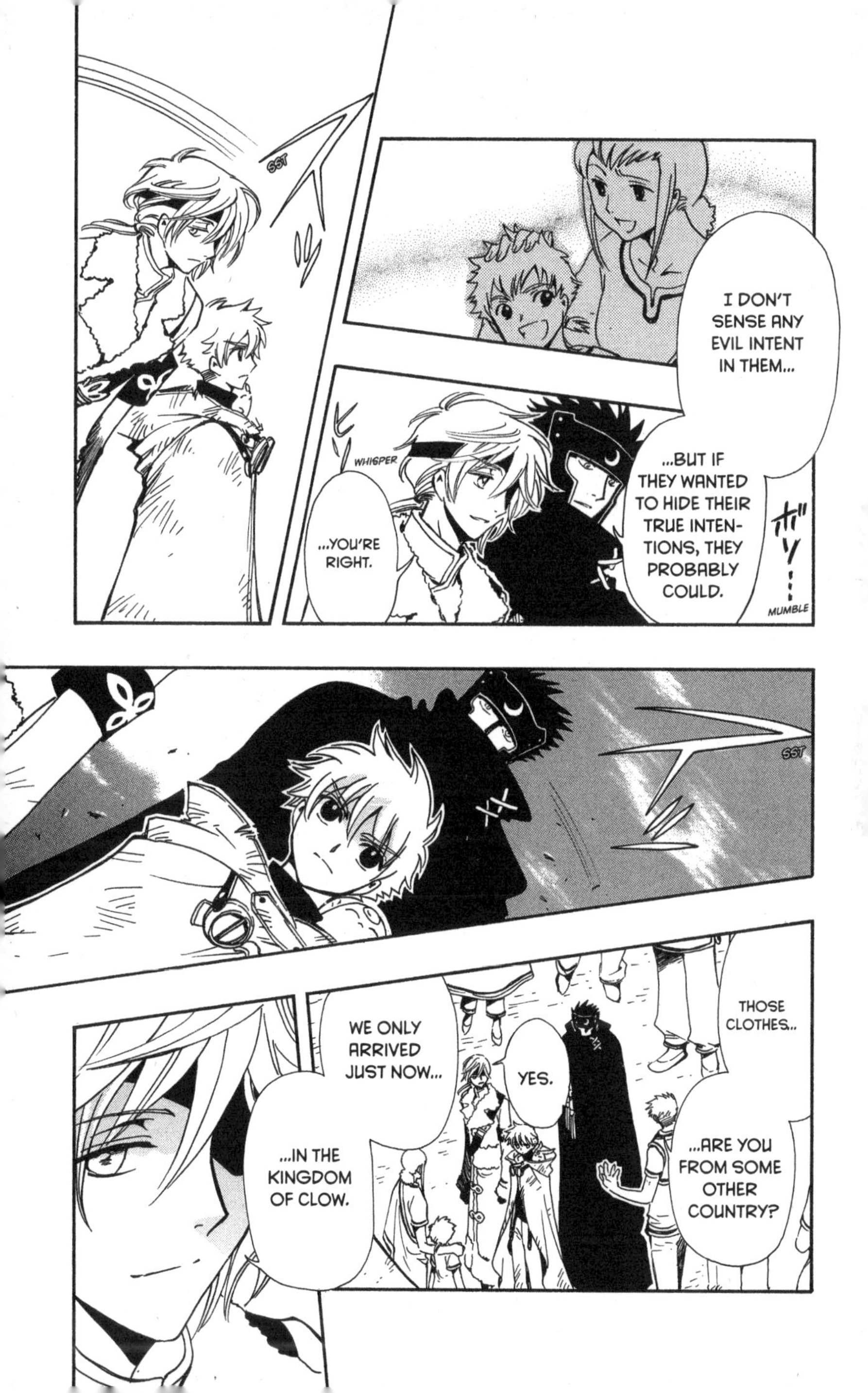
I DON'T SENSE ANY EVIL INTENT IN THEM...
...BUT IF THEY WANTED TO HIDE THEIR TRUE INTEN-TIONS, THEY PROBABLY COULD.
MUMBLE
WHISPER
...YOU'RE RIGHT.
SST
SST
THOSE CLOTHES...
...ARE YOU FROM SOME OTHER COUNTRY?
YES.
WE ONLY ARRIVED JUST NOW...
...IN THE KINGDOM OF CLOW.

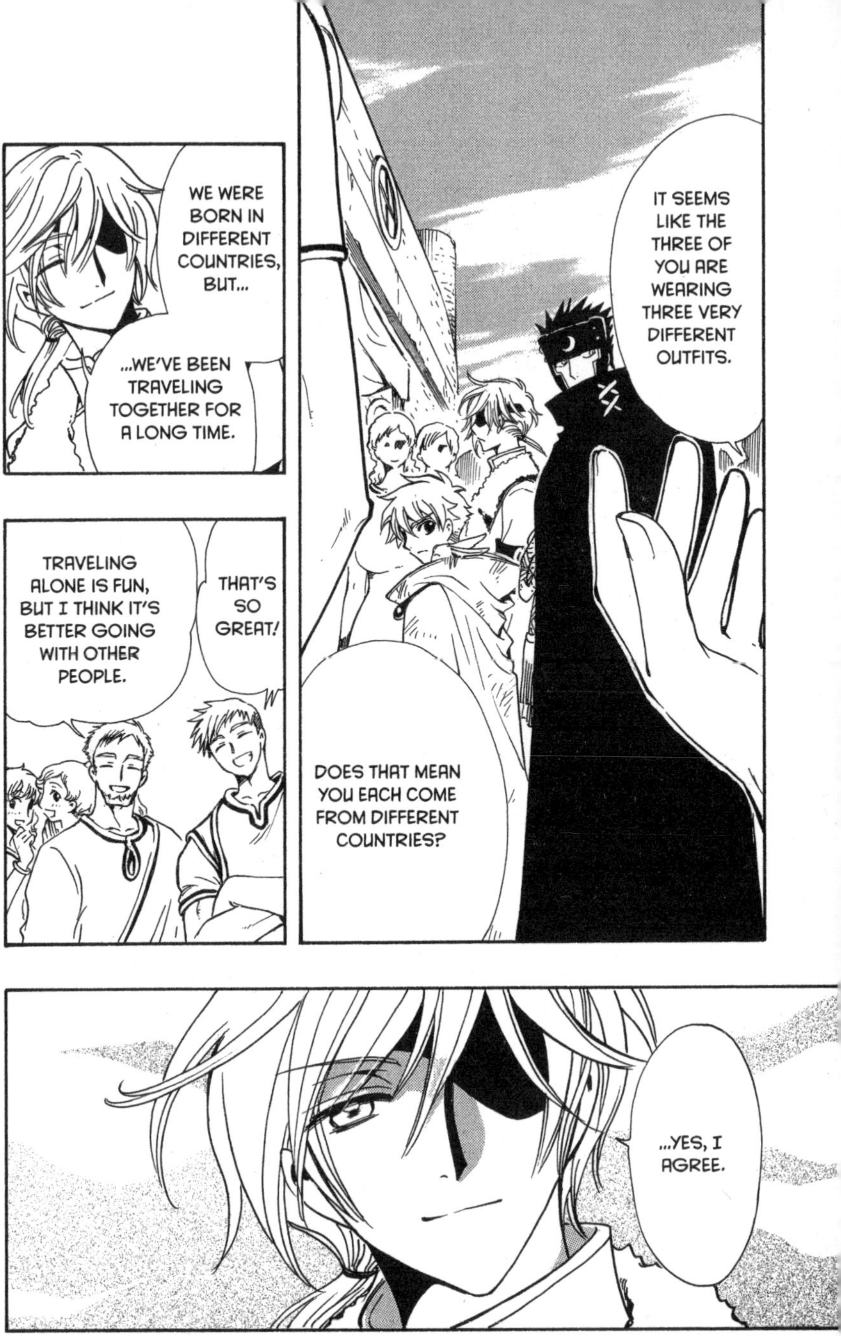
IT SEEMS LIKE THE THREE OF YOU ARE WEARING THREE VERY DIFFERENT OUTFITS.
DOES THAT MEAN YOU EACH COME FROM DIFFERENT COUNTRIES?
WE WERE BORN IN DIFFERENT COUNTRIES, BUT...
...WE'VE BEEN TRAVELING TOGETHER FOR A LONG TIME.
THAT'S SO GREAT!
TRAVELING ALONE IS FUN, BUT I THINK IT'S BETTER GOING WITH OTHER PEOPLE.
...YES, I AGREE.

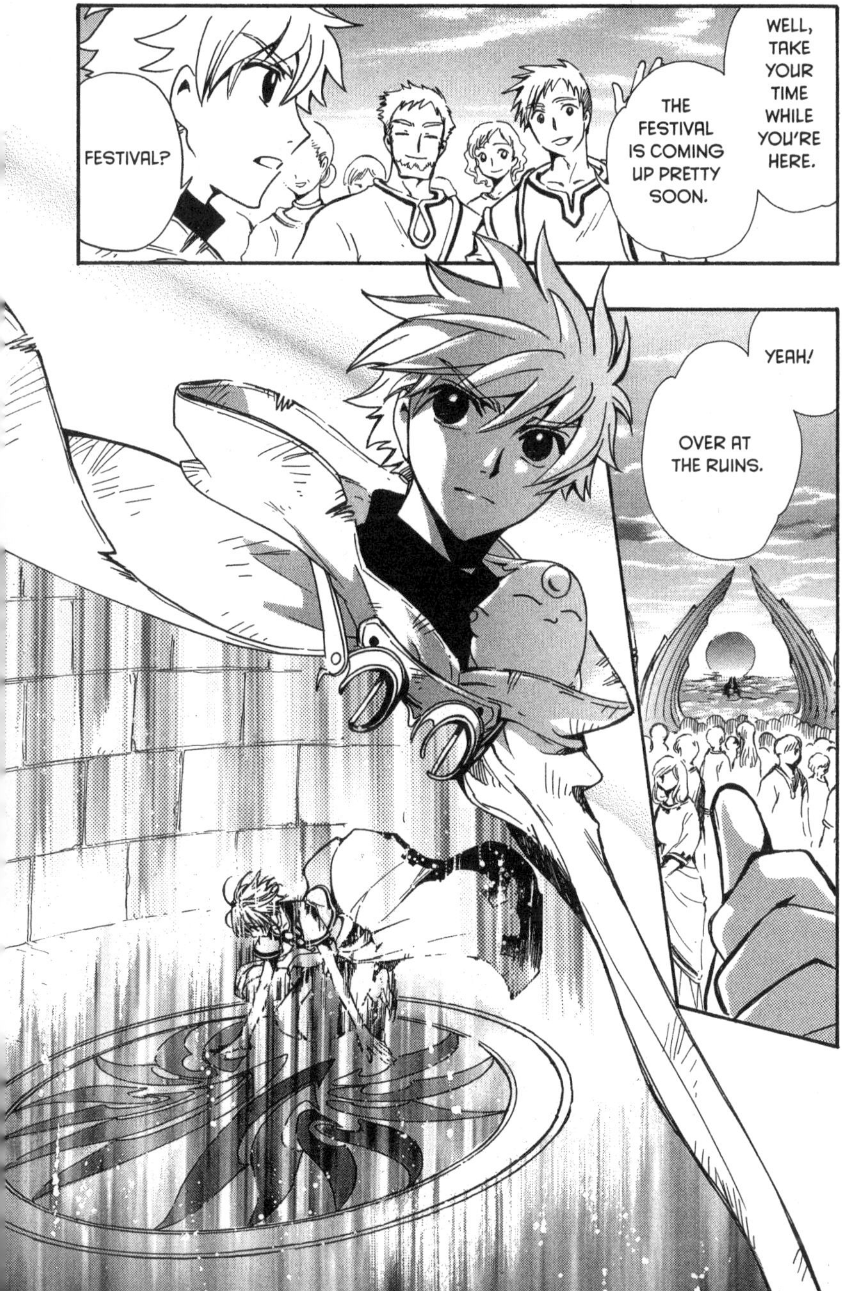
WELL, TAKE YOUR TIME WHILE YOU'RE HERE.
THE FESTIVAL IS COMING UP PRETTY SOON.
FESTIVAL?
YEAH!
OVER AT THE RUINS.

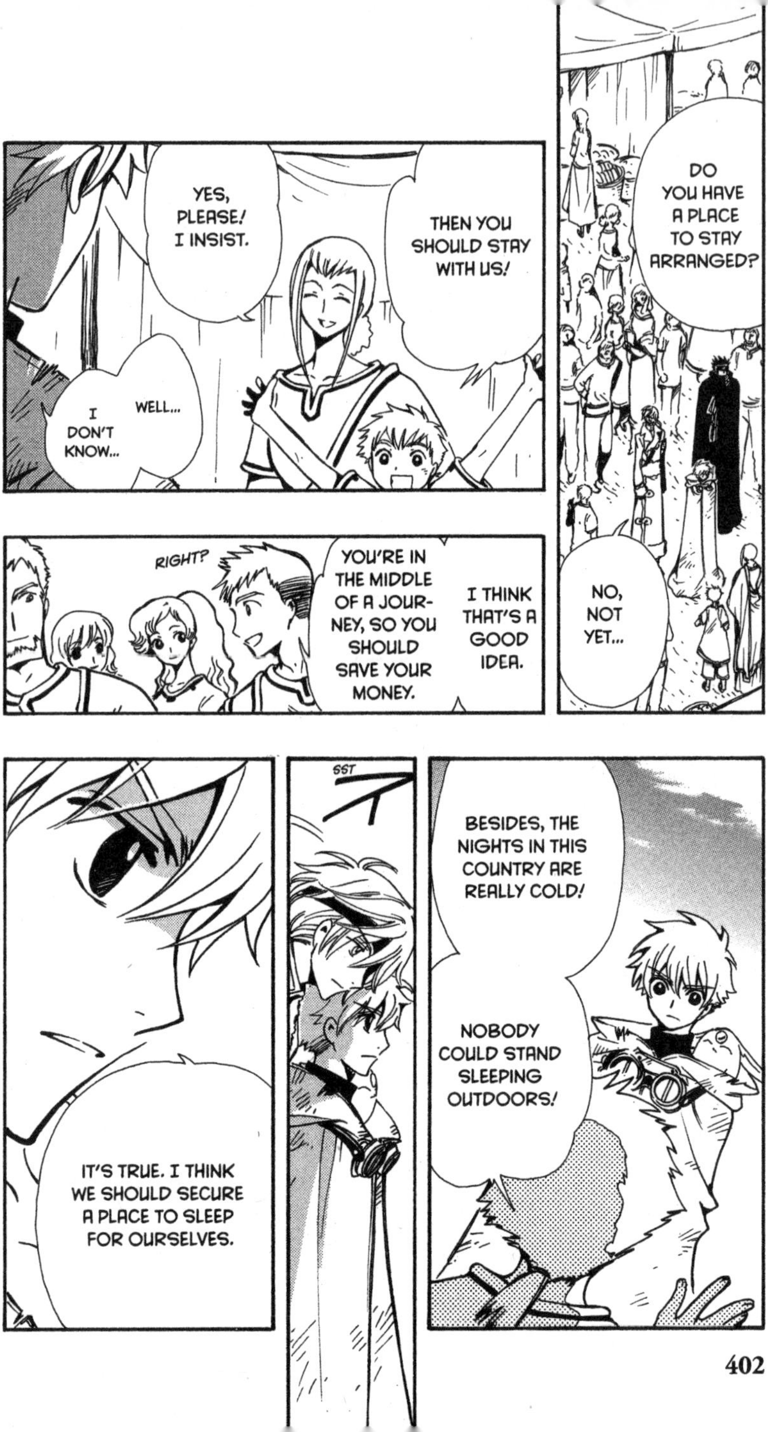
DO YOU HAVE A PLACE TO STAY ARRANGED?
NO, NOT YET...
THEN YOU SHOULD STAY WITH US!
YES, PLEASE! I INSIST.
WELL...
I DON'T KNOW...
I THINK THAT'S A GOOD IDEA.
YOU'RE IN THE MIDDLE OF A JOURNEY, SO YOU SHOULD SAVE YOUR MONEY.
RIGHT?
BESIDES, THE NIGHTS IN THIS COUNTRY ARE REALLY COLD!
NOBODY COULD STAND SLEEPING OUTDOORS!
SST
IT'S TRUE. I THINK WE SHOULD SECURE A PLACE TO SLEEP FOR OURSELVES.

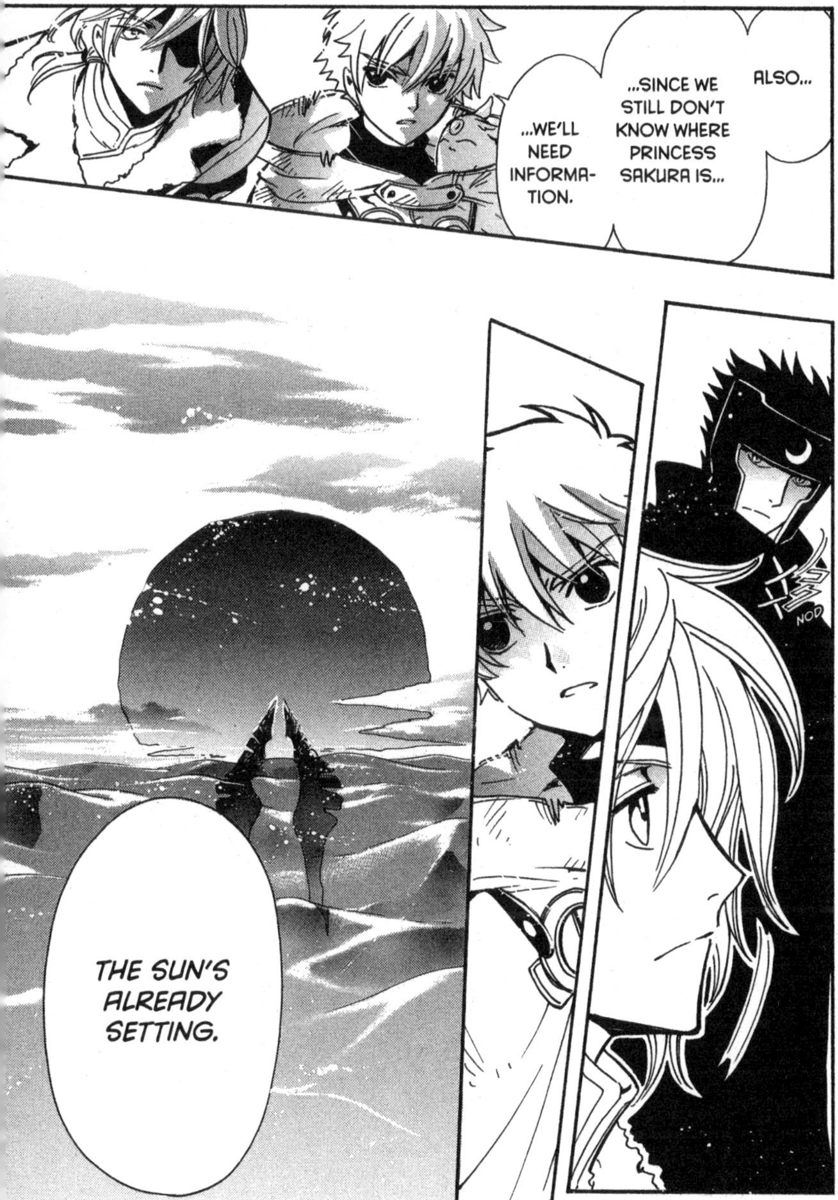
ALSO...
...SINCE WE STILL DON'T KNOW WHERE PRINCESS SAKURA IS...
...WE'LL NEED INFORMA-TION.
NOD
THE SUN'S ALREADY SETTING.

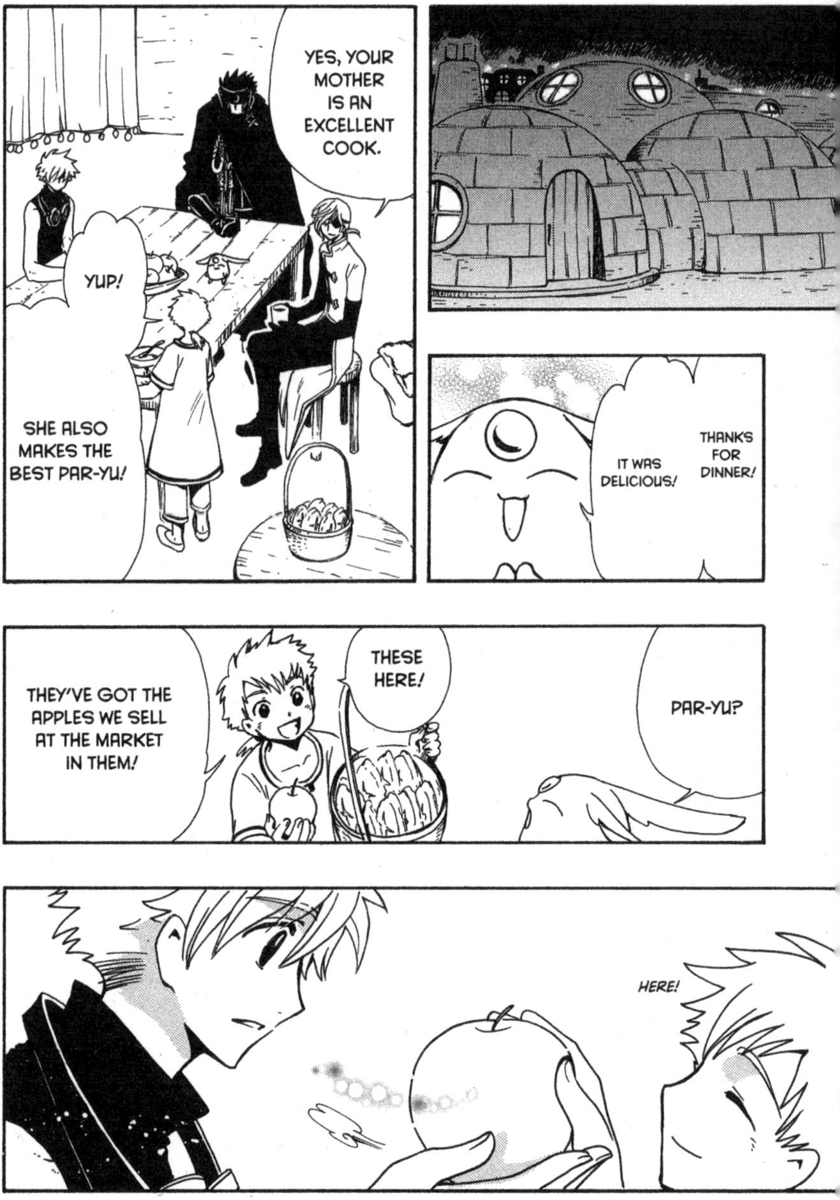
THANKS FOR DINNER!
IT WAS DELICIOUS!
YES, YOUR MOTHER IS AN EXCELLENT COOK.
YUP!
SHE ALSO MAKES THE BEST PAR-YU!
PAR-YU?
THESE HERE!
THEY'VE GOT THE APPLES WE SELL AT THE MARKET IN THEM!
HERE!

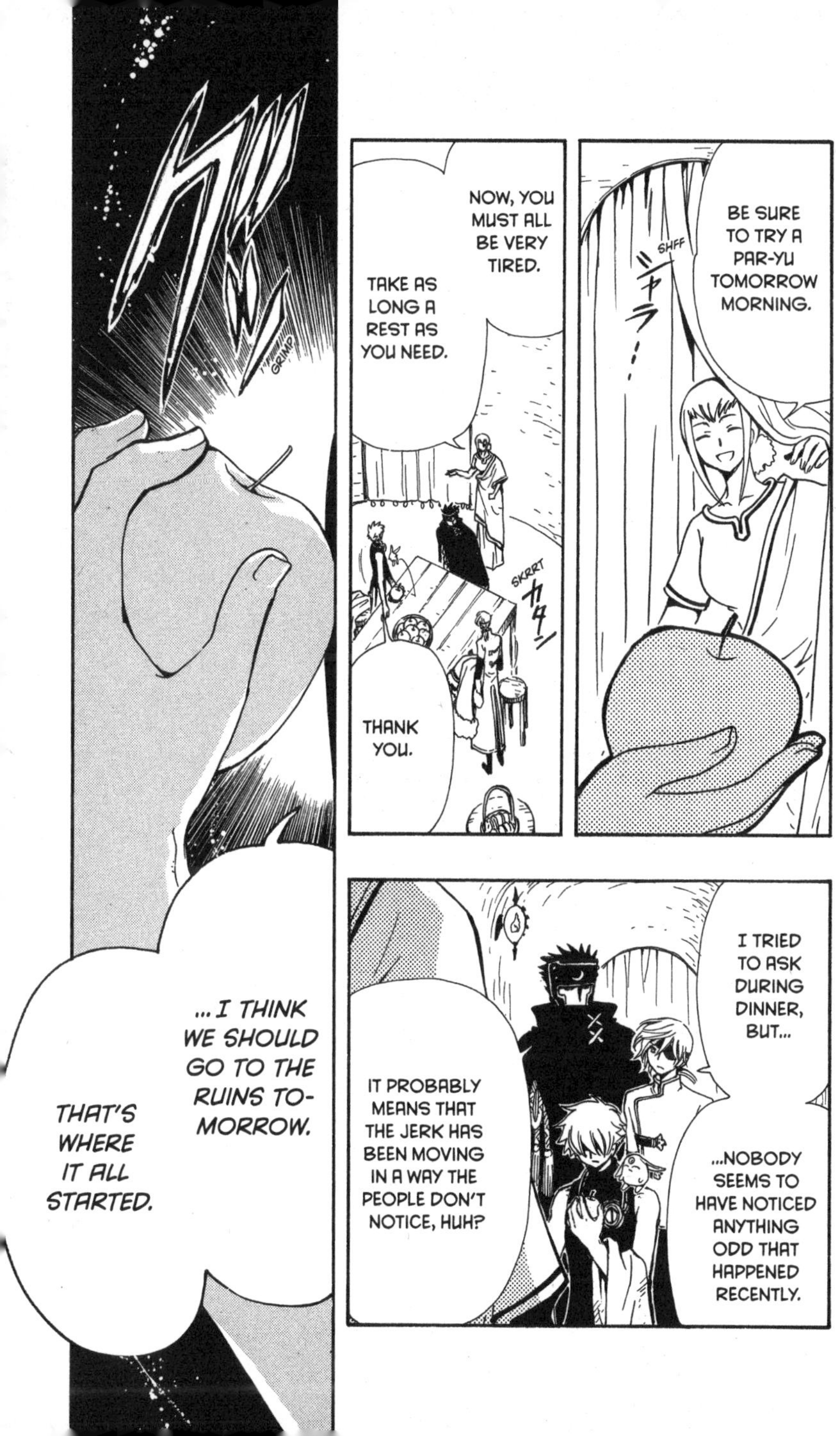
BE SURE TO TRY A PAR-YU TOMORROW MORNING.
SHFF
NOW, YOU MUST ALL BE VERY TIRED.
TAKE AS LONG A REST AS YOU NEED.
SKRRT
THANK YOU.
I TRIED TO ASK DURING DINNER, BUT...
...NOBODY SEEMS TO HAVE NOTICED ANYTHING ODD THAT HAPPENED RECENTLY.
IT PROBABLY MEANS THAT THE JERK HAS BEEN MOVING IN A WAY THE PEOPLE DON'T NOTICE, HUH?
GRIMP
...I THINK WE SHOULD GO TO THE RUINS TO-MORROW.
THAT'S WHERE IT ALL STARTED.

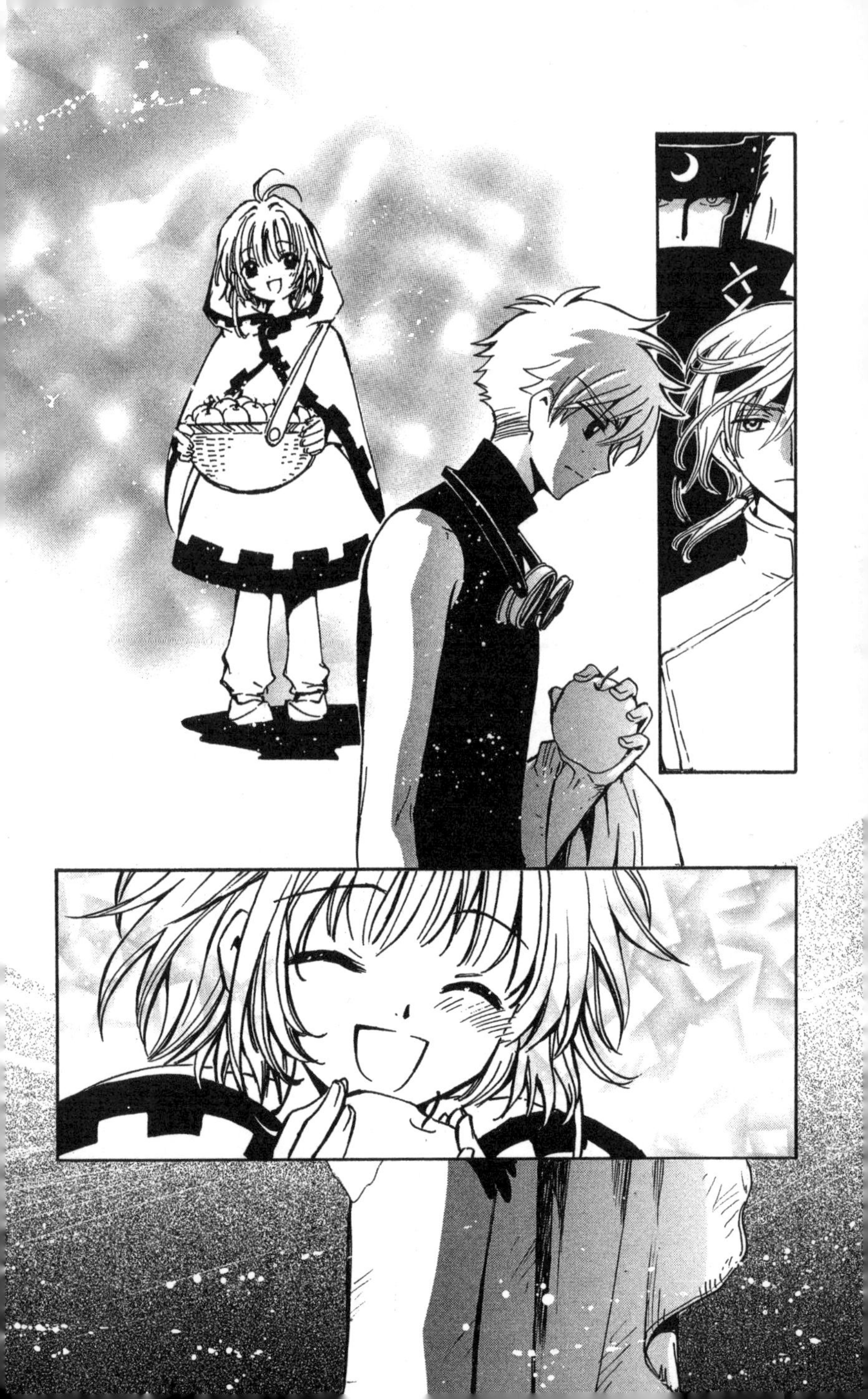

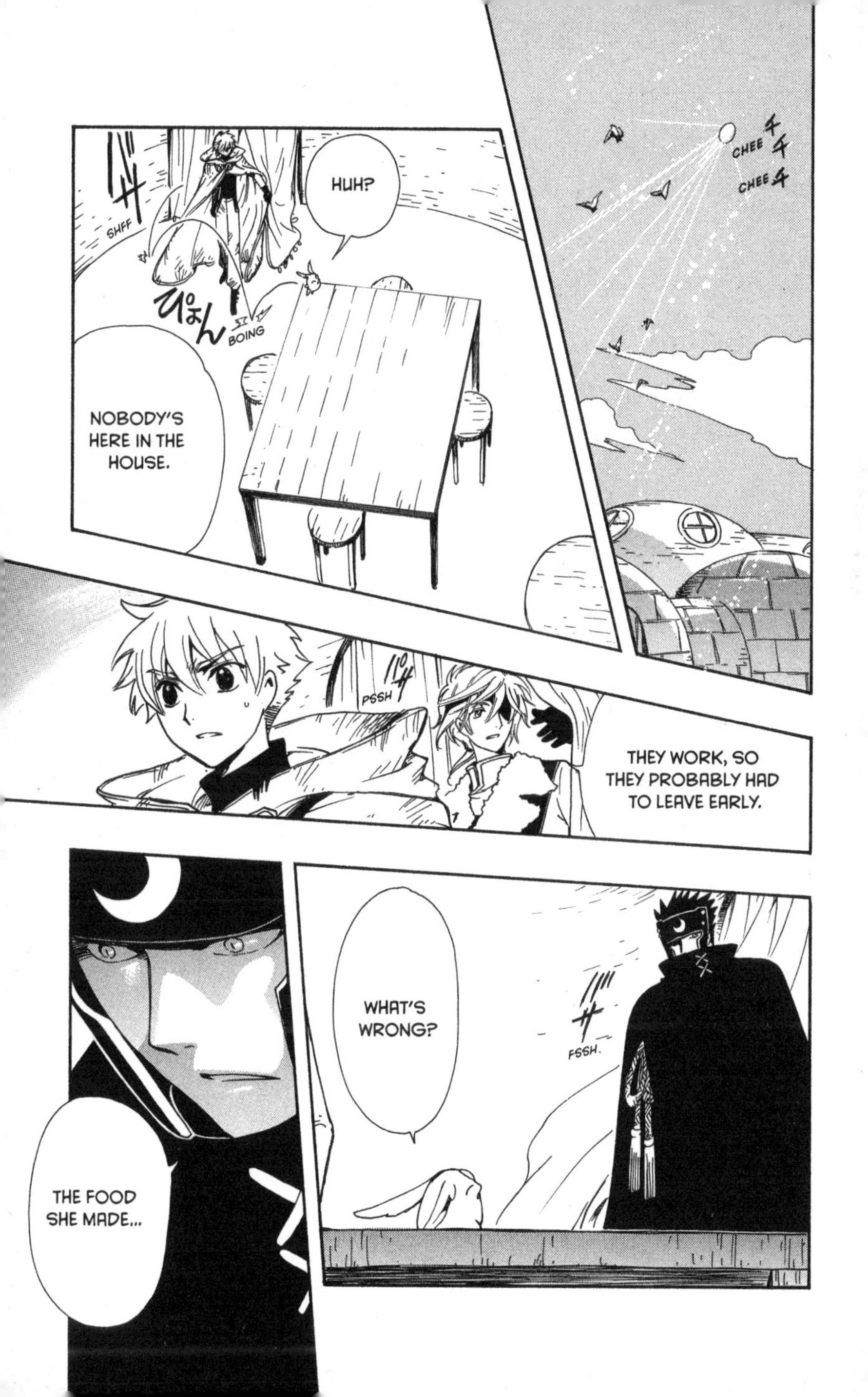
チ CHEE
チ CHEE
HUH?
バサ SHFF
ぴょん BOING
NOBODY'S HERE IN THE HOUSE.
パサ PSSH
THEY WORK, SO THEY PROBABLY HAD TO LEAVE EARLY.
WHAT'S WRONG?
FSSH.
THE FOOD SHE MADE...

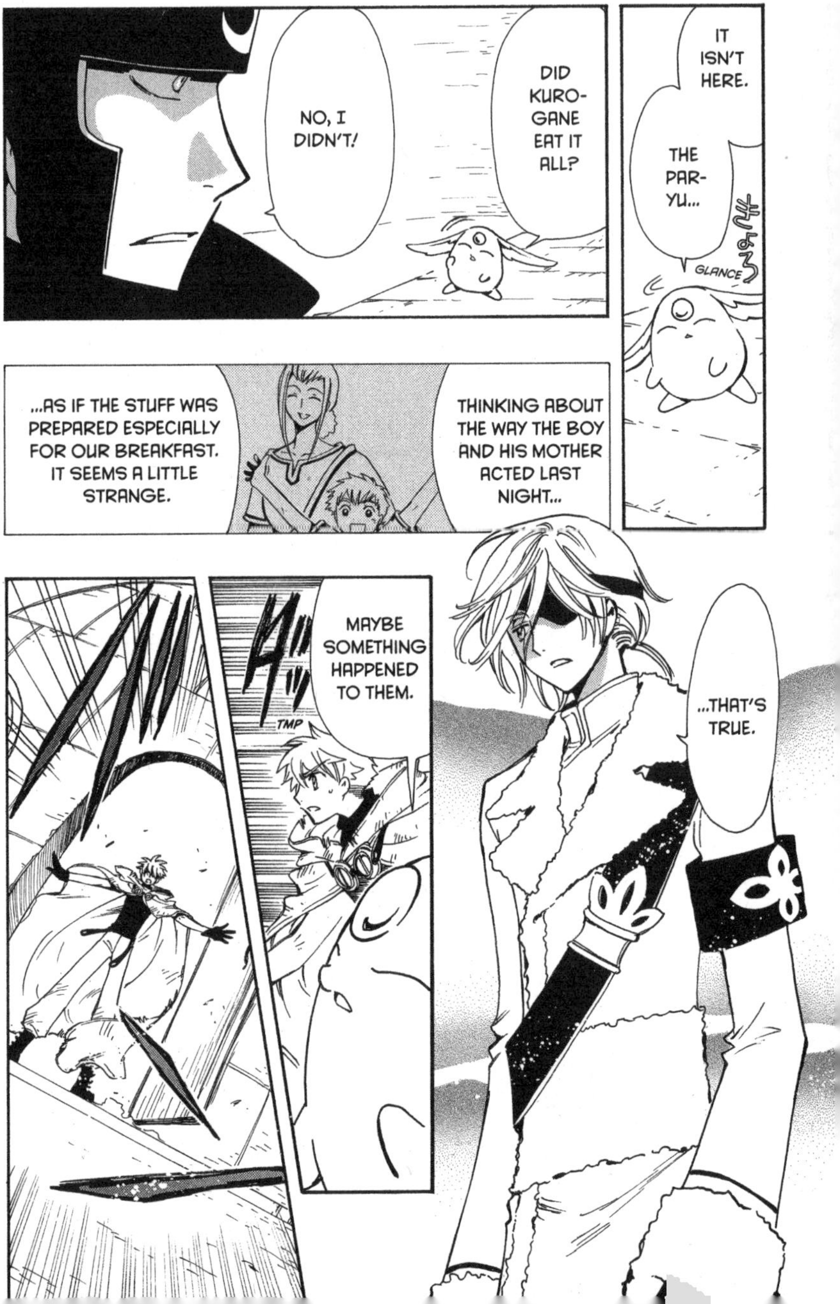
IT ISN'T HERE.
THE PAR-YU...
GLANCE
DID KURO-GANE EAT IT ALL?
NO, I DIDN'T!
THINKING ABOUT THE WAY THE BOY AND HIS MOTHER ACTED LAST NIGHT...
...AS IF THE STUFF WAS PREPARED ESPECIALLY FOR OUR BREAKFAST. IT SEEMS A LITTLE STRANGE.
...THAT'S TRUE.
MAYBE SOMETHING HAPPENED TO THEM.
TMP

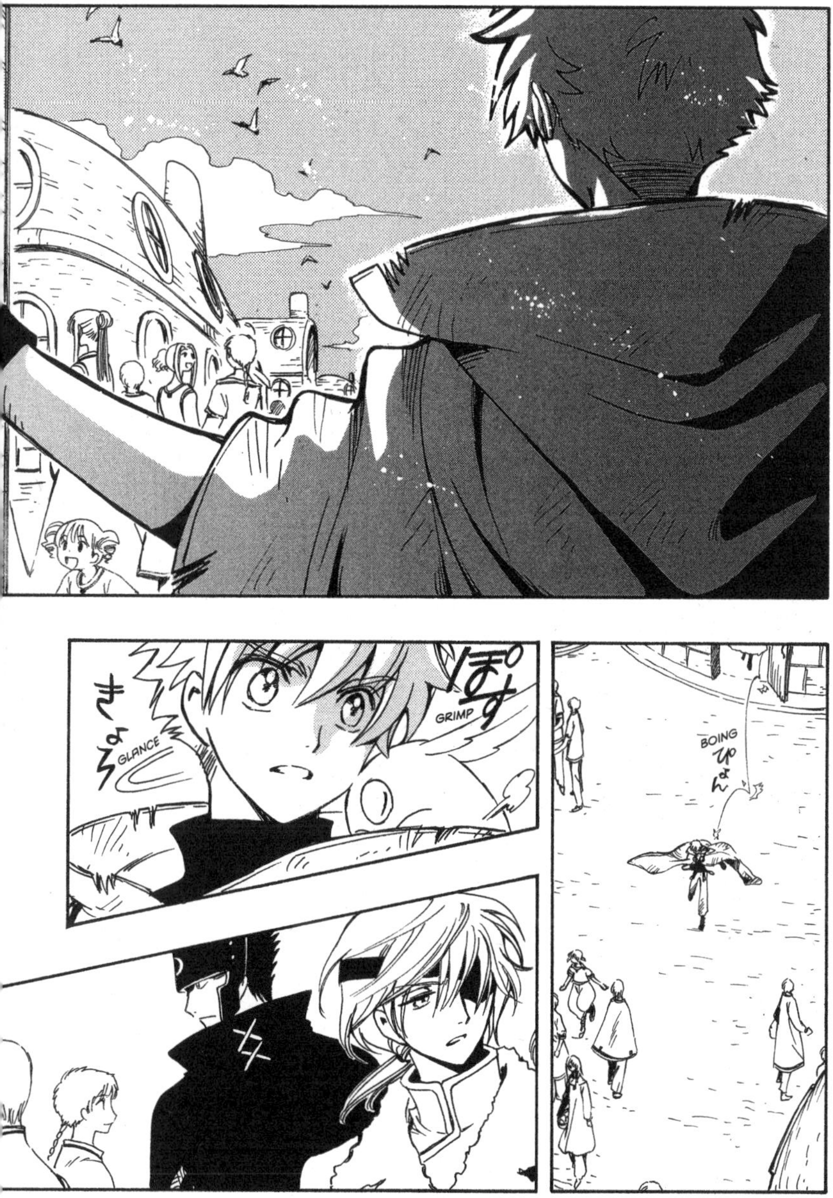
BOING
ぴょん
ぽす
GRIMP
きょろ
GLANCE

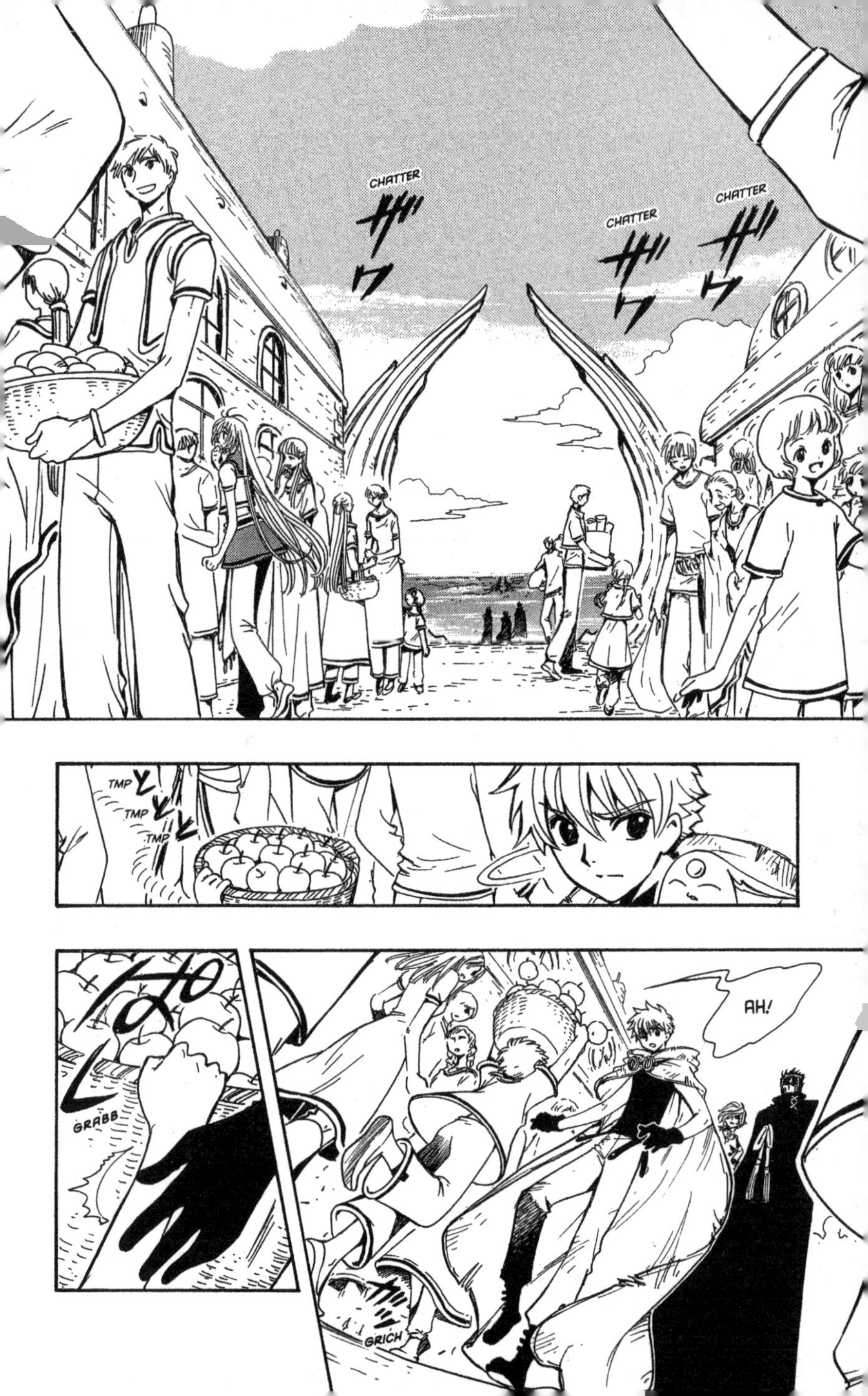
CHATTER
ザワ
CHATTER
ザワ
CHATTER
ザワ
TMP
TMP
TMP
AH!
GRICH
GRABB

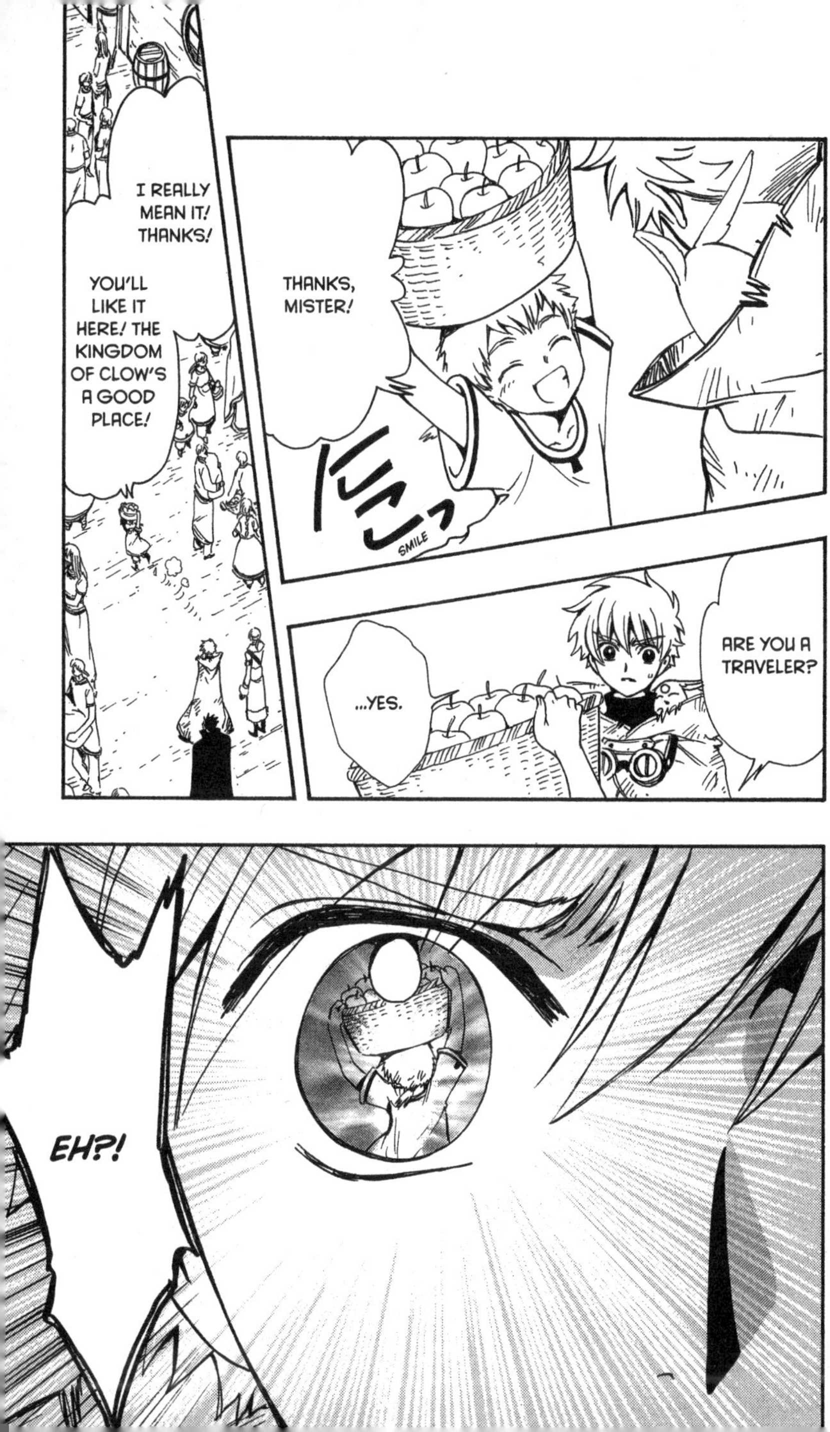
THANKS, MISTER!
SMILE
ARE YOU A TRAVELER?
...YES.
I REALLY MEAN IT! THANKS!
YOU'LL LIKE IT HERE! THE KINGDOM OF CLOW'S A GOOD PLACE!
EH?!

ツバサ

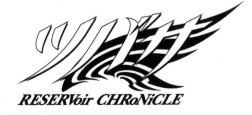

RESERVoir CHRoNiCLE

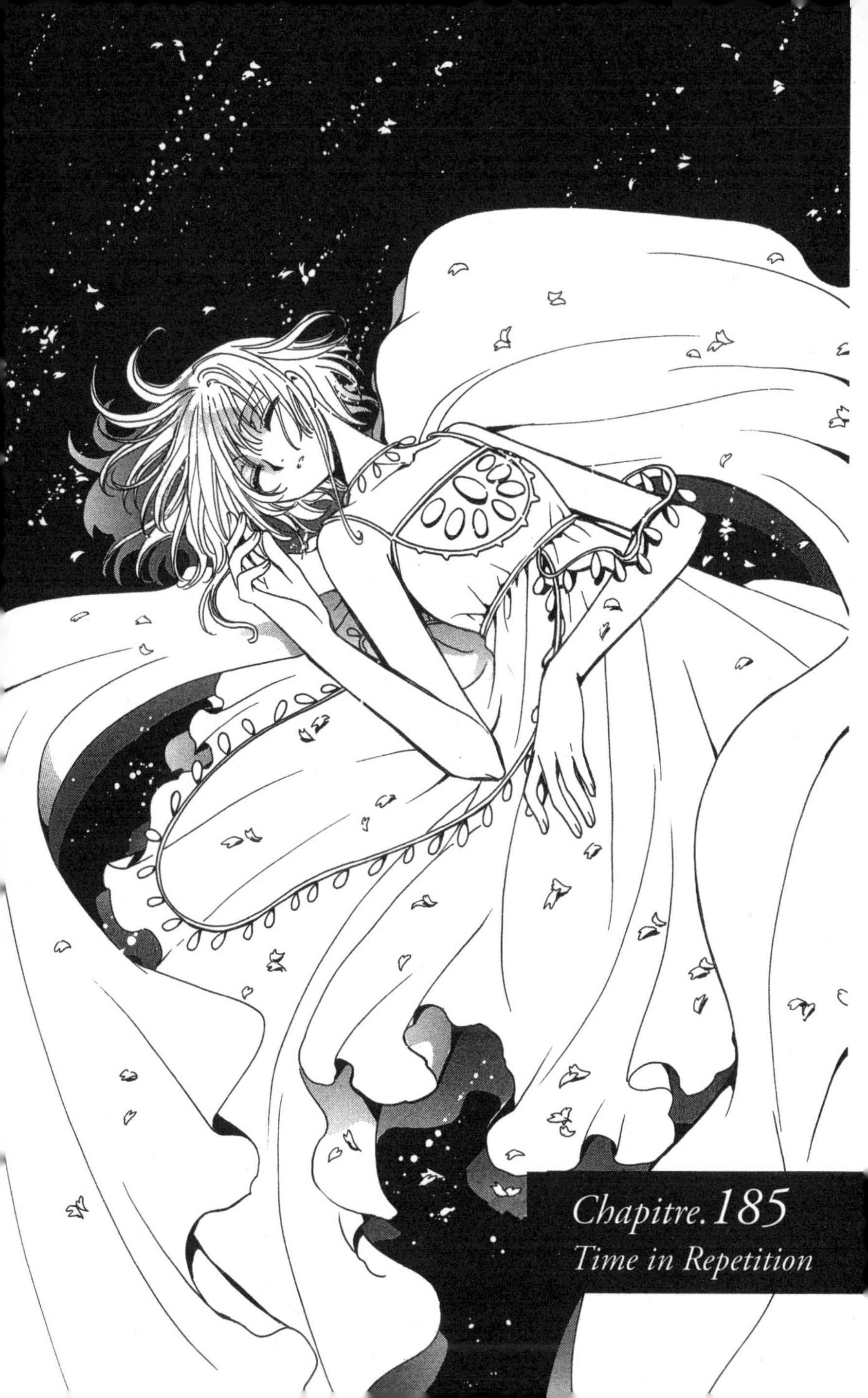

Chapitre. 185
Time in Repetition

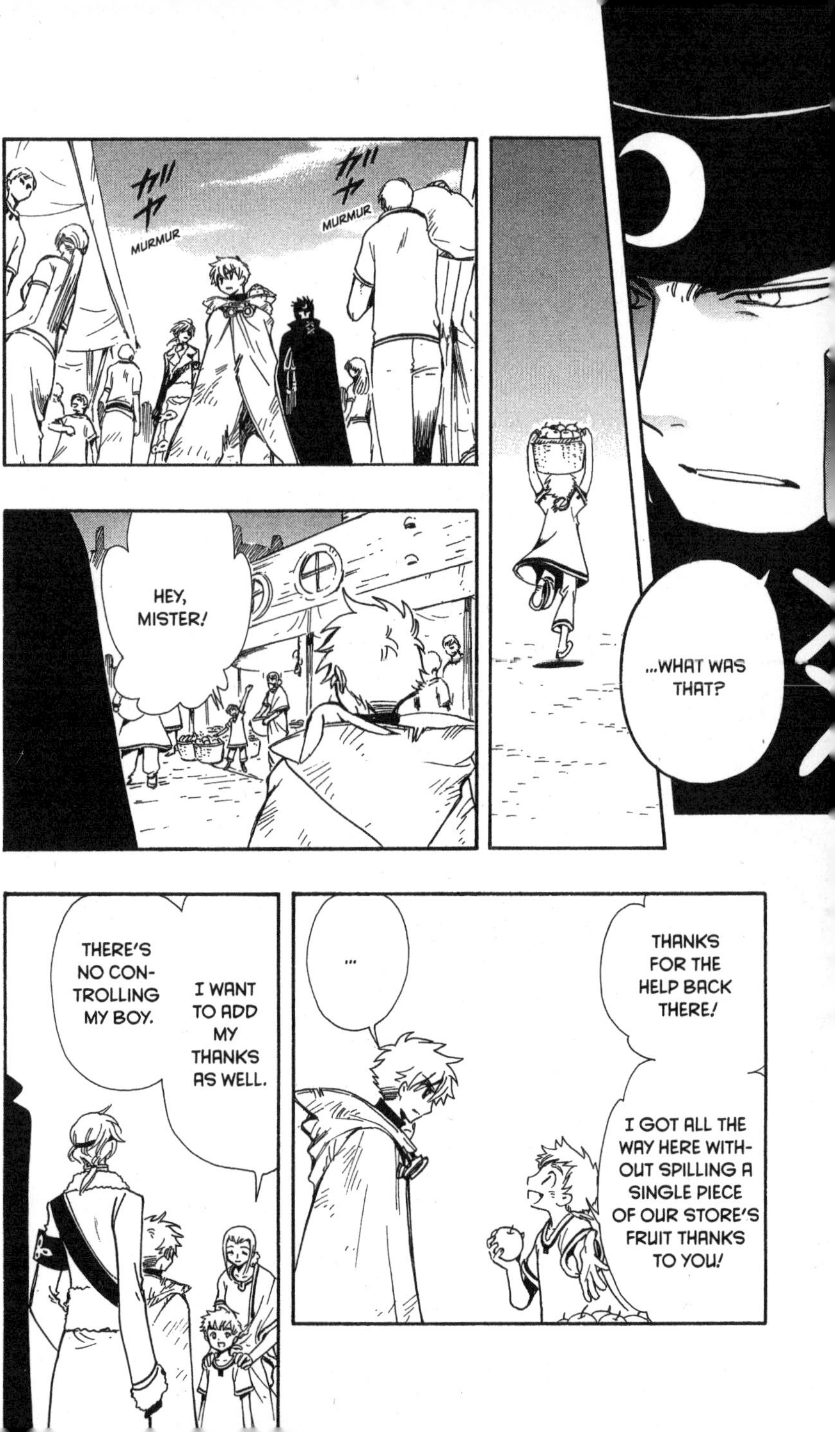
...WHAT WAS THAT?
MURMUR
MURMUR
HEY, MISTER!
THANKS FOR THE HELP BACK THERE!
I GOT ALL THE WAY HERE WITHOUT SPILLING A SINGLE PIECE OF OUR STORE'S FRUIT THANKS TO YOU!
...
THERE'S NO CONTROLLING MY BOY.
I WANT TO ADD MY THANKS AS WELL.

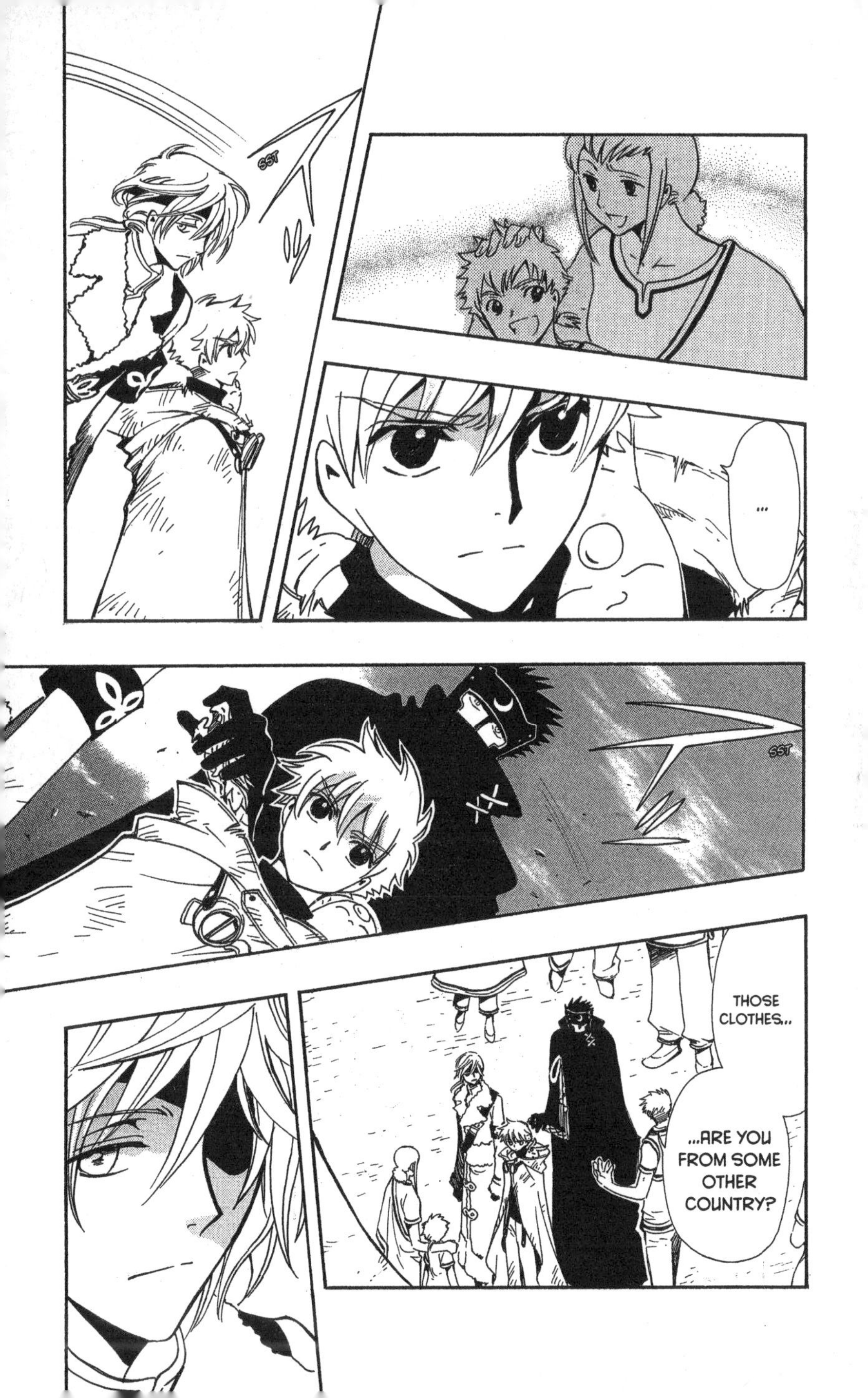
SST
...
SST
THOSE CLOTHES...
...ARE YOU FROM SOME OTHER COUNTRY?

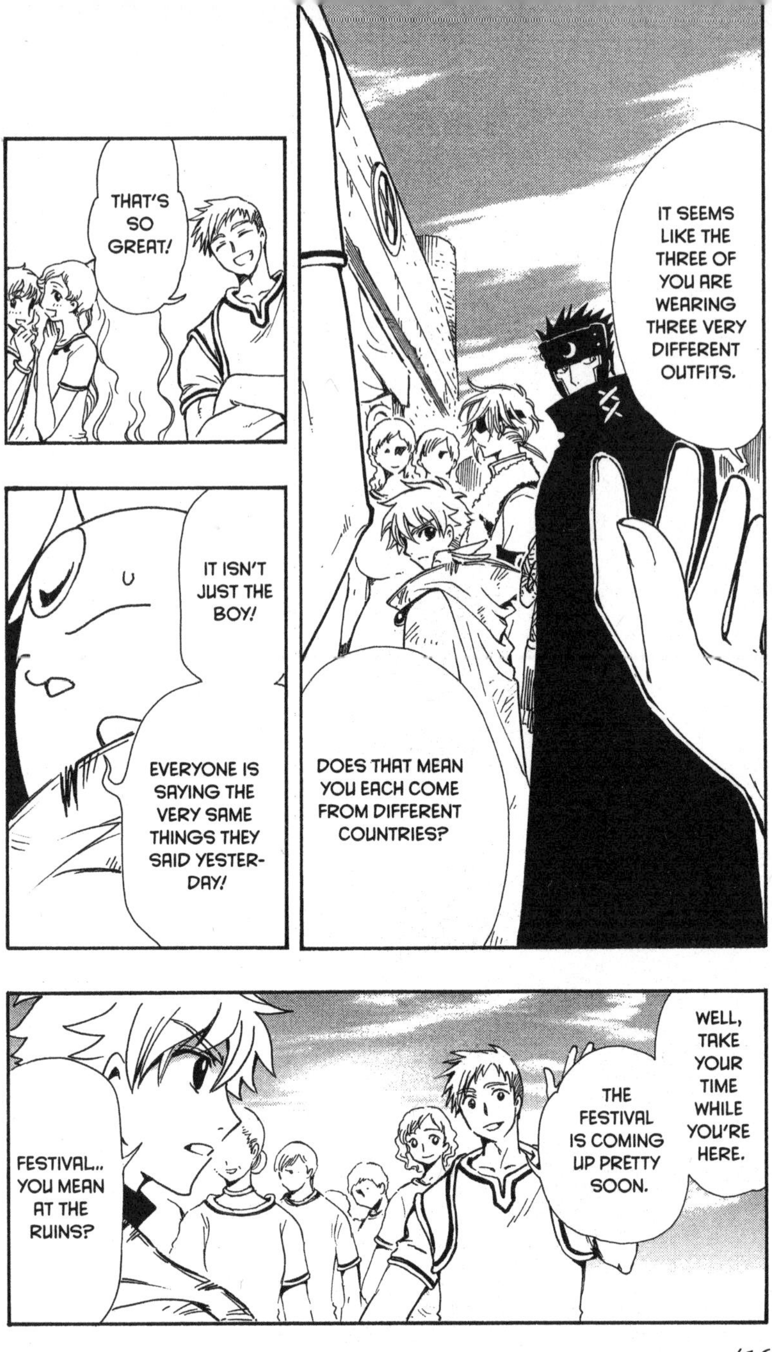
IT SEEMS LIKE THE THREE OF YOU ARE WEARING THREE VERY DIFFERENT OUTFITS.
DOES THAT MEAN YOU EACH COME FROM DIFFERENT COUNTRIES?
THAT'S SO GREAT!
IT ISN'T JUST THE BOY!
EVERYONE IS SAYING THE VERY SAME THINGS THEY SAID YESTER-DAY!
WELL, TAKE YOUR TIME WHILE YOU'RE HERE.
THE FESTIVAL IS COMING UP PRETTY SOON.
FESTIVAL.. YOU MEAN AT THE RUINS?

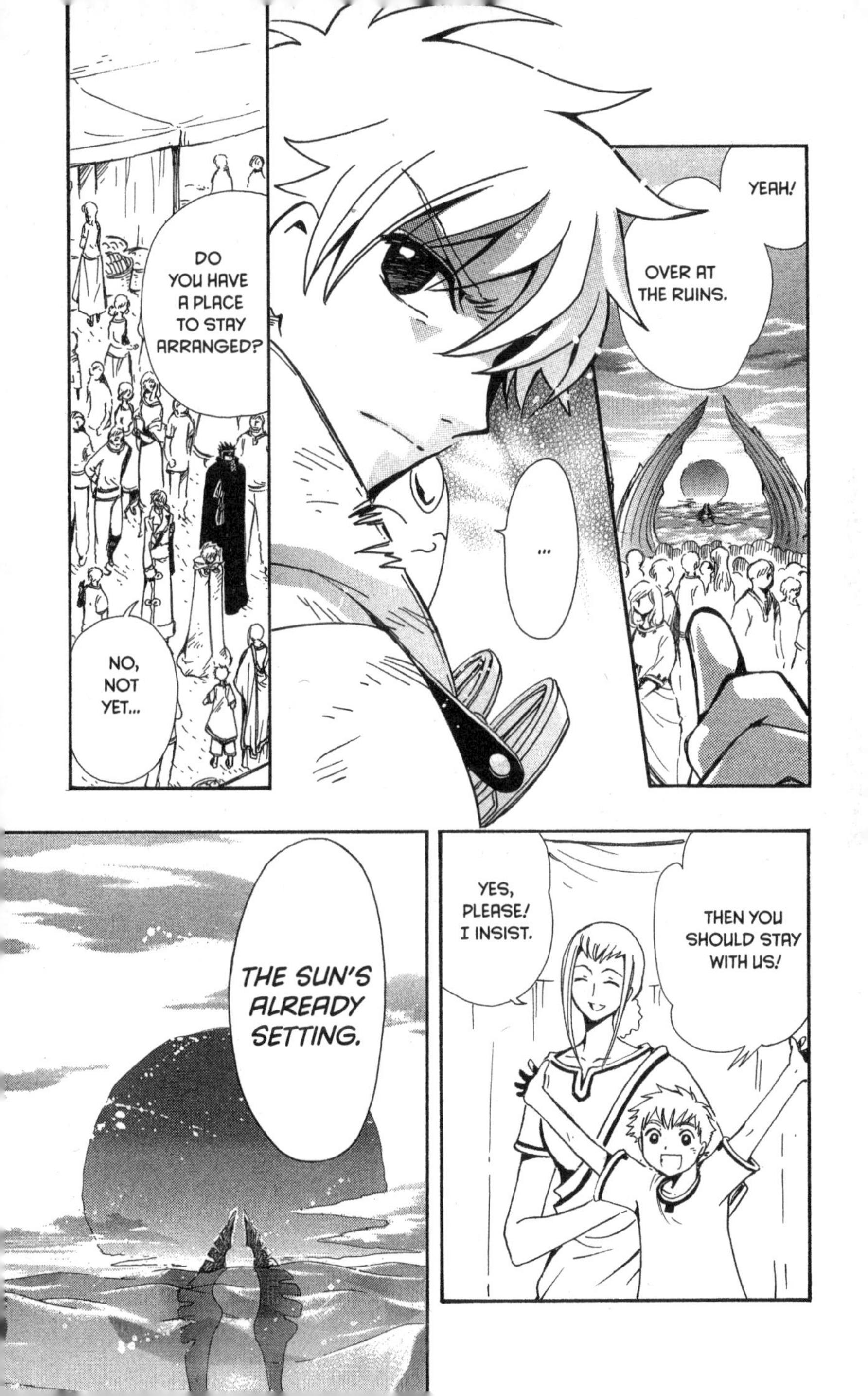
YEAH!
OVER AT THE RUINS.
...
DO YOU HAVE A PLACE TO STAY ARRANGED?
NO, NOT YET...
THEN YOU SHOULD STAY WITH US!
YES, PLEASE! I INSIST.
THE SUN'S ALREADY SETTING.

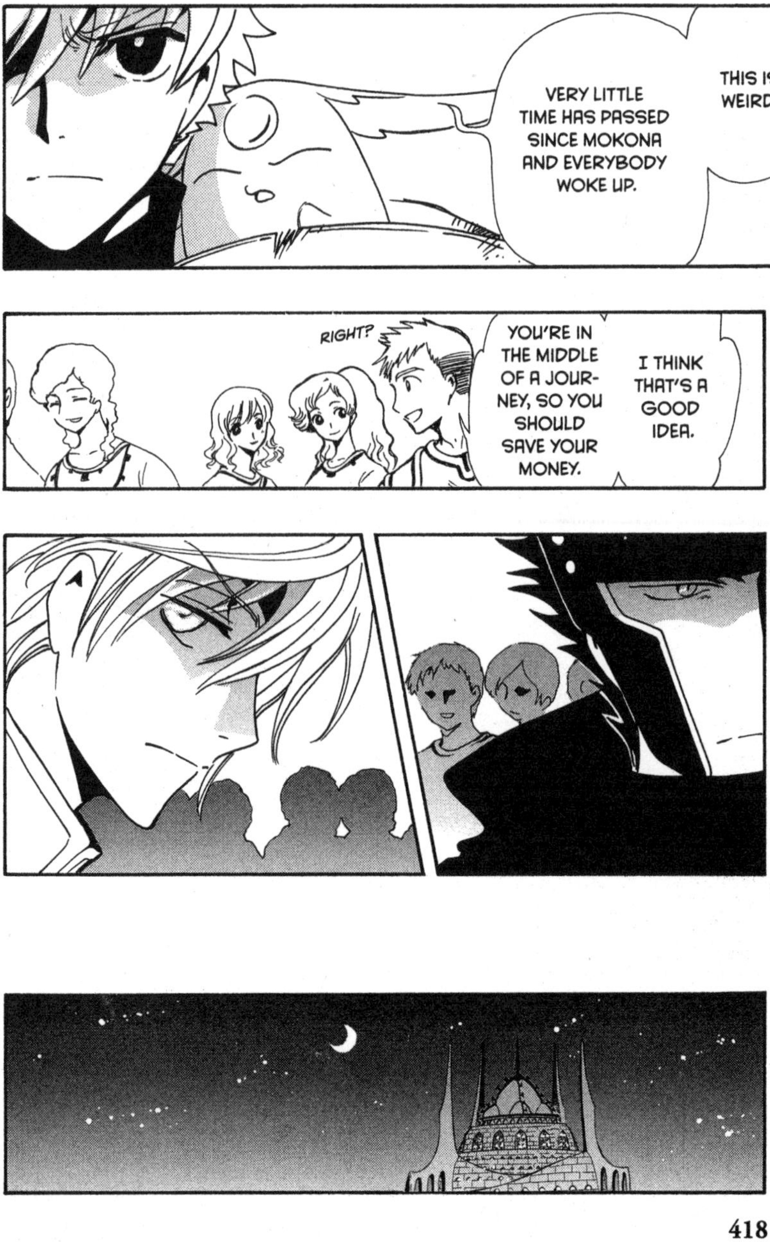
THIS IS WEIRD!
VERY LITTLE TIME HAS PASSED SINCE MOKONA AND EVERYBODY WOKE UP.
I THINK THAT'S A GOOD IDEA.
YOU'RE IN THE MIDDLE OF A JOURNEY, SO YOU SHOULD SAVE YOUR MONEY.
RIGHT?

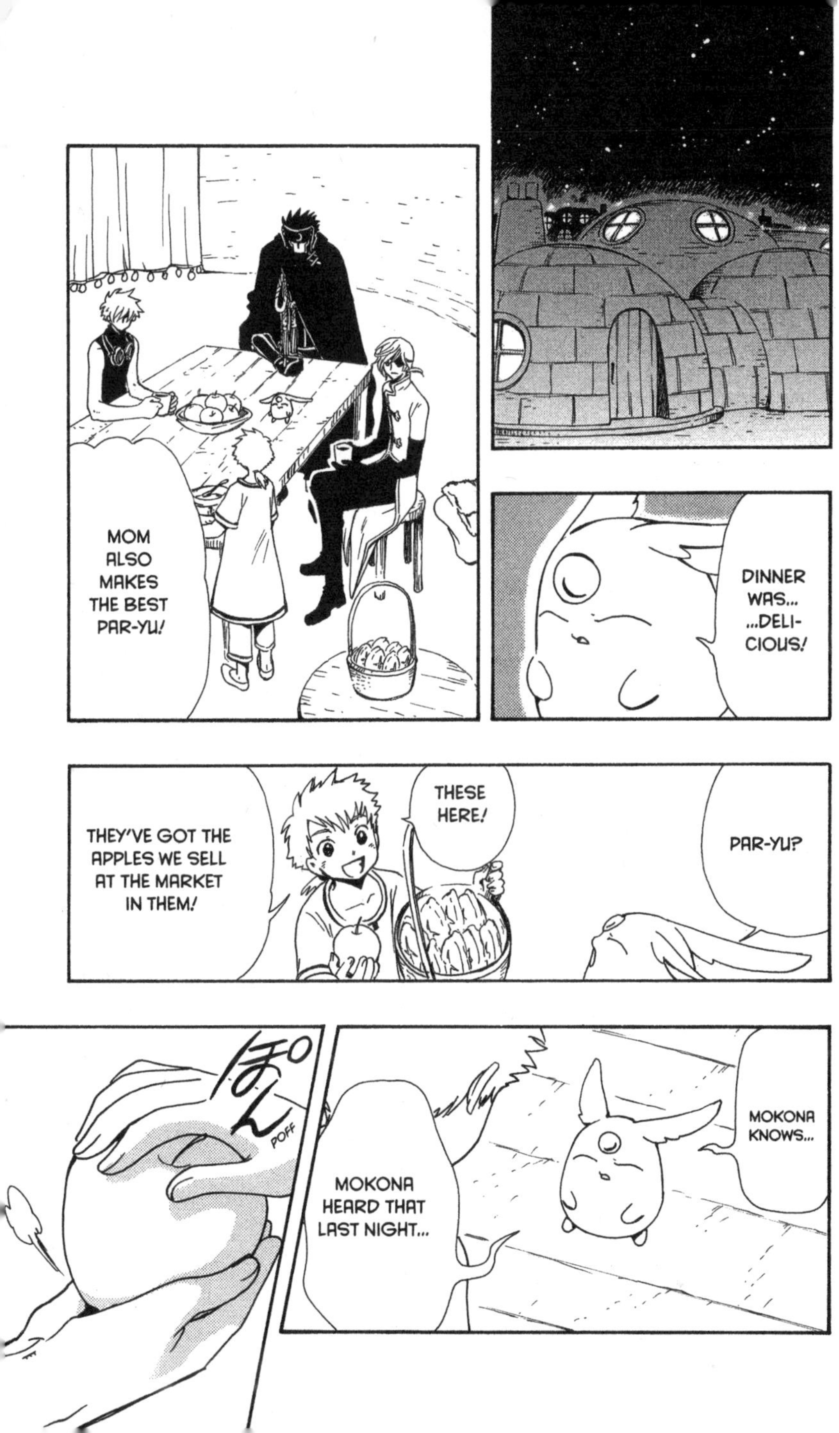
DINNER WAS... ...DELI- CIOUS!
MOM ALSO MAKES THE BEST PAR-YU!
PAR-YU?
THESE HERE!
THEY'VE GOT THE APPLES WE SELL AT THE MARKET IN THEM!
MOKONA KNOWS...
MOKONA HEARD THAT LAST NIGHT...
ぽん
POFF

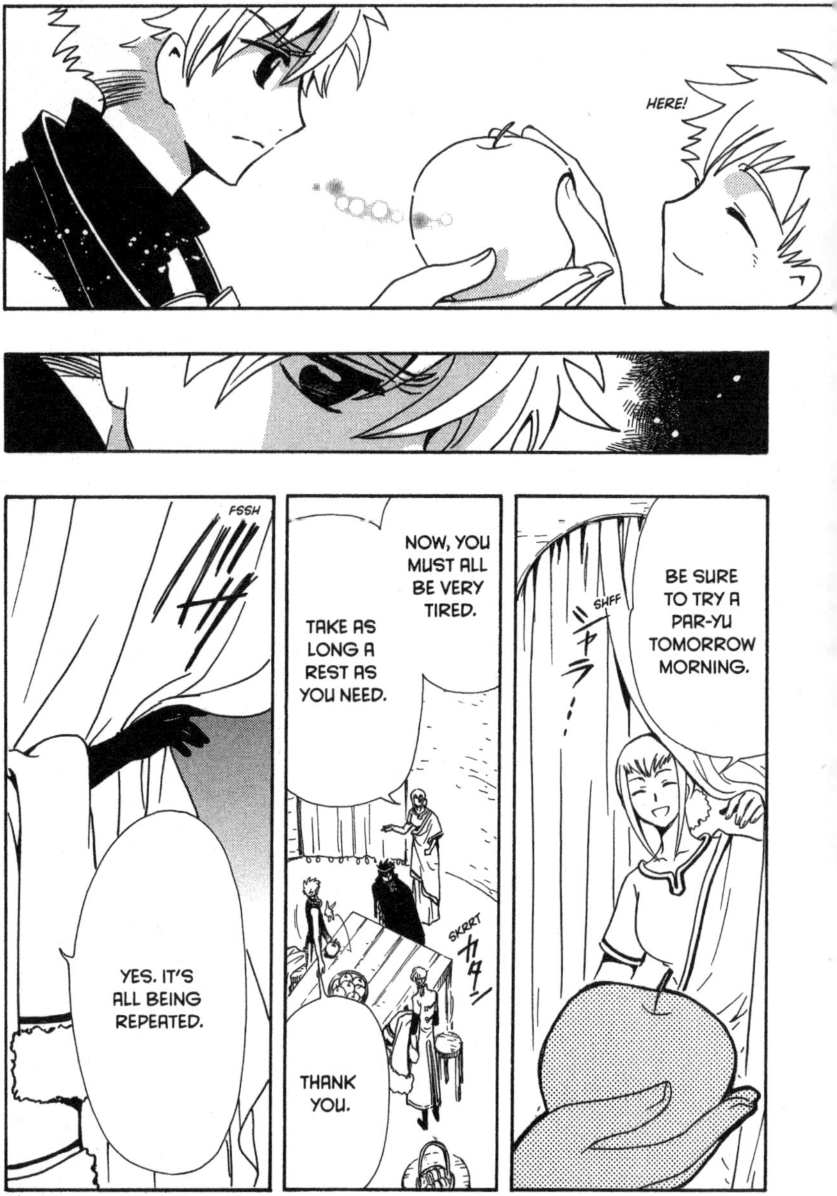
HERE!
SHFF
BE SURE TO TRY A PAR-YU TOMORROW MORNING.
NOW, YOU MUST ALL BE VERY TIRED.
TAKE AS LONG A REST AS YOU NEED.
SKRRT
THANK YOU.
FSSH
YES. IT'S ALL BEING REPEATED.

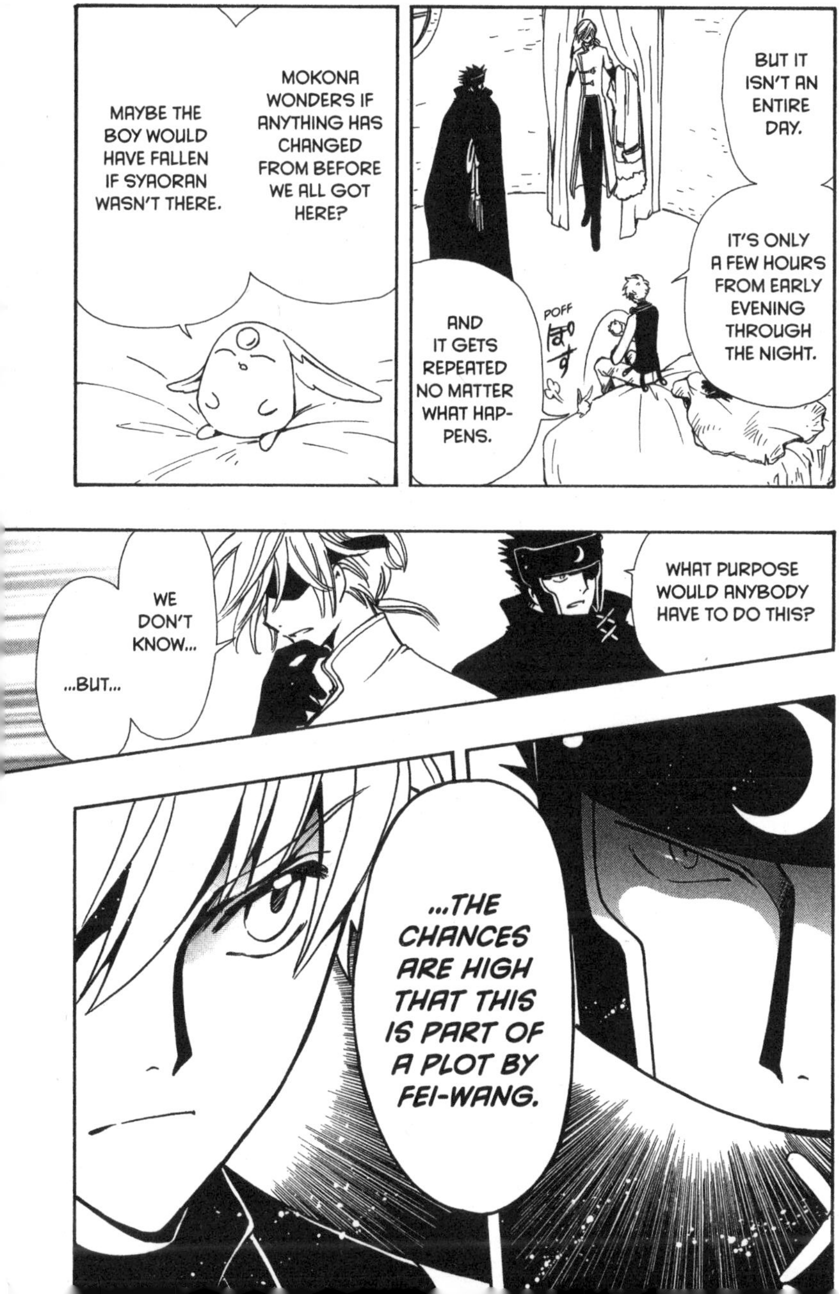
BUT IT ISN'T AN ENTIRE DAY.
IT'S ONLY A FEW HOURS FROM EARLY EVENING THROUGH THE NIGHT.
POFF
AND IT GETS REPEATED NO MATTER WHAT HAP-PENS.
MOKONA WONDERS IF ANYTHING HAS CHANGED FROM BEFORE WE ALL GOT HERE?
MAYBE THE BOY WOULD HAVE FALLEN IF SYAORAN WASN'T THERE.
WHAT PURPOSE WOULD ANYBODY HAVE TO DO THIS?
WE DON'T KNOW...
...BUT...
...THE CHANCES ARE HIGH THAT THIS IS PART OF A PLOT BY FEI-WANG.

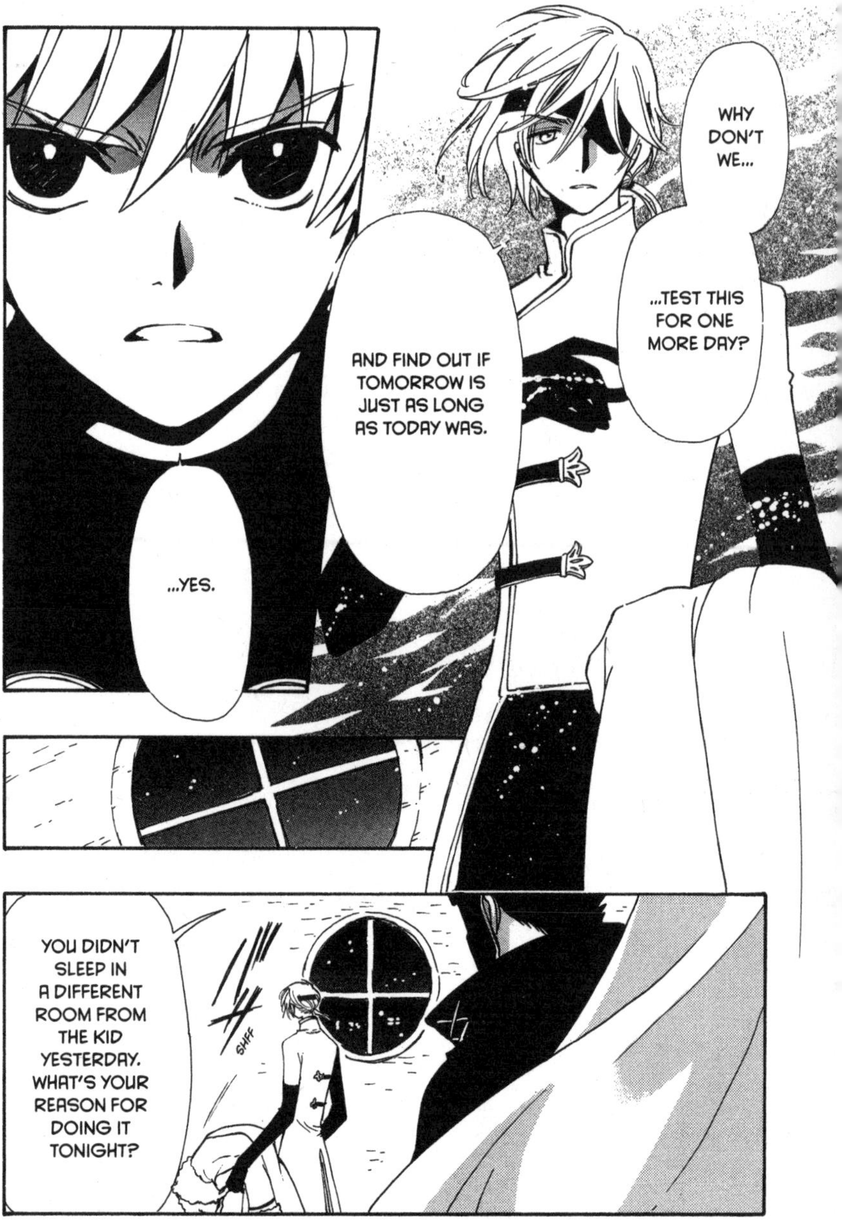
WHY DON'T WE...
...TEST THIS FOR ONE MORE DAY?
AND FIND OUT IF TOMORROW IS JUST AS LONG AS TODAY WAS.
...YES.
YOU DIDN'T SLEEP IN A DIFFERENT ROOM FROM THE KID YESTERDAY. WHAT'S YOUR REASON FOR DOING IT TONIGHT?
SHFF

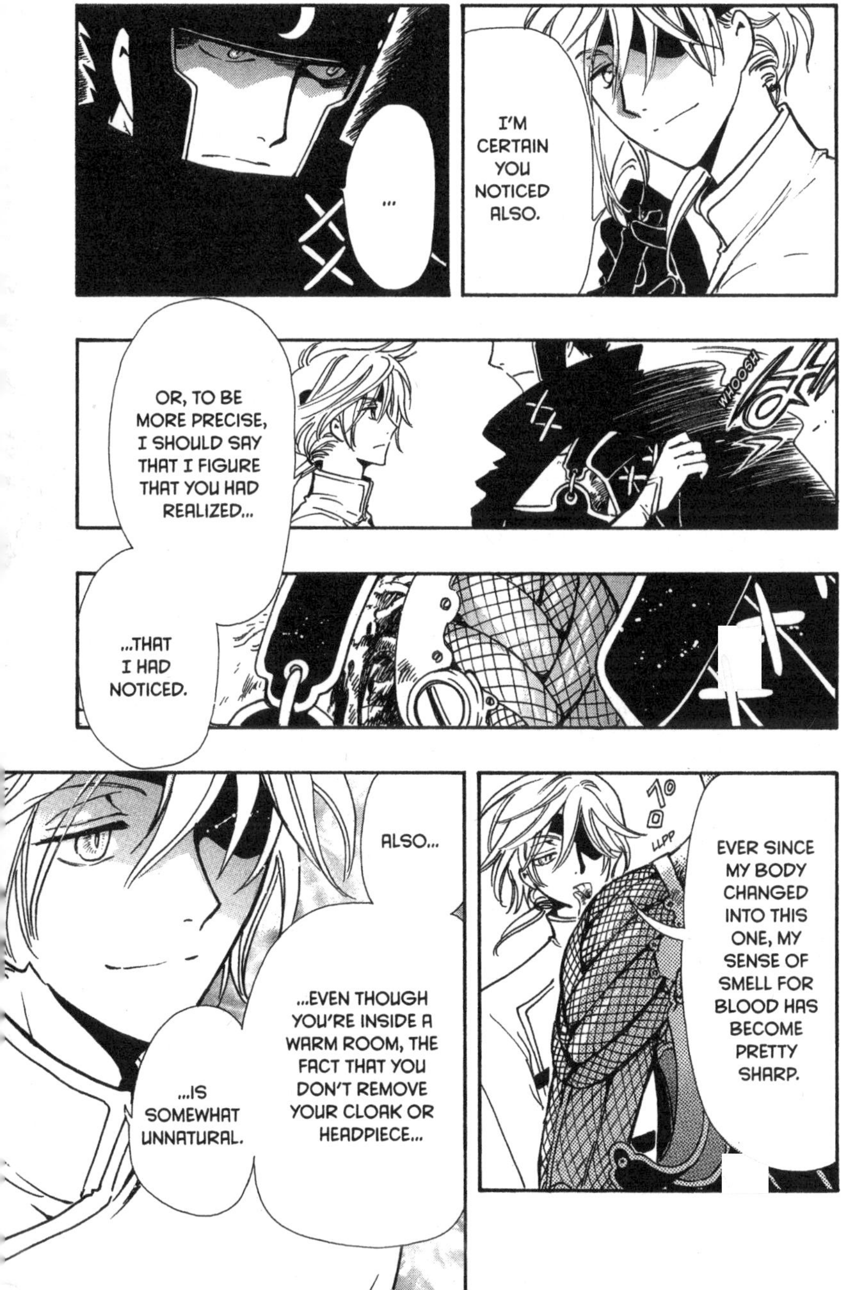
I'M CERTAIN YOU NOTICED ALSO.
...
WHOOSH
OR, TO BE MORE PRECISE, I SHOULD SAY THAT I FIGURE THAT YOU HAD REALIZED...
...THAT I HAD NOTICED.
LLPP
EVER SINCE MY BODY CHANGED INTO THIS ONE, MY SENSE OF SMELL FOR BLOOD HAS BECOME PRETTY SHARP.
ALSO...
...EVEN THOUGH YOU'RE INSIDE A WARM ROOM, THE FACT THAT YOU DON'T REMOVE YOUR CLOAK OR HEADPIECE...
...IS SOMEWHAT UNNATURAL.

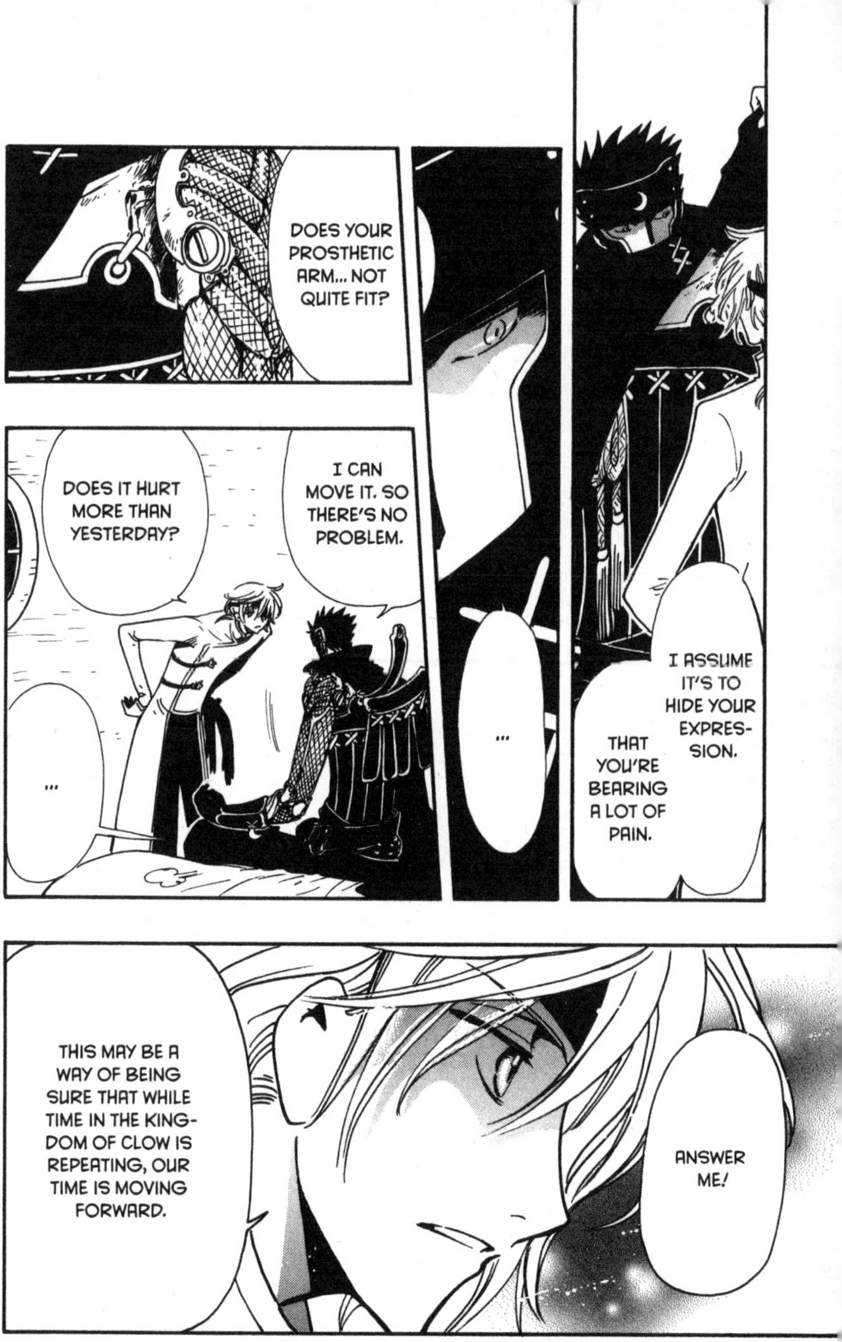
DOES YOUR PROSTHETIC ARM... NOT QUITE FIT?
DOES IT HURT MORE THAN YESTERDAY?
I CAN MOVE IT. SO THERE'S NO PROBLEM.
...
...
I ASSUME IT'S TO HIDE YOUR EXPRESSION.
THAT YOU'RE BEARING A LOT OF PAIN.
THIS MAY BE A WAY OF BEING SURE THAT WHILE TIME IN THE KINGDOM OF CLOW IS REPEATING, OUR TIME IS MOVING FORWARD.
ANSWER ME!

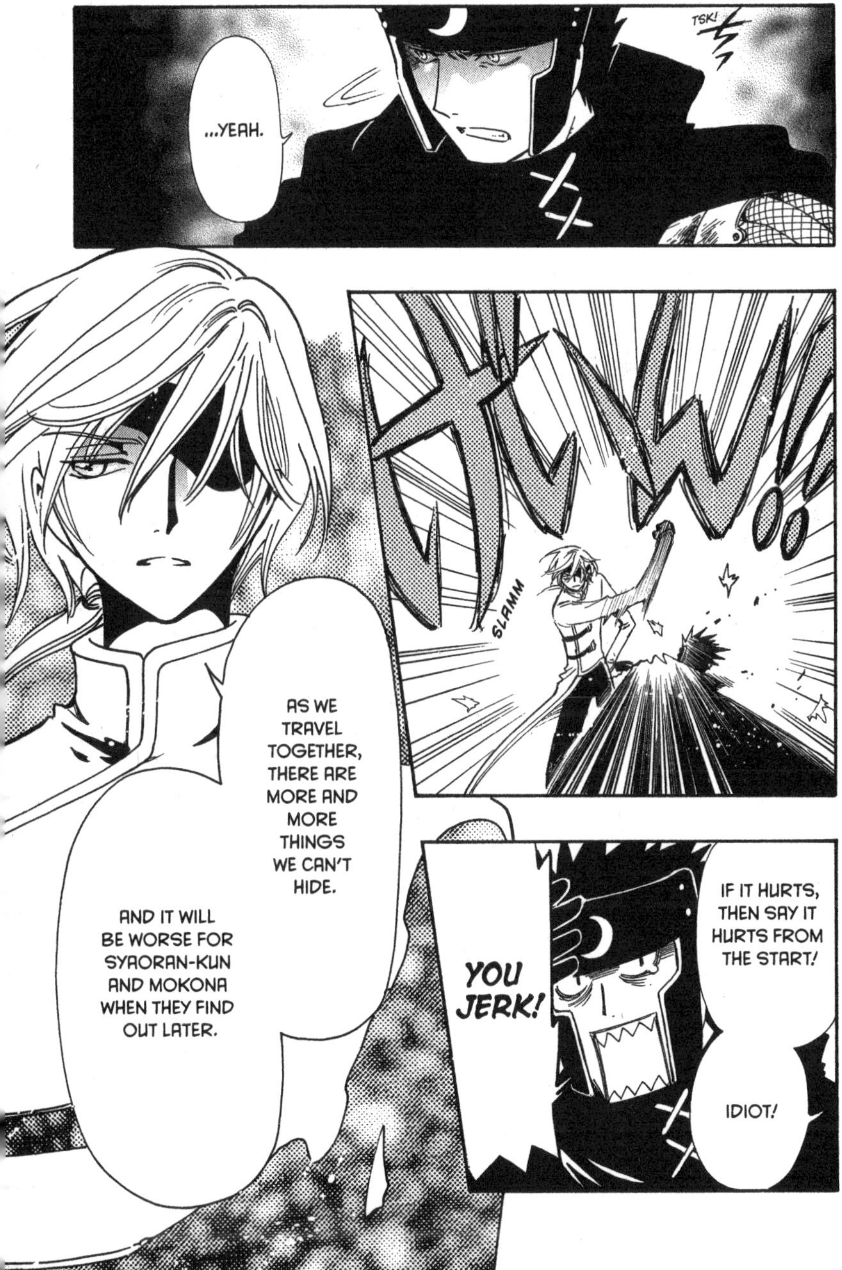
TSK!
...YEAH.
AS WE TRAVEL TOGETHER, THERE ARE MORE AND MORE THINGS WE CAN'T HIDE.
AND IT WILL BE WORSE FOR SYAORAN-KUN AND MOKONA WHEN THEY FIND OUT LATER.
SLAMM
IF IT HURTS, THEN SAY IT HURTS FROM THE START!
YOU JERK!
IDIOT!

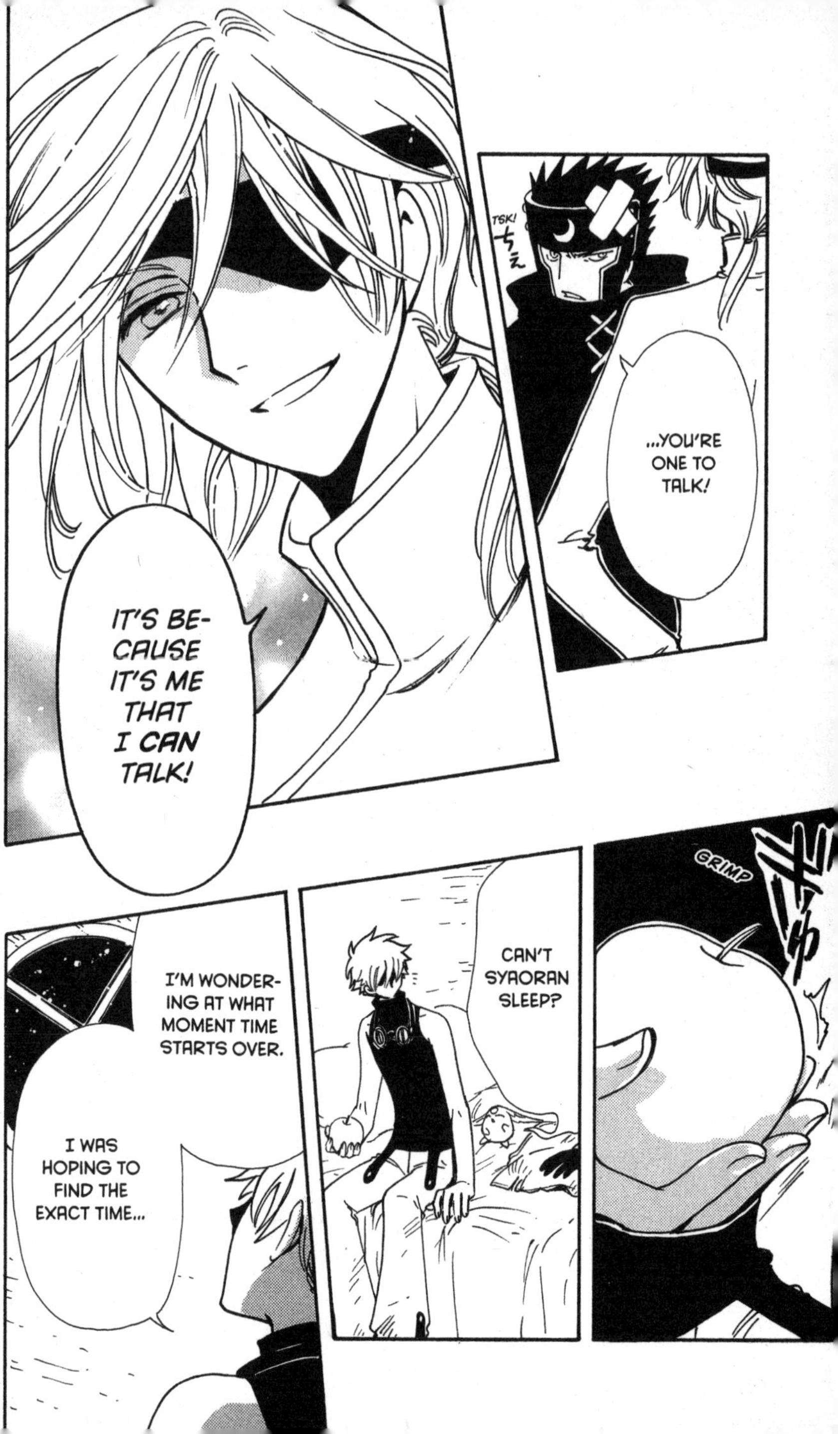
TSK!
...YOU'RE ONE TO TALK!
IT'S BE- CAUSE IT'S ME THAT I CAN TALK!
GRIMP
CAN'T SYAORAN SLEEP?
I'M WONDER- ING AT WHAT MOMENT TIME STARTS OVER.
I WAS HOPING TO FIND THE EXACT TIME...

...WHAT WAS THAT?

MOKONA'S EYES CAN'T STAY OPEN...

ⱅⱅⱅ
PLIP

⊃ロロロ..
ROLLLLL

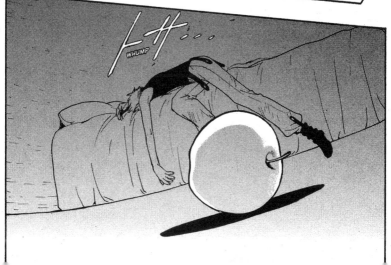

⊦⊦...
WHUMP!

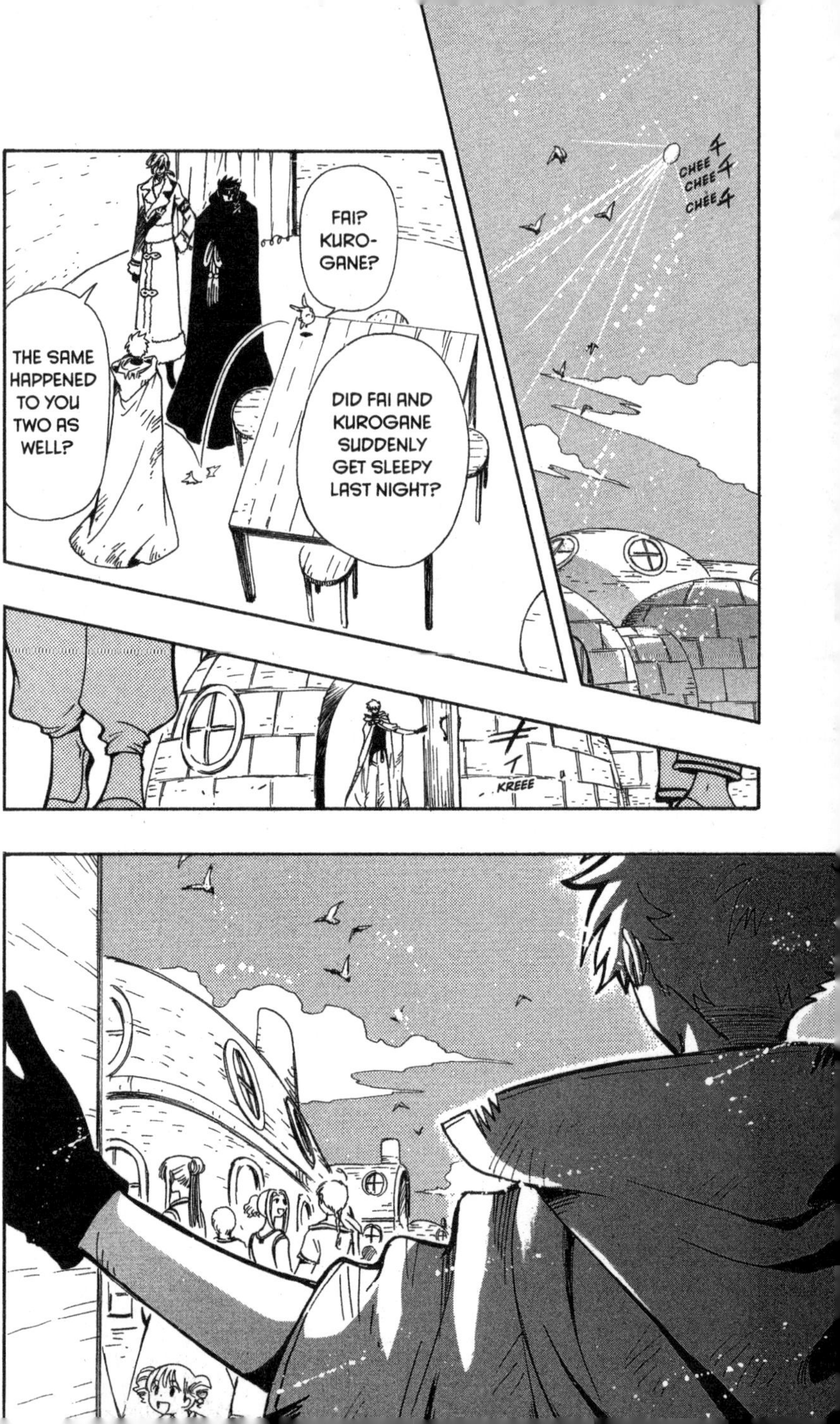
CHEE CHEE CHEE
FAI? KURO-GANE?
DID FAI AND KUROGANE SUDDENLY GET SLEEPY LAST NIGHT?
THE SAME HAPPENED TO YOU TWO AS WELL?
KREEE

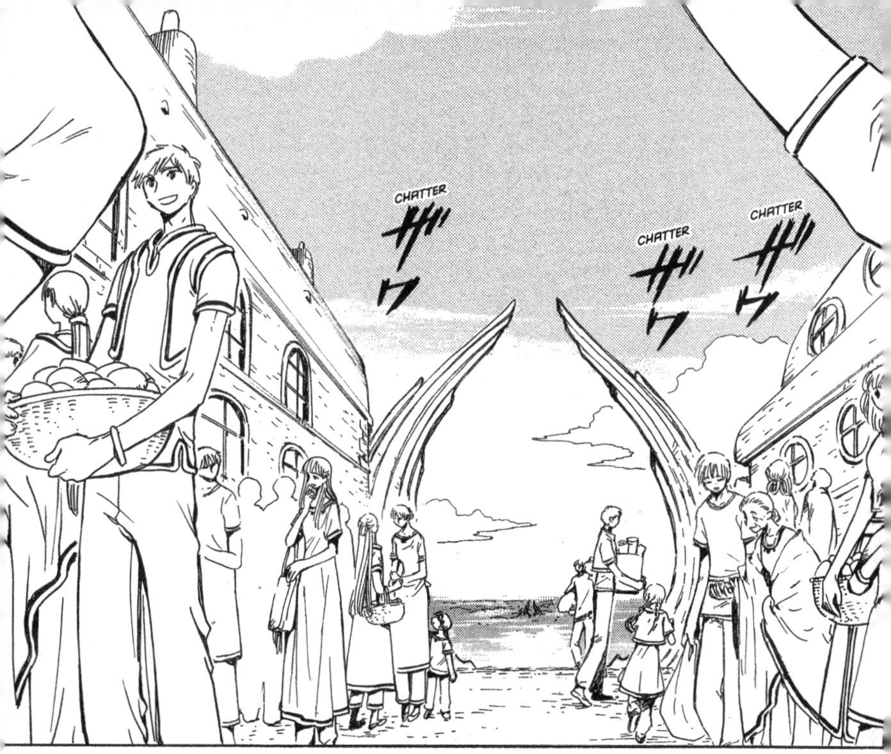
CHATTER
ザワ
CHATTER
ザワ
CHATTER
ザワ

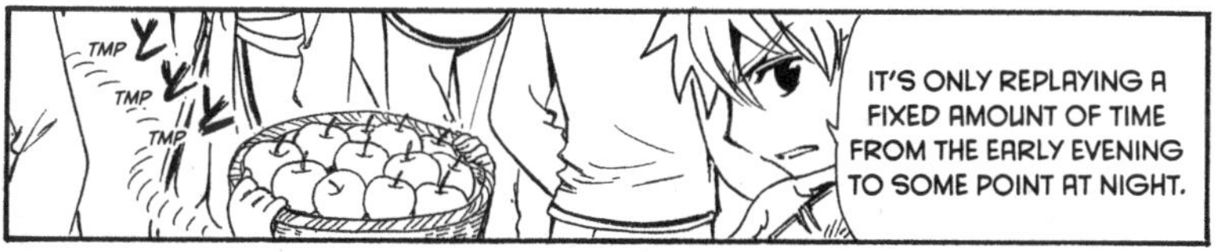
IT'S ONLY REPLAYING A FIXED AMOUNT OF TIME FROM THE EARLY EVENING TO SOME POINT AT NIGHT.
TMP
TMP
TMP

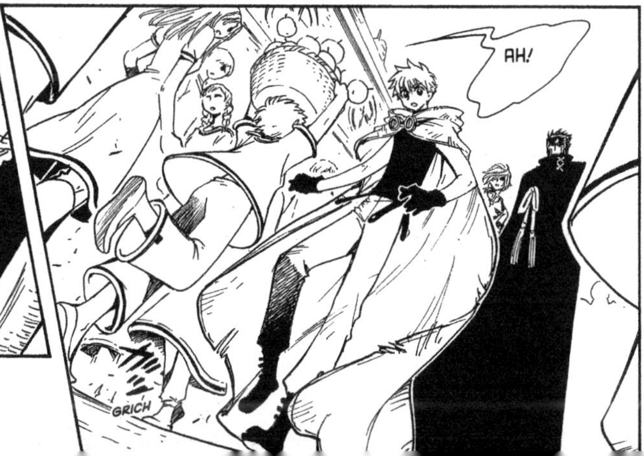
AH!
GRICH

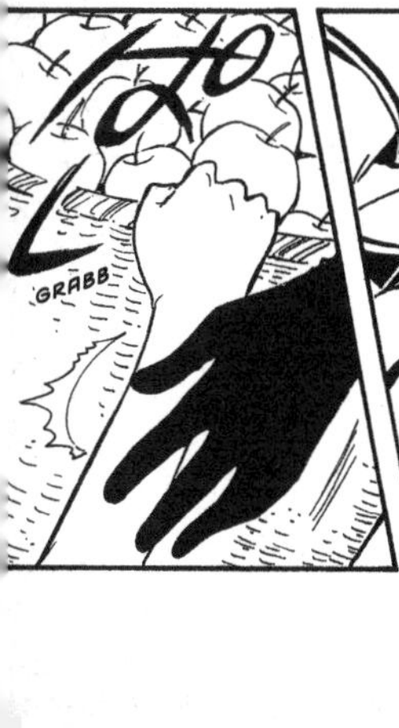
GRABB

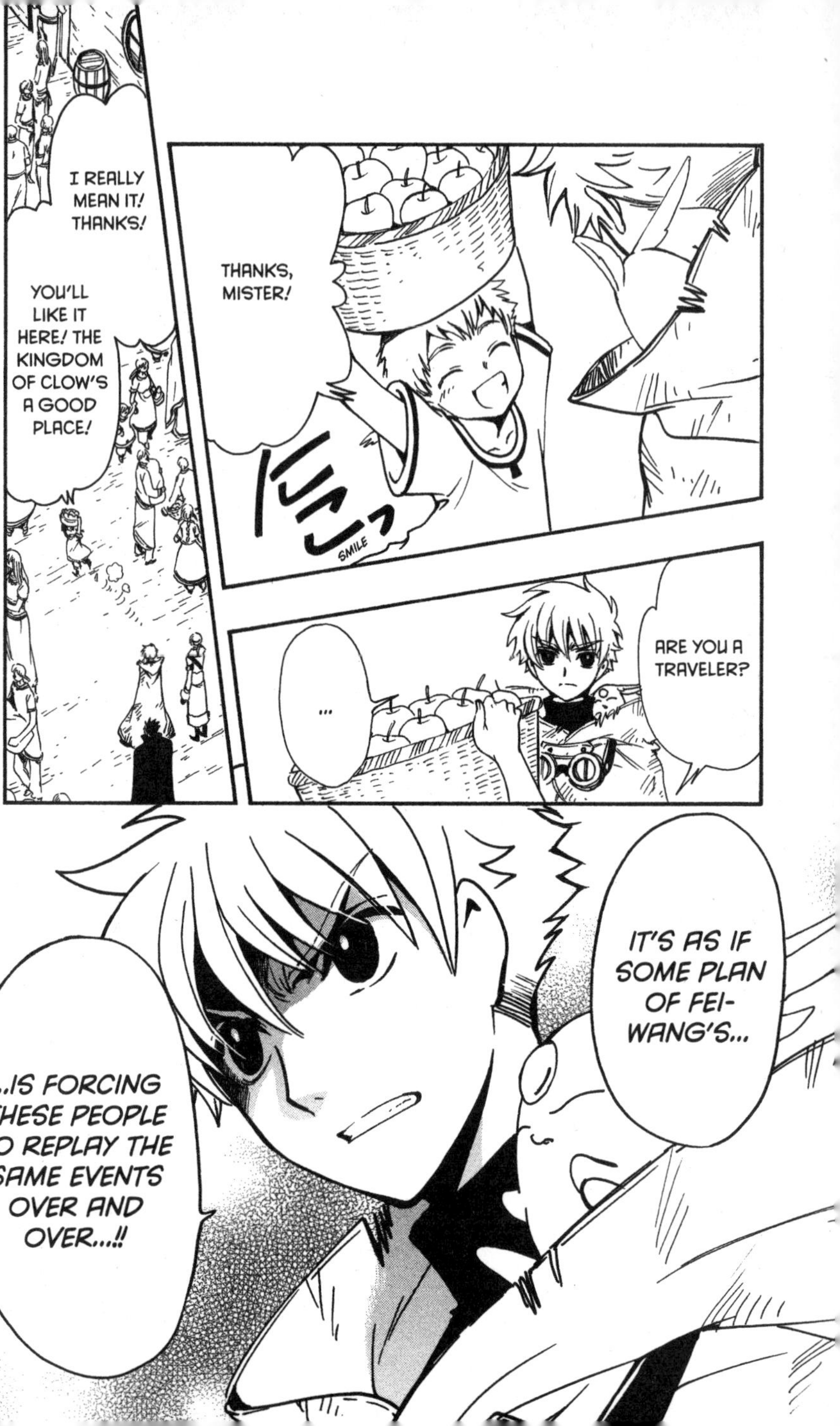
THANKS, MISTER!
SMILE
ARE YOU A TRAVELER?
...
I REALLY MEAN IT! THANKS!
YOU'LL LIKE IT HERE! THE KINGDOM OF CLOW'S A GOOD PLACE!
IT'S AS IF SOME PLAN OF FEI-WANG'S...
...IS FORCING THESE PEOPLE TO REPLAY THE SAME EVENTS OVER AND OVER...!!

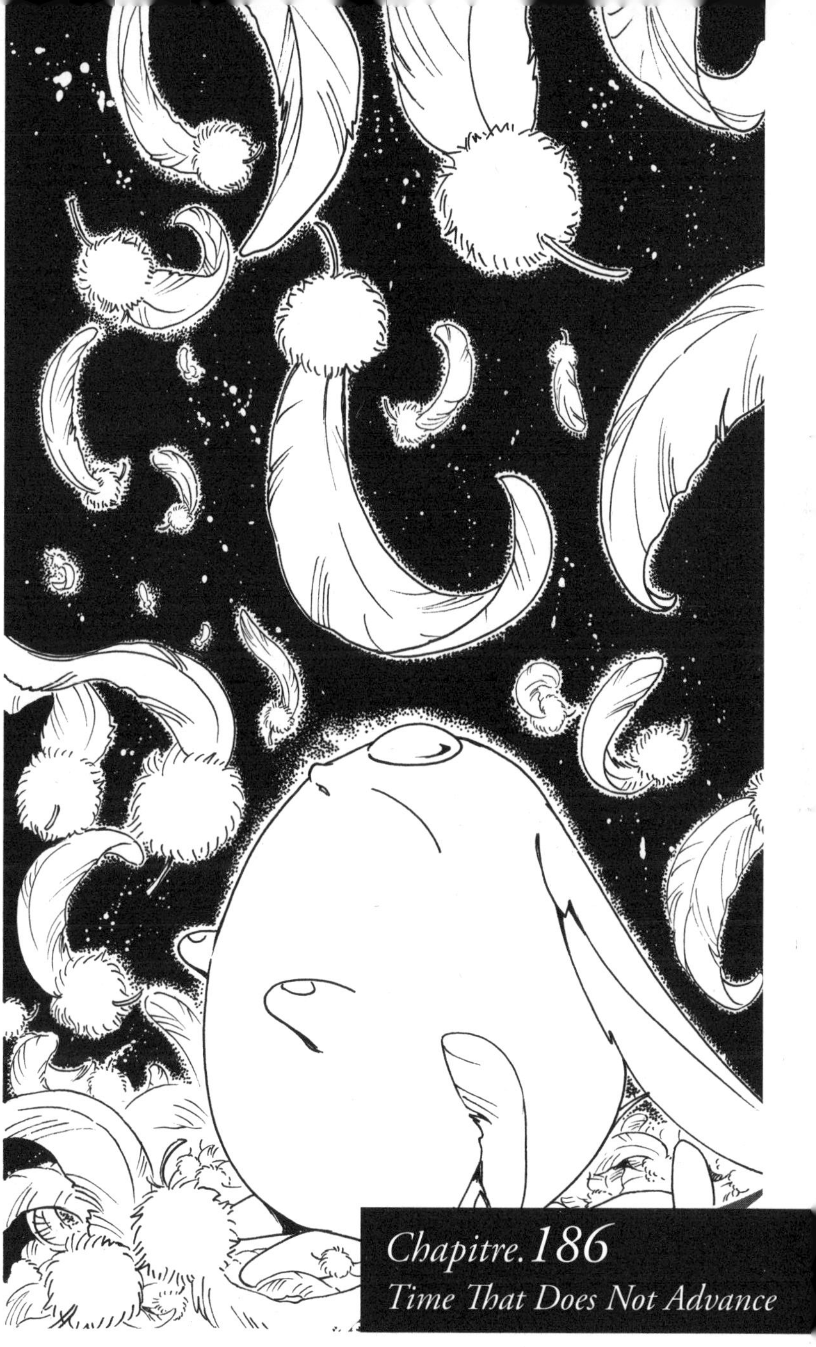

Chapitre. 186
Time That Does Not Advance

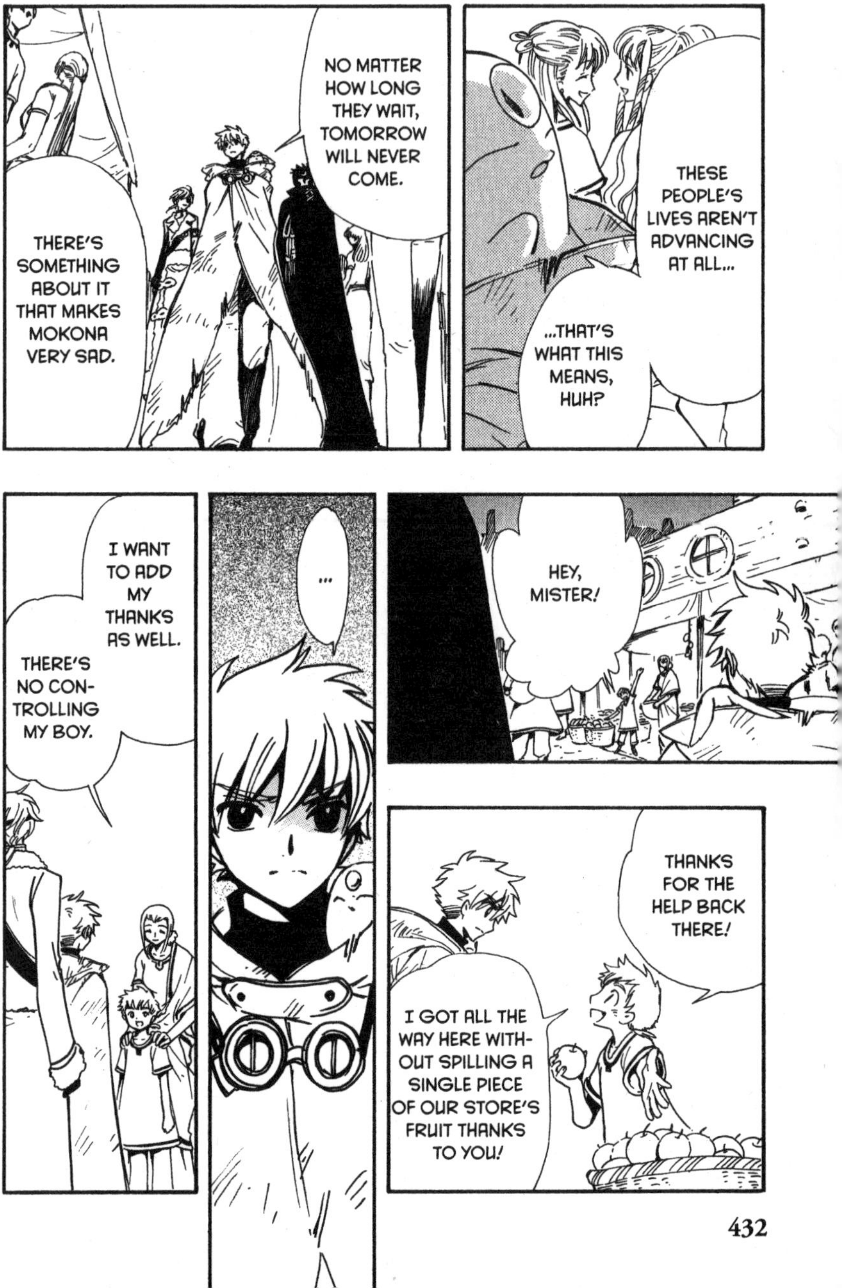
THESE PEOPLE'S LIVES AREN'T ADVANCING AT ALL...
...THAT'S WHAT THIS MEANS, HUH?
NO MATTER HOW LONG THEY WAIT, TOMORROW WILL NEVER COME.
THERE'S SOMETHING ABOUT IT THAT MAKES MOKONA VERY SAD.
HEY, MISTER!
THANKS FOR THE HELP BACK THERE!
I GOT ALL THE WAY HERE WITH-OUT SPILLING A SINGLE PIECE OF OUR STORE'S FRUIT THANKS TO YOU!
...
I WANT TO ADD MY THANKS AS WELL.
THERE'S NO CON-TROLLING MY BOY.

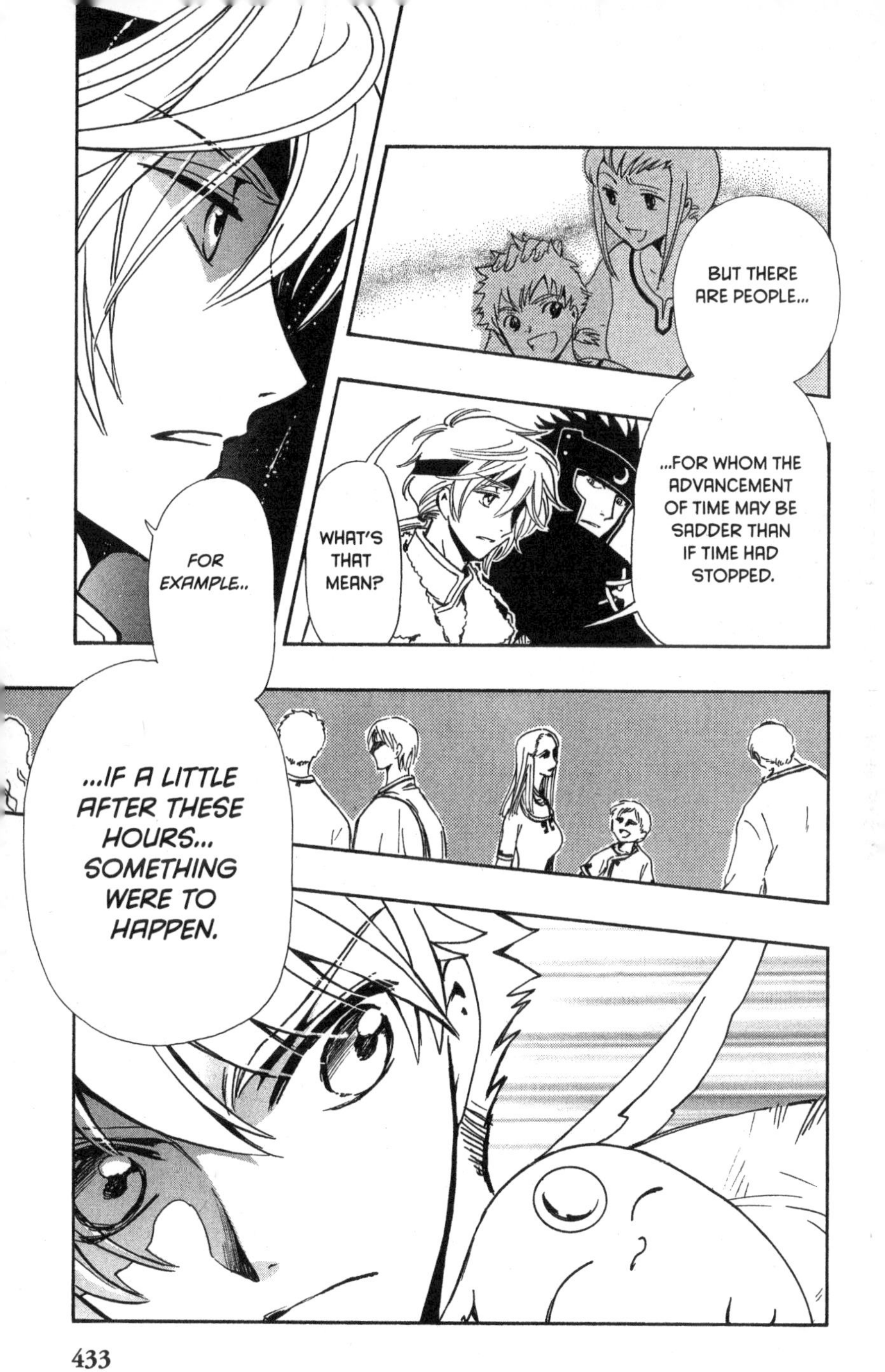
BUT THERE ARE PEOPLE...
...FOR WHOM THE ADVANCEMENT OF TIME MAY BE SADDER THAN IF TIME HAD STOPPED.
WHAT'S THAT MEAN?
FOR EXAMPLE..
...IF A LITTLE AFTER THESE HOURS... SOMETHING WERE TO HAPPEN.

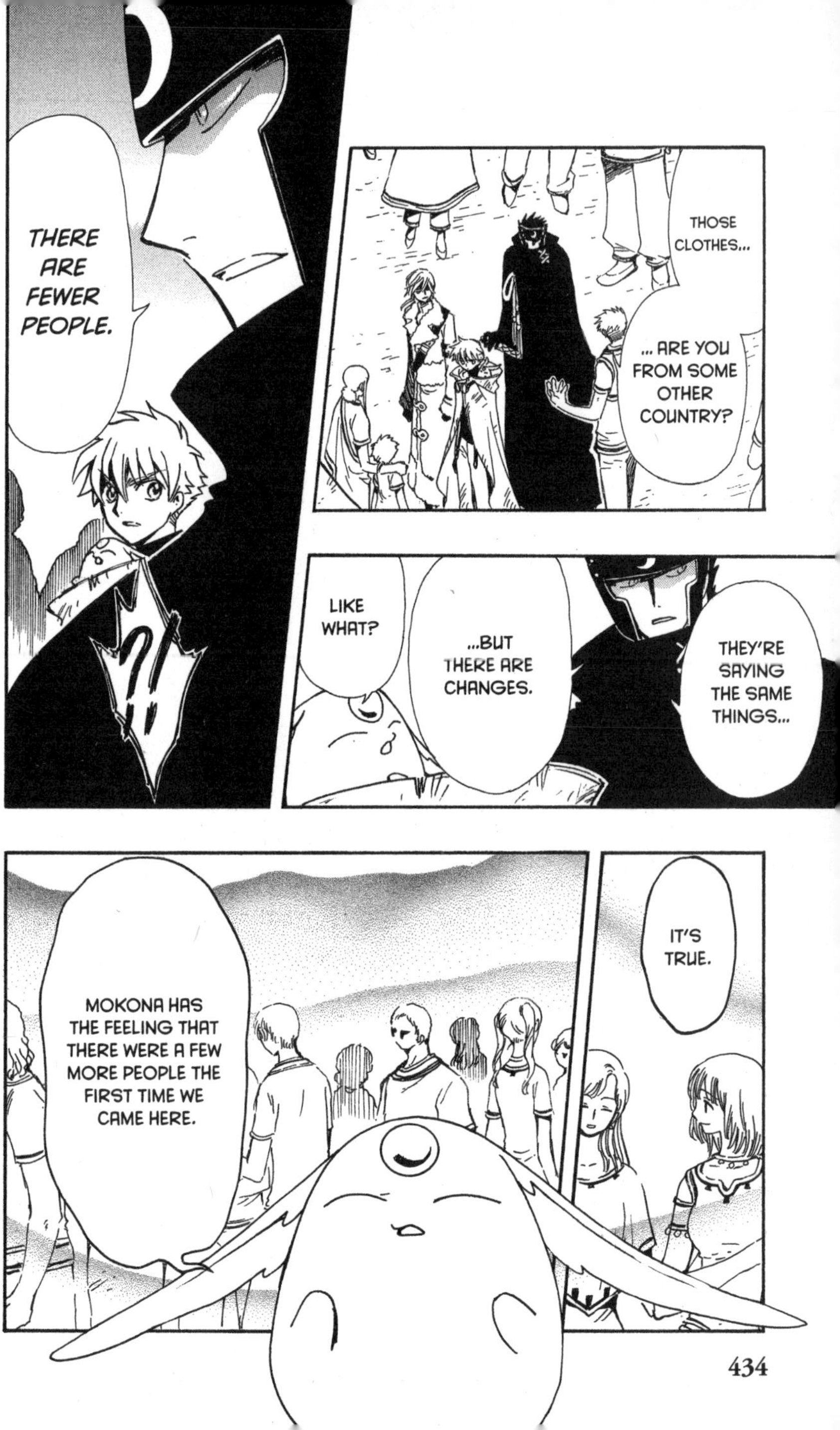
THOSE CLOTHES...
... ARE YOU FROM SOME OTHER COUNTRY?
THEY'RE SAYING THE SAME THINGS...
...BUT THERE ARE CHANGES.
LIKE WHAT?
THERE ARE FEWER PEOPLE.
?!
IT'S TRUE.
MOKONA HAS THE FEELING THAT THERE WERE A FEW MORE PEOPLE THE FIRST TIME WE CAME HERE.

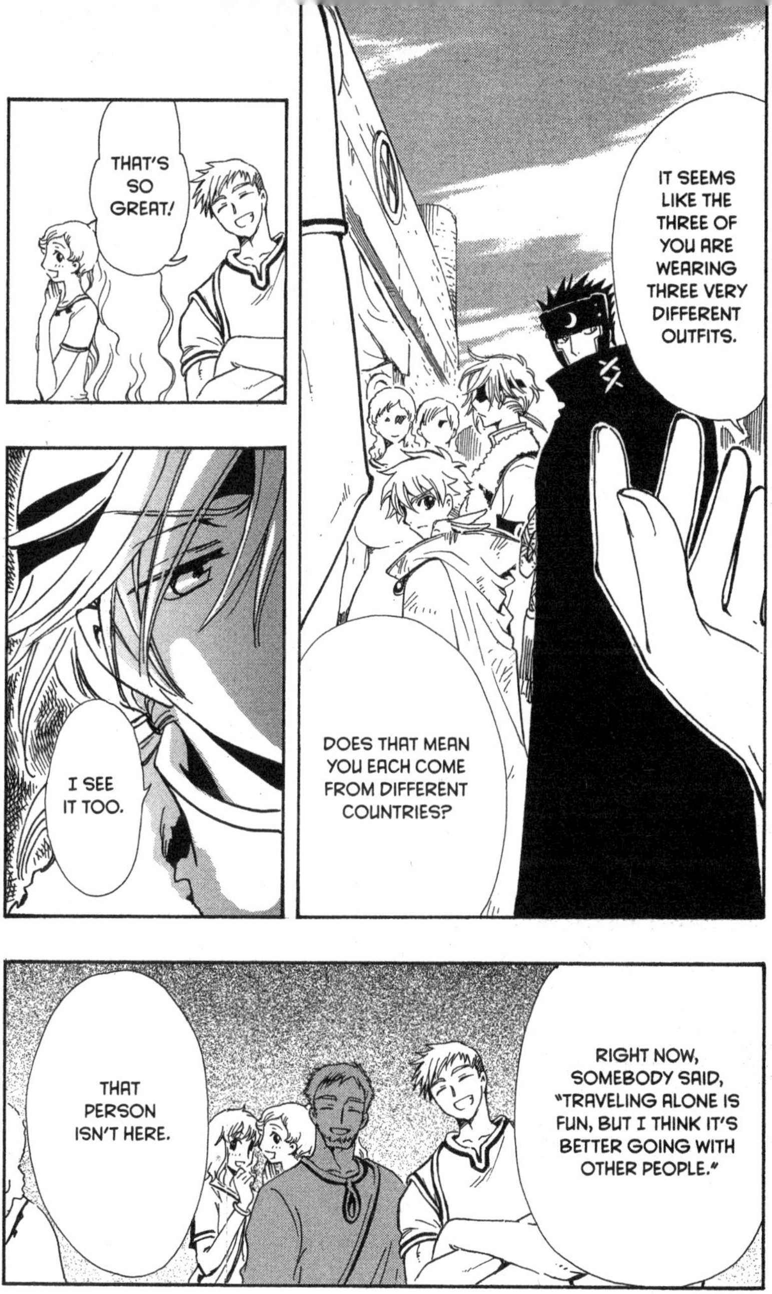
IT SEEMS LIKE THE THREE OF YOU ARE WEARING THREE VERY DIFFERENT OUTFITS.
DOES THAT MEAN YOU EACH COME FROM DIFFERENT COUNTRIES?
THAT'S SO GREAT!
I SEE IT TOO.
RIGHT NOW, SOMEBODY SAID, "TRAVELING ALONE IS FUN, BUT I THINK IT'S BETTER GOING WITH OTHER PEOPLE."
THAT PERSON ISN'T HERE.

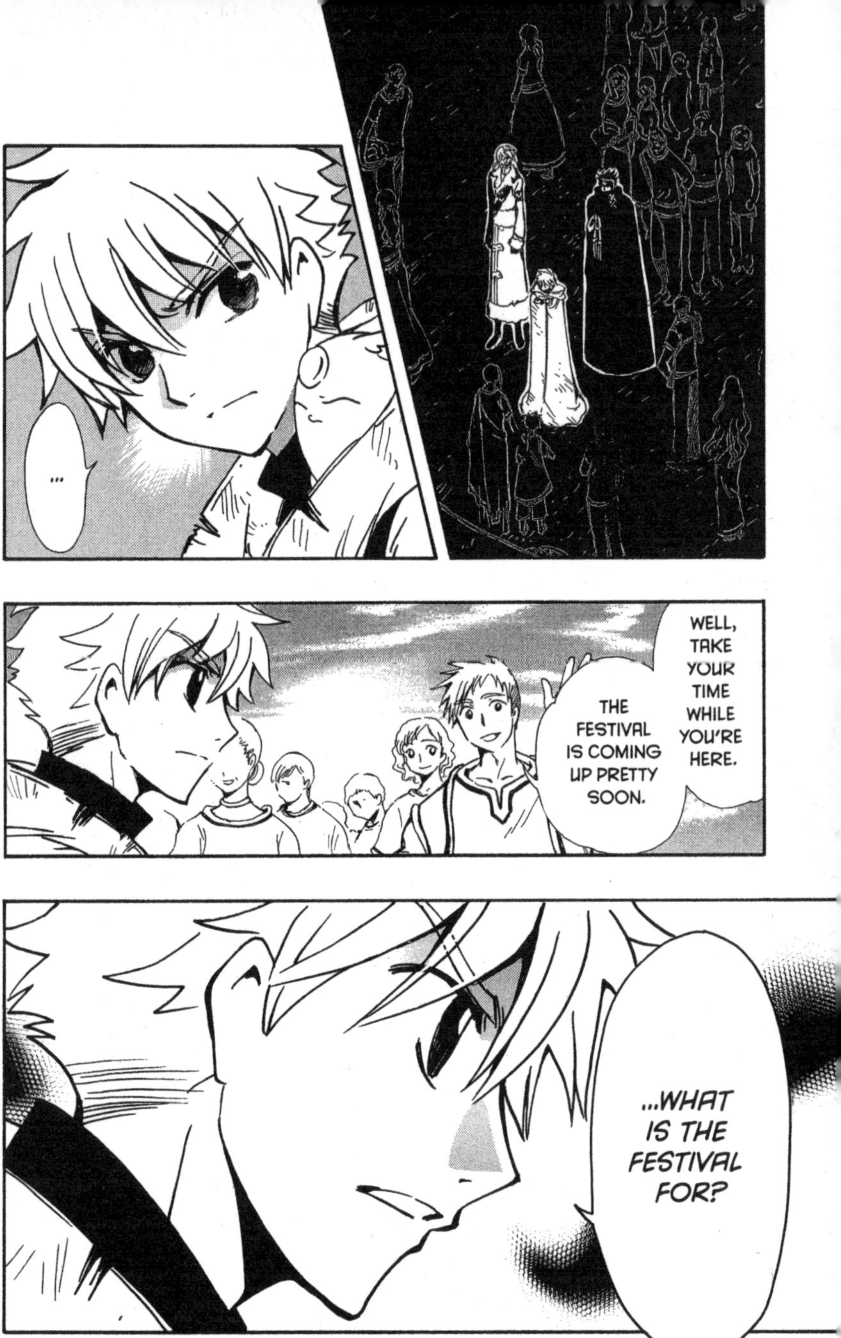
...
WELL, TAKE YOUR TIME WHILE YOU'RE HERE.
THE FESTIVAL IS COMING UP PRETTY SOON.
...WHAT IS THE FESTIVAL FOR?

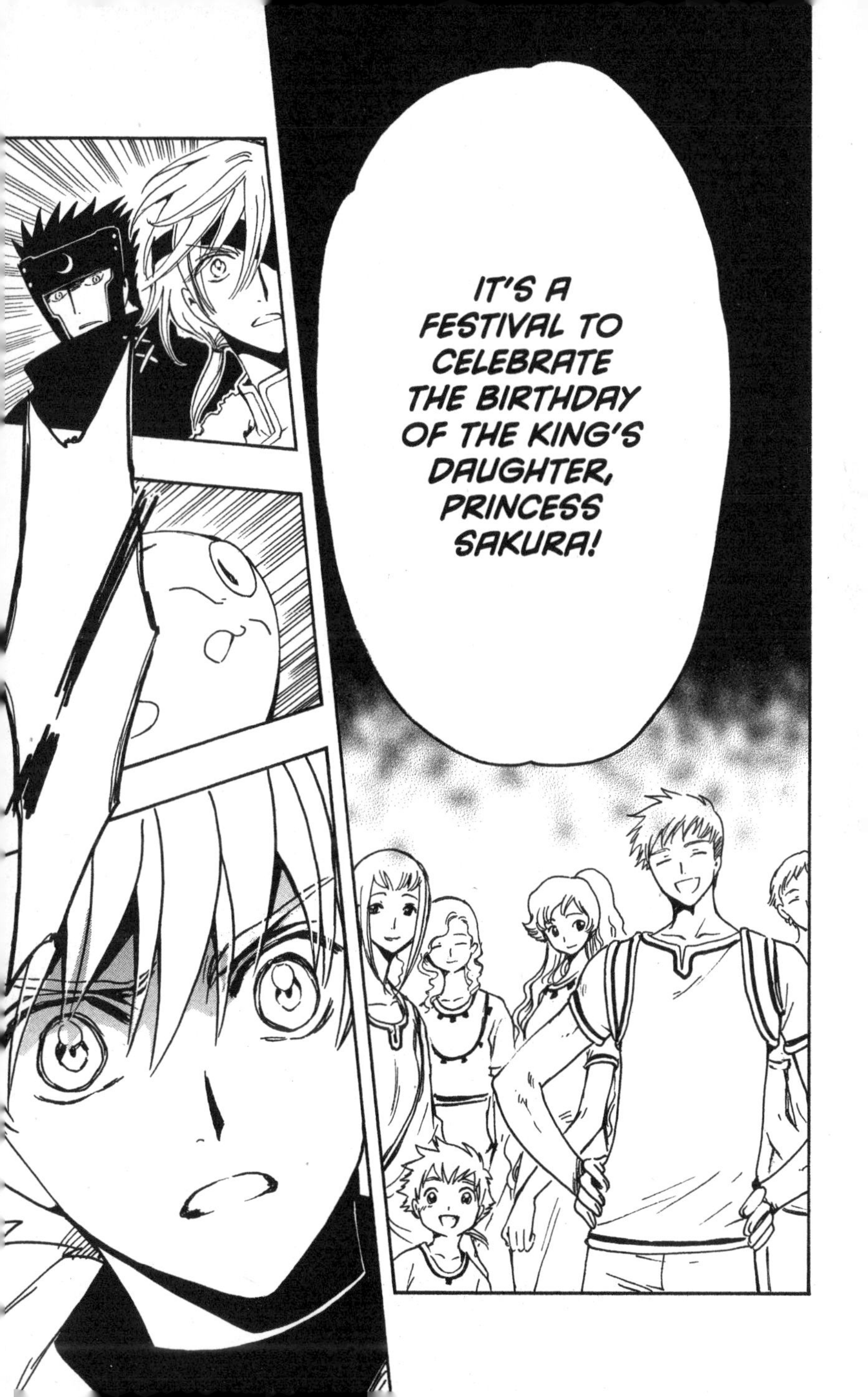
IT'S A FESTIVAL TO CELEBRATE THE BIRTHDAY OF THE KING'S DAUGHTER, PRINCESS SAKURA!

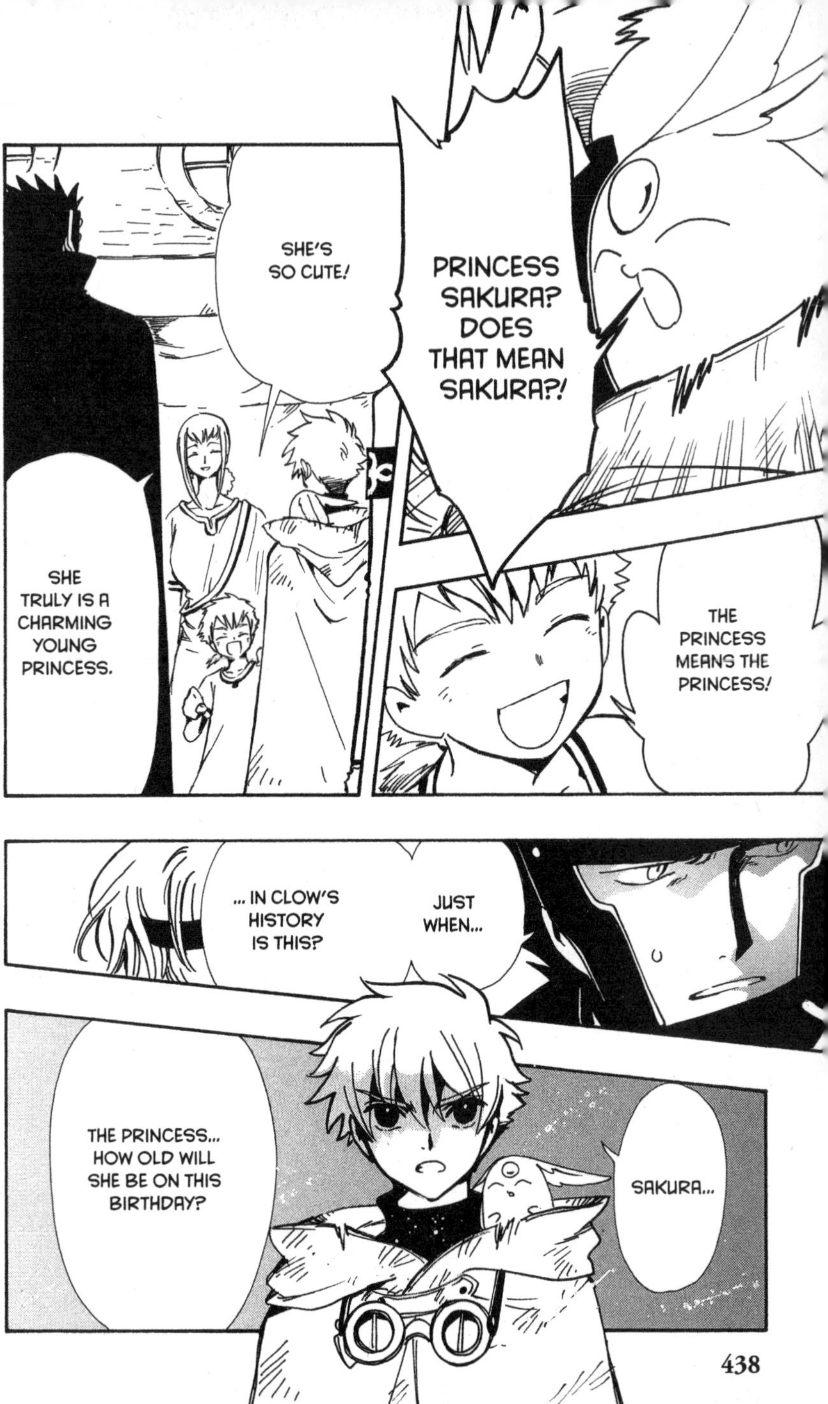
PRINCESS SAKURA? DOES THAT MEAN SAKURA?!
THE PRINCESS MEANS THE PRINCESS!
SHE'S SO CUTE!
SHE TRULY IS A CHARMING YOUNG PRINCESS.
JUST WHEN...
... IN CLOW'S HISTORY IS THIS?
SAKURA...
THE PRINCESS... HOW OLD WILL SHE BE ON THIS BIRTHDAY?

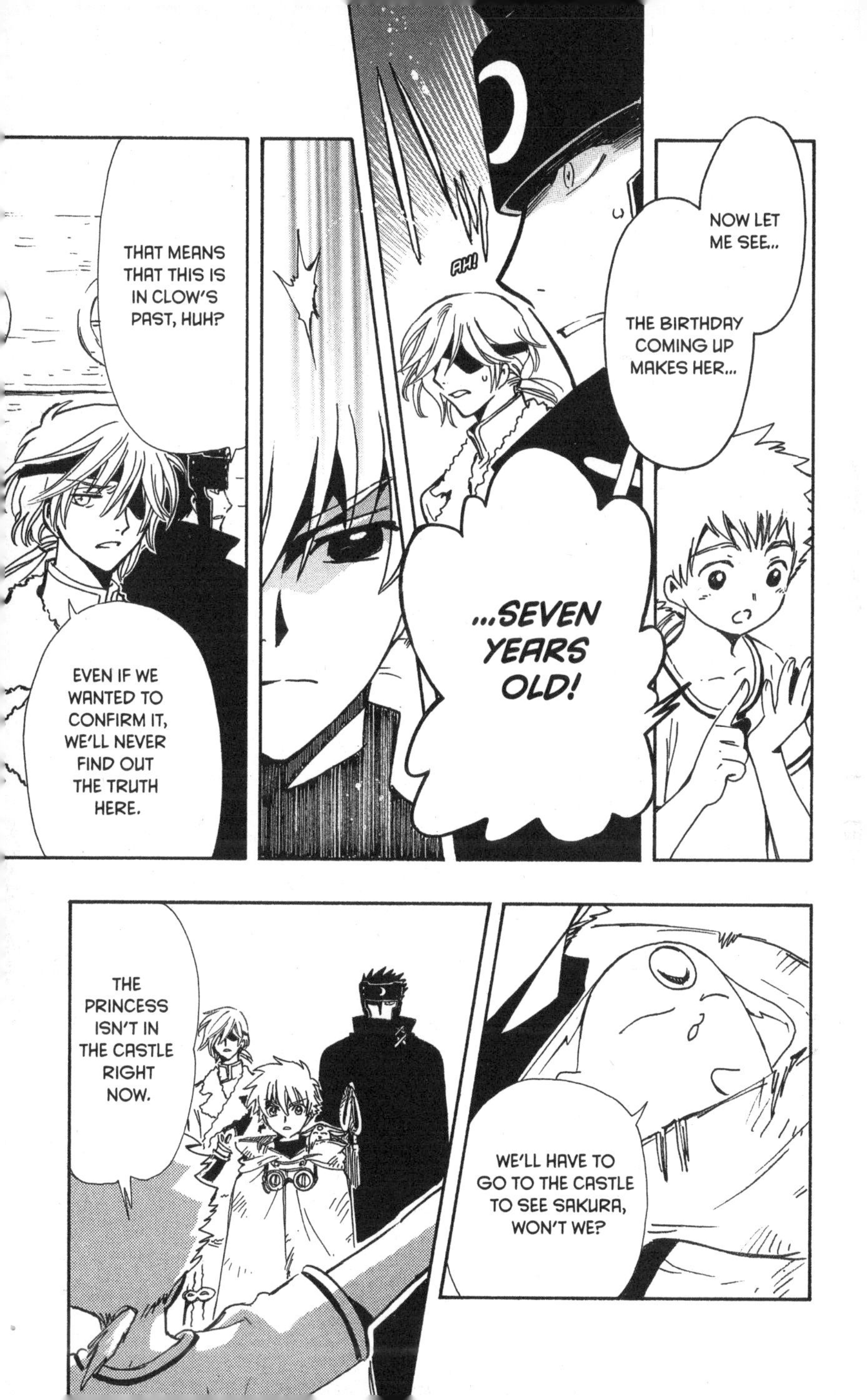
NOW LET ME SEE...
THE BIRTHDAY COMING UP MAKES HER...
AH!
...SEVEN YEARS OLD!
THAT MEANS THAT THIS IS IN CLOW'S PAST, HUH?
EVEN IF WE WANTED TO CONFIRM IT, WE'LL NEVER FIND OUT THE TRUTH HERE.
WE'LL HAVE TO GO TO THE CASTLE TO SEE SAKURA, WON'T WE?
THE PRINCESS ISN'T IN THE CASTLE RIGHT NOW.

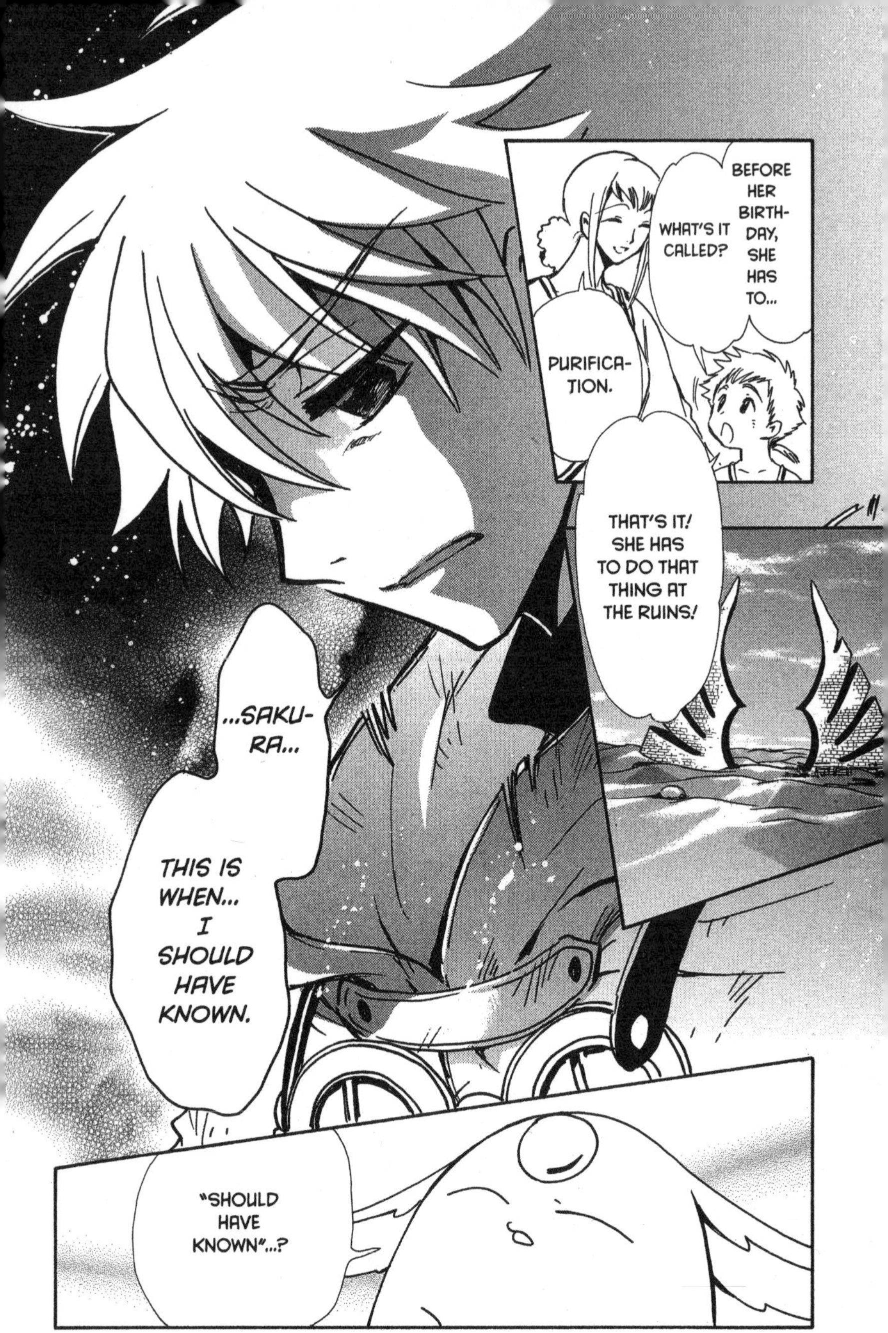
BEFORE HER BIRTH-DAY, SHE HAS TO...
WHAT'S IT CALLED?
PURIFICA-TION.
THAT'S IT! SHE HAS TO DO THAT THING AT THE RUINS!
...SAKU-RA...
THIS IS WHEN... I SHOULD HAVE KNOWN.
"SHOULD HAVE KNOWN"...?

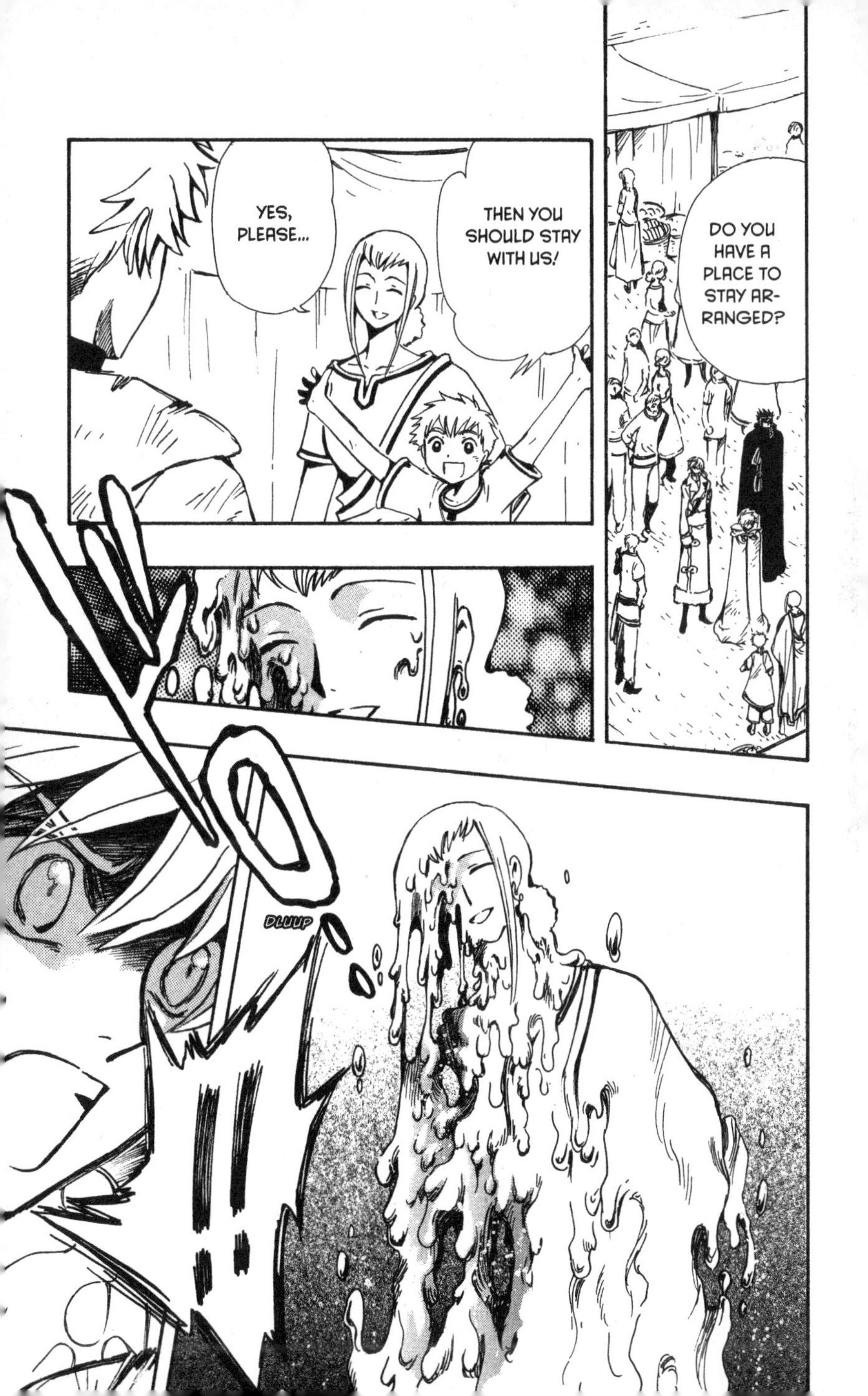
DO YOU HAVE A PLACE TO STAY AR-RANGED?
THEN YOU SHOULD STAY WITH US!
YES, PLEASE...
DLUUP

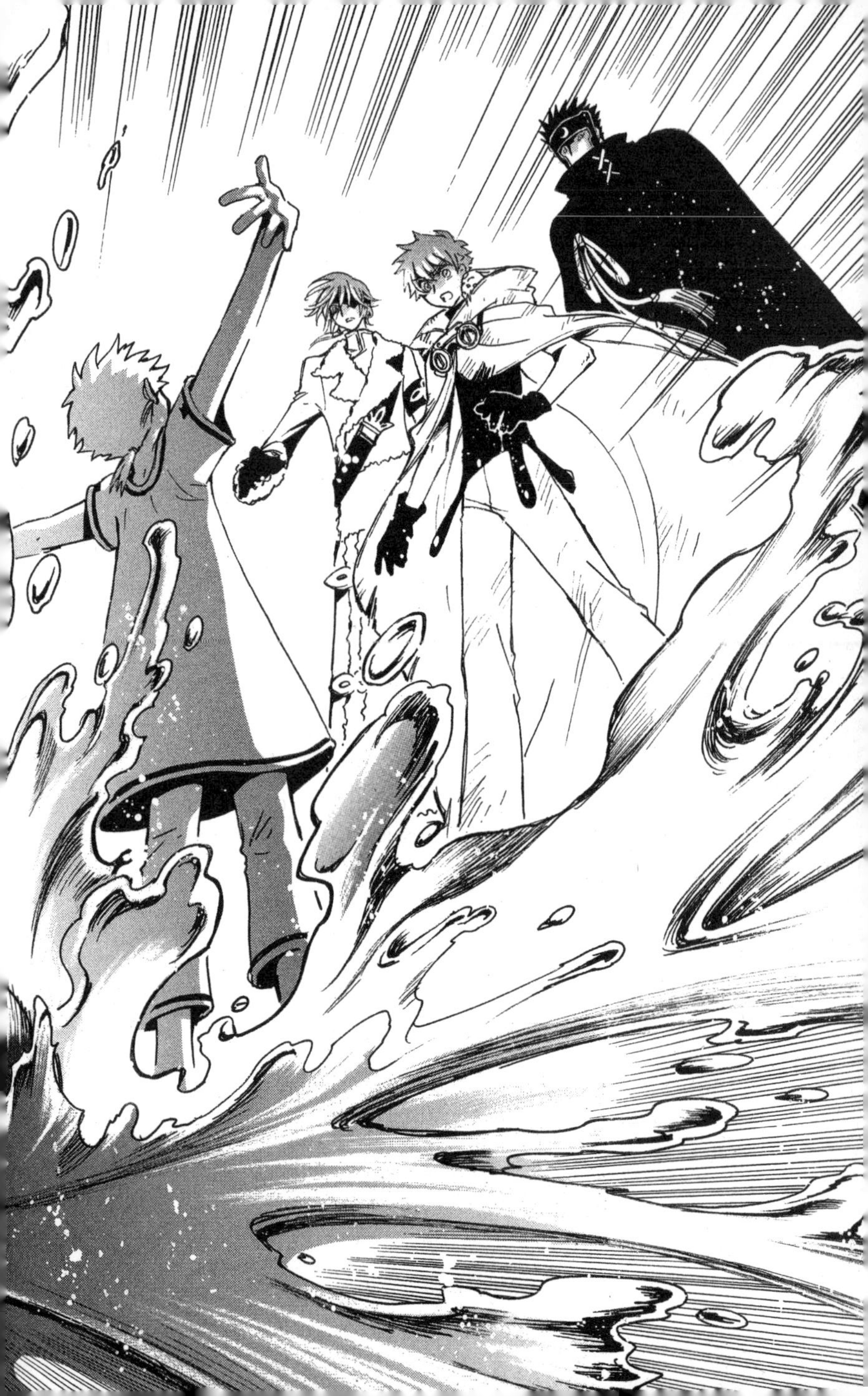

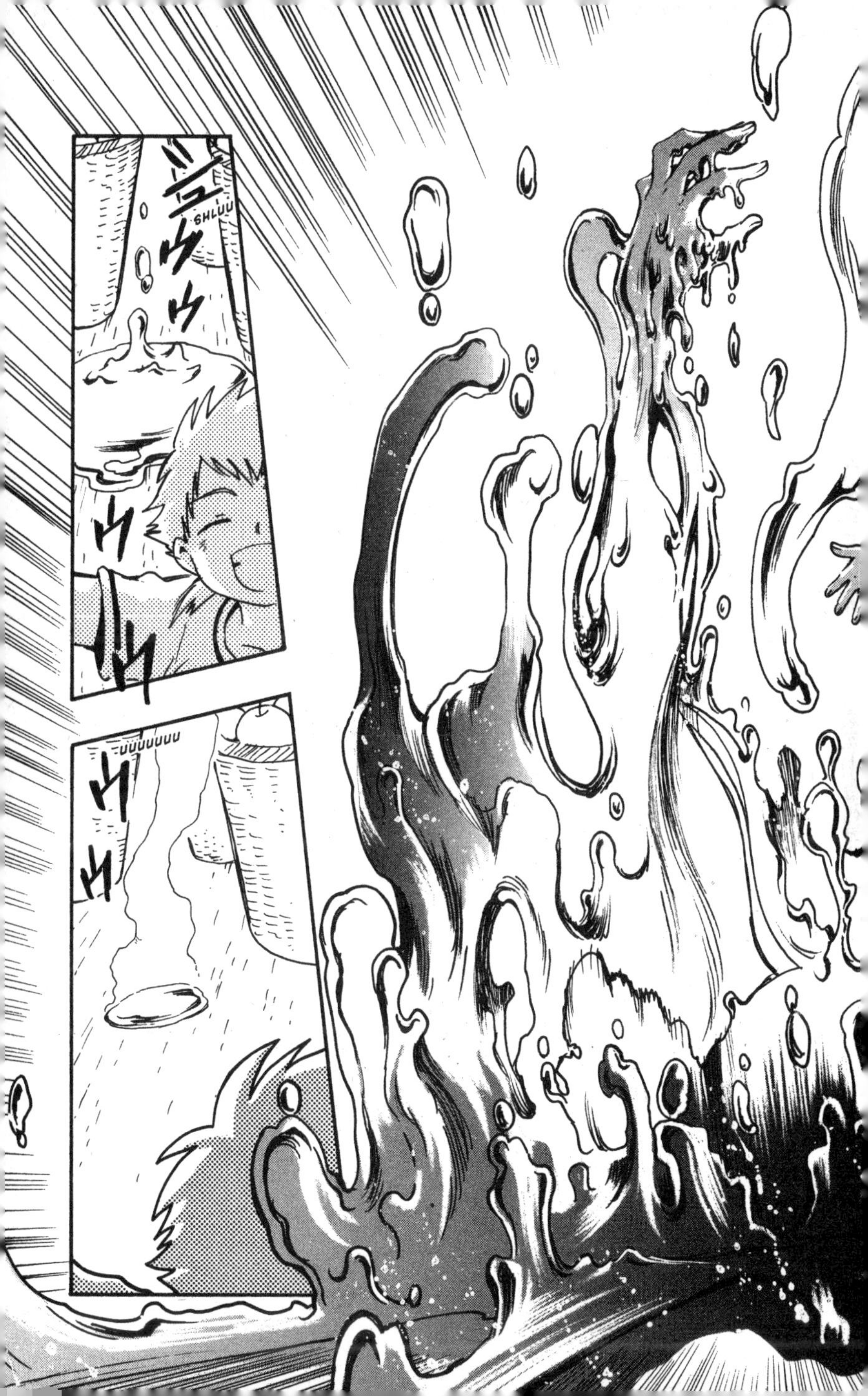
SHLUU
UUUUUUUU

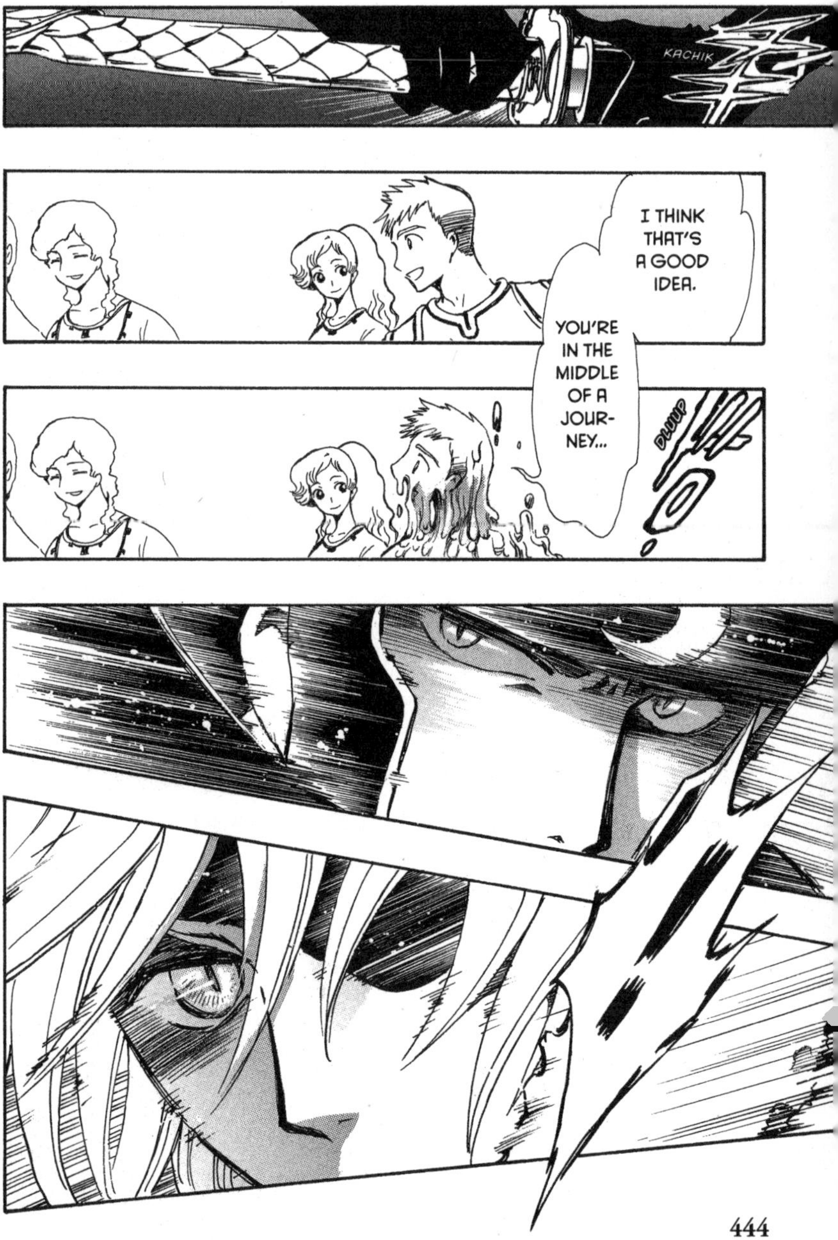
KACHIK
I THINK THAT'S A GOOD IDEA.
YOU'RE IN THE MIDDLE OF A JOURNEY...
DUUUP

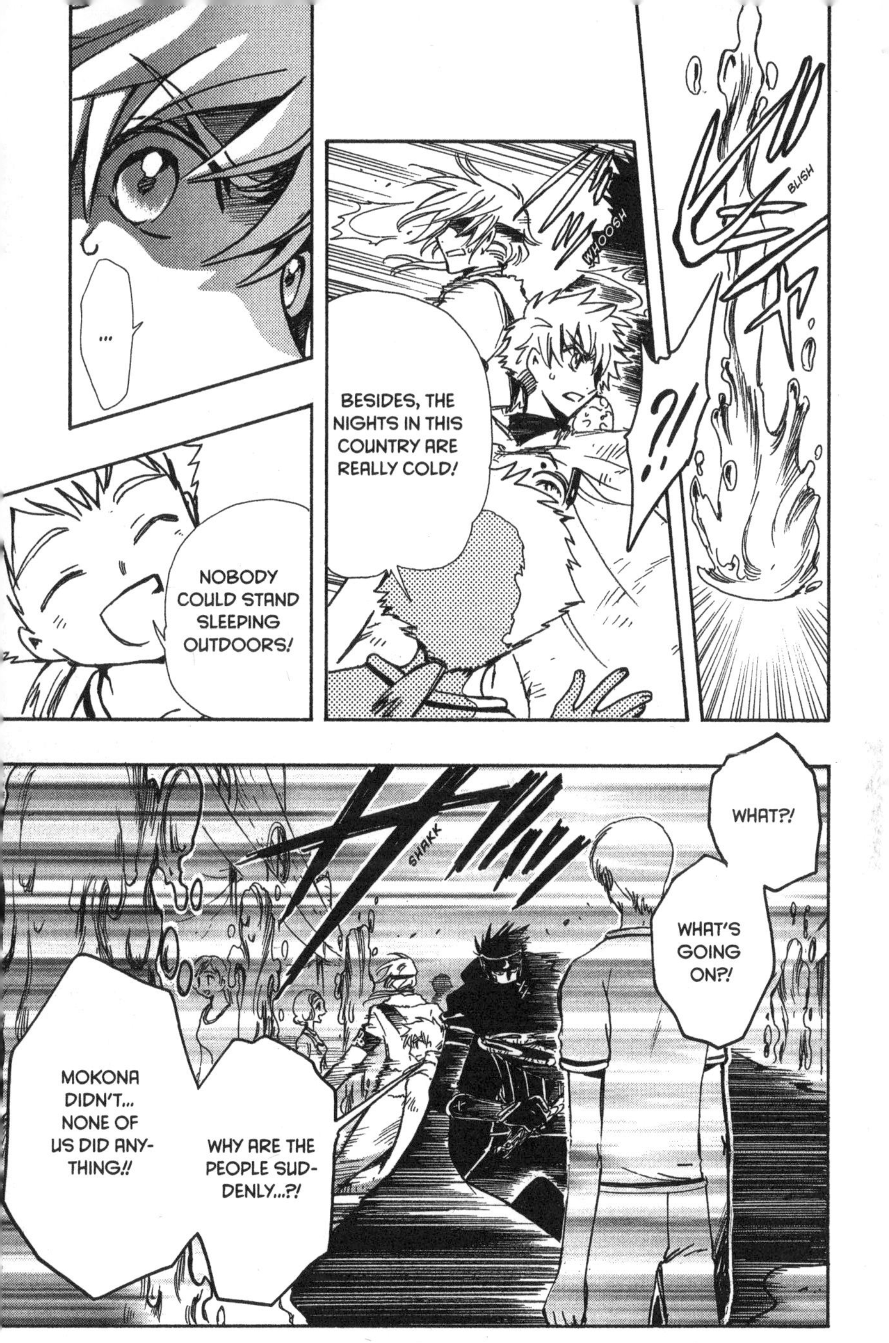
...
NOBODY COULD STAND SLEEPING OUTDOORS!
BESIDES, THE NIGHTS IN THIS COUNTRY ARE REALLY COLD!
WHOOSH
BUSH
?!
MOKONA DIDN'T... NONE OF US DID ANY-THING!!
WHY ARE THE PEOPLE SUD-DENLY...?!
SHAKK
WHAT?!
WHAT'S GOING ON?!

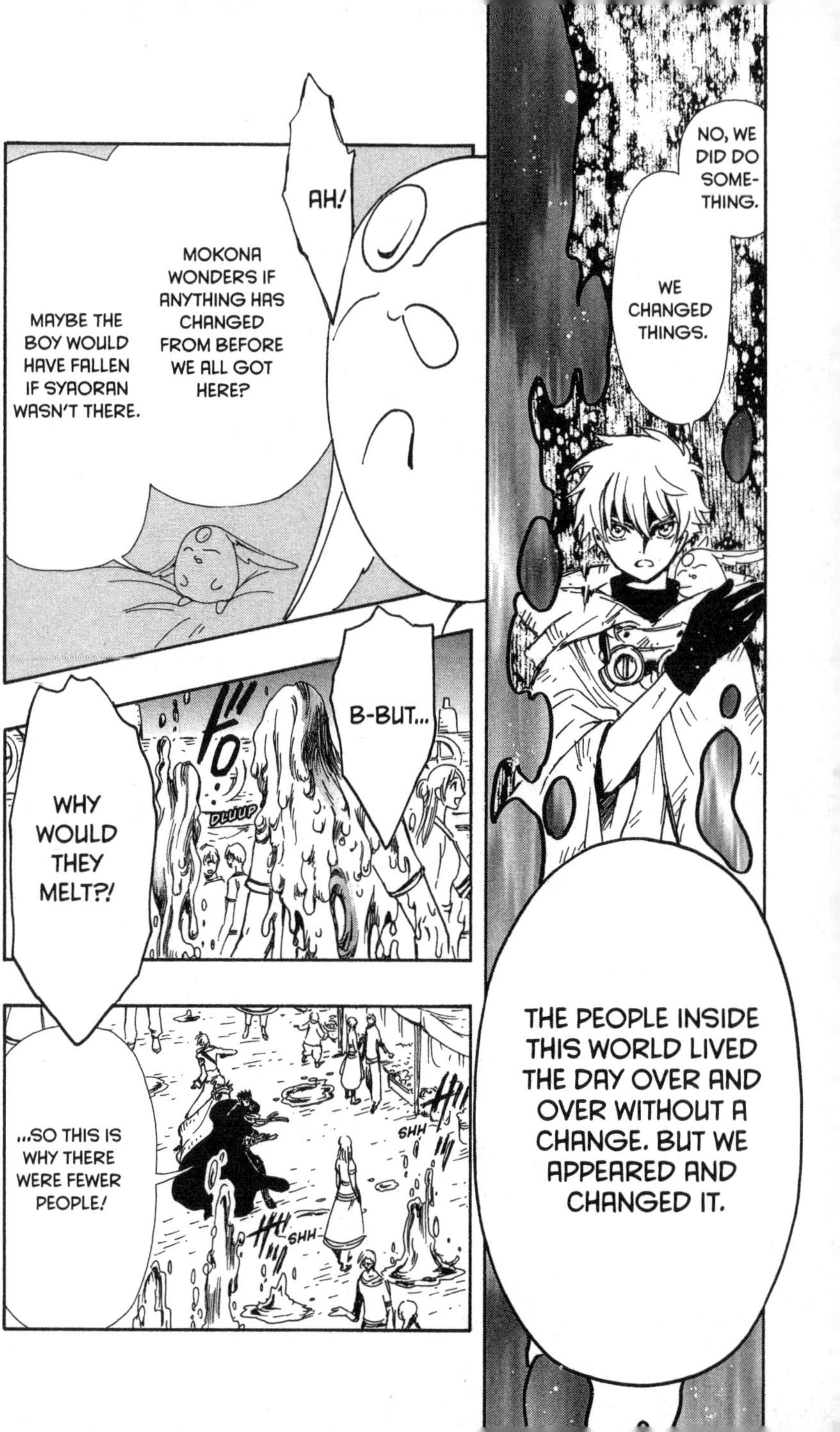
AH!
MOKONA WONDERS IF ANYTHING HAS CHANGED FROM BEFORE WE ALL GOT HERE?
MAYBE THE BOY WOULD HAVE FALLEN IF SYAORAN WASN'T THERE.
B-BUT...
DLUUP
WHY WOULD THEY MELT?!
SHH
SHH
...SO THIS IS WHY THERE WERE FEWER PEOPLE!
NO, WE DID DO SOMETHING.
WE CHANGED THINGS.
THE PEOPLE INSIDE THIS WORLD LIVED THE DAY OVER AND OVER WITHOUT A CHANGE. BUT WE APPEARED AND CHANGED IT.

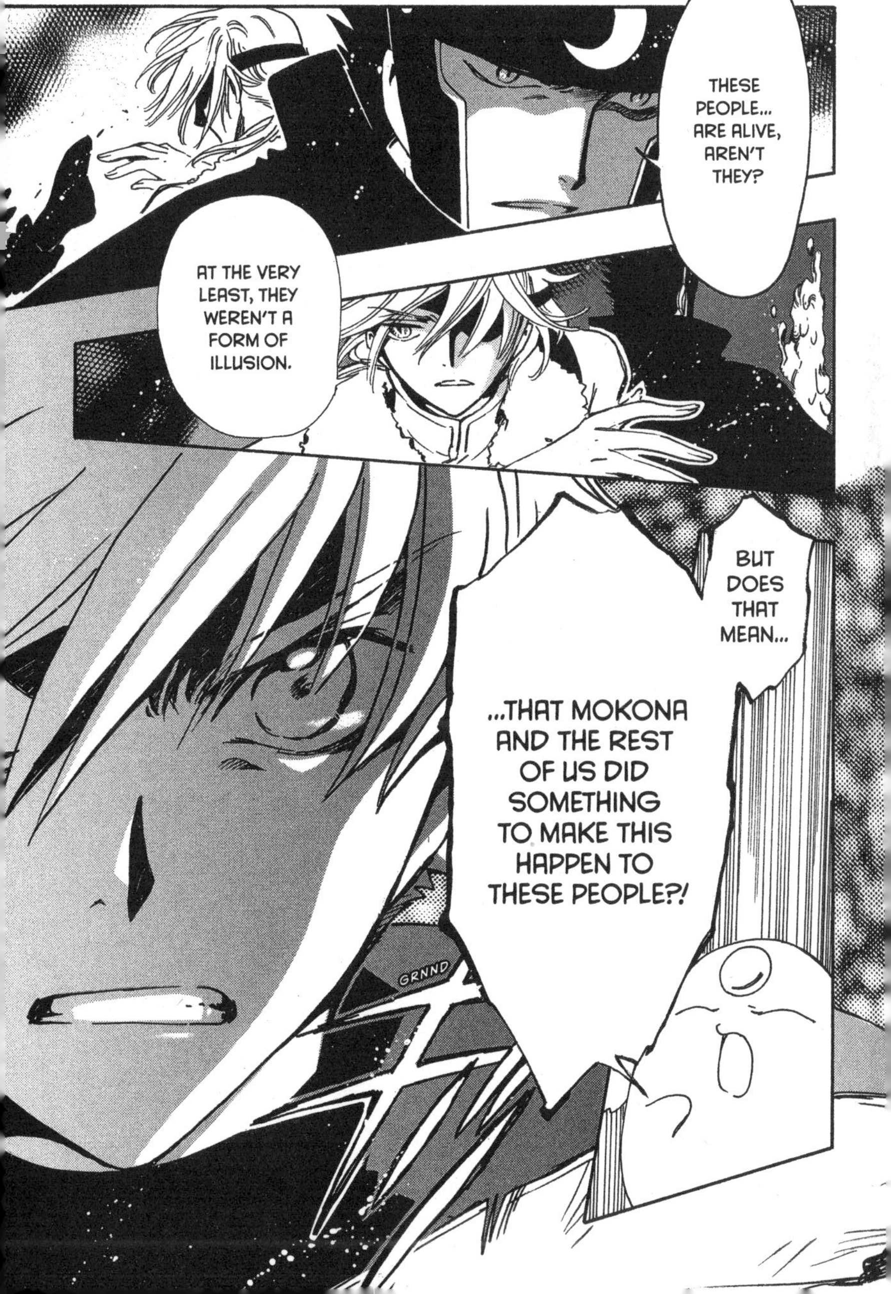
THESE PEOPLE... ARE ALIVE, AREN'T THEY?
AT THE VERY LEAST, THEY WEREN'T A FORM OF ILLUSION.
BUT DOES THAT MEAN...
...THAT MOKONA AND THE REST OF US DID SOMETHING TO MAKE THIS HAPPEN TO THESE PEOPLE?!
GRNND

RESERVoir CHRoNiCLE

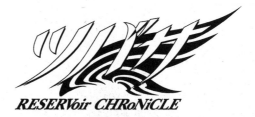

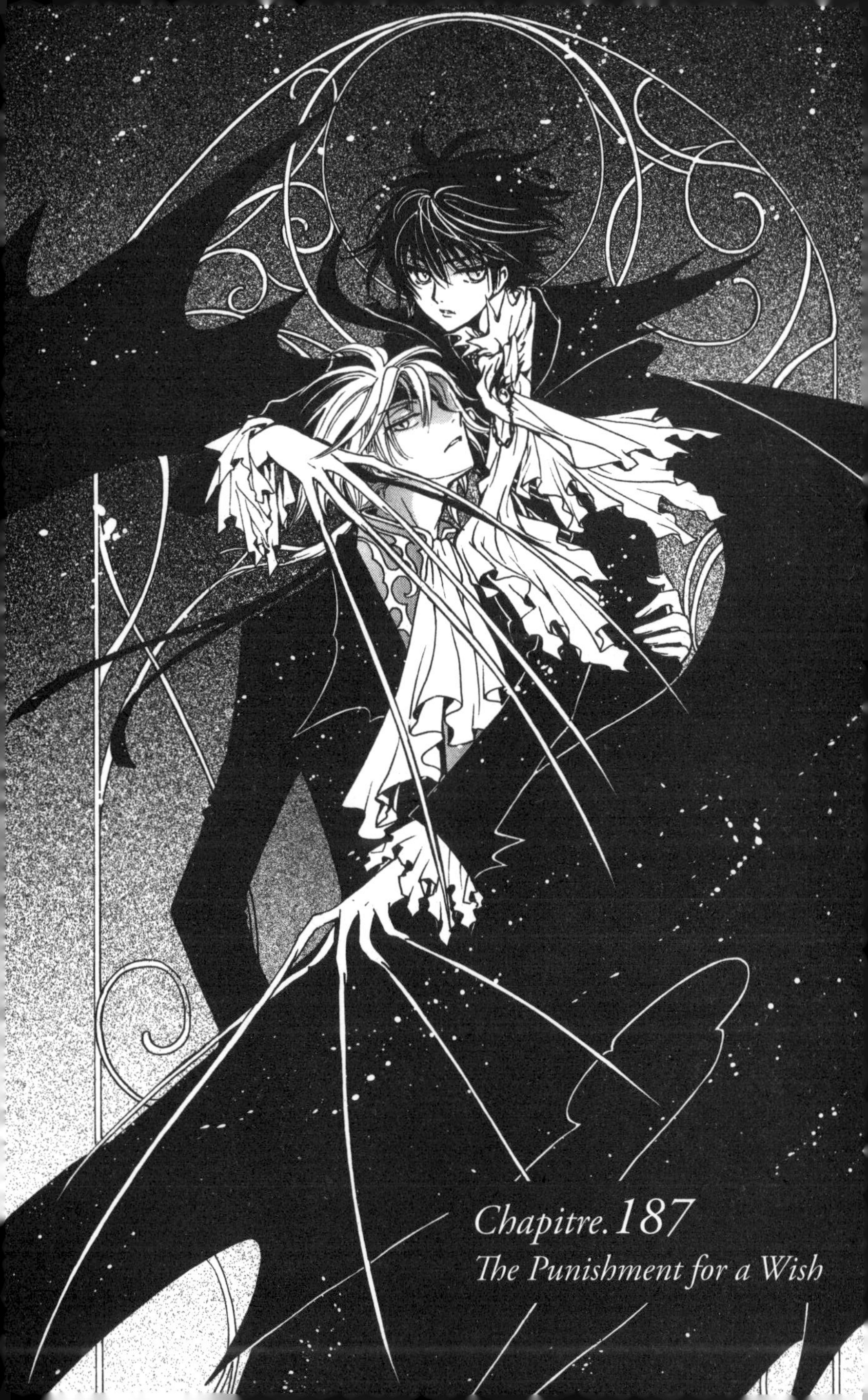
Chapitre.187
The Punishment for a Wish

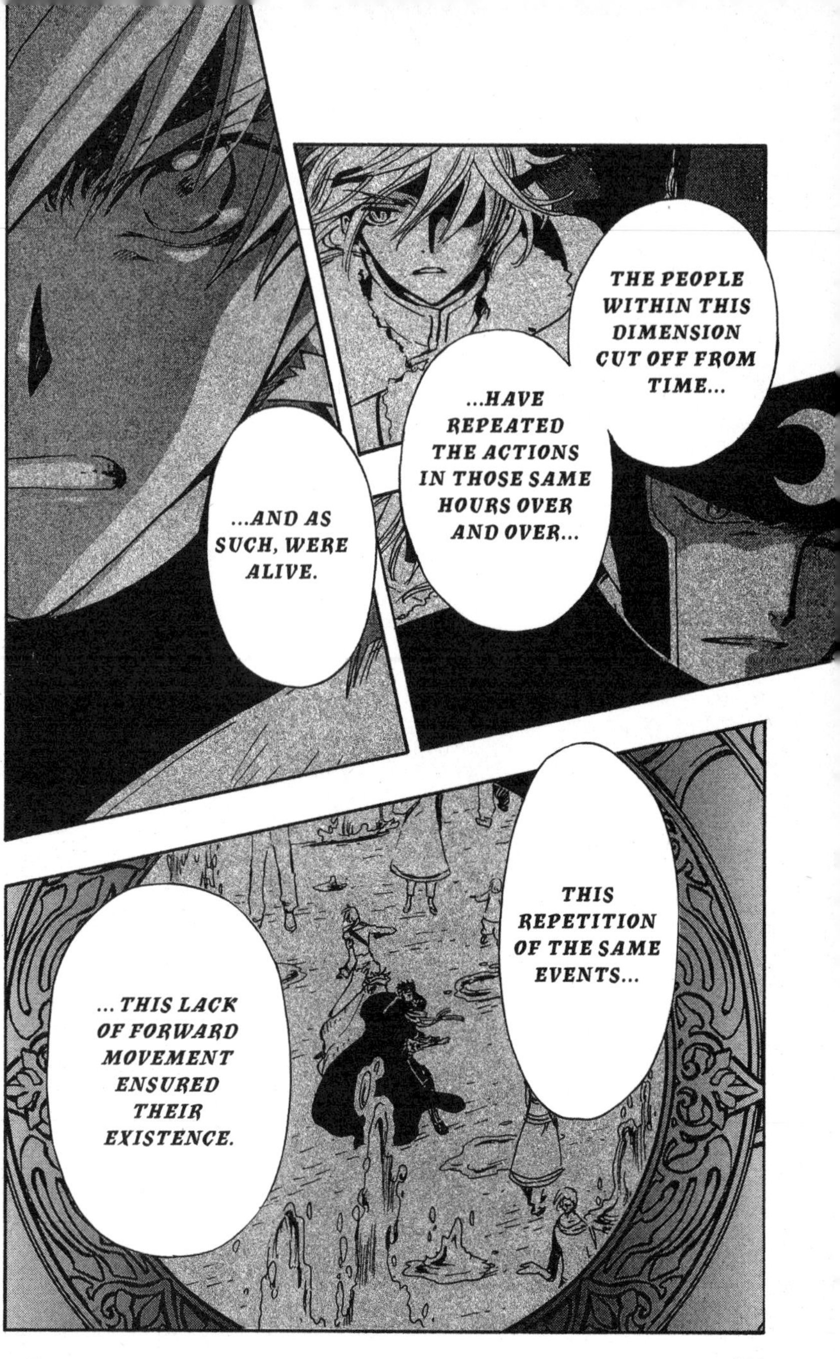
THE PEOPLE WITHIN THIS DIMENSION CUT OFF FROM TIME...
...HAVE REPEATED THE ACTIONS IN THOSE SAME HOURS OVER AND OVER...
...AND AS SUCH, WERE ALIVE.
THIS REPETITION OF THE SAME EVENTS...
... THIS LACK OF FORWARD MOVEMENT ENSURED THEIR EXISTENCE.

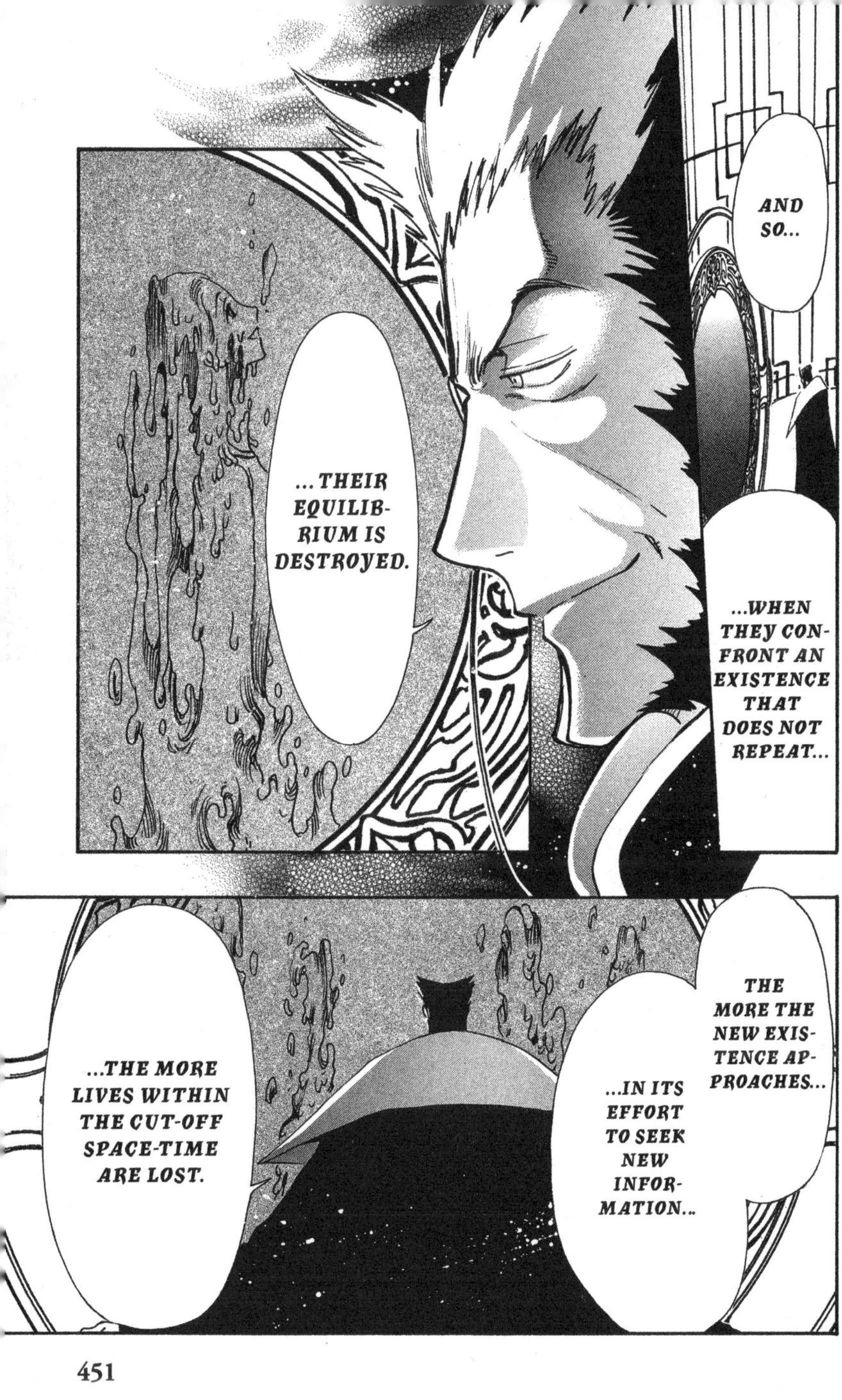
AND SO...
...WHEN THEY CON- FRONT AN EXISTENCE THAT DOES NOT REPEAT...
...THEIR EQUILIB- RIUM IS DESTROYED.
THE MORE THE NEW EXIS- TENCE AP- PROACHES...
...IN ITS EFFORT TO SEEK NEW INFOR- MATION...
...THE MORE LIVES WITHIN THE CUT-OFF SPACE-TIME ARE LOST.

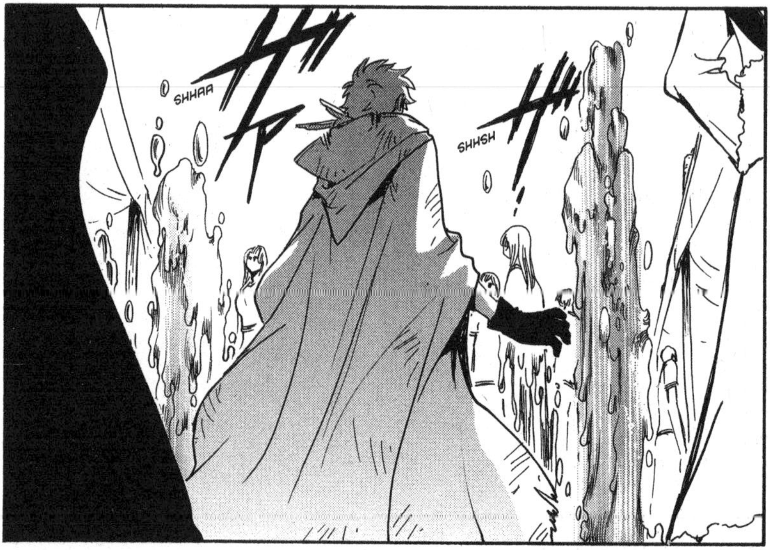
SHHSH
SHHAA
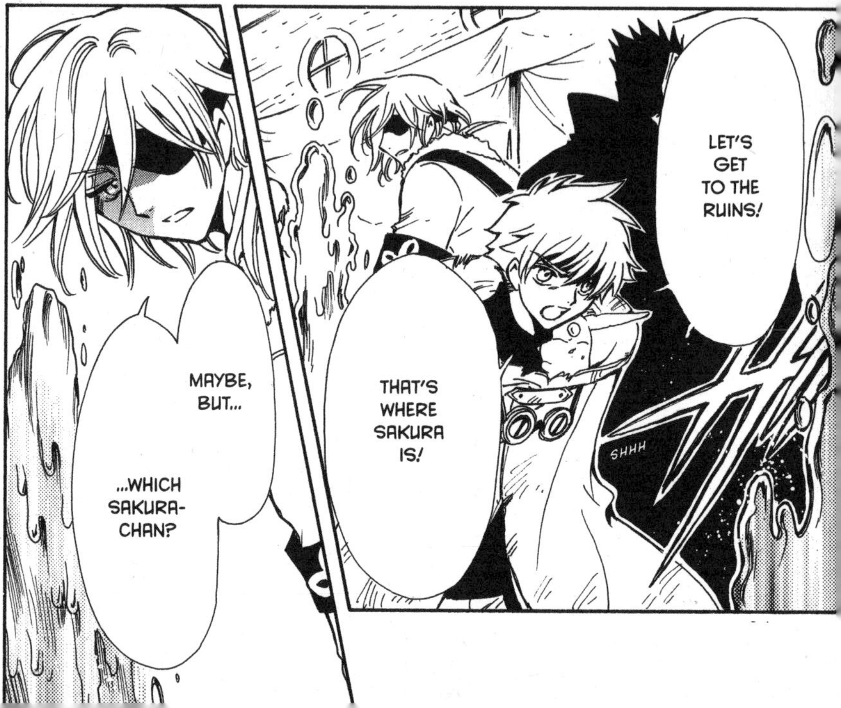
LET'S GET TO THE RUINS!
SHHH
THAT'S WHERE SAKURA IS!
MAYBE, BUT...
...WHICH SAKURA-CHAN?

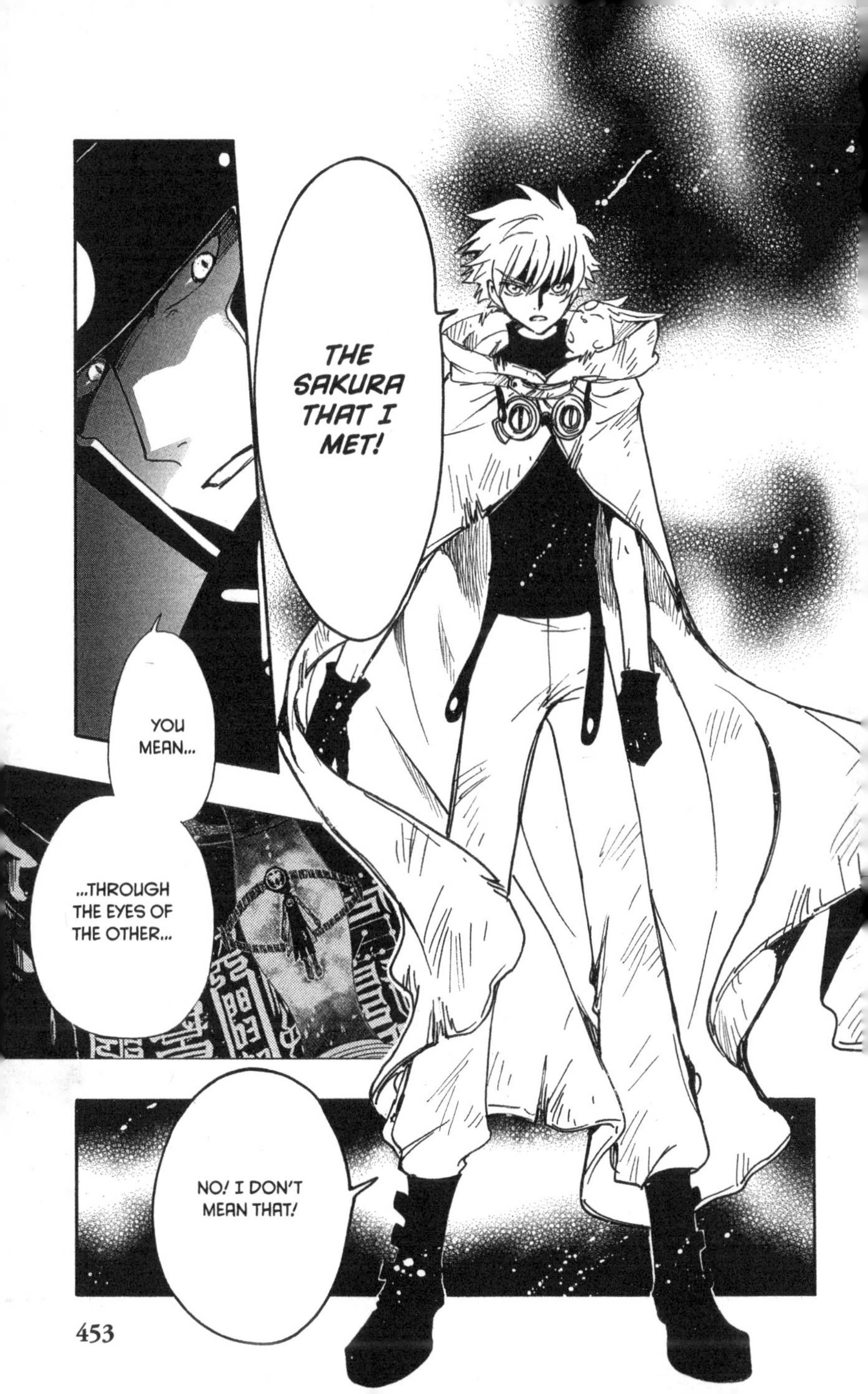
THE SAKURA THAT I MET!
YOU MEAN...
...THROUGH THE EYES OF THE OTHER...
NO! I DON'T MEAN THAT!

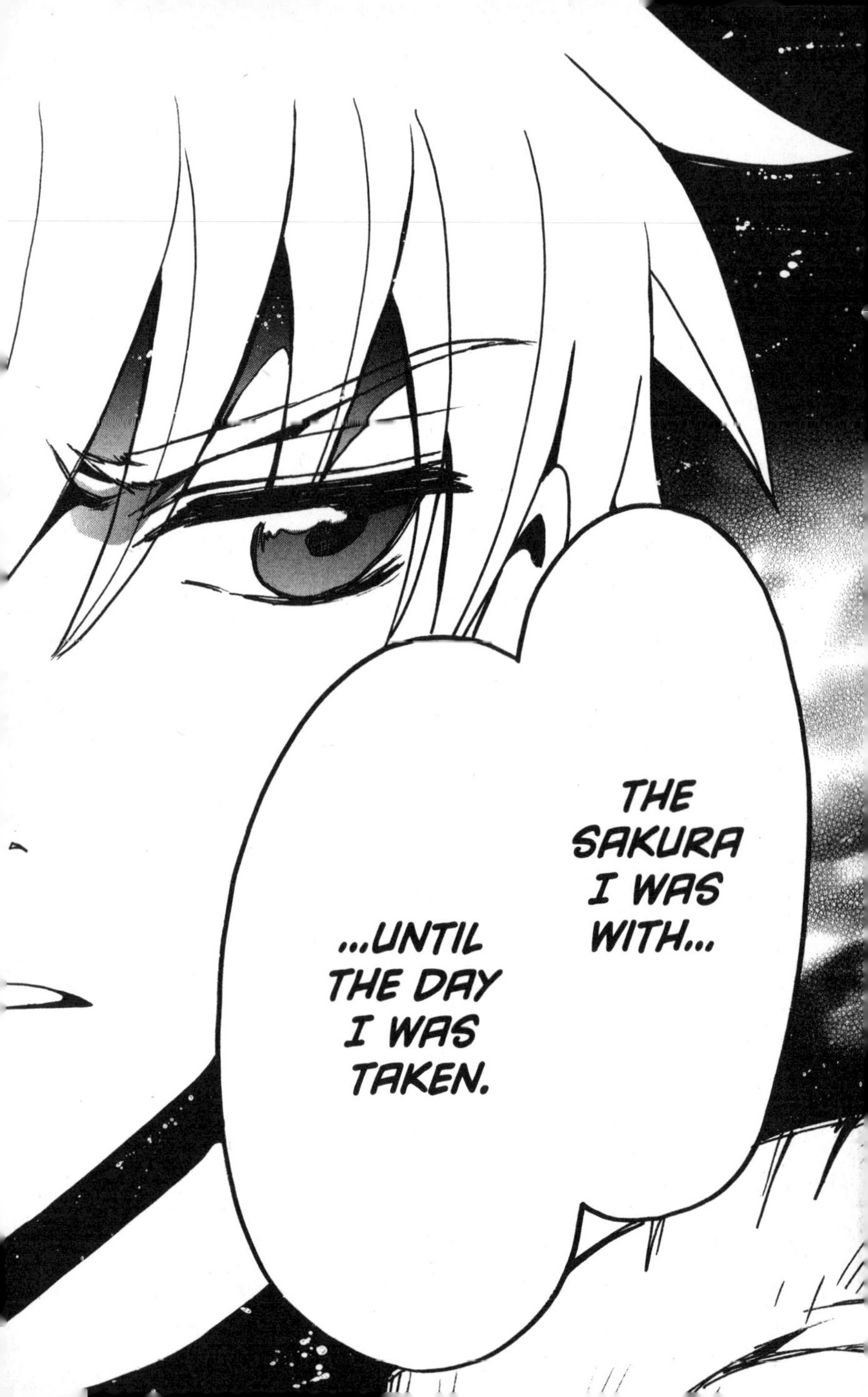
THE SAKURA I WAS WITH...
...UNTIL THE DAY I WAS TAKEN.

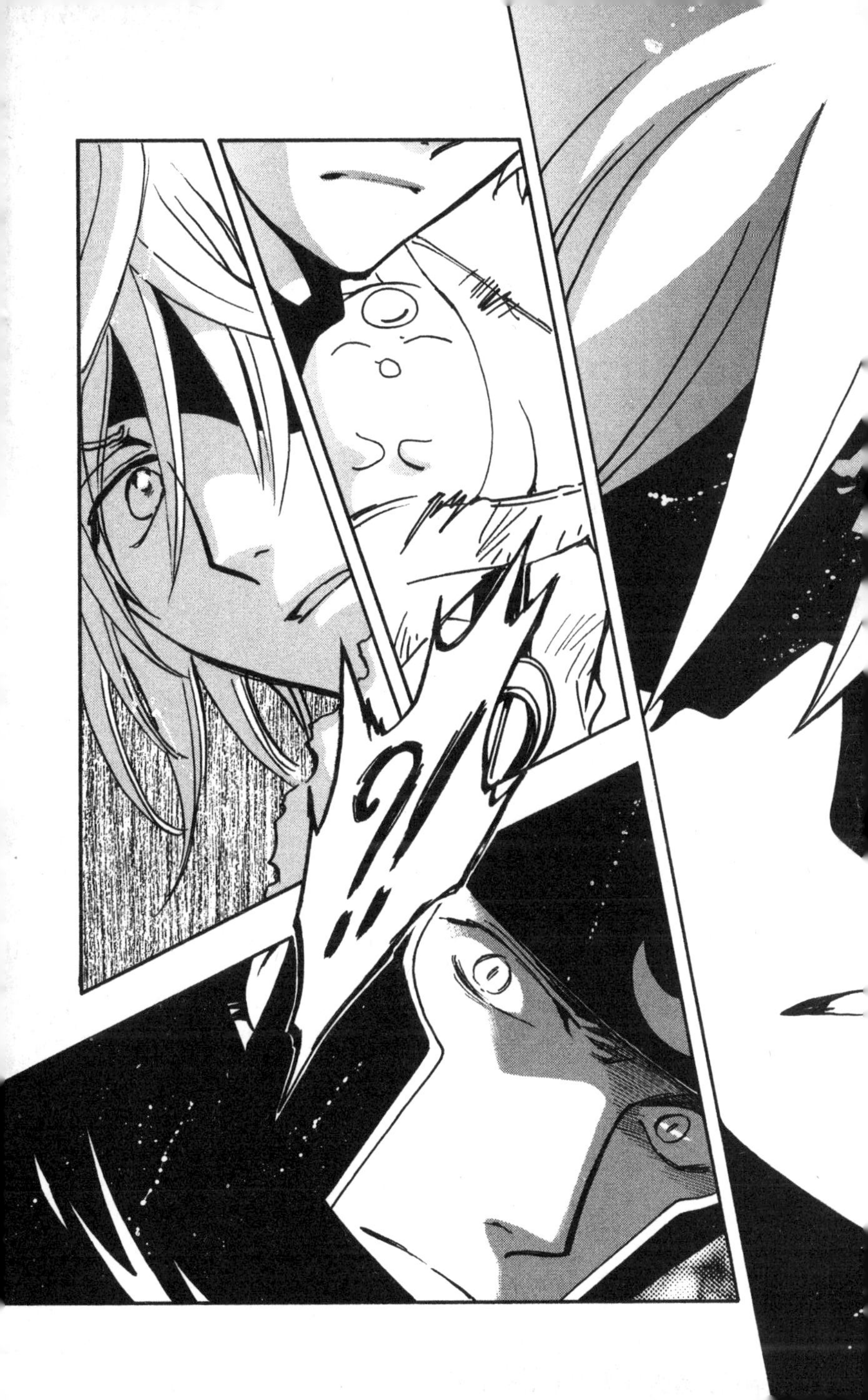

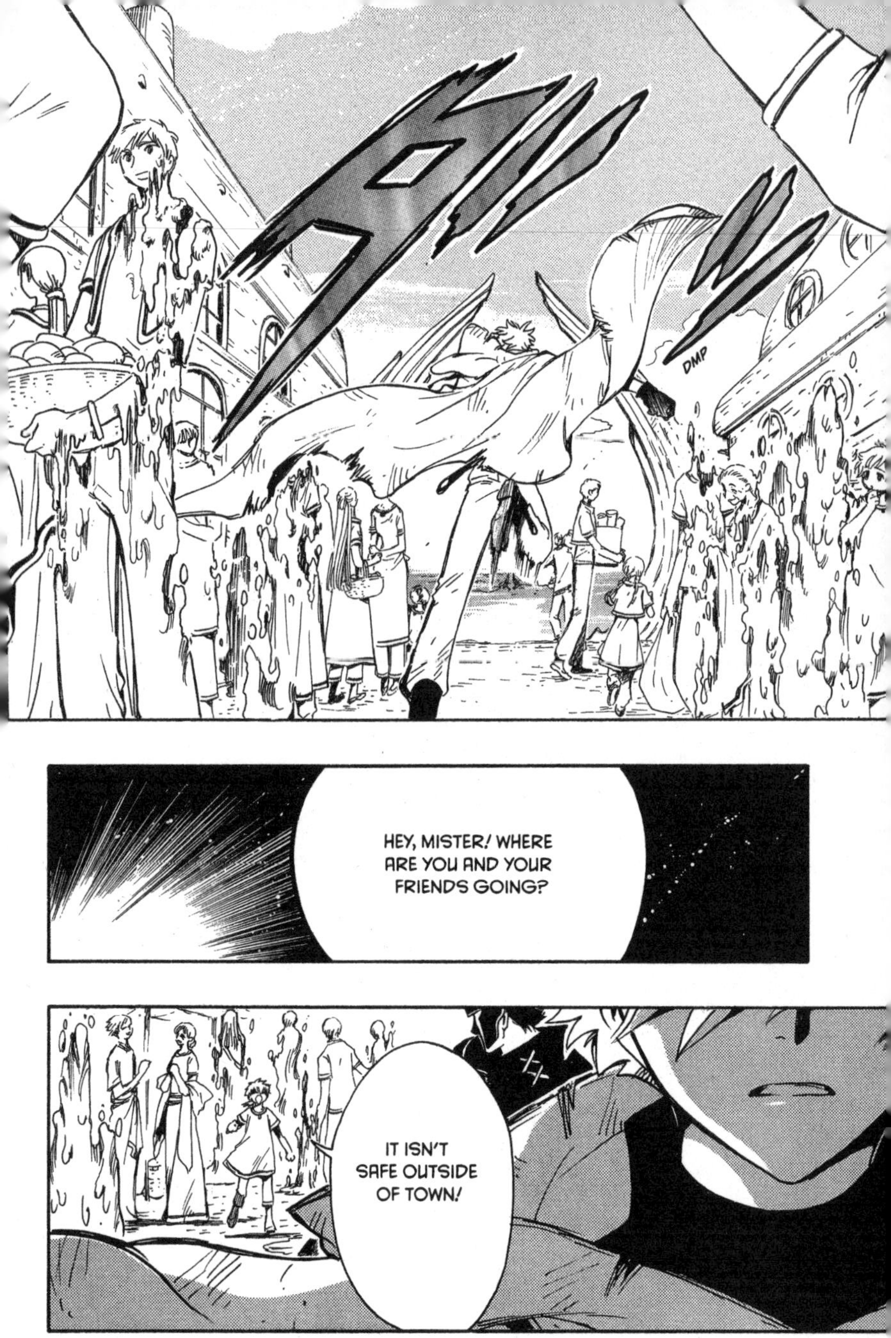
DMP
HEY, MISTER! WHERE ARE YOU AND YOUR FRIENDS GOING?
IT ISN'T SAFE OUTSIDE OF TOWN!

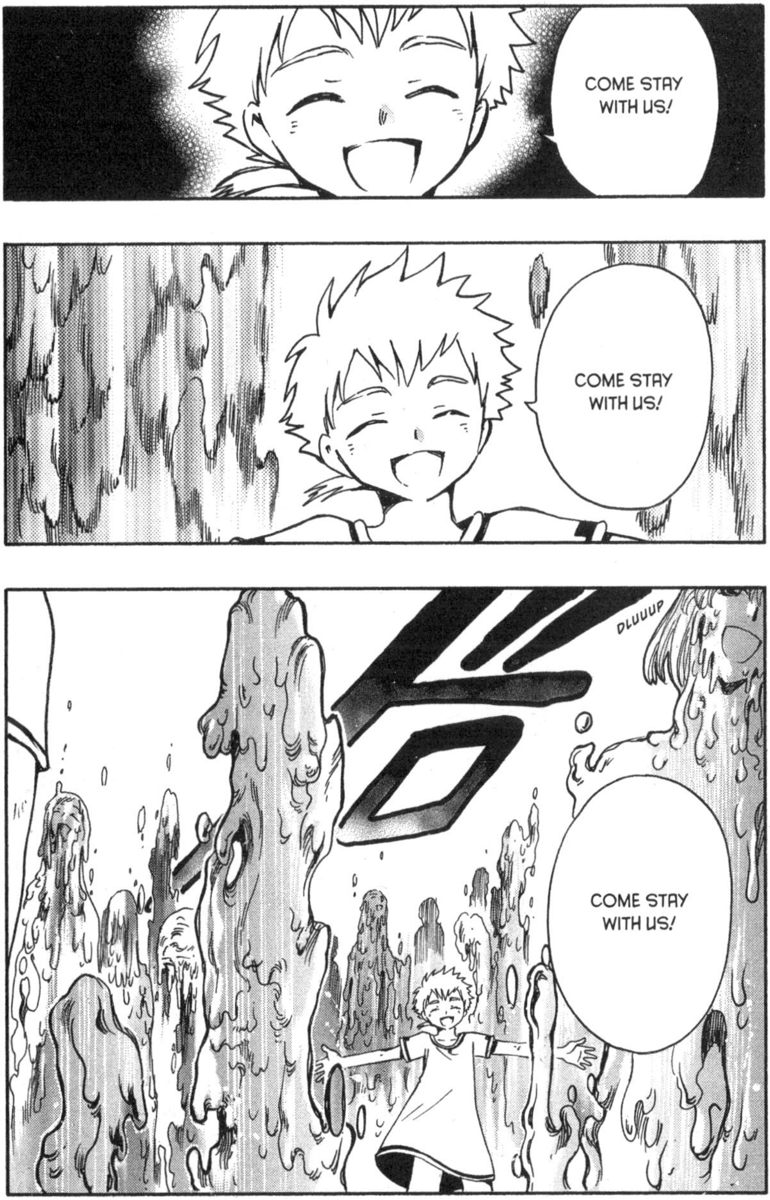
COME STAY WITH US!
COME STAY WITH US!
DLUUUP
COME STAY WITH US!

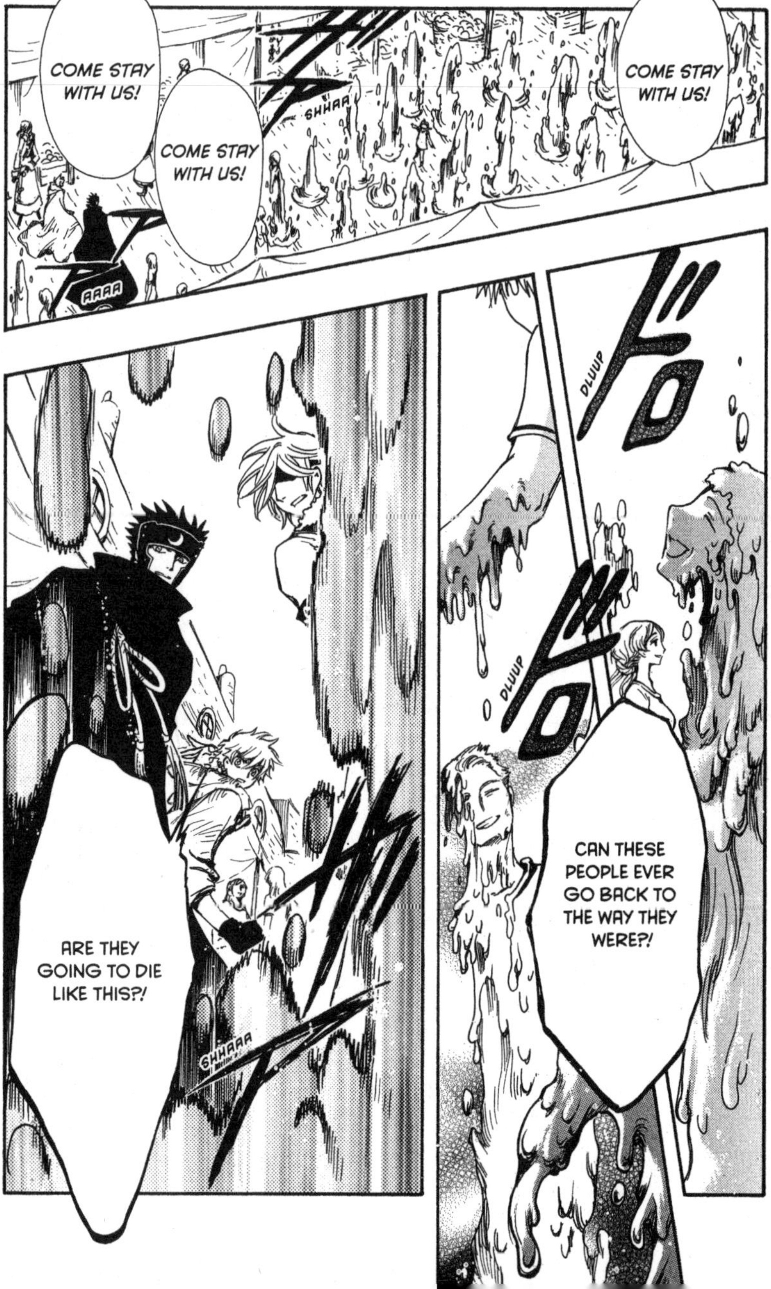
COME STAY WITH US!
COME STAY WITH US!
COME STAY WITH US!
SHHAA
AAAA
DLUUP
DLUUP
CAN THESE PEOPLE EVER GO BACK TO THE WAY THEY WERE?!
ARE THEY GOING TO DIE LIKE THIS?!
SHHAAA

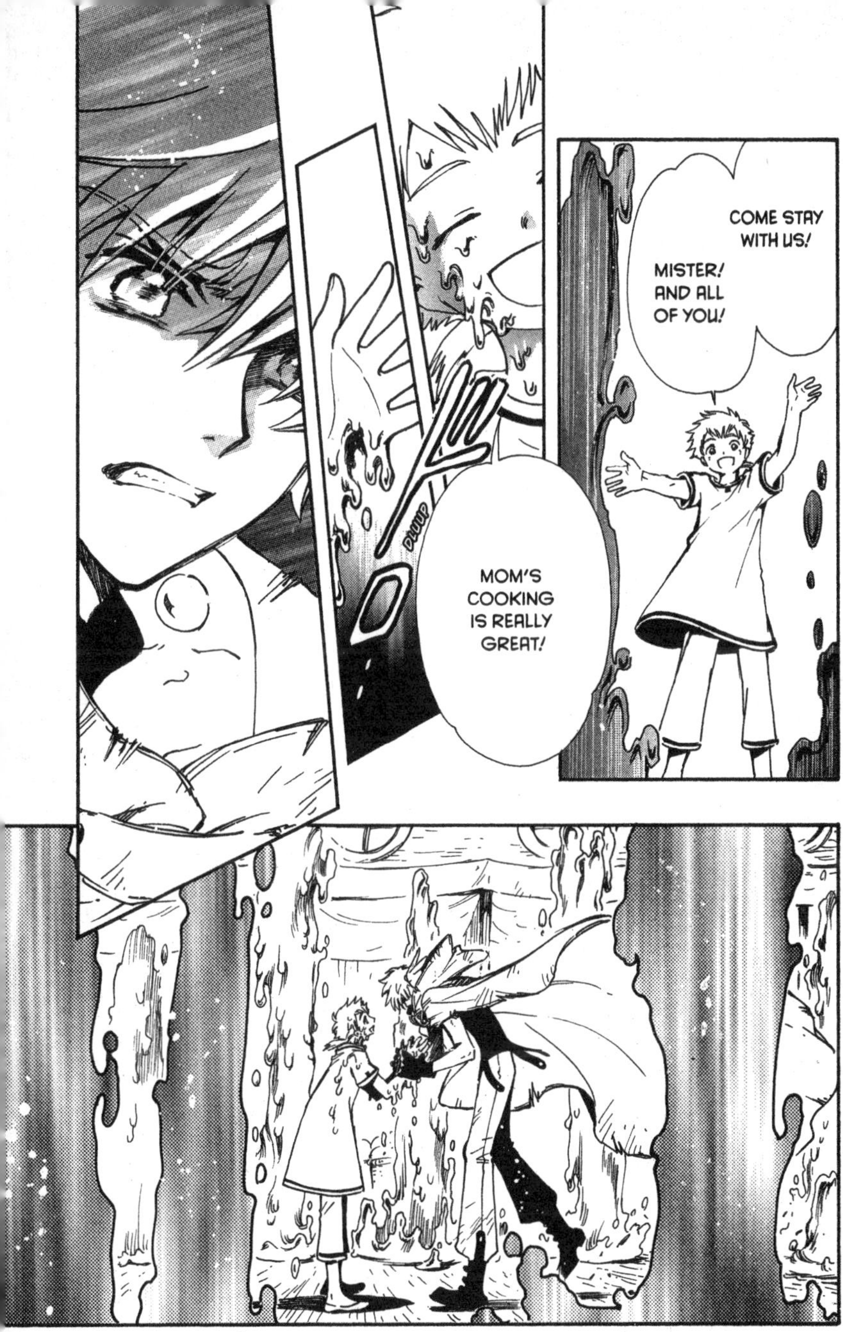
COME STAY WITH US!
MISTER! AND ALL OF YOU!
MOM'S COOKING IS REALLY GREAT!
DWUUP

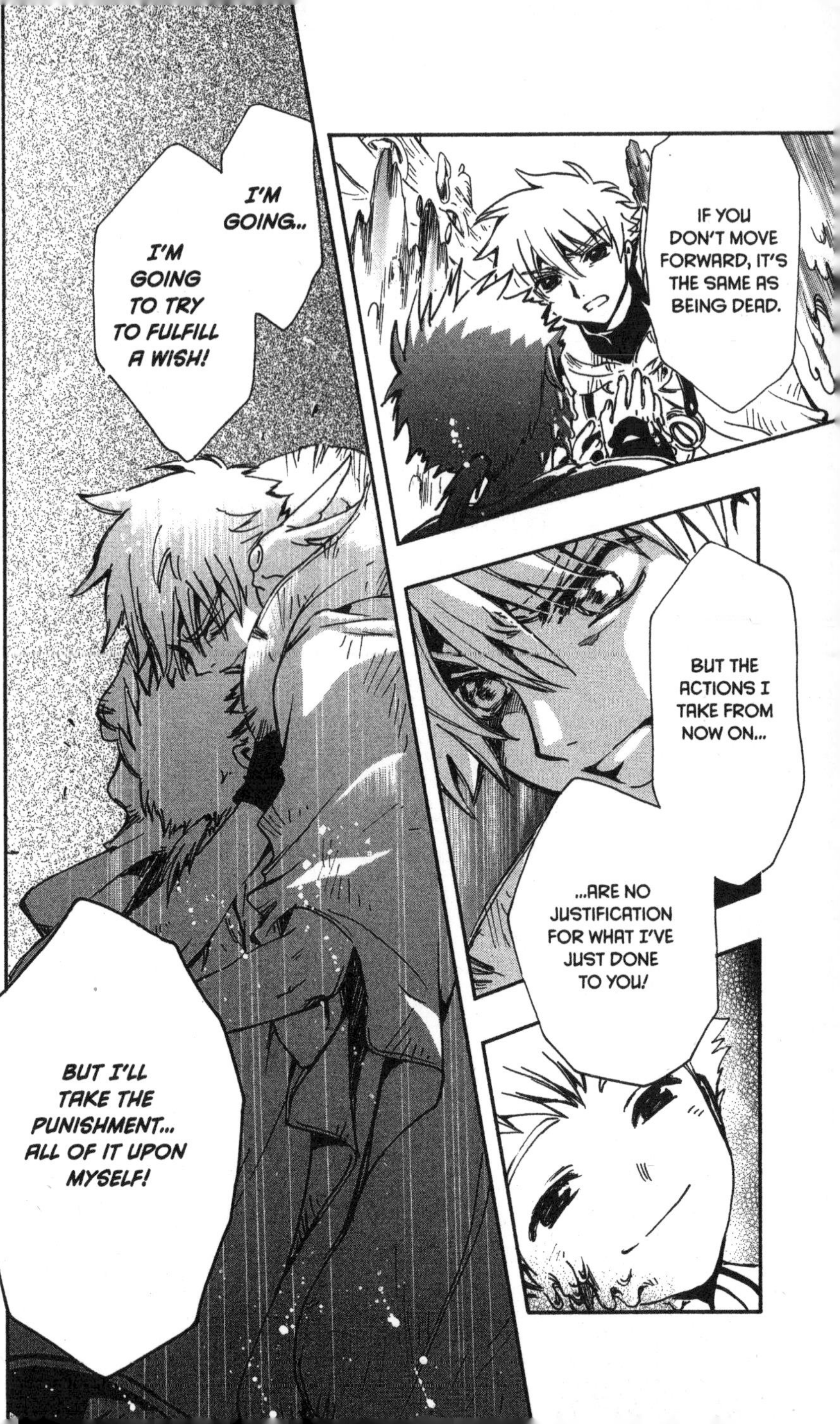
IF YOU DON'T MOVE FORWARD, IT'S THE SAME AS BEING DEAD.
BUT THE ACTIONS I TAKE FROM NOW ON...
...ARE NO JUSTIFICATION FOR WHAT I'VE JUST DONE TO YOU!
I'M GOING..
I'M GOING TO TRY TO FULFILL A WISH!
BUT I'LL TAKE THE PUNISHMENT... ALL OF IT UPON MYSELF!

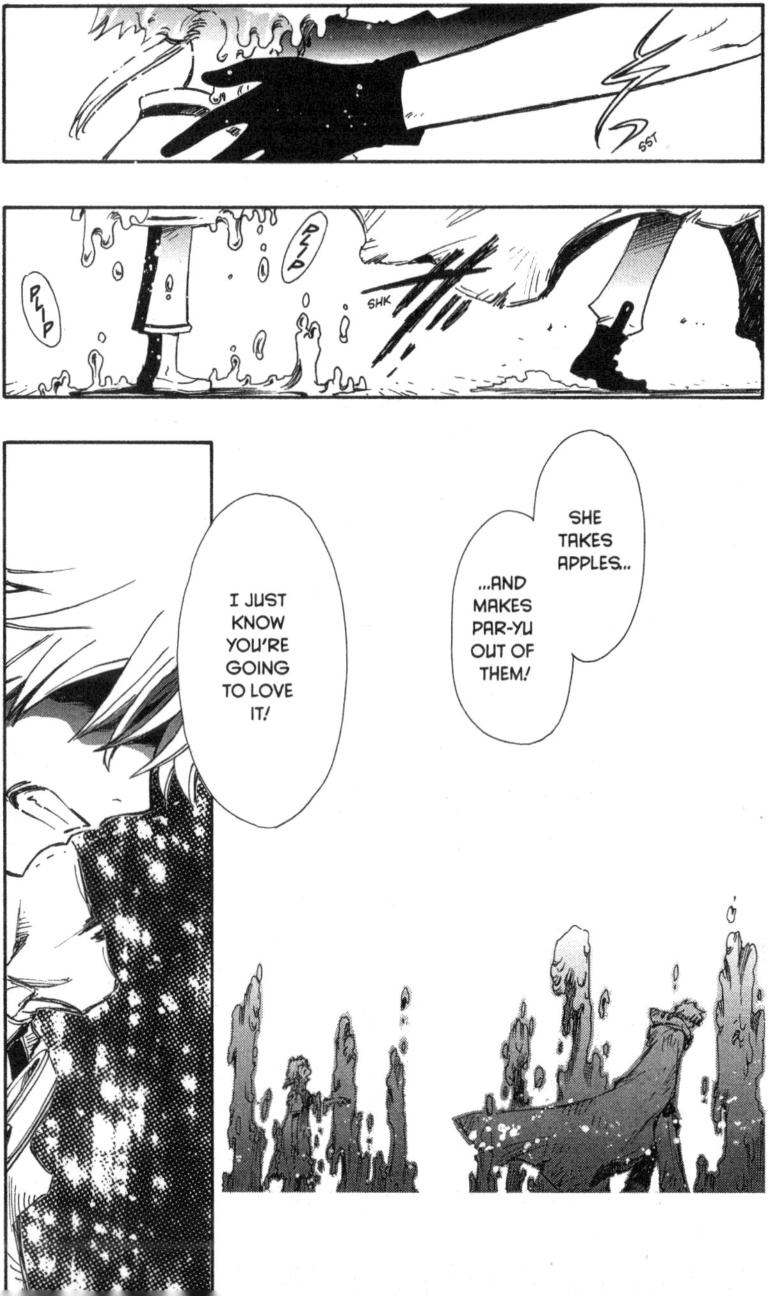
SST
SHK
PLIP
PLIP
SHE TAKES APPLES...
...AND MAKES PAR-YU OUT OF THEM!
I JUST KNOW YOU'RE GOING TO LOVE IT!

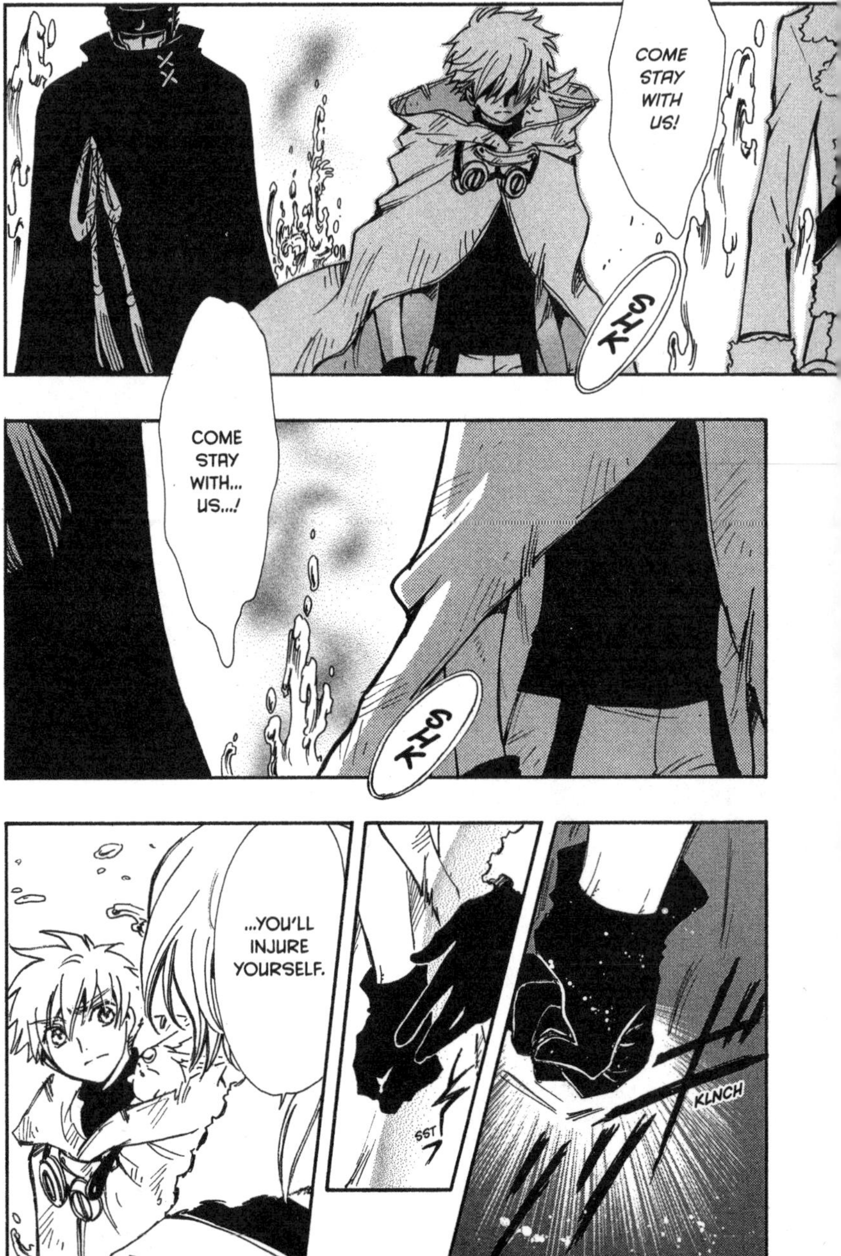
COME STAY WITH US!
SHK
COME STAY WITH... US...!
SHK
KLNCH
SST
...YOU'LL INJURE YOURSELF.

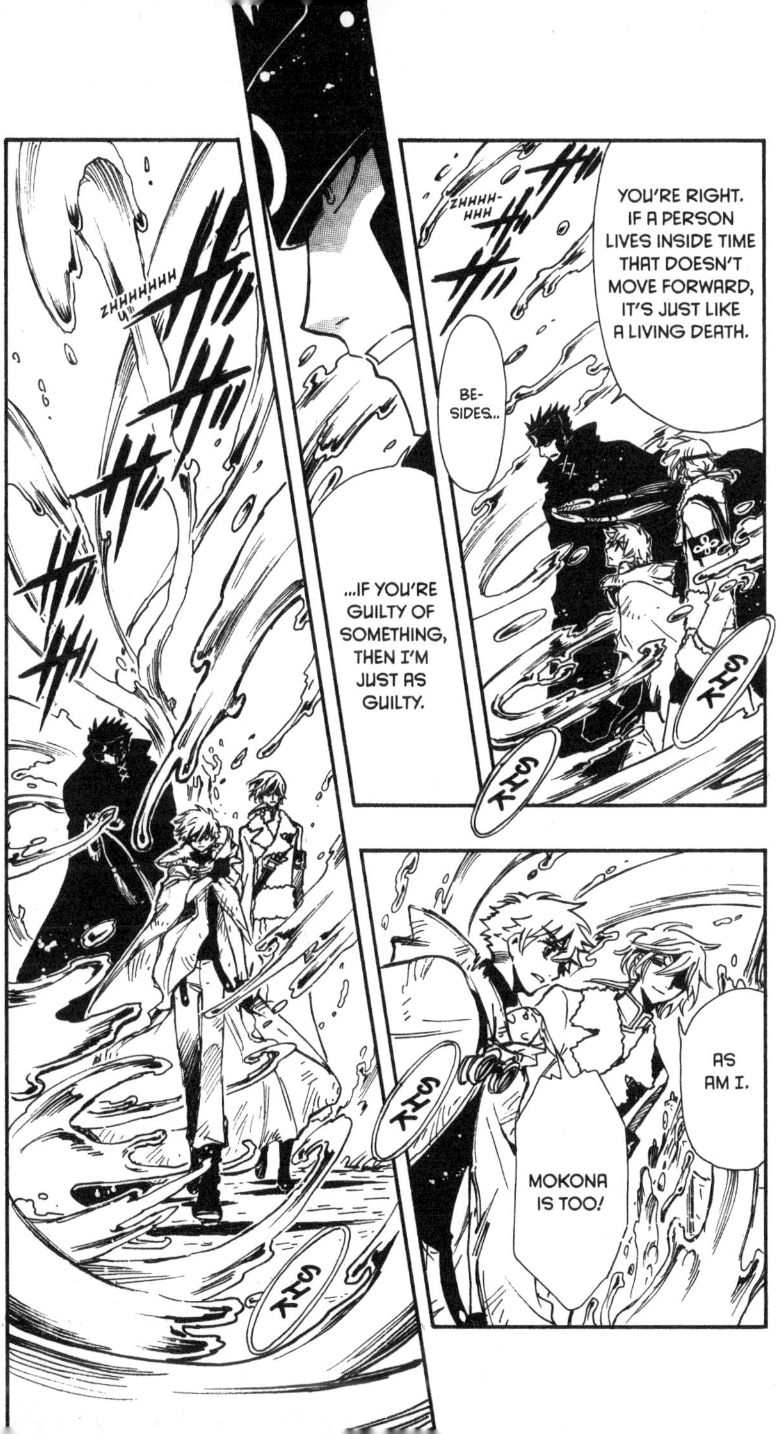
ZHHHH-HHH
YOU'RE RIGHT. IF A PERSON LIVES INSIDE TIME THAT DOESN'T MOVE FORWARD, IT'S JUST LIKE A LIVING DEATH.
BE-SIDES...
SHK
SHK
...IF YOU'RE GUILTY OF SOMETHING, THEN I'M JUST AS GUILTY.
AS AM I.
MOKONA IS TOO!
SHK
ZHHHHHHHH
SHK

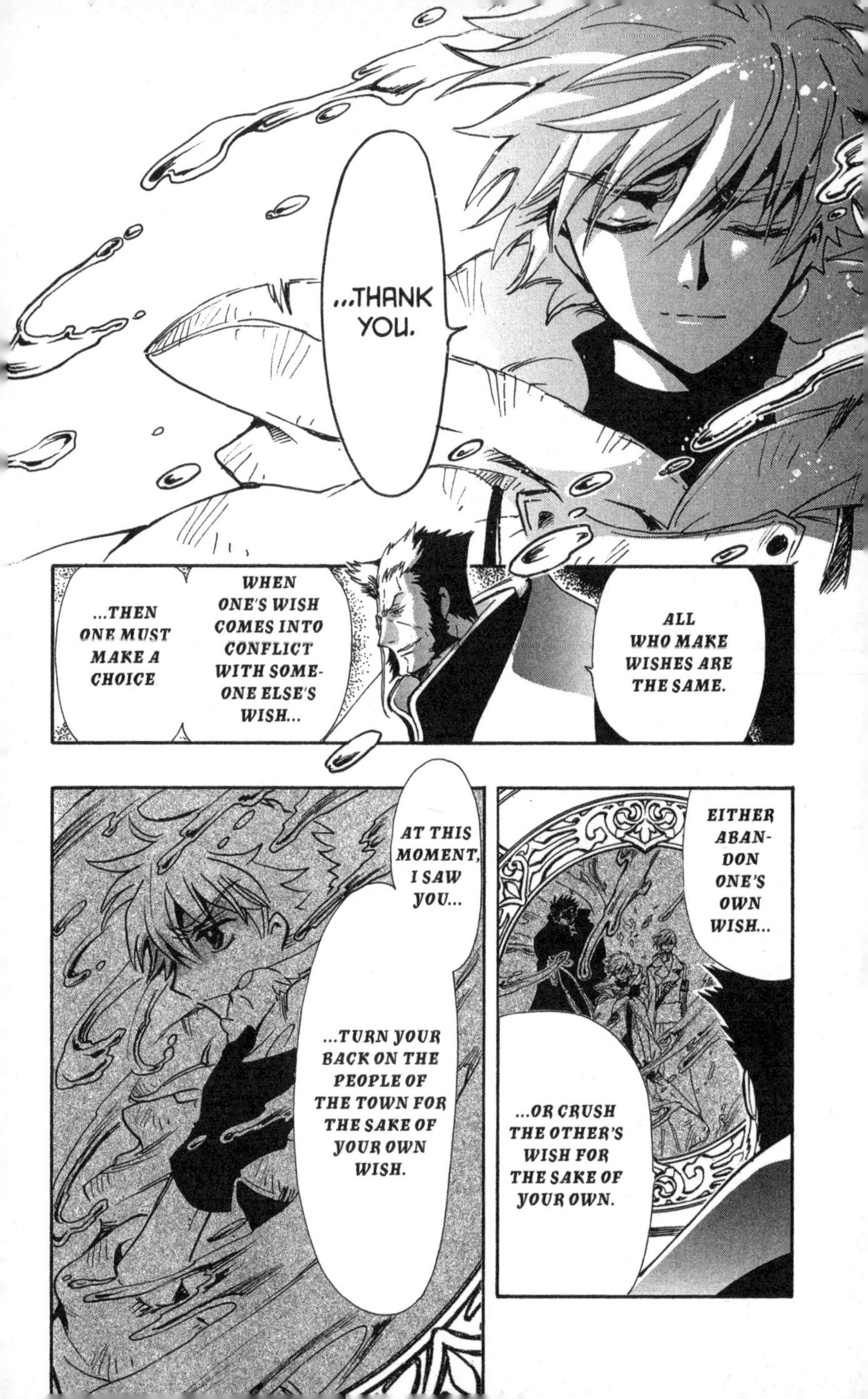
...THANK YOU.
ALL WHO MAKE WISHES ARE THE SAME.
WHEN ONE'S WISH COMES INTO CONFLICT WITH SOME-ONE ELSE'S WISH...
...THEN ONE MUST MAKE A CHOICE
EITHER ABAN-DON ONE'S OWN WISH...
...OR CRUSH THE OTHER'S WISH FOR THE SAKE OF YOUR OWN.
AT THIS MOMENT, I SAW YOU...
...TURN YOUR BACK ON THE PEOPLE OF THE TOWN FOR THE SAKE OF YOUR OWN WISH.

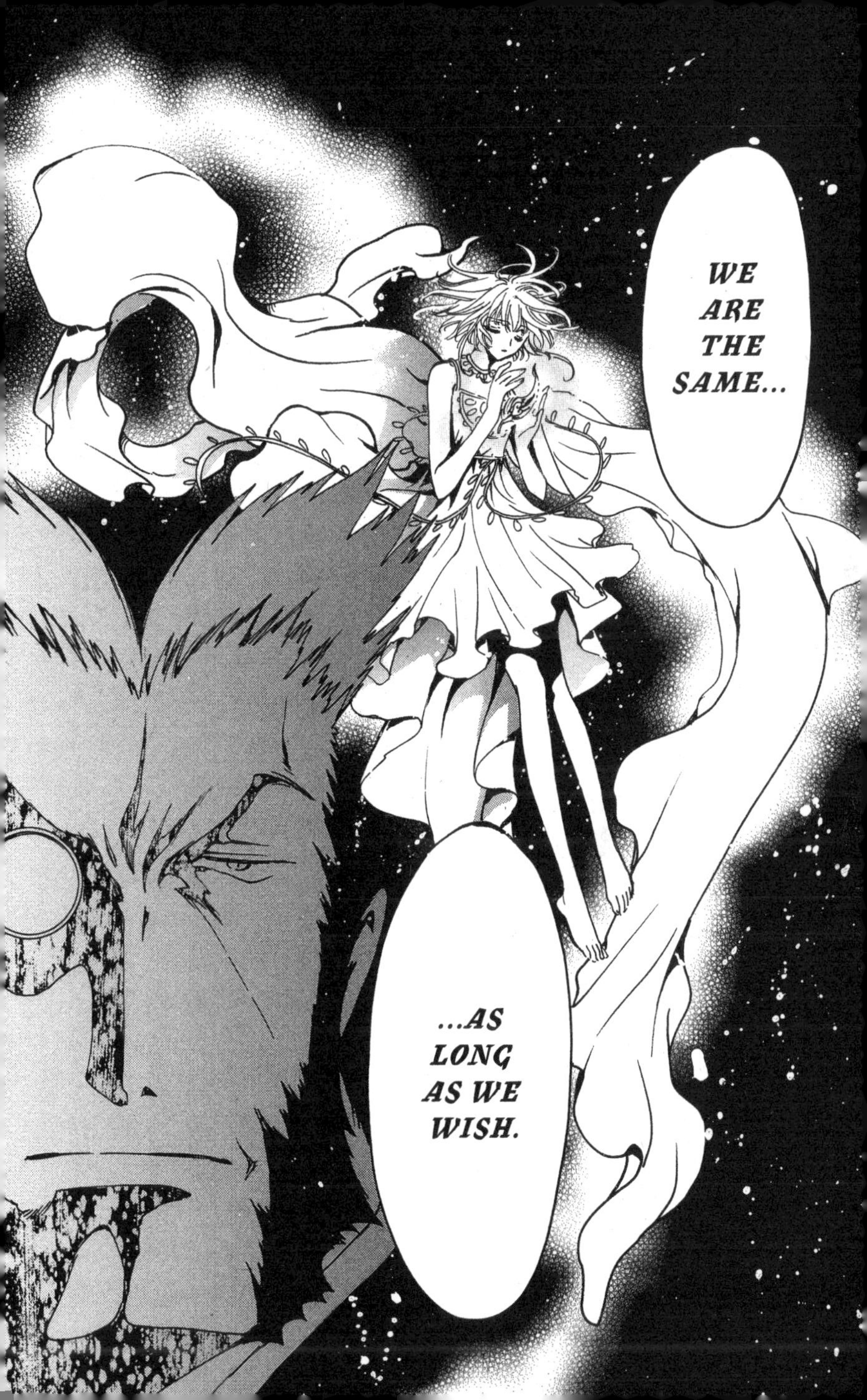
WE ARE THE SAME...
...AS LONG AS WE WISH.

ツバサ

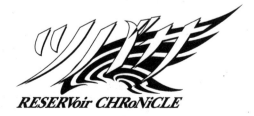

RESERVoir CHRoNiCLE

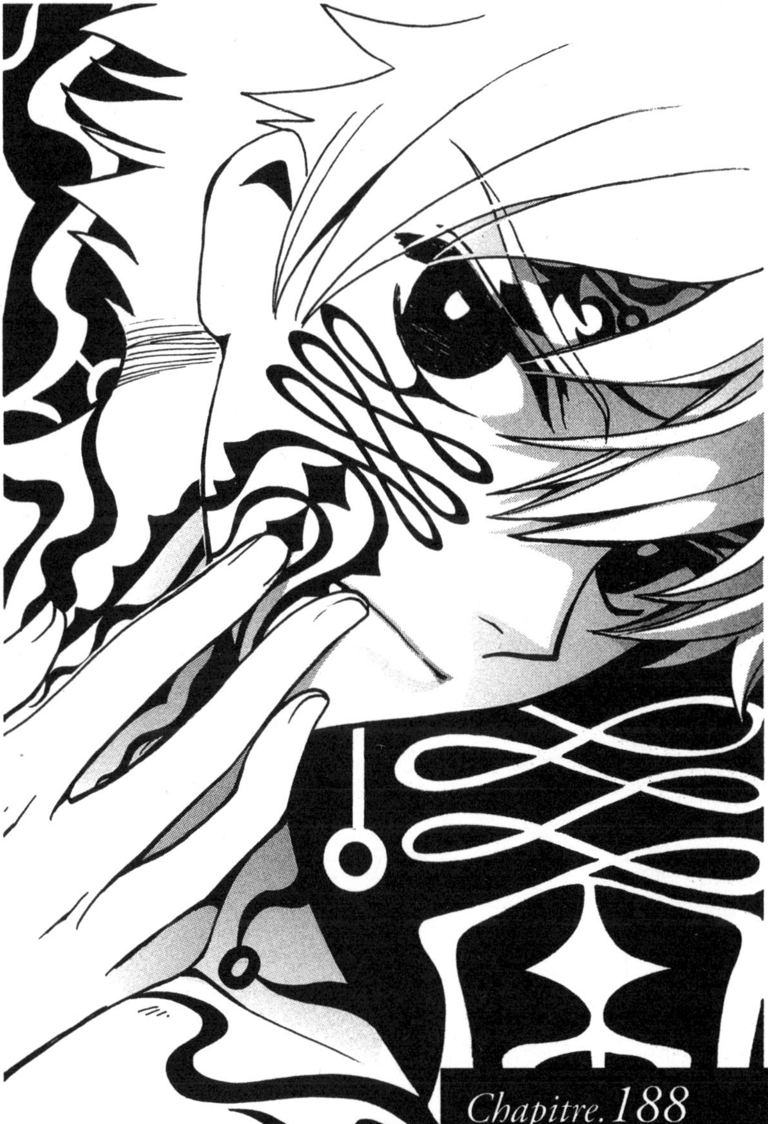

Chapitre. 188
The Ruins on That Day

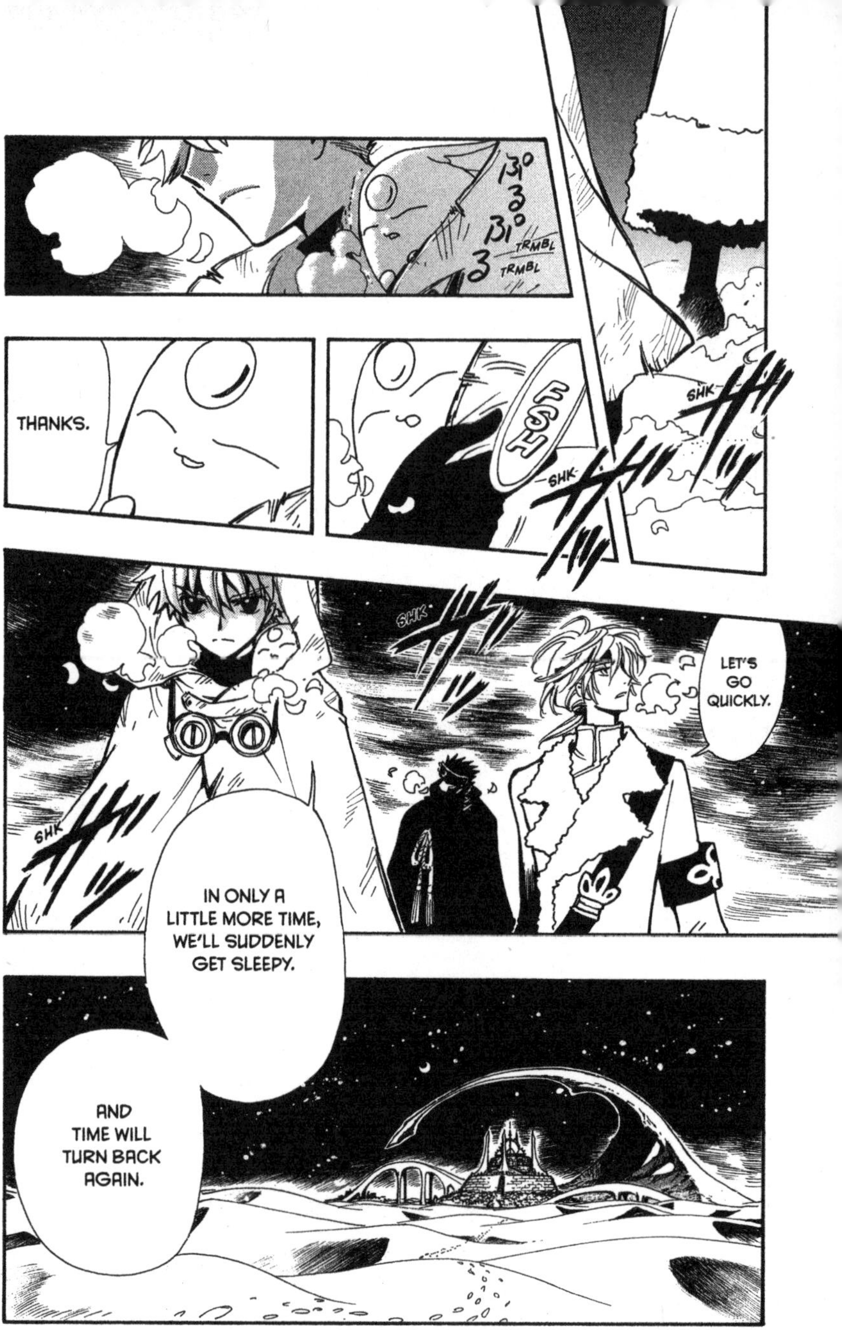
ぷるぷる
TRMBL
TRMBL
SHK
SHK
FSH
THANKS.
SHK
LET'S GO QUICKLY.
SHK
IN ONLY A LITTLE MORE TIME, WE'LL SUDDENLY GET SLEEPY.
AND TIME WILL TURN BACK AGAIN.

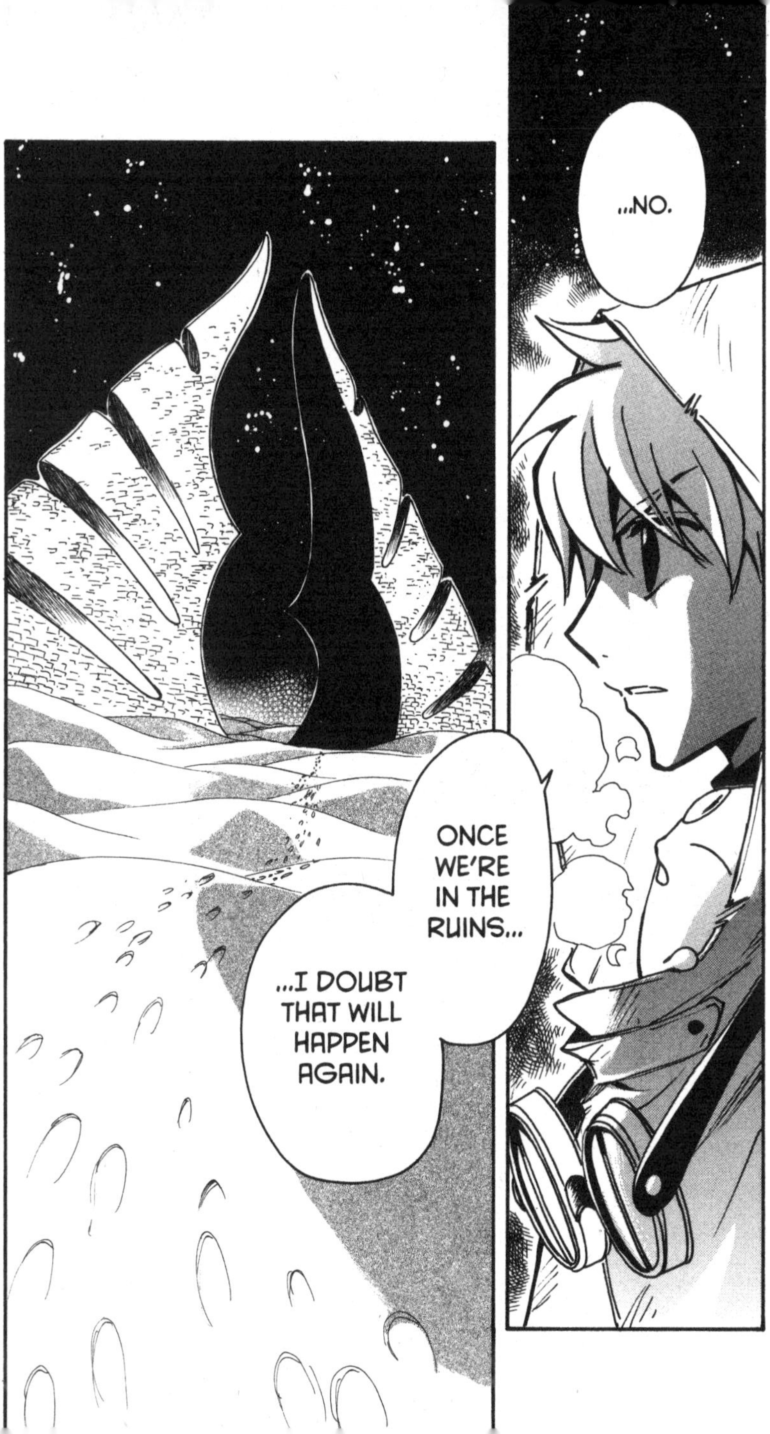
...NO.
ONCE WE'RE IN THE RUINS...
...I DOUBT THAT WILL HAPPEN AGAIN.

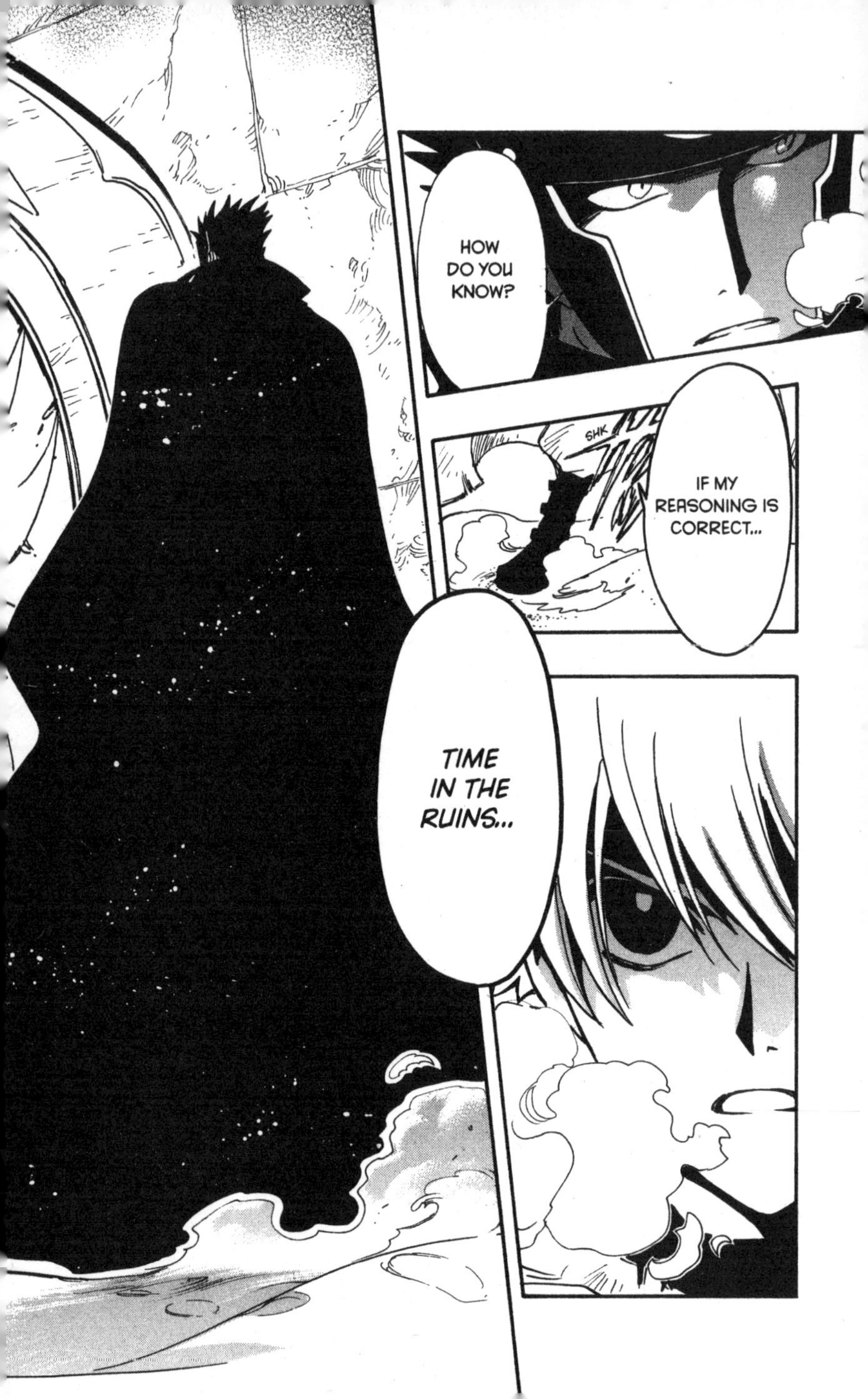
HOW DO YOU KNOW?
SHK
IF MY REASONING IS CORRECT...
TIME IN THE RUINS...

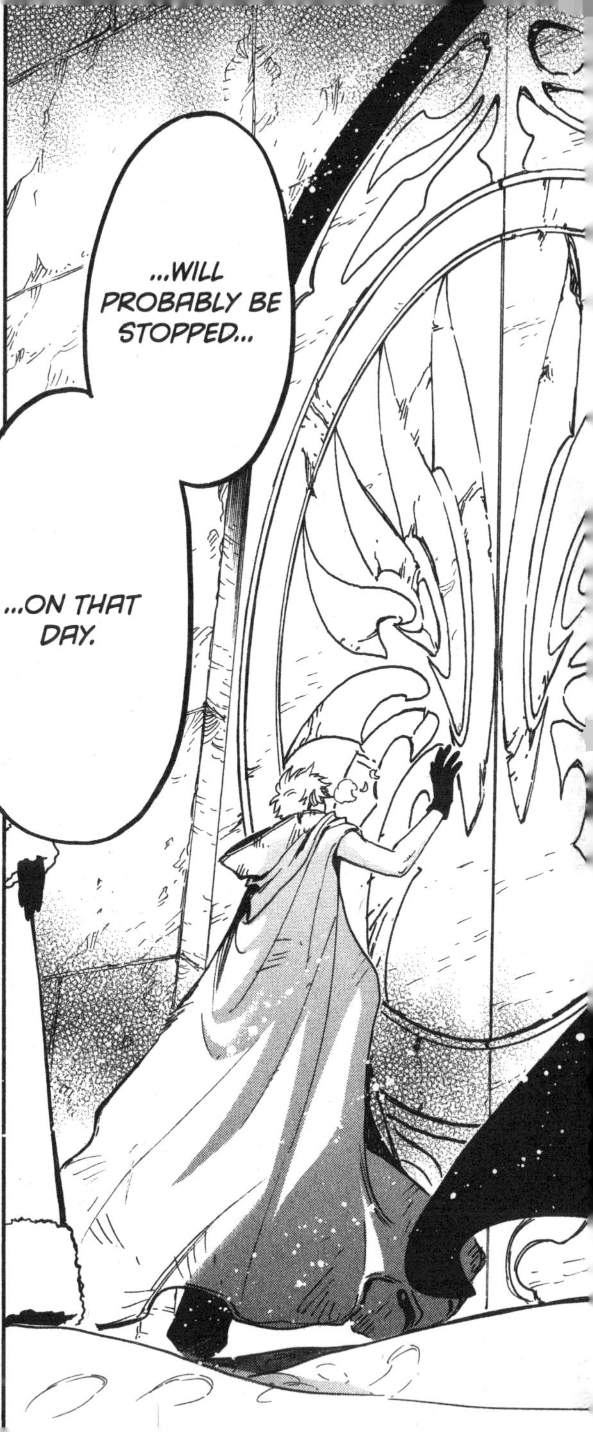
...WILL PROBABLY BE STOPPED...
...ON THAT DAY.
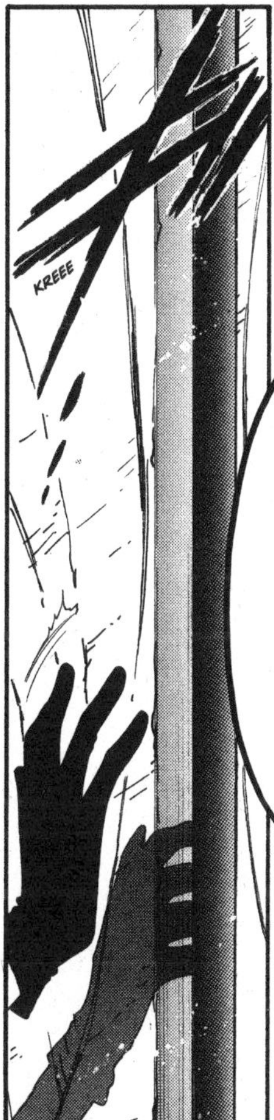
KREEE

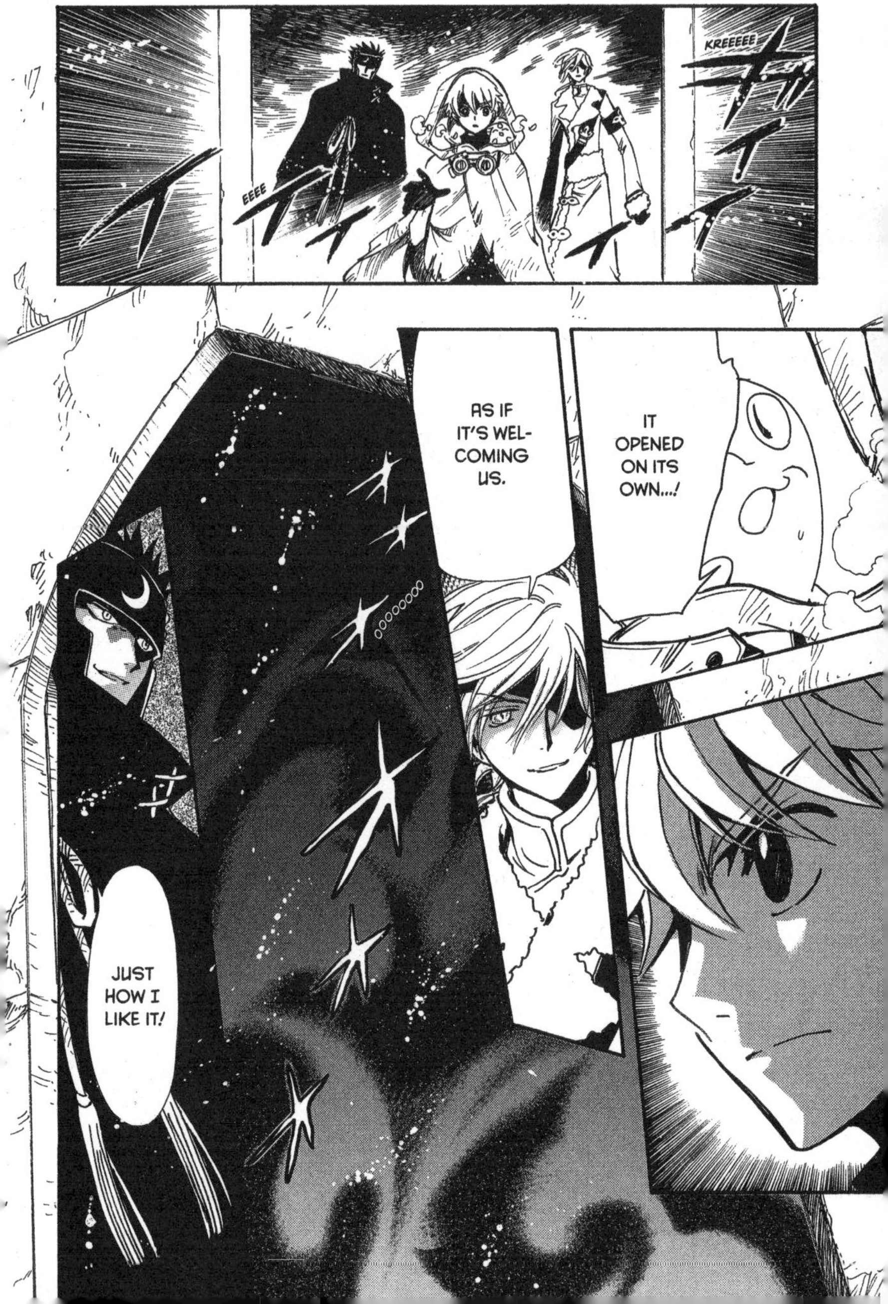
KREEEEE
EEEE
IT OPENED ON ITS OWN...!
AS IF IT'S WEL-COMING US.
JUST HOW I LIKE IT!

ISN'T...

...ANY-BODY HERE?

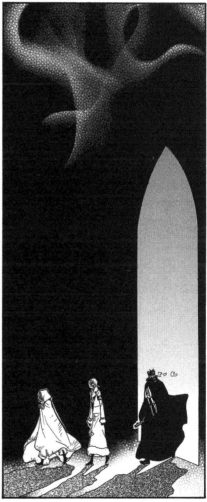

THE ONLY PEOPLE ALLOWED IN THE RUINS DURING THE PURIFICATION RITES ARE THE HIGH PRIEST...

...AND THE MEMBER OF THE ROYAL FAMILY TAKING PART IN THE CEREMONY.

BY "MEMBER OF THE ROYAL FAMILY," YOU MEAN THE SAKURA-CHAN...

...THAT YOU KNEW?

473

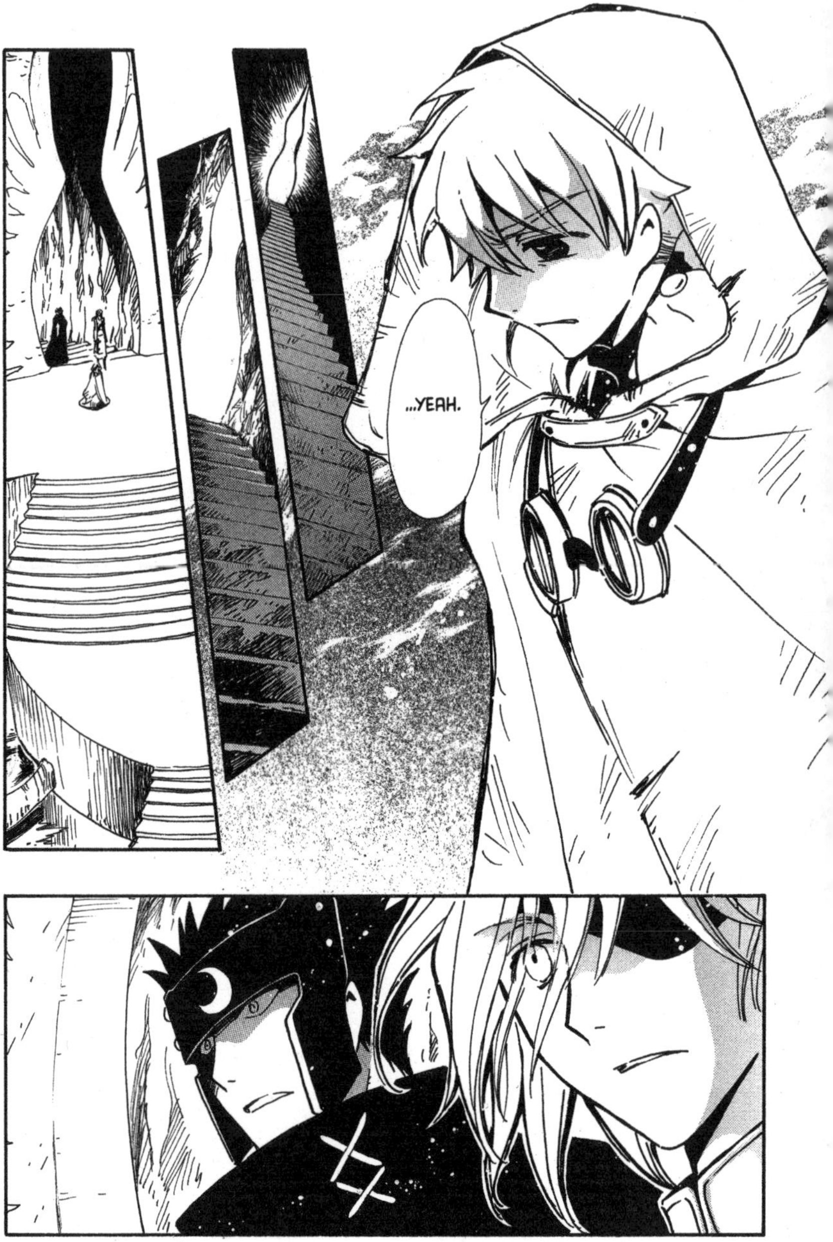
...YEAH.

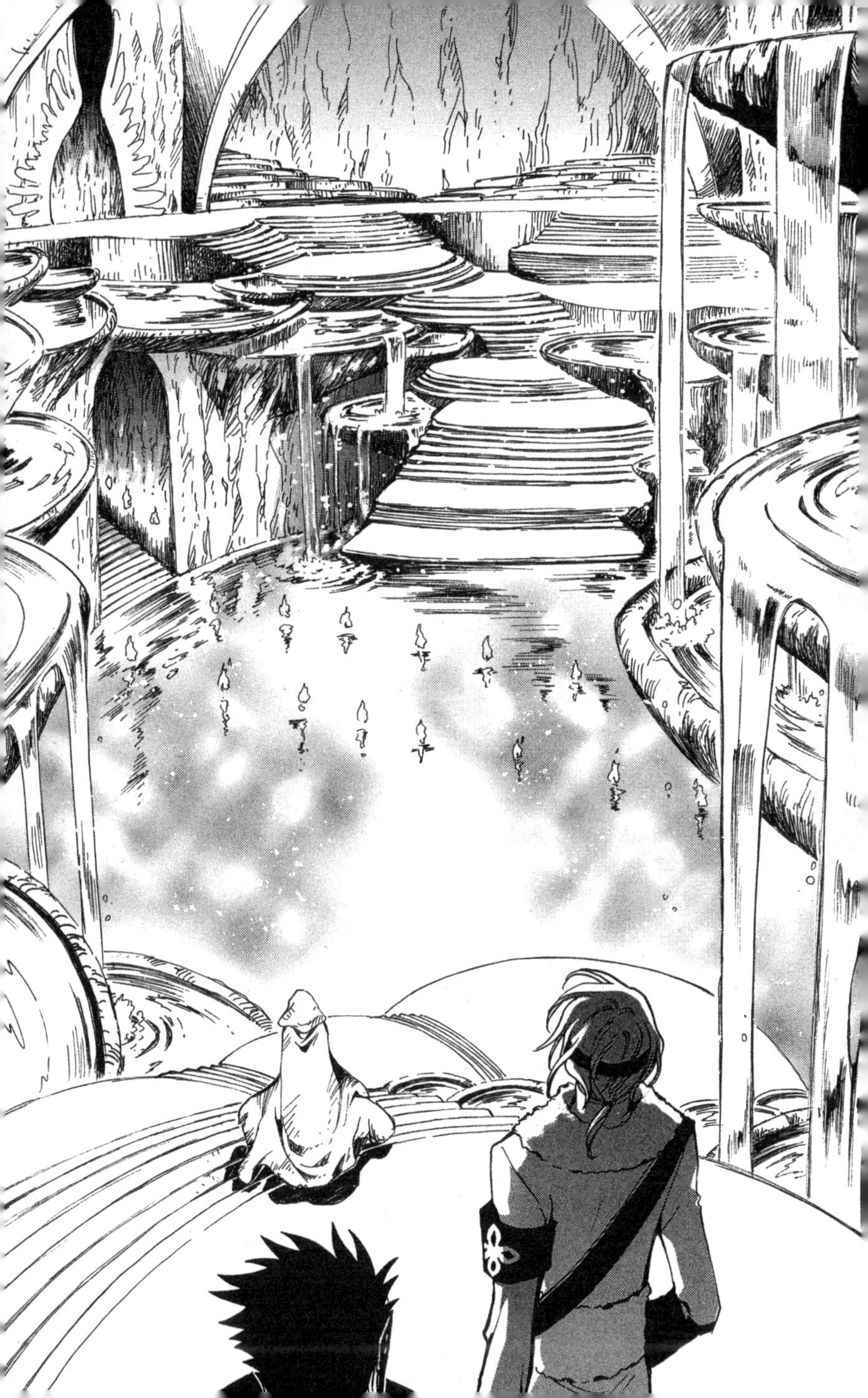

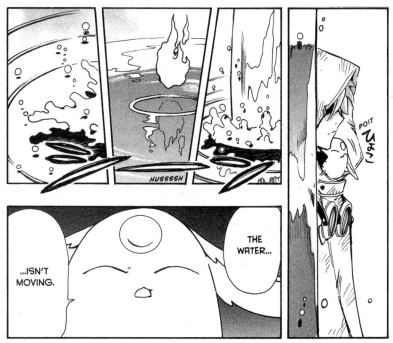

POIT

HUSSSSH

THE WATER...

...ISN'T MOVING.

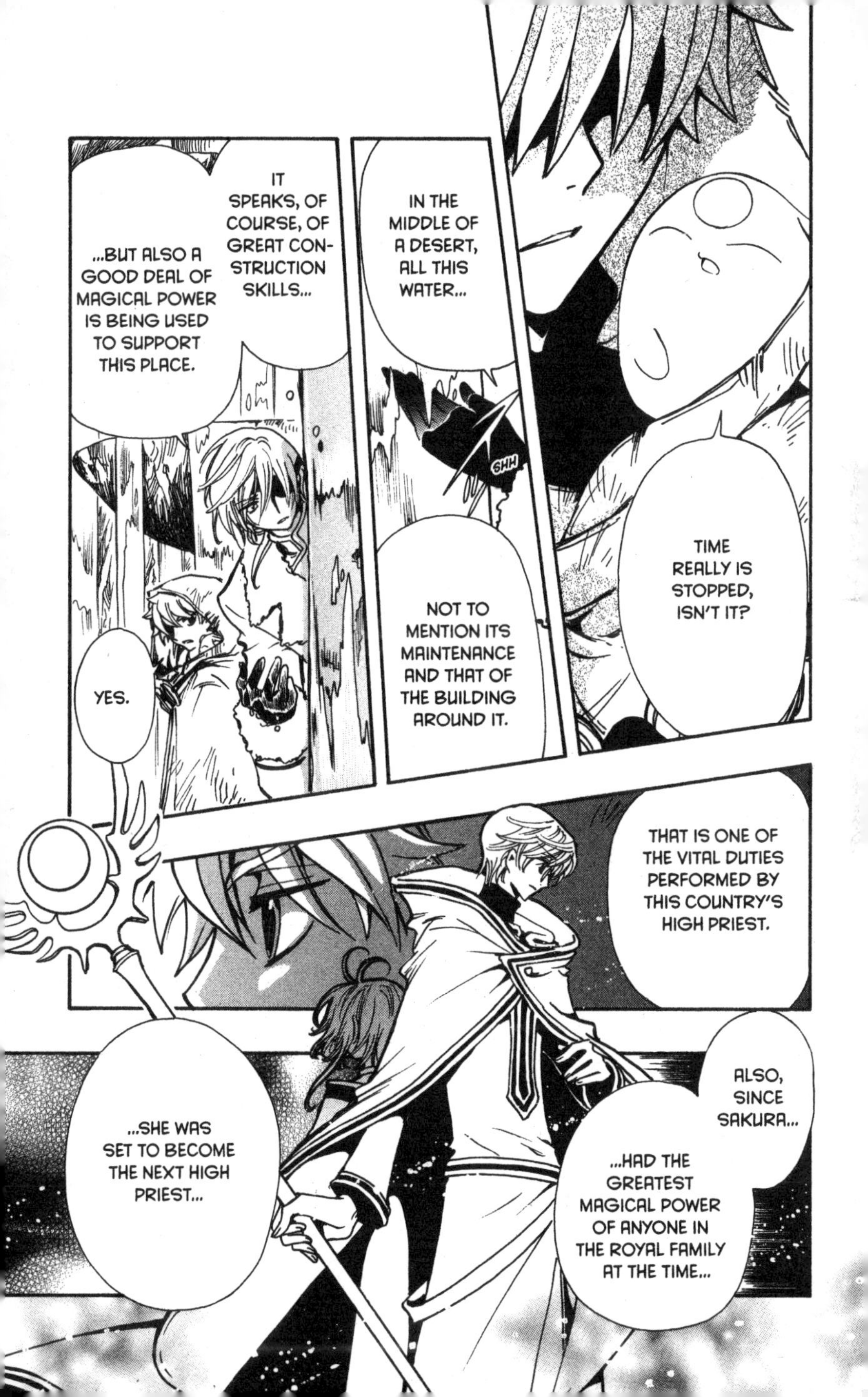
TIME REALLY IS STOPPED, ISN'T IT?
IN THE MIDDLE OF A DESERT, ALL THIS WATER...
SHH
NOT TO MENTION ITS MAINTENANCE AND THAT OF THE BUILDING AROUND IT.
IT SPEAKS, OF COURSE, OF GREAT CONSTRUCTION SKILLS...
...BUT ALSO A GOOD DEAL OF MAGICAL POWER IS BEING USED TO SUPPORT THIS PLACE.
YES.
THAT IS ONE OF THE VITAL DUTIES PERFORMED BY THIS COUNTRY'S HIGH PRIEST.
ALSO, SINCE SAKURA...
...HAD THE GREATEST MAGICAL POWER OF ANYONE IN THE ROYAL FAMILY AT THE TIME...
...SHE WAS SET TO BECOME THE NEXT HIGH PRIEST...

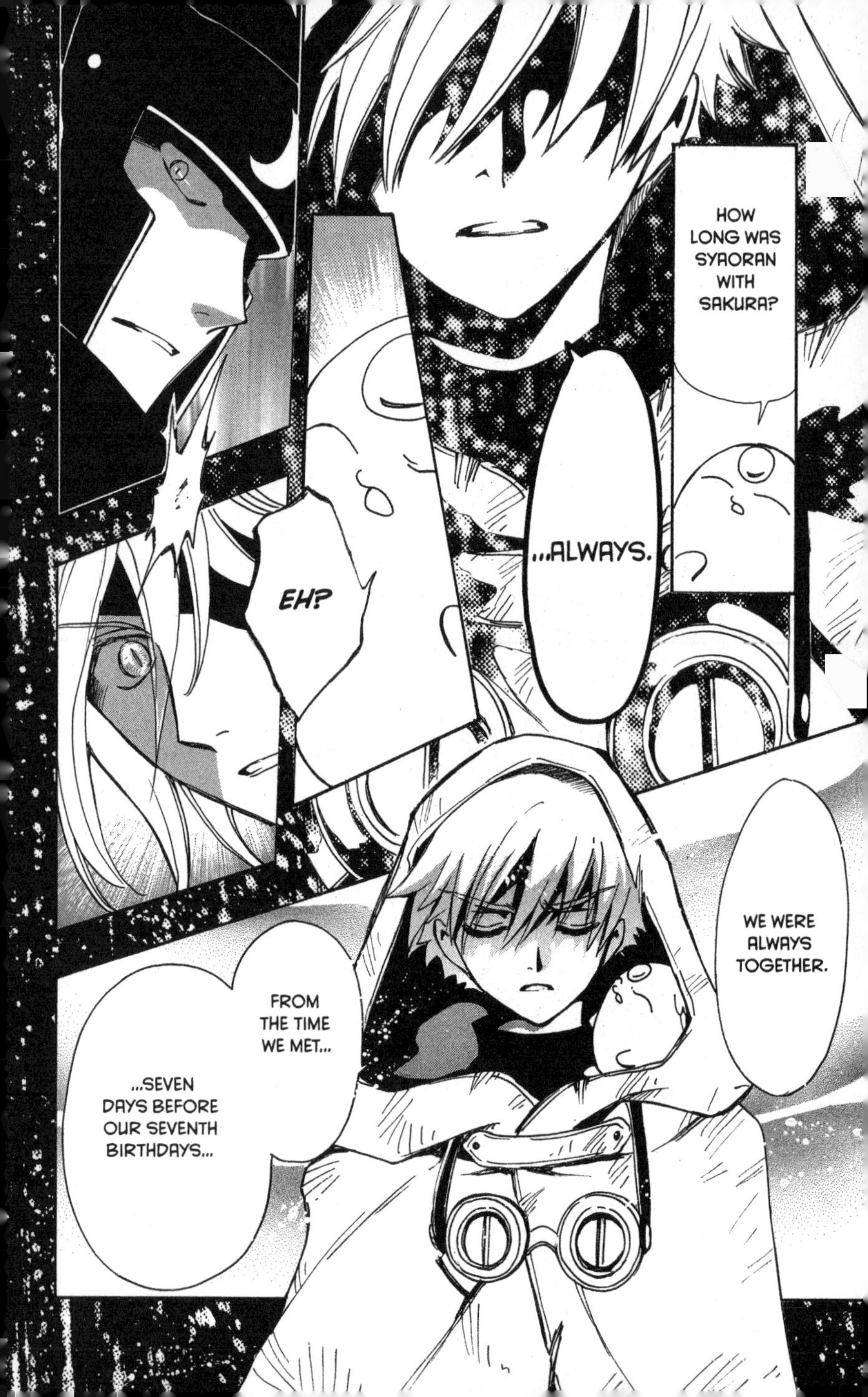
HOW LONG WAS SYAORAN WITH SAKURA?
...ALWAYS.
EH?
WE WERE ALWAYS TOGETHER.
FROM THE TIME WE MET...
...SEVEN DAYS BEFORE OUR SEVENTH BIRTHDAYS...

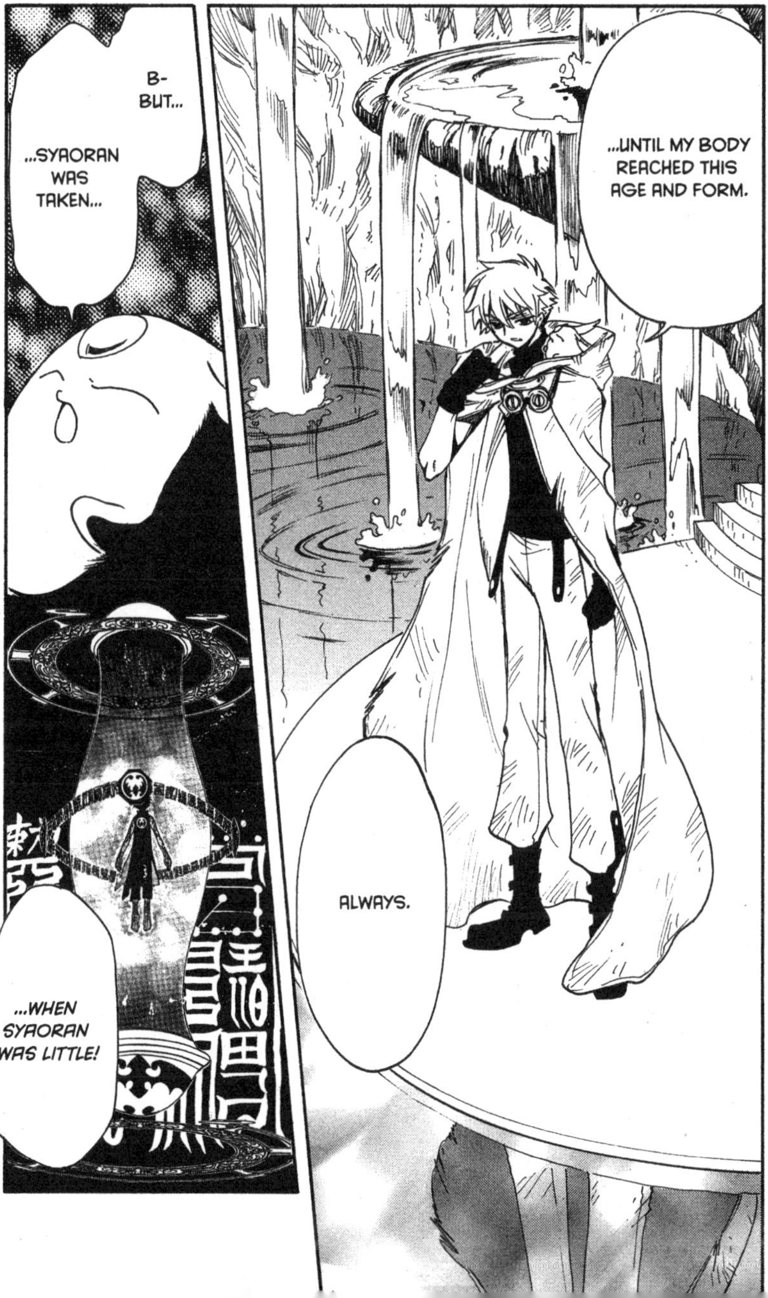
...UNTIL MY BODY REACHED THIS AGE AND FORM.
ALWAYS.
B-BUT...
...SYAORAN WAS TAKEN...
...WHEN SYAORAN WAS LITTLE!

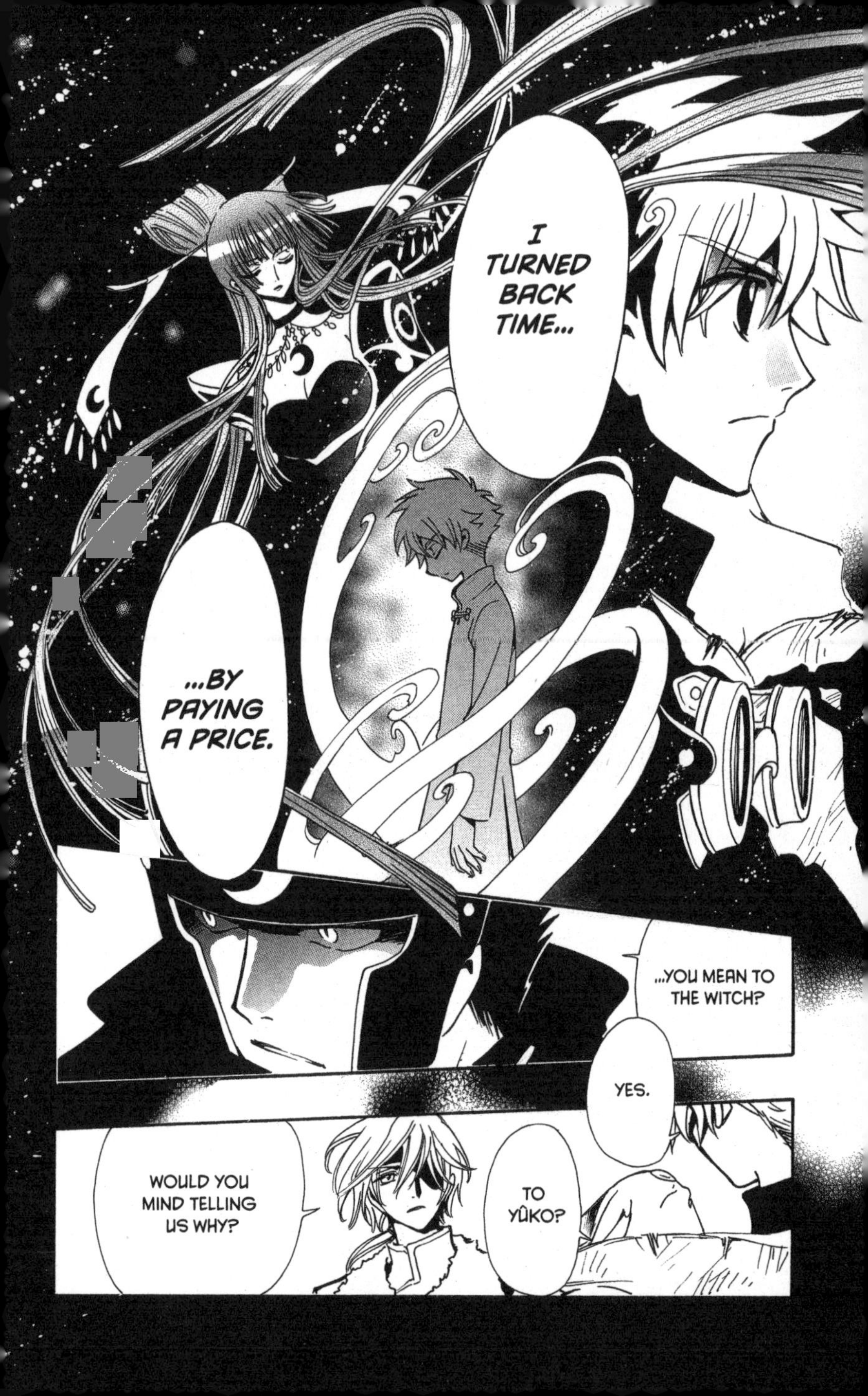
I TURNED BACK TIME...
...BY PAYING A PRICE.
...YOU MEAN TO THE WITCH?
YES.
TO YÛKO?
WOULD YOU MIND TELLING US WHY?

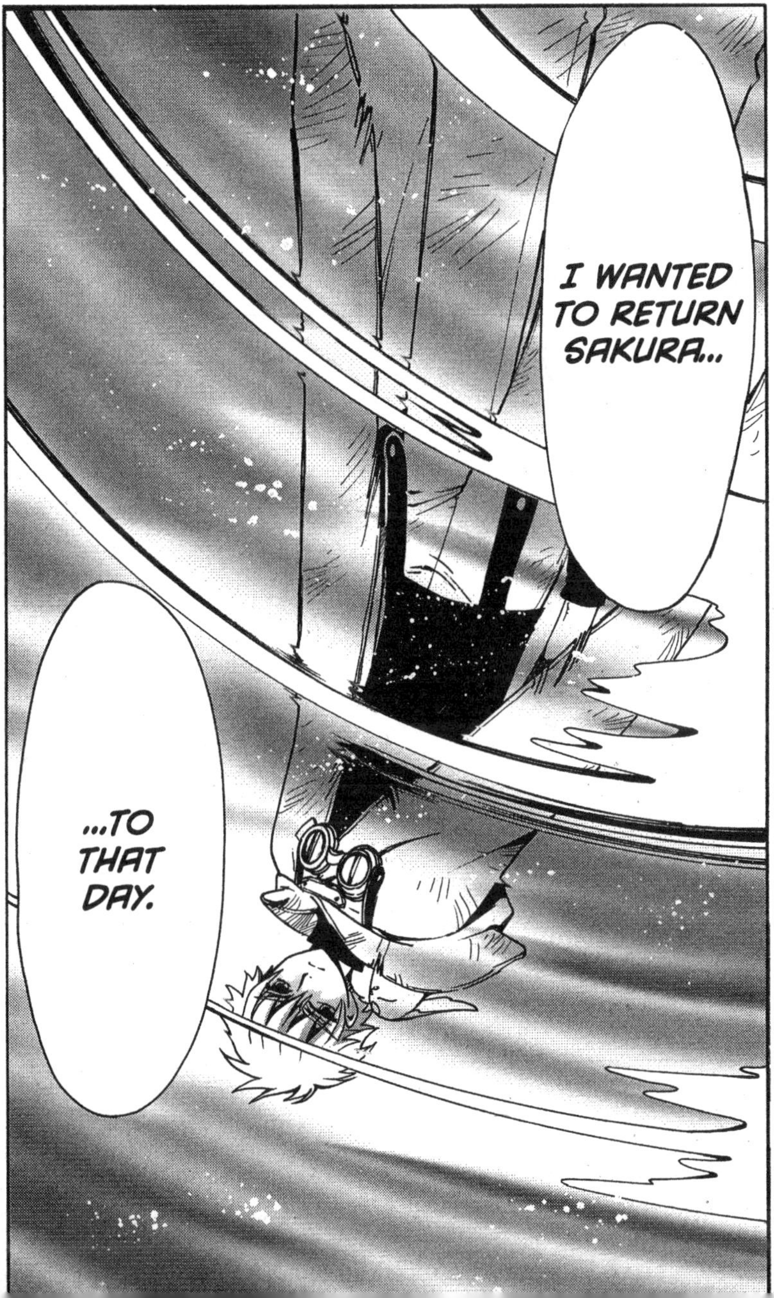
I WANTED TO RETURN SAKURA...
...TO THAT DAY.

RESERVoir CHRoNiCLE

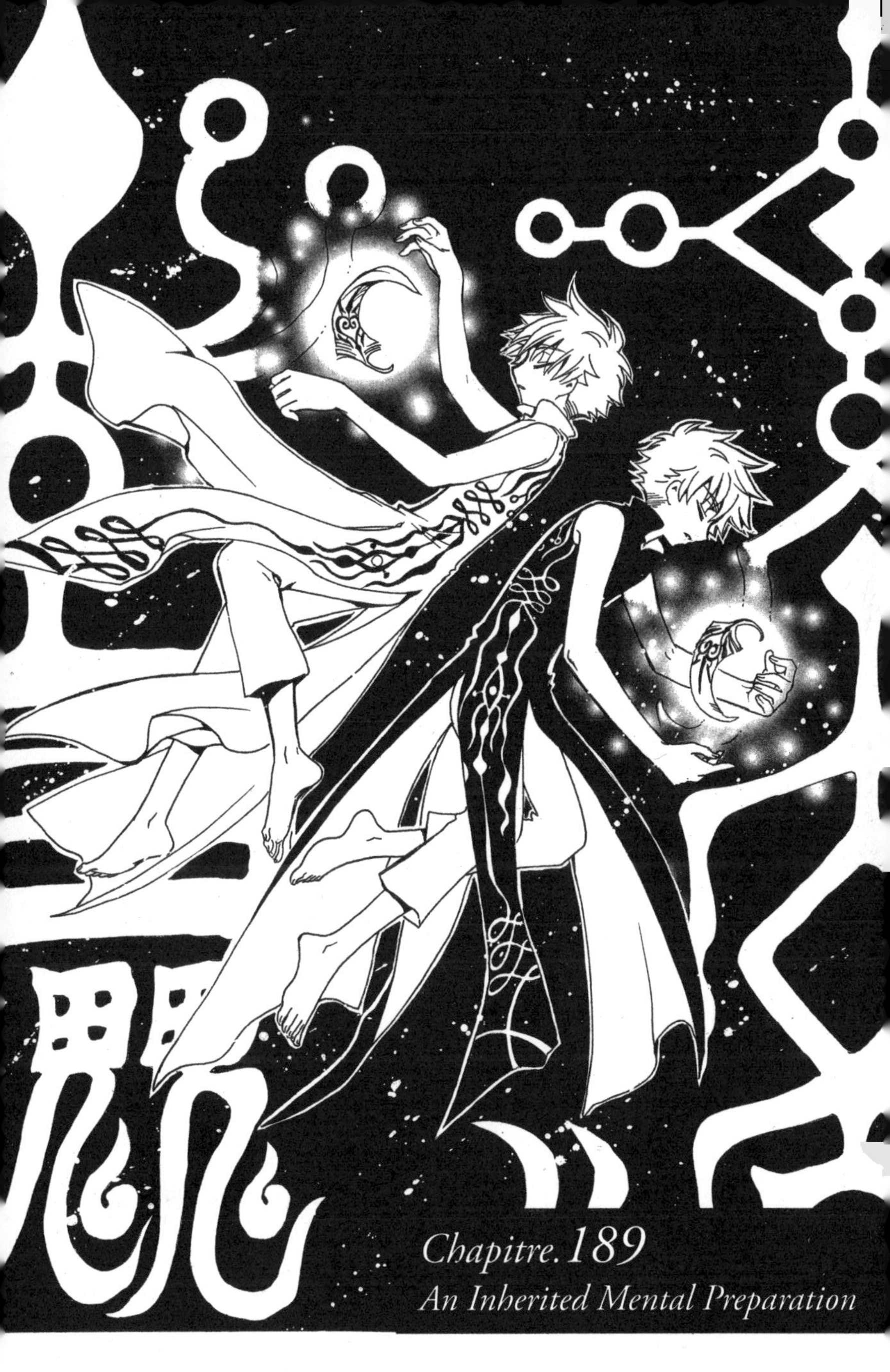
Chapitre. 189
An Inherited Mental Preparation

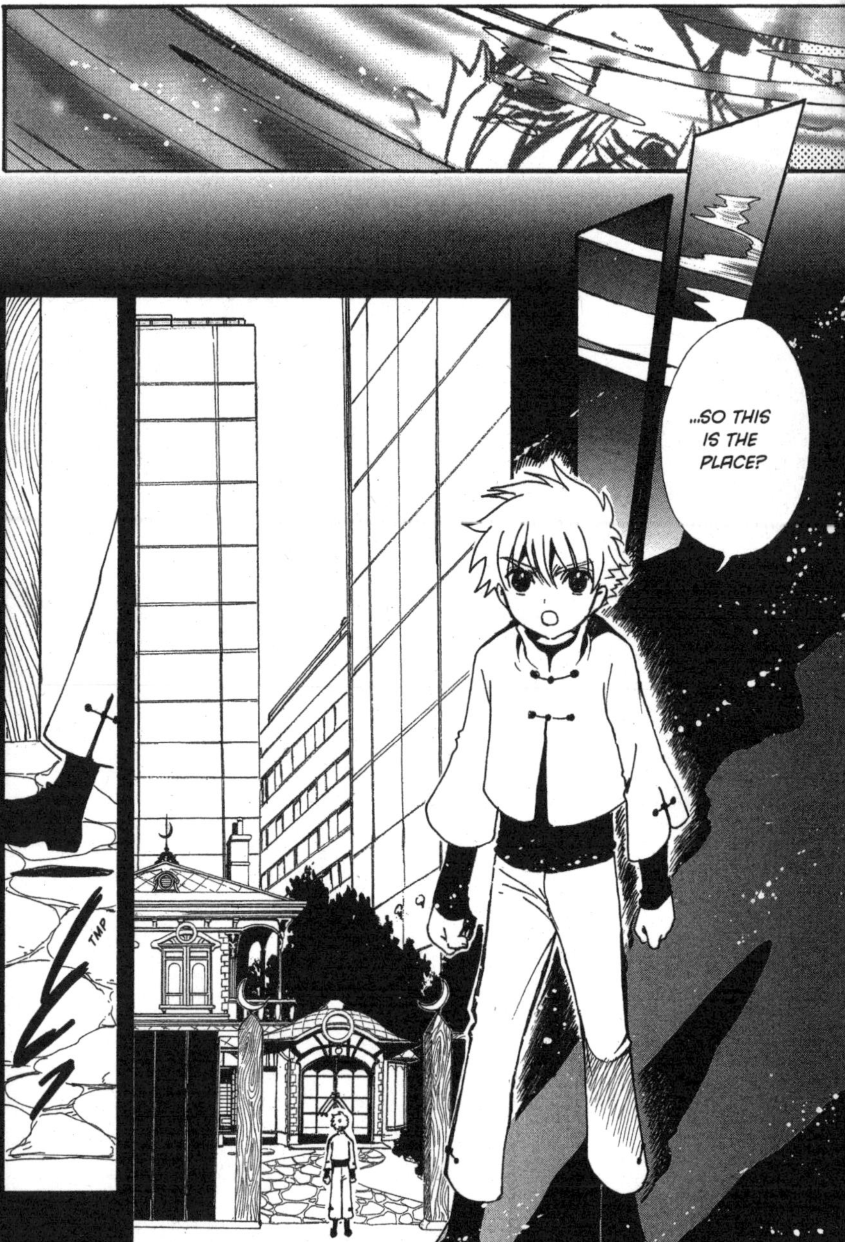
...SO THIS IS THE PLACE?
TMP

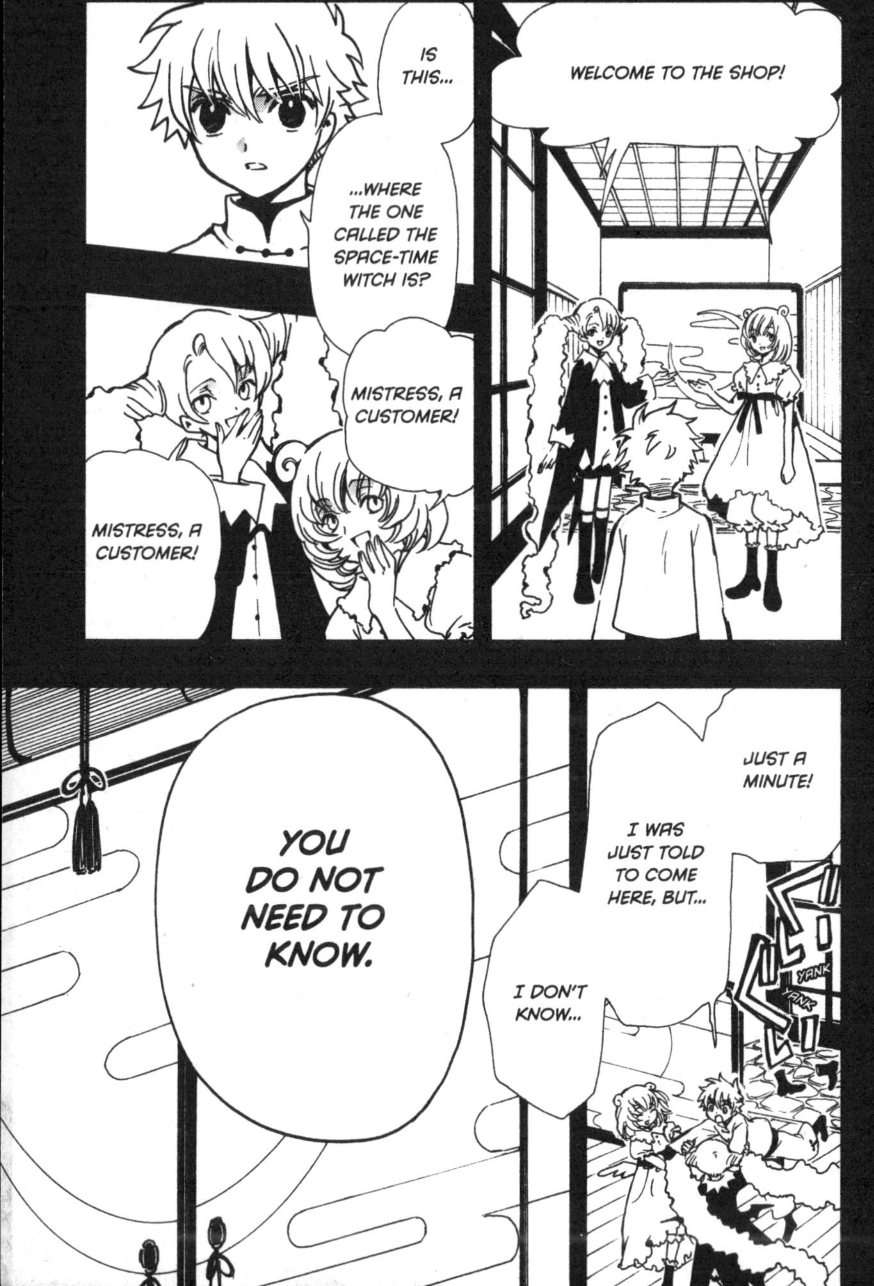
WELCOME TO THE SHOP!
IS THIS...
...WHERE THE ONE CALLED THE SPACE-TIME WITCH IS?
MISTRESS, A CUSTOMER!
MISTRESS, A CUSTOMER!
JUST A MINUTE!
I WAS JUST TOLD TO COME HERE, BUT...
I DON'T KNOW...
YANK
YANK
YOU DO NOT NEED TO KNOW.

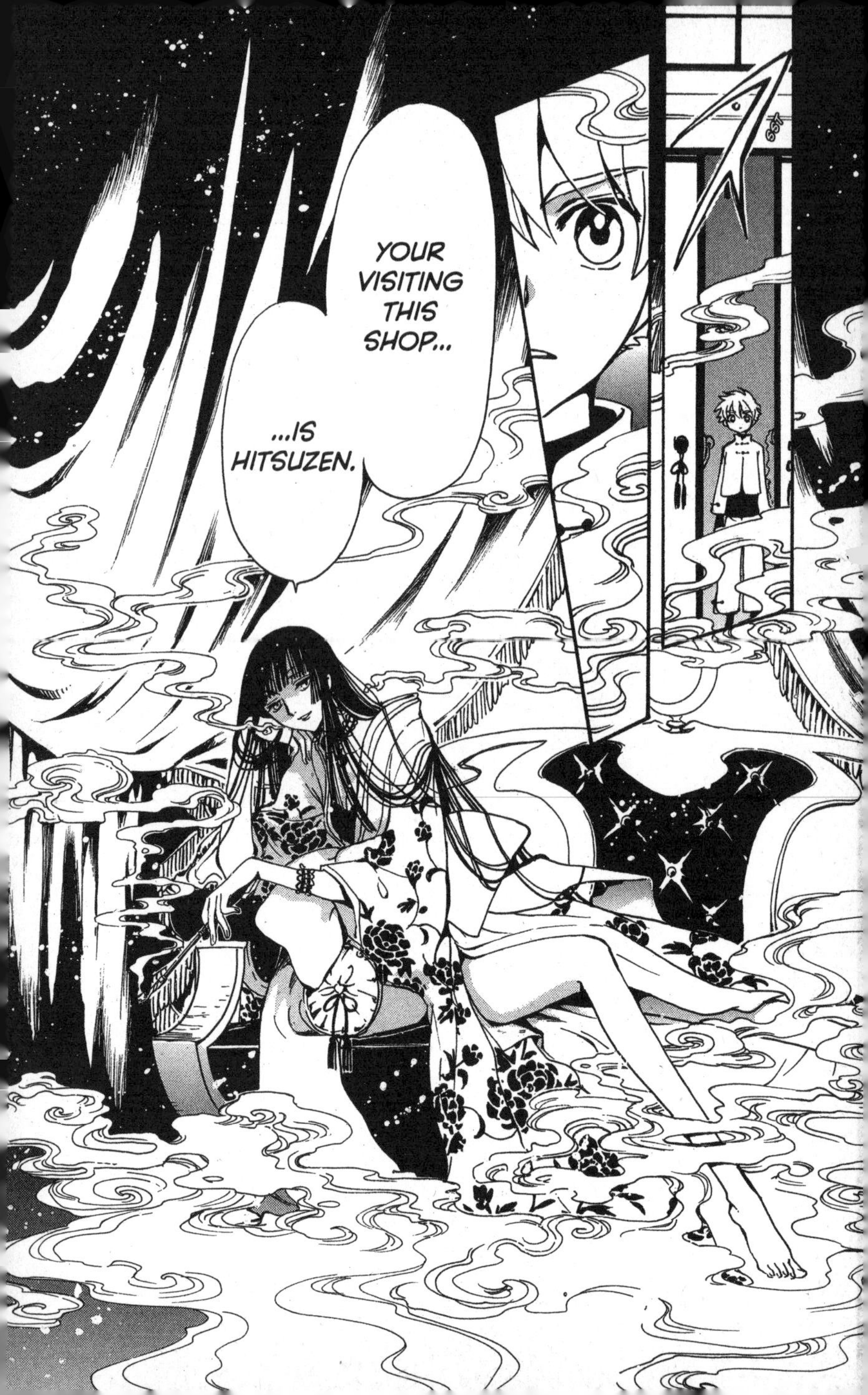
YOUR VISITING THIS SHOP...
...IS HITSUZEN.

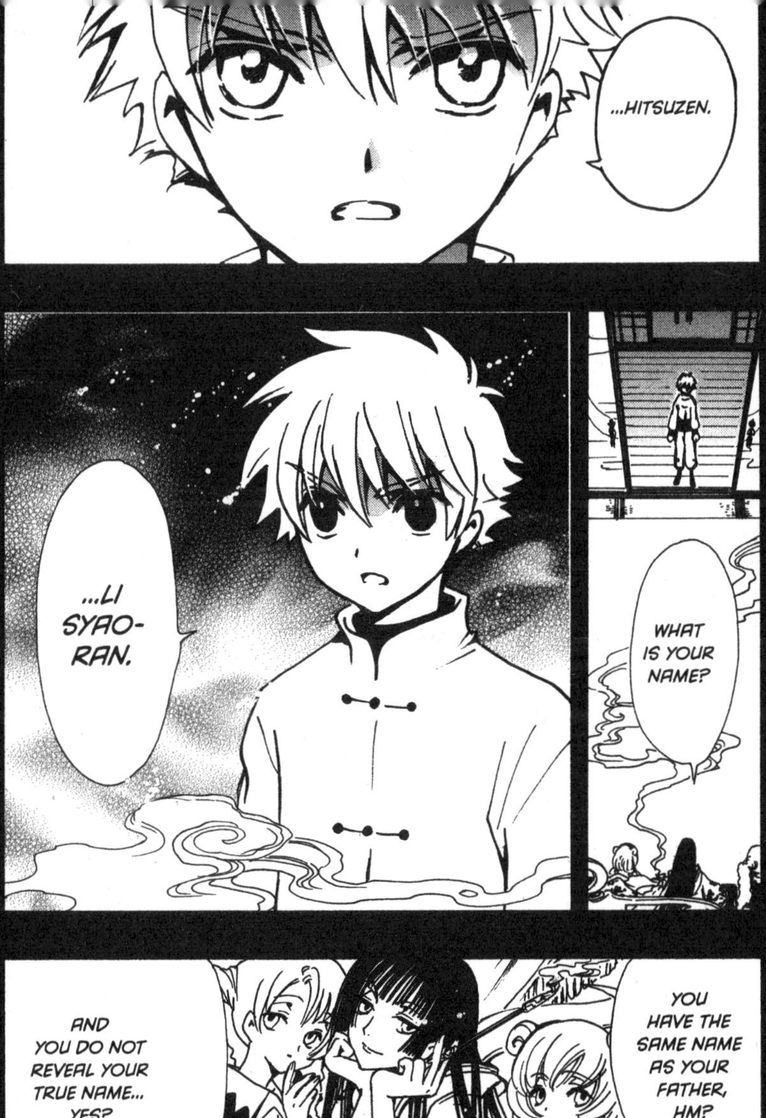
...HITSUZEN.
WHAT IS YOUR NAME?
...LI SYAO-RAN.
YOU HAVE THE SAME NAME AS YOUR FATHER, HM?
AND YOU DO NOT REVEAL YOUR TRUE NAME... YES?

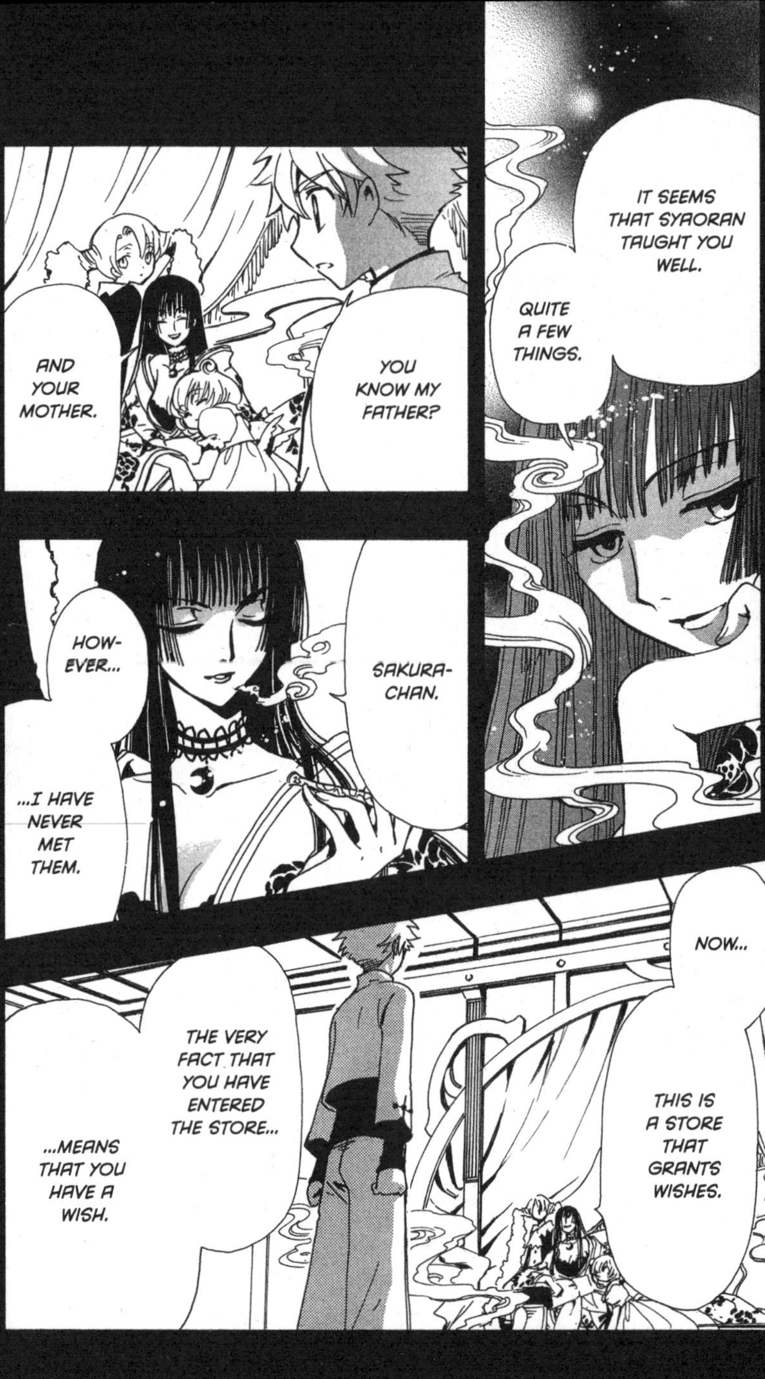
IT SEEMS THAT SYAORAN TAUGHT YOU WELL.
QUITE A FEW THINGS.
YOU KNOW MY FATHER?
AND YOUR MOTHER.
SAKURA-CHAN.
HOW-EVER...
...I HAVE NEVER MET THEM.
NOW...
THIS IS A STORE THAT GRANTS WISHES.
THE VERY FACT THAT YOU HAVE ENTERED THE STORE...
...MEANS THAT YOU HAVE A WISH.

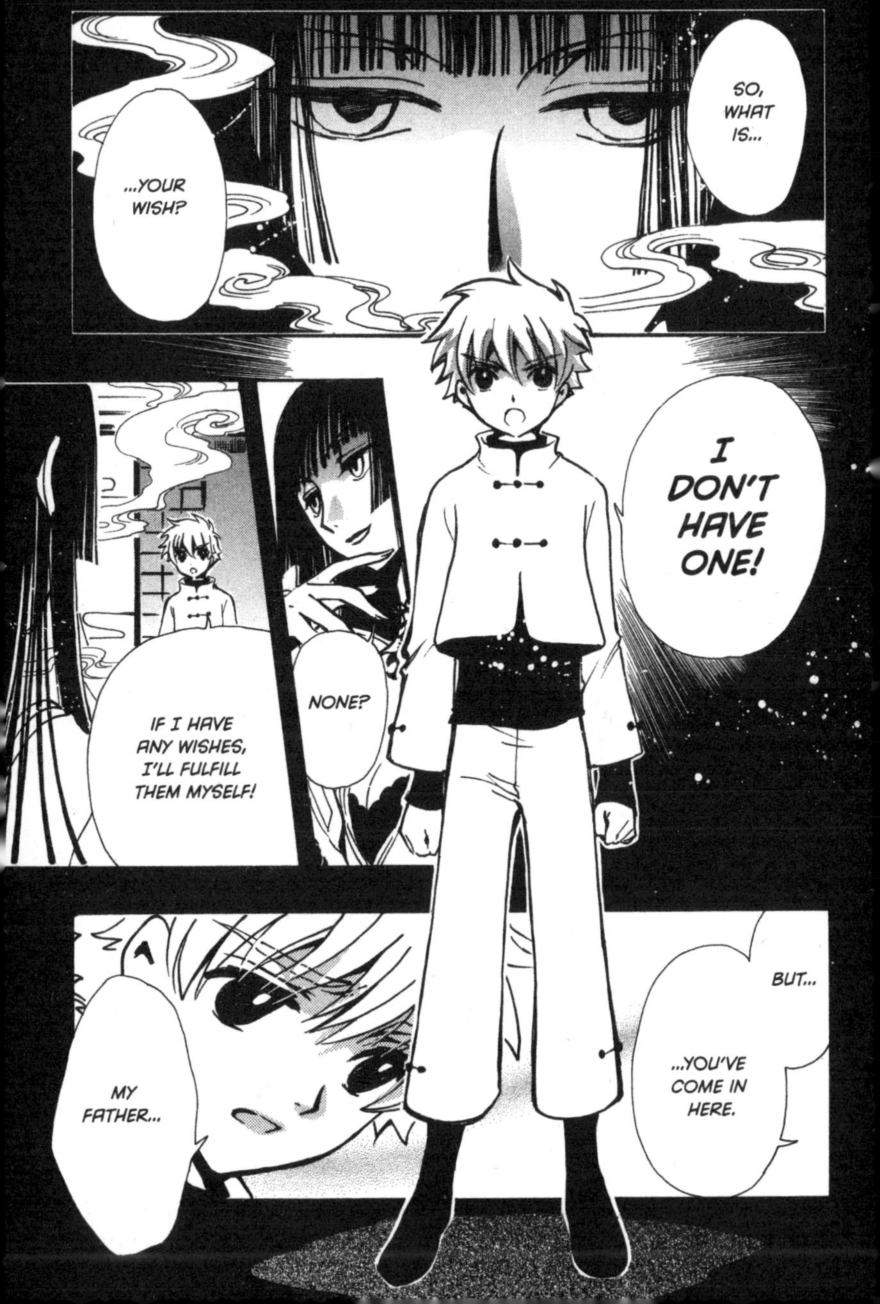
SO, WHAT IS...
...YOUR WISH?
I DON'T HAVE ONE!
NONE?
IF I HAVE ANY WISHES, I'LL FULFILL THEM MYSELF!
BUT...
...YOU'VE COME IN HERE.
MY FATHER...

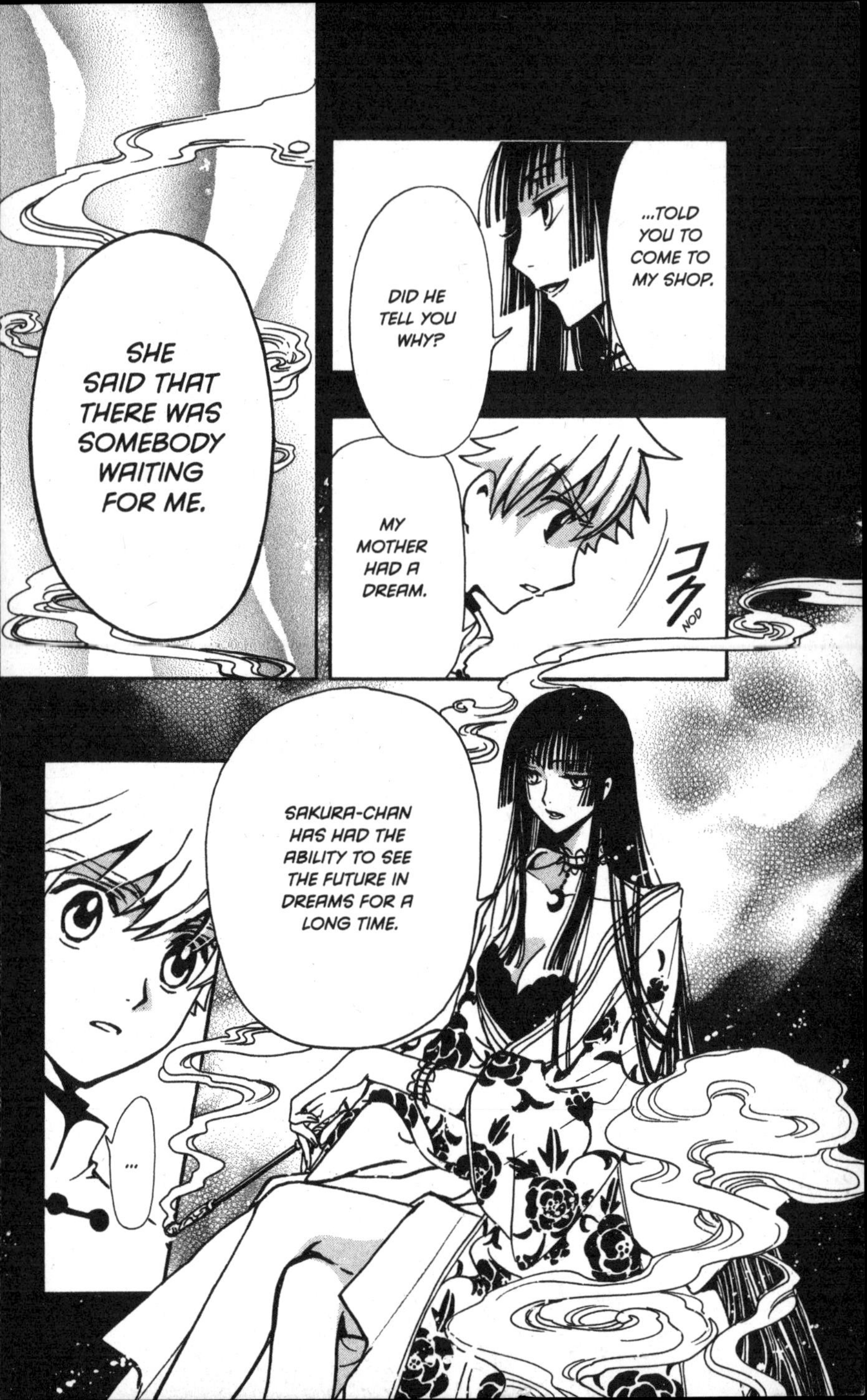
...TOLD YOU TO COME TO MY SHOP.
DID HE TELL YOU WHY?
MY MOTHER HAD A DREAM.
コク
NOD
SHE SAID THAT THERE WAS SOMEBODY WAITING FOR ME.
SAKURA-CHAN HAS HAD THE ABILITY TO SEE THE FUTURE IN DREAMS FOR A LONG TIME.
...

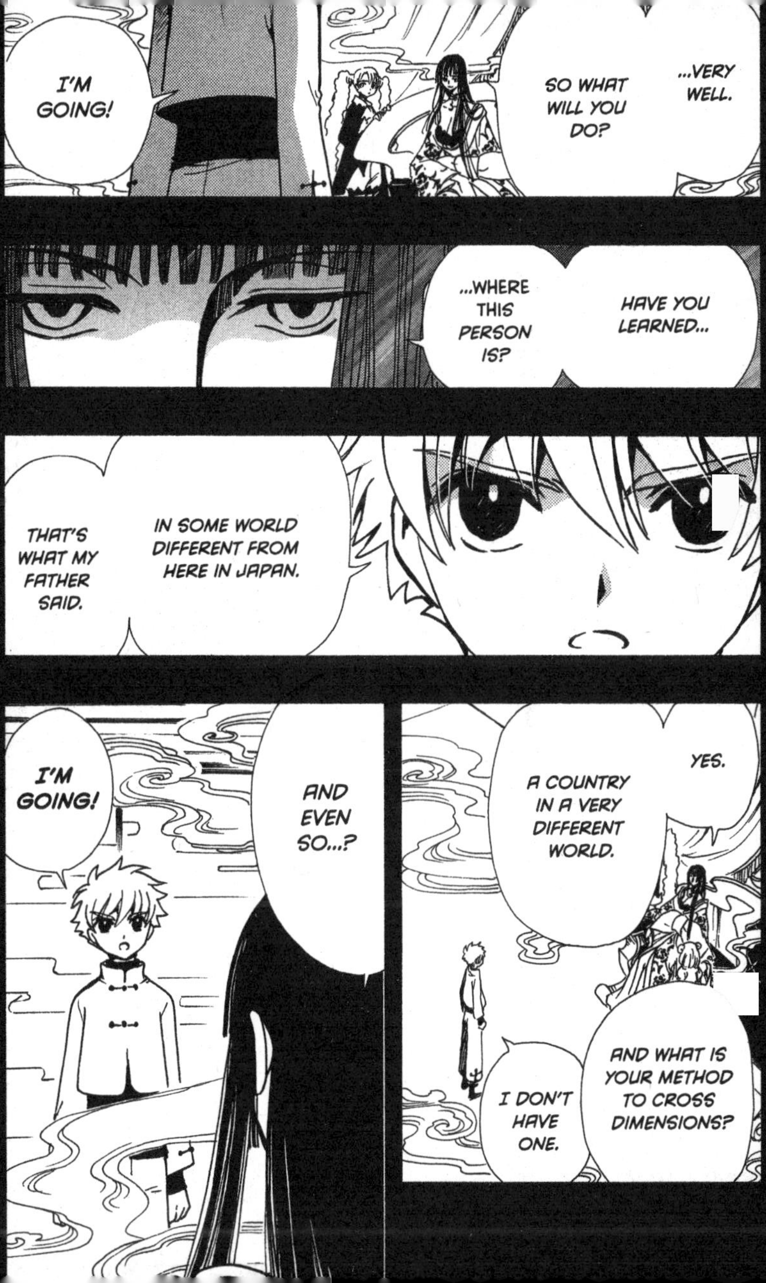
...VERY WELL.
SO WHAT WILL YOU DO?
I'M GOING!
HAVE YOU LEARNED...
...WHERE THIS PERSON IS?
IN SOME WORLD DIFFERENT FROM HERE IN JAPAN.
THAT'S WHAT MY FATHER SAID.
YES.
A COUNTRY IN A VERY DIFFERENT WORLD.
AND WHAT IS YOUR METHOD TO CROSS DIMENSIONS?
I DON'T HAVE ONE.
AND EVEN SO...?
I'M GOING!

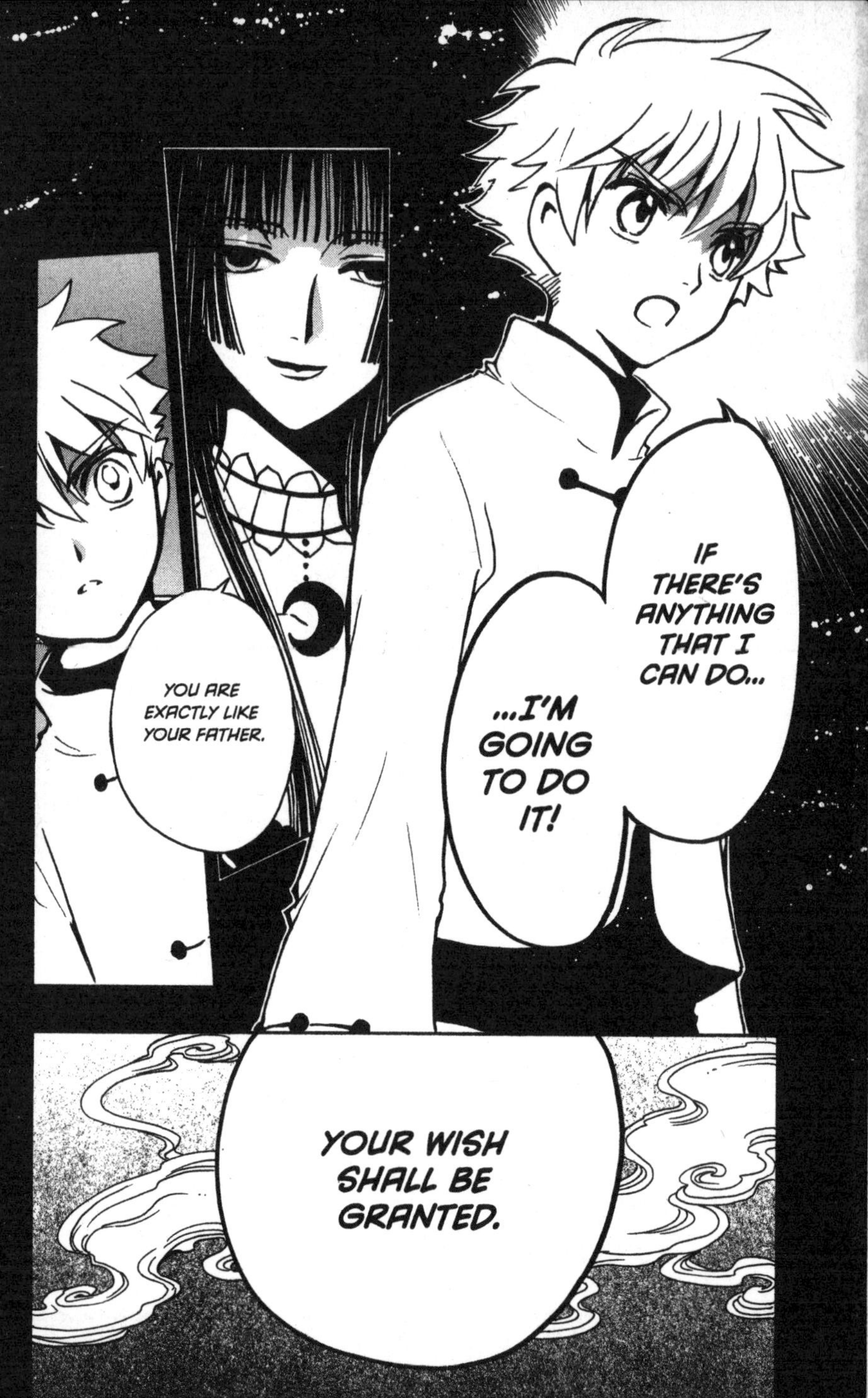
IF THERE'S ANYTHING THAT I CAN DO...
...I'M GOING TO DO IT!
YOU ARE EXACTLY LIKE YOUR FATHER.
YOUR WISH SHALL BE GRANTED.

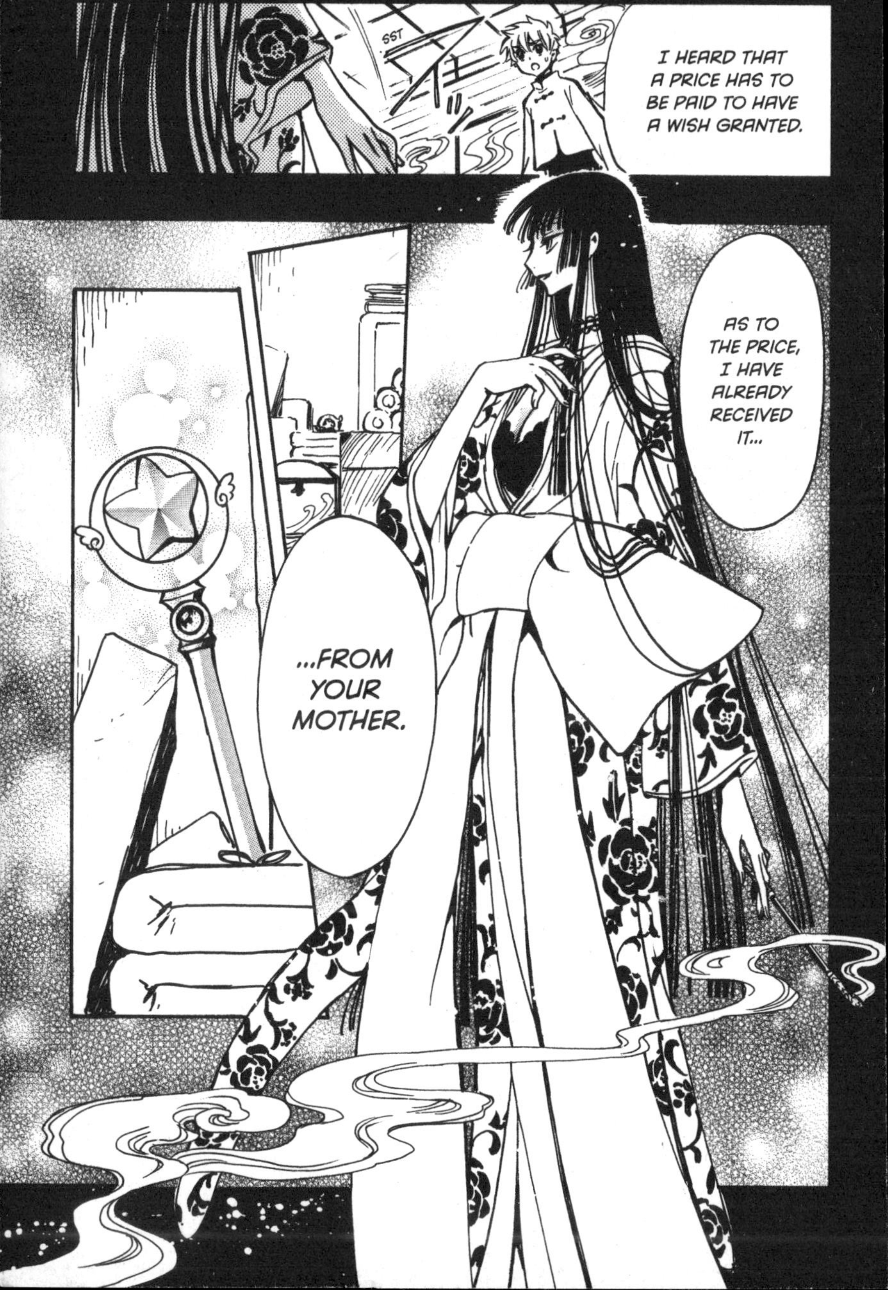

I HEARD THAT A PRICE HAS TO BE PAID TO HAVE A WISH GRANTED.
SST
AS TO THE PRICE, I HAVE ALREADY RECEIVED IT...
...FROM YOUR MOTHER.

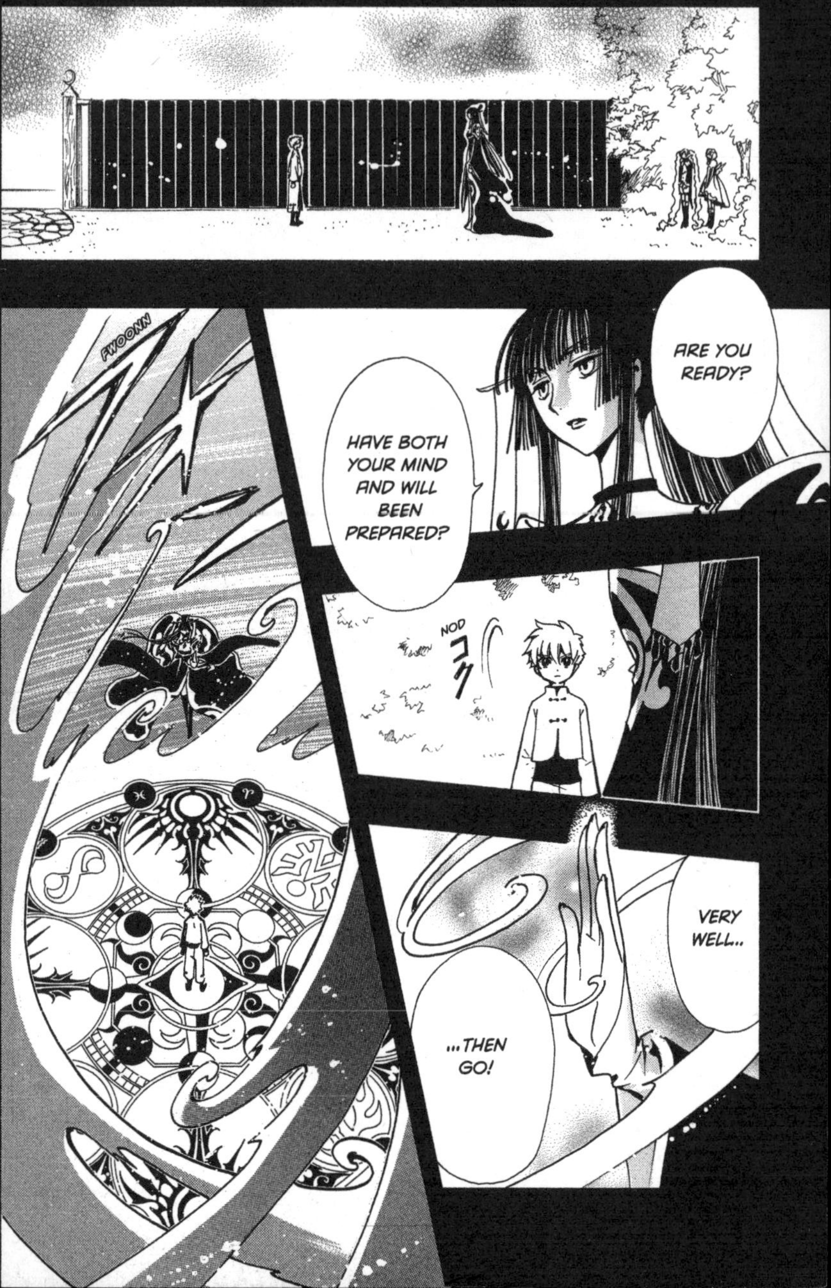
ARE YOU READY?
HAVE BOTH YOUR MIND AND WILL BEEN PREPARED?
NOD
VERY WELL...
...THEN GO!
FWOONN

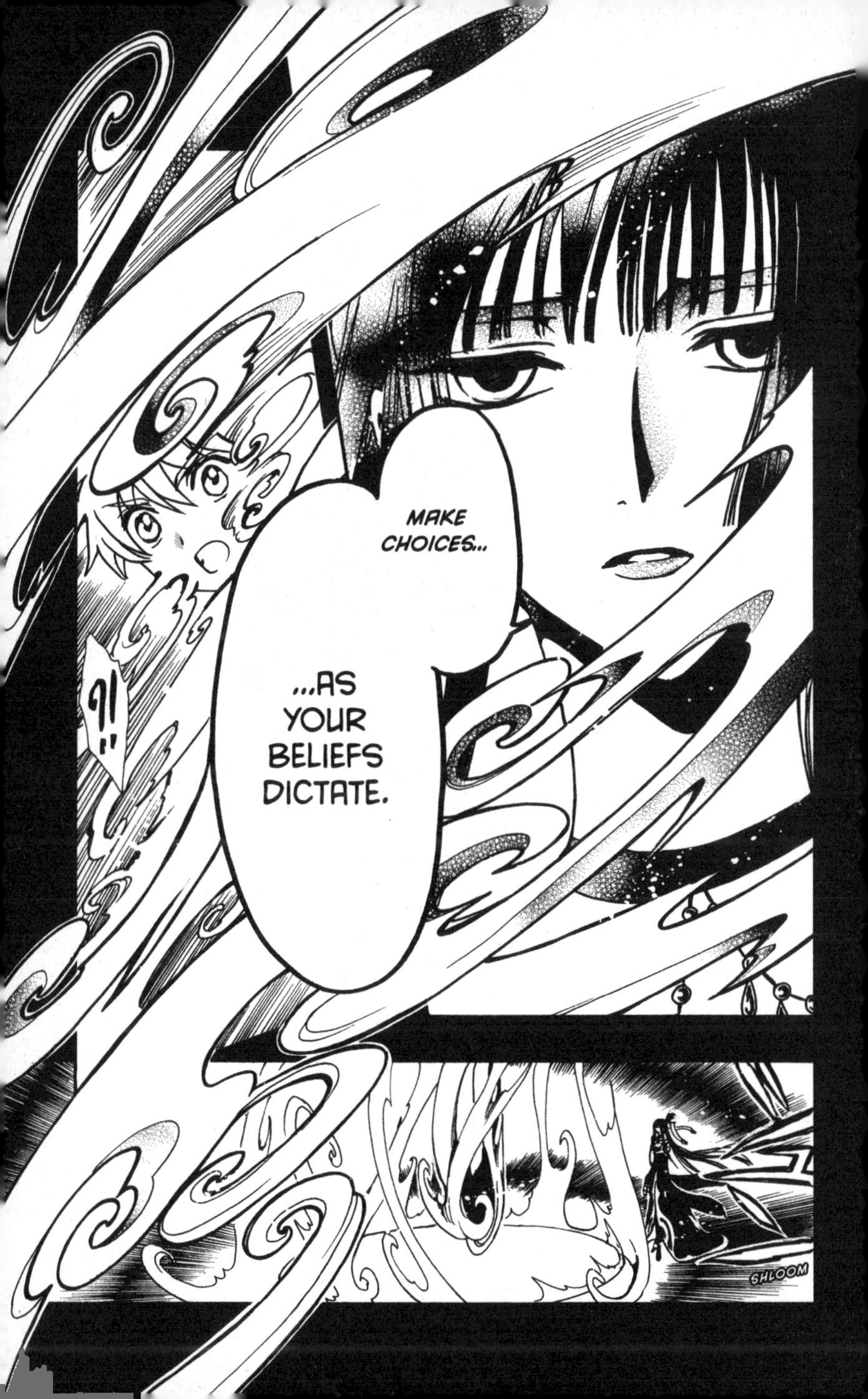
MAKE CHOICES...
...AS YOUR BELIEFS DICTATE.
?!!
SHLOOM

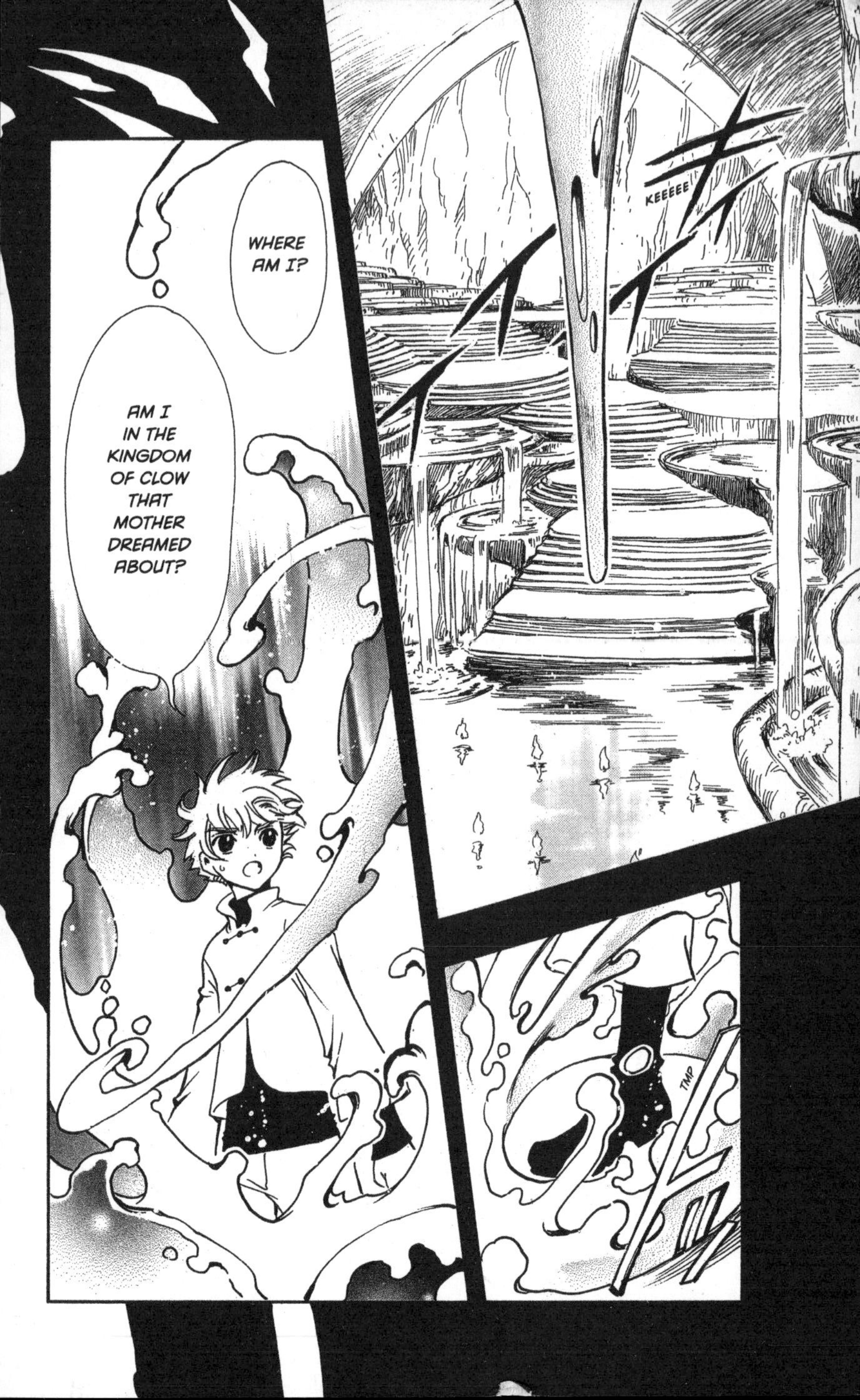
KEEEEE
WHERE AM I?
AM I IN THE KINGDOM OF CLOW THAT MOTHER DREAMED ABOUT?
TMP

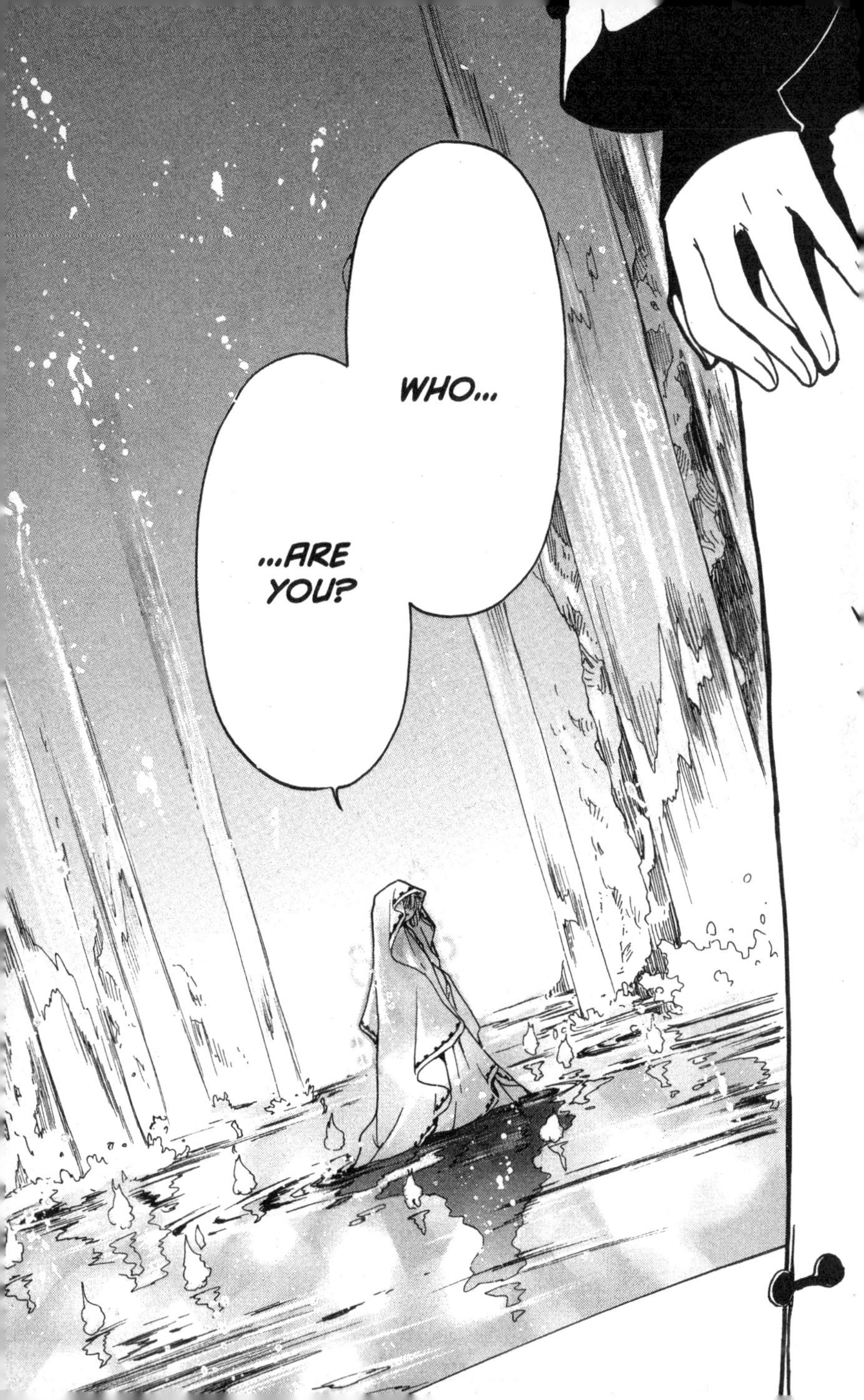
WHO...
...ARE YOU?

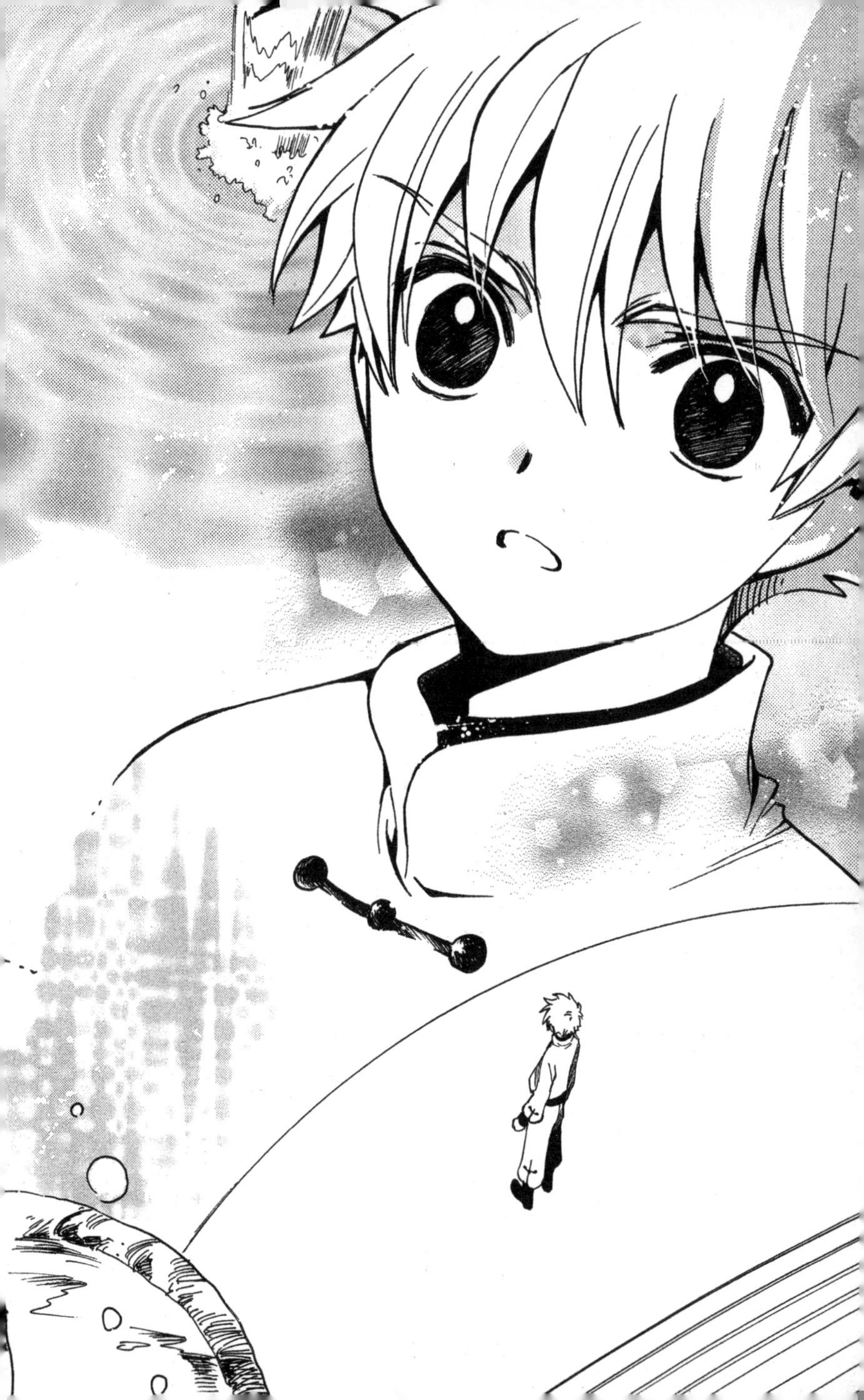

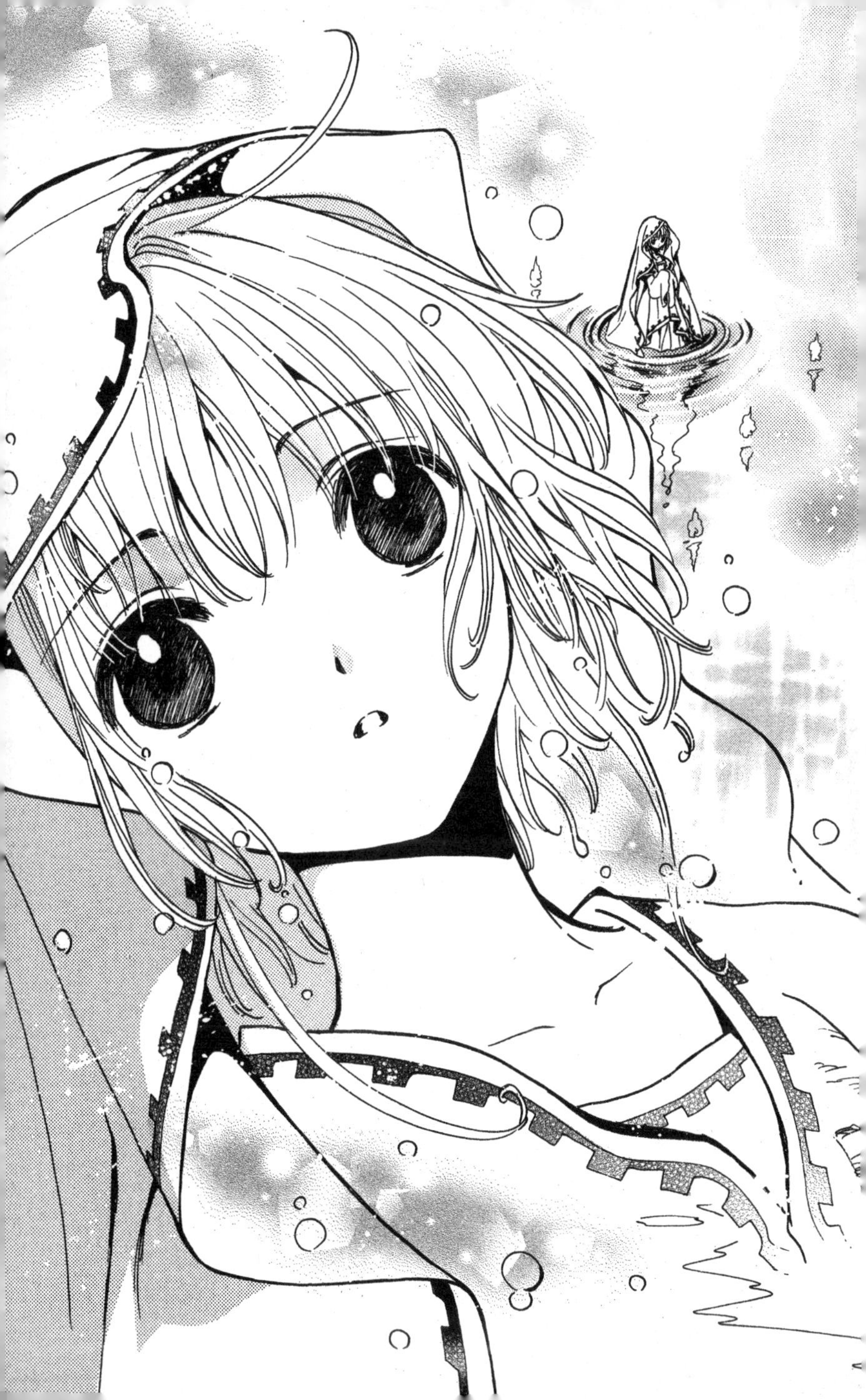

ツバサ

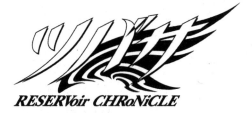

RESERVoir CHRoNiCLE

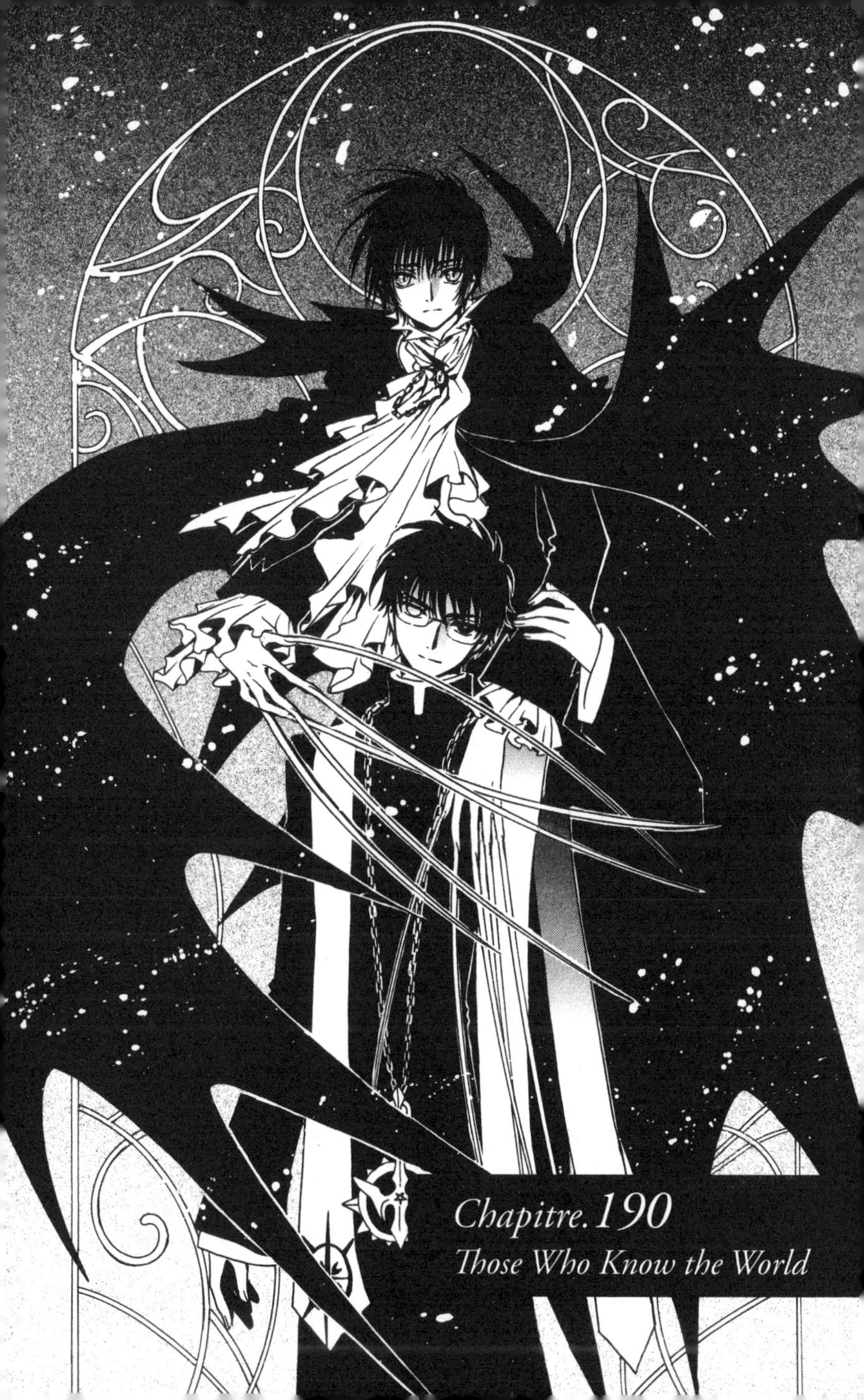
Chapitre.190
Those Who Know the World

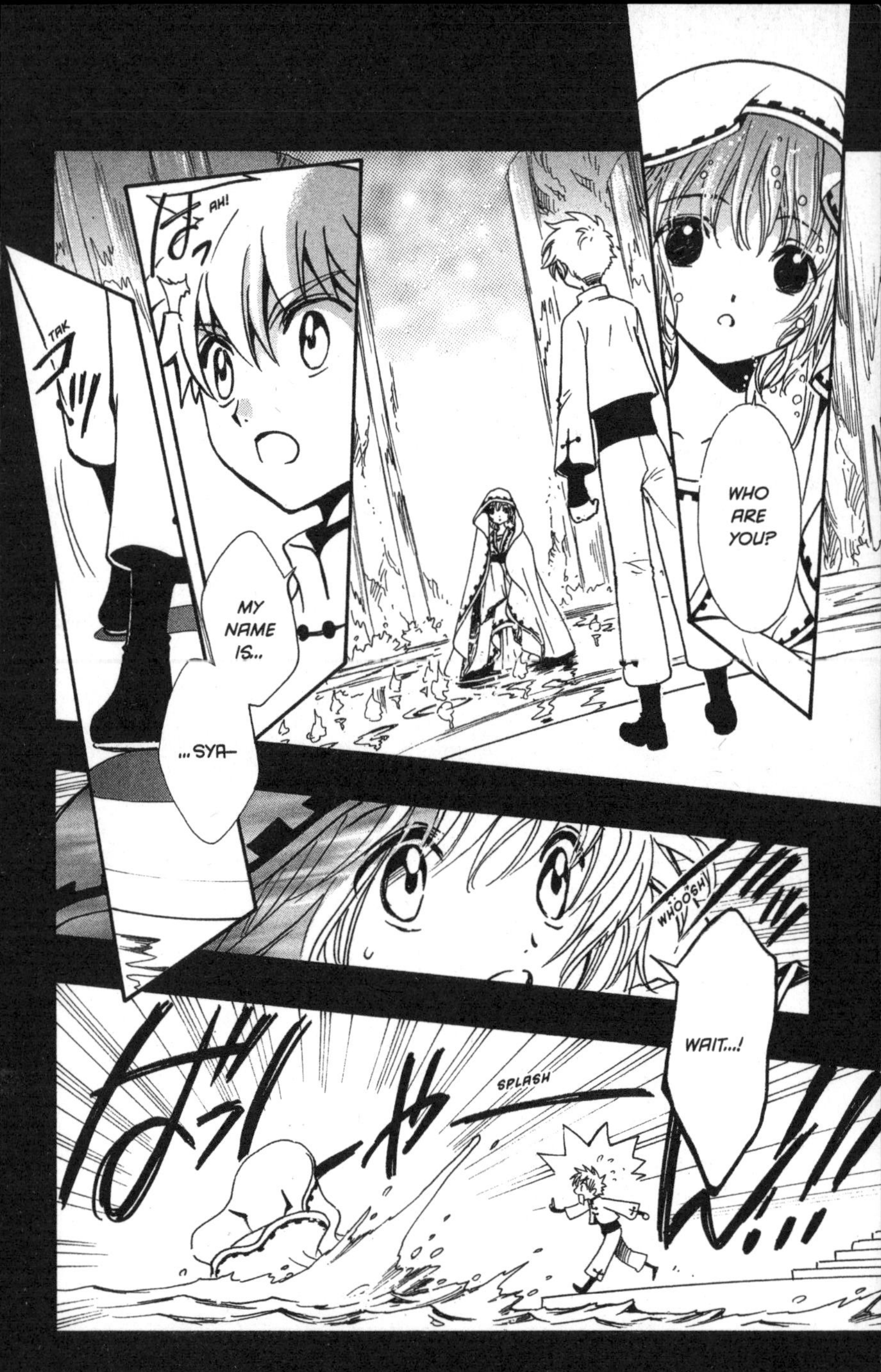
WHO ARE YOU?
AH!
MY NAME IS...
...SYA—
TAK
WHOOSH
WAIT...!
SPLASH

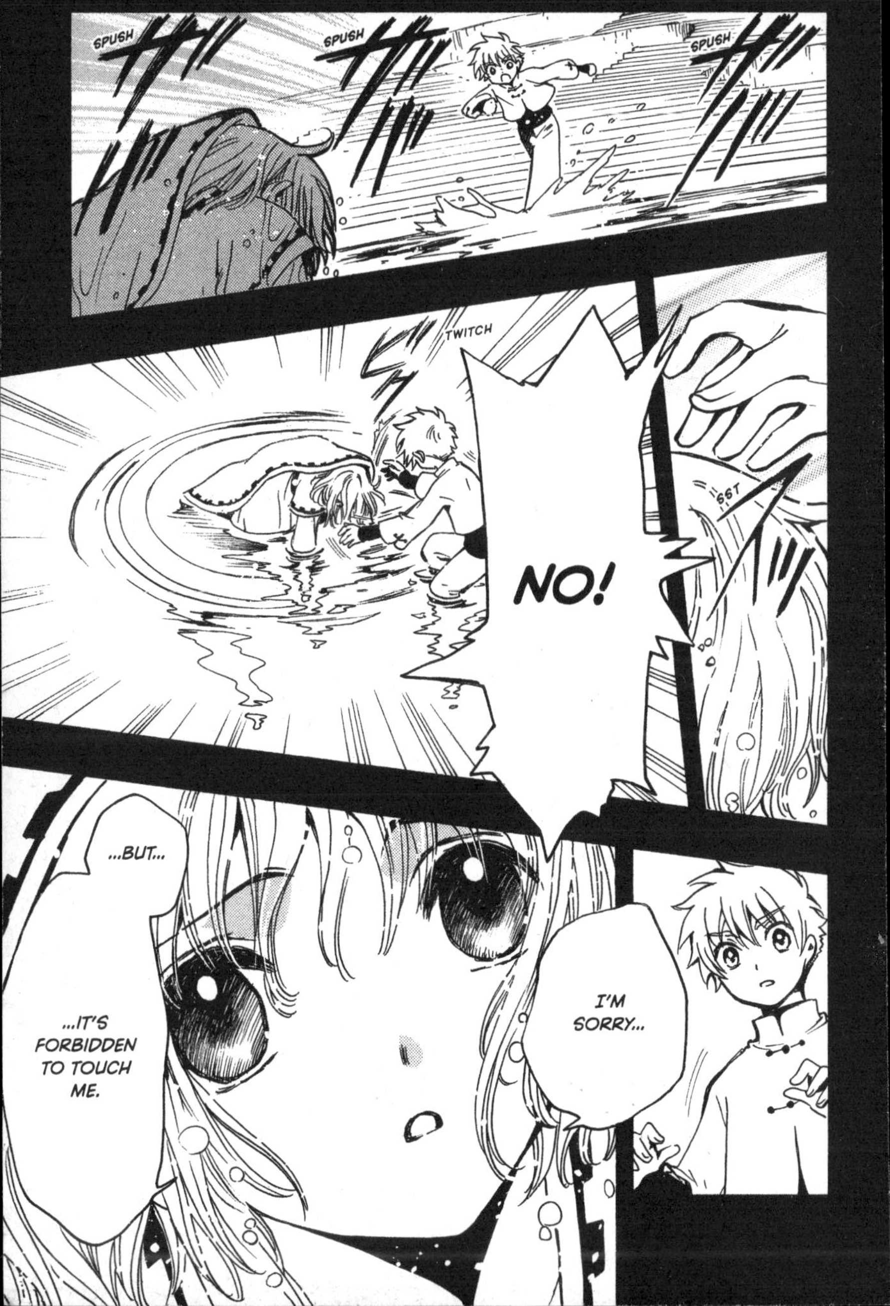
SPUSH
SPUSH
SPUSH
TWITCH
SST
NO!
I'M SORRY...
...BUT...
...IT'S FORBIDDEN TO TOUCH ME.

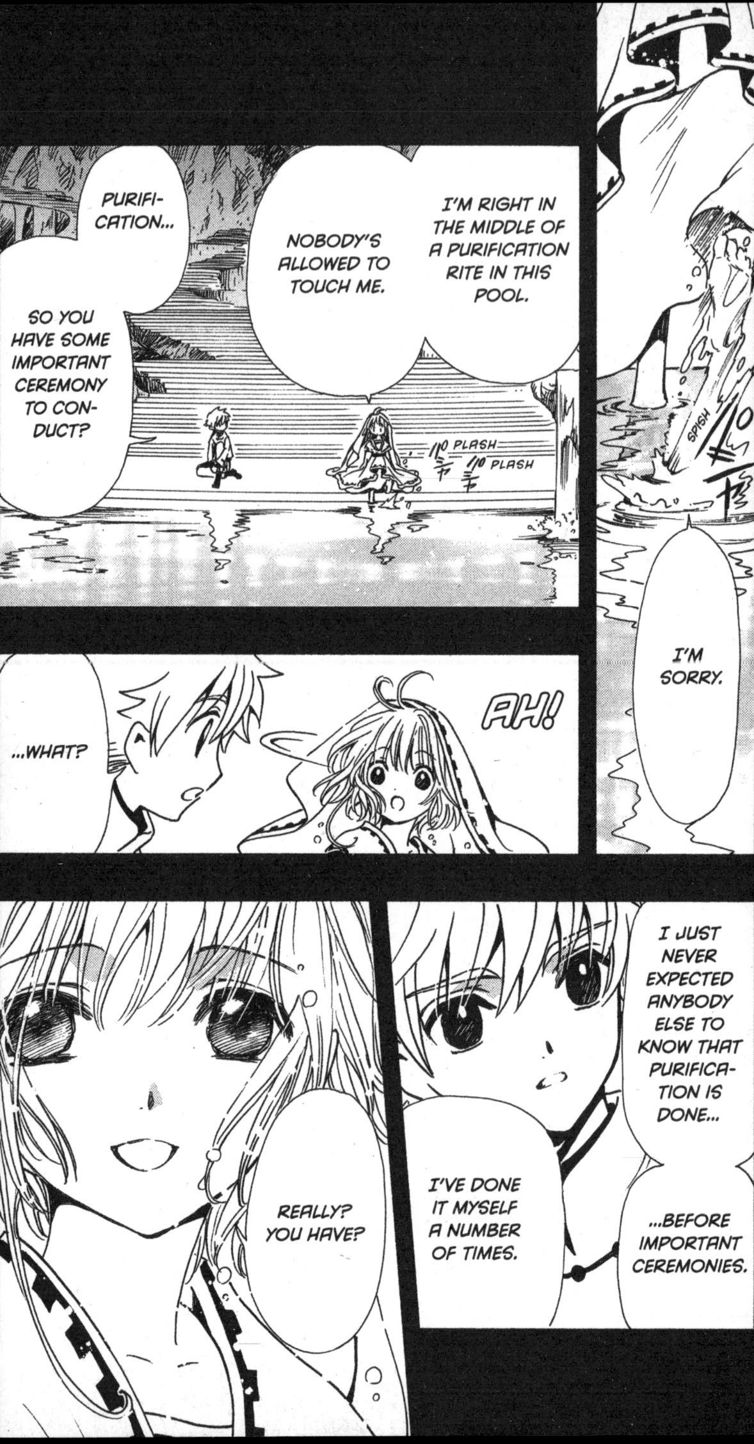
I'M RIGHT IN THE MIDDLE OF A PURIFICATION RITE IN THIS POOL.
NOBODY'S ALLOWED TO TOUCH ME.
PLASH
PLASH
PURIFI-CATION...
SO YOU HAVE SOME IMPORTANT CEREMONY TO CON-DUCT?
AH!
...WHAT?
SPISH
I'M SORRY.
I JUST NEVER EXPECTED ANYBODY ELSE TO KNOW THAT PURIFICA-TION IS DONE...
...BEFORE IMPORTANT CEREMONIES.
I'VE DONE IT MYSELF A NUMBER OF TIMES.
REALLY? YOU HAVE?

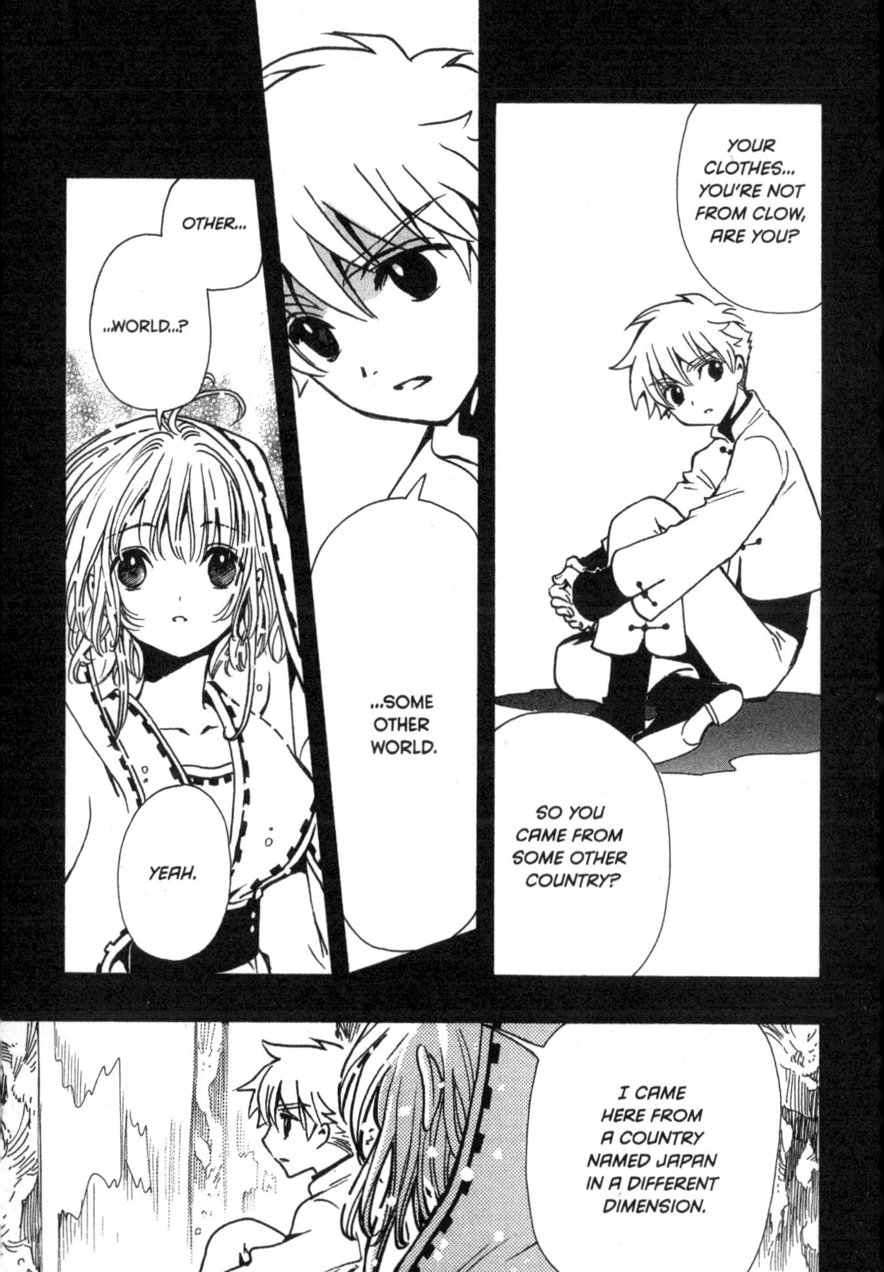
YOUR CLOTHES... YOU'RE NOT FROM CLOW, ARE YOU?
SO YOU CAME FROM SOME OTHER COUNTRY?
...SOME OTHER WORLD.
OTHER...
...WORLD...?
YEAH.
I CAME HERE FROM A COUNTRY NAMED JAPAN IN A DIFFERENT DIMENSION.

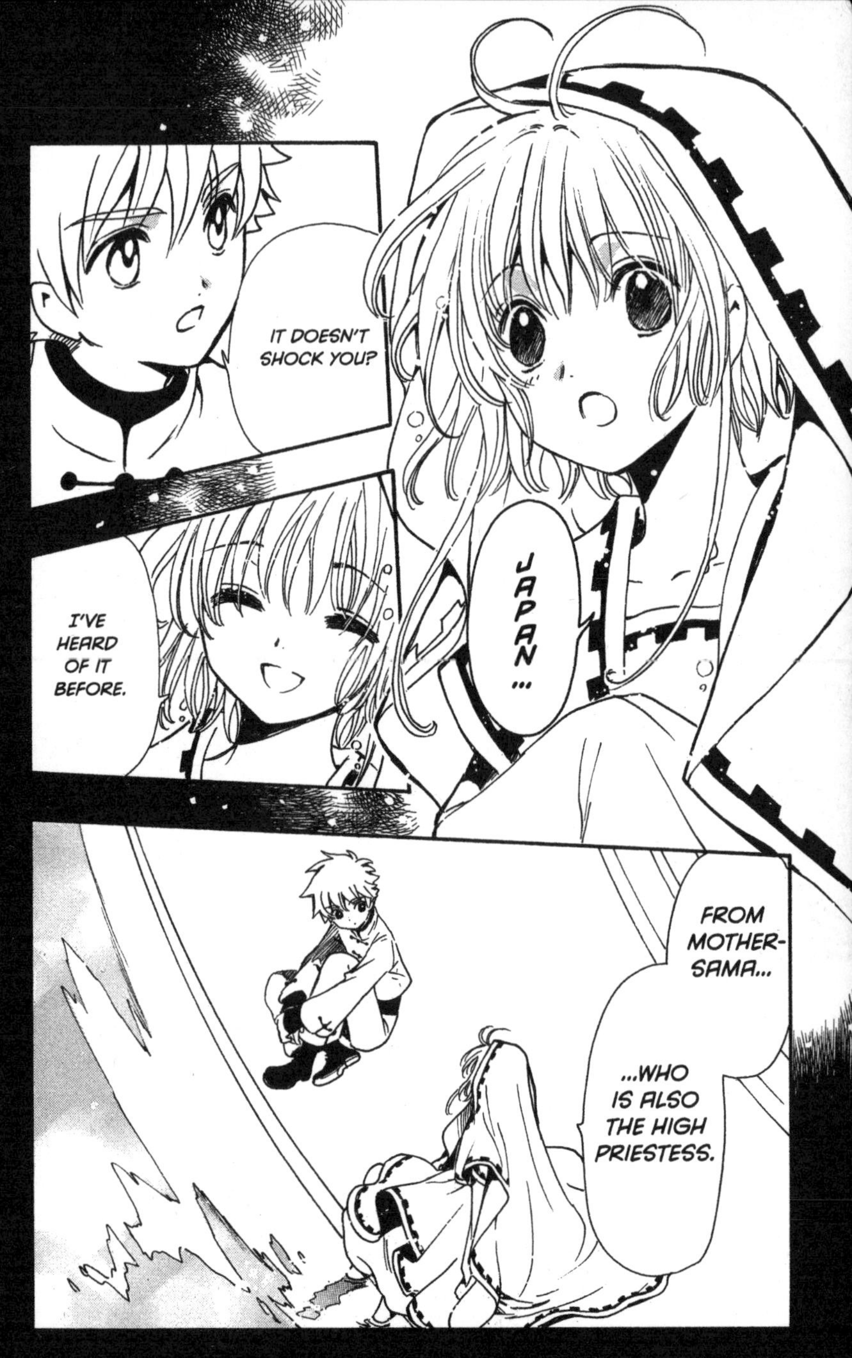
JAPAN...
IT DOESN'T SHOCK YOU?
I'VE HEARD OF IT BEFORE.
FROM MOTHER-SAMA...
...WHO IS ALSO THE HIGH PRIESTESS.

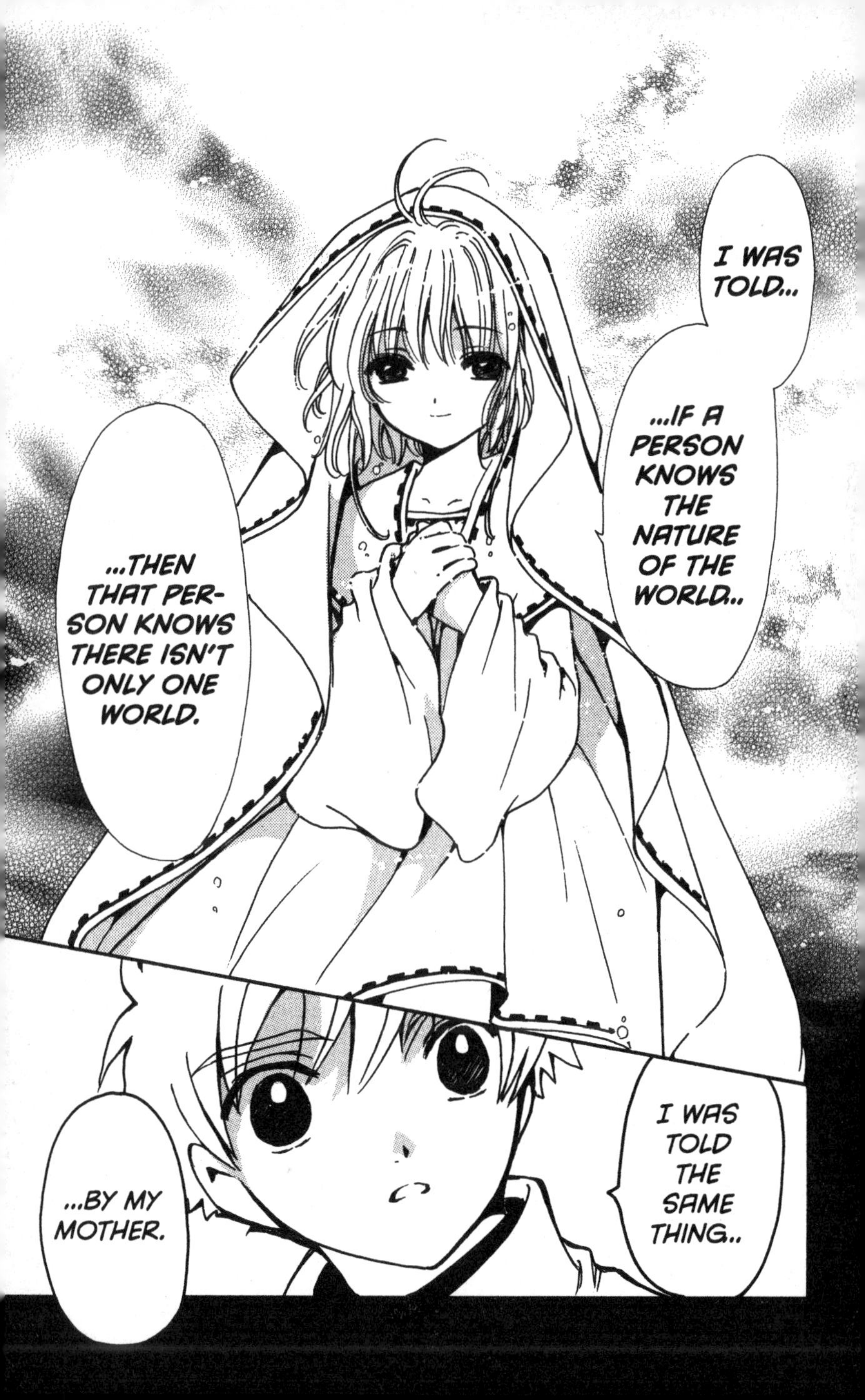
I WAS TOLD...
...IF A PERSON KNOWS THE NATURE OF THE WORLD..
...THEN THAT PER-SON KNOWS THERE ISN'T ONLY ONE WORLD.
I WAS TOLD THE SAME THING..
...BY MY MOTHER.

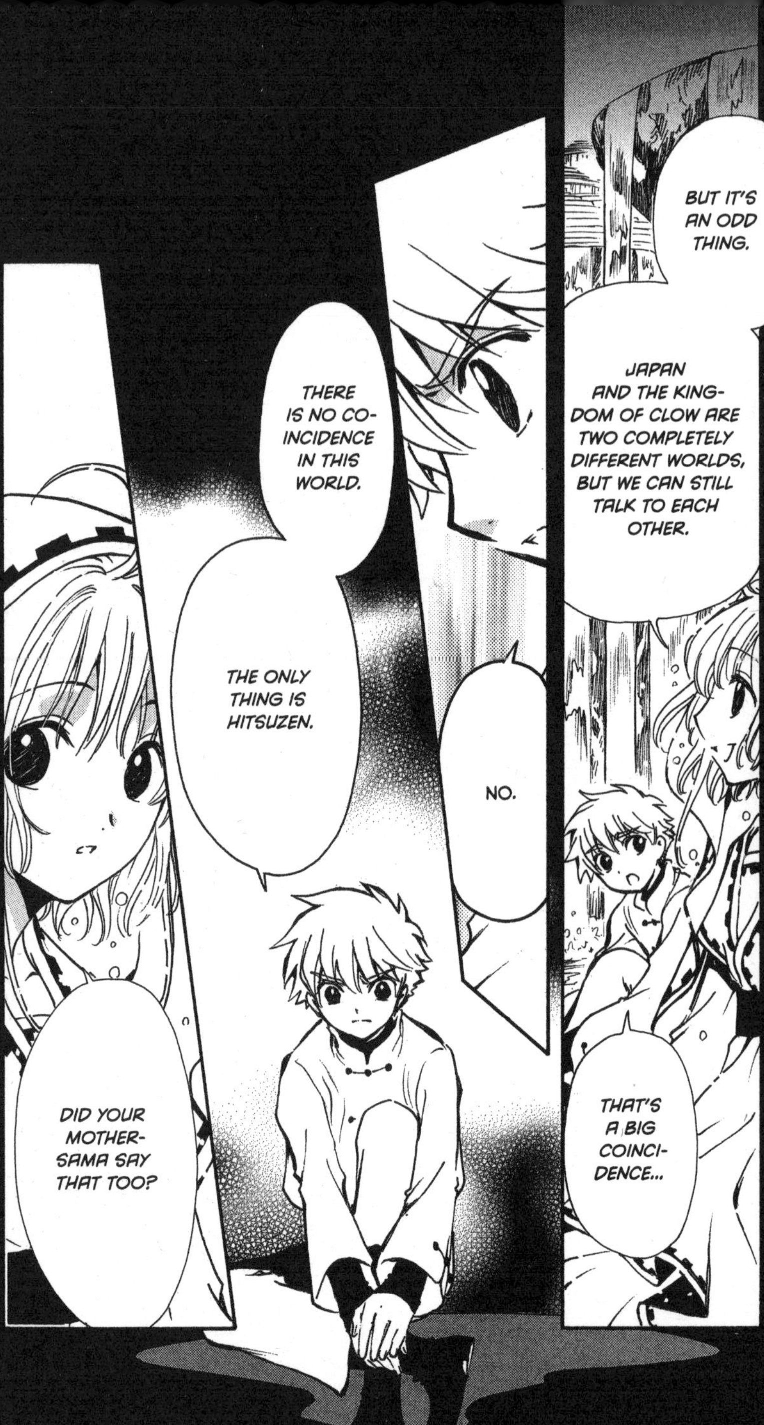
BUT IT'S AN ODD THING.
JAPAN AND THE KING-DOM OF CLOW ARE TWO COMPLETELY DIFFERENT WORLDS, BUT WE CAN STILL TALK TO EACH OTHER.
THAT'S A BIG COINCI-DENCE...
NO.
THERE IS NO CO-INCIDENCE IN THIS WORLD.
THE ONLY THING IS HITSUZEN.
DID YOUR MOTHER-SAMA SAY THAT TOO?

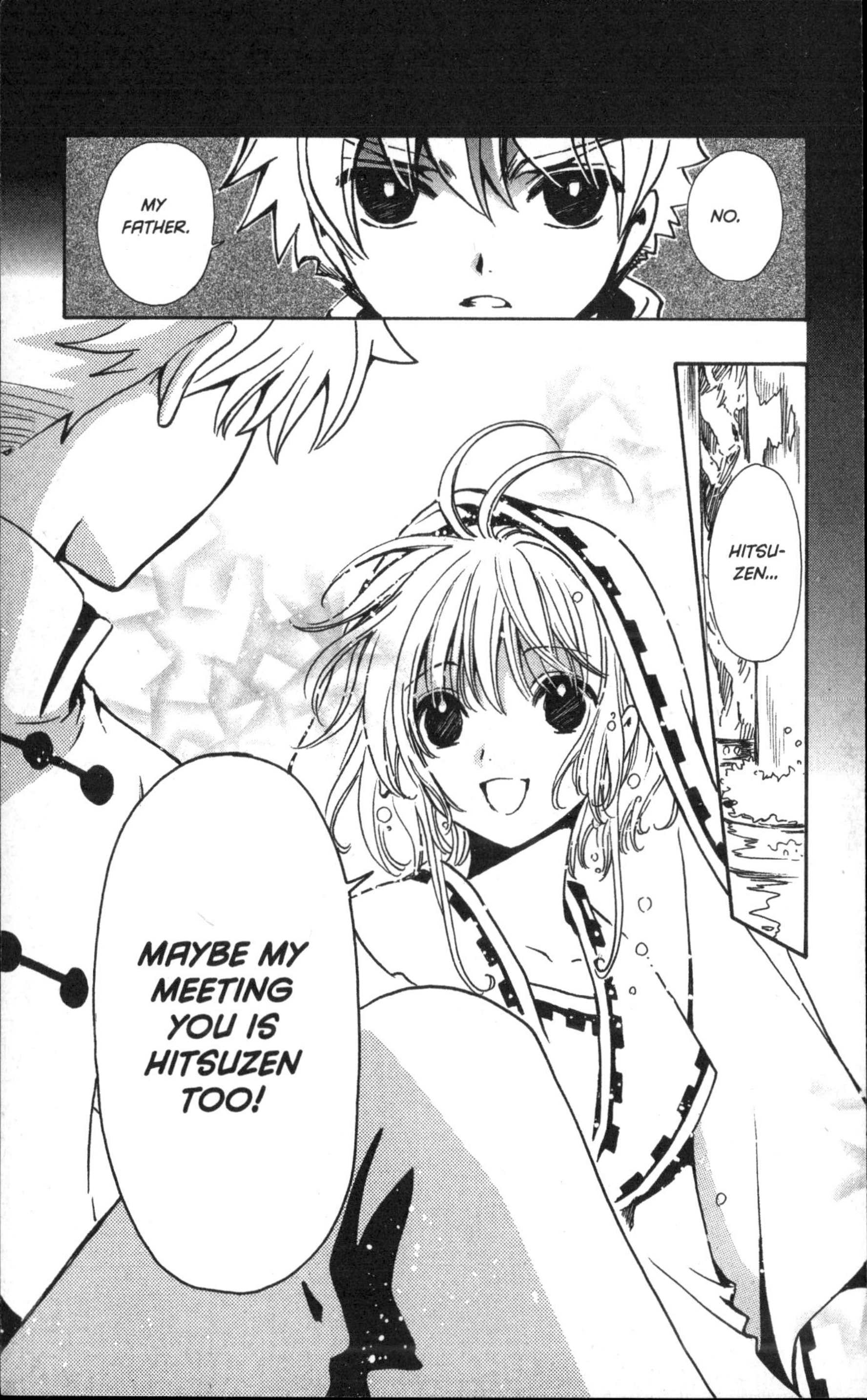
NO.
MY FATHER.
HITSU-ZEN...
MAYBE MY MEETING YOU IS HITSUZEN TOO!

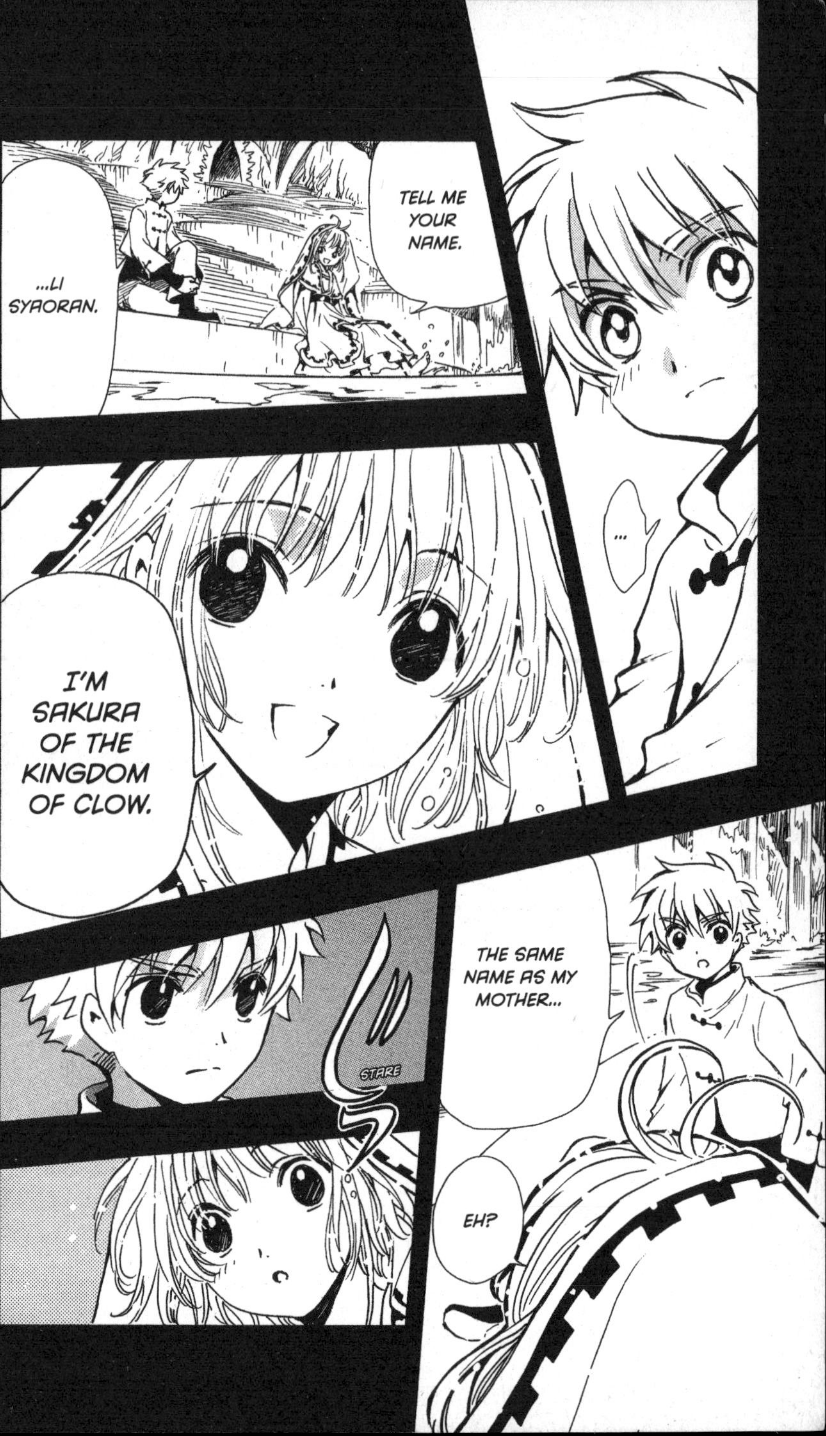
TELL ME YOUR NAME.
...LI SYAORAN.
I'M SAKURA OF THE KINGDOM OF CLOW.
...
THE SAME NAME AS MY MOTHER...
EH?
STARE

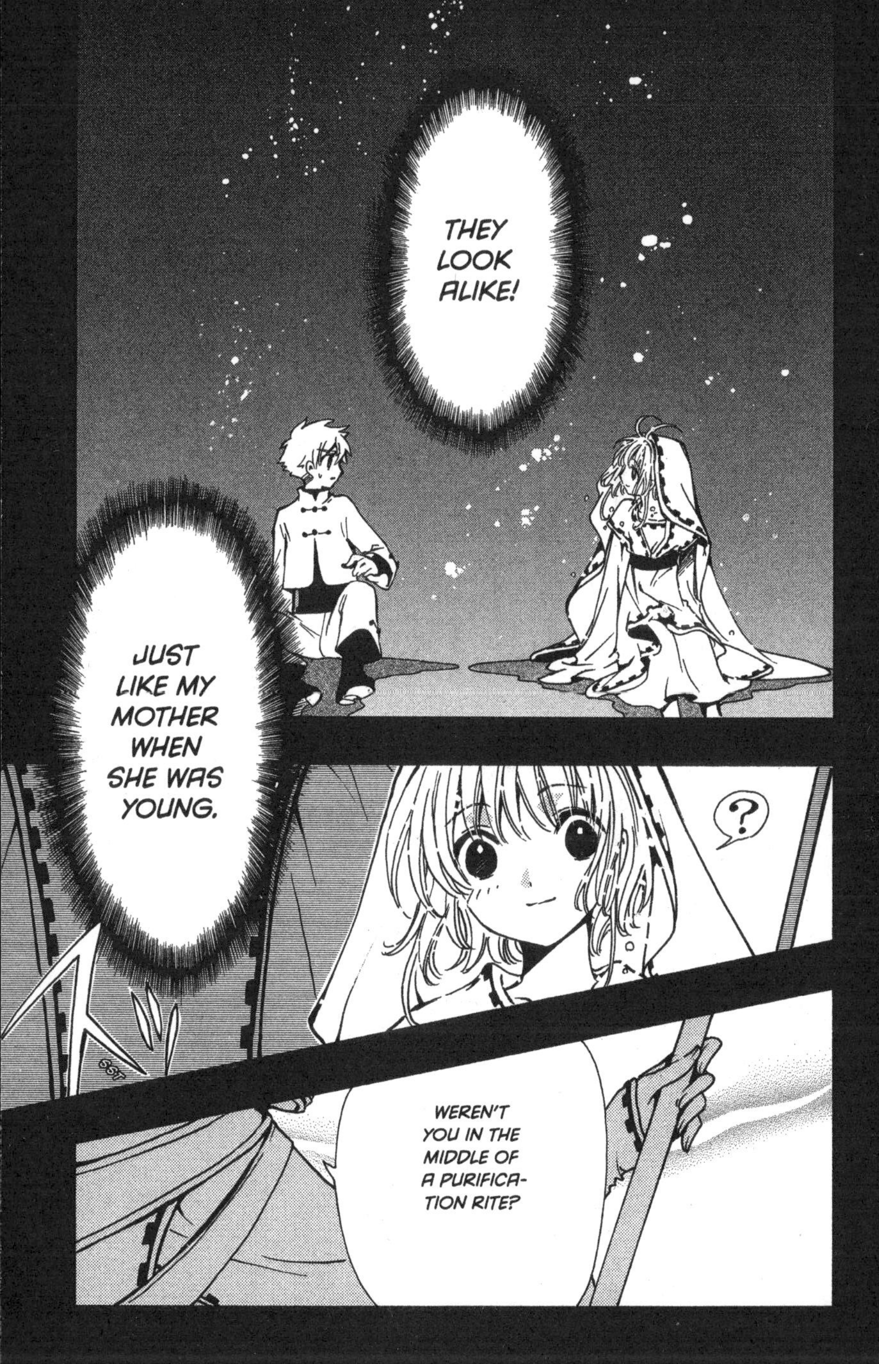
THEY LOOK ALIKE!
JUST LIKE MY MOTHER WHEN SHE WAS YOUNG.
?
WEREN'T YOU IN THE MIDDLE OF A PURIFICATION RITE?

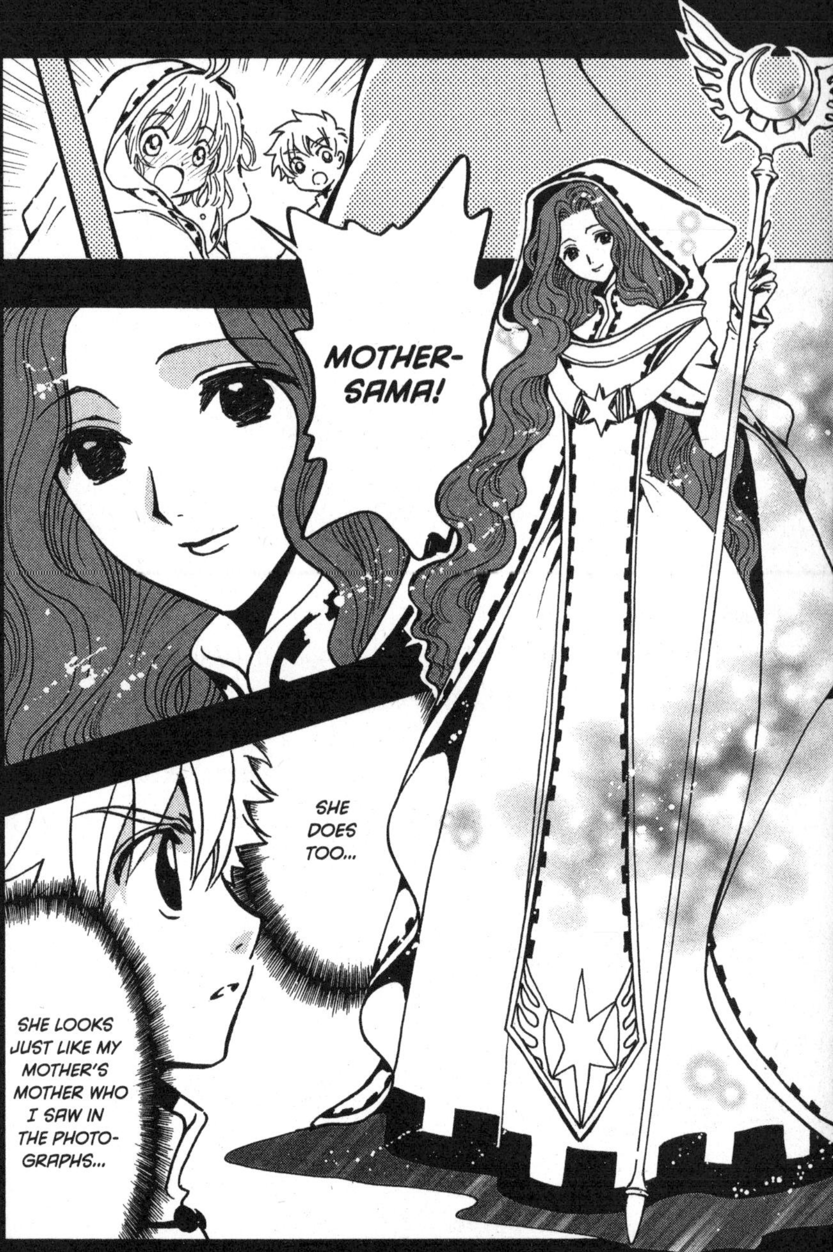
MOTHER-SAMA!
SHE DOES TOO...
SHE LOOKS JUST LIKE MY MOTHER'S MOTHER WHO I SAW IN THE PHOTOGRAPHS...

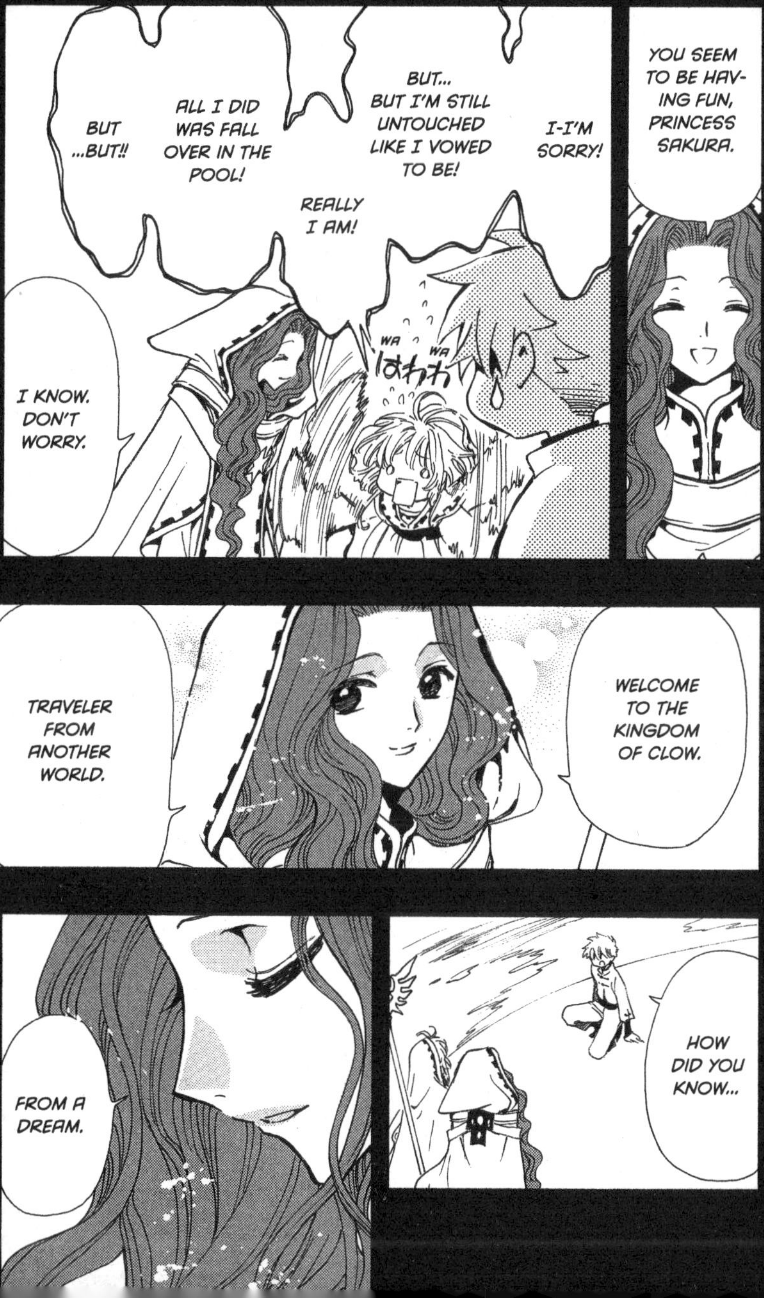
YOU SEEM TO BE HAV-ING FUN, PRINCESS SAKURA.
I-I'M SORRY!
BUT... BUT I'M STILL UNTOUCHED LIKE I VOWED TO BE!
REALLY I AM!
ALL I DID WAS FALL OVER IN THE POOL!
BUT ...BUT!!
WA WA
I KNOW. DON'T WORRY.
WELCOME TO THE KINGDOM OF CLOW.
TRAVELER FROM ANOTHER WORLD.
HOW DID YOU KNOW...
FROM A DREAM.

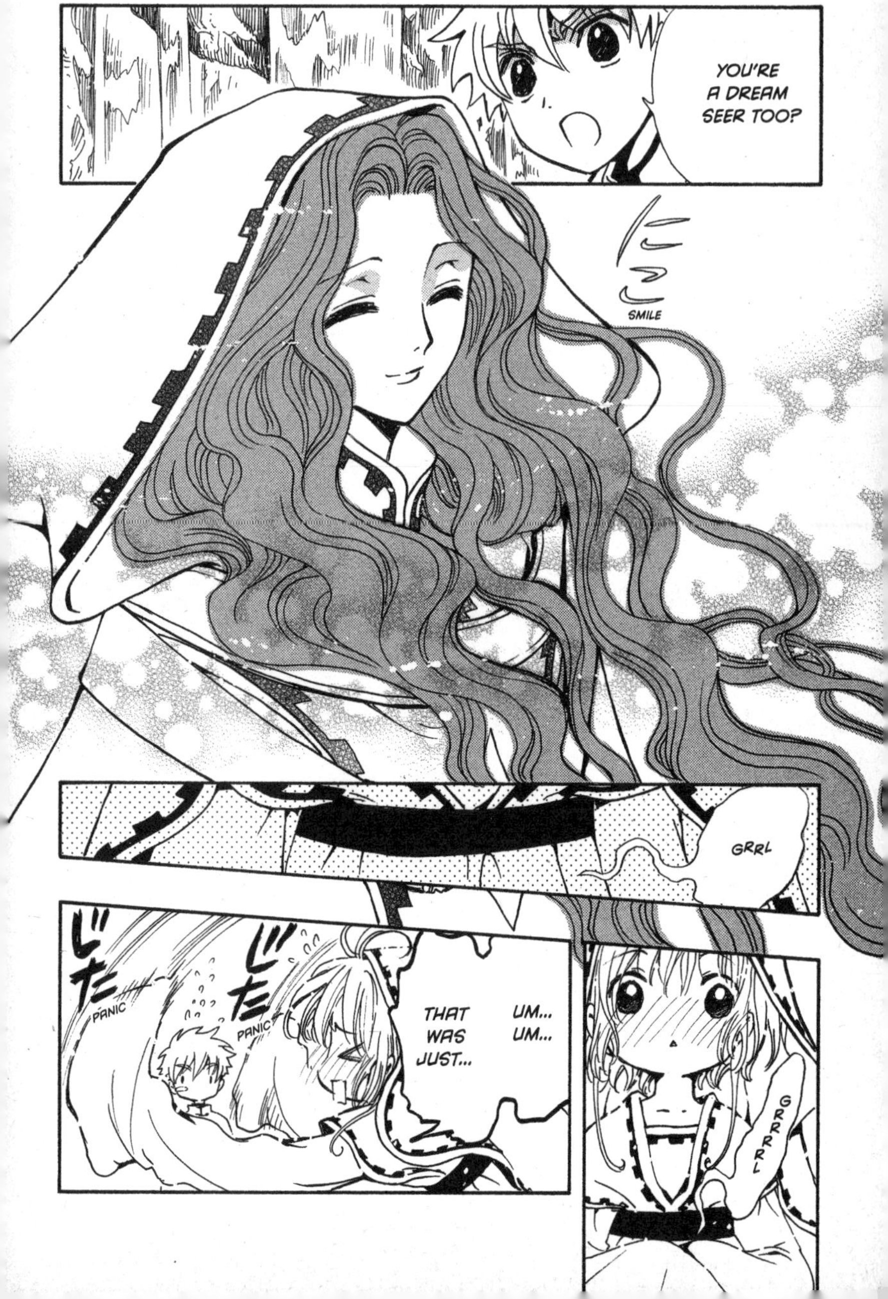
YOU'RE A DREAM SEER TOO?
SMILE
GRRL
GRRRRL
UM... UM...
THAT WAS JUST...
じた
PANIC
じた
PANIC

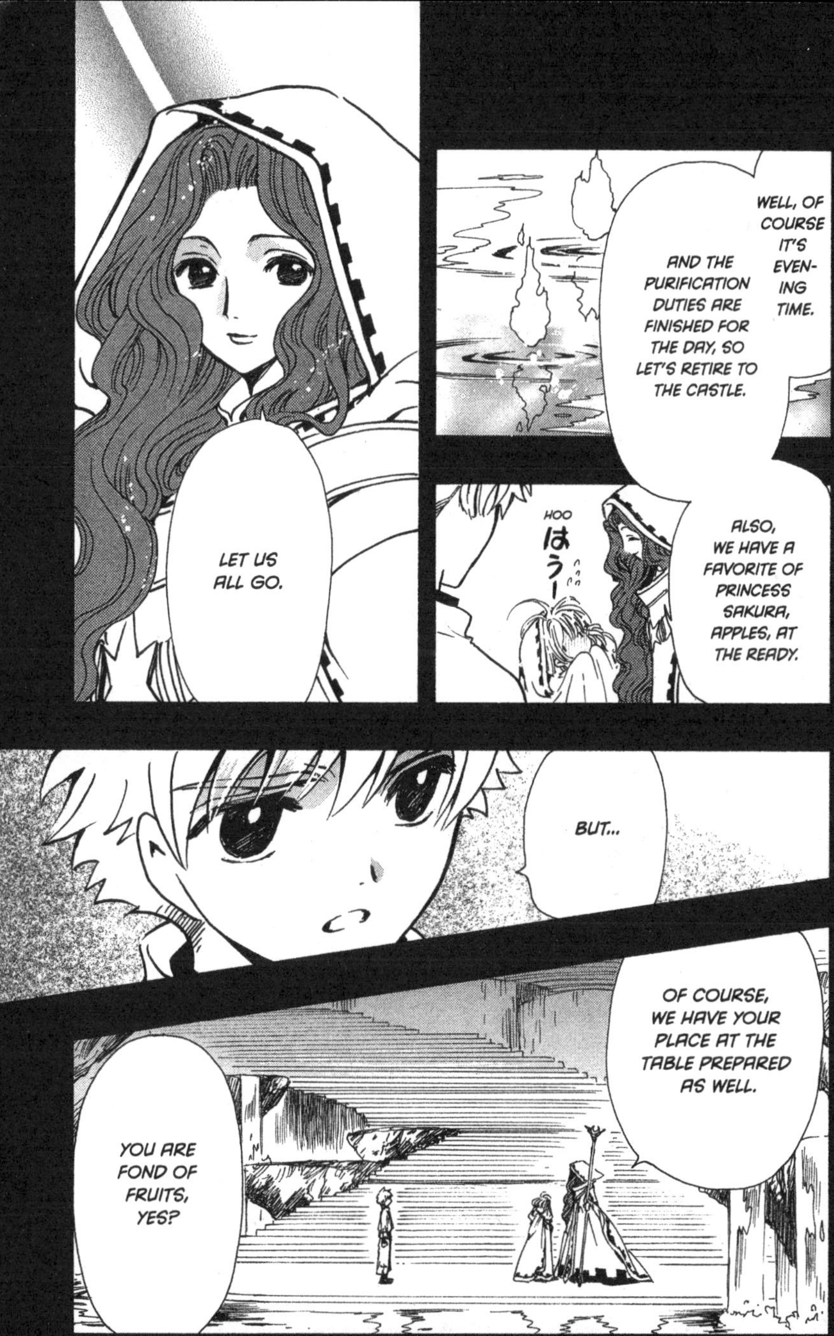
WELL, OF COURSE IT'S EVENING TIME.
AND THE PURIFICATION DUTIES ARE FINISHED FOR THE DAY, SO LET'S RETIRE TO THE CASTLE.
HOO
はうー
ALSO, WE HAVE A FAVORITE OF PRINCESS SAKURA, APPLES, AT THE READY.
LET US ALL GO.
BUT...
OF COURSE, WE HAVE YOUR PLACE AT THE TABLE PREPARED AS WELL.
YOU ARE FOND OF FRUITS, YES?

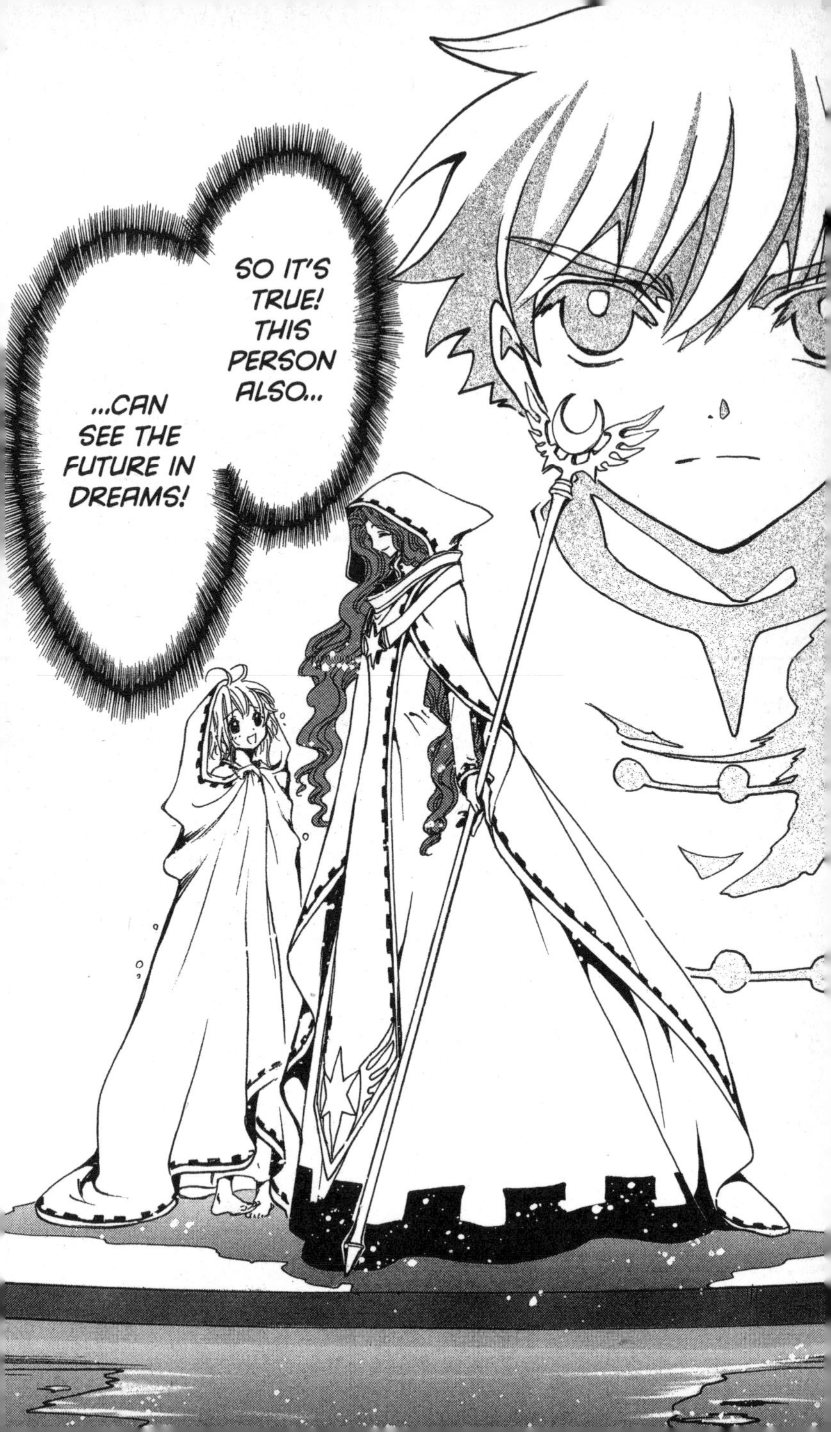
SO IT'S TRUE! THIS PERSON ALSO...
...CAN SEE THE FUTURE IN DREAMS!

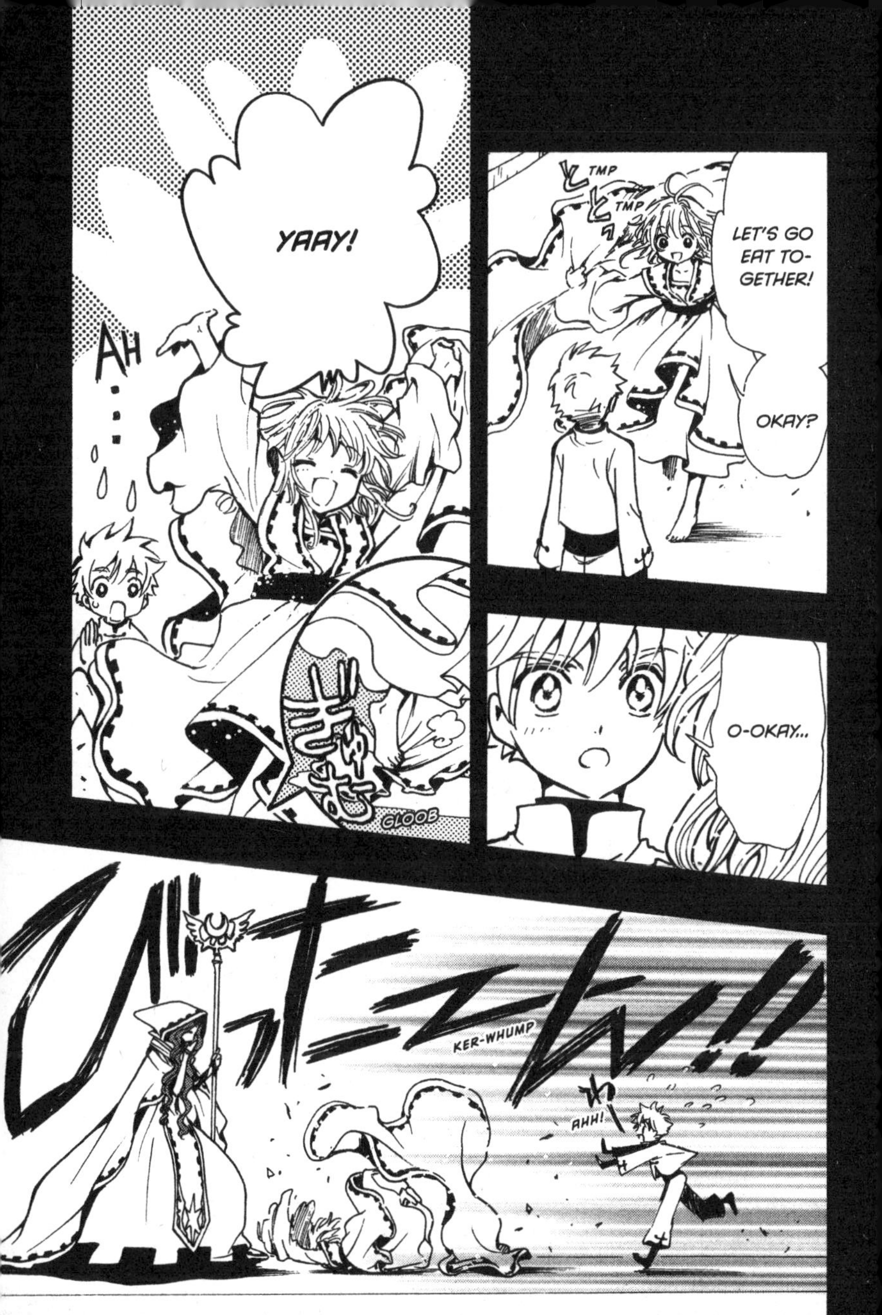
TMP
TMP
LET'S GO EAT TO-GETHER!
OKAY?
O-OKAY...
YAAY!
AH...
GLOOB
KER-WHUMP
AHH!

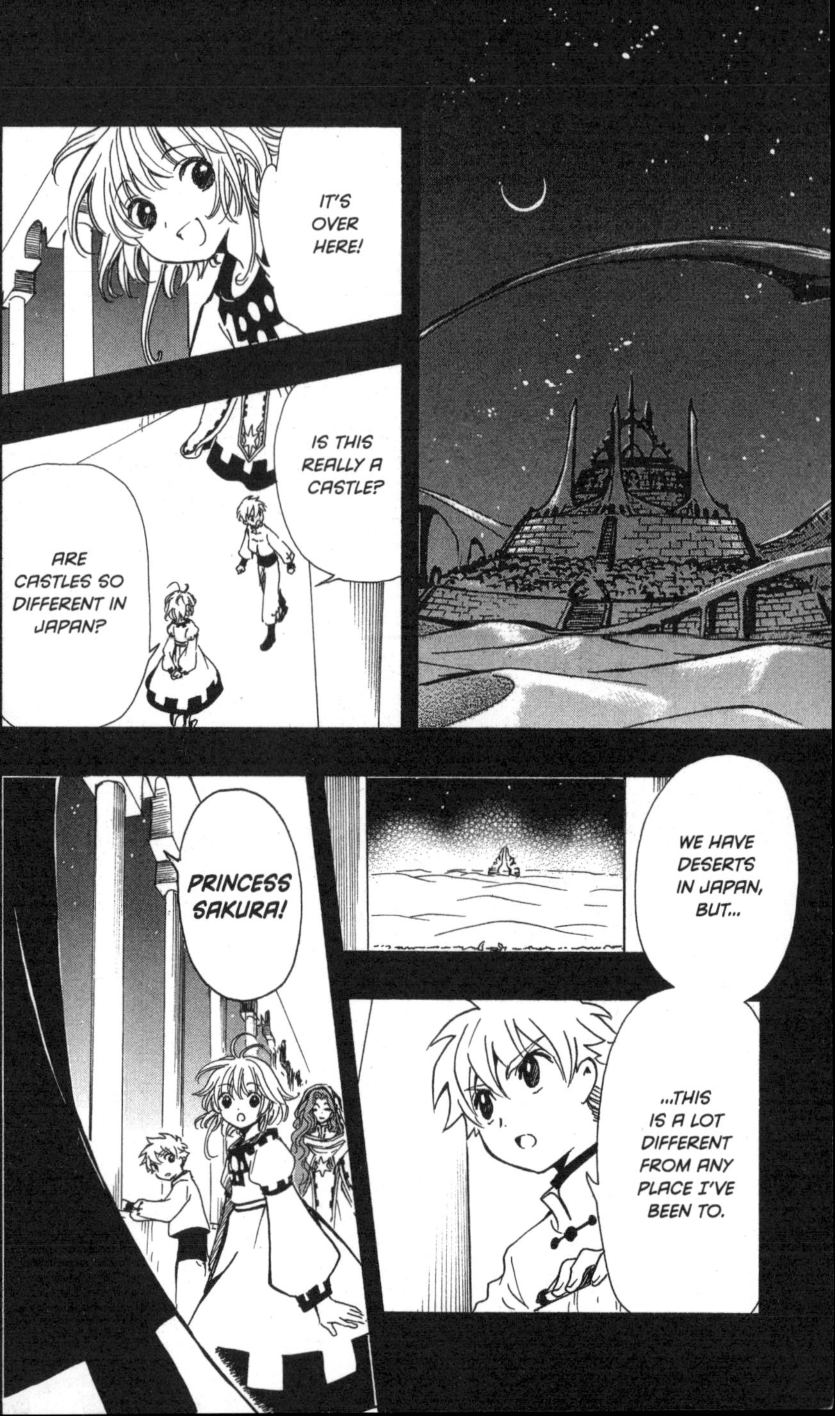
IT'S OVER HERE!
IS THIS REALLY A CASTLE?
ARE CASTLES SO DIFFERENT IN JAPAN?
WE HAVE DESERTS IN JAPAN, BUT...
...THIS IS A LOT DIFFERENT FROM ANY PLACE I'VE BEEN TO.
PRINCESS SAKURA!

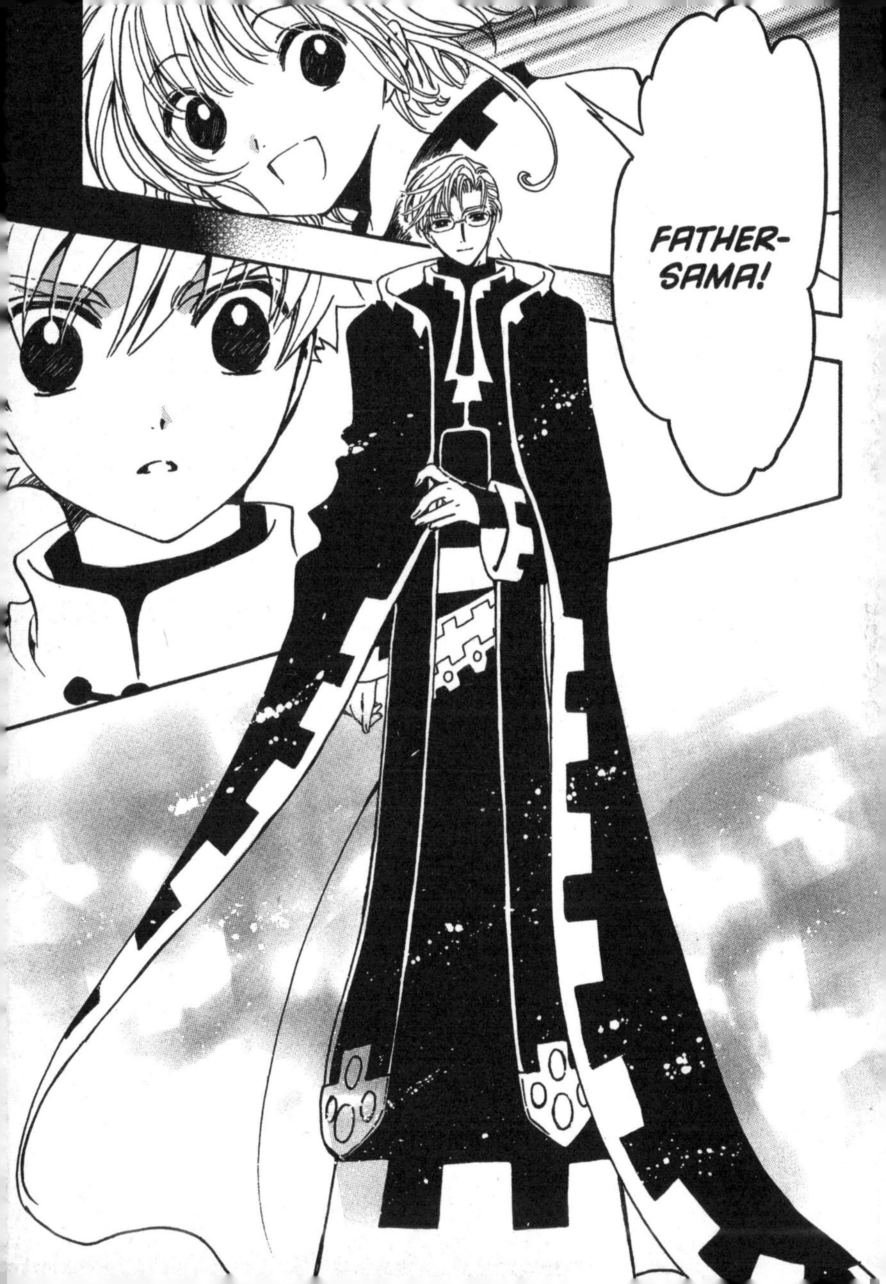
FATHER-SAMA!

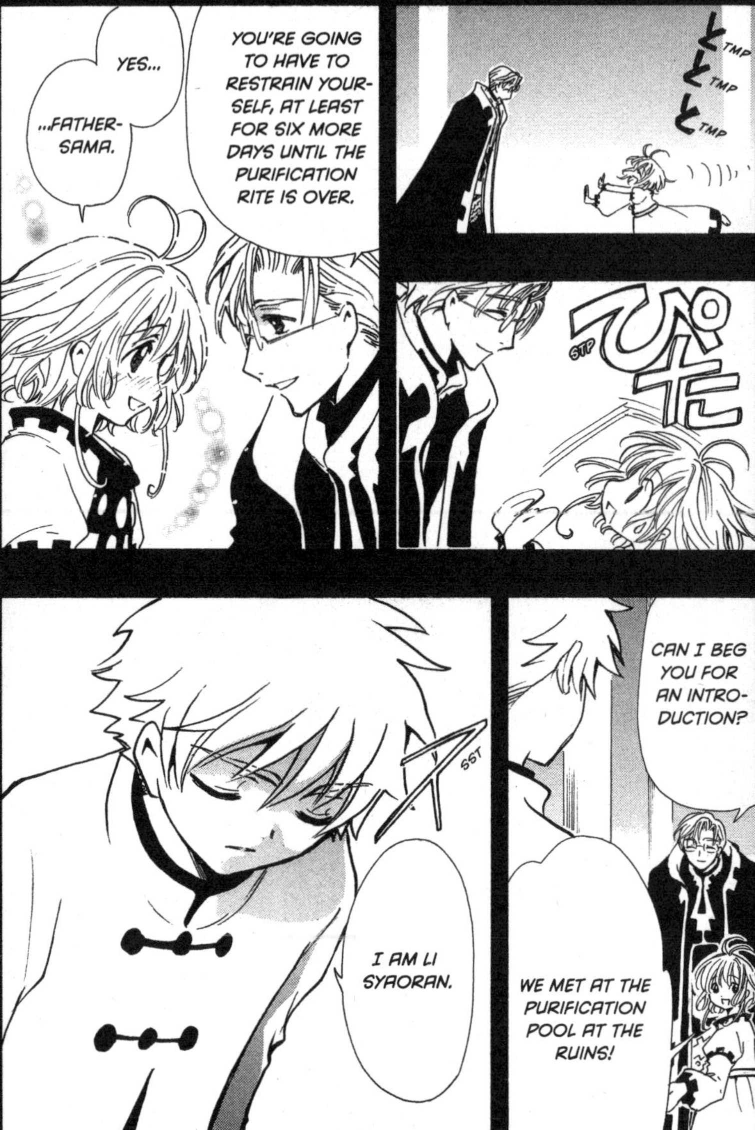

と TMP
と TMP
と TMP
ぴた STP
YOU'RE GOING TO HAVE TO RESTRAIN YOURSELF, AT LEAST FOR SIX MORE DAYS UNTIL THE PURIFICATION RITE IS OVER.
YES... ...FATHER-SAMA.
CAN I BEG YOU FOR AN INTRODUCTION?
WE MET AT THE PURIFICATION POOL AT THE RUINS!
SST
I AM LI SYAORAN.

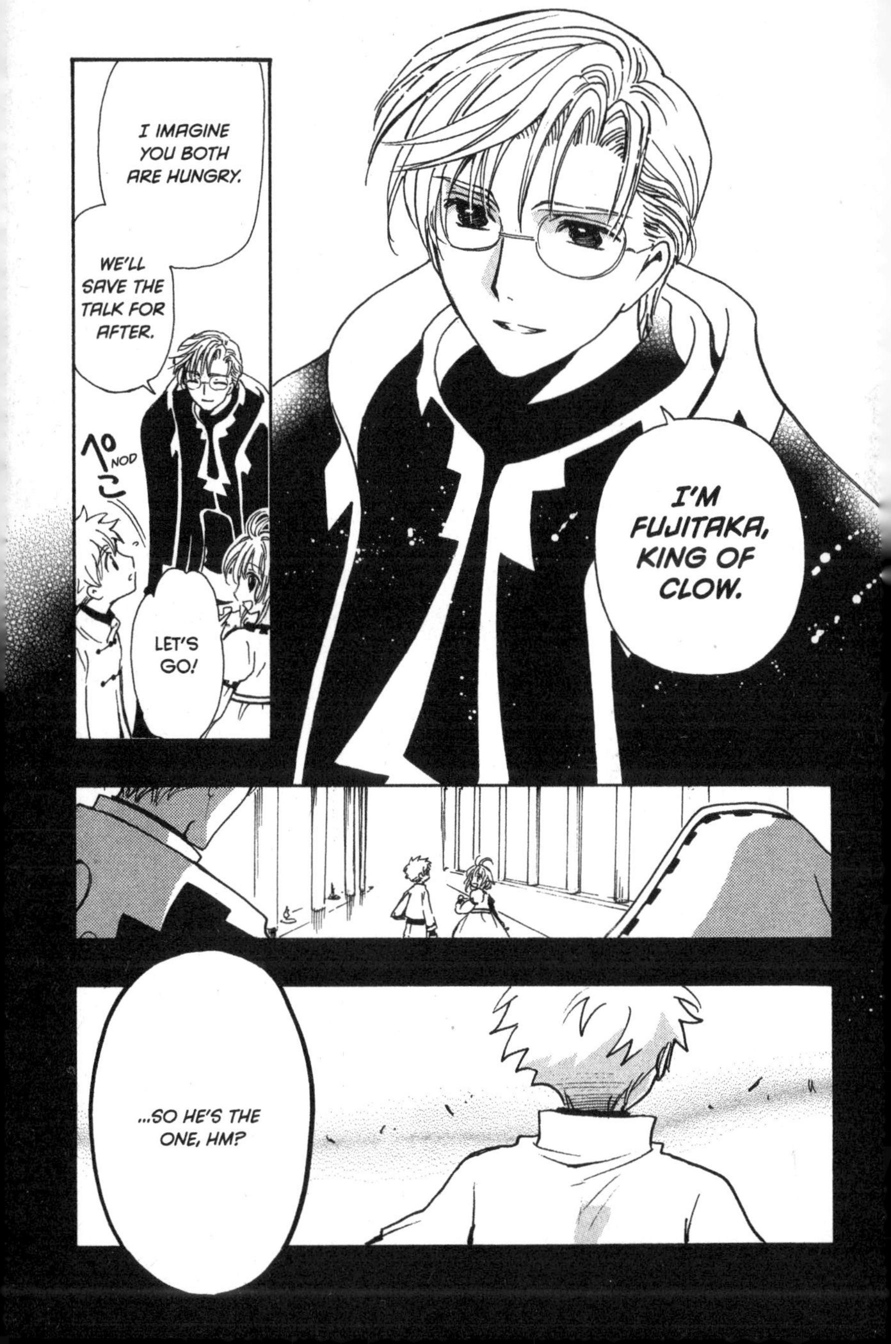
I'M FUJITAKA, KING OF CLOW.
I IMAGINE YOU BOTH ARE HUNGRY.
WE'LL SAVE THE TALK FOR AFTER.
NOD
LET'S GO!
...SO HE'S THE ONE, HM?

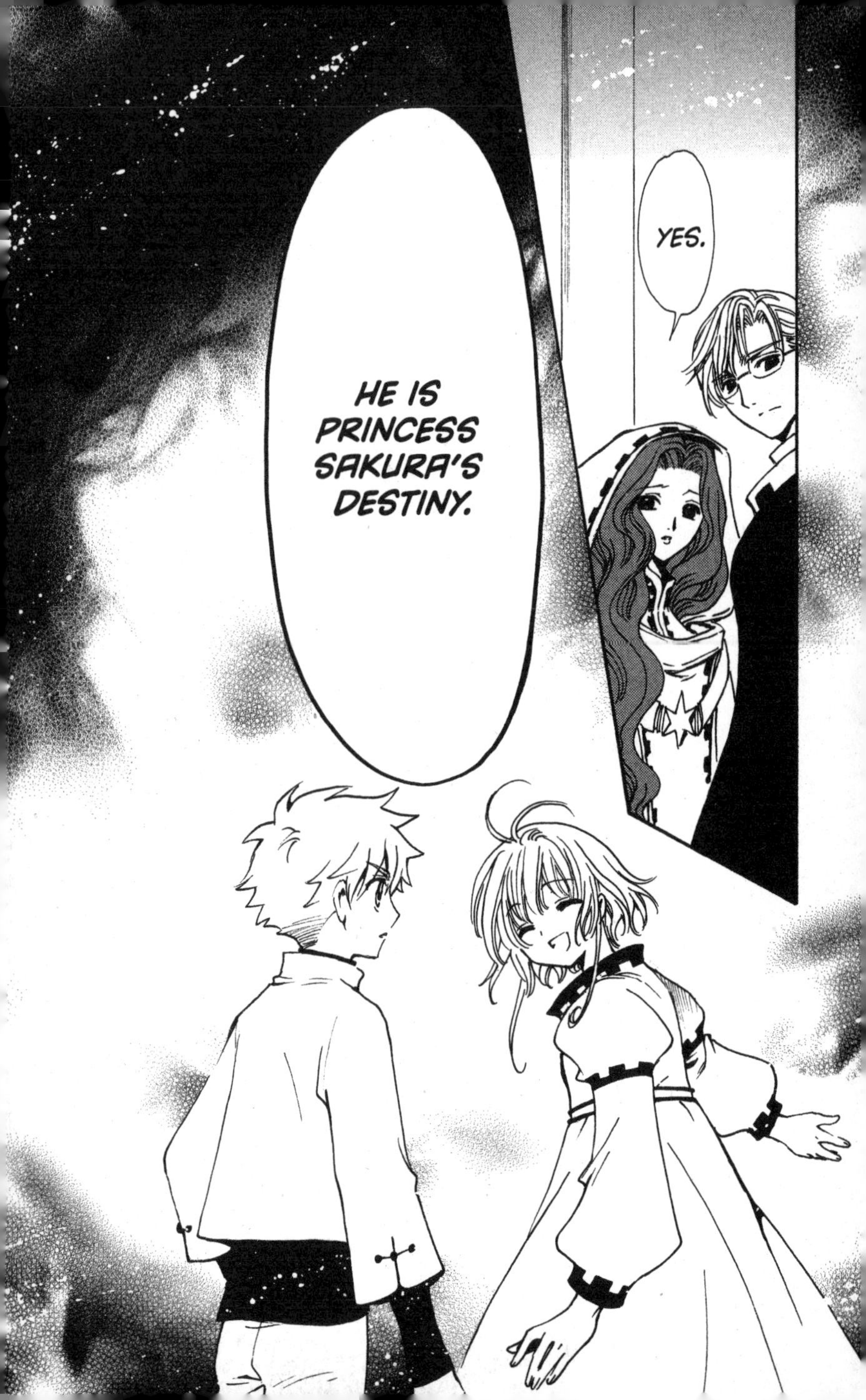
YES.
HE IS PRINCESS SAKURA'S DESTINY.

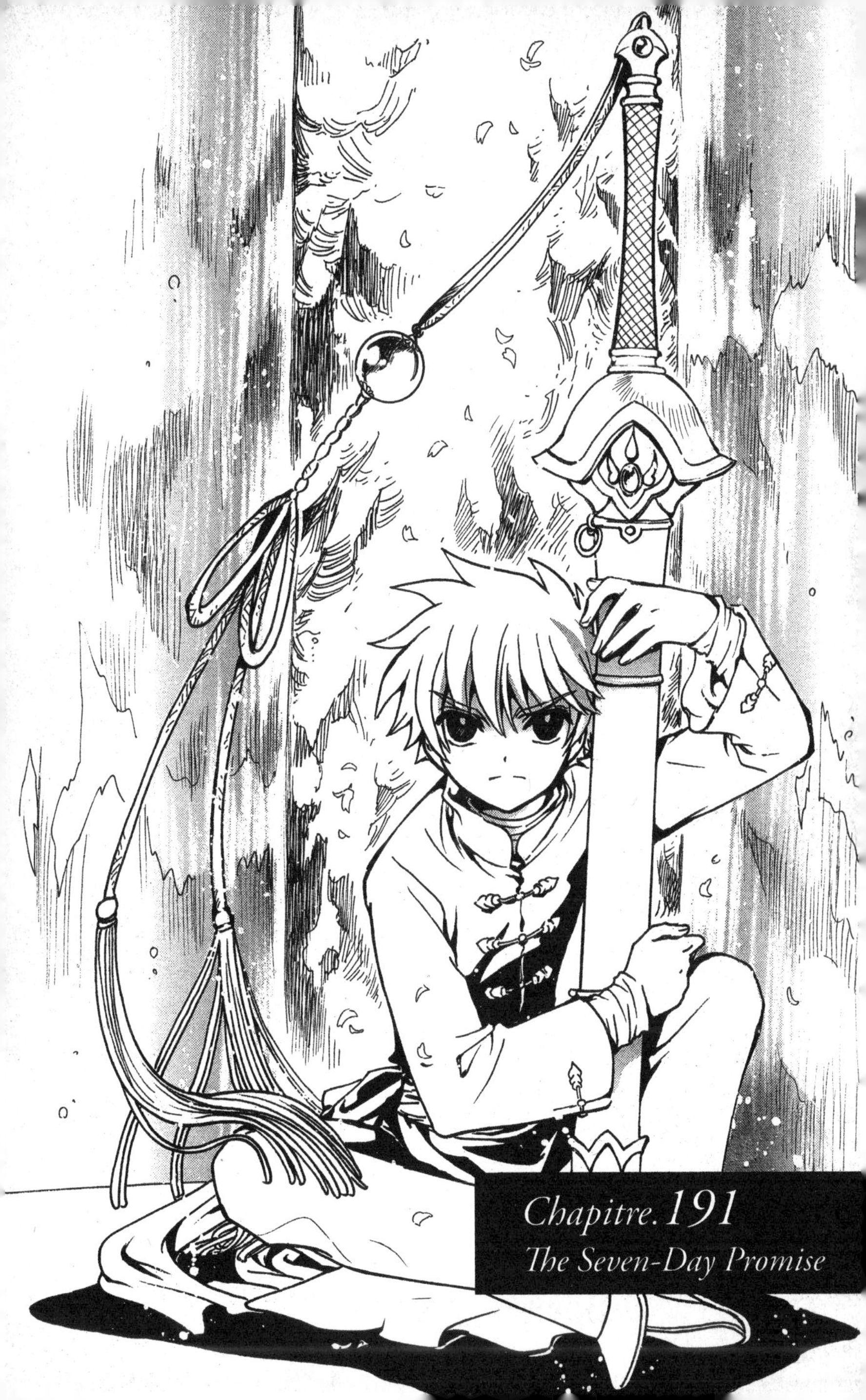
Chapitre. 191
The Seven-Day Promise

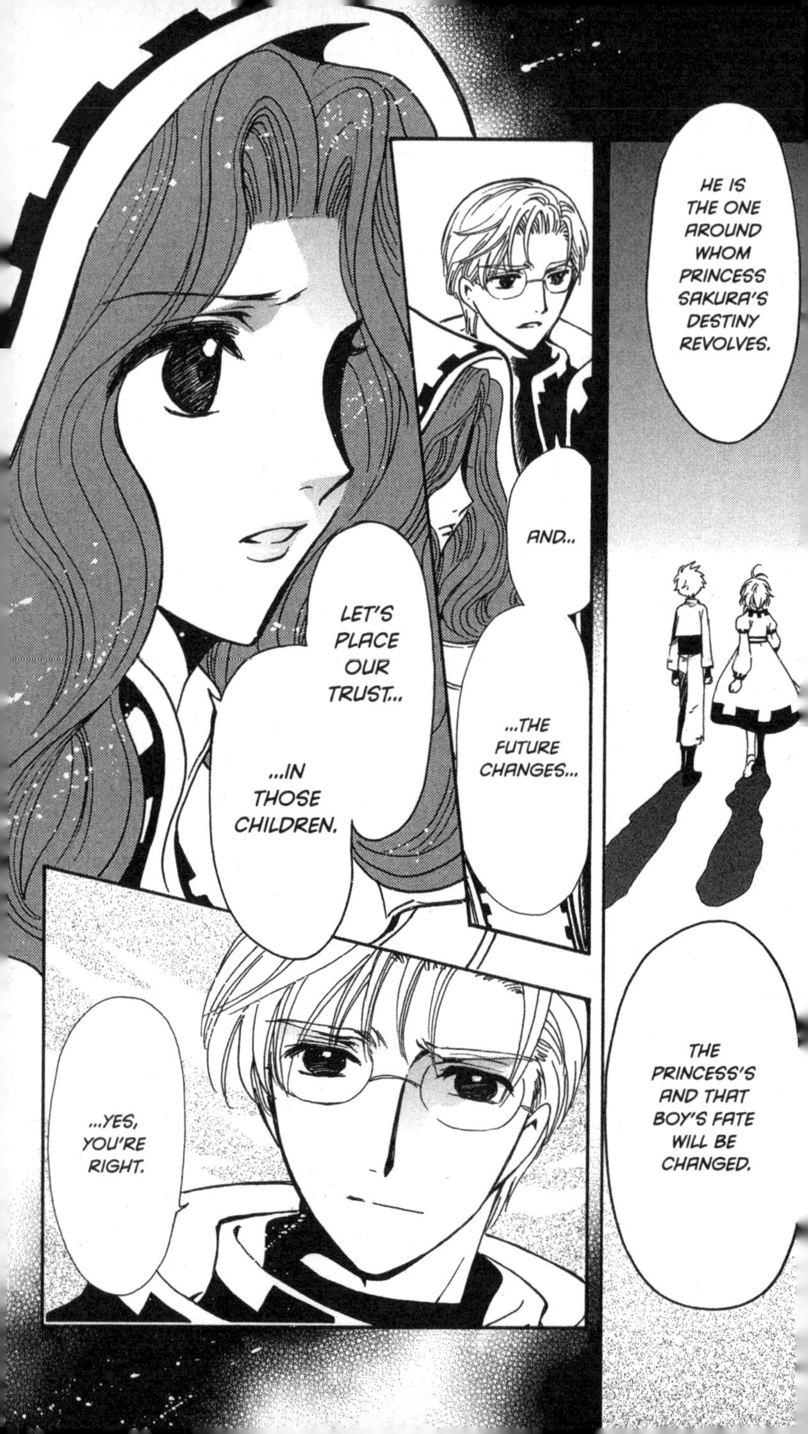
HE IS THE ONE AROUND WHOM PRINCESS SAKURA'S DESTINY REVOLVES.
AND...
...THE FUTURE CHANGES...
THE PRINCESS'S AND THAT BOY'S FATE WILL BE CHANGED.
LET'S PLACE OUR TRUST...
...IN THOSE CHILDREN.
...YES, YOU'RE RIGHT.

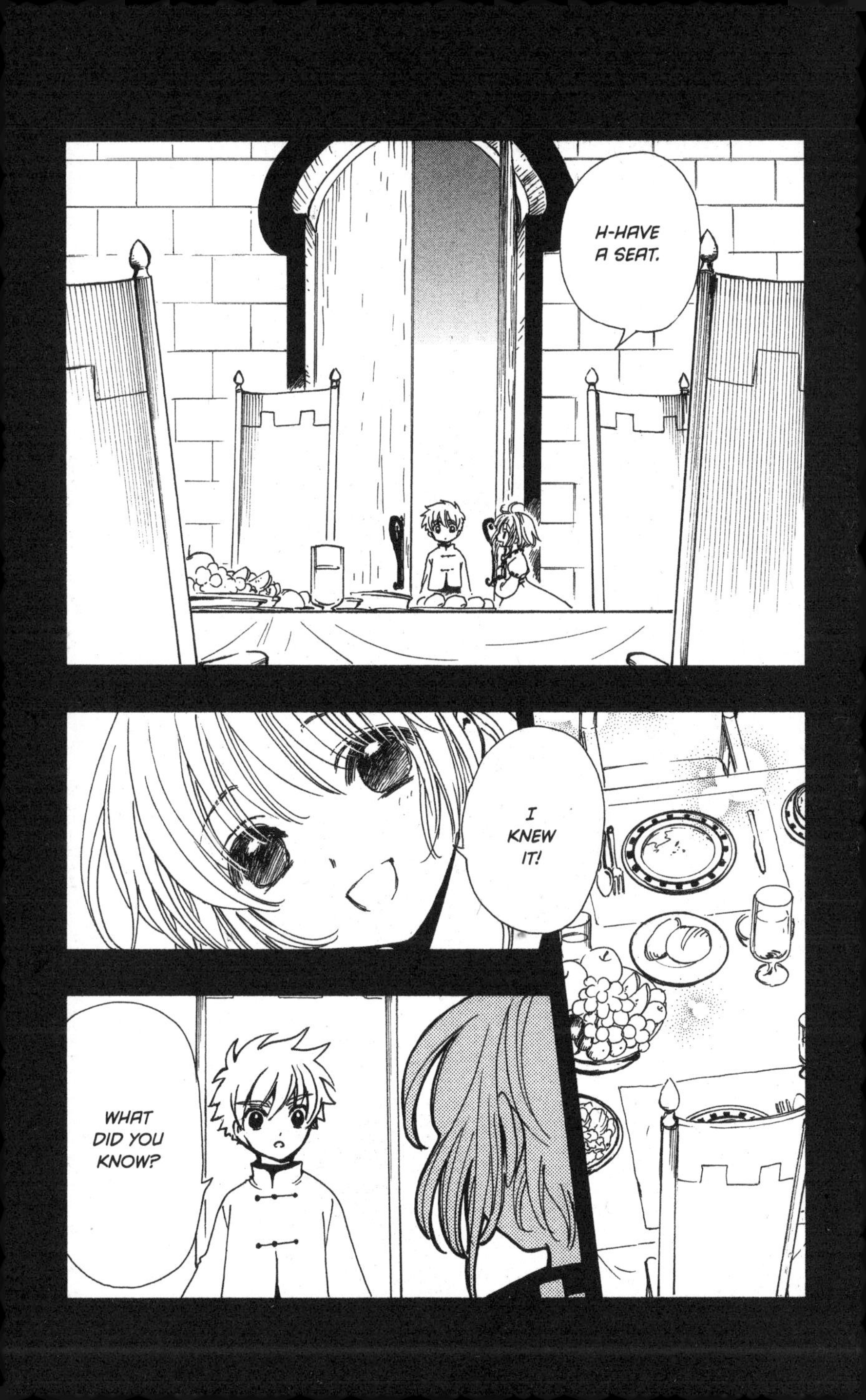
H-HAVE A SEAT.
I KNEW IT!
WHAT DID YOU KNOW?

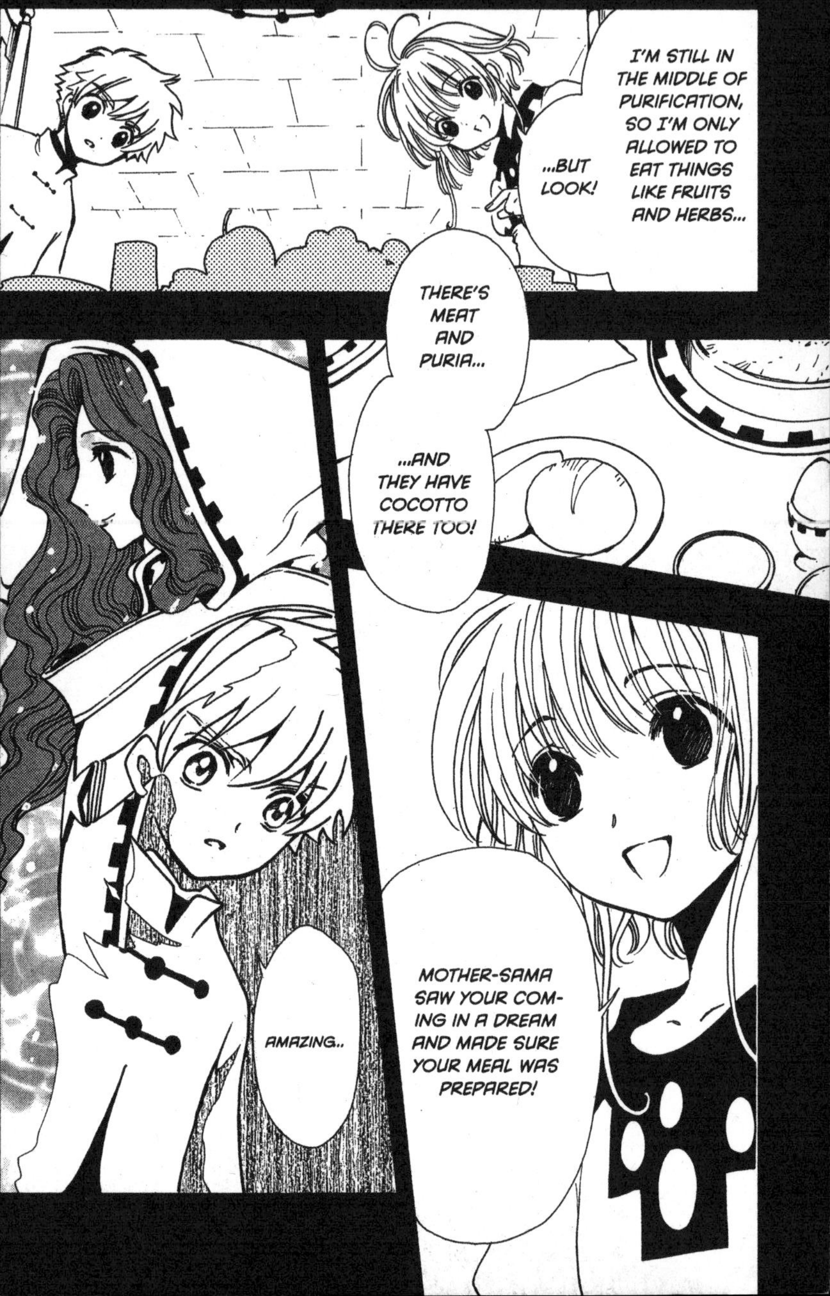
I'M STILL IN THE MIDDLE OF PURIFICATION, SO I'M ONLY ALLOWED TO EAT THINGS LIKE FRUITS AND HERBS...
...BUT LOOK!
THERE'S MEAT AND PURIA...
...AND THEY HAVE COCOTTO THERE TOO!
MOTHER-SAMA SAW YOUR COMING IN A DREAM AND MADE SURE YOUR MEAL WAS PREPARED!
AMAZING..

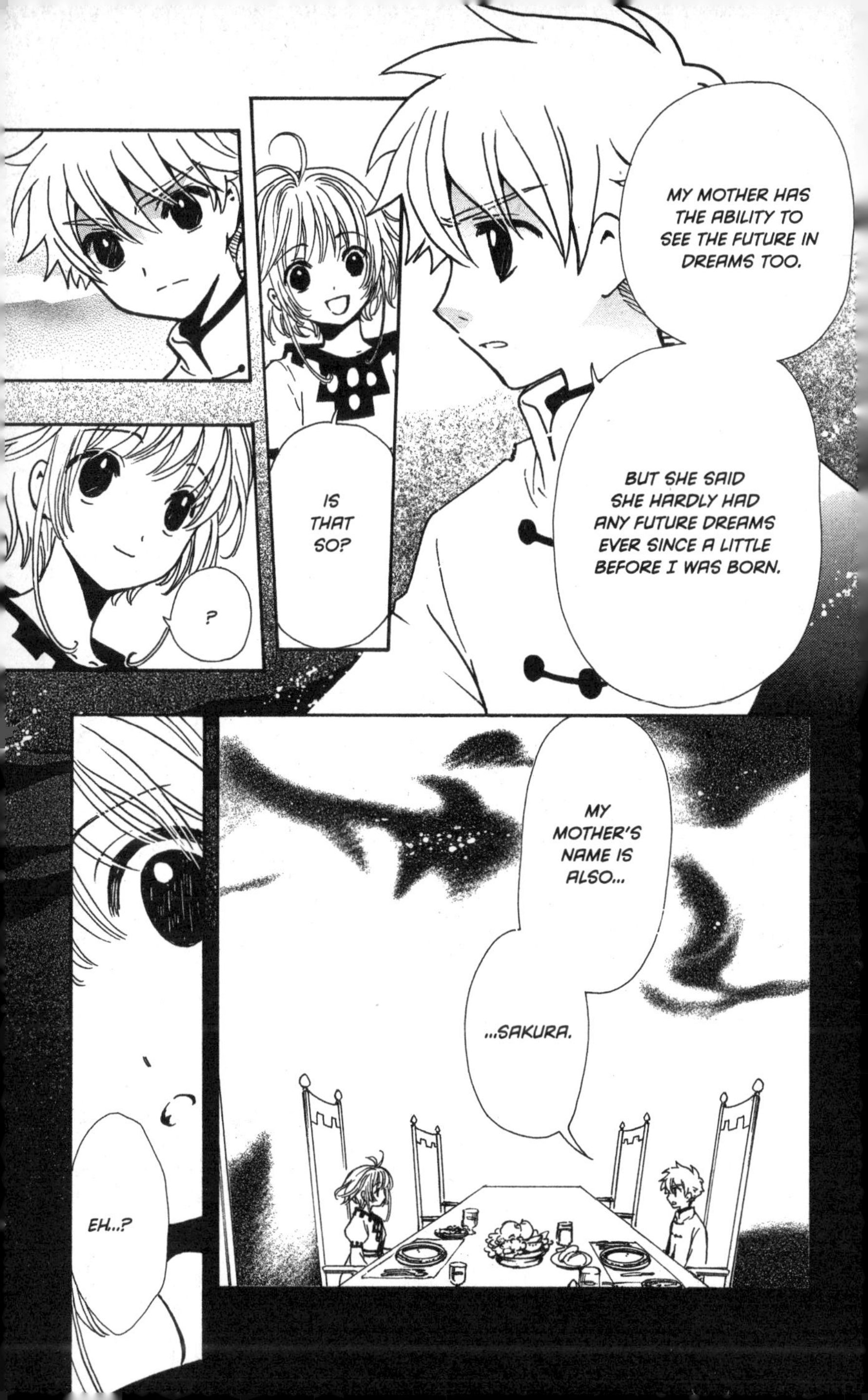
MY MOTHER HAS THE ABILITY TO SEE THE FUTURE IN DREAMS TOO.
BUT SHE SAID SHE HARDLY HAD ANY FUTURE DREAMS EVER SINCE A LITTLE BEFORE I WAS BORN.
IS THAT SO?
?
MY MOTHER'S NAME IS ALSO...
...SAKURA.
EH...?

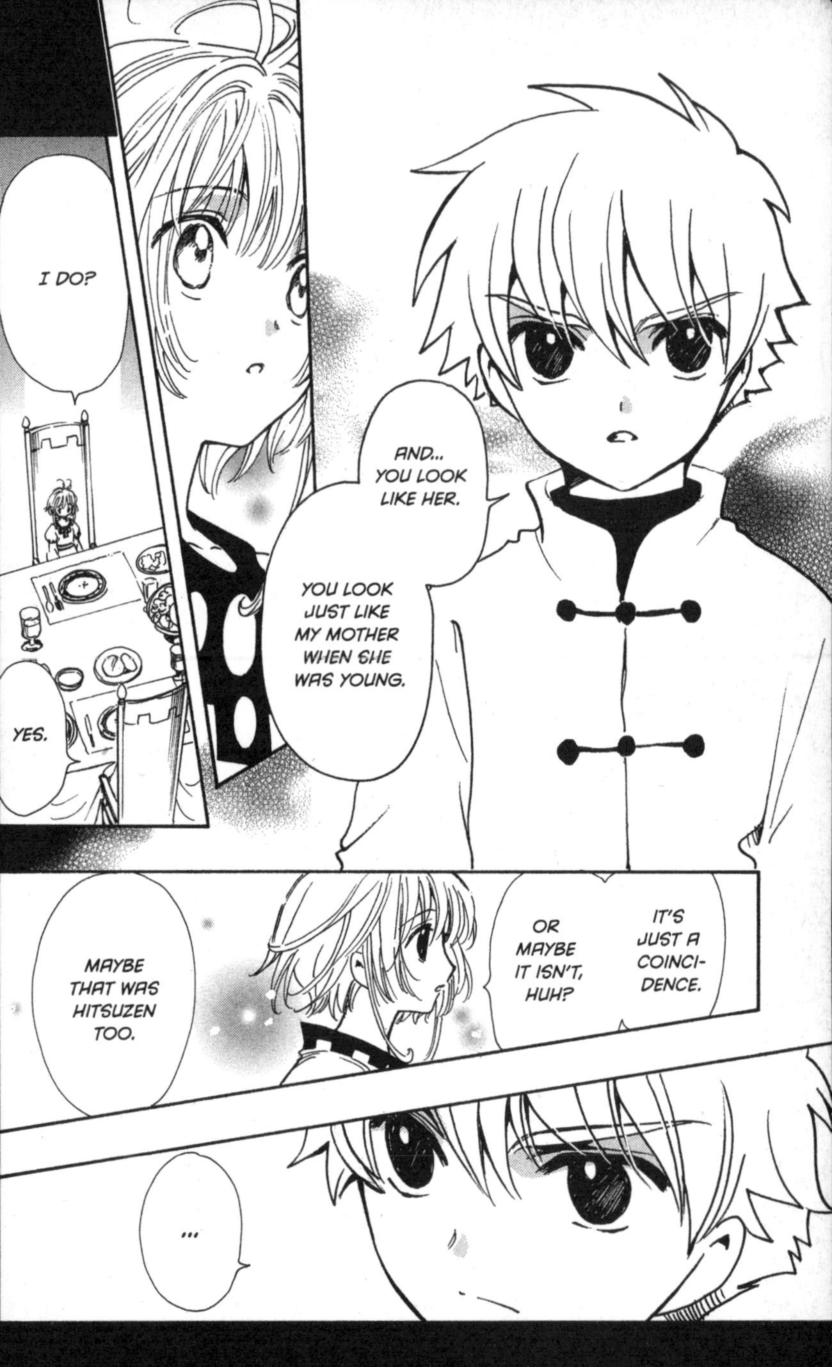
AND... YOU LOOK LIKE HER.
YOU LOOK JUST LIKE MY MOTHER WHEN SHE WAS YOUNG.
I DO?
YES.
IT'S JUST A COINCIDENCE.
OR MAYBE IT ISN'T, HUH?
MAYBE THAT WAS HITSUZEN TOO.
...

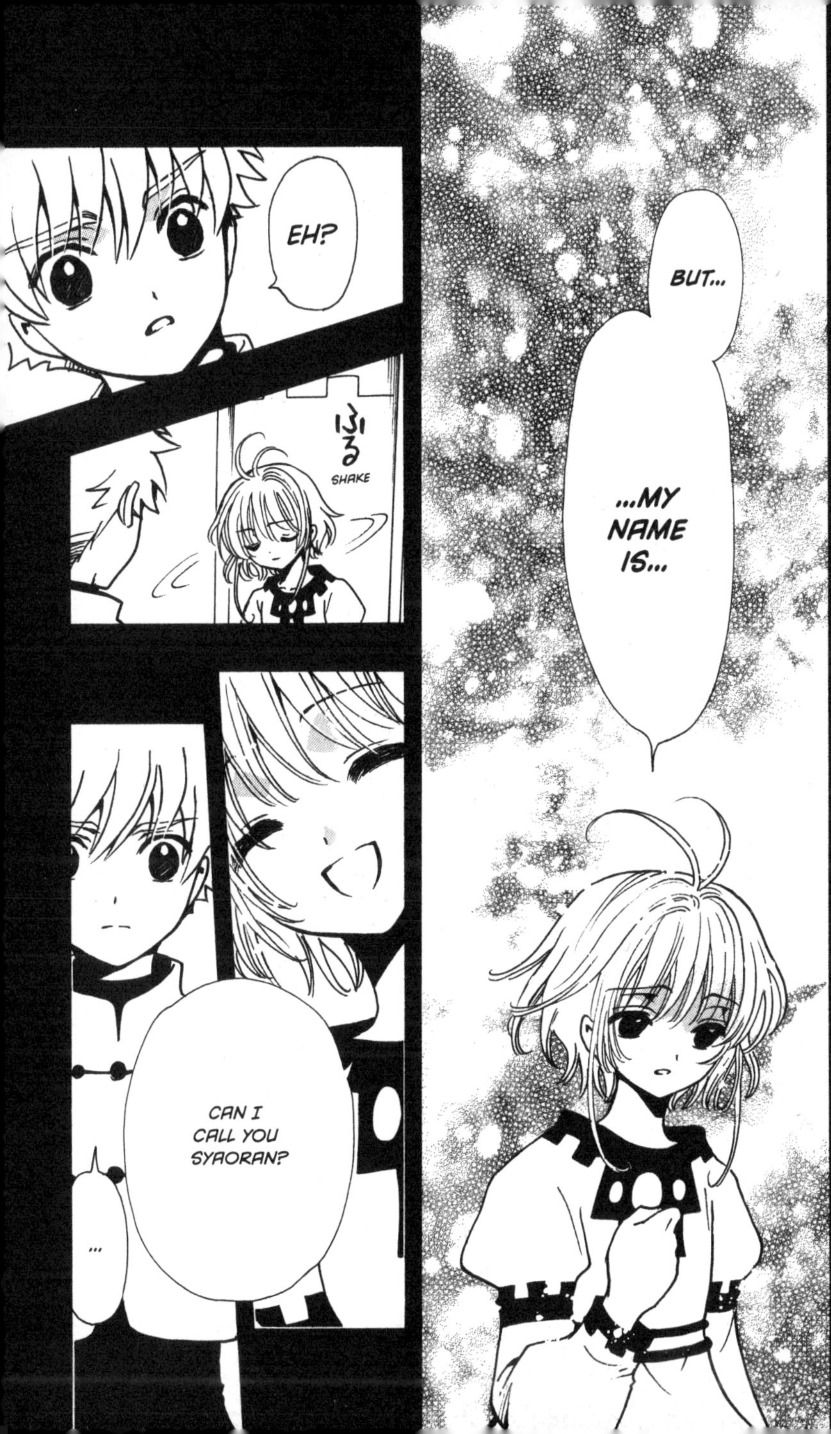
BUT...
...MY NAME IS...
EH?
ふる
SHAKE
CAN I CALL YOU SYAORAN?
...

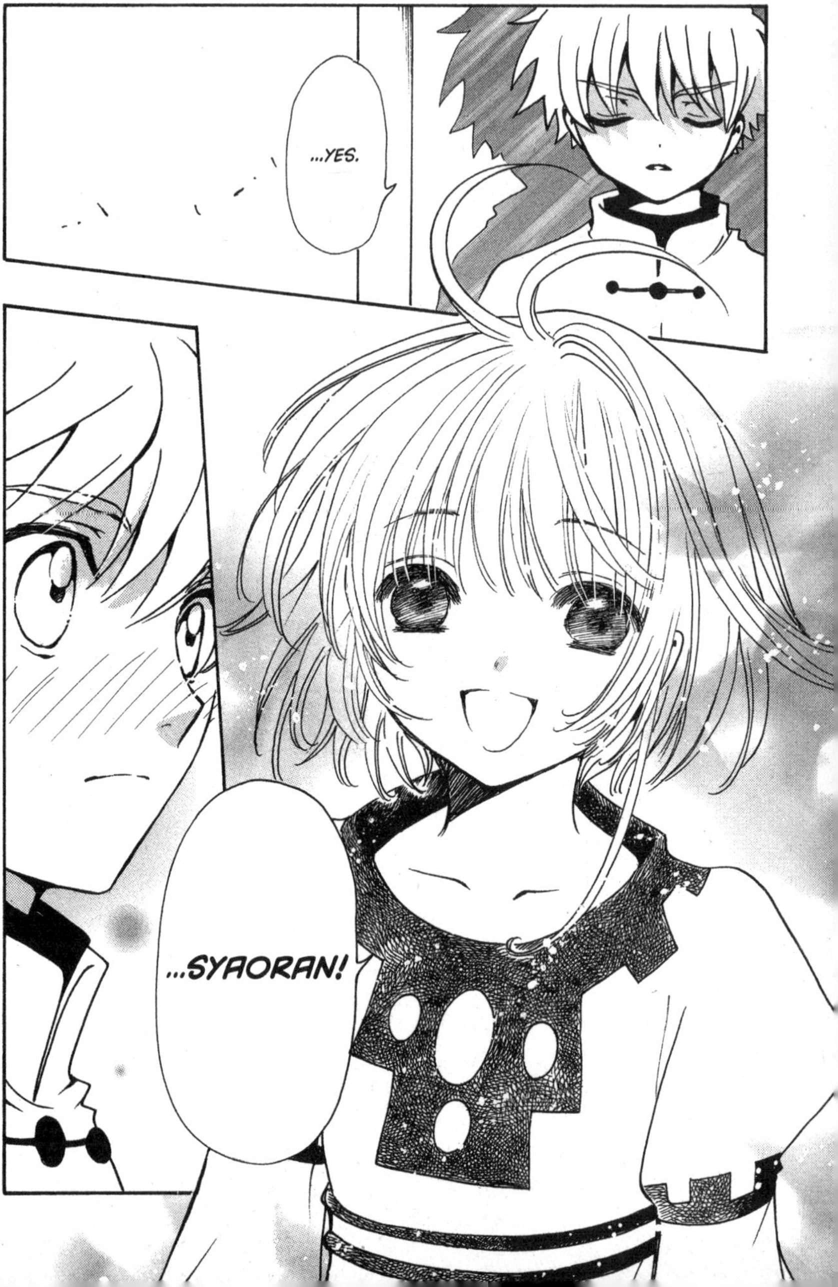
...YES.
...SYAORAN!

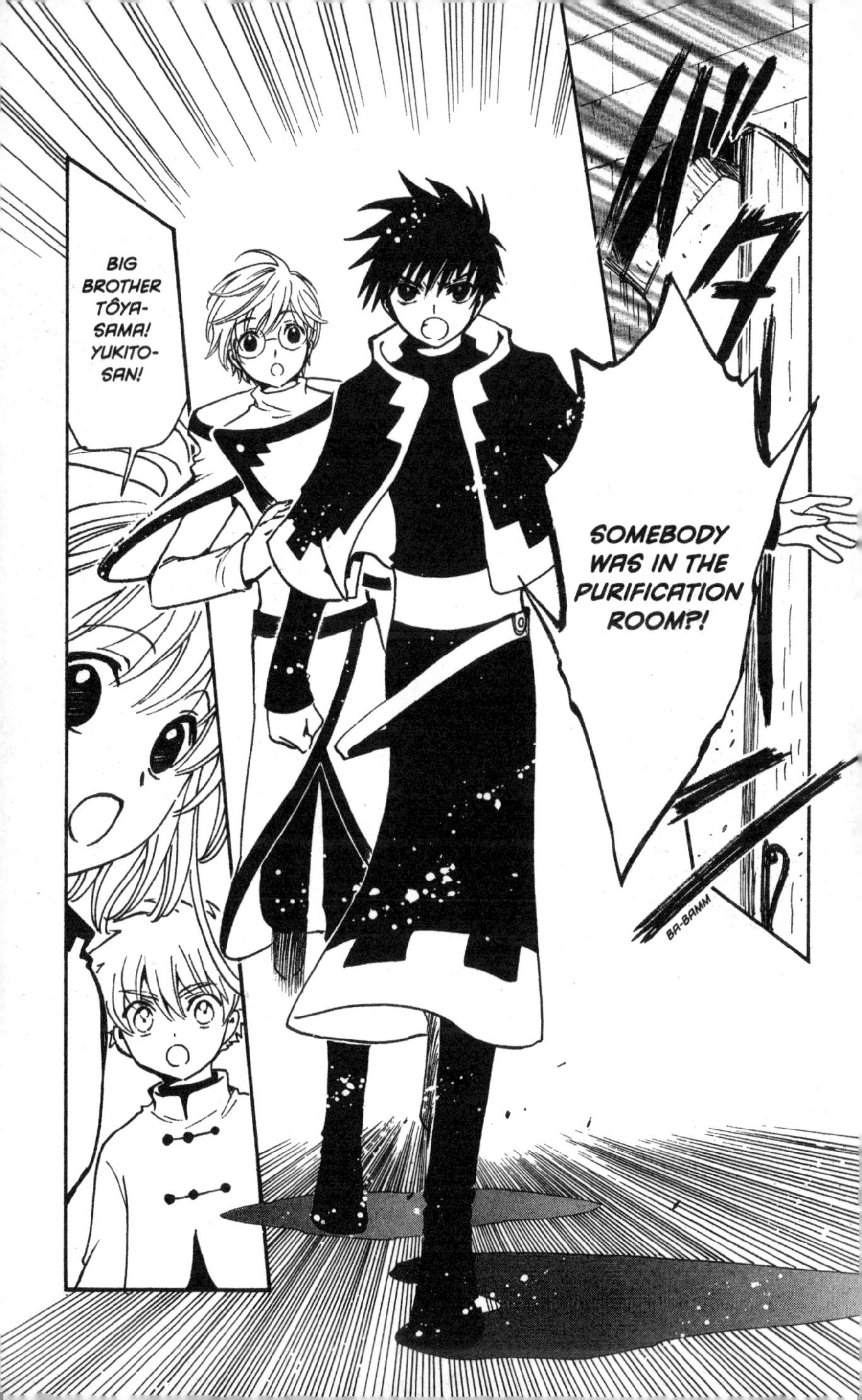
SOMEBODY WAS IN THE PURIFICATION ROOM?!
BA-BAMM
BIG BROTHER TÔYA-SAMA! YUKITO-SAN!

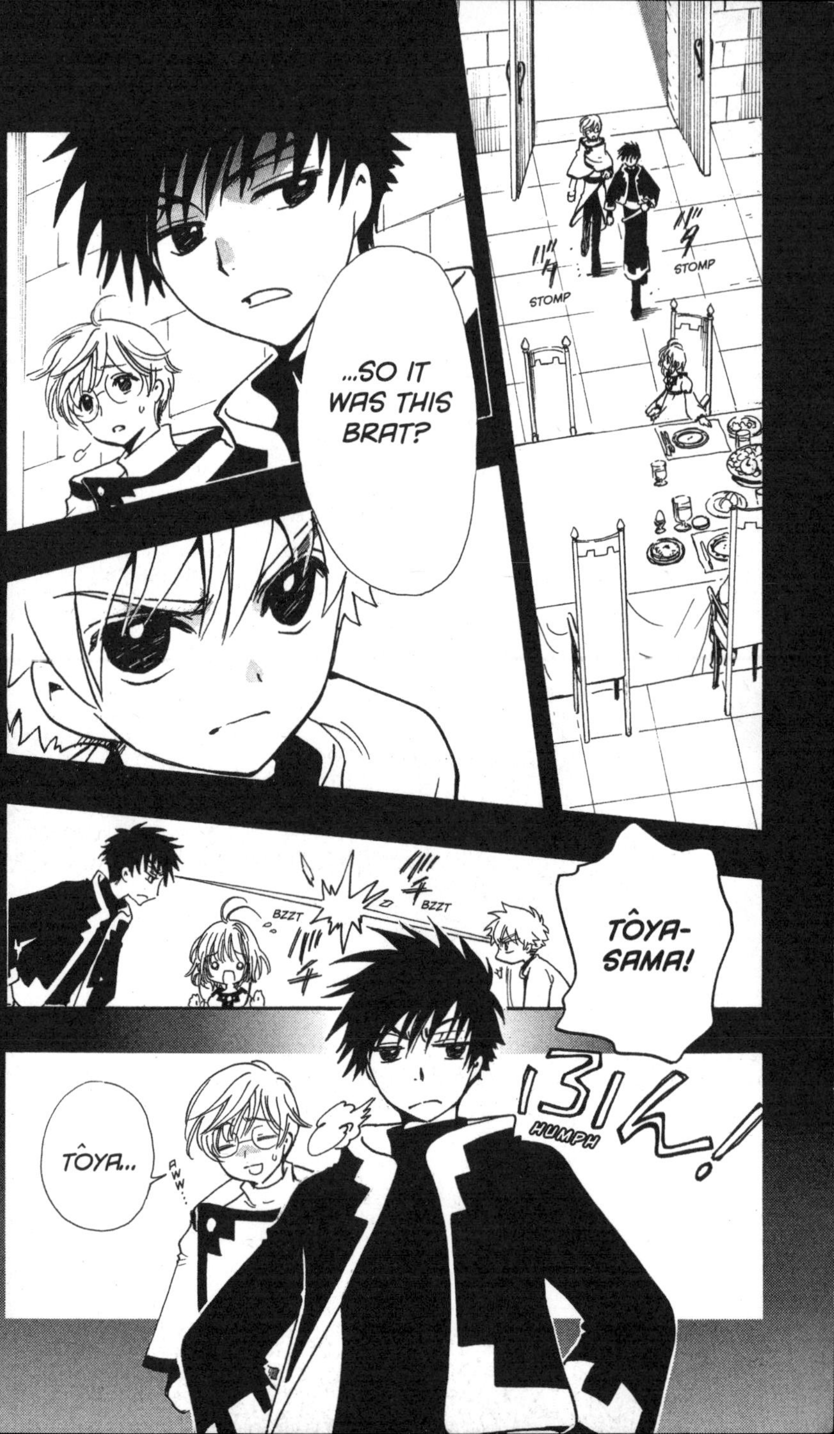
STOMP
STOMP
...SO IT WAS THIS BRAT?
BZZT
BZZT
TÔYA-SAMA!
HUMPH
TÔYA...
AWW...

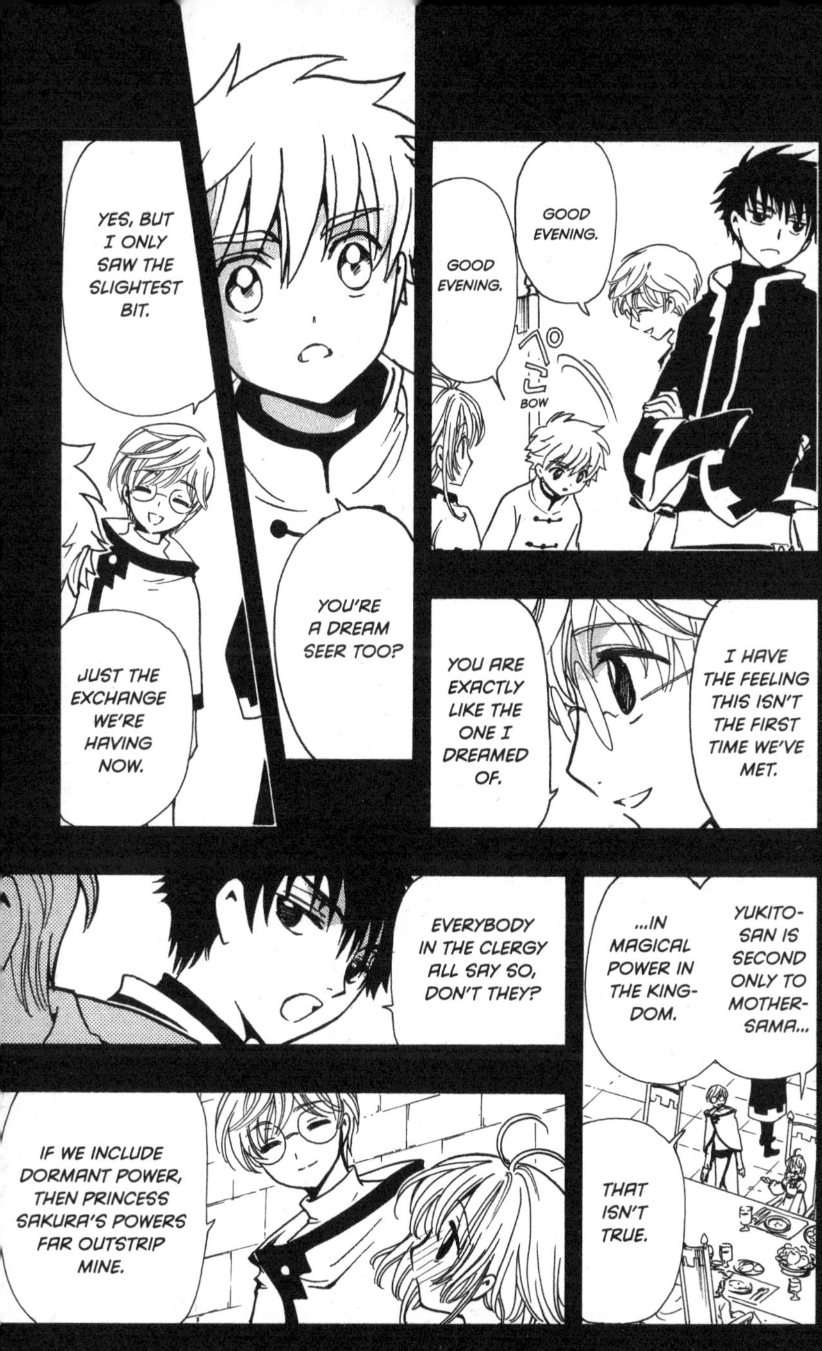
GOOD EVENING.
GOOD EVENING.
BOW
I HAVE THE FEELING THIS ISN'T THE FIRST TIME WE'VE MET.
YOU ARE EXACTLY LIKE THE ONE I DREAMED OF.
YOU'RE A DREAM SEER TOO?
YES, BUT I ONLY SAW THE SLIGHTEST BIT.
JUST THE EXCHANGE WE'RE HAVING NOW.
YUKITO-SAN IS SECOND ONLY TO MOTHER-SAMA...
...IN MAGICAL POWER IN THE KING-DOM.
EVERYBODY IN THE CLERGY ALL SAY SO, DON'T THEY?
THAT ISN'T TRUE.
IF WE INCLUDE DORMANT POWER, THEN PRINCESS SAKURA'S POWERS FAR OUTSTRIP MINE.

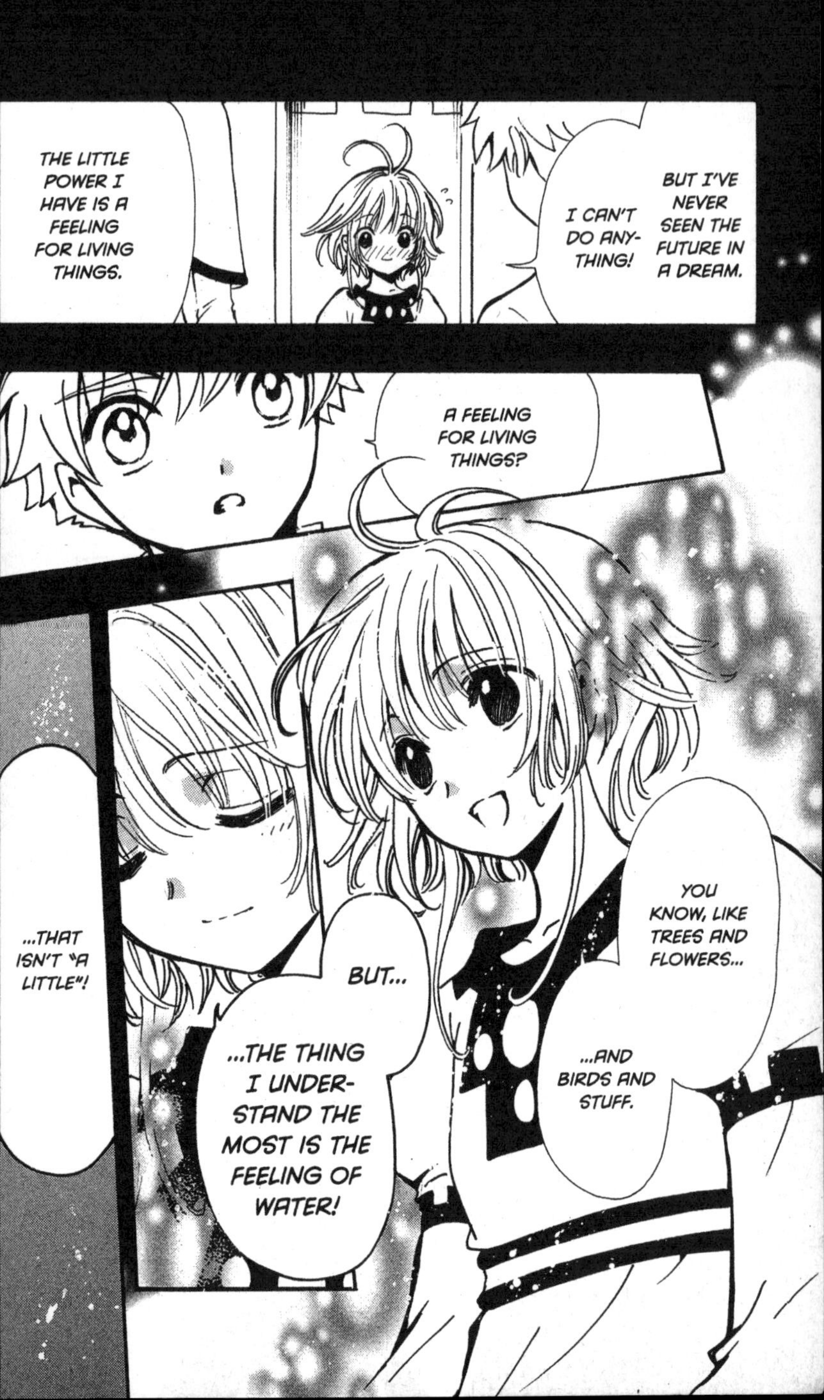
BUT I'VE NEVER SEEN THE FUTURE IN A DREAM.
I CAN'T DO ANY-THING!
THE LITTLE POWER I HAVE IS A FEELING FOR LIVING THINGS.
A FEELING FOR LIVING THINGS?
YOU KNOW, LIKE TREES AND FLOWERS...
...AND BIRDS AND STUFF.
BUT...
...THE THING I UNDER-STAND THE MOST IS THE FEELING OF WATER!
...THAT ISN'T "A LITTLE"!

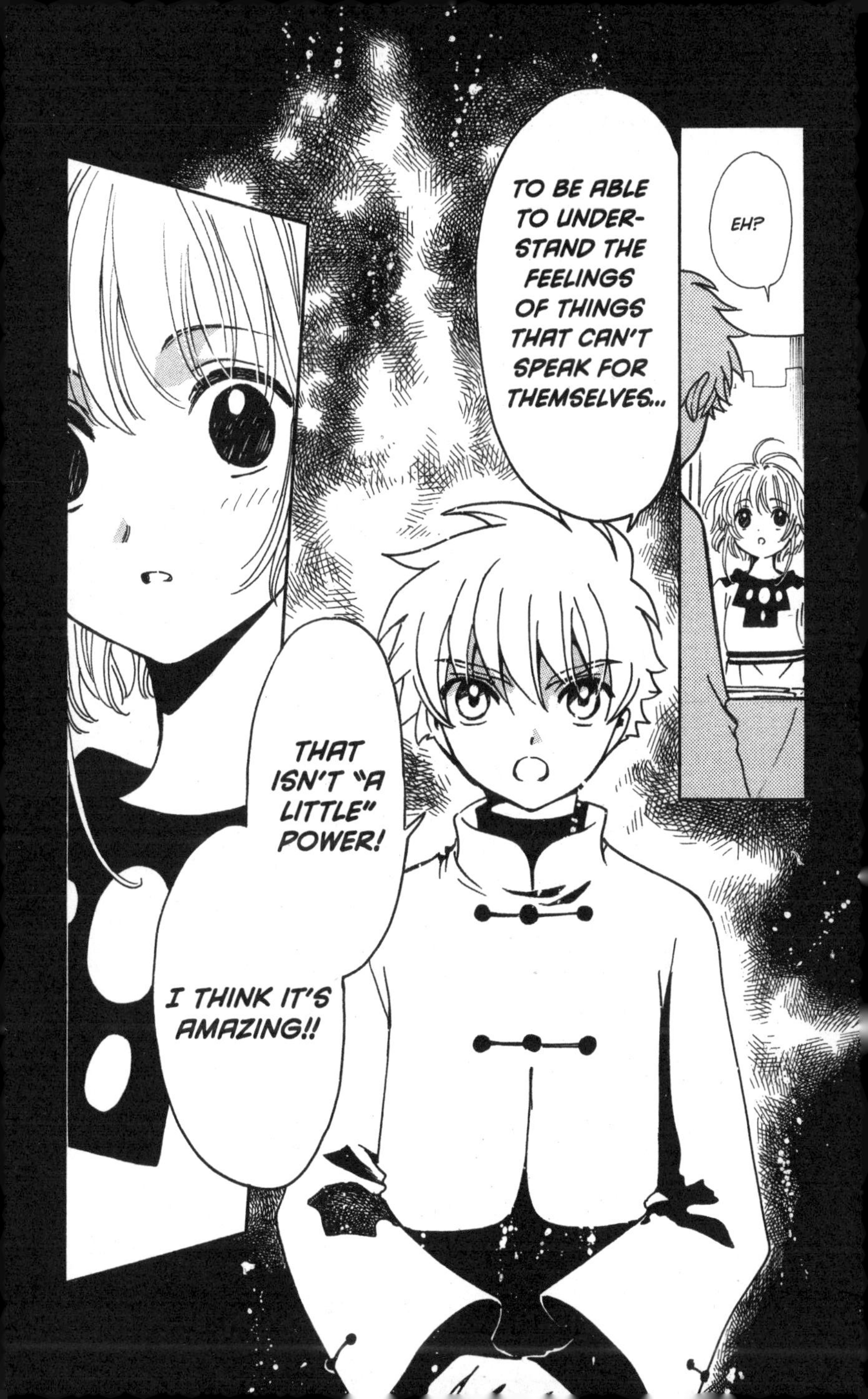
EH?
TO BE ABLE TO UNDER-STAND THE FEELINGS OF THINGS THAT CAN'T SPEAK FOR THEMSELVES...
THAT ISN'T "A LITTLE" POWER!
I THINK IT'S AMAZING!!

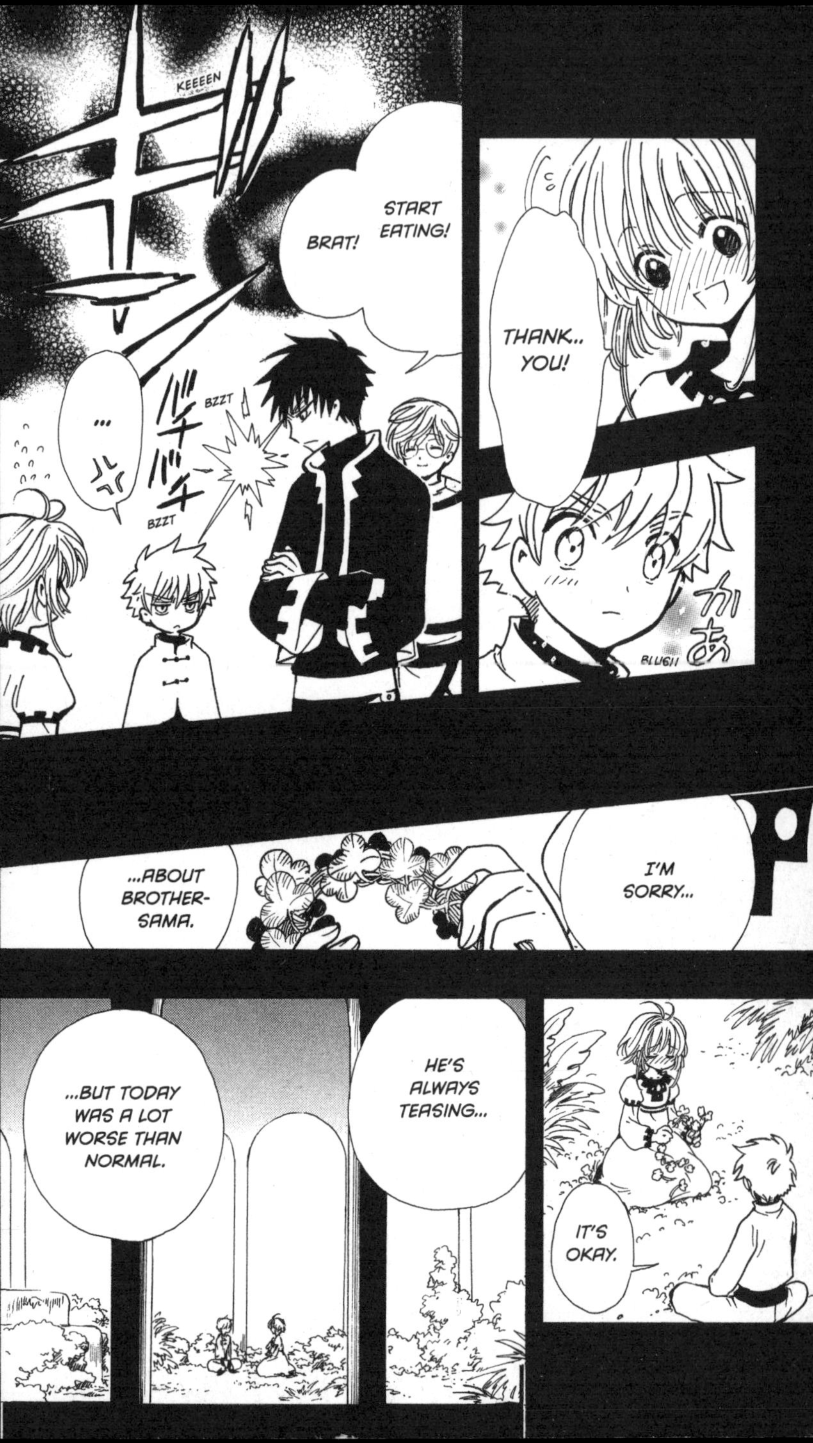
THANK.. YOU!
BLUSH
KEEEEN
START EATING!
BRAT!
...
BZZT
BZZT
I'M SORRY...
...ABOUT BROTHER-SAMA.
IT'S OKAY.
HE'S ALWAYS TEASING...
...BUT TODAY WAS A LOT WORSE THAN NORMAL.

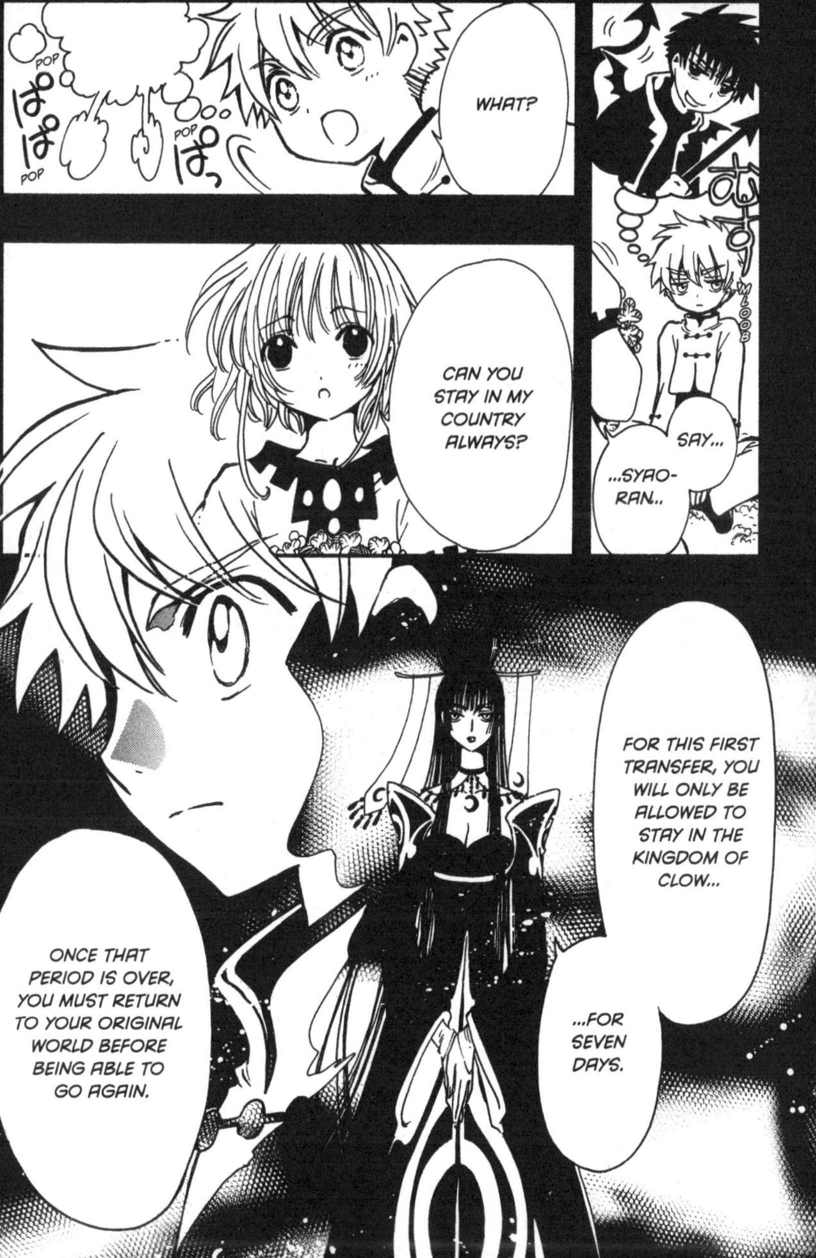
むすっ
MLOOB
SAY...
...SYAO-RAN..
ぱ POP
ぱ POP
ぱっ POP
WHAT?
CAN YOU STAY IN MY COUNTRY ALWAYS?
FOR THIS FIRST TRANSFER, YOU WILL ONLY BE ALLOWED TO STAY IN THE KINGDOM OF CLOW...
...FOR SEVEN DAYS.
ONCE THAT PERIOD IS OVER, YOU MUST RETURN TO YOUR ORIGINAL WORLD BEFORE BEING ABLE TO GO AGAIN.

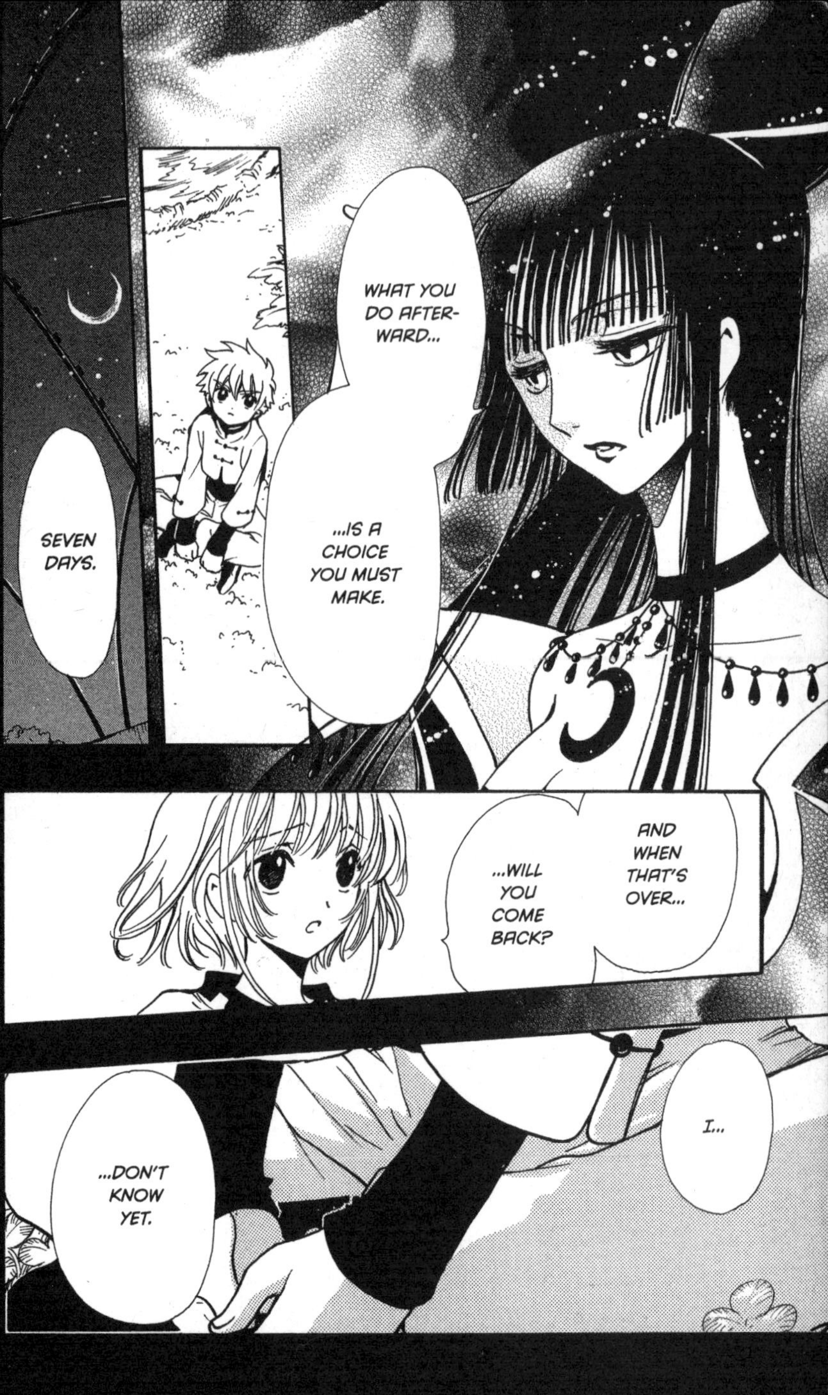
WHAT YOU DO AFTER-WARD...
...IS A CHOICE YOU MUST MAKE.
SEVEN DAYS.
AND WHEN THAT'S OVER...
...WILL YOU COME BACK?
I...
...DON'T KNOW YET.

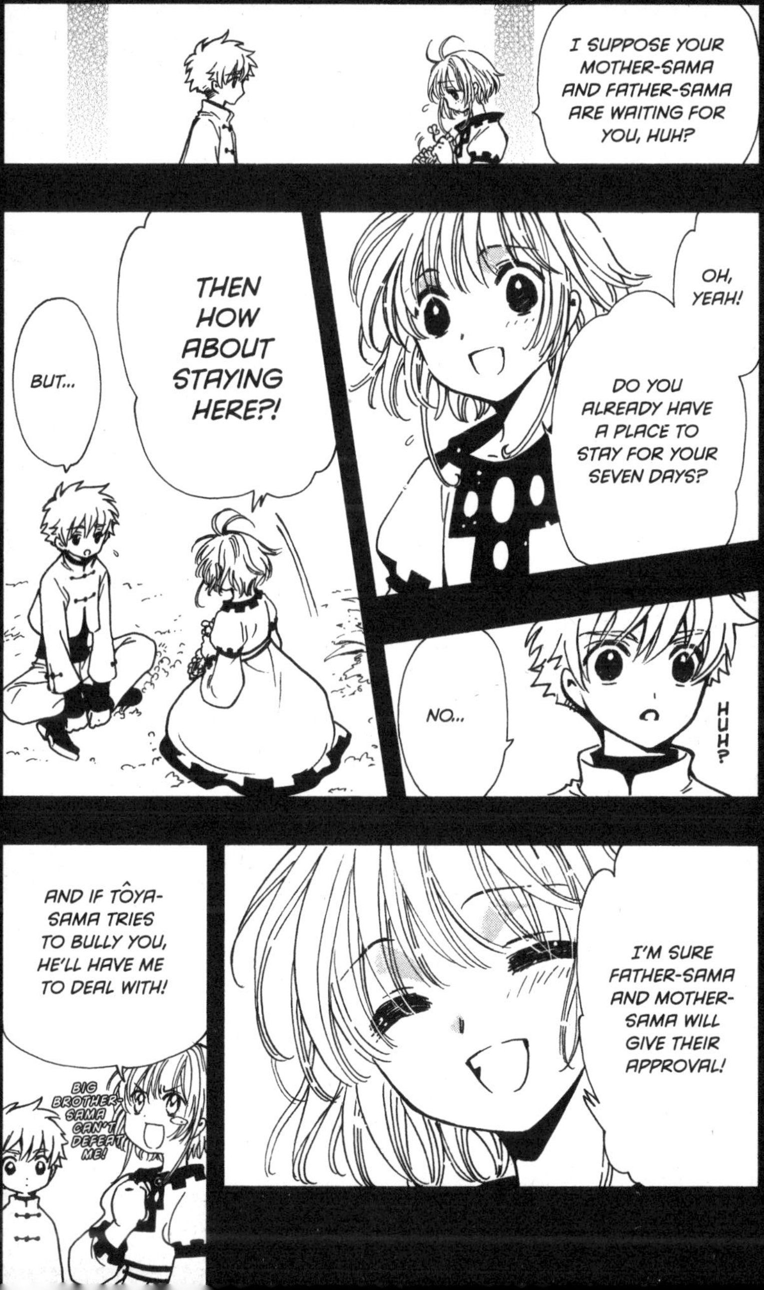
I SUPPOSE YOUR MOTHER-SAMA AND FATHER-SAMA ARE WAITING FOR YOU, HUH?
OH, YEAH!
DO YOU ALREADY HAVE A PLACE TO STAY FOR YOUR SEVEN DAYS?
HUH?
NO...
THEN HOW ABOUT STAYING HERE?!
BUT...
I'M SURE FATHER-SAMA AND MOTHER-SAMA WILL GIVE THEIR APPROVAL!
AND IF TÔYA-SAMA TRIES TO BULLY YOU, HE'LL HAVE ME TO DEAL WITH!
BIG BROTHER-SAMA CAN'T DEFEAT ME!

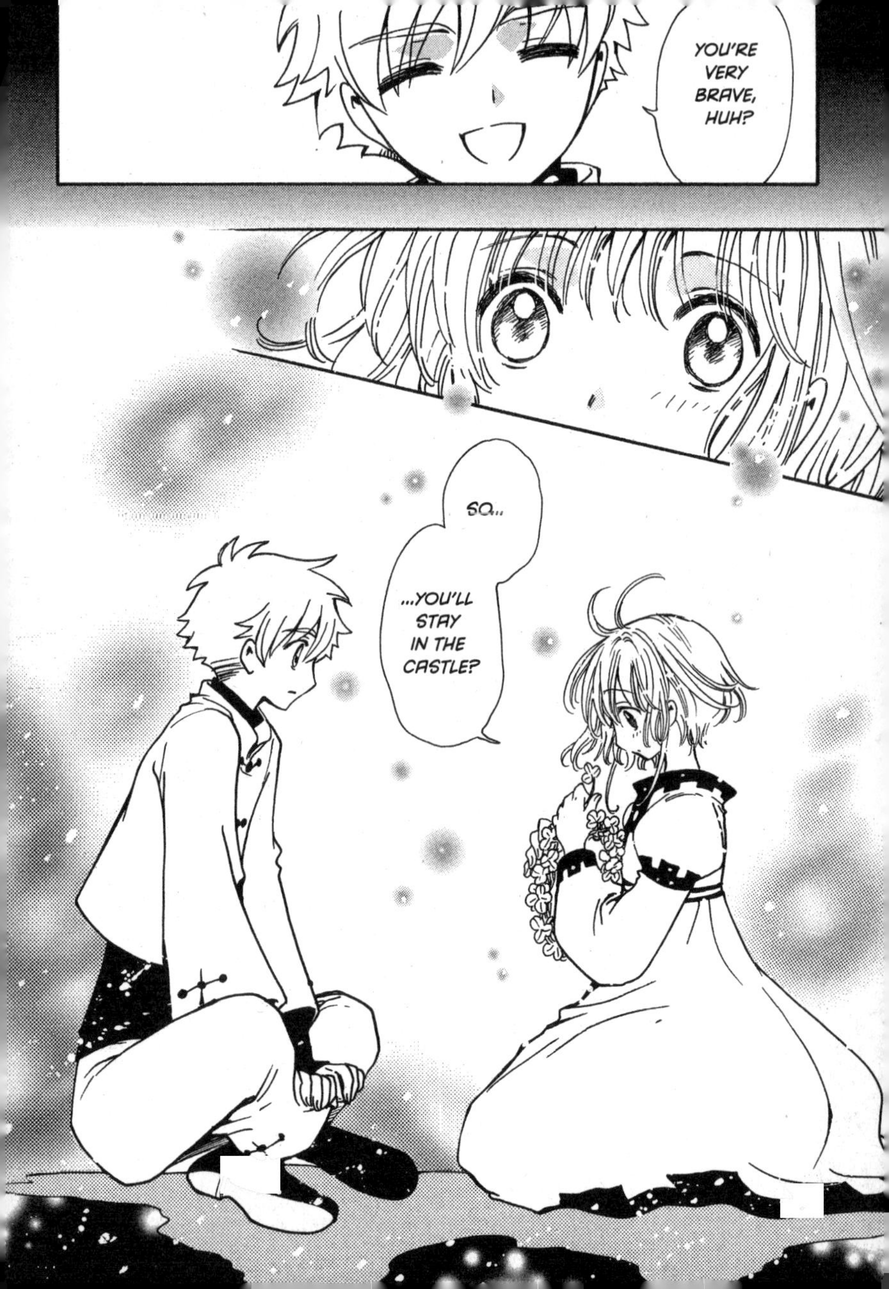
YOU'RE VERY BRAVE, HUH?
SO...
...YOU'LL STAY IN THE CASTLE?

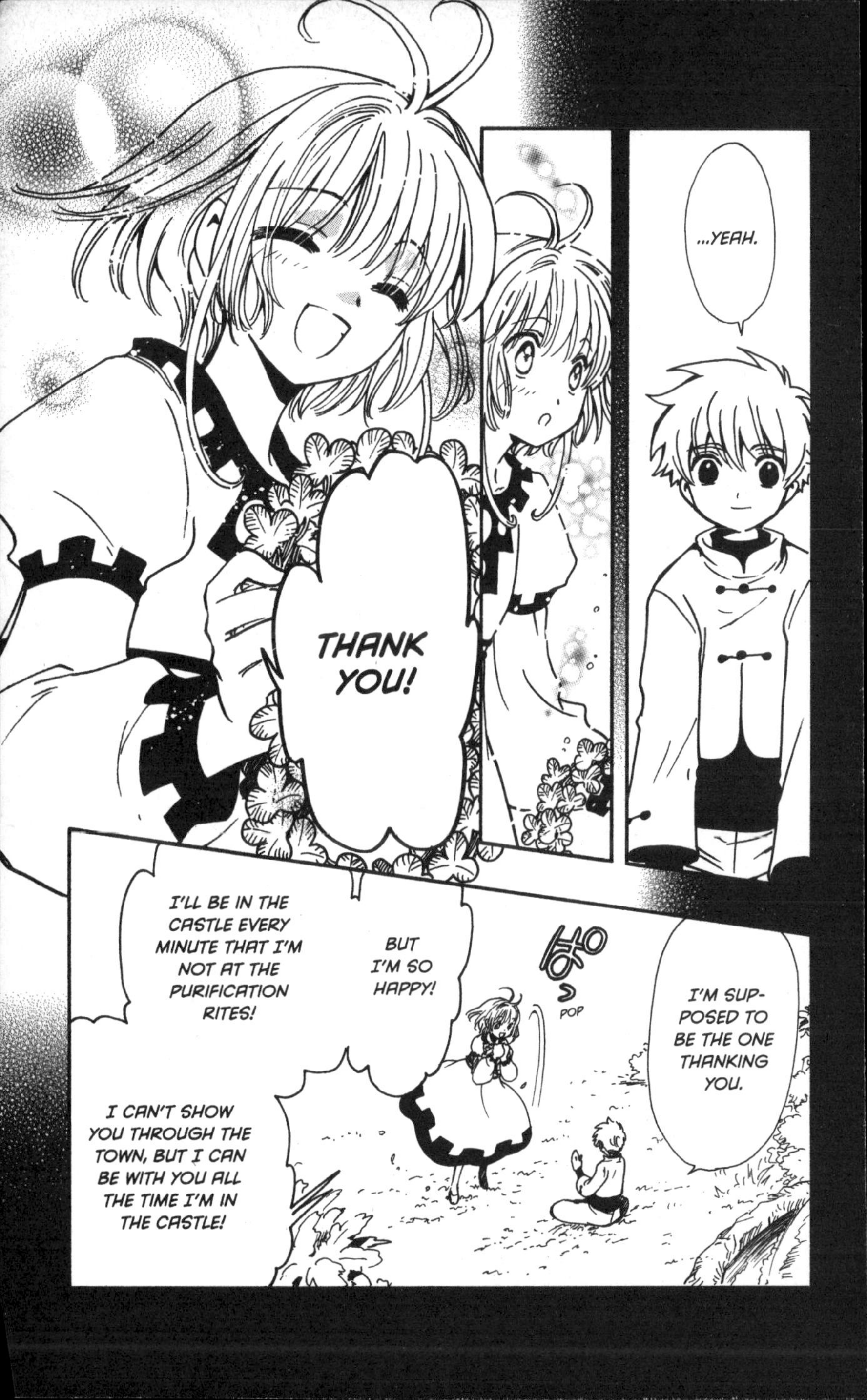
...YEAH.
THANK YOU!
I'M SUP-POSED TO BE THE ONE THANKING YOU.
POP
BUT I'M SO HAPPY!
I'LL BE IN THE CASTLE EVERY MINUTE THAT I'M NOT AT THE PURIFICATION RITES!
I CAN'T SHOW YOU THROUGH THE TOWN, BUT I CAN BE WITH YOU ALL THE TIME I'M IN THE CASTLE!

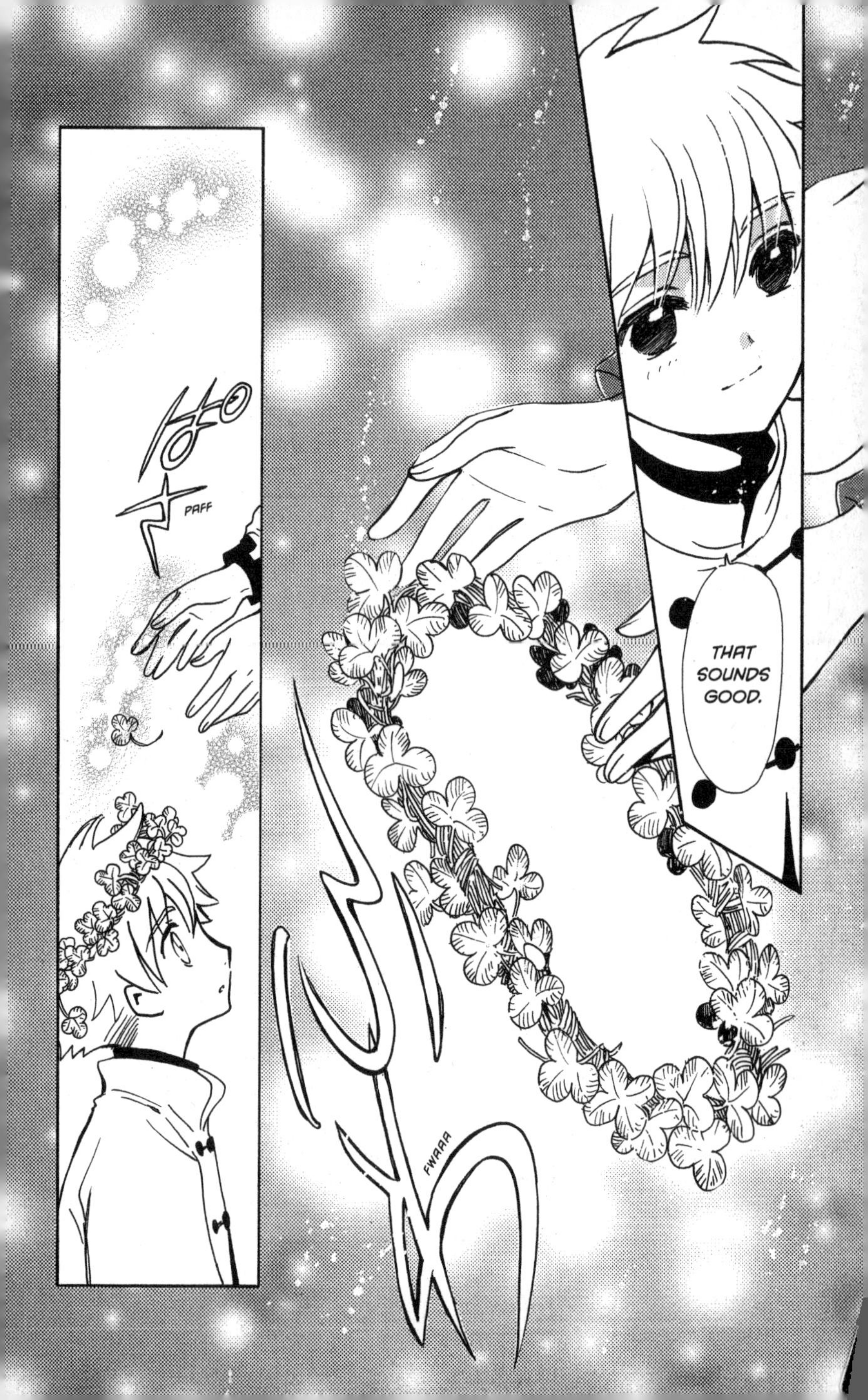
THAT SOUNDS GOOD.
FWAAA
PAFF

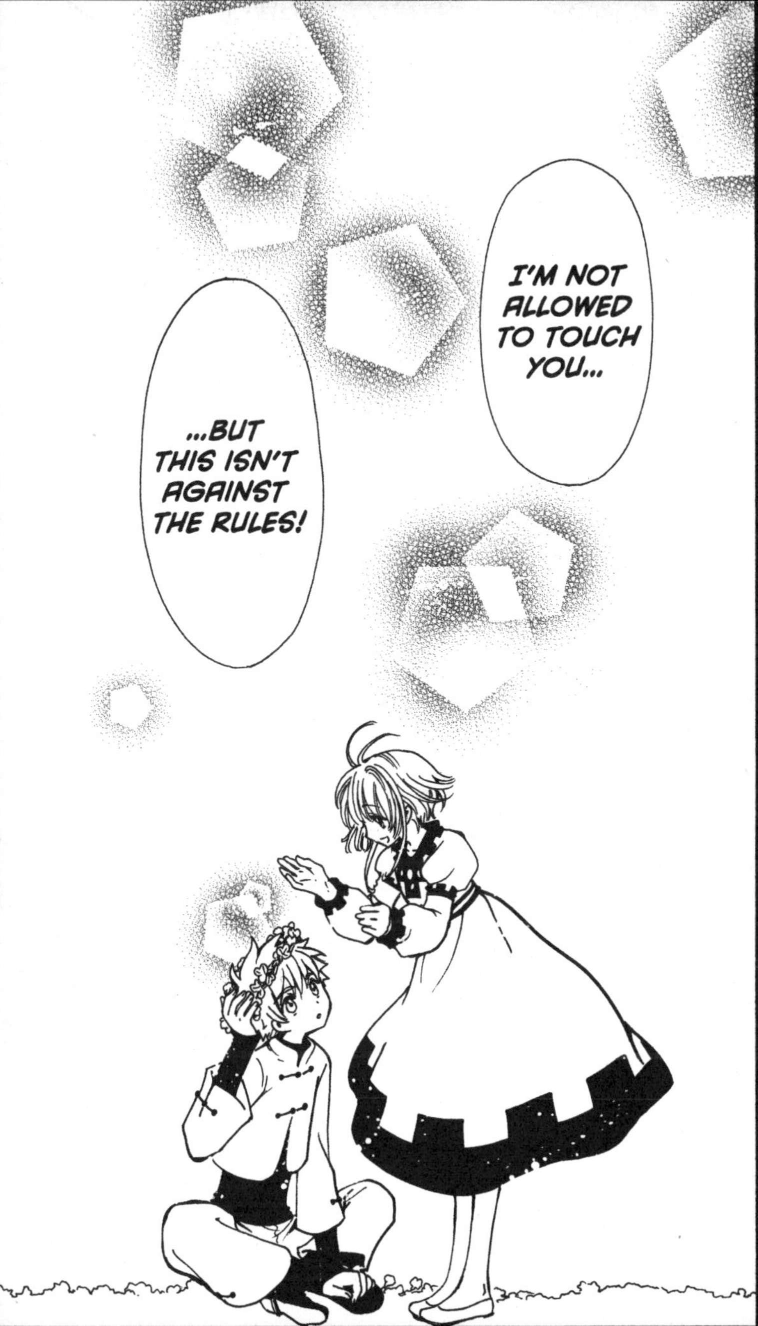
I'M NOT ALLOWED TO TOUCH YOU...
...BUT THIS ISN'T AGAINST THE RULES!

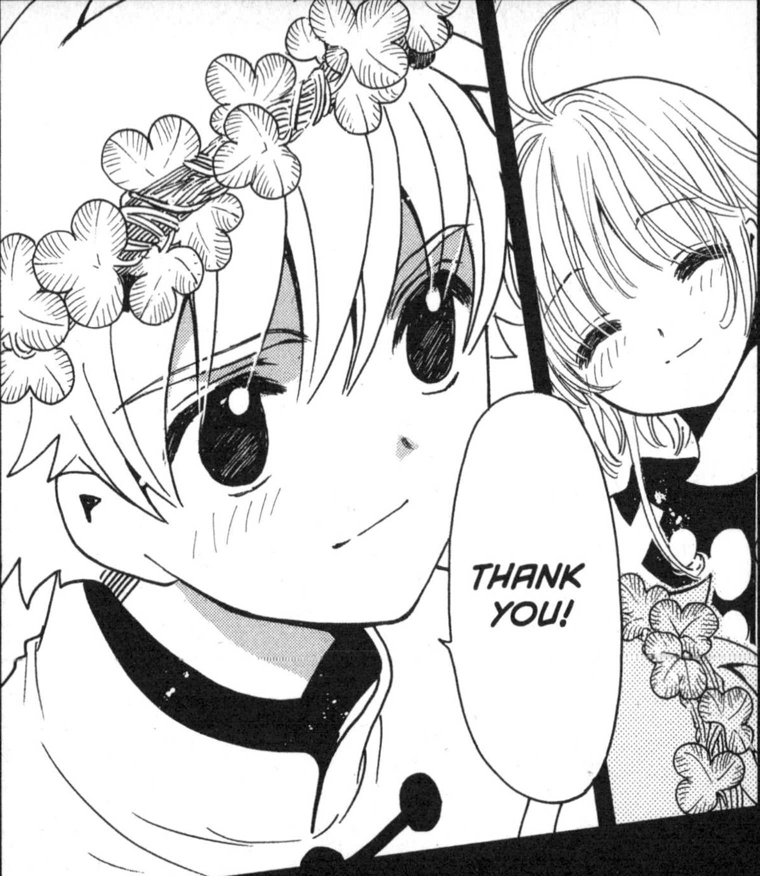
THANK YOU!
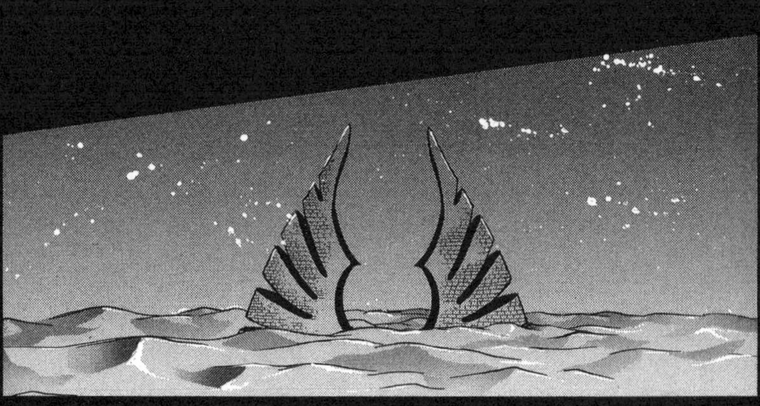

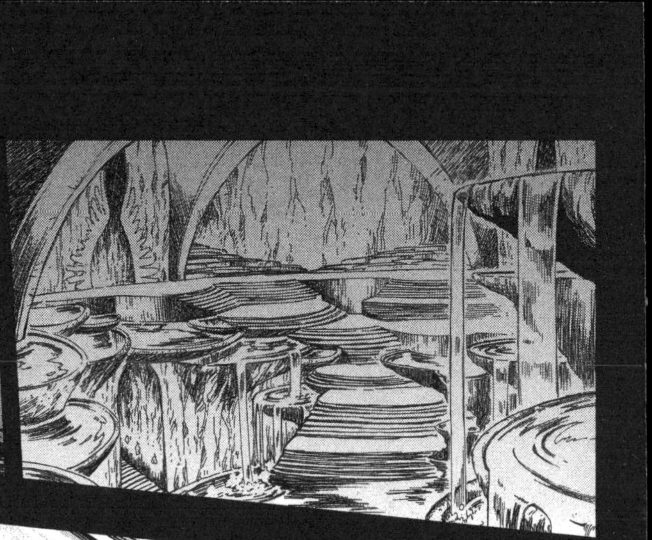
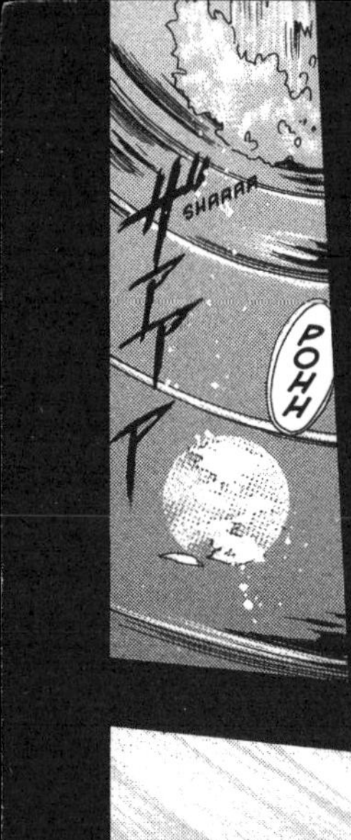
ザァァァ
SHARRR
POHH
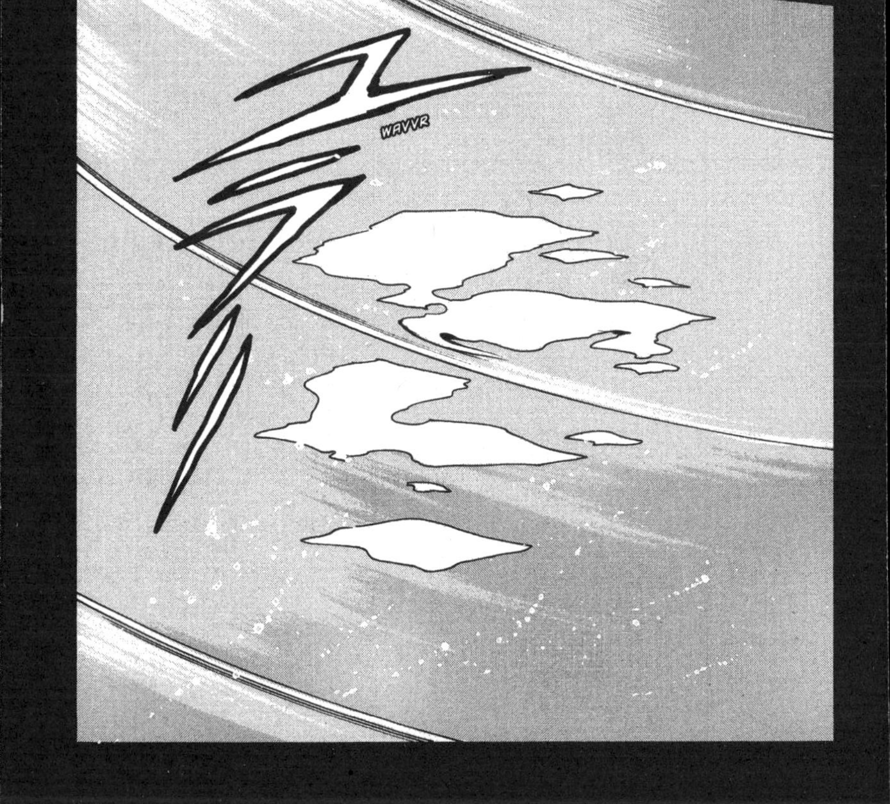
WAVVR

To Be Continued

Translation Notes

Japanese is a tricky language for most Westerners, and translation is often more art than science. For your edification and reading pleasure, here are notes on some of the places where we could have gone in a different direction in our translation of the work, or where a Japanese cultural reference is used.

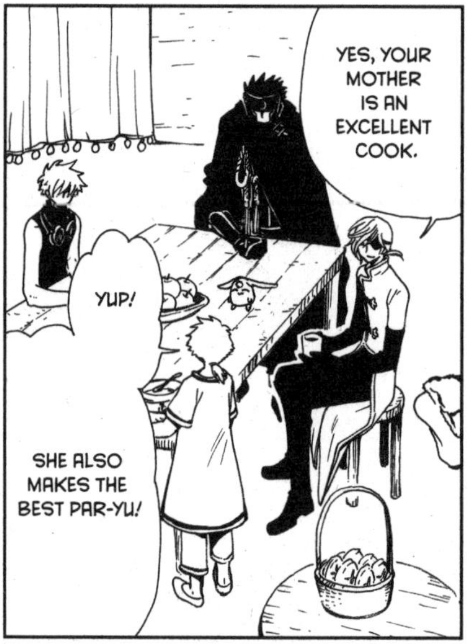
YES, YOUR MOTHER IS AN EXCELLENT COOK.
YUP!
SHE ALSO MAKES THE BEST PAR-YU!

Par-yu, page 404

As has been mentioned in notes from previous volumes, when names or titles (or in this case, food names) come up spelled in *katakana* (the Japanese "alphabet" usually reserved for foreign words) with no Western spelling, the translator must choose a spelling that seems to fit the situation. In this case the word was *paayu*. The elongated "a" sound often indicates an "r" sound in the word. Quite a few other spellings are available, but this one (at least for me) seemed to fit the word best.

Purification, page 440

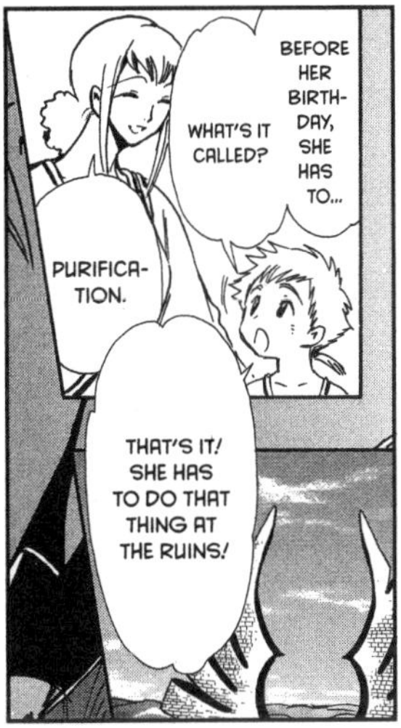
BEFORE HER BIRTH-DAY, SHE HAS TO...
WHAT'S IT CALLED?
PURIFICA-TION.
THAT'S IT! SHE HAS TO DO THAT THING AT THE RUINS!

Although ritual purification rites in Japan are not full-body purifications in pools of water (as in Sakura's case), most large Japanese temples and shrines have places for ritual purification. The spots on the temple/shrine grounds are troughs, usually made of stone, of running water with wooden dippers placed in a row above the water. The rules of the custom vary from place to place, but in all cases, one dips the dipper into the water and pours it over one's hands. Other customs include drinking or quickly washing one's mouth with the water. Since these spots can be found in the majority of large temples and shrines in Japan, nearly everyone raised in Japan would be familiar with purification rites.

Mother-sama, Father-sama, Brother-sama, page 512

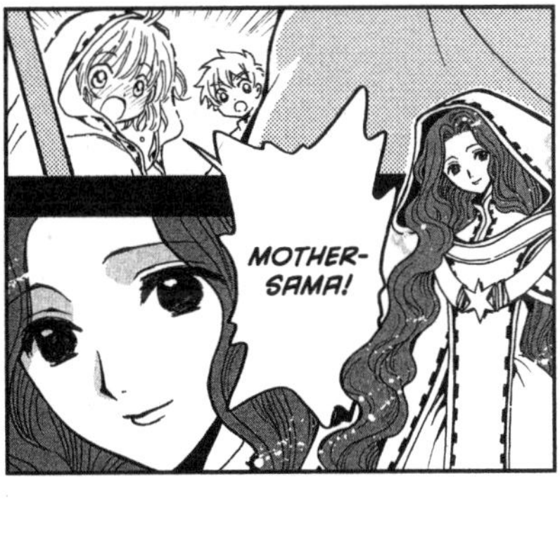
MOTHER-SAMA!

In fiction, the Imperial family and other rich or well-placed families tend to call one another by their family title followed by the -sama honorific. This is meant to be a show of respect, but it also gives off a nuance of people growing up in a privileged world apart from normal life.

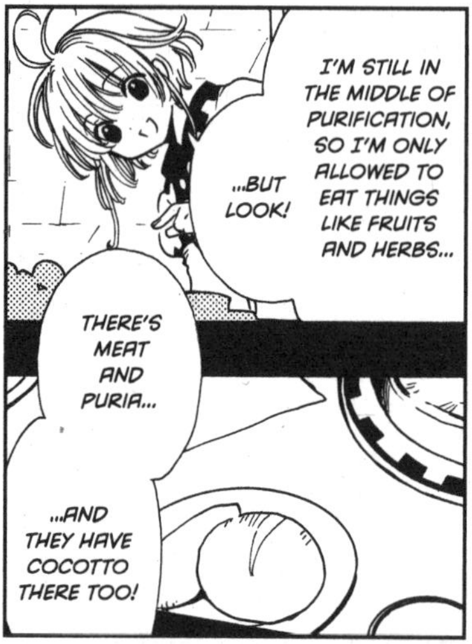
I'M STILL IN THE MIDDLE OF PURIFICATION, SO I'M ONLY ALLOWED TO EAT THINGS LIKE FRUITS AND HERBS...
...BUT LOOK!
THERE'S MEAT AND PURIA...
...AND THEY HAVE COCOTTO THERE TOO!

Puria, Cocotto, page 526

In much the same way as explained in the note on par-yu, these are more food names spelled in *katakana* and left for the translator to find an appropriate spelling. I did my best based on the Japanese pronunciation. It is always possible that a different, official spelling for these dishes will be released by CLAMP after the publication of this book.

Can I call you Syaoran?, page 529

To Western ears, this sounds like a strange question. In Western nations, if a person introduces himself by his first name only, it is implied that one has permission to use that name. But in Japan, one does not use honorifics when saying one's own name in a self-introduction, so when using the name, the other person adds an honorific to it. Sakura is actually asking if she can leave off the honorific when calling Syaoran by name—an intimacy reserved only for family and close friends. It means she wants to become close to Syaoran.

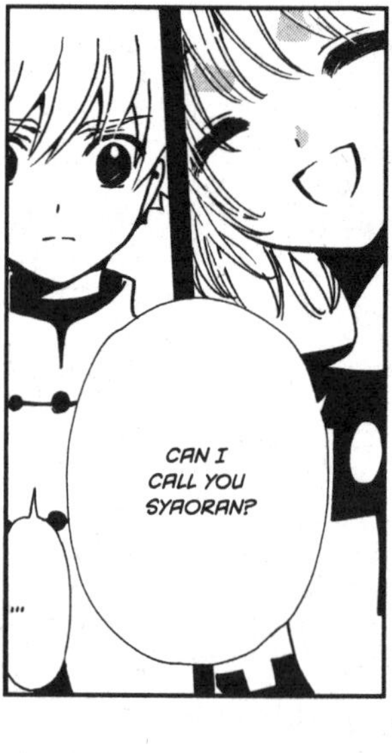
CAN I CALL YOU SYAORAN?
...

KODANSHA COMICS

THE HEROIC LEGEND OF ARSLAN

READ THE NEW SERIES FROM THE CREATOR OF FULLMETAL ALCHEMIST, HIROMU ARAKAWA! NOW A HIT TV SERIES!

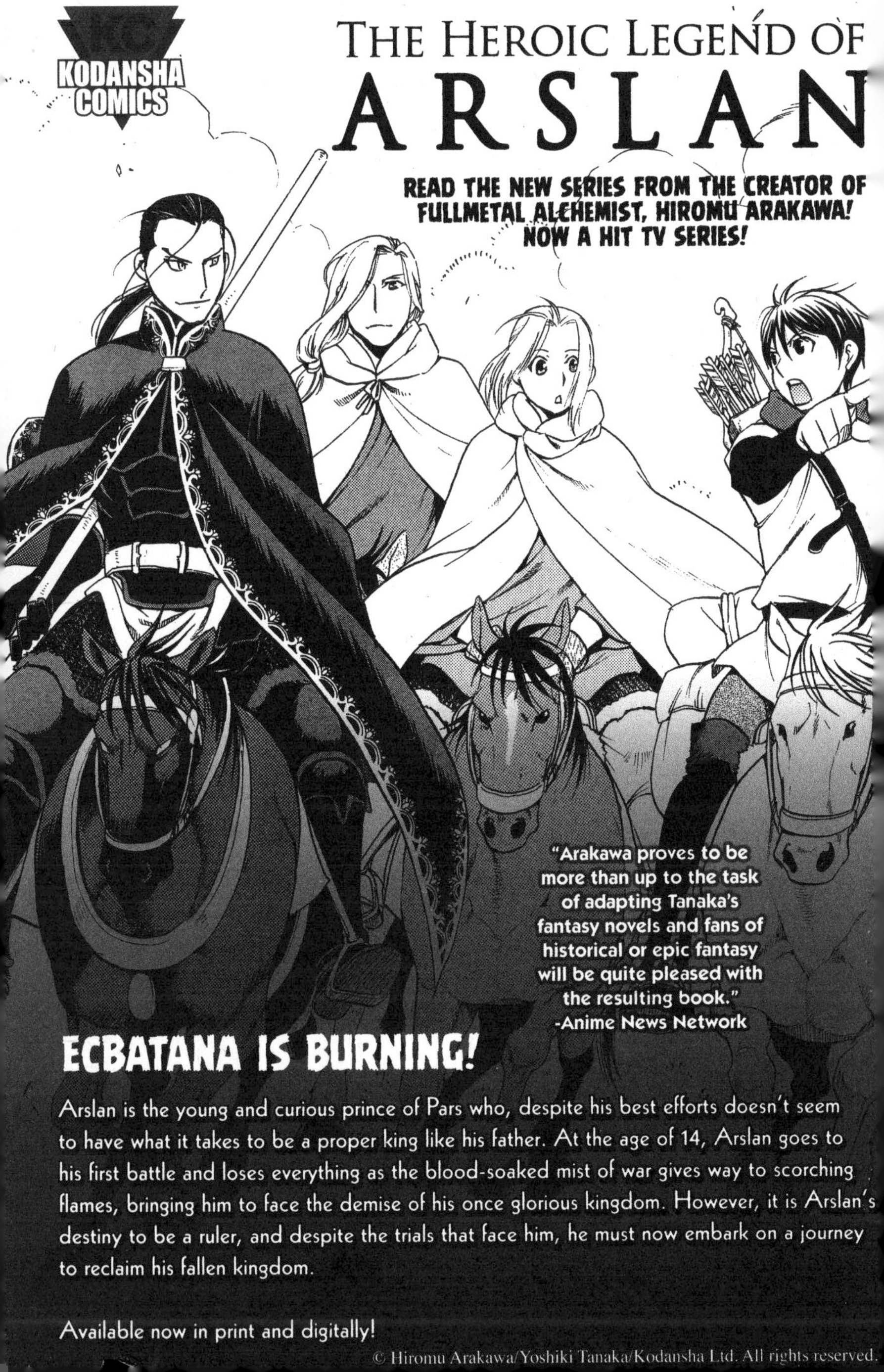

"Arakawa proves to be more than up to the task of adapting Tanaka's fantasy novels and fans of historical or epic fantasy will be quite pleased with the resulting book."
-Anime News Network

ECBATANA IS BURNING!

Arslan is the young and curious prince of Pars who, despite his best efforts doesn't seem to have what it takes to be a proper king like his father. At the age of 14, Arslan goes to his first battle and loses everything as the blood-soaked mist of war gives way to scorching flames, bringing him to face the demise of his once glorious kingdom. However, it is Arslan's destiny to be a ruler, and despite the trials that face him, he must now embark on a journey to reclaim his fallen kingdom.

Available now in print and digitally!

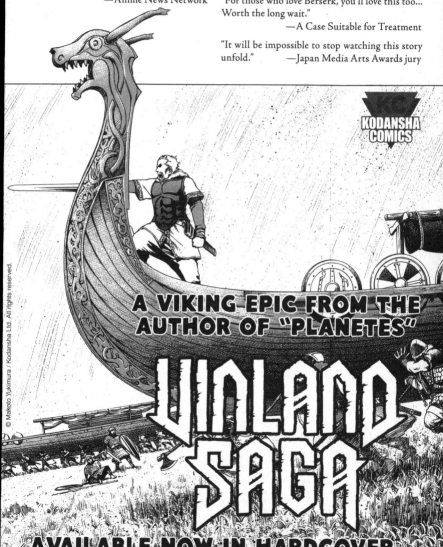